FROMMER'S
DOLLARWISE GUIDE TO ENGLAND & SCOTLAND

by Stanley Haggart and
Darwin Porter

1981-1982 Edition

Copyright © 1969, 1971, 1973, 1975, 1977, 1979, 1981
by Simon & Schuster

All rights reserved
including the right of reproduction
in whole or in part in any form

Published by Frommer/Pasmantier Publishers
A Simon & Schuster Division of
Gulf & Western Corporation
380 Madison Avenue
New York, New York 10017

ISBN 0-671-41424-0

Manufactured in the United States of America

*Although every effort was made to insure the accuracy
of price information appearing in this book,
it should be kept in mind that prices
can and do fluctuate in the course of time.*

CONTENTS

Introduction	**DOLLARWISE GUIDE TO ENGLAND AND SCOTLAND**	1
Chapter I	**GETTING THERE**	7
	1. Plane Economics	7
	2. By Ship	10
	3. Traveling Within Britain	11
Chapter II	**LONDON: HOTELS FOR EVERY BUDGET**	21
	1. Deluxe Hotels	24
	2. St. James's	27
	3. Piccadilly Circus	30
	4. The Strand and Covent Garden	32
	5. Westminster	33
	6. Chelsea	35
	7. Belgravia and Knightsbridge	37
	8. Kensington, South Kensington, and Earl's Court	40
	9. Bayswater	46
	10. Paddington and Little Venice	49
	11. St. Marylebone	49
	12. Mayfair	52
	13. Bloomsbury	54
	14. Euston Station and King's Cross	56
	15. On the Fringe	57
	16. Alternatives to Hotels	59
Chapter III	**LONDON: RESTAURANTS AND PUBS**	64
	1. The Top Restaurants	65
	2. The West End	66
	3. Other Locales	93
	4. Suggestions for Sunday	98
	5. The Pubs of London	100
	6. The Wine Bars	106
	7. Country Dining Near London	109

CHAPTER IV	**LONDON: WHAT TO SEE AND DO**	**111**
	1. Getting Around Town	111
	2. Seeing the Sights	115
	3. Shopping for Value	141
	4. London After Dark	152
	5. Taking the Tours	167
	6. One-Day Trips from London	171
Chapter V	**WINDSOR, OXFORD, AND THE HOME COUNTIES**	**177**
	1. Windsor	178
	2. Oxford	188
	3. Hertfordshire	198
	4. Buckinghamshire	201
	5. Bedfordshire	204
Chapter VI	**KENT, SURREY, AND THE SUSSEXES**	**206**
	1. Kent's Country Houses and Castles	209
	2. Canterbury	211
	3. Dover	215
	4. Tunbridge Wells	217
	5. Richmond	219
	6. Haslemere	220
	7. Rye	224
	8. Winchelsea	225
	9. Hastings and St. Leonard's	226
	10. Battle	228
	11. Alfriston and Lewes	229
	12. East Grinstead	231
	13. Brighton	231
	14. Arundel	236
	15. Chichester	237
Chapter VII	**HAMPSHIRE AND DORSET**	**242**
	1. Portsmouth	245
	2. Southampton	247
	3. Isle of Wight	251
	4. Winchester	253
	5. Bournemouth	256
	6. Shaftesbury	259
	7. Wool	260
	8. Wareham	260

	9.	Dorchester	**261**
	10.	Bridport	**263**
	11.	Chideock	**264**
	12.	Charmouth	**265**
	13.	Lyme Regis	**265**
	14.	Donyatt	**266**
Chapter VIII		**DEVON AND CORNWALL**	**268**
	1.	Beer	**269**
	2.	Exeter	**271**
	3.	Dartmoor	**274**
	4.	Torbay	**277**
	5.	Totnes	**279**
	6.	Dartmouth	**282**
	7.	Plymouth	**283**
	8.	Clovelly	**285**
	9.	Lynton-Lynmouth	**287**
	10.	Combe Martin	**288**
	11.	Looe	**290**
	12.	Polperro	**293**
	13.	Fowey	**295**
	14.	Truro	**295**
	15.	Portloe	**296**
	16.	St. Mawes	**296**
	17.	Falmouth	**297**
	18.	Penzance	**299**
	19.	The Scilly Isles	**302**
	20.	St. Hilary, Newlyn, and Mousehole	**303**
	21.	St. Ives	**305**
	22.	St. Columb Major	**307**
	23.	Port Isaac	**307**
	24.	Tintagel	**308**
Chapter IX		**WILTSHIRE, SOMERSET, AND AVON**	**310**
	1.	Salisbury	**311**
	2.	Castle Combe	**318**
	3.	Lacock	**319**
	4.	Wells	**320**
	5.	Bleadney	**322**
	6.	Glastonbury	**322**
	7.	The Caves of Mendip	**325**
	8.	Bath	**327**

	9. Bristol	333
Chapter X	**THE COTSWOLDS**	**335**
	1. Burford	336
	2. Clanfield	337
	3. Minster Lovell	338
	4. Bibury	338
	5. Cirencester	339
	6. Painswick	341
	7. Cheltenham	342
	8. Royal Sudeley Castle	345
	9. Malmesbury	346
	10. Tetbury	347
	11. Wotton-under-Edge	347
	12. Shipton-under-Wychwood	348
	13. Chipping Norton	349
	14. Bourton-on-the-Water	350
	15. Lower Swell	351
	16. Upper and Lower Slaughter	351
	17. Stow-on-the-Wold	352
	18. Moreton-in-Marsh	353
	19. Broadway	355
	20. Chipping Campden	357
Chapter XI	**STRATFORD AND THE HEART OF ENGLAND**	**359**
	1. Stratford-upon-Avon	360
	2. Warwick	370
	3. Kenilworth Castle	373
	4. Coventry	374
	5. Hereford and Worcester	376
	6. Salop (Shropshire)	379
	7. Straffordshire	381
Chapter XII	**CAMBRIDGE AND EAST ANGLIA**	**383**
	1. Cambridge	385
	2. Ely	392
	3. Thaxted	394
	4. Saffron Walden	395
	5. Finchingfield	395
	6. Dedham	396
	7. Clare	397
	8. Long Melford	399

	9. Lavenham	399
	10. Woodbridge	401
	11. Aldeburgh	402
	12. East Bergholt	403
	13. Norwich	404
	14. Tottenhill	407
	15. North Norfolk	407
	16. English Country Cottages	411
Chapter XIII	**EAST MIDLANDS**	**413**
	1. Northamptonshire	413
	2. Leicestershire	415
	3. Derbyshire	417
	4. Nottinghamshire	420
	5. Lincolnshire	424
Chapter XIV	**CHESHIRE, LIVERPOOL, AND THE LAKES**	**428**
	1. Chester	429
	2. Nantwich	432
	3. Liverpool	434
	4. Kendal	436
	5. Windermere	436
	6. Ambleside	439
	7. Rydal	440
	8. Grasmere	441
	9. Hawkshead and Coniston	443
	10. Keswick	443
	11. Bassenthwaite	445
	12. Ullswater	445
Chapter XV	**YORKSHIRE AND NORTHUMBRIA**	**447**
	1. York	447
	2. North Yorkshire	455
	3. West Yorkshire	460
	4. Durham	462
	5. Tyne and Wear	463
	6. Northumberland	465
Chapter XVI	**SCOTLAND**	**471**
	1. The Border Country	471
	2. Edinburgh	477
	3. Day Trips from Edinburgh	492
	4. The Kingdom of Fife	498

5.	Exploring Tayside	**504**
6.	The Trossachs and Loch Lomond	**515**
7.	Aberdeen and Royal Deeside	**520**
8.	Aviemore, Speyside, and Elgin	**527**
9.	Inverness and Loch Ness	**535**
10.	Fort William and Lochaber	**542**
11.	Kyle of Lochalsh and Skye	**547**
12.	Oban, Mull, and District	**552**
13.	Kintyre, Arran, and Islay	**561**
14.	Glasgow and the Clyde	**566**
15.	Ayr, Prestwick, and District	**574**
16.	Dumfries and Galloway	**580**

Appendix   **CURRENCY EXCHANGE**   **596**

MAPS

Counties of England and Wales	12
Tourist Areas	19
London Areas	23
Westminster, Whitehall, St. James's, and Victoria	28
The Heart of London	31
Chelsea	35
Belgravia and Knightsbridge	37
Earl's Court, West Kensington, and West Brompton	41
Paddington, Bayswater, Lancaster Gate	47
Regent's Park and Marylebone	50
Mayfair	53
Bloomsbury and Holborn	55
Euston Station, St. Pancras, King's Cross	57
Soho	86
Fleet Street and the City	92
Kensington and Holland Park	97
London Subway	112
Oxford	189
Surrey, the Sussexes, and Kent	207
Southern Counties	243
Cornwall and Devon	270
Salisbury	312
Gloucester, Worcester, and Warwick	343
Cambridge	384
East Anglia	398
The Lake District	437
Scotland	472
Edinburgh	478
Glasgow	567

Britain's VAT

On June 18, 1979, Great Britain raised its standard Value Added Tax (called VAT for short) from 8% to 15%. Most Common Market countries already have a tax similar to VAT (France, for example, a paralyzing 23%). In Britain, hotel rates and meals in restaurants are now taxed 15%. This extra VAT charge will show up on your bill unless otherwise stated. It is in addition to the service charge. Should the service charge be 15%, you will, in effect, be paying 30% higher than the prices quoted. The service charges, if included as part of the bill, are also taxable!

As part of an energy-saving scheme, the British government has also added a special 25% tax on gasoline ("petrol")!

Inflation Alert!!!

It is hardly a secret that a wave of inflation has battered the countries of northern Europe, and Britain has been hard hit. The authors of this book have spent laborious hours researching to try and ensure the accuracy of prices appearing in this guide. As we go to press, we believe we have obtained the most reliable data possible. However, in a system that in 1980 alone saw one London hotelier raise his prices three times in one season, we cannot offer guarantees for the tariffs quoted. In the lifetime of this edition—particularly its second year (1982)—the wise traveler will add *at least* 20% to the prices quoted.

A Question of Borders

England and Scotland have changed their counties or "shires," carving out new ones, such as Humberside, and cutting up big ones, such as Yorkshire. Greater London has gobbled up many land areas of neighboring counties such as Surrey. The famous counties of Angus and Perthshire are now called "Tayside." However, many jolly innkeepers are keeping their old addresses—and threaten to continue to do so! In the transition there may be some confusion.

Introduction

DOLLARWISE GUIDE TO ENGLAND AND SCOTLAND

The Reason Why

ENGLAND, AND SCOTLAND, too, sent her children across the waves to settle North America, Australia, New Zealand, and a host of other lands. Today the offspring of those children are returning to visit their mother lands at a rate that is practically an invasion.

What's the big attraction?

England, as in Restoration days, has thrown out the Puritan and is experimenting in all sorts of imaginative, creative ways. Vigorous and exciting changes are taking place, and England today is, in a word, fun. The island may be small, but, like Mighty Mouse, it packs a powerful punch.

On the other hand, Scotland fulfills romantic myths—a land of shimmering lochs, pepper-pot towers and crow-stepped castles, clans with bagpipes, and balladeers. Scotland is very different from England. When English people go to Scotland, they are, in effect, "going abroad."

Connecting you with the life forces of both countries is one of the aims of this book.

We have set for ourselves the formidable task of seeking out the best of England and Scotland and condensing it between the covers of a guide. The best includes not only descriptions of hotels, restaurants, pubs, and nightspots, but descriptions of cities, towns, and sightseeing attractions. Part of the philosophy of this book is based on the fact that the best need not be the most expensive. Hence, our ultimate aim—beyond that of familiarizing you with the offerings of merrie old England and romantic Scotland—is to stretch your dollar power, to show you that you need not always pay scalper's prices for charm, top-grade comfort, and food.

In this guide, we'll devote a great deal of attention to the tourist meccas of London, Edinburgh, Stratford-upon-Avon, and Oxford. But these ancient cities and towns are not the full "reason why" of the book. Important as they are, they simply do not fully reflect the complexity and diversity of both countries. Unlike most nations of Europe, England and Scotland defy a clear, logical, coherent plan of sightseeing. Both lands are a patchwork quilt of treasures, with many of the most scenic items tucked away in remote corners—

an Elizabethan country estate in Devon, a half-timbered thatched cottage by the sea in Cornwall, a Regency manor in the Lake District, an old whitewashed coaching inn at Loch Ness.

Meeting the English and the Scots is perhaps the most important reason for making the trip. If possible, try to arrive with few preconceived ideas. For example, generalizing about the character of the English in a land filled with "soopah" swinging dukes, Cockney porters, Rudyard Kipling adventurers, and Miss Marple-type ladies is fraught with hazards. Suffice it to say, they'll surprise you—particularly if you think of the English as a cold, snobbish, withdrawn people. A few visits to the haunts of Soho, or to a local pub for a "lager and lime," or even a look at the racy London tabloids, will cure you of stereotypes.

SOME NEW REASONS WHY: It may be presumptuous to give you "reasons why" to go to England and Scotland. Dozens may have already occurred to you, ranging from doing a brass rubbing on a church floor to tracing your ancestors to determine if you're descended from royalty or highwaymen. We'll merely add a few you may not have thought of:

To go pub crawling

The English pub is a unique institution. Its special charms will win you instantly, making you abandon the jaded cocktail hour forever. You can begin your crawl in the heart of Piccadilly Circus, eating "bangers and mash" with the young "blokes" from the East End in a "chirpy" Victorian atmosphere; then proceed to a pub in "The City" in the footsteps of Samuel Johnson, with Boswell writing down every word: "This man (Lord Chesterfield) I thought had been a Lord among wits; but, I find, he is only a wit among Lords"; then on to exclusive Belgravia to mix with London bluebloods in the stamping ground of the Iron Duke himself; finally, end your adventure with elegantly dressed operagoers in a pub off Covent Garden, Eliza Doolittle territory.

But don't stop there. You can go all over England, staking out your own "local"—be it the Mermaid in Rye, basking in its associations with a band of cutthroat smugglers, the Hawkhurst Gang; the Fox & Hounds on the outskirts of Southampton where you'll drink the legendary mead from a silver mazer (the Saxons considered it an elixir); the Ship Inn in Exeter, beloved ("next to mine own shippe") by Sir Francis Drake; and finally, the Sloop, an artists' pub at St. Ives on the Cornish coast, where you're likely to hear some Welsh folk singing.

To discover if Victoria was a wicked old witch or a nice old lady

Perhaps no woman in history ever dominated an era—at least symbolically —as much as the Empress of India and the Queen of Great Britain and the Dominions. One historian wrote: "She seemed the richest and most impressive monarch since Cyrus the Great or Augustus Caesar." Interest in her today hasn't dimmed—nor has controversy about her. Wherever you go in England, her influence permeates the air. At a theater club in London, members still drink a mock toast to the chubby queen, whose influence on morality still affects people even today.

To sample the country life

Involve yourself in the rural life, the very heart of England. There's still quite a bit of it left. Dine in an ancient hall with a walk-in fireplace (inglenook), eat off an old blackened oak table, gobble up huge portions of roast beef and Yorkshire pudding, followed by hot deep-dish fruit pies smothered in thick Devonshire cream. At night crawl into a Tudor four-poster and dream of the England of yore. The next day go for a walk through a meadow, down a crooked lane lined with hedges and wild roses, until you eventually find your way to a tiny hamlet and ruined castle, with a tall stone tower and surrounding moat. Later go to one of the nearby inns where you can order a pint of cider in a pewter mug, sit in a 300-year-old settle, and listen to and talk to the villagers.

To be lord or lady of the manor

Burdened with taxes, the descendants of the privileged class are having to rent out their estates to paying guests. Many of the grand homes have been discreetly turned into manor house hotels that usually, for the price of a good seat at a Broadway show, will house you in a spacious room and provide three bountiful meals a day. By all means, take advantage of this unique opportunity to act the lord or lady of the manor—playing croquet on the well-rolled green, riding horseback, attending a hunt ball, fishing for speckled trout, having afternoon tea in a formal garden.

To look into your dark family history

You may be eligible to wear a tartan! Up in Aviemore, a little resort town in Scotland, a computer spews out family histories to inquirers. If you're a MacWhy, MacKnee, MacFun, MacPoke, MacRabbit, MacCash, or a Mac-Goon, you may find some interesting background about your clan. For example, the MacDuffs once boiled an unpopular sheriff into soup and drank him! If you're a MacVanish, you're out of luck. The clan lived up to the promise of its name—and just vanished.

DOLLARWISE—WHAT IT MEANS: This is a guidebook giving specific, practical details (including prices) about the hotels, restaurants, pubs, sightseeing attractions, and nightlife of England and Scotland. First-class to rock-bottom-budget establishments have been documented and described, from the elegant May Fair Hotel in London to a bed-and-breakfast house in an old fishing village in Scotland. Each establishment has been judged by the strict yardstick of value.

The major focus of the book is on the average voyager who'd like to patronize the almost wholly undocumented establishments of England and Scotland—that is, the second-class hotels and some of the better, although less heralded, restaurants where you can often get a superb dinner.

The sights of England and Scotland have been set forth in what we believe is a human, personal, and practical style. In both England and Scotland, the bewildered visitor is faced with a staggering number of attractions from the most catholic collection of art and artifacts in the world (the British Museum), to George Washington's ancestral home, to Anne Hathaway's Cottage of Stratford-upon-Avon, to some of the Scottish castles where Mary Queen of Scots lived during her brief, tragic reign.

What the Dollarwise Guide attempts is to lead the reader through the maze of important sights, such as the Tower of London and Edinburgh Castle, then introduce him or her to a number of lesser known locales, such as the little hamlets, flint churches, and historic houses of East Anglia, perhaps the mellow old towns of the Scottish "Borders." The hours and prices of admission to these attractions have been detailed.

SOME DISCLAIMERS: No restaurant, inn, hotel, guest house, or shop paid to be mentioned in this book. What you read are personal recommendations—in many cases, proprietors never knew their establishments were being investigated.

A word of warning: Unfortunately, prices change, and they rarely go downward, at least not in Britain. The government does not control hotel prices, as is customary in Spain and Italy. Nearly all British hotels are fond of quoting a rate of "from so many pence up," and many establishments simply refuse to quote anything else. The hotelier, anxious about inflation or a sudden tax imposed by the government, doesn't want to commit himself or herself too far in advance to a specific price. However, the "from" rate often—but not always—means the average price you're likely to be charged.

Always, when checking into a hotel, inquire about the price—and agree on it. This policy can save much embarrassment and disappointment when it comes time to settle the tab. In no circumstances can you invariably demand to be charged the price quoted in this book, although every effort has been made to state the accurate tariff as much as it was foreseeable when this guide was published.

This guide is revised every other year, yet even in a book that appears fresh every year it may happen that that cozy little family dining room changes colors, blossoming out with cut-velvet walls and dining tabs that include the decorator's fee and the owner's new Bentley. It may be that some of the people, animals, and settings we've described are no longer there or have been changed beyond recognition.

AN INVITATION TO READERS: Like all the Dollarwise books, *Dollarwise Guide to England and Scotland* hopes to maintain a continuing dialogue between its writers and its readers. All of us share a common aim—to travel as widely and as well as possible, at the best value for our money. And in achieving that goal, your comments and suggestions can be of tremendous help. Therefore, if you come across a particularly appealing hotel, restaurant, store, even sightseeing attraction, please don't keep it to yourself. We'll send free copies of the next edition of *this* book to readers whose suggestions are used. Unfortunately, we cannot send copies of other guides to other countries published in the series, but only the book in which your specific recommendation appears. The solicitation for letters applies not only to new establishments, but to hotels or restaurants already recommended in this guide. The fact that a listing appears in this edition doesn't give it squatter's rights in future publications. If its services have deteriorated, its chef grown stale, its prices risen unfairly, whatever, these failings should be known. Even if you enjoyed every place and found every description accurate—that, too, can cheer many a gray day. Send your comments to Stanley Haggart and Darwin Porter, c/o Frommer/Pasmantier Publishing Corp., 380 Madison Avenue, New York, NY 10017.

THE $15-A-DAY TRAVEL CLUB: In just a few paragraphs, you'll begin your exploration of England and Scotland. But before you do, you may want to learn about a device for saving money on all your trips and travels; we refer

INTRODUCTION 5

to the now widely known $15-a-Day Travel Club, which has gone into its 18th successful year of operation.

The Club was formed at the urging of readers of the $15-a-Day Books and the Dollarwise Guides, many of whom felt that such an organization could bring financial benefits, continuing travel information, and a sense of community to economy-minded travelers in all parts of the world. We thought—and have since learned—that the idea had merit. For by combining the purchasing power of thousands of our readers, we've been able to obtain a wide range of exciting travel benefits—including occasional discounts to members from auto rental agencies, restaurants, sightseeing operators, hotels, and other purveyors of tourist services throughout the United States and abroad.

In keeping with the budget concept, the membership fee is low and is immediately exceeded by the value of your benefits. Upon receipt of U.S. $12 (U.S., Canadian, and Mexican residents), or $14 (other foreign residents) to cover one year's membership, we will send all new members by return mail (book rate) the following items:

(1) The latest edition of any *two* of the following books (please designate in your letter which two books you wish to receive).

Europe on $20 a Day
Australia on $15 & $20 a Day
England and Scotland on $20 a Day
Greece and Yugoslavia on $15 & $20 a Day
Hawaii on $25 a Day
Ireland on $25 a Day
Israel on $20 a Day
Mexico and Guatemala on $15 & $20 a Day
New Zealand on $15 & $20 a Day
Scandinavia on $25 a Day
South America on $15 & $20 a Day
Spain and Morocco (plus the Canary Is.) on $15 & $20 a Day
Washington, D.C. on $25 a Day

Dollarwise Guide to the Caribbean (including Bermuda and the Bahamas)
Dollarwise Guide to Canada
Dollarwise Guide to Egypt
Dollarwise Guide to England and Scotland
Dollarwise Guide to France
Dollarwise Guide to Germany
Dollarwise Guide to Italy
Dollarwise Guide to Portugal (plus Madeira and the Azores)
Dollarwise Guide to California and Las Vegas
Dollarwise Guide to New England
Dollarwise Guide to the Southeast and New Orleans
(Dollarwise Guides discuss accommodations and facilities in all price ranges, with emphasis on the medium-priced.)

The Caribbean Bargain Book
(A one-of-a-kind guide to the "off-season" Caribbean—mid-April to mid-December—and the fabulous resorts that slash their rates from 20% to 60%; includes almost every island group in the Caribbean, and the Bahamas too.)

The Alternative Guide to China
(A unique guide to the latest opportunities for group, individual, and business travel to and around China; includes hotels, restaurants, sights, and shopping; history and culture plus a substantial phrase book section.)

How to Live in Florida on $10,000 a Year
(For the resident or anyone contemplating the move, this book provides all the information needed to live economically but well in the Sunshine State.)

Where to Stay USA
(By the Council on International Educational Exchange, this extraordinary guide is the first to list accommodations in all 50 states that cost anywhere from $2 to $20 per night.)

(2) A copy of **Arthur Frommer's Guide to New York,** a newly revised pocket-size guide to hotels, restaurants, night spots, and sightseeing attractions in all price ranges throughout the New York area.

(3) A one-year subscription to the quarterly Club newsletter—**The Wonderful World of Budget Travel** (about which more below)—which keeps members up-to-date on fast-breaking developments in low-cost travel to all areas of the world.

(4) A voucher entitling you to a $5 discount on any Arthur Frommer International, Inc. tour booked by you through travel agents in the United States and Canada.

(5) Your personal membership card, which, once received, entitles you to purchase through the Club all Arthur Frommer Publications for a third to a half off their regular retail prices during the term of your membership.

Those are the immediate and definite benefits, which we can assure to members of the Club at this time. Further benefits, which it has been our continuing aim to achieve for members, are announced to members in *The Wonderful World of Budget Travel (WWBT).* An eight-page, full-size newspaper, *WWBT* carries such continuing features as "The Traveler's Directory" (a list of members all over the world who are willing to provide hospitality to other members as they pass through their home cities) and "Share-a-Trip" (offers and requests from members for travel companions who can share costs); worldwide travel news and feature stories by our acclaimed expert travel writers; plus tips and articles on specific plans and methods for travel savings.

If you would like to join this hardy band of international budgeteers and participate in its exchange of travel information and hospitality, simply send your name and address, together with your membership fee of $12 (U.S., Canadian, and Mexican residents), or $14 (other foreign residents) in U.S. currency to: $15-a-Day Travel Club, Inc., 380 Madison Avenue, New York, NY 10017. Remember to specify which *two* books in section (1) above you wish to receive in your initial package of members' benefits. Or, if you prefer, use the last page of this book, simply checking off the two books you want and enclosing $12 or $14 in U.S. currency.

Chapter I

GETTING THERE

1. Plane Economics
2. By Ship
3. Traveling Within Britain

A FEW YEARS AGO this chapter was fairly simple to write, because, prior to 1979, airfares were strictly regulated by the International Air Transport Association (IATA) and therefore uniform: if British Airways's round-trip fare from New York to London was $626, let's say, then you could be sure that Pan Am, TWA, Air India, and the rest offered the identical fare.

Since deregulation under the Carter administration, such simplicity and uniformity have disappeared as the airlines have competed fiercely with one another for air traffic. To many destinations, an airline now proposes a fare structure; another airline then files a competing and different fare structure. A process of jockeying occurs which may or may not result in a uniform price structure for all airlines flying to that particular city.

It all adds up to chaos—but often *beneficial* chaos for the alert traveler willing to study and consider all the various alternative fares available. The key to bargain airfares is to shop around.

1. Plane Economics

It's never been cheaper—and more complicated—to fly to London. In what follows we'll try to unravel the current options available by classifying the fares according to their basic function.

Please note that all fares appearing on these pages are those available at press time in autumn 1980 and are subject to change and/or government approval. Doublecheck all fares with the airlines or your travel agent.

LEAST EXPENSIVE "REGULAR" FARES: Currently your cheapest options with the regular airlines fall into two categories

Standby Fares

Every airline flying to London offers standby fares sold at the airport on the day of departure, and subject to availability. You'll have to chance (in many cases, you can call the airline the night before to find out what those chances are) waiting hours to find out whether you're confirmed, and being "stranded" for one to several days on the return leg of your trip.

If you're emotionally ready to hazard those risks and your travel plans are flexible enough, then you can take advantage of the lowest "regular" fares

8 □ DOLLARWISE GUIDE TO ENGLAND AND SCOTLAND

available. British Airways offers standby seats between New York and London at a roundtrip price of $392 in basic season, $418 peak season (May 15 through September 14). The same standby opportunities to London are available on Delta from Atlanta for $460 roundtrip in basic and $540 in peak season; on Braniff from Dallas for $462 and $562 respectively.

Budget Fares

Introduced by Pan Am and matched by several airlines, these can be less expensive—from some cities—than even a standby fare; Pan Am offers standby and budget fares at identical prices. And what you do is, simply, designate at least 21 days in advance the week when you wish to travel to London. At least seven to ten days in advance of departure, the airline will then assign you to a particular date and flight within that week. You later repeat the process in England for your return flight.

Roundtrip budget fares are as follows, low and high season respectively, between the following sample U.S. cities and London: New York, $394 and $460 (via Pan Am); Dallas, $462 and $566 (via Braniff); Atlanta $422 and $530 (via Delta).

Super-Apex and Apex Fares

The most heavily used fare to London is the super-apex, known also (by British Airways) as the Dollar Stretcher. It's valid for a stay abroad of from seven days to six months, must be purchased at least 21 days in advance of your outbound flight to London, and, with slight variations among the airlines, is priced from New York roundtrip to London at $409 in low winter (November and February), $429 in winter (December, January, March, April), $469 low shoulder (September 15 to October 31), $549 high shoulder (May, September 1–14), and $599 peak (June, July, August).

What if all super-apex seats are sold out (their capacity being limited)? You then ask for just plain apex, priced at from $40 to $50 above super-apex levels; apart from price, their terms and conditions are identical.

THE EXPENSIVE FARES: If you can't take advantage of any of the above fares, which should be unlikely, here are the regular economy, Club, first-class, and Concorde fares offered by British Airways between New York and London: economy $754 basic, $890 peak; Club $910 basic, $1110 peak; first class, $2188; Concorde $2522—the last two year-round.

THE CHOICE OF AIRLINE: Since all the major international airlines other than Icelandic charge approximately the same fares, why not go to England or Scotland aboard the British airline, **British Airways?** It boasts an outstanding record for reliability and comfort; and, most important, its personnel are British. Flying with them is like a preview of your British vacation—or an extension of your holiday, as the case may be.

As soon as you step aboard a British Airways plane, you'll encounter the famed British courtesy, the good humor and calm intelligence, and the painstaking attention to your comfort and needs that characterize the hotel and restaurant selections that appear later in this guide. All of this makes the transatlantic flight as exciting and enjoyable as your later adventures on land.

This sense of graciousness isn't confined just to first-class, where the steward seemingly becomes your private butler ("Yes, Madame, it's my pleasure," you hear when the roast beef is carved by your seat). Throughout the trip, important extras are brought to your seat such as alcoholic or soft drinks, newspapers, magazines, even a writing portfolio. Older guests are tucked in—presented, if they so desire, with soft slippers and an extra cushion.

En route to England, first-time visitors can be introduced to the English ritual of afternoon tea, with a properly steeped brew, open-faced sandwiches, and cake. First-class meals are luxurious all the way, beginning with a *"ferris wheel"* of hors d'oeuvres that invariably includes caviar, then a selection of main dishes, perhaps partridge or curried chicken with delectable condiments —topped off with other extras. Meals in Club and economy class aren't to be belittled either—and include, for example, smoked Scotch salmon for an appetizer, with many English specialties, such as grilled lamb cutlets, game pie, or "Lancashire hot pot."

The second major reason for flying British Airways is the jet plane itself. You can choose the Concorde, 747, L1011, 707, or the VC10, all Rolls Royce powered. The latter is called the "velvet-voiced jet," as its motors are at the rear, the noise literally left behind. The motors are so well built they could properly function for 10½ hours a day for 365 days a year, but British Airways insists on a total overhaul after every 975 flying hours. Of course, you may wish to book a seat on "the largest airplane ever designed for commercial service," the Boeing 747, complete with upper-deck cocktail lounge for first-class passengers.

Another major advantage of flying via British Airways: it is the only carrier with daily service from the U.S. and Canada to Scotland and the Midlands (the planes on these flights land at Prestwick and Manchester). Many budget-minded tourists like to take advantage of the less expensive fares to these cities, and then tour their way down to London. Prestwick, of course, is a perfect point for starting such a tour, and it is also a gateway to Northern Ireland. Manchester is, among other things, the natural gateway to Wales. British Airways planes take off from New York City, Boston, Chicago, Detroit, Miami, San Francisco, Los Angeles, Philadelphia, Washington, D.C., Seattle, Anchorage, Montreal, and Toronto; naturally, they offer the greatest number of flights to the United Kingdom of any airline.

There are British Airways offices in cities throughout the United States, and there are thousands of travel agents as well, who are authorized to book you on a flight. Needless to say, the British Airways offices, and their staffs, are unusually well-qualified to discuss touring in England and to make whatever arrangements—hotels, sightseeing, escorted bus trips, and the like—you need.

OTHER POSSIBILITIES: Sir Freddie Laker is still forging ahead with his cut rate airfares. Laker Airways now flies from three destinations in the U.S.—New York, Los Angeles, and Miami—to London's Gatwick Airport. Three tiers of service are offered. First there is the Skytrain Standard service, which is the original standby concept—if today's flights are sold out, seats may be booked for the next available flight, and meals are extra. Economy service offers unrestricted sales and reservations anytime. Excursion service requires 21-day *roundtrip* advance purchase, with a minimum stay of seven days. For standard and economy service (except from Miami), peak season runs from May 15 to September 14, off-peak from September 15 to May 14. Excursion service prices change more often; therefore in the table below we give the price *ranges* for the equivalent periods.

Roundtrip fares to London are:

	Standard	Economy	Excursion
From New York			
Peak	$418	$660	$539–$589
(up to 3 flights daily)			
Off-Peak	374	572	$399–$459
(1/2 flights daily)			
From Los Angeles			
Peak	572	1012	$659–$712
(up to 2 flights daily)			
Off-Peak	506	880	$529–$609
(1 flight daily)			
From Miami			
Peak	435	618	$569–$599
(June 16-Sept. 14)			
Off-Peak	368	518	$499–$569
(Sept. 15-June 15)			
(1 flight daily year-round)			

For Standard Service information call 212/459-7323 or 212/995-2113 in New York; 213/646-9650 in Los Angeles; 305/871-4595 in Miami. For all other information call 212/459-6092 or 800/221-0374 (New York); 213/646-9600 (Los Angeles); 305/871-5450 (Miami).

World Airways has now joined the carriers flying routes from all over the U.S. to Britain: Pan Am, TWA, Braniff, Delta, National, Northwestern, Air India, and El Al. Check with your travel agent for the airline which flies the most direct and cheapest route.

2. By Ship

Traveling to England by ship is only for those who crave a sea experience —either on a luxury liner, with resort-level facilities, or else on a more relaxed, time-consuming freighter. For traveling by air is both quicker and cheaper.

Here is a brief description of some of the major services offered from the Atlantic seaboard to various ports in England (most often Southampton, where you'll pay a small debarkation fee):

Cunard Line, 555 Fifth Ave., New York, NY 10017 (tel. 212/880-7500), boasts the *Queen Elizabeth 2* as its flagship—self-styled, quite accurately, as "the most advanced ship of the age." It is the only ocean liner providing regular transatlantic service—23 sailings from April to November—between New York and Cherbourg, France, and Southampton, England. Designed for super cruises, the *Queen Elizabeth 2* is reaching a younger market, those leery of the traditional liner-type crossing. Hence, you'll find four swimming pools, a sauna, nightclubs, a theater with a balcony, an art gallery, cinemas, even chic boutiques.

The vessel is a two-class ship, with both first and transatlantic classes. Each class has a number of public rooms for its exclusive use. However, most public rooms, such as the Casino, are used in common.

Throughout the year lively and fascinating entertainment is provided aboard. Called "Festival of Life," a series introduces you to such personalities as Lauren Bacall, Lillian Gish, or Clive Barnes.

The prices quoted are per person, but based on double occupancy. In transatlantic class, the fares are from $895 in thrift season, $995 in intermediate, and $1050 in high season. Fares include a one-way air ticket in the opposite direction, via British Airways. Round-trip excursion rates of up to 50% are available. Youth fare is $355.

New tours include the "Explorer's Special," which is a week's vacation combining a *QE2* crossing and a weekend in London or Paris. Fares are from $949.

In addition, discount programs include special excursions throughout the year. These complicated and often changing dates will be provided by writing Cunard or else dealing directly with your travel agent.

3. Traveling Within Britain

BY TRAIN: There is something magical about traveling on a train in Britain. You sit in comfortable compartments, on upholstered seats, next to the reserved and well-dressed British; you're served your meal in the dining car like an aristocrat; and the entire experience can become a relaxing interlude.

You should, of course, be warned that your Eurailpass is not valid on trains in Great Britain. But the cost of rail travel in England, Scotland, Northern Ireland, and Wales can be quite low—particularly if you take advantage of certain cost-saving travel plans, some of which can only be purchased in North America, before leaving for Great Britain.

BritRail Pass

This pass gives unlimited rail travel in England, Scotland, and Wales, and is valid on all British Rail routes, on Lake Windermere steamers, and on Sealink ferry services to the Isle of Wight. It is not valid on ships between Great Britain and the continent, the Channel Islands, or Ireland. A seven-day **economy class pass**, as of 1980, cost $85 for one person, rising to $120 in first class, for U.S. travelers. Canadians, on the same arrangement, pay $96 in economy, $140 in first class. Children under 3 years of age travel free, and children from 3 to 14 pay approximately half fare. BritRail also offers a **Youth Pass** to people ages 14 through 22. On this arrangement, U.S. citizens pay $75 for a seven-day pass while Canadians are charged $86. On the Youth Pass ticket, seats are in the economy section only.

In addition, a **Senior Citizen pass** is offered to those aged 65 or more. For the economy rate, those eligible can travel in first-class accommodations on trains where this passage is available.

BritRail and Youth Passes cannot be obtained in Britain, but should be secured before leaving North America either through travel agents or by writing or visiting BritRail Travel International, 630 Third Ave., New York, NY 10017; 510 West Sixth St., Los Angeles, CA 90014; or 333 North Michigan Ave., Chicago, IL 60601. Canadians can write to BritRail Travel International, 55 Eglinton Ave., East Toronto M4P 1G8, ON; or 409 Granville St., Vancouver V6C 1T2, BC.

BritRail Passes do not have to be predated. Validate your pass at any British Rail station when you start your first rail journey.

Britrail Seapass—Continent

In general terms, purchasers of a BritRail Pass wishing to travel one way or round trip between Britain and Ireland and Britain and continental Europe by Sealink services can purchase an extension of their BritRail Pass carrying

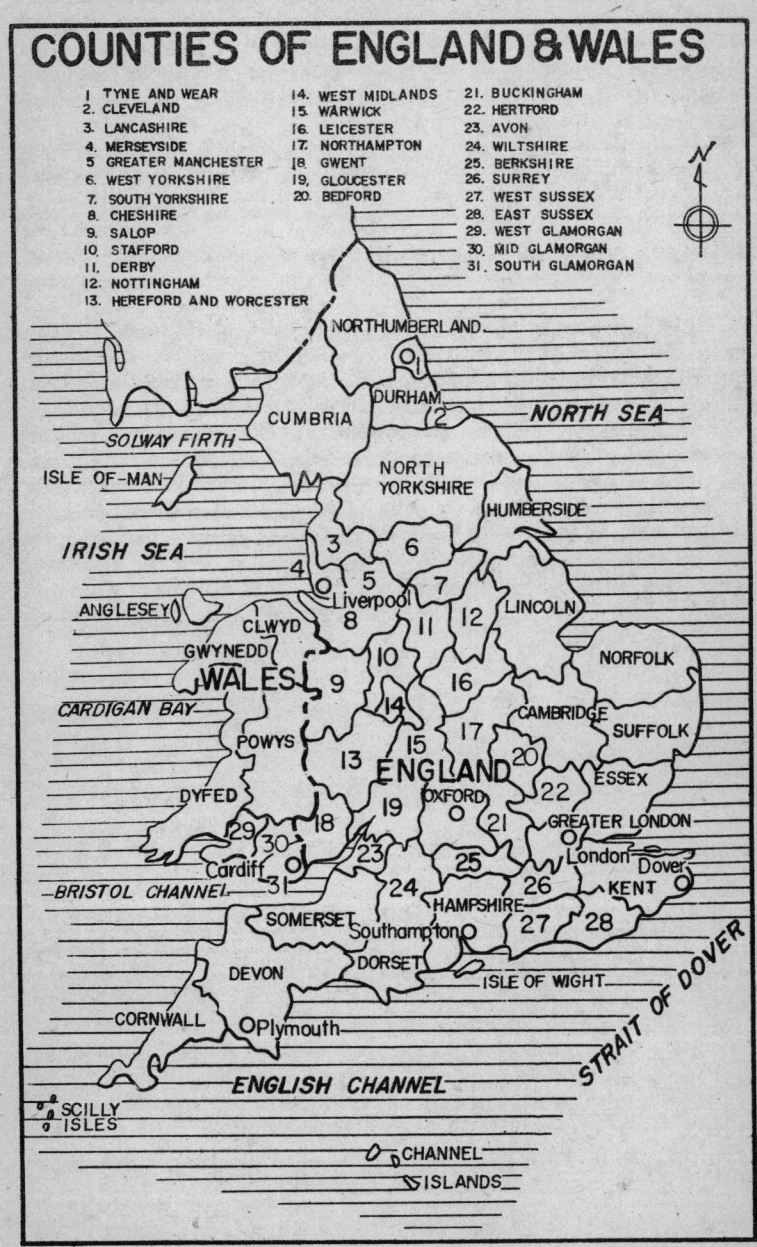

one or two coupons, according to requirements. The one-way fare to continental Europe, for example, is $23.80, and if a round-trip is required, then two coupons are made available for $47.60. In the case of Ireland, equivalent amounts of $35 and $70 are required. However, one-way trips can be purchased for either route—that is, Ireland to Britain for $35 one way, and then on into Europe for $23 one way.

Furthermore, if the appropriate supplement is paid, the coupons are valid for all services operated by Sealink or Seaspeed, and are not tied to the validity of the associated BritRail Pass. For example, a traveler may arrive in Ireland, use one coupon for the journey to London, stay several days, validate the BritRail Pass and travel for its duration, and then return to London for another period of time before traveling from London to a continental European port.

Special Bargain Fares

British Rail from time to time offers special round-trip fares for optional travel and weekend travel, which may only be purchased in Great Britain. Because of the changing nature of these fares and facilities, it is not possible to give advance information about them to travelers from abroad. Information can be obtained from travel agents and British Rail stations in Great Britain.

If you're in London, and want more information on transportation rates, schedules, or facilities, go to the **British Rail Travel Centre** on Lower Regent Street, only a few minutes' walk from Piccadilly Circus. You can also make reservations and purchase rail tickets there and at British Rail Travel Centres at Oxford Street, Victoria Street, the Strand, King William Street, Heathrow Airport, and the main London stations.

CAR RENTALS: No doubt about it, though—the best way to see the real England and Scotland is to travel by car. It gives you the freedom to visit that out-of-the-way antique shop that doesn't know about tourist prices, and to picnic wherever you like. And for two or more persons, economy can be a major advantage of traveling by car.

There are many car-rental services available in England and Scotland, including **Hertz, National, Kemwel,** and **Avis.** There are also dozens of British-owned car-rental firms, most of them charging rates to match their American competitors.

For our purposes, an ideal car-rental firm is **E & P Self-Drive Limited,** Sloane Avenue Mansions Garage, Sloane Avenue, S.W.3 (tel. 581-2255). It offers high-quality, well-serviced vehicles at tariffs considerably cheaper than the better known car-rental firms. The highest tariffs are charged from April 1 to November 30. At that time, the least expensive car is £9 ($20.70) per day, or £51 ($117.30) per week. Larger cars go for anywhere from £13.50 ($31.05) to £25 ($57.50) per day, or £75 ($172.50) per week. Rates do not include insurance or VAT, but all mileage is free. Clients must be more than 21 years old, and the estimated cost of the rental is required at the beginning. It's most important to *reserve in advance,* and all major credit cards are accepted. The company doesn't maintain an (expensive) office at the airports, but you can be picked up or returned to London's Heathrow Airport for a charge of £12 ($27.50), plus VAT. This same procedure applies to London's Gatwick Airport, where the pickup or delivery fee is £15 ($34.50), plus VAT.

Unless you are an experienced operator of right-hand-drive cars on left-hand-drive roads, E & P personnel will go with you for a drive around the block to instruct you in possible problems of making the changeover, a helpful gesture.

Driving Requirements

To drive a car in Britain, your passport and your own driver's license must be presented along with your deposit; no special British license is needed. The prudent driver will secure a copy of the *British Highway Code,* available from almost any stationer or news agent.

Although not mandatory, a membership in one of the two major auto clubs in England can be helpful: the **Automobile Association** and the **Royal Automobile Club.** The headquarters of the AA are at Fanum House, Basingstoke, Hampshire (tel. Basingstoke 20123); the RAC offices are at 83 Pall Mall, London, S.W.1 5HW (tel. 01/839-7050). Membership in one of these clubs is usually handled by the agent from whom you rent your car. Upon joining, you'll be given a key to the many telephone boxes you see along the road, so that you can phone for help in an emergency.

Motorized Caravan Rentals

This is an excellent way to defray costs and tour the countryside.

Penta Motorhomes, Bridge Road, Chertsey, Surrey KT16 8JX (tel. Chertsey 66821), rents five- and six-berth motorhomes that are fully stocked with refrigerators, cutlery, and cookers, as well as crockery, cooking utensils, camping gas, a shower, and a flushing toilet. Delivery charges are £15 ($34.50) to the various London airports (except free on rentals of more than 14 days, 7 days for Heathrow). In high season, a motorhome costs £195 ($448.50) per week. Various discounts are granted for long or off-season rentals. A deposit of £40 ($92) is required on booking, and full payment before the beginning of the rental. That deposit is refunded on completion if the vehicle is undamaged, clean, and delivered on time.

The company also rents out sleeper motor caravans with an elevating roof at £165 ($379.50) per week—the same conditions. The vehicles appear to be kept in good condition, considering the heavy wear and tear they suffer. In addition, the company also rents out Leyland and Ford minibuses—12 seats at £105 ($241.50) per week on an unlimited-mileage basis. A 15-seater costs £145 ($333.50). This may be good to know about, as almost all other car-rental firms have ceased renting minibuses, because of the heavy wear on the vehicles and their high cost of replacement.

Godfrey Davis, Davis House, Wilton Road, S.W.1 (tel. 828-7700), rents Ford Motorhomes with two full-size doubles and a child's bunk which are fully equipped with hot and cold water plus a shower. They cost from £100 ($230) per week in low season, rising to £210 ($483) per week in high season, including unlimited mileage. For those who plan to cover part of their travels by train and part by car, Godfrey Davis is the best equipped, having in excess of 70 offices at rail stations and more than 100 other locations, including airports. They offer such bargains as a weekend cost-cutter when a small Ford rents for £25.95 ($59.69), plus VAT, from Friday at 5 p.m. to Monday at 9 a.m. with 500 miles free. Excess miles are 7p (16¢) a mile. Cost-cutters are from set locations only.

BUSES IN ENGLAND: For the traveler who wants to see the country as even a train cannot reveal it, but who can't afford to rent a car, the old, reliable, and inexpensive (half the cost of railway fares) bus offers a fine form of transportation. While the trains do go everywhere, passing through towns and villages, they rarely bring you into contact with country life, and they almost never carry you across the high (main) streets of the villages, as the buses do. Moreover, distances between towns in England are usually short, so your chances of tiring are lessened. Every remote village is reachable by a bus.

The express motorcoach network covers the greater part of Britain. It links villages, towns, and cities with frequent schedules, convenient timetables, and efficient operation in all seasons. Most places located off the main route can be easily reached by stopping and switching to a local bus. Fares are relatively cheap, making travel on the express motorcoach network economical.

The departure point from London for most of the bus lines is **Victoria Coach Station,** which is a block up from Victoria Railroad Station. You'll be well advised to have reservations for the express buses; the locals can usually be boarded on the spot.

Coach Master

This bargain pass is rather like the BritRail pass, but it offers unlimited travel for a specified period on Britain's express coach network. You can stop wherever you wish for as long as you like on any journey. The Coach Master is issued for periods of 8, 15, 22, or 29 days. If you buy at least a 15-day ticket, you're entitled to use the direct express services between Edinburgh and London. This latter trip was highly endorsed by reader Ron Taylor of Ontario, Canada. "It saves you a night's hotel," he writes, "and the buses are quiet, clean, comfortable, the drivers friendly and considerate. Large windows let you look out and see dawn over the Border Country." It also covers about 40 local excursions from London, including Canterbury, Cambridge, Windsor Castle, Blenheim Palace, and the Shakespeare Country. The Coach Master pass should be bought at a travel agency before you go, but it can be bought in London by presenting your passport at the Victoria Coach Station, Buckingham Palace Road, London, SW1W 9TP.

Green Line Buses

For trips to the immediate suburbs of London, and the towns nearby, you needn't go to Victoria Coach Station, however. Most of the spots are serviced by the Green Line Coaches, which you can board throughout the city wherever you see green bus signs. To the south, these buses go as far as Reigate, Westerham, East Grinstead, and Tunbridge Wells, all 30 to 40 miles from the center of London. To the north, they go as far as Dunstable, Luton, Hitchin, or Bishops Stortford—all around 20 to 25 miles from Piccadilly Circus. To the west, they reach Guildford, High Wycombe, Windsor, and Aylesbury, within 20 to 40 miles from London. And to the east, they go to Brentwood, Grays, or Gravesend, approximately 15 to 26 miles from the center of London.

A **Golden Rover Ticket** costs £1.70 ($3.91) per person, purchased as you board your first bus. Pick up a map of the system to plan your journey. An **Outback Ticket,** off-peak day return, will save up to 40% on two tickets.

For more precise information on the Green Line routes, fares, and schedules, write to the **London Country Bus Service Ltd.,** Bell Street, Reigate, Surrey, RH2 7LE (tel. Reigate 4-2411).

Country Buses

The Country Bus Lines ring the heart of London. They never go into the center of London itself, although they hook up with the routes of the red buses and the Green Line Coaches which do. You can get free maps of Country Buses from London Country Bus Services Ltd., Bell Street, Reigate, Surrey (see above). For more information about this form of touring, refer to "One-Day Trips from London," Chapter IV.

MOTORCYCLES: These are real money savers in this land of steep gas prices, if you don't mind getting drenched occasionally. **Rent-A-Scooter**, 7 Broadwell Parade, Broadhurst Gardens, N.W.6 (tel. 624-8491 and 328-4060; nearest underground, West Hampstead), has Hondas and gives free unlimited mileage, plus free safety helmets and free membership in the Royal Automobile Club which gives roadside assistance anywhere in the British Isles. These cycles go up to 200 miles per gallon. The one-seater Honda Moped rents for £4.50 ($10.35) per day, or £22 ($50.60) per week. More expensive Hondas can cost from £13.55 ($31.17) per day. A valid license endorsed for motorcycles is required for every vehicle except a Honda Moped, for which only a car license is necessary. Advance reservations are advised.

DAY CRUISES ON THE THAMES: This is a venture for those who have visited London before, and want to spend a day—or even a week—cruising the Thames. The idea is to show overseas visitors a side of England they might not otherwise see.

The craft used are slipper-stern riverday launches, designed especially for their elegance and grace. They are privately owned, and this is not an advertised hire service. The boats have awnings in case of rain.

Passengers are collected from their London hotel in the morning by car and driven to Runnymede where they embark. There they cruise downstream through Runnymede Fields past Magna Carta Island, where King John is reputed to have signed the famous document. Then they turn upstream and cruise through Windsor, under the shadow of the castle, Eton College, and Bray, to Maidenhead, so popular in Edwardian times with young sportsmen and their ladies.

Lunch is taken either as a picnic while moored in some quiet backwater or else in a riverside hotel or pub. At Maidenhead, Skindles Hotel grounds run down to the river, making it a popular stopping-off place.

Passengers then turn downstream again during the afternoon, disembarking at Windsor Town Quay within yards of the railway station. From there, the journey back to London is quick, cheap, and easy.

The cost for up to four people is $60 (U.S.), increasing to $80 for five to eight people. A picnic lunch is provided at an extra cost of £4 ($9.20) per person.

Extended cruises can be arranged to suit the time available and the passengers' inclination. The journey from Oxford to Hampton Court takes three or four days, but shorter or longer cruises can be planned. They are carefully arranged so that not more than four or five hours a day are spent traveling. There is time for everyone to go ashore and explore riverside towns and villages, shop for antiques, walk in the fields, or talk to the locals in pubs.

Overnight accommodation must be arranged in advance, as many of the riverside hotels are small, although they do provide accommodations with private facilities. All are personally selected and offer good food with a fine standard of accommodation. Baggage is transferred between hotels by taxi, as there is no room for cabin trunks in the dayboats.

Passengers are transferred from and to London at the start and finish of the cruise. They are expected to pay their own overnight expenses and all meals during the day.

These extended cruises cost $80 per day for up to six persons, excluding all meals and accommodations.

Advance booking is essential. Write to **Peter J.E. Barnes,** Willow Point, Friary Island, Wraysbury Staines, Middlesex TW19 5JR (tel. Wraysbury 983-2259).

SELF-DRIVE HOUSEBOATS AND HOTEL BOATS: At various places on the Thames, it's possible to rent a self-drive houseboat (the English call them river cruisers). Using this unique form of sightseeing—ideal for a family—you can visit Hampton Court, Windsor Castle, the city of Oxford, and stop off at attractive riverside towns, known for their antique shops. The Thames Valley abounds in restaurants and pubs. The facilities on these boats vary, but you can usually expect to find a gas cooker with an oven, hot and cold water, cooking utensils and cutlery, a refrigerator, blankets and pillows, and chemical toilets. The larger boats are also equipped with showers. Navigational aids, other than a map of the river, aren't needed.

Houseboats are also available on the Norfolk Broads and on much of the network of canals covering the country.

The bulk of the self-drive cruisers on the Thames, and on the canal network throughout the country, are available through two central booking agencies. They are: **Boat Enquiries,** 7 Walton Well Rd., Oxford, OX2 6ED; and **Hoseasons Holidays,** Sunway House, Lowestoft, Suffolk, NR32 3LT. Hoseasons, the larger of the agencies offering a wide choice of boats, has various telephone numbers for whichever part of the system you want to hire a boat in. Try Lowestoft 0502/66622. A four-berth cruiser on the Thames costs from £85 ($195.50) to £260 ($598) in high season, but do inquire around as there are many large and small boats available, and at varying prices, depending on the season.

When you book, you can get a plan of the boat you're to have and a description of its facilities—many have showers, even TV if you wish and all contain hot and cold running water, toilets, and central heating. In addition, the boatyard will often arrange (upon request) a supply of victuals for your breakfast and other meals. All are fully equipped with bed and table linen, dishcloths, cutlery, cooking utensils, and crockery.

Becoming more popular these days—particularly on canals where self-drive hirers have to work the locks themselves—are hotel boats, beautifully decorated canal barges with snug but basic cabins, local fare, and congenial company. They are run by people who know their waterways, and this is an ideal way of seeing a good deal of the country totally lost to the motorist or coach-tourist. Full details are available upon application, of course.

Actief is a converted Dutch barge with a private shower and toilet for each cabin. The barge spent most of her 70 years carrying cargo on the waterways of Europe before being brought to England and converted by Jonathan Parratt into the sort of hotel boat in which he himself liked to travel. He and his wife Kate have the backing of most of the river people and have carefully arranged moorings for themselves at the vital stopping places along the river. They are now the only ones on the river who operate their own boat and eat their own delightfully cooked food.

In the spacious lounge and dining saloon, pictures of the Thames by Michael Vicary adorn the walls. Two long wooden tables with benches and cane-backed chairs accommodate visitors. You'll also find an antique sofa and a classical roll-top desk, plus plenty of fresh flowers and a vast selection of books and taped music. Wall-to-wall carpeting and paneled walls of contrasting pine and mahogany give a warm, luxurious, well-kept air. Regency print curtains frame the large windows. At the end of the saloon there is a small, well-stocked bar. Out through the door is a sundeck with plenty more seats and tables with bright umbrellas—abundant room for the dozen passengers carried. Down a staircase from the saloon are the cabins, neat and compact with comfortable bunk beds, toilet, shower, and washbasin, 240-volt shaver points, and flyscreens in each cabin to protect you from mosquitoes.

Actief makes one leisurely voyage from Oxford to Kingston and back each month, and you can join her for 3, 6, 9, or 12 days. It takes 12 days to make the entire round trip. A small dinghy is carried for excursions up peaceful backwaters and around little islands and bicycles for trips to riverside villages and pubs. Excursions are also arranged to the oldest mill on the river, a vineyard, a trout farm, to the City of Oxford, and other interesting places. The upper reaches are rural England at its best, and from Henley down to Kingston is more commercial, with large, elegant houses with gardens sweeping down to the river between riverside towns where you can shop and wander.

Meals are a highlight of the voyage. Kate, a Cordon Bleu-trained chef, and her team provide sumptuous food. There is also a good selection of wines on board.

On a three-day cruise, the single rate is £162 ($372.60), the cost increasing to £139 ($319.70) in a twin or double. Tariffs quoted are per-person rates, and include VAT. The only other extras are purchases from the bar. Tickets are free for the theater at Windsor, one of the best repertory theaters in the country. Children under 14 and animals cannot be accommodated. For further information and reservations, write to **Actief Barge Cruising Holidays,** Hilton House, Norwood Lane, Meopham, Gravesend DA13 OYE (tel. Meopham 0474/812-171).

Those who do not have three days to spare can join *Actief* (subject to availability) for a 24-hour cruise by getting in touch with the booking office when they arrive in London and not more than seven days in advance. Full instructions on where the boat will be and how to get there will be given; passengers must pay their own rail or road costs to join her. You find your own way to Windsor Riverside Station by train or other means, and there a car will collect you and take you wherever the barge is.

PLANNING YOUR ITINERARY: If you require or prefer assistance in planning your itinerary for your self-drive tour of England or Scotland, a useful and, from all reports, popular service is offered by **Peter J.E. Barnes** who for many years has assisted many of the world's top travel writers and journalists in their researches throughout the land.

Mr. Barnes decided to use his knowledge to help overseas visitors get to know parts of his country that they might not otherwise think of visiting and will prepare an individual itinerary according to the number of days you have at your disposal and the sort of things you like to see and do—stately homes, ruined castles, churches and cathedrals, or just plain countryside or seaside resorts. It helps, too, if you tell him of the things you've seen before or don't want to see.

TRAVELING WITHIN BRITAIN 19

All you have to do is send him a letter with the outline of your plans, plus your check for £10 ($23) for seven days and £1 ($2.30) per day thereafter. If payment is not made in sterling, add £3 ($6.90) to cover clearance and make sure that the current rate of exchange is used, as these are rock-bottom prices. The itinerary will be mailed back to you or delivered to your London hotel. Mr. Barnes will make recommendations on places to stay each night, but unfortunately he is unable to make reservations in budget accommodations, as they frequently require deposits on advance bookings. However, on your acceptance of the itinerary, preliminary reservations for you to confirm can be made in nonbudget hotels at a cost of 50p ($1.15) per reservation. Write early, as all this takes time. Each route is prepared individually.

Also, Mr. Barnes will meet you at the airport on your arrival and take you to your London hotel. The rate for up to three persons is £15 ($34.50) from Heathrow, £28.50 ($65.55) from Gatwick. Even if your plane is delayed, he will still be there to meet you, but you may have to pay a little more for his waiting time.

For a party up to three persons, he will conduct full-day guided tours of Oxford, Windsor, Cambridge, or Canterbury at a cost of £45 ($103.50) daily. For Stratford-upon-Avon, Salisbury, and Stonehenge, the charge is £66 ($151.80) daily.

Mr. Barnes also does a few special tours which he arranges and conducts personally during, say, two or three weeks and covering the major sights of England, Scotland, and Wales. The main advantage of this is that you get to see the places you want to see, at your own pace. All overnight accommodations are at your own expense but will be arranged in advance according to your budget and requirements. The cost for seven people, for example, comes to about £62 ($142.60) per person per week for transportation and Mr. Barnes's personal services. Hotels, admission charges, meals, and the like are extra. The snag is that you must make up your own party and select your own traveling companions.

For more information, write to Peter J.E. Barnes, Willow Point, Friary Island, Wraysbury, Staines, Middlesex TW19 5JR (tel. Wraysbury 983-2259).

Chapter II

LONDON: HOTELS FOR EVERY BUDGET

1. Deluxe Hotels
2. St. James's
3. Piccadilly Circus
4. The Strand and Covent Garden
5. Westminster
6. Chelsea
7. Belgravia and Knightsbridge
8. Kensington, South Kensington, and Earl's Court
9. Bayswater
10. Paddington and Little Venice
11. St. Marylebone
12. Mayfair
13. Bloomsbury
14. Euston Station and King's Cross
15. On the Fringe
16. Alternatives to Hotels

LONDON IS A HYBRID, a gathering place for people from the far corners of a once-great Empire. Both the country gentry and the blue-collar worker from the provinces visit London somewhat in the mood of going abroad.

The true Londoner—usually from the East End—is called a Cockney, the name for a person born within the sound of the Bow Bells, the chimes of a church in Cheapside. But the city is also the home of the well-bred English lady who has had to sell her family estate of 400 years and take meager lodgings in Earl's Court; of the expatriate Hollywood actress living in elegance in a Georgian town house; of the islander from Jamaica who comes seeking a new life and ends up collecting fares on one of London's red double-decker buses; of the young playwright from Liverpool whose art reflects the outlook of the working class.

Cosmopolitan or not, Europe's largest city is still like a great wheel, with Piccadilly Circus at the hub and dozens of communities branching out from it. Since London is such a conglomeration of sections—each having its own life (hotels, restaurants, pubs)—the first-time visitor may be intimidated until he gets the hang of it. In this chapter, we'll concentrate on the so-called West End, although nobody has been able to come up with a satisfactory explanation as to what that entails. For the most part, a visitor will live and eat in the West End, except when he or she ventures into the old and historic part of London known as "The City," or goes on a tour to the Tower of London, or seeks lodgings in the remote villages such as Hampstead Heath.

The East End—the docks, the homes of the Cockney working class, the commercial and industrial districts—is rarely visited by tourists, except the more adventurous travelers bent on discovering the true London.

A LIVABLE METROPOLIS: The government has moved strongly against pollution. For example, residents can't burn anything but smokeless fuel. The legendary smog that hung over the city is gone. When a trout was caught in the Thames, it made headlines in the world press. Nostalgia buffs miss the fogs, but eight million Londoners are getting 50% more winter sunshine than they used to.

In this day of energy crisis and inflation, London has many problems she's yet to tackle. But she has made inroads to create a better city in which to live.

She's wrinkled with age and was severely scarred by the war, but her presence is impressive. Tradition is maintained in the face of world change nd upheaval. Mutton-chopped veterans of World War I still exist—hiding behind the Dickensian, dark-mahogany walls of their gentlemen's clubs, poring over the memoirs of long-forgotten generals.

But they are clichés. London today is filled with vital people, both young and old, pursuing their interests. Gambling clubs, discos, strip shows, and experimental theater make London an adventure all night long, as art galleries, museums, curiosity shops, and historic monuments fill the day.

THE HOTEL OUTLOOK: The hotel picture has changed drastically since the 19th century, when the Hotel Victoria had only four bathrooms for its 500 guests! London now offers accommodations to satisfy all purposes, tastes, and pocketbooks—ranging from the deluxe suites required by the late King Saud and his entourage (his bed-and-breakfast charge, £500 a night) to army cots that rent to students in hostels for $3 a night.

One or two hotels sprout up every year, and others are on the drawing boards. For too long London hotels seemed lost in the days of Victoria (many still are). Now, increased pressure from overseas has brought about a discernible upgrading. Of course, in the name of progress, Edwardian architectural features have often given way to the worst and most impersonal of modern; and showers (even bedrooms) are placed in broom closets best left to serve their original functions. Nevertheless, a hotel revolution is in the air, as evidenced by low-budget town-house hotels now forced to install central heating.

Before launching into actual recommendations, we should issue a . . .

Warning: July and August are the vacation months in England, when nearly two-thirds of the population—every Jaguar maker, Liverpudlian dockworker, and Manchester textile worker—strikes out for a long-awaited holiday. Many head for the capital itself, further exacerbating what has become a crowded hotel situation. Every room is rented out to make way for the human tide of English, along with the colonials, the Yanks, the Canadians, the Australians, and the New Zealanders.

LONDON: HOTELS 23

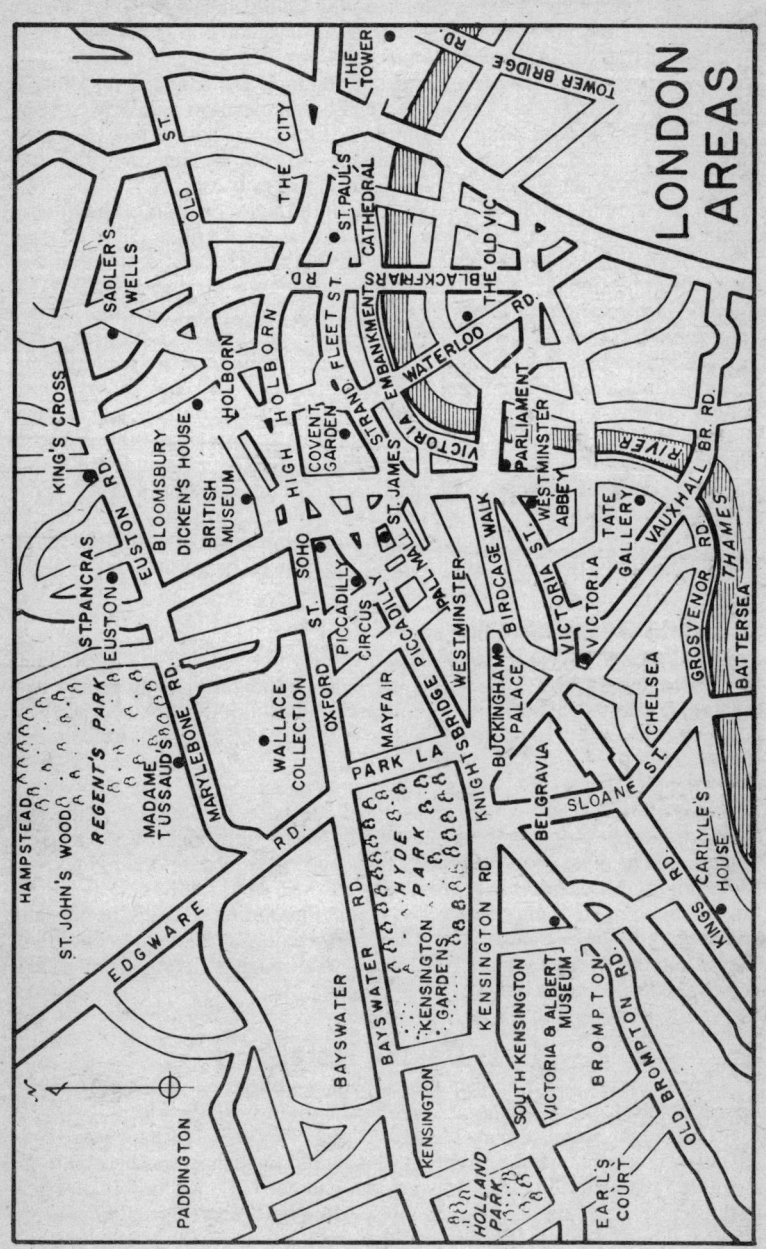

When the holidays are over, the season in London begins, lasting through October. Even in September and October, as in June, hotels are tight—although nothing like they are in the peak summer months. It is recommended that you nail down a reservation before arriving in London. If you're a personal shopper who doesn't like to book a blind date, then by all means arrive early to begin your search for a room. Many of the West End hotels have a few vacancies, even in peak season, between 9 a.m. and 11 a.m., but by noon they are often packed solidly again with fresh arrivals from London Airport.

In the sections to follow, we'll explore all the major districts of the English capital of interest to tourists. But first we'll devote our attention to the pressing problem of finding a room—be it the Oliver Messel Suite at "The Dorch," or a beautifully decorated, comfortable guest house—privately owned—near Kensington Gardens and Hyde Park, charging about $15 a night for a big bed and a large English breakfast with "all the works."

All hotels, motels, inns, and guest houses in Britain, with four bedrooms or more (including self-catering accommodations), are required to display notices showing minimum and maximum overnight charges. The notice must be displayed in a prominent position in the reception area or at the entrance. The prices shown *must* include any service charge and *may* include VAT, and it must be made clear whether or not these items are included. If VAT is not included, then it must be shown separately. If meals are provided with the accommodation, this must be made clear, too. If prices are not standard for all rooms, then only the lowest and highest prices need be given.

STORAGE OF LUGGAGE: You may want to make excursions throughout England, taking only your essentials along. Very few bed-and-breakfast hotels in London have space to store luggage, and you might want to return to a different hotel. It's possible to store suitcases at most railway stations, but there is a place in central London where it's even cheaper and the service much friendlier.

Michael Gibbons & Co., Ltd., 25 Great Windmill St., W.1, off Shaftesbury Avenue (tel. 437-2866), will store personal effects on its premises at the rate of 25p (58¢) per day, per item, plus VAT. Maximum weight per item is 30 kilograms. The office is open Monday through Friday from 8:45 a.m. to 5 p.m. Most important, clients have free access to their stored effects during those hours. The company's main business is freight forwarding, and it is the officially appointed London port clearing and shipping agents for the Automobile Association and the Royal Automobile Club. Its services cover the shipment of cars, personal effects, and antiques.

1. Deluxe Hotels

For the lucky few who can afford them, we'll lead off with a selection of luxury hotels, some of which are among the finest in the world.

Connaught Hotel, Carlos Place, W.1 (tel. 499-7070), perhaps more than any other hotel in London captures an elegant old English atmosphere. It ranks at the top with Claridge's for prestige and character. Its position is supreme, in the center of Mayfair, two short blocks from both Berkeley and Grosvenor Squares. The Connaught is a 19th-century architectural treasure house of a way of life fast disappearing. It's a brick structure, with a formal Rolls-Royce entrance, and its tall French windows overlook two curved, tree-lined streets.

As you enter, the staircase reminds you of an estate in the English countryside. Throughout the hotel you'll find excellent antiques, such as in the drawing room with its formal fireplace, soft lustrous draperies at high windows, and bowls of fresh flowers. The cost of staying here is the same year round: a single with bath from £45 ($103.50) to £55 ($126.50); a double with bath from £71 ($163.30 to £80 ($184); inclusive of VAT. All meals are extra, and the service charge is 15%. The bedrooms vary in size but all are furnished with well-selected antiques and tasteful reproductions. All of the rooms have well-equipped bathrooms and niceties galore. It is imperative to reserve well in advance.

The paneled bar-lounge is old-school-tie conservative; the fashionable (everybody from movie stars to bestselling novelists) dining room is also wood paneled, but it glitters with mirrors and crystal. The chef has perfected the English cuisine and a selection of French dishes. The bowing and attentive waiters, the fresh flowers, set the proper mood. A table d'hôte luncheon is offered for £15 ($34.50) to £22 ($50.60), depending on your choice of a main course.

At four o'clock at the Connaught guests head for the circular sun room just off the entry lounge, where the English ritual of afternoon tea is practiced at its best, with all the proper accoutrements.

The Connaught is constantly taking top awards for its restaurant.

The Dorchester, Park Lane, W.1 (tel. 629-8888), sits facing Hyde Park on the fringe of Mayfair. As it was built in 1931, it enjoys many of the benefits of 20th-century design. The management has been involved in a long-range modernization and refurbishing program, much of which has been quite successful. Lined up at its prestigious corner entry is usually a row of old Bentleys and Rolls-Royces.

The celebrated attraction is the Oliver Messel suite, just like one of the late designer's stage settings. Other leading English decorators were employed to adorn the roof garden suites on the ninth floor. The average room (if there is such a thing) is brightly adorned with traditional themes. Singles start at £86 ($197.80), doubles at £96 ($220.80), including tax and service.

As a deluxe hotel, "The Dorch" offers numerous services, such as personal maid service (mending and pressing), hairdressing salons, a theater booking office, a florist, and a garage. The Dorchester Bar is a popular rendezvous, and both the air-conditioned Terrace Restaurant (dancing in the evening overlooking Hyde Park) and the Grill Room attract both the English and overseas visitors.

Ritz Hotel, Piccadilly, W.1 (tel. 493-8181), along with its namesake on the Place Vendôme in Paris, made the word "Ritzy" synonymous in the English vernacular with luxury. Of the Ritz in the "other city," a French writer once said, "It isn't a hotel, it isn't even a big hotel, it's a monument." Much the same can be said of the London Ritz, built when Edward VII and Lily Langtry were slipping around London. For the incurable romanticist, it remains the leading choice in the capital, seemingly cut off from busy Piccadilly, especially if you get a room overlooking Green Park. The Ritz world is one of sparkling crystal, gleaming gilt, rich Italian marble, all dear to the heart of the Edwardian belle époque.

After two years of renovation, Cunard Leisure has restored the lovely old place to much of its former elegance. Many of the old staff have remained, and the Ritz today is still the finest place in London to order afternoon tea in bone-china cups, accompanied by cucumber and paste sandwiches. The repainting, cleaning, and recovering has been much in the original scheme, the way César Ritz would have wanted it back in 1906—a predominantly pastel world of pink, dusty rose, and cream with gold-leafed molding, cupids and garlands, and forests of potted palms.

Staying here costs from £56 ($128.80) to £68 ($156.40) in a single, from £90 ($207) to £102 ($234.60) in a double, VAT and service included. Each bedroom has its own character, generally furnished in an old-fashioned manner, the champagne brocade with beige or pale blue seemingly preferred by every generation of English aristocracy. Everybody from Jacqueline Onassis to Mick Jagger is discreetly slipped in without fanfare. Ornately carved beds, marble fireplaces, and crystal lighting fixtures are found in many of the bedrooms.

The public rooms are spacious and dramatic. The restaurant has been refurbished, its elegant Louis XVI decor of the 1900s restored to its former splendor. It lies at the far end of the gallery. On the way there you'll pass through the Palm Court where tea is served. It's like a stage setting, an oval-shaped room dominated by a gold-leafed fountain with a seven-foot-high Edwardian nude. The ceiling is a gingerbread confection.

The Savoy, The Strand, W.C.2 (tel. 836-4343), is a landmark. Lucius Beebe maintained that its position has "ranked with the great hotels of all time." He went on to say that it "is perfumed with an aura lingering from the rich and regal England of Edward VII." The London institution looks to Richard D'Oyly Carte, the Victorian impresario who managed the first Gilbert and Sullivan operas, as its founding father. Through it have walked many of the famous personages of yesterday and today, everybody from the Divine Sarah, to acting partners Dame Ellen Terry and Sir Henry Irving, to rock stars.

Its position is choice, right on the Strand overlooking the Thames. The lounges of the Savoy are comfortable and restrained, with intimate nooks. Bedrooms are skillfully planned and furnished with color-coordinated accessories; the furnishings are a blend of antiques, an eclectic combination of such pieces as gilt mirrors, Queen Anne chairs, and Victorian sofas. Singles cost from £60 ($138), doubles from £80 ($184), VAT and service charge included. Every chambermaid, every waiter, is groomed for attentive service; the Savoy has long been a training ground for employees desiring to learn top-level hotel service. The Savoy Grill and the Savoy Restaurant are world famous.

Churchill, Portman Square, W.1 (486-5800), is a 500-room luxury hotel in Mayfair. It's leased for 99 years to a subsidiary of the Loew's chain and Yankee know-how in design and taste are combined here with the best of traditional London hotel keeping. Interior designer Ellen Lehman McCluskey has dipped into England's great periods to give the hotel style and flair. At No. 10, a restaurant, the decor is Regency, the tented effect reminiscent of the field headquarters of the Iron Duke; all is glamorous, with much gilt and marble, columns and Egyptian-style paintings. You dine in a simpler fashion in the Greenery, with its skylit roof. Drinks are served in the swank Churchill Bar, where soft piano music plays in the background; afternoon tea is taken in the sunken lounge. The bedrooms tastefully blend traditional pieces with classic modern. Every room has individually controlled temperature, two phones (one in the bath), radio, TV, and bath. Singles rent for around £55 ($126.50); doubles, £70 ($161); plus service and VAT.

Brown's, Dover Street and Albemarle Street, W.1 (tel. 493-6020), is the London base of many of the gentry who desert their stuffy manors for "the season" in the capital, quietly booking into their "usual" room. They know that Brown's resists the brassy new and doesn't appeal to flashy tourists.

This traditional hotel was the creation of Lord Byron's manservant, James Brown, who wanted to go into business for himself. He accepted "fine gentlemen only." The location is appropriate—in Mayfair, just off Berkeley Square. Singles here cost from £63 ($144.90), doubles from £85 ($195.50), including VAT and service.

The bedrooms vary considerably, and are a tangible record of the past history of England. Even the wash basins are semiantiques. The rooms have restrained taste, with good soft beds and telephones. The lounges on the street floor are inviting and cozy. There's a paneled lounge for the drinking of "spirits," another for afternoon tea.

The dining room has a quiet dignity and unmatched service. À la carte meals are served, plus a set luncheon menu at £10 ($23).

HOTELS IN THREE PRICE RANGES

After this look at life at the top, we'll now discuss our remaining recommendations, the bulk of those in this guide. These establishments are divided into districts, such as Mayfair, Belgravia, Bloomsbury. All of the hotels have one thing in common: they are less expensive than the deluxe, but even they reveal wide price differences. Therefore, we've broken them down into categories, beginning with the upper bracket, with first-class amenities. The medium-priced range follows with a listing of the best of London's moderately priced hotels with or without private baths. In this category a full English breakfast is usually (but not always) included in the rates quoted. Finally, for those who want to keep travel costs bone-trimmed, we'll list budget range choices wherever possible. Establishments in this category are most often converted town houses with only a handful of rooms with private baths, if any.

First-class hotels in London have generally abandoned the time-honored English tradition of serving you a full English breakfast (bacon and eggs) for the price of the room. The hotels in the medium-priced range are a toss-up—the majority still maintain this custom, although many establishments rely on skimpy continental fare instead of the works.

Most budget hotels in London, with many exceptions, still provide a full English breakfast for the price of the room. Because the policy of charging extra for breakfast is so erratic, always inquire before checking in.

Further, nearly all upper and middle-bracket hotels, and even some budget accommodations, charge a service fee ranging from 10% to 15%. Again, inquire about all such hidden extras *before* checking in so as to avoid a surprise when the bill's presented.

2. St. James's

This section, the beginning of Royal London, starts at Piccadilly Circus and moves southwest. It's frightfully convenient, as the English say, enclosing a number of important locations such as American Express on Haymarket, many of the leading stores (Burberry's of raincoat wear), and Buckingham Palace itself (see Royal London in Chapter IV).

It basks in its associations with royalty—it was the "merrie monarch" himself, Charles II, the famous skirt chaser (Nell Gwynne the favorite), who founded St. James's Park. And it was in St. James's Palace that his father, Charles I spent his last troubled night, awaiting his beheading the following morning. At one time the palace was a hunting lodge of Henry VIII and his wife of the moment, Anne Boleyn.

For the traditionalist in particular, living in the heart of aristocratic London has many advantages—none more important than its well-run and discriminating hotels themselves. Their number is limited, but their addresses are most fashionable, just as they were in the society heyday of the 18th century.

28 DOLLARWISE GUIDE TO ENGLAND AND SCOTLAND

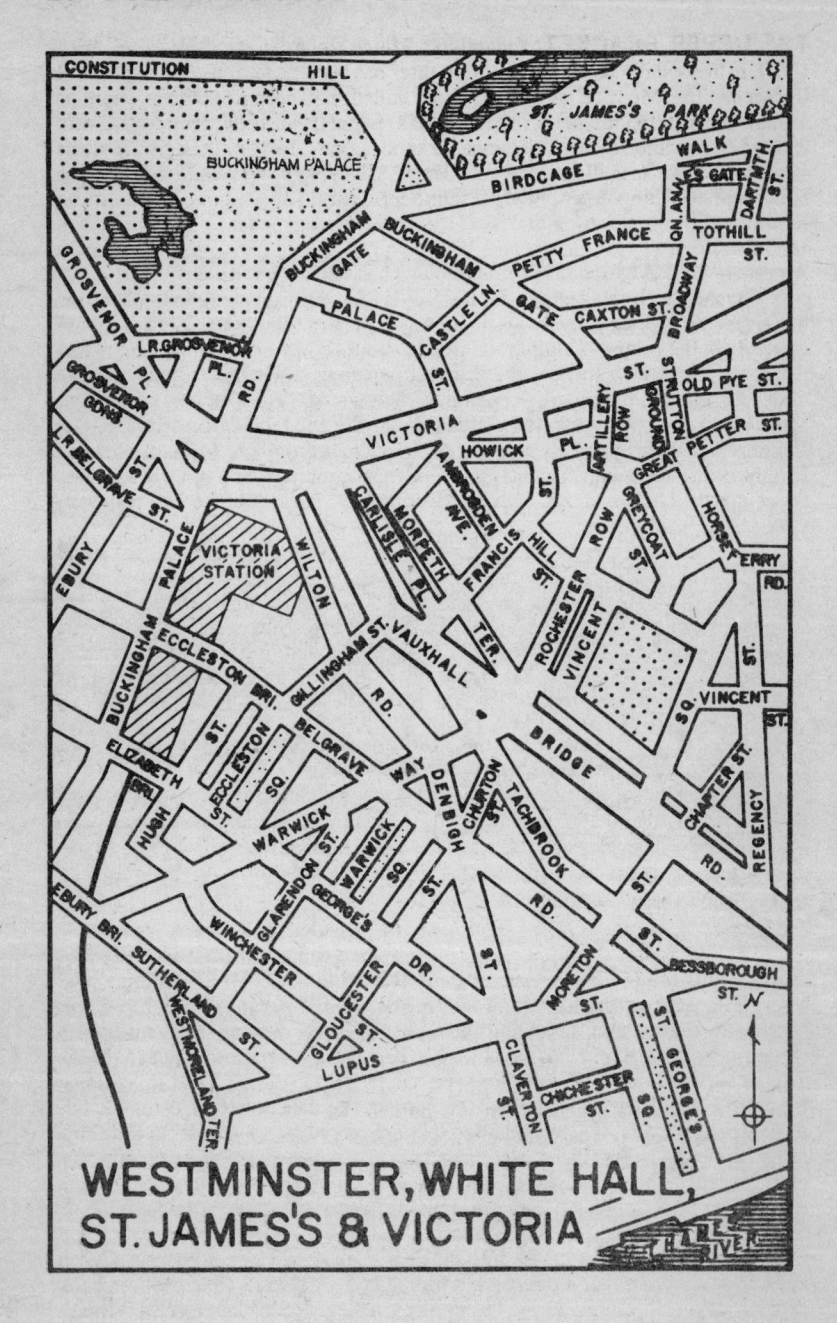

WESTMINSTER, WHITE HALL, ST. JAMES'S & VICTORIA

LONDON: HOTELS

THE UPPER BRACKET: **Quaglino's Hotel,** Bury Street, S.W.1 (tel. 930-6767), is like a stage mother whose daughter has become famous and dominates the scene. The Meurice, as it used to be called, has been known for years as a small but prestigious hotel in St. James's, popular with the pound-wise who wanted charm and subdued elegance for their money. Its restaurant is the scene stealer, however (see "London After Dark"). The bedrooms—all with private bath—are well appointed, with semimodern furnishings; some have sitting room areas. A single starts at £60 ($138), doubles and twins at £75 ($172.50). Included are a service charge and VAT. Thirsty guests meet for drinks in the American Bar. A garage and private car park are available.

Cavendish Hotel, Jermyn Street, S.W.1 (tel. 930-2111), has an old name, but a new body with a lively spirit. It was built in 1966 on the site of the old Cavendish, the subject of numerous stories about the days of Edward VII, when it was thronged with theatrical and royal personages. The hotel grew to fame under its colorful proprietor Rosa Lewis, known as "The Duchess of Jermyn Street" in a biography written about her. In the St. James's district ("Royal London"), just off Piccadilly and a five-minute walk from Pall Mall, this former landmark has been transformed into an ultra-contemporary hotel. Its first two floors are devoted to shops, lounges, restaurants, bars, and the 250-bedroom tower is set back, rising above it.

The rooms are bright and airy, with wall-to-wall curtains, a sitting area, and TV. Double-thickness windows keep out traffic noises. All rooms have private baths. A single rents for £55 ($126.50), doubles for £70 ($161).

The second-floor lounge and drinking bar are approached by a curious "floating staircase." The Sub Rosa bar-lounge, named in honor of the former proprietor, captures some of the flavor of the Edwardian era with brass lamps and black tufted banquettes. The Cavendish Restaurant is suitable for an after-theater supper (special menu from 11:30 p.m. to 7 a.m.) and also offers an alternative menu in the style of *cuisine minceur* (cooking without fats) during the lunch and dinner service.

The **Goring Hotel,** Beeston Place, Grosvenor Gardens, S.W.1 (tel. 834-8211), achieves the seemingly impossible—it provides the charm of traditional, dignified English living, but at the same time offers all modern comforts. Hotelier Goring built the establishment in 1910 with "revolutionary ideas"—that is, that every room should have a private bath, foyer, and central heating. His grandson, George Goring, continues to provide top service.

The 100 rooms (here they are called apartments) rent for £40 ($92) in a single, £52 ($119.60) in a double or twin. Rates include color TV, service, and VAT. The most practical way of lodging at the Goring is to take the demi-pension (breakfast and dinner) for £51 ($117.30) per person. You can have a three-course table d'hôte luncheon for £7 ($16.10) and dinner from £8 ($18.40). The menu includes such selections as chef's pâté, sole Véronique, chicken Maryland, and beef Stroganoff. Fires burn in the ornate fireplaces in the paneled drawing room, where afternoon teas are served by a butler from a trolley, Many prefer to enjoy this ritual in the adjacent sunroom, with its view of the rear gardens. The Goring's situation is choice—close to Victoria Station, a ten-minute walk to Westminster Abbey and the Houses of Parliament.

Stafford Hotel, 16 St. James's Pl., S.W.1 (tel. 493-0111), is left over from Edwardian days, hidden away from the pulse beat of Piccadilly, near Green Park. You'll need either a compass, divining rod, or the aid of an oldtime hack driver to locate it. The hotel can be entered via St. James's Place or else through the more colorful Blue Ball Yard (but only when the hotel's cocktail bar is open). Many of the original architectural details remain, although there have been attempts at modernizations. All the bedrooms—described by an English friend as "comfy and homey"—have private bathrooms. A single rents for £54 ($124.20), a double for £64 ($147.20) to £71 ($163.30), plus VAT. Breakfast is also extra. A restaurant serving both lunch and dinner is on the premises. The Stafford is often used by those who need a place near court, as well as the embassy and political life of London.

Duke's Hotel, 35 St. James's Pl., S.W.1 (tel. 491-4840), is a small, turn-of-the-century hotel in the St. James's district, only a five-minute walk from Piccadilly, a hundred feet or so from Green Park (which abuts Buckingham Palace) and near to St. James's Palace. A bit of leftover Victorian architecture, it sits on a postage stamp square lit by gas lamps and gay with flowers. It's all pure Regency, and frequented mainly by gentry who avoid the large impersonal hotels and gravitate to an establishment where the staff knows their quirks ("Welcome back, Lady Cooper-Plympton, will you want your morning tea at the usual time?").

There is central heating throughout, every bedroom has its own private bath and direct-dial telephone, and each suite is named after a duke. A single rents for £53 ($121.90), a double for £67 ($151.10), a twin for £78 ($179.40) to £100 ($230), inclusive of service and VAT. Light refreshments are available in a charming little bar or in the sitting room at all times. Main meals are served in the St. James's Room restaurant from 12:30 to 2:30 p.m. and from 6:30 to 10:30 p.m. Room service functions 24 hours a day.

Royal Westminster, Buckingham Palace Road, S.W.1 (tel. 834-1821), has one of the most fashionable addresses in London, within minutes of Buckingham Palace (in fact, this hotel is passed during the Changing of the Guard). A shining concrete and glass structure, the Royal Westminster charges from £59 ($137.50) in a double or twin, £50 ($115) in a single. Rates are inclusive of service charge and VAT, although breakfast is extra. Each bedroom is spacious, with many fine touches; you get private baths, radio and TV, and there's a free ice machine on every floor. Thatcher's, the Royal Westminster's à la carte restaurant, is designed on a charming English rustic theme and offers an exciting English and international menu appealing to business persons and tourists alike. The attractive cocktail bar, conveniently situated next to Thatcher's Restaurant, is ideal for a relaxing prelunch or dinner drink. Light refreshments and drinks are also served to residents in the comfortable, elegant lounge-bar, adjacent to the reception. The notable feature of the hotel is its collection of 18 "royal suites," each portraying a different theme—you go from Braganza and Botticelli to Victoria and Gladstone to Sayonara to Du Barry.

Hamilton House, 62 Warwick Way, S.W.1 (tel. 821-7113), is composed of early Victorian houses, joined and recently modernized. James Burns, the owner, was born in Pimlico, a few yards from the hotel. Since buying the property with his Danish wife, who was a TWA stewardess, he has constantly improved the facilities. There are now 45 rooms of which 30 have private baths and toilets, renting for £30 ($69) per night, breakfast and tax included. All rooms have telephone, radio, and TV. There is a residents' bar on the premises, and a fine restaurant for 60 people. Open to the public, it serves traditional English dishes and American fast foods. American guests are particularly welcome.

3. Piccadilly Circus

If you want to be in the middle of the West End, right at Piccadilly Circus and Leicester Square, then the following will appeal to you. Most of London's theaters, Soho, Regent Street, and many famous restaurants and pubs will be at your doorstep.

LONDON: HOTELS 31

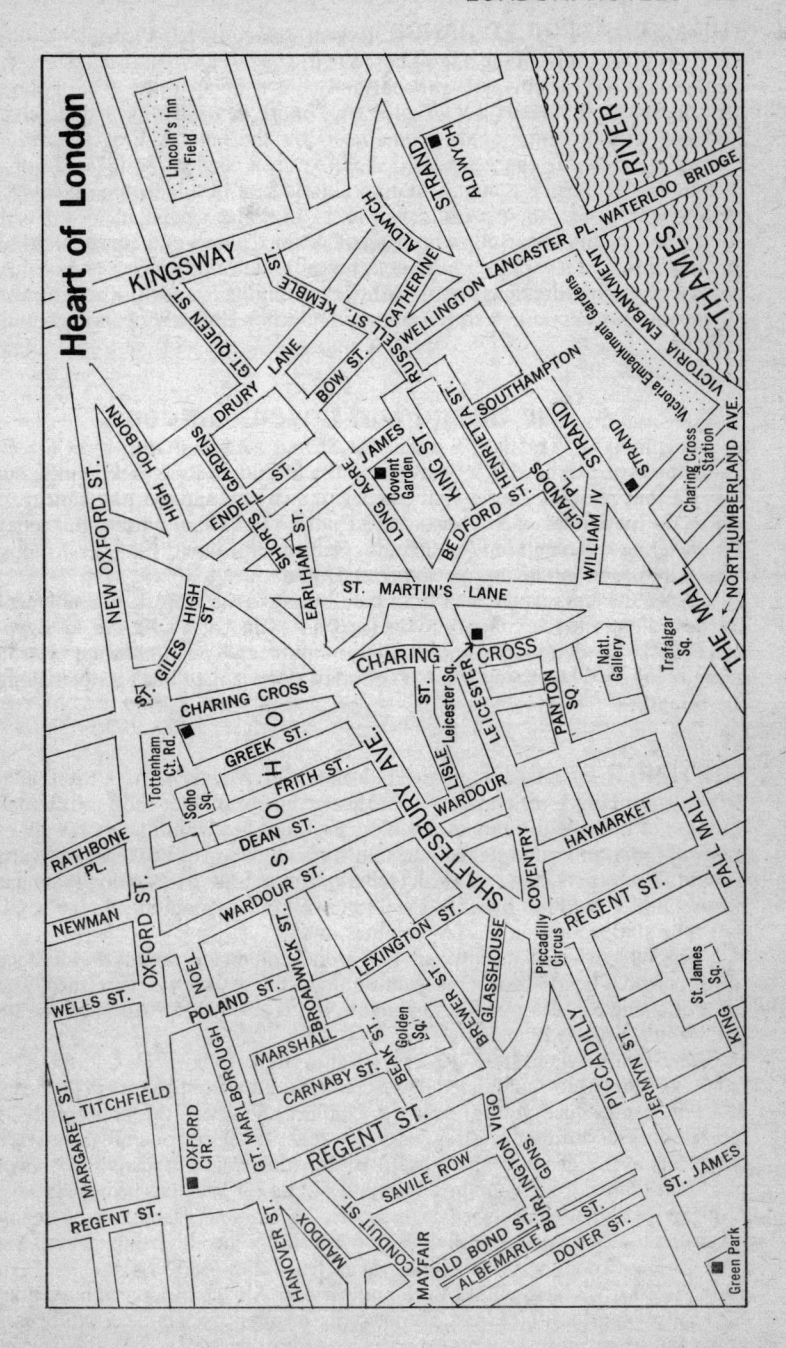

THE MEDIUM-PRICED RANGE: Regent Palace Hotel, Piccadilly Circus (tel. 734-7000), is one of the largest hotels in Europe. It's a mammoth establishment, some 1068 rooms, all with hot and cold running water (i.e., without private baths) and color TV. There is no more centrally located hotel in London—in fact, some of its rooms overlook the famous Eros statute on Piccadilly Circus. It charges £22.50 ($51.75) for a single, £34 ($78.20) for a double. Prices include a continental breakfast. Best of all, there is plenty of well-brewed coffee, an item which makes the Palace popular with North Americans. Facilities include a booking office for theaters and concerts, pressing, cleaning, and laundry service, shops for gifts, clothing, jewelry, and confectionery, and a hairdressing salon. Within the building is a Grill Room and an all-you-can-eat Carvery. A third restaurant, Garry's Coffee Shop, is open until 1:30 a.m.

4. The Strand and Covent Garden

Beginning at Trafalgar Square, the Strand runs east into Fleet Street. Londoners used to be able to walk along the Strand and see the Thames, but the river has receded. In the 17th century, the elegant and wealthy built their homes on the Strand, their gardens stretching to the Thames itself. But today it's changing to something less grand—flanked as it is with theaters, shops, hotels, and such landmarks as Somerset House.

Peaceful lanes jut off from the Strand, leading to the Victoria Embankment Gardens along the river. Opposite the gardens is Cleopatra's Needle, an Egyptian obelisk, London's oldest (and dullest) monument. You might want to stroll along the river if weather permits. You may also want to book a hotel along the Strand.

THE UPPER BRACKET: The **Waldorf Hotel,** Aldwych, W.C.2 (tel. 836-2400), is our choice for travelers on a theater binge. It's not only surrounded by some of the best theaters in the West End, but lies within a quick walk of many of the most visited sights—the Old Curiosity Shop of Dickens fame (just around the corner), the National Gallery, Horse Guards Parade, Trafalgar Square, and Piccadilly. Buses to the Tower of London stop outside the hotel, and tube stations are only a few minutes away.

The Waldorf, with its now-rare Edwardian colonnade, retains the elegance of yesteryear. The 310 bedrooms, from suites to singles, are well furnished. The price of a single is £40 ($92), a double or twin is £50 ($115). All have private bathrooms. VAT is included.

The **Drury Lane Hotel,** 10 Drury Lane, High Holborn, W.C.2 (tel. 836-6666), a Grand Metropolitan hotel, is a concrete and glass structure in the heart of theaterland. Once you're inside its confines, however, the atmosphere is relaxed and subdued, suggesting neither a chain hotel nor one of such severe modernity as the facade might indicate. Built with terraced gardens and its own plaza, the hotel is a self-contained entity. All of its 128 spacious bedrooms have good views and are furnished in a subtle, harmonious fashion, with many luxurious touches, such as individually controlled central heating, color TVs, even 24-hour room service. Singles range from £35 ($80.50), doubles from £52 ($119.60). Tariffs include VAT and service. All the bedrooms have fully tiled baths kept sparkling clean. The decor in the public rooms successfully uses green and beige, and plants evoke a garden atmosphere. Maudie's Restaurant is named after Sir Osbert Lancaster's famous arbiter-of-chic cartoon character

Maudie Littlehampton, and offers a French cuisine. Maudie's Bar makes a good posttheater rendevous. Tube: High Holborn.

Strand Palace Hotel, The Strand, W.C.2 (tel. 836-8080), is ideally situated for those who want to be in the theater district, near points such as Trafalgar Square, yet within a block of the Thames Embankment. Rooms have baths, wall-to-wall draperies, innerspring mattresses, comfortable furnishings. Sunbright colors contrast vividly with chalk-white walls. Behind the scenes is a staff of more than 700, standing by to provide personalized service. Rates are £35 ($80.50) in a single, £50 ($115) in a double or twin, and £65 ($149.50) in a triple. VAT and service are included, and all rooms have private baths or showers.

One of the assets of the Strand Palace is its restaurants, including a Carvery where every day but Sunday you can gorge yourself on England's finest roasts at £6.50 ($14.95). There's also the Gaiety Bar, a coffeeshop with curving red booths and frosted lights which attracts show people. Favored also is the intimate Mask Bar, with a collection of Saul Steinberg cartoons decorating the wall. To complete the dining possibilities, there is the sedate Carriage Room, where you can select from an à la carte menu.

THE MEDIUM-PRICED RANGE: The **Fielding Hotel,** 4 Broad Court, Bow Street (tel. 836-8305), is like a small country inn on a lane closed to traffic at the back of Covent Garden and the Opera House. This restored 300-year-old pub hotel is named after a famous guest, novelist Henry Fielding. It has a mellowed look with shutters and potted plants, as well as benches and tables set outside. Inside the Fielding is a tiny pub with room for only a dozen or so drinkers, and a reception area so small there's hardly space to set down your luggage. Yet its quaintness attracts singers and musicians appearing at the Opera House. The owner-manager has keyed his little 30-room establishment to their tastes. The bedrooms, although often quite dark, are sometimes colorfully decorated, with good use made of antiques and reproductions. Singles rent for £25.27 ($58.12); and twins, £34 ($78.20). Tube: Covent Garden.

5. Westminster

This section has been the seat of British government since the days of Edward the Confessor. Dominated by the Houses of Parliament and Westminster Abbey, Parliament Square symbolizes the soul of England. Westminster is a big name to describe a large borough of England, including Whitehall itself, headquarters of many government offices. A good part of the sprawling area in and around Victoria Station with its many budget hotels is also a part of Westminster. Known as the gateway to the continent, Victoria Station is where you get boat trains to Dover and Folkestone for that trip across the Channel. The area also has other advantages: the British Airways Air Terminal, the Green Line Coach Station, and the Victoria Coach Station are just five minutes from Victoria. From the bus stations, you can board many a Green Line coach for the suburbs. And an inexpensive bus tour of London departs from a point on Buckingham Palace Road, just behind Victoria Station.

THE MEDIUM-PRICED RANGE: Dolphin Square, Dolphin Square, S.W.1 (tel. 834-9134), is what dollarwise is all about. One of the largest blocks of flats (apartments) in all of Europe, it offers one of the best values in the city. The location, if not prestigious, is interesting—set back from Thames-bordering Grosvenor Road, between Chelsea and the Tate Gallery. Its past closed-door policy has changed to admit transient guests, many of whom want to create an instant home in London. To do so, you can book, say, a one-room apartment with a double bed for £30 ($69) nightly. A two-room apartment with twin beds goes for £37 ($85.10). Three- and four-room apartments are available also. You get handsome reductions with minimum stays of one week, even better bargains if you stay a month. Besides the fully equipped and furnished apartments, all of which have color TV, guest rooms, including early-morning tea and biscuits, are also rented at £10 ($23) in a single, £15 ($34.50) in a double, plus VAT. Dolphin Square was created to provide luxury living and has a vast inner courtyard and acres of gardens and lawns. The reception lounge is impressive, and a restaurant overlooking the heated swimming pool serves meals from breakfast until after the theater is out. Luxurious sauna baths for both men and women are available. For those who want to go English all the way, eight squash courts beckon.

St. Ermin's Hotel, Caxton Street, S.W.1 (tel. 222-7888), is the supreme choice for those who love opulent Victoriana. The palatial hotel, with a formal courtyard entry, was created for distinguished visitors from the world over—sultans, maharajahs, etc.—who had business to transact with the government. Modernization hasn't destroyed the splendor, certainly not in public rooms such as the front reception lounge, with its curving balcony and marble staircase.

The bedrooms vary considerably in size—some of them cavernous—and degree of modernization (many of the restyled singles and doubles have sleek, Nordic-inspired furnishings, with desks, television, bedside lights, and telephones). A single with bath goes for £28 ($64.40). You pay £52 ($119.60) in a double or twin, also with bath. Rates include a continental breakfast, VAT, and service. Modern installations include the Griffin Bar and Caxton Grill, the latter a contemporary setting for such traditional English fare as steak and chops, steak-and-kidney pie, Scottish salmon, and Welsh lamb.

The hotel is opposite New Scotland Yard, halfway between Victoria Station and Big Ben.

St. James Hotel, Buckingham Gate, S.W.1 (tel. 834-2360), is another great old Victorian hotel built in the heart of diplomatic London, only a few minutes' walk from 10 Downing Street, Whitehall, and the Houses of Parliament. Like St. Ermin's, St. James clings to the glory of the past. A world unto itself, it is an ornate group of brick buildings with a courtyard. Its towers make for spacious sunny bedrooms.

The bedrooms—520 in all—have been streamlined and contain built-in headboards, private baths, and radios. The rooms vary in size and degree of modernization (indicate your needs when reserving). All the following rates include service, VAT, and continental breakfast. A bathless single goes for £18 ($41.40), £26 ($59.80) with a bath or shower. Bathless twins cost £25 ($57.50), £34 ($78.20) with a bath or shower. The American Diner is open till 11:30 p.m. You can order steak-and-kidney pie at the Happy Casserole. Tube: St. James's Park.

Ebury Court, 26 Ebury St., S.W.1 (tel. 730-8147), was created out of a group of small town houses. You notice the country-house flavor right away; it's brightly painted (turquoise and white), with railings to match and flower-filled window boxes. The little reception rooms are informal and decorated with flowery chintz and quite good antiques. Best of all, it has a cordial and informal staff. The hotel is close to the airline terminals. Terms quoted include an English breakfast, service charge, and VAT. The rate in a single ranges from £18.50 ($42.55), from £28.50 ($65.55) in a bathless twin-bedded room or a double. Doubles with private bathrooms cost from £38.50 ($88.55). Recent improvements, which gained the hotel its official Fire Certificate, include the installation of a small elevator. Each of the rooms has hot and cold running water, as well as a telephone and radio. An asset is the night porter, handy for late arrivals. In the small restaurant, you can order either a lunch or dinner.

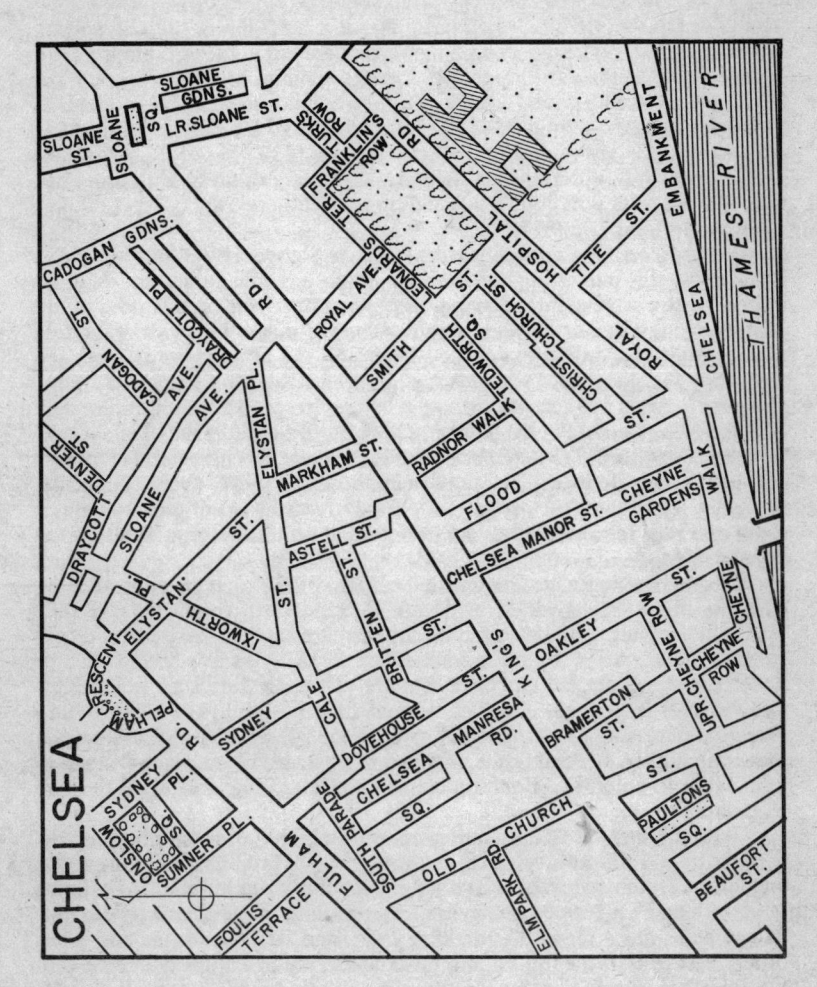

6. Chelsea

This stylish district stretches along the Thames, south of Hyde Park, Brompton, and South Kensington. Beginning at Sloane Square, it runs westward toward the periphery of Earl's Court and Brompton. Its spinal cord: King's Road, center for boutique hopping. The little streets and squares on either side of King's Road have hundreds of tiny cottages used formerly by the toiling underprivileged of the 18th and 19th centuries (although Carlyle lived there—see "Homes of Famous Writers and Artists" in Chapter IV). Now, except for Belgravia and Mayfair, Chelsea couldn't be more chic. To become a part of the scene, you can, like Carlyle, "take up abode" in one of the following recommendations.

THE MEDIUM-PRICED RANGE: Royal Court Hotel, Sloane Square, S.W.1 (tel. 730-9191), is a Jacobean monument erected in the last century, right in the hub of Chelsea. The lower-floor lounges are mini and contemporary; the bedrooms are well planned, with built-in pieces, adequate lighting, and TV. Many doubles have sitting areas. Twins with bath go for £25 ($57.50) to £32 ($73.60), singles with bath for £36 ($82.80) to £42 ($96.60). Rates include service and VAT. You must pay an extra £3 ($6.90) for an English breakfast. On the premises is a traditional pub and a restaurant serving good food, offering a set dinner for £7.50 ($17.25).

Fenja Hotel, 69 Cadogan Gardens, Sloane Square, S.W.3 (tel. 589-1183), is an unusually interesting town house which has maintained much of its individualistic architecture. Some modern amenities have been slipped in, including a tiny elevator between a pair of marble pillars in the entry. A true English way of living is maintained here, and the atmosphere is quiet (no children), the clientele discriminating. Many embassy personnel stay here, along with owners of country manors who like to spend a season in London. Mr. and Mrs. Kaulback charge from £21 ($48.30) to £26 ($59.80) in a single, from £30 ($69) to £42 ($96.60) in a double, the more expensive tariffs for those rooms with private baths. The rates include VAT, service, and a continental breakfast. The rooms themselves are cheerily furnished, and each contains a radio or TV (if requested), plus a telephone and central heating. Tube: Sloane Square.

Sloane Hall, 6 Sloane Gardens, S.W.1 (tel. 730-9206), is an authentic 1888 Victorian mansion converted by Derek R. Jones to accommodate visitors, especially families. Some rooms have private baths and all have hot and cold running water. A few rooms accommodate as many as five persons in two doubles and one single. The chambers are pleasantly furnished, renting for £13 ($29.90) in a single. Doubles without bath go for £19 ($43.70) to £21 ($48.30), increasing to £21 ($48.30) to £23 ($52.90) with bath. Rates include breakfast and VAT. Breakfast is provided in a paneled room which doubles as a lounge with color TV. Courtesy tea and coffee are available at all times in all bedrooms.

Willett Hotel, 32 Sloane Gardens, S.W.1 (tel. 730-0634), opening onto the gardens, is a 19th-century town house with many architectural curiosities, including a Dutch-style roof and varying styles of bay windows. It's an intimate hotel with many luxurious and stylish features. Each of the pleasantly decorated bedrooms has a radio, TV, dressing table, and facilities for making coffee or tea. Best of all is the full English breakfast served in a club-style room with black leather chairs. Most of the accommodations contain private baths. Including breakfast, singles rent for £18.50 ($42.55); doubles and twins, £23.50 ($54.05) to £26 ($59.80). An extra single bed in a family room costs an additional £7 ($16.10). VAT and the service charge are included in these tariffs as well. Tube: Sloane Square.

11 Cadogan Gardens, Sloane Square, S.W.3 (tel. 730-3426), is a Victorian house—or two—converted into comfortable service apartments, single rooms, doubles, and suites. It is well furnished and elegant. Bed and an English breakfast, served in the rooms with morning papers of the guest's choice, costs £30 ($69) in a single, £44 ($101.20) in a double. Suites go for £60 ($138) for two. There is no license for liquor, but the porters will gladly send out for a

bottle. TV can be arranged in your room at a small extra cost. Laundry and dry cleaning as well as shoe cleaning can be taken care of. Theater tickets, car rentals, and sightseeing excursions are in the hands of the porters. Charles Harbord is the owner, and his managers, Peter G. de Loriol and Mark A. Fresson, will look after you.

THE BUDGET RANGE: Culford Hall, 7 Culford Gardens, off Sloane Square, S.W.3 (tel. 581-2211), is a small, well-run hotel in one of the most fashionable parts of Chelsea. It's quiet, comfortable, and attractively furnished with contemporary pieces. Singles without bath cost from £11.35 ($26.11) nightly, and bathless doubles go from £18 ($41.40). However, the double rate in a unit with private bath and TV begins at £21 ($48.30). Breakfast, at no extra charge, is served in the rooms (which contain phones and radios). The rooms have won the approval of many a visiting American, who cited the shaving outlets, the intercom, the good beds, central heating, and cleanliness. The hotel attracts people connected with embassies, universities, airlines, and foreign office personnel. The atmosphere is friendly. A short walk from the hotel will take you to some of the best restaurants along King's Road.

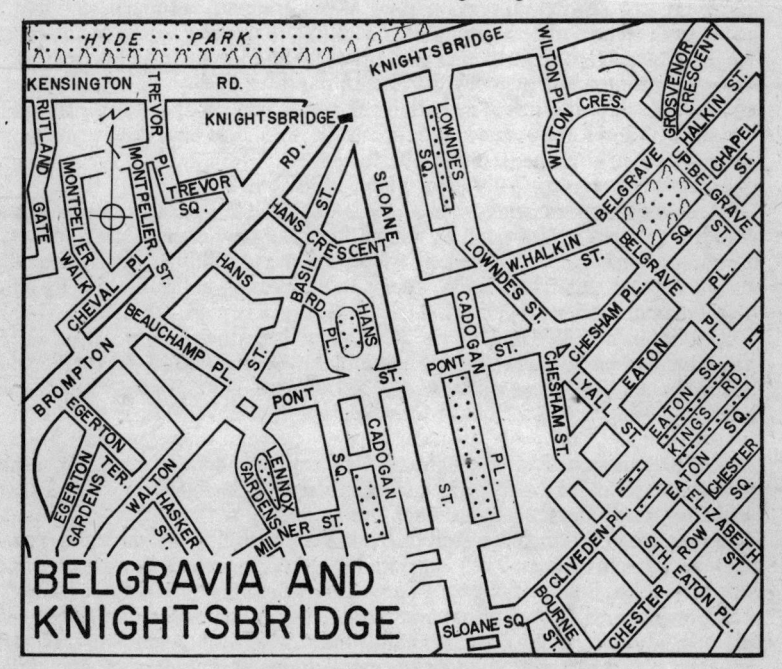

7. Belgravia and Knightsbridge

Belgravia, south of Hyde Park, is the so-called aristocratic quarter of London, challenging Mayfair for grandness. It reigned in glory along with Queen Victoria, but today's aristocrats are likely to be the top echelon in foreign embassies, along with a rising new money class of actors and models.

Belgravia is near Buckingham Palace Gardens and Brompton Road. Its center is Belgrave Square, one of the more attractive plazas in London. A few town houses once occupied by eminent Edwardians have been discreetly turned into moderately priced hotels (others were built specifically for that purpose). For those who prefer a residential address, Belgravia is choice real estate.

Adjoining Belgravia is Knightsbridge, another top residential and shopping district of London. Just south of Hyde Park, Knightsbridge is close in character to Belgravia, although much of this section to the west of Sloane Street, is older—dating back in architecture and layout to the 18th century. Several of the major department stores, such as Harrods, are here (take the Piccadilly subway line to Knightsbridge). Since Knightsbridge is not principally a hotel district, our recommendations are limited.

THE UPPER AND MEDIUM-PRICED RANGE: The **Ladbroke Belgravia Hotel,** 20 Chesham Pl., S.W.1 (tel. 235-6040), is a 1971 hotel entry, in Belgravia, home of most of London's diplomatic corps. Eleven stories—nearly all glass—rise from its foundation, and provide airy, well-lit bedrooms. Each room contains color TV, a bath with a shower-tub combination, and air conditioning. The rooms are luxuriously comtemporary, with pure white walls, vividly colored carpets, chairs, and bedcovers. You even get a telephone in your tiled bath, 24-hour room service, and a helpful concierge. A single costs £50 ($115); a double or twin £60 ($138). VAT and breakfast are extra, although service is included. On the premises is the Terrace Restaurant opening from Pont Street. The decor is cool, and the menus both practical and inexpensive. Service and VAT are included in the prices. At lunchtime, three fixed-price meals and a superb buffet are offered. The specialty is rib of beef on the trolley. In the evening, a limited à la carte and buffet are available, and, as always, a mouthwatering selection from the dessert trolley.

Wilbraham Hotel, Wilbraham Place, off Sloane Street, S.W.1 (tel. 730-8296), is as dyed-in-the-wool British as you can get. On this quiet little street, just a few hundred yards from busy Sloane Square, three Victorian town houses have been joined together as one hotel. The hotel has two intimate sitting rooms and a reception hall. There are 57 rooms in all, plus 34 baths. Depending on the plumbing, singles range from £18 ($41.40) to £21 ($48.30); doubles, £26 ($59.80) to £33 ($75.90). VAT is added, and breakfast is also extra. The Wilbraham owns a choice little restaurant, Le Beurre Fondu, serving both luncheons and dinners.

The **Cadogan Hotel,** Sloane Street, S.W.1 (tel. 235-7141), is a colorful Edwardian hotel, one of the few older hotels in London whose modernization has not been destructive. Untouched is its fussy belle époque facade, corner towers, and mansard roof. Its interior architecture—designed by the Adam brothers—is also untouched, although brightened by red velvet and gilt. The furnishings are traditional, as seen in the lounge, with its gold, mirrored, and colored walls and ceilings. The lounge leads to the Lily Langtry Bar, which was once part of the London home of "Jersey Lily," mistress of Edward VII. The bedrooms have been modernized and provide plenty of comfort. Singles with bath start at £45 ($103.50), doubles and twins at £60 ($138), including service. Breakfast is extra. Oscar Wilde was arrested in one of the suites, by the way, a fact recorded in a poem by John Betjeman.

Capital Hotel, Basil Street, Knightsbridge, S.W.3 (tel. 589-5171), is one of the most personalized hotels in the West End. Small and modern, it's a stone's throw from Harrods. The proud owner, David Levin, sat down and listed all the niceties he could offer guests. For example, it's one of the few hotels anywhere that will provide an emergency pack for the stranded traveler —robe, toothbrush, razor. From the modest lobby, an elevator will take guests to each floor, each corridor and staircase being treated as an art gallery, with original oil paintings. In all, 60 rooms are offered, the singles having more space than the doubles. The furniture is handmade, with color-coordinated fabrics. Singles rent for £50 ($115). Doubles go for £55 ($126.50) to £60 ($138). The Capital Restaurant is among the finest in London, offering such exquisitely prepared main dishes as poupotte de pigeonneaux and carré d'agneau persillé. Fresh vegetables are used, and a sachertorte is often the featured dessert. Tube: Knightsbridge.

Basil Hotel, Basil Street, Knightsbridge, S.W.3 (tel. 581-3311), has long been a favorite little hotel of discerning English, who make an annual pilgrimage to London to shop at Harrods and perhaps attend the Chelsea Flower Show. This Edwardian charmer, totally unmarred by pseudo-modernization, is managed by Stephen Korany, who prefers guests who can appreciate his highly individualistic hotel. The open mahogany staircase seems ideal as a setting for the entrance line of a drawing room play: "You're just in time for tea, Braddie." There are several spacious and comfortable lounges, appropriately furnished with 18th- and 19th-century decorative accessories. Off the many rambling corridors are smaller sitting rooms.

The pleasantly furnished bedrooms are priced according to size and location. Single rooms range from £28 ($64.40) to £42 ($96.60), the latter with private baths. Doubles without bath go for £42 ($96.60), increasing to £55 ($126.50) with bath. The dining room serves a three-course lunch for about £6 ($13.80), and dinner is around the same price. The Upstairs Restaurant is suitable for lighter meals and snacks, and the Downstairs Wine Bar serves a wide selection of wines and cheap food.

The Diplomat, 2 Chesham St., off Belgrave Square, S.W.1 (tel. 235-1544), provides an opportunity to stay in the converted town house of a lord. As such, it attracts many high-ranking military officers, diplomats (in honor of its namesake), and professional persons. Many of the original architectural features have been retained. The entrance is marble floored, and the circular staircase is illuminated by a frieze-covered dome. All rooms have appropriately tasteful furnishings as well as private baths, phones, color televisions, and radios. Singles range from £19 ($43.70) and doubles start at £28 ($64.40). VAT is added, and breakfast at no extra charge is served in the rooms.

Knightsbridge Hotel, 10 Beaufort Gardens, S.W.3 (tel. 589-9271), sandwiched between the trendy restaurants and fashionable boutiques of Beauchamp Place and Harrods, still retains the feeling of a traditional British hotel. On a tree-lined square that is peaceful and tranquil, and free from traffic, it has a subdued Victorian charm. The place is small—only 18 bedrooms—and personally run by the manager, Robert A. Novella. Units have phones, radios, and central heating, and there's a lounge with a color "telly" and a bar on the premises. Most expensive are rooms with private baths, costing £16.90 ($38.87) in a single, from £25.90 ($59.57) in a double. The best for the budget are the bathless specials—from £13.55 ($31.17) in a single and from £19.90 ($45.77) in a double. A family room for three guests rents for about £30 ($69) per night. All tariffs include a continental breakfast and VAT, although a 12% service charge is added.

THE BUDGET RANGE: Bucks Hotel, 33 Beaufort Gardens, S.W.3 (tel. 584-5252), is the product of architectural evolution. Originally converted from two Georgian houses, the hotel has recently been completely renovated right down to the very entrance doors. Each of the 34 rooms has either a private bath or shower. Visitors can relax in the attractive bar, the comfortable lounge, or the small, pleasant garden. The rooms themselves are cozy, not large, but well furnished. Carpeting and central heating are used throughout. The bed-and-breakfast rate begins at £26 ($59.80) in a single, rising to £37 ($85.10) in a double, including an English breakfast, VAT, and service.

Claverley House Hotel, 13-14 Beaufort Gardens, Knightsbridge, S.W.3 (tel. 589-4740), offers fair value for the dollar, considering its chic location. Many guests are regulars, including two millionaires who drop in occasionally. The hotel has been extensively renovated and decorated. Fifteen of its 31 rooms have private baths, although none contains a toilet. The cost of a room with bath or shower is from £12.50 ($28.75) to £13.50 ($31.05) for a single, from £18.50 ($42.55) to £20.50 ($47.15) for a double or twin-bedded room, including VAT, service, and an English breakfast.

8. Kensington, South Kensington, and Earl's Court

Although the Royal Borough draws its greatest number of visitors from shoppers (Kensington High Street), it also attracts with a number of fine, medium-priced hotels, for the most part on Kensington Gardens itself. In Victoria's day, the rows of houses along Kensington Palace Gardens were inhabited by millionaires (although Thackeray also lived there). Today the houses are occupied largely by ambassadors.

South Kensington, south of Kensington Gardens and Hyde Park, is essentially a residential area, not as elegant as bordering Belgravia and Knightsbridge. However, the section is rich in museums, and it has a number of colleges.

Staying in South Kensington has much to recommend it. Besides its proximity to the Kensington Museums, such as the Victoria and Albert, the area encompasses Albert Hall, and is within walking distance of Kensington Gardens and Harrods department store. At the South Kensington station, you can catch trains for Kew Gardens and the Thames River town of Richmond.

For the most part, the hotels in this area recall yesterday more than today, although contemporary furnishings and modern amenities are grudgingly creeping in. It's an ideal spot for the traditionalist.

Earl's Court, below Kensington and bordering the western half of Chelsea, is one of the most popular middle-class hotel and rooming-house districts. A 15-minute subway ride from Earl's Court station will take you into the heart of Piccadilly, via either the District or Piccadilly Lines. The area is convenient to the West End Air Terminal.

THE UPPER BRACKET: Kensington Palace Hotel, De Vere Gardens, W.8 (tel. 937-8121), although built in 1951, now rates as one of London's "newest," having been comprehensively refurbished and remodeled. It is ideally situated just opposite Kensington Gardens and two minutes' walk from Kensington High Street shopping center. The elegant and spacious foyer is decorated with a Regency theme. For formal wining and dining, there is the Kensington Chelsea Piano Bar and Restaurant which offers a comprehensive menu. More relaxed meals can be taken in the continental atmosphere of the Pavilion Coffee House. The 320 bedrooms have stylish, color-coordinated decor, and each has its own bathroom, radio, and TV. Singles rent from £37 ($85.10) nightly, with doubles going for £45 ($103.50).

Royal Kensington, 380 Kensington High St., W.14 (tel. 603-3333), supplies a near-luxurious accommodation at less-than-luxurious prices. It's in the fashionable Kensington area, near parks, museums, and shopping. You can enjoy the comforts of the handsomely styled bedrooms which include color TV,

LONDON: HOTELS 41

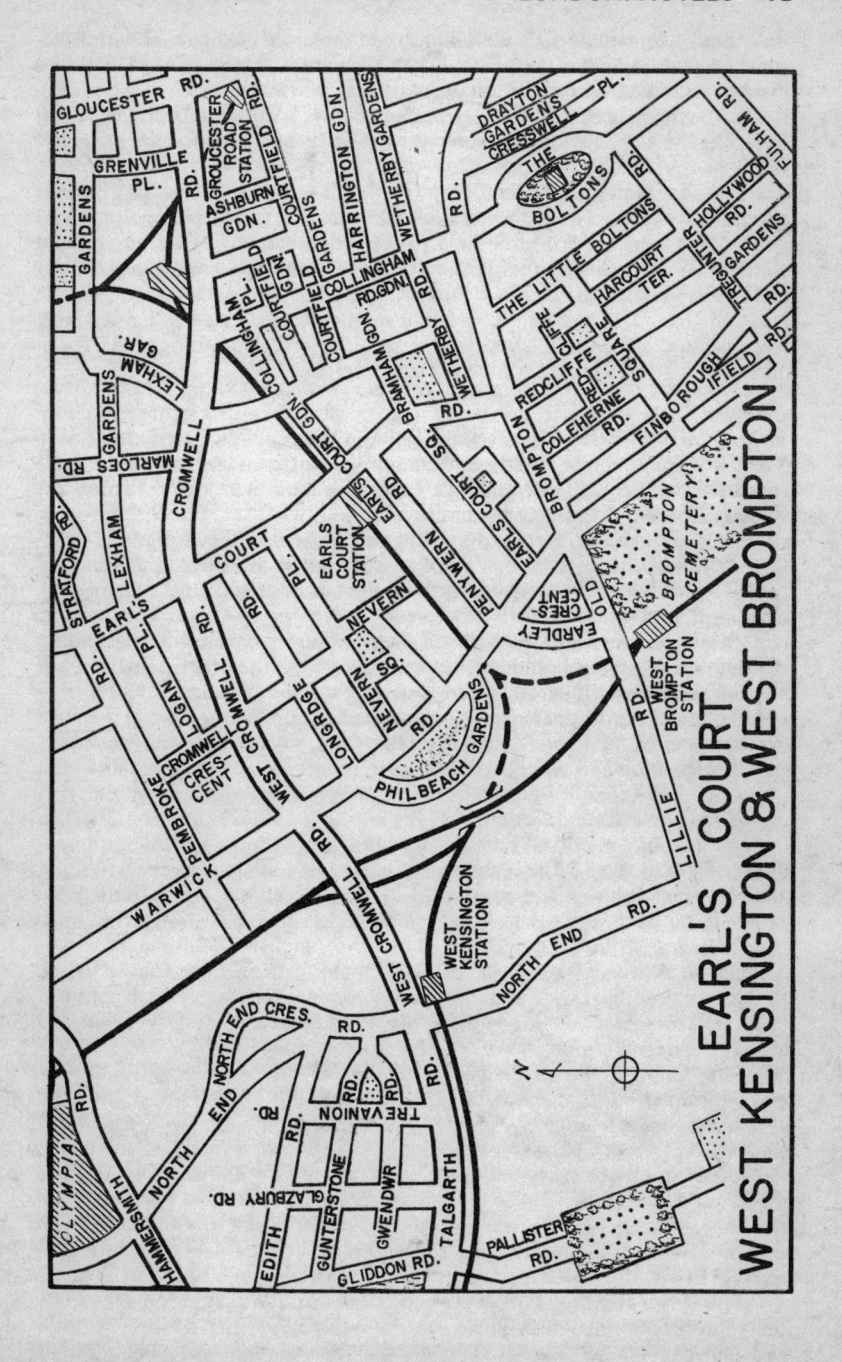

EARL'S COURT, WEST KENSINGTON & WEST BROMPTON

individually controlled air conditioning, and direct-dial telephones with bathroom extensions. Singles go for £35 ($80.50), doubles or twins are £43 ($98.90), including service. VAT and a continental breakfast are extra. The Flaming Ox Restaurant offers a choice of steaks or flambés, while in the coffeeshop you can have a light snack. Twenty-four-hour room service and garage space are available.

De Vere Hotel, Hyde Park Gate, W.8 (tel. 584-0051), takes you back to another day—you'll know it when you're served tea in the Adam drawing room overlooking Kensington Gardens. It's a Victorian building, with much of the old maintained, although the spacious bedrooms, with their fine paneled walls and occasional "tufted boudoir" furnishings, have been updated with all the required amenities, such as hot and cold running water. In a single room with bath, the rate is £35 ($80.50). A double with bath costs from £50 ($115). Rates include VAT, but service and breakfast are extra.

THE MEDIUM-PRICED RANGE: Bailey's Hotel, Gloucester Road, S.W.7 (tel.373-8131), to quote the management, was a "firm favourite with the squirearchy" when it was built back in the 1880s—but now caters to the tourist, both foreign and domestic, along with budding executives. This brick corner establishment in South Kensington, with its formal arched entrance and mansard roof, was one of those first revolutionary hotels to install an "ascending room"—that is, an elevator. The ground floor is paneled in oak, mixing antiques with reproductions. All 155 bedrooms have a private bathroom/shower, remote-control color TV, radio, direct-dial telephones, and facilities including wake-up calls, messages, and an electronic door-locking system. The hotel has finished an extensive upgrading program, and many new amenities have been added, such as automatic elevators, a good coffeeshop, a hotel bar, and a wine bar, with a restaurant specializing in foreign food. There's also a fully computerized reservation and billing system. Single rooms are £34 ($78.20), and twin rooms are £49 ($112.70) per night. All prices include VAT and service.

Number Sixteen, 16 Sumner Pl., S.W.7 (tel. 589-5232), is considered a luxury "pension" in central London. Just off Old Brompton Road, it's a three-minute walk to the South Kensington underground station. Michael Watson is the creator of this offbeat hotel, built in 1860, which is much patronized by people in the performing arts. The twin building is classically Victorian, with high-ceilinged period rooms converted to self-contained bed-sitting accommodations, with private shower/bathrooms (some of them have tubs as well). Rooms are decorated with antiques and Victorian pieces, along with pictures, Hans Holbein prints, and lithographs. Mr. Watson prefers guests who will stay at least three nights or more. Singles range from £18.50 ($42.55) to £23 ($52.90), doubles and twins from £25.50 ($58.65) to £43 ($98.90).

Milestone Hotel, Kensington Court, W.8 (tel. 937-0991), is a great old building facing Kensington Gardens. There's an ornate roof with decorative gables and chimneys, plus large bay windows. The decor is modified neoclassic, the best example the glass-ceilinged dining room with its paneled walls, red draperies, and red chairs. The bedrooms, each with radio and telephone, are spacious. A bathless single rents for £12 ($27.60); a single with bath is £16 ($36.80). Bathless doubles or twins range from £18 ($41.40). A twin with bath costs £21 ($48.30). Rates include service and tax, although breakfast is extra.

The **Town House,** 44–48 West Cromwell Rd., S.W.5 (tel. 568-1361), is a small, privately owned place made over from three Victorian houses. Friendly and informal, it is well suited to younger tourists. All rooms have hot and cold running water, radio, and phone, and most are also equipped with shower and toilet. Color TV is standard in most units or else available at a small extra charge in others. There is a cozy, comfortable bar-lounge and a larger games bar with dartboard, pool table, fruit machines, dominos, backgammon, and bridge.

Singles range in price from £18 ($41.40) to £23 ($52.90) a night, and doubles or twins run from £26 ($59.80) to £32 ($73.60), these tariffs including service, although VAT is extra. The staff also offers some family rooms which work out at about £40 ($92) per night for four persons. Laundry and dry-cleaning can be taken care of, and there's also a Telex service available to guests.

Breakfast can be served in your room or else in the main dining room. Snacks are available throughout the day, and in the evenings a three-course dinner is offered, costing from £6.50 ($14.95). The fare is simple, traditional English cookery.

The **Regency Hotel**, 100–105 Queen's Gate, S.W.7 (tel. 370-4595), is a skillful conversion of six lively old houses to provide 200 simply furnished, comfortable rooms with bathroom or shower, color TV, radio, and telephone. There are elevators to all floors and 24-hour porterage. The high-ceilinged, warm red-walled dining room serves a set lunch or dinner, three courses for around £5 ($11.50). They also do a limited à la carte menu where a meal will cost around £10 ($23) per person. The bar is large and cheerfully decorated with green walls, dark wood, and button chairs, and serves coffee, tea, and sandwiches as well as drinks. The tariffs are a very good value at £18 ($41.40) single, £24 ($55.20) twin or double, £30 ($69) triple, including a continental breakfast, service, and VAT. South Kensington museums are close by, as well as the South Kensington and Gloucester Road underground stations to the West End or Heathrow Airport.

Albany Hotel, Barkston Gardens, S.W.5 (tel. 370-6116), has combined five Victorian town houses on tree-shaded Barkston Gardens—secluded, yet only one minute from Earl's Court Road and conveniently near the West London Air Terminal. Rebuilding and tasteful furnishing have transformed these former private residences into attractive public places in which to stay. Most of the 100 rooms contain private bath and toilet, and all have color TV, radio, and telephone. A single without bath rents for £16 ($36.80); a single with bath, £21.75 ($50.03); a bathless twin or double, £24 ($55.20); a double or twin with bath, £32 ($73.60). These tariffs include a continental breakfast, service, and VAT. Highly popular is an old-style pub, with a beamed ceiling, rough brick walls, and Windsor chairs. The dining room is stylish and airy. Tube: Earl's Court.

Burns Hotel, Barkston Gardens, S.W.5 (tel. 373-3151), stands near its sister, the already recommended Albany, in the vicinity of the West London Air Terminal. Small and intimate, it was once the home of Ellen Terry (1848–1928), who was especially acclaimed for her Shakespearean roles and was also known for her correspondence with G. B. Shaw. Most of the rooms overlook the trees of Barkston Gardens. With private bath, singles rent for £20 ($46) nightly, doubles or twins for £30 ($69). Tariffs include VAT, service, and a full English breakfast. You can also use the sauna at the nearby Albany. Tube: Earl's Court.

Airways Hotel, 16 Collingham Rd., S.W.5 (tel. 373-1075), is a neat, bandbox-modern hotel, in Earl's Court near the West London Air Terminal. It's only a short block away from the heavy Cromwell Road traffic, where finding a quiet room is almost impossible. Its bedrooms are as compact and as utilitarian as some motels in America—built-in headboards, radios, telephones, dressing tables. Every room has a private bath. The rates, including continental breakfast, in a single are £18.70 ($43.01), £30 ($69) in a double or twin, including a continental breakfast, service, and VAT. One of the reasons for staying here is the ease with which you can settle in—you can check in anytime, day or night. On the premises is a restaurant serving lunch and dinners.

Onslow Court Hotel, 109–113 Queen's Gate, S.W.7 (tel. 589-6300), is a long-established family hotel. The plain but comfortable rooms have radio, telephone, and central heating, and there is an elevator to all floors. Many units have private bathrooms as well. A single goes from £15 ($34.50) to £20 ($46), a double from £23 ($52.90) to £30 ($69), and a triple from £32 ($73.60) to £38 ($87.40). All rates include a full breakfast, VAT, and service. Add £5 ($11.50) per person per night for half board. Otherwise, a set three-course lunch costs £3.50 ($8.05) and four courses is £5 ($11.50); a set dinner is from £6 ($13.80). The hotel is not licensed, but they are quite happy for you to bring your own supplies of wine or liquor. They have a good range of mixes and sodas and will provide ice for you in your room, or the headwaiter will purchase wines, liquor, and beer for you on request.

Stanhope Court Hotel, 46–52 Stanhope Gardens, S.W.7 (tel. 370-2161), belongs to the same group as the previously recommended Onslow Court. The facilities offered are the same. This place looks out over a delightful London square garden just off Cromwell Road and around the corner from the Gloucester Road underground station. Rates are the same as for the Onslow Court and, in fact, reservations can be made through the central reservations office, The North Hotels, 58 Cromwell Rd., London S.W.7 5BZ (tel. 01/589-1212; Telex: 262180). This is an advantage, as it saves your having to try a second hotel if the first one is full. The group has several other hotels in the area which are totally adequate but from a point of view of location and facilities these two are the ones we recommend the most. The chain is owned by a Quaker, Sir Cyril Black. Hence, the lack of bars.

THE BUDGET RANGE: Strathmore House, 12 Strathmore Gardens, W.8 (tel. 229-3063). You'd never guess this is a hotel. There's no sign, only a street number, and its location near Embassy Row and Kensington Palace make it appear like a private town house. It's a corner house, with a low wall and shrubbery. Mr. and Mrs. Haskell, the proprietors, charge £9 ($20.70) per person per night inclusive. Terms include a complete English breakfast, but don't expect private baths. The bed-sitting rooms, opening off the central hallway, are large and comfortable. There are some nice old pieces mixed in with the nondescript furniture, and the total effect is homey and immaculate. You get hot and cold running water in the rooms, as well as the free use of the corridor baths. Breakfast is brought to your room, and you have a gas ring and kettle so you can make your own tea or coffee. Tube: Notting Hill Gate.

Princes Lodge Hotel, Prince of Wales Terrace, W.8 (tel. 937-6306), is a family hotel in the literal meaning of the word. A number of rooms have been specially designed to accommodate families; there are also family suites, rooms for parents and children separated by private bath. There are day and night "baby-watching" and "child-minding" services; the hotel has cribs and cots. Large families are never met with a sigh here, but are always given a welcoming smile. Singles range in price from £20 ($36) to £24 ($55.20), and doubles go from £30 ($69) to £34 ($78.20). The difference in price depends on location, plumbing, and season, and all tariffs include a continental breakfast, service, and VAT. The Princes Lodge is opposite Kensington Palace Gardens.

Vicarage Private Hotel, 10 Vicarage Gate, W.8 (tel. 229-4030), is the domain of Ellen and Martin Diviney, who charge £7.50 ($17.25) per person double occupancy, and £8.50 ($19.55) in a single. All rates include breakfast, and as of November 1 charges are reduced slightly. The rooms have pleasant furnishings. All have water basins, and there's a good supply of showers. Mrs. Diviney makes each breakfast individually, and introduces her guests to each other. Vicarage Gate is handy for boutiques and restaurants on Kensington Church Street, and a laundromat is nearby. The nearest tube stops are Kensington High and Notting Hill Gate.

Clearlake Hotel, 19 Prince of Wales Terrace, W.8 (tel. 937-3274), is an ideal family hotel on a residential street facing Kensington Gardens. Remodeled from a row of early Victorian houses, the hotel offers every possible convenience for the traveler weary of typical hotel life. You can, of course, rent the comfortable single and double rooms, costing from £6.75 ($15.53) to £12.50 ($28.75) for one, or from £12.50 ($28.75) to £23 ($52.90) for two persons. However, the real finds are the two-room suites with bath and kitchenettes, housing up to five persons for anywhere from £14.50 ($33.35) to £28 ($64.40) nightly; and three-room suites, with baths and separate kitchens, accommodating four persons at a cost of £24 ($55.20) to £36 ($82.80). All rooms and suites have color TV sets. If you don't use the room's cooking facilities, you get your breakfast free. Andrew Herskovitz and his wife, Diana, have been managers here for many years.

Mr. and Mrs. A. Demetriou, 9 Strathmore Gardens, W.8 (tel. 229-6709), operate this small, privately owned guest house very close to Kensington Gardens and Hyde Park. Reader Joseph A. Wilson, a sergeant in the army, wrote, "They are without a doubt the most helpful, courteous, and gracious pair of hosts you could ever have the good fortune to meet. These kind people went out of their way to make me feel at home. The accommodations were immaculately clean. To use a cliché, 'You could literally eat off the floor.'" Beautifully kept and decorated, the rooms are rented at a rate of £8 ($18.40) per person for a bed and a breakfast served in a sun-filled basement dining room.

Hotel One Two Eight, 128 Holland Rd., W.14 (tel. 602-3395), is a somewhat offbeat place at which to live, located as it is in Holland Park to the north of Kensington High Street and to the south of Holland Park Avenue. Here the converted town houses still retain spacious gardens in the rear. The white facade of the hotel greets you with its small wrought-iron balconies and abundant flowers in summer. Of the 36 colorful, well-equipped bedrooms, 13 have private showers and 16 have private showers and toilets. All have bed lights, radio, TV, and telephone. Rates, including a complete English breakfast, are as follows: from £19 ($43.70) to £24 ($55.20) in a double, from £12.50 ($28.75) to £16 ($36.80) in a single, depending on the plumbing. Ask the owners, Mr. and Mrs. D. Novakovic, for one of the quieter rooms in the rear. Besides two guest lounges and a breakfast room, guests in the warmer months can also enjoy the rear garden, with its large lawn, stone walls, and towering trees. Tube: Shepherd's Bush.

Camellia Hotel, 16 Longridge Rd., S.W.5 (tel. 373-3848), lies in an unspoiled section of Kensington, on the better side of Earl's Court Road. The exterior is graced with an abundance of flowers in boxes and urns and baskets hanging from the windows. The lounge and breakfast room are made more inviting with Austrian pine furnishings. Central heating and color television add to the amenities. Singles cost £9 ($20.70). Doubles with private bath cost £16 ($36.80), although a few with hot and cold running water go for £14 ($32.20). A continental breakfast, VAT, and service are included. A full English breakfast is available at an extra charge. Tube: Earl's Court.

Hotel 167, 167 Old Brompton Rd., S.W.5 (tel. 373-0672), is a converted corner town house, maintaining its Victorian architectural features, although the decor has been considerably updated by Christina Rasmus, a Finnish designer. In clean, comfortable rooms, the hotel charges £11 ($25.30) in a bathless single, £16.69 ($38.39) in a bathless double or twin, and £18.36 ($42.23) in a double or twin with private bath or shower. A short walk from the hotel will take you to boutique-strewn King's Road. Tube: Gloucester Road.

READER'S HOTEL SELECTION: "I stayed in a delightful family hotel, **Coronet Hotel,** 59 Nevern Square, Earl's Court (tel. 373-6396), in a quiet residential area of London. Being well within walking distance of the underground, buses, exhibitions, and museums, it is an ideal base for any type of overseas visitor wishing to see and do as much as possible during a short stay. I found the rates offered most acceptable, and the accommodation of a very high standard. A single rents for £10.50 ($24.15), a bathless twin or double for £14.50 ($33.35), and a twin or double with private bath or shower for £18 ($41.40). A full English breakfast is included in all prices, and the service is personal and friendly. The proprietors are Mr. and Mrs. James, who ensure that the needs of their guests are attended to with promptness and courtesy" (W. Bowker, Manama, Bahrain).

9. Bayswater

North of Bayswater Road, west of Hyde Park and north of Kensington Gardens, is Bayswater, another unofficial district of London, with many well-recommended, moderately priced hotels, plus a number of low-budget bed-and-breakfast lodgings. Many of these former town houses, converted into hotels, date back to the days when Bayswater spelled the good life to a prosperous, upper middle class. Some of the town houses, often lined up in rows, open onto pleasant squares. Serving Bayswater Road are buses 12, 88, and 289. Both the Central and District undergrounds run to Bayswater tube station.

THE MEDIUM-PRICED RANGE: Portobello, 22 Stanley Gardens, W.11 (tel. 727-2777), makes us green with envy, as it fulfills a secret desire to take over a couple of antiquated, threadbare, 19th-century town houses and restore them to their former luster. Under the leadership of Tim Herring, his wife Cathy, and designer Julie Hodgess, a 30-room miracle was created. It has all that cool sophistication that goes with an eclectic collection of furnishings harmoniously blended. A single room costs £30 ($69); a double room, £35 ($80.50); a twin-bedded room, £40 ($92)—plus VAT and service. A continental breakfast is provided in your room and included in the cost. Each bedroom has a private bath, as well as color TV and individually controlled air contitioning. Natural wood pieces are upholstered in bright colors, an oval gilt mirror in the lounge hangs over a gleaming white marble fireplace, and the reception area echoes the Edwardian era. Shuttered doors in the bedrooms hide do-it-yourself equipment for preparing light fare and mixing drinks. At a beautiful restaurant, again designed by Julie Hodgess, good food and drink can be obtained at any hour. Tube: Notting Hill Gate.

Henry the Eighth, 19 Leinster Gardens, W.2 (tel. 262-0117), is a glamorous remake of an older, more conservative hotel. Its fine facade, with Ionic-style columns, and the lime trees out front have been preserved, and inside the restoration has been carried out with good taste. The lounges and dining rooms open onto a covered courtyard, with its own heated swimming pool and semitropical plants; the entry lounge has a ceiling-high wall of modern ceramic sculpture and a collage from London University. The "Strikes 1926" Restaurant specializes in a large variety of hamburgers, also providing steaks. The

LONDON: HOTELS 47

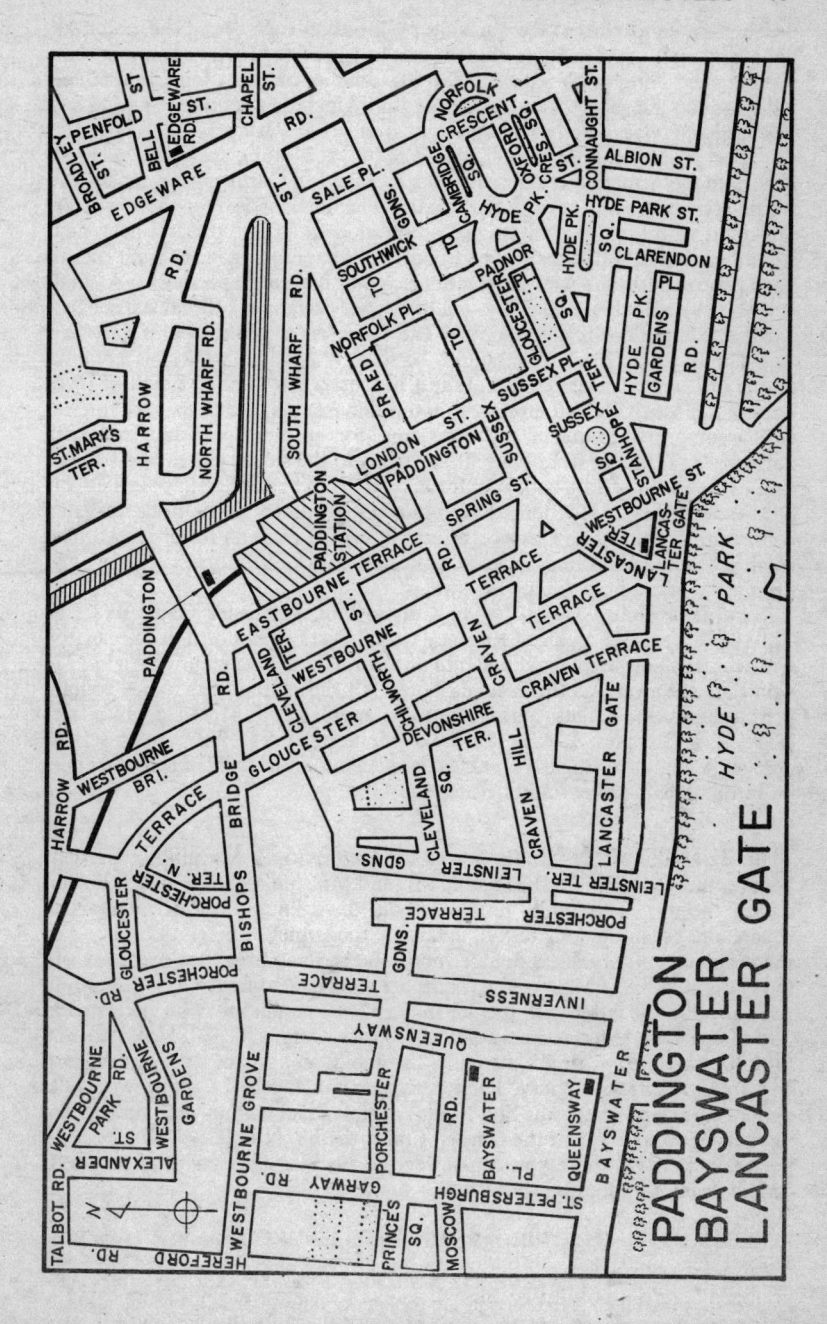

bedrooms are most attractive; each has push-button control of radio, color TV, lights and maid service. Some contain sofa beds, making for a bed/sitting room arrangement. Singles go for £25 ($57.50), doubles or twins for £35 ($80.50). All units contain showers and toilets, and rates include a continental breakfast, VAT, and service. The hotel is just north of Hyde Park.

Post House, 104 Bayswater Rd., W.2 (tel. 262-4461), contains nine floors of ultramodern rooms. It's across from Kensington Gardens, and most of its studio-style bedrooms open onto the park. The hotel is ideal for those who are impatient with London's antiquated accommodations, and prefer a neat, new, streamlined look. All of the 175 bedrooms (air conditioning in the front rooms) have private baths, as well as telephones, color TV sets, and radios. A single is £30 ($69); a double, £40 ($92)—including service and tax. Breakfast is extra. On the second floor is a restaurant. The hotel has a free car park.

The Senator Hotel, Westbourne Terrace, W.2 (tel. 262-4521), is a remake of one of London's classic old hotels; it lies just a few minutes north of Hyde Park and close to Oxford Street. Although the front is traditional, the interior is contemporary. Many of the bedrooms, for example, are duplexes, with narrow stairs leading from your sitting room to the sleeping area and bath. A single room with private bath goes for £20.50 ($47.15); £28 ($64.40) in a double or twin with bath. All rooms have color TV included in the price, as are a continental breakfast and service, although VAT is extra. A lower-level dining room is "ye olde England"—wood settles, Windsor chairs, trestle tables, and decorative bric-a-brac. Tube: Bayswater.

Cordova House Hotel, 14–16 Craven Hill, Lancaster Gate, W.2 (tel. 723-1065), was once a pair of Regency town houses lying north of Kensington Gardens. It's now been converted into an informal establishment which in 1976 won the area award as the best run hotel. All the redecorated rooms contain private baths and toilets, and single rates are £18.25 ($41.98); doubles, £25 ($57.50); and triples, £28.30 ($65.09),—including VAT. There is no service charge. A complete English breakfast is included in the tariff. The hotel offers an intimate bar. Tube: Paddington.

THE BUDGET RANGE: Garden Court Hotel, 30–31 Kensington Gardens Square, W.2 (tel. 229-2553), is run by Mr. and Mrs. Stefan Lis, who fled Poland during the war. The family found this old town house on a private garden square and began the long task of making it the homelike hotel it is today. For the occupants of a bathless double room, the bed-and-breakfast charge is £18 ($41.40), plus VAT. Most of the rooms are singles, renting for £11 ($25.30) to £13 ($29.90), the latter with private showers, but families may be interested in one of the four triple rooms ranging in price from £24.50 ($56.35) to £28 ($64.40), the latter with private bath. The ten double rooms with private bath cost from £20 ($46) nightly. Each room has a water basin, along with telephone, radio, and intercom. You'll enjoy meeting and talking with guests from many lands who frequent the Garden Court; there's a bar-television lounge on the ground floor, where you can lower the stock of beer on hand and hear candid opinions about world affairs.

READERS' HOTEL SELECTION: "Redland House Hotel, 52 Kendal St., Hyde Park, W.2 (tel. 723-7118), is a double town house just off Edgware Road. The proprietors Mr. and Mrs. H. Newlands, who charge £12 ($27.60) for singles, £11 ($25.30) per person for doubles or twins, plus VAT. This is just at the edge of the W.1 area. A two-minute walk from buses serving the Strand, this is a first-rate choice for budgeting time as well as money. Nearby are teashops and a variety of restaurants, plus laundromats. Further, one can walk to Oxford and Regent Streets and the parks. Redland House is attractive, clean, centrally heated, and most efficiently operated. No private baths are available, but there are ample facilities near all rooms. Reservations are desirable; in our experience inquiries were promptly answered. It is but a short walk to Selfridge's and the Marble Arch tube stop, but the Newlandses point out that using buses saved money. They are Welsh, intelligent, and interesting people. The establishment is well ordered and quiet for sleeping" (Mr. and Mrs. Arthur Thurner, Chicago, Ill.).

10. Paddington and Little Venice

Another popular hotel area, particularly for budget travelers, is the Paddington section, around Paddington Station, just to the northwest of Kensington Gardens and Hyde Park. Here you'll be within walking distance of the great Marble Arch, the entrance to Hyde Park. The main Paddington avenue, Sussex Gardens, has been known for years to pence-shy travelers who seek out its bed-and-breakfast houses. But as more and more town houses are being razed on Sussex Gardens to make way for expensive flats, Norfolk Square is gaining importance as the area in which to shop for budget hotels. Allowed to deteriorate after World War II, the square was formerly one of the most prestigious squares of London, especially in the reign of Victoria when the eminent built large, beautiful town houses ideal for big families, maids, and nannies.

On the periphery of Paddington is an unofficial district dubbed Little Venice, a seldom-visited hideaway off Edgware Road, north of Paddington Station. Little Venice gets its name because two branches of the Grand Union canal meet at Blomfield Road and Warwick Avenue. Bus 6 from the West End runs to Warwick Avenue, or else you can take the Bakerloo line to the Warwick Avenue station. From this district, you can book a ride on Jason's boat through Regent's Park, or board a boat in summer to the London Zoo.

THE MEDIUM-PRICED RANGE: Colonnade Hotel, 2 Warrington Crescent, W.9 (tel. 286-1052), is an imposing town house in a pleasant residential area, just a block from the Warwick Avenue tube station. Owned and managed by the Richards family, the hotel is run in a personal and friendly manner. The bedrooms are spacious (some with balconies), and are equipped with either private bath or hot and cold water. The rates, including a full English breakfast, are: £16 ($36.80) in a single without bathroom, £22 ($50.60) in a bathless double. For a single with private bath, the charge is £20 ($46) to £24 ($55.20); for a double with private bath, £24 ($55.20) to £30 ($69). VAT is extra. Tipping is left to your discretion. Mr. Richards emphasizes: "Every bedroom, bathroom and corridor is centrally heated 24 hours a day of every day from the first chill wind of autumn until the last breath of retreating winter, even in summer if necessary." He's installed a water-softening plant as well. All rooms have TV, radio, and telephone, and one even has a four-poster bed.

READER'S HOTEL SELECTION: "We stayed at the **Dylan Hotel,** 14 Devonshire Terrace, Lancaster Gate, W.2 (tel. 723-3280). The rates with breakfast are from £18 ($41.40) to £20.50 ($47.15) in a double, the latter with private shower. Singles rent from £10 ($23) to £12 ($27.60). The rooms are large, cheery, and very clean, and the breakfast delicious and more than adequate. The hotel has been redecorated and recarpeted from top to bottom. Accommodations have radio intercoms, shaver points, and central heating. Guests gather in the lounge to watch color TV. The hotel is convenient to the Paddington underground and Hyde Park" (Ann Calhoun, Los Angeles, Calif.).

11. St. Marylebone

Below Regent's Park, northwest of Piccadilly Circus, is the district of St. Marylebone (pronounced Mar-li-bone), a residential section which faces May-

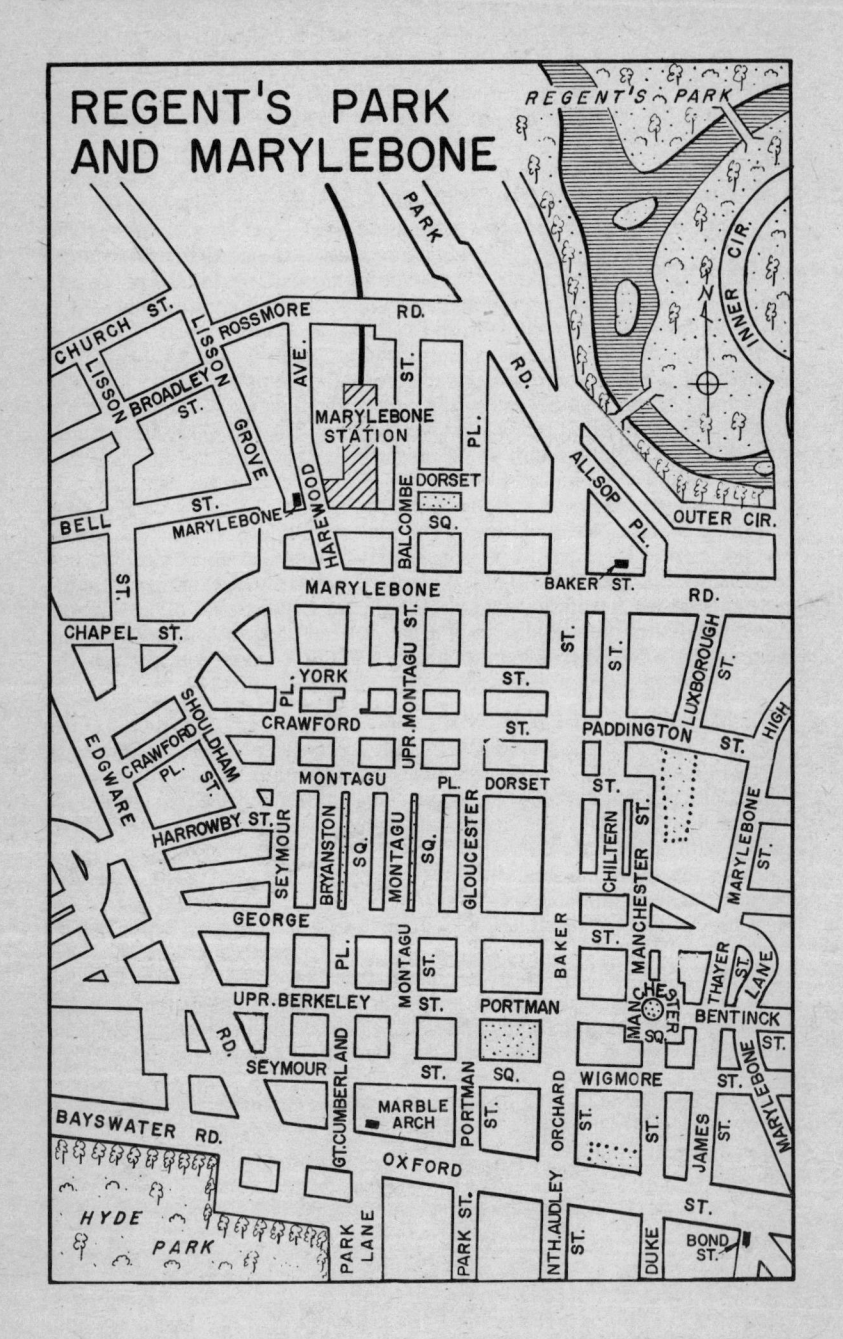

REGENT'S PARK AND MARYLEBONE

fair to the south and extends north of Marble Arch. A number of simple but gracious town houses in this section are being converted into private hotels. Many visitors arriving in London in peak season without a reservation go hotel shopping in this relatively undiscovered area, letting the crowds fight it out in Bloomsbury.

THE UPPER BRACKET: Cumberland Hotel, Marble Arch, W.1 (tel. 262-1234), will please those who want to be in the center—at Marble Arch, at the corner of Hyde Park, with its Speakers' Corner, and at the beginning of Oxford Street and Mayfair. It's a modern, well-equipped hotel, which in North America would be described as a top-notch business persons' place. You may get lost in the corridors, as the Cumberland is a colossus, containing 900 bedrooms! Those rooms are furnished with built-in units, bedside lights, TV sets, telephones, radios, private baths with showers, color television, trouser pressers, mini-bars, and small sitting areas. The rates include service charge and VAT. From April to October, a twin-bedded room rents for £55 ($126.50), a single for £44 ($101.20). Off-season prices are lower.

A plus is the ownership: Trust Houses Forte. Also, in the hotel is one of the best bargain restaurants in the capital, the all-you-can-eat Carvery, costing £6.80 ($15.64). And there's a quick-meal coffeeshop. The hotel's newest restaurant, Wyvern, offers traditional recipes from the 18th and 19th centuries. Specialties include such dishes as sirloin steak in "wow wow sauce," a recipe which includes pickled walnuts, capers, and port. Another offering is sole with prawn sauce, based on a dish devised by the head cook to Queen Victoria in the first year of her marriage to Albert. Yet another specialty is salmagundy, a salad from *The British Housewife,* a book published in 1749.

THE MEDIUM-PRICED RANGE: Hotel Concorde, 50 Great Cumberland Pl., Marble Arch, W.1 (tel. 402-6169), is a five-story brick building with a carriageway leading through to a quaint mews, little houses once reserved for servants, but now attracting the chic. The location is prestigious, just off a park and within walking distance of Marble Arch. The nightly charges, with a continental breakfast included, are £20 ($46) in a single with full bath, £29 ($66.70) in a twin or double with bath. VAT is extra. The rooms are attractively furnished, the lounge a mixture of antiques and leather chairs. Tube: Marble Arch.

Bryanston Court Hotel, Great Cumberland Place, Marble Arch, W.1 (tel. 262-3141), is three 19th-century town houses joined together by a central reception lounge, decorated with Delft Blue canvas. Just off restful Bryanston Square, with its well-tended gardens and trees, the hotel is only a short walk from Marble Arch and a rarity in central London in that it maintains a moderate price level. It is furnished with a good combination of antiques and traditional pieces. All rooms have bath or shower. Singles rent for £25 ($57.50), doubles or twins for £32 ($73.60), and triples for £38 ($87.40), these tariffs including a continental breakfast, service, and VAT. It's a good choice year round, as it's centrally heated, and each room has a radio and telephone. Tube: Marble Arch.

THE BUDGET RANGE: Merryfield House, 42 York St., off Baker Street, W.1 (tel. 935-8326), is a refreshingly pleasant remake of a 19th-century pub, the Lord Keith. Ale drinkers of old would look askance at the bright facade and the flower boxes filled with red geraniums. Owned by Mr. and Mrs.

Tyler-Smith, the hotel is a haven for those who cling to the old English ways. Resisting continental breakfasts, the manager, Bridget, serves a "jolly good breakfast" right in your room. Radio and TV can be had on request. According to the season and location, doubles (no twins or singles) range in price from £20 ($46) to £23 ($52.90), and every room has its own private bath and toilet. The house is small enough so that a tiny staff can keep everything shiny, polished, scrubbed, and laundered. The location is also convenient for budget-conscious shoppers, as it lies near Selfridges and Marks and Spencers. York Street is just two blocks south of Marylebone Road. Tube: Baker Street.

12. Mayfair

Mayfair, bounded by Piccadilly, Hyde Park, and Oxford and Regent Streets, is an elegant section of London. Luxury hotels exist side by side with Georgian town houses and swank shops. Here are the parks, names, and streets that have snob appeal the world over, including Grosvenor Square (pronounced Grov-nor) and Berkeley Square (pronounced Bark-ley). If you can't afford Claridge's try:

THE UPPER BRACKET: May Fair Hotel, Berkeley Street, W.1 (tel. 629-7777), is a remade, redecorated hotel that's a world unto itself. The circular cantilevered lobby staircase sets the pace. If you're not of international celebrity material, and can't afford either the Maharajah or Monte Carlo Suites, then you may settle for one of the decorator bedrooms. Those we've inspected have been colorfully and tastefully conceived. All the bedrooms contain private baths, and rent for £35.50 ($81.65) to £44 ($101.20) in a single, £53 ($121.90) to £58 ($133.40) in a double, service included. All rooms have color TV.

There are two major restaurants: Chateaubriand, with its excellent French cuisine, and the Beachcomber, with its Polynesian atmosphere and cuisine (dancing to two bands until 2 a.m.). In addition, there's a coffeehouse, really a grill, open from 10 a.m. until midnight. The facilities seem endless: bars, a movie house that operates as a private club (but is available to all hotel residents), a theater, and the Palm Beach Casino Club next door.

The **Europa,** Grosvenor Square, W.1 (tel. 493-1232), right by the American Embassy, is one of the leading hotels in the Grand Metropolitan Hotel chain. Its bedrooms—nearly 300 in all—have been furnished in the modern manner—but all in good taste, with an emphasis placed on simplicity. All rooms have private baths. Singles rent for £43 ($98.90); doubles or twins, £56 ($128.80). VAT is extra. Facilities include color TV, radios, and central heating. On the premises are the well-known Diplomat Restaurant and the Coffee Exchange.

THE MEDIUM-PRICED RANGE: Piccadilly Hotel, Piccadilly, W.1 (tel. 734-8000), is a union of the old and new. A classically designed building with a contemporary entrance, it is just one minute from Piccadilly Circus and close to many of London's fine stores. Opened in the spring of 1908, the hotel has attracted kings, queens, and ministers of state among other celebrated guests. Built at a tremendous cost, it became famous in the '20s for its tea dances. The bedrooms, 290 in all, have been modernized and furnished with Danish-style utilitarian furniture. A single with bath rents from £40 ($92), a twin with bath from £55 ($126.50). You can help yourself to delicious roasts from the Carver's Table Restaurant, where visitors can admire the magnificent Australian oak paneling. The Lounge Bar also creates an atmosphere of bygone days.

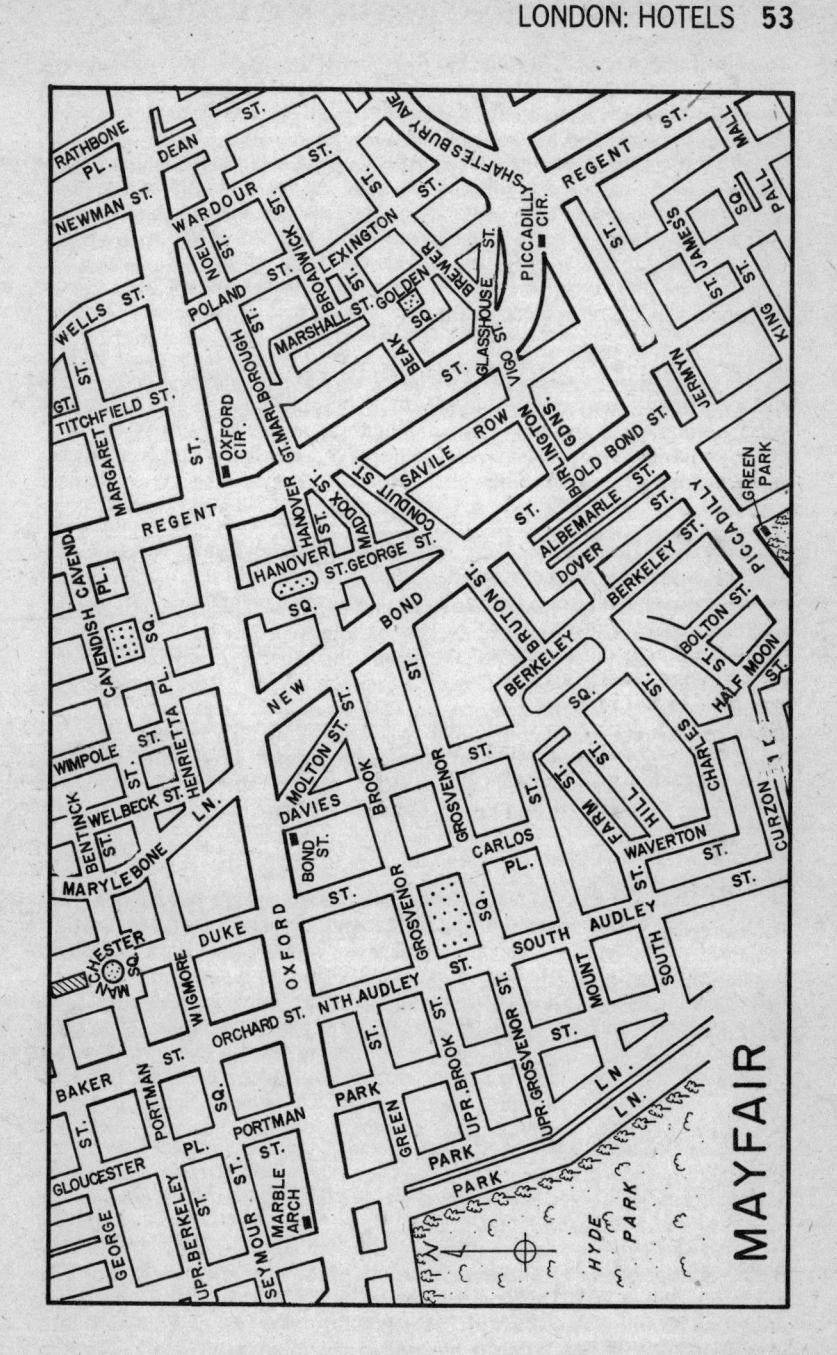

LONDON: HOTELS 53

The **Londoner** and **Clifton Ford,** Welbeck Street, W.1 (tel. 935-4442), stand next to each other and share a joint reservation service. They are members of the Grand Metropolitan chain, dedicated to rejuvenating aging London hotels. Tucked away in Mayfair, off Wigmore Street (near Cavendish Square and Wigmore Hall), the hotels are excellent remakes of older buildings. Spaciousness is the mood, especially in the clean-cut and uncluttered reception areas. The bedrooms have been furnished in shipshape Nordic fashion. Each one has its own shower bath. Singles rent for £30 ($69), doubles for £40 ($92). A continental breakfast, VAT, and service are included. All rooms have TV, radio and 24-hour room service. At the Londoner, Oliver's Tavern serves traditional English dishes, and in the Chesterfield Room the martinis are dry.

13. Bloomsbury

To the northeast of Piccadilly Circus, beyond Soho, is Bloomsbury, a world unto itself. It is, among other things, the academic heart of London, where you'll find London University, several other colleges, the British Museum, and many bookstores. Despite its student overtones, the section is fairly staid and quiet. Its reputation has been fanned by such writers as Virginia Woolf (it figures in her novel, *Jacob's Room*). She and her husband, Leonard, were once the unofficial leaders of a coterie of artists and writers known as the Bloomsbury Group, nicknamed Bloomsberries.

The exact heart of Bloomsbury is difficult to pinpoint. There are those who say it is Russell Square, with its university buildings, private homes, and hotels. Others feel it is the nearby British Museum. Still others are convinced it's the sprawling University of London, which also contains the Royal Academy of Dramatic Art on Gower Street. In any case there are at least four other old tree-filled squares—Bloomsbury, Bedford, Gordon, and Tavistock—each one an oasis of green in the midst of some of London's finest buildings. The unquestioned northern border is Euston Road, with its three railway stations—St. Pancras, King's Cross, and Euston—and its southern border is New Oxford Street.

THE UPPER BRACKET: Hotel Russell, Russell Square, W.C.1 (tel. 837-6470), is a late Victorian hotel facing the gardens of Russell Square and within easy reach of theaters and shopping. It is run by Trust Houses Forte and offers 300 rooms, all with private baths or showers. Rates for a single are from £35 ($80.50) and from £45 ($103.50) for a twin. The public rooms have been refurbished, and include an excellent restaurant which offers a full range of dishes and a Gaiety Bar with quick grills and drinks at pub prices in an Edwardian atmosphere. In the restaurant, you can order a continental breakfast at £3 ($6.90) or an English one at £4 ($9.20). Other facilities include a theater ticket agency, secretarial services, and a car-rental agency.

THE MEDIUM-PRICED RANGE: "Y" Hotel, 112 Great Russell St., W.C.1 (tel. 637-1333), is actually a modern hotel in the heart of London. Single rooms with shower rent for £19 ($43.70) a night, prices rising to £28 ($64.40) in a double or twin-bedded room with shower. It was built by the London Central Young Men's Christian Association for men and women of all ages. At the Oxford Street end of Tottenham Court Road, this new "Y" Hotel may not be like any you've ever seen before. Its facilities include squash courts, a gymnasium, an Olympic-size swimming pool, a shop, and an underground garage for car parking. Other facilities include a lounge and bar, plus two restaurants.

LONDON: HOTELS 55

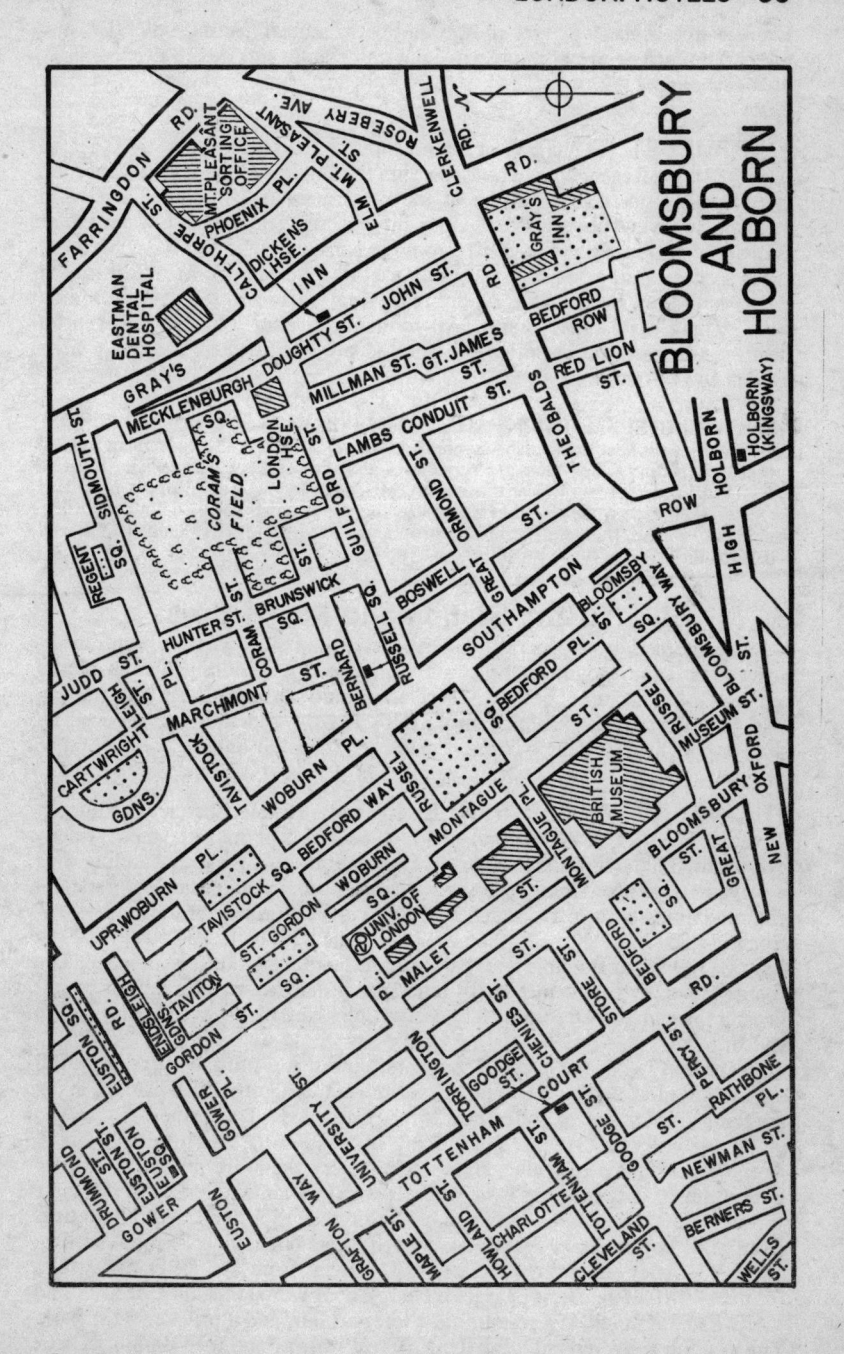

Every bedroom has a private shower and bath, central heating, color TV, and radio. The furnishings are modern and comfortable, and there's even wall-to-wall carpeting.

THE BUDGET RANGE: Lonsdale Hotel, 9-10 Bedford Pl., W.C.1 (tel. 636-1812), is a Regency town house, within the shadow of the British Museum. It's elegantly positioned on one of the most attractive tree-lined streets in London, midway between Russell and Bloomsbury Squares. It is a particular favorite of professors and scientists from the continent who find it a convenient place to stay while researching at the museum. The bed-and-breakfast rate in a double or twin is £25 ($57.50), although singles pay £15 ($34.50), including VAT. There is no other charge. All rooms have razor outlets—and central heating assures cozy warmth. The hotel is privately owned and has a little garden in the rear.

READERS' HOTEL SELECTION: "Staunton Hotel (B&B), 13-15 Gower St., W.C.1 (tel. 580-2740), stands near the British Museum and many shops. It is also convenient to good city transportation. The rooms are very clean, and the breakfast is excellent. The rate is £8 ($18.40) per person (lower off-season). Mr. and Mrs. W.G.D. Morgan permitted us to leave luggage while on other tours, keeping the lodgings for us upon our return. Anxious to please, they are personable proprietors" (Mr. and Mrs. Samuel C. Levin, Chicago, Ill.).

14. Euston Station and King's Cross

Accommodations generally less expensive than those we have been considering so far can be found in these rather nondescript sections just a few blocks north of Bloomsbury. The hotels here are mainly around three large railway stations—Euston, St. Pancras, and King's Cross—and they are serviced by three tube stations. King's Cross, Euston, and Euston Square.

THE MEDIUM-PRICED RANGE: Kennedy Hotel, Euston, Cardington Street, N.W.1 (tel. 387-4400), opened in 1968 and is perhaps the most American-inspired hotel in London. Next to Euston Station, it is a gray building with a drive-in entrance. Inside, everything is bright and you'll find top-grade accommodations with many touches of luxury. Yet the prices are moderate—from £24.50 ($56.35) to £29 ($66.70) in a single with bath, £34.50 ($79.35) to £39.50 ($90.85) in a double with bath. A continental breakfast is included. The rooms are expertly designed, with innerspring mattresses, TV, and air conditioning throughout. Decorator fabrics and colors are used—even the lamps are stylish.

The hotel's novelty is its Planters Restaurant. A profusion of greenery, full air conditioning, and an intriguing decor make this an attractive place to enjoy anything from a cup of coffee to a three-course meal with wine.

London Ryan, Gwynne Place, King's Cross Road, W.C.1 (tel. 278-2480), is one of London's new efficiency hotels, where there are no hidden extras. Everything in the bedrooms is streamlined and self-contained, that is, complete private baths, telephones, TV, radios, color television, and central heating. Even your continental breakfast is served in your chamber. From April to October, singles rent from £30.50 ($70.15), twins from £40 ($92), and triples from £45 ($103.50). These charges include a continental breakfast, service, and VAT. Facilities include a restaurant, Victorian Bar, and a private 50-car park. The location is convenient, near King's Cross railway and tube station, in back of Sadler's Wells, and within walking distance of the Dickens house.

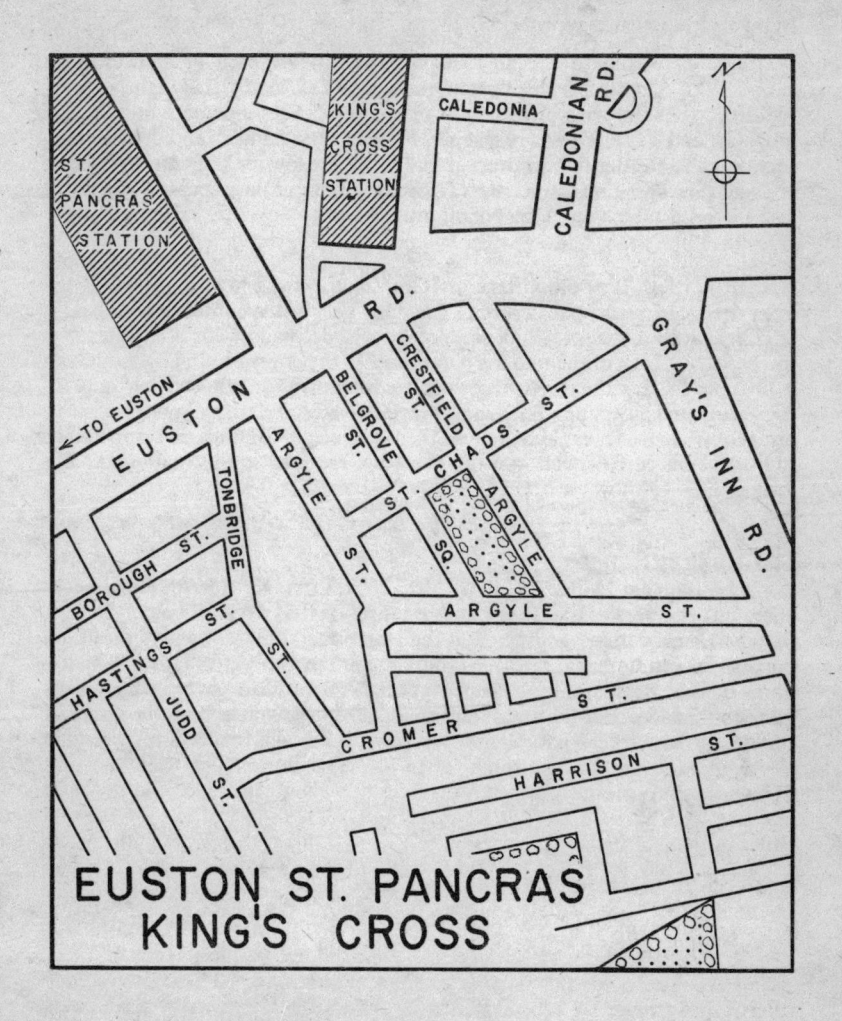

15. On the Fringe

SOUTHEAST LONDON: Time was when no one would think of building a hotel in unchic Elephant and Castle, across the Thames in Southeast London. But this is a new day and a new London—and here it is . . .

The Budget Range

London Park Hotel, Brook Drive, S.E. 11 (tel. 735-9191), is an enormous warehouse across the Thames that has been completely overhauled and turned into a streamlined modern hotel. It now boasts 380 bedrooms, most with showers or tubs, plus a large restaurant, coffeeshop, and two bars. Rooms are very comtemporary and contain built-in headboards with telephones and radios (some even have "baby-listening" devices). Bathless singles go for £11.90 ($27.37), increasing to £13.30 ($30.59) with private bath or shower. In a twin-bedded or double-bedded room, the cost is £18.75 ($43.13) nightly, rising to £20.90 ($48.07) with private bath or shower. Prices include a full English breakfast and VAT. There are fast elevators, express laundry and dry-cleaning service, and a theater ticket bureau. Meal prices are low for London: a set lunch is £5.50 ($12.65); a set dinner, £6 ($13.80). Numerous buses pass by the hotel, and there's a tube stop at Elephant and Castle.

HAMPSTEAD: The old village of Hampstead, sitting high on a hill, is the most desirable residential suburb of London. The village borders a wild heathland, which contains sprawling acres of wooded dells and fields of heather. Yet the Northern Line of the underground reaches the edges of the heath, making it possible for Londoners to enjoy isolated countryside while living only 20 minutes from city center. These advantages have caused many young artists to discover what Keats could have told them years ago—Hampstead is the place to live. The little Georgian houses have never received so much attention and love as they get now.

The Budget Range

Sandringham Hotel, 3 Holford Rd., N.W.3 (tel. 435-1569). You'd never guess this is a hotel, because it stands on a residential street in one of the best parts of London. After getting off at the Hampstead tube station, you walk up the hill past interesting shops, pubs, and charmingly converted houses. Shortly, at the Turpin Restaurant, you turn right into Hampstead Square which leads into Holford Road. A high wall and trees screen the house from the street (if you have a car, you can park in the driveway). It is a well-built, centrally heated house, and the comfortable rooms often house professional people who want to be near the center of London, yet retain the feel of rural life. The bed-and-breakfast charge is £8.50 ($19.55) in a single, increasing to £16 ($36.80) in a twin or double if bathless, but rising to £18 ($41.40) with private bath. A few triple rooms rent for £20 ($46). The breakfast room overlooks a walled garden; from the upper rooms you have a panoramic view over the heath of the center of London. You'll find a homelike lounge furnished with a color TV. Owners Mr. and Mrs. Dreyer and their two sons live on the premises.

SWISS COTTAGE: If you prefer life on a tree-lined residential street in north London, the following choice may appeal to you. It lies only ten minutes by underground from the heart of the West End.

Swiss Cottage Hotel, 4 Adamson Rd., N.W.3 (tel. 722-2281). This is rather an intriguing sort of place, an elegant family house furnished with paintings and antique furniture, Persian rugs, and chandeliers. The glass-fronted reception desk contains a fine collection of porcelain figures, and each bedroom has an old-fashioned bureau or writing desk. The lounge boasts a fine grand piano, a select place for afternoon tea. There is a pleasant quiet bar and a handsome dining room where à la carte meals are served.

Behind the hotel is a small formal town garden with trees, ferns, and geraniums, plus the Tea House area. This is the honeymoon suite, but you need not be on honeymoon to rent it. Bedrooms in the main hotel are very comfortable and, except for some singles, have modern showers or bathrooms. All have TV and telephone. The whole place is centrally heated. Singles go from £20

($46) to £34 ($78.20) for sole occupancy of a large double with bathroom. Doubles are £32 ($73.60) to £40 ($92), and the Tea House rents for £28 ($64.40). All rates include a full breakfast and VAT.

FULHAM: This is a pleasant part of West London. A tree-lined road stretches from St. Ethelred's Church (that's the bus stop you should ask for) to Bishop's Walk, a shady park running down to the river where in the afternoons a band often plays. And just around the corner is Fulham Palace, home of the bishop of London. In such a setting you're likely to discover London's most elegant bed and breakfast.

Off Fulham Palace Road, which runs from Hammersmith to Putney Bridge, at 10 Doneraile St., Fulham, S.W.6 (tel. 731-2192), **Lady Hartley** has two comfortable doubles available at £15 ($34.50) single occupancy, £20 ($46) double occupancy. In this elegant Edwardian house, renovated by Lady Hartley herself, you can come and go as you please.

The rooms are well furnished with comfortable beds. Guests share a bathroom but have their own tea- and coffee-making equipment. Knowing North American tastes, Lady Hartley willingly provides ice for your drinks.

Guests have the use of the front room to sit in, and this is where breakfast with hot croissants is served. Lady Hartley decided to take in guests purely because she and her two pug dogs enjoy meeting people. She does all she can to make you comfortable.

NEAR HEATHROW: For those who arrive jaded after an overnight flight to Heathrow, but have enough energy still left to rent a self-drive car and head north to Lincoln and York, this is just far enough to go.

Thatched Barn Hotel, Borehamwood, Elstree (tel. 953-1622), sits beside the A1 to the north, some 12 miles from Heathrow and the center of London. The original building dates from the 16th century, but much has been added and modernized to provide a very pleasant motel. Furnished with oak paneling and reproductions of antiques, all 60 bedrooms contain baths, color TVs, radios, telephones, and tea- and coffee-making facilities. Single occupancy costs £27 ($62.10). In a double or twin, the rate per person is £17 ($39.10). There are also rooms for three persons at £12 ($27.60) per person. All tariffs include service, VAT, and a large English breakfast. The dining room serves simple but well-prepared meals and hot grills, and there are also two bars which provide snacks besides the usual range of drinks. Close by is St. Albans and the remains of the Roman city of Verulanium. Also nearby is Eyot St. Lawrence where Sir George Bernard Shaw lived.

16. Alternatives to Hotels

STAYING WITH A FAMILY: At least ten agencies in Britain can arrange stays with a private family, either in London or in the country. As much as is possible, interests are matched. This program is an intriguing way to involve yourself in the social life of a country, seeing it from the inside. Also it's a great bargain. Some agencies limit themselves to teenagers, others welcome older readers.

Try one of the following: **Family Friendships Service,** 22 Palmerston Crescent, Palmers Green, London N.13 (tel. 882-5572), arranges accommodations with families in both London and throughout the United Kingdon (ages 12 and over), at prices that range from £50 ($115) to £65 ($149.50).

Or perhaps **Host & Guest Service,** 592a King's Rd., S.W.6 (tel. 731-5340), will provide a place for you at a cost that begins at £35 ($80.50) weekly for bed and breakfast.

In addition, **Family Holidays,** 2 Kirklands Ave., Baildon, Shipley, Yorkshire (tel. Bradford 584-848), owned by Douglas Cummins, has a well-screened list of Britishers who ordinarily don't accept paying guests and who are not accessible from any other source. These include professional people, owners of London apartments or country estates. Upon application, you'll receive information about your host, his or her interests, age, and family. The cost of all accommodations is the same: about £100 ($230) per person weekly for full board. Mr. Cummins adds a 15% service charge, and you'll pay no more. There's even an arrangement for what to do if you and your host don't get on too well.

E.T.S., 9 Norbury Ave., Thornton Heath, CR4 8AH (tel. 653-8467), arranges accommodations throughout the year for any length of visit with selected families living in the southwest suburbs of London. These locations are about 15 to 18 minutes by suburban train to the center of London, and there are also frequent buses. These pleasant residential suburbs have many recreational and cultural facilities. There is also good train service from Heathrow and Gatwick Airports. Accommodation is also available in various other towns in the United Kingdom. London fees: £6 ($13.80) per person per night for accommodation with English breakfast, or £7.60 ($17.48) per person per night for a room, an English breakfast, and an evening meal. Prices include the booking fee and tax.

London Tourist Holiday Flatlets, 4 Cornwall Mews West, S.W.7 (tel. 937-1011), is run by the very helpful Bill Wiggins and Chris Kauntze, who will secure readers "flatlets" (small apartments) in the Fulham and Chelsea area. They charge from £25 ($57.50) per week for a single room, from £38 ($87.40) per week in a double. However, doubles with private kitchens and baths cost from £55 ($126.50) per week. Letters from "flat-hunters" should be accompanied by a stamped, self-addressed envelope.

Hotel and Personal Accommodation Ltd., 10 Lower Belgrave St., S.W.1 (tel. 730-6181), will find suitable hotel accommodations for you in London and throughout the United Kingdom. As an alternative to a hotel, this agency can arrange short-term accommodation in serviced apartments, but only in the London area. Apartments in central London are all of first-class standard, and those in the suburbs are of economy standard. Try to give as much notice as possible, stating dates, types of rooms, standard, area required, and your maximum budget. This company charges no fees.

ACCOMMODATION SERVICE: The **London Tourist Board,** at 26 Grosvenor Gardens, Victoria, S.W.1 (tel. 730-0791), will make same-day bookings in a wide range of accommodations, from guest houses to hotels, for a basic price of £4.50 ($10.35) per person, including bed, breakfast, and VAT. At this price, though, the accommodation would be shared in a guest house or a hostel. Singles are available, beginning at £6.50 ($14.95). The board performs this service from its information centers at Victoria Station and at Heathrow Underground station. You're charged a booking fee of £1 ($2.30), regardless of the number of persons in your party, plus a refundable deposit of £4 ($9.20).

LONDON: HOTELS

In addition, the centers supply information on accommodations at campsites and in dormitories, plus other types of accommodations below the minimum price of £4.50 ($10.35). However, staff members will not book such accommodations through their centers.

BED AND BREAKFAST: A London firm offers B&B for $10 (U.S.) to $15 per night per person, and visitors who don't mind staying with an English family a bit away from the center of town can save a lot of money. **Stayaway Abroad** promises that all homes are within easy reach of public transport to central London. Much of the accommodation is in the northwest London Area, toward Hampstead and Golders Green. The price depends on the nearness to central London. There are a few "in town" rooms at $15 a night, and some budget accommodations with large rooms at only $10 a night per person. For information, write Stayaway Abroad, 71 Fellows Rd., London, NW3 3JY, England, or telephone 586-2768. Your reservations must be made six weeks before your trip.

LIVING LIKE A LORD AND LADY: If you have always wanted to spend the night inside a castle, **Country Homes and Castles**, 138a Piccadilly, W.1 (tel. 491-2584), may be able to arrange just the suitable abode for you. More than 250 houses, ranging from cottages to historic manor houses to turreted fortresses, are available to paying guests through this program. Since the owners naturally vary in their interests, ages, and professional backgrounds, the agency makes every effort to match you with suitable hosts so that both will benefit from an enjoyable experience.

The organization will arrange a one- or two-night stay in a single house to fit in with your travel plans, or it will try to arrange a complete tour with stops throughout the country, bearing in mind your personal interests. Prices for accommodations range from £63 ($144.90) to £105 ($241.50) per couple per night. The rate includes drinks, dinner with wine, accommodations with private bath and breakfast. All payments are made in advance to the agent so that you can enjoy your guest-host relationship without embarrassment.

STAY ON A FARM: Country Farm Holidays, The Place, Ham Lane, Powick, Worcester (tel. Worcester 0905/830899). For two or three nights in the country, all you have to do is get in touch with Country Farm Holidays who will fit you up with a lovely Elizabethan farm in Salop, amid paneled walls and old oak beams, or with a 15th-century moated farmhouse in Suffolk where you can enjoy the country life, dinner, bed, and breakfast for as little as £10 ($23) a night per person. They have a wide selection of attractive and often historic farms on their books, and will give you details of how to get there, what to see and do. Many of the places allow guests to help with the animals and the working of the farm. They also have a list of self-catering cottages and apartments available for rentals of seven nights or more, sleeping from two to ten persons in comfort. Prices vary, obviously, but in June four to five persons can have an accommodation for around £70 ($161) for seven nights, including VAT.

YOUR OWN APARTMENT: The **South London Tourist Accommodation**, 428 Southcroft Rd., Streatham, S.W.16 (tel. 769-3225), is a family-run business, serving some 5000 visitors to London yearly who are looking for nice and inexpensive "self-catering" accommodation. Michael or John Slade will try to provide you with a fully equipped, private, clean, cozy, modern flatlet, flat, or house, depending on the number in your party and your needs for seven days or more. Mini-flatlet prices start at £60 ($138) a week. Family mini-flatlets are from £90 ($207) a week. Accommodations are in quiet, pleasant suburbs only about five miles from the center of London, reached by excellent public transport service. Upon arrival you will be presented with a free "Welcome Pack" containing: bus and train maps, things to do, places to see, and how to get there. Advance bookings can be made. Discounts are available if you mention that you obtained the address from the Arthur Frommer *Dollarwise Guide to England and Scotland.* The bureau also offers a free pickup service from the local station to take you to the accommodation upon arrival. The offices are open Monday through Friday from 9 a.m. to 4 p.m. and Saturday from 9 a.m. until noon; closed Sunday and bank holidays. A free airmail brochure by return mail is available upon request. If you do not have time to book, simply telephone the bureau when you arrive. The staff will usually be able to help you. Rentals are for a minimum of seven days, plus any number of additional days or weeks you require, and start on any day and end on any day. No lease is required, no extra fees, no fuss—in fact, it's as simple as booking into a hotel, but it only costs about half the price of comparable accommodations.

The **Regency Suites,** 130 Queen's Gate, S.W.7 (tel. 370-4242), are well-furnished apartments. Style varies from rather masculine brown leather buttoned chairs, indoor plants, and sober carpeting to warm apricot and white net curtains, flowery armchairs, and soft lights. The kitchens are fully equipped with modern electrical appliances and kitchen utensils, the glass is good, and all the china comes from Wedgwood. The penthouse suites even have a dishwasher to cope with your entertaining program, and all suites are serviced daily. There is 24-hour porterage as well. A very wide range of provision shops are just around the corner so you should have to lack for nothing. Several of the larger apartments have their own terraces, equipped with garden furniture and electrically operated sunblinds. All have direct-dial telephone and a doorlock with a TV monitor. There is remote-control TV in all bedrooms and in the lounges. Bathrooms are very well equipped, and all linen is provided. A studio flat with large reception and bedroom, bath and kitchen costs from £250 ($575) per week; a double room, lounge, kitchen, and bath from £350 ($805). Three-room flats run from £400 ($920) per week; and the penthouses, each with enormous living rooms, three bedrooms each with bath, kitchen, and entrance lobby, are from £1500 ($3450) per week. All rates include VAT and service, and rentals of 22 days or more are preferred.

Draycott House, 10 Draycott Ave., S.W.3 (tel. 584-4659), and its fellow block, 41 Draycott Pl., just across the street, offer what may seem the ultimate in the way of facilities. The old London houses are well converted to provide self-contained luxury apartments and studio flats, furnished in Edwardian style but with modern kitchens and bathrooms. All have private telephone lines and color TV. There are a resident porter and housekeeper, plus maid service five days a week. On your arrival the refrigerator will be stocked with basic provisions and daily milk and newspapers will be delivered to you. Garage parking is also available. Rates compare very favorably with London hotels. A two-bedroom apartment is about £425 ($977.50) per week, and a three-bedroom apartment from £575 ($1322.50) to £625 ($1437.50) per week. Studios with room for two range from £225 ($617.50) to £325 ($847.50) per week. No service charge or VAT is added. The rub is that minimum rental is for three weeks. Miss Linda Coulthard is the resident administrator, young and highly experienced in the travel, hotel, and catering industry. In addition to the more domestic details, they can provide Telex, secretarial, and translation services for the business person, and will recommend eating places.

46 Lennox Gardens, Knightsbridge, S.W.1 (tel. 584-0665), stands in a lovely Victorian square just behind Harrods, the famous store. Mrs. Annie Chinner, assisted by Patricia Goodman, her receptionist, runs a block of "holiday apartments" of excellent standard and much patronized by regular visitors to London. The flats are simply but adequately furnished. Extra beds can be pulled from cupboards. Linen is supplied, and the kitchen/dinettes are excellently provisioned with all cooking and eating equipment. There are plenty of shops in the area to provide the ingredients of a do-it-yourself breakfast, and nearby Beauchamp Place will provide enough varied evening eating for your stay even if you don't wish to venture further. Prices range from £30 ($69) per night for a penthouse studio to £38 ($87.40) for two or three persons, up to £54 ($124.20) per night for two bedrooms, a lounge, kitchen, bath, and shower room. All rates include VAT and service. A deposit of £150 ($345) is required to secure a flat, but this will be refunded upon departure when the inventory has been checked and telephone accounts settled. All apartments have phones, TV sets, and central heating.

HOUSE SWAPPING: This custom is becoming more and more popular among those who spend three weeks or more in Great Britain. In exchange for a caretaker for your New York apartment or California bungalow, you might end up in a vine-covered country cottage.

Home Swap Overseas, P.O. Box 28, Pinner, Middlesex HA5 1DH (tel. 868-8254), has about 400 properties on their books in the United Kingdom, Europe, U.S.A., and Canada. They have a very simple application form, and for a subscription fee of £10 ($23), they will send you a list of properties suitable to your needs, as well as hints to make your exchange smooth and trouble-free. They require payment in sterling, or if you pay in any other currency, they will convert at current rates and add £2 ($4.60).

FOR GOLFERS ONLY: The Golfers Club was started in 1893. It has now opened its doors to overseas members, and an annual subscription of £20 ($46) will give you access to more than 50 golf clubs in England and Scotland, as well as privileged greens fees of around half the normal rates. Membership also permits you to use the Sloane Club in London where accommodations are available at around £18 ($41.40) a night. The 400 or so United Kingdom members will arrange introductions for overseas visitors in the particular area they are visiting. Matches and friendly games are also arranged, and members will even help in lending clubs and equipment. Members are often able to obtain concessionary rates for car hire, restaurants, and hotels. The club also makes up special golf packages for aficionados of the game. Write to Alan Jupp, Golfers Club, International House, Windmill Road, Sunbury-on-Thames, Middlesex (tel. 09327/85666).

Chapter III

LONDON: RESTAURANTS AND PUBS

1. The Top Restaurants
2. The West End
3. Other Locales
4. Suggestions for Sunday
5. The Pubs of London
6. The Wine Bars
7. Country Dining Near London

WHEN QUEEN ELIZABETH I was released from the Tower, with her stiff neck intact, she feasted on loin of pork and overcooked English peas. Up until the last few years, most of the English agreed with Queen Bess's idea of a feast, sometimes varying the peas with gray cabbage and boiled-to-death brussels sprouts. But the England of Elizabeth I is not the England of Elizabeth II, as your palate will quickly reveal to you if you sample some of the wares in the upcoming restaurants.

A new wave of skilled cooking, inspired by the continent and visitors' demands, has swept the country, but is most noticeable in London. Of course, the trend toward continental dishes is not without its pretensions. As novelist-historian-gourmet Raymond Postgate pointed out, boiled beef and carrots are still served, passed off as "la pièce de boeuf salée londonienne." A striking feature of the dining scene in London and the country is the emergence of the personality restaurant—that is, a dining spot based on the character, charm, and individual recipes of one exceptional chef.

Many Americans accustomed to spices and mixing and blending of foods find English cooking dull. Of course, the French show their disdain by calling anything plain, boiled, or cooked in the blandest way possible "à l'anglaise." However, simplicity doesn't mean bad food, and it's good to keep that in mind as you dine in London and elsewhere in England and Scotland.

All restaurants and cafes in Britain are required to display the prices of the food and drink they offer, in a place where the customer can see them before entering the eating area. If an establishment has an extensive à la carte menu, the prices of a representative selection of food and drink currently available must be displayed as well as the table d'hôte menu, if one is offered. Charges for service and any minimum charge or cover charge must also be made clear. The prices shown must be inclusive of VAT.

1. The Top Restaurants

Waltons, 121 Walton St., S.W.3 (tel. 584-0204). Dish after dish reflects the professionalism, enthusiasm, and creative skill of a fine chef, Murdo McSween. He is inspired. Not only is the cooking inventive, but the presentation is enchanting against a backdrop of an intimate modern decor. For an utterly delightful dining experience, go upstairs first and order an apéritif while looking over the menu leisurely.

As you're shown to your seat, you pass through a setting that blends Trianon gray with buttercup yellow and mauve tiles. The china is Royal Copenhagen; the cutlery, Georg Jensen.

A four-course dinner is featured at prices ranging from £18 ($41.40). We'd suggest beginning with the green vegetable pâté or else a pâté of hare and wood pigeon, if either of these openers are featured on the night of your visit. Main courses are likely to include rainbow trout poached in a whiskey cream sauce, saffron chicken (based on an 18th-century recipe), or chicken suprême, even collops (fried slices of meat) in the pan. The wine list includes selections from the aristocratic vintages of France, but also some modest choices as well. Although the prices are among the loftiest in the United Kingdom, the quality of the service and cuisine seem to merit them. You must make a reservation unless you plan to appear unannounced with the Queen of England on your arm.

This dinner of four courses, with international dishes, is served daily except Sunday. However, you might prefer "simply Waltons" at £9.50 ($21.85), a light lunch which changes frequently (again, not on Sunday). A three-course luncheon menu at £15.50 ($35.65) is featured daily except Sunday as well. On Sunday the traditional English weekend lunch of roast meats is offered for £11 ($25.30). In addition to the regular dinner, a late supper, costing £11 also, is presented after the theater, including a selection of principal dishes along with petit fours. The late supper is served daily except Sunday from 10:30 p.m. Lunch is from 12:30 to 2:30 p.m. (from 11:30 a.m. to 1:30 p.m. on Saturday) and dinner is from 7:30 to 11:30 nightly except Sunday.

Parkes and Mr. Benson's Bar, 4 Beauchamp Pl., S.W.3 (tel. 589-1390), is the pioneer of the new sort of gourmet restaurants that have sprung up in London; it has turned its back on the classic, dignified setting, the traditional French cooking, and has forged ahead to create a unique cuisine. Founded in the '50s by the late Ray Parkes, it was subsequently taken over by his assistant, Tom Benson, who not only carries on, but improves standards yearly.

It's on a short street of boutiques off Brompton Road, reached by a deceivingly small entrance, Inside is a *Town & Country* setting for portraying appetizing foods.

There are three intimate rooms for dining. Your host, Peter Dunn, will usher you to an upper-level drinking lounge where menu selections are made. Dinners all cost the same: £22 ($50.60), plus service and VAT. You pay extra for wines. The menu is highly personal and just a few dishes are prepared daily; the combinations reflect great imagination. A recent sampling: blackberry melon, or figs and smoked salmon as appetizers, followed by mussels in Pernod sauce. Main dishes include boned chicken with spinach and almonds, and roast partridge. Accompanying such plates is a green salad or a cheese pâté and freshly made herb bread. Among dessert listings, you're likely to find a grapefruit sorbet, and other items to tempt you. Last, you'll be served coffee and bittersweets. Dinner is from 7:30 to 11:15 p.m., except Sunday.

Lunch, offered from noon to 2:45 p.m., is à la carte, costing about £12 ($27.60) per person. A truly delicious recent midday meal began with a pheasant pâté en brioche, followed by loin of lamb en croûte, and ended with a peach in champagne, and coffee.

Carrier's, 2 Camden Passage, The Angel, N.1 (tel. 226-5353), is the special domain of Robert Carrier, one of the leading cookbook writers in the British Isles. His restaurant's location is unique—in a tiny antique row district of Islington, where little shops and booths are crammed to the ceiling with antiques and bric-a-brac. Everybody makes the trip, and Mr. Carrier proves a point—if you serve exciting food, the world will find its way to your door.

To simplify matters, both the lunch and dinner have set prices, the former costing from £12.50 ($28.75), the latter from £14 ($32.20), both plus VAT. Service and wine are extra. Starters are likely to include the house specialty, brandade of smoked trout. You might follow with leek and pumpkin soup. For your main course, you can make selections from "the open fire" or else "the great dish of the day." All the main dishes are served with a choice of gratin Dauphinois or saffron rice, as well as a green salad with herb dressing. A dessert treat, when featured, is a cold chocolate soufflé. The wine list is modest, but sufficient. Carrier's is open Monday through Saturday from 12:30 to 2:30 p.m. and from 7:30 till 11:30 p.m. Tube: Angel.

2. The West End

We'll begin the pleasant task of exploring the cuisine in the major districts of the West End:

ST. JAMES'S: In the former playground of royalty is a well-recommended French restaurant.

The Upper Bracket

À l'Ecu de France, 111 Jermyn St., S.W.1 (tel. 930-2837), offers the quintessence of French cuisine. It's not cheap, but then you wouldn't expect it to be. A short block from Piccadilly, the restaurant attracts Londoners with bowlers and briefcases, as well as numerous well-heeled visiting French diners. The atmosphere is traditional, without ostentation. On the right of the menu, there is a prix-fixe luncheon choice for £10.25 ($23.58). Dinner is à la carte and prices range from £15 ($34.50). Singled out for special praise are the coquilles St. Jacques (scallops baked in their shells) the crêpe de volaille (poultry) princess, and the boeuf en croûte (filet of beef cooked in pastry and served with truffle sauce). There is a good selection of desserts, including soufflé aux liqueurs and gâteau fromage. Dinner is served until 11:30 p.m. No lunch is served on Saturday or Sunday.

PICCADILLY CIRCUS: Garish, neon, crowded, but exciting, Piccadilly Circus keeps time with the heartbeat of a mighty city. Here, from all sections of the city, come the aristocrat, the housewife, the revolutionary, the government official, the secretary, the pimp, the financier. They converge around the statue of Eros.

Much of your London activity will center here, so finding the right restaurant is important, as many establishments are unabashed tourist traps or sleazy joints. The following restaurants have been selected not only for the quality of their food but because they offer the best value for the money.

The Upper Bracket

The **China Garden,** 66 Brewer St., W.1 (tel. 437-6500), is probably the most sophisticated and richly adorned Chinese restaurant in the West End. The bar entrance is dramatically conceived, with a stairway railed with brass bamboo poles leading down to the softly lit dining room, the stage center of which is reserved for dancing, with a 50p ($1.15) cover charge. The mood is set for a seductive evening, and the lure is the food itself, an authentically prepared selection of more than 200 dishes.

Owner Raymond Yu has carefully planned various groups of meals for one to four persons. For example, a dinner for two ranges from £6.50 ($14.95) to £9 ($20.70) per person. Among the more interesting items on the à la carte menu are sharkfin soup at £3.50 ($8.05) and Peking duck, £15 ($34.50) for five persons, including all the trimmings. The chef also does an excellent dish of prawns in sesame seed (called elephant eye) for £4.20 ($9.66). A good selection of desserts includes the house specialty, a fruit salad, £1.20 ($2.76). The restaurant is open daily, except Sunday, from noon to 3 p.m. and from 6 p.m. to 1 a.m.

The Budget Range

Rowley's, 113 Jermyn St., W.1 (tel. 930-2707), off Piccadilly Circus, gives one the impression of having just walked into Visconti's *"Death in Venice."* In what used to be an old meat market, today you'll find decorative tiled walls, potted palms, carved bentwood chairs, and hanging frosted globes. A slowly whirling overhead fan completes the picture—a successful recreation of a turn-of-the-century cafe. Didier Milinaire, son of the Duchess of Bedford, is managing director. A fashionable man not unused to leisurely meals, he insists the table is yours for the evening. When you arrive, the waiter will bring a bowl of tossed salad to your table. The main course itself is limited to only one item, a deliciously tender entrecôte of the finest quality sirloin, cooked to your specifications and served with a spicy butter. Fried potatoes—all you can eat—accompany the meat course. With your coffee you may choose from an interesting selection of puddings and cheeses. The total tab for this bill of fare comes to £7 ($16.10), including VAT. House wines served in magnums and champagnes are also available at moderate prices. Rowley's is open seven days a week from 12:15 to 2:30 p.m. and from 6 to 11:30 p.m.

The Granary, Albermarle Street, W.1 (tel. 493-2978), is open from 10 a.m. to mid-evening, serving throughout this time a delicious variety of hot dishes, all of which have a real home-cooked flavor. Chicken provencale costs £1.80 ($4.14); egg and prawn Florentine, £1.50 ($3.45); braised liver with bacon and onions, £1.80 ($4.14); and cottage pie, £1.40 ($3.22). Everything can be taken in foil containers to eat elsewhere. (Remember, no VAT is charged for food carried away.) A number of puddings and homemade cakes are offered at 75p ($1.73) a serving.

The Carvery, on the ground floor of the Regent Palace Hotel, Glasshouse Street, W.1, is just 20 feet from Piccadilly Circus. Who'd think that for £6.50 ($14.95) you could have all that your plate can hold of fabulous roasts and be able to go back for seconds, even thirds? Yet that's the policy of this renowned, all-you-can-eat establishment, a winner with visitors seeking rib-sticking food. The first course, perhaps a large slice of chilled melon, is served at your table. After that, you can go to the buffet table, where roast prime ribs of beef (choice of rare or well done), Yorkshire pudding, roast leg of Southdown lamb with mint sauce, and a roast leg of pork with apple sauce are spread before you.

You carve the meat yourself, slicing off as much as you want, although carvers stand by to assist and give instructions on how to wield the knife. You can then heap your heated plate with buttered peas, roast potatoes, new carrots, and gravy. In another area is a display of cold joints and assorted salads—whatever is in season. A plate of fresh fruit and a pitcher of thick cream are brought in for dessert, or you can select from the sweet trolley such desserts as meringue or chocolate and pineapple gâteaux, perhaps a strawberry mousse. Well-brewed coffee for "afters" is included in the price. The Carvery is open Monday to Saturday from noon to 3 p.m. and 5:30 to 9 p.m., and on Sunday from 12:30 to 2:30 p.m. and 6 to 9 p.m.

Good news department: There are four more Carvery establishments in London, with the same policy and the same menu. The newest is within the Tower Hotel, an ideal place to lunch when you visit the Tower of London. The tab here will run £7.60 ($17.48), however. Then there is one at the Strand Palace Hotel, on the Strand. Here the decor is fetching: black tufted booths, a wood-paneled ceiling, decorative artifacts on the walls, a hugh old wine press, modern paintings, rare Italian engravings, and converted baroque kerosene lanterns. At the Cumberland Hotel, at Marble Arch, the Carvery is more clublike, with tables on two levels, where you dine in low-lit, seductive atmosphere. It's convenient for Paddington and the West End area. Finally, a Carvery is at the Kingsley Hotel, Bloomsbury Way, close to the British Museum.

Hard Rock Cafe, on Piccadilly at Hyde Park Corner, W.1 (tel. 629-0382), is as close as London comes to having a roadhouse diner or truck stop, reminiscent of the American South. Naturally, two Americans, one from Memphis, the other from Chicago, opened it. Popular with the young English, it is open from noon to the early hours of the morning. Pop music is played in the background. The Hard Rock soup of the day goes for 75p ($1.73). A half-pound "Down Home" double-burger is served for £3.20 ($7.36), including a salad. Hot chili (in winter) and crackers is priced at £2.50 ($5.75). Ice cream is homemade, costing £1.20 ($2.76) a dish.

LEICESTER SQUARE: Named for the Earl of Leicester, and once the site of the home of Sir Joshua Reynolds, Leicester Square has since become the movie center of London. The 19th-century square is a congested area of stores, theaters, movie houses, even churches. It also has some inexpensive restaurants and pubs (popular with West End actors) in its little offshoot lanes and alleyways.

The Medium-Priced Range

Stone's Chop House, Panton Street, off the Haymarket, S.W.1 (tel. 930-0037), is a legend. Of course, what you see today is a reproduction of the old place—the original was bombed in 1941. During the 19th century, this was a meeting place for London society (men only), a world of handlebar mustaches and cut-velvet walls. In Edwardian days, the food was highly praised. The Dover sole was said to bring "tears to the eyes for grief that anything so innocent and tender should have to yield up its life." The stuffy male diners were shocked in 1921 at a sudden female invasion, but women are now most welcome in both restaurants. The tradition of serving good English food is maintained. Offered are the traditional Dover sole, £6.85 ($15.76); roast saddle of lamb, £6.95 ($15.99); roast pheasant, £17.60 ($40.48) for two diners. Roast sirloin from the trolley goes for £6.95 ($15.99). Fresh pineapple at £1.35 ($3.11) makes a good finish. Closed Sunday but otherwise open from noon to 2:30 p.m. and from 6 to 11:15 p.m.

London Swiss Centre Restaurant, New Coventry Street, W.1 (tel. 734-1291), is a showcase four-in-one restaurant where Switzerland wins friends and influences palates. Opened in 1968 and dedicated to bettering people-to-people relationships between England and Switzerland, this group of restaurants prepares Swiss cuisine with consummate skill. You can dine either in the Chesa, Rendez-Vous, Taverne, or the Locanda. Hot meals are served until midnight. The Chesa is the most expensive, the Locanda and Taverne medium priced, and Rendez-Vous the cheapest.

In the Taverne, the excellent cheese fondue is served for £4 ($9.20). In the Locanda you can sample tasty dishes, including marinated lamb grilled on a skewer, £3.50 ($8.05). The informal Rendez-Vous serves an interesting range of snacks and light meals as well as hamburgers and steak tartare. Finally, in the Chesa you can enjoy specialties such as Züri-Gschnätzlets, a spectacular émincé of veal served with rösti potatoes, £6.10 ($14.03).

There is also a coffee bar open seven days a week, 8:30 a.m. to 11:30 p.m. (on Sunday, 11:30 a.m. to 11:30 p.m.).

J. Sheekey Ltd., 29–31 St. Martin's Court, W.C.2 (tel. 240-2565), is an 1896 restaurant-fishbar that over the years has been a gathering place for show people (autographed celebrity photos on the wall). Trying to get a table may make you feel like a salmon going upstream, but it's worth it. Sheekey serves a pre- and after-theater meal. For a beginning, we'd suggest the smoked fish pâté at £1.10 ($2.53). A regular dish of the day, such as fish pie, is usually offered at about £3.50 ($8.05). Naturally, the chef features jellied eels, costing £3.50 also. Most fish dishes are either grilled or poached. The large Dover sole, at this writing, goes for £6 ($13.80). The restaurant is open Monday through Saturday from 12:30 to 3 p.m. and from 5:30 to 11:30 p.m. It faces the stage doors of the Albury and Wyndham's theaters.

Manzi's, 1–2 Leicester St., off Leicester Square, W.C.2 (tel. 437-5131), is London's oldest seafood restaurant. Here you can get that jellied eel you've heard so much about, or else real Dover sole which overflows your platter. This lively Soho seafood restaurant doesn't waste much effort on decor, but the fish is fresh and it's proved so reliable that a loyal clientele has patronized Manzi's for years. Perhaps the waiters aren't English any more, but otherwise the recipes are much the same. You can begin with a prawn cocktail at £1.30 ($2.99) or perhaps half a dozen Whitstable oysters at £1.75 ($4.03). Recently we sampled the legendary jellied eels at £1.80 ($4.14); fresh sardines, £1.75 ($4.03); and crab salad, £3.80 ($8.74). Other recommendable courses include the Dover sole at £5.10 ($11.73) and grilled turbot, £5.10 also. If you don't prefer the ground-floor restaurant, then you can ask to go up to the Cabin Room on the next floor. Hours are from noon to 3 p.m. and from 5:30 till 11:45 p.m.

San Martino, 46 St. Martin's Lane, W.C.2 (tel. 240-2336), is a typical Italian eating place, the entrance hall with its enormous mouthwatering display of cold delicacies leading to the lounge where a piano softly plays while you sip your apéritif. They do a set pre- or post-theater meal for £5.60 ($12.88), offering a choice of appetizers, followed by osso buco, a cold buffet, grilled trout, or chicken with two vegetables, then fruit salad, trifle, cassata, or crème caramel, and coffee.

But the à la carte menu has a wide range of appetizers, including an enormous plate of mixed hors d'oeuvres of sardine, squid, whitebait, vegetables, and salads for £2.50 ($5.75). This is to be avoided if you plan a substantial main course. There are the usual spaghetti, cannelloni, and lasagne dishes for between £1.50 ($3.45) and £2 ($4.60). Main courses include fagottino San Martino at £4 ($9.20), veal filets with cheese and ham filling, wine and mushroom sauce. Most vegetables are 65p ($1.50) a portion. There is a good trolley of desserts for around 90p ($2.07) a serving. House wine is £4 ($9.20) a bottle, or you can chose from a selection of more expensive Italian vintages. The restaurant is open Monday to Saturday for lunch from noon to 3 p.m. and then from 5:30 p.m. to 11:30 p.m. Closed on Sunday.

READER'S RESTAURANT SELECTION: "The Leicester Square Restaurant is actually just off the square, at 16 Irving St., W.C.2 It served the best char-broiled steaks that we had in London, priced at £4 ($9.20) to £5 ($11.50). The menu, which is à la carte, lists veal, fish, lamb, chicken, salads, vegetables, and, surprisingly, baked potatoes. The fresh flowers on the tables and profusion of potted plants provide a relaxing decor. After a large steak dinner, the many fruit and pastry desserts may be too much, but a sweet is provided even if dessert is not ordered. Glace fruit is served with the coffee" (Edward Pasahow, San Diego, Calif.).

ON THE STRAND: In another major geographic and tourist center, the Strand, you'll probably want to consider what we view as the most English restaurant in the world:

The Medium-Priced Range

Simpson's-in-the-Strand, 100 The Strand, W.C.2, is more an institution than a restaurant. All this very Victorian place needs is an Empire; it has everything else—Adam paneling, crystal, and an army of grandly formal waiters hovering about. On most visitors' lists there is this notation: "See the changing of the guard, lunch at Simpson's." It's that popular. Consequently, you must call in advance for reservations (tel. 836-9112).

There is one point most diners agree on: Simpson's serves the best roasts (joints) in London. Huge roasts are trolleyed to your table and you can have slabs of beef carved off and served with traditional Yorkshire pudding. The classic dishes are: roast sirloin of beef, £6.85 ($15.76); roast saddle of lamb with red currant jelly, £6.85 also; roast Aylesbury duck with apple sauce, £6.05 ($13.92); steak, kidney, and mushroom pie, £4.30 ($9.89). All dishes include the near-legendary Simpson's cabbage, as well as potatoes and rolls. Remember to tip the carver so you won't get one of those frightening, contemptuous British stares. The classic dessert is the boiled treacle roll at £1.05 ($2.42). There is a cover charge of 85p ($1.96), and all prices are inclusive of VAT and service charge.

Joe Allen's, 13 Exeter St., W.C.2 (tel. 836-0651), has invaded London with his red-checked tablecloths and spinach salad, not to mention barbecued ribs and bowls of chili. Londoners, of course, by now are long familiar with American invasions, so Mr. Allen didn't create a revolution. The decor is actually an improvement on its New York namesake, the London Restaurant appearing more openly inviting. We even enjoy the food better in the English eatery. The food is solid, reliable, uninspired, but, on the other hand, rarely disappointing. Try the familiar specialties: black bean soup at 80p ($1.84); barbecued ribs at £3.50 ($8.05); the regular spinach salad, £1.50 ($3.45); a bowl of chili, £2 ($4.60); calf liver and onions, £4 ($9.20); and the really delicious carrot cake, 95p ($2.19). The items of the day are listed on a blackboard menu. Naturally, show business posters adorn the walls. Service is by friendly waiters and waitresses who just may be out-of-work actors and actresses. The guests are often people connected with the world of the theater. Joe Allen's is open until 1 a.m. every day (till midnight on Sunday). The bar closes from 3 to 5:30 p.m. (from 2 to 7 p.m. on Sunday).

COVENT GARDEN: In 1970, London's flower, fruit, and veg market celebrated its 300th anniversary. But Auld Land Syne should have been the theme song that day, as the historic, congested market was transferred in 1974 to a $7.2-million, 64-acre site at Nine Elms, in the suburb of Vauxhall, 2½ miles away, across the Thames.

Covent Garden dates from the time when the monks of Westminister Abbey dumped their surplus home-grown vegetables there. In 1670 Charles II granted the Earl of Bedford the right to "sell roots and herbs, whatsoever" in the district. The king's mistress, Nell Gwynne, once peddled oranges on Drury Lane (and later appeared on the stage of the **Drury Lane Theatre**).

Before that, in the 1630s, Inigo Jones designed the square. He hoped to complete a plaza in the Florentine style, but the work on it got bogged down. Even his self-tabbed handsomest barn in England, **St. Paul's Covent Garden**, burned down in the late 18th century and was subsequently rebuilt. The English actress, Dame Ellen Terry (noted in particular for her letters to G. B. Shaw), is buried there, incidentally. St. Paul's eastern face looks down on the market where Pygmalion's Professor Higgins met his "squashed cabbage leaf," Eliza Doolittle.

Also in the area is the **Royal Opera House** on Bow Street, housing the Royal Ballet and the Covent Garden Opera Company. On nearby Russell Street, Samuel Johnson met his admirer, Boswell, and coffeehouses in the district were once patronized by Addison and Steele. Just as chicly dressed people once flocked to Les Halles in Paris to have onion soup, so London revelers used to drop in at Covent Garden's pubs to drink with Cockney barrow boys in the early dawn hours. The tradition will be sadly missed.

What will happen to Covent Garden? One plan being discussed is to turn the area into a commercial and entertainment district, complete with restaurants, hotels, maybe a convention center. But conservationists won a major battle in 1973, when the Department of Environment ruled that 250 buildings near the market site must be preserved as historic, plus 80 already designated. Geoffrey Rippon, environmental minister, said: "We can't preserve everything. The plan will go forward, but on a reduced scale. We want to avoid the look of a concrete jungle. And we want to be sure there is proper harmony between the new and the old. What we really want to achieve is something like the preserved character of Bourbon Street in New Orleans."

Recently an old cabbage warehouse was reopened as the Jubilee Street Market. Cockney costermongers (vegetable traders) have moved in in force, including Barry Teeden, the fastest apple polisher in the business, and Ginger Hurd, purveyor of jellied eels.

There are new exlcusive clubs here, such as the **Zanzibar** and the **Rock Garden**. The **Blitz** offers snacks, and **Brahms and Liszt** offers drinks.

And the area has begun to attract art galleries, such as the Acme, the Hammond Lloyd, the Covent Garden, and the William Drummond. A new plant shop, the Neal Street, specializes in Chinese vases used as planters.

It's appropriate that art galleries should be returning to Covent Garden. In the 18th century it was a beehive of artists, including Lely and Kneller (famous portrait painters, the latter of whom is buried at St. Paul's Church around the corner). Others who lived here were Thornhill, Richard Wilson, Fuseli, Daniel Mytens, the sculptor Roubiliac, Zoffany, and Flaxman. The

American painter Benjamin West also lived here after he got out of jail for trying to study in London during the Revolution.

The Upper Bracket

Inigo Jones, 14 Garrick St., W.C.2 (tel. 836-6456), offers a mainly French menu and superbly cooked fresh vegetables, in a romantic setting, a former stained-glass studio in Covent Garden. It appears that you're arriving at a chapel door. During the reconstruction of the building, five stained-glass windows were discovered, and they were used decoratively in the present establishment. Listening to gentle harpischord music, you are served while seated on a soft brown woolen banquette placed against a rough-textured brick wall. Filtered light focuses on wooden carved gargoyles and saints placed on the walls. Service by waiters in leather aprons is friendly and efficient. It's costly, but then you would expect it to be. For a beginning, why not one of the soups in the £2.20 ($5.06) to £2.60 ($5.98) range? For a main dish, we'd recommend the boned saddle of English lamb, baked in puff pastry, £18.60 ($42.78) for two persons although you may prefer Dover sole meunière at £9.30 ($21.39). As a side course, we especially like the shredded lettuce and spinach salad with bacon at £2 ($4.60). The restaurant is closed for lunch on Saturday and all day Sunday. Otherwise, hours are from 12:30 to 2:30 p.m. and from 6 to 11:45 p.m.

The Medium-Priced Range

Poons of Covent Garden, 41 King St., W.C.2 (tel. 240-1743), is one of the best Chinese restaurants in London. The place is run by Wai-Lim (Bill) and his wife, Cecilia Poon. Mr. Poon's great-great-grandfather cooked for the Chinese emperors, and succeeding generations of the family have all interested themselves in traditional Chinese cookery. The decor is reminiscent of *The World of Susie Wong.* Tables surround an island see-through kitchen which has been the subject of some controversy. We personally like it, as it's fascinating to stand and watch the chefs go through their intricate steps. The house specializes in wind-dried sausage and duck, which is quite different in flavor from smoked. Two of the most recommendable courses include Poons special wind-dried duck at £4.20 ($9.66) and Poons special wind-dried bacon with seasonal greens at £3.50 ($8.05). For a beginning, you might select the sharkfin broth at £2.20 ($5.06) or the bird's-nest soup at £2 ($4.60). Other preferred specialties include Poons special crispy chicken (one half) for £5.50 ($12.65); braised pigeon, Cantonese style, £5.80 ($13.34); and sweet-and-sour pork based on an original recipe, £2.70 ($6.21).

Poons also runs a much smaller and more ethnic restaurant in Soho at 27 Lisle St., W.1 (tel. 437-1528), but we infinitely prefer the Covent Garden one, and we think you will, too. If you're a serious and dedicated gourmet of the Chinese cuisine, as are many people these days, you'll find Poons willing to provide you with some rare and delectable specialties, providing you give them 24 hours' notice. Ever had stewed duck's feet with fish lips? Mr. Poon gives Chinese cooking lessons on the premises, and Cecilia is usually on hand to explain the niceties of the menu and to discuss the ingredients of any particular dish. They also do a set lunch at £12 ($27.60) for two persons or £15 ($34.50) for four diners. The restaurant is open from noon to midnight daily except Sunday.

Rules, 35 Maiden Lane, off the Strand, W.C.2 (tel. 836-5314), dates back to 1798 when it made its debut as an oyster bar. Over its long and legendary history, it has been the steady haunt of actors and actresses, newspaper columnists, and barristers. In the Gay '90s, the Prince of Wales (later Edward VII) was its most famous patron, accompanied, as always, by the Jersey Lily. The prince dined on the second floor, now the Edward VII Room. Pictures of Lily hang in the alcove where they used to sit. Another alcove honors Charles Dickens, who used to dine and do some of his writing at Rules. The restaurant is under the care of Cyril Taylor.

You enter via the front bar, with its red plush settees. The walls are hung with cartoons George Whitelaw did in the '20s and '30s. Rules specializes in dishes such as jugged hare at £6 ($13.80); grilled Dover sole at £8 ($18.40); grouse, steak, and kidney pie at £6 ($13.80); and Rules duckling, £10 ($23) for two persons. In season, hare soup costs £1.50 ($3.45). Apple and black currant pie with fresh cream makes a good finish at 80p ($1.84). Rules is closed on Saturday and Sunday.

Boulestin, 25 Southampton St., W.C.2 (tel. 836-7061). This famous old restaurant, founded by Marcel Boulestin, the first Fleet Street restaurant critic, more than half a century ago has had a facelift. It's reached by a side door which goes down into the basement beneath a bank. The decor is warmly gold and tortoiseshell. Sober pictures of cattle and deer adorn the walls in a very British manner, but the menu is entirely French. Appetizers include soups and pâtés, although you'll have to pay around £4 ($9.20) for the more elaborate "starters." For a main course, we'd recommend such dishes as sole Véronique or liver served with orange, both costing from £4 ($9.20). Desserts include fresh fruit salad, mousses, and sorbets, and there is a wide choice of house wines (half bottles available as well). The cover charge and VAT are included in the prices quoted, although a 15% service charge is added. The restaurant serves Monday to Friday from noon to 2:30 p.m. and from 7 to 11 p.m. (from 7 to 11:30 p.m. only on Saturday).

Tuttons, 11–12 Russell St., W.C.2 (tel. 836-1167), sits on the side of Covent Garden's piazza with wide windows overlooking the square and the Opera House. The restaurant has stone floors and clean wooden tables. It opens from 9 a.m. for breakfast, works through morning coffee, lunch, and tea to dinner, closing around 11:30 p.m. The atmosphere is businesslike, and the service quick and cheery. Various quiches go for £1.25 ($2.88) to £2 ($4.60), pâtés and mousses for £1.20 ($2.76). Main courses include steak-and-kidney pie at £3.20 ($7.36), game pie and salad at £3 ($6.90), and salmon trout mayonnaise at £5 ($11.50). Desserts start at 65p ($1.50) and rise to £1.20 ($2.76) for profiteroles. Down below the snackbar is another restaurant, serving gazpacho at £1.10 ($2.53), or oyster pâté at £1.40 ($3.22). A Barnsley chop costs £4 ($9.20); rump steak with bananas, £4.20 ($9.66); and a baby chicken in mushroom sauce, £4 ($9.20). Vegetables fresh in season are 75p ($1.73) a portion. Downstairs, it's better to book a table for dinner as it gets quite full.

The Grange, 39 King St., W.C.2 (tel. 240-2939). There's a small cocktail bar at the entrance in which to decide on which of the set menus you will embark upon. Then you go into a warm brown restaurant, with soft lights and bright white table linen. There are two set menus, one at £8.50 ($19.55), the other at £12 ($27.60) for three courses, £13 ($29.90) for four courses. All include half a bottle of the house wine to be chosen from quite a wide selection of French-bottled whites and reds.

The most reasonable menu is a choice from the ten or so appetizers—cream of artichoke soup, whiting in cucumber shells, a selection of pâtés, shrimp, celery and apple cocktail, seafood cocktail, leek and bacon flan, followed by skate in black butter, loin of pork with red cabbage, kidneys in mustard sauce, Shrewsbury lamb, chicken with scampi, Irish stew, veal with mushrooms, and peppersteak. The meal is rounded off with coffee.

The more expensive list includes salmon and turbot pâté, fresh raw vegetables with dips, and artichokes with taramasalata. Then roast saddle of venison, rack of lamb, filet of beef, or poached turbot. Desserts include fruit fools and mousses, apple and hazelnut tart, Nesselrode pudding, or various sorbets. There is Stilton cheese and coffee. The Grange is open Monday to Friday from 12:30 to 2:30 p.m. and from 7:30 to 11:30 p.m.; on Saturday from 6:45 to 11:30 p.m. Closed Sunday.

The Budget Range

Penny's Place, 6 King St., W.C.2 (tel. 836-4553), is a wine and food bar in an old Victorian pub still with the mirrors and the antique mahogany woodwork. Snacks include various pâtés, crab, taramasalata, and chicken liver at £1.20 ($2.76) to £1.50 ($3.45). There is a wide selection of wines, a glass costing around 55p ($1.27). The place is open for lunch and from 6 p.m. to very late. There is live music Friday nights.

Calabash Restaurant, 38 King St., W.C. 2 (tel. 836-1976), is the only African restaurant in London, underneath the African Centre (where you can buy carved wood statutes, straw baskets, and bead necklaces). A simply furnished place with a bar, it has an informal atmosphere. Dishes from all over Africa are offered, with fish and chicken a speciality. Pepperpot soup with bread costs £1 ($2.30). Also offered are Egusi (Nigerian) beef stew with melon seeds; spinach, dried shrimps, and fresh peppers; firire of fish (Senegal) with tomato sauce and potatoes; Nyama yo Phika (Malawi) beef stew with sweet peppers; or stew from the Ivory Coast with okra in palm oil—each going for £2 ($4.60). Pineapple fritters with rum round off the meal at £1.20 ($2.76). The restaurant is open Monday to Friday from noon to 3 p.m. and from 5:30 to 11 p.m.; on Saturday from 6 to 11:30 p.m. Closed Sunday.

READER'S RESTAURANT SELECTION: "Food for Thought, 31 Neal St., W.C.2 (tel. 836-0239), is a very small place with inexpensive vegetarian food. Better go at odd hours—perhaps in the middle of the afternoon. Otherwise, it's likely to be crowded. Everybody ends up sitting with and often talking with everybody else. It's most congenial. The establishment is a tiny basement cafe in the heart of the theater and movie district. From the Covent Garden tube station, walk along Neal Street toward Shaftesbury Avenue. The restaurant will be in the second block on the left. It's open Monday through Friday from noon to 8 p.m. The price of a meal for two is around £5 ($11.50)" (Vicki Banks, London, England).

HIGH HOLBORN: In "legal London," you can join barristers, solicitors, and law clerks at the following recommendation.

The Budget Range

My Old Dutch, 132 High Holborn, W.C.1 (tel. 242-5200), is a cheerful, friendly place, resembling a Dutch kitchen with scrubbed pine tables at which you can be served 101 different pancakes—all enormous—on huge Delft plates. Fillings and garnishes include cheese, meats, and vegetables, as well as sweet fillings such as Adam's Downfall—that is, figs and avocado. The cost is around £2 ($4.60), and one of these dishes makes a good meal. Fresh ground coffee and hot chocolate are available to wash it all down. My Old Dutch stays open from 11 a.m. to midnight Sunday through Wednesday, and 11 a.m. to 1 a.m. on Thursday, Friday, and Saturday. Other branches are in London at 31 Dover St., W.1, and in Brighton at 56 Ship St., if you're heading down there.

WESTMINISTER: Our dining expedition to Westminister begins in one of London's famous fish houses:

The Medium-Priced Range

Overton's, 4 Victoria Buildings, S.W.1 (tel. 834-3774), may not have been visited by Queen Victoria (it was founded in her day), but her image is indelibly imprinted on this famous second-floor restaurant overlooking Victoria Station (another branch is at 5 St. James's). The specialties of the house, the fish dishes, are worth getting excited about. If it swims, Overton's has it. You can devour some Whitstable oysters for £8 ($18.40) per dozen. Main-dish specialties include sole Overton at £6.50 ($14.95) and poached halibut at £5.25 ($12.08). Well recommended is the bouillabaisse Marseilles, £8 ($18.40) for two. The bisque de homard at £1.25 ($2.88) is a good beginning, and desserts in the 85p ($1.96) to £1.25 ($2.88) range provide the finale. You can order a carafe of wine for £2.50 ($5.75) to £5 ($11.50). A little oyster bar adjoins the main restaurant. The place is closed on Sunday.

Bumbles, 16 Buckingham Palace Rd., S.W.1 (tel. 828-2903), gives you a chance to dine just 300 yards from Buckingham Palace. John D. Forbes places emphasis on cooking originality, above-average though moderately priced food, and gracious service by young women once described as "very sweet." There is a full wine list, including English wines, from £4 ($9.20), including VAT. The staff will make menu suggestions. Hours of opening are Monday to Friday from noon to 2:15 p.m. and from 6 to midnight (last orders at 10:30 p.m.). Saturday hours are from 6 p.m., with the last orders placed at 10:30 p.m. The restaurant is closed all day Sunday and on bank holidays.

Both luncheon and supper choices are written on a super-large sheet of brown wrapping paper. Bumbles soup of the day costs 95p ($2.19), followed by a large selection of main courses, which average about £4 ($9.20) in price. On our most recent visit we enjoyed a leg of lamb stuffed with mushrooms, onions, and rosemary, then roasted and cut into steaks, caramelized with red-currant jelly and served with sauteed potatoes and cauliflower. Tube: Victoria Station.

Le Steak Nicole, 72/73 Wilton Rd., S.W.1 (tel. 834-7301), is a bistro run on French lines, with tables placed on the pavement in summer. There's a tiny dining room on the ground floor and more room in the basement. You can have your usual "tipple" at the bar while deliberating about your meal. Try a Kir, white wine and cassis, or one of the essentially French apéritifs, St. Raphael or Suze, so as not to destroy your tastebuds.

The owners, Graham Collard and Tony Clane, offer entrecôte, cut finely in strips and served in a creamy garlic sauce (no garlic if you say so beforehand), with unlimited french fries and a choice of two salads (a green one with french dressing and a raw one with vinaigrette). Your main course costs £5.50 ($12.65). A large bottle of the house wine is placed on your table, and you pay for what you drink, a whole bottle costing from £5 ($11.50). Desserts include caramelized oranges at 85p ($1.96), or else you may prefer just cheese and coffee. VAT and service are extra. The restaurant serves from noon to 2:30 p.m. Monday to Friday, and from 6:30 to 11 p.m. Monday to Saturday.

Pomegranates, 94 Grosvenor Rd., S.W.1 (tel. 828-6560). The owner, Patrick Gwynn-Jones, has traveled far and collected dishes from throughout the world. Asian and Indonesian delicacies vie for a place on the menu with European dishes, spiced pickled salmon with sweet mustard sauce, leg of lamb with herbs, veal kidneys deviled lightly. The decor is purely European—soft lights, mirrors, and well-laid tables. Bread is baked fresh twice a day, and vegetables are cooked when fresh, adding to the pleasure of a good meal. You should get away for about £12 ($27.60) a person, but if you start in on the more exotic dishes or the delicious desserts—grapefruit and gin sorbet, honey and brandy ice cream, it will probably cost more. The place is open for lunch from 12:30 to 2:15 p.m. Monday to Friday, and for dinner from 7:30 to 11:15 p.m. Monday to Saturday. There is a very good wine list and some reasonable house wines. A set lunch of three courses costs from £6 ($13.80), excluding wines.

BELGRAVIA: Belgravia after dark used to be a gastronomic wilderness. Happily, that situation has changed.

The Medium-Priced Range

Drones, 1 Pont St., S.W.1 (tel. 235-9638), was labeled by one newspaper columnist the "unofficial club for the bright people, at least half of whom seem to know each other." David Niven & Friends launched this two-floor restaurant, and its reputation for charm and chic has long ago spread. Reservations are imperative, preferably a day in advance. There's no elaborate menu, no fancy sauces, just simple but good food. At lunch have the Droneburger at £2.20 ($5.06), a favorite. For dinner, the calf liver with bacon at £4.25 ($9.78) is delicious (have it cooked pink if you prefer). As an appetizer, the chef's pâté is worthy—£1.10 ($2.53). A main-dish specialty is the chili, £1.90 ($4.37). Our heartiest recommendation goes to the entrecôte chasseur, £5.75 ($13.23). Hot apple pie at £1.05 ($2.42) and cheesecake at 95p ($2.19) vie for your attention in the dessert department. The menu is wisely limited, and it never changes, although plats du jour are featured.

You sit on bentwood armchairs with green velvet cushions at white wrought-iron tables. The simple white walls are perfect foils for oil paintings and framed copies of children's comics and magazines. Try to get a table downstairs. If you're lingering in the bar while waiting for a table (a likely possibility), take a look at the collection of movie-star photos. But John Wayne as a baby is hardly recommended as an appetizer! Open seven days a week, Drones serves lunch from 12:30 to 3 p.m., dinner from 7:30 p.m. to midnight.

Papillon, at the Chelsea Holiday Inn, Sloane Street, S.W.1 (tel. 235-4377), is a restaurant built around the pool. In good weather the clear roof rolls back for al fresco eating. Around the pool are bamboo tables and chairs, there is a guitarist lunchtime, a piano player in the evening, and on Sunday a jazz band entertains from noon to 4 p.m. when those who come to eat and drink may also use the pool free. A wide menu of appetizers is offered, then omelets, lasagne, or spaghetti. Steaks and grills are served with french fries, baked or croquette potatoes, or rice. A mixed grill Chelsea will cost £5 ($11.50).

If this is all too much for you, hamburgers go at around £3 ($6.90). Sandwiches, too, are filling, and you can have a very ample snack meal, a club sandwich, steak sandwich, or buck rarebit (cheese with fried egg on top), for around £3.50 ($8.05). The place is fully licensed and specializes in quite an impressive list of cocktails and apéritifs. All prices include VAT and service.

The **Terrace Coffee House,** Pont Street, S.W.1 (tel. 235-6041), is the coffeeshop of the Ladbroke Dragonara Hotel, in the old place of the Grand Vefour Restaurant, long gone. On good days the whole of the front is opened up to create an almost Parisian-style street cafe. The decor is cool, with wooden tables and wicker-backed chairs. A wide menu is served throughout the day—good value and very pleasant. Service is included in the prices but VAT is added to all bills. A set lunch costs from £8 ($18.40), including a hot soup, a choice from the cold buffet of meats and salads, followed by dessert and coffee. At lunchtime there is also an à la carte selection, and this runs through the evening session, lasting from 7 to 10 p.m. Main courses include beef Stroganoff at £8 ($18.40), including a vegetable, or chicken suprême at £5 ($11.50). Desserts from the trolley go for around £2 ($4.60).

KNIGHTSBRIDGE-BROMPTON ROAD: After splurging at the high-priced shops of Knightsbridge, these choices will make you feel better:

The Medium-Priced Range

Shezan, 16 Cheval Pl., off Montpelier Street, S.W.7 (tel. 589-7918), is generally considered the finest Pakistani restaurant in London, and we heartily concur. In a cul-de-sac behind Harrods, this brick-and-tile establishment in Kensington turns out exquisite dishes from its clay tandoor ovens. By all means, order murgh tikka lahori (marinated tandoori chicken), which is usually served slightly pink and is delicious, £2.65 ($6.10). Another specialty is bhuna gosht (lamb cooked with tomatoes and spices), £2.70 ($6.21). Tandoori charcoal barbecues and grills are usually priced at £2.65 ($6.10), and most kebabs begin at £2.65 also. The tandoori breads are excellent, especially roti, a dark whole-wheat bread. The restaurant is one of the most sophisticated in the city, and the service is flawless. Lunch is from noon to 3 p.m. and dinner from 7 p.m. to midnight. Closed Sunday and bank holidays. Tube: Knightsbridge.

In a small street, just off Knightsbridge, the **Upper Crust,** 9 William St., S.W.1 (tel. 235-8444), is a modest, simply decorated country sort of place with bare brick walls, wheel-back chairs, and warm lights. Pies, rather obviously, are the house specialty, and they are served filled with steak and giblets, savory chicken, curried fish, and a magnificent steak and pickled walnut, an ample portion going for about £3.25 ($7.48). Main dishes, which average around £3 ($6.90) in price, are accompanied, for the cover charge of 80p ($1.84), by fresh country bread and herb butter, plus a selection of fresh seasonal vegetables. Cold dishes with salads are also available, beginning at £3.50 ($8.05). Puddings have a definitely old-world air, including traditional plum with custard or Yorkshire pudding with mincemeat, costing from £1.50 ($3.45). The Franks family, who own and run the place, have a secret in that Mr. Franks also owns the superbly entitled butchershop, Wainwright and Daughter. Naturally, they select meat of prime quality for their restaurant showcase. Hours are 11:30 a.m. to 3 p.m. and 6 to 11 p.m., Monday to Saturday. On Sunday, hours are only from 6 to 11 p.m.

Paper Tiger, 10 and 12 Exhibition Rd., S.W.7 (tel. 584-3737). The dishes here are Szechuan rather than Peking cuisine, more spiced and beginning to be closer to Malaysian dishes than the blander Japanese ones. At this basement restaurant in South Kensington a Szechuan feast will cost £9.50 ($21.85) for a minimum of two persons. Dishes include "bang-bang" sesame chicken salad, pickle soup, prawns, pork and peppers, chili chicken, and bamboo shoots. A less piquant Peking feast for the same price includes duck with trimmings, sweet-and-sour pork, chicken and almonds, fried dumplings, and hot-and-sour soup.

There is an extensive à la carte menu of reasonably priced dishes—soups going at £1.20 ($2.76), entrees such as seaspice chicken shreds with peppers, chicken with yellow bean sauce and almonds, lemon chicken, each costing £2.20 ($5.06). Vegetable dishes include stir-fried bean sprouts and Mother-

Ma's hot pork mince and bean curd. Toffee apples and bananas cost £1.10 ($2.53), followed by Chinese tea or coffee at 55p ($1.27).

Lunchtimes they have platters—pork loin slices, meat and noodles, sweet-and-sour pork, beef slices and spring onions, all at £2.50 ($5.75). In the off-season, they have a gourmet winter menu for £11.50 ($26.45), including a sharp Chinese salad, a fish dish, spring rolls and wanton, three meat dishes (chicken, pork, and lamb), vegetables, rice, and a dessert. All prices include VAT. You should go there to sample the house specialty, aromatic crispy duck with pancakes, hoisin, and cucumber, or with green ginger and spring onions.

The Budget Range

Great American Disaster, Beauchamp Place, S.W.3 (tel. 589-0992), is the answer to the fervent hope that someday the English would get to taste what a real hamburger is like. A few years ago, a curly-haired young North American finally succeeded in shaming the English "pseudo-burgers" by giving London a true American burger. Reportedly, some 2000 burgers were rejected before the final achievement was created with a sesame bun. The press call GAD "the apotheosis of the hamburger." The original Disaster is at 335 Fulham Rd., S.W.10, but the one at Beauchamp Place is much more fashionable and interesting. An exterior sign shows a man jumping presumably from a high building with a calendar in hand dated October 29, 1929. Uncle Sam is pondering, and King Kong is holding an airplane. Inside the restaurant, the tables are tightly packed, crowded, and noisy, the service cheerful. A quarter-pound hamburger with french fries costs £2 ($4.60), although you can order the half-pound Disaster special with french fries at £4 ($9.20). Barbecued spare ribs with GAD sauce, french fries, and coleslaw costs £3 ($6.90); and homemade American apple pie is yet another 96p ($2.21).

Harveys, the rooftop restaurant above Harvey Nichols store, S.W.1 (tel. 235-5000, ext. 149 for table reservations), is a light, airy place among the rooftops of Knightsbridge. In summer you can eat in the open air, but there is also a large restaurant inside. The day starts with an English breakfast at 9:30 a.m., costing £3.50 ($8.05), or just tea or coffee at about 60p ($1.38). The staff serves morning coffee, luncheon, and then afternoon tea until 5:30 p.m. when the store closes (6:30 p.m. on Wednesday). Lunch has a minimum charge of £4 ($9.20).

There is a selection of appetizers, then you choose your main dish from the long buffet of hot dishes or from the salad table. The meal ends with dessert or cheese and coffee. The cost is around £7 ($16.10) unless you have an omelet with one of the many fillings, salad, and vegetables for £4 ($9.20). Wine by the glass is £1 ($2.30). They also do a real old cream tea £2 ($4.60) with homemade scones, strawberry jam, and clotted Devon cream to revive the flagging shopper. Waitresses offer pleasant service in this nice atmosphere. It's rather Knightsbridge and British.

KENSINGTON: If Meg didn't ask you to stay to dinner at Kensington Palace, you'll be just as happy with:

The Medium-Priced Range

The **Twin Brothers Restaurant,** 51 Kensington Church St., W.8 (tel. 937-4152), is run by two identical twin brothers, who hail from Berlin. Tall and blond, they create an attraction in themselves, and they offer excellent and friendly service, good food, and a relaxed and happy atmosphere. Detlef and

Helge are master cooks and master carpenters. They made the chairs and benches. The decor is enhanced by a collection of oil paintings. The restaurant is small, ideal for a tête-à-tête dinner. The dinner menu is international—Bismarck herring ("our mother's recipe"), 95p ($2.19); chicken à la Kiev served with paprika rice, £2.75 ($6.33); wienerschnitzel, also £2.75. The salads have been called entertaining, and the vegetables are fresh, included in the price of the main dish. A slice of apple strudel goes for 85p ($1.96). Every dish is freshly prepared for you.

Flanagans, 11 Kensington High St., W.8 (tel. 937-2519), recaptures the splendor of turn-of-the-century dining. One of London's bounciest restaurants, it offers bountiful food in a fun-loving atmosphere. It's a trip back through the years to a world of handlebar mustaches, cut-velvet walls, a honky-tonk piano player, gas lights, sawdust on the floor—and the inevitable sing-alongs. All the Florrie Forde favorites are aired here, everything from "Has Anybody Seen Kelly?" to "Flanagan" itself.

The pièce de résistance is Lobster Lily Langtry, Edward VII's favorite, at £8.50 ($19.55). The shelled lobster is sauteed in chablis with tarragon and thyme and covered with a piquant cream sauce, then sprinkled with parmesan cheese and grilled. The Dover sole at £7.50 ($17.25) is so huge it extends over the edges of your plate; it is accompanied by a large helping of french fries. For an adventure in old English fare, order the homemade game pie, with mashed potatoes, for £4.50 ($10.35), and perhaps a side dish of pease pudding at 70p ($1.61), for those who want to go Cockney all the way. A large dish of Irish stew, big enough for two, costs only £4 ($9.20). For starters there's an order of cockles at £1.50 ($3.45), and for dessert, there's the original golden sponge pudding at 80p ($1.84). The original Flanagans is at 100 Baker St., W.1. Both are open from noon to 3 p.m. and from 6 p.m. to midnight, daily. Just mind your manners, and "Please Do Not Expectorate."

SOUTH KENSINGTON: When you're exhausted from South Kensington's museums, try a feast at the following:

The Upper Bracket

Elizabethan Rooms, Gore Hotel, 190 Queen's Gate, S.W.7 (tel. 584-6616), is where you'll meet with a hey, and a ho, and a hey nonino. It's right out of *The Six Wives of Henry VIII,* although it doesn't go back that far—being dedicated instead to his daughter, Bess. The unique rooms evoke Elizabethan England, complete with "bifurcated daggers" and "tyg cups" for mead, claret, and ale, and long candlelit wooden trestle tables.

A minstrel accompanying himself on a lute plays and sings Elizabethan ballads throughout the meal. Since it's a banquet, the head of each table is "knighted," and there are many toasts of mead, even kisses by the serving girls. If you finish your plate—and don't leave something for the poor—you'll be fined. The recipes are from 400 years ago and your "first remove" might consist of anything from baked seafood served in the shell to cucumbers in Canary wine. For the second remove, you're likely to have a boar's head or "salmagundy." The cost of this return to Shakespeare's time is £20 ($46), which includes service and VAT. Reservations are required, and banquets are held seven nights a week.

Eleven Park Walk, 11 Park Walk, S.W.10 (tel. 352-3449), is a high-key, airy, two-level restaurant, with a winding staircase for "entrances." Coming down that staircase nightly is a bevy of chic Londoners, including many from the art, fashion, and photographic worlds. A smart establishment, modern and beautiful, it is a haven for the sophisticated and glamorous. In addition to being seen, you can also order some good food. Even the service is friendly.

The restaurant serves mainly Italian dishes, beginning with minestrone primavera at £1.10 ($2.53), and a number of good pasta dishes, principally taglierini verdi at £1.80 ($4.14). Fish specialties include calamari fritti at £3.50 ($8.05). Main meat courses include roast baby chicken, bollito misto with green sauce, and calf liver veneziana, all at £3.50 also. For dessert, try a zabaglione, £1.50 ($3.45).

The Medium-Priced Range

Chanterelle, 119 Old Brompton Rd., S.W.7 (tel. 373-5522), used to be a part of the South Kensington Public Library. But times have changed. The smell is not of old books, but of highly original English and continental cookery in a restrained setting of wood paneling. The personable Stewart Grimshaw oversees the restaurant, and his partner, Fergus Provan, organizes the kitchen. They are open every day of the week for both lunch and dinner, including Sunday. The à la carte menu changes every three weeks, and it is supplemented by a fixed-price lunch of three courses for £5 ($11.50). On one recent occasion, we enjoyed watercress soup, beef braised with black walnuts, and a grape-and-orange salad. The à la carte menu is likely to include such well-prepared items as huntsman's beef at £4 ($9.20); saddle of rabbit with mustard and shallots, £3.50 ($8.05); and pigeon, £3.50 also. A cold soufflé costs £1 ($2.30), and most puddings and ices average the same. VAT is included in all prices. Wines are limited, but well selected, the house wine going for £3.75 ($8.63). Reservations are necessary. Dinner is nightly from 7 p.m. to midnight.

The Budget Range

Chompers, 2 Exhibition Rd., S.W.7 (tel. 589-8947), is probably the oldest established bistro in town. It boasts an art nouveau decor, but doesn't get lost in its stage setting. Chompers serves good food prepared on the premises at low prices. Helpings are generous. You can order barbecued spare ribs for £1 ($2.30), onion soup for 80p ($1.84), and pâté maison for £1 ($2.30). The main-course specialties include chicken ratatouille, £2.20 ($5.06); kidneys in sherry, £2.20 also; and trout with capers, £2.50 ($5.75). Chompers sells a lot of filet, about £4.85 ($11.16), and sirloin steak, about £3.95 ($9.09) a serving. Chompers is open for dinner from 6 p.m. to 1 a.m. Monday to Saturday (on Sunday from 6 p.m. to midnight), and for lunch seven days a week from noon to 2:30 p.m. On Sunday it offers a traditional English roast lunch. Reservations are recommended between 8 and 10:30 p.m. It's fully licensed. Tube: South Kensington.

CHELSEA: This area, comparable to the Left Bank of Paris and parts of Greenwich Village, is fashionable. Here diplomats and wealthy-chic, stars of stage and screen, and successful sculptors and painters live alongside a decreasing number of poor and struggling artists. To reach the area, take the Circle or District lines to Sloane Square.

King's Road (named for Charles II) is the principal street of Chelsea, and it's lively both day and night. On Saturday mornings, Chelsea boutiques blossom with London's latest "achievers."

Chelsea has long attracted artists. Oscar Wilde found refuge here; so did Henry James, Whistler, and many more. The Chelsea Embankment, an esplanade along the Thames, is also here. Homes of famous writers, such as the one once occupied by George Eliot, line the street. The best known and most interesting part of the embankment is called Cheyne Walk (pronounced chainy), containing some Georgian town houses. It's a delightful place to stroll around about dusk. The most popular residents here are the Chelsea Pensioners, who live at the Royal Chelsea Hospital. These uniformed veteran and invalid soldiers can be seen walking up and down the riverfront.

This charming district contains some of the city's finest, but not the cheapest, restaurants.

The Medium-Priced Range

Au Fin Bec, 100 Draycott Ave., S.W.3 (tel. 584-3600), is an intimate, high-level, French-style medium-priced bistro, serving some of the best food in Chelsea. The chef selects only the best of fresh vegetables from the markets, the finest of meats and fish, and he prepares dishes according to his favorite recipes from the continent. You don't have a wide selection of main dishes, but perhaps that's why everything tastes so fresh. Sometimes the waiter will tell you the day's specials that might not be on the menu.

The oeufs bénédicte make a good appetizer at £1.50 ($3.45). The trick is to pop the egg into the oven at the last moment so that a filmy crust is formed. You might want to follow this with scampi frits, fried lightly in butter, with sprigs of parsley, £5.25 ($12.08). The house specialty is Dover sole, prepared in at least six different ways, and costing £5 ($11.50) if you prefer it plain. Otherwise, with one of the chef's sauces, the charge is £6 ($13.80). Bananas flambés at £1.65 ($3.80) make a delicious dessert. Hours are from 12:30 to 2:30 p.m. and from 7 to 10:45 p.m. The restaurant is closed Sunday.

ST. MARYLEBONE: In Mar-li-bone you're in for a treat when you visit:

The Medium-Priced Range

The **Baker & Oven,** 10 Paddington St., W.1 (tel. 935-5072), may be in an out-of-the-way neighborhood, but it's a big success—a little corner bakery, with a sales shop converted into a tavern with a genuine pub atmosphere. The neighborhood people mingle with the fashionable West End visitors. Meals are served in the cellar kitchens, attractively done in a rustic style. The very English food often pleases the most critical; the portions are enormous, the tabs moderate. With a bit of luck, you'll be given a bare wooden table in one of the brick cove-ceilinged nooks, the former ovens.

The onion soup is a fine beginning at 75p ($1.73), as is the country pâté at 95p ($2.19). For the main course, there are several good choices, including roast Aylesbury duckling with stuffing and apple sauce for £3.95 ($9.09) and jugged hare with red currant jelly, £4.25 ($9.78). All entrees include vegetables. For dessert, you can order a thoroughly English hot fruit pie and cream at 75p ($1.73). The restaurant is open Monday to Friday from noon to 3 p.m. and from 6:30 to 11 p.m. On Saturday, it's open only in the evenings.

London Steak Houses, Ltd., with its main offices at Cadby Hall, W.14 (tel. 603-2040), operates 16 restaurants in metropolitan London, all with similar menus and prices, but with varying decors. The restaurant at 116 Baker St., W.1 (tel. 935-1932) is an attractive example, with small tables stretched in a single row through a long, narrow room decorated cheerfully in green and lemon yellow. Simulated gaslight plays across the oak-beamed ceiling. Framed French magazine prints add interest to the walls. The menu is extensive, with plenty of beef, pork, and seafood dishes available. Steak is, of course, the specialty, with rump, sirloin, and filet steaks offered in three sizes: standard, medium, and large. Steak Diane, served with shallots and parsley, costs about £4 ($9.20). Other steaks go from £3.75 ($8.63) to £5.50 ($12.65). Vegetables are extra. Appetizers, such as fresh avocado stuffed with prawns, go for about £1.65 ($3.80). After an enjoyable repast you can enjoy a cup of rich coffee for 65p ($1.50), accompanied by a complementary tray of sugared Turkish delights. A 60p ($1.38) cover charge is added to the tab, which does not include the tip. All London Steak Houses are open for lunch and dinner every day of the week. Other locations include 10 Broadway, Westminster; 29 Ebury St.; and 17-20 Kendal St.

READER'S RESTAURANT SELECTION: "We discovered a restaurant in London where we had one of the best meals we've ever eaten. It's **Trattoria Parioli,** 129 Crawford St., W.1 (tel. 935-3791), just around the corner one block south of the Baker Street tube station. The menu is à la carte, no service charge included, and there is one of those mysterious 45p ($1.04) cover charges. Nevertheless, we had everything—soup, entree, a magnificent salad, excellent pasta, dessert, coffee, and the fine house white wine—all for £10.50 ($24.15) per person, including tax and tip. It's gourmet Italian, with fine service, an attractive decor, and even the ubiquitous Muzak was soft" (Patricia Muller, Denver, Colo.).

NOTTING HILL GATE: From a gourmet treat to fish 'n' chips, our choice in this area is wide ranging.

The Upper Bracket

Leiths, 92 Kensington Park Rd., W.11 (tel. 229-4481). Prudence Leith, a lovely young woman from South Africa, has brought her culinary talents to the most unlikely Notting Hill Gate district of London, a few blocks from the Portobello Road Market and near the Portobello Hotel. Pru, as she is called, discovered "how good food could really be" when she worked as an *au pair* girl in a French family. In time, she studied at the Cordon Bleu in Paris and also at the Cordon Bleu in London. Nowadays she relies on her managing director, French-born Jean-Baptiste Reynaud, who was a chef by trade until joining her as a manager in 1973, to produce the menus and to maintain the established high quality. Like the Four Seasons in New York, there are four seasonal menus. A fixed-price meal costs £18 ($41.40), including service and VAT. One recent spring menu included such dishes as trout stuffed with chicken and ham, tarragon chicken, stuffed quail in pastry, and poached salmon with a hollandaise sauce. There is an ambitious wine list. To end your meal, you can make a selection from the dessert trolley, perhaps a lemon soufflé. Open daily, 7:30 p.m. to midnight.

The Medium-Priced Range

Hungry Viking, 44 Ossington St., W.2 (tel. 727-3311), is a modern restaurant on a street of mews houses. You descend past flower-draped boxes into a Scandinavian parlor, where waitresses in national costume will help you select from a gigantic smörgåsbord for a set price of £7.75 ($17.83). It's called the traditional Viking table, and includes the usual array of delicacies, such as prawns, herring, smoked fish, aspics, salads, cheeses, and meats, both hot and cold. The salads are especially good. The amount of food you can eat is your own capacity. The restaurant is closed on Monday but open otherwise Tuesday to Saturday from 6:30 to 11 p.m. (Sunday, 7 to 11 p.m.). Tube: Queensway or Notting Hill Gate.

The Budget Range

Geale's, 2 Farmer St., W.8 (tel. 727-7969), is worth the investment in a subway ride to the western part of London if you're seeking some of the best fish and chips in the English capital—all at prices for around £1.75 ($4.03). The fish is bought fresh daily, and it's not greasy as it is in most establishments in London. Cod, hake, and plaice are the featured mainstays of the menu. This corner restaurant, at the end of a mews street, is owned by Christopher A. Geale, who is proud, and rightly so, of his offerings. The place is run on very informal lines, and is open Tuesday to Saturday from noon to 3 p.m. and from 6 to 11 p.m. Tube: Notting Hill Gate.

MAYFAIR: Stick a few extra pounds in your pocket and join the swells for a memorable meal in Mayfair (less expensive Mayfair restaurants coming up, too):

The Upper Bracket

Langan's Brasserie, Stratton Street, W.1 (tel. 493-6437), has become quite the "in" place in London since its opening in late 1976. Owned by restaurateur Peter Langan and actor Michael Caine, along with the chef de cuisine, Richard Shepherd, the cafe is reminiscent of a Parisian bistro. The walls are covered with pictures, and the combination of overhead fans and potted palms creates a 1930s atmosphere. The food is very French, even though the chef is English, and a complete meal, including wine, VAT, and service, comes to about £15 ($34.50). Live music is played during the dinner hour. Lunch is served Monday to Friday from 12:30 to 3 p.m. and dinner is offered from 7 p.m. to midnight, Monday through Friday. On Saturday, hours are from 8 p.m. to 1 a.m., and the restaurant is closed on Sunday. Upstairs is a more intimate dining room with silver service, although prices are the same as downstairs. The Venetian decor was the work of Patrick Proctor, the artist.

Café-Royal Grill Room, 68 Regent St., W.1 (tel. 930-2473). One columnist called the Café Royal "champagne-from-slipper" country. And so it is. Mirrored walls, painted ceilings, a sea of white linen and plush red velvet—enough to warm the heart of Oscar Wilde, one of its most illustrious former patrons. But then everybody famous, including Noël Coward, at one time or another since 1865 has dined at the Café Royal. The wine list continues to merit acclaim, remaining as comprehensive as ever. Get ready for a mile-long list Frank Harris called "The best on earth!" The food? A well-prepared haute cuisine. The ingredients are high quality, the vegetables fresh. The menu features such dishes as filets de sole sur le plat, Rochellaise (filets of sole braised with vermouth, tarragon, shallots, and sliced fresh tomatoes, pan reduced with butter, and covered with hollandaise sauce); and mignonettes d'agneau elysée (prime leg of lamb, sauteed in butter, coated with a madeira and port sauce with foie gras, chicken liver, and noisette potatoes). The restaurant offers a Sunday brunch at a set price of £6.95 ($15.99), plus a 12½% service charge. Our most recent meal started with a soup of the day and was followed by a kipper, then scrambled eggs, mushrooms, kidney, tomato, and bacon washed down by a bottle of Pouilly Fuisse (an extra charge). Of course, "lashings" of toast were included, along with Cooper's Oxford marmalade and coffee. Whistler used to sign his bill with a mark of the butterfly. The brunch, from noon to 2:30 p.m., is frequented by a wide variety of Londoners—some rounding out a night's revelry. It's an amusing break in a London Sunday.

Bentley's, 11–15 Swallow St., W.1 (tel. 734-4756), is one of the most prestigious fish restaurants in London; tradition permeates the place. There's a certain type of Mayfair gentleman, with bowler and cane, who heads for Bentley's at sunset. There, standing at the shellfish bar, he slowly and deliberately downs one oyster after another, a ritual unchanged in years. Then he fades away, seemingly having no life before or after swallowing those oysters until he shows up the following evening.

This clublike restaurant is on a tiny street connecting Regent Street with Piccadilly (a three-minute walk from Piccadilly Circus). On the ground floor, you'll find the Oyster Bar, usually crowded with men feasting on the riches from Bentley's own oyster beds near Colchester, Essex. Upstairs is a dining room filled with devotees of good fish dishes. A half-dozen oysters go for £4 ($9.20), but you may prefer iced lobster soup, the house specialty, at £1.40 ($3.22). Each weekday, there's a different specialty from the chef. On Monday it's a sole Véronique, poached in white wine and garnished with grapes, for £5.85 ($13.46). You'll find exciting menu selections from the scampi, scallop, lobster, mussel, plaice, trout, turbot, and sole families. Scottish salmon, grilled or poached, comes to £6.50 ($14.95), and the lobster thermidor, £9 ($20.70). Less expensive offerings include the scampi meunière for £4 ($9.20). Prices include VAT. Closed Sunday.

The Medium-Priced Range

Gaylord, 16 Albemarle St., W.1 (tel. 629-9802), has established an enviable reputation among local connoisseurs of Indian cuisine in spite of its relative youth—it just opened in 1974. An elegant Oriental atmosphere pervades the restaurant, creating an air of festive expectancy. The ornate hanging lamps, the gold-studded door, and the unusual glass ceiling imported from India set off the rich color scheme of royal purple and gold. And the delicacies upon which you dine do not disappoint you.

So many regional dishes are available that one hardly knows where to begin. The restaurant features three different types of regional cooking: Tandoori centers on the tandoor, an oven of Indian clay which is used for cooking foods while retaining the flavor and natural moisture. A good example of this cooking style is tandoori fish, at £3.40 ($7.82).

Mughlai cooking dates from the Moghul period of Indian history in which exotic dishes were prepared with rich combinations of spices. If you like curried foods, you may wish to try the chicken noor jehani, a chicken, minced lamb, and egg dish cooked in a thick curry sauce, at £2.45 ($5.64).

Kashmiri specialties frequently include combinations of lamb and yogurt, as exemplified in the roghan josh, pieces of lamb cooked alternately between smoking butter and beaten yogurt to develop a unique flavor, also costing £2.45. Vegetarian entrees are also available for about £1.65 ($3.80). As a dessert treat, try an Indian sweet from the trolley, for £1.10 ($2.53). All prices include VAT. The Gaylord is open daily for lunch and dinner.

The Budget Range

Cranks Salad Table, Marshall Street (around the corner from Carnaby Street), took its name from "cranks." But instead of the colloquial meaning of an eccentric, impractical person, the Salad Table defines the word as those "who have the courage to pursue a line of thinking against the general stream of orthodox belief." Their "line," by the way, is excellent—the best of natural soups, salads, and breads made from whole-meal, compost-grown, stone-ground English flour. Cranks became famous when it operated on Carnaby Street, and first drew its young health-conscious clientele. The food-reform restaurant even tempts full-fledged carnivores by its fresh-tasting selections—such as the mix-it-yourself salad platter at lunch. If you've got a small waist, you can order a bowl of choice salads for £1.25 ($2.88), although if you've already lost the battle of the bulge, you may prefer a large plate at £1.60 ($3.68). Homemade cakes range from 45p ($1.04). Cranks serves the best tiger's milk and dandelion coffee in town. It's open Monday to Friday from 10 a.m. to 8:30 p.m., on Saturday from 10 a.m. to 4:30 p.m. Warning: At lunchtime, it's extremely crowded.

My Old Dutch, 31 Dover St., W.1 (tel. 499-4316), is back in the West End in new premises with a clean, cheerful decor. There are 101 different savory and sweet pancakes to choose from. Served on enormous Delft plates, one pancake is a good meal, covered with ratatouille, peppers and salami, mushrooms and cheese, cheese and tomatoes or pineapple, black cherries, or peaches and cream. The cost is about £1.75 ($4.03) each. You can wash the pancakes down with beer, cider, lager, tea, coffee, or house wines, at about £3.50 ($8.05) a bottle or around 65p ($1.50) a glass. They also do a delicious continental breakfast of meats, eggs, cheeses, bread, rusks, and rolls, with juice and coffee. The place is open from 8 a.m. Monday through Saturday, from 10 a.m. on Sunday, closing at midnight except on Thursday, Friday, and Saturday, when closing is at 1 a.m.

Justin de Blanc, 54 Duke St., W.1 (tel. 629-3174), stands just off Oxford Street by Selfridges. It serves breakfast, then runs into lunchtime when it is very popular with tired shoppers. Choose your meal from a variety of hot dishes: lamb and eggplant casserole, £2 ($4.60); barbecued spare ribs, £1.70 ($3.91); or roast beef and three vegetables, £4 ($9.20). The dishes of the day are written over the bar, and it can be quite a problem to select among them. The array of salads, rice and celery, cucumber and yogurt, orange and beetroot go for around £1.75 ($4.03) for a large plateful. Desserts are all homemade, including fruit pies, cheesecakes, and fruit salad from around £1 ($2.30) a portion. They bake their own bread, and the fresh granary rolls are delicious. A glass of wine costs 65p ($1.50). It is open from 9 a.m. to 3:30 p.m., then from 4:30 to 9:30 p.m. on weekdays (on Saturday from 9 a.m. to 3:30 p.m. only). Closed on Sunday.

SOHO: This wedge-shaped section of narrow lanes and crooked streets is the main foreign quarter of London, where the city's best international restaurants reside. The life of the continent echoes throughout Soho. Large numbers of French people are found here, and so are Italians and all other European nationalities, as well as Orientals.

One writer wrote of Gerrard Street: "The smell of pickled ginger and roast duckling seeps from restaurant doors. The men scurry into stores from afternoon games of fan-tan and mah-jongg. A lilting twang of Chinese rock 'n' roll envelops the downtown street." Gerrard Street has succeeded in becoming London's Chinatown. Strip shows and honky-tonk clubs have given way to Chinese restaurants and bookstores keeping you informed of the latest developments in Hong Kong and the wisdom of Mao.

Soho starts at Piccadilly Circus, spreading out like a peacock and ending at Oxford Street. One side borders the theater center on Shaftesbury Avenue. From Piccadilly Circus, walk northeast and you'll come to Soho, to the left of

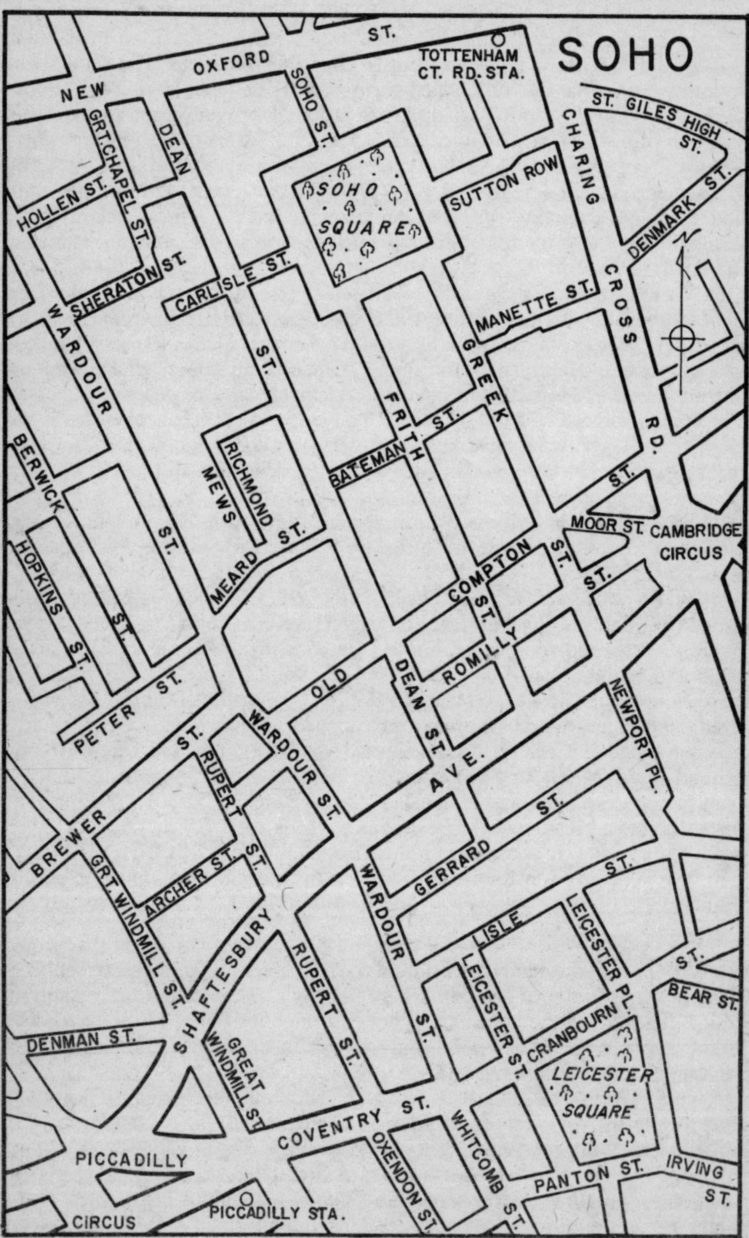
SOHO
OXFORD ST.
TOTTENHAM CT. RD. STA.
NEW
DEAN
SOHO ST.
SOHO SQUARE
ST. GILES HIGH ST.
CHARING CROSS RD.
DENMARK ST.
SUTTON ROW
GRT. CHAPEL ST.
HOLLEN ST.
SHERATON ST.
CARLISLE ST.
MANETTE ST.
WARDOUR ST.
ST.
GREEK ST.
FRITH ST.
BATEMAN ST.
BERWICK ST.
RICHMOND MEWS
MEARD ST.
MOOR ST.
CAMBRIDGE CIRCUS
HOPKINS ST.
COMPTON ST.
ST.
DEAN ST.
ROMILLY ST.
OLD
PETER ST.
NEWPORT PL.
WARDOUR ST.
RUPERT ST.
AVE.
BREWER ST.
GERRARD ST.
GRT. WINDMILL ST.
ARCHER ST.
WARDOUR ST.
LISLE ST.
LEICESTER PL.
SHAFTESBURY
RUPERT ST.
LEICESTER ST.
BEAR ST.
DENMAN ST.
GREAT WINDMILL ST.
CRANBOURN ST.
LEICESTER SQUARE
COVENTRY ST.
WHITCOMB ST.
OXENDON ST.
PICCADILLY CIRCUS
PANTON ST.
IRVING ST.
PICCADILLY STA.

Shaftesbury. This jumbled section can also be approached from the Tottenham Court Road tube station. Walk south along Charing Cross Road and Soho will be to your right.

The Upper Bracket

The Ivy, 1–5 West St., W.C.2 (tel. 836-4751). It's difficult to concentrate on the top-notch French cuisine here; diners are too busy star gazing in what is often a celebrity-filled dining spot. The Ivy is strong on tradition, an entrenched London restaurant since World War I. In the past it drew such regulars as Prime Ministers Lloyd George and Sir Winston Churchill, who knew his French viands and wines. Over the years, it became a rendezvous for show folk—Noël Coward, Gracie Fields, Dame Sybil Thorndike, Rex Harrison used to be habitués. The interior gleams with the luster of Paris—paneled walls with old paintings, bronze lamps, cut-plush chairs, art nouveau bronze figures set in window ledges. In the front drinking lounge you can wait for your table while making menu selections.

The Ivy had been getting a bit désuet, but with the arrival of Sir Leslie Grade's wife, Kathleen, who now owns the Ivy, the old tradition of theatrical star-spotting is coming back. The paintings, paneling, and luxurious furnishings remain, and the menu tends to be a little old-fashioned in its length and detail.

Sole is available with 13 different sauces and garnishes, but the table d'hôte luncheon or dinner is what you'll probably go for at £10 ($23). If you don't see anything you like, then order one of the lunchtime plats du jour, including a gigot of lamb at £4.20 ($9.66) or roast beef with the trimmings, £5 ($11.50).

In the evening you can try a chateaubriand steak for two, costing £17 ($39.10), or else duck in orange sauce at £7.50 ($17.25) per portion. Desserts average around £1.50 ($3.45), although you'll pay £3.50 ($8.05) for crêpes suzette. There's a cover charge of 90p ($2.07) and a minimum charge of about £5 ($11.50), but this is quite amusing for a night out among the celebrities.

Terrazza, 19 Romilly St., W.1 (tel. 437-8991), at one time was considered the chicest restaurant in London. But the West End theater crowd and "society" are, alas, fickle. Whether in or out of fashion, Terrazza remains one of the best places in the capital for authentic Italian food. If you visit, you'll have a choice of four different dining rooms, both upstairs and down.

The food is classic, beginning with cocktail Amalfi, £2 ($4.60). House specialties include spaghetti with clams, £2 also; fritto misto mare (scampi, octopus, and other sea products deep-fried), £4.60 ($10.58); and rolled and stuffed breast of chicken, £4.20 ($9.66). You pay £1.20 ($2.76) for a smooth zabaglione. Lunch is served from noon to 3 p.m.; dinner from 6 p.m. to midnight. Open Sunday.

Au Jardin des Gourmets, 5 Greek St., W.1 (tel. 437-1816), draws many a discriminating diner to some of the best French food in Soho. The restaurant has a Frenchman as its chef, and the traditional Gallic cuisine reflects the highest standards of his country. For appetizers, you can have such a treat as pâté maison for £1.05 ($2.42). The soups are exceptionally good: vichyssoise for 90p ($2.07); soupe à l'oignon gratinée, the same. House specialties include carré d'agneau at £4 ($9.20); red snapper with fennel sauce, £2.70 ($6.21); and a hot seafood dish in wine sauce at £2.90 ($6.67). Vintage wines are available, but you can also order by the glass. The restaurant is open from 12:30 to 2:15 p.m. and from 6:30 to 11:30 p.m. Closed Sunday.

The Budget Range

Romano Santi, 50 Greek St., W.1 (tel. 437-2350), established in 1886, in the very heart of Soho, is one of the best values in this district, considering the grade of its cuisine. It's run by a friendly and polite international staff, under the direction of a distinguished and charming woman manager, Miss Farida of Mauritius. The management has made it a duty to keep this building, which was erected in 1735, in its original condition. The continental restaurant features an excellent three-course luncheon for £5.50 ($12.65). A typical meal might include an assortment of hors d'oeuvres, followed by chicken chasseur, with a green vegetable, and peach Melba for dessert. The helpings are generous, and there are several main dishes from which to choose. Expect to spend at least £12 ($27.60) for an à la carte dinner. Main courses include tournedos Romano Santi, veal piccatine al Marsala, chicken Kiev, and trout San Remo (with prawns and tomatoes). You'll find the lack of elbow room either a plus or a minus—depending on the person you're elbowing at the next table. Romano Santi's is open from noon to 3 p.m. and from 6 to 11:45 p.m.; closed Sunday and bank holidays.

The **Dumpling Inn,** 15a Gerrard St. (tel. 437-2567), in the small Chinese district of Soho, attracts a number of devoted regulars. Don't be fooled by the name or the Venetian murals—this is an elegant Chinese restaurant serving classical Mandarin dishes. The haute cuisine of China, Mandarin cooking dates back nearly 3000 years, and employs a number of unique cooking rituals, including the Mongolian hot pot. The fact that this restaurant serves somewhat small portions can be turned into an advantage because it gives you an opportunity to sample a variety of this delectable cuisine. You can savor the special tastes of Mandarin cooking in the sharkfin soup, at £4 ($9.20); the beef in oyster sauce, £3.20 ($7.36); or the grilled pork or beef dumplings, at £2.20 ($5.06). Pancakes stuffed with discreetly flavored minced meat are a house specialty. Dinner reservations are recommended, and you should allow plenty of time for dining here since most dishes are prepared to your special order.

Chiu-Chow Inn, 21 Lisle St., W.C.2 (tel. 437-8919), is a little Pekinese restaurant on two floors that serves the best dumplings in Soho. Especially good are the fried dumplings, crescent-shaped, made with pork, beef, and coriander. Some are shaped like a mound and filled with both meat and soup. A good bargain is one of the set meals, costing anywhere from £4 ($9.20) to £9 ($20.70) per person. There must be two or more diners to avail yourself of these meals. These dinners are likely to feature the house specialties, sweet-and-sour fish slices, crispy duck, chicken and cashew nuts, North Chinese dumplings, quick-fried beef with scallions, and sliced chicken with a black bean sauce. Surely, the Chiu-Chow Inn represents one of the best food values in Soho, considering the quality of its offerings. For £4 ($9.20) you can order the chef's special, a bowl of mixed meats simmered at your table. The restaurant is open seven days a week from noon to 2:30 p.m. and from 5:30 p.m. to midnight.

Chuen Cheng Ku, 17 Wardour St., W.1 (tel. 437-1398), is one of the finest eateries in Soho's "New China." A large restaurant, Chuen Cheng Ku is noted for its Singapore noodles. Specialties are paper-wrapped prawns, rice in lotus leaves, steamed spare ribs in black bean sauce, shredded pork with cashew nuts, all served in generous portions. Dim sum (dumplings) are served from 11 a.m. to 6 p.m. The Singapore noodles, reflecting one of the Chinese-Malaysian inspirations, are thin rice noodles, sometimes mixed with curry and pork or else shrimp with red and green peppers. A set dinner costs £5 ($11.50) per person. Featured à la carte dishes include fried oysters with ginger and scallions, £4

($9.20); sliced duck with chili and black bean sauce, £3 ($6.90); and steamed pork with plum sauce, £3 also. The restaurant is open daily until midnight.

NORTH SOHO: In this district we have one lone recommendation in:

The Upper Bracket

Lacy's, 26 Whitfield St., W.1 (tel. 636-2323 or 636-2411), is run by award-winning husband-and-wife team, William Lacy and Margaret Costa. He was the chef des cuisines at the Empress in Berkeley Street, and trained under the last living disciples of Escoffier. She is the author of *The Four Seasons Cookery Book* and *London at Table.* On the ground level is a small reception and cocktail area. Reached by going down a flight of stairs, the dining room is in the Moorish style, with tiled floors and white arches. Fresh food is prepared in unusual and imaginative ways. For hors d'oeuvres, we'd recommend the fish pâté with a yogurt sauce, £2.85 ($6.56). A truly heavenly soup is the watercress, lettuce, and almond at £1.45 ($3.34). Main dishes begin at £5.20 ($11.96). We particularly enjoyed the seafood pancakes and the lamb kidneys flambéed with Dutch gin in a juniper berry-flavored sauce, £5.20 also. Desserts begin at £1.60 ($3.68). Reservations are essential. Meals are served from 12:30 to 2:30 p.m. and from 7:30 to 11 p.m. The luncheon menu is wonderful value for present-day London. It starts at about £11 ($25.30) for a three-course meal, including tax, cover charge, and coffee, but not service. The price of the main course is the price of the whole meal. In addition, they offer a wide range of excellent, low-priced wines.

TOP OF THE TOWER: This dining adventure takes place on a revolving stage way atop the Post Office Tower.

The Upper Bracket

Top of the Tower Restaurant, Maple Street, W.1 (tel. 636-3000), revolves completely three times an hour. When it bills itself "the top restaurant in London," it really means it! The 620-foot Post Office Tower was designed by the Ministry of Public Buildings and Works (it's a sightseeing attraction as well: see the following chapter). The managers resisted the temptation to turn it into a mere gimmick and hired as the chef de cuisine, Mario Van-Putt from Belgium. Reservations are most important here, as there are only 130 seats. You enter the reception area on the ground floor where you're given a ticket to ride up in the elevator, providing your reservation's in order; the lift, incidentally at 1000 feet a minute, is supposed to be the speediest in Britain. You're delivered to a cocktail bar where you can have a predinner drink before going into the restaurant.

A three-course table d'hôte lunch is served Monday through Friday, for £9.90 ($22.77), plus VAT and service charge. Otherwise, you order from the à la carte menu which changes seasonally. Two specialties are filets de sole sur les toits (one covered with lobster sauce, the other with a champagne sauce with lobster and caviar) for £9.65 ($22.20), and the entrecôte "La Tour Ronde"—garnished with pommes Anna, French green beans, braised celery, tomate clamart, and sauce chasseur, £9 ($20.70). The restaurant is open Monday to Saturday from 12:30 until 2:30 p.m. On Sunday it serves lunch from 12:30 to 2 p.m. Dinner, Monday to Saturday, is from 6:30 till 11:30 p.m., on Sunday from 7 to 10 p.m. Tube: Goodge Street.

BLOOMSBURY: Although the center of much sightseeing and a complex of hotels, Bloomsbury is relatively shy on really good restaurants. There are a few, of course, and one of the best is previewed below in—

The Medium-Priced Range

Tagore, 8 Brunswick Centre, off Russell Square, W.C.1 (tel. 837-9397), is one of the finest Indian restaurants in London. It has an unobtrusive and rather unattractive entrance in this modern complex of apartments and shops. Hardly what you'd expect if you're seeking delicate Indian cookery, including the best of tandoori dishes. Colored lights inside gently illuminate a display of art objects and paintings. Sitar music is provided nightly, and there is dancing as well, so it becomes somewhat like a nightclub.

Specialties include pan-fried herring, heavily spiced, at 90p ($2.07) per helping; lamb pasanda, £3 ($6.90); and tandoori king prawn masalla at £4.50 ($10.35). Tagore is an ideal center for vegetarians who will find a special menu of tempting dishes. The special vegetable thali is £2.80 ($6.44). Incidentally, if you're in the neighborhood, perhaps sightseeing at the British Museum, you might want to visit and sample the executive luncheon at £3.50 ($8.05). At the entrance is a large portrait of namesake Tagore, the Hindu poet and prose writer who died in 1941. The restaurant is open daily, including Sunday, from noon to 3 p.m. and from 6 p.m. till midnight. Tube: Russell Square.

REGENT'S PARK: When in Regent's Park you have an opportunity to dine in London's first floating restaurant.

The Medium-Priced Range

Barque & Bite, opposite 15 Prince Albert Rd., Regent's Park, N.W.1 (tel. 485-8137), as London's first floating restaurant, makes a unique contribution to the continuing parade of dining oddities in the English capital. Like the Top of the Tower, it doesn't rely on the sheer novelty of its location, although that alone might sustain it. You'll find the moored restaurant at the dock pier, down the steps from the road encircling the northern periphery of Regent's Park; and the excellent meals are served on two decks with views of the waterway.

There are many classic French dishes on the set-price menu, great value at £9.50 ($21.85) for three courses. For starters we recommend the avocado Tunisienne or the celery and almond soup. Among the fish dishes try the trout Grenobloise or filets de sole Dieppoise. Good desserts are the homemade strawberry cake or profiteroles and chocolate sauce. Lunch is served Monday to Friday from noon to 3 p.m.; dinner, daily from 7 p.m. until the last orders go in at 11:30 p.m. (closed Sunday and bank holidays). Reservations are essential.

HYDE PARK: If you crave greenery, this choice in the center of Hyde Park is welcome:

The Medium-Priced Range

The **Serpentine,** Hyde Park, W.2, is like a World's Fair exhibition center. It's in the center of Hyde Park, with an unobstructed view of the Serpentine Lake; the restaurant is a free-form glass structure built on different levels, with a separate area for drinks. The food is decidedly good, beginning with a selection of freshly prepared soups at from 80p ($1.84) or a full range of fish and fruit starters from £1.20 ($2.76). The menu features a full range of seafood and grilled meats. Main-course specialties include smoked and poached finnan haddock at £4 ($9.20) and roast beef and Yorkshire pudding at £6.25 ($14.36). Meals are served daily from noon to 3 p.m. and from 6 to 11 p.m.

THE CITY: When the English talk about The City, they don't mean London. The City is the British version of Wall Street. Not only is it an important square mile of finance and business, but it contains many sights. Here are the buildings known the world over: the **Bank of England** on Threadneedle Street (entrance hall open to the public); the **Stock Exchange,** where you can watch transactions from a special gallery; **Lloyd's of London,** on Leadenhall, one of the world's great insurance centers. Lloyd's will insure anything from a stamp collection to a giraffe's neck.

Typical English food—shepherd's pie, mixed grills, roast beef—is dished up in dozens of the old pubs of The City. Here you can eat inexpensively along with the English, whether they be the man in the bowler worried about his country's inflation, or a Cockney secretary anxious to get back to the sound of the Bow Bells.

The Budget Range

The **George & Vulture,** 3 Castle Court, Cornhill, E.C.3 (tel. 626-9710), is for the Dickens enthusiast, ye olde Pickwickian hostelrie, etc. This chophouse, founded in 1660, claims that it is "probably" the world's oldest tavern, and refers to an inn on this spot back in 1175. The George & Vulture no longer puts up overnight guests (although Dickens himself used to bed down here), but its three floors are still used for serving truly English meals. The Pickwick Club meets here now, by the way. Come here for lunch, Monday through Friday, noon to 2:45 p.m. No tables are booked after 1:20 p.m. Besides the daily specials, the George & Vulture features a mixed grill for £2.50 ($5.75); a "loin chop, chump chop," £2.55 ($5.87); or fried filets of Dover sole with tartar sauce, £6 ($13.80). Potatoes or buttered cabbage costs 52p ($1.20) per portion. The apple tart is 58p ($1.34), always reliable. The system is to arrive and give your name, then retire to the Jamaica pub opposite for a drink. You are then fetched when your table is ready. The staff claims the wait is no more than 20 minutes. After lunch, explore the intricate nearby passageways, and discover the maze of shops, wine houses, pubs, and old buildings surrounding the tavern.

FLEET STREET: This street of ink, as it is called, is the gateway to The City. It is the center of London's newspaper and publishing world. The chances are that the person you're rubbing shoulders with in one of the old pubs is a writer or editor. Men and women of letters gather here, as they have for centuries.

The Budget Range

Cheshire Cheese, Wine Office Court, 145 Fleet Street, E.C.4 (tel. 353-6170), is one of the greatest of the old city chophouses, running since 1667. It is the place where Dr. Johnson supposedly entertained Boswell with his acerbic wit. This is quite possible, as the good doctor's house is practically within shouting distance of the Cheese. The two specialties of the house cost £3.25 ($7.48) each. The first is "ye famous pudding"—(steak, kidney, mushroom, and game)—and the other is Scottish roast beef, with Yorkshire pudding and horseradish sauce. The carving wagon holds a giant joint of the roast beef, and

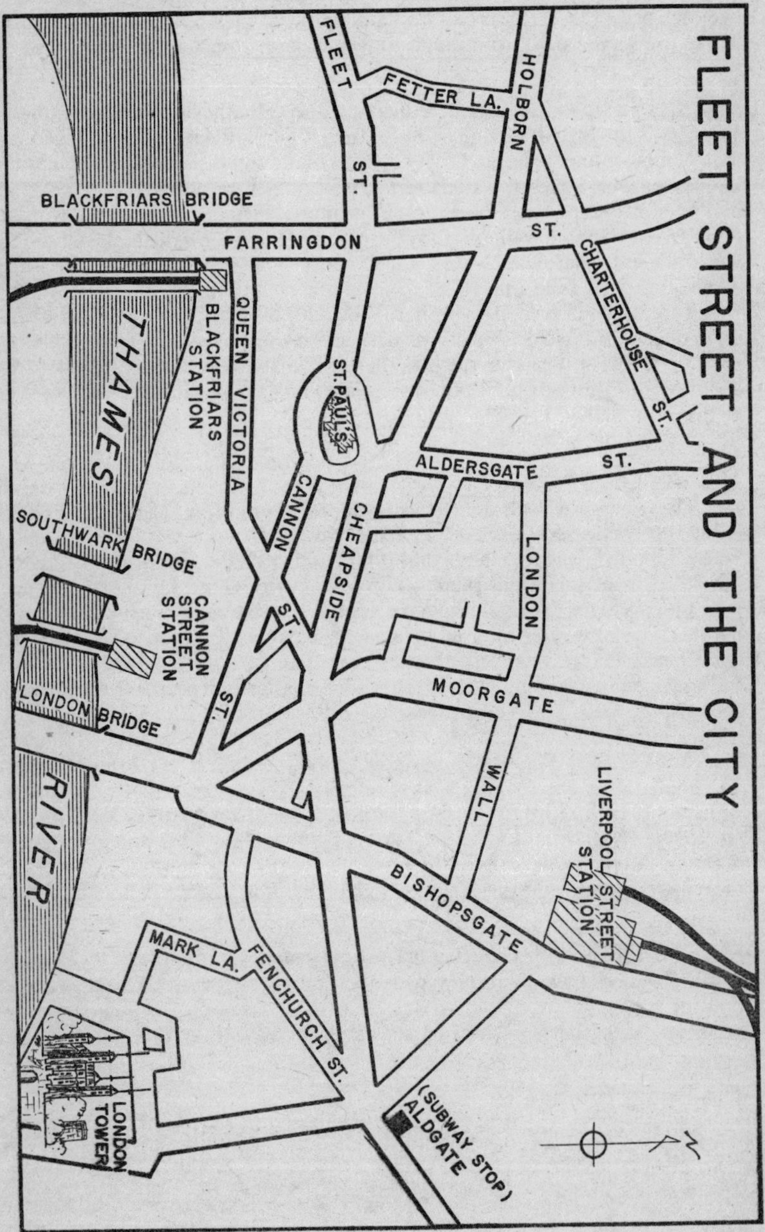

FLEET STREET AND THE CITY

the waiters will occasionally give you additional helpings (on your Wedgwood plate) warning you "not to waste it." For dessert, "ye famous pancake" is £1 ($2.30). Lunch is served from noon to 2:30 p.m. (last orders), and dinners from 6 to 9 p.m. Closed Saturday nights and all day Sunday.

FULHAM: In this home territory for the bishop of London, you'll find the following good eating:

The Medium-Priced Range

Provans, 306b Fulham Rd., S.W.10 (tel. 352-7343). Down the Fulham Road in a narrow building where they used to make gravestones for the neighboring churchyard and then stored ladders, Stewart Grimshaw has established a delightfully informal eating place where famous actors rub shoulders with dwellers from the nearby flats and bed-sits. The whole building is no more than 12 feet wide, but it's 100 feet long. They have cleverly contrived to seat 45 people without making the place cramped, and it is still possible to hold a private conversation without being overheard.

The set four-course dinner at £9.50 ($21.85) includes VAT. Intriguing offerings include cherry and red currant soup, vegetable pâté or consommé, followed by smoked salmon mousse or some other light fish dish. Main dishes are lamb, veal, or chicken, served with fresh vegetables, then a dessert of fruit salad, fruit tart, or Stilton cheese. Coffee is included.

The à la carte menu carries a 60p ($1.38) cover charge, offering leg of lamb with mushrooms, loin of veal with kidneys and bean salad, £5.50 ($12.65), or chicken in tarragon cream sauce or ox tongue with puree of green peas, £5.40 ($12.42). All are served with fresh vegetables in season. A salad on the side costs 70p ($1.61). Desserts include cherry and almond tart, £1.70 ($3.91), or fresh fruit ice creams, £1.20 ($2.76). VAT is included but not service. Wine of the house begins at £4 ($9.20) a bottle.

3. Other Locales

THE EAST END: You may want to plunge into the drab East End of London at least once. Much of it looks like slice-of-life background shots from countless films. But in restaurants it has a few potent drawing cards.

London's Most Famous Jewish Restaurant

Bloom's, 90 Whitechapel High St., E.1 (tel. 247-6835), is worth the crossover to the wrong side of the tracks. Although overcrowded, with frantic service, Bloom's continues to tempt with kosher delights. Sunday lunch, however, is completely impossible, so try to schedule your visit at some other time. A chicken blintz is 90p ($2.07), cabbage borscht in your bowl for 80p ($1.84). The main dishes are reasonably priced, with specialties such as sauerbraten and salt beef (corned) at £4 ($9.20). For dessert, you can order apple strudel at £1 ($2.30). The restaurant is open 11:30 a.m. to 10 p.m., except on Friday when it closes at 3 p.m. (closed all day Saturday).

Chinese Food in Limehouse

Remember "Limehouse Blues"? The limekilns, from which the East End parish takes its name, were abolished before the war, but the legend lives on.

On the North Bank of the Thames, the district is unattractive, with lots of ugly buildings—but therein lies its charm. Populated by broken-down or retired seamen by day, Limehouse at night is often filled with fashionable West Enders on a slumming spree. The big attractions are the Chinese restaurants known as "The Friends" (a few originals and a host of imitators).

New Friends Chinese Restaurant, 53 West India Dock Rd., E.14 (tel. 987-1139), is so popular, it's adopted a reservations only policy. The pocket-sized licensed restaurant, open noon to midnight, doesn't concern itself with decoration—just food and a reputation for some of the best quality Cantonese dishes in England. Although the menu is filled with surprises (many diners call in advance to order special dishes), you will fare handsomely just by sticking to the routine listings: items such as beef fried with green peppers, £3 ($6.90); crunchy yet tender spare ribs for £3 also; sweet-and-sour pork for £2.90 ($6.67); and Kupar prawn for £4.20 ($9.66). If you want a truly special dinner, ask for Mr. Cheung. West India Dock Road lies off Commercial Road and Burdett Road.

Young Friends, 11 Penny Fields, Poplar, E.14 (tel. 987-4276). This is the domain of Raymond Low, and many West Enders cross the city to sample his gray mullet (on 24-hour notice). From the tiniest kitchen imaginable come excellent meals, served in a dining room that couldn't be more basic. Here are our suggestions for a memorable dinner: wonton soup, £1.65 ($3.80); sharkfin soup, £1.50 ($3.45); sweet-sour wonton, £2 ($4.60); stuffed chicken wings in oyster sauce, £2 also. You can top your dinner with lichee nuts for 65p ($1.50). Bring your own wine, as the restaurant is unlicensed. Penny Fields lies just off West India Dock Road. Lost? Call Raymond Low for directions.

READER'S RESTAURANT SELECTION: "Slender's Health Food Restaurant, 41 Cathedral Pl., E.C.4, is exactly in front of St. Paul tube station. The menu at this fine eating place includes such items as tomato and watercress soup, 50p ($1.15); lasagne verdi, £1.10 ($2.53); baked potato with butter, 40p (92¢). Herb teas and decaffeinated coffee cost 22p (51¢). They serve luscious desserts, such as apple-date pie, apricot meringues, and cheesecake, all at reasonable prices. The young people serving you are most pleasant, the food very well prepared and attractive. One may either eat in the restaurant or take food out. Beans, whole grains, and dried fruits are also sold. Hours are 8:30 a.m. to 6:15 p.m., Monday through Friday" (Jean See, Spokane, Wash.).

SOUTH OF THE THAMES: The **George Inn,** 77 Borough High St., S.E.1 (tel. 407-2056), across the bridge at Southwark, is a National Trust property, the only remaining London pub with an outside gallery. A touch of old England safely tucked away in an alley, the present building dates back some 300 years. Some claim that Shakespeare and his troupe performed in an old inn that stood on the same ground. Dickens not only frequented the George, but he also wrote about it in *Little Dorrit.* Recently the building next door was acquired by the owners and the pub has been enlarged to include a new wine bar.

You enter the George through a gateway into the "old bar," noteworthy for its functioning beer engines, which are nearly as old as the building itself, and a bar area complete with a fire for nippy days and the famous Act of Parliament clock. This bar offers a variety of hot snacks, while the newer wine bar has a large cold buffet counter. The remaining bar on the first floor is for more serious drinkers. Two original staircases lead to each of the two restaurants, where a traditional three-course English luncheon costs £4.50 ($10.35). Lunch is served Monday through Friday from noon to 2 p.m., and dinner Monday through Saturday from 6 to 9 p.m.

The **Royal Festival Hall Restaurant,** Belvedere Road, S.E.1 (tel. 928-2829), is on the third floor of this concert hall, with big picture windows overlooking the river and the floodlit buildings on the other side. In this dramatic setting, well-prepared food is served efficiently. Opening courses include deviled whitebait at £1.50 ($3.45) and smoked salmon at £3.50 ($8.05). Main dishes feature chicken Maryland at £3.25 ($7.48), although you may prefer the chateaubriand for two at £14.50 ($33.35). For your dessert, you can make a selection from the trolley at £1.10 ($2.53). Lunch is offered Monday to Friday from noon to 3 p.m.; dinner, Monday to Saturday, from 6 to 11:30 p.m. Tube: Waterloo.

South of the Border, 8–10 Joan St., S.E.1 (tel. 928-6374). The name reflects the attitude a lot of people have toward London "South of the River" as the locals say, and it is rare to find a fashionable place to eat after a visit to the nearby Festival Hall, National Theatre, and Young Vic Theatre. Joan Street is at the junction of the Cut and Blackfriars, within easy reach of all. Once a mattress factory, the ground floor and gallery can seat more than 80 people and, in summer, there are also tables on the outdoor terrace.

The menu consists of a choice of various appetizers. There's always a homemade soup such as minestrone at £1.10 ($2.53) or white bean at 95p ($2.19). Main dishes include a variety of chicken, lamb, beef, and fish dishes, such as chicken escalope, carbonnade of beef cooked in beer with potatoes and onions and served in its own pot, and fish pie stuffed with cod, shellfish, mullet, and crab. The price range is from £2.20 ($5.06) to £3.50 ($8.05). Desserts have such succulent names as Belvoir pudding steamed with fruits and custard costing £1 ($2.30). There is a good selection of wines and a choice from seven house wines at a cost of £4 ($9.20) per bottle. The menu is frequently changed so a return visit can be recommended. The restaurant is open Monday to Saturday from 6 to 11:30 p.m. and from Monday to Friday from noon to 2:30.

555, 555 Battersea Park Rd., S.W.11 (tel. 228-7011), is a most unprepossessing cafe (in looks only) in a dreary commercial sector of London, south of the Thames. But surprise! The food is delicious, the ingredients extremely fresh. A gemütlich feeling prevails at night, and soon you're joining in the fun. The posters on the walls are more permissive than ever. You can get a number of really good Baltic dishes here. Vera, the owner, oversees everything. By all means, try the homemade sausage. The pâté is also delicious, a bit crude but good. The suckling pig is highly recommended, and seems to be a house specialty. Vegetables come with everything; red cabbage is often featured. An entire meal will run about £7 ($16.10) to £8 ($18.40). Meals are served to a very cosmopolitan crowd against a background of taped music. Vera says it's all in great fun, and we agree. It is closed Sunday and Monday, but open otherwise for dinner only from 7:30 p.m. till midnight. Take a taxi: you'll never find the place if you don't.

HAMPSTEAD: Keats, Downshire Hill, Hampstead, N.W.3 (tel. 435-1499), is a "small, serious restaurant for committed gourmets," just around the corner from Keats's house. The well-prepared food is the best in Hampstead. Considering the size of the restaurant—it has a capacity of only about 50 diners—the French menu is exceedingly ambitious, containing some 40 delectable dishes which are varied every five weeks. Proprietor Aron Misan's special pride is his wine cellar, which houses at least 100 varieties, including a collection of "Dr. Barolet" burgundies with vintages as old as 1926. An average dinner at Keats comes to about £12 ($27.60), not including wine. Keats is open every evening except Sunday. Reservations are a must.

Oslo Court, Prince Albert Road, N.W.8 (tel. 722-8795), is oddly situated for a restaurant, with an entrance on Charlbert Street, to the west of Regent's Park. But the food offered here, a combination Balkan and Scandinavian, is so good and so well prepared that it merits a taxi ride from Central London. We were there the night Richard Burton discovered the place, and he threatened to send all his friends. Rajko Katnic, a Yugoslav, rules the establishment in an apartment complex like an emperor, but you are likely to have his sweet and charming daughter take your order. She's a hearty Welsh woman and is ingratiating in her friendliness and spirit. The waiters employed are highly skilled, and will even call you a cab at the end of the evening. Always reserve a table. It's easy to obtain space for lunch, more difficult in the evening.

The specialties are many and varied. We prefer for openers the Kvarnerv fish soup at £1.75 ($4.03), or else crab La Rochelle at £3.25 ($7.48). Main-dish specialties include duck Bosnaka; veal cutlet trapiste; and sole Papa Augustine, each £6.75 ($15.53). Fresh vegetables are served at £1.10 ($2.53) a portion, and desserts begin at £1.30 ($2.99). In addition to the high standard of cooking, the wine list is also outstanding. The restaurant is open for lunch from 12:30 to 2 p.m. and for dinner from 6:30 to 10:30 p.m. It is closed all day on Monday and for lunch on Saturday.

Le Cellier du Midi, Church Row, N.W.3 (tel. 435-9998), is a basement French bistro, off Hampstead Heath Street. It's decorated with odd Victorian knickknacks, with bunches of garlic and onions hanging from the roof beams. Rough wooden tables are covered with red cloths. It's run by Henri Saux, who offers classical French cooking with the day's specialties shown on the blackboard. For £11 ($25.30), you're given a four-course meal with a choice of some 16 appetizers, including pâté and mussels marinière, then 20 main dishes such as pot au feu or boeuf Alaric. A tempting array of at least 15 desserts is offered nightly. It is wise to reserve, particularly on weekends. Le Cellier is well recommended for the quality of its cuisine and its general ambience.

Pippin, 83/84 Hampstead High Street, N.W.3 (tel. 435-6434), offers a fine array of strictly vegetarian dishes to tempt even the most skeptical non-vegetarian. Prices begin at £1.50 ($3.45). The delicious freshly baked breads and cakes are prepared from Pippin's own organically grown wheat flour. The restaurant's Copella pure apple juice is the favorite beverage to accompany any dish. Open daily from 10 a.m. to 11:30 p.m., Pippin offers morning coffee, lunch, afternoon tea, or dinner on its terrace restaurant.

NEAR OLYMPIA EXHIBITION HALL: Jonathan's Restaurant, 71 Blythe Rd., W.14 (tel. 602-2758). In an almost suburban street behind Olympia Exhibition Hall, you may feel you need a passport to divert so far from the normal tourist paths. But once you have parked your car or paid off the taxi, rung the bell at number 71, and been ushered into the small informal bar, you will be quite at home. Sink into a deep sofa, sip your drink, and discuss with Jonathan Keyne the merits of the various dishes on the extensive French menu prepared by the Spanish chef. Downstairs, the restaurant is cozy, with candles and fresh flowers on the linen tablecloths.

A hot avocado Jonathan, stuffed with seafood, is £2 ($4.60); seafood pancakes, £2.20 ($5.06); and a mushroom tart, £1.75 ($4.03). Entrecôte steak with cream and pepper sauce, mushroom and wine sauce, or crusted with mustard and sugar goes for £5 ($11.50). Beef Stroganoff is £4.75 ($10.93); grilled chicken with honey and rosemary, £4 ($9.20). There is a nice selection of desserts, plus an excellent wine list with house wines at £4 ($9.20) a bottle. VAT is included but you should add a 50p cover charge plus 10% for service.

LONDON: RESTAURANTS 97

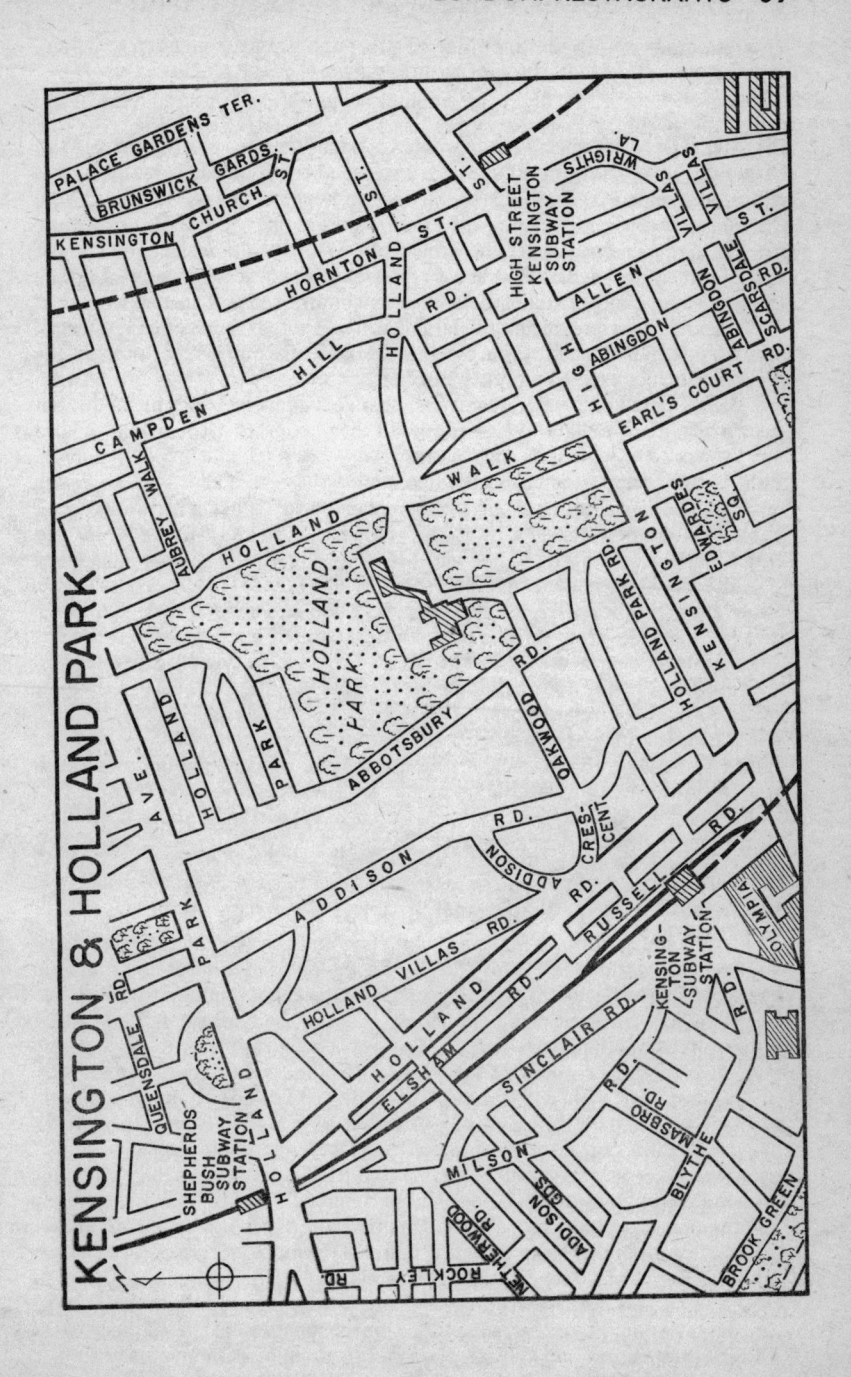

The restaurant is open for lunch Tuesday through Friday from noon to 2 p.m., and for dinner Tuesday through Saturday from 7 to 11 p.m.

ISLINGTON: Frederick's Restaurant, Camden Passage, N.1 (tel. 359-2888). Originally, in 1789, the building was a pub called the Gun. Then in 1834 it was rebuilt and renamed "The Duke of Sussex" in honor of George III's sixth son, Prince Augustus Frederick. So when the restaurant opened in 1970, what more natural than to name it after the prince? As well as tables inside, you can eat in the Garden Room, designed like a Victorian glasshouse with a domed ceiling of many small panes of tinted glass. It is air-conditioned and heated, with glass doors leading to a terrace and the large garden. There is much open brickwork and tropical plants to create a pleasant, relaxed place in which to enjoy the delicacies of the excellent French cuisine.

Jean-Louis Pollet, chef de cuisine, changes the menu every fortnight, but there are so many delightful alternatives to each course that you would be hard put to work through it in two weeks. Appetizers include smoked salmon, French onion soup, snails, and fried camembert cheese. There are several fish dishes including turbot with buttered spinach, chicken, duck with orange, pork or lamb chops, peppersteaks, or, from the charcoal grill, a variety of steaks and cutlets served with garlic butter and béarnaise sauce.

Frederick's specialties include scampis St. Tropez and liver Berlinoise. Vegetables are always freshly prepared, and you can choose your own salad, specifying what you would like in it. Desserts are all homemade, and there is a good cheese board of French cheeses. A three-course meal with coffee will cost around £12 ($27.60) including VAT, but it is quite possible to dine for around £9 ($20.70) per person.

There is a long and excellent wine list and a very palatable French claret can be as little as £5 ($11.50), or the house wine is £3.50 ($8.05) a bottle. If you are in the area on Saturday, they do a set luncheon for £6 ($13.80). This is the area for the antique hunter, so you may very well find yourself up there with time to enjoy a delicious meal. Tube: Angel.

4. Suggestions for Sunday

When much of the West End is closed on Sunday, you'll find more life—if you take a taxi, tube, or bus to Aldgate East and spend a hectic hour or so at **Petticoat Lane.** That's the street market where, even if you don't want to buy the goods, you can see the full wit and expertise of the Cockney street vendors. Look for the one who sells tea services, buy a toffee apple or a hot dog, and then go around the corner to **Club Row,** a street market for animals and birds.

Then a short walk will bring you down to the Tower of London and, right beside it, just below Tower Bridge, **St. Katharine's Dock.** This is a new development, created out of the old London dock area where the "breakfast ships," carrying bacon and eggs from Holland, used to tie up. It is gradually becoming a vast open-air pleasure area—but with a difference. At the dock lie many old and famous vessels, the old **Nore Lightship** (admission 10p or 23¢ for adults, 5p or 12¢ for children), an Isle of Wight ferry which once acted as tender to a battleship in wartime, Thames sailing barges, a Chinese junk, and among these the elegant craft of visiting yachtsmen from all over the world.

By now, you should be ready for a splurge luncheon at the **Carvery** of the **Tower Hotel.** For £7.60 ($17.48), you can retaliate by eating yourself silly on delicious hot roast beef, lamb, and pork.

Or you can have a very English meal at the **Captain's Cabin,** St. Katharine-by-the-Tower, East Smithfield, E.1 (tel. 480-5907), opened in the Ivory House, where ivory was once stored upstairs, slaves in the cellar. The menu features game soup at £1.50 ($3.45), venison at £5.50 ($12.65), Captain Cook's Eastern Island chicken at £4 ($9.20), and snacks such as the barge master's special at £2 ($4.60). The cabin is decorated tavern style, with a flagstone floor and fishnets draped about. It is open daily from 11 a.m. to 11 p.m., including public holidays. Live music is featured every evening.

Perhaps the main attraction is the **Dickens Inn by the Tower,** St. Katharine's Way, E.1 (tel. 488-2208), a very carefully reconstructed 19th-century warehouse. Incorporating the original redwood beams, stock bricks, and ironworks, it is a balconied pub/restaurant on three levels. Sitting on a wooden chair and an old table, you can enjoy such bar snacks as cockles at 60p ($1.38); mussels, 75p ($1.73); rollmops at 55p ($1.27); even a ploughman's lunch at £1 ($2.30).

For more elegant dining, go upstairs to the **Pickwick Room,** where old-fashioned English-style meals are available beginning at £15 ($34.50) per head. Specialties include a braised whole pigeon with button onions and red wine sauce and sirloin of Scottish beef. The inn's dessert specialty is Betsy Trotwood's tipsy cake.

In the top-floor **Dickens Room** fish restaurant, you can order an unusual range of fish, making your selection from a slab at one end of the restaurant. For a traditional cockney dish, try the jellied eels at £1.10 ($2.53), or perhaps the cockles and mussels at £1.40 ($3.22). Fish dishes, including whitebait, John Dory, salmon, and crayfish tails, range in price from £2 ($4.60) to £5.50 ($12.65).

The tavern keeps regular pub hours; otherwise, the Pickwick Room is open Monday to Friday from 12:30 to 2 p.m. and from 7:30 to 10 p.m., on Saturday from 7:30 to 10 p.m. only, and on Sunday from 12:30 to 2 p.m. The Dickens Room serves Monday to Saturday from noon to 3 p.m. and from 5 to 10 p.m. (Sunday, noon to 5 p.m.).

It's essential to book (tel. 488-2208).

EATING AFLOAT: An increasingly popular London activity is dinner aboard. On Wednesday, Saturday, and Sunday lunchtimes, **Catamaran Cruises** leave Westminster Pier, S.W.1 (tel. 839-2349). The cost is £8.30 ($19.10) per passenger. Evening floodlit supper cruises are also offered on Wednesday and Sunday at 9 p.m. (you're back at 10:30 p.m.). Tours leave from Westminster Pier, and the cruise costs £2.50 ($5.75). If you purchase supper, the cost goes up to £6.50 ($14.95), including a basket containing French bread, cheese and butter, chicken, a lettuce and tomato salad, rice, sherry trifle, and a piece of fresh fruit. The boat is licensed to serve drinks, and there is a commentary on the historic buildings as you ply between Albert Bridge and Tower Bridge.

The Regents Canal which winds and twists through London is the home of **The Fair Lady,** departing from 250 Camden High St., N.W. 1, two minutes from the Camden Town tube station. There are cruises most nights (but never on Monday) starting at 7:30 p.m. and costing £12 ($27.60) per person for a three-hour trip. Searchlights illuminate the banks and buildings, and often there is live entertainment, perhaps a singer with a guitar. Dinner is a choice of three appetizers, then a choice of meat, poultry, or fish, dessert or cheese, and coffee. House wines go for £3 ($6.90) a bottle. The Sunday lunch is presented at 12:30 p.m. at a cost of about £8.50 ($19.55). Advance reservations are imperative (tel. 485-4433).

The Packet Boat is a traditional painted narrow boat, very attractive, leaving from Portobello Dock, Ladbroke Grove, near the Portobello Road market. For reservations, telephone 960-5456. A lunch cruise, featuring a large cold buffet, leaves at 12:30 p.m., costing £6 ($13.80), plus VAT. Barbecue cruises are also bookable, leaving at 7:30 p.m. and costing £8 ($18.40) for a cruise, barbecue supper, and dancing in the dock supper club.

The paddle steamer **Princess Elizabeth** is berthed at Swan Pier, Upper Thames Street, E.C.4 (tel. 623-1805), and is, once again, open to the public. She is entirely genuine, and you can view her massive engines and explore her narrow alleyways before a drink and a snack in the Chartroom Wine Bar. Or else you can order a cocktail in the Ward Room Bar before lunch in the Winston Churchill Restaurant, where a meal will cost around £6 ($13.80) per person. The simple menu includes the more exotic shrimps paddle steamer for £2.20 ($5.06), served with mushrooms in a butter and sherry sauce, and steak, kidney, and oyster pie for £4.50 ($10.35). The steamer is open Monday to Friday only for lunch from noon to 2:30 p.m.

LUNCHTIME THEATER: There is drama on the menu these days in many of the small theaters and pubs of London. The actors often include well-known names, and the plays the work of established writers, although this is an outlet for many a would-be Olivier, Ayckbourn, or Stoppard. With the play, which usually lasts about an hour, the audience can often enjoy a light, inexpensive meal, and prices are deliberately kept low so that the spectacle is available to all.

The **King's Head Theatre Club,** 115 Upper St., N.1 (tel. 226-1916), run by American-born Don Crawford, charges 75p ($1.73) for your ticket. You pay a little extra for beer or wine and collect your meat and salad or steak-and-kidney pie on the way into the theater.

The **Soho Poly Theatre Club,** 16 Riding House St., W.1 (tel. 636-9050), also charges 75p ($1.73), with lunch at 40p (92¢) extra.

After your visit to the Changing of the Guard ceremony, the **Institute of Contemporary Arts,** Nash House, The Mall, S.W.1 (tel. 930-6393), charges 80p ($1.84) and is rapidly gaining a reputation for avant-garde productions.

The **Young Vic Theatre,** across the river near Waterloo, charges £1 ($2.30) for their lunchtime performances. There is a bar, and light snacks are offered.

At Richmond, the **Orange Tree Pub,** just opposite Richmond Station, concentrates on new authors and plays, and tickets cost 50p ($1.15). Productions are remarkably sophisticated. You may be able to say that you saw the latest Broadway or West End hit months or even years before, and appreciated its brilliance even then!

5. The Pubs of London

No activity is more typically British than to head for that venerated institution, the Public House, affectionately known as pub. Many are dreary Victorian monstrosities, patronized by the working men and women in the neighborhood. Others, particularly those in the West End, have glamor, basking in associations real (Charles Dickens, Samuel Johnson) or imagined (Sherlock Holmes). Pub crawling, as previewed in our introduction, is a real part of your English experience.

LONDON: PUBS

Many North American visitors who don't usually go to bars at home become rabid enthusiasts of the English pub. And most single women feel comfortable in pubs.

Licensing hours are unpopular in England—generally from 11 a.m. to 3 p.m. and from 5:30 to 11 p.m. On Sunday the hours are usually from noon to 2 p.m. and from 7 to 10:30 p.m. Persons under 18 are not allowed in licensed bars.

The most noticeable change in English pubs, especially those in the West End, is in the improved standard of food served. However, many pubs still rely on snacks, as typified by the little meat pies, drab dough wrapped around last week's pork roast. Others serve superb sandwiches (fresh salmon stuffed between healthy slices of brown bread), even hot dishes, such as shepherd's pie. Some London pubs are pursuing a fine cuisine in a separate dining room on their premises—the fare ranging from lobster soup to river trout grilled in butter to roast Aylesbury duckling in orange sauce.

Our pub recommendations in all major tourist centers of the West End follow, the emphasis placed on those having historic interest (the Prospect of Whitby, Ye Olde Cock Tavern) or else those catering to special-interest groups, such as theater buffs and actors (Salisbury).

ST. JAMES'S: The **Red Lion**, 2 Duke of York St., St. James's Square, S.W.1, is only a short walk from Piccadilly Circus. Ian Nairn compared its spirit to that of Edouard Manet's painting *A Bar at the Folies-Bergère* (see the collection at the Courtauld Institute Galleries). Try to avoid peak hours, so that you'll be able to introduce yourself to the friendly owners, Roy and Corinne Hamlin, who pride themselves on the number of friends they have made. They offer pub luncheons at noon: steak pie with vegetables, 95p ($2.19), and a wide variety of sandwiches—all on healthy brown bread—at 40p (92¢) a "cutting," as they say. All roasts are £1.10 ($2.53), vegetables included. Everything is washed down with Ind Coope's fine ales in this little Victorian pub, with its posh turn-of-the-century decorations—patterned glass, deep-mahogany curlicues—that recapture the gin-palace atmosphere. It is open six days a week from 11 a.m. to 3 p.m. and from 5:30 to 11 p.m. (on Sunday from noon to 2 p.m.). Mr. and Mrs. Hamlin rule their little kingdom in a way that would have pleased Queen Victoria—that is, with style and elegance. Single women can be at ease here.

The **Captain's Cabin**, 4 Norris St., S.W.1 (tel. 930-3979), just off Haymarket and close to Piccadilly Circus, is an old high London building on a narrow street with a narrow pavement—unremarkable from the outside. The ground floor and snackbar are busy at lunchtime. Here, try the Director's Bitter, which is pure English beer, and have a meat salad for £2 ($4.60) to £2.50 ($5.75). Other offerings include steak-and-kidney pie, curried beef, and shepherd's pie, at around £1.25 ($2.88) to £2.50 ($5.75).

The Dive Bar in the basement is a small, paneled, quiet bar with a regular clientele. Dimly lit, it was famous during the last world war as a rendezvous for airmen and servicemen on leave. Mementos from those days are still on the walls.

PICCADILLY CIRCUS: The **Cockney Pride**, at Piccadilly Circus, W.1 (tel. 930-5339), occupies the same spot as the formerly celebrated Criterion Restaurant. It is a clever reproduction, a latter-day tribute to the glory of Victoriana: tufted velvet banquettes, cut-glass mirrors, and converted brass oil lanterns.

When ordering food, better take along a friend born within the sound of the Bow Bells; you'll need one for translations. For example, you can select such Cockney cuisine oddities as "bangers and mash" at 85p ($1.96) or cottage pie at £1.25 ($2.88).

LEICESTER SQUARE: The **Salisbury,** 90 St. Martin's Lane, W.C.2, is one of the most famous Victorian pubs of London, attracting today a largely gay patronage. Its glittering cut-glass mirrors reflect the faces of English stage stars (and would-be stars), sitting around the curved buffet-style bar, having a cold joint snack. A plate of the roast leg of pork on the buffet, plus a salad, costs from £2 ($4.60) to £3 ($6.90). If you want a less prominent place to dine or to nibble oysters, choose the old-fashioned wall banquette with its copper-topped tables, and art nouveau decor. The light fixtures, veiled bronze girls in flowing togas holding up clusters of electric lights concealed in bronze roses, are appropriate. In the saloon, you'll see and hear the Olivier of yesterday and tomorrow.

TRAFALGAR SQUARE: The **Sherlock Holmes,** 10 Northumberland St., W.C.2 (tel. 930-2644), is for fans of the legendary English detective and his creator, Arthur Conan Doyle. You can order your mug of beer and then look at the recreation upstairs of 221B Baker Street's living room, where get-togethers of "The Baker Street Irregulars" are held. Such "Holmesiana" are included as the cobra of the *Speckled Band* and the head of the *Hound of the Baskervilles.* The food served upstairs reflects both an English and continental influence. Appetizers run from 95p ($2.19) to £1.35 ($3.11). Main-dish specialties include Dover sole at £6.50 ($14.95); trout, £3.50 ($8.05); and veal escalope Cordon Bleu, £5 ($11.50). Desserts from the trolley begin at 95p ($2.19). Downstairs you can order sandwiches for 52p ($1.20), salads from £1.25 ($2.88), and shepherd's pie at £1 ($2.30).

SOHO: **Maison Berlemont,** 49 Dean St., W.1 (tel. 437-2799), is popularly known as York Minster. Run by Monsieur G. R. Berlemont, it once was the unofficial headquarters of the French resistance in exile in London during the war. Nostalgic Frenchmen still come here, talking about the old days and purchasing outstanding "vins" by the glass. The pub has a plain exterior, and the decor itself is not remarkable. However, the hospitality of the patron is laudable, as are his bar-room snacks, especially the pâté and the excellent quiche Lorraine. A lot of authors, theater and film people are also attracted to "the Minster."

CHELSEA: **King's Head & Eight Bells,** 50 Cheyne Walk, S.W.2 (tel. 352-1820), is a historic Thames-side pub in a fashionable residential area of London, that has reopened after extensive redecoration and some reconstruction. It's popular with stage and TV personalities as well as writers. Many distinguished personalities once lived in this area. A short stroll in the neighborhood will take you to the former homes of such famous personages as Carlyle, Swinburne, and George Eliot. Press gangs used to roam these parts of Chelsea seeking lone travelers who were abducted for a life at sea. The snackbar has been upgraded to Cordon Bleu standards at pub prices. Rosie and Jilly are in charge of catering, buying, preparing, and cooking everything. The best English beers are served here, as well as a goodly selection of wines and liquors. Soups begin at

60p ($1.38), and traditional English fare includes such main dishes as shepherd's pie at £1.25 ($2.88), followed by desserts costing from 65p ($1.50). More elegant offerings would include lobster soup at £1.50 ($3.45), trout at £3 ($6.90), or perhaps chicken à la crème, also costing from £3.

BELGRAVIA: The **Grenadier**, Wilton Row, S.W.1 (tel. 235-3400), is an old-time pub on a cobblestoned street, sheltered by higher buildings, and protected from the noise of traffic. The Grenadier is one of the special pubs of London—associated with the Iron Duke. But today the smell is not of the horses of Wellington's officers. The scarlet front door of the one-time officers' mess is guarded by a scarlet sentrybox and shaded by a vine. The bar is nearly always crowded with blue-bloods and their thin, pale girlfriends. Very English meals are served in front of fireplaces in two of the small rooms behind the front bar. Luncheons and dinners are offered daily, including Sunday, from noon to 3 p.m. and from 7 to 11 p.m. A soup of the day costs 90p ($2.07). Main courses include such dishes as baked Virginia ham at £3.50 ($8.05), followed by desserts including apple pie and cream, £1.15 ($2.65).

There is a gentle ghost, that of an officer who died after being flogged for cheating at cards. The decor is definitely Wellingtonian. At the entrance to Wilton Row (in the vicinity of Belgrave Square), a special guard ("good evening, guv'nor") is stationed to raise and lower a barrier for those arriving by "carriage." May British tradition never die. Pub enthusiasts are fanatic about the Grenadier. If anyone tries to tear it down, he may meet his Waterloo.

The **Antelope**, 22 Eaton Terrace, S.W.1 (tel. 730-7781), on the fringe of Belgravia, at the gateway to Chelsea, caters to a hotchpotch of clients, aptly described as "people of all classes, colours and creeds who repair for interesting discussion on a whole gamut of subjects, ranging from sport to medieval history, wicker-work, bed-bug traps, and for both mental and physical refreshment." 'Nuff said? You can wine and dine upstairs, or else have lunch in a ground-floor chamber offering a cold buffet. For openers, try the Antelope soup, followed by steak-and-kidney pie, and topped off by red currant pie and cream. The trappings have long ago mellowed, as the history of the Antelope goes back to 1780.

IN PADDINGTON: The **Victoria Tavern**, Strathearn Place, W.2 is a three-in-one house, beginning with an old street-level tavern, a real Victorian pub. Sit back over a lager and enjoy the polished mahogany, the cut and etched glass, a working fireplace, and the window seats with their soft cushions. The upper-level salon, called the Theatre Bar, is a delightful place at which to entertain friends in the evenings. Here are the nostalgic memorabilia of the defunct Gaiety Theatre, including a playbill of the last performance, on July 4, 1903.

On the basement level, reached by an outer stairway, you enter the **Victorian Cellars Wine Bar**. To describe its atmosphere would make it sound artfully corny, but it isn't. The small dining room is placed in a simulated narrow street of 19th-century London, including an Old Curiosity Shop and a gas lamppost. The food is typical of wine-bar society—steak-and-kidney pie, smoked mackerel, or barbecued pork for around £1.75 ($4.03). Quiches and salads go for the same price. Pâté or cheese with French bread costs £1.10 ($2.53); a glass of wine begins at 70p ($1.61). The restaurant is open from 11:30 a.m. to 3 p.m., and from 6:30 p.m. to midnight, Monday to Saturday. The restaurant is closed on Sunday, although the bar upstairs opens to serve drinks. For restaurant seating, telephone 262-4554 for reservations.

SHEPHERD MARKET (MAYFAIR): Shepherd's Tavern, 50 Hertford St., W.1 (tel. 499-3017), is a nugget, considered the pub of Mayfair. It attracts a congenial mixture of English, from those who read *The Times* every morning to a rather pacey set of young 'uns. There are many fine touches, including an exceptional collection of antique furniture. Attention is focused on the sedan chair which once belonged to the son of George III, the Duke of Cumberland (it's now fitted with a telephone for those very private "ring ups"). Many of the locals like to recall the tavern's associations with the pilots in the Battle of Britain. Bar snacks and hot dishes include shepherd's pie, curry or fish pie with vegetable, the prices beginning at £1.25 ($2.88) per serving.

BLOOMSBURY: The Museum Tavern, 49 Great Russell St., W.C.1 (tel. 242-8984), opposite the British Museum, is a turn-of-the-century pub, with all the trappings: velvet, oak paneling, and cut glass. It's right in the center of the London University area, and popular with writers and publishers. At lunch you can order real, good-tasting, low-cost English food. Such standard English fare is featured as shepherd's pie at 75p ($1.73) or "sausages and mash" at 50p ($1.15). Hot pies are 70p ($1.61). A cold buffet is offered, running from £1 ($2.30) to £2 ($4.60), including herring, Scottish eggs, and veal and ham pies, as well as salads and cheese.

THE CITY: Old King Lud, 78 Ludgate Circus, E.C.4 (tel. 236-6610), is a Victorian pub built in 1855 on the site of the Old Fleet Prison. The former dungeons are now the cellars of this old-world pub, which bills itself as the home of the original Welsh rabbit. However, it no longer serves that specialty for which it became famous. Rather, it offers a selection of pâtés at 95p ($2.19) which ranges from venison to duck with orange. Both hot and cold dishes are dispensed. One of the hot plates, such as beef curry with two vegetables, costs £1.60 ($3.68). Wine is sold by the glass, selections including claret at 68p ($1.56) or Anjou at 68p also. You can also order good Marlow Bitter here. The decor is in varying shades of green, including the tufted banquettes. Tube: Blackfriars.

Ye Olde Watling, 29 Watling St., E.C.4, is associated with Sir Christopher Wren; it was built after the Great Fire of London in 1666. On the ground level is a mellow pub, with an intimate and stuffy restaurant upstairs which serves lunch from noon to 2:15 p.m., Monday through Friday. Under oak beams and on trestle tables, you can have a good choice of English food, with such traditional dishes as steak, kidney, and mushroom pudding, £2.35 ($5.41), the house specialty. Steak and oyster pie is the same price, although most main dishes begin at £3 ($6.90).

FLEET STREET: Ye Olde Cock Tavern, 22 Fleet St., E.C.4, boasts a long line of ghostly literary comrades, such as Dickens, who have favored this ancient pub. After having a half pint on the ground floor, diners go upstairs to have lunch in a former horse stall. "Ye fare" is served from 12:30 to 3 p.m. Of course, the food is traditionally English. A bowl of rich tomato soup costs 65p ($1.50); a steak-and-kidney pie, £1.75 ($4.03); a delicious fruit trifle, 65p ($1.50).

ALONG THE THAMES: The Prospect of Whitby, 57 Wapping Wall, E.1 (tel. 481-1095), is one of London's oldest riverside pubs, having been founded originally in the days of the Tudors. The Prospect has many associations—it was visited by Dickens, Turner, Whistler, in search of local "colour." Come here for a "tot," a "noggin," or whatever it is that you drink. The Pepys Room honors the diarist, who may—just may—have visited the Prospect back in its rowdier days, when the seamy side of London dock life held sway here. The pub is named after a ship, the *Prospect,* which sailed from its home port of Whitby and used to drop anchor outside the pub. Live music is heard every night, 8:30 to 11.

Take the Metropolitan Line to Wapping Station. When you emerge onto Wapping High Street, turn right and head down the road along the river. Wapping Wall will be on your right, running parallel to the Thames. It's about a five-minute walk.

The **City Barge**, Strand-on-the-Green, Chiswick, W.4. Londoners head here for an outing and an evening pint of ale on a summer night. A little country pub, a nostalgic link with the past—it can be reached in 45 minutes from the center of London. Take the tube to Hammersmith, then change to bus 27 and get off at the beginning of Kew Bridge (during the day this can be combined with a visit to Kew Gardens). Then walk down a towpath (about a five-minute jaunt), past moored boats and a row of little Regency, Queen Anne, Georgian, and Dutch houses, till you reach the pub. Or you can go by boat from Westminster Pier to Kew Gardens, then visit the City Barge, and return to London by train. Regulars often bypass the little tables set outside (in summer) so as to have their pint while sitting on the embankment wall under a willow tree, and enjoying the boats chugging or gliding by.

The **Anchor**, 1 Bankside, Southward, S.E.1 (tel. 407-1577), is steeped in atmosphere, standing near what used to be the infamous debtors' prison, Clink (hence, the expression—"putting a man in the clink"). The original Anchor burned down in 1676 but was rebuilt and survived the bombs of World War II. Much of the present tavern, however, is aptly described by the management as "Elizabeth II." After getting off at the tube stop, you pass by Southwark Cathedral through a warehouse district that looks at night like Jack the Ripper country till you reach the riverside tavern. There's a viewing platform—especially popular during the day—right on the Thames. You'll find a number of bars named after the historical associations of the inn (Thrale Room, Dr. Johnson's Room, the Globe Bar, the Clink Bar, and the Boswell Bar). In addition, you can dine either upstairs or down in such "parlours" as the Boswell Grill or the Elizabethan Long Gallery Restaurant. The food is good, and meals begin at £5 ($11.50). The Anchor is open from noon to 2 p.m. for lunch and from 7 to 10 p.m. for dinner Monday through Saturday. On Sunday, lunch is from noon to 1 p.m.; dinner, 7 to 9 p.m.

The **Old Caledonia** (tel. 242-3280), a paddle steamer built in 1889, is London's only floating pub. It's opposite the Savoy Hotel moored below Waterloo Bridge. It can be reached by taking either the Circle or District Line of the tube to Charing Cross. Before arriving at her present berth, the steamer saw wartime service in June 1944, when it was recruited as part of the Western Task Force in the Normandy landings.

You have a choice of three bars. The Thirties Bar retains its original decor of 1930, when the ship was in passenger trade. The Saloon Bar on the main deck was once the first-class dining room; the Promenade Bar above the Saloon Bar offers an opportunity for a stroll on the deck. In the bars, you can obtain a salad roll at 85p ($1.96), pork sausage at 50p ($1.15), and assorted sandwiches at 75p ($1.73). There's also a restaurant, affording views of the Houses of Parliament and Big Ben. Appetizers are in the £1.75 ($4.03) to £2.25 ($5.18) range, including pâté, smoked mackerel, and a prawn cocktail. Main dishes run to grills, which are well prepared, and desserts from the trolley begin at £1.35 ($2.88). A meal will cost about £6.50 ($14.95), a bottle of house wine going for £5 ($11.50). All bills are subject to a 15% service charge. Although children under 16 aren't allowed in the main bars, they are welcome in the restaurant and on the surrounding decks. They may also visit the floodlit engine room, where the original steam engines and paddles are on display through glass observation panels.

ELEPHANT & CASTLE: South of the Thames, the following pub is easily reached by underground train to Elephant & Castle. From the station where you get off, it's a five-minute walk.

The **Goose and Ferkin**, 47-48 Borough Rd., S.E.1 (tel. 403-3590), is a pub which brews its own beer. The owner of this unique enterprise is David Bruce, who worked as a brewer for one of the big companies for many years until his chance came to buy the Goose and Ferkin. He obtained his own license to brew, and set about producing his own beers. A large mirror proclaims "Bruce's Brewery, established 1979." He brews three special strengths, Borough Bitter, 26p (60¢) for a half pint, Dog Bolter, 35p (81¢) for a half, and, for special occasions, Earth Stopper, 50p ($1.15), and only served in halves. Be warned: This one is a real man's beer, and your 50p worth is the equivalent of three measures of whiskey in strength.

Food is also available in this lovely old London pub. Each day there is a different hot dish costing from around £1.50 ($3.45). Or else you can order extra-large baps (bread buns) filled with your choice of meat and salad, costing from 90p ($2.07).

The whole operation is managed by the buxom Tint Watson and her husband Alistair. Son Neil is David's assistant brewer. From 8 p.m. onward, Crazy Jimmy plays the piano in the good old "knees up" style, and on Sunday at lunchtime the pub's group of Morris dancers entertain, another traditional item.

HAMPSTEAD: The **Old Bull and Bush**, North End Way, N.W.3, is one of London's most famous pubs. Although built in this century, it traces its origins back to the mid-17th century. Hogarth's home was near the site (so it is believed) of the present pub. Florrie Forde's famous song did much to fan its fame far and wide. The pub is in the center of the Heath, away from the commercial areas. It is a gathering spot for the young set of Hampstead, and weekend trippers from London. The drinking favorite is draft beer, and a fantastic number of mugs are consumed here. You can also get an assortment of sandwiches for around 80p ($1.84) and salads for around £1.25 ($2.88). It's not help yourself. You select and a waitress serves. A fire burns on nippy evenings.

6. The Wine Bars

For years, the stark, atmospheric, and ancient wine cellars of the old City have been patronized by businessmen in bowlers, and were almost a well-kept secret, as you never ran into a tourist or a woman there. However, that has changed now. Wine bars are the fashion, and the pub no longer completely dominates the drinking scene in the English capital.

With the coming of newer and trendier wine bars, London's drinking habits have undergone significant change. Wine bars are not only places at which to drink, but also to meet friends and enjoy good food. A few of the older, more established ones still offer only wine, but in today's terms a wine bar is likely to mean anything, including a disco!

The English taste for wine has increased, hence the number of wine bars springing up in all parts of the city. Nearly all the establishments recommended below sell wine by the glass, although if you're traveling in a party you may want to order by the bottle and share as it's less expensive that way.

We'll lead off with the most interesting collection of wine bars which still lie in the City and are best visited weekdays for lunch. In the other sections of town you can go for both lunch and dinner.

THE CITY: Olde Wine Shades, 6 Martin Lane, off Cannon Street, E.C.4 (tel. 626-6876), is the oldest wine house in the City, dating from 1663. It was the only City tavern to survive the Great Fire of 1666, not to mention the blitz of 1940. Only 100 yards from the Monument, the Olde Wine Shades used to attract Charles Dickens who enjoyed its fine wines. In the smoking room the old oil paintings have appropriately darkened with age, and the 19th-century satirical political cartoons remain enigmatic to most of today's generation. Some of the fine wines of Europe are served here, and port and sherry are drawn directly from an array of casks behind the counter. The owners, El Vino, the famous City wine merchants, boast that they can satisfy anyone's taste in sherry. A candlewick bar and restaurant is found downstairs, but upstairs, along with your wine, you can order French bread with ham off the bone at £1.10 ($2.53), Breton pâté at 80p ($1.84), and sandwiches beginning at 50p ($1.15). Hours are from 11:30 a.m. to 3 p.m. and from 5 to 8 p.m. Closed Saturday, Sunday, and bank holidays. Tube: Monument.

Mother Bunch's Wine House, Arches F & G, Old Seacoal Lane, E.C.4 (tel. 236-5317), is a maze of vaults underneath the arches of Ludgate Circus. Our favorite of all the wine houses, Mother Bunch's is one of the most atmospheric places for dining in the City, boasting a "well-stocked larder," with the best of hams and all manner of cheeses as well as game and other pies. Port wines of the most noted vintages are decanted daily "for gentlemen in the proper manner." In season, grouse, partridge, pheasant, and Scottish salmon are featured. Guests can dine in the mellow room downstairs or perhaps in the elegantly furnished upstairs room where many are seated around a large table and served family style. Sherry, port, and Madeira "from the wood" begin at 60p ($1.38), and table wines by the glass start at 60p also. The favorite dish is a plate of smoked ham off the bone, although game pie is also praised. Strawberries and raspberries in season make fine dessert. Main lunchtime dishes cost around £2 ($4.60), and cheese and French bread go for 75p ($1.73). The wine house is open from 11:30 a.m. to 3 p.m. and from 5:30 to 8:30 p.m., Monday to Friday. Tube: Blackfriars.

Bow Wine Vaults, 10 Bow Churchyard, E.C.4 (tel. 248-1121), has existed long before the current wine bar fad. The atmosphere is staunchly masculine, and the vaults attract a loyal following of business and professional people who somehow manage to find their way back to their offices after a heavy eating and drinking session here. Sherries, port, and Madeira are available by the glass, as are an assortment of table wines at prices ranging from 64p ($1.47) to £3.50 ($8.05), the latter price for a 1901 vintage Madeira. A cold buffet with a salad will run you £2.25 ($5.18); there's a minimum charge of £2 ($4.60). The vaults are open from 11:30 a.m. to 3 p.m. and from 5 to 7 p.m. but closed weekends and bank holidays. Tube: Mansion House.

Jamaica Wine House, St. Michael's Alley, off Cornhill, E.C.3 (tel. 626-9496), lies in a tangle of City alleyways, and if you do manage to find it, you'll be at one of the first coffeehouses to be opened in England. In fact, the Jamaica Wine House is reputed to be the first coffeehouse in the Western world. Pepys used to visit it and mentioned the event in his Diary. The coffeehouse was destroyed in the Great Fire of 1666, rebuilt in 1674, and has remained, more or less, in its present form ever since. For years London merchants and daring sea captains came here to lace deals with rum and coffee. Nowadays, the two-level house dispenses beer, ale, lager, and fine wines to appreciative drinkers. The oak-paneled bar on the ground floor is more traditional, as the downstairs bar has been modernized. The Bank of England is only a stone's throw away. Tube: Bank.

NEAR LEICESTER SQUARE: Slatters, 3 Panton St., S.W.1 (tel. 839-4649), lies off Haymarket, a split-level wine bar convenient for theater-goers. It makes a good rendezvous for pretheater and after-theater suppers. A stylish informality reigns. Classical music plays in the background and the paintings on the wall are for sale. The house wine is from France, and you can drink it at 65p ($1.50) a glass, along with food offered by owner Kenneth Slatter. The smoked trout goes for £2.25 ($5.18); the underdone pink roast beef, £3 ($6.90); a mackerel pâté served with French bread, £1.40 ($3.22); baked ham or chicken, £3 ($6.90); or the soup of the day, 85p ($1.96). Closed on Sunday, Slatters is open otherwise for lunch or dinner until midnight. Tube: Leicester Square.

NEAR COVENT GARDEN: Blitz, 4 Great Queen St., W.C.2 (tel. 405-6598), evokes a nostalgic World War II atmosphere. The walls are lined with newspaper clippings, telling you what to do if the country is invaded or commanding you to "Hide Your Food from the Nazis." Downstairs is a quick service bar and tables for wine drinking, and upstairs on the mezzanine is a restaurant for more intimate dining. Recorded music is played. You can order a charcoal-grilled hamburger and chips, along with a salad, for £2.50 ($5.75), followed by chocolate fudge cake, 95p ($2.19). The staff also serves chicken Kiev, veal Holstein, and grills in the £5 ($11.50) to £6 ($13.80) price range. Many reasonably priced clarets and Burgundies are offered, costing from £4 ($9.20) to £6 ($13.80) a bottle or from 80p ($1.84) to 95p ($2.19) a glass (house wine only). Hours are from 11 a.m. to 3 p.m., Monday to Friday. The Blitz is open nightly, except Sunday, from 5:30 to midnight. Tube: Holborn.

MAYFAIR: Downs Wine Bar, 5 Down St., W.1 (tel. 491-3810), attracts "the beautiful people" of Mayfair, who live in and around that square mile at the Hyde Park end of Piccadilly, near the Athenaeum Hotel. In fair weather, there are sidewalk tables. Every evening you can descend a spiral staircase to a simple, admission-free disco. Nearly 100 wines are available, each bottled in its country of origin. The food specialty is ham cooked in marmalade, costing £2 ($4.60) for a large platter with garnishes. On Sunday, a set lunch is featured for £4 ($9.20). The upstairs dining room is decorated in a modern style with chrome and cane chairs, along with banquettes. Hours are from 11:30 a.m. to 3 p.m. and from 5:30 to midnight daily, from noon to 3 p.m. and from 7 p.m. to 12:30 a.m. on Sunday. Tube: Green Park.

IN BLOOMSBURY: Entrecôte, 124 Southampton Row, W.C.1 (tel. 405-1466), invites you to go downstairs to its Edwardian precincts. Attractive women students are the waitresses, and they will serve you the house specialty, an entrecôte with french fries, for £4 ($9.20). Selections from the cheese board go for 95p ($2.19). Other daily specials are offered as well—perhaps coq au vin at £3.50 ($8.05) or beef bourgignonne at £3.50 also. In fact, the food is generally French inspired, and the wine list includes some Haut Médoc selections. In the evenings, a small disco atmosphere prevails. Hours are from 11:30 a.m. to 3:30 p.m. and from 5:30 p.m. to 1 a.m. daily (till midnight on Sunday). Tube: Russell Square.

IN BELGRAVIA: Motcomb's, 26 Motcomb St., S.W.1 (tel. 235-6382), opposite Sotheby's Belgravia, is one of the handsomest and most charming wine bars in London. A small, friendly place above the main restaurant, it is run by Betty and Don Phillips. The bar is decorated with family paintings and pews. A complete range of food is served, and there is an excellent choice of wine as well, including several sold by the glass. Dishes are cooked to order, and recorded music is played at lunch along with occasional live music in the evenings. Specialties include gazpacho at 85p ($1.96); tipsy chicken, £3.80 ($8.74); kipper pâté, £1.25 ($2.88); calf liver with bacon, £4 ($9.20). To finish, coffee goes for 55p ($1.27). Motcomb's is open from noon to 3:30 p.m. and from 7 to midnight daily except Sunday and bank holidays. Tube: Knightsbridge.

Bill Bentley's, 31 Beauchamp Pl., S.W.3 (tel. 589-5080), stands on this restaurant- and boutique-lined street near Harrods. A small Georgian house, it offers tiny ground-floor rooms and a little sun-filled patio in back. Cozy and atmospheric, it presents a varied list of reasonably priced wines, including a fine selection of Bordeaux. If you're in the neighborhood for lunch, you can enjoy a pub-style lunch, such as ham and salad, for £2.20 ($5.06). Hot main dishes are likely to include skate in black butter with capers for £3.20 ($7.36) and grilled lemon sole at £4 ($9.20). It's open daily from 11:30 a.m. to 3 p.m. and from 5:30 to 11 p.m., on Saturday from 6:30 to 11 p.m. Closed Sunday and bank holidays. Tube: Knightsbridge.

CHELSEA: Charlie's, 52 King's Road, S.W.3 (tel. 589-6640), stands across from the Duke of York's headquarters. Behind its red and white facade, it is usually busy in the evenings, attracting a lively young King's Road crowd, drawn to its array of salads, quiches, and hot dishes, from around £1.25 ($2.88) a portion. The choice of wine is fair and reasonably priced, and drinks are served on two floors. Hours are from noon to 3 p.m. and from 6 to 11 p.m. daily (Sunday, from noon to 2:30 p.m. and from 7 to 10:30 p.m.). Tube: Sloane Square.

Charco's/Searcy's, 1 Bray Pl., S.W.3 (tel. 584-0765), has an entrance on two streets in Chelsea, lying right off King's Road. A very bright crowd patronizes this establishment, enjoying the reasonably priced wines and the good and inexpensive food, such as salads, cold meats on the buffet, and such hot dishes as moussaka. Prices begin at £1.50 ($3.45) per portion. In summer you may dine at one of the sidewalk tables. The wine bar is open from 11 a.m. to 3 p.m. and from 5:30 to 11 p.m. daily (Sunday, noon to 2 p.m. and from 7 to 10:30 p.m.). Tube: Sloane Square.

7. Country Dining Near London

The **Bell Inn,** Aston Clinton, Buckinghamshire (tel. Aylesbury 630-252), is a coaching inn and believed to have been built at the end of the 18th century. Under the guidance of the Harris family, the inn has won extraordinary acclaim for its cuisine. Advertised by a large bell instead of an inn sign, it stands unobtrusively by the road, 40 miles from London and four miles from Aylesbury. It's a mossy brick structure, with crisp white windows and a Georgian portico. Inside, antiques are used liberally. The dining room in olive green is coolly elegant, with polished wood and sparkling glass and silver. You select your meal in a large stone-floored bar while having a drink. Lunch or dinner is a special event. The Bavarian chef, Jacques Dick, is a perfectionist. For a beginning, try his "smokies" or his pâté maison, each £2.50 ($5.75). Main dishes include poached salmon (in season only) and roast duck with apple sauce from the trolley, a specialty at £11 ($25.30) for two diners. On Saturday nights, a menu with six courses is presented at £15 ($34.50), service included.

There are six bedrooms in the original inn, all with private baths, and all tastefully decorated. Converted from a stable block are 15 more comfortable rooms, arranged around a courtyard across a narrow road from the inn. Rooms are priced at £33 ($75.90) in a single, rising to £43 ($98.90) in a double. Prices include a continental breakfast and service. VAT is extra.

Chapter IV

LONDON: WHAT TO SEE AND DO

                1. Getting Around Town
                2. Seeing the Sights
                3. Shopping for Value
                4. London After Dark
                5. Taking the Tours
                6. One-Day Trips from London

DR. JOHNSON SAID: "When a man is tired of London, he is tired of life, for there is in London all that life can afford." And that holds true today.

Come along with us as we survey only a fraction of that life: ancient monuments, boutiques, debates in Parliament, art galleries, Soho, dives, museums, theaters, flea markets, and castles. Some of what we're about to see was known to Johnson and Boswell, even Shakespeare, but much of it is new.

1. Getting Around Town

If you know the ropes, transportation within London can be unusually easy and cheap because London enjoys one of the best underground and bus systems in the world.

THE UNDERGROUND: The electric subways are, to begin with, comfortable—the trains have cushioned seats, no less. You purchase your ticket in advance either at a ticket booth or from an automatic ticket machine. Fares vary according to distance, from 15p (35¢) for short rides to a high of £1.85 ($4.26) to the outer extremities of Greater London. The fare from Heathrow to Piccadilly Circus is £1.55 ($3.57), and the average fare is 50p ($1.15). Be sure to keep your ticket: it must be presented at the end of the line. If you owe extra, you'll be billed then by an attendant.

Each subway line has its own distinctive color, and all you need follow is the clearly painted arrows. On every stairway, at every corridor turning, on every platform, are additional diagrams in color, giving the routes of the various trains. More diagrams are inside the trains themselves.

The Heathrow Central, an extension of the Piccadilly line, opened in late 1977, giving London Transport the world's first connection between an airport and a major underground transportation system. Built with special considera-

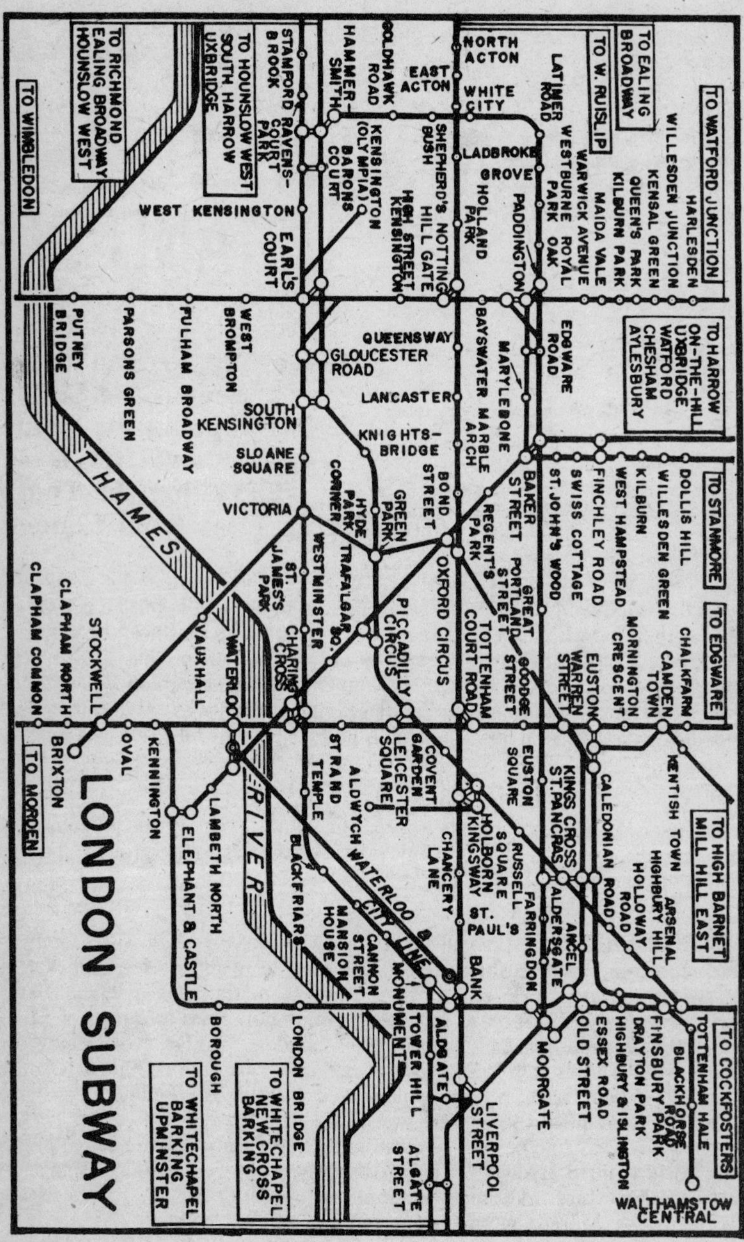
LONDON SUBWAY
TO WATFORD JUNCTION
TO EALING BROADWAY
TO W. RUISLIP
HARLESDEN
WILLESDEN JUNCTION
KENSAL GREEN
QUEEN'S PARK
KILBURN PARK
MAIDA VALE
WARWICK AVENUE
WESTBOURNE PARK
ROYAL OAK
LATIMER ROAD
NORTH ACTON
EAST ACTON
WHITE CITY
LADBROKE GROVE
PADDINGTON
HOLLAND PARK
SHEPHERD'S BUSH
NOTTING HILL GATE
HIGH STREET KENSINGTON
KENSINGTON (OLYMPIA)
GOLDHAWK ROAD
HAMMER-SMITH
BARONS COURT
STAMFORD BROOK
RAVENS-COURT PARK
WEST KENSINGTON
EARL'S COURT
TO RICHMOND
EALING BROADWAY
HOUNSLOW WEST
TO HOUNSLOW WEST
SOUTH HARROW
UXBRIDGE
TO WIMBLEDON
PUTNEY BRIDGE
PARSONS GREEN
FULHAM BROADWAY
WEST BROMPTON
GLOUCESTER ROAD
QUEENSWAY
BAYSWATER
LANCASTER
SOUTH KENSINGTON
MARYLEBONE
EDGWARE ROAD
TO HARROW ON-THE-HILL
UXBRIDGE
WATFORD
CHESHAM
AYLESBURY
KNIGHTS-BRIDGE
MARBLE ARCH
SLOANE SQUARE
BOND STREET
HYDE PARK CORNER
GREEN PARK
VICTORIA
BAKER STREET
REGENT'S PARK
TO STANMORE
DOLLIS HILL
WILLESDEN GREEN
KILBURN
WEST HAMPSTEAD
FINCHLEY ROAD
SWISS COTTAGE
ST. JOHN'S WOOD
THAMES
ST. JAMES'S PARK
WESTMINSTER
TRAFALGAR SQ.
PICCADILLY CIRCUS
OXFORD CIRCUS
GREAT PORTLAND STREET
TOTTENHAM COURT ROAD
GOODGE STREET
WARREN STREET
EUSTON
TO EDGWARE
CHALKFARM
CAMDEN TOWN
MORNINGTON CRESCENT
CLAPHAM COMMON
CLAPHAM NORTH
STOCKWELL
VAUXHALL
WATERLOO
CHARING CROSS
TO MORDEN
BRIXTON
OVAL
KENNINGTON
STRAND
TEMPLE
COVENT GARDEN
LEICESTER SQUARE
EUSTON SQUARE
KENTISH TOWN
ALDWYCH
LAMBETH NORTH
BLACKFRIARS
WATERLOO & CITY LINE
CHANCERY LANE
HOLBORN KINGSWAY
RUSSELL SQUARE
KINGS CROSS ST. PANCRAS
CALEDONIAN ROAD
TO HIGH BARNET
MILL HILL EAST
ELEPHANT & CASTLE
RIVER
MANSION HOUSE
CANNON STREET
ST. PAUL'S
FARRINGDON
ALDERSGATE
ANGEL
HOLLOWAY ROAD
HIGHBURY HILL
ARSENAL
MONUMENT
BANK
BOROUGH
LONDON BRIDGE
TOWER HILL
ALDGATE
MOORGATE
OLD STREET
ESSEX ROAD
HIGHBURY & ISLINGTON
DRAYTON PARK
FINSBURY PARK
BLACKHORSE ROAD
TOTTENHAM HALE
TO COCKFOSTERS
TO WHITECHAPEL
BARKING
UPMINSTER
TO WHITECHAPEL
NEW CROSS
BARKING
ALGATE STREET
LIVERPOOL STREET
WALTHAMSTOW CENTRAL

tion for airline travelers, the Heathrow extension has trains with additional luggage space as well as moving walkways from the airport terminals to the underground station. The link enables incoming passengers to dash from Heathrow to Piccadilly Circus in only 40 minutes.

The Piccadilly line has increased its service to accommodate the demand created by the Heathrow extension, but be warned: if you're out on the town and are dependent on the underground, watch your time carefully—many of the subways stop running at midnight (11:30 p.m. on Sunday).

On Sunday and public holidays there is a maximum fare to anywhere (except Heathrow) on the network of £1.10 ($2.53) for a single journey and £1.25 ($2.88) for a round trip. These are not Rover tickets and therefore each ticket can be used only once.

BUSES: The comparably priced bus system is almost as good. To find out about current routes, pick up a free bus map at the BTA, 64 St. James's St., Piccadilly, or at any London Transport Travel Enquiry office.

After you have lined up (queued) for the bus, and picked a seat either downstairs or on the upper deck (where you can smoke, and where you'll see more of the city), a conductor will come by to whom you tell your destination. He or she then collects the fare and gives you a ticket. As with the subways, the fare varies according to the distance you travel. If you want to be warned when to get off, simply ask the conductor.

BARGAIN TRAVEL PASSES—SUBWAYS AND BUSES: London Transport, which operates one of the world's biggest urban transport systems, offers many special facilities for the visitor. Information on bus and underground services and sightseeing tours can be obtained by calling at London Transport's Travel Enquiry Offices (at Heathrow Central, Victoria, Piccadilly Circus, Oxford Circus, St. James's Park, Euston, and King's Cross underground stations, or in the British Rail Travel Centre at Waterloo main line station). These offices are open every day from 8:30 a.m. to 9:30 p.m. (Heathrow Central is open from 5 a.m. to midnight Monday through Saturday, 6 a.m. to midnight on Sunday.) They sell Go-As-You-Please tourist tickets and take bookings for London Transport's guided coach tours. They can also supply free underground and bus maps and other information and leaflets designed to help visitors.

Of special value to tourists are:

Go-As-You-Please Tourist Tickets, very useful bargains for visitors to London. They give four or seven days of unlimited travel on London's red buses and most of the underground, and can be bought at underground stations or Travel Enquiry Offices. They cost £11.50 ($26.45) for adults, £4.50 ($10.35) for children for four days; £16.50 ($37.95) for adults, £6.50 ($14.95) for children for seven days.

Central Tube Rovers. These are available for unlimited travel for one day between more than 50 Central London stations on or inside the Circle Line, plus some important ones just outside. They can be bought from any underground station or Travel Enquiry Office in the Central Tube Rover area. They cost £2.60 ($5.98) for adults, £1.10 ($2.53) for children.

Red Bus Rovers. These tickets give unlimited travel on London's red buses for one day and can be bought at any Travel Enquiry Office, most underground stations, bus garages, and agents of National Travel. They cost £1.80 ($4.14) for adults, 50p ($1.15) for children.

TAXIS: You can get a cab in London either by heading for a cab stand, hailing one in the street, or telephoning 837-8800, 636-8771, 289-1133, 272-3030, or 286-4848. The minimum fare is 50p ($1.15). On weekends and at night a surcharge of 10p (23¢) is added, these tariffs including VAT. It's recommended that you tip about 20% of the fare, and never less than 10p (23¢).

BOAT TRIPS: Touring boats operate on the Thames between April and September, taking you various places within London and also to nearby towns along the Thames. Main embarkation points are **Westminster Pier, Charing Cross Pier,** and **Tower Hill Pier**—a system that enables you, for instance, to take a "water taxi" from the Tower of London to Westminster Abbey. Not only are the boats energy-saving, bringing you painlessly to your destination, but they permit you to sit back in comfort as you see London from the river.

Several companies operate these boats, which vary from large launches to smaller speedboats. Many offer service every 20 minutes from 10:20 a.m. until dusk. Because of tides, however, no exact schedule is given; you simply go to the pier and take your chances. But the wait is usually short. From Westminster Pier to Tower Hill generally costs 90p ($2.07) one way. You can even cruise up to Hampton Court for £3.80 ($8.74) for adults, £2.40 ($5.52) for children, round trip, but it's a full day's excursion, leaving in the morning and returning at night. There are deck chairs on board these water taxis, and beer is sold even during the hours when the pubs of London are closed. Westminster Pier (for information, phone 930-4097), near Westminster Bridge, is reached by taking the tube to Westminster. Charing Cross Pier (for information, phone 930-0921 on weekdays, 839-5320 on Saturday and Sunday), on the Thames Embankment, is reached from the Charing Cross tube stop.

OTHER VITAL DATA: Banking hours: In general, hours are from 9:30 a.m. to 3:30 p.m., Monday through Friday. Many exchange bureaus in the West End are open from 9 a.m. to 5:30 p.m. You get a better rate at exchange bureaus and banks than at your hotel.

Medical services: All medical treatment in the United Kingdom is free, except when you consult a physician privately. Hotels will get in touch with their house doctor should you need one.

Telephone services: In addition to being able to reach anywhere in the world, the telephone service offers the weather forecast (dial 246-8091); the time (dial 123); motoring conditions (dial 246-8021); daily information about main events in and around London (dial 246); activities concerning children's London (dial 246-8007); and the Financial Times Share Index and business news summaries (dial 246-8206).

To operate a telephone in London, pick up the receiver and dial your number. Have your money ready. When the person on the other end answers, insert 5p (12¢) for local calls. If you don't insert the coin, the party you are calling cannot hear your voice. You are granted two minutes per 5p coin. For long distance (known as a trunk call), you must insert 10p (23¢) when the call is answered. Coinboxes take only 5p and 10p coins, although many 50p ($1.15) coinboxes are now being installed. Dialing codes are shown in the notice frame in telephone kiosks. After you dial your number, or code and number, you will either hear a regularly interrupted single tone, which means the line is busy, or a repeated brr-brr sound which means the exchange is trying to connect you. When the call is answered, you will hear rapid pips. Immediately put a coin into the slot and speak. If you hear the pips again and wish to continue speaking, put another coin in the slot at once. Long-distance calls are cheaper between 6 p.m. and 8 a.m. Monday to Friday and all day Saturday and Sunday.

Note: Calls through a hotel switchboard will have a surcharge added to the normal post office cost of the call. Pay telephones are available in most hotel foyers.

The **Westminster International Telephone Bureau,** 1 Broadway, S.W.1, is open daily from 9 a.m. to 5:30 p.m., including Sunday. The bureau allows you to call all countries not available through call boxes (that is, outside Europe). There is a receptionist to help and to take your money once you've finished your call.

2. Seeing the Sights

London is not a city to visit hurriedly. It is so vast, so stocked with treasures that the visitor does himself or herself a disservice if he or she plans to "do" London in two or three days. Not only will a person miss many of the highlights, he or she will also fail to grasp the spirit of London and to absorb fully its special flavor, which is unique among cities. Still, faced with an infinite number of important places to visit and a time clock running out, the tourist will have to concentrate on a manageable group. We'll survey a personal list of the indispensable sights for those with a minimum of time, then follow in this section with "The Best of the Rest." But first, a digression.

BARGAIN TIP: The **Department of the Environment,** 25 Savile Row, W.1 (tel. 734-6010), offers a **Season Ticket to History** which allows the holder free and unlimited entry to all those places in England, Scotland, and Wales which are maintained by the British government. The cost of the ticket, payable only by international money order (sterling only) is £4 ($9.20) for adults, £2 ($4.60) for children under 16. Also available are special tickets for families. The price of the first ticket is £4 ($9.20), but further tickets are £1.50 ($3.45) per family member. However, there's a minimum order of £7 ($16.10) per family. Valid for one year, it can be purchased at the address given above or at any of the Ancient Monuments which have custodians. A list of sights to be seen, including the Tower of London, Hampton Court Palace, Stonehenge, and Edinburgh Castle, giving opening times and available facilities is given free with each ticket order.

An **Open to View** ticket sells for $13 for adults, $6 for children, and includes free admission to more than 500 properties in Britain, including Edinburgh Castle, Churchill's Chartwell, Woburn Abbey, Hampton Court Palace, Windsor Castle, and Warwick Castle. It is good for one month after you first use it, and covers all properties in care of Britain's National Trust and those run by the Department of the Environment. It is estimated that anyone visiting as many as five of these sightseeing attractions will get back the initial outlay. In the U.S., inquire at **BritRail Travel International Inc.,** 630 Third Ave., New York, NY 10017; 333 North Michigan Ave., Chicago, IL 60601; or 510 West Sixth St., Los Angeles, CA 90014.

Before you rush into London's many sightseeing attractions, we have this suggestion for the first-time visitor. It's an easy way to begin an almost impossible task, the discovery of London. "Breakfast first, business next," wrote Thackeray.

BREAKFAST TO REMEMBER: The **Albert,** Victoria Street, S.W.1 (tel. 222-5577), is a real bit of old Victorian England nestling among modern office blocks near Victoria Station where already at 8 a.m. the town is bustling and noisy. The door stands open and you enter the deserted bar past a sign directing you upstairs for breakfast, served from 8 a.m. to 10:30 a.m.

Up the staircase, hung with pictures of past prime ministers and Queen Victoria, treading on red carpet, past dark wood paneling, you arrive at the dining room. If you are lucky enough to get a window seat on the right day, you can watch dignitaries and even members of the Royal Family passing in the course of their duty. Perhaps the Queen will take her coach down to Victoria Station to meet another royal visitor.

It is not necessary to reserve a table at the Albert. Once there, you'll be greeted by a cheerful waitress who plies you with either coffee or tea, fresh hot toast, and butter. The ritual then starts. On the bar is a vast array of juice, grapefruit, cereal, and porridge. Help yourself—several times if you wish—but leave room for the contents of huge platters on the hot plate. For some, giant sausages, bacon, kidneys, tomatoes, mushrooms, kippers, fried eggs, and baked beans will evoke memories of childhood. You can order as much as you wish. Then more toast with old English marmalade, more coffee or tea. All for only £2.50 ($5.75), including tax, but don't forget the attentive waitress who has kept your cup filled throughout your meal.

Having well fortified yourself, take a few minutes' walk up Victoria Street which will bring you to Westminster Abbey, not crowded at this hour. Then at 10:30 a.m. after a short walk down Whitehall, you can see the Changing of the Guard at Horseguards Parade. Walk through St. James's Park and up to Buckingham Palace where the guard is changed most days at 11:30 a.m.

Along the Embankment, past the Houses of Parliament and the statue of the Burghers of Calais, turn into Dean Bradley Street for a drink in the **Marquis of Granby**. Here, during lunch, you can rub shoulders with members of Parliament, officers of the Conservative and Labour parties chatting together and proving that their party allegiance is not so strong, although doubtless they will have their daggers drawn when they return to the House.

Later, hop on a bus to Westminster Pier and take a boat ride to the Tower of London—so sinister from the river as you drift past Traitors' Gate. See the Tower and the Crown Jewels and then, if you have an appetite again, drop in to the **Dickens Inn** at St. Katharine's Dock for a pint of ale and a snack. Return to the West End again by boat or else take the tube from Tower Hill.

And now, the Top 10:

THE TOWER OF LONDON: This ancient fortress on the north bank of the Thames continues to pack 'em in because of its macabre associations with all the legendary figures who were either imprisoned or executed here, or both. James Street once wrote, ". . . there are more spooks to the square foot than in any other building in the whole of haunted Britain. Headless bodies, bodiless heads, phantom soldiers, icy blasts, clanking chains—you name them, the Tower's got them."

Back in the days of the axman, London was "swinging" long before *Time* magazine discovered that fact. Ranking in interest are the colorful attending Yeoman Warders, the so-called Beefeaters, in Tudor dress, who look as if they are on the payroll for gin advertisements (but don't like to be reminded of it).

Many visitors consider a visit to the Tower to be the highlight of their sightseeing in London—so schedule plenty of time for it. You don't have to stay as long as Sir Walter Raleigh (released after some 13 years), but give it an afternoon. Take either the Circle or District line to Tower Hill Station (the site is only a short walk away). You will be admitted March 1 to October 31 from

9:30 a.m. to 5 p.m. Admission prices vary according to the season, but count on spending around £2 ($4.60) for adults, £1 ($2.30) for children in July and August. Otherwise, charges are £1.50 ($3.45) for adults, 70p ($1.61) for children. In winter the hours are from 9:30 a.m. to 4 p.m. The Tower is also open on Sunday from March to October, in the afternoon only (2 to 5 p.m.), but these times tend to be overcrowded.

Don't expect to find only one tower. The fortress is actually a compound, with the oldest and finest structure being the White Tower, begun by William the Conqueror. Here you can view the Armories, the present collection dating back to the reign of Henry VIII. A display of instruments of torture and execution will be spread before you, recalling some of the most ghastly moments in the history of the Tower. At the Bloody Tower, the Little Princes (Edward V and the Duke of York) were allegedly murdered by their uncle, Richard III.

The hospitality today far excels that of years ago, when many of the visitors left their cells only to walk to the headsman's block on Tower Hill. Through Traitors' Gate passed such ill-fated, but romantic, figures as Robert Devereux, a favorite of Elizabeth I, known as the second Earl of Essex. Elizabeth herself, then a princess, was once imprisoned briefly in Bell Tower. At Tower Green, Anne Boleyn and Katharine Howard, two wives of Henry VIII, lost their lives. The nine-day queen, Lady Jane Grey, and her husband, Dudley, also were executed, along with such figures as Sir Thomas More.

According to legend, the disappearance of the well-protected ravens at the Tower will presage the collapse of the British Empire (seen any around lately?).

For a well-spent 50p ($1.15) for adults, 20p (46¢) for children, you can see the Jewel House, where the Crown Jewels are kept, but go early in summer, as long lines usually form by late morning. Get a Beefeater to tell you how Colonel Blood almost made off with the crown and regalia in the late 17th century. Of the three English crowns, the Imperial State Crown is the most important—in fact, it's probably the most famous crown on earth. Made for Victoria for her coronation in 1838, it is today worn by Queen Elizabeth when she opens Parliament. Studded with some 3000 jewels (principally diamonds), it contains the Black Prince's Ruby, worn by Henry V at Agincourt, the battle in 1415 when the English defeated the French. In addition, feast your eyes on the 530-carat Star of Africa, a cut diamond on the Royal Sceptre with Cross. The Jewel House is closed for four to six weeks early in each year for the annual cleaning and overhaul.

The Tower of London has an evening ceremony called the **Ceremony of the Keys.** It begins with visitors who have tickets being admitted by a Beefeater around 9:40 p.m. It is, in fact, the changing of the guard and the ceremonial locking up of the Tower for yet another day in its 900 years. Nothing stops the ceremony. During World War II, a bomb fell within the castle walls during the ceremony, and nobody flinched—but the Tower was locked up two minutes late. Rumor has it that the guard that night was censured for tardiness, the pilot of the plane which dropped the bomb blamed as the culprit. The Beefeater will explain to guests the significance of the ceremony. For tickets, write to the Governor, Tower of London, London, E.C.3, England, requesting a specific date but also giving alternate dates you'd like to attend. One-week notice is preferred. With ticket in hand, you will be admitted by a Beefeater around 9:40 p.m.

WESTMINSTER ABBEY: No less than such an illustrious figure as St. Peter is supposed to have left his calling card at the abbey. If it's true, we wouldn't be surprised—for nearly everybody else, at least nearly everybody in English history, has left his mark. But what is known for certain is that in 1065 the Saxon king, Edward the Confessor, founded a church on this spot, overlooking Parliament Square (tube to Westminster).

Edward's cousin, William the Conqueror, was crowned at the abbey; the coronation tradition has continued to the present day, broken only twice (Edward V and Edward VIII). The essentially Early English Gothic structure existing today owes more to Henry III's plans than to any other sovereign, although many architects, including Wren himself, have dabbled at the abbey.

Adults pay 80p ($1.84) and children pay 10p (23¢) to visit the Royal Chapel, the Royal Tombs, the Coronation Chair, and the Henry VII Chapel. Hours are Monday to Friday from 9:20 a.m. to 4:45 p.m.; Saturday from 9:20 a.m. to 2:45 p.m. and 3:45 to 5:45 p.m. On Wednesday, the abbey, including the Royal Chapel, is open with free admission from 6 to 8 p.m. It's closed Sunday.

Built on the site of the ancient Lady Chapel, in the early 16th century, the Henry VII Chapel is the loveliest in the abbey, with its fan vaulting, colorful Knights of Bath banners, and Torrigiani-designed tomb of the king himself over which is placed a 15th-century Vivarini painting of *Madonna and Bambino*. The chapel represents the flowering of the Perpendicular Gothic style. Also buried here are those feuding sisters, Elizabeth I and Mary Tudor ("Bloody Mary"). Elizabeth I was always vain and adored jewelry. The effigy which lies on top of her tomb has been fitted out with a new set of jewelry, a gilded collar and pendant, a modern copy derived from a painting now at Hatfield House. The originals were stolen by souvenir hunters in the early 18th century. A London stockbroker donated the pounds to replace the queen's lost finery. Her orb and sceptre were added earlier. In one end of the chapel you can stand on Cromwell's memorial stone and view the R.A.F. chapel containing the Battle of Britain memorial stained-glass window, unveiled in 1947 to honor the R.A.F.

You can also visit the most hallowed spot in the abbey, the shrine of Edward the Confessor (canonized in the 12th century). In the saint's chapel is the Coronation Chair, made at the command of Edward I in 1300 to contain the Stone of Scone. Scottish kings were once crowned on this stone (in 1950 the Scots stole it back, but it was later returned to its position in the abbey). Nearby are the sword and shield of Edward III.

Another noted spot in the abbey is Poets' Corner, to the right of the entrance to the Royal Chapel, with its monuments to everybody from Chaucer on down—the Brontë sisters, Shakespeare, Tennyson, Dickens, Kipling, Thackeray, Samuel Johnson, "O Rare Ben Johnson" (his name misspelled), even the American Longfellow. The most stylized and controversial monument is Sir Jacob Epstein's sculptured bust of William Blake.

Statesmen and men of science—such as Disraeli, Newton, Charles Darwin—are also either interred in the abbey or honored by monuments. Near the west door is the 1965 memorial to Sir Winston Churchill. In the vicinity of this memorial is the tomb of the Unknown Soldier, symbol of British dead in World War I. Surprisingly, some of the most totally obscure personages are buried in the abbey, including Westminster janitors.

Many visitors overlook such sights in the western sector as the 13th-century Chapter House, where Parliament used to convene (special shoes must be worn to walk across the 700-year-old floor). The Chapter House is open from 10:30 a.m. till 6 p.m. (closed Sunday), March through September. It shuts down at 3:30 p.m. off-season.

Even more fascinating are the treasures in the museum in the Norman undercroft (crypt), part of the monastic buildings erected between 1066 and 1100. The collection includes effigies—figures in wax, such as that of Nelson, and wood carvings of early English royalty. Along with the wax figures—the abbey's answer to Madame Tussaud—are ancient documents, seals, replicas of coronation regalia, old religious vestments (such as the cope worn at the coronation of Charles II), the sword of Henry V, and the famous Essex Ring that Elizabeth I is supposed to have given to her favorite earl. The museum, which charges 11p (25¢) for adults, 5p (12¢) for children, is open daily from 9:30 a.m. till 6 p.m., April 1 to September 30; 9:30 a.m. till 4 p.m. (except Sunday), from October 1 to March 31.

For tours of the abbey with an expert guide, the cost is £2.50 ($5.75) per person. These tours operate Monday through Friday at 10:15 and 10:45 a.m., 2:15 and 2:45 p.m. On Saturday, the hours are 10:15 and 10:45 a.m. Inquire at the West Door for the meeting point.

For times of services and any special events, telephone the Chapter House, 222-5152.

Off the Cloisters, **College Garden** is the oldest garden in England, under cultivation for more than 900 years. Surrounded by high walls, flowering trees dot the lawns, and park benches provide comfort where you can hardly hear the roar of passing traffic. It is open on Thursday throughout the year, from 10 a.m. to 4 p.m. in winter, to 6 p.m. in summer. In August and September, band concerts are held at lunchtime from 12:30 to 2 p.m. Admission is free.

HOUSES OF PARLIAMENT: You may want to visit the Palace of Westminster at least twice. First, to see Western democracy at work (a debate in the House of Lords or the House of Commons), and again to explore the buildings themselves. The first is difficult, the second relatively easy.

Although we can't assure you of the oratory of a Charles James Fox or a William Pitt the Elder, the debates are often lively and controversial (seats are at a premium during crises). The chances of getting into the House of Lords when it's in session are generally better than they are in the more popular House of Commons (even the Queen herself isn't allowed there). The old guard of the palace informs us that the peerage speak their minds more freely and are less likely to adhere to party line than their counterparts in the Commons.

The general public is admitted to the Strangers' Gallery in the House of Commons on "sitting days"—normally about 4:15 p.m. on Monday to Thursday (about 10 a.m. on Friday). Often there is considerable delay before the head of the public queue is admitted. You can speed up matters somewhat by applying at the American Embassy or the Canadian High Commission for a special pass—but this is too cumbersome for many. Besides, as reader Richard Grant put it, "The U.S. Embassy has only four tickets for daily distribution. Forget it and stand in line."

The head of the queue is normally admitted to the Strangers' Gallery in the House of Lords after 2:40 p.m. from Monday to Wednesday (often at 3 p.m. on Thursday). Line up at the St. Stephen's entrance. It is usually easier to get in after about 6 p.m.

The Houses of Parliament can also be visited when the members of Parliament are not meeting—that is, from 10 a.m. to 4:30 p.m. on Saturday (also on Easter Monday and Tuesday, spring and late summer bank holidays). You enter by the Norman Porch at Victoria Tower (when the Union Jack flies overhead, Parliament is in session). Guests can hook up with a guide who'll give them a running commentary, while escorting them through the handsome ly decorated Robing Room and the Royal Gallery, with the sunburst theme on the ceiling, and the Princes' Chamber, with portraits of Henry VIII and his many wives. Incidentally, it was Henry VIII who packed up his linen and moved to Whitehall. From the days of Edward the Confessor to Henry VIII, the palace was a royal residence.

The House of Commons was destroyed by a German air attack on May 10, 1941, and was rebuilt by 1950. The famous Churchill Arch to the House of Commons remains in the damaged state in which it was found after the fire which destroyed the chamber. The stonework was cleaned but not restored in any way. The palace has been razed once before, in a fire in 1834.

Westminster Hall, scene of the trials of Guy Fawkes and of Charles I, is the oldest surviving structure in the complex. It is known for its hammerbeam roof built in the late 14th century by Richard II. Westminster Hall is open Monday to Thursday, and Saturday (unless the House of Commons is sitting) from 10 a.m. to 1:30 p.m. When both Houses are recessed, the time of opening is extended on Monday to Friday until 4 p.m. (5 p.m. on Saturday).

There is no charge for admission to the Palace of Westminster, but guides will expect remuneration. the usual tip is 50p ($1.15). Further information about the work of the House of Commons is available by phoning 219-4272; House of Lords, 219-3107; or on the Post Office Prestel Viewdata system, frame 5000.

THE BRITISH MUSEUM: Within its imposing citadel on Great Russell Street in Bloomsbury (tube to Holborn or Tottenham Court Road), the British Museum shelters one of the most catholic collections of art and artifacts in the world, containing countless treasures of ancient civilizations. To storm this bastion in a day is a formidable task, but there are riches to see even on a cursory first visit. Basically, the overall storehouse splits into the National Museum of Antiquities and Ethnography and the Prints and Drawings division —each of which, in its own way, has much to offer.

As you enter the front hall, you may want to head first to the Assyrian Transept on the ground floor, where you'll find the winged and human-headed bulls and lions that once guarded the gateways to the palaces of Assyrian kings, along with a rare Black Obelisk from about 860 B.C. From here you can go into the angular hall of Egyptian sculpture to see the Rosetta Stone, whose discovery led to the deciphering of the mysterious hieroglyphics (on the opposite side of the stone is a booklet outlining the method).

Also on the ground floor is the Duveen Gallery, housing the famed Elgin Marbles, consisting chiefly of sculpture from a frieze on the Parthenon showing a ceremonial procession that took place in Athens every four years. Of the 92 metopes from the Parthenon, 15 are housed today in the British Museum. The metopes depict the to-the-death struggle between the handsome Lapiths and the grotesque, drunken Centaurs (see, in particular, the head of the horse from the chariot of Selene, goddess of the moon).

The classical sculpture galleries hold *The Caryatid* from the Erechtheum, a temple started in 421 B.C. and dedicated to Athena and Poseidon. Also displayed here is a statue of Mausolus, Prince of Caria in 353 B.C., whose tomb at Halicarnassus was listed among the seven wonders of the world. Look also for the blue and white Portland Vase, considered the finest example of ancient cameo carving, having been made between 27 B.C. and 14 A.D.

The department of Medieval and Later Antiquities has its galleries on the first floor, reached by the main staircase. Of its exhibitions, the Sutton Hoo funeral deposit, discovered at Ipswich, Suffolk, is, in the words of an expert, "the richest treasure ever dug from English soil"—containing gold jewelry, armor, weapons, bronze bowls and cauldrons, silverware, and the inevitable drinking horn of the Norse culture. No body was found, although the tomb is believed to be that of a king of East Anglia who died in the seventh century A.D. You'll also see the bulging-eyed Lewis Chessmen, Romanesque carvings by the Scandinavians of the 12th century, and the Ilbert collection of clocks and watches.

The featured attractions of the Upper Floor are the Egyptian Galleries, especially the mummies. The fourth Egyptian room is extraordinary, looking like the props for *Cleopatra,* with its cosmetics, domestic utensils, toys, tools, and other work. Some rare gems of Sumerian and Babylonian art—unearthed from the Royal Cemetary at Ur (southern Iraq)—lie in the room beyond: a bull-headed queen's harp (oldest ever discovered); a queen's sledge (oldest known example of a land vehicle); and a figure of a he-goat on its hind legs, crafted about 2500 B.C.! In the Persian Landing rests "The Treasure of Oxus," a hoard of riches, probably from the fifth century B.C.—containing a unique collection of goldsmith work, such as a nude youth, signet rings, a fish-shaped vase, and votive plaques.

One of the most popular attractions is a battered marble head which for years rested relatively forgotten in the gloomy basement of the museum. These days, dusted off, the one-foot-high head is displayed prominently, its identification by a U.S. scholar the subject of controversy. Dr. Iris Love of New York identified the head as that of the fourth century B.C. *Aphrodite* by Praxiteles. The head arrived at the British Museum in 1859 from an excavation site at Cnidus, in southwestern Turkey, on a peninsula overlooking the Aegean Sea. The Praxiteles *Aphrodite* had generally been regarded as lost. Some archeologists and scholars believe it still is—but not Iris Love and a host of believers.

The museum is open weekdays from 10 a.m. till 5 p.m. (Sunday, 2:30 to 6 p.m.). It is closed Good Friday, Christmas Eve, Christmas Day, Boxing Day, and New Year's Day.

Incidentally, the Ethnography Department is housed at 6 Burlington Gardens, W.1, where the galleries are open to the public during the same hours as above. Here are displayed the tools of early man. Seek out, in particular, the Benin bronze sculpture of Nigeria.

The British Library

In the east wing the galleries form part of the British Library. In the Grenville Library you'll see the Benedictional (in Latin) of St. Ethelwold (963–984 A.D.), written by a monk for the bishop of Winchester, and regarded as one of the most splendid medieval works of art in England. The library also contains the Manuscript Salon, with its collection of autographs by such men as Cromwell, Disraeli, Sir Walter Raleigh, Newton, Pepys, Wren, Milton, Dr. Johnson, Pope, Fielding, and Swift.

There are also seven major exhibits (at least) of world interest: the Codex Sinaiticus (a Greek version of the Bible, written in the fourth century A.D.); the Lindisfarne Gospels (a masterpiece, viewed by experts as one of the important treasures from early Northumbria, written and illustrated about 698 A.D.); Shakespeare's mortgage deed (with his signature, of course) to the Blackfriars Gate House; Captain Robert Scott's journals telling of his attempt to reach the South Pole in the expedition of 1910–12; a memorandum by Admiral Nelson explaining his plans for engaging the allied French and Spanish fleet, taken from the *Victory* logbook, and a letter to Lady Hamilton written two days before he died in the Battle of Trafalgar; and, finally, documents relating to the Magna Carta, including the Articles of the Barons, demands accepted by King John at Runnymede in June 1215, along with John's seal of white wax and two of the four surviving exemplifications of Magna Carta issued over his seal.

In the King's Library rests a First Folio (1623) of the comedies, histories, and tragedies of Mr. Shakespeare. In addition, don't miss the Gutenberg Bible, the first substantial book ever printed from movable type (of the copies known, the British Library possesses one printed on paper, another on vellum—circa 1455).

Like the museum, the British Library often changes part of its permanent gallery displays to set up special exhibitions in rotation, for example, to mark a centenary. The opening times of the British Library's exhibition galleries are the same as those of the museum. Admission is free.

The Museum of Mankind

The Museum of Mankind, the Ethnography Department of the British Museum, is housed at 6 Burlington Gardens, W.1, where the galleries are open to the public during the same hours as those of the Bloomsbury museum. It has the world's largest collections of art and material culture from tribal societies. A dazzling selection of treasures from five continents is displayed, and a number of large exhibitions show the life, art, and technology of selected cultures. New exhibitions are mounted every year. Seek out, in particular, the Benin bronze sculpture of Nigeria. Weekday hours are from 10 to 5; on Sunday, 2:30 to 6; and there is no admission charged.

MADAME TUSSAUD'S: Strasbourg-born Marie Tussaud was to become world-famous as the madame of the macabre. She went to Paris at the age of six to join her uncle, Dr. Curtius. In 1770, he opened an exhibition of life-size wax figures. During the French Revolution, the head of almost every distinguished victim of the guillotine was molded by Madame Tussaud or her uncle.

After the death of Curtius, Madame Tussaud inherited the exhibition, and in 1802 she left France for England. For 33 years she toured the United Kingdom with her exhibition, and in 1835 she settled on Baker Street. The exhibition was such a success that it practically immortalized her in her day; she continued to make portraits until she was 81 (she died in 1850). The perennially popular waxworks are visited by some tourists even before they check out Westminster Abbey or the Tower of London.

Some of the works displayed came from molds cast by the incomparable Madame Tussaud herself. But to keep from becoming stilted the waxworks continue to make new figures, whoever is *au courant*. Of course, good old reliables, such as Sir Winston, can always be counted on to be there. Some of the figures—that of Voltaire, for example—were taken from life!

In the not-to-be-missed and entirely new Chamber of Horrors, opened in 1980, you can have the vicarious thrill of meeting such types as Dr. Crippen, and walking through a Victorian London street where special effects include the shadow presence of Jack the Ripper. The instruments and victims of death penalties contrast with present-day criminals portrayed within the confines of prison.

An enlarged Grand Hall, as well as high-speed elevators and air conditioning, are welcome improvements. In "Heroes," with a sequence of sound, light, and projection, each hero is presented in turn, including Elton John, Humphrey Bogart, and Elvis Presley. On the ground floor, you can relive the Battle of Trafalgar, complete with Nelson's recreated flagship (built at the cost of

£75,000). Madame Tussaud's costs £2.10 ($4.83) for adults, £1.10 ($2.53) for children under 16. You can visit the neighboring **Planetarium** for £2.90 ($6.67), £1.50 ($3.45) for children under 16. Take the tube to Baker Street (entrance on Marylebone Road). Madame Tussaud's is open daily from 10 a.m. till 6 p.m. (5:40 p.m. October to March), including Saturday and Sunday. It's closed only on Christmas Day.

TATE GALLERY: This building, beside the Thames on Millbank, houses the best collection of British paintings from the 16th century on, as well as England's finest collection of modern art, from the French impressionists to pop. The Tate is open from 10 a.m. to 6 p.m. weekdays (Sunday, 2 to 6 p.m.). To reach it, take the tube to Pimlico or bus 88 or 77. The number of paintings is staggering. If time permits, try to schedule at least two visits—the first to see the classic English works, the second to take in the modern collection (circa 1870 to the present). Since only a portion of the collections can be shown simultaneously, the works on display vary from time to time. However, the most time-pressed individual may not want to miss the following which are almost invariably on view:

The first giant among English painters, William Hogarth (1697–1764), is well represented, particularly by his satirical *O the Roast Beef of Old England, Calais Gate,* with its distorted figures, such as the gluttonous priest. The ruby-eyed *Satan, Sin, and Death* remains one of his most enigmatic works.

Two other famous British painters of the 18th century (exhibited in Galleries 4 and 17) are Sir Joshua Reynolds (1723–1792), and Thomas Gainsborough (1727–1788). Reynolds, the portrait painter, shines brightest when he's painting himself (two self-portraits hang side by side). Two other portraits, that of Francis and Suzanna Beckford, are typical of his work. His rival, Gainsborough, is noted for his portraits, too, and also landscapes ("my real love"). His landscapes with gypsies are subdued, mysterious; *The View of Dedham* is more representative. One of Gainsborough's most celebrated portraits is of Edward Richard Gardiner, a handsome boy in blue (the more famous *Blue Boy* is in California). Two extremely fine Gainsborough portraits have recently been acquired: *Giovanna Baccelli* (1782), who was well known both as a dancer and as the mistress of the third Earl of Dorset, and *Sir Benjamin Truman,* the notable brewer. The latter painting had been sold to Mr. Paul Mellon, but an export license was denied.

In the art of J. M. W. Turner (1775–1851), the Tate possesses its greatest collection of the works of a single artist. Most of the paintings and watercolors exhibited here were willed to the nation by Turner (collection divided between the Tate, the National Gallery, and the British Museum). Of his paintings of stormy seas, none is more horrifying than *Shipwreck* (1805). In the Petworth series, he broke from realism (see his *Interior at Petworth*). His delicate impressionism is best conveyed in his sunset and sunrise pictures, with their vivid reds and yellows. Turner's vortex paintings, inspired by theories of Goethe, are *Light and Color—the Morning After the Deluge,* and *Shade and Darkness—the Evening of the Deluge.*

In a nation of landscape painters, John Constable (1776–1837) stands out. Some of his finest works include *Vale of Dedham* and *Flatford Mill, on the River Stour,* painted in 1817—both scenes from East Anglia.

American-born Sir Jacob Epstein became one of England's greatest sculptors, and some of his bronzes are owned and occasionally displayed by the Tate. Augustus John, who painted everybody from G. B. Shaw to Tallulah Bankhead, is also represented here with portraits and sketches.

The Tate owns some of the finest works of the Pre-Raphaelite period of the late 19th century. One of the best of the English artists of the 20th century, Sir Stanley Spencer (1891-1959) is best represented by his two versions of *Resurrection* and a remarkable self-portrait (1913).

The Tate has many major paintings from both the 19th and 20th centuries, including Syndham Lewis's portraits of Edith Sitwell and of Ezra Pound, and Paul Nash's *Voyages of the Moon*. But the sketches of William Blake (1757-1827) attract the most attention. Blake, of course, was the incomparable mystical poet and illustrator of such works as *The Book of Job*, *The Divine Comedy*, and *Paradise Lost*.

In the modern collections, the Tate contains Matisse's *L'Escargot* and *The Inattentive Reader*, along with works by Dali, Chagall, Modigliani, Munch, Ben Nicholson (large collection of his works), and Dubuffet. The different periods of Picasso bloom in *Woman in a Chemise* (1905), *Three Dancers* (1925), *Nude Woman in a Red Armchair* (1932), and *Goat's Skull, Bottle, and Candle* (1952).

Truly remarkable is the area devoted to the sculpture of Giacometti (1901-1966), and the paintings of two of England's most famous modern artists, Francis Bacon (especially gruesome, *Three Studies for Figures at the Base of a Crucifixion*), and Graham Sutherland (see his portrait of W. Somerset Maugham).

Rodin's *The Kiss* and Marino Marini's *Cavaliere*—both world-famous pieces of sculpture, are on show. In addition, sculptures by Henry Moore and Barbara Hepworth are displayed.

Downstairs is an inexpensive self-service cafeteria, offering tea, coffee, sandwiches, cakes, and ice cream.

Admission to the general gallery is free, but for special exhibitions, a charge of approximately £1 ($2.30) is made (half price for children).

For the **Tate Gallery Restaurant**, Millbank, S.W.1, telephone 834-6754 for reservations. The menus, at least the main dishes, are selected from the vast array of dishes, some of which were concocted from old recipes handed down from Cromwellian or Elizabethan times. For example, you can order Elizabethan veal kidneys Florentine at £4.95 ($11.39); Hindle Wakes (a medieval dish of stuffed chicken from Lancashire), £4.50 ($10.35); or Windsor veal pie made to an original recipe, £4.85 ($11.16). "Accompanying salads" are large enough for a main course. The Joan Cromwell's Grand Sallet for £3.30 ($7.59) includes almonds, shrimp, raisins, pickled cucumbers, and French beans in a cream sauce. Desserts from the trolley cost £1.50 ($3.45) and include another traditional Pye with Fruyt Ryfshews. Wine by the glass is available. It is essential to book, as this place is very popular with Tate visitors as well as local business people. It's still the choice for taking a maiden aunt out to lunch, as the service, by pleasant young women, is good and polite, the dishes delicious.

NATIONAL GALLERY: On the north side of Trafalgar Square, in an impressive neoclassic building, the National Gallery houses one of the most comprehensive collections of European paintings, representing all the major schools from the 13th to the early 20th centuries. The largest part of the collection is devoted to the Italians, including the Sienese, Venetian, and Florentine masters.

Of the early Gothic works, the *Wilton Diptych* in Room 1 (French school, late 14th century) is the rarest treasure. It stands in a niche by itself, and depicts Richard II being introduced to the Madonna and Child by such good contacts as John the Baptist and the Saxon king, Edward the Confessor.

A Florentine gem—a Virgin and grape-eating Bambino—by Masaccio (one of the founders of modern painting) is in Room 3. In Room 4 are notable works by Piero della Francesca, particularly his linear *The Baptism*.

In a specially lighted hall, Room 7, is the famous cartoon (in the fine arts sense) of *The Virgin and Child with Saint John and Saint Anne* by Leonardo da Vinci. Matter and spirit meet in the haunting nether world of the *Virgin of the Rocks*, a famous Leonardo painting, now hung in Room 8. Also in Room 8 are two other giants of the Renaissance—Michelangelo (represented by an unfinished painting, *The Entombment*), and Raphael (*The Ansidei Madonna*, among others).

The Venetian masters of the 16th century, to whom color was paramount, fill Room 9. The most notable works include a rare *Adoration of the Kings* by Giorgione; *Bacchus and Ariadne* by Titian; *The Beginning of the Milky Way* by Tintoretto (a lush galaxy, with light streaming from Juno's breasts); and *The Darius Family Kneeling Before Alexander the Great* by Veronese (one of the best paintings at the National). Surrounding are a number of satellite rooms, filled with works by major Italian masters of the 15th century—artists such as Andrea Mantegna of Padua (*Agony in the Garden*); his brother-in-law, Giovanni Bellini (his portrait of the Venetian doge, Leonardo Loredano, provided a change of pace from his many interpretations of Madonnas); finally, Botticelli, represented by *Mars and Venus*, *Adoration of the Magi*, and *Portrait of a Young Man* in Room 5.

The painters of northern Europe are well displayed. In Room 24, for example, is Jan van Eyck's portrait of G. Arnolfini and his bride, and Pieter Brueghel the Elder's Bosch-influenced *Adoration* (Room 25), with its unkingly kings and ghoul-like onlookers. In Room 28 the 17th-century pauper, Vermeer, is rich on canvas in a *Young Woman at a Virginal*, a favorite theme of his. Fellow Delft-ite Pieter de Hooch comes on sublimely in a *Patio in a House in Delft* (Room 28).

One of the big drawing cards of the National is its collection of Rembrandts in Rooms 15, 19, 26, and 27. Rembrandt, the son of a miller, became the greatest painter in the Netherlands in the 17th century. His *Self-Portrait at the Age of 34* shows him at the pinnacle of his life, his *Self-Portrait at the Age of 63* is more deeply moving and revealing. For another Rembrandt study in old age, see his *Portrait of Margaretha Trip* (Room 27). *The Woman Taken in Adultery* shows the artist's human sympathy. Rembrandt's portrait of his mistress, Hendrickje Stoffels, last displayed in public in the 1930s, has been bought and is now displayed by the National Gallery (Room 26). The picture is signed and dates from 1659. The purchase price has not been disclosed, but the market value is believed to be in the region of $2,000,000. Part of the prolific output of Peter Paul Rubens is to be seen in Room 20, notably his *Peace and War* and *The Rape of the Sabine Women*.

Five of the greatest of the home-grown artists—Constable, Turner, Reynolds, Gainsborough, and Hogarth—share their paintings with the Tate. But the National owns masterpieces by each of them. Constable's *Cornfield* is another scene of East Anglia, along with *Haywain*, perhaps his best-known work, a harmony of light and atmosphere. Completely different from Constable is the work of Turner, including his dreamy *Fighting Téméraire* and *Rain, Steam, and Speed*. Room 34 is essentially a portrait gallery, hung with several works by Sir Joshua Reynolds, along with a Gainsborough masterpiece, *The Morning Walk*, an idealistic blending of portraiture with landscape. Finally, in a completely different brush stroke, Hogarth's *Marriage à la Mode* caricatures the marriages of convenience of the upper class of the 18th century.

The three giants of Spanish painting are represented in Room 41 by Velázquez's portrait of the sunken-faced Philip IV; El Greco's *Christ Driving the Traders from the Temple;* Goya's portrait of the Duke of Wellington (once stolen) and his mantilla-wearing *Dona Isabel de Porcel.*

Room 33 is devoted to 18th-century French painters such as Watteau and Fragonard; Room 40, 19th-century French painters such as Delacroix and Ingres; Room 44, 19th-century French impressionists such as Manet, Monet, Renoir, and Degas; and Room 45, 19th-century French post-impressionists such as Cézanne, Seurat, and Van Gogh.

The National Gallery (tube to Charing Cross) is open weekdays from 10 a.m. to 6 p.m.; Sunday, 2 to 6 p.m. Closed January 1, Good Friday, Christmas Eve, Christmas Day, Boxing Day, and bank holidays. Admission is free.

KENSINGTON PALACE: Home of the State Apartments, some of which were used by Queen Victoria, this is another of the major attractions of the city, at the far western end of Kensington Gardens. The palace was acquired by asthma-suffering William III (William of Orange) in 1689, and was remodeled by Sir Christopher Wren. George II, who died in 1760, was the last king to use it as a royal residence.

The most interesting chamber to visit is Queen Victoria's bedroom. In this room, on the morning of June 20, 1837, she was aroused from her sleep with the news that she had ascended to the throne, following the death of her uncle, William IV. Thus, the woman who was to become the symbol of the British Empire and the Empress of India began the longest reign in the history of England. In the anteroom are memorabilia from Victoria's childhood—a dollhouse and a collection of her toys.

In Queen Mary's bedroom, you can see her mid-17th-century writing cabinet with its tortoise-shell surface. Incidentally, Mary II reigned with William III, and is not to be confused with the late Queen Mary (1867–1953), who also has many relics at Kensington. The late Queen Mary was born in Victoria's bedroom.

As you wander through the apartments, you can admire many fine paintings, most of which are from the Royal Collection. The State Apartments are open Monday through Saturday, 9 a.m. to 5 p.m.; on Sunday, 1 to 5 p.m. Adults pay an admission of 40p (92¢); children, 20p (46¢) January through March and October through December; 60p ($1.84) for adults and 30p (69¢) for children April through September. You enter from the Broad Walk, and you reach the building by taking the tube either to Queensway or Bayswater on the north side of the gardens, or High Street Kensington on the south side. You'll have to walk a bit from there, however.

The palace gardens, originally the private park of royalty, are also open to the public for daily strolls around Round Pond, near the heart of Kensington Gardens. The gardens adjoin Hyde Park. Also in Kensington Gardens is the Albert Memorial to Queen Victoria's consort. Facing Albert Hall, it is a wart on the face of London, a statue that reflects all the opulent vulgarity of the Victorian era—it's fascinating, nonetheless.

ST. PAUL'S CATHEDRAL: During World War II, newsreel footage reaching America showed the dome of St. Paul's Cathedral lit by bombs exploding all around it. That it survived at all is miraculous, as it was hit badly at least twice in the early years of the Nazi bombardment of London. But St. Paul's is accustomed to calamity, having been burned down at least three times and destroyed once by invading Norsemen. It was in the Great Fire of 1666 that the old St. Paul's was razed, making way for a new Renaissance structure designed (after many mishaps and rejections) by Sir Christopher Wren.

The masterpiece of this great architect was erected between 1675 and 1710. Its classical dome dominates The City's square mile. Inside, the cathedral is laid out like a Latin cross, containing few art treasures (Grinling Gibbons choir stalls an exception) and many monuments, including one to the "Iron Duke" and a memorial chapel to American servicemen who lost their lives in the United Kingdom in World War II. Encircling the dome is the Whispering Gallery, where discretion in speech is advised. In the crypt lie not only Wren himself, but the Duke of Wellington and Lord Nelson. The funeral carriage of the Iron Duke—focal point of one of the greatest of all Victorian funerals—is displayed here.

The cathedral (tube to St. Paul's) is open daily from 8 a.m. to 7 p.m. from mid-April to September. The crypt and galleries, including the Whispering Gallery, are open only from 10:45 a.m. to 4:15 p.m. in summer. The rest of the year the cathedral's hours are from 8 a.m. to 5 p.m. The crypt and galleries, on the other hand, are open only from 11 a.m. to 3:15 p.m. Guided tours, lasting 1½ hours, and including the crypt, the Chapter House, and other parts of St. Paul's not normally open to the public, take place daily when the cathedral is open and cost £2 ($4.60) for adults, £1 ($2.30) for children.

VICTORIA AND ALBERT MUSEUM: When Queen Victoria asked that this museum be named after herself and her consort, she could not have selected a more fitting memorial. The Victoria and Albert is one of the finest museums in the world, devoted to fine and applied art of many nations and periods, including the Orient. In many respects, it's one of the most difficult for viewing, as many of the most important exhibits are so small they can easily be overlooked. To reach the museum on Cromwell Road, take the tube to the South Kensington stop. The museum is open weekdays, except Friday, from 10 a.m. to 5:50 p.m., on Sunday from 2:30 till 5:50 p.m.

We have space only to suggest some of its finest art. The early medieval art in Room 43 includes many treasures, such as the Eltenberg Reliquary (Rhenish, second half of the 12th century). In the shape of a domed, copper-gilt church, it is enriched with champlevé enamel and set with walrus-ivory carvings of Christ and the Apostles. Other exhibits in this same salon include the Early English Gloucester Candlestick, and the Byzantine Veroli Casket, with its ivory panels based on Greek plays. Devoted to Islamic art, Room 42 contains the Ardabil carpet from 16th-century Persia (320 knots per square inch).

In the Gothic art exhibition (Rooms 22 through 25), there are some fine pieces—such as the Syon Cope, made in the early 14th century, an example of the highly valued embroidery produced in England at that time; a stained-glass window from Winchester College (circa 1400); a Limoges enameled triptych for Louis XII. The Gothic tapestries, including the Devonshire ones depicting hunting scenes, are in Room 38.

Renaissance art in Italy, Rooms 11 through 20, include such works as a Donatello marble relief, *The Ascension;* a small terracotta statue of the Madonna and Child by Antonio Rossellino; a marble group, *Samson and a Philistine*, by Giovanni Bologna; a wax model of a slave by Michelangelo. The highlight of the 16th-century art from the continent is the marble group, *Neptune with Triton*, by Bernini (Room 21).

In Room 48 are displayed the cartoons by Raphael, which are owned by the Queen. These cartoons—conceived as designs for tapestries for the Sistine

Chapel—include scenes such as *The Sacrifice of Lystra* and *Paul Preaching at Athens.*

Of the rooms devoted to English furniture and decorative art during the period from the 16th to the mid-18th century, the most outstanding exhibit is the Bed of Ware (Room 52), big enough for eight. In the galleries of portrait miniatures, two of the rarest ones are in Room 55—both by Hans Holbein the Younger (one of Anne of Cleves, another of a Mrs. Pemberton). In the painting galleries (8 and 9) are many works by Constable. His *Flatford Mill* represents a well-known scene from his native East Anglia. The museum's phone number is 589-6371.

THE BEST OF THE REST: Now, for those with more time to get acquainted with London, we'll continue our exploration of this sight-filled city.

Royal London

From Trafalgar Square, you can stroll down the wide, tree-flanked avenue known as **The Mall.** It leads to **Buckingham Palace,** the heart of Royal London (English kings and queens have lived here since the days of Victoria). Three parks—St. James's, Green, and the Buckingham Palace Gardens (private)—converge at the center of this area, where you'll find a memorial honoring Victoria.

London's most popular daily pageant, particularly with North American tourists, is the **Changing of the Queen's Guard** in the forecourt of Buckingham Palace. The regiments of the Guard's Division, in their bearskins and red tunics, actually are five regiments in one—including the Scots, Irish, and Welsh. The guards march to the palace from either the Wellington or Chelsea barracks, arriving around 11:30 a.m. for the half-hour ceremony. To get the full effect, go somewhat earlier. There is usually no ceremony when the weather is what the English call "inclement." But remember that your idea of inclement may not be a weather-toughened Londoner's idea of inclement. When in doubt, ring up 222-1234 for information; tube to St. James's Park or Green Park. In winter the ceremony is on alternate days, so check by telephone.

You can't visit the palace, of course, without an invitation, but you can inspect the **Queen's Gallery** (entrance on Buckingham Palace Road). It may be visited from 11 a.m. to 5 p.m. Tuesday through Saturday (from 2 to 5 p.m. on Sunday) for an admission of 70p ($1.61) for adults, 40p (92¢) for children. As is known, all the royal families of Europe have art collections—some including acquisitions from centuries ago. The English sovereign has one of the finest, and has consented to share it with the public. Of course, we can't predict what exhibition you're likely to see, as they are changed yearly at the gallery. You may find a selection of incomparable works by old masters, and sometimes furniture and objets d'art.

You can get a close look at Queen Elizabeth's coronation carriage at the **Royal Mews,** on Buckingham Palace Road. Many other official carriages are housed here as well, including the Scottish and Irish state coaches. The Queen's horses are also housed here. The mews is open to the public on Wednesday and Thursday from 2 to 4 p.m. and charges an admission of 45p ($1.04) for adults, 20p (46¢) for children. It is closed during Ascot week in June.

Official London

Whitehall, the seat of the British government, grew up on the grounds of Whitehall Palace, turned into a Royal residence by Henry VIII, who snatched it from its former occupant, Cardinal Wolsey. Beginning at Trafalgar Square, Whitehall extends southward to Parliament Square (Houses of Parliament and Westminster Abbey described earlier). On this street you'll find the Home Office, the Old Admiralty Building, and the Ministry of Defence.

At the **Cenotaph** (honoring the dead in two World Wars), turn down unpretentious Downing Street to the modest little town house at **No. 10**, flanked by two bobbies. Walpole was the first prime minister to live here; Churchill the most famous.

Nearby is the **Horse Guards Building**, where the changing of the Queen's Life Guard takes place daily at 11 a.m., 10 a.m. on Sunday. The ceremony lasts 20 minutes—a spectacle provided by the Life Guards and the Royal Horse Guards, combined to form the Household Cavalry. Mounted on their black horses, the guards in their white and red plumes, red and blue tunics, make for an exciting and dramatic show.

Across the street is Inigo Jones's **Banqueting House**, site of the execution of Charles I. William and Mary accepted the crown of England here, but preferred to live at Kensington Palace. The Banqueting House was part of Whitehall Palace, which burned to the ground in 1698, although the ceremonial hall itself escaped razing. Its most notable feature today is an allegorical ceiling painted by Peter Paul Rubens. The Banqueting House may be visited weekdays from 10 a.m. to 5 p.m., except Monday, on Sunday, 2 to 5 p.m. Admission is 30p (69¢) for adults, 15p (35¢) for children.

Finally, you may want to stroll to Parliament Square for a view of Big Ben, the world's most famous timepiece.

Legal London

The smallest borough in London, bustling **Holborn** (pronounced Hoburn) is often referred to as Legal London, the home of the city's barristers, solicitors, and law clerks. It also embraces the university district of Bloomsbury. Holborn, which houses the ancient Inns of Court, was severely damaged in World War II bombing raids. The razed buildings were replaced with modern offices housing insurance brokers, realtors, whatever. But the borough still retains quadrangle pockets of its former days.

Turn south from busy Fleet Street down Middle Temple Lane, leading to the Embankment. You'll come to an area known as **The Temple**, named after the medieval order of the Knights Templar (originally formed by the Crusaders in Jerusalem in the 12th century). Here you'll find the Temple Church, one of four Norman "round churches" left in England. First completed in the 12th century, it was restored. Look for the knightly effigies and the Norman door anytime from 10 a.m. to 5 p.m. (4 p.m. in winter). Readers Manly and Mary Johnson, from Tulsa, Oklahoma, were impressed with "a circle of grotesque carved portrait heads which have to be seen to be believed—a goat in a mortar board, characters making faces, rolling their eyes, lolling tongues, and even a couple of them with little fierce creatures biting their ears! There's also a 'dungeon' one flight up—ask the caretaker to show you."

The **Middle Temple** contains a Tudor hall completed in 1570 with a double hammer-beam roof. It is believed Shakespeare's troupe played *Twelfth Night* here in 1602. A table on view is said to have come from timber from Sir Francis Drake's *The Golden Hind*. The hall may be visited from 10 a.m. to noon and from 3 to 4:30 p.m. weekdays.

While in this district, you may also want to explore the area north of Fleet Street and the Temple. **Staple Inn**, near the Chancery Lane tube stop, is the last of the old Tudor fronts to be found in London. The inn, lined with shops, was constructed and reconstructed many times, originally having come into existence between 1545 and 1589. Dr. Johnson moved here in 1759, the year *Rasselas* was published.

On Chancery Lane itself you can visit the **Public Record Office** (see Other Museums), or else walk through a Tudor gateway into **Lincoln's Inn**, dating back to 1422. Another of the ancient Inns of Court, Lincoln's Inn forms an important link in the architectural maze of London. In the 17th century Inigo Jones erected a chapel here; Cromwell lived here at one time. To the east of Lincoln's Inn is the large square known as Lincoln's Inn Fields, with the Soane Museum (see Other Museums). Near the south of the fields on Kingsway is the **Old Curiosity Shop**, immortalized by Charles Dickens.

North of Lincoln's Inn in High Holborn stands the last of the four great Inns of Court—**Gray's**, restored after being heavily damaged by World War II bombings. Francis Bacon was the most eminent tenant to have resided here. Off Gray's Inn Road, it contains a rebuilt Tudor hall.

Other Museums

The present **Guildhall**, on King Street in Cheapside (The City, E.C.2; tube to Bank), was built in 1411. But the Civic Hall of the Corporation of London has had a rough time, notably in the Great Fire of 1666 and the 1940 blitz. The most famous tenants of the rebuilt Guildhall are *Gog and Magog*, two giants standing over nine feet high. The original effigies, burned in the London fire, were rebuilt only to be destroyed again in 1940. The present giants are third generation. Restoration has returned the Gothic grandeur to the hall—replete with a medieval porch entranceway; monuments to Wellington, Churchill, and Nelson; stained glass commemorating lord mayors and mayors; the standards of length; a 15th-century crypt; and colorful shields honoring fishmongers, haberdashers, merchant tailors, ironmongers, and skinners—some of the major Livery Companies. The Guildhall and Crypt may be visited Monday through Saturday, 10 a.m. to 5 p.m. (on Sunday, May to September only, from 10 a.m. to 5 p.m.).

The museum of the **Public Record Office**, on Chancery Lane (tube to the Temple or Chancery Lane), is one of the finest of the small museums of London, deserving far more attention than it gets. A mere recitation of some of its exhibits is all the selling it needs. To the left as you enter, you'll find two volumes of the *Domesday Book*, a general survey of England ordered by William the Conqueror in 1085. Here also are the navy log of the H.M.S. *Victory*, showing Nelson's dispatches relating to the Battle of Trafalgar; Elizabeth II's signed oath "to govern Great Britain"; exemplars of Magna Carta (Case VIII); John Bunyan's preaching license; one of the six authentic signatures known of Shakespeare, along with his Last Will and Testament, dated March 25, 1616; a letter from George Washington (Case XII) to his "great and good friend," King George III; letters from Maria Theresa, Frederick the Great, Catherine the Great, Marie Antoinette, and Metternich; the first confession of Guy Fawkes about the gunpowder plot to blow up the king, signed November 9, 1605; scads of royal autographs—Richard II, Edward IV, Catherine Parr, Anne Boleyn. The museum is open Monday through Friday from 1 to 4 p.m.

Sir John Soane's Museum, 13 Lincoln's Inn Fields, W.C.2, is the former home of a knight who lived from 1753 to 1837. Sir John, who rebuilt the Bank of England (not the present structure, however), was a "spaceman" in a different era. With his multilevels, fool-the-eye mirrors, flying arches, and domes, Soane was a master of perspective, a genius of interior space (his art gallery, for example, is filled with three times the number of paintings a room of similar dimensions would be likely to hold). That he could do all this—and still not prove a demon to claustrophobia victims—was proof of his remarkable talent. Even if you don't like Soane (he was reportedly a cranky fellow), you may still want to visit this museum to see William Hogarth's satirical series, *The Rake's Progress,* containing his much reproduced *Orgy,* and the less successful satire on politics in the mid-18th century, *The Election.* Soane also filled his house with paintings (Watteau's *Les Noces,* Canaletto's large *Venetian Scene*), and classical sculpture. Finally, be sure to see the Egyptian sarcophagus found in a burial chamber in the Valley of the Kings. Soane turned his house over to his country for use as a museum. It is open Tuesday through Saturday from 10 a.m. till 5 p.m. Take the tube to Chancery Lane or Holborn.

Just across the Thames in Lambeth Road, S.E.1, is the **Imperial War Museum** (tube to Lambeth North or Elephant and Castle). This large domed building, built around 1815, the former Bethlehem Royal Hospital for the Insane, or Bedlam, houses the museum's collections relating to the two World Wars and other military operations involving the British and the Commonwealth since 1914.

A wide range of weapons and equipment is on display: aircraft, armored vehicles, field guns, small arms, and models, decorations, uniforms, posters, photographs, and paintings. You can see a Mark V tank, a Battle of Britain Spitfire, a German one-man submarine, and the rifle carried by Lawrence of Arabia, as well as the German surrender document, Hitler's political testament, and a German V2 rocket. There is an exhibition on trench warfare in the First World War and a show of uniforms, medals, and accouterments which belonged to the Duke of Gloucester. Paintings on display include works by well-known war artists such as William Orpen, Paul Nash, Stanley Spencer, and Jacob Epstein. There is also a collection of propaganda posters from the First and Second World Wars, plus Field Marshal Montgomery's three campaign caravans. The museum is open Monday to Saturday, 10 a.m. to 5:50 p.m.; on Sunday, 2 to 5:50 p.m. It is closed on Good Friday, Christmas Eve, Christmas Day, Boxing Day, New Year's Day, and the first Monday in May. Admission is free.

The **National Army Museum,** Royal Hospital Road, S.W.3, in Chelsea (tube: Sloane Square), is one of London's newest museums. It traces the history of the British, Indian, and Colonial forces from 1485. (The Imperial War Museum above concerns itself with World Wars I and II.)

The National Army Museum stands next door to Wren's Royal Hospital. The museum backers agreed to begin the collection at the year 1485, because that was the date of the formation of the Yeomen of the Guard. The saga of the forces of the East India Company is traced, beginning in 1602 and going up to Indian independence in 1947. The gory and the glory—it's all here, everything from Florence Nightingale's lamp to the French Eagle captured in a cavalry charge at Waterloo, even the staff cloak wrapped round the dying Wolfe at Quebec. Naturally, there are the "cases of the heroes," mementos of such outstanding men as the Dukes of Marlborough and Wellington. But the field soldier isn't neglected either. The museum is open weekdays from 10 a.m. to 5:30 p.m., Sunday from 2 to 5:30 p.m. It is closed on New Year's Day, Good Friday, from December 24 to 26, and on the May bank holiday.

The **Wellington Museum,** at Apsley House, 149 Piccadilly, Hyde Park Corner, W.1, takes us into the former town house of the Iron Duke, the British general (1769–1852) who defeated Napoleon at the Battle of Waterloo. Wellington's London residence was opened as a public museum in 1952. Once Wellington had to retreat behind the walls of Apsley House—even securing it in fear of a possible attack from Englishmen, outraged by his autocratic opposition as prime minister to reform. In the vestibule you'll find a colossal statue in marble of Napoleon by Canova—ironic, to say the least. Completely idealized, it was presented to the duke by King George IV. In addition to three good paintings by Velázquez, the Wellington collection includes Correggio's *Agony in the Garden,* Jan Steen's *The Egg Dance,* and Pieter de Hooch's *A Musical Party.* You can see the gallery where Wellington used to invite his officers for the annual Waterloo banquet (the banquets were originally held in the dining room). The house also contains a large porcelain and china collection—plus many Wellington medals, of course. The residence was designed by Robert Adam and built in the late 18th century. The museum is open Tuesday, Wednesday, Thursday, and Saturday from 10 a.m. to 6 p.m.; on Sunday from 2:30 to 6 p.m. Admission is free. Tube: Hyde Park Corner.

The **Commonwealth Institute,** Kensington High Street (tube to Kensington High Street or no. 9 bus from Piccadilly Circus), is a center of information on the 40 or so countries of the modern Commonwealth. There are continuous exhibitions on each country, and you can capture some of the atmosphere and flavor of places as different as Sri Lanka and Papua, New Guinea, Malaysia, and Trinidad. Admission is free and there are also free film shows, an attractive and inexpensive restaurant called Flags, and a shop selling Commonwealth crafts, gifts, and books. The institute also has a free library and art gallery. The institute plays host to many cultural events, including dance, drama, music, and exotic food-tastings and festivals. Many, perhaps most, of these events are free. In addition, the institute offers gallery guides who come from a selection of the countries of the Commonwealth and who are on hand to meet the public, answer questions, and talk about their homelands. It's open Monday through Saturday from 10 a.m. to 4:30 p.m., on Sunday from 2 to 5.

In London's Barbican district, in the bombed-out World War II area around St. Paul's Cathedral, the **Museum of London** allows visitors to trace the history of London from prehistoric times to the present—through relics, costumes, household effects, maps, and models. Exhibits are arranged so that visitors can begin and end their chronological stroll through 250,000 years at the main entrance to the museum. Of special interest to Anglophiles is a large number of relics, possessions, and costumes of the monarchs of England, including such gruesome items as a vest supposedly worn by Charles I at his execution and the death mask of Oliver Cromwell. But the pièce de résistance is the Lord Mayor's coach, built in 1757 and weighing in at three tons. This gilt and red, horse-drawn vehicles is like a fairytale coach. Visitors can also see the Great Fire of London in living color and sound; a Roman dinner, including the kitchen and utensils; a cell in Newgate Prison made famous by Charles Dickens; and, most amazing of all, a shop window with pre-World War II prices on the items.

The museum overlooks London's Roman and medieval walls and, in all, has something from every era before and after—including little Victorian shops and recreations of what life was like in London in the Iron Age. Anglo-Saxons, Vikings, Normans—they're all there, arranged on two floors around a central garden. With quick labels for museum sprinters, more extensive ones for those who want to study, and still deeper details for scholars, this new museum—built at a cost of some $18 million—is an enriching experience for *everybody.*

A small coffeeshop helps sustain the visitor with various soft drinks, tea and coffee, plus sandwiches and other cold snacks. At least an hour should be allowed for a full (but still quick) visit to the museum, which will surely rank as one of the most worthwhile hours you'd spend in any museum in London. Free lectures on London's past are given during lunch hours. These aren't given daily, but it's worth inquiring at the entrance hall. In addition, the museum sponsors Dickens evenings five times a week. You can reach the museum by going up to the elevated pedestrian precinct at the corner of the London Wall and Aldersgate, five minutes from St. Paul's. It is open Tuesday through Saturday from 10 a.m. to 6 p.m., on Sunday from 2 to 6 p.m.; admission free.

The **London Transport Museum,** 39 Wellington St., W.C.2., exhibits a collection of historic vehicles displayed in a splendid Victorian building which formerly housed the Flower Market at Covent Garden. The museum shows how London's transport systems evolved, and exhibits include a representative collection of road vehicles, featuring a reconstruction of George Shillibeer's Omnibus of 1829.

Nearly two centuries of London's public transport are represented by these historic buses, trams, trolleybuses, locomotives, rolling stock, posters, models, working exhibits, and audio-visual displays. A steam locomotive which ran on the world's first underground railway, a knifeboard horse bus, the "B"-type motor bus, London's first trolleybus, and the Feltham tram are of particular interest.

The museum is open every day of the year except Christmas and Boxing Day from 10 a.m. to 6 p.m. Admission charges are £1.40 ($3.22) for adults, 60p ($1.38) for children.

The **R.A.F. Museum,** Hendon Aerodrome, Colindale Avenue, N.W.9, shelters what must be the largest and most comprehensive collection of airplanes and equipment from every stage of British aviation. All but the largest aircraft are housed in a gigantic hangar, and there is also a special section, the Battle of Britain Museum, with souvenirs, photographs, and exhibits explaining and portraying those days when "so much was owed by so many, to do few." The museums are open Monday to Saturday from 10 a.m. to 6 p.m., on Sunday from 2 to 6 p.m. Admission is £1 ($2.30); children pay 50p ($1.15). Tube: Colindale.

The **National Postal Museum,** King Edward Building, King Edward Street, E.C.1, contains the post office's collection of British postage stamps, a worldwide stamp collection from 1878 and a philatelic correspondence archives covering postage stamps of 200 countries from 1855 onward. The museum is open Monday to Friday from 1 to 4:30 p.m.

A unique private museum in London, the home of **Denis Seevers,** 18 Folgate St., E.1 (tel. 247-4013), is a delight. Denis is a young Californian who has lived in London since he was 16 years old and is utterly involved with England, the history and the culture of the place. He has restored a house on the edge of the City. Originally built in 1725, no. 18 was occupied by the Huguenot family Jerris, who were silk weavers.

Now the home belongs to Denis and his black cat Whitechapel (who claims to have been born on the grounds of Buckingham Palace). The six rooms of the house recreate with sound and vision the world of the 18th century. You walk into the kitchen of Beatrix Potter, with its blackened range holding simmering pots, the gleaming coppers, and china glinting in the candlelight on the Welsh dresser. You explore the Dickens Room, the master bedroom (with Bob Cratchett's high desk in the corner). The withdrawing room with highbacked chairs and ornaments all add up to a fascinating picture of bygone times.

To visit the house and its charming occupants, telephone 247-4013. Two tours are planned for Sunday, at 4 p.m. and 8:15 p.m., and a tour each weekday evening. It is not practical for more than six people to try to tour together, and this is only really suitable for historians and those who wish to step back into the past world of candlelight, in a nonelectric, nongasoline age. The cost is £10 ($23) per person. The house is five minutes from Liverpool Street underground at the back of Spitalfields Market.

Another unique London museum is **Whitbread's Brewery,** Chiswell Street, E.C.1 (tel. 606-4455). Although beer is no longer brewed in Chiswell Street, the old brewery remains the headquarters of Whitbread's which has opened the magnificent old building to the public. The most impressive of the rooms is the Porter Tun Room, completed in 1784 and renowned for its massive unsupported King Post timber roof, the second largest of its kind in Europe. The lower part of this room is now renamed the Overlord Room and houses the remarkable Overlord embroidery, depicting the story of the invasion on June 6, 1944, of the Normandy beaches during World War II. The appliqued embroidery, probably the largest of its kind—272 feet long and 3 feet high— was designed by Miss Sandra Lawrence and took 20 ladies of the Royal School of Needlework five years to complete. It is a remarkably complete record of the Allied Forces' progress into France.

Also on display in the brewery is the Speaker's Coach. A magnificent affair of gold and finery, it was built in 1698 and is still used, drawn by dray horses, to convey the Speaker of the House of Commons on state occasions. The stables can be visited by appointment.

The coffeeshop is open Monday to Friday from 8:30 a.m. to 4:30 p.m. and provides light snacks from 65p ($1.50) to £1.20 ($2.76) or a three-course meal from £5 ($11.50).

Across the road on the north side of Chiswell Street, in the vaults below the Georgian terraces, is a cellar wine bar. The vaults are a honeycomb of tunnel-like rooms with curved brick ceilings, sawdust on the floor, and tables and benches set between old wine barrels. From the vast selection of wines a glass will cost about 60p ($1.38). Bottles start at £3 ($6.90) up to around £6 ($13.80). Champagne is £12 ($27.60) a bottle. In one of the vaults, snacks are available. There is also a small restaurant area with tables and chairs and waitress service.

Other Galleries

National Portrait Gallery, St. Martin's Place, W.C.2 (entrance around the corner from the National Gallery on Trafalgar Square), gives you a chance to outstare the stiff-necked greats and not-so-greats of English history. In a gallery of remarkable and unremarkable portraits, a few paintings tower over the rest, including Sir Joshua Reynolds's first portrait of Samuel Johnson ("a man of most dreadful appearance"). Among the best are Nicholas Hilliard's miniature of a most handsome Sir Walter Raleigh (Room 1); a full-length Elizabeth I (painted to commemorate her visit to Sir Henry Lee Ditchley in 1592), along with the Holbein cartoon of Henry VIII (sketched for a family portrait that hung, before it was burned, in the Privy Chamber in Whitehall Palace)—both in Room 1. In Room 1, also, is a portrait of William Shakespeare (with gold earring, no less!). The artist is unknown, but the portrait bears the claim of being the most "authentic contemporary likeness" of its subject of any work yet known. The John Hayls portrait of Samuel Pepys adorns Room 4. Whistler could not only paint a portrait, he could also be the subject of one (Room 24). One of the most unusual portraits (Room 17) in the gallery—a group of the three Brontë sisters (Charlotte, Emily, Anne)—was painted by their brother, Branwell. An idealized portrait of Lord Byron by Richard Westall is pleased with itself in Room 13. For a finale, treat yourself to the likeness of the incomparable Aubrey Beardsley (Room 24). For sheer volume of portraiture, Queen Victoria reigns supreme. The gallery is open from 10 a.m. to 5 p.m. Monday to Friday, from 10 a.m. to 6 p.m. on Saturday, and from 2 to 6 p.m.

on Sunday. Special exhibitions are held at the gallery from time to time.

The **Wallace Collection,** Manchester Square, off Wigmore Street (tube to Bond Street), has an outstanding collection of works of art of all kinds bequeathed to the nation by Lady Wallace in 1897 and still displayed in the house of its founders. There are important pictures by artists of all European schools, including Titian, Rubens, Van Dyck, Rembrandt, Hals, Velázquez, Murillo, Reynolds, Gainsborough, and Delacroix. Representing the art of France in the 18th century are paintings by Watteau, Boucher, and Fragonard, and sculpture, furniture, goldsmiths' work, and Sèvres porcelain. Valuable collections also are found of majolica and European and Oriental arms and armor. Frans Hals's *Laughing Cavalier* is the most famous in the collection, but Pieter de Hooch's *A Boy Bringing Pomegranates* and Watteau's *The Music Party* are also well known. Other notable works include Canaletto's views of Venice (especially *Bacino di San Marco*); Rembrandt's *Titus;* and Gainsborough's *Mrs. Robinson (Perdita).* Worthy also is Boucher's portrait of the Marquise de Pompadour. The Wallace Collection may be viewed daily from 10 a.m. to 5 p.m., on Sunday from 2 to 5 p.m. Closed Christmas Eve, Christmas Day, Boxing Day, New Year's Day, Good Friday, and the first Monday in May. Nearly half the rooms will be shut until 1982 because of the installation of air conditioning.

The **Courtauld Institute Galleries,** Woburn Square (tube to Russell Square), is the home of the art collection of London University—noted chiefly for its superb impressionist and post-impressionist works. It has eight works by Cézanne alone, including his *A Man with a Pipe.* Other notable works include Seurat's *La Poudreuse,* Van Gogh's self-portrait (with ear bandaged), a nude by the great Modigliani, Gauguin's *Day-Dreaming,* Monet's *Fall at Argenteuil,* Toulouse-Lautrec's most delicious *Tête-à-Tête,* and Manet's *Bar at the Folies Bergère.* The galleries also feature classical works, including a *Virgin and Child* by Bernardino Luini, a Botticelli, a Giovanni Bellini, and a Veronese. The collection may be viewed Monday to Saturday from 10 a.m. to 5 p.m., on Sunday from 2 to 5 p.m. Admission is free.

The **Hayward Gallery,** South Bank, S.E.1, presents a changing program of major exhibitions organized by the Arts Council of Great Britain. The gallery forms part of the South Banks Arts Centre, which also includes the Royal Festival Hall, the Queen Elizabeth Hall, the Purcell Room, the National Film Theatre, and the National Theatre. Admission to the gallery varies according to exhibitions, with cheap entry on Monday and in the evening on Tuesday and Thursday. Opening hours are Monday to Thursday from 10 a.m. to 8 p.m.; Friday and Saturday, 10 a.m. to 6 p.m.; and Sunday, noon to 6 p.m. The gallery is closed between exhibitions, so check the listings before crossing the Thames.

The **Serpentine Gallery,** Kensington Gardens, W.1. The Old Teahouse, near the Albert Memorial, was an inspired choice for the Arts Council's London platform for professional artists whose work has not been seen in commercial galleries. Its four large rooms, spacious and adaptable, are well suited to the experimental, and large-scale works are often shown here. The fact that the gallery is in popular parkland not only means that there are excellent adjacent outdoor facilities for sculpture and events, but that it draws a crowd who generally would not think of going to a Bond Street exhibition. Usually a minimum of four artists is shown at a time and given freedom to use the space as they wish. The exhibitions are principally for those interested in the most outstanding contemporary trends and tendencies, and are carefully watched by the more far-sighted commercial gallery owners. The gallery now has a winter program as well, and stages some international shows, exhibitions by more established artists, and occasional retrospectives devoted to just one artist. The gallery is open daily from 10 a.m. to 7 p.m., April through October, and 10 a.m. to 15 minutes before dusk during November through March. Admission is free. Closed Good Friday, Chirstmas Eve, Christmas Day, Boxing Day, and New Year's Day.

Homes of Famous Writers

Dr. Johnson's House: The Queen Anne house of the famed lexicographer is at 17 Gough Square. It'll cost you 40p (92¢), and it's well worth it. Students and children pay only 20p (46¢). It was there that Dr. Johnson and his copyists compiled his famous dictionary. The 17th-century building has been painstakingly restored (surely "Dear Tetty," if not Boswell, would approve). Although Johnson lived at Staple Inn in Holborn and at a number of other houses, the Gough Square house is the only one of his residences remaining in London. He occupied it from 1748 to 1759. It is open from 11 a.m. to 5:30 p.m., Monday through Saturday, May through September, closing half an hour earlier off-season. Take the tube to Blackfriars, then walk up New Bridge Street, turning left onto Fleet. Gough Square is a tiny, hidden square, north of the "street of ink."

Carlyle's House: 24 Cheyne Row, in Chelsea (bus 11, 19, 22, or 39). For nearly half a century, from 1834 to 1881, the handsome author of *The French Revolution* and other works, along with his letter-writing wife, took up abode in this modest 1708 terraced house, about three-quarters of a block from the Thames, near the Chelsea Embankment. Still standing and furnished essentially as it was in Carlyle's day, the house was described by his wife as being "of most antique physiognomy, quite to our humour; all wainscotted, carved and queer-looking, roomy, substantial, commodious, with closets to satisfy any Bluebeard." Now who could improve on that? The second floor contains the drawing room of Mrs. Carlyle. But the most interesting chamber is the not-so-soundproof "soundproof" study in the skylit attic. Filled with Carlyle memorabilia—his books, a letter from Disraeli, a writing chair, even his death mask—this is the cell where the author labored over his *Frederick the Great* manuscript. The Cheyne (pronounced chainey) Row house may be visited weekdays, except Monday and Tuesday, from 11 a.m. to 5 p.m.; on Sunday from 2 to 5 p.m. Admission is 70p ($1.61) for adults, 35p (81¢) for children up to 16 years of age. Closed November through March.

Dickens's House: In Bloomsbury stands the house of the great English author Charles Dickens, accused in his time of "supping on the horrors" of Victoriana and read by Russians today to find out "what Britain is really like." Born in 1812 in what is now Portsmouth, Dickens is known to have lived at 48 Doughty St., W.C.1 (tube to Russell Square) from 1837 to 1839. Unlike some of the London town houses of famous men (Wellington, Soane), the Bloomsbury house is simple, the embodiment of middle-class restraint.

The house contains an extensive library of Dickensiana, including manuscripts and letters second in importance only to the Forster Collection in the Victoria and Albert Museum. In his study are his desk and chair from the study at Gad's Hill Place, Rochester, on which he wrote his last two letters before he died (also the table from his Swiss chalet on which he wrote the last unfinished fragment of *The Mystery of Edwin Drood*). The basement contains a remodeled Dingley Dell kitchen from *Pickwick Papers,* also the wash house as it was when Dickens lived in the house. Open daily, except Sunday and bank holidays, from 10 a.m. to 5 p.m. Admission is 75p ($1.73) for adults, 60p

($1.38) for students, and 35p (81¢) for children.

Keats's House: The darling of romantics, John Keats lived for only two years at Wentworth Place, Keats Grove, Hampstead, N.W.3 (tel. 435-2062). Take the tube to Belsize Park or Hampstead or bus 24 from Trafalgar Square. But for the poet, that was something like two-fifths of his creative life, as he died in Rome of tuberculosis at the age of 25 (1821). In Hampstead, Keats wrote some of his most celebrated *Odes*—in praise of a Grecian Urn and to the Nightingale. In the garden stands an ancient mulberry tree which the poet must have known. His Regency house is well preserved, and contains the manuscripts of his last sonnet *("Bright star, would I were steadfast as thou art")*, a final letter to the mother of Fanny Brawne (his correspondence to his Hampstead neighbor, who nursed him while he was ill, forms part of his legend), and a portrait of him on his death bed in a little house on the Spanish Steps in Rome. Wentworth Place is open weekdays 10 a.m. to 6 p.m. On Sunday, Easter, and spring and summer bank holidays hours are from 2 to 5 p.m. Closed Christmas Day, Boxing Day, New Year's Day, Good Friday, Easter Eve, and May Day. Admission is free.

Churches

St. Martin-in-the-Fields, overlooking Trafalgar Square, is the Royal Parish Church, dear to the hearts of many an English person, and especially the homeless who have found shelter in its crypt during many a cold winter night. The present classically inspired church, with its famous steeple, dates back to 1721. James Gibbs, a pupil of Wren's, is listed as its architect. The origins of the church go back to the 11th century. Among the congregation in years past was George I, who was actually a churchwarden, unique for an English sovereign. From St. Martin's vantage position in the theater district, it has drawn many actors to its door—none more notable than Nell Gwynne, the mistress of Charles II. On her death in 1687, she was buried here. Throughout the war, many Londoners rode out an uneasy night in the crypt, while blitz bombs rained down overhead. One, in 1940, blasted out all the windows.

Floating History

The Maritime Trust's **Historic Ship Collection** is at St. Katharine's Dock, E.1, which has been for some years the home of the old Nore lightship. That vessel has now been joined by the Thames sailing barge, *Cambria,* a schooner, an East Coast herring drifter, a steam coaster the *Robin,* and now the R.R.S. *Discovery,* the royal research ship which was removed from its berth at Victoria Embankment.

The Trust provides walk-around guide leaflets to help visitors interpret what they see, and souvenirs are sold aboard the *Cambria.* While the *Discovery* is in dock, it will be possible to see restoration work carried out on her massive timbers by traditional shipwrights and riggers. There are plenty of places for a snack lunch or a pint in a pub, and, of course, the Tower of London is just across the road. The ships are open daily from 10 a.m. to 5 p.m. (until dusk in winter), charging an admission of 75p ($1.73) for adults, 30p (69¢) for children.

A floating museum, H.M.S. *Belfast,* Symons Wharf, Vine Lane, S.E.1, is an 11,500-ton cruiser, the last of the great British warships. She's moored on the opposite bank of the Thames, looking out onto the Tower of London. The first shots were fired during the sinking of the *Scharnhorst* from her guns, and she saw distinguished service during the D-Day bombardment of Normandy. She also was in action in Korea. Exhibitions show the history not only of the

H.M.S. *Belfast* but of cruisers in general. The huge engine and boiler rooms can be seen, together with many other working and living spaces. The price of admission is £1.40 ($3.22) for adults, half price for children. The hours are 11 a.m. to 5:50 p.m. daily. In winter the ship closes at sunset. Nearest tube stations: Tower Hill, Monument, and London Bridge. Boats run from Tower Pier in summer and on weekends in winter.

The Dungeon

The **London Dungeon,** 34 Tooley St., S.E.1 (tel. 403-0606), simulates a ghoulish atmosphere designed deliberately to chill the blood while reproducing faithfully the conditions which existed in the Middle Ages. Set under the arches of London Bridge Station, the dungeon is a series of tableaux, more grizzly than Madame Tussaud's, depicting life in Old London. The rumble of trains overhead adds to the spine-chilling horror of the place. Bells toll and there is constant melancholy chanting in the background. Dripping water and live rats make for even more atmosphere.

The heads of executed criminals were stuck on spikes for onlookers to observe through glasses hired for the occasion. The murder of Thomas à Becket in Canterbury Cathedral is also depicted. Naturally, there's a burning at the stake, as well as a torture chamber with racking, branding, and fingernail extraction.

If you survive, there is a souvenir shop selling certificates which testify that you have been through the works. The dungeon is open from 10 a.m. to 6 p.m. daily, charging £1.60 ($3.68) for adults, 80p ($1.84) for children.

A Royal Tournament

The **Royal Tournament** at Earl's Court, Warwick Road, S.W.5, is a military and athletic spectacular with a century-long history. The tournament is put on each summer by various branches of the British service. You'll see exhibitions by the King's Troop Royal Horse Artillery, the London Metropolitan Police with their dogs, and the Red Caps with their daring performances combining horsemanship and motorcycle feats. The Royal Navy Field Gun Competition is an audience favorite in which two teams struggle with heavy field artillery across a rough, obstacle-laden terrain.

The Massed Bands of the Royal Air Force will perform throughout the tournament. Guests from foreign nations, such as the Carrousel de la Gendarmerie from Belgium, and the Oman Bank from South Arabia frequently make appearances. Performances are held daily, except Sunday, at 2:30 p.m. and 7:30 p.m. (no matinees on Monday). Seat prices range from £1.50 ($3.45) and up. For tickets or further information, write to: The Royal Tournament, Horse Guards, Whitehall, London, S.W.1, U.K. Dates of the tournament for 1981 are July 14 through July 31 and for 1982, July 15 through August 1.

Highgate Cemetery

At last, the ideal setting for a collection of Victorian sculpture. Described as everything from "walled romantic rubble" to "an anthology of horror," the 20-acre cemetery in North London's old Highgate section is a real treat for tombstone fanciers. The unkempt look of overgrown weeds combined with the clutter of obelisks and crosses give the graveyard a rare, Gothic kind of beauty. Several of the tombstones are masterpieces in themselves, including the full-size concrete grand piano, its top opened as if ready for a concert, marked only with the name Thornton and a poetic phrase by Puccini. Another grave, that of a sporting goods manufacturer, is decorated with crossed tennis rackets, cricket bats, and balls. The most tender marker is a life-like statue of a small boy with a ball, placed over the grave of a five-year-old boy. Highgate's most famous grave is that of Karl Marx, the founder of modern Communism, who died in Hampstead in 1883. On his tomb is a huge bust of Marx, inscribed with his quotation, "Workers of all lands, unite." The grave is seldom without a wreath or bouquet of red flowers, usually placed there by an Eastern embassy or a local Communist group. The cemetery adjoins attractive Waterlow Park, a 29-acre landmark of Highgate. In the nearby community are also several historic houses, including the Cromwell House, dating from 1638, and the home of Samuel Taylor Coleridge.

Free Sights—London in Action

Those who have grown museum-weary might like to see workaday London engaged in its task of, say, trying to start a revolution at Speakers' Corner or sentencing a modern-day Jack the Ripper at Old Bailey. Here are a few of the action items available:

First, at the northwest extremity of Mayfair, head for **Marble Arch,** an enormous *faux pas* that the English didn't try to hide but turned into a monument. Originally it was built by John Nash as the entrance to Buckingham Palace, until it was discovered that it was too small for carriages to pass through. If you see a crowd of people nearby who look as if they are plotting revolution, you might be right. In this part of Hyde Park (tube to Marble Arch) is **Speakers' Corner,** where you will see English free speech in action. Everybody from Communists to Orgone theorists mounts the soapbox to speak his or her mind. The speeches reach their most violent pitch on Sunday, the best day to visit Marble Arch.

If you are intrigued with the operation of the courts, you may want to include a visit to the **Central Criminal Court** while you are in the area of St. Paul's. On the corner of Old Bailey and Newgate Street, E.C.4, the court was built on the site of the infamous Old Newgate Prison. Affectionately called Old Bailey, it has witnessed some great—and some dubious—moments in the history of British justice. The public is permitted to enter from 10:20 a.m. to 1 p.m. and from 1:50 to 4 p.m. Monday through Friday. Entry is strictly on a first arrival basis. Guests queue up outside (where, incidentally, the final public execution took place in the 1860s). Courts 1 to 4, 17, and 18 are entered from Newgate Street, and the balance from "Old Bailey." No persons under 14 are admitted, and teenagers from 14 to 17 must be accompanied by a responsible adult. No cameras are allowed. If you prefer civil cases to criminal ones, you can visit the **Law Courts** on The Strand, W.C.2 (tube to Temple), which are open Monday through Friday from 10 a.m. to 4 p.m.

The **Stock Exchange** has replaced New York as the world's leading money mart. On the trading floor of this famous money center, one of the most modern in the world, you can catch a glimpse of brokers and jobbers. Guides explain what the furious action means, and later you are shown a film in an adjoining cinema, giving you an insight into the world of high finance. T͎ Visitors' Gallery entrance is in Old Broad Street, and the nearest underg͛ station is Bank. Admission is free, and visiting hours are weekdays ͟ a.m. to 3 p.m.

London Zoo

One of the greatest zoos in the world, the London Zoo celebrated its 150th birthday in 1976. Among the thousands of animals, the most famous are the two giant pandas, Ching-Ching and Chia-Chia, a gift to Britain from the People's Republic of China. One of the most fascinating exhibits is the Snowdon Aviary. Many families budget almost an entire day to spend with the animals, watching the sea lions being fed or the elephants bathed on fine summer days. Also of interest is the Moonlight World, where animals of the night—the "nocturnal beasties"—wander in their special world, everything from Australian fruit bats to primitive echidnas.

The London Zoo occupies 36 acres of Regents Park, and is open every day except Christmas Day from 9 a.m. in summer and from 10 a.m. in winter, till 6 p.m. or dusk, whichever is earlier. You can go by underground to Baker Street or Camden Town and then take the no. 74 bus (Camden Town is nearer and an easy ten-minute walk). On the grounds are two fully licensed restaurants, one self-service, the other with waitresses. Admission is £2.50 ($5.75) for adults, £1.50 ($3.45) for children.

The Jewish Museum

The major communal building for English Jewry is **Woburn House,** Upper Woburn Place, W.C.1, near Euston Station. In these precincts you'll also come upon the hard-to-find Jewish Museum (tel. 387-3081), tucked away on a lovely square. Walk along Euston Road, and turn right onto Upper Woburn Place. Look for a sign referring to the head rabbi. After entering, you're invited to sign a guest book, then you're guided up to the museum itself, a large salon filled with antiques relating to the history of the Jews. You'll come across many artifacts used in Jewish rituals. All the exhibits, in fact, are of interest to those concerned with Anglo-Judaica. It is open Monday to Thursday from 2:30 to 5 p.m. and on Friday and Sunday from 10:30 a.m. to 12:45 p.m. It is closed on bank and Jewish holidays. The Jewish Historical Society runs the **Mocatta Library and Museum** at the neighboring University College on Gower Street.

The London Experience

Almost a million visitors have seen this warm and wonderful story of London's history and character at Piccadilly Circus (entrance on Coventry Street), W.1 (tel. 734-6155). You see and experience the great events of London's past and present from the Roman city of Londinium through 2000 years of history. Using seven screens, 42 projectors, multichannel sound, and special effects, the show depicts the Plague, the Great Fire, the Blitz, and other scenes of the pageantry and splendor of England. Shows are presented every day except Christmas Day, on the hour from 11 a.m. to 10 p.m. Admission is £1.80 ($4.14) for adults, 90p ($2.07) for children.

LONDON INFORMATION: The **British Tourist Authority** operates a telephone tape which is changed daily, giving details of all sorts of things to do each day. On the day we tried it, the service reported there was a free jazz concert in Battersea Park, a flower show in Chelsea, and, in addition, it suggested we visit the new gallery at the National Maritime Museum at Greenwich. The tape gives prices and visiting hours and also tells you how to get there. For this information, telephone 246-8041.

There are several official information centers around The City and West End, providing particular data about a certain part of town. These centers

LONDON: SHOPPING   141

know of exhibitions and places to visit which are seldom open to the public—the Livery Halls in The City, for example.

Centers include the **City of London Information Centre,** St. Paul's Churchyard, E.C.4 (tel. 606-3030), which is open Monday to Friday from 9:30 a.m. to 5 p.m. (Saturday and holidays from 10 a.m. to 6 p.m.). Others are operated by the London Tourist Board as follows: 26 Grosvenor Gardens, S.W.1, open during office hours for general advice and sale of tourist tickets, sightseeing tours, theater tickets, and guide books (this is the head LTB office to which mail inquiries should be sent); Victoria Station near platform 15, open daily from 9 a.m. to 8:40 p.m., a tourist information and accommodation center; Travel Information Center, Heathrow Central Station, London Airport, open daily from 8 a.m. to 7:30 p.m., providing tourist information, hotel accommodations, and publications; Selfridges, Oxford Street, W.1; Harrods, Knightsbridge, S.W.3; Tower of London, E.C.3, by the main gate, tourist information, leaflets, and other publications, open from 9 a.m. to 5 p.m. Monday through Saturday and 2 to 5 p.m. on Sunday in summer; and telephone information service, 730-0791 from 9 a.m. to 6 p.m. Monday through Friday or call Teletourist, 246-8041, 24 hours a day for a selection of attractions and events.

Also providing information are the **British Tourist Authority,** 64 St. James's St., S.W.1 (tel. 629-9191), Easter to September 30, Monday through Friday, from 9 a.m. to 6 p.m.; Saturday from 9 a.m. to 2:30 p.m.; October to Easter, Monday through Friday, 9:15 a.m. to 5:30 p.m.; Saturday, 9:15 a.m. to 12:30 p.m.

3. Shopping for Value

In London, this "nation of shopkeepers" displays an enormous variety of wares. You can pick up bargains ranging from a still-functioning hurdy-gurdy to a replica of the crown jewels. For the best buys, search out new styles in clothing, as well as traditional and well-tailored men's and women's suits, small antiques and curios, woolens, tweeds, tartans, rare books, Liberty silks, Burberrys, English china, silver, even arms and armor, to name just a few.

Here is a brief survey of some of the more attractive merchandise offered:

ANTIQUE MARKETS—FOR CURIOS: Chelsea Antique Market, 245–253 King's Rd., S.W.3, is billed as the world's largest covered antique market. It's a gold mine where you can pan for some hidden little treasure. Sheltered inside a rambling old building, it offers endless browsing possibilities for the curio addict. In this ever-changing display you're likely to run across Staffordshire dogs, shaving mugs, Edwardian buckles and clasps, ivory-handled razors, old velours and lace gowns, wooden tea caddies, antique pocket watches, wormy Tudoresque chests, silver snuff boxes, grandfather clocks, and jewelry of all periods. The market is open Monday through Saturday from 10 a.m. to 6 p.m. Closed Sunday.

The **Antique Hypermarket,** 26–40 Kensington High St., W.8, is London's choicest antique mart, with more than 100 stalls owned by leading dealers. As a trading center of excellence, it is often called the Stock Exchange of the Antique World. Each stallkeeper is a specialist in his or her field. If you don't find what you want, chances are you'll be directed to someone who has. You'll find rare books, bronzes from Tibet, Tudor (often Tudoresque) inlaid boxes, rare china and jewelry, silver-tipped canes, old Engli model ships, tole tea caddies, and on the lower ground floor is of antique furniture and fabulous silver vaults. At the rear of the ground floor is an amusing place for a quick snack, the Pullman Train, a Victorian railroad dining car where you sit on plush seats and order sandwiches and salads.

Antiquarius, 135-141 King's Rd., S.W.3, is the most varied of the indoor markets of London, with more than 200 stalls leased to collectors as a showcase for their wares: souvenir spoons, silver decanter labels, old books, authentic Tudor and Elizabethan furniture, rare helmets, antique guns and swords, silver pillboxes, snuff boxes, fine bone china, Roman glass, pocket watches, teapots, ornate wooden boxes, lead toy soldiers, military buttons, Oriental cannisters, dolls of every size, age, and character, mechanical toys, unusual walking sticks, and an amusing collection of art nouveau statuary. There's also a large selection of 1920s and 1930s fashion. Antiquarius is open from 10 a.m. till 6 p.m., Monday to Saturday. But it's closed Sunday.

Alfies Antique Market, 13-25 Church St., N.W.8 (tel. 723-6066), is one of the cheapest covered markets in London. The dealers come to buy here, inspecting more than 150 stalls, showrooms, and workshops on 20,000 square feet of floor.

Bond Street Antique Centre, 126 New Bond St., W.1, consists of 66 stands with more than 30 dealers selling antique jewelry, silver, watches, clocks, paintings, porcelain, glass, some small furniture, and Oriental antiques and antiquities. Prices are lower than those usually associated with Bond Street.

BEAUCHAMP PLACE: This is one of London's top shopping streets. Beauchamp Place (pronounced Beecham) is a block off Brompton Road, near Harrods Department Store. The *Herald Tribune* called it "a higgledy-piggledy of old-fashioned and trendy, quaint and with-it, expensive and cheap. It is deliciously unspecialized." Whatever you're looking for—a pâté de marcassin to a carved pine mantelpiece—you are likely to find it here. Reject china, second-hand silver, old alligator bags, collages, custom-tailored men's shirts—whatever. It's pure fun even if you don't buy anything.

BOOKS: Foyles, 119-125 Charing Cross Rd., W.C.2, claims to be the world's largest bookstore, with an impressive array of hardcovers and paperbacks. The shop includes records and stationery as well.

The **Children's Book Centre Ltd.,** 229 Kensington High St., W.8 (tel. 937-6314), is a must for both children's books and toys. It is thought to be the largest children's book shop in the world and has thousands of titles, including volumes from both France and Germany. A feature of the book shop is that fiction, both hardback and paperback, is arranged according to age. The large toy department, which has been described as the most imaginative in London, offers a wide selection of toys, games, and stationery for all ages. The store is open from 9 a.m. to 7 p.m. Monday through Friday, 9 to 6 on Saturday.

READER'S TIP: "The most concentrated gathering of out-of-print bookstores in England has to be **Cecil Court,** W.C.2, just north of Trafalgar Square and east off of Charing Cross Road. It represents a gold mine of inexpensive gift items with a 'from our home to yours' feeling"(Robert F. Fera, Orchard Lake, Mich.).

THE BURLINGTON ARCADE: Opposite Fortnum and Mason on Piccadilly is the **Royal Academy of Arts** (tel. 734-9052), where there are remarkable art shows throughout the year. A door west of the Royal Academy is the **Burlington Arcade,** a glass-roofed passage from Piccadilly north for several hundred feet to the next street. It houses dozens of shops, all with tiny upper floors, devoted solely to the sale of luxuries almost beyond imagination. You can take a short stroll through, or spend a day wandering up and down, protected from the weather—no small item in rainy London. You will see some of the best that London has to offer in the way of jewelry, both antique and modern, clothing for both men and women, fine arts, linen, bric-a-brac, all in profusion. It is possibly the greatest single concentrated bit of luxury shopping in London. Pomp and ceremony may be departing, but if you linger in the arcade until 5:30, you can watch the beadles, those ever-present attendants, in their black and yellow livery and top hats, ceremoniously put in place the iron grills which block off the arcade until 9 the next morning, when they just as ceremoniously remove them, marking the start of the new business day.

CHINA: **Lawleys,** 154 Regent St., W.1, offers a wide range of English bone china, as well as crystal and ovenware (more than 400 different open-stock patterns, the management proudly states). The firm specializes in Royal Doulton, Minton, Royal Crown Derby, Wedgwood, Denby, Aynsley, and Webb Corbett, Stuart, Waterford, Edinburgh, and Lalique crystal, plus Hummel and Lladro figures.

The **Reject China Shop,** 33–35 Beauchamp Pl., S.W.3 (tel. 584-9409), is really three shops at Knightsbridge, near Harrods Department Store. Offering a wide choice of china seconds, the shops were started almost on a whim by the Marquess of Queensberry and D'Arcy Conyers, a designer and film director, respectively. From a lowly basement dive, they have grown into a hit. They offer excellent china at prices at least 25% lower than most other stores. The merchandise changes constantly and what you don't find today most likely will show up tomorrow. Offered are good buys in bone china dinner and coffee sets, earthenware, and ornamental china birds, flowers, and boxes. The shop is open from 9 a.m. to 7 p.m., seven days a week.

At Beauchamp corner, the establishment has opened a new shop.

In addition, **Wedgwood** has a large shop at 249 Oxford St., W.1 (tel. 734-5656), at the corner of Regent Street. The staff there will explain their export plan to save you money on your souvenir buying. Even if you do find their porcelains expensive, the shop does offer small and inexpensive ashtrays in the traditional blue and white or in sage green and white. In any case, the store is like a miniature museum and well worth a visit. It also carries a collection of china, jewelry, pendants, earrings, and brooches. There are also Wedgwood shops at 158 Regent St. and 173 Piccadilly.

CHOCOLATES: **Charbonnel et Walker Lts.,** 28 Old Bond St., W.1 (tel. 629-4396), makes probably the best chocolates in the world and will send messages of thanks or love, spelled out on the chocolates themselves. Mr. and Mrs. Wallace, who run the bow-fronted shop on the corner of the Royal Arcade off Old Bond Street, will help you choose from the variety of centers. A quarter-pound selection will cost £2.50 ($5.75), and the box will be priced according to what you decide to put in it. They have ready-made presentation boxes at £20 ($46).

CIGARETTES: **Fribourg & Treyer,** 34 Haymarket, S.W.1, will produce cigarettes personalized by your own name or monogram. The company has been making and selling snuff and tobacco in their quaint old bow-fronted shop since 1720.

CLOCKS: Strike One Ltd., 1a Camden Walk, N.1 (tel. 226-9709), offers clocks for collectors. It's in the heart of the Camden Passage Antique Village in Islington (tube: Angel). Strike One clearly dates and prices each old clock; qualified horologists are on the premises to advise on repairs, and every clock is guaranteed for a year against faulty workmanship. A wide selection of clocks is displayed, ranging from Victorian dial clocks to early English long-case. Strike One specializes in Act of Parliament clocks. The shop is owned by John Mighell, a former mining executive who loved clocks more than his job. He gave up his business more than a decade ago to found Strike One. The shop is open daily, except Sunday, from 9 a.m. to 5 p.m. (9 a.m. to 6:30 p.m. on Saturday).

CONTEMPORARY ART: Christie's Contemporary Art, 8 Dover St., W.1 (tel. 499-3701), offers original etchings and lithographs, landscapes, and other works by up-and-coming artists for around £30 ($69) to £50 ($115). You will certainly not end up with an absolute "pup," and your holiday purchase may turn out to be a first work of a second Picasso. The gallery also has the works of such masters as Henry Moore and John Piper. Each work is an authentic original, numbered and signed by the artist, then stamped with Christie's seal of authentication before delivery. You can send for a catalogue or just go along.

COVENT GARDEN ENTERPRISE: What will happen to Covent Garden? This area is developing fast. In the Central Market Building an impressive array of shops, pubs, and other attractions will be opening. Judging from the already-existing enterprises in the area, the new Covent Garden will prove exciting for the visitor. After all, who would expect to find in central London a kite shop?

The **British Crafts Center,** 43 Earlham St., Covent Garden (tel. 836-6993), is a gallery and display center promoting the best of British crafts through exhibitions, information, and events. Many of the leading crafts people in Britain exhibit their work through the center, much of which is for sale. A program of changing exhibitions attempts to cover all the craft disciplines and their various applications, with the emphasis on contemporary original and professional work. The exhibition program is complemented by a smaller display area with a range of work changed each month. The ceramics, glass, jewelry, leather, metal, silver, textiles, and wood shown in the center have an appeal for the serious collector of fine crafts through to the person wanting an individual gift for a friend. Information is available about craft organizations, galleries, and studios throughout Britain. The center is open Monday to Friday 10 a.m. to 5:30 p.m., on Saturday from 10 a.m. to 4 p.m.

The **Covent Garden Information Centre,** run by the Greater London Council, is at 1-4 King St., and will give information about the local whereabouts of any particular craft (such as Indian crafts and saris, batik lengths, beads, and shell necklaces, sandals, handbags, and wooden and cane goods).

The following are places which have caught our interest.

The **Covent Garden General Store,** 1 Neal St., W.C.2, offers a conglomeration of household items, ranging from pots, pans, glass and china, cups, mugs, money boxes, packing boxes, walking sticks, handbags, and shopping bags. It's ideal for browsing to find that odd souvenir which will have some use. Prices range from a few pence to several pounds, and they also sell herb teas, sea salt, spices and country jam, as well as natural soaps.

At 21 Neal St., W.C.2, the **Natural Shoes Store** sells all manner of footware from thong sandals to climbing boots made of natural leather.

The **Neal Street Shop,** 29 Neal St., W.C.2, sells herbal and traditional soaps, artificial flowers, cookery books, which jostle with pottery, baskets, glassware, chinoiserie, and Victoriana.

The Warehouse, 39 Neal St., W.C.2, specializes in beads and stones, providing the fittings, clasps, and strings to make necklaces and earrings.

Guy Norris, Ltd., 47 Neal St., W.C.2, boasts 2000 square feet of classical discs, and also has loads of jazz. All records are discounted, and also offered are boxed sets, rare singles, and imported LPs.

Naturally British, 13 New Row, W.C.2, specializes in items made in Britain, including handmade pottery from Devon and Cornwall, tweed and knitwear from Scotland, leather goods, wrought-iron work, and carved woodwork. A perfectly carved rocking horse will cost upward of £350 ($805), but a three-dimensional jigsaw puzzle monkey, dog, or cat will go for only about £9 ($20.70).

The Glasshouse, 65 Long Acre, W.C.2, sells beautiful glass, and also invites visitors into the workshops to see the crafts people producing their wares.

Penhaligon's, 41 Wellington St., W.C.2, will blend a perfume to suit your taste for around £55 ($27.50), or else sell you an exclusive bath soap for £3 ($6.90) in their dark, gleaming shop where the air is heavy with exotic scents.

And **Robert White & Sons,** 25 Shelton St., W.C.2, will make you a full suit of armor to size for around £600 ($1380), or a miniature set with sword for about £80 ($184) on a stand three feet high. These are the people who make theatrical jewelry. In the workshop in Neal's Yard, they'll make you a fine copy of the crown jewels at a cost of £3500 ($8050).

Behind the Warehouse off Neal Street runs a narrow road leading to the already-mentioned **Neal's Yard,** a mews of warehouses which seem to retain some of the old London atmosphere. The open warehouses display such goods as vegetables, health foods, fresh-baked breads, cakes, sandwiches, and in an immaculate dairy, the largest variety of flavored cream cheeses you are likely to encounter.

At the top of Burleigh Street, off The Strand, beside the old Flower Market, is the **Covent Garden Flea Market.** This is a real browser's paradise, with its good, bad, and indifferent clothing, fruit, and vegetables—you name it. The stalls are mainly under cover, and stallholders range from the aristocratic through punk.

And **Coppershop,** 48 Neal St., W.C.2 (tel. 836-2984), is another one of the enthusiastic enterprises to blossom in the market, this one selling a wide range of English-manufactured copper goods. For the kitchen, you'll find jelly molds depicting rabbits, flowers, whatever, along with frying and omelet pans, plus more exotic sauté pans, pomme anna pans, and zabaglione pans. In addition to fish kettles, jardinières, and traditional coal scuttles, ideal as flower-pot holders, Coppershop has a wide range of other copper ornaments, lamps, miniatures, and watering cans. The shop is run by Sally and Michael Crosfield.

There are a multitude of tiny shops, mostly of a specialized nature, where artists and crafts people seem to have gathered to form a new community. In Bedfordbury, one of the tiny streets, Cherry Saltzer specializes in—not surprisingly—cats, in her shop called **Catz.** There are model cats, teapot cats, ashtray cats, cat calendars, cat badges, books, poster, and cat umbrellas. **Paradox,** in the same street, deals in unusual ceramics and pottery; and **Nubia,** 29 Bedfordbury, sells clothing and accessories from the '30s through the '60s. Elsewhere there are silversmiths, pewter, and copperware shops, and several small snackbars and restaurants. It's well worth making your own voyage of discovery and enjoy finding odd shops and souvenirs to take home.

While in the area, you might drop in at the **Rock Garden Theatre Co.**, corner of James Street and King Street, W.C.2 (tel. 240-3961), which offers live music in the evenings. American groups are sometimes featured, and sets are at 9:45 and 11 p.m. Admission is £1 ($2.30) or more, depending on the group. In addition, the company offers lunchtime theater at 1:15 p.m., tickets costing 85p ($1.96), with presentations lasting up to an hour, having high standards of acting and using new plays and entertainments. In the restaurant you can order ratatouille, £1 ($2.30); salad of cheese, fruit, and nuts, £3 ($6.90); spare ribs, £1.75 ($4.03). Various hamburgers with relishes and french fries go for around £2 ($4.60). The restaurant is open from noon to midnight.

DEPARTMENT STORES: Harrods, Brompton Road, at Knightsbridge, S.W.1, is the department store to end all department stores. As firmly entrenched in English life as Buckingham Palace and the Ascot Races, it is an elaborate emporium, at times as fascinating as a museum. In a magazine article about Harrods, a salesperson was quoted as saying: "It's more of a sort of way of life than a shop, really." Aside from the fashion department (including high-level tailoring and a "Way In" section for young people), you'll find such incongruous sections as a cathedral-ceilinged and arcaded meat market, even a funeral service. Harrods has everything: men's custom-tailored suits, tweed overcoats, cashmere or lambswool sweaters for both men and women, hand-stitched traveling bags, raincoats, mohair jackets, patterned ski sweaters, scarves of hand-woven Irish wool, pewter reproductions, a perfumery department, "lifetime" leather suitcases, pianos.

Much more economical, however, is **Selfridges,** on Oxford Street, W.1, one of the biggest department stores in Europe, with more than 550 divisions, selling everything from artificial flowers to groceries. The specialty shops are particularly enticing, with good buys in Irish linen, Wedgwood, leather goods, silver-plated goblets, cashmere and woolen scarves. There's also the Miss Selfridge Boutique, for the young or those who'd like to be. To help you travel light, the Export Bureau will air freight your purchases to anywhere in the world, completely tax free. On the ground floor, the London Tourist Board will help you find your way around London's sights with plenty of maps, tips, and friendly advice.

Liberty & Company Limited celebrated its centenary in 1975. In 100 years the store became known worldwide for its exquisite fabrics. One whole floor of the department store is devoted to fabrics of all kinds from all over the world, including Liberty printed cottons, silks, and pure wool. Liberty printed Tana lawn costs approximately £3.20 ($7.36) a meter, and Liberty printed silk around £10 ($23) a meter. Liberty printed silk squares in all sizes and colors, for both men and women, can be found in the country's largest scarf department. Twenty-seven-inch squares cost approximately £7 ($16.10).

Other exciting departments include treasures from the Orient, a wide range of modern furniture, an extensive furnishing fabric department, including Liberty's own fabrics and wallpapers, plus the best china and glass from all over the world.

Marks & Spencer has several branches in London, attracting the thrifty British, who get fine buys, especially in woolen goods. The main department store is at 458 Oxford St., W.1, three short blocks from Marble Arch. Cashmere sweaters for women are in the £25 ($57.50) to £30 ($69) range, women's suits from £30 ($69) to £45 ($103.50). Cashmere sweaters for men cost from £35 ($80.50) to £40 ($92), and men's suits go for around £50 ($115).

In addition, you might visit **British Home Stores**, on Oxford Street, W.1, near the Oxford Circus tube station, between John Princes Street and Holles Street. Similar to Marks & Spencer, it is patronized almost exclusively by the English themselves, and is known for its buys in woolens. Look for bargains. British Home Stores also operates next to the Marks & Spencer building on Kensington High Street, just a few minutes from the tube station.

THE WORLD'S MOST ELEGANT GROCERY STORE: Fortnum and Mason Ltd., 181 Piccadilly W.1 (tel. 734-8040), down the street from the Ritz, draws the carriage trade, the well-heeled dowager from Mayfair or Belgravia who comes seeking such tinned treasures as pâté de foie gras or a boar's head. She would never set foot in a regular grocery store, but Fortnum and Mason, with its swallow-tailed attendants, is no mere grocery store; it's a British tradition dating back to 1707. In fact, the establishment likes to think that Mr. Fortnum and Mr. Mason "created a union surpassed in its importance to the human race only by the meeting of Adam and Eve." In the Mezzanine Restaurant, you can mingle at lunch with the caviar and champagne shoppers. The "country cousin" (cheddar and cottage cheese blended with egg on brown bread) costs £2.80 ($6.44); a Danish pastry, 60p ($1.38). The pastries are calorie loaded, but divine. The chocolate and confectionery department is also on the mezzanine. The Fountain Restaurant has both store and street entrances (Jermyn Street), and is open from 9:30 a.m. until 11:30 p.m., Monday to Saturday, for the benefit of theater-goers. The St. James's Room Restaurant on the fourth floor is open during normal store hours. Two departments of interest are luxury goods, downstairs from the main shopping area, and an enchanting children's carousel on the second floor. Look for the Fortnum and Mason clock outside.

IRISH WARES: The **Irish Shop**, 11 Duke St., W.1 (tel. 935-1366), unites northern and southern Ireland by stocking so much stuff in such a small area. Directed by Charles Bruton and Anthony Tarrant, it is a useful place for those who missed buying souvenirs in Ireland. All products are genuine. Prices are reportedly as close to those you'd pay in Ireland as possible. Merchandise ranges from china to woolens, from "tea-cosies" to Celtic-designed jewelry set with precious stones, to Irish linen bedsheets. Waterford crystal comes in all styles and types. Belleek china and Gaelic coffee glasses—single or in a set—are also featured. You can purchase hand-woven tweed at £4.75 ($10.93) a yard, a 45″ and 45″ Irish linen tablecloth, hand-embroidered, will be yours for £26 ($59.80). As the jerseys are all hand-knitted, you have to rummage to find the exact one to suit your particular shape and size. Women's skirts and dresses in fine wool are offered as well. Duke Street is off Wigmore, a street running alongside Selfridges from Oxford Street.

Ireland House Shop Limited, 150–151 New Bond St., W.1 (tel. 493-6219), can eliminate a trip to Ireland, if you were planning to go there just to pick up some of those wonderful Irish tweeds. Opened in conjunction with the Irish Tourism Bureau, this colorful shop provides hand-loomed tweeds, as well as handmade apparel and accessories for both men and women. Some quality merchandise here includes Aran sweaters starting at £50 ($115); all-wool dresses, around £50, too; as well as blouses at £4.75 ($10.93) and jumpers at £21 ($48.30).

JEWELRY: **Gary Mark of London Ltd.**, 3 Station Approach Baker St., N.W.1 (tel. 935-3170), is a modern jewelry shop adjacent to Madame Tussaud's. Its owner, Gary M. Edelman, sells the latest designs in gold and silver jewelry from Paris, Amsterdam, Rome, and London as well, with many exclusive styles at reasonable prices. The shop has an excellent reputation for design and value for money, and is so patronized by people worldwide when visiting London, and by Londoners themselves, that it is open every day. The shop also carries Swiss watches and a wide collection of gifts.

Another Gary Mark store is at the Mount Royal Hotel, Bryanston Street, W.1 (tel. 491-8502), inside the hotel, specializing in a complete range of Swiss and Japanese watches in the latest designs of gold and silver at reasonable prices.

MEN'S CLOTHING—TRADITIONAL: Cassidy's, 114–116 King's Rd., S.W.3, presents the Old English look, but with a very up-to-date twist. Here for the young gentleman are velvet suits in almost every color under the sun, tweed jackets, ready-to-wear suits, sweaters, a wide choice of slacks, and a good collection of shirts. Cassidy's offers good variety at good prices.

MILITARY MINIATURES: Tradition, 5a Shepherd St., W.1, sells a bewildering array of military miniatures—perfect in every detail. You name it, Tradition makes it. It has a vast stock of French cavalry figures, all sorts of British soldiers from the Napoleonic Wars, U.S. Cavalrymen from the War of 1812 and the Civil War, to name but a few. What more fitting souvenir of London than a British Grenadier, a Beefeater, or a Chelsea Pensioner? The range is enormous, and the shop will sell you figures painted or unpainted, marching, running, firing, kneeling, even dying.

OLD MAPS: The Map House, 54 Beauchamp Pl., S.W.3, sells antique maps and engravings. The shop also has a vast selection of old prints of London and England, both in the original and in reproduction. It's an ideal place to find an offbeat souvenir of your visit. An original engraving, guaranteed genuinely more than 100 years old, can cost from as little as 75p ($1.73) to a massive £1400. The Map House is open from 9:45 a.m. to 5:45 p.m., Monday to Friday, and from 10:30 a.m. to 4 p.m. on Saturday.

County Hall, headquarters of the Greater London Council, is just across Westminster Bridge on the south side of the Thames. It houses the Greater London History Library which contains an extensive collection of books on London history, and topography and maps, prints, and photographs of the Greater London area from the 16th century to the present day. The library is open to the public for reference purposes between 9:15 a.m. and 5 p.m. Monday to Friday, and photocopies or photographs of most documents can be ordered. More than 40 lithographic reproductions of maps and prints are on sale in the bookshop adjoining County Hall, with prices ranging from 50p ($1.15) to £2.50 ($5.75). Incidentally, this shop contains the largest collection of books on London in London.

OLD SILVER AND PLATE: Stanley Leslie, 15 Beauchamp Pl., S.W.3, is a tiny shop stacked to the roof with a mass of mostly small old pieces of silver, plate, and pewter. It's just the place to spend hours ferreting around for a special present. It may look like junk, but the quality is very high—and it's amazing that Mr. Leslie knows what he's got there and how much is a fair price.

He's a lovely London character, hovering ready to help in his glasses and jeweler's apron.

RAINCOATS: The word **Burberry** (store at 18 Haymarket, S.W.1, near American Express, and at 165 Regent St., W.1), is synonymous with raincoats. Going far beyond the traditional designs that earned the firm a world-wide reputation, the store also features a wide range of apparel for both men and women. Don't think you'll get anything cheap. A Burberry will cost around £200 ($460) unless you're prepared to settle for a man-made fiber one at around £165 ($379.50).

SILVER: The **London Silver Vaults,** Chancery Lane, W.C.2, were established in Victoria's day (1882), and soon became the largest silver vaults in the world. You can actually go shopping in vault after vault for that special treasure. The vaults are open Monday to Friday from 9 a.m. to 5:30 p.m., on Saturday from 9 a.m. to 12:30 p.m. Closed on bank holiday weekends. Tube: Chancery Lane.

SOUVENIRS: The **Old Curiosity Shop,** 13-14 Portsmouth St., off Lincoln's Inn Fields, W.C.2, was used by Charles Dickens as the abode of Little Nell. One of the old Tudor buildings still remaining in London, dating from 1567, the shop crams every nook and cranny with general knickknackery, whatnots, china, silver, pewter, prints, and souvenirs—even Charles Dickens first editions. A popular item is an unframed silhouette of Little Nell's grandfather at 25p (58¢). Horse brasses go for £1.20 ($2.76), Old Curiosity Shop bookmarks cost only 10p (23¢), and ashtrays with Dickensian engravings are £1 ($2.30) to £2.50 ($5.75). The shop is open every day of the week, including Sunday and holidays.

SPORTS GOODS: Lillywhites Ltd., off Piccadilly Circus, S.W.1, has been around for more than a century, and some claim it's the most famous store in Europe. In times gone by, elegant Britishers came here for those tweedy things one wore on a fox hunt weekend. But Lillywhites has kept abreast of the times, and now offers everything for those ski weekends in Norway and Switzerland, as well as all types of athletic clothing, golf wear, country and sports shoes, not to mention tennis and scuba equipment.

STAFFORDSHIRE FIGURES: **Exhibition Galleries,** 4-12 Exhibition Rd., S.W.7, is an antique shop opposite the Contented Sole restaurant. It offers a mishmash of items—an unusually large collection of Staffordshire figures—at fair prices. The figures were once given by traveling peddlers as prizes. They were usually of well-known personalities of the period, and are items for serious collectors. The location is one minute from South Kensington Station.

STEAM ENGINE MINIATURES: Steam Age, 59 Cadogan St., S.W.3 (tel. 584-4357), is for steam engine buffs, and offers a rare selection of miniature, but accurately scaled, models of locomotives and stationary, marine, and traction engines permanently on display. They also stock a large range of steam fittings for model engineers. It's open Tuesday through Friday from 9:30 a.m. till 5:30 p.m., on Saturday from 9 a.m. till 1:30 p.m.

STREET MARKETS: Street markets have played an important part in the life of London. They are recommended not only for bric-a-brac but as a low-cost adventure. In fact, you don't have to buy a thing. But be warned—some of the stallkeepers are mighty convincing. Here are the best ones:

Portobello Road Market: This Saturday market is one of the city's most popular flea markets. Take the tube to Ladbroke Grove Station, then walk east. Here you'll enter a hurly-burly world where stall after stall selling curios may tempt you. Items include everything from the military uniforms worn by the Third Bavarian Lancers to English soul food. Some of the stallholders are antiquarians, with shops in fashionable Kensington, Belgravia, and Chelsea—and they know the price of everything. Feel free to bargain, however. A pastime is dropping in for a pint of ale at one of the Portobello pubs. The best time to visit is on a Saturday between 9 a.m. and 6 p.m.

New Caledonian Market: Commonly known as the **Bermondsey Market** because of its location, it's on Long Lane, commencing on the west at the Borough underground station. At its extreme east end, it begins at Tower Bridge Road. It is also approachable by a longer walk from the tube stop at Elephant and Castle. The stalls are well known, and many dealers come into London from the country. The market gets under way at 5 a.m.! This is even before the underground opens. Antiques and other items are generally lower in price than at Portobello Road and other street markets.

Petticoat Lane: On Sunday morning (go before noon), throngs of shoppers join the crowds on Petticoat Lane (also known as Middlesex Street, E.1). The lanes begin at the Liverpool Street Station on the Bishopsgate side. Here you can buy clothing, food, antiques, and plenty of junk.

Camden Passage: This antique bric-a-brac market in Islington, N.1 (in back of the Angel), northeast of Bloomsbury, is open all week—but the best time to visit is on Saturday market day. On all days, the emphasis is on paintings, antiques, and similar hard items. Prices are not inexpensive, but there are bargains to be found if you look carefully through the more than 50 shops and 20 boutiques. Take the tube to the Angel Station stop.

Church Street: Along Church Street, N.W.8, you'll have to search through a wide assortment of junk, but you'll often come across a great buy. There's a lot of secondhand furniture that won't fit under your airplane seat, but you'll find smaller purchases as well. Business is conducted Tuesday through Saturday from 8 a.m. to 6 p.m. (mornings only on Thursday); on Saturday there is more merchandise from which to select. North of Marble Arch, Church Street crosses Edgware Road, one street beyond Harrow Road, and is reached by taking the tube to either Edgware Road or Marylebone.

READERS' MARKET SUGGESTIONS: "**Leather Lane** is a daily market. The best time to go to this bustling street market is at noon, as the vendors begin to pack up at 2 p.m. A great variety of things is sold: carts bearing fruits, vegetables, books, men's shirts and sweaters, and women's clothing. There are no try-ons (obviously, because this is an outdoor market), so there is a certain amount of risk involved in buying clothing. Even if you don't buy anything, it is interesting to have a look around" (Linda Aminoff, Kew Gardens, N.Y.).... "If you want to visit a London street market, but won't be in town for Saturday's Portobello Road or Sunday's Petticoat Lane, there are three everyday markets within or close to the West End: **Shepherd's Bush,** between the Shepherd's Bush and Goldhawk Road stations of the Metropolitan Line (heavy on clothes and sundries); **The Cut,** behind Waterloo Station (small but fairly bustling in the morning); and **Berwick Street,** in the heart of Soho, which is heavy on fresh fruits and busiest around noon" (G. Berkowitz, DeKalb, Ill.).

STYLISH CLOTHING: Carnaby Street, just off Regent, is a legend, and legends take time to build. Often, by the time they are entrenched, fickle fashion has moved on elsewhere. Alas, Carnaby no longer dominates the world of pace-setting fashion. But the street is still visited by the curious, and some of its shops display lots of claptrap and quick quid merchandise. For value, style, and imagination in design, the **Chelsea** (King's Road) and **Kensington** boutiques have left Carnaby behind.

WELSH HANDICRAFTS: The **Welsh Craft Centre**, 36 Parliament St., S.W.1 (tel. 839-5056), is a gallery of things Welsh, ranging from hand-woven rugs, tapestries, and tweeds to Welsh loving spoons, brass miners' lamps, horse brasses, pottery, and stoneware. You can learn about the people and the history of the goods before buying at very genuine prices.

WOOLENS: See Harrods, where the standards are high. But for a specialty shop, **Estridge**, with stores at 61A Piccadilly, W.1, opposite the Ritz Hotel, and at 62 Regent St., next to the Cafe-Royal Grill Room, is a good choice (and it's not as expensive as one would judge from its location). Cashmere, camel's hair, shetlands, tartan kilts and skirts—Estridge is a virtual showcase of Scottish crafts. Good values are to be found in cashmere sweaters for around £35 ($80.50). Lambswool sweaters are around £17 ($39.10); shetland Fair Isle, £14 ($32.20). Authentic tartans cost £26 ($59.80). Cashmere and lambswool scarves sell for from £4 ($9.20).

READERS' SHOPPING SUGGESTIONS: "In London an outdoor (weather permitting) art show takes place on Saturday and Sunday on Piccadilly at Green Park (underground stop is Hyde Park or Green Park). The show extends for almost half a mile, and you can pick up good-quality drawings, watercolors, oils, and crafts" (Ray R. Conley).... "In London combine a Sunday afternoon outing at the Hyde Park Speakers' Corner with a stroll down Bayswater Road. Along the edge of the park, from Marble Arch for four blocks toward Lancaster Gate, stretches an outdoor art fair. Every possible type of art and craft is exhibited, from paintings on velvet to handmade pottery—and most at reasonable prices" (Phyllis and Steve Wilson, Chicago, Ill.).... "For those interested in posters, a visit to **London Transport Poster-Shop**, 280 Old Marylebone Rd., Griffin House, N.W.1 (tube: Edgware Road), is a must. Here you can choose out of hundreds of posters, at prices much lower than usual. Most are £2 ($4.60). As a special souvenir of London, for example, you might buy a map of the London Underground in its original size, as it is to be seen on every tube station, for £2.50 ($5.75). You can also buy books, souvenirs, and photos" (Rolf Hopke, Achim, West Germany).

"My husband and I want to add a suggestion about shopping for gifts that we found helpful on our trip to England. We restricted our buying to museum and cathedral shops. This is a good idea for several reasons. We found many wonderful people in these shops and learned a good deal about local history, their family backgrounds, and their historic ties. The items bought were well priced and quite lovely, e.g., note paper in the Jewish Museum in London; placemats and trivets in Warwick Castle; paperweights in the Ashmolean Museum at Oxford; and a facsimile of Wordsworth's 'Tintern Abbey' at the abbey. Also we felt that in making such purchases we contributed to the preservation of these sights and made it possible for other visitors to follow" (Henry and Gertrude Langsam, Malverne, N.Y.).

READER'S SUGGESTION: "The **London Brass Rubbing Centre** is at St. James's Church, Piccadilly, W.1 (tel. 437-6023), a two-minute walk from Piccadilly Circus. I visited it to discover a dozen or more young Americans who had walked by, seen the sign, and entered. For those parents who want to rest a bit while teenagers are vigorously occupied, and for those grownups who are interested in making their own brass rubbings at little expense, this center is ideal. Sixty exact copies of celebrated bronze portraits are ready for use. The center furnishes the paper, rubbing materials, and instruction on how to begin your own rubbing. There are also some books and pamphlets for sale on the subject. I did a bronze rubbing (gold on black) of a medieval knight about three feet high. The charges range from 40p (92¢) to £6.50 ($14.95). For those who become bitten by the bug, they also sell materials to take with you. There is a similar center in an annex to Westminster Abbey, with different bronzes. However, tourists flow through the large hall, and the general environment is much more distracting. I would strongly recommend the center at St. James's Church (in the basement) as an inexpensive way to pass several hours and obtain a personal work of art which would cost considerably more if purchased. Classical music plays all day for the 'rubbers.' Hours are from 10 a.m. to 6 p.m. Monday to Saturday; noon to 6 p.m. Sunday" (William A. Knowlton, West Springfield, N.H.).

Authors' Note: During the summer, from May to October inclusive, the center runs a second brass-rubbing center at All Hallows Church by the Tower of London. It is open from 11 a.m. to 5:45 p.m. Monday to Saturday, and from 12:30 to 5:45 p.m. on Sunday. The church itself has the finest brasses in London, and a special feature of the center is that it includes the only facsimiles of these great brasses. All Hallows Church has a little-known museum beneath it which displays the Roman pavement of the villa on which the church was built, together with many artifacts of the church's early history and its connections with Roman times, the Great Fire of London, the executions at the Tower, World War II, and other historic events. It's well worth visiting.

4. London After Dark

London is crammed with nighttime entertainment. You'll have a wide choice of action—from the dives of Soho to elegant clubs. So much depends on your taste, pocketbook, and even the time of year. Nowhere else will you find such a panorama of legitimate theaters, operas, concerts, gambling clubs, discos, vaudeville at Victorian music halls, striptease joints, jazz clubs, folk-music cafes, nightclubs, and ballrooms. For information about any of these events, ask a newsstand dealer for a copy of *What's on in London*.

THEATERS: The fame of the English theater has spread far and wide. In London, you'll have a chance to see it on its home ground. You may want to spend a classical evening with the National Theatre Company (formerly the Old Vic), or you may settle for a new play by Harold Pinter. You might even want to catch up on that Broadway musical you missed in New York, or else be an advance talent scout for next year's big Stateside hit.

You can either purchase your ticket from the theater's box office (the most recommended method), or else from a ticket agent, such as the one at the reservations desk of American Express (agent's fee charged, however). In a few theaters, you can reserve your spot in the gallery—the cheapest seats of all—but in some cases the inexpensive seats are sold only on the day of performance. This means that you'll have to buy your ticket earlier in the day, and—as you don't get a reserved seat—return about an hour before the performance and queue up for the best gallery seats. Occasionally you can enjoy a preshow staged by strolling performers called "buskers," next year's Chaplin—or last year's (the theater has its peaks and valleys).

If you want to see two shows in one day, you'll find that Wednesday, Thursday, and Saturday are always crammed with matinee performances. Many West End theaters begin their evening performances at 7:30.

Students and older people stand a chance of getting London theater tickets at half price under a new scheme which offers seats at nine of the British capital's most prominent theaters.

Ticket vouchers cost £2.50 ($5.75) and guarantee theater-goers at least a 50% discount off the regular ticket price. The vouchers must be picked up on the day of the performance, between 5 and 7 p.m., Monday through Friday, for evening shows, from noon to 2 p.m. for midweek matinees. The special box office is at the "Avenue" Ticket Office in the Queen's Theatre Foyer, on Shaftesbury Avenue, which leads out of Piccadilly Circus.

Of London's many theaters, these are particularly outstanding:

The **National Theatre**, a concrete cubist fortress—a three-theater complex that stands as a $32-million landmark beside the Waterloo Bridge on the south bank of the Thames. It was first suggested in 1848, and it took Parliament 101 years to pass a bill vowing government support. Flaring out like a fan, the most thrilling theater in this complex is the **Olivier**, named after Lord Laurence Olivier, its first director when the company was born in 1962. (Olivier was succeeded in 1973 by Peter Hall, who created the Royal Shakespeare Company.) The Olivier Theater bears a resemblance in miniature to an ancient Greek theater. It's an open-stage, 1160-seat theater which is intended primarily for the classics. The **Cottesloe** is a simple box theater for 400 people, offering experimental plays. Finally, the 890-seat **Lyttelton** is a traditional proscenium arch house that doesn't have one bad seat for any theater-goer. In the foyers there are two bookshops, eight bars, a restaurant, and five self-service buffets (some open all day except Sunday), and many outside terraces with river views. For everyone, with or without tickets for a play, there is live foyer music, free, before evening performances and Saturday matinees, and free exhibitions. The foyers are open 10 a.m. to 11 p.m. except Sunday. Also guided theater tours are available daily, including backstage areas, for about £1.25 ($2.88).

Tickets range from £2.80 ($6.44) to £6 ($13.80), but midweek matinees are cheaper. Group bookings can be arranged in advance. Credit cards are accepted. You can book through a travel agent or with the theater in advance, and some tickets are available on the day of performance at £2.80 ($6.44).

The National Theatre Restaurant will serve you a good meal for around £7 ($16.10), but at one of the coffee bars a snack will run around £1.90 ($4.37). If the weather is good, you can just sit and look out over the river and the London skyline spread before you. Tube: Waterloo Station.

The **Royal Shakespeare Company** has its famous theater in Stratford-upon-Avon and is also housed in the Aldwych Theatre, Aldwych, W.C.2 (tube to either Holborn or Temple; phone 836-6404 or Stratford 292-271). A program of new plays and Shakespearean and other classics is performed here. Plays run in repertoire and are presented two or three times a week each. The company also has two smaller theaters where new and experimental plays are performed as well as classics: **The Other Place**, in Stratford, and **The Warehouse**, near the Aldwych Theatre.

Royal Court Theatre, Sloane Square, S.W.1 (tel. 730-1745); tube to Sloane Square. The English Stage Society has operated this theater for more than two decades. The emphasis is on new playwrights (John Osborne got his start here with the 1956 production of *Look Back in Anger*). Also on the premises is the Theatre Upstairs, a large room without a proper stage, which was once the site of the famous nightclub run by Clement Freud. For the box office, phone 730-1745. Tickets in the main theater range in price from £1.50 ($3.45) to £3.50 ($8.05). At the Theatre Upstairs, the tickets go for £1.50 ($3.45) Monday to Wednesday, increasing to £2 ($4.60) from Thursday to Saturday.

The **Young Vic**, The Cut, Waterloo, S.E.1 (tel. 928-6363), aims primarily at the 15 to 25 age group, with some productions specifically for younger audiences. The Young Vic's repertoire includes such authors as Shakespeare, Ben Jonson, O'Casey and Pinter, as well as specially written new plays. Performances begin normally at 7:45 p.m. Seats cost an average of £1.40 ($3.22), plus VAT.

Sadler's Wells Theatre is on Rosebery Avenue, E.C.1 (tel. 837-1672). Apart from its resident company, Sadler's Wells Royal Ballet, it also plays host to other outstanding companies. Prices fluctuate from £1.50 ($3.45) to £9 ($20.70). Take the underground to Angel Station (Northern Line). The theater is a three-minute walk. Or you can go by bus direct from Piccadilly (no. 19 or 38); from Holborn (no. 19, 38, or 172); to the Angel (no. 30, 43, 73, 104, 214, 277, or 279); and from Waterloo (no. 171 or 188), and change at Holborn.

Many theaters will accept bookings by telephone if you give your name and American Express card number when you ring. Then all you have to do is go along before the performance to collect your tickets which will be sold at the theater price. All theater booking agencies charge a fee. Once confirmed, the booking will be charged to your account even if you don't use the tickets. Only card holders can collect the tickets charged to their accounts.

THEATER CLUBS: Besides the productions in the regular theaters, several theater clubs have been established, originally to avoid the censorship of the Lord Chamberlain, although that is no longer necessary. These clubs are where the most experimental and avant-garde productions are staged. By stopping by at their box offices and paying a nominal fee, you can become a temporary member. The clubs include the **Mountview Arts Centre** and **Mountview Theatre School,** with two theaters, the Mountview Theatre and the Judi Dench Theatre, both at 104 Crouch Hill, N.8 (tel. 340-5885), have been established for some 35 years. Sixty plays and musicals are presented annually, plus 30 films. Membership is free. Many courses are offered, mainly full time, although some evening parttime courses are also offered. Affiliated theaters include the New Arts Theatre Club in London, the Hampstead Theatre Club, and the Traverse Theatre Club, Edinburgh. Performances on weekday evenings begin at 8 p.m., on Sunday at 8 p.m. Matinees are at 2:30 p.m. There is no charge for seats, although donations are invited for the students' scholarship fund. Take the subway on the Piccadilly Line to Finsbury Park and then a W2 or W7 bus (terminus). The theater is on the main road.

The **Holland Park Court Theatre** is a charming open-air stage in Holland Park, W.8, close to the Commonwealth Institute. It really has the air of a court theater in some Renaissance palace yard. There is a weekly program in June and July of opera and drama. Concerts and chamber music are presented on Sunday evenings. Tickets are £2 ($4.60) Tuesday through Saturday, £1.75 ($4.03) on Sunday. Shows begin at 7:30 nightly, at 2:30 p.m. for Saturday matinees. The Dutch Garden is floodlit until midnight, and the theater is closed on Monday. For program inquiries, telephone 633-1707. Tube: Kensington High Street.

The **Almost Free Theatre** has finally been forced to abandon its "pay what you can afford" policy, although it is still "almost free" in the sense that it provides a vehicle for young and established actors, writers, and directors to try new ideas without financial pressures. Admission is currently £1 ($2.30), inclusive of membership (which is reciprocal with most other London fringe theaters). The Almost Free is currently operating "in exile" while its home theater is being rebuilt. Details can be obtained from Inter-Action by telephoning 267-9421.

MUSIC HALLS: Players, Villiers Street (formerly the famous Gatti's "Under the Arches"), W.C.2 (tel. 839-1134). Nowadays, the Players is a Victorian music hall variety club. Top-notch entertainers often perform here. The presentation is professionally staged, with the appropriate settings and costumes. The master of ceremonies, the chairman, asks members to introduce their guests, who stand for a bow (and comments). Insults are exchanged in jest, especially if a guest is from one of the "colonies."

You can enjoy the entire show, having drinks only, although it's best to make an entire evening of it, have dinner, and stay for the dancing session after the show. To do that, you can have a generous dinner, à la carte. Temporary membership is available for overseas members for £4 ($9.20) a week, £10 ($23) quarterly. It is essential that 48 hours elapse before a membership becomes valid. Incidentally, memberships must be paid in sterling. Application must be made in person. While members don't have to pay for a seat, guests are charged £2.30 ($5.29). Dinner is served in the restaurant from 6:45 p.m. (book a table ahead). The show starts nightly at 8:30. On Friday and Saturday nights, each member is limited to 11 guests. Performances are given every night, except Sunday, but check in advance by calling the box office. Tube: Charing Cross Station. (Directly across the street from the Players, incidentally, is a house with a plaque commemorating the fact that Rudyard Kipling lived there between 1889 and 1891.)

Cockney Cabaret and Music Hall, 18 Charing Cross Rd., W.C.2 (tel. 408-1001), recaptures the atmosphere of a Victorian music hall. At the whiskey and gin reception, you'll have the cockles of your heart warmed and learn about "mother's ruin" (large gins). The lively waiters and waitresses join the guests to sing along to the sounds of a honky-tonk piano. An East End meal, four courses of Cockney nosh, is served, along with unlimited beer and wine. Music to sing and dance to mark the evening. The show itself is divided into two parts, featuring cabaret with both production numbers and solo performances. Seven nights a week you can join in the revelry at a cost of £18 ($41.40) inclusive, plus a £1.50 supplement on Sunday, a £2.50 ($5.75) supplement on Saturday. The club is open from 8 p.m.

Aba Daba, 328 Gray's Inn Rd., W.C.1 (tel. 722-5395), near King's Cross underground station, is not a club, like the Players' Theatre, and its admission charges are £3.50 ($8.05) per person. In winter the club is especially popular, and reservations are suggested. The place is more like a pub than a supper club, although in addition to drinks from its well-stocked bar, you can also order typically British meals. Decorated in red, Aba Daba seats more than 100 guests at tiny tables. On show nights about half a dozen performers entertain, exchanging banter with members of the audience. This music hall presents shows on Thursday, Friday, and Saturday nights.

The **Pindar of Wakefield,** 328 Gray's Inn Rd., W.C.1 (tel. 722-5395 for bookings), perpetuates the convivial world of the Victorian music hall. Aided by tankards of foaming ale and authentic Cockney entertainment, the boisterous days of communal friendliness live on. As your chairman, the "garrulous glossarist" puts it, the Pindar is for "booze, ballads, and bonhomie," not to forget "bangers & mash and faggots." The admission charge is £3 ($6.90). In the pub you can order chicken, sausage, or scampi in the basket, at a cost ranging from £1.50 ($3.45) to £3 ($6.90). The show is billed as "a gargantuan garish gala gloriously gathered for your gracious gratifications." Usually six performers belt out tearjerkers, and you're given a song-sheet to help in the sing-alongs. Tube: King's Cross Station.

The **Rheingold Club,** Sedley Place at 361 Oxford St., W.1 (tel. 629-5343), has brought the old-world charm of an ancient Rhineland inn to the heart of Mayfair. Appropriately housed in a 100-year-old wine cellar, this nightspot provides a relaxed atmosphere where the strains of popular and Latin music are freely mingled with German drinking songs and Viennese waltzes. Wrought-iron lanterns cast a soft glow across Rhenish coats-of-arms, dark wooden beams, and historical copper etchings. Although celebrities frequently perform at the midnight cabaret, the patrons themselves are responsible for most of the entertainment.

The temporary membership you purchase at the entrance costs £4 ($9.20) for men and £3 ($6.90) for women, and entitles you to one free admission. The menu offers such wholesome German dishes as pickled knuckle of pork and sauerkraut served with pease pudding and boiled potatoes for £2.85 ($6.56). It also has a strong German draft beer at 50p ($1.15) for a half pint, and excellent German and French wines, from £3.50 ($8.05) for a simple qualitatswein to £7 ($16.10) for an Auslese. The Rheingold is open every night except Sunday from 7:30 p.m., closing at 1:30 a.m. on Monday and Tuesday, at 2 a.m. on Wednesday and Thursday, and remaining open until 2:30 a.m. on Friday and Saturday.

The Rheingold is also open for lunch between 12:30 and 3 p.m. Monday through Friday, and offers then a wider range of Western European (mainly German and French) dishes and an ample choice of hot and cold buffet meals. A three-course lunch starts from approximately £3.75 ($8.63), including taxes and cover charge. No membership is required for lunchtime visits.

NIGHTCLUBS: There are several kinds of nightclubs where you can eat or drink, be entertained, dance—even gamble. Most often these clubs are private—but don't turn away yet. To avoid the unpopular early closing hour of 11 p.m. for licensed public establishments, the private club has come into existence and may stay open till 3 and 4 a.m. In most cases, the clubs welcome overseas visitors, granting them a temporary membership—often for anywhere from £1 ($2.30) to £6.40 ($14.72) or more. Many clubs offer dinner, a show, and dancing from £10 ($23) to £20 ($46) per person, including entertainment. No visitor to London should be afraid to ask about membership in a private club. After all, most of the clubs are in business to make money and welcome foreign patronage.

For Dancing and Late-Night Suppers

Quaglino's Restaurant, 16 Bury St., S.W.1 (tel. 930-6767), is an established nighttime citadel, holding forth under the roof of the Hotel Quaglino. Haute cuisine suppers are served; two bands play nightly and there is a cabaret. Dinner is £14 ($32.20) Monday through Thursday, £15 ($34.50) on Friday and Saturday, from 7:30 p.m. Dancing starts at 8:30. The doors are open from 7:30 p.m. to 1:30 a.m. (on Saturday till 2 a.m.). Closed Sunday.

The Top Nightclubs

Churchills, 160 New Bond St., W.1 (tel. 493-2626), named after a certain prime minister, opened its doors at the end of World War II. The setting was auspicious: the town house of the Earl of Clarendon, who was a friend to Charles II. The building was the home of Emma, Lady Hamilton, Lord Nelson's friend. Eartha Kitt made her debut in London there. Time was when you could see Judy Garland or Frank Sinatra. Churchills remains one of London's leading clubs, run by the man with the handlebar mustache, Harry Meadows, who has, along with Paul Raymond, a talent for selecting some of the loveliest showgirls from Britain and the continent. He claims he is a gallon a day man—champagne, of course—a claim substantiated by many outside sources. You can see two spectacular floor shows nightly: at 11 p.m. and 1 a.m. You don't have to pay a membership, although there is a cover charge of £4 ($9.20). You can order a banquet for from £12 ($27.60) and up.

Eve, 189 Regent St., W.1 (tel. 734-0557), has long remained one of the leading supper clubs of London. There is continuous entertainment till 3:30 a.m. Lavish and spectacular floor shows are presented at 10:45 p.m., 12:30 a.m., and 1:45 a.m.—all different. Between shows a variety of musical talent, usually trios, performs. It's open Monday to Friday from 10 p.m. to 3:30 a.m. The restaurant serves a champagne supper until midnight, including the entrance fee, an apéritif, a three-course meal, a half bottle of champagne, brandy, and coffee for £20 ($46). All prices include VAT. Admittance is by membership only. There is an annual subscription of £5 ($11.50), but a special temporary membership for overseas visitors—valid for one night only—is granted for £1 ($2.30). The entrance fee is an additional £3 ($6.90).

Royal Roof, Royal Garden Hotel, Kensington High Street, W.8 (tel. 937-8000), is a sophisticated à la carte restaurant overlooking Hyde Park, the lights of Kensington and Knightsbridge, with a spectacular view of the West End skyline. In a candlelit atmosphere, you can order three-course dinners between £18 ($41.40) and £22 ($50.60), with a £4 ($9.20) entertainment charge. Joe Stein and the international Royal Roof violins serenade clientele at their tables, and a quartet plays for dancing as the night passes away. The roof is open Monday to Saturday, 8 p.m. to 2 a.m. Reservations are necessary.

L'Hirondelle, Swallow Street, W.1 (tel. 734-6666), is a small but popular nightspot just off Regent Street. The spectacular hour-long stage shows put together by producer Chris Daniel are performed in what appears to be an all-gold environment, complete with golden-colored wallpaper, accessories, and sparkling chandeliers to reflect the entire scene. The company of glamorous showgirls go skillfully through their routines in colorful—and often scanty—costumes with overwhelming headdresses. Singers and dancers add their talents to the hour of variety and music. Two bands assure you of constant music for dancing throughout the rest of the evening.

You'll pay a minimum charge of £5.75 ($13.23) if you don't dine here, but L'Hirondelle offers a very good three-course meal package for about £12 ($27.60), which allows you to choose from a number of items in each course. There's also a more expensive à la carte menu. Wines are expensive, ranging from £12 ($27.60) for the house wine. A service charge and VAT are added to the tab. The entire staff of L'Hirondelle is courteous and efficient, assuring you of an enjoyable evening of dining, dancing, and entertainment. The club is open from 7:30 p.m. to 3:45 a.m., and dancing is from 8 p.m. to two live bands. The floor shows are at 11 p.m. and at 1:30 a.m. It's closed Sunday.

Bouzouki and Plate Smashing

The **Elysse,** 13 Percy St., W.1 (tel. 636-4804), is for *Never on Sunday* devotees who like the reverberations of bouzouki and the smashing of plates. The domain of the Karegeorgis brothers—Michael, Ulysses, and the incomparable George—it offers hearty fun at moderate tabs. You can dance nightly (until 3 a.m.) to music by Greeks. At two different intervals (last one at 1 a.m.) a cabaret is provided, highlighted by brother George's altogether amusing act of balancing wine glasses (we'd hate to pay his breakage bill). You can book a table either on the ground floor or the second floor, but the Roof Garden is a magnet in summer. The food is good, too, including the house specialty, the classic moussaka, and the kebabs from the charcoal grill. Expect to pay about £15 ($34.50) for a complete meal, including a bottle of wine.

Clubs with Shows

The **Talk of the Town,** Hippodrome Corner of Leicester Square, W.C.2 (tel. 734-5051), is a popular nightspot choice, and has been since its opening in the autumn of 1958. The stage is big enough for the presentation of three big musicals—all at the same time. Pitched at those wanting to witness an extravaganza, with Rockette-type showgirls galore, it's a gimcrack theater-restaurant, sheltering about 750 on-the-towners who want a whole evening's entertainment for a comparatively low price. From Monday to Thursday, the cost per person is about £17 ($39.10), about £20 ($46) for Friday and Saturday splashes. Add 10% for service.

For this you get a three-course table d'hôte dinner (including coffee, but drink extra), followed by a floor show at 9:30 p.m. and later by dancing (three bands featured), plus the windup, the appearance at 11 p.m. of the headliner—often from the best of the international cabaret talent, but occasionally a local known exclusively within the British Isles.

Club Fantastic, 18 Charing Cross Rd., W.C.2 (tel. 408-1001), has been described as "exquisitely bizarre and very, very different." A semierotic revue, it doesn't have the nudity of Raymond's Revuebar, but it does offer enough flesh to provide mild titillation. Two shows are presented nightly Monday to Saturday, each one lasting 1½ hours and featuring exotic dance routines, comedy, and "specialty" acts. Arrive at 8:15 p.m. for the early show, 11 p.m. for the late show. At its opening the revue was choreographed by Molly Malloy, known for her work in Paris. The price for the show is £10.45 ($24.04), although you're charged a £2.50 ($5.75) supplement on Saturday. Drinks are available at bar prices.

A Theater Restaurant

The **London Room,** at the New London Centre, Parker Street, Drury Lane, W.1 (tel. 408-1001), is a theater restaurant set appropriately in the heart of London's theater district. The unique stage is fully automated with varying floor levels. This, combined with the circular arrangement of the dining area, guarantees every guest a perfect view of all the action. The productions are all elaborately staged, with spectacular sets, colorful costumes, and glamorous showgirls. Emcees present revues often focusing on the musicals for which the Drury Lane district is so famous. Each evening there's a "star time," when international and British celebrities perform. A cabaret begins each night at 10:30 p.m., and you can dance right up to closing time at 1 a.m. All this and the superb four-course dinner, consisting of seasonal specialties, will cost you about £20 ($46), plus a £1.50 ($2.45) supplement on Friday and Sunday, a £3 ($6.90) supplement on Saturday. Call in advance for reservations.

From Madrigal to Modern

Tiddy Dols, 2 Hertford St., W.1 (tel. 499-2357), is a cluster of five connected buildings in Mayfair's Shepherd Market. It's become one of London's hottest choices for dinner and entertainment, costing about £13 ($29.90) per head, including everything. The ground floor is restored and furnished in the Georgian manner, although the downstairs is more rustic, with exposed beams and brick walls. Women in period dress serve you with a personal flair. Tiddy Dols is open seven nights a week for dinner and entertainment, serving from 6 p.m. to 2 a.m. (noon to 3 p.m. for lunch Monday through Friday). The cuisine is old English, featuring such dishes as jugged hare, steak in a copper pot, beef Wellington, and the famous gingerbread from which the establishment takes its name. Tiddy Dols is named after an eccentric seller of gingerbread who attended May Fair in the 18th century, singing, "Tiddy ti-ti, tiddy tiddy dol!" as he sold the product of his special recipe, which the restaurant still makes today. Tiddy Dols also features Elizabethan minstrels playing early English music as they stroll through the many small dining rooms. After dinner you can listen to Victorian and more modern music in the bar and music room, and there is dancing every night from 11 until the restaurant closes at 3 a.m.

A Night in Covent Garden

The first club to open in Covent Garden is **Next Door,** 17 Russell St., W.C.2 (tel. 836-0303), next to Brahms and Liszt Wine Bar. It is open for lunch from noon to 2:30 p.m. and for a swinging evening from 7:30 p.m. to 3 a.m. There is a pianist at lunchtime, and disco evenings after dinner finishes at 1 a.m. to about 3 a.m. They claim 30 different cocktails, including Next Door's own at £2.75 ($6.33) (ingredients unknown). Happy Hour (drinks at almost half price) is from 6 to 8:30 p.m. The menu ranges from hamburger, salad, and french fries for £2.50 ($5.75) to rack of lamb or beef Stroganoff at £4.50 ($10.35). American chocolate fudge cake, fruit salad, and sorbets are among the desserts at around £1.25 ($2.88). You must add VAT and service to all bills. Club membership goes for £35 ($80.50) a year. They are open Monday to Friday for lunch, and Monday to Saturday evenings. Closed all day Sunday.

Mediaeval Feestes

Beefeater by the Tower of London, Ivory House, St. Katharine's Dock (tel. 408-1001), is housed in the historic vaults alongside the Thames where ivory was stored in days of yore. During the Napoleonic wars, the vaults served as a prison for captured French soldiers.

In this historic setting, Merrie Olde England comes alive every night from 8 p.m. to midnight in the form of an enormous, rollicking, medieval feast. When you first arrive, you'll be led down into the vaults where you're greeted by no less a personage than Henry VIII, surrounded by serving wenches, jester, and madrigal singers. In no time at all you'll be caught up in the spirit of the celebration and forget that these are actors playing the parts of characters who lived 400 years ago.

Entertainment begins at the reception, where you sip honeyed wine to the tune of a few fa-la-lahs and hey-nonny-noes, and continues between courses ("removes") during the meal. Your party will be led in procession to the long trestle tables, where you'll dine in typical Tudor fashion, using no utensils except a knife. The leader of each procession becomes the "head boy" who is host for the table, filling all the plates and calling for more bread or wine as necessary. If you are lucky enough to be chosen, you'll be given a tall white hat to mark your distinguished position.

The dinner consists of a five-course sumptuous feast, topped off by all the wine and ale you can drink. During the meal, the entertainment, in the forms of magicians, acrobats, and musicians continues. There's even a very believable duel between two knights. Be sure to hiss the villain! Dinner is followed by dancing. The cost for the entire evening of food, entertainment, and dancing comes to about £18 ($41.40) per person. There's a £1.50 ($3.45) supplement on Sunday, £2.50 ($5.75) on Saturday. Tube: Tower.

King Arthur's Court, Northumberland Avenue, off Trafalgar Square, W.C.2 (tel. 408-1001), is one of London's newest "medieval" night-out package operations. Well thought out and presented, the show is available seven nights a week from 8 p.m. on. A five-course "Round Table" banquet is served, and you can join the company of King Arthur and his Queen Guinevere, along with Merlin the magician, jesters, knights, musicians, and wenches. The cost, exclusive of drinks, is from £12 ($27.60), plus a £2.50 ($5.75) supplement on Saturday, a £1.50 ($3.45) supplement on Sunday. Tube: Trafalgar Square.

1502 A.D. Tudor Rooms, 80–81 St. Martin's Lane, W.C.2 (tel. 240-3978). If you want to eat, drink, and be merry, then this is the place to be. A sumptuous five-course feast awaits you in the true atmosphere of the Tudor period, with King Henry VIII, his queen Anne Boleyn, sister Mary Tudor, assorted strolling minstrels, and his majesty's dancing bear, all while being served by charming wenches. The banquet is made up of Olde English soups, pâté, Tudor chicken with Henry's pie, sirloin of beef or roasted lamb cutlets. Then for your dessert, enjoy syllibub, consisting of fresh fruit and cream flavored with wine and brandy. It's the fastest, most tuneful musical in London.

There's a star cabaret at 11 p.m., including belly dancers, jugglers, and comedians, followed by disco dancing from 12:30 a.m. to 2 a.m. The cost is £12 ($27.60) per person for the evening, or £15 ($34.50), including a bottle of wine or a carafe of mead, all rates including VAT. In the peak season, a surcharge is levied on Friday, Saturday, and Sunday nights in the amount of £1 ($2.30). The rooms are open from 8 p.m., Monday to Thursday, and from 7:30 p.m. on Friday, Saturday, and Sunday.

Additionally, King Henry's luncheon is now available Monday to Friday from noon to 3 p.m. At that time for £4 ($9.20), plus VAT, you can sample a 16th-century Olde English soupe, Tudor chicken, Henry's beef, kidney-and-mushroom pie, pork or sirloin, followed by a fruit trifle. From 3 to 5 p.m. the staff serves a traditional English tea with sandwiches and pastries in medieval surroundings.

A Scottish Fling

The **Caledonian,** Hanover Street, W.1, in Mayfair (tel. 408-1001), not only treats you to a "Tilt o' the Kilt," but fills you with a fine Scottish meal as well—all for £18 ($41.40). A supplement of £1.50 ($3.45) is levied on Sunday, £2.50 ($5.75) on Saturday. The atmosphere of the Highlands has been recreated in London—you're greeted by a Scottish host who offers a welcoming dram of whiskey, the kilted staff swirls, the bagpipes sound out their melodies. Your dinner begins with cock-a-leekie soup, which is followed by salmon "frae the river." Then you're given "haggis and a' the honours," followed by roasted succulent steak, garnished with "fruits o' the soil." Finally a trifle wi' sherry or guid Scots cheese wi' oatcakes rounds out the repast. The whiskey, by the way, is unlimited before the meal, and you're given all the wine you want during dinner. After the plates are swept away, the evening's entertainment begins, featuring Highland dancing, "the skills and nimbleness of Scottish feet." Kilts and sporrans for men are available for the evening. The club is open from 8 p.m. to midnight, including Sunday. Tube: Oxford Circus.

Eroticism in Soho

Raymond Revuebar Theatre, Walkers Court, Brewer Street, W.1 (tel. 734-1593), is a world center of erotic entertainment. The stage show, Festival of Erotica, is presented three times nightly, Sunday included, at 7, 9, and 11 p.m. There are licensed bars, and patrons can take their drinks into the theater. The price of admission is £6.50 ($14.95), and there is no membership fee. Whiskey is around 10p ($2.07) per large measure.

The **Gargoyle-Nell Gwynne,** 69–70 Dean St., W.1, entrance on Meard Street (tel. 437-2378), is a showcase for some of the most interesting and novel striptease acts in London. The show at the Nell Gwynne Club begins at 6 p.m. and runs until midnight. It is noted for the unique sensual routines and comedy striptease. Audience participation is also there, but the management likes to keep it subtle. A typical double-measure drink costs about £1.80 ($4.14). The entrance fee of £5 ($11.50), including VAT, also admits you to the Gargoyle Night Club, open from 10:30 p.m. until 3:30 a.m. In addition to its strip floor show, the Gargoyle offers drinks and moderately priced dinners.

THE DISCO: A firmly entrenched London institution, the disco is nevertheless as vulnerable as the Stone of Scone. Many of them open, enjoy a quick but fast-fading popularity, then close. Some possible favorites that may still be going strong upon your arrival are the following.

The **Marquee,** 90 Wardour St., W.1 (tel. 437-6630), is considered one of the best-known centers for rock in Europe. Its reputation goes back to the '50s, but it remains forever young, in touch with the sounds of the future. Famous groups such as the Stones played at the Marquee long before their names spread beyond the shores of England. Fortunately, you don't have to be a member— you just pay at the door. If you have a Student Union Card from any country, it will cost you less to enter. The entrance fees vary, but usually fall in the £1 ($2.30) to £2.50 ($5.75) range, depending on who is appearing. There's a coffee and a Coke bar for light snacks; those 18 or older can order hard drinks. Many well-known musicians frequent the place regularly on their nights off. The quite small and very crowded club is one of the few which features live music. Hours are from 7 to 11 p.m.

The **Chelsea Birds Nest,** 197 King's Rd., S.W.3 (tel. 352-9255), is one of the largest and most jam-packed of the disco-pubs of Chelsea. The DJ booth is a center pulpit dominating the dance floor. The entrance on Tuesday and Wednesday is 60p ($1.38) from 8:30 p.m. to midnight. On Thursday you pay £1.50 ($3.45) for admission from 9:30 p.m. to 2 a.m. On Friday and Saturday the charge is £1.50 ($3.45) up to 10 p.m., increasing to £2.50 ($5.75) thereafter (the pub is open to 2 a.m.). On Sunday, admission is free for the session from 8 to 10:30 p.m. Closed Monday. A pint of beer will cost 57p ($1.32), and lager goes for 62p ($1.43) a pint. Bar snacks and pizzas are in the 75p ($1.73) to £1.25 ($2.88) range. The **Six Bells** pub is reached by a separate front entrance and provides a quiet drink in old-fashioned surroundings. In summer, any night of the week, you may want to take your mug of lager and stroll out into the garden where you'll seemingly meet half the young guys and gals of London.

Tiffany's, 22 Shaftesbury Ave., W.1 (tel. 437-5012), is a leading disco in the theater district, featuring live groups and top-drawer DJs into the early hours. It is open nightly from 8, closing at 2 a.m. except on Friday and Saturday when it's open till 3 a.m. On Sunday the last record is played at midnight. The entrance fee ranges from £1.50 ($3.45) to £2.60 ($5.98), depending on the time of the week and the hour of the evening. Kinetic lighting is the craze here. Tiffany's is easy to find, within walking distance of Piccadilly Circus along Shaftesbury Avenue.

La Valbonne Club, 62 Kingly St., off Regent Street, W.1 (tel. 439-7242), is a crazily beautiful melange of disco, supper club, and fun fair, with a swimming pool thrown in for good measure. The place looks like a cross between a Mediterranean beach resort and Trader Vic's: bamboo roofbeams, Chinese lanterns, palm trees, tile flooring, armchairs around the heart-shaped pool, and "lovebird" waitresses serving drinks, dressed in white bikinis. There are four bars, one of them a straw hut, another a mock boat, a third a cave beneath a waterfall. Also there are taped soul music, an arcade with amusement machines, an outstanding dance floor, a continual slide or film show, and occasionally go-go girls dancing in the swimming pool. Full à la carte meals are served in the restaurant, from which you can watch all the action. This is certainly the most wildly versatile disco we've ever visited. No membership is required for out-of-town and overseas visitors. The cover charge is £2 ($4.60) for women, £3 ($6.90) for men. The club is in action Monday through Saturday from 9 p.m. to 3:30 a.m.

Samantha's, 3 New Burlington St., W.1 (tel. 734-6249), just off Regent Street, has been one of London's most popular discos and nightspots since it opened about two decades ago. The central feature of the club is, of course, the disco, with its sound and light system controlled by a disc jockey who has taken up residence inside an E-type Jaguar. Flashing colored lights and curved mirrors create a surrealistic setting for the endless parade of youthful, energetic dancers. Besides the two bars which flank the disco, Samantha's offers several other facilities for those who require a momentary escape from the hectic vibrations of the main dance floor.

"Samantha's Playroom" is the favorite gathering spot for pinball or pool enthusiasts. A second area of bars and a smaller dance floor with quieter music are set apart from the disco so that even the highest decibels do not penetrate. Upstairs is one of Samantha's newer creations, Sir Harry's Bar, where you can sip cocktails in a tropical atmosphere of cane furniture and animal skins. Admission to Samantha's is £2.50 ($5.75) per person, which gives you access to any part of the club. Drinks average about £1.20 ($2.76) but you'll pay more for the "super cocktails" in Sir Harry's.

Trafalgar, 200 King's Rd., S.W.3 (tel. 352-1072), in the heart of Chelsea, combines a pub atmosphere with sophisticated club-style entertainment. Weekday lunch hours are spiced up with entertainment by topless dancers and a disc jockey who plays disco music. Beginning at 7 p.m. Monday through Saturday, you can listen to live music, from soul to country to pop. The music lasts until 11 p.m. Jazz is played on Saturday at lunchtime. Good food is available at lunchtime and in the evening, and there's no admission charge for the entertainment. For a pint of draft beer, you pay 60p ($1.38). And of course you can always play the typical pub games, pool and darts.

JAZZ: Ronnie Scott's, 47 Frith St., W.1 (tel. 439-0747), has long been the citadel of modern jazz in Europe. Featured on almost every bill is an American band, often with a top-notch singer. The best English and American groups are booked. It's in the heart of Soho, a ten-minute walk from Piccadilly Circus via Shaftesbury Avenue, and worth an entire evening. You can not only saturate yourself in the best of jazz, but get reasonably priced drinks and dinners as well. There are three separate areas: the Main Room, the Upstairs Room, and the Downstairs Bar. You don't have to be a member, although you can join if you wish. The nightly entrance fee averages around £4 ($9.20) for members, £5 ($11.50) for nonmembers, depending on who is appearing. If you have a student ID you are granted considerable reductions on entrance fees, providing you come before 9:30 p.m., Monday through Thursday, without making a reservation beforehand. Drinks cost around 65p ($1.50) for whiskey. The Main Room is open Monday through Saturday from 8:30 p.m. to 3 a.m. You can either stand at the bar to watch the show or sit at a table, where you can order a three-course dinner for around £7 ($16.10). The Downstairs Bar is more intimate, a quiet rendezvous where you can meet and talk with the regulars, usually some of the world's most talented musicians. The Upstairs Room is a disco, with unusual sculptured foam seating, where you can either dance or drink. On most nights a live band is featured. Incidentally, if you bypass the other two floors, you can get in here at a reduced entrance fee of around £2 ($4.60).

The **100 Club,** 100 Oxford St., W.1 (tel. 636-0933), is a serious contender for the title of London's finest jazz center. The emphasis here is strictly on the music, which begins each evening at 7:30 p.m. and lasts until 11 p.m. or later. Membership in the club costs £3 ($6.90) per year, and admission is usually between £2 ($4.60) and £2.50 ($5.75). Without membership you'll pay an additional 50p ($1.15). On Thursday nights, West Indian reggae is presented, but jazz—all kinds of jazz—is performed on the other six nights. The scheduled performers vary every night, so you'll have to phone ahead for that evening's program. However, you're sure to see the cream of jazz at the 100 Club, including such bands as Ken Colyer's All Star Jazzmen, Brian White's Magnolia Jazz Band, and Mr. Acker Bilk and his Paramount Jazz Band. The club's menu features Chinese food. There's also a fully licensed bar, serving cocktails, wine, and beer. Tube: Tottenham Court Road.

A much cheaper way to hear jazz is at one of the many pubs in the West End offering it on certain nights of the week. Some charge admission; others allow you to listen for the price of your drink.

One of the best is the **White Hart,** 2 Drury Lane, off High Holborn, W.C.2. Said to be the oldest licensed pub in London, it traces its history back to its ancient site, the original White Hart dating from 1216. Imported sherries are available on draft, and carafe wines are sold by the glass. At the very edge of the Covent Garden area, the pub also offers a cold buffet. A different jazz group plays nightly between 8:45 and 11 p.m. Tube: Holborn.

The **Bull's Head,** Barnes Bridge, S.W.13 (tel. 876-5241), offers live jazz all week, with musical happenings that sometimes get very lively indeed. The modern jazz is said by many to be the best in town. Weekdays it attracts shoppers and fashion designers to its old English snackbar, which is a fine place to meet for lunch.

GAMBLING: You may be prepared to risk a "quid" or so under the steely eye of a croupier. The British are a sporting lot. Gambling is legal in their country, and they are out to go for broke—regardless of whether they can afford it. Visitors must register at the casino of their choice and then wait 48 hours before their membership becomes effective. In addition, visitors must register separately at each casino they wish to attend.

Ladbroke Park Towers Casino, 101 Knightsbridge, S.W.1 (tel. 235-6161), is open from 2 p.m. to 4 a.m. seven days a week. Life membership costs £25 ($57.50), and the usual 48 hours must elapse before you're considered a member. The decor is dark blue and rust, with paneling and soft lighting. This is not part of the Park Tower Hotel. The entrance is on Knightsbridge and totally separate, although the casino is beneath the tower of the hotel. Games offered are Punto Banco and blackjack, among others. A four-course meal is served during the evening, with wine, at a cost ranging from £15 ($34.50) per gambler.

International Sporting Club, Berkeley Square, W.1 (tel. 629-1657), right in the heart of elegant Mayfair, is an exciting casino, a combination of a private members' club and a top London nightspot. As you descend the stairway to the large bar, you're greeted by an attractive "International Girl." The membership fee is £3.50 ($8.05), which automatically entitles you to membership in the Palm Beach Casino. The restaurant serves an extensive à la carte European selection as well as a Middle Eastern menu. In addition to serving a weekday table d'hôte menu, it is open seven nights a week from 7 p.m. to 3:30 a.m. The club specializes in American roulette and blackjack, and is open for gaming from 2 p.m. until 4 a.m. each day except Saturday night and Sunday morning when gaming ceases at 3 a.m.

Palm Beach Casino Club, 30 Berkeley St., W.1 (tel. 493-6585), is the sister club to the International Sporting Club, and membership in one entitles you to visit the other as well. This casino has one of the largest gambling floors in Britain. It's laid out in the former grand ballroom of the May Fair Hotel and is cosmopolitan in style. For a membership fee of £3.50 ($8.05), you can participate in a wide variety of gaming from the popular French and American roulette to blackjack and Punto Banco. Gaming is available from 2 p.m. to 4 a.m. daily, except for Saturday night and Sunday morning when it ceases at 3 a.m. The elegant, elevated restaurant offers an extensive international menu, as well as a variety of popular Middle Eastern specialty dishes.

The **Sportsman Club**, 3 Tottenham Court Rd., W.1 (tel. 636-9622), is a favorite gathering spot for prominent personalities in the world of sports. You're likely to see players, trainers, and sportswriters alike meeting in the luxurious bar and Pavilion Lounge or in the Sportsman's Restaurant, renowned for its cuisine and high quality. The casino itself offers American roulette, blackjack, baccarat, and dice games during the evening hours. In the card rooms you can indulge in poker or kalooki. The club is open daily from 2 p.m. to 4 a.m., and admission is free to American visitors.

The **Victoria Sporting Club**, 150–162 Edgware Rd., W.2 (tel. 262-2467), north of Marble Arch, is one of the biggest, finest, and slickest gambling casinos—and it won't be expensive unless Lady Luck turns against you. No entrance fee is required, and there is no charge for overseas membership. Types of gambling include baccarat, blackjack, poker, roulette, chemin-de-fer, dice, gin rummy, and kalooki. There are two floors, restaurants, a small bar and lounge. The top floor is for poker and other card games. The club is open seven days a week, from 2 p.m. till 4 a.m. (Saturdays, 2 p.m. till 2 a.m.). Jackets are required after 6 p.m.; you can order drinks in the bar till 11 p.m.

CHESS: If you consider yourself a buff and wish to challenge the English or whomever, then Sunday from 10 a.m. to 10 p.m. is your time, and the venue is **Prompt Corner**, the Hampstead Restaurant, 1 South End Rd., N.W.3 (tel. 794-2846).

FOLK MUSIC: The 20th-century troubadour makes his way to a smoke-gets-in-your-eyes candlelit haven called the **Troubadour Coffee House**, 265 Old Brompton Rd., S.W.5 (tel. 373-1434). The Troubadour is open to nonmembers. At one time, this club was young at heart, a pacesetter in a new kind of unpretentious, natural entertainment. It still offers many happy nights to an attractive young crowd (if you can squeeze in).

You can dine upstairs, again if you can find a seat. From the ceiling hang musical instruments of every shape and size; the walls are covered with unusual trade signs of the Victorian era. Prices are quite reasonable: omelets for £1.10 ($2.53); spaghetti Bolognese, £1.40 ($3.22); and salads, 75p ($1.73).

FOR DANCING: Café de Paris, Coventry Street, off Piccadilly Circus (tel. 437-2036), W.1, is a legend. Once Robert Graves considered it a worthy subject for a book; the Duke of Windsor went there to see Noël Coward perform. Now part of the Mecca chain, it is elaborately decorated with chandeliers. Changing lights set the mood. Two bands alternate every night. Dancing is seven nights a week from 7:30 p.m. to 1 a.m. (later on weekends). Admission charges range from £1.75 ($4.03) to £3 ($6.90), but it's always cheaper before 9:30 p.m. and most expensive on Friday and Saturday. There's a reasonable three-course meal offered for about £6.50 ($14.95), a bottle of wine costing another £5.50 ($12.65). Cabaret shows, however, are no longer featured. A tea dance is staged seven days a week from 3 to 5:45 p.m. when guests dance to both live and recorded music.

A CULTURAL COMPLEX: In the old **Riverside Studios,** Crisp Road, Hammersmith, W.6, an enterprising young group has developed a complex of theaters and exhibition rooms where, under the directorship of Peter Gill, unknown and not-so-unknown artists can demonstrate their skills. In the film theater seasons of movies demonstrate the producer's art or that of the cameraman; visiting orchestras and dance teams perform nightly, and, in the restaurant, there is generally an exhibition of paintings or collages.

The restaurant is open from 11 a.m. to 11 p.m. Tuesday through Saturday, 12:30 to 11 p.m. on Sunday, and 11 a.m. to 6 p.m. on Monday, serving mostly homemade meals. A filling repast will cost about £2.50 ($5.75). The bar serves real ale among other beverages during licensing hours. Current programs are available throughout London, and the studios are well worth a visit, lying just a five-minute walk from Hammersmith underground station. Telephone the box office at 748-3354. Tickets for concerts, films, and plays cost about £3.50 ($8.05), but are increased on occasions when well-known performers appear.

VAUDEVILLE: This lives on in London on a grand scale.
Palladium, Argyle Street, W.1 (tel. 437-7373). World-famed for the best of vaudeville, it is equivalent to the former Palace in New York. Performers from America, the continent, and England can be seen here in acts that sometimes border on the spectacular. Seats normally range from around £2.50 ($5.75) to £8 ($18.40) for orchestra stalls, but it depends on who's appearing. Prices can go much higher. Tube: Oxford Circus.
Victoria Palace, Victoria Street, S.W. 1 (tel. 834-1317), near Victoria Station, presents comedy, variety, and light entertainment, all at popular prices.

EAST END DRAG PUBS: In the East End is a series of pubs offering entertainment nightly. Drag acts (female impersonators) are the chief form of amusement. The English, especially the Cockneys of the East End, love to giggle and scream over the caricatures of men satirizing women. Many female impersonator acts find their way into the posh West End clubs which many of our readers will find too expensive. However, talent without all the fancy trappings appears almost nightly in some of these Victorian pubs. You pay no admission, no cover, no minimum—one of the bargain entertainment values in London.

One of the best is the **Union Tavern,** 146 Camberwell New Road, S.E.5 (tel. 735-3605)—Oval tube or bus 36 from Marble Arch. Some of London's top drag artists perform here. You should arrive earlier to get a comfortable seat. The "ladies" tend to make for a hysterical night. Two of the favorites (by now all the habitués know their acts) are bejeweled, begowned, bewigged, even breasted—a couple of sex sirens who do mime recordings of stars. Hopefully, you'll hear their rendition of Shirley Temple in *Animal Crackers* or Carol

Channing in *Gentlemen Prefer Blondes*. A half pint of lager costs only 28p (64¢). Drag shows with gay disco or live groups are presented from 8 p.m. on Wednesday, Friday, and Saturday. There are also performances at 12:30 p.m. on Sunday and again at 8 p.m. The tavern closes nightly at 11 (at 10:30 on Sunday).

READER'S DRAG CLUB SUGGESTION: "I've often recommended two drag clubs to North American visitors. The **Black Cap**, 171 Camden High St., N.W.1 (tel. 485-1742), features a different drag act each night—some are hilarious, others grotesque, but it's excellent for a fun evening. The **Royal Vauxhall Tavern**, 372 Kennington Lane, S.E.11 (tel. 582-0833), lies on the south of the Thames, over the Vauxhall Bridge and near the Vauxhall tube station. It offers drag acts nightly—some of them original, some in pantomime to records. There's no cover charge—just the drinks you buy" (Howard Archer, London, England).

OPERA AND BALLET: London has treasures to offer the opera and ballet lover. The **Royal Opera House**, at Bow Street, is the center of the Royal Opera Company and the Royal Ballet. The Opera House advance box office, at 48 Floral St., is open from 10 a.m. to 7:30 p.m., Monday to Saturday (tel. 240-1066). A good seat can be had for £5.50 ($12.65), and sometimes one of the finest seats in the house will cost you no more than £11 ($25.30). Sixty-five rear amphitheater seats will be available for sale at 10 a.m. on the day of performance.

English National Opera, London Coliseum, St. Martin's Lane, W.C.2 (tel. 836-3161 for reservations; 240-5258 for credit-card booking and inquiries), is the state-supported opera company that performs in English and draws many enthusiastic audiences. Light operas are often included in the repertory, and tickets can cost as little as £2 ($4.60). These cheap seats are in the balcony and may be booked in advance, although a limited number are available on the day of the performance only. The average tourist may find the upper circle seats preferable, with prices ranging for most performances from £5 ($11.50).

The **D'Oyly Carte Company** has no permanent home in London or elsewhere. When in London, the company usually presents Gilbert and Sullivan operettas at Sadler's Wells Theatre. The rest of the time is spent touring the provinces. Theater booking agencies can provide up-to-date information. The company's office address is 261-3 East Block Savoy, W.C.2 (tel. 836-1533). At **Gilbert's House,** which is now run as a hotel and restaurant, Gilbert and Sullivan concerts are given every Sunday night during dinner. It is called Grim's Dyke Country Hotel, Old Redding, Harrow Weald, Middlesex.

CONCERTS: There are at least five major orchestras performing in London. They are: the London Philharmonic, the Royal Philharmonic, the BBC, the London Symphony, and the New Philharmonia.

These orchestras are to be heard mainly in the **Royal Festival Hall,** while in the adjoining **Queen Elizabeth Hall** and **Purcell Room** there are concerts of chamber music, lieder recitals, and poetry readings, among other presentations. In all, roughly 100 events take place each month in these three concert halls. Tube to Waterloo Station. Tickets are available from the Royal Festival Hall box office (tel. 928-3191), or the usual booking agents.

Royal Albert Hall, Kensington Gore, S.W.7 (tel. 589-8212). Acoustic improvements and other alterations have made this one of the world's finest auditoriums. The BBC Promenade Concerts are held here for eight weeks in summer. Throughout the year there are performances by top orchestras and artists, brass bands, and all manner of events ranging from covered court lawn tennis to the annual Royal British Legion Festival of Remembrance. Ticket prices vary according to the type of event.

Wigmore Hall, 36 Wigmore St., W.1 (tel. 935-2141). At this intimate auditorium, you'll hear excellent recitals and concerts. The singers and musicians of London often make their debuts here, and numerous international artists of renown also entertain. Many good seats are in the £1.75 ($4.03) range. A free list of the month's concerts is available from the hall. Tube: Bond Street and Oxford Circus.

At **Victoria Embankment Gardens,** adjacent to Charing Cross underground station, bands from Her Majesty's Guards and Regiments as well as the London Police and Fire Brigade give twice-daily concerts from late May to early September. Special concerts by visiting bands from high schools in the United States, Canada, and Australia are occasionally arranged between the regular concerts. Details of concert times and programs are displayed in the gardens. A charge is only made when a deck chair is used.

City of Westminster Arts Council, Marylebone Library, Marylebone Road, N.W.1, sponsors concerts, recitals, and exhibitions throughout the year. These are held in small and often little-known halls around the city. For current information, refer to the address above. The average entrance charge is around £1.50 ($3.45) and some promotions, such as exhibitions, are free. In most cases, payment is at the door, and no advance reservations are necessary. *What's On in Westminster* lists a wide range of such promotions. Free copies can be collected from the above address.

5. Taking the Tours

In addition to the sights you can see in London by foot, or by using the tubes, there are numerous attractions that can be reached via several inexpensive coach tours. As an added bonus, there are dozens of fascinating trips that can be made on the Thames.

EASIEST WAY TO SEE LONDON: For the first-timer, the quickest and most economical way to bring the big city into focus is to take a two-hour, 20-mile circular tour of the West End and The City, the **'Round London Sightseeing Tour,** which is offered by London Transport, the city's official bus company. The cost is £2 ($4.60) for adults, £1.30 ($2.99) for children under 16. Some journeys are by open-top buses. Tours pass virtually all the major places of interest in Central London. There is no guide. Passengers are given an illustrated diagram of the route, showing points of interest.

The one drawback is that seats cannot be reserved, but the buses run with great frequency every day (except Christmas). From March to October, tours are at hourly intervals from 10 a.m. to 8 p.m. (10 a.m. to 4 p.m. in the winter). The starting points for the tour are Piccadilly Circus, Marble Arch, and Victoria.

LONDON'S WEST END AND THE CITY: If you prefer a more detailed look at the city's sights, then **London Transport** offers two highly regarded conducted coach tours.

For a look at the West End, a three-hour tour is offered, passing Westminster Abbey (guided tour), Houses of Parliament, Horse Guards, Trafalgar Square, and Piccadilly Circus, including the changing of the guard. The tour starts at 10 a.m. every day except Sunday from mid-March to mid-October, and the fare is £5 ($11.50) for adults, £3.70 ($8.51) for children under 14.

London Transport's other popular three-hour tour is of The City, and includes guided trips to the Tower of London and St. Paul's Cathedral. The fare for this is £6.70 ($15.41) for adults, £4.60 ($10.58) for children. The tour is operated from March to October, leaving daily at 2 p.m. In summer the tour also leaves on Sunday.

These two tours are combined to form the London Day tour, which costs £12.70 ($29.21) for adults, £9.40 ($21.62) for children under 14, including lunch. The tour leaves at 10 a.m.

The tours begin at Victoria Coach Station, at the corner of Buckingham Palace Road and Elizabeth Street. To reserve seats, go to the London Transport Travel Information Offices at: St. James's Park, Piccadilly Circus, King's Cross, Euston, Oxford Circus, Charing Cross, or Victoria tube stations. Reservations cannot be made over the phone.

EVENING CRUISE TO GREENWICH: Thames Launches Limited offers a two-hour evening scenic cruise, leaving at 7:30 p.m. from Charing Cross pier on the Thames (tube to Embankment). The boat ride costs £1.75 ($4.03) round trip, and takes you on a cruise by the Houses of Parliament, Scott's *Discovery*, the Tower—all the way to Greenwich, where the last of the great clippers, *Cutty Sark*, is in drydock. The tour is operated May through September.

There's also a Disco Cruise, costing £6.95 ($15.98), including a free drink, a two-course buffet meal, and, of course, disco dancing while you drift past the sights. A dinner-dance cruise goes for £12.95 ($29.78), including your meal and a half bottle of wine. A luncheon cruise for £8.95 ($20.58) includes a three-course meal and a commentary on the famous landmarks of London's river. Telephone 870-6158 for further information and reservations for these three cruises.

A CANAL BOAT IN LITTLE VENICE: When you get tired of fighting the London traffic, you might want to come here and take a peaceful trip (1½ hours) aboard the traditionally painted Narrow Boat *Jason* and her butty boat *Serpens*. Come for lunch along the most picturesque part of the Regent's Canal in the heart of London. The boat is moored in Blomfield Road, just off Edgware Road in Maida Vale. Little Venice is the junction of two canals and was given its name by Lord Byron.

To inquire about bookings, including the Boatman's Basket Luncheon Trip, get in touch with **Jason's Trip,** Opp. No. 60 Blomfield Rd., Little Venice, W.9 (tel. 286-3428). Advance booking is essential during high season. If you come by tube, take the Bakerloo Line to Warwick Avenue. Face the church, turn left, and walk up Clifton Villas to the end and turn right (about two minutes). If you arrive early, you can browse around the shop which sells many brightly colored traditionally painted canal wares.

On the trip you'll pass through the long Maida Hill tunnel under Edgware Road, through Regent's Park, the Mosque, the Zoo, Lord Snowdon's Aviary, past the Pirate's Castle to Camden Lock and return to Little Venice. The season begins Good Friday and lasts through September. During April and May, the boats run at 2 and 4 p.m. In June, July, August, and September, there is an additional morning trip at 11, as well as trips at 2 and 4 p.m., but always telephone first. Refreshments are served on all trips, including a prebooked lunch on the 2 p.m. trip. The fare for a day trip is £1.25 ($2.88) for adults and 65p ($1.50) for children.

A DAY IN BELGIUM: Three times a day, from the terminal at British and Foreign Wharf, just by Tower Bridge, **P & O's Jet Ferry** leaves for the 3½-hour journey to Ostende. The jetfoil skims down the Thames, through the Pool of London, past Greenwich and the *Cutty Sark*, then out to sea for the short channel crossing, the only link between the heart of London and the continent. And what a wealth of history to see on the way.

On the early-morning flight at 8:15 a.m., a light continental breakfast is served. On the later services, 12:30 p.m. and 5:30 p.m., a light snack meal with salad will sustain you. Or you can just enjoy a duty-free drink in the comfort of your seat, taking in the view from the wide, spray-free windows.

Once landed at Ostende, a free coach link takes you to the railway station, and Bruges is only 30 minutes away by train. Visit the lace-makers on Peperstraat or just walk off the effects of a gargantuan lunch at the Hotel des Ducs de Bourgogne before returning on the 6 p.m. crossing and slipping up the Thames among the twinkling lights.

A day return ticket costs £41 ($94.30), £45 ($103.50) from July to September. Reservations should be made in advance with P. & O. Jet Ferries, British and Foreign Wharf, St. Katharine's Way, London E1 9LJ (tel. 488-0461). There are several very good small hotels and pensions in Bruges, among them the Pannenhuis, if you wish to stay overnight, and three services daily to bring you back again.

THE WORLD OF BREWING: At 226 Tower Bridge Rd., S.E.1 (tel. 403-1129), you can see how draft beer is made from yeast and hops. The museum contains a display of brewing tools and cooperage (the art of making barrels), and in the shop you can buy drayhorse brasses for £4 ($9.20), beer tankards for £1 ($2.30), or in copper for £8 ($18.40). Liquor measures are £10 ($23), and a Yard of Ale measure will set you back £9 ($20.70). More modestly, model inn signs, waiters' knives with corkscrew, T-shirts, and beermats go from around £1 ($2.30) to £3 ($6.90).

There are also tours, starting from the museum, of a traditional brewery and a modern bottling plant. The cost of £1 ($2.30) per person includes one free beer. You will be taken between the two factories by dray to see the total process from raw material to bottled product or, if you are a draft drinker, to barreled product. The museum is open from 10 a.m. to 5:30 p.m. Monday to Friday, on Saturday from 10:30 a.m. to 5:30 p.m., and on Sunday from 2 to 5:30 p.m.

OFFBEAT WALKS: J. W. Travel, 66 St. Michael's St., W.2 (tel. 262-9572). John Wittich, who owns J. W. Travel, started walking tours of London in 1960. He is a Freeman of the City of London and a member of two livery companies as well as having written six books on London walks. He is also director of the London History Fellowship. There is no better way to search out the unusual, the beautiful, and the historic, than to take a walking tour. The walks are conducted by guides who really know their business, and you don't need an advance booking. Tours take place whatever the weather. The cost is £1 ($2.30) for adults, 50p ($1.15) for students with ID cards, and free to children with adults. Some of the titles of the organized tours are "Steeple-chasing," "Dick Whittington," and "The Great Fire of London Walk."

Hunt for ghosts or walk in the steps of Jack the Ripper, the infamous East End murderer of prostitutes in the 1880s. Relive Britain's monarchist past by wandering through the Royal Parks and Belgravia, or discovering the relics of

Tudor London. Investigate the London of Dickens and Sherlock Holmes, or taste the delights of an evening's drinking in four historic pubs. These and many other walks (Roman London; 1660s: Great Plague and Great Fire; Dockland) are included in the program of unusual and historical walks organized by **London Walks,** 139 Conway Rd., Southgate, London N14 7BH (tel. 882-2763). Walks take place on weekends all through the year and during the week throughout the summer. The cost is £1 ($2.30) for adults; children under 16 go free. No booking is required. Get in touch with the above address for details.

Another small and enthusiastic company offering a vast variety of London walks is **Discovering London.** It's operated by a Scot, Alex Cobban, a historian of some note who insists that his guides are knowledgeable and sympathetic, and who, perhaps, looks at the London which the Londoners take for granted. Mainly on Sunday, but during the week as well, scheduled walks are planned, starting at easily found underground stations—to Dickens's London, Roman London, Sinister London, Ghosts of the City, Legal and Illegal London. Mr. Cobban's knowledge of Sherlock Holmes is immense. No advance booking is necessary, and the walks themselves cost 70p ($1.61); children under 16 go free, and students with ID cards are charged 50p ($1.15). Each walk takes about 1½ to 2 hours, except for the pub walks which usually are in the evening and last about three hours. At these you pay for whatever you wish to drink, and enjoy the pleasure of jostling at the bar with the locals. Write, enclosing an international reply coupon, for a detailed sheet of the walks available during your stay in London. The address is 11 Pennyfields, Warley, Brentwood, Essex CM14 5JP (tel. Brentwood 0277/213-704).

Theatreland Tours, 10 St. Martin's Ct., St. Martin's Lane, W.C.2 (tel. 836-8591), give you the exclusive opportunity to visit London's theaterland and to go backstage at a West End theater. After coffee at the Reception Centre at 10 St. Martin's Ct., off St. Martin's Lane, you leave in the company of an actor/guide on foot through Covent Garden and theaterland. You visit the city's oldest street, now the home of many of London's theatrical managers, as well as the Actors' Church with its many memorials to famous personages, including Ellen Terry.

The tour continues past many well-known theaters and pubs frequented by actors and theater managers, and also includes a visit to one of the theaters in the area, a behind-the-scenes preview. The tour finishes either with lunch at the Albery Theatre or with tea at the Waldorf Hotel. The cost is £7.50 ($17.25) per person, and the hours are from 10:30 a.m. to 2 p.m. The organizer is Josephine Burke.

TOURS FOR CHILDREN: Junior Jaunts, 4A William St., S.W.1 (tel. 235-4750), is a responsible organization which will take children over 12 years old off your hands for the entire day. The service provides tours for parties of no more than six children at a time to various points of interest in London. The small number in each group assures you that your child will be carefully supervised and that his or her interests will be taken into consideration. Tours range from a visit to the Regent Park Zoo to a trip to Buckingham Palace or the Tower of London to a museum tour which includes no less than six popular museums in London. Tours are flexible, and suggestions from the children are often incorporated into the activities. Tours cost from £15 ($34.50), and children are collected from their London hotel and returned to it.

6. One-Day Trips from London

It would be sad to leave England without ever having ventured into the countryside, at least for a day. The English are the greatest excursion travelers in the world, forever dipping into their own rural areas to discover ancient abbeys, 17th-century village lanes, shady woods for picnic lunches, and stately mansions. From London, it's possible to take advantage of countless tours—either by conducted coach, boat, or via a do-it-yourself method on bus or train. On many trips, you can combine two or more methods of transportation; for example, you can go to Windsor by boat and return by coach or train.

In this section, you'll find a sampling of what is available—but, first, some general tips.

DO-IT-YOURSELF: Many hidden sightseeing surprises are in store for the adventurous traveler who doesn't depend on guides and scheduled routes. And this is possible even if you don't rent a car. Several means of transportation are available: coach, train, or boat.

Highly recommended are the previously described Green Line Coaches, operated by London Country Bus Services. You can go to the Green Line Enquiry Office at Victoria (Eccleston Bridge) and pick up Green Line timetables giving specific details on routes.

For longer tours, say to Stratford-upon-Avon, you will find the trains much more convenient. Often you can take advantage of the many bargain tickets outlined in Chapter I. For further information about trains to a specific location, go to the British Rail offices at Lower Regent Street, off Piccadilly, S.W.1.

THE BRITAINSHRINKERS: This is a bonanza for travelers who want to make several quickie trips into the heart of England, without having to check out of their hotel room in London. Scheduled full-day tours are operated by Road 'n' Rail Tours Ltd. in cooperation with British Rail. You're whisked out of London by train to your destination, where you hop on a waiting bus to visit the various sights during the day. You have a light lunch in a local pub, and there is also free time to shop or explore. A guide accompanies the tour from London and back to London. Your return is in time for dinner or the theater. Included in the rates are entrance fees and VAT.

For more information, telephone 589-0156. It's possible to call this number, even on weekends, providing you do so before 4:30 p.m.

On one day trip, you can visit Warwick Castle, Stratford-upon-Avon, and Coventry Cathedral, at a cost of £18.30 ($42.09) for adults, £16.80 ($38.64) for children under 14. Overnight trips to the Lake District cost £67.50 ($155.25) for adults, £64.80 ($149.04) for children under 14. It's also possible to visit Devon and Cronwall on an overnight trip, at a cost of £68.50 ($157.55) for adults, £65.80 ($151.34) for children under 14. One of the most heavily booked tours is to Oxford and the Cotswolds, taking in Blenheim Palace, costing £17.40 ($40.02) for adults, £16 ($36.80) for children under 14.

It's better to write **Britainshrinkers**, 22 Hans Pl., London, S.W.1, than to get in touch with British Rail.

London Transport Tours

The official bus company, **London Transport**, take the lead in conducted coach tours to the places of interest in and around London. The coach tours are accompanied by an experienced guide, and they start from Victoria Coach

Station. It is necessary to reserve seats; this is done at the London Transport Travel Enquiry Offices at the St. James's Park, Piccadilly Circus, Oxford Circus, Victoria, King's Cross, and Euston underground stations.

An outstanding coach tour is offered to **Windsor Castle** and **Hampton Court Palace**, a half day's adventure that also includes Eton College, Runnymede, and the Kennedy Memorial. The tour departs daily at 10 a.m., getting back at 4:15 p.m. Adults pay £9.20 ($21.16); children under 14, £7.80 ($17.95). Rates include lunch and the admission charge to the State Apartments at Windsor. The tours are operated daily in summer and four times a week from October to March.

HAMPTON COURT: On the Thames, 13 miles west of London, this 16th-century palace of Cardinal Wolsey can teach us a lesson. Don't try to outdo your boss—particularly if he happens to be Henry VIII. The rich cardinal did just that. But the king had a lean and hungry eye. Wolsey, who eventually lost his fortune, power, and prestige, ended up giving his lavish palace to the Tudor monarch. In a stroke of oneupmanship, Henry took over, even outdoing the Wolsey embellishments. The Tudor additions included the Anne Boleyn gateway, with its 16th-century astronomical clock that even tells the high water mark at London Bridge. From Clock Court, you can see one of Henry's major contributions, the aptly named Great Hall, with its hammer-beam ceiling.

To judge from the movie *"A Man for All Seasons,"* Hampton Court had quite a retinue to feed. Cooking was done in the Great Kitchen, which may be visited today. Henry cavorted through the various apartments with his wives of the moment—everybody from Anne Boleyn to Catherine Parr (the latter reversed things and lived to bury her erstwhile spouse). Charles I was imprisoned at one time, and temporarily managed to escape his gaolers.

Although the palace enjoyed prestige and pomp in Elizabethan days, it owes much of its present look to William and Mary of Orange—or rather to Sir Christopher Wren. You can parade through the apartments today, filled as they are with porcelain, furniture, paintings, and tapestries. The King's Dressing Room is graced with some of the best art. In Queen Mary's closet, you'll find Pieter Brueghel the Elder's macabre *"Massacre of the Innocents."* Tintoretto and Titian deck the halls of the King's Drawing Room. Finally, be sure to inspect the Royal Chapel (Wolsey wouldn't recognize it). To confound yourself totally, you may want to get lost in the serpentine shrubbery Maze in the garden.

The State Apartments may be visited year round—April to September, weekdays from 9:30 a.m. to 6 p.m., on Sunday from 11 a.m. to 6 p.m.; October to March, weekdays from 9:30 a.m. to 5 p.m., on Sunday from 2 to 5 p.m. The admission is £1.20 ($2.76) for adults, 60p ($1.38) for children. The off-season admission is 60p ($1.38) for adults, 30p (69¢) for children. There is an extra charge for admission to any special exhibition held at the palace. Entrance to the Maze is 5p (12¢).

Frequent trains run from Waterloo to Hampton Court Station. To come by boat, apply to Thames Passenger Services, Westminster Pier, S.W.1 (tel. 01-930-0921). Or take bus 201, 206, 216, or 264 weekdays; 267 on Saturday and Sunday only. Green Line coaches 716, 716A, and 718 will deliver you to Hampton Court in about half an hour from London.

Where to Eat

After visiting the palace, lunch at **Bastians,** Hampton Court Road, in East Molesey, Surrey (tel. 977-6074), an attractive old building with a large stone-floored hall, roaring log fire, and comfortable chairs. Here you order an apéritif and select your meal. Then you go into the simple dining room or, in summer, into the tiny garden to eat al fresco.

The French menu includes such appetizers as moules marinières in season, £2 ($4.60) for an enormous platter, or else avocado mousse, £1.75 ($4.03). Main dishes include filet steak, £6 ($13.80); a whole small chicken, £3.50 ($8.05); and lamb cutlets in a light mustard sauce, £4 ($9.20). These courses are served with a delicious variety of sauces and well-cooked vegetables, depending on the season and availability. Desserts include crème brulée, sorbets, and chocolate mousse, and there is a good cheese board. A carafe of housewine costs £4 ($9.20), and there is a cover charge of 50p ($1.15). Prices include VAT but not the 12½% service charge. The restaurant is open Monday to Friday from 12:30 to 2:30 p.m. for lunch, Monday to Saturday from 7 to 10:45 p.m. for dinner (until 11:15 p.m. Saturday evenings).

KEW GARDENS: Nine miles southwest of central London at Kew, near Richmond, are the **Royal Botanic Gardens,** among the best known in Europe, containing thousands of varieties of plants. But Kew is no mere pleasure garden—rather, it is a vast scientific undertaking that happens to be beautiful. A pagoda, erected in 1761, represents the "flowering" of chinoiserie. One of the oddities of Kew is a Douglas fir flagstaff, more than 220 feet high. The Palm House, built in the heyday of Victoria by Decimus Burton, is replete with torrid temperatures and cannibalistic-looking vegetation—a sort of south of Pago Pago setting.

Much interest focuses on the red-brick **Kew Palace** (dubbed the Dutch House), a former residence of King George III and Queen Charlotte. It is reached by walking to the northern tip of the Broad Walk. Now a museum, it was built in 1631 and contains memorabilia of the reign of George III, along with a royal collection of furniture and paintings. It is open only from April to October, 11 a.m. to 5:30 p.m. daily (on Sunday from 2 to 6 p.m.). Admission is 40p (92¢) for adults, 20p (46¢) for children over 10. The gardens themselves may be visited from 10 a.m. to 8 p.m. in summer, to 4 p.m. in winter. Admission is 10p (23¢). Closed Christmas Day, New Year's Day, and May bank holiday.

At the gardens, **Queen Charlotte's Cottage** has been restored to its original splendor. Built in 1772, it is half-timbered and thatched. George III is believed to have been the architect. The house has been restored in great detail, including the original Hogarth prints which hung on the downstairs walls. The cottage is open on weekends and bank holidays. The least expensive and most convenient way to visit the gardens is to take the District Line subway to Kew. The most romantic way to come in summer is via a steamer from Westminster Bridge to Kew Pier.

GREENWICH: Greenwich Mean Time, of course, is the basis of standard time throughout most of the world, the zero point used in the reckoning of terrestrial longitudes since 1884. But Greenwich is also home of the Royal Naval College, the National Maritime Museum, and the Old Royal Observatory. In drydock at Greenwich Pier is the clipper ship *Cutty Sark,* as well as Sir Francis Chichester's *Gipsy Moth IV.*

174 □ DOLLARWISE GUIDE TO ENGLAND AND SCOTLAND

About four miles from The City, Greenwich is reached by a number of methods, and part of the fun of making the jaunt is getting there. Ideally, you'll arrive by boat, as Henry VIII preferred to do on one of his hunting expeditions. In summer, launches leave at regular intervals from either the Charing Cross or Westminster piers. Actually, Westminster is preferred, because the boats from Charing Cross are usually filled with tour group passengers. You can take the tube to New Cross, then buses 171a or 177. Buses 70 and 188 run from the Surrey Docks tube station. The boats leave daily to Greenwich every 20 minutes from 10 a.m. to 7 p.m., costing only £1.90 ($4.37) for adults, £1 ($2.30) for children for a return ticket.

Unquestionably, the *Cutty Sark*—last of the great clippers—holds the most interest, having been seen by millions. At the spot where the vessel is now berthed stood the Ship Inn in the 19th century (Victorians came here for whitebait dinners, as they did to the Trafalgar Tavern). Ordered built by Captain Jock Willis ("Old White Hat"), the clipper was launched in 1869 to sail the China tea trade route. It was named after the Witch Nannie in Robert Burns's *Tam o'Shanter* (note the figurehead). Yielding to the more efficient steamers, the *Cutty Sark* later was converted to a wool-clipper, plying the route between Australia and England. Before her retirement, she knew many owners, even different names, eventually coming to drydock at Cutty Sark Gardens, Greenwich Pier, S.E.10, in 1954. For 60p ($1.38) for adults, 30p (69¢) for children, the vessel may be boarded weekdays from 11 a.m. to 6 p.m., on Sunday from 2:30 to 6 p.m. It closes at 5 p.m. in winter.

A neighbor to the *Cutty Sark*—and also in drydock—is Sir Francis Chichester's *Gipsy Moth IV*, in which he circumnavigated the world in 1967. He single-handedly fought the elements in his vessel for 119 days. For 25p (58¢) you can go aboard (same hours as *Cutty Sark*). It's usually closed on Friday.

The **Royal Naval College** grew up on the site of the Tudor palace in which Henry VIII and Elizabeth I were born. William and Mary commissioned Wren to design the present buildings in 1695 to house naval pensioners, and these became the Royal Naval College in 1873. The buildings are a baroque masterpiece, in which the Painted Hall (by Thornhill 1708-27) and the chapel are outstanding. It is open to the public every day, except Thursday and Christmas, from 2:30 until 5 p.m.

The **National Maritime Museum,** built around Inigo Jones's 17th-century Palladian Queen's House, portrays Britain's maritime heritage. Actual craft, marine paintings, ship models, and scientific instruments are displayed, including the full-dress uniform coat that Lord Nelson wore at the Battle of Trafalgar. Other curiosities include the chronometer (or sea watch) used by Captain Cook when he made his Pacific explorations in the 1770s. The museum is open from 10 a.m. to 6 p.m. in summer and from 10 a.m. to 5 p.m. in winter (on Saturday from 10 a.m. to 6 p.m., on Sunday from 2:30 to 6 p.m. all year). It's closed Christmas Eve, Christmas Day, Boxing Day, New Year's Day, Good Friday, and May bank holiday. Admission is free. Just off the Navigation Room, in the west wing, is a licensed restaurant.

Eating in Greenwich

Trafalgar Tavern, Park Row, S.E.10 (tel. 858-2437), overlooks the Thames at Greenwich and is surrounded by many tourist attractions. Directly opposite the tavern is the Royal Naval College, and nearby are the *Cutty Sark*, the National Maritime Museum, Greenwich Royal Observatory, and the *Gypsy Moth IV*. The Trafalgar was mentioned by Charles Dickens in his book *Our Mutual Friend*, and was also the scene of the ministerial whitebait dinners.

Mr. Gladstone was a frequent visitor to the tavern. Nobility and gentry flocked down to Greenwich to dine at the Trafalgar on local whitebait, fresh out of the Thames, washed down with iced champagne.

Traditional English dishes and seafood specialties are featured. Many of the fish have never seen the Thames, and, consequently, dishes such as whitebait do not appear on table d'hôte menus, but only on the à la carte. To begin your meal, you can order deep-fried whitebait at £2.20 ($5.06). You might follow with Dover sole at £8.90 ($20.47) or else roast goose cooked in a cider sauce at £7.30 ($16.79). Also good is English lamb roasted with rosemary and carved at your table, £5.60 ($12.88).

In its most recent redecoration, the tavern retained all the original artist's designs, and it has many antique and historical pieces of naval equipment. All its rooms are named after famous sea admirals. For example, there is the Nelson Room, the Hardy and the Hawke and Howe Bars, the Duncan Room, also the Collingwood Room, and the Rodney and Hood Bars.

Lunch is served from noon to 2:30 p.m.; dinner, from 6:30 to 10:30 p.m. (only lunch is served on Sunday). If a visitor to the tavern wants only to eat a snack pub-grub type lunch, he or she can enjoy this in the Hawke and Howe Bar, or else come in simply for a drink.

The **Cutty Sark Free House,** Ballast Quay, Lassell Street, S.E.10 (tel. 858-3146), has plenty of local color on its Thames-side perch. About a half mile from the railway station, this English riverside tavern will dispense drinks in an atmosphere in which you can eavesdrop on the conversation of oldtime salts (head to the second floor for the Captain's Bar). At lunch and dinner, traditional English fare, such as whitebait suppers and English roast beef, is featured. Dinner costs around £8 ($18.40), exclusive of wine and service charge, and lunches go for around £5 ($11.50).

RUNNYMEDE: Two miles outside Windsor is the meadow on the south side of the Thames, in Surrey, where King John put his seal on the Great Charter. John may have signed the document up the river on a little island, but that's being technical. Today, Runnymede is also the site of the John F. Kennedy Memorial, one acre of English ground given to the United States by the people of Britain.

In accommodations, the **Runnymede Hotel,** Egham (tel. Egham 6171), stands in ten acres of landscaped grounds on the Thames, bordering the famous Mede. The setting, near the spot where King John signed the Magna Carta, is just 17 miles from the heart of London (Waterloo can be reached by fast train in about half an hour). The water-view garden hotel is newly built, but not blatantly contemporary, providing a clean-cut freshness, open-plan lounges, plus 90 well-equipped bedrooms, each with its own private bath or shower, renting for £28 ($64.40) nightly in a single, £36 ($82.80) in a double, a full English breakfast and VAT included.

English and continental cuisines are served in the River Room which is built on two levels, giving every table a view of the garden and river. Music for dancing is played nightly except Sunday. Live jazz and folk music are heard in the Magna Carta Bar. A hot and cold buffet is served in this same bar every day for lunch. At night the Anglers Bar is one of the most attractive along the Thames.

SYON PARK: Just nine miles from Piccadilly Circus, on 55 acres of the Duke of Northumberland's Thames-side estate, is one of the most beautiful spots in all of Great Britain. There's always something in bloom. Called "The Showplace of the Nation in a Great English Garden," Syon Park was opened to the public in 1968. A nation of green-thumbed gardeners is dazzled here, and the park is also educational, showing amateurs how to get the most out of their small gardens. The vast flower- and plant-studded acreage betrays the influence of "Capability" Brown, who laid out the grounds in the 18th century.

Particular highlights include a six-acre rose garden—12,000 plants in 500 varieties—and the Great Conservatory, one of the earliest and most famous buildings of its type, housing everything from cacti to fuchsias. In it is also housed a walk-through aviary full of exotic and brilliantly colored tanagers and hummingbirds. In the old dairy you will find an interesting seawater aquarium. There is a quarter-mile-long ornamental lake studded with waterlilies and silhouetted by cypresses and willows, even a huge gardening supermarket and a doll museum.

Operated by the Gardening Center Limited, Syon was the site of the first botanical garden in England, created by the father of English botany, Dr. William Turner. Trees include a huge black walnut from North America planted in 1740; a 200-year-old Chinese juniper; an Afghan ash; an Indian bean tree; and a "Liquidambar." The gardens are open all the year (except for Christmas and Boxing Day). The gates open at 10 a.m. and close at 6 p.m. In winter, after October 31, gates close at 4 p.m. Admission is 70p ($1.61) for adults, 35p (81¢) for children.

On the grounds is **Syon House,** built in 1547, the original structure incorporated into the Duke of Northumberland's present home. The house was later remade to the specifications of the first Duke of Northumberland in 1766. The battlemented facade is that of the original Tudor mansion, but the interior is from the 18th century, the design of Robert Adam. Basil Taylor said of the interior feeling: "You're almost in the middle of a jewel box." In the Middle Ages, Syon was a monastery, later suppressed by Henry VIII. Katharine Howard, the king's fifth wife, was imprisoned in the house before her scheduled beheading in 1542. The house may be visited from noon to 5 p.m. from Good Friday until the end of September. (It is closed every other Friday but Good Friday, and every Saturday, because the duke is in residence during the summer. Adults can purchase a combined ticket to the park and house at a cost of £1.20 ($2.76), and children are charged 60p ($1.38). For the park alone, adults pay 70p ($1.61); children, 60p ($1.38). There is a restaurant for light meals and snacks.

Chapter V

WINDSOR, OXFORD, AND THE HOME COUNTIES

**1. Windsor
2. Oxford
3. Hertfordshire
4. Buckinghamshire
5. Bedfordshire**

WITHIN EASY REACH of London, the Thames Valley and the Chilterns are a history-rich part of London, and they lie so close to the capital they can be easily reached by automobile or Green Line coach. You can explore here during the day and return in time to see a show in the West End.

Here are some of the most-visited historic sites in England: the former homes of Disraeli and Elizabeth I, the estate of the Duke of Bedford, and, of course, Windsor Castle, 22 miles from London, one of the most famous castles in Europe and the most popular day trip for those visitors venturing out of London for the first time.

Of course, your principal reason for coming to Oxfordshire, our second goal, is to explore the university city of Oxford, about an hour's drive from London. But Oxford is not the only attraction in the county, as you'll soon discover as you make your way through Henley-on-Thames. The shire is a land of great mansions, old churches of widely varying architectural styles, and rolling farmland.

In a sense, Oxfordshire is a kind of buffer zone between the easy living in the southern towns and the industrialized cities of the heartland. In the southeast are the chalky Chilterns, and in the west you'll be moving toward the wool towns of the Cotswolds. In fact, Burford, an unspoiled medieval town, lying west of Oxford, is one of the traditional gateways of the Cotswolds (dealt with in a later chapter). The Upper Thames winds its way across the southern parts of the county.

The "Home Counties" are characterized by their river valleys and gentle hills. The beech-clad Chiltern Hills are at their most beautiful in spring and fall. This 40-mile chalk ridge extends in an arc from the Thames Valley to the old Roman city of St. Albans in Hertfordshire. The whole region is popular for boating holidays, as it contains a 200-mile network of canals.

1. Windsor

If you hop aboard a 701 or 704 Green Line coach at Victoria Station, you'll be delivered in little more than an hour to Windsor, site of England's greatest castle and its most famous boys' school.

You can also take an express nonstop bus (no. 700). Before 9 a.m., the single fare is £1.20 ($2.76), although you'll pay £1.55 ($3.57) to return.

Windsor was originally called "Windlesore" by the ancient Britons who derived the name from winding shore—so noticeable as you walk along the Thames here.

THE SIGHTS: Your bus will drop you near the Town Guildhall, to which Wren applied the finishing touches. It's only a short walk up Castle Hill to the following sights:

Windsor Castle

It was William the Conqueror who founded a castle on this spot, beginning a legend and a link with English sovereignty that has known many vicissitudes. King John cooled his heels at Windsor while waiting to put his signature on the Magna Carta at nearby Runnymede; Charles I was imprisoned here before losing his head; Queen Bess did some renovations; Victoria mourned her beloved Albert, who died at the castle in 1861; the royal family rode out much of World War II behind its sheltering walls. When Queen Elizabeth II and her entourage are at Windsor, a Royal Standard flies, which means the State Apartments are off limits then. Otherwise, they may be visited weekdays from 10:30 a.m. to 5 p.m. from March to October; 10:30 a.m. to 3 p.m. November to Febtuary; also on Sunday from 1:30 to 5 p.m. The price of admission is 60p ($1.38) for adults, 30p (69¢) for children. The apartments are closed for about six weeks at Easter and for around three weeks in June when the Queen and Philip come here for the Ascot races. The apartments themselves contain many works of art, porcelain, armor, furniture, three Verrio ceilings, and several Gibbons carvings from the 17th century. The world of Rubens adorns the King's Drawing Room and in his relatively small dressing room is a Dürer, along with Rembrandt's portrait of his mother, and Van Dyck's triple look at Charles I. Of the apartments themselves, the grand reception room, with its Gobelin tapestries, is the most spectacular.

The guard is changed daily at 10:30 a.m., except on Sunday. The Windsor changing of the guard is a much more exciting and moving experience, in our opinion, than the London exercises. In Windsor, the guard marches through the town, stopping the traffic as it wheels into the castle to the tune of a full regimental band when the court is in residence. When the Queen is not there, a drum and pipe band is mustered.

Old Master Drawings

The royal family possesses a rare collection at Windsor of drawings by old masters—notably Leonardo da Vinci. One Leonardo sketch, for example, shows a cat in 20 different positions; another is a study of a horse; still a third is that of Saint Matthew, a warmup for the head used in *The Last Supper*. In addition, you'll find sketches by William Blake, Thomas Rowlandson, and 12 Holbeins (don't miss his sketch of Sir John Godsalve). The drawing exhibition may be visited at the same time as the State Apartments for a 30p (69¢) for adults, 10p (23¢) for children admission. It remains open, unlike the State Apartments, when the Court is in residence.

WINDSOR 179

Queen Mary's Dollhouse

Just about the greatest dollhouse in all the world is at Windsor. Presented to the late Queen Mary as a gift, and later used to raise money for charity, the dollhouse is a remarkable achievement and recreation of what a great royal mansion of the 1920s looked like—complete with a fleet of cars, including a Rolls-Royce. The house is perfect for Tom Thumb and family, and a retinue of servants. All is done with the most exacting detail—even the champagne bottles in the wine cellar contain vintage wine of that era. There's a toothbrush suitable for an ant. A minuscule electric iron really works. For late-night reading, you'll find volumes ranging from Hardy to Housman. In addition, you'll see a collection of dolls presented to the monarchy from nearly every nation of the Commonwealth. The dollhouse may be viewed for an admission of 30p (69¢) for adults, 10p (23¢) for children, even when the State Apartments are closed.

St. George's Chapel

A gem of the Perpendicular style, this chapel shares the distinction with Westminster Abbey of being a pantheon of English monarchs (Victoria is a notable exception). The present St. George's was founded in the late 14th century by Edward IV on the site of the original Chapel of the Order of the Garter (Edward III, 1348). You enter the nave first with its fan vaulting (a remarkable achievement in English architecture). The nave contains the tomb of George V and Queen Mary, designed by Sir William Reid Dick. Off the nave in the Urswick Chapel, the Princess Charlotte memorial provides an ironic touch. If she had survived childbirth in 1817, she—and not her cousin, Victoria—would have ruled the British Empire. The Edward IV "Quire," with its imaginatively carved 15th-century choir stalls (crowned by lacy canopies and colorful Knights of the Garter banners), evokes the pomp and pageantry of medieval days. In the center is a flat tomb, containing the vault of the beheaded Charles I, along with Henry VIII and one of his wives (no. 3, Jane Seymour), Henry's tomb has long been stripped of its former embellishments. Finally, you may want to inspect the Prince Albert Memorial Chapel, reflecting the opulent taste of the era of Victoria. The chapel is closed during services, and it's advisable to telephone to check opening hours at other times (tel. Windsor 65538). The chapel is usually open from 10:45 a.m. to 3:45 p.m. Monday to Thursday, from 1 to 3:45 p.m. on Friday and Saturday, and from 2:15 to 3:45 p.m. on Sunday. The price of admission is 80p ($1.84) for adults, 30p (69¢) for children.

Footnote: Queen Victoria died on January 22, 1901, and was buried beside her beloved Prince Albert in a mausoleum at **Frogmore** (a private estate), near Windsor (open only three days a year, in May). The Prince Consort died in December 1861.

Sunday Entertainment

There are often polo matches in **Windsor Great Park**—and at Ham Common—and you may see Prince Charles playing and Prince Philip serving as umpire. The Queen herself often watches. For more information, telephone Windsor 60633.

The Town Itself

Windsor is largely a Victorian town, with lots of brick buildings and a few remnants of Georgian architecture. In and around the castle are two cobblestoned streets—**Church** and **Market**, with their antique shops, silversmiths, and pubs. One shop on Church Street was supposedly occupied by Nell Gwynne who needed to be within call of Charles II's chambers. After lunch or tea, you may want to stroll along the three-mile, aptly named Long Walk.

For our final sight, we cross over a bridge spanning the Thames.

STAYING OVER AT WINDSOR: If you don't have an engraved invitation to overnight at the castle, there's always room at one of the inns—except during Ascot Races and the Windsor Horse Show.

For those who decide to stay in Windsor and use it as a base for London sightseeing, trains run from Windsor Town Station and from Windsor and Eton Riverside Station to London. A second-class day return ticket costs £2.50 ($5.75), and trains leave London as late as 10:30 or 11 p.m., so it is quite easy to take in an early theater and dinner before returning to Windsor for overnight.

Alternatively, the **Windsor Theatre** has nightly performances of weekly productions. Run by John Counsel and his wife Mary Kerridge, this is one of the best repertory companies around London. Best seats are £4.60 ($10.58); the cheapest, 95p ($2.19).

The Upper Bracket

The **Old House Hotel** (tel. Windsor 61354) was designed and lived in by Christopher Wren in 1676. Between Eton and Windsor, the former town house occupies a prime position on the Thames, its gardens overlooking the swans and boats. The owners, Wren House Ltd., have maintained the beauty of the past, keeping the same architectural detail, furnishing the hotel with a collection of antiques. The central hall is impressive, with a Queen Anne black marble refectory table. Inviting is Wren's former study in apricot and white paneling, with his Empire desk, along with a fireplace and shield-back Hepplewhite chairs. Another area is a small apple-green salon, with linenfold walls, Tudor oak and chintz-covered chairs. The bay-windowed main drawing room, decorated with mirrors, sconces, and a formal marble fireplace, opens into a garden and a riverside flagstone terrace for after-dinner coffee and drinks. You can also drink in the Bamboo Room, ordering one of the specials, such as Planter's Punch.

All bedrooms have private baths. Singles range from £32.50 ($74.75) to £36.50 ($83.95); twins cost from £40 ($92) to £50 ($115). Most of the older and larger rooms have some select pieces of furniture. Some of the more recently built accommodations are compact, pleasantly decorated, and color coordinated. The food is among the best in Windsor (many nonresidents come in just to dine). Dinner is à la carte only, costing about £16 ($36.80) for two persons.

The Medium-Priced Range

Castle Hotel, High Street (tel. Windsor 51011), a small link in the Trust House Forte circuit, sits in a prominent position facing the Guildhall, across from the castle. Formerly a Georgian posting house, it enjoyed many prestigious visitors, such as second-string royal cousins, in its heyday in the 18th century. Nowadays, it's more likely to be patronized by parents visiting their sons at Eton. Its classic facade is a "parchment color." The interior may not contain the splendid furnishings of its former days, but the hotel is nevertheless comfortable and immaculate, with central heating throughout. A ballroom suite is its most attractive feature. All of the well-furnished rooms (new wing added) contain private baths, along with television and radio. A single room with bath rents for £28.50 ($65.55); it's £34 ($78.20) in a double with bath. Prices include tea- and coffee-making facilities, service charges, and VAT. Breakfast is extra.

Harte and Garter Hotel. High Street (tel. Windsor 63426), stands right opposite the castle, beside the Castle Hotel. Modest rooms are simply furnished; some have private baths and all have tea- or coffee-making facilities, radios, TV sets; and the daily newspaper is brought to you free. Singles rent from £15 ($34.50) to £22 ($50.60), doubles from £26 ($59.80) to £31 ($71.30), including VAT and a full English breakfast. The four grill rooms serve a ten-ounce rump steak with garnish at £5 ($11.50), a mixed grill at £5 also, or scampi with peas and jacket potato at £4 ($9.20).

Royal Adelaide Hotel, Kings Road (tel. Windsor 63916), is opposite the famous Long Walk leading to Windsor Castle. An old Victorian hotel, it offers single rooms from £14 ($32.20) to £19 ($43.70), and doubles from £22 ($50.60) to £26 ($59.80), including a continental breakfast and service. There is good car parking at the rear for guests, and the hotel is warm and well furnished. The staff, used to a quick turnover of guests, may be a little offhand. A set lunch or dinner is available at £5 ($11.50) for a three-course meal. Some of the rooms have private bathrooms, but there are adequate public facilities.

LUNCH AT WINDSOR: For lunch in Windsor, try the **William IV Hotel,** Thames Street, 100 yards from Eton Bridge (tel. Windsor 51004). This lovely old place (circa 1500) with its armor, beams, and log fire, invites visitors in with its friendly and local atmosphere. Just outside is the Chapter garden where the Windsor martyrs were burned at the stake in 1544 for their religious beliefs. It was from this inn that they received their last cups of strong ale "in gratification of their last wish." The house built by Sir Christopher Wren for his own use is opposite the William IV, and the great architect of St. Paul's was reputedly a regular visitor to the old tap room, as were diarists Evelyn and Pepys. The present landlord is Ken Gardner, award-winning journalist and writer. Rub shoulders here with newspaper people and actors (nearby is the Theatre Royal), artists and rivermen, and drink traditional ale which is still pulled by old-fashioned beer engines.

The food is home cooked, and the portions are guaranteed to satisfy gargantuan appetites. Scottish beef is served by two motherly locals, Lottie and Gert, who are quick and accurate. Try a steak or one of the house regional specials. A three-course luncheon costs £3.50 ($8.05), and might consist of soup, followed by a roast topside of beef with Yorkshire pudding, served with a selection of vegetables, and followed by a homemade apple pie with cream. In the evening you might prefer a sirloin steak with potatoes and peas at a cost of £3.20 ($7.36), or perhaps fried scampi at £1.80 ($4.14). Bar meals are also available. You can sit at sidewalk tables in a pedestrian area by the Eton Bridge, gazing up at the castle while enjoying lunch. The William IV lies at the bottom of Windsor Hill on the approach road to the bridge, which is now open to pedestrians only.

The house also rents out three double bedrooms, one with shower, charging £7.50 ($17.25) for single occupancy, from £16 ($36.80) to £19 ($43.70) for two persons, these tariffs including a good English breakfast.

For those to whom a town is not a town without its Chinese restaurant, Windsor offers **Windsor's Peking,** 14 High St. (tel. Windsor 66217). Downstairs is a small disco and bar. Upstairs, the restaurant specializes in Peking dishes. They have three set dinners at £6.15 ($14.15), £6.75 ($15.53), and £8 ($18.40) per person. Poultry and meat dishes include shredded beef with onion, grilled pork Peking style, and sliced duck with mushrooms at £2.50 ($5.75) each. The specialty is barbecued Peking duck for £12 ($27.60). Peter Lam and his staff are very friendly and knowledgeable about the dishes. The restaurant is open daily from noon to 2:30 p.m. and from 6 to 11:30 p.m., on Sunday from noon until 11:30 p.m.

The **Ship Hotel,** Church Lane (tel. Windsor 64257), is a pub that is quite popular with the locals. Publican Geoff Holmberg looks after the lager, and Mrs. Holmberg is famous in these parts for her farmhouse pie. Only pub lunches are served. For that main dish, plus soup, a salad, and vegetables, even homemade apple pie, the charge is £3 ($6.90) per head. Or you might try the more traditional roast beef with soup as a starter and apple pie for dessert, at £3.50 ($8.05). Bed-and-breakfast terms are £8.50 ($19.55) per person, including morning tea or coffee. The Ship is well recommended for that "down home" feeling.

ETON: For our final sight, from Windsor Castle we must cross over a bridge spanning the Thames:

Eton College

Largest and best known of the public (private) schools of England, Eton College was founded by a teenage boy himself, Henry VI in 1440. Some of England's greatest men, notably the Duke of Wellington, have played on the fields of Eton. Twenty prime ministers were educated at Eton, as well as such literary figures as George Orwell and Aldous Huxley. Even the late Ian Fleming, creator of James Bond, attended. The traditions of the school have had plenty of time to become firmly entrenched (ask a young gentleman in his Victorian black tails to explain the difference between a "wet bob" and a "dry bob"). For 60p ($1.38) admission, the School Yard and Cloisters may be visited daily, 2 to 5 p.m., throughout the year, and also from 10:30 a.m. to 2 p.m. on school holidays, including most of July and all of August. If it's open, take a look at the Perpendicular chapel, with its 15th-century paintings and reconstructed fan vaulting.

Bernard Weinraub wrote, "Eton, the Gothic school on the Thames that has symbolized starched exclusiveness, is quietly lifting its cloak of privilege." In the future, along with the sons of diplomats and prime ministers, boys from poorer families will also be educated there, the tuition funded by scholarships. All of this represents the movement in England toward a classless society. One man put it this way, "The lifestyle of the young cuts across all classes—they're wearing the same clothes, listening to the same music, engaging in the same activities." However, the administration (at the moment) doesn't plan to go coed.

Lunch at Eton

There is no better place to have lunch here than at the **Cock Pit,** 47 Eton High St. (tel. 95/60944). The place dates back to 1420 and it is a rendezvous for Eton students. The inn is owned by Italian Vittorio Bianchi and his English wife, Janet. Together they have considerably upgraded and internationalized the menu, although lunch still retains some fairly traditional English dishes. Light meals are served at lunch only in the upstairs bar where you can order sandwiches from £1.05 ($2.42) or else pasta dishes such as cannelloni or lasagne at £1.50 ($3.45). At dinner a set menu is featured at £11.75 ($27.03), a three-course meal, or else you may prefer to select from an extensive à la carte menu, including roast beef at £4.95 ($11.39). On nippy days, a fire burns in an old fireplace, but when the weather's warmer you'll be tempted to have lunch under an umbrella in the rear courtyard. Specialties include veal on the bone (cooked in butter and breadcrumbs) and saddle of lamb roasted with fennel, sage, rosemary, and cooked in white wine. A set afternoon tea here is served from 3:30 till 5:30 p.m., on Saturday and Sunday only. The restaurant is closed all day Monday. Dining hours are from 12:30 to 2:15 p.m. and from 7:30 to 10:30 p.m. Ask to be shown the knucklebone yard out back. Then you'll know why the restaurant is called the Cock Pit. The restaurant is licensed for alcohol, and has a varied wine list.

Eton Wine Bar (tel. Windsor 54921) is owned and run by William and Michael Gilbey of the Gilbey's gin family, although no gin in served here. Just across the bridge from Windsor, it is a charming place set among the antique shops with pinewood tables and old church pews and chairs. There is a small garden out back. It is open seven days a week from 11:30 a.m. to 2:30 p.m. and from 6 to 10:30 p.m., but on Friday and Saturday they remain open until 11 p.m. Soups of the day are often imaginative and sophisticated (ever had watercress vichyssoise?). Another "starter" might be mussels marinated in a roquefort dressing. Main dishes include such treats as stuffed eggplant with a Provençal tomato sauce and rice. For a main dish and appetizer, expect to pay from £6 ($13.80). Each day two special dishes are featured, and desserts include pineapple and almond flan and damson crunch, ranging from 85p ($1.96) to £1.10 ($2.53). Wine can be had by the glass or the bottle.

Antico, 42 High St. (tel. Windsor 63977), is an old building with beams spreading through several rooms. On your way to the tiny bar you cannot help but pass the magnificent cold table, displaying a vast array of hors d'oeuvres, fresh fish, and cold meats. Grilled fresh sardines are £1.20 ($2.76). There is a wide choice of fish dishes, such as sole grilled, colbert, or with mushrooms, capers, and prawns, each costing around £4 ($9.20). Beef filet goes for £5 ($11.50), and a kidney brochette for £3.50 ($8.05). Desserts from the trolley begin at £1.50 ($3.45). VAT and service are added to all bills, and there is a cover charge of 30p (69¢). The restaurant is open for lunch daily, except Saturday, from noon to 2:30 p.m. Dinner is nightly from 7 to 11 p.m.

Eton Buttery, 73 High St. (tel. Windsor 54479), is just on the Eton side of the bridge from Windsor, a new building among the boathouses of the college with magnificent views over the river and up toward the town and the castle. Open seven days a week from 9:30 a.m. to 7 p.m., it is decorated with plain red brick walls, brown carpets and tables, caneback chairs, and a mass of potted plants. This is an up-market self-service buffet owned by Mrs. Ron Stanton, owner of the House on the Bridge restaurant, opposite. Marion Peck is the manager.

Food is well displayed along spotless counters. There are waitresses to clear away and to bring you wine and drinks; otherwise, you help yourself to the variety of quiches, 75p ($1.73); cold sliced meats, £1.75 ($4.03); and specialty salads and pâtés, from 75p ($1.73). There is also a hot dish of the day at £2.75 ($6.33).

SHOPPING IN WINDSOR: For those who have time to spare, Windsor offers a great variety of attractive shops for browsing or more serious souvenir hunting.

Scots Corner, High Street (tel. Windsor 51695), has Shetland sweaters for £6.50 ($14.95), women's fairisle jumpers for £12 ($27.60), and Cairngorm brooches, cufflinks, and necklaces from £5 ($11.50) to £15 ($34.50).

Woods of Windsor Ltd., at the Castle Perfumers, Queen Charlotte Street (tel. Windsor 55777), established in 1770, right beside the Guildhall, is a heady experience where you can buy a scented leaf of paper to slip between your hankies for 50p ($1.15) or an elegant potpourrie for £12 ($27.60). In between are lavender and herb bags from £1 ($2.30) to £1.50 ($3.45), and oil to refresh potpourrie for £1.50 ($3.45).

Opposite, the **Token House** has one of the best selections of china and porcelain of all well-known makes, and further down the High Street, **Le Sac** has a wide selection of leather goods, handbags, wallets, scarves, and gloves.

A short walk down Peascod Street, opposite the Queen Victoria Statue, brings you to King Edward's Court. On the corner is **Hammick's Books and Bistro,** 1 King Edward's Court (tel. Windsor 56456). Charles Hammick, ex-army, now runs a string of bookshops where you can get the latest paperbacks and guidebooks, maps, and illustrated historical documentation on the town and the country.

Upstairs, over the bookshop, is a small bistro which is open daily from 10 a.m. to 3:30 p.m. for coffee, luncheon, or afternoon tea. Coffee is 25p (58¢); Chinese or Indian tea, 20p (46¢). Cakes go for about 35p (81¢) a portion. The dishes of the day are displayed on a blackboard and might include chicken breast in puff pastry with mushroom and tarragon sauce, salad, and jacket potato for £2.50 ($5.75). All the cooking is done by a team of local housewives who produce genuine home-cooked dishes to go with the carefully chosen wine list.

All wines are bottled in their country of origin and Charles claims to have tasted each one and will take full responsibility for them. The manager is Joan Booth, whose husband is a housemaster at Eton College. There is a salad table where you pick your choice, and the whole thing is brought to your table. Good quick service and a friendly atmosphere are found here.

At 34 King Edward's Court is **Le Pot,** a paradise of traditional cooking utensils, tableware, herbs, and spices. The large, once-bare shop is stuffed with cooking pots, garlic presses, earthenware casseroles, pepper mills at £3.50 ($8.05), oven gloves at £2 ($4.60), napkin rings and egg cups at 75p ($1.73). There is a large selection of kitchen knives from £1.50 ($3.45) to £10 ($23) and wooden spoons from 50p ($1.15), to a gigantic stirring spoon at £2.25 ($5.18). We counted 41 different herbs and spices from 30p (69¢) to £1 ($2.30), all small and easy to slip into a pocket. Blue-and-white-striped butchers' aprons go for £4 ($9.20), and there is a mass of basket work and an excellent selection of cookbooks. This is the domain and brainchild of Graham Cooper and actor friend Anthony Davidson. They are helped by several young women who are always willing to discuss the merits of various pots and utensils. It's a lovely place in which to buy souvenirs at prices lower than in Central London.

ROUND WINDSOR SIGHTSEEING TOUR: The Royal Heritage Drive by open-top double-decker bus is operated by Windsorian Coaches (tel. Windsor 56841). The 1¼-hour, 25-mile drive starting from Castle Hill just outside Windsor Castle passes through Windsor town and then across the river to Eton, then Datchet, Runnymede, and the Magna Carta and Kennedy Memorials, to Virginia Water and Fort Belvedere where King Edward VIII wrote his abdication speech. The tour continues past Ascot Racecourse and through the Great Park. As a complement to the London sights, this drive combines many historical venues with a glimpse at the countryside in which royalty has relaxed, and spent many anguished hours, over the past years.

From the beginning of April until the end of September, there are three departures daily, at 11:30 a.m., and 1:30 and 3:30 p.m., augmented from the end of May to mid-September by two more at 12:30 and 2:30 p.m. The tour costs £2 ($4.60) for adults, £1.25 ($2.88) for children. Tickets are available from the Tourist Office in Windsor Central Station, from 17 Alma Rd., Windsor, or on departure from the tour-bus driver. A joint Green Line/Royal Heritage Drive excursion ticket costs adults £4 ($9.20); children, £2 ($4.60). These can be bought at Eccleston Bridge, Victoria, London, S.W.1, and they include the ride from London and back.

NEARBY SIGHTS: Two attractions of interest are located in the surrounding area.

One of England's Great Gardens

The **Savill Garden,** Wick Lane, Englefield Green, is in Windsor Great Park and clearly signposted from Windsor, Egham, and Ascot. Started in 1932, the garden is now considered one of the finest of its type in the northern hemisphere. The display starts in spring with rhododendrons, camellias, and daffodils beneath the trees; then throughout the summer there are spectacular displays of flowers and shrubs all skillfully presented in a natural and wild state. It is open March 1 to December 24 from 10 a.m. to 6 or 7 p.m., and the admission is 75p ($1.73) for adults, 45p ($1.04) for children. There is also a restaurant and snackbar on the premises.

Adjoining the Savill Garden are the **Valley Gardens,** full of shrubs and trees in a series of wooded natural valleys running down to Virginia water. It is open daily, free, throughout the year.

Windsor Safari Park and Seaworld

In the safari craze sweeping the world, even the Royal Borough of Windsor hasn't been spared. The Safari Park and Seaworld is open just two miles from Windsor Castle on a site 23 miles from London. Take the M4 motorway and leave it at Junction 6. The park is on the B3022 road. There you can watch the performing dolphins and a killer whale, and drive through reserves of lions, tigers, baboons, giraffes, camels, and many other wild animals. It is open from 10 a.m. There are catering facilities, but you can picnic on acres of green. If you have a soft-top car or come on public transport from Windsor, take the safari bus through the reserves. Admission to Safari Park is £2.50 ($5.75) for adults, £1.25 ($2.88) for children. The dolphin and killer whale show is 50p ($1.15) for all ages.

INNS ALONG THE THAMES: For those who want to anchor into riverside villages with old inns along the Thames, we offer the following suggestions for the motorist.

Cookham-on-Thames

King's Arm Inn, Cookham-on-Thames in Berkshire (tel. Bourne End 2146), is a charming old inn in a riverside village where Stanley Spencer lived and painted for many years. The inn has an early 17th-century staircase, low beams, and plastered walls. In the gardens, which are floodlit at night, are the owner's two Pyrennean wolfhounds, great soft animals with thick white fur and a tendency to pose under the floodlights for the diners.

The small dining room is warm and softly lit, and the menu includes a very good chef's pâté, as well as the soup of the day made from fresh ingredients. Main dishes include roast duckling with orange and cherry sauce, chicken poached in wine, and sliced filet of beef with mushrooms cooked in beer. There are also T-bone steaks, entrecôte, and grilled sole. Desserts include fruit pies and tarts. A meal will cost around £8 ($18.40), including VAT and service. A very good light red wine goes for £5 ($11.50) a bottle.

On Sunday, there is a traditional English lunch with roast joint and all the trimmings. The inn serves food from noon to 1:45 p.m. and from 7 to 10 p.m. Closed Sunday evenings and Monday all day.

The landlord, Martin Cummings, and his wife Joy, also have rooms in the hotel which go for £15 ($34.50) in a single, £25 ($57.50) in a double or twin. Some units are in the main building, and some in the Cummings's own house just across the narrow street, beside another inn. The place is comfortably furnished, with many antiques and good beds, but none of the rooms has a private bath, however. The nightly rate includes VAT, service, and a breakfast of almost whatever you wish to have in the traditional English style.

Streatley-on-Thames:

This Thameside village has some old buildings and a fine Priory church. And it has the **Swan Hotel,** Streatley-on-Thames, Berkshire (tel. Goring 3737), a pleasant riverside inn. The hotel Swan has now been much enlarged, but still it retains much of its old charm. It would take a lot to ruin the tranquility and eternity of the River Thames. Gardens slope down to the water, and your hire-cruiser will nestle happily alongside while you have dinner. The menu is unstartling, mainly grills, steaks, roast chicken, and desserts from the trolley. A meal will cost around £9 ($20.70), excluding drinks. If you are touring, or spending a last night before Heathrow Airport and departure, single rooms go from £16 ($36.80) to £29 ($66.70) (with or without bath); doubles from £24 ($55.20) to £35 ($80.50). All prices are subject to a service charge, and breakfast is extra.

Bray-on-Thames

Twenty-eight miles from London, you come upon this attractive Thames-side village, with its beautiful old almshouses, timbered cottages, and small period houses. Windsor Castle is but just a short jaunt away. The town was once famous for its 16th-century "Vicar of Bray" who couldn't make up his mind about his religious or political affiliations.

Into such a town, with its gliding swans and willows bordering the Thames, the Roux brothers of Le Gavroche fame have opened the **Waterside Inn,** with its impeccable cooking but astronomical prices. Those who cannot afford such a place will be amply rewarded at the following, more modestly priced recommendation.

The **Hinds Head Hotel,** Bray-on-Thames, Berkshire (tel. Maidenhead 26151), lies on the bend of a very busy, narrow road, but there's ample parking in front of the restaurant. Although calling itself a hotel, the Hinds has no rooms to rent. There is a bar and you can take your pint in with you if you wish, as the wine list is expensive. A three-course lunch costs £8 ($18.40) and a four-course lunch is £9 ($20.70), plus VAT and service. A three-course dinner goes for £9 ($20.70); a four-course dinner, £10 ($23). There is a fish course before the roast beef, pork, or lamb, with all the trimmings. Be warned, the friendly waitresses bring around three sorts of potatoes and then about four different green vegetables. A carafe of the house wine is £4 ($9.20). Hours are from 12:30 to 2 p.m. and from 7:30 to 10 p.m. This is the sort of place to come to on a nice Sunday for a good old English "blow-out" lunch. The portions are large and the standard of cuisine pretty high on the plainer dishes.

Henley-on-Thames

At the eastern edge of Oxfordshire, only 35 miles from London, Henley-on-Thames is a small town and resort on the river. At the foothills of the Chilterns, it is the headquarters of the Royal Regatta held annually in July, the Number One event among European oarsmen. The regatta dates back to the first years of the reign of Victoria.

The Elizabethan buildings, the tearooms, and inns along the town's High Street live up to one's conception of what an English country town looks like—or should look like

The life here is serene, and Henley-on-Thames makes for an excellent stopover en route to Oxford. Warning: During the Royal Regatta, rooms are virtually impossible to get at the fashionable inns of Henley, unless you've made reservations months in advance.

The **Red Lion**, Henley Bridge (tel. Henley-on-Thames 2161), is a former coaching inn, dating from the 16th century. A bedchamber used to be kept ready for the Duke of Marlborough, who would stop over on his way to his palace at Blenheim. The guest list reads like a hall of fame, including such notables as Johnson and Boswell, even George IV who, it is said, downed more than a dozen lamb chops one night. The red brick facade, with its climbing wisteria, remains untouched, but most of the interior has been renovated and modernized. Nowadays, wayfarers enjoy central heating and private baths in most of the rooms, some of which are named after famous personages who have stopped over. The decor in most of the bedrooms has been brightened with contemporary furnishings and color-coordinated pieces. A bathless single costs £18 ($41.40), rising to £24 ($55.20) with bath, and bathless doubles go for £28 ($64.40), increasing to £34 ($78.20) with bath, these tariffs including an English breakfast and VAT. Guests congregate in the low-beamed lounge. Opening onto views of the Thames, the Riverside Restaurant is cozy in green and gold. A three-course lunch goes for £4.50 ($10.35). On Saturday nights, a pianist plays, and a four-course meal is priced at £7 ($16.70).

The Cherub, 49–51 Market Pl. (tel. Henley-on-Thames 3060), is an intimate restaurant, offering a French cuisine, prepared under the watchful eye of Mrs. Lesley Strojecki. Inside, it's true to its namesake—pen-and-ink sketches of baby-fat cherubs bestow their blessings on romantically inclined guests. You can first have a drink in the informal Apéritif Bar. The menu is selectively limited, with such fare as beef Stroganoff, lobster Cherubin, and steak Diane. For appetizers, try a smooth vichyssoise. A desert specialty is meringue chantilly. The average price of a meal is in the £6 ($13.80) to £7 ($16.10) range. Usually, it's necessary to book a table. The Cherub entertains for lunch from noon to 2 p.m.; for dinners, from 7 till 11 p.m. Closed Monday.

EN ROUTE TO OXFORD: Between Henley-on-Thames and Oxford (a 24-mile drive) lies the following recommendation.

The **Swan Inn**, Tetsworth, Oxfordshire (tel. Tetsworth 281), is an old inn which has been in business for at least 700 years. Over the centuries it has been added to, and examples of the various architectural styles can been seen around the house. Elizabeth I and then Queen Victoria stayed here. It is reputed to be haunted and could very well be, as it has had many occupants since the monks who ran the first hostelry left in the 14th century. Singles go for £15 ($34.50); doubles, £26 ($59.80) to £31 ($71.30); including a full breakfast and VAT. Lunch can be ordered for £5.50 ($12.65), and a set dinner begins at £6 ($13.80), depending on your choice from a selection of well-cooked roasts, grills, and salads. If you're ordering à la carte, expect to pay from £10 ($23). The Swan makes an ideal last-night stopover on the way back to Heathrow or for someone leaving the Cotswolds and Oxford and wanting to stop over before plunging into London.

2. Oxford

A walk down the long sweep of The High, one of the most striking streets in England; a mug of cider in one of the old student pubs; the sound of a May Day dawn when choristers sing in Latin from Magdalen Tower; the Great Tom bell from Tom Tower, whose 101 peals traditionally signal the closing of the college gates; towers and spires rising majestically; the barges on the upper reaches of the Thames; nude swimming at Parson's Pleasure; the roar of a cannon launching the bumping races; a tiny, dusty bookstall where you can pick up a valuable first edition. All that is Oxford—57 miles from London and home of one of the greatest universities in the world. An industrial city, the center of a large automobile business, as well as a university town, Oxford is better for sightseeing in summer. The students are wherever Oxford scholars go in the summer (allegedly they study more than they do at term time), and the many bed-and-breakfast houses—vacated by their gown-wearing boarders —will be happy to offer you an accommodation. But you'll be missing a great deal if you view Oxford without glimpsing its life blood.

However, at any time of the year, you can enjoy a tour of the colleges—many of them representing a peak in England's architectural kingdom, as well as a valley of Victorian eyesores. Just don't mention the other place (Cambridge), and you shouldn't have any trouble.

The city predates the university—in fact, it was a Saxon town in the early part of the tenth century. And by the 12th century, Oxford was growing in reputation as a seat of learning—at the expense of Paris. The first colleges were founded in the 13th century. The story of Oxford is filled with conflicts too complex and detailed to elaborate here. Suffice it to say, the relationship between town and gown wasn't as peaceful as it is today. Riots often flared, and both sides were guilty of abuses.

Nowadays, the young people of Oxford take out their aggressiveness in sporting competitions, with the different colleges zealously competing in such games as cricket and soccer. However, all colleges unite into a powerful university when they face matches with their traditional rival, Cambridge.

Ultimately, the test of a great university lies in the men it turns out. Oxford can name-drop a mouthful: Roger Bacon, Samuel Johnson, William Penn, John Wesley, Sir Walter Raleigh, Edward Gibbon, T.E. Lawrence, Sir Christopher Wren, John Donne, William Pitt, Matthew Arnold, Arnold Toynbee, Harold Macmillan, Graham Greene, A. E. Housman, Lewis Carroll, and even Dean Rusk.

Many Americans arriving in Oxford ask, "Where's the campus?" If an Oxonian shows amusement when answering, it's understandable. Oxford University is, in fact, made up of 28 colleges, including five just for women (scholars in skirts in years past staged, and won, the battle for equal rights). To tour all

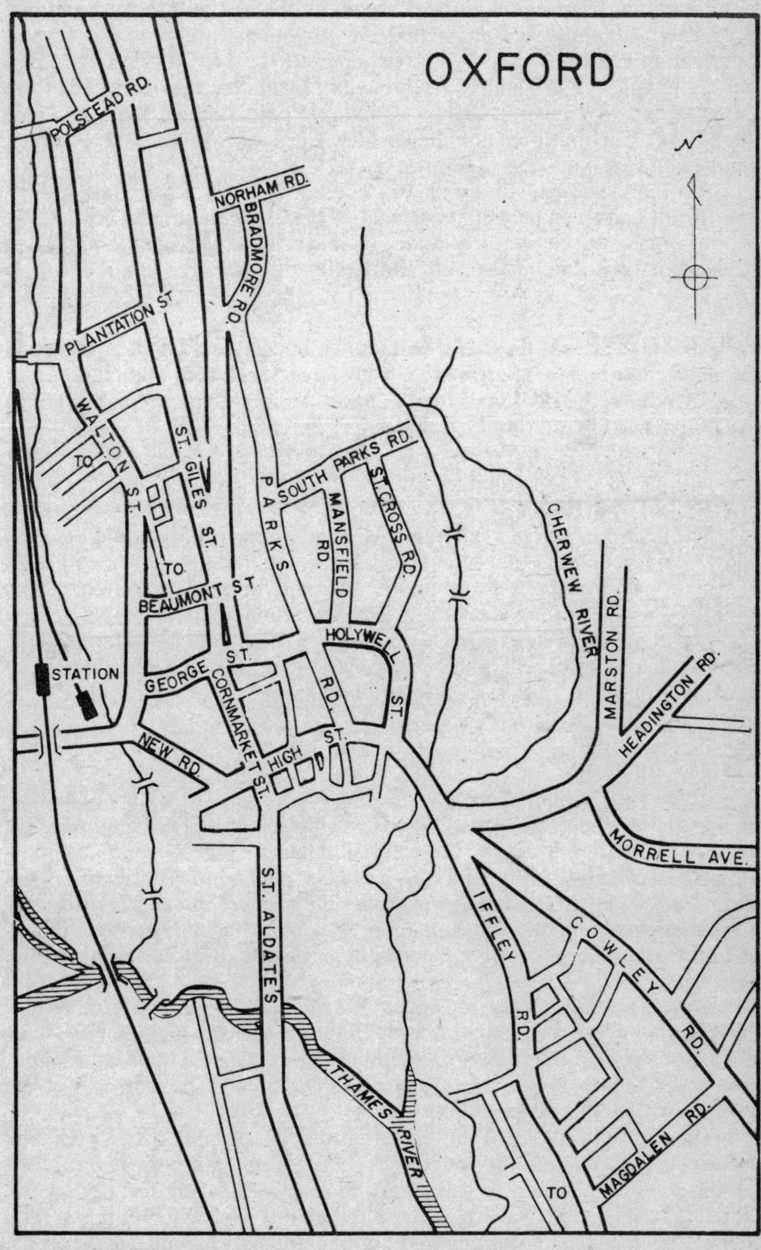
OXFORD
N
POLSTEAD RD.
NORHAM RD.
BRADMORE RD.
PLANTATION ST
WALTON ST.
TO
ST. GILES ST.
SOUTH PARKS RD.
PARKS
MANSFIELD RD.
ST. CROSS RD.
CHERWEW RIVER
TO
BEAUMONT ST
HOLYWELL ST.
MARSTON RD.
STATION
GEORGE ST.
CORNMARKET ST.
RD.
HEADINGTON RD.
NEW RD.
HIGH ST.
MORRELL AVE.
ST. ALDATE'S
IFFLEY RD.
COWLEY RD.
THAMES RIVER
MAGDALEN RD.
TO

of these would be a formidable task. Besides, a few are of such interest they overshadow the rest.

In season (from Easter through October), the best way to get a running commentary on the important sightseeing attractions is to go to the **Oxford Information Centre,** St. Aldate's Street, opposite the Town Hall, near Carfax (tel. Oxford 48707). Walking tours through the major colleges leave daily from Easter to mid-November at 10:45 a.m. and 2:15 p.m., last two hours, and cost 80p ($1.84). The tour does not include New College or Christ Church, which charge 20p (46¢) and 35p (81¢), respectively.

At **Punt Station,** Cherwell Boathouse, Bardwell Road (tel. Oxford 55978), you can rent a punt at a cost of £1.70 ($3.91) per hour, plus a £10 ($23) deposit which must be posted. Similar charges are made on rentals at Magdalen Bridge Boathouse and at the Folly Bridge Boathouse.

WHAT TO SEE: Of the many well-known buildings in Oxford—Radcliffe Camera, whose dome competes in a city of spires; Sheldonian Theatre, an early work of Wren's; the Bodleian Library, one of the most important in the world —we have narrowed down the sights to a representative list of a few colleges.

A Word of Warning

The main business of a university, is, of course, to educate—and unfortunately this function at Oxford has been severely interfered with by the number of visitors who have been disturbing the academic work of the university. So, with deep regret, visiting is now restricted to certain hours and small groups of six or less. In addition, there are areas where visitors are not allowed at all, but your tourist office will be happy to advise you when and where you may "take in" the sights of this great institution.

Christ Church

Begun by Cardinal Wolsey as Cardinal College in 1525, Christ Church, known as The House, was founded by Henry VIII in 1546. Facing St. Aldate's Street, Christ Church has the largest quadrangle of any college in Oxford.

Tom Tower houses Great Tom, the 18,000-pound bell referred to earlier. It rings at 9:05 nightly, signaling the closing of the college gates. The 101 times it peals originally signified the number of students at the time of the founding of the college. The student body number changed, but Oxford traditions live on forever.

In the 16th-century Great Hall, with its hammer-beam ceiling, are some interesting portraits, including works by those old reliables, Gainsborough and Reynolds. Prime ministers are pictured, as Christ Church was the training ground for 13 prime ministers: men such as Gladstone and George Canning. There is a separate picture gallery.

The cathedral, dating from the 12th century, was build over a period of centuries. (Incidentally, it is not only the college chapel, but the cathedral of the diocese of Oxford.) The cathedral's most distinguishing features are its Norman pillars and the vaulting of the choir, dating from the 15th century. In the center of the Great Quadrangle is a statue of Mercury mounted in the center of a fish pond. The college and cathedral can be visited between 9:30 a.m. and noon and from 2 to 4:30 p.m. Entrance fee is 50p ($1.15).

Magdalen College

Pronounced "maud-len," this college was founded in 1458 by William of Waynflete, bishop of Winchester and later chancellor of England. Its alumni range all the way from Wolsey to Wilde. Opposite the botanic garden, the oldest in England, is the bell tower, where the choristers sing in Latin at dawn on May Day. The reflection of the 15th-century tower is cast in the waters of the Cherwell below. On a not-so-happy day, Charles I—his days numbered—watched the oncoming Roundheads. But the most celebrated incident in Magdalen's history was when some brave Fellows defied James II. Visit the 15th-century chapel, in spite of many of its latter-day trappings. The hall and other places of special interest are open when possible. The College Shop in Cloisters Quadrangle issues tickets for entrance to these areas.

A favorite pastime is to take Addison's Walk through the water meadows. The stroll is so named after a former alumnus, Joseph Addison, the 18th-century writer and poet noted for his contributions to *The Spectator* and *The Tatler*. The grounds of Magdalen are the most extensive of any Oxford college, even containing a deer park. You can visit Magdalen each day from 2 to 6:15 p.m. There is a gift shop in the Cloisters.

Merton College

Founded in 1264, this college is among the trio of the most ancient at the university. It stands near Corpus Christi College on Merton Street, the sole survivor of Oxford's medieval cobbled streets. Merton College is noted for its library, said to be the oldest in England, having been built between 1371 and 1379. In keeping with tradition, some of its most valuable books were chained. Now only one book is so secured, to show what the custom was like. One of the treasures of the library is an astrolabe (astronomical instrument used for measuring the altitude of the sun and stars), thought to have belonged to Chaucer. You pay only 20p (46¢) to visit the ancient library, as well as the Max Beerbohm Room (the satirical English caricaturist who died in 1956). Both are open from 2 to 4 p.m. (4:30 p.m. March 2 to October 1) daily, and, in addition, from 10 a.m. to noon on Saturday and Sunday only. You can also visit the chapel, dating from the 13th century, at these times.

University College

On The High, the University College is the oldest one found at Oxford, tracing its history back to 1249 when money was donated by an ecclesiastic called William of Durham. More fanciful is the old claim that the real founder was Alfred the Great! Don't jump to any conclusions about the age of the buildings when you see the present Gothic-esque look. The original structures have all disappeared, and what remains today represents essentially the architecture of the 17th century, with subsequent additions in Victoria's day, as well as in more recent times. For example, the Goodhart Quadrangle was added as late as 1962. Its most famous alumnus, Shelley, was "sent down" for his part in collaborating on a pamphlet on atheism. However, all is forgiven today, as the romantic poet is honored by a memorial erected in 1894. The hall and chapel of the University College can be visited during university vacations from 10 a.m. to noon and from 2 to 4 p.m. (otherwise, 2 to 4 p.m.).

New College

New College was founded in 1379 by William of Wykeham, bishop of Winchester and later lord, chancellor of England. The college at Winchester itself supplied a constant stream of candidates. The first quadrangle, dating from before the end of the 14th century, was the initial quadrangle to be built in Oxford, forming the architectural design for the other colleges. In the ante-chapel is Sir Jacob Epstein's remarkable modern sculpture of *Lazarus,* and a fine El Greco painting of St. James. One of the treasures of the college is a crosier (pastoral staff of a bishop), belonging to the founding father. In the garden, you can see the remains of the old city wall and the mound. The college (entered at New College Lane) can be visited from 2 to 5 p.m. weekdays at term time (otherwise, 11 a.m. to 6 p.m.). On weekends, it is open from noon to 6 p.m.

WHERE TO STAY: The accommodations in Oxford are limited, although the addition of a couple of motels on the outskirts has aided the plight of those who require modern amenities. Recently, some of the more stalwart candidates in the city center have been refurbished as well. In addition, motorists may want to consider two grand old country houses on the outskirts, which offer the best living in Oxford if you don't mind commuting.

When the tourist rush is on, why tire yourself further? The **Oxford Association of Hotels and Guest Houses** has provided an efficient accommodation secretary, Mr. J. O'Kane, who also operates the Earlmont Guest House at 322/4 Cowley Rd. (tel. Oxford 40236). If Mr. O'Kane cannot accommodate you himself, he will spare no effort in helping you to find the kind of accommodation you require. Advance single or party bookings can also be made, long or short term, single person or party booking. No fees are charged. Bed-and-breakfast prices begin at £6.50 ($14.95) per person.

The **Oxford Information Centre** (tel. Oxford 48707) operates a room-booking service for personal callers for a fee of 50p ($1.15) from Easter to September. If you'd like to seek out lodgings on your own, the staff at the center will provide a list of accommodations, or you may try one of the following recommendations:

The Upper Bracket

Randolph Hotel, Beaumont Street (tel. Oxford 47481), is a recently refurbished Gothic-Victorian monument, dating back to 1864. For more than a century, it has been Oxford's prestige hotel, centrally situated and commanding an impressive vantage point overlooking St. Giles, the Ashmolean Museum, and the Cornmarket. The lounges, although modernized, are still cavernous enough for dozens of separate conversational groupings; and the furnishings are bright and contemporary. Run as a member of Trust Houses Forte Ltd., the hotel contains 111 rooms, all with private bath, telephone, radio and color TV. The price for a single is from £30 ($69), from £38 ($87.40) for a double. The Randolph Restaurant boasts a high standard of cuisine, and specializes in flambé dishes. A set lunch goes for £6 ($13.80), a set dinner for £8 ($18.40), and there's a very good à la carte menu as well. A wide selection of wines is also available. The restaurant is open from 12:30 to 2:30 p.m. and from 7 to 9:45 p.m. Service charge and VAT are included in the tariffs.

The Medium-Priced Range

The **TraveLodge,** Peartree Roundabout, Woodstock Road (tel. Oxford 54301), is ideal for motorists who want to be within easy reach of the university and shopping districts of Oxford, yet set apart at the city edge for a quiet night's sleep. Easy to spot, near a large bus stop, the lodge invites with international flags fluttering in the breezes. Its lower-level bedrooms open onto private terraces. The furnishings are in the typical motel style, with compact, built-in necessities. Each of the rooms has a picture-window wall, a private bath with shower, a television and radio, individually controlled heating and tea-making facilities. Room rates in a single are £20 ($46), £28 ($64.40) for a double. Some family rooms for three or four persons cost the double rate, plus £2 ($4.60) per extra bed. In the Autogrill (open at 7:30 a.m.), you can order an English breakfast. Otherwise, a continental breakfast is included in the room rates, as are service and VAT. On the grounds are a swimming pool, the fully licensed Blenheim Bar, a 24-hour cafeteria, and a garage.

The **Oxford Lodge Hotel**, Godstow Road, Wolvercote Roundabout (tel. Oxford 59933), one of the Grand Metropolitan chain members, incorporates the principles of advanced motel design, with an emphasis on spacious, glassed-in areas and streamlined bedrooms. Its position is ideal, hidden from the traffic at the northern edge of Oxford, two miles away, at the junction of the A40 and the A34. Although generally patronized by motorists, it can also be reached by bus. In a double or twin, with a full breakfast, you pay £33 ($75.90) for two, £20.40 ($46.92) in a single. On the second floor is a restaurant, and there are drinking bars as well, with traditional entertainment on most nights.

Eastgate Hotel, Merton Street, off The High (tel. Oxford 48244), is a hotel of character, exquisitely placed opposite Merton College and on The High. It's smallish—in fact, it is a group of older buildings joined together and modernized. The bedrooms are clean-cut, borrowing their inspiration from the compact, serviceable designs of Scandinavia. Singles without bath cost from £16.25 ($37.38) nightly, rising to £21 ($48.30) with bath; and doubles without bath rent from £25.50 ($57.50), going up to £33 ($75.90) with bath. All units have color TV sets, and tariffs quoted include a full English breakfast, although VAT is extra. The lounge opening onto The High is pleasantly furnished; the dining room is airy and comfortable.

Royal Oxford Hotel, Park End Street (tel. Oxford 48432), is an oldish establishment given a new lease on life by a drastic renovation of its interior. Near Oxford Station, about a ten-minute walk from the center of the city, it is a comfortable and convenient place at which to stay. Of its 23 bedrooms, 10 have private baths, and all have color TV, phone, and radio. A bathless single goes for £18.50 ($42.55); with bath, £23.50 ($54.05). A bathless twin or double rents for £28 ($64.40), increasing to £30 ($69) with bath. Prices include service, VAT, and breakfast. The bedrooms are well kept, with modern, compact furnishings, and all have television.

The Budget Range

The **Turf Tavern**, 4–5 Bath Pl. (tel. Oxford 43235), is recommended separately as a dining establishment. However, the owner, Wally Ellse, a jovial Yorkshireman with a handshake like a vice, has acquired two old cottages from around the 13th century. He has converted these into nine accommodations, offering bed and breakfast for £11.50 ($26.45) per person. The bedrooms are smallish but pleasantly furnished in chintz. Baths and toilets are adjacent. The rooms are decorated to preserve the atmosphere. A dining room is between the two cottages, and it's paneled with rough wood, giving it a warm appearance. Breakfast is the only meal served here. If you want a big breakfast, ask and ye shall get. Mr. Ellse would prefer to give you an extra egg rather than see you go hungry. For anyone seeking atmosphere in Oxford, it would be hard to beat the Turf Tavern for the price.

The **Old Parsonage Hotel,** 3 Banbury Rd. (tel. Oxford 54843), is so old it looks like an extension of one of the ancient colleges. Originally a 13th-century hospital named Bethleen, it was restored in the early 17th century. Today, it's slated for designation as an ancient monument. Near St. Giles Church, it is set back from the street behind a low stone wall and sheltered by surrounding trees and shrubbery. However, most of the rooms are in a modern wing which is more institutional in character. The owners charge from £12 ($27.60) per person nightly for bed and breakfast in a single, from £22 ($50.60) in a twin or double. Should you want a private shower, the price is increased to £23 ($52.90) for two persons. Twenty rooms have been added to the accommodations. Some of the large front rooms, with leaded-glass windows, are set aside for tourists. Many rooms are big enough to have a living-room area, armchairs, antique chests, and soft beds. You have breakfast in a pleasant Swedish-style dining room, overlooking the garden. A licensed restaurant and bar are on the premises.

Ascot Guest House, 283 Iffley Rd. (tel. Oxford 40259), is ideally located in the quiet outskirts of Oxford, yet only minutes away by bus or car from the city center. The owners, Mr. and Mrs. Fraser, have performed the difficult task of combining friendliness, high standards, and reasonable prices in their recently refurbished home. All rooms have wall-to-wall carpeting, telephones, and hot and cold running water. The per-person charge of £6.50 ($14.95) per night includes breakfast and VAT. Parking facilities are plentiful here, and it's usually less expensive and more convenient to leave your car at the guest house and take the frequent buses into the city proper. When the Frasers are unable to accommodate any more guests, they cheerfully will recommend other guest houses in the area.

Belmont Guest House, 182 Woodstock Rd. (tel. Oxford 53698), is on a tree-lined avenue in the residential part of Oxford, about one mile from the city center. It's on the main road and close to Blenheim Palace, Stratford-upon-Avon, the Midlands, and the Lake District. All rooms have central heating and hot and cold running water. Bath, showers, and a good English breakfast are supplied. Most rooms can be used as either doubles, twins, or family rooms. The charge is £6 ($13.80) per person for bed and breakfast.

LIVING ON THE OUTSKIRTS: Weston Manor, Weston-on-the-Green (tel. Bletchington 621), is a moated stone manor house, only eight miles from Oxford (on the A43 Oxford-Northampton road)—ideal as a center for touring the district (Blenheim Palace is only five miles away). The manor, owned and run by the Price family, is rooted in the 11th century; portions of the present building date back to the 14th and 16th centuries, with later additions in Victoria's day. Although long owned by noblemen, the estate was an abbey until abolished by Henry VIII. Of course, there are ghosts, such as Mad Maude, the naughty nun who was burned at the stake for her "indecent and immoral" behavior. She returns to haunt the Oak Bedrooms. Prince Rupert, son of Charles II, hid from Cromwell's soldiers in one of the fireplaces, eventually escaping in drag as the "maiden of the milk bucket."

As you enter the driveway, you pass two elm trees, dating back to 1672, and proceed into a formal car-park area. The reception lounge is furnished with antiques, dominated by a Tudor fireplace and a long refectory table, the latter glowing from centuries of polishing. The various lounges have fine old pieces. Most of the bedrooms are spacious, furnished with antiques (often four-posters), old dressing tables, and chests. The cost of staying here is £34 ($78.20) in a single without bath. Doubles without bath go for £35 ($80.50), increasing to £44 ($101.20) with bath. All these tariffs include an English breakfast, VAT, and service. Breakfast is served in the yellow morning room, with your table set in front of the stone-mullioned and leaded windows. The view is of the formal garden, edged with animal and bird figures trimmed out of the old yew hedges.

In the Great Hall, one of the most beautiful dining rooms in England, you'll be served your lunch and dinner. It's like a chapel, with an open raftered and beamed ceiling, the lower portion solidly paneled with a rare example of linenfold. There's a minstrels' gallery and a large wrought-iron chandelier. The food is first rate. A cold buffet is featured in the bar for £3 ($6.90). On any given dinner menu, you're likely to find roast Aylesbury duckling, spring chicken, sirloin steak, Scottish salmon, or rainbow trout. Dinner ranges in price from £8.50 ($19.55) to £12 ($27.60), depending on your choice of a main course, and the big Sunday lunch costs £8 ($18.40). In warm weather, you can enjoy the open-air swimming pool, surrounded by its gardens.

Studley Priory Hotel, Horton-cum-Studley (tel. Stanton St. John 203), may be remembered by those who saw *A Man for All Seasons*. The former Benedictine priory—now a hotel—was used for background shots for the private residence of Sir Thomas More. It is really a stunning example of Elizabethan architecture, although it originally dates from the 12th century. Lived in for around 300 years by the Croke family, it was brought by Mr. and Mrs. E. E. Parke in 1961. They receive bed-and-breakfast guests for £25 ($57.50) in a single, from £32.50 ($74.75) to £46 ($103.50) in a double. All of the rooms have private baths.

Only seven miles from Oxford, the manor is protected from noise by its gardens and lawns. Stone built, in the manorial style with large halls and long bedroom wings, Studley is gabled with mullioned windows. The rooms are large, the beds soft, and the furnishings tasteful. Even if you're not staying over, you may want to drop in for lunch or dinner, with a four-course meal averaging around £10 ($23). Getting here is a bit complicated—so be armed with a good map when you strike out from Oxford.

WHERE TO EAT: Restaurant Elizabeth, 84 St. Aldate's (tel. Oxford 42230), is an intimate and special restaurant that (in spite of its name) owes the inspiration of its cuisine to the continent, notably Spain, France, and Greece. Under the watchful eye of Antonio Lopez, it attracts Oxonians who appreciate good food served in a friendly, inviting atmosphere. For appetizers, try either the ttoro (a Basque fish soup served with aioli) or avgolemono (the Greek national soup—chicken bouillon laced with a beaten egg and lemon juice). Favorite main dishes which we highly recommend include moussaka, charcoaled prawns with aioli, and coq au vin. For dessert, the syllabub is a winner. Including wine and coffee, plus all the extras, the cost of a dinner is about £14 ($32.20) per person. Wine by the liter, both Bourgogne and Bordeaux, is available. The restaurant is open for dinner from 6:30 to 11 p.m. every day, except Monday. Sunday lunch is from 12:30 to 2:30 p.m. and dinner from 7 to 10:30 p.m.

La Sorbonne, 130A The High (tel. Oxford 41320), is tucked away on a narrow lane off The High. True to its name, it provides typically French meals from time-tested recipes. A good beginning is the chef's special, moules marinières, offered from October to March only. An alternative suggestion is escargots bourguignonnes. Mr. Chavagnon, the chef de cuisine and proprietor, offers not only the usual French dishes, but the following specialties as well: jugged hare and suprême de volaille estragon. A soufflé for two costs £7 ($16.10). Mr.

Chavagnon says: "We charge a lot for soufflés because they require a lot of care and attention. When we tried to charge less, everybody wanted one and we couldn't cope." Expect to pay, on an average, about £15 ($34.50) per head. The restaurant is open from noon to 2:30 p.m. and from 7 to 10:30 p.m. It's closed on Sunday.

The **Turf Tavern,** 4–5 Bath Pl. (tel. Oxford 43235), is on a very narrow passage near the Bodleian Library, off New College Lane. A 13th-century tavern, it is surely the find of the year. It's run by a Yorkshireman, Wally Ellse, a former Royal Marine and boxer. His greeting is so enthusiastic it's like a tonic to cure even the most miserable soul. Thomas Hardy used the place for the setting of part of *Jude the Obscure.*

Inside the low-beamed hospice, you can order such hot dishes as fish and chips, shepherd's pie, pizza, and risotto in the £1.25 ($2.88) to £2 ($4.60) range. More impressive, however, is a table about eight feet long and four feet wide, covered with meats, fish, fowl, eggs, rum babas, bread puddings, sausages, and vegetables (all cold)—a spread of hors d'oeuvres, freshly prepared daily. You can fill your plate for about £2 ($4.60). Ask for the special "beer from the wood," brewed by a father-son combine. They don't advertise, preferring to put their money into the brew. If you're there on a cold day, ask for Wally's special Old English punch, made with rum, cider, red wine, cinnamon, cloves, and nutmeg. If you like it dry, lemon is added; otherwise, brown sugar. Also available is a large selection of country wines, including dandelion, cowslip, and rhubarb.

The **Cherwell Boathouse Restaurant,** Bardwell Road (tel. Oxford 52746), is owned by the people who rent out the punts, and it's run by a cheerful committee of amateurs who cater to impoverished undergraduates. The menu contains items which have obviously come from friends (Di's pork with mushrooms, for example). Two fixed menus which are rarely repeated are offered at each meal, and the cooks admit they try out new dishes all the time. Appetizers include soups or fish or meat pâtés, followed by casseroles, pies, and hot pots, then some exotic dessert—cikolatak pasta, rum soufflé, or fruit fool.

There is a very reasonable wine list, including brandy after dinner. The restaurant is open every evening from 8 to 10 p.m. and for Sunday lunch. For a regular dinner, the charge is £7.10 ($16.33), although Sunday lunch is only £6.70 ($8.51), plus VAT. It's recommended that you make a reservation. Children, if they don't order a full meal, are granted half price. In summer the restaurant also does an all-day cold buffet in the Marquee for thirsty punters. This place surely must be one of the most English, most attractive, and least known of the eating establishments of Oxford. It also provides an opportunity to observe a most important aspect of Oxford undergraduate life.

THE SPECIAL PUBS OF OXFORD: The **Bear Inn,** Alfred Street, is an Oxford tradition, a short block from The High overlooking the north side of Christ Church College. It's the village pub. Its swinging inn sign depicts the bear and ragged staff, old insignia of the Earls of Warwick, who were among the early patrons. Built in the 13th century, the inn has been known to many famous people who have lived and studied at Oxford. Over the years, it's been mentioned time and time again in English literature.

The Bear has served a useful purpose in breaking down social barriers, bringing a wide variety of people together in a relaxed and friendly way. You might talk with a rajah from India, a university don, a titled gentleman—and Dave and Des Beeson, who are the latest in a line of owners that goes back more than 700 years.

They may explain to you their astonishing hobby: collecting ties! Around the lounge bar you'll see thousands of snipped portions of neckties, which have been labeled with their owners' names. For those of you who want to leave a bit of yourself, a thin strip of the bottom of your tie will be cut off (with your permission, of course) with a huge pair of ceremonial scissors. Then you, as the donor, will be given a free drink on the house. After this initiation, you may want to join in some of the informal songfests of the undergraduates.

The shelves behind the bar are stacked and piled with delicious items to nibble on: cheese, crisp rolls, cold meats, flans. Homemade pie with french fries and beans costs 90p ($2.07); a ploughman's lunch, 60p ($1.38); and many salads are offered, from 80p ($1.84).

The **Trout Inn,** 195 Godstow Rd., near Wolvercote (tel. Oxford 54485), lies on the outskirts of Oxford. Ask any former or present student of Oxford to name his most treasured pub, and his answer is likely to be the Trout. Hidden away from tourists and townspeople, the Trout is a private world where you can get ale and beer—and top-notch meals. Have your drink in one of the historic rooms, with their settles, brass, and old prints, or go out in sunny weather to sit on a stone wall, where you can feed crumbs to the swans that swim in the adjoining weir pool. Take an arched stone bridge, stone terraces, architecture that has wildly pitched roofs and gables, throw in the Thames River, and you have the Trout. If you don't have a car, take bus 520 or 521 to Wolvercote, then walk.

Daily specials are featured for lunch. The seafood platter's popular, as is a tempting seven-ounce entrecôte. For dessert, try the fruit tart with cream. The pub is open from noon to 2 p.m. and from 7 to 10 p.m. Salads are served during the summer and grills in winter. Expect to pay about £6 ($13.80) for a meal, unless you settle for just a plate of smoked trout or salmon with brown bread and butter. If so, you're likely to pay £2 ($4.60).

On your way there and back, look for the view of Oxford from the bridge. And go ahead and talk with the undergraduates, who usually like telling about their university. They may even ask you to have tea at one of their colleges, where the average visitor rarely penetrates.

EATING AND DRINKING NEAR TO OXFORD: White Hart, Fyfield, seven miles along the A420 Oxford/Swindon/West Country (tel. Frilford Heath 390585), is high on the list of Oxford students who want to celebrate by taking their friends to a romantic inn—once the Fyfield Chantry—for a superb dinner. It's a public house, dating from the early 15th century, and owned since 1580 by St. John's College (although the present building is leased). In the 1960s the college renovated the inn, successfully restoring its old-world charm. It was once the home of a chantry priest and five almsmen until it was dissolved under Henry VIII. What was the lower chamber for the priest has now been transformed into a raftered dining room; and the ancient kitchen is the beamed lounge bar. The menu consists of house specialties, plus the dishes of the day. A lunch costs £4.75 ($10.93); a three-course dinner, from £6.50 ($14.95) to £8.50 ($19.55), including VAT, the difference in price depending on your selection of a main dish. The wines—an excellent selection—are extra. Specialties of the White Hart include traditional English food, with emphasis on game. The restaurant is open daily, and reservations are advised.

BLENHEIM PALACE: This extravagant baroque palace regards itself as England's answer to Versailles. Blenheim is the home of the 11th Duke of

Marlborough, a descendant of the first Duke of Marlborough (John Churchill), an on-again, off-again favorite of Queen Anne. In his day (1650-1722), the first duke became the supreme military figure in Europe. Fighting on the Danube near a village named Blenheim, Churchill defeated the forces of Louis XIV. The lavish palace of Blenheim was built for the duke as a gift from the queen. It was designed by Sir John Vanbrugh, who was also the architect of Castle Howard. Landscaping was carried out by Capability Brown.

The palace is loaded with riches: antiques, porcelain, oil paintings, tapestries, and chinoiserie. But more North Americans know Blenheim as the birthplace of Sir Winston. Today, the former prime minister lies buried in Bladon Churchyard, near the palace.

Blenheim Palace is open every day from April to October, inclusive, from 11:30 a.m. to 5 p.m. The last tour is at 5 p.m., and the last admittance to the palace is at 4:45 p.m. On spring bank holidays, Sundays, and Mondays charity events take place in the park, when different prices and times apply. The admission fee is £1.50 ($3.45) for adults, 90p ($2.07) for children.

In the park is the Bleinheim Model Railway, second longest in Britain, which you can usually ride on weekends in season. The palace is at Woodstock, eight miles north of Oxford on the A34 Road to Stratford-upon-Avon. From Oxford, do-it-your-selfers take bus 44 from the Gloucester Green Bus Station, which make the run to Woodstock.

3. Hertfordshire

Like a giant jellyfish, the frontier of Greater London spills over into this county, once described by Charles Lamb as "hearty, homely, loving Hertfordshire." This fertile land lies northwest of London and supplies much of that city's food, although industry has crept in. Hertfordshire is sometimes called "the market basket of England."

Its most important tourist attraction, which is usually visited on a day trip from London, follows.

HATFIELD HOUSE: One of the chief attractions of Hertfordshire, and one of the greatest of all English country houses, Hatfield House is just 21 miles north of London on the A1. To build what is now the E-shaped Hatfield House, the old Tudor palace at Hatfield was mostly demolished. The Banqueting Hall, however, remains.

Hatfield was much a part of the lives of both Henry VIII and his daughter Elizabeth I. In the old palace, built in the 15th century, Elizabeth romped and played as a child. Although Henry was married to her mother, Anne Boleyn, at the time of Elizabeth's birth, the marriage was later nullified (Anne lost her head and Elizabeth her legitimacy). Henry also used to stash away his oldest daughter, Mary Tudor, at Hatfield. But when Mary became Queen of England, and set about earning the dubious distinction of "Bloody Mary," she found Elizabeth a problem. For a while she kept her in the Tower of London, but she eventually let her return to Hatfield (Elizabeth's loyalty to Catholicism was seriously doubted). In 1558, while at Hatfield, Elizabeth learned of her ascension to the throne of England.

The Jacobean house that exists today contains much antique furniture, tapestries, and paintings as well as three much-reproduced portraits, including the famed ermine "rainbow portraits" of Elizabeth I. The Great Hall is suitably medieval, complete with a minstrel's gallery. One of the rarest exhibits is a pair of silk stockings, said to have been worn by Elizabeth herself, the first lady in

England to don such things. The park and the gardens are also worth exploring. The Riding School and Palace Stables contain a number of interesting historical and costume exhibitions.

Hatfield is usually open from March 25 through October 7, daily, except on Monday and Good Friday, from noon to 5 p.m.) on Sunday, from 2 to 5:30 p.m., and on bank holiday Mondays from 11 a.m. to 5 p.m.). Admission is £1.20 ($2.76). The house itself is across from the station in Hatfield. From London, take Green Line coach 716, 716a, or 724, or the fast trains from King's Cross. Luncheons and teas are available in the converted coach house in the Old Palace yard.

Elizabethan banquets are staged Tuesday, Thursday, Friday, and Saturday, and also Wednesday from May to September, with much gaiety and music. Guests are invited to drink in an anteroom, then join the long tables for a feast consisting of typical English food, ending with the classic syllabub. Wine is included in the cost of the meal, but you're expected to pay for your predinner drinks yourself. The best way to get there from London is to book a coach tour for an inclusive fee from £13.50 ($31.05). The Evan Evans agency has tours leaving from Russell Square or even from 41 Tottenham Court Rd. The coach returns to London after midnight. If you get there under your own steam, the cost is £10.50 ($24.15) on Tuesday, Wednesday, and Thursday, £12.50 ($28.75) on Friday and Saturday. For reservations, telephone Hatfield 62055.

In Old Hatfield, a fine place for light lunches and good lager is **Eight Bells,** a pub on Park Street. For Dickens fans, it was the inn where Bill Sikes and his dog found temporary refuge after the brutal murder of Nancy, It's a rickety old corner inn with a central bar for drinks and dining nooks—in all, a forest of time-blackened beams, settles, and pewter tankards. A bowl of homemade soup costs 30p (69¢), and the cook's specialty is smoked mackerel filet at £1.10 ($2.53).

HERTFORD: This old Saxon city is the county town, containing many fine examples of domestic architecture, some of which date back to the 16th century. Hertford is reached via the A1 or A10 from London. Samuel Stone, founder of Hartford, Connecticut, was born here. The town's Norman castle has long been in ruins, although part of the still-standing keep dates from the 16th century.

For food and lodgings, try the **Salisbury Arms Hotel,** Fore Street (tel. Hertford 53091), which has been called "always Hertford's principal inn." For 400 years it's been feeding and providing lodgings to wayfarers, or giving a hot grog to the coachman, a stable for his horses. Although the stables have long given way to a car park, a sense of history still prevails. In the cellar is medieval masonry predating the 16th-century structure around it. Cromwell is said to have lodged here, and both Royalists and Roundheads have mounted the Jacobean staircase. Bedrooms now spill over into a modern extension, a total of 22 functionally furnished rooms added to the 10 more antiquated original ones. Rates depend on the room occupied—single, double, or twin. Singles start at £13 ($29.90), going up to £15.20 ($34.96) for those requiring a private bath. Two persons pay from £20.50 ($47.15) to £23 ($52.90). Good, wholesome English "fayre" is provided. At lunch, when most visitors stop by, a cut from the roast of the day goes for £3 ($6.90) with vegetables. The dining room is paneled and intimately partitioned. There is, as well, a well-stocked cellar. Dinners are from £6 ($13.80).

ST. ALBANS: This cathedral city, just 21 miles northeast of London, dates back 2000 years. It was named after a Roman soldier, the first Christian martyr in England. Don't ask a resident to show you to the **Cathedral of St. Albans.** Here it's still known as "The Abbey," even though Henry VIII dissolved it as such in 1539. Construction on the cathedral was launched in 1077, making it one of the early Norman churches of England. The bricks, especially visible in the tower, came from the old Roman city of Verulamium at the foot of the hill. The nave and west front date from 1235.

The **Verulamium Museum** at St. Michael's stands on the site of the Roman city. Here you'll view some of the finest Roman mosaics in Britain. Part of the Roman town wall, a hypocaust, and a theater and its adjoining houses and shops are still visible. Visit in summer from 10 a.m. to 5:30 p.m. weekdays (on Sunday from 2 to 5:30 p.m.), and in winter from 10 to 4 weekdays, 2 to 4 on Sunday, paying 40p (92¢) for adults, 20p (46¢) for children.

The **Clock Tower** at Market Place was built in 1402, standing 77 feet high, a total of five floors.

From St. Albans you can visit **Gorhambury House,** a classic-style mansion built in 1777, containing 16th-century enameled glass and historic portraits. It's open, May to September, only on Thursday (2 to 5 p.m.), charging adults 80p ($1.84) for admission; children 40p (92¢). The location is 2½ miles north of St. Albans near the A5.

Salisbury Hall, a 17th-century house surrounded by a Norman moat, lies five miles south of St. Albans on the A6. Nell Gwynne, Charles II, even Jenny Churchill and her son Winston, have all stayed here. Inside, the fireplaces are of exceptional beauty. Also displayed is the prototype of the de Havilland "Mosquito" aircraft which was designed and built at Salisbury Hall in World War II. Visits are possible from Easter Sunday to October 1 on Sunday from 2 to 6 p.m. It is also open on Thursday from 2 to 6, from July 6 till around the end of September. Admission is 80p ($1.84) for adults, 35p (81¢) for children.

Back in St. Albans, we offer the following low-cost recommendations for food and lodgings:

Food and Lodging

St. Michael's Manor Hotel, Fishpool Street (tel. St. Albans 64444), stands on five acres of landscaped gardens, with a private reflection lake, about a ten-minute walk from the heart of St. Albans. At its core is an original manor house dating from the 16th century. The dedicated Newling Ward family run the hotel with flair and grace. To the original structure a William and Mary bow-fronted center section has been added, along with a Georgian-style extension.

The grounds of the hotel contain such trees as cedars of Lebanon and hornbeam, and all the attractively furnished bedrooms are named after the trees in the garden. Bathless singles cost £18 ($41.40) nightly, bathless twins going for £24 ($55.20). A twin room with a private bath and shower costs £30 ($69), including a full English breakfast. The Lilac Honeymoon Suite is most impressive, with its four-poster bed and lilac-colored bath.

In the Georgian-style dining room, lit by candlelight, a well-prepared international menu is presented nightly to both residents and nonresidents. At lunchtime, the chef serves a table d'hôte menu with coffee at £5 ($11.50) per head. For dinner, a three-course meal is offered at £7 ($16.10) per head, but the restaurant also has a reasonable à la carte menu at around £13 ($29.90) per person.

The **White Hart Hotel,** Holywell Hill (tel. St. Albans 53624), is a timbered inn of uncertain origin. It may have been a 13th-century coaching inn. At the White Hart, formerly called the Hartshorn, Hogarth painted the picture of himself which hangs in London's National Portrait Gallery. Of architectural interest is a lounge with a minstrels' gallery, oak timbering, and a collection of copper and antiques. The old-world dining room has Windsor chairs and paneled walls, and there are two lounge bars, all in the old English style. Bedrooms come with hot and cold running water, but none of the ten units has a private bath. Singles are expensive—£18 ($41.40) for bed and breakfast, although doubles or twins go for a more moderate £22 ($50.60) nightly, these tariffs including VAT, service, and a full English breakfast. In the dining room you can order from a table d'hôte menu and an à la carte selection. The White Hart stands opposite the cathedral and a short walk through the abbey grounds leads to the ruins of Roman Verulamium.

For dining, **Zorba's Greek Restaurant,** 3 French Row (tel. St. Albans 60609), seems an incongruous choice in such an historic English town, but it is a good and fairly inexpensive eating place. Right in the old part of town, it is reached by going along a pedestrian mall. The Theocharides family welcome you if you've come to dine, although we've seen them politely turn away English ladies who drop in just for afternoon tea, which they don't serve, incidentally. The house specialty, served with rice, is a kebab at £3.50 ($8.05). You might prefer to begin with a Greek salad at £1 ($2.30) or humus (ground chick peas with garlic) at £1.10 ($2.53). Pita bread is also served, as is the classic Greek moussaka at £2.85 ($6.56). Another house specialty is stuffed vine leaves, at £2.85 also. Although closed for lunch on Sunday and holidays, the restaurant is open otherwise until 3 p.m., and for dinner from 6 to 11:30 p.m.

SHAW'S CORNER: Just southwest of Ayot St. Lawrence, three miles northwest of Welwyn, stands the home where George Bernard Shaw lived from 1906 to 1950. The house is practically as he left it at his death. In the hall, for example, his hats are still hanging, as if ready for him to don one. His personal mementos are in his study, drawing room, dining room, and writing hut, which can be visited in March and November on Saturday and Sunday, and from April 1 to October 31 on Wednesday through Sunday from 11 a.m. to 1 p.m. and from 2 to 6 p.m. (or sunset if it comes before 6). Admission is 80p ($1.84) for adults, half price for children.

4. Buckinghamshire

This is a leafy county, lying north of the Thames and somewhat to the west of London. Its identifying marks are the wide Vale of Aylesbury, with its sprawling fields and tiny villages, and the long chalk range of the Chilterns. Going south from the range, you'll find what is left of a once-great beech forest.

A good center for touring the Chilterns is—

AYLESBURY: Gourmets still speak of its succulent ducks, a prize-winning dish on any table, although ducks bearing that name are usually raised elsewhere these days. The county town, Aylesbury has a number of timbered inns, old houses, and a wide Market Square. Although less than 40 miles from London, it remains cozily old world.

Six miles northwest of Aylesbury, **Waddeson Manor** contains an outstanding collection of decorative art of the 17th and 18th centuries. Among the paintings are portraits by Reynolds, Gainsborough, and Romney. Visiting times are from March 22 to October 29, Wednesday to Sunday, from 2 to 6 p.m. Admission to the grounds, aviary, and house is £1 ($2.30). The manor was built in the late 19th century for the Baron Ferdinand de Rothschild.

Back in Aylesbury itself, you can find food and lodgings at the **Kings Head,** Market Square (tel. Aylesbury 5158), a half-timbered hotel that was once a 15th-century coaching inn. It is one of the finest examples of Tudor architecture in Buckinghamshire. Its 15 bedrooms overlook a cobbled courtyard. Because of its heavy patronage by business people on weekdays, we've never been able to get a room unless reserved well in advance. Rooms, incidentally, cost from £23 ($52.90) in a double, plus VAT, and from £15 ($34.50) in a single, plus VAT. No unit has a private bath. Lunch is served from noon to 2 p.m. and dinner from 7 to 9 p.m. (from 7:30 to 10 p.m. on Saturday). Try to have a predinner drink in the cozy pub in back, with its collection of weapons. A three-course luncheon goes for £5.50 ($12.65), plus VAT. A set dinner is offered for £7 ($16.10), although there is an à la carte menu as well. The inn was much frequented by Cromwell, and his chair is still on view in the lounge bar. He slept in the Cromwell Room upstairs with its extra-large bed.

BUCKINGHAM: This old market town on the River Ouse was once the county town of Buckingham. It has a fine 13th-century Chantry Chapel and some 18th-century houses.

If you're motoring through, try to plan a luncheon or dinner stopover at **Old Market House,** Market Hill (tel. Buckingham 2385), housed in one of the town's most interesting buildings, a black-and-white timbered structure with leaded-glass windows. A three-course set luncheon is offered at £4 ($9.20) from noon to 2:15 p.m. If you arrive earlier, you can order morning coffee from 9:30 to 11 a.m. Dinner is à la carte, beginning at £7 ($16.10), and features the chef's specialty—chicken chasseur. Dinner is served every evening from 7 to 9:15 p.m. except Sunday and Monday. Wine is sold by the glass.

Food and Lodging

White Hart, Market Square (tel. Buckingham 2131), is an oldish market-town hotel, with 18th-century origins, although the plaster facade and portico are Victorian additions. In recent years the hotel has been remodeled and equipped for modern comfort, its renovation bringing simplicity to the interior. Of the hotel's 20 bedrooms, four have private baths and two come equipped with showers, although all units have television sets and coffee-making facilities. Bathless singles rent for £21 ($48.30), increasing to £24 ($55.20) with private bath; and bathless doubles cost £25 ($57.50), rising to £30 ($69) with private bath. The hotel's dining room, called the Georgian Room, has its own small dance floor, and there is a lounge bar as well.

MILTON'S COTTAGE: The modern residential town of Gerrards Cross is often called the Beverly Hills of England, as it attracts the wealthy-chic who settle here in many beautiful homes. Surrounding this plush section are several tucked-away hamlets, including **Chalfont St. Giles,** where the poet Milton lived during the Great Plague in 1665. He completed *Paradise Lost* here, and the cottage he lived in contains a small museum of Miltoniana. It is open daily, except Tuesday, from February 1 to November 1 from 10 a.m. to 1 p.m. and from 2:15 to 6 p.m. (on Sunday from 2:15 to 6 p.m.), charging 30p (69¢) for adults, 15p (35¢) for children. Off-season it is open on weekends only.

West of Gerrards Cross, the town of Beaconsfield, with its broad, tree-lined High Street, enjoys many associations with Disraeli. Visitors pass through here en route to—

HUGHENDEN MANOR: Outside High Wycombe, in Buckinghamshire, sits a country manor that gives us not only an insight into the age of Victoria, but acquaints us with a remarkable man. In Benjamin Disraeli we meet one of the most enigmatic figures of 19th-century England. At age 21, Dizzy published anonymously his five-volume novel *Vivian Grey*. But it wasn't his shining hour. He went on to other things, marrying an older widow for her money, although they developed, apparently, a most successful relationship. He entered politics and continued writing novels, his later ones meeting with more acclaim.

In 1848 Disraeli acquired Hughenden Manor, a country house that befitted his fast-rising political and social position. He served briefly as prime minister in 1868, but his political fame rests on his stewardship as prime minister during 1874-80. He became Queen Victoria's friend, and in 1877 she paid him a rare honor by visiting him at Hughenden.

In 1876 Disraeli became the Earl of Beaconsfield: he had arrived. Only his wife was dead, and he was to die in 1881. Instead of being buried at Westminster Abbey, he preferred the simple little graveyard of Hughenden Church.

His library is preserved much as he left it. In fact, Hughenden contains an odd assortment of memorabilia, including a lock of Disraeli's hair. The letters from Victoria, the autographed books, and especially a portrait of Lord Byron, known to Disraeli's father.

If you're driving to Hughenden Manor on the way to Oxford, continue north of High Wycombe on the A4128 for about 1½ miles. If you're relying on public transportation from London, take coach 711 to High Wycombe, then board an Alder Valley bus (27, 27a, 31, or 34a). The manor house and garden are open daily except Monday and Tuesday from April to October, from 2 to 6 p.m. (from 12:30 to 6 p.m. on Sunday and bank holidays). In March and November, they're open on Saturday and Sunday only from 2 to 5 p.m. (or sunset if earlier). Admission for adults is 90p ($2.07), half price for children. It is closed all December, January, and February, and on Good Friday.

WEST WYCOMBE: Snuggled in the Chiltern Hills 30 miles west of London, the village of West Wycombe still has an atmosphere of the early 18th century. The thatched roofs have been replaced with tiles, and some of the buildings have been removed or replaced, but the village is still two centuries removed from the present day.

In the Mid-18th century, Sir Francis Dashwood began an ambitious building program at West Wycombe. His strong interest in architecture and design led Sir Francis to undertake a series of monuments and parks which are still among the finest in the country today. He also sponsored the building of a road using the chalk quarries on the hill to aid in the support of the poverty-stricken villagers. The resulting caves became the meeting place of "The Knights of St. Francis of Wycombe," later known as **"The Hellfire Club."** The knights consisted of a number of illustrious men drawn from the social circle surrounding the Prince of Wales. Its members "gourmandized," swilling claret and enjoying the company of women "of a cheerful, lively disposition. . .who considered themselves lawful wives of the brethren during their stay."

You can tour the caves today, wandering through a quarter mile of winding passages, past colorful waxwork scenes brought to life by sound and light effects. The caves are open from 11 a.m. to 6 p.m. daily from March through September, and from noon to 4 p.m. on weekends only during the rest of the year. Admission is £1 ($2.30) for adults, 50p ($1.15) for children.

Other sights at West Wycombe include the **Church of St. Lawrence,** perched atop West Wycombe Hill. Parts of the church date from the 13th century; its richly decorated interior was copied from a third-century Syrian sun temple. The view from the church tower is worth the trek up the hill. Near the church stands the Dashwood Mausoleum, designed in the style of Constantine's Arch in Rome.

A visit to **West Wycombe House,** home of the Dashwoods, is of both historical and architectural interest. Both George III and Ben Franklin stayed here, although not at the same time. The house is one of the best examples of Palladian-style architecture in England. The interior is lavishly decorated with paintings and antiques from the 18th century.

During your tour, you may also wander freely through the village, stopping for lunch at one of the public houses, or browsing through the gift shop. Four miles of nature trails also meander about the village, through forests and farmlands.

Although the Dashwood house is open only from June 1 to August 30, the rest of the village may, of course, be visited all year. The house is open Monday to Friday from 2:15 to 6 p.m. and charges an admission of £1 ($2.30) for adults and 50p ($1.15) for children. If you just want to visit the grounds, the cost is reduced to 80p ($1.84).

5. Bedfordshire

This county contains the fertile, rich Vale of Bedford, crossed by the River Ouse. Most visitors from London head here on a day trip to visit historic Woburn Abbey (previewed below). Others know of its county town—

BEDFORD: On the Ouse, Bedford contains many riverside parks and gardens, but is better known for its associations with Bunyan. In Mill Street stands the 1850 **Bunyan Meeting House,** erected on the site of a barn where Bunyan used to preach. The bronze doors, considered to be artistically outstanding, illustrate ten scenes from *Pilgrim's Progress.* The Bunyan Meeting House contains the surviving relics of Bunyan and a famous collection of the *Pilgrim's Progress* in 165 languages. Open Tuesday to Saturday from 2 to 4 p.m., it charges 20p (46¢) for admission.

About 1½ miles south of Bedford lies Elstow, Bunyan's reputed birthplace. Here you can visit **Elstow Moot Hall,** a medieval market hall containing exhibits depicting the life and times of John Bunyan. It is open Tuesday through Saturday, 10 a.m. to 1 p.m. and 2 to 5 p.m. (on Sunday from 2 to 5:30 p.m., or dusk in winter), charging 10p (23¢) for adults, 5p (12¢) for children, and 25p (58¢) for a family ticket.

WOBURN ABBEY: Few tourists visiting Bedfordshire miss the Georgian mansion of **Woburn Abbey,** the seat of the Dukes of Bedford for nearly three centuries. The much-publicized 18th-century estate is about 42 miles from London outside Woburn. Its State Apartments are rich in furniture, porcelain, tapestries, silver, and a valuable art collection, including paintings by Van Dyck, Holbein, Rembrandt, Gainsborough, and Reynolds. A series of paintings by Canaletto, showing his continuing views of Venice, grace the walls of the dining room in the Private Apartments (Prince Philip said the duke's collection was superior to the Canalettos at Windsor—but Her Royal Highness quickly corrected him!). Of all the paintings, one of the most notable from an historical point of view is the *Armada Portrait* of Elizabeth I. Her hand rests on the globe, as Philip's invincible armada perishes in the background.

Queen Victoria and Prince Albert visited Woburn Abbey in 1841. Victoria slept in an opulently decorated bedroom (her night dress is still there). In 1954, another queen—this one of the cinema, Marilyn Monroe—slept in the same bed as a publicity stunt. Victoria's Dressing Room contains a fine collection of 17th-century paintings from the Netherlands. Among the oddities and treasures at Woburn Abbey are a Grotto of Shells, a Sèvres dinner service (gift of Louis XV), a China Salon, and a chamber devoted to memorabilia of "The Flying Duchess." Wife of the 11th Duke of Bedford, she was a remarkable woman, who disappeared on a solo flight in 1937 (the same year as Amelia Earhart). The duchess, however, was 72 years old at the time.

In the 1950s, the present Duke of Bedford opened Woburn Abbey to the public to pay off some $15 million in inheritance taxes. In 1974 he turned the estate over to his son and daughter-in-law, the Marquess and Marchioness of Tavistock, who reluctantly took on the business of running the 75-room mansion. And what a business it is, drawing more than a million visitors a year and employing more than 300 persons to staff the shops and grounds.

Today, Woburn Abbey is surrounded by a 3000-acre park containing many rare and exotic animals (ten varieties of deer). Some visit just to see the animals. While seated in one of 57 gondolas on the two-mile cable lift, you pass over lions, elephants, and giraffes. What would Humphrey Repton, the designer of the estate's park in the 18th century, say?

Woburn Abbey is outside Woburn, near Dunstable. It is hard to reach by public transportation from London, so you may prefer to take one of the organized tours.

From January to Easter the park is open from noon to 3:45 p.m., the house from 1 to 4 p.m. From Easter on, the park is open from 10 a.m. to 4:45 p.m., the house from 11 a.m. to 5 p.m. The abbey is closed from December 22 to Boxing Day, but everything else is open all year. Admission to the park is only 50p ($1.15) for adults, 25p (58¢) for children. A combined ticket to the park and abbey goes for £1.50 ($3.45) for adults, only 25p (58¢) for children. The Animal Kingdom is open daily throughout the year. If you take one of the safari bus tours, you pay £1 ($2.30) per adult, 50p ($1.15) per child. If you drive yourself, the car and all occupants will cost £3.40 ($7.82).

After visiting the abbey, a good spot for both food and lodgings is the **Bedford Arms,** George Street (tel. Woburn 441). This is a Georgian coaching inn with a checkered history which blends the old and new at the gates of the estate of the Duke of Bedford. Tastefully modernized, it still preserves a mellow charm. Its 80-seat Georgian dining room was designed by Henry Holland, architect of the Woburn estate. Guests are housed in one of 41 pleasantly furnished bedrooms, more than half of which contain private baths or showers. Bathless singles rent for £25 ($57.50), going up to £27.25 ($62.68) with private bath. Bathless twins cost from £31.50 ($72.45), or else £34.50 ($79.35) with private bath, each unit containing coffee-making facilities, radio, phone, automatic alarm system, and color TV. A bar adjoining the hotel's main restaurant has been restored, its old beams exposed, as well as its inglenook fireplaces.

Chapter VI

KENT, SURREY, AND THE SUSSEXES

1. Kent's Country Houses and Castles
2. Canterbury
3. Dover
4. Tunbridge Wells
5. Richmond
6. Haslemere
7. Rye
8. Winchelsea
9. Hastings and St. Leonard's
10. Battle
11. Alfriston and Lewes
12. East Grinstead
13. Brighton
14. Arundel
15. Chichester

LYING TO THE SOUTH and southeast of London are the shires (counties) of Kent, Surrey, and the Sussexes. Combined, they form a most fascinating part of England to explore, and are easy to reach, within commuting distance of the capital.

Of all the centers, **Canterbury** in Kent is of foremost interest, but the old Cinque ports of **Rye** and **Winchelsea** in East Sussex are equally exciting, as is **Brighton** in its own distinctive way. In and around these major meccas are dozens of castles and vast estates, monuments, homes of famous men, cathedrals, yachting harbors, and little villages of thatched cottages.

The range of accommodations varies from an old-world smugglers' inn at the ancient seaport of Rye to a 16th-century house in Canterbury featured in *David Copperfield*. Throughout the counties of the south coast, you'll discover some superb bargains, as the English themselves come to these coastal shires for the sun and are accustomed to paying reasonable rates.

In the fog-choked cities of Northern England, the great dream for retirement is to find a little rose-covered cottage in the south, where the living's easier.

SURREY/SUSSEX/KENT 207

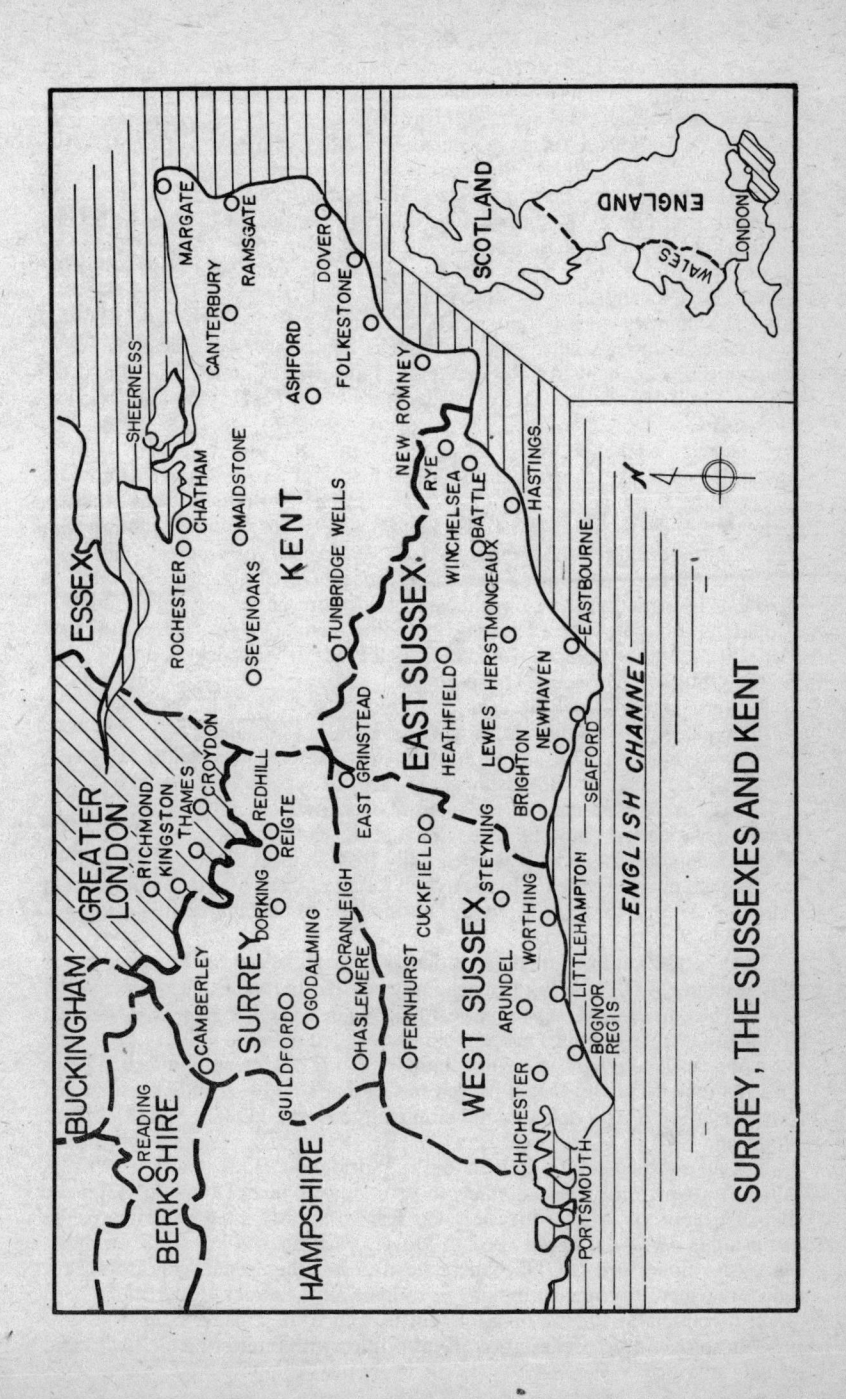

SURREY, THE SUSSEXES AND KENT

KENT

Fresh from his cherry orchard, the Kentish farmer heads for his snug spot by an inglenook, with its bright-burning fire, for his glass of cherry brandy. The day's work is done. All's right with the world.

We're in what was once the ancient Anglo-Saxon kingdom of Kent, on the fringes of London itself, yet far removed in spirit and scenery. Since the days of the Tudors, cherry blossoms have pinkened the fertile landscape. Not only orchards, but hop fields abound. The conically shaped oasthouses with kilns for drying the hops dot the rolling countryside. Both the hops and orchards have earned for Kent the title of the garden of England. And in England the competition's rough for that distinction.

The country is also rich in Dickensian associations—in fact, Kent is sometimes known as Dickens Country. His family once lived near the naval dockyard at Chatham. At **Rochester**, 30 miles from London, you'll find his home, Gad's Hill, at the edge of town (in *Pickwick Papers* is a description of the Bull Inn).

Charles Dickens Centre, Eastgate, High Street, in Rochester, is open seven days a week, from 10 a.m. to 12:30 p.m. and 2 to 5:30 p.m. Admission is 50p ($1.15) for adults, 25p (58¢) for children. The museum has tableaux depicting various scenes from Dickens's novels, including a Pickwickian Christmas scene, then the fever-ridden graveyard of *Bleak House*, scenes from *The Old Curiosity Shop* and *Great Expectations, Oliver Twist*, and *David Copperfield*. Information is also available at the centre on various other sights in Rochester associated with Dickens, including Eastgate House and, in the garden, the chalet, transported from Gad's Hill Place, where Dickens died, as well as the Guildhall Museum, Rochester Cathedral, and the mysterious "6 Poor Travellers' House." Pick up a brochure which includes a map featuring the various places and the novels with which each is associated.

Canterbury, the road to Dover, the byways of Kent, were all known to the Victorian novelist. At Broadstairs, his favorite seaside resort, what is now **Dickens House Museum** (on the main seafront) was once the home of Mary Pearson Strong, on whom he based much of the character of Betsey Trotwood, David Copperfield's aunt. It is open daily from 2:30 to 5:30 p.m. from April to October, charging 40p (92¢) admission for adults, 15p (35¢) for children. On Tuesday, Wednesday, and Thursday, from June to September, it is also open from 7 to 9 in the evening.

An attraction for Canadian readers is the square, red brick, gabled home where James Wolfe, the English general who defeated the French in the battle for Québec, lived until he was 11 years old. Called **Québec House**, a National Trust property, it contains memorabilia associated with the military hero, who was born in Westerham (Kent) on January 2, 1727. The house which Wolfe's parents rented may be visited March to October—daily except Thursday and Saturday, 2 to 6 p.m., for an admission charge of 90p ($2.07), 50p ($1.15) for children.

Kent suffered severe destruction in World War II, as it was the virtual alley over which the Luftwaffe flew in its infamous blitz of London. After the fall of France, a German invasion was feared. Shortly after becoming prime minister in 1940, Churchill sped to Dover, with his bowler, stogie, walking cane, and pin-striped suit. Once there, he inspected the coastal defense and gave encouragement to the men digging in to fight off the attack. But Hitler's "Sea Lion" (code name for the invasion) turned out to be a paper tiger.

In spite of much devastation, Kent is filled with interesting old towns and stately homes.

1. Kent's Country Houses and Castles

CHURCHILL'S HOME: For many years, Sir Winston lived at **Chartwell**, which lies 1½ miles south of Westerham in Kent. Churchill, a descendant of the first Duke of Marlborough, was born in grand style at Blenheim Palace on November 30, 1874. Chartwell doesn't pretend to be as grand a place as Blenheim, but it's been preserved as a memorial, administered by the National Trust. The rooms remain as Churchill left them, including maps, documents, photographs, pictures, and other personal mementos. In two rooms are displayed a selection of gifts that the prime minister received from people all over the world. There is also a selection of many of his well-known uniforms. Terraced gardens descend toward the lake with its celebrated black swans. In a garden studio are many of Churchill's painting. Go if you want to see where a giant of a man lived and worked. The house is open from March 1 to November 30 on Tuesday, Wednesday, and Thursday from 2 to 6 p.m.; Saturday and Sunday from 11 a.m. to 6 p.m. Entrance to the house and gardens costs £1.20 ($2.76) for adults, 60p ($1.38) for children. There's a restaurant, serving snacks, tea, and coffee.

KNOLE: Begun in the mid-15th century by Thomas Bourchier, archbishop of Canterbury, Knole is one of the largest private houses in England, and is considered one of the finest examples of the purely British Tudor style of architecture.

Henry VIII confiscated it along with other church property in 1537, and it was later granted to Thomas Sackville, Earl of Dorset, by Queen Elizabeth I. Sackville, whose descendants reside in Knole to the present day (although the building was donated to the National Trust in 1946), extended the mansion by adding long gabled wings and the great hall.

The completed house is huge, with 365 rooms, seven courts, and more than 50 staircases. The elaborate paneling and friezework provide a background for the 17th- and 18th-century tapestries and rugs, the Jacobean furniture, and the collection of family portraits.

Knole, in the village of Sevenoaks, about five miles north of Tonbridge, is open to the public from April through November, Wednesday to Saturday, from 11 a.m. to dusk (on Sunday from 2 p.m. to dusk). Admission is £1.60 ($3.68), with no reductions for children.

HEVER CASTLE: The 13th-century moated castle just three miles southeast of Edenbridge has the distinction of having been the residence of two of the wives of Henry VIII. The family home of Anne Boleyn, it was forfeited by Henry's second wife—along with her head. Later, Henry gave Hever Castle to his proxy wife, the "great Flanders mare," Anne of Cleves when he discovered that this mail-order bride did not live up to her Holbein portrait. Anne did not mind, however, since she was perfectly happy to settle into a comfortable castle with plenty of money. It was certainly better than the king's usual alternative.

The forecourt of the castle and the gardens were used during the filming of *Anne of a Thousand Days* in 1969. The fortress-like Hever Castle is open to the public from April through September. Hours are 1:30 to 6:15 p.m. on Tuesday, Wednesday, Friday, Sunday, and bank holidays. Admission is £1 ($2.30) for adults and 50p ($1.15) for children, except on Tuesday and Friday, when the charge is £1.50 ($3.45) for adults, 70p ($1.61) for children. On these days, additional rooms are on view, and the extra charge is intended to give visitors an opportunity to view the castle under the best possible conditions.

The estate, now the home of Lord and Lady Astor of Hever, was redesigned around the turn of the century to include a formal Italian garden, complete with fountains, classical statuary, and shrubbery trimmed into fantastic shapes. The grounds also include a 35-acre lake through which the Eden River flows. The gardens are open from 1 to 6 p.m. on the same days as those listed for the castle. Admission is 80p ($1.84) for adults, 30p (69¢) for children. Admission to the castle grounds is required before you can purchase your additional ticket to the castle.

CHILHAM CASTLE GARDENS: This former royal property can be reached from the M2 Faversham turnoff—the A252 (Canterbury–Maidstone road) or the Folkestone–London road (the A20). It was used as a hunting lodge by more than one royal personage until King Henry VIII sold it. The castle is closed on Monday and Friday. From April 1 to May 4 and September 29 to October 31, the hours are 2 to 6 p.m., and admission is £1 ($2.30) for adults, 50p ($1.15) for children, going up to £1.10 ($2.53) for adults and 55p ($1.27) for children from May 5 to September 28, when the castle is open from noon to 7 p.m.

Falconry displays are given hourly, and the Battle of Britain Museum is open all day. On Sunday, jousting is staged, and the charge is £1.50 ($3.45) for adults, 75p ($1.73) for children. If the jousting is canceled because of weather, the weekday rates apply. On holiday Sundays and Mondays when there are medieval jousting exhibitions, the cost for an adult is £2.20 ($5.06); for children, £1.10 ($2.53).

There is also a display by Woodwings Flying Circus of scale-model airplanes doing aerobatics and a display of the "dogfights" and bombings of the Battle of Britain.

PENSHURST PLACE: This magnificent English Gothic-style mansion, one of the outstanding country houses in Britain, lies 33 miles from London and 3½ miles west of Tonbridge on the Tunbridge Wells Road. A house of some importance seems to have stood on the site since 1085. Sir John de Pulteney, four times mayor of London, built the stone house whose Great Hall forms the heart of Penshurst, even after more than 600 years. The boy king, Edward VI, presented the house to Sir William Sidney, and it has remained in this family ever since, becoming, in 1554, the birthplace of the soldier-poet, Sir Philip Sidney. In the first half of the 17th century, Penshurst was known as a center of literature, attracting such personages as Ben Jonson.

Visitors are shown through the premises, including the splendid State Dining Room and Queen Elizabeth's Room. In the Stable Wing is an interesting Toy Museum. The site is open daily, except Monday and Friday, from April 1 to October 5, and each bank holiday. The gardens and home park are open noon to 6 p.m., April to June, and from 11:30 a.m. to 6 p.m., July to October 5. Inclusive tickets to the house, grounds, toy museum, and exhibition are £1.50 ($2.30) for adults, 75p ($1.73) for children.

LEEDS CASTLE: This castle at Maidstone, dating from A.D. 857, was once described by Lord Conway as the loveliest castle in the world. Originally built of wood, it was rebuilt in 1119 in its present stone structure. It is surrounded by a moat and is an almost impregnable fortress.

The castle has strong links with America through the sixth Lord Fairfax who, as well as owning the castle, owned five million acres in Virginia and was a close friend and mentor of the young George Washington.

Within the surrounding parkland, there is a wild wood garden and duckery where rare swans, geese, and ducks can be seen, and the aviaries contain a superb collection of birds, including parakeets and cockatoos. Dogs are not allowed here, but dog lovers will enjoy the Great Danes of the castle and the unique collection of dog collars dating from the Middle Ages. A nine-hole golf course is open to the public daily.

The castle is open from April 1 to October 30 on Tuesday, Wednesday, Thursday, and Sunday (every day during August) from noon to 5 p.m. Admission is £1.90 ($4.37) to the castle and grounds.

Every Saturday from 7:15 to 11 p.m., a Kentish evening takes place in the Jacobean Tithe Barn, the Fairfax Hall, when a five-course meal is served with wine and musical entertainment for £15 ($34.50) per person. Advance booking is essential. Telephone Maidstone 65400 for reservations.

Postscript: **Violet Bourne,** 70 High St., Milton Regis, near Sittingbourne (tel. Sittingbourne 23762 in the evenings), owns the Elizabethan house in which she lives and has filled it with Victoriana. Each room has been furnished absolutely to period down to the last ornament and trinket—a tiny purse made of shells, polished and lacquered musical boxes, and chiming clocks. She is delighted to take visitors around, charging 50p ($1.15) to see her lovely collection. She prefers afternoon visitors.

2. Canterbury

Under the arch of the ancient West Gate journeyed Chaucer's knight, solicitor, nun, squire, parson, merchant, miller, and cook—spinning racy tales. They were bound for the shrine of Thomas à Becket, archbishop of Canterbury, who was slain by four knights of Henry II on December 29, 1170. (The king later walked barefoot from Harbledown to the tomb of his former friend, where he allowed himself to be flogged in penance.) The shrine was finally torn down in 1538 by Henry VIII, as part of his campaign to destroy the monasteries and graven images. Canterbury, then, had already been an attraction of long standing.

The medieval Kentish city, on the Stour River, is the mother city of England, its ecclesiastical capital. Mother city is an apt title, as Canterbury was known to have been inhabited centuries before the birth of Christ. Julius Caesar, once went on a rampage near it. Although its most famous incident was the murder of Becket, the medieval city witnessed other major moments in English history—including Bloody Mary's ordering of nearly 40 victims to be burned at the stake. Richard the Lionhearted came back this way from crusading, and Charles II passed through on the way to claim his crown.

Canterbury was once completely walled, and many traces of its old fortifications remain. In the 16th century, weavers—mostly Huguenots from northern France and the Low Countries—fled to Canterbury to escape religious persecution. They started a weaving industry that flourished until the expanding silk trade with India ruined it.

The old city is much easier to reach today than it was in Chaucer's time. As it lies 56 miles from London, it is within a 1½-hour train ride from Victoria Station.

Now, as in the Middle Ages, the goal of the pilgrim remains:

CANTERBURY CATHEDRAL: The present Gothic structure, erected on the site of an even earlier church, dates back 100 years (1070) before the murder of Becket. From the outside, the Perpendicular tower in the center (known locally as Bell Harry) comes into view first. Inside, the Perpendicular Gothic nave was built in the 14th century with a fan-vaulted ceiling. It soars. The early Gothic 12th-century choir—considered revolutionary in the history of English architecture—represents mainly the guiding talent of William of Sens (the building of the choir cost the master mason his life, as he suffered a fall that eventually caused his death).

As mentioned before, Becket's shrine was destroyed by the Tudor king, but the site of that tomb is in Trinity Chapel, near the High Altar. The saint is said to have worked miracles and the cathedral contains some rare stained glass depicting those feats. Perhaps the most miraculous thing is that the windows escaped Henry VIII's agents of destruction and Hitler's bombs as well (part of the cathedral was hit in World II).

Near Becket's shrine is an effigy marking the grave of Edward, "The Black Prince," who died in 1376 and is famed chiefly for his role in the Battle of Poitiers when he netted the French king, John II. Also in the area is the tomb of Henry IV (who died in 1413), and that of his queen, Joan of Navarre. Behind Trinity Chapel is "Becket's Crown," in which you'll find St. Augustine's Chair, one of the symbols of the archbishop of Canterbury's authority.

WHERE TO STAY: Before you can begin any serious exploring, you'll need to find a hotel. You have several possibilities, both in the city itself, and on the outskirts, ranging from craggy Elizabethan houses of historic interest to modern studio-type bedrooms with private baths. We'll proceed in descending order of cost.

The Upper Bracket

Slatters, St. Margaret's Street (tel. Canterbury 63271), is a record of the city's changing past. Originally, its Jolly Miller Restaurant was built in the 17th century, and many of its old beams and stones are intact. But today the hotel has branched out, erecting a new structure on ground once occupied by buildings bombed in World War II. Slatters, as a result, has emerged as one of the most up-to-date establishments in the shire. The contemporary bedrooms, most with private baths, are motel-like in their efficiency. Most of the rooms convert into sitting areas during the day, with armchairs, a radio, and television. All rates include breakfast. A bathless single rents for £18 ($41.40), going up to £20 ($46) with bath. A bathless double is tabbed at £25 ($57.50), rising to £30 ($69) with bath, these tariffs including an English breakfast, service, and VAT. A set lunch costs around £4 ($9.20); a table d'hôte dinner, about £5.50 ($12.65), depending on your choice of a main dish. Parking is available even though you're in the heart of congested Canterbury, a five-minute stroll from the cathedral. The fully licensed Jolly Miller Restaurant serves lunch and dinner.

Chaucer, Ivy Lane (tel. Canterbury 64427), harmonizes modern features with its original Regency character. It's within strolling distance of the cathedral in the old part of the city. The bedrooms are well furnished, with good central heating, adequate storage space, and comfortable beds. The hotel has 51 bedrooms, 31 with private bathrooms. Facilities for making your own morning coffee or tea are available in the rooms, as well as color TV, radio, and telephone. A bathless single rents for £20 ($46) nightly, increasing to £23

($52.90) with private bath. Bathless doubles go for £26 ($59.80), rising to £31 ($71.30) with bath. The Pilgrim's Bar is comfortable and tastefully decorated and offers a variety of bar snacks. The Dickensian restaurant is famed for its local specialties, such as filet of beef Chaucer and Pilgrim's lamb. Service and VAT are included in the tariffs.

The Medium-Priced Range

The **County Hotel,** High Street (tel. Canterbury 66266), has been a hotel since the closing years of the reign of Victoria. But its recorded history goes back to the end of the 12th century, when Jacob the Jew built a private town house on the spot. Over the years, it has undergone many changes and alterations, in both its structure and its name. It was first licensed in 1629. Today, it offers 73 luxury bedrooms fully equipped with private bathrooms and showers, color TV, tea- and coffee-making facilities, radios, and telephones. The intimate restaurant offers a full à la carte menu, or for a more informal meal the coffeeshop is open from 11 a.m. to 11 p.m. The rate for a single room is £28 ($64.40) and for a twin or double room, £37 ($85.10). All prices include a full English breakfast and VAT. The service charge is left to the customer's discretion. The average cost of a meal in the restaurant is £6.50 ($14.95) for lunch and £10 ($23) for dinner.

Abbots Barton Hotel, New Dover Road (tel. Canterbury 60341), was built to order in the 19th century to simulate a French château. Adorned with chimneys, turrets, gables, and towers, it is at the edge of the city, surrounded by gardens (yews, cypress, fir, walnut, and copper beech). The interior is close to the heart of Victoriana; there are no special antiques, but pleasantly comfortable pieces. More than half of the 40 bedrooms contain private baths, and all of them have hot and cold running water. A single goes for £9.50 ($21.85) without bath, £10 ($23) with bath. A twin costs £18 ($41.40) without bath, £19.50 ($44.85) for two persons with bath. The rates quoted include an English breakfast; service is added. Abbots Barton is mostly a hotel catering to families. You can order a table d'hôte dinner for £4.75 ($10.93). Afternoon tea is served in the drawing room in the classic English tradition.

The **Falstaff Hotel,** St. Dunstan's Street (tel. Canterbury 62138), is a restored coaching inn (you drive in where coaches from London to Dover used to unload their passengers). Just outside Westgate, near the River Stour, it is easy to spot, with its black and white timbered gables. Its street floor is devoted to pub-style lounges, the soul of Falstaff even after 500 years. On the floors above are a dining room, with its collection of antique clocks and framed Dutch tiles, and the well-kept bedrooms. Each of the rooms has hot and cold running water; private baths are rare. The rate in a single is £14 ($32.20). Twins range from £28 ($64.40) to £31 ($71.30), depending on the plumbing. Tariffs include an English breakfast. A three-course lunch or dinner costs from £5 ($11.50).

Queen's Head Hotel, Walting Street (tel. Canterbury 62373), is a well-renovated 15th-century inn, right in the center of Canterbury, within walking distance of the cathedral. It is on the site of the largest amphitheater built outside of Rome (500–300 B.C.). For the tidy and immaculate rooms upstairs, the charge is £10.50 ($24.15) per person for bed and breakfast. Three-course lunches at the pub's well-stocked, fully licensed bar can cost as little as £2 ($4.60), and dinner in the Old Granary restaurant is table d'hôte or à la carte, going for around £6 ($13.80). The restaurant, incidentally, contains a priest escape hole, connected via a tunnel to the cathedral. Like the rest of the building, it is part of one of the oldest coaching inns in Britain, a great deal of its timber coming from ships wrecked on the Goodwin Sands outside nearby

Dover (15 miles away). London is just one hour and 20 minutes away, and the hotel makes a good base from which to explore the southeast coast of England, and, of course, the atmosphere of the old English inn makes it just the place for relaxing after a day's sightseeing. George and Kay Howes, your hosts, do their best to make your stay comfortable.

The Budget Range

Cathedral Gate Hotel and Restaurant, 37 Burgate (tel. 64381), is for the modern-day pilgrims who want to rest their bones at an inn shouldering up to the cathedral's gateway. In 1620 this former hospice became one of the earliest of the fashionable coffee and tea houses of England. Its facade was added in the 19th century, however. The interior reveals many architectural features of the 17th century. Ms. Adsett is devoted to the hotel, and has done much to furnish it as authentically as possible. Two curved bay windows in the living room overlook the little square in front of the gateway. On chilly nights, log fires burn in an old fireplace, although the bedrooms are heated electrically. Each of the 33 bedrooms has hot and cold running water. Some contain private baths. The single rate goes from £9 ($20.70) to £11 ($25.30); the double tariff runs from £12 ($27.60) to £17 ($39.10), plus 10% for service. A full English breakfast is an additional £3 ($6.90). The ground-floor restaurant serves morning coffee, luncheon, afternoon teas, and evening snacks, and is licensed.

The **House of Agnes Hotel**, 71 Saint Dunstan's St. (tel. Canterbury 65077), remains much as Dickens described it in *David Copperfield*, as the home of Agnes Wickfield, heroine of the novel. Built in the 16th century, the House of Agnes is an authentic, Tudor black-and-white-timbered building—historic surroundings at budget prices. The Frost family, who run it, quote bed-and-breakfast terms (depending on the room and the time of year) ranging from £9 ($20.70), inclusive. Some of the bedrooms are handsome and cozy; all ye olde chambers have hot and cold running water. The hotel has its own car park, TV lounge, and full central heating.

WHERE TO EAT: The **Castle Restaurant**, 71 Castle St. (tel. Canterbury 65658), is frequented by in-the-know "Canterburians" as the choicest dining spot in the medieval city (the building itself dates back to 1485)—choice not only because of its refined cuisine, but because of economy, too. It is directed by Mr. and Mrs. Benjamin, who keep it unpretentious and unspoiled. For suggestions: The soups have rarely been found disappointing—a choice of two is offered daily for 45p ($1.04). The specialties run to grills and fish dishes (prices include chips and garden peas), with such favorites as large Dover sole going for £5.50 ($12.65) and rainbow trout, £3.50 ($8.05). Two grilled lamb cutlets cost £2.80 ($6.44). The desserts are especially good and widely varied, often featuring a gooseberry tart with fresh cream, costing 90p ($2.07). The restaurant is open from 10 a.m. to 10 p.m. On Saturday, it's imperative to book before 4 p.m.

Adelaide Silver Grill, Adelaide Place (tel. 65658), is part of the Castle Restaurant recommended above. It, too, is run by the Benjamins. Mr. Benjamin flits between one restaurant and the other via the "coalhole." The grill room has a slower turnover and higher prices. The food is good, and the place has a fine reputation among locals. Both restaurants are joined by a common kitchen, although much of the cooking in the Adelaide is on a grille in the dining room. The average price of a meal is £8 ($18.40), including drinks. For starters try a selection of hors d'oeuvres from the trolley, which holds 18 different varieties, at £1.80 ($4.14). Grilled fish is a main dish specialty, ranging in price from £4 ($9.20) to £6 ($13.80). A meat specialty at £3.40 ($7.82) is grilled Barnsley chop with mint sauce (a double loin lamb chop). Incidentally, steaks and chops are on display, and you can select your own if you wish. A choice from the sweets trolley will cost you an additional £1.25 ($2.88). With its reds and browns, the dining room is inclined to give one the feeling of a nightclubbish place. You need to reserve for Saturday luncheons.

On the Outskirts

The **Abbot's Fireside,** Elham (tel. Elham 265), has been a famous restaurant for many years. The Prebble family has owned the inn for the past decade or so, although the family's roots in the village go back to the 14th century. The building itself is circa 1480, an example of pre-Renaissance architecture. Its wooden mullions and transoms have been well preserved. The whole structure leans forward, as if it's been standing too long. Latticed windows and grotesquely carved wooden brackets give an old-world aura. In one room is a great old fireplace, carved by a monk, from which the establishment takes its name. The Duke of Wellington made this his garrison headquarters when he was mustering his army for battle against Napoleon. Charles II and the Duke of Richmond are reported to have hidden in the chimney while pursued by Roundheads. The inn also has a rare Parliament Clock, thought to be 16th century, and in the restaurant a "coat of chain mail" from the 14th century, reputedly worn by the Black Prince.

Try to schedule at least a luncheon visit, enjoying a three-course meal for £3.65 ($8.40), featuring standard English fare. If you fall in love with the place, you can stay over. For your bed, breakfast, and evening meal, you're charged £12 ($27.60) nightly. Bed and breakfast only is £8 ($18.40). All prices include VAT.

In the area is the **Romney, Hythe & Dymchurch Light Railway Co.,** the world's smallest public railway. The engines are all steam driven, the carriages covered so there is no fear of getting wet. It operates daily from Easter to the end of September and on weekends from March 1 through October. The railway is reached by road along the A259.

To go to Elham itself, leave Canterbury on the Dover road, five miles out turn right and Elham's five miles further.

3. Dover

Dover, one of the ancient Cinque ports, is famed for its white cliffs. In Victoria's day, it basked in popularity as a seaside resort. Today it is of importance mainly because it is a port for major cross-Channel car and passenger traffic between England and France (usually Calais). Sitting in the open jaws of the white cliffs, Dover was one of England's most vulnerable and easy-to-hit targets in World War II and suffered repeated bombings that destroyed much of its harbor.

Hovering nearly 400 feet above the port is **Dover Castle,** one of the oldest and best known in England. Its keep was built at the command of Becket's fair-weather friend, Henry II, in the 12th century. You can visit the keep year round, generally from 9:30 a.m. to 5:30 p.m. in summer (it closes earlier off-season), for an admission of 50p ($1.15); children and pensioners pay 20p (46¢). Admission to the underground works is 25p (58¢), 10p (23¢) for children and pensioners. Admission to the castle grounds is free. The ancient castle was called back to active duty as late as World War II. The "Pharos" on the grounds is a lighthouse built by the Romans in the first half of the first century. The Romans landed at nearby Deal in 55 B.C. and 54 B.C. The first landing was not successful. The second in 54 B.C. was more so, but after six months they departed, and did not return until nearly 100 years later, 43 A.D., when they occupied the country and stayed 400 years.

WHERE TO STAY: The **White Cliffs Hotel,** Sea Front (tel. Dover 203-633), is the traditional choice, with many of its bedrooms facing the Channel. Clinging tenaciously to the past, its facade is impressive, built like a string of attached town houses, with an unbroken sea front balcony and a glass-enclosed front veranda. The bedrooms are comfortable and tranquil. The rooms facing the sea carry the higher price tag, of course. A waterfront double with private bath rents for £28.50 ($65.55). A bathless double costs £25.50 ($58.65). A single without bath is £14.50 ($33.35), rising to £16.50 ($37.95) with bath. Tariffs include a full English breakfast, service, and VAT. Late supper service and a covered garage are available. The hotel is close to the eastern and western docks and the hoverport for travel to and from France and Belgium.

The **Dover Stage Coachotel,** Sea Front (tel. Dover 201-001), is for those who desire streamlined motel efficiency. Set back from the sea, it opens onto its own miniature plaza with flowers and fountain. Six floors of the most up-to-date bedrooms attract cross-Channel overnighters. The entire waterfront facade zig-zags, with angular bayview bedrooms and individual balconies. The studio-style rooms have built-in furnishings, and hot and cold running water—but no private baths. Price for bed and breakfast is £16 ($36.80) in a single, £25 ($57.50) in a twin, including breakfast, service, and VAT. On the ground floor are a breakfast room and a drinking lounge. In addition, appetizing meals are served, featuring a three-course luncheon for £6 ($13.80). Dinner is à la carte.

East Cliff Hotel, Marine Parade, Eastern Docks (tel. Dover 202-299), stands serenely on the promenade under the White Cliffs of Dover, at the entrance to the leading line of the ferry and hovercraft to Calais. It's a well-kept establishment. Some of the rooms have a dramatic view of the harbor, and all come well equipped although without private baths. The bed-and-breakfast rate is approximately £10.50 ($24.15) per person, inclusive of service and VAT. Bar meals include a T-bone steak, served with salad and french fries, for £5 ($11.50), and it's available at both lunch and dinner.

The **Holiday Inn,** Townwall Street (tel. Dover 203-270), stands in the center of town, just a few minutes away from the railway station, the seafront, and the international ferry and hoverport terminals. Small as Holiday Inns go in England, it offers 83 rooms, designed in the typical utiltarian chain motif, each with a private bath, color TV, radio, in-house movies, direct-dial phones, plus individually controlled air conditioning and heating. Singles rent for £24 ($55.20) nightly, the tariff increasing to anywhere from £30 ($69) to £34 ($78.20) in a double. On the premises is an attractive heated indoor swimming pool, along with a fitness center. You can dine in a modern restaurant at the inn or else order a snack in the coffeeshop, perhaps a drink in the Lord Warden bar.

WHERE TO EAT: **Britannia,** Townwall Street (tel. Dover 203-248), across from the Dover Stage Coachotel, near the seafront, brings imagination and flair to an otherwise dull restaurant town. In a modern pub setting, you can sample good English food: Canterbury lamb cutlets, grilled Dover sole. But the chef reaches out to France and Spain as well for inspiration. On our latest rounds, we spotted six Spanish specialties on the menu, including such treats as Valencian paella. The appetizers are tempting as well, including pâté maison and lobster soup with brandy. Among the desserts, we prefer the Tia Maria walnut parfait. A three-course lunch is offered for £4.40 ($10.12), a set three-course dinner for around £6 ($13.80). However, to sample the specialties, you'll have to order from the à la carte menu, with main dishes priced from £3.75 ($8.63) to £7 ($16.10).

For our next and final stopover in Kent, we go inland—37 miles from London—to a once-fashionable resort.

4. Tunbridge Wells

Dudley, Lord North, courtier to James I, is credited with the discovery in 1606 of the mineral spring that started it all. His accidental find led to the creation of a fashionable resort that reached its peak in the mid-18th century under the foppish leadership of "Beau" Nash. Beau or Richard Nash (1674–1761) was a dandy in his day, the final arbiter of what to wear and what to say—even how to act (for example, he got men to take off their boots and put on stockings). But, of course, most of his time was devoted to Bath. Even so, Tunbridge Wells enjoyed a prime spa reputation from the days of Charles II through Victoria. Because so many monarchs had visited it, Edward VII named it Royal Tunbridge Wells in 1919. Over the years the cure was considered the answer for everything from too many days of wine and roses to failing sexual prowess.

The most remarkable feature of Tunbridge Wells is its Pantiles, a colonnaded walkway for shoppers, tea-drinkers, and diners, built near the wells. At the Assembly Hall, entertainment (opera, vaudeville) is presented.

Alas, there's nothing sadder in tourism than a resort that's seen its day. Still, it's worth a visit—just for a fleeting glimpse of the 18th century.

Canadians touring in the area may want to seek out the grave of the founder of their country's capital. Lt. Col. John By of the Royal Engineers (1779–1836) died at Shernfold Park in Frant East Sussex, near Tunbridge Wells, and is buried in the churchyard there. His principal claim to fame is that he built the Rideau Canal in Upper Canada and established what was later to be the capital of the Dominion of Canada—the city of Ottawa.

The Rideau Canal, some 124 miles long, links the city of Kingston on the St. Lawrence River with the city of Ottawa on the Ottawa river. Between 1826 and 1832 John By successfully constructed this canal through an unexplored wilderness for the British government. At the northern end of the canal he laid out "Bytown." Twenty years later this was renamed Ottawa, and it became the capital of a united Canada. His grave near Tunbridge Wells is marked with a plaque erected by the Historical Society of Ottawa in 1979.

Food and Lodging

Calverley Hotel, Crescent Road (tel. Tunbridge Wells 26455), is an old stone hotel facing Calverley Park, gardens of special interest in themselves. The hotel's enormous lounge, furnished with comfortable chairs and decorated in relaxing colors, opens onto the terrace and gardens. The dining room also overlooks the gardens, from which come many of the fresh vegetables you may enjoy at your table. The bedrooms, on the upper floors, are reached by elevator. Each room has central heating, telephone, radio, and many have private bath or shower. Guests frequently meet in the warm and friendly cocktail bar for drinks before dinner. Overnight rates at the Calverley range from £15 ($34.50) for a bathless single to £30 ($69) for a double with private bath. Breakfast is included, but you'll pay an additional £5 ($11.50) for the table d'hôte luncheon, and about £6 ($13.80) for dinner. VAT is added to all charges.

The **Spa Hotel,** Mount Ephraim Road (tel. Tunbridge Wells 20331), is for those who insist on gracious living. Far superior to any other in the vicinity, the Spa is like a sprawling manor house successfully converted to receive guests. The interior has been updated, with comfortable furnishings. The great drawing rooms, as well as the cathedral high-ceilinged dining room, open onto the rear gardens, with their spreading lawns, groves of trees, and beds of flowers. It's a peaceful oasis, only 30 miles from London, but miles away from London prices. The Spa was built in 1766 as a private house.

Throughout the hotel are more than 80 well-furnished and centrally heated bedrooms, reached by elevator. Most of them contain private bathrooms, TV, and radio. You pay around £22 ($50.60) per person in a room with bath. The terms include breakfast, service, and taxes. To be quoted pension terms, you must stay a minimum of four days or more. Otherwise, you can order meals separately, with a table d'hôte luncheon going for £6 ($13.80), a set dinner for £8 ($18.40). Garage facilities are available.

Wellington Hotel, Mount Ephraim Road (tel. Tunbridge Wells 20286), enjoys a regal position, with a grassy Common as its front domain. From every side, there is a veiw of the sprawling countryside. The old hotel suggests a Charles Addams drawing, with a mansard roof, rows of dormers, and Regency balconies. Catering mostly to families and business people, it also attracts motorists passing through Tunbridge Wells. For a superior double room with private bath, the charge is from £28 ($64.40) nightly, including breakfast, VAT, and service. The full-board terms are an additional £7.50 ($17.25) per person daily.

Instead of leaving London for Kent, you might head directly south of the capital to inviting Surrey.

SURREY

This tiny county has for some time been in danger of being gobbled up by the growing boundaries of London and turned into a sprawling suburb. Already some of the densely populated area in Surrey is now part of Greater London. But Surrey still retains much unspoiled countryside, largely because its many heaths and commons do not make good land for postwar suburbanite houses. Essentially, Surrey is a county of commuters (Alfred, Lord Tennyson was among the first), since a worker in the city can practically travel to the remotest corner of Surrey from London in anywhere from 45 minutes to an hour.

Long before William the Conqueror marched his pillaging Normans across its chalky North Downs, Surrey was important to the Saxons. In fact, early Saxon kings were once crowned at what is now **Kingston-on-Thames** (their Coronation Stone is still preserved near the Guildhall).

LIVING IN TUDOR SPLENDOR: The best of England—the best living accommodations, in particular—are to be found in the countryside. There you can sometimes live like a duke or duchess for the same amount you'd pay for only a fairly good room in London. Transportation facilities are often so good that you can enjoy the best of two worlds, darting into London for all its attractions, while enjoying the lower costs and better surroundings of rural England. For those who want to be in the vicinity of Heathrow Airport, yet within easy access of central London, we have the following recommendation in the upper bracket:

Great Fosters, Egham (tel. Egham 3822), is one of the most impressive old manor houses of England. It was built in 1550 and in its day belonged to Elizabeth I and was a hunting lodge in Windsor's Royal Forest. Although only 18 miles from London, it still preserves the link to its past. A red brick Tudor building, with stone-mullioned windows, many gables and towering chimneys, it is placed in a private garden, where paths cut through formal grounds of clipped yew hedges, roses, and rhododendrons—and a swimming pool. The architectural features of the interior are in the grand style, as witness the main hall with its carved black oak Jacobean fireplace. In the 15th-century Tithe Barn, with its high-vaulted and raftered oak beams, excellent English meals are served and an orchestra plays for dancing on Saturday nights. Some of the master bedrooms are worthy of royalty. For example, the gilt-paneled Italian bedroom contains an overscale bed with hand-carved cherubs on the posts. Period twins or doubles rent from £45 ($103.50) per night, increasing to £48 ($110.40) in a single. Period and second-floor singles cost from £28 ($64.40) per night, increasing to £41 ($94.30) in second-floor twins or doubles. These room rates include a full English breakfast, service, and VAT. Great Fosters is only a half mile from Runnymede and the Kennedy Memorial, and only seven miles in different directions from Windsor Castle and Hampton Court Palace.

5. Richmond

Want to spend an afternoon in a Thames river town? Richmond in Surrey is only a 30-minute ride from London, and can be easily reached by the underground trains, or else Green Line coaches 716 or 716a from Hyde Park Corner. The old town, popular in Victorian times, has good public rail links with London, costing about £2 ($4.60) for a return ticket, and it offers the escape many seek from the rush and bustle of the metropolis. If you're feeling lighthearted, take the boat trip down the Thames. Turner himself—art materials in hand—came here for inspiration.

Richmond is only one mile from Kew and its botanical gardens. You may prefer a combined excursion to Kew Gardens and Richmond on the same day. One of the attractions of the Thames town is the 2500-acre **Richmond Park,** first staked out by Charles I in 1637. It is filled with photogenic deer and waterfowl. Richmond has long enjoyed associations with royalty, as Henry VII's Richmond Palace stood there (an even earlier manor was razed). Queen Elizabeth I died in the old palace in 1603. Somebody's short-sightedness led to the palace's being carted away, and only a carriageway remains.

If you want to be like the English, you'll climb **Richmond Hill** for a view of the Thames considered by some to be one of the ten best views in the world. The scene reminded William Byrd of a similar view near his home on the James River in Virginia, inspiring him to name the city founded there in 1737 Richmond.

There are good shops and an excellent theater facing the green on which, in summertime, cricket matches are played. Boating happens on the river. Richmond Park has a public golf course, and you can rent a horse from the local stables. The Richmond Ice Skating Rink has been the nursery of many of England's skating champions. Wimbledon and the Tennis Championships are within easy reach, as is Hampton Court Palace.

At Petersham, the 13th-century St. Peter's Church is the burial place of Captain George Vancouver. The Queen Mother's parents, Lord and Lady

Glamis, were married there. It also has some very old wooden box pews. At St. Anne's Church at Kew Green, the painters Gainsborough and Zoffany were buried.

WHERE TO EAT: Londoners often go down to Richmond for the day, browse through its art galleries, and then dine out—which must account for the town's number of good restaurants. Our recommendation follows:

Richmond Rendezvous, 1 Paradise Rd. (tel. 940-5114), bills itself with some justification as "the leading Peking-style restaurant in the United Kingdom." You would never suspect it, however, to judge from the unprepossessing decor. The food is superb, especially if you stick to the chef's specialties, and avoid the routine Chinese restaurant fare. Three dishes, designed to delight, include barbecued Peking duck, duck steamed and deep fried, or a variety of meats in a chafing dish. Also recommended are hot-and-sour Peking soup at £1 ($2.30); scampi Peking style, £3.20 ($7.36); sliced beef in oyster sauce, £2.40 ($5.52); and diced chicken in yellow bean sauce, also £2.40. If there are six persons in your party, you can forego the above and leave it to the chef, who will prepare you a Peking dinner at £6.20 ($14.26) per head. The restaurant has overflowed to an annex at 1 Wakefield Rd. (tel. 940-6869). In London itself, the chain has opened two more restaurants, one the **Soho Rendezvous,** 21 Romilly St., W.1 (tel. 437-1486), specializing in a Peking-style cuisine, and another, the **Chiu Chow Inn,** 21 Lisle St., W.C.2 (tel. 437-8919), also specializing in Peking-style cooking. Both of these establishments are in the moderately priced bracket.

WHERE TO STAY: The **Richmond Gate,** Richmond Hill (tel. 940-0061), and the **Petersham,** Richmond Hill (tel. 940-7471), are two privately owned hotels, 200 yards apart, which are operated and managed as one unit. Both are old houses, modernized and refurbished to provide pleasant accommodations, with bathrooms, color TV sets, radios, and phones. A full English breakfast is included in the tariff, and snacks can be had during most of the day in the Terrace Bar of the Richmond Gate. Room service is available in both hotels, but the main restaurant is Nightingales, at the Petersham. Here, lunch or dinner from the set menu will cost from £5 ($11.50), or else you can order from an à la carte menu in this delightful room overlooking the river. There is a courtesy car service between the two buildings so you don't have to worry about the weather. Singles rent for £25 ($57.50), doubles from £33 ($75.90). However, for a large room and river view the charge is £40 ($92) nightly.

6. Haslemere

A quiet, sleepy town, Haslemere attracts because early English musical instruments are made by hand there. Ever hear a harpsichord concert? An annual music festival (see below) is the town's main drawing card. Over the years, the Dolmetsch family has been responsible for the acclaim that has come to this otherwise unhearalded little Surrey town, which lies in the midst of some of the shire's finest scenery. Haslemere is only an hour's train ride from Waterloo Station in London, about 42 miles away.

THE FESTIVAL: It isn't often that one can hear such exquisite music played so skillfully on the harpischord, the recorder, the lute, or any of the instruments designed so painstakingly to interpret the music of earlier centuries. Through-

HASLEMERE 221

out the year, the Dolmetsch family makes and repairs these instruments, welcoming visitors to their place on the edge of Haslemere. They rehearse constantly, preparing for the concerts that are held in July, and last nine days.

You can get specific information by writing to the **Haslemere Festival Office,** Jesses, Grayswood Road, Haslemere (or telephone Haslemere 2161 between 9 a.m. and 12:30 p.m. daily). During the festival, matinees begin at 3:15 p.m., evening performances 7 p.m. For seats in the balcony, prices range from £1.20 ($2.76) to £2.20 ($5.06), with stall seats going from 50p ($1.15) to £1.50 ($3.45).

WHERE TO STAY: The **Georgian Hotel,** High Street (tel. Haslemere 51555), is in the middle of the town, within walking distance of the Dolmetsch Center. Antiques and period accessories are well placed throughout. The bed-and-breakfast rate per person ranges from £12.50 ($28.75) to £15.25 ($35.08) nightly, the latter for a single with private bath. (Of the hotel's 22 pleasingly furnished bedrooms, 13 have private baths.) The hotel, although Georgian itself, is actually named after the U.S. State of Georgia. James Edward Oglethorpe, a member of Parliament in the 18th century, who owned the hotel, founded the state of Georgia. The establishment is licensed, and you can have healthy-size drinks before dinner. The garden is a favorite spot for afternoon tea.

A Hotel on the Outskirts

Lythe Hill Hotel, Petworth Road, near Haslemere (tel. Haslemere 51251), is a 14th-century farmhouse of historic interest set in 14 acres of beautiful parkland overlooking National Trust woodlands and just one hour from London, Heathrow, and Gatwick. Across the courtyard is the newer part of the hotel in converted 16th-century farm buildings which offer a luxurious accommodation, 28 rooms and suites, handsomely decorated public rooms, and a restaurant serving international and English dishes, both table d'hôte and à la carte. In the Italian garden, a dinner dance is staged on Saturday evenings.

The black and white timbered farmhouse has six period bedrooms with all modern comforts, and in the Tudor room stands a four-poster bed dated 1614. Downstairs in the oak-beamed and paneled dining room is the renowned **Auberge de France** restaurant, offering a fine French cuisine at candlelit, polished oak tables. Specialties include escalope de veau Jeanette, suprême de volaille Souvaroff, crêpes suzette, and a cellar of fine wines. Dinner for two in the auberge costs around £17 ($39.10).

The table d'hôte menu in the main hotel restaurant is around £5.50 ($12.65) to £7.50 ($17.25); and a twin room with private bath for two, including a continental breakfast and VAT, plus the service charge, is £40 ($92).

Madame Colonna, the patronne of the Lythe Hill Hotel, started with a farmhouse and now owns what is really a French hamlet in Surrey, offering peace and comfort as well as a genuine French cuisine. The auberge is closed for lunch on Tuesday and all day on Monday.

READER'S HOTEL SELECTION: "Trumble's Hotel and Restaurant on Stanhill (the road to Newdigate), Charlwood, Surrey (tel. Crawley 862212), is a wonderful place to stay overnight, or just to dine, if your plane comes in at Gatwick Airport. The hotel is only ten minutes by car from there, in lovely rolling country. Its rooms are large and beautiful, some furnished with fine antiques (one bedroom even has a 200-year-old canopied four-poster bed). All bedrooms have private bathrooms. There's nothing gloomy—everything's airy and cheerful and comfortable, and the 'full' heat is really that. Proprietors Sue and Peter Trumble provide all kinds of services, including arranging for car rentals and booking theater tickets for you in London. Or they let you alone if that's your wish. Dinner here averages about £10 ($23) per person and is of gourmet quality. We had black currant pie that was the best pie we had ever tasted. House specialties are traditional roast beef for Sunday lunch, roast duckling with orange sauce and fresh wheels of orange, very tender steaks, and plenty of fresh English fish. Also try the homemade lemon meringue pie. Excellent wines and liqueurs are available. There's a small Victorian bar. Trumble's would be a splendid place to spend a week or two. With a car, you could travel to Canterbury, Oxford, the South Coast, or Winchester, to name a few good spots, and get back in time for a memorable dinner. Also you can drive to Gatwick Airport, leave your car, and take the short train ride to London for the day. Trains run every 15 minutes during the day, every hour at night. Charlwood village is full of historic houses, some more than 500 years old. The church has a wall pre-William the Conqueror and 1066. My husband and I thought this the nicest place and the best buy on our 1000-mile tour of England" (Mrs. Janet Kay, Rochester, N.Y.).

GUILDFORD: The old and new meet in the county town on the Wey River, 40 minutes by train from Waterloo Station in London. Charles Dickens believed that its High Street, which slopes to the river, was one of the most beautiful in England. The Guildhall has an ornamental projecting clock which dates back to 1683.

Lying 2½ miles southwest of the city, **Loseley House,** a beautiful and historic Elizabethan mansion visited by Queen Elizabeth I, James I, and Queen Mary, has been featured on TV and in five films. Its works of art include paneling from Henry VIII's Nonsuch Palace, period furniture, a unique carved chalk chimneypiece, magnificent ceilings, and cushions made by the first Queen Elizabeth. The mansion is open from the end of May to the end of September on Wednesday, Thursday, Friday, and Saturday from 2 to 5 p.m., charging 80p ($1.84) for adults, 45p ($1.50) for children.

Food and Lodging

Angel Hotel, High Street (tel. Guildford 64555), is an old coaching inn in the middle of the steep main street of town. Its entrance and part of its courtyard are Tudor, and many other original features of this once-busy hostelry have been maintained. Inside, there is lavish paneling, plus a huge, open fireplace as well as exposed beams. Great oak timbers from old ships at Portsmouth were used to support the gallery.

Most of the two dozen bedrooms, including two family rooms, are simply furnished, although some are quite attractively decorated (these disappear first to those who reserve ahead). Each has a private bath, as well as a phone, radio, TV, and coffee-maker. Rates begin at £22 ($50.60) in a single, going up to £30 ($69) in a double. In addition to a well-decorated bar, the hotel has a quick-service Buttery as well as a unique 13th-century bistro in the crypt, with medieval architecture making for cozy surroundings.

DORKING: This country town lies on the Mole River, at the foot of the North Downs. Within easy reach are some of the most scenic spots in the shire, including Silent Pool, Box Hill, and Leith Hill. Three miles to the northwest stands **Polesden Lacey,** a former Regency villa containing the Greville collection of antiques, paintings, and tapestries. The 18th-century garden contains herbaceous borders, a rose garden, and beech walks. It's open in March and November on Saturday and Sunday from 2 to 5 p.m.; April to the end of October, daily, except Monday and Friday from 2 to 6, charging adults £1.10 ($2.53) to visit both the house and gardens; children 55p ($1.27).

Back in Dorking, you can find accommodations at the following:

Burford Bridge Hotel, Box Hill (tel. Dorking 4561), offers stylish living in a rural town from which a train will zip you into London in less than half an hour. At the foot of the famous beauty spot of Box Hill, the hotel has a lot of Historical associations. Lord Nelson was a frequent patron, and Keats completed *Endymion* here in 1817. Everyone from Wordsworth to Robert Louis Stevenson also frequented the place. You get the best of both the old and the new here, including a tithe barn (circa 1600) as well as 30 large, colorfully decorated bedrooms, renting for £22 ($50.60) in a single, from £25 ($57.50) to £30 ($69) in a double. Each room has its own bath or shower, plus a phone and color TV. The restaurant serves good English food, and a bar opens onto a flowered patio with a fountain. Pub snacks are served in the Nelson Bar. Concerts are held regularly in winter, and in summer you can enjoy the hotel's own swimming pool.

White Horse Hotel, High Street (tel. Dorking 81138). Just ten miles from Gatwick Airport, you can dine or lodge at a hotel which dates in part from 1500. Once the vicarage of Dorking, the White Horse by tradition was supposed to have been the "Marquis of Granby" in the *Pickwick Papers.* At least Dickens was known to have frequented the bar parlor.

An atmospheric place of creaking timbers and low beamed ceilings, the inn offers 70 bedrooms, including 18 family units, each with private baths or showers, plus phones, radios, TV sets, and coffee makers. A single with bath costs from £25 ($57.50), a double renting for £34 ($78.20). Often called "the most interesting house in Dorking," the inn has a restaurant, decorated in shades of green and red, as well as a Boot Hole bar serving hot and cold snacks.

After visiting Surrey, you can head south toward the English Channel and the sprawling shires of Sussex.

THE SUSSEXES

If King Harold hadn't loved Sussex so much, the course of English history might have been changed forever. Had the brave Saxon waited longer in the north, he could have marshaled more adequate reinforcements before striking south to meet the Normans. But Duke William's soldiers were ravaging the countryside he knew so well, and Harold rushed down to counter them.

Harold's enthusiasm for Sussex is understandable. The landscape rises and falls like waves. The country is known for its Downlands and tree-thickened Weald, from which came the timbers to build England's mighty fleet in days gone by. The shires lie south of London and Surrey, bordering Kent in the east, Hampshire in the west, and opening directly onto the sometimes sunny, resort-dotted English Channel.

Like the other sections in the vulnerable south of England, the Sussexes witnessed some of the most dramatic moments in the country's history. Apart from the Norman landings at Hastings, the most life-changing transfusion of plasma occurred in the 19th century, as middle-class Victorians flocked to the seashore, pumping new spirit into Eastbourne, Worthing, Brighton, even old Hastings itself. The cult of the saltwater worshippers flourished, and has to this day. Although **Eastbourne** and **Worthing** are much frequented by the English, we'd place them several fathoms below **Brighton** and **Hastings,** which are much more suitable if you're seeking a holiday by the sea.

Far more than the resorts, the old towns and villages of the Sussexes are intriguing, particularly **Rye** and **Winchelsea,** the ancient towns of the Cinque Port Confederation. No Sussex village is lovelier than **Alfriston** (and the innkeepers know it, too!); **Arundel** is noted for its castle; the cathedral city of **Chichester** is a mecca for theater buffs. Traditionally, and for purposes of government, Sussex is divided into East Sussex and West Sussex. We've adhered to that convenient dichotomy.

We'll begin in East Sussex, where you'll find many of the inns and hotels within commuting distance of London.

7. Rye

"Nothing more recent than a Cavalier's Cloak, Hat and Ruffles should be seen in the streets of Rye," said Louis Jennings. He's so right. This ancient town, formerly an island, was chartered back in 1229. Rye, 65 miles below London, near the English Channel, and neighboring Winchelsea were once part of the ancient Cinque Ports Confederation. Rye flourished as a smuggling center, its denizens sneaking in contraband from the marshes to stash away in little nooks (even John Wesley's firm chastisements couldn't stop what was a strongly entrenched tradition).

But the sea receded from Rye, leaving it perched like a giant whale out of water. Its narrow, cobblestoned streets twist and turn like a labyrinth. It has long been considered a special place, having attracted any number of famous men, including Henry James, who once lived in the Lamb House on Mermaid Street.

Attacked several times by French fleets, Rye was practically razed in 1377. But it rebuilt sufficiently, decking itself out in the Elizabethan style so that Queen Elizabeth I, during her visit in 1573, bestowed upon the town the distinction of Royal Rye.

Today the city has any number of specific buildings and sites of architectural interest, notably the 13th-century **Ypres Tower** (sheltering the Rye Museum), and the 15th-century **St. Mary's Parish Church,** with its unusual clock.

WHERE TO STAY: The **Mermaid Inn,** Mermaid Street (tel. Rye 3065), is one of the most famous of the old smugglers inns of England, known to that band of cutthroats, the real-life Hawkhurst Gang, as well as to Russell Thorndike's fictional character, Dr. Syn. One of the present rooms, in fact, is called Dr. Syn's Bedchamber, and is connected by a staircase—set in the thickness of the wall—to the bar. That room, with a private bath, rents for £14 ($32.20) per person nightly, as does the Elizabethan Chamber (with four-poster and private bath). Two other special rooms—the Fleur-de-Lys Chamber and the Tudor Rose Chamber—contain private baths and twin beds, and rent for £13.50 ($31.05) per person. Terms include breakfast, and a 10% service charge is added. Other less expensive rooms are equipped with hot and cold running water, some with baths, attractive furnishings, and are available in single, double, or twin. The charge is from £12 ($27.60) per person, including breakfast. The Mermaid has sheltered everybody from Queen Elizabeth I to George Arliss. When Elizabeth came to Rye in 1573, the inn had already been operating nearly 150 years. A covered carriageway leads to the car park. In the center of the hotel is a courtyard, where you'll see a pedestal fountain with water flowing down on the heads of water lilies. The Mermaid has also taken over the 16th-century Ship Inn at the foot of Mermaid Street which, with its 12 bedrooms and restaurant on the first floor, complements the Mermaid very well. The Mermaid also makes a good dining and pub choice (see below).

Monastery Hotel, 6 High St. (tel. Rye 3272), is an early 17th-century building that grew up over the ruins of a 13th-century friary of the Augustinian order. Its own monastic garden backs up against the walls of the old friary. Nowadays, the house offers seven modernized double- and twin-bedded rooms (with hot and cold running water, private showers, central heating, and razor points), renting at £10.50 ($24.15) per person for bed and breakfast. There is a comfortable lounge, with color television, and a restaurant installed in an attractive room overlooks the Old Friary Chapel. For more than 45 years, the Monastery has been receiving guests, the welcome today provided by the resident manager, Mr. Jon Culverhouse.

WHERE TO EAT: The **Mermaid Inn,** Mermaid Street, doesn't depend totally on its Elizabethan atmosphere and smuggling associations—it also serves good food, and has the most charming tavern in Rye. The cooking is English with frills. For £5 ($11.50) you can have a table d'hôte luncheon such as this typical one: a rich kidney soup, followed by poached salmon with hollandaise (superb), accompanied by three vegetables, including beans. Imported cheese or fruit pies such as black currant and apple round out the meal. Lunch is served from 12:45 to 2 p.m. At the dinner, from 7:30 to 9 p.m., your tab will average £6.50 ($14.95). The dining room itself, with its linenfold paneling, Caen stone fireplaces, and oak-beamed ceiling, makes for an ideal setting. Even if you're not dining at the Mermaid, drop in to the old Tudor pub, with its 16-foot-wide fireplace (look for a priest's hiding hole).

The **Flushing Inn,** Market Street (tel. Rye 3292), is in a 16th-century inn on a cobblestoned street. It has preserved the best of the past, including a wall-size fresco in the restaurant dating from 1544 and depicting "a menagerie of birds and heraldic beasts." A rear dining room overlooks a carefully tended flower garden. A special feature is the Sea Food Lounge Bar, where sandwiches and plates of seafood are available from £1.50 ($3.45) to £5 ($11.50). In the main restaurant, luncheons are offered for from £5.60 ($12.88); dinners run from £8 ($18.40). Besides these lunches and dinners, gastronomic evenings are held at regular intervals between October and April. For one of these specially prepared meals, including your apéritif, wine, and after-dinner brandy, you pay £15 ($34.50) per person. Fine Wine evenings cost £18 ($41.40) per person. The inn is closed Monday nights and all day on Tuesday, three weeks in October, two weeks after Christmas, and one week after Easter.

8. Winchelsea

The sister Cinque Federation port to Rye, Winchelsea has also witnessed the water's ebb. It traces its history back to Edward I, and has experienced many dramatic moments, such as sacking by the French. Today it is a dignified residential town (Ellen Terry's former cottage can be seen huddling up to Strandgate, on the road to Rye). In the words of one 19th-century writer, Winchelsea is "a sunny dream of centuries ago." Its finest sight is a badly damaged 14th-century church, containing a number of remarkable tombs.

WHERE TO STAY: The **New Inn** (tel. Winchelsea 252) is an old hostelry in the middle of this picture-postcard village, across the road from the 14th-century church. It has all the mellow associations of a country inn of England —pleasant, comfortable rooms, a tavern, good food, a garden in the rear, a fireplace, old settles (high enough to keep the draft off), plenty of battered, but polished, brass and copper steins hanging from the ceiling, even a dart game going. Run by John Wood, the New Inn rents its well-furnished (many quite large) doubles for £19 ($43.70) per night (innerspring mattresses) including a big English breakfast and VAT—plus 10% for service. All the rooms have hot and cold water. A three-course dinner is served for around £6 ($13.80) to £7 ($16.10), depending on your main dish.

On the Outskirts

Justins Hotel, Bodiam, near Robertsbridge (tel. Staplecross 372), is a Tudor-style estate set in a well-tended two-acre garden, surrounded by tall trees and a view of the Sussex Downs. Only 12 miles from Rye and Winchelsea, it is very close to Bodiam Castle, built in 1386 and considered one of the most magnificent castles of its kind in England.

Your resident owners are Thalia and Bob Turner, who have installed private baths in eight of their ten attractively furnished bedrooms, charging from £10.50 ($24.15) per person nightly for bed and breakfast, or else £15.50 ($35.65) per person for half board. After enjoying a drink and friendly conversation in the cocktail bar, guests can order good cookery served in the oak-paneled dining room. Personal service is a hallmark of the establishment.

9. Hastings and St. Leonard's

The world has seen bigger battles, but few are as well remembered as the Battle of Hastings in 1066. When William, Duke of Normandy, landed on the Sussex coast and lured King Harold (already fighting Vikings in Yorkshire) southward to defeat, the destiny of the English-speaking people was changed forever. It was D-Day in reverse. The actual battle occurred at what is now Battle Abbey (nine miles away), but the Norman duke used Hastings as his base of operation.

Hastings suffered other invasions—it was razed by the French in the 14th century. But after that blow a Tudor town grew up in the eastern sector, and it makes for a good stroll today. The more recent invasion threat—that of Hitler's armies—never came to pass, although the dragons' dentures put up across the countryside stood waiting to bite into Nazi tanks.

Linked by a three-mile promenade along the sea, Hastings and St. Leonard's were given a considerable boost in the 19th century by that eminent tripper Queen Victoria, who visited several times. Both towns no longer enjoy such royal patronage; rather, they do a thriving business with Midlanders on vacation. Hastings and St. Leonard's have the usual shops and English sea-resort amusements. Only 63 miles from London, they are serviced by fast trains from Victoria Station.

The two chief attractions are:

HASTINGS CASTLE: In ruins now, the first of the Norman castles to be built in England sprouted up on a western hill overlooking Hastings, circa 1067. Precious little is left to remind us of the days when proud knights, imbued with a spirit of pomp and spectacle, wore bonnets and girdles. The fortress was ordered torn down by King John in 1216, and later served as a church and monastery until it felt Henry VIII's ire. Owned by the Pelham dynasty from the latter 16th century to modern times, the ruins have been turned over to Hastings. It is open from 10 a.m. to 5 p.m. daily from Easter to September, charging an admission of 22p (51¢) for adults, 11p (25¢) for children. From the mount, you'll have a good view of the coast and promenade.

THE HASTINGS EMBROIDERY: A commemorative work, the Hastings Embroidery was first exhibited in 1966. It is a remarkable achievement that

HASTINGS/ST. LEONARD'S

traces 900 years of English history through needlework. Depicted are some of the nation's greatest moments (the Battle of Hastings itself, the coronation of William the Conqueror) and its legends (Robin Hood). In all, 27 panels, 243 feet in length, depicting 81 historic scenes, are exhibited at the Town Hall (tel. Hastings 425-855). The history of Britain comes alive—the murder of Thomas à Becket, King John signing the Magna Carta, the Black Plague, Chaucer's pilgrims going to Canterbury, the Battle of Agincourt with the victorious Henry V, the War of the Roses, the Little Princes in the Tower, Bloody Mary's reign, Drake's *Golden Hind,* the arrival of Philip's ill-fated Armada, Guy Fawkes's gunpowder plot, the sailing of the *Mayflower,* the disastrous plague of 1665 and the great London fire of the following year, Nelson at Trafalgar, the Battle of Waterloo, the Empress of India, Victoria, the Battle of Britain, and the D-Day landings at Normandy. In the center is a scale model of the battlefield at Battle, depicting Wiliam's one-inch men doing in Harold's mini-soldiers. Also displayed is a colection of dolls in period costumes. Admission is 40p (92¢).

WHERE TO STAY: Royal Victoria Hotel, Marina (tel. Hastings 433-300), is peacock-proud of its seafront prominence. It owes its fame to Queen Victoria, who visited here several times. Most of its bedrooms face the sea, but others look onto St. Leonard's Gardens. Inside, the furnishings are fairly modern, although many of the grandest architectural features are still intact. It offers nearly 90 bedrooms, only 15 of which have private baths. Many of the rooms are quite large—good beds, sound comfort. The highest prices are charged from June 1 to September 30. A bathless single rents for £11 ($25.30), going up to £12.50 ($28.75) with bath. A bathless double is £18 ($41.40), rising to £20 ($46) with complete bath. These prices include breakfast, service charge, and VAT. Special rates for stays of more than three days are offered. Guests gather evenings in the Crown Bar, which has many fine old touches. Lunch is £4 ($9.20); dinner, £6 ($13.80). The chef's specialty is the local sole.

Beauport Park Hotel, Route A2100 (tel. Hastings 51222), is one of the best places to stay in the Hastings–Battle district. It looks much older than it is. It was originally erected as the private estate of General Murray, once the governor of Québec (he had previously served under General Wolfe). However, a fire in 1923 swept over it, and it was later reconstructed in the old style. Now run as a hotel accommodating 30 guests, it is surrounded by beautiful gardens (the Italian-style grounds in the rear contain statuary and vivid flowering shrubbery). The living room and drinking lounge are tastefully furnished, and the French windows in the dining room open onto the park-like rear. The bed-and-breakfast rate ranges from £12 ($27.60) to £16.50 ($37.95) per person daily. All first-floor rooms have private bathrooms with shower, direct-dial telephone, and TV.

The hotel offers an ambitious cuisine, well prepared and handsomely served. Some of the produce comes from the hotel's own gardens. A set lunch is featured for £4.80 ($11.04) at which a varied choice is available. The set dinner is £5.80 ($13.34), and again the choice is wide. The à la carte menu offers such tempting dishes as a half dozen escargots for £2.60 ($5.98); real turtle soup, 95p ($2.19); chateaubriand for two, £15 ($34.50). A rich and creamy dessert is the zabaglione.

10. Battle

Nine miles from Hastings is the old market town, famed in history as the site of the Battle of Hastings in 1066. William the Conqueror founded Battle Abbey (some of the stone was shipped from Caen) to commemorate his victory over Harold, the last of the kings of the English. The town grew up around the abbey. Regrettably, stucco has been plastered over many of Battle's half-timbered buildings, a notable exception being the Pilgrims' Restaurant (see below). Even the church was torn down as part of the act approved by Henry VIII in 1537 to dissolve the monasteries.

But some buildings and ruins remain in what Tennyson called: "O Garden, blossoming out of English blood." The principal building is the Abbots' House, at present rented to a public (private) school for girls (not open to visitors). Of architectural interest is the Gatehouse, with its octagonal towers, standing at the top of the Market Square. All of the north precinct wall still stands, and one of the most interesting sights of the ruins themselves is the ancient Dorter Range, where the monks once slept.

Harold was killed and dismembered by William, Duke of Normandy. Encircled by his house-carls, Harold battled bravely not only for his kingdom but his life. The abbey is open year round—from 9:30 a.m. to 5:30 p.m. (on Sunday from 2 to 5:30 p.m.) in summer; from 9:40 a.m. to 4 p.m. in winter (on Sunday from 2 to 4). The admission is 50p ($1.15) for adults, 20p (46¢) for children.

WHERE TO STAY: **George Hotel,** High Street (tel. Battle 2844), was an early 18th-century coaching inn. A Trust House, it charges high-season rates from April to October. In a single without bath, the bed-and-breakfast tariff is £18 ($41.40), increasing to £22 ($50.60) in a twin without bath and £27 ($62.10) in a twin with bath, including an English breakfast, tax, and service. The rooms are comfortable, although not imaginatively furnished. Lunch, available to nonresidents as well, costs £4.50 ($10.35), and includes such English fare as game soup and roast leg of pork with apple sauce. Dinner is from £6 ($13.80).

WHERE TO EAT: **Pilgrim's Restaurant,** Battle Village Green, High Street (tel. Battle 2314), adjacent to Battle Abbey, is an early 14th-century, black and white timbered house—the preferred place for lunch or afternoon tea while in town. You'll not only receive good portions of homemade food, but you'll encounter an authentic atmosphere. Recommended is the set lunch for £4 ($9.20), which is likely to include the soup of the day, hot roast shoulder of lamb with vegetables, and a special English dessert. A 10% service charge is added. An afternoon tea costs £1.20 ($2.76), and features toasted buttered scones (biscuits) and assorted cakes. The more elaborate Sunday lunch costs £4.50 ($10.35).

Owned by Mr. and Mrs. Peter and Heather Randall-Nason, the Pilgrim is a treasure house of antiquity. Peter and Heather gave up the pressure of commercial life for the pleasure of restaurant life. They both enjoy preparing and serving food—Peter had his first job at the age of six working on Saturday for his grandfather, a master confectioner. There is also a separate light meal restaurant where you can have a continental platter of cold meats and salad for £2.20 ($5.06), or an egg and cheese salad for the same price. A hamburger and chips cost £1.40 ($3.22). You may have lunch in the two-story, high-pitched main room with its open brick hearth, exposed beams, and collection of antiques, or you may prefer the smaller adjoining room where the tables are placed in front of an old open fireplace. The licensed restaurant is open seven days a week until 5:30 p.m.

11. Alfriston and Lewes

Nestled on the Cuckmere River, **Alfriston** is one of the most beautiful villages of England. Its High Street, with its old market cross, looks like one's fantasy of what an English village should be. Some of the old houses still have hidden chambers where smugglers stored their loot. Alfriston has several old inns, the best known of which is the Star, now a Trust House hotel with its heraldic carvings outside.

During the day, Alfriston is likely to be overrun by coach tours (it's that lovely, and that popular). The village lies about 60 miles from London, northeast of Seaford on the English Channel, in the general vicinity of the resort of Eastbourne and the modern port of Newhaven.

Only about a dozen miles along the A27 toward Brighton lies **Lewes**, an ancient Sussex town, worth exploring. Centered in the South Downs, Lewes lies 51 miles from London. Since the home of the Glyndebourne Opera is only five miles to the east, the accommodations of Lewes are often frequented by cultured guests.

The county town has many historical associations, listing such residents as Thomas Paine and Anne of Cleves. The fourth wife of Henry VIII, Anne of Cleves was Queen of England for about six months before her marriage was annulled. She was not beheaded, but managed to get herself a pension instead. The half-timbered **Anne of Cleves House**, cared for by the Sussex Archaeological Society, is found on High Street (Southover), and is open weekdays, February to November, from 10 a.m. to 5 p.m.; on Sunday, April to October, 2 to 5 p.m. Charge is 35p (81¢) for adults, 20p (46¢) for children. Lewes, of course, grew up around its Norman castle. From the tower you can obtain a fine view of the countryside. To visit **Lewes Castle and Museum**, a joint ticket costs adults 45p ($1.04); children, 25p (58¢). To visit the castle costs only 30p (69¢) for adults, 20p (46¢) for children. The castle and museum are open all year from 10 a.m. to 5:30 p.m., Monday through Saturday (also Sunday from April to October, from 2 to 5:30 p.m.). Accommodations are impossible during the Glyndebourne Opera festival, but adequate at other times.

WHERE TO STAY IN ALFRISTON: If you're spending the night, try to get a room at one of the old inns.

The **Star Inn** (tel. 870495) answers the craving of those who want all the charm of Tudor living without having to sacrifice 20th-century comfort. The present building dates from 1450, although it was originally founded in the 1200s, perhaps to house pilgrims en route to Chichester and the shrine of St. Richard. The timbered inn is a gem. In the center of the village, its carved front still unchanged, it boasts an overhanging second story of black and white timbers and bay windows. The lounges are on several levels, a veritable forest of old timbers, seasoned by the centuries. The furnishings and decorations blend well, with a Tudor refectory table, a bowl of English garden flowers, Windsor armchair, wrought-iron ceiling lights, old engravings, and several fireplaces.

Out back is a motel-type wing, with every studio-style room offering a private bath. Each is simply furnished in a tasteful style, well designed, with radio and telephone, heating, and built-in wardrobes. In rooms with bath, the rate in a single is £25 ($57.50), £33 ($75.90) in a double or twin. Tariffs include breakfast as well as service and VAT. A set luncheon goes for £5.50 ($12.65), a set dinner for £6.50 ($14.95).

Deans Place Hotel (tel. 870248) is a vine-covered country house, dating from the early 18th century and sitting under great old shady trees in its own gardens bounded by the Cuckmere River. At the edge of the village of Alfriston, it is a good introduction to gracious English life. You can play croquet, knocking those wooden balls around the green lawns, or you can relax by the heated (in summer only) outdoor swimming pool. A single with bath is £10 ($23); a double or twin with bath, £18 ($41.40). A continental breakfast, service, and VAT are included.

The meals are excellent, with a regular table d'hôte lunch going for £4 ($9.20), a three-course dinner for £5 ($11.50). Deans Place is open from February to December.

WHERE TO STAY IN LEWES: White Hart Hotel, High Street (tel. Lewes 3794), was labeled by Thomas Paine as "the cradle of American Independence," owing to his founding of the volatile and aptly named Headstrong Club there in 1761. Originally, it was the town house of the Pelhams, a kind of first family of Lewes. Later, it became a coaching inn, although the facade today dates from the 19th century. In yet another century, the representative of the Soviet Union met here with the British foreign secretary as a prelude to the resumption of diplomatic relations between the two countries.

A single with bath costs £30 ($69); a double with bath, £34 ($78.20); including an English breakfast, service, and VAT. Rooms without bath go for a bit less. Units in the annex have individual color TV sets, but if you're in the main building you have to watch TV in the lounge. All the tidily kept bedrooms have hot and cold running water and are comfortably furnished. The Sheriff's Room on the second floor is like a private club, with 16th-century timbers and cozy armchairs for quiet talks and drinks. The wine cellars once whispered with the sighs of 16th-century Protestant martyrs (many were buried there).

The dining room, with its view of the Downs, is warmly decorated with paneling and a hand-carved formal fireplace. Here, while sitting on red banquettes, you can order some of the finest viands in Lewes. A table d'hôte lunch costs £5.50 ($12.65), a set dinner going for £6.50 ($14.95).

The **Shelleys Hotel** (tel. Lewes 2361) is a manor house dating back to 1526. In its day, it was owned by the Earl of Dorset, before it was sold to the Shelley family, distant relatives of the poet. Radical changes were made to the architecture in the 18th century. Nowadays, the standards of the management are reflected in the fine antiques, the bowls of flowers, the paintings and prints, the well-kept garden, and, most important, the staff. In the rear is a sun terrace and lawn for tea and drinks. Horse chestnuts and copper beech shade the grounds.

The central hall is characterized by Ionic columns, a Welsh cupboard full of antique plates, a domed ceiling, and the coat-of-arms of the Shelley family. The bay windows of the front drawing room open onto the rear gardens, and the drinking lounge is paneled. The bedrooms themselves are personal, individually furnished, usually spacious and most comfortable. Singles with shower cost from £28.50 ($65.55); doubles with bath/shower, from £39 ($89.70). Service and VAT are included in all charges. Room 11 has a 16th-century frieze of Bacchanalian figures and a design of entwining grapes and flowers. You can, by the way, order meals at Shelleys. Lunch costs from £4.50 ($10.35); dinner is from £6 ($13.80).

12. East Grinstead

Twenty-four miles from Lewes and you're at East Grinstead on the A22 Eastbourne Road, 30 miles south from London. It has much charm, especially in its well-preserved, half-timbered buildings, Jacobean almshouses, and the Church of St. Swithin, built in the Perpendicular style. As a base for exploring the North Downs and Ashdown Forest, it attracts many English visitors. We prefer it, however, because of Gravetye Manor (see below), one of the finest accommodations in the south of England. East Grinstead can be reached by the Green Bus Line from London.

WHERE TO STAY: Gravetye Manor (tel. Sharpthorne 810-567). Your own room is in an Elizabethan manor, part of an estate set in the hills, standing in its own 30 acres of woods, orchards, and a trout lake. It's approached by a mile-long winding driveway leading into an entrance courtyard. Later, you can discover the restored formal gardens, the lifetime creation of one of England's leading horticulturists, William Robinson.

The spacious drawing room has tasteful furnishings, with many antiques. The bedchambers are individual, each one named after trees on the estate: ash, bay, beech, whatever. Medium-size and large double- or twin-bedded rooms range in price from £44 ($102.20) to £60 ($138) nightly. One is the former master bedroom, with a massive carved four-poster, as well as wood-carved portraits of the original owners over the fireplace (Richard and Katharine Infield in 1598). Other smaller doubles with private showers go for £40 ($92). The rates in a single with private bath are from £38 ($7.40). A full English breakfast costs extra. Write well in advance for reservations in high season.

Dinner is to be savored, not rushed. Jacketed waiters are trained by the restaurant manager, Helmut Kircher. He supervises what some wine experts claim to be the best cellar in England, some 500 listings. The kitchen is the domain of a true Englishman, a native of Yorkshire, Michael Quinn. He delights not only with his British dishes, but also he has been trained in imaginative French cuisine—a happy combination.

13. Brighton

Back in 1753, when Dr. Russell propounded the seawater cure—even to the point of advocating the drinking of an "oceanic cocktail"—he launched a movement that was to change the life of the average English person, at least his or her vacation plans. Brighton was one of the first of the great seaside resorts of Europe.

The original swinger who was to shape so much of its destiny arrived in 1783, after just turning voting age; he was the then Prince of Wales, whose presence and patronage gave immediate status to the seaside town.

Fashionable dandies from London, such as Beau Brummell, began turning up. The construction business boomed, as Brighton blossomed with charming and attractive town houses, well-planned squares and crescents. From the Prince Regent's title came the voguish word "Regency," which was to characterize an era, but more specifically refers to the period between 1811 and 1820. Under Victoria—and in spite of her cutting off the patronage of her presence—Brighton continued to flourish.

Alas, in this century, as the English began to discover more glamorous spots on the continent, Brighton lost much of its old joie de vivre. It became more aptly tabbed as tatty, featuring the usual run of fun-fair-type English seaside amusements ("let's go down to Brighton, ducky"). Happily, that state of affairs is today changing rapidly, owing largely to the huge numbers of Londoners moving in (some of whom have taken to commuting, as Brighton lies only one hour—frequent train service—from Victoria Station). The invasion is making Brighton increasingly lighthearted and sophisticated.

The Lanes, a closely knit section of alleyways off North Street in Brighton (many of the present shops were formerly fisherman's cottages) were frequented in Victoria's day by style-setting curio and antique collectors. Many are still there, although sharing space with boutiques.

THE ROYAL PAVILION: Among the royal residences of Europe, the Pavilion at Brighton—a John Nash version of an Indian mogul's palace—is unique. Ornate and exotic, it has been subjected over the years to the most devastating wit of English satirists and pundits. But today we can examine it more objectively as one of the outstanding examples of the Orientalizing tendencies of the romantic movement in England.

Originally, the Pavilion was built in 1787 by Henry Holland. But it no more resembled its present look than a caterpillar does a butterfly. By the time Nash had transformed it from a simple classical villa into an Oriental fantasy, the Prince Regent had become King George IV. He and one of his mistresses, Lady Conyngham, lived in the palace until 1827.

A decade passed before Victoria, then queen, arrived in Brighton. Although she was to bring Albert and the children on a number of occasions, the monarch and Brighton just didn't mix. The very air of the resort seemed too flippant for her—and the latter-day sea-bathing disciples of Dr. Russell trailed Victoria as if she were a stage actress. Further, the chinoiseries of the interior and the mogul domes and cupolas on the exterior didn't set too well with her firm tastes—even though the pavilion would have been a fitting abode for a woman who was to bear the title Empress of India.

By 1845 Victoria and Brighton had had it. She began packing, and the royal furniture was carted off. Its tenants gone, the Pavilion was in serious peril of being torn down. By a narrow vote, Brightonians agreed to purchase it. Gradually, it has been restored to its former splendor, enhanced in no small part by the return of much of its original furniture on loan by the present tenant at Buckingham Palace.

The caretakers put out the silverware, gold plate, and porcelain during the annual Regency Exhibition from June to September. But at any time you can walk through the world of crustacean ceilings, winged dragons, silk draperies, lacquered furniture, water-lily chandeliers, gilt dolphins, Chinese mythological figures, and serpents who hold everything up.

Of exceptional interest is the domed **Banqueting Hall,** with a chandelier of bronze dragons supporting lily-like glass globes. In the Great Kitchen, with its old revolving spits, is a collection of Wellington pots and pans—his *batterie de cuisine*—from his town house at Hyde Park Corner. In the State Apartments, particularly the domed Salon, dragons wink at you, serpents entwine, lacquered doors shine. The Music Room, with its scalloped ceiling, is a salon of water lilies, flying dragons, sunflowers, reptilian paintings, bamboo, silk, and satin. In the second-floor gallery, look for Nash's views of the Pavilion in its elegant heyday. Finally, don't miss the sitting room of the king's "wife," Mrs. Fitzherbert, with some of her former furniture.

From June to early October the Pavilion is open daily from 10 a.m. to 7:30 p.m. It closes at 5 p.m. off-season. The admission charges are: July to October (Regency Exhibition), adults, £1.20 ($2.76); children, 55p ($1.27). For the rest of the year, adults pay £1 ($2.30); children, 40p (92¢).

WHERE TO STAY: Hundreds of accommodations are to be found in all price ranges. Regrettably, many are establishments, to quote Norman Mailer, "where elderly retired India colonels brood through dinner...." However, that situation is changing now, as the most celebrated relics of yesteryear are experiencing (or have experienced) extensive overhauling. We'll survey the leading hotels, then proceed to a representative sampling of the accommodations awaiting those who must keep expenses trimmed.

The Upper Bracket

Grand Hotel, Kings's Road (tel. Brighton 26301), unquestionably has grandeur. Built in 1864, it is listed as a building of architectural and historical importance by the Department of Environment. The interior is impressive, the outstanding features being the wrought-iron staircase and the dome. The Victorian era has been skillfully recreated on the ground floor, but the bedrooms, all with private bath, radio, and TV, are modern. There are 166 bedrooms, plus seven luxury suites for VIPs.

Singles range from £30 ($69). Doubles go from £59 ($135.70) facing the sea. Terms include an English breakfast and VAT. En pension terms are quoted as well. The Grand also offers a table d'hôte luncheon for £10 ($23) and a set dinner for £8 ($18.40), both inclusive. There are special weekend rates available throughout the year, excluding public holidays.

The Medium-Priced Range

Royal Albion Hotel, Old Steine (tel. Brighton 29202), stands right on the seafront, opposite the Palace Pier. As a hotel, it is one of the traditional choices of Brighton, with lots of Regency character and history, dating back to 1826. Inside, the hotel has been luxuriously decorated and furnished to a very high standard. All rooms have private bath/shower, color television, radio, telephone, and a tea- and coffee-making machine. The majority of the rooms have a superb sea view. Sir Harry's Bar, with a nautical theme, is named after the late Sir Harry Preston, who owned the hotel in the early 1900s. There is also a spacious lounge with magnificent views onto the seafront and a large Regency-style restaurant. The rates are £36 ($82.80) for a single and £50 ($115) for a twin or double room, inclusive of VAT and service. Table d'hôte menus range from £7.50 ($17.25) per person.

Courtlands, The Drive, Hove (tel. Brighton 731-055), emerges as a comfortable and wise choice for a Brighton stopover. A short block and a half from the waterfront, it is a traditional hotel with adequate facilities, including the Golden Dolphin lounge bar and a dining room opening onto gardens. A good cuisine, both international and English, is assured. Bedrooms are spacious and harmonious, with prices set according to plumbing. Per-person rates include a full English breakfast, service, and VAT. Bathless singles cost £18.50 ($42.55), rising to £26 ($59.80) with bath. Bathless doubles go for £17.25 ($39.68) per person, increasing to £23.25 ($53.48) per person with bath.

The **Old Ship Hotel** (tel. Brighton 29001), on the seafront, midway between the two piers, combines a fascinating history with modern comfort. The oldest hotel in Brighton, dating from the 17th century, the Ship was owned by Captain Tettersell, who in 1651 saved the life of Charles II after the battle of Worcester by taking him across the Channel to France in his boat, the *Surprise,* renamed the *Royal Escape* after the Restoration. The Old Ship boasts the original Regency assembly rooms where the Prince Regent (later George IV) dined, danced, and played cards with his friends, and where he held his birthday and coronation celebrations. Frequent visitors included Mrs. Fitzherbert (the Prince Regent's illegal wife), the Duke of York, Fanny Burney, Paganini (see the famous balcony where the maestro played in 1831), Dr. Samuel Johnson, Sir Henry Irving, and William Thackeray, who wrote *Vanity Fair* when he stayed at the Old Ship.

Most rooms have private bathrooms, all have color TV, and many have balconies overlooking the sea. Prices range from £24 ($55.20) to £28 ($64.40) for singles, from £34 ($78.20) to £40 ($92) for two persons, inclusive of service charge, an English breakfast, and VAT. The hotel has a superb restaurant, with a table d'hôte luncheon going for £6 ($13.80) and dinner for £8 ($18.40). There is also a Buttery, open from 10:30 a.m. to 10:30 p.m., serving grills and light snacks.

The Budget Range

Ellesmere Private Hotel, 8 New Steine (tel. Brighton 607812), is one of the best low-cost establishments in the resort. Run by Mr. and Mrs. Colin Muzzall, it is friendly, warm, and clean, lying 100 yards from the sea in the center of Brighton, immediately off Marine Parade, close to Palace Pier and the Royal Pavilion. Fourteen bedrooms—neat, though unremarkably furnished—are complete with hot and cold running water. They cost from £5 ($11.50) per person nightly. Included in this tab is a full English breakfast cooked by Colin Muzzall, who is fully experienced in the culinary arts. The standard of food at the Ellesmere is high. A complete four-course dinner costs from £3.25 ($7.48). The hotel is closed from the end of November until the end of January.

Kennedy Palace Hotel, 11/12 Marine Parade (tel. 604928), honors the assassinated American president, and is also a good place for bed and breakfast or else full board. The proprietors, A. and Y. Stylianou, charge £9 ($20.70) per person for bed and breakfast. Their fully licensed restaurant and bar is open to nonresidents as well. Their house, a Regency treasure, with an authentic bow front and an encircling balcony, has tables out on the patio so that guests may enjoy the view of the sea. The service is personal, the welcome friendly at the family-run establishment.

The **Regency Hotel,** 28 Regency Sq. (tel. Brighton 202690), is a charming Regency building with bow windows, carved doors, and a canopied balcony facing south across the square toward the pier and the sea. It was recently refurbished in a traditional style, yet incorporating modern comforts such as central heating and baths. Most units face the sea. For that romantic splurge night, you can reserve the Regency Suite, overlooking the water. This is an enormous room with a canopied bed, private sun balcony, and tented bathroom "just like something out of the Royal Pavilion." The rest of the hotel is comfortably furnished. Chris Turner and his Irish-born collaborator, Brian Nugent, have made sure that decorations are in period. The chandeliers are pure sparkling Waterford crystal in deference to Brian. Overnight will cost from £12 ($27.60) per person, including a continental breakfast.

Ryford Private Hotel, 6 and 7 New Steine (tel. Brighton 681576), on a Regency square adjacent to the Marine Parade, is within minutes of the seafront, the Palace Pier and the Aquarium. The comfortable lounge and some of the guest rooms offer views of the sea. All the rooms are carpeted and immaculate, complete with hot and cold running water. Bed-and-breakfast rates per person per night are about £8.50 ($19.55). Dinner is also available in the spacious dining room where excellent cuisine is prepared and served under the personal supervision of the resident proprietors.

DINING OUT IN BRIGHTON: **English's Oyster Bar and Seafoods Restaurant,** 29 East St. (tel. Brighton 27980), is our leading choice for superbly cooked fish, served in a well-preserved, 19th-century building conveniently opening onto "The Lanes." It combines a romantic setting with good food. For years, diners have been making such wise selections as a half dozen small Colchester oysters for £4 ($9.20) or a delicious hot lobster pâté at £2.50 ($5.75) per serving. The chef is known for such specialties as Dover sole (plate-size) for £6.50 ($14.95) and fresh locally caught plaice, £4 ($9.20). The pièce de résistance is the bouillabaisse at £3.60 ($8.28) per person. The chef also offers set two- and three-course table d'hôte menus at £5.75 ($13.23) and £6.55 ($15.07), respectively, which are available for luncheon and dinner every day. You're given a selection of appetizers, plus a choice of five main courses. The restaurant is open for lunch every day, including Sunday, from noon to 2:20 p.m., and for dinner from 6 to 10:20 p.m. every day except Sunday.

French Connection, 11 Little East St. (tel. Brighton 24454), occupies a Georgian fisherman's cottage. Mr. and Mrs. Brian Howell run this elegant and comfortable little place, offering a short menu of imaginative dishes, both French and English. Several flambé dishes are featured, and fresh ingredients are used whenever possible. The wine list is well chosen, and the service is among the best at the resort. Expect to pay from $30 per person for a three-course dinner with both wine and coffee. Only dinner is served, and it is offered nightly except Sunday from 7 to 11. Reservations are suggested.

The **Pump House,** 44–46 Market St. (tel. Brighton 26864), is a Regency chop and steak room combined with a coffeehouse that's one of the favorite rendezvous points in Brighton for morning coffee or afternoon tea. In the Lanes area, the Pump House stands in one of the oldest parts of Brighton. The establishment's grill room is richly paneled, with a genuine Adam door. On the second landing is the steak and chop house. The food is "distinguished English," with a three-course luncheon going for £4.75 ($10.93), a three-course dinner for £6.25 ($14.36). Specialties on the à la carte menu include real turtle soup at £1 ($2.30), smoked Scottish salmon at £3.25 ($7.48), and steak tartare at £6.25 ($14.36). A sirloin steak menu, costing £4.75 ($10.93), is also offered at luncheon daily and from 6 to 8 every evening (except Saturday). The restaurant is closed on Sunday, but the bar is open seven days a week.

Christopher's, 24 Western St. (tel. Brighton 775048), is a favorite bistro in Brighton. Operated by a former chef at London's Carlton Tower and his banker partner, the restaurant is a champion of creative cookery. Given sufficient notice, the chef will endeavor to prepare any dish you request. Appetizers include a delicious homemade pâté for £1.10 ($2.53). Main dishes are à la carte, and are likely to feature filet maison, a filet steak with wine and mushroom sauce served in a light puff pastry, for £5.10 ($11.73), or côte de pork Julietta, pork chops cooked with prawns and asparagus and served in a cherry brandy sauce, for £3.80 ($8.74). Vegetables are served separately and cost about 45p ($1.04) per portion. All desserts are homemade and average about £1.20 ($2.76). Dinner is served from 7 p.m. to 10:45 p.m. daily except Wednesday. Reservations are recommended.

The **Swiss Restaurant** (also called the William Tell), 11–12 Queen's Rd. (tel. Brighton 26865), is a miniature Alpine world, tucked away in a building a block north of the clock tower. In this pine-paneled room, run by Alan and Pamela Jones, you'll be served top-notch Swiss dishes, along with French fare. The national dish of Switzerland, fondue Neuchatelloise, costs £7 ($16.10) for two persons. For more elaborate dining, you can order the fondue bourguignonne for two persons at £10.50 ($24.15). Other specialties include rösti, a Swiss potato dish, at 80p ($1.84). For dessert, try the pineapple with kirsch at

£1.50 ($3.45). The place is open daily, except Sunday, from noon to 2 p.m. and from 6 to 10 p.m.

Henekeys, Ship Street (tel. Brighton 27492), is the leading pub (established in 1695), which makes it big on atmosphere. Even if it didn't serve good food and drinks (which it does), it'd make an interesting stopover, inviting with its old timbers, bricks, stones, and leaded glass windows. In the center is a beer garden (open in summer only), and there's a lounge bar upstairs. Behind the Old Ship Hotel, it's especially popular at lunch. The fare is very English, and includes locally caught plaice, £3 ($6.90); a grilled sirloin, £4.50 ($10.35); and scampi, £4.50 also. These main dishes, all served in the Steak Bar, come with pie or cheese. Henekeys keeps regular pub hours.

Tureen, 31 Upper North St. (tel. Brighton 28939), is one of our favorite Brighton bistros, a rare one that makes available (see the blackboard for daily specials) some of the best of the English and continental dishes at low prices—including an always-delicious soup "from the tureen" for 85p ($1.96) or a cheese and prawn vol-au-vent at £1.50 ($3.45). Main courses include such delectable fare as a whole pigeon and walnut casserole, £3.65 ($8.40); filet steak wrapped in pastry, mushrooms, and onion, £5.75 ($13.23); and lamb sweetbreads in a mushroom and white wine sauce, £3.50 ($8.05). In addition, the restaurant does a budget Sunday traditional family lunch at £5 ($11.50), including three courses, plus coffee. The Tureen is hot from noon to 2 p.m. Tuesday to Sunday, and from 7 p.m. to midnight (last orders at 9:30) Tuesday to Saturday.

Browns Restaurant and Coffee House, 3-4 Duke St. (tel. Brighton 23501), is a charming, rather 1930s place with plain tables and hoop-backed chairs. There is no bar so the staff prefers diners to wait in the Victory Inn at 7 Duke St. where they collect eaters when tables become available. Dishes have imaginative accompaniments. For example, spaghetti dishes are served with hot cheese bread and a salad; pies, including chicken and chestnut, pork, apple, and cider, come with cottage fried potatoes (sauteed) rather than the obiquitous chips. Salads and grills make up the small but tasty menu. Followed by thick dark-chocolate cake and coffee, a meal will cost around £5 ($11.50) a person. House wine goes for 75p ($1.73) a glass.

14. Arundel

This small and beautiful town in West Sussex, only 58 miles from London, four miles from the English Channel, nestles at the foot of one of England's most spectacular castles. The town itself was once an Arun River port, its denizens enjoying the prosperity of considerable trade and commerce. The harbor traffic is gone, replaced by coaches filled with visitors who come to visit Le Castle.

ARUNDEL CASTLE: The ancestral home of the Dukes of Norfolk, this baronial estate is a much-restored mansion of considerable importance. Its legend is associated with some of the great families of England—the Fitzalans and the powerful Howards of Norfolk. Arundel Castle traces its history back to King Alfred; its keep goes back to around the Conquest.

Over the years, Arundel Castle suffered destruction, particularly during the Civil War when Cromwell's troops stormed its walls, perhaps in retaliation for the 14th Earl of Arundel's (Thomas Howard) sizable contribution to Charles I. In the early 18th century, the castle virtually had to be rebuilt. In late Victorian times, it was remodeled and extensively restored again. Today it is filled, as you'd expect, with a good collection of antiques, along with an assortment of paintings by old masters such as Van Dyck and Holbein.

The castle is open from the week before Easter until the end of October, Monday to Friday from noon to 5 p.m. for £1.40 ($3.22) admission charge for adults, 90p ($2.07) for children. The last admission is at 4 p.m. Surrounding the castle is an 1100-acre park (scenic highlight: Swanbourne Lake).

READER'S SIGHTSEEING TIP: "The little **Museum of Curiosity,** 6 High St., will delight children (and their parents) with its displays of small animals in storybook tableaux. It is open daily Easter through October. Admission is 15p (35¢) for children; 35p (81¢) for adults" (Ralph Williams, Falls Church, Va.).

WHERE TO STAY: Norfolk Arms, High Street (tel. Arundel 882-101), is a former Georgian coaching inn set in the center of the town, just a short walk from the castle. The lounges and dining room are in the typically English country-inn style—that is, unostentatious but unquestionably comfortable. The hotel has been restored with many modern amenities blending with the old architecture. The bedrooms are handsomely maintained and furnished—each with personal touches. Most rooms have private bathrooms, and all have color television. It is a medium-priced place. The bed-and-breakfast rate is £15.50 ($35.65) per person without bath, £17 ($39.10) per person with bath, VAT included. No service is charged.

In the restaurant you can order good English cooking with Host's Luncheon for £4.25 ($9.78). When available, fresh local produce is offered. You can also dine à la carte. Specialties include lobster soup with brandy, local Arundel trout £2 ($4.60), and jugged hare at £5.50 ($12.65). Desserts of the day are £1.10 ($2.53).

Bridge Hotel, Queen Street (tel. Arundel 882242), is a substantial inn on the banks of the Arun River run by a Portuguese man, Orlando Simoes. The bedrooms have views of the castle, and the location's only a minute or two from the town center. In all, the Bridge rents out 13 well-maintained bedrooms, with hot and cold running water and soft beds. The bed-and-breakfast rate is from £12 ($27.60) per person, including VAT and service. The lounges and bedrooms are comfortable and roomy. Ask for a breakfast table opening toward the river view. Snacks begin at 75p ($1.73), complete meals at £5 ($11.50). You'll find a car park and a lock-up garage.

15. Chichester

According to one newspaper, Chichester might have been just a market town if the Chichester Festival Theater had not been established in its midst. One of the oldest Roman cities in England, Chichester is in vogue—drawing a chic crowd from all over the world who come to see its theater's presentations.

Only a five-minute walk from the Chichester Cathedral and the old Market Cross, the 1400-seat theater, with its apron stage, stands on the edge of Oaklands Park. It opened in 1962 (first director: Lord Laurence Olivier), and its reputation has grown steadily, pumping new vigor and life into the former walled city. Of course, in some quarters there is still resentment, and occasionally you hear suggestions that the pounds could have been better spent on a municipal swimming pool. But others point to the success of the Chichester theater in having given fresh stimulus to the living theater in England.

THE FESTIVAL THEATER: Booking generally opens in the middle of March, although the season might not start till the middle of May (it continues until late September). The price of seats ranges from £1 ($2.30) to £5.50 ($12.65) for the finest tickets in the house. A limited number of £1 ($2.30) seats go on sale at the box office on the day of each performance, and are sold on a first-come, first-served basis. Reservations made over the telephone will be held for a maximum of four days (call Chichester 781-312). It's better to mail inquiries and checks to the box office, **Chichester Festival Theatre,** Oaklands Park, Chichester. Matinee performances begin at 2 p.m., evening shows at 7 p.m.

How to get there: If you would like to come down from London, 62 miles away, for a matinee, then catch the 11:28 train from Victoria Station which will deliver you to Chichester by 1:05 p.m., in plenty of time. For an evening performance, board the 4:28 p.m. train from Victoria Station, arriving at 6:07 p.m. Regrettably, there is no direct late train back to London after the show. Visitors who must return can make a connection via Brighton, arriving at Victoria Station shortly after midnight.

WHERE TO STAY: In Chichester, you have a choice of living either at one of the old inns inside the city, or else at a motel on the outskirts.

The **Ship Hotel,** North Street (tel. Chichester 782028), is for those who enjoy a formal, yet gracious, lodging. A five-minute walk from the Festival Theatre, it is surrounded by attractive antique shops. An example of Georgian architecture, it invites with its red brick facade, white portico, and its tall, wide windows. The focal point inside is the Adam staircase, giving flair and style to the entire establishment. The management has achieved many improvements in the bedroom decor. The rooms are comfortable, with hot and cold running water (many with private baths as well). Singles begin at £12 ($27.60); doubles start at £20 ($46); breakfast included. Modern touches include an elevator and central heating. Here you'll find the Victory Bar, and in the rear, a dining room of simple attractiveness which serves good meals. The fixed-price luncheon is £4 ($9.20); dinner, £6.25 ($14.36).

Dolphin & Anchor, West Street (tel. Chichester 785-121), is two old inns joined together and run as a Trust House. The situation is prime, right at the historic 15th-century Market Cross and opposite the Chichester Cathedral, a ten-minute walk from the Festival Theatre. The tradition of good innkeeping is honored here, in a setting that blends 19th-century architectural features with 20th-century comforts, including an old coaching entrance, but a new wing of handsomely furnished bedrooms as well. A Forte Trust House, the two-in-one inn has 54 bedrooms, all with baths, TV, radio, and telephone. A single with bath is £24 ($55.20), increasing to £32 ($73.60) in a twin with bath, these tariffs including service and VAT. There are lounges, bars, a Finnish sauna, the Whig and Tory Restaurant, and the Roussillon Buttery, which serves light meals and grills until 10:30 p.m.

Chichester Lodge Hotel, Westhampnett, Chichester (tel. Chichester 786351), is a boon to motorists because it's a mile from the city center on the main A27 with large car parking facilities. A covered passageway connects it to the older White Swan Inn nearby. The attractively styled hotel offers 43 modern bedrooms tastefully furnished, containing private bathrooms, telephone, radio, tea-making facilities, and color TV. The rate is £34 ($78.20) for a double and £24 ($55.20) for a single, including VAT, service, and a full English breakfast. The hotel has an attractive cocktail bar and restaurant serving a set lunch for £5.50 ($12.65), a table d'hôte dinner for £6.50 ($14.95), including VAT and service.

WHERE TO EAT: Unlike its limited number of accommodations, Chichester abounds with good restaurants. We find the following establishments superior, both for food and value.

    Little London Restaurant, Little London, off East Street (tel. Chichester 784-899), nestles in a charming little building. The fully licensed restaurant serves a fine cuisine, each dish prepared individually. The service and reception are friendly as well. In an atmosphere of subdued taste, you can order from one of the small, but very select, menus, while seated on an upholstered chair at a pink-clothed table. At lunch, a three-course table d'hôte meal is served for £5 ($11.50), including, for example, pears with tarragon mayonnaise, roast rolled rib of beef, and profiteroles in chocolate sauce. In the evening, there is a small à la carte menu which varies during the year, serving such delicacies as caviar cream, nut cutlets, sweetbread pie, or guinea fowl in red wine and herbs. Coffee is an additional 50p ($1.15), and there is a cover charge of 30p (69¢). The vegetables of the day are included in the price of the main dishes. The desserts are homemade and mouthwatering. You must reserve. The restaurant is closed all day Sunday and Monday, but open otherwise from noon to 2 p.m. and from 7 to 10 p.m. On Saturday nights and also during the May to September Festival Theatre season, there are two sittings, at 7:30 and 9:45 p.m. The place is usually closed for one week in February.

    Also on the premises is the fully licensed, self-service **Savourie,** offering a variety of soups at 60p ($1.38), pâtés at 75p ($1.73), and hot pies at £1.60 ($3.68). Salads are priced at £1 ($2.30), and jacket potatoes go for 30p (69¢). Such desserts as chocolate gâteau cost £1 ($2.30). This place is well worth recommending for its good service and the high standard of its food. Wicker chairs are placed before clean white tables. As East Street is a pedestrian way, you must be prepared to walk to the restaurant, only a short distance.

    The **Roussillon Buttery,** Dolphin & Anchor, West Street, serves light meals and grills. Standard English fare includes such dishes as scampi and fried potatoes at £2.20 ($5.06); sausage with beans and fried potatoes, £1.75 ($4.03); and a baked potato, 60p ($1.38). Hamburgers at £2.20 ($5.06) make good luncheon fare, and various salads are priced at £1.85 ($4.26).

    The **Coffee House,** West Street (tel. Chichester 784-799), stands right beside the Dolphin & Anchor, opposite the cathedral. It has a good reputation for satisfying food at low prices. A small place, it provides plats du jour including a shrimp salad at £2 ($4.60). Hot snacks, such as Welsh rarebit with bacon at £1 ($2.30), are offered from 10 a.m. to closing. A soup of the day goes for 35p (81¢), and sandwiches, beginning at 50p ($1.15), are served on the ground floor only between noon and 2 p.m. In the licensed restaurant you can order good-tasting omelets beginning at £1.10 ($2.53), or else a selection from the cold buffet, costing from £1.60 ($3.68).

THE LOCAL PUB: The **Old Punch House,** East Street, by the Market Cross, is a pub built in 1576 and restored to its full Elizabethan glory by its hosts, Michael and Valerie Reilly. They offer a full range of hot and cold foods ranging from a simple snack at 75p ($1.73) to a full meal, obtained both at lunch or in the evening, with prices starting at £4 ($9.20).

THE OPEN-AIR MUSEUM: On a 40-acre site at Singleton, six miles north of Chichester on the A286 (London Road), Old England is being recreated. In a natural setting of mature woodland and meadows, buildings in which men and women lived and worked from the Middle Ages to the 19th century are being assembled. It's part of the **Weald & Downland Open-Air Museum,** open every day except Monday and bank holidays from April through September (but including Monday in July and August), 11 a.m. to 6 p.m. Admission for adults is 85p ($1.96); children and students, 50p ($1.15). Although still in the growing stage, the museum includes the 17th-century Market Hall from Titchfield in Hampshire; a 15th-century farmhouse; a 1731 granary; a timber-framed medieval house with wattle and daub walls; a treadwheel of 1600; a reconstruction of a Saxon weaver's hut considered to date from 500 A.D.; a charcoal burner's hut; a weather-boarded toll cottage from Sussex.

FISHBOURNE: A worthwhile visit only two miles from Chichester is the **Roman Palace,** the largest yet discovered in Britain. Built around 75 A.D. in Italianate style, it has many mosaic-floored rooms and even an underfloor heating system. The gardens have been restored to their original first-century plan. There is free parking, and on the site is a cafeteria. The museum is open March through November. Admission for adults is 75p ($1.73). Students and senior citizens pay 50p ($1.15), and children are charged 20p (46¢).

LIVING ON THE OUTSKIRTS: One of the most interesting ways to attend the theater in Chichester is from a base on the outskirts. That way, you get to enjoy the best of English village life, but can conveniently go into the city whenever you want. Some recommendations follow.

Old Bosham

One of the most charming little villages of West Sussex, Bosham was a Saxon hamlet (King Harold lived near here in a now disappeared palace). Its little church was depicted in the Bayeux Tapestry. Near the harbor, it is reached by a narrow lane. Its graveyard overlooks the boats (a daughter of King Canute is buried inside). The church is filled with ship models and relics, showing the villagers' link to the sea. Bosham today is principally a sailing resort, linked by good bus service to Chichester.

The **Millstream Hotel,** Bosham (tel. Bosham 573-234), is set on the road to the village of Bosham and its harbor, off the A27. Completely redecorated, the rooms have different colors, but all are outfitted with floral-patterned wallpaper. The decor is in keeping with the country cottage-type hotel. Beds are new and comfortable. Of the 16 rooms, 12 have baths, costing couples £30 ($69) nightly. However, two persons in a bathless room pay £25 ($57.50). Singles in bathless rooms are charged £13 ($29.90). The cocktail bar at the entrance to the restaurant is tastefully furnished with white bamboo chairs and tables, plus green carpeting. At the adjoining restaurant, you can order such à la carte dishes as moules marinières, roast duck braised with petits pois, £4.25 ($9.78); and desserts for around £1 ($2.30). A set luncheon is £5 ($11.50).

Incidentally, Mr. Goodman, of the Bosham Sea School, next to the Millstream Hotel, hires out sailing dinghies of the Wayfarer type. Of course, you should be experienced before taking a boat out. Those who aren't can generally get a local person to go with them if they'd like to go sailing for the day.

AT HOME WITH AN AMERICAN COUPLE: At Home, Arundel Holt Court, Bedham, Fittleworth, Pulborough (tel. Fittleworth 079-882-221). Bill and Gretchen Stevens, an American couple, live at Arundel Holt Court and offer two private bedrooms in their own house. The guest suite has a library lounge and tea- and coffee-making equipment. There is another bedroom under the roof, with a comfortable sitting area and drinks cupboard. Both have private bathrooms. The Stevenses will provide breakfast and evening meals either in your own suite or en famille in their own charming dining room. They are both good cooks and feature traditional American farmhouse, Italian, and Mexican dishes, with barbecues for hot summer evenings.

They will gladly give information on the various local sights and arrange for excursions to the coast, to Brighton, or Chichester for the theater, Goodwood for the racing, or to Glyndebourne for the opera. They charge £35 ($80.50) for one person, £58 ($133.40) for two, or £70 ($161) for three, including a full English breakfast. Lunch is available at £4 ($9.20); dinner at £7 ($16.10) to £9 ($20.70) with wine.

Chapter VII

HAMPSHIRE AND DORSET

1. Portsmouth
2. Southampton
3. Isle of Wight
4. Winchester
5. Bournemouth
6. Shaftesbury
7. Wool
8. Wareham
9. Dorchester
10. Bridport
11. Chideock
12. Charmouth
13. Lyme Regis
14. Donyatt

STONE FARMHOUSES—Burke's Landed Gentry—all this belongs to the countryside of the 17th century. Fireplaces where stacks of logs burn gaily. Wicker baskets of apples freshly brought in from the orchard (ever had homemade apple butter?). Chickens stuffed with dressing and roasted with strips of bacon on top to keep them tender and juicy. Milk that doesn't come from bottles. Old village houses, now run as hotels, possessing quality and charm. Beyond the pear trees, on the crest of a hill, the ruins of a Roman camp. A village pub, with two rows of kegs filled with varieties of cider, where the hunt gathers.

You're in Hampshire and Dorset, two shires guarded zealously by the English, who protect their special rural treasures. Everybody knows of Southampton and Bournemouth, but less known is the undulating countryside lying inland. Your car will take you through endless lanes, revealing tiny villages and thatched cottages untouched by the industrial invasion.

HAMPSHIRE

This is Jane Austen country—firmly middle class, largely agricultural, its inhabitants doggedly convinced that Hampshire is the greatest spot on earth.

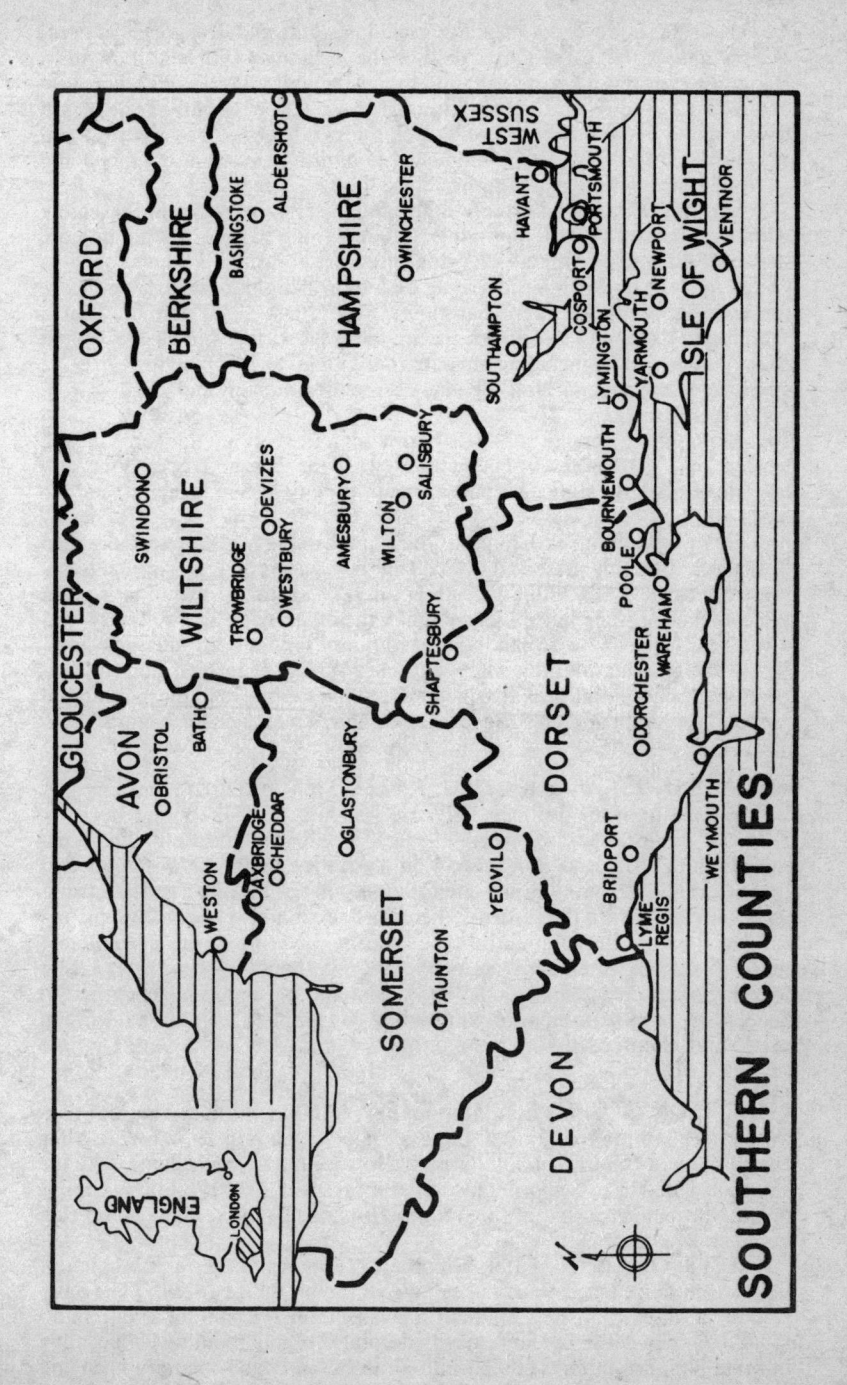

HAMPSHIRE 243

SOUTHERN COUNTIES

Austen wrote six novels of manners, including *Pride and Prejudice* and *Sense and Sensibility*, that earned her a room at the top among 19th-century writers. Her books provided a keen insight into the solid middle-class English who were to build such a powerful Empire. Although the details of the life she described have now largely faded ("At five o'clock the two ladies retired to dress, and at half-past six Elizabeth was summoned to dinner"), much of the mood and spirit of Hampshire depicted in her books remains.

Born in 1775, Jane Austen was the daughter of the rector of Steventon. Although she lived in Bath for a while, and for a troubled time in Southampton, she spent most of her life at **Chawton**, near Alton, where her home may be visited today. You can see the writing desk on which she penned such memorable novels as *Emma* (her "handsome, clever, and rich" heroine, Emma Woodhouse). About a mile from the station, Ms. Austen's home (tel. Alton 83262) is open daily, including Sunday from 11 a.m. to 4:30 p.m. for 40p (92¢) admission; children under 14, 20p (46¢). It is closed Monday and Tuesday from November 1 to March 31.

Hampshire embraces the **New Forest** (don't expect anything in England labeled "new" to be new), the **South Downs**, the **Isle of Wight** (Victoria's favorite retreat), the passenger port and gateway city of **Southampton**, and the naval city of **Portsmouth**.

Going west from Southampton, you'll come to the New Forest, more than 90,000 acres selfishly preserved by William the Conqueror as a private hunting ground (poachers met with the death penalty). William lost two of his sons in the New Forest—one killed by an animal, the other by an arrow. Today, it is a vast and unspoiled woodland and heath, ideal for walking and exploring.

Although Hampshire is filled with many places of interest, for our purposes we've concentrated on two major areas that seem to hold the most appeal for tourists: Southampton for convenience and Winchester for history.

BROADLANDS: At **Romsey** (tel. Romsey 516878), Earl Mountbatten of Burma lived until his death in 1979. He lent his beautiful country house to H.M. the Queen when, as Princess Elizabeth, she married Prince Philip. Originally built in 1536 as an adjunct to Romsey Abbey, the house was purchased by Lord Palmerston in 1736 and later decorated in fine Palladian style. Capability Brown landscaped the gardens. There is a fine exhibition and show depicting the highlights of Lord Mountbatten's brilliant career as sailor and diplomat until his partial retirement from public life. The house is open daily, except Monday (daily including Monday in August and September), from April to September, from 10 a.m. to 6 p.m. Admission is £1 ($2.30) for adults, 50p ($1.15) for children.

LUNCHEON STOPOVERS ON THE WAY: For those driving down to Winchester and the New Forest, there is a good lunch stop at **Selborne**. After taking the A31 from London to Chawton to see Jane Austen's home, take the signposted B3006 to Selborne, five miles away. In the 18th century, Gilbert White, the famous author of the *Natural History of Selborne* and a pioneering botanist, lived here.

At the **Queens Hotel** (tel. Selborne 272) you can order a pub lunch of homemade soup, Queensburger, and Welsh rarebit for £1 ($2.30). The daily traditional dish from the restaurant is available in the bars for about £1.50 ($3.45). Or else eat in the fantastically decorated dining room under a canopy of brass jugs, bits of farm equipment, corncobs, and "god-whattery" hanging from the old oak beams. David, son of the owner, Blake Paton, ladles out the special Peggy Paton's homemade soup (his mother's recipe), plus large portions of freshly roasted beef with all the trimmings, such as Yorkshire pudding, roast potatoes, and properly cooked cabbage (that is, al dente with a little butter and some pepper). On other days there is lamb with mint sauce and red currant jelly. Desserts are homemade, and the fruit pies and cream are especially good. The bill, including VAT, will come to around £4 ($9.20) per person. If you can drive after leaving the place, Winchester is not too far away if you retrace your steps on the A31. The hotel is open for lunches from 12:30 to 1:45 p.m. and for dinners from 7:30 to 8:45 p.m. Accommodation with a full English breakfast is available from £8 ($18.40) per night. Six of the nine bedrooms have private bath or shower and toilets.

Similarly at Hurstbourne Priors, between Andover and Whitchurch—on the B3400—stands the **Portsmouth Arms** (tel. Whitchurch 2000), another country pub serving marvelous food. The range of hot dishes isn't large, but there are usually two choices as appetizers—smoked mackerel, soup, pâté—followed by pork chops, ham steaks, or lamb, all served with freshly picked and freshly cooked vegetables in season. Cheese, homemade pie, or trifle finishes the meals which, with coffee, comes to about £4 ($9.20) per person. The "Arms" is open for lunch from noon to 2:30 p.m. and for dinner from 7 to 10:30 p.m.

1. Portsmouth

Virginia, New Hampshire, even Ohio, may have their Portsmouths, but the daddy of them all is the old port and naval base on the Hampshire coast, 70 miles south of London. German bombers in World War II virtually leveled the city, hitting about nine-tenths of its buildings. But the seaport has recovered admirably.

Its maritime associations are famous. From Sally Port, the most interesting district in the Old Town, "Naval heroes innumerable have embarked to fight their country's battles." That was certainly true on June 6, 1944, when Allied troops set sail to invade occupied France.

Of chief interest is Lord Nelson's flagship, H.M.S. *Victory,* a 104-gun, first-rate ship of the line, now at No. 2 Dry Dock in Portsmouth Naval Base. Although she first saw action in 1778, her fame was earned on October 21, 1805, in the Battle of Trafalgar when the English scored a victory over the combined Spanish and French fleets. It was in this battle that Lord Nelson lost his life. The flagship, after being taken to Gibraltar for repairs, returned to Portsmouth with Nelson's body on board (he was later buried at St. Paul's in London). It is open March 1 to November 1 weekdays, 10:30 a.m. to 5:30 p.m. on Sunday from 1 to 5 p.m. From November 1 to March 1, weekdays, 10:30 a.m. to 4:30 p.m. and on Sundays 1 to 4:30 p.m.

The **Portsmouth Royal Naval Museum** stands opposite H.M.S. *Victory,* in her unique setting in the old naval dockyard, and houses many naval relics that are complementary to the ship. These include personal items which belonged to Lord Nelson and his officers, a fine collection of figureheads and ship models, and a special display of Nelson memorabilia given by Mrs. John McCarthy, C.B.E., an American citizen. A recent addition is an exhibition of naval campaign medals showing the history of the British navy in the Victorian era, after which the visitor is returned to the present by a graphic portrayal of the navy of today, which includes a mock-up of an operations room aboard a modern warship.

The museum is open daily from 10:30 a.m. to 5:30 p.m. (on Sunday from 1 to 5 p.m.) in summer, closing at 5 p.m. in winter. Admission is 20p (46¢) for adults, 10p (23¢) for children. The museum complex also includes a small snackbar and souvenir shop.

Portsmouth was the birthplace of Charles Dickens, and the small terrace house of 1805 in which the famous novelist made his appearance on February 7, 1812, and lived for a short time, has now been restored and furnished to illustrate the middle-class taste of the early 19th century. Called **Charles Dickens' Birthplace Museum**, it is at 393 Old Commercial Rd., Mile End. It is open daily from 10:30 a.m. to 5:30 p.m., except Christmas Day and Boxing Day. Admission is 25p (58¢) for adults, 12p (28¢) for students and children. Family tickets (four persons) are available for 50p ($1.15). Last tickets are sold at 5 p.m.

Jutting out into the harbor, **Portchester Castle** has one of the finest examples of early Saxon timber work in all of England. It was here that Henry V assembled his men for the assault on Agincourt in 1415. In addition, Portsmouth also has one of the best surviving Roman forts in England.

WHERE TO STAY: Overnighting in Portsmouth? If so, try the following:

Keppel's Head Hotel, The Hard (tel. Portsmouth 21954), is an impressive Victorian brick monument facing the train ferry pier. A prestigious hotel for generations, the inn preserves its traditional niceties, with good old-style bedrooms, some with private baths. Bathless singles rent for £18 ($41.40), increasing to £24 ($55.20) with private bath. Bathless doubles go for £28 ($64.40), the tariff going up to £33 ($75.90) with private bath, these rates including breakfast, service, and VAT. Some travelers to the Isle of Wight stop off here to dine at the Captain's Table. The cuisine is English, including such dishes as thick slices of ribs of beef with Yorkshire pudding, or roast loin of pork with apple sauce.

WHERE TO EAT: The **Lone Yachtsman** at The Point (tel. Portsmouth 24293) (head up Broad Street) is a revamped pub that is the center of the local life of old Portsmouth. Decorated in a nautical theme, it commands a view of the harbor from its perch on the end of a promontory. You can drink in the Sir Alec Rose bar (popular with yachting people) or else dine at the Lively Lady (hot luncheons Monday to Friday from noon to 2:30 p.m.). Among the usual entrees are such tempting items as the soup of the day for 55p ($1.27), and steak, kidney, and mushroom pie at £1.75 ($4.03). A tradition is the hot fruit pie, served with thick cream, for 70p ($1.61).

The Hungry One, 15 Arundel Way, Arundel Street (tel. Portsmouth 817-114), is a simple, clean snackbar, offering a wide range of salads from plain cheese to fresh salmon from £1.50 ($3.45) to £2.60 ($5.98), plus well-cooked chicken and chips, plaice and chips, scampi and chips (with everything—it's that sort of place) for about the same prices. Desserts are about 75p ($1.73).

IN THE ENVIRONS: **The Old House**, The Square, Wickham, near Fareham (tel. Wickham 833-049), is a tiny village-square hotel built in 1702, in the time of Queen Anne. It is personally run by its owners, Mr. and Mrs. Skipwith. The hotel stands in a preserved Georgian square of Wickham, and is noted for its good restaurant, which is closed at lunchtime on Monday and Saturday (all day on Sunday).

The hotel's bedrooms, each with private bath, are not rented on Saturday and Sunday, and therefore it is open on weekdays only. Prices are from £25

($57.50) in a single, from £35 ($80.50) in a double, these tariffs including a full English breakfast and the service charge, although VAT is extra.

The garden overlooks the Meon River, and the restaurant specializes in a French provincial cuisine, a complete meal costing from £10 ($23). The menu changes frequently, and care goes into the selection of the vegetables as well. On one occasion, local spring greens, with butter and black pepper, were excellent. Lunch is served from 12:30 to 2 p.m. and dinner from 7:30 to 9:30 p.m. Always reserve well in advance.

2. Southampton

To many North Americans, England's No. 1 passenger port, home base for the *Queen Elizabeth 2*, is the gateway to Britain. Southampton is a city of wide boulevards, parks, and shopping centers. It was rebuilt after German bomb damage, which destroyed hundreds of its old buildings.

In World War II, some 3½ million men embarked from here (in the First World War, more than twice that number passed through Southampton). Its supremacy as a port has long been recognized and dates from Saxon times when the Danish conqueror, Canute, was proclaimed king here in 1017.

Southampton was especially important to the Normans and kept them in touch with their homeland. It shares the dubious distinction of having imported the bubonic plague in the mid-14th century that wiped out a quarter of the English population. Near the docks is a memorial tower to the Pilgrims, who set out on their voyage to the New World from Southampton on August 15, 1620.

If you're waiting in Southampton between boats, you may want to use the time to explore some of the major sights of Hampshire that lie on the periphery of the port—the New Forest, Winchester, the Isle of Wight, even Bournemouth in neighboring Dorset.

WHERE TO STAY: The **Post House,** Herbert Walker Avenue (tel. Southampton 28081), is a Trust House Forte oasis of style and taste, the pacesetter of modern hotels on the south coast. Ten floors tall, it was built near the New Docks to overlook the harbor, but is only five minutes away from the city center. You can unload your luggage under a sheltered drive, and walk straight into the reception area. The rooms themselves, 132 in all (nine studio and eight syndicate accommodations), are handsome and spacious, decorated in strong bold colors, with fine built-in pieces, picture-window walls, private baths, telephones, radio, and television. Twin or double rooms cost £26 ($59.80) per person; a single, £36 ($82.80). Your breakfast is extra, but all rates include service and VAT. The facilities of the hotel are exceptional, especially the heated open-air swimming pool. The residents' lounge has a color television. The Harbour Bar adjacent to the restaurant has a intimate atmosphere. For dining in the Solent Room, see our restaurant recommendations.

Dolphin Hotel, High Street (tel. Southampton 26178), was Jane Austen's choice, even Thackeray's when he was writing *Pendennis*. In time, Queen Victoria arrived in a horse-drawn carriage at this Georgian inn and coaching house. A classic brick building, with a pair of bow windows, it is in the center of the city, and is approached through an arched entrance, over which rests a coat-of-arms of William IV and Queen Adelaide. The 73 bedrooms vary widely in size, but are generally spacious and well furnished. All have baths. Singles cost £25 ($57.50); doubles and twins, £34 ($78.20). The lounge is dignified, nicely paneled, and tidily kept. The open staircase holds a rare collection of naval uniform prints. Meals at the Dolphin are quite good, with a table d'hôte dinner beginning at £6 ($13.80). Drinks are served in the Nelson Bar.

Polygon Hotel, Cumberland Place (tel. Southampton 26401), 15 minutes to the Ocean Terminal, is the ideal hotel for transatlantic passengers just off the *Queen Elizabeth 2.* Set quietly back overlooking West Park and the Civic Centre, it is run as a member of Trust House Forte Hotels Ltd. It offers 119 well-furnished bedrooms, all with private baths, telephones, radios, and color TV sets. A single is £28 ($64.40), and a twin is £36 ($82.80), including service and VAT. A bar and restaurant are on the premises; there is ample parking space, plus near-instant taxi service.

Cotswold Hotel, Highfield Lane (tel. Southampton 559-555), is a modern hotel, offering plain, comfortable overnight accommodations. All rooms have telephone, radio, color TV, tea- and coffee-making equipment, and most have bathrooms or showers. There is a good car park and a night porter. A good feature is that a supper menu takes over from dinner at 9 p.m. and goes on until last orders are given at 11 p.m. Gilley's restaurant is open daily, virtually all day—a coffeeshop-type place with bench seats around "stall" tables. At lunchtime, including Sunday, roast ribs of beef, served from a majestic trolley salvaged from the transatlantic liner R.M.S. *Queen Mary,* are the specialty, accompanied by horseradish sauce and Yorkshire pudding. In season fresh local salmon is an added attraction, caught by Frank Gilley, the hotel's chairman. Lunch or dinner will cost you around £6 ($13.80) a person for three courses. Supper includes kebabs, barbecued chicken, beefburgers, and mixed grill for around £3 ($6.90). Most Saturday nights they have a dinner dance. Rooms go for £18 ($41.40) to £23 ($52.90) in a single, from £30 ($69) to £34 ($78.20) in a double, including an English breakfast, VAT, and service.

County Hotel, 11 Hulse Rd., off The Avenue (tel. 24236), was once a substantial private, brick-built Victorian residence, and is now one of the leading unlicensed hotels of Southampton. For bed and breakfast, it charges from £8 ($18.40) per person in high season, plus VAT. Bus 15 goes from here into the center of the city. Next to the Hampshire County Cricket Field, the hotel offers ten tastefully furnished doubles, four singles—but only three public baths. However, the rooms themselves have hot and cold running water, and are heated. Dinners begin at £4 ($9.20). There's a space for your car, too.

WHERE TO DINE: The **Solent Room,** Post House, Herbert Walker Avenue (tel. Southampton 28081), is a distinguished restaurant in a colorful setting. On the ground floor of this ten-story modern hotel, top-notch meals are served against a background of bright-red floors and walls. The service is friendly and attentive and the cuisine is international. A three-course lunch is £7 ($16.10), and a three-course dinner begins at £9 ($20.70). All charges are inclusive of service and VAT. The headwaiter will present you with a comprehensive list of wines, from £4.50 ($10.35).

Cobbett's Restaurant, The Square, Botley (tel. Botley 2068), is run with flair by Mr. and Mrs. Charles Skipwith, who prepare French dishes with skill, using fresh ingredients whenever possible. Even the vegetables—too often neglected in restaurants in England—are well prepared, tender and crisp. Mr. Skipwith's wife, Lucie, comes from Bordeaux, France, and she does the cooking, taking pride in selecting original and unusual dishes. To her the words "deep freeze" are dirty words. Seating 40, the snug restaurant has a 16th-century beamed bar where pre- and postdinner drinks are served. The menu and prices change seasonally, so we can't recommend particular specialties. However, recent main courses included tournedos Curnonsky and a regional cassoulet. Fresh vegetables in season go at £1 ($2.30) per single portion. The hors d'oeuvres were good, especially the salade des crudités. Although the list varies, depending on what's available at the market, a recent plate featured celery, tomatoes, fennel, watercress, chicory, cucumber, egg, artichoke hearts, and other vegetables. Expect to pay about £30 ($69) for two persons, including VAT. Lunch is served from 12:30 to 2 p.m.; dinner, 7:30 to 10 p.m. Closed Sunday and for a two-week summer vacation.

London Steak House, Civic Center Road (tel. Southampton 24394), is the favored choice for general all-around dining. These chain steakhouses, operated by Lyons, are becoming a byword in many English towns. The specialties run to grills and steaks, backed up by a selection of fine wines. A medium-size sirloin goes for £3.20 ($7.36), a large order (cooked as you desire it) for £4 ($9.20). Desserts include such selections as crème caramel, 65p ($1.50). Saturday nights, it's necessary to book a table. The steakhouse serves from noon to 3 p.m. and from 6 fo 11 p.m. daily, except Sunday when it's open from 12:30 to 3 p.m. and 6:30 to 10:30 p.m.

The Best Pub in Town

The **Red Lion,** High Street, is one of the few architectural jewels that survived World War II. The pub is rooted in the 12th century (a Norman cellar), but its high-ceilinged and raftered Henry V Court Room is in a later style. The room was the scene of the trial of the Earl of Cambridge and his accomplices, Thomas Grey and Lord Scrope, who were condemned to death for treason in plotting against the life of the king in 1415. The Court Room is adorned with coats-of-arms of the noblemen who served as peers of the trio. All this bloody history needn't deter you. The Red Lion is a friendly, fascinating place at which to stop in for a drink, a good old English pub lunch, and a chat.

SIDE TRIPS FROM SOUTHAMPTON: If postwar Southampton is too modern for your taste, and you want to capture the flavor of old England, then strike out for the **Fox and Hounds Inn,** Hungerford Bottom, Old Bursledon (tel. Bursledon 2784), between Southampton and Portsmouth—not far from the ferry to the Isle of Wight, and close to the Bursledon Railroad Station. It would take the writing ability of Dickens and the visual techniques of Hogarth to capture the spirited image of this inn, which dates back to 1338. You can have your wine-tasting experience in either the Hunter's Bar or the Farmer's Kitchen. Against a backdrop of horse brasses, a heavily beamed ceiling, and an open fireplace, the legendary mead—known to both the English and the Vikings—is dispensed. The Saxons considered it an elixir, and it is believed that the honey-based drink was the customary toast following a wedding—hence, the term honeymoon. Between lifting your maple and silver "mazer," you can sample Hampshire farm cheese served with good-tasting cottage bread. The Fox and Hounds, run by Bill and Joy Rout, is also noted for its English wines, which can be ordered on draft. If you've tasted cowslip before, you surely haven't sampled damson dandelion! From your beer-barrel seat, you can also take your chance on some sloe gin. English wines cost 45p ($1.04) per glass; a half pint of draft cider or beer, 29p (67¢). At the rear of the inn is a timbered barn serving as both a museum of farming artifacts (old farm wagons, carts, and smithy tools) and a self-service dining room. Here you dine on benches at one of the longest, oldest tables in England. During winter, the table nearest the ten-foot-wide fireplace is favored. Summertime, tables are also available in the courtyard beside an ancient wine press, under a rose arbor. Soups are 45p ($1.04); sandwiches, 95p ($2.19) and up. Helpings of fresh fruit salad cost 65p ($1.50).

Directions: Go on road A27 from Southampton, toward Portsmouth. Go past Lowford, turn right onto Long Lane, pass the school on School Road, and you'll reach a road called Hungerford Bottom. The Fox and Hounds is on your right.

BEAULIEU ABBEY: This stately home in the New Forest draws more visitors than Woburn Abbey. The abbey and palace house, as well as the National Motor Museum, are on the property of Lord Montagu of Beaulieu, at Beaulieu, five miles southeast of Lyndhurst and 14 miles south of Southampton. Originally, a Cistercian Abbey was founded on this spot in 1204, and the ruins can be explored today. The palace house itself was the gate house of the abbey before it was converted into a private residence in 1538. The house is surrounded by gardens. On the grounds one of the best and most comprehensive motor museums in the world, with more than 200 vehicles, was opened to the public. It traces the story of motoring from 1895 to the present day. Famous autos include four land-speed record holders, among them Donald Campbell's "Blue Bird." The museum was based on the Montagu family's collection of vintage cars. All the facilities are open every day from 10 a.m. to 6 p.m. (till 5 p.m., November to March). Inclusive admission to the museum, house, abbey ruins, and gardens is £1.80 ($4.14) for adults, 90p ($2.07) for children.

Food and Lodging

Montagu Arms, in Beaulieu (tel. Beaulieu 612-324), was built with locally made bricks and tiles as well as timbers from the New Forest. This time-tested favorite combines the comfort of a country manor house with the cozy hospitality of a mellow wayside inn. The hotel staff keeps up an old English garden which is well sheltered and filled with some rare plants. The main lounge overlooks this garden, and the dining room, serving good food and wine, is oak beamed and paneled. In one of the three bars, the counter was fashioned from an old wine press.

The bedrooms are immaculately kept and modernized, most of them containing private baths and wall-to-wall carpeting. Singles rent from £20 ($46), and doubles range from £30 ($69) to £38 ($87.40), including a full English breakfast.

A COUNTRY PLACE: Chewton Glen Hotel, New Milton, Hampshire (tel. Highcliffe 5341), is a gracious old country house on the fringe of the New Forest. It's within easy reach of Southampton and Bournemouth for those who want to escape from the bustle of the 20th century. Follow the signpost off the B3055, New Milton/Christchurch Road, through well-kept parkland to a private car park. The staff will arrange for you to be met if you intend to arrive by ship or train at Southampton.

Rooms are either in the old house or else in the new wing. In your bedroom you'll find "a tot" of sherry along with a bowl of fresh flowers to greet you. In the old house, you will either take the magnificent staircase to one of the well-furnished chambers, decorated with chintz armchairs, good beds, and lovely views over the spacious grounds, or find yourself on the ground level with French doors opening onto your own private patio. Here the decor is in muted colors, the rooms named for the heroes of novels written by Captain

Marryat (he was the author of *The Children of the New Forest*). There is full room service so you can retire fully from the world if that is your wish. In the old part, the rooms have eaves and dormer windows, and some have been combined to provide family accommodations.

Settle in and wander downstairs to explore the many lounges, arranged so that you can join the small crowd in the bar, or sit and talk in the big drawing room. Everywhere log fires burn and fresh flowers add fragrance. In the hall an information office provides details of local excursions, golf, sailing, and horse-riding. Guests can also swim in an open-air heated swimming pool. The garden sweeps down to a stream and then to rhododendron woods. In addition there are tennis courts and a croquet and putting green.

In the dining room, the standard of cooking and the presentation of the food is high. Particular emphasis is placed on fresh ingredients. Christian Delteil, the young French chef, came via the Connaught and Le Gavroche. Toni Ferrario is one of the most efficient restaurant managers in the country. Your dinner will be a treat. The set meal of three magnificent courses is changed daily, costing about £12 ($27.60), no hidden extras. The à la carte menu includes such delicacies as sweetbreads and Scottish salmon, and such daily specialties as lobster in season. But you will probably find the set meal delicious and adequate for the best of trenchermen. A simpler but equally excellent luncheon is provided, and the kitchen will also prepare a succulent picnic for you to take on an excursion. The wine cellar contains a choice of well-chosen French and German wines—and some Italian ones, too.

The price for all this begins at £35 ($80.50) per person for a double room, including VAT, service, and a continental breakfast. The Marryat suite costs £60 ($138) a night.

The hotel is owned by Martin Skan and his family, and their influence and that of their general manager, David Brockett, can be seen in the many thoughtful touches, the friendly attitude of the efficient staff, and the spotless condition of the hotel and grounds.

3. Isle of Wight

Four miles across the Solent from the South Coast towns of Southampton, Lymington, and Portsmouth, the Isle of Wight is known for its sandy beaches and its ports, favored by the yachting set. The island, which long attracted such literary figures as Alfred Tennyson and Charles Dickens, is compact in size, measuring 23 miles from east to west, 13 miles from north to south. You can take regular ferryboats over, although hydrofoils cross the Solent in just 20 minutes from Southampton.

Long a favorite of British royalty, the island has as its major attraction **Osborne House,** Queen Victoria's most cherished residence, lying a mile southeast of East Cowes. Prince Albert himself designed the Italian-inspired mansion which stands in lush gardens, right outside the village of Padmore. The rooms have remained as Victoria knew them, right down to the French piano she used to play and with all the cozy clutter of her sitting room. Grief-stricken at the death of Albert in 1861, she asked that Osborne House remain as it was, and so it has been. Even the turquoise scent bottles he gave her, decorated with cupids and cherubs, are still in place. It was at her bedroom in Osborne House that the queen died on January 22, 1901. Times of admission are April 7 to June 28 from 11 a.m. to 5 p.m. (same hours from September 8 to October 11). From June 30 to September 6, hours are 10 a.m. to 5 p.m. Price of admission is £1 ($2.30) for adults, 50p ($1.15) for children.

A completely different attraction, **Carisbrooke Castle** is where Charles I was imprisoned by the Roundheads in 1647. This fine medieval castle is in the center of the island, 1½ miles southwest of Newport. Everybody heads for the Well House, concealed inside a 16th-century stone building. Donkeys take turns treading a large wooden wheel connected to a rope which hauls up buckets of water. The castle is open all year, in March, April, and October, weekdays from 9:30 a.m. to 5:30 p.m., and on Sunday from 2 to 5:30 p.m. From May to September, hours are weekdays 9:30 a.m. to 7 p.m., and on Sunday from 2 to 7. From November to February, hours are weekdays from 9:30 a.m. to 4 p.m., on Sunday from 2 to 4. Summer admission prices are 75p ($1.73) for adults, 25p (58¢) for children.

You have a choice of several bases on the Isle of Wight unless you're what the English call a "day-tripper."

Cowes is the premier port for yachting in Britain. Henry VIII ordered the castle built there, but it is now the headquarters of the Royal Yacht Squadron. The seafront, the Prince's Green, and the high cliff road are worth exploring.

Along the southeast coast are the twin resorts of **Sandown**, with its new pier complex and theater, and **Shanklin**, at the southern end of Sandown Bay which has held the British annual sunshine record more times than any other resort. Keats once lived in Shanklin's Old Village.

Further along the coast, **Ventnor** is called the "Madeira of England," because it rises from the sea in a series of steep hills.

On the west coast, the sand cliffs of **Alum Bay** are a blend of many different colors, a total of 21 claimed. The Needles, three giant chalk rocks, and the Needles Lighthouse, are further features of interest at this end of the island. If you want to stay at the western end of Wight, refer to our recommendations under **Totland Bay, Ullcase,** and **Freshwater Bay.**

Newport is the capital, a bustling market town lying in the heart of the island.

Visitors who'd like to explore the Isle of Wight just for the day can take an **"Around the Island"** six-hour bus tour which leaves from the Cowes Bus Station (and, in summer, from Yarmouth Quayside) daily at 11 a.m. The price is £3.50 ($8.05) for adults, £2 ($4.60) for children. For further information, telephone 0983/524-221.

The ferry from Southampton to the Isle of Wight costs £2.30 ($5.29) for a return ticket, or else you can take a ferry/hydrofoil combination, a return ticket going for £3.40 ($7.82).

VENTNOR: **Madeira Hall,** Trinity Road (tel. Ventnor 852-624), is perhaps one of the nicest places to stay on the Isle of Wight. In an estate garden of lawns, tall trees, and flowering shrubs stands this stone manor house, with mullioned windows, gables, and bay windows. It has housed interesting people, such as Lord Macaulay, who wrote some of his well-known essays here. And there are associations with Charles Dickens and some of his characters. On the grounds is a heated swimming pool and an 18-hole putting course. All bedrooms are fitted with bed lights and wash basins. There are ample baths and toilets in the corridors. Mr. and Mrs. Waring prefer most guests to stay a week, although they quote a bed-and-breakfast rate ranging from £10 ($23) per person nightly. Half board begins at £13 ($29.90) per person nightly.

SANDOWN: **St. Catherine's Hotel,** 1 Winchester Park Rd. (tel. 402-392), stands in its own garden a few minutes' walk from Sandown's sandy beach and pier complex, with its sun lounges and theater. St. Catherine's was built in 1860 of creamy Purbeck stone and white trim, for the dean of Winchester College; a modern extension was added for streamlined and sunny bedrooms. Bright colors have been generously used in the interior—the living room has a cherry-red carpet and draperies to match at the wide bay windows. The walls are soft sage green, and the dining room is done in rose pink and olive. Bedrooms have bright bedspreads, white furniture, and built-in headboards. Most of the bedrooms face the sun and are centrally heated. Tucked away in your bedroom are tea- and coffee-making facilities. Many of the rooms contain private baths or showers en suite. Jim and Maureen Hitchcock welcome you, charging a peak rate of £19 ($43.70) per person for room with bath or shower, breakfast, and dinner, including VAT and service. Bathless rooms are cheaper, costing only £17 ($39.10) per person, based on double occupancy, and including only breakfast.

FRESHWATER BAY: Farringford Hotel, Bedbury Lane, Freshwater (tel. Freshwater 2500), once the home of Lord Tennyson, has a pleasant, old-fashioned country ambience. A holiday, recreational estate, it has at its core a fine stone manor house and is surrounded by cottages on attractively landscaped grounds. It's adapted to the taste of the English who are accepted from Easter until its closing in November. We prefer the rooms in the main house, although families often ask for one of the simpler furnished cottages, each equipped with private bath. In high season bed and breakfast costs £22 ($50.60) per person, although you can take full-pension terms for £26 ($59.80) per person daily, plus service.

4. Winchester

The most historical city in all of Hampshire, Winchester is big on legends —it's even associated with King Arthur and the Knights of the Round Table. In the Great Hall, all that remains of Winchester Castle, a round oak table, with space for King Arthur and his 24 knights, hangs on the wall. But all that spells undocumented romance. What is known, however, is that when the Saxons ruled the ancient kingdom of Wessex, Winchester was the capital.

The city is also linked with King Alfred, who is honored today by a statue, and is believed to have been crowned here. The Danish conqueror, Canute, came this way, too, as did the king he ousted, Ethelred the Unready (Canute got his wife Emma in the bargain). The city is the seat of the well-known Winchester College, whose founding father was the bishop of Winchester, William of Wykeham. Established in 1382, it lays claim to being the oldest public (private) school in England.

Traditions are strong in Winchester. It is said (although we've never confirmed the assertion) that if you go to St. Cross Hospital, now an almshouse, dating from the 12th century, you'll get ye olde prilgrim's dole of ale and bread (and if there's no bread, you can eat cake!). Winchester, 65 miles from London, is essentially a market town, on the Downs on the Itchen River.

WINCHESTER CATHEDRAL: For centuries Winchester Cathedral has been one of the great mother churches of England. The present building, the longest cathedral in Britain, dates from 1079, and its Norman heritage is still in evidence. When a Saxon church stood on this spot, St. Swithin, bishop of Winchester and tutor to young King Alfred, suggested modestly that he be buried outside. When he was later buried inside, it rained for 40 days. The legend lives on: just ask a resident of Winchester what will happen if it rains on St. Swithin's Day, July 15.

Of the present building, the nave with its two aisles is most impressive, as are the chantries, the reredos (late 15th century), and the elaborately carved choir stalls. Of the chantries, that of William of Wykeham, founder of Winchester College, is perhaps the most visited (it's found in the south aisle of the nave). The cathedral also contains a number of other tombs—notably those of Jane Austen and Izaak Walton (exponent of the merits of the pastoral life—*The Compleat Angler*). The latter's tomb is to be found in the Prior Silkestede's Chapel in the South Transept. Jane Austen's grave is marked with a commemorative plaque. Winchester Cathedral contains in chests the bones of many of the Saxon kings and the remains of the Viking conqueror, Canute, and his wife, Emma, in the presbytery. The son of William the Conqueror, William Rufus (who reigned as William II), is also believed to have been buried at the cathedral.

The Crypt is flooded for a large part of the year, and at such times is closed to the public. When it's not flooded, there are regular tours at 10:30 a.m. and 2:30 p.m. The Library, in which is displayed the Winchester Bible and other ancient manuscripts, is open for limited hours throughout the summer season (except Monday mornings and Sunday, and on Wednesday and Saturday for the rest of the year). In January the library is open on Saturday only. The Treasury is open during the summer season from 11 a.m. to 5 p.m. It is small and does not require a guide.

WHERE TO STAY: Accommodations are limited, but adequate. We'll survey the most expensive recommendations first.

The Upper Bracket

Wessex Hotel, Paternoster Row (tel. Winchester 61611), has won over critics who protested such a modern structure adjacent to the grounds of Winchester Cathedral. Three stories high, built of natural brick, it turns most of its walls of windows toward a view of the Norman Tower. The lounges and reception areas are built on several open levels, using such elements as colored tiles, plastic and wood paneling, and simple hand-woven fabrics. The bedrooms —93 in all, each with private bath—are warmed by soft materials and Scandinavian-style furnishings, with such amenities as telephones and bedlamps. A single rents from £32 ($73.60), a double from £38 ($87.40). The Buttery is open from 10 a.m. until 10 p.m. daily, and the hotel's main restaurant has large picture windows overlooking the cathedral and its grounds.

The Medium-Priced Range

Royal Hotel, St. Peter Street (tel. Winchester 2031), is a fine, old hotel, built at the end of the 17th century as a private house. For 50 years, it was used by nuns from Brussels as a convent before being turned into a hotel. As a hotel, though, it soon became the center of the city's social life. It's only a few minutes' walk to the cathedral, yet still enjoys a secluded position. Best of all is the garden hidden behind high walls. If you like a hotel where old-fashioned values and comfort predominate, you'll appreciate the Royal. Bathless singles go for £16 ($36.80), doubles for £25 ($57.50). With bath, a single is £18 ($41.40); a double, £30 ($69). For a double room with a four-poster and private bath, the charge is £35 ($80.50) a night. These prices include a traditional

English breakfast, VAT, and service. Meals are served in a small, formal dining room, with a view of the private garden.

The Budget Range

Southgate Hotel, Southgate Street (tel. Winchester 51243), is a brick house in the center of Winchester. It opens onto a rear garden with flowerbeds and an old walnut tree. Christopher Wren designed and built Southgate in 1715, and many of the original architectural details remain (note the front entry with the glass lights over the doorway). All the bedrooms are equipped with hot and cold running water. The bed-and-breakfast rate is £12 ($27.60) per person, to which 10% is added for service. There is an excellent cuisine, an à la carte meal in the dining room costing from £6.50 ($14.95).

WHERE TO EAT: The Elizabethan, 18–19 Jewry St. (tel. Winchester 3566). In an atmosphere of another century, under hand-hewn timbers, you dine by candlelight, on sparkling white linen. You have a choice of cozy nooks or a galleried main dining room. Well run under the personal supervision of the Harrison family, the kitchen offers an excellent Anglo-French cuisine. The licensed restaurant serves table d'hôte lunches at around £4.50 ($10.35), as a full à la carte menu. The extensive choice of dishes provides for an interesting lunch or dinner at about £9 ($20.70) per person. Flambé dishes are a specialty. Light refreshments are served at lunchtime in the fully licensed modern bar. The restaurant is open from noon to 2 p.m., and from 7 to 10 p.m. On Sunday, only lunch is served. Closed Monday.

The **Old Chesil Rectory Restaurant,** Chesil Street (tel. Winchester 3177), is just a short walk from the cathedral. Once a rectory, the unusual timber and stucco building dates from the 15th century. Inside and out the Old Chesil exudes an air of merrie Old England, but the food served in the heavily beamed dining room is the finest quality northern Italian cuisine. The menu is a wonderful melange of creative and classical dishes, including pollo sorpresa (chicken "surprise"), rolled, stuffed chicken breasts flavored with garlic and herbs, costing £5.25 ($12.08), or scaloppa alla Boccaccio, a delightful combination of veal, lobster, and cheese cooked with Orvieto wine, at £5.95 ($13.69). Appetizers include a prawn and melon cocktail at £2.40 ($5.52) or seafood hors d'oeuvres at £3.55 ($8.17). The tasty Italian desserts cost about £1.50 ($3.45). The Old Chesil is open daily except Sunday evenings and Monday. Otherwise, it serves lunch from noon to 2:30 p.m. and dinner from 7 to 10:30 p.m.

Splinters, 9 Great Minster St. (tel. Winchester 64004). Downstairs in the Edwardian bar, soup of the day with roll and butter is 75p ($1.73), and there are several hot dishes, such as quiche with salad, moussaka, or cottage pie at around £1.50 ($3.45). Desserts are about 75p ($1.73). Upstairs, the elegant plushy restaurant serves delicious à la carte meals, including coq au vin and other French stalwarts, or grills and roasts. A meal will cost around £9 ($20.70) a person, or you can just have a light meal from the same sort of things as are available downstairs. A glass of wine costs 60p ($1.38), and there is a very good selection of more expensive French and German wines available by the bottle. Mike Sherret and his wife, Fiona, are the owners. It is open lunchtime only from 11 a.m. to 2:30 p.m., Monday to Saturday.

A Pub Crawl

Instead of lunching at one of the above restaurants, you may want to drop in at the **Royal Oak Pub,** which is to be found in a passageway leading from the High Street and next door to the God Begot House. The Royal Oak serves lunches at the bar from noon to 2 p.m. daily, Monday through Saturday. Various hot and cold snacks, hot meals, and an extensive serve-yourself cold buffet are available. The pub also contains the oldest bar in England, which is worth a visit, as indeed is the pub itself—a busy, friendly hostelry with lots of atmosphere. For those with a liking for live traditional or New Orleans jazz, this can be enjoyed in the bar on Monday and Thursday from 8:30 to 10:30 p.m. at no extra charge apart from the cost of your drinks.

The **Old Market Pub,** The Square, is ideal for those who enjoy a local. It offers a relaxed, friendly, unself-conscious atmosphere, a proper background in which to enjoy a pint. The corner pub sits opposite the cathedral in the oldest and most historic district of Winchester. It's mellowed enough to have timbers galore, cozy nooks, and a collection of oddments. The owners are always pleased to see travelers who wish to sample traditional ales drawn by hand pumps, and sample snacks either from the cold buffet or hot snacks menu.

DORSET

This is Thomas Hardy country. By now, you've probably seen *Far from the Madding Crowd,* or read *Tess of the D'Urbervilles,* and know Dorset is the Wessex of Hardy novels. Some of the towns and villages, although altered considerably, are still recognizable from his descriptions. However, he changed the names to protect the innocent. Bournemouth, for example, became Havenpool, Weymouth converted to Budmouth. "The last of the great Victorians," as he was called, died in 1928 at the age of 88. While his tomb rests in a position of honor in Westminster Abbey, his heart was cut out and buried in his beloved Dorsetshire.

One of England's smallest shires, Dorset stretches all the way from the old seaport of **Poole** in the east to **Lyme Regis** in the west (known to Jane Austen). Dorset is a southwestern county, bordering the English Channel. It's big on cows, and Dorset butter is served at many an afternoon tea. Mainly, it is a land of farms and pastures, with plenty of sandy heaths and chalky downs.

The most prominent tourist center of Dorset is the Victorian seaside resort of Bournemouth. If you don't anchor there, you might also try a number of Dorset's other seaports, villages, and country towns. For the most part, we've hugged closely to the impressive coastline.

Incidentally, Dorset, as the vacation-wise English might tell you if they wanted to divulge a secret, is a friend of the budget traveler.

5. Bournemouth

The south coast resort at the doorstep of the New Forest didn't just happen: it was carefully planned and manicured, a true city in a garden. Flower-filled, park-dotted, Bournemouth contains great globs of architecture inherited from those arbiters of taste, Victoria, and her son, Edward. Its most distinguished feature is its Chines (shrub-filled, narrow steep-sided ravines) along the zig-zag coastline. The real walking English strike out at, say, Hengistbury Head, making their way past sandy beaches, both the Boscombe and Bournemouth Piers, to Alum Chine, a distance of six miles, and a traffic-free walk to remember.

It is estimated that of the nearly 12,000 acres which Bournemouth claims for its own, about one-sixth is turned over to green parks and flowerbeds, such as the Pavilion Rock Garden, through which amblers pass both day and night. The total effect, especially in spring is dramatic, and helps explain

DORSET: BOURNEMOUTH

Bournemouth's long-established popularity with the garden-loving English. Bournemouth was discovered back in Victoria's day, when seabathing became a firmly entrenched institution, often practiced with great ritual. Many of the comparatively elegant villas that exist today (now largely bed-and-breakfast houses and hotels) were once private homes.

Bournemouth, which along with Poole and Christchurch, forms the largest urban area in the south of England, is not as sophisticated as Brighton. Increasingly, it is becoming a retirement place for widowed or single English ladies. But Bournemouth and its neighbors also have some 20,000 students attending the various schools or colleges, who explore, in their off-hours, places written about or painted by such poets and artists as Shelley, Beardsley, and Turner.

The resort's amusements are wide and varied. At the Pavilion Theatre, for example, you can see West End–type productions from London. The Bournemouth Symphony Orchestra is justly famous in Europe. And there's the usual run of golf courses, band concerts, variety shows, and dancing.

Bournemouth is about 104 miles from London, easily reached in about one hour 40 minutes on an express train from Waterloo Station. It makes a good base for exploring a historically rich part of England. On its outskirts are the New Forest, Salisbury, and Winchester, and the Isle of Wight (15 miles away, the former seaside retreat of Victoria).

WHERE TO STAY: Bournemouth offers accommodation choices in all price ranges. We'll begin with—

The Upper Bracket

Royal Bath Hotel, Bath Road (tel. Bournemouth 25555), was built in the Victorian era to simulate a French château, with towers and bay windows looking out over the bay and Purbeck Hills. In its own three acres of cliff-top gardens is a heated swimming pool. The rate is £33 ($75.90) per person per day, inclusive of service and taxes. The table d'hôte lunch and dinner prices start at £8 ($18.40). The resident band plays for a dinner-dance Saturday evenings. Also available for your nightly entertainment is a casino. For health enthusiasts, there is a sauna bath, as well as Swedish massages and special diets. Every bedroom, 135 in all, has a private bath and television (the large accommodations contain sitting areas as well).

The Medium-Priced Range

Norfolk Hotel, Richmond Hill (tel. Bournemouth 21-521), is one of the oldest prestige hotels of the resort, built a few blocks from the seafront and the shopping area in the center of town. Disregarding what lies on its periphery, it is like a country estate, with a formal entrance and a rear garden and fountain shaded by trees. The public rooms are geared to holiday guests, with two drinking bars and a ballroom (in the evenings, patrons gather in the Richmond Room where a trio plays for listening and dancing). The bedrooms—more than half with private baths—are furnished with traditional, serviceable pieces, comfortable and satisfactory. The Norfolk charges its highest rates from April 1 to the end of October.

In a room without bath, the rate is £18 ($41.40) per person nightly, rising to £21 ($48.30) in a unit with bath, these tariffs including an English breakfast, dinner that evening, VAT, and service. The set dinner-dance on Saturday is included in the above rates. However, if you're a nonresident and wish to attend, expect to pay from £7 ($16.10) for dinner and nothing extra on Saturday when you can disco dance.

Langtry Manor Hotel, 26 Derby Rd., East Cliff (tel. Bournemouth 23887), was built in 1877 for Lillie Langtry, the famous Jersey Lily, as a gift from Edward VII to his favorite mistress. The house contains all sorts of reminders of its illustrious inhabitants, including initials scratched on a windowpane and carvings on a beam of the entrance hall. On the half-landing is the peephole through which the prince could scrutinize the assembled company before coming down to dine, and one of the fireplaces bears his initials.

Mrs. Pamela Hamilton Howard, the present owner, has carefully furnished the hotel in the Edwardian style, and on Saturday she has six-course Edwardian dinner parties. There is no menu; the dishes are just produced for inspection. Other evenings dinner is a more usual four-course affair at £6 ($13.80).

Bedrooms range from ordinary twins with bathroom from £11.75 ($27.03) per person to £15.50 ($35.65) per person, including breakfast. The Lillie Langtry suite, Lillie's own room, with a four-poster bed draped in Nottingham lace and a double heart-shaped bathtub (not to mention the more modern refinements of color TV, refrigerated bar, and modern toilet), goes from £20 ($46) to £26 ($59.80) per person. All rates are subject to VAT.

The Budget Range

Belgravia Hotel, 56 Christchurch Rd., East Cliff (tel. Bournemouth 20857), is a gracious brick mansion in a smart section of the resort, set in 1½ acres of ground. Terms are from £7.50 ($17.25) per person per day, according to the season, for bed and a full English breakfast. Dinner is available on request, costing from £4 ($9.20) per person. The Belgravia is a five-minute walk along a zig-zag path to the beach. It is a pleasant house with a mansard roof, and all rooms are bright and sunny. Reservations of only one or two nights are almost impossible during high season, when one-weekers are given priority, of course.

Apartments by the Week

Miami Court, 27a Surrey Rd., Westbourne, Bournemouth (tel. Bournemouth 764-329), will intrigue travelers tired of hotels and guest houses. Here, at these luxury holiday flats, guests can enjoy a private life, preparing their own kind of food. This, of course, is an increasingly popular way of traveling in Europe. The apartments or "flats" are ideally situated, allowing you to explore the coast, inland country villages, and stately homes.

The new block of eight apartments has its own garden; and, best of all, there is a woods in the rear with a stream, as well as a pathway leading to the seafront and Bournemouth Square.

Owners Howard Archer and Michael Marshall used to run the Camelot Hotel in London, where they made many friends among American travelers and, incidentally, won an award as the best small hotel of the year. To the Miami Court in Bournemouth, they bring the same highly personal flair that distinguished them in London.

At their new location, they provide one-, two-, and three-bedroom apartments which are completely furnished. The flats are centrally heated as well and contain TV sets and refrigerators. The highest tariffs are charged from June to September, £45 ($103.50) per person weekly. Between October and April, the rates are slashed in half. Then the flats rent for only £22 ($50.60) per person weekly.

Write to them for a reservation and the amount of deposit required.

WHERE TO DINE: Restaurant San Marco, 148 Holdenhurst Rd. (tel. Bournemouth 21-132), has a small and intimate atmosphere, and is run by Angie and Ettore Longi. He is an English-born Italian, and she is from Parma, where the best salami and Parmesan cheese come from. The cost of the menu varies with the season and availability of certain produce. Specialties include minestrone, suckling pig, stracciatella, salami, prosciutto con melone, piccatini (veal pieces), saltimbocca, and pasta. In other words, there's something for everybody at a cost of about £8 ($18.40) to £9 ($20.70) per person for a three-course meal, plus wine, which begins at £5 ($11.50) per bottle. They won't serve cheap wines—"it should be used for cooking." The restaurant is open daily, except Monday and bank holidays, from noon to 2:30 p.m. and from 6:30 p.m. to midnight.

Fisherman's Haunt Hotel, Salisbury Road, Route B3347, Winkton, near Christchurch (tel. Christchurch 484-071), is an ancient inn (built in 1673) just two miles from the English Channel. Authentic regional British dishes are the fare in the dining room which overlooks the River Avon. Open from 12:30 p.m., Fisherman's Haunt offers a set luncheon for £3.50 ($8.05). Weeknight dinners are served from 7 to 10 p.m., costing from £6 ($13.80). A special feature of the restaurant is the traditional family-style Sunday midday meal. If you decide to bed down here for the night, your breakfast on the following morning is the classic, full English breakfast.

6. Shaftesbury

The origins of this typical Dorsetshire market town date back to the ninth century when King Alfred founded the abbey and made his daughter the first abbess. King Edward the Martyr was buried there, and King Canute died in the abbey but was buried in Winchester. Little now remains of the abbey, but the ruins are beautifully laid out. The museum adjoining St. Peter's Church at the top of Gold Hill give a good idea of what the ancient Saxon hilltop town was like.

Today, ancient cottages and hostelries cling to the steep cobbled streets, thatched roofs frown above tiny paned windows, and modern stores vie with the street market in the High Street and the cattle market off Christy's Lane.

The town, right on the A30 from London, is an excellent center from which to visit the Hardy Country (it appears as Chaston in *Jude the Obscure*), Stourhead Gardens, and Longleat House.

FOOD AND LODGING: The Royal Chase Hotel (tel. Shaftesbury 3355) is a Georgian house with Victorian additions, and as such has had varied occupants. Once a button-making factory and then a monastery, it is now a delightfully informal hotel run by George and Rosemary Hunt with their assistant, Liz Thomas. Most rooms have baths and go for £24 ($55.20) per person per night, including a full breakfast, early-morning tea, newspaper, service, and VAT. A meal in the Country Kitchen Restaurant, with its gingham cloths and hoop-backed chairs, will cost around £7 ($16.10), and includes several local dishes—pork filet cooked in cider or bluevinney cheese and Dorset knobs. House wine is £4 ($9.20) a bottle.

From November to March they also offer bargain rates, among which is the Real Ale Break at around £11.50 ($26.45) per person per night, including accommodation, a full English breakfast, five pints of traditional ale, plus a free bottle of Thomas Hardy's Ale, featured in the *Guinness Book of Records* as the strongest beer brewed in a bottle. Even for less fanatical drinkers, the bar, dominated by an open-kitchen range and decorated with Dorsetshire bygones, is an attraction. There are traditional bar games, shove ha'penny, and table skittles at which to pitch your skill. On weekends, the Cellar Bar also offers snacks and a wide selection of wines at lunchtime, and in the evenings if you don't want a full meal in the restaurant.

Milestones, at Compton Abbas, lies between the church and the village post office, 2½ miles south of Shaftesbury on the A350. Just the telephone exchange of this ideal English tearoom is enough to make one curious about it (tel. Fontmell Magna 811-360). Two delightful old ladies, Mrs. Smith, the owner, and her friend, preside over the spotless, beamy little place with views over the Dorset hills. Their farmhouse teas, with boiled eggs, fresh sandwiches, homemade scones, and cakes are accompanied by tea or coffee. Expect to pay from £1.20 ($2.76) per person. They serve from 11 a.m. to 6 p.m.

7. Wool

Set in the midst of pastoral scenery, known to readers of Hardy, the sleepy hamlet of Wool is one of the most charming in East Dorset. On the Frome River, it has thatched cottages on either side of the road. The stream that winds its way through the maze of streets and lanes lures potential waders.

The district was also known to T. E. Lawrence, Lawrence of Arabia, who died in a motorcycle crash in 1935. His former home, **Clouds Hill,** lies four miles to the northwest (one mile north of Bovington Camp). It is open Wednesday to Friday (also Sunday) from April until the end of September, from 2 to 5 p.m. (from October until the end of March, it is open only on Sunday, from 1 to 4 p.m.), charging an admission of 60p ($1.38).

WHERE TO STAY AND EAT: Woolbridge Manor Hotel (tel. Bindom Abbey 462-313) is a small manor house edging up to the village. It owes its present fame to its Thomas Hardy associations, having been a setting in *Tess of the D'Urbervilles.* The owners, Mr. and Mrs. Peter Maddocks, have furnished the place attractively. The manor, which dates from medieval times, is a good backdrop for all the copper, brass, and oak. Most of the basic food cooked here comes from the manor farm itself, and you know what that means—fresh berries, thick cream, pears, apples, pheasant, local venison, and salmon from the river. You can enjoy a dinner starting at £7 ($16.10). A single rents for £18 ($41.40) per night, the tariff increasing to £24 ($55.20) in a double, inclucing VAT and breakfast.

8. Wareham

This historic little town on the Frome River is about a mile west of Poole Harbor. Many find it a good center for touring the south Dorset coast and the Purbeck Hills. It contains remains of early Anglo-Saxon and Roman town walls, plus the Saxon church of St. Martin with its effigy of Lawrence of Arabia.

FOOD AND LODGING: The Old Granary, The Quay (tel. Wareham 2010), is a riverside country pub, where you dine either inside or on a terrace overlooking the boats and swans. The interior dining room has a charm of its own, with bentwood chairs, a wine rack, a natural wood sideboard, and white walls displaying a collection of locally painted watercolors. A gracious and informal atmosphere prevails. The secret behind the success of the Old Granary is its fine cuisine; the owners, Mr. and Mrs. Michael Hipwell, try hard to stick to natural country foods. Homemade soups go for 55p ($1.27); pâté for £1 ($2.30); a filet of pork in a barbecue sauce, £4.20 ($9.66); Dorset lamb chops with cheese and onion, £4.25 ($9.78). A hefty portion of homemade fruit pie with cream is 65p ($1.50). The restaurant is open every day. If you wish to overnight here, the charge is £20 ($46) per person, including a full English breakfast, dinner, and taxes.

A COUNTRY MANOR: At Culeaze, near Wareham, **Col. and Mrs. Anthony Barne,** along with two Labrador retrievers, welcome you to this manor house, standing in the center of the estate known as Culeaze. They offer two double rooms and two single rooms, with private bath, charging £20 ($46) per person per night, including everything except lunch. Liquor is not served, but wine is offered at dinner. As their pillared manor house lies off the beaten track, a car is essential. For their own reasons, they don't encourage first-time visitors to stay more than three days, but they have friends in Somerset, Wiltshire, and Norfolk who would be pleased to welcome you. During the day you can visit Salisbury Cathedral, Wilton House, Abbotsbury, and Portland Bill, along with Stonehenge. Here is a rare chance to experience a fast-fading English way of life. For more information or reservations, write to Col. A. M. Barne, O.B.E., Culeaze, Wareham, Dorsetshire, BH20 7NR, England.

9. Dorchester

Thomas Hardy, in his 1886 novel *The Mayor of Casterbridge,* gave Dorchester literary fame. But it was known to the Romans; in fact, its Maumbury Rings, south of the town, is considered the best Roman amphitheater in Britain, having once resounded with the shouts of 12,000 spectators screaming for gladiator blood. Dorchester, a country town, was the setting of another bloodletting, the "Bloody Assize" of 1685, when Judge Jeffreys condemned to death the supporters of the Duke of Monmouth's rebellion against James II.

But it is mostly through Hardy that the world knows Dorchester. Many of his major scenes of love and intrigue took place on the periphery of Dorchester. The land was best known to Hardy, since he was born in 1840 at **Higher Bockhampton,** three miles northeast of Dorchester. His home, now a National Trust property, may be visited by the public from March to October, from 11 a.m. to 6 p.m. or dusk, whichever is earlier. But to go inside, you must make an appointment with the tenant. You may write in advance to **Hardy's Cottage,** Higher Bockhampton, Dorchester, Dorset, England, or telephone Dorchester 2366. You approach the cottage on foot, a ten-minute walk after parking your vehicle in the space provided in the wood. The admission is 60p ($1.38).

You may also want to browse around the **Dorset County Museum** on High West Street (next to St. Peter's Church), with its gallery devoted to memorabilia of Thomas Hardy. In addition, you'll find prehistoric and Roman relics, plus natural history exhibits and others pertaining to the geology of the region. The museum is open weekdays from 10 a.m. to 1 p.m. and from 2 to 5 p.m.; admission is 30p (69¢) for adults, 15p (35¢) for children.

WHERE TO STAY: The **Wessex Hotel,** High West Street (tel. Dorchester 2660), is an architecturally interesting Georgian structure built on medieval foundations. In the town center, the quiet hotel offers 17 bedrooms with full residential services. Room rates range from £8 ($18.40) for a single room to £14.50 ($33.35) for a double or twin. Prices include a full English breakfast, but you can add to the tab a service charge and VAT. The Wessex also offers a small cozy bar for guests as well as a public restaurant.

The **Antelope Hotel,** South Street (Cornhill; tel. Dorchester 3001), was known in medieval times. Subsequently, it has received a Victorian overlay. The high point (or low) in its history was when Judge Jeffreys held his Bloody Assize here. Old and traditional, it's been the wayfarer's choice for generations.

It charges £21 ($48.30) nightly for a double, including breakfast. It's £12.50 ($28.75) for singles, these tariffs including an English breakfast, VAT, and service. A table d'hôte dinner costs £5 ($11.50).

WHERE TO EAT: **Judge Jeffreys' Restaurant,** High West Street, opposite the County Museum, is an attractive stop on your cross-country jaunt. Dating back to the 14th century, it had the dubious distinction of lodging that "cantankerous alcoholic," Judge Jeffreys, during the Bloody Assize. The restaurant today offers different services in each room. In the Judge's Room, a traditional three-course lunch costs £4 ($9.20). In the Tudor Room, an à la carte steak and trout menu features a main-course steak at £4.10 ($9.43). In the bar and lounge, snacks and salads go from 75p ($1.73) to £2.20 ($5.06). Evening meals are served from mid-June to mid-October on Wednesday, Friday, and Saturday, the final orders taken at 10 p.m. The proprietor, Mr. Bean, takes pride in the old English atmosphere of massive oak beams, an oak spiral staircase, stone-mullioned windows, paneled rooms, Tudor fireplaces. Most important, the restaurant's haunted! During its restoration in 1928, parts of a human skeleton were discovered in a bricked-up part of the east wall.

A HOTEL AT CERNE ABBAS: The **Old Market House,** Cerne Abbas (tel. Dorchester 2660), is the sister hotel to Dorchester's Wessex. On the main street of the village of Cerne Abbas, seven miles north of Dorchester, this historic building offers a peaceful alternative for those wishing to get away from the busier coastal resort towns. Although smaller than the Wessex, the Old Market House provides guests with the same basic hotel services. In addition, guests at Cerne Abbas are invited to take advantage of the bar and restaurant facilities of the Wessex during the day and evening.

A single rents for £8 ($18.40), a double for £14 ($32.20), these tariffs including an English breakfast, although VAT and service are extra. There are no meals provided other than breakfast. If you're staying at the Old Market House, you can rent a horse for riding at £4 ($9.20) an hour, but you must make prior arrangements, as you'll need an escort from among the stable staff.

INNS ON THE OUTSKIRTS: **Brace of Pheasants,** Plush (tel. Piddletrenthide 357). Jack and Joan Chandler have transformed this row of two adjoining thatched cottages and a village forge, dating from the 16th century, although rebuilt in the old style after a fire. The two of them—he, a director in the paper industry; she, the owner of a toy factory—sought and found a new way of life in this tiny hamlet, 15 miles from the coast. The major activity takes place in the all-purpose living, dining, and drinking room—a cozy setting with inglenooks, antiques, comfortable armchairs and old decorative objects. Mr.

Chandler is an informal host, helping with drinks. He and his wife are well known in the area for their delicious homemade meals. They offer a five-course meal for a set price of £7 ($16.10). Game is a specialty. In the restaurant upstairs, beautiful views can be enjoyed from the little dormer windows, and many guests prefer to dine "under the thatch." They accept 50 guests per meal (reservations are imperative), and the table is yours for the evening. There is only one sitting per evening, at 8:30. Varied bar snacks are available midday and evenings from Tuesday to Sunday, and you can enjoy them in a beautiful old room with a log fire and a bar serving counter. This is separate from the main bar which means you can bring in children. In summer you can also enjoy a lovely big garden. How to get there: Take the B3143 out of Dorchester to Piddletrenthide, turning off at the sign to Plush. The inn will be on your left. It is open Monday through Saturday.

Summer Lodge, Evershot (tel. Evershot 424), is a country-house hotel, where its resident owners, Nigel and Margaret Corbett, provide care, courtesy, and comfort. Once the home to the heirs of the Earls of Ilchester, the country house, in the attractive village of Evershot, stands on four acres of secluded gardens. Evershot itself appears as Evershed in *Tess of the D'Urbervilles*.

In this relaxed, informal atmosphere, guests rent rooms with views either of the garden or over the village rooftops to the fields beyond. Although centrally heated, the hotel offers log fires in winter. Guests sit around the fire getting to know each other in a convivial atmosphere. Units contain hot and cold running water, and private baths are being installed. Rates range from £21 ($48.30) to £24 ($55.20) per person, including not only a bedroom with private bath, but a full-course English breakfast and a five-course dinner. There is a 25% supplement for single occupancy of a double room.

Mrs. Corbett, who does the cooking, specializes in traditional English dishes the way they should be done, placing the emphasis on home-grown and local produce. In addition to the dining room with its French windows opening onto a terrace, the Corbetts have a bar and a TV room. They will direct you to places of local interest, including National Trust houses.

READER'S HOTEL SELECTION AT FRAMPTON: "Our very favorite place on our entire trip was **The Court** at Frampton, a tiny village in Dorset, near Dorchester in the Thomas Hardy country. The Court is a beautiful manor house, elegantly furnished, run by two lovely women. It's on a secluded lane and contains 60 acres of woods and fields, a pond, and a charming menagerie of ducks, chickens, a golden retriever, a Siamese cat, and a pair of peacocks. There are ample bathrooms and a shower room. Our breakfast, served in their first floor dining room overlooking the garden and pond, included hot homemade rolls, fresh milk and homemade butter from their Jersey cows, and generous servings of sausage, bacon, and eggs, with, of course, marmalade and tea. We had electric kettles in our rooms, and Mrs. Goddard brought us a doily-lined tray with a bone china cup and saucer and teapot for our early morning tea. There was also a small covered pitcher of cream, sugar, and tea bags. Dinner, bed, and breakfast (no children) in the best English manor tradition are £15 ($34.50) per person" (Alice L. Jones, Au Sable Forks, N.Y.).

10. Bridport

On Thomas Hardy's fictional Wessex terrain, Bridport was "Port Bredy." The town lies inland, although there is a harbor one mile away at the holiday resort of West Bay, near the end of Chesil Beach. Ropes and fishing nets are Bridport specialties. Many a man dangled from the end of a "Bridport dagger" that is, a rope—especially when Hanging Judge Jeffreys was around.

WHERE TO STAY AND EAT: The Bull Hotel, East Street (tel. Bridport 22878), a 16th-century coaching inn, now houses modern wayfarers in its 22 bedrooms, all with hot and cold running water, many overlooking the old courtyard. Bed-and-breakfast rates range from £9.25 ($21.28), per person nightly, including an English breakfast and VAT. The atmosphere is definitely old-worldish, complete with a minstrels' gallery and enough bars to satisfy anybody. The bedrooms themselves are simply, but comfortably, furnished. In 1939, George VI stopped off at the Bull. The hotel remains open all year and is run under the close personal supervision of the Terleski family. Fresh local food and fish dishes are a specialty. Luncheons range from £2 ($4.60) and dinners from £5 ($11.50).

Eype's Mouth Hotel, Eype, 1½ miles west of Bridport and one mile south of the A35 Bridport/Lyme Regis road (tel. Bridport 23300), is a gracious country house, right on the sea, surrounded by its own grounds, a five-minute walk from the beach. Most of the public rooms and bedrooms open south toward the water. At times, Eype's Mouth seems like an English version of a villa on the Riviera, with a sea-view front terrace, where you can relax and have drinks or tea. The hotel's managed by Mrs. Ian Forbes, who also provides meals for nonresidents. The rooms are centrally heated, containing hot and cold water basins. There are convenient corridor toilets and baths, plus nine private bathrooms. Generally a guest stays here on what is called inclusive terms, meaning bed, breakfast, luncheon (perhaps a packed picnic variety), and dinner. The rate (minimum of three days) is from £18 ($41.40) per person daily, going slightly higher in June, July, August, and September. For straight bed and breakfast, you pay from £11 ($25.30) to £13 ($29.90) per person nightly, the latter in a room with private bath. The rooms are plain, but comfortable. There is a lounge bar and cellar bar with live entertainment, along with a dinner-dance every Saturday night.

11. Chideock

Chideock is a charming village one mile west of Bridport. It's a hamlet of thatched houses, with a dairy farm found in the center itself. About a mile away from the coast, it's a gem of a place for overnight stopovers, or even longer stays. The countryside, with its rolling hills, makes excursions a temptation.

WHERE TO STAY: Chideock House Hotel (tel. Chideock 242) is perhaps the prettiest thatched house in Chideock, a village of winners. Set near the road, with a protective stone wall, the house opens onto a rear garden of flowers, shrubs, and fruit trees. A driveway through the gardens leads to a large car park (wood-burning fires on cool days). You can stay here on a bed-and-breakfast basis at a cost beginning at £12 ($27.60) per person nightly. The hotel has been extended, and most of its bedrooms have baths en suite. The cuisine reflects the skill of a Swiss chef. In addition to the à la carte restaurant, a Copper Grill has opened, decorated with antique pieces of copper and featuring large steaks and fish dishes. Especially interesting is the Tudor part of the house, and the Adam fireplace in the lounge. The house quartered the Roundheads in 1645, and the ghosts of the village martyrs still haunt, as their trial was held at the hotel. Resident owners are Brian and Ruth Munday.

The **Thatch Cottage** (tel. Chideock 473). You'd never suspect that under the thatch of this 17th-century cottage are the comforts of home. The owner, Reena O'Rourke, accepts paying guests year round. While this is essentially a summer resort, there are those who welcome the idea of staying winter weekends, snugly sitting in front of the fireplace after enjoying good home cooking. Fresh local produce is a specialty. Most of the year, the charge is £7.50 ($17.25) per person for bed and breakfast. If you want to walk to the beach, you can ask your hostess to pack a picnic lunch. It's best to make Chideock your center for a week, exploring the many sights in the area on day trips. Weekly costs for bed and breakfast range from £48 ($110.40). Reservations are necessary from June to September.

12. Charmouth

On Lyme Bay, Charmouth is another winner. A village of Georgian houses and thatched cottages, Charmouth contains some of the most dramatic coastal scenery in West Dorset. The village itself lies to the west of Golden Cap, which is—according to the adventurers who measure such things—the highest cliff along the coast of southern England.

WHERE TO STAY: The **Queens Armes Hotel** (tel. Charmouth 60339). Catherine of Aragon, the first of Henry VIII's six wives and the daughter of Ferdinand and Isabella of Spain, is believed to have stayed in this hotel near the sea. It also figured in the flight of King Charles II, who spent the night here, with the Roundheads in hot pursuit. Since the Queens Armes is right on the road, you may not suspect its inner charm: a rear flower garden, oak beams, pewter, old doors with creaky hardware, a dining room with dark oak tables and Windsor chairs, the living room with its Regency armchairs and antiques. Records don't reveal what the hotel charged for housing royalty. But you can stay here in one of the simply furnished rooms for £12.50 ($28.75) per person for bed and breakfast. If you wish, you can also take all your meals. Lunch costs depend on your choice; dinner, £5.95 ($13.69). The hotel specializes in well-prepared, delicious English fare, such as succulent roast beef. The owners, Mr. and Mrs. Rendell and Mrs. and Mrs. Rolfe, have pleasantly added their own touches to the house.

Charmouth House Hotel (tel. Charmouth 319) is an old thatched house, its origins going back to 1575. It faces the main village road, although many of its under-the-eaves bedrooms open onto formal gardens at the rear. The interior rooms have special charm, with beams and antiques. The bedrooms come in every size, but all are country-clean and homelike, containing good beds and hot and cold running water. Singles go from £10 ($23), doubles from £20 ($46), including breakfast and service, although VAT is extra. Dinner is from £6 ($13.80). The proprietors prepare very good meals.

13. Lyme Regis

On Lyme Bay near the Devonshire border, the resort of Lyme Regis is one of the most attractive centers along the south coast. For those who shun such big, commercial holiday centers as Torquay or Bournemouth, Lyme Regis is ideal—the true English coastal town, with a highly praised mild climate. Sea gulls fly overhead; the streets are steep and winding; walks along Cobb Beach brisk and stimulating; the views, particularly of the craft in the harbor, photogenic. Following Lyme Regis's career as a major seaport (the Duke of Monmouth landed here to begin his unsuccessful attempt to become king), one finds it was a small spa for a while, catering to such visitors as Jane Austen.

WHERE TO LODGE AND EAT: The **High Cliff Hotel,** Sidmouth Road (tel. Lyme Regis 2300), is an impressive Regency house, placed in the midst of surrounding gardens on the edge of a cliff, providing views of the coast. Formerly the home of Lord Lister, the doctor who pioneered antiseptic surgery, it now accepts paying guests. Inside, the central formal hallway, lounges, and dining room are tastefully decorated, with a sprinkling of good antiques. Bedrooms are appropriately homelike, with good beds, hot and cold running water, and comfortable furnishings. The charge is from £14.75 ($33.93) per person for bed and breakfast from May to October; from £11.75 ($27.03) October to December and March to May. The per-week inclusive (all meals) rate is from £120 ($276) per person from May to October, from £110 ($253) October to December and March to May. Ordered separately, a dinner costs £6.25 ($14.36). All rates include VAT.

The **Mariners Hotel,** Silver Street (tel. Lyme Regis 2753), has been a coaching inn since 1641, and now it's owned by Leo and Mary Featherstone. They are proud, and rightly so, of the view from their lounge of the Dorset coastline—all the way around to the lighthouse at Portland Bill. This view of approximately 25 miles is considered the best in Lyme Regis. Modern plumbing has been installed, including hot and cold running water in all 16 bedrooms (12 with private bath or shower). Of course, the 17th-century rooms retain their special charm, crooked and irregular. Full fire precautions have been implemented.

In the low-ceilinged dining room, you are served excellent food. For bed, breakfast, and a four-course evening meal, the daily rate ranges from £22 ($50.60), including service and VAT.

The building was immortalized by Beatrix Potter in her painting of "Susan the Cat and Stumpy the Dog," in *The Tale of Little Pig Robinson,* published in 1902. The tulip tree in the garden is one of the five oldest in England, more than 300 years old.

Kersbrook, Pound Road (tel. Lyme Regis 2596), lives up to its boast of being the "dream house of the Dorset Riviera." Stone built in 1790, Kersbrook is crowned by a thatched roof and sits on a ledge above the village, which provides a panoramic view of the coast. Mr. and Mrs. James Robshaw are the proprietors of Kersbrook, charging from £9 ($20.70) for bed and breakfast, £11 ($25.30) for bed, breakfast, and an evening meal. Many of the rooms have private baths and showers available at a small extra cost.

Bell Cliff, Broad Street (tel. Lyme Regis 2459), is a miniature white house set like a jewel upon a cliff edge, overlooking the sea and near the bottom of the main street. Whether for morning coffee, lunch, afternoon tea, or dinner, it's a good choice, specializing in good home cooking. A complete meal at noon costs from £3 ($6.90) to £3.50 ($8.05), increasing to about £6 ($13.80) at dinner. Lunch specialties include homemade steak-and-kidney pie, plus apple tart and clotted cream. Dinner might be scampi or steak. Fish dishes are recommended heartily, and the french-fried potatoes accompanying them are crisp and done to order. In the afternoon, order the Dorset cream tea at £1.10 ($2.53). Bell Cliff is open throughout the year seven days a week. Reservations are advisable in summer.

14. Donyatt

After Lyme Regis, you may want to journey to Donyatt, a village near Ilminster. Just outside the village of Donyatt, between the A303 and the A30 London/West Country roads, stands the following recommendation:

Thatchers Pond, Donyatt, near Ilminster (tel. Ilminster 3210), is a 15th-century thatched limestone farmhouse where Michael and Pamela Smith, both experienced caterers, offer a vast cold table for lunch and dinner daily except Monday. The house is warm and welcoming, with old clocks, guns, and swords adorning the walls of the flagstoned hall and dining room. Meals are served from a vast table laden with fresh lobster, salmon, crab, and prawns, cold roast beef, ham, tongue, homemade pâté, quiches, and mousse. You're offered a choice of any two meats and then are allowed to help yourself from a selection of 25 different salads. The dessert trolley is laden with succulent sweets, and there is cheese if you prefer it. The bar offers beers and wines, and coffee is available, but no tea. The main course is large enough, but if you're a good trencher person an appetizer can be provided at an extra £1.75 ($4.03). Lunch from the buffet costs £6.50 ($14.95); dinner, £7 ($16.10). Thatchers is open from noon to 2 p.m. for lunch. There are two sittings for dinner, one at 7:30, another at 9 p.m.

Chapter VIII

DEVON AND CORNWALL

1. Beer
2. Exeter
3. Dartmoor
4. Torbay
5. Totnes
6. Dartmouth
7. Plymouth
8. Clovelly
9. Lynton-Lynmouth
10. Combe Martin
11. Looe
12. Polperro
13. Fowey
14. Truro
15. Portloe
16. St. Mawes
17. Falmouth
18. Penzance
19. The Scilly Isles
20. St. Hilary, Newlyn, and Mousehole
21. St. Ives
22. St. Columb Major
23. Port Isaac
24. Tintagel

THE GREAT PATCHWORK QUILT area of the southwest of England, part of the "West Countree," abounds with cliffside farms, rolling hills, foreboding moors, semitropical plants, and fishing villages—all of which combine to provide some of the finest scenery in England. The British themselves approach the sunny countries of Devon and Cornwall with the same kind of excitement one would normally reserve for hopping over to the continent. Especially along the coastline, the British Riviera, many of the names of the little seaports, villages, and resorts have been synonymous with holidays in the sun: Penzance, Looe, Polperro.

Many small towns and fishing villages do not allow cars to enter. These towns provide car parks on their outskirts, but this can involve a long walk to reach the center or the harbor. In high season, from mid-July to mid-September, the more popular villages get quite crowded, and one needs reservations in the limited number of hotels available.

It's easy to involve yourself in the West Country life, as lived by the British vacationers. Perhaps you'll go pony trekking across moor and woodland, past streams and sheep-dotted fields, stopping at local pubs to soak up atmosphere and ale. Chances are your oddly shaped bedroom will be in a barton (farm) mentioned in the Domesday Book or in a thatched cottage neither straight, level, nor true.

Fishermen can catch their lunch (salmon and trout in such rivers as the Dart), then take it back to the kitchen of their guest house to be grilled. Life is usually very informal. The hosts here, many of farming stock, don't like to "muck about" putting on airs for tourists. In the morning, your landlady might be out picking runner (string) beans for your dinner. Later, she'll bring up pails from the milk house, and you can watch her create her own version of clotted Devonshire cream—cooked on the back of the stove. For dessert that night, you'll get a country portion heaped on your freshly picked gooseberries.

When a Devonian invites you to walk down the primrose path, he or she means just that. The primrose is practically the shire flower of this most beautiful of counties. Devon is a land of jagged coasts—the red cliffs in the south facing the English Channel, the gray cliffs in the north opening onto the Bristol Channel.

Aside from the shores, a great many of the scenic highlights appear in the two national parks, **Dartmoor** in the south, **Exmoor** in the north. First, we'll explore:

SOUTH DEVON

It's the lazy life in South Devon, as you sit in the orchard, enjoying the view of the coast from which Raleigh and Drake set sail. Almost every little hamlet, on some level, is geared to accommodate tourists, who flock here in great numbers from early spring to late fall. There is much to see and explore (although a minimum of historical sights), but mainly the tranquil life prevails.

1. Beer

Only seven miles from the last stopover in Dorset (Lyme Regis), is the town of **Beer,** no longer a center for smugglers, but still colorful with its small fleet of fishing craft, sandy beach, white cliffs, and pebbly cove. We can think of no better way to acquaint you with the fine accommodations of Devon than to introduce:

Bovey House, Beer, near Seaton (tel. Branscombe 241), on the edge of the village, about 1½ miles away. Picture the sort of dreams you're likely to have at Bovey House, sleeping in the Charles II room, with its designed ceiling which tells the story of how the king finally escaped the Roundheads by hiding in an oak tree. After poking about, knocking, and old-fashioned snooping, you're likely to find a concealed door leading to an underground passageway to the sea—a mile and a half away.

A 12th-century manor with an avenue of trees leading to the village road, Bovey was presented to Queen Catherine Parr by King Henry VIII as part of her dowry following the dissolution of the monasteries. It is the favorite property of its present owner, Lord Clinton. In one of his off-moments, he was

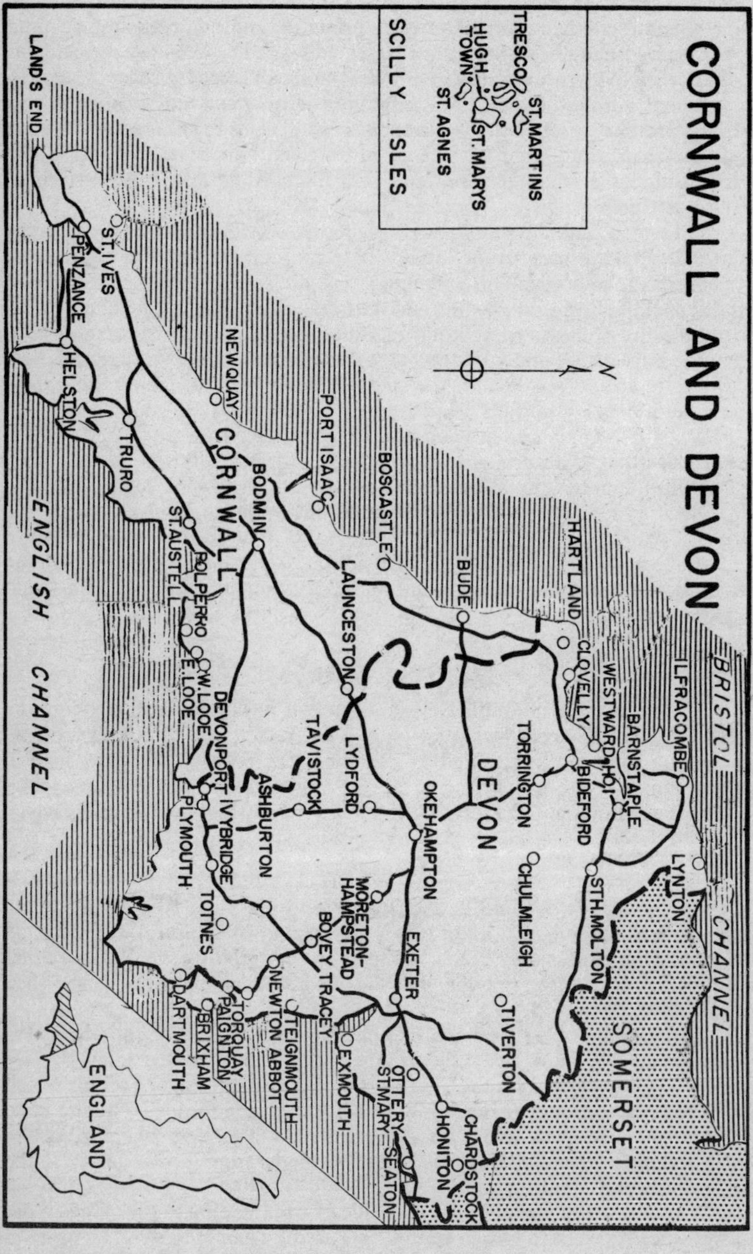
CORNWALL AND DEVON
SCILLY ISLES
TRESCO
HUGH TOWN
ST. MARTINS
ST. MARYS
ST. AGNES
N
BRISTOL CHANNEL
ENGLISH CHANNEL
LAND'S END
ST. IVES
PENZANCE
HELSTON
NEWQUAY
TRURO
CORNWALL
PORT ISAAC
BODMIN
ST. AUSTELL
POLPERRO
E. LOOE
W. LOOE
BOSCASTLE
LAUNCESTON
BUDE
HARTLAND
CLOVELLY
WESTWARD HO!
BIDEFORD
ILFRACOMBE
BARNSTAPLE
LYNTON
TORRINGTON
DEVON
OKEHAMPTON
LYDFORD
TAVISTOCK
DEVONPORT
ASHBURTON
IVYBRIDGE
PLYMOUTH
TOTNES
MORETON-HAMPSTEAD
BOVEY TRACEY
NEWTON ABBOT
TORQUAY
PAIGNTON
BRIXHAM
DARTMOUTH
TEIGNMOUTH
EXETER
EXMOUTH
OTTERY ST. MARY
SEATON
HONITON
CHARDSTOCK
CHULMLEIGH
STH. MOLTON
TIVERTON
SOMERSET
ENGLAND

persuaded to let his tenants, Mr. and Mrs. Alan Roberts, accept paying guests under the guise of house parties.

When you see the antique furnishings in the drawing room, you'll want to whisk them away into the night. Adam, Chippendale, Georgian—all the important furniture periods are represented here. The linenfold paneling in the dining room is museum caliber. There are collections of old china, silver, paintings, and sculpture. The spacious bedrooms contain antiques and beds that blend in with the atmosphere. A famous playwright once used the house as the model for the setting in one of his plays. In the drawing room you'll occasionally meet political leaders of England, perhaps stage stars—those who love this way of life.

Tea- and coffee-making facilities are provided in the bedrooms. You can also arrange to have a lunch packed for a later meal near the shore or on a picnic walk. Be sure to find a secluded, protected spot—this is hunting country, and one often sees a pack of hounds and hunters chasing a fox.

We've deliberately held off telling you the price till last. It's the nicest surprise of all! For your bed, breakfast, and evening dinner, you are charged from £10.41 ($23.94) per person, depending on the location of the room, plus a small service charge and VAT. Bovey House is open mid-March to mid-November. This is one of the best values in England.

2. Exeter

The county town of Devonshire, on the banks of the Exe River, Exeter was a Roman city founded in the first century A.D. Two centuries later, it was encircled by a mighty stone wall, traces of which remain today. Conquerors and would-be conquerors, especially the Vikings, stormed the fortress in the centuries to come. None was more notable than William the Conqueror. Irked at Exeter's refusal to capitulate (perhaps also at the sheltering of Gytha, mother of the slain Harold), the Norman duke brought Exeter to its knees on short notice.

Under the Tudors, the city grew and prospered. The cocky Sir Walter Raleigh and Sir Francis Drake cut striking figures strolling through Exeter's streets. In May 1942, the Germans bombed Exeter, destroying many of the city's architectural treasures. Exeter was rebuilt, but the new, impersonal-looking shops and offices couldn't replace the Georgian crescents and the black-and-white timbered buildings with their plastered walls. Thankfully, much was spared, including the major architectural treasure—

EXETER CATHEDRAL: Owing its present look to the Decorated style of the 13th and 14th centuries, the Exeter Cathedral of St. Peter actually goes back to Saxon times. Even Canute, the Viking conqueror, got in on the act of rebuilding around 1017. The cathedral of Bishop Warelwast came into being in the early 12th century, and the north and south towers serve as reminders of the Norman period. The remarkable feature of the present Gothic building is the nave, with its tierceron vaulting, stretching out for some 300 feet, broken only by an organ. The cathedral did suffer damage in the 1942 German bombings, losing its St. James's Chapel, which subsequently has been restored. But most of the treasures remained intact, including the rows of sculpture along the west front; the 14th-century Minstrels' Gallery, its angelic figures with Early English musical instruments in hand; and the carved oak 14th-century bishop's throne.

OTHER MONUMENTS: Much of the old remains. The **Exeter Guildhall**, a colonnade building on The High, is regarded as the oldest municipal building in the kingdom. The earliest reference to the Guildhall is contained in a deed of 1160. The Tudor front which straddles the pavement was added in 1593. Inside is a fine display of silver in the gallery. It contains a number of paintings as well, including one of Henrietta Anne, daughter of Charles I (she was born in Exeter in 1644). The ancient hall is paneled in oak. The Guildhall is open throughout the year, Monday to Saturday, from 10 a.m. to 5:30 p.m., and admission is free.

Rougemont Castle, with its Norman gateway, is now largely a memory. Rougemont was created for William the Conqueror. Over the centuries the castle fell into ruins. Now there has been some consolidation of masonry, and it is pleasant to stroll through Rougemont Gardens.

If time remains, see also **St. Nicholas Priory,** The Mint, lying off Fore Street, a 15th-century craft building; and the underground passageways at **Princesshay,** off The High (the subterranean water supply channels of medieval times).

READERS' SIGHTSEEING TIP: "One of Exeter's best attractions is the **Exeter Maritime Museum** at the Quay. This museum is a must for all boat lovers as it has a collection of more than 80 small craft and contains the world's largest collection of British and foreign boats" (Mr. and Mrs. Eric Ruff, Yarmouth, Nova Scotia, Canada).

WHERE TO STAY: In accommodations, Exeter has a number of comfortable choices.

Rougemont Hotel, Queen Street (tel. Exeter 54982), is imbued with a stylish flair that none of its competitors provides. Fairly recently, this great, old-fashioned hotel, opposite the Central Railway Station, underwent a metamorphosis, emerging as a solid place at which to stay. Its neoclassic architecture is a background for the contemporary furnishings. The bone-white walls in the reception lounge are a foil to the golds and oranges. Much of the comfort and tasteful decor are found in the bedrooms. Singles rent from £25 ($57.50); doubles, from £30 ($69), including VAT and an English breakfast. Amenities include telephones, radios, TV, and private baths.

Dinner is à la carte, beginning at £7 ($16.10). Guests gather in the Adam-styled Cavendish Bar for drinks—sparkling with crystal and vibrant in gold and white. An excellent stock of wines comes from the cellar, which, incidentally, was once used as a debtor's prison.

Royal Clarence Hotel, Cathedral Yard (tel. Exeter 58464), a Georgian-style building, miraculously escaped destruction during the war. A hotel full of history, it possesses modern amenities: all of the 63 bedrooms have private bathrooms, and many overlook the Cathedral Green. Comfortable lounges display a mixture of antiques, gilt mirrors, and modern pieces. The restyled restaurant is open to the public, and a table d'hôte luncheon costs from £4.95 ($11.39), and a table d'hôte dinner from £5.95 ($13.69). A single room with bath rents from £20.50 ($47.15), a double with bath from £29.50 ($67.85). Prices include all taxes. The general manager is Arthur E. Barnes.

The **Devon Motel,** Exeter Bypass, Matford (tel. Exeter 59268), lies on the outskirts of the city at the western sector of the bypass on the A38. Convenient to the airport and as a stopping-off point for those headed for the West Country, it is one of the Watney Lyons properties, built in a style familiar to most North Americans. You drive your car into your own open garage, and your bedroom and private bath are directly overhead. Singles pay £20 ($46); doubles, £30 ($69); including breakfast, service, and VAT. Some cheaper singles are in the old part of the hotel and are without bath, costing from £18 ($41.40) nightly. However, all doubles and units in the new wing have private baths. Inside, all is compact and built-in, with a picture window overlooking the meadows beyond. On the premises are a restaurant and drinking bars, serving a set lunch for £3.50 ($8.05) and dinner from £6 ($13.10).

WHERE TO EAT: The **Ship Inn**, Martin's Lane (tel. Exeter 72040), a short walk from the cathedral, was often visited by Sir Francis Drake, Sir Walter Raleigh, and Sir John Hawkins. Of it Drake wrote: "Next to mine own shippe, I do most love that old 'Shippe' in Exon, a tavern in Fyssh Street, as the people call it, or as the clergie will have it, St. Martin's Lane." The pub still provides tankards of stout and lager and is still loved by both young and old. The reconstructed dining room on the second floor also retains the early English atmosphere: settles, red leather and oak chairs. The fare is hearty English, the service friendly. At either lunch or dinner, you can order such temptations as onion soup, 55p ($1.27); grilled rainbow trout, £2.80 ($6.44); or grilled rump steak, £4 ($9.20). The price of the main courses includes vegetables, roll and butter. The portions, as in Elizabethan days, are large. The restaurant is open from noon to 2 p.m. and from 6:30 to 10:30 p.m., Monday through Saturday. Closed Sunday, and all bank holidays. The bars are open from 10:30 a.m. to 2 p.m. and 5 to 10:30 p.m. weekdays.

Coolings Wine Bar, 11 Gandy St. (tel. Exeter 34183). In one of the older and more interesting little streets of the city, this is a friendly place with beams above the checked cloths of the tables. Some of the dining space is in the cellars of the old building. All the food is prepared on the premises, and that includes a good selection of cold meats, pies, and quiches, as well as chicken Waldorf, sugar-baked ham, each served with a variety of salads, then two or three daily hot dishes, chalked up on the blackboard. A plateful, either hot or cold, will cost about £1.75 ($4.03). Desserts are available at 55p ($1.27) to 75p ($1.73). House wine is 50p ($1.15) a glass. It is open daily except Sunday from noon to 2:15 p.m. and from 5:30 to 11:30 p.m.

WHERE TO STAY AND EAT OUTSIDE EXETER: In the Exe Valley, four miles south of Tiverton and ten miles north of Exeter, lies **Bickleigh**, a hamlet with a river, an arched stone bridge, a mill pond, and thatched-roof cottages—a cliché of English charm, one of the finest spots in all of Devon. In this village, we have a recommendation in the medium-priced range:

The **Fishermen's Cot Hotel** (tel. Bickleigh 237) sits like a picture postcard across the way from Bickleigh Bridge. Even though it's thatched and blends beautifully into the local setting, it is newer than most of the houses here, and has all the heating and plumbing necessary. The bed-and-breakfast rate is £21 ($48.30) nightly in a bathless double room, £26 ($59.80) in a double with bath. Chances are you'll be served some of the best food in Devon. Ask if the cook will make you a chocolate mousse—light and airy, of country-fresh eggs. The Cot serves excellent trout dishes. Fishermen particularly like the place, because they can catch salmon and trout right in front of the hotel on the banks of the Exe. The hotel is fully licensed. There are dinner dances on Saturday.

Trout, on the main Tiverton/Exeter Road, A396, four miles south of Tiverton (tel. Bickleigh 339), is a former 17th-century coaching inn, transformed skillfully into three pubs and a gourmet restaurant. The long, low thatched roof with tiny leaded windows encloses the former stables, converted into a spacious and dramatic restaurant, with heavy dark beams and oak furniture. A collection of copper and glittering horse brasses, turkey-red table linens, and ladderback chairs provide a warm atmosphere for dining. Pre-dinner drinks are provided in one of the pubs, the most popular one containing an old open fireplace, made from the original bridge stone. A sign indicates that the inn was built in 1630 as a trout hatchery.

A buffet lunch and evening snacks are available in the bar seven days a week. A meal for less than £3 ($6.90) includes smoked trout, Austrian cheese, chicken or pâté, with a salad, and homemade desserts. The restaurant does only à la carte dinners. Appetizers might include pâté and a Cumberland sauce at £1.40 ($3.22), or else whitebait at £1.40 also, perhaps a homemade soup at £1 ($2.30). Main-dish specialties are beef Stroganoff at £4.95 ($11.39); veal Marsala at £4.85 ($11.16); chicken mornay at £3.85 ($8.86); and lamb cutlets at £3.75 ($8.63). On Sunday, lunch in the restaurant features a four-courser at £5 ($11.50), with such main dishes offered as roast beef and Yorkshire pudding.

An Old Manor at Ottery St. Mary

The sleepy little market town, where the incomparable Coleridge *(The Rime of the Ancient Mariner, Kubla Khan)* was born, lies in the Otter River Valley, only ten miles east of Exeter. See the almost perfectly preserved church from the 14th century. The old cloth town makes a good base for exploring the South Devon coastline—particularly if you center at the following medium-priced recommendation.

Salston Hotel (tel. Ottery St. Mary 2310), an old manor house, lies 1½ miles off the main A30 London road, and a mile from Ottery St. Mary. The hotel is officially listed as a building of historical and architectural interest. Even though it's lost most of its acreage and original furnishings, the exterior is intact—a rambling three-story brick hotel with dozens of chimneys and gables. The lounge is large, with a bay window opening onto the gardens. A ballroom, built for the visit of Princess Alexandra of Teck (that name will send you rushing to your history books), has a Tudor fireplace. Open all year, the Salston charges peak season (July to October) bed-and-breakfast rates of £18.65 ($42.90) to £21 ($48.30) per person, the latter price for rooms with private baths. Weekly demi-pension terms are also quoted. Spa fans will find a health studio run in conjunction with the Salston. There is a 20- by 48-foot swimming pool, plus an adjoining Norwegian pine cabin with sauna, solarium, and a massage and relaxing room, available at an extra charge. There is also a swimming instructor. Most Friday evenings, the years roll back to 1530. In front of the Henry VIII fireplace, a medieval banquet is spread, complete with costumed serving "wenches," minstrel singers, and a jester. Featured at a "six-remove" banquet are such items as game soup based on a 16th-century recipe, Tudor-style pâté, ribs of oxen, and lots of mead and ale.

READER'S HOTEL SELECTION: "Louisiana-born James Henry and his English wife own one of the oldest (1487) continuously licensed pubs in England, the **Oxenham Arms**, South Zeal, Devon (tel. Sticklepath 244). The carefully preserved inn itself was originally built in the 12th century and used as a monastery. A cob-walled double room is £11 ($25.30) per person, tax included, with a choice of breakfast menus. Seventeen miles west of Exeter, the inn is just a short hike into the bracken and gorse-covered hills of Dartmoor National Park" (A. Emerson Smith, Columbia, S.C.).

3. Dartmoor

Antiquity-rich Dartmoor lies in the southern part of the shire. The Tors (huge rock formations) of this granite mass sometimes soar to a height of 2000 feet. The national park is a patchwork quilt of mood changes: gorse and purple heather ... Dartmoor ponies ... a foreboding landscape for the experienced walker only ... gorges with rushing water.

Some 13 miles west from Exeter, the peaceful little town of **Moreton Hampstead,** perched on the edge of Dartmoor, makes a good center. The heavily visited Dartmoor village of **Widecombe-in-the-Moor** is only seven miles from the town. Moreton Hampstead contains much that is old, including a market cross and several 17th-century colonnaded almshouses.

WHERE TO STAY AND EAT: **Manor House Hotel** (tel. Moreton Hampstead 355), at the edge of Dartmoor, is a converted, gabled, Jacobean manor. It is in the midst of 200 acres of parkland, much of which has been cultivated for the pleasure of guests. This upper bracket hotel is a favorite with fishermen (trout in the Bovey and Bowden Rivers, salmon in the Teign), and with golfers as well who are drawn to the 18-hole course. Built for a distinguished family, the manor has lost its old grandeur, but added the new lure of modern amenities. The halls, reception lounge, drawing and dining rooms are for life on a large scale; the bedrooms are often outsize (some suitable for a diplomatic reception); the furnishings are comfortable, with good beds, and all the rooms have private baths. Expect to pay from £35 ($80.50) for bed and breakfast in a single room. In a double, two persons are charged anywhere from £60 ($138) for bed and breakfast. VAT and service are included in all tariffs. The cuisine blends some of the best English dishes with fine continental fare. A dinner costs around £10 ($23) per person.

Gidleigh Park Hotel, Chagford (tel. Chagford 2225), is set one mile from the edge of Dartmoor in beautiful countryside. A visit to this hotel is highly recommended, if you can find it! Its owners, Kay and Paul Henderson, have renovated and refurnished the house with flair and imagination.

In a park of 30 acres, the mansion is Tudor style, lying just two miles from Chagford. Large beech and oak trees abound. Inside, the oak-paneled public rooms and the open log fires invite a return to yesterday. The windows open onto views of the garden and the Teign Valley, with Dartmoor lying beyond.

Most of the bedrooms, 11 in all, are on the second floor and are approached by a grand staircase. All rooms contain private bath, color TV set, and phone. Demi-pension ranges from £35 ($80.50) per person nightly, plus VAT.

Delicious meals are served in an oak-paneled dining room. The menu is changed daily, and only the best and freshest products are used. Cheeses are supplied by Paxton & Whitfield of London, and the wine cellar is one of the most extensive and reasonably priced in England. Kay Henderson trained at Cordon Bleu in London and Paris. She believes it is better to make up a meal from the freshest produce available each day from local farmers, fishermen, and the hotel's own garden, than to offer a large choice of indifferently prepared à la carte dishes.

How to get there: From Chagford Square turn into Mill Street, leaving Lloyds Bank on your right. After 200 yards, fork right and down the hill to the crossroads. Cross straight over into Holy Street, following the lane passing Holy Street Manor on your right and shifting into low gear to negotiate two sharp bends on a steep hill. Over Leigh Bridge turn a sharp right into Gidleigh Park. A half-mile drive will bring you to the hotel.

Teignworthy Hotel, Frenchbeer, near Chagford (tel. Chagford 3355), is an attractive granite and slate country house where John and Gillian Newell and their family welcome you as guests. All bedrooms have baths (one is only a shower), color TVs, and phones, and there is room to relax in privacy. They have a drawing room with an open log fire and a small bar for predinner drinks.

John does most of the cooking, aided by the Newells' daughters, Debbie and Rebecca, plus various local girls. His individual style is becoming very popular in the area, and dinner can include poached brill with dill hollandaise, trout with Pernod, or filet of pork with date and red wine sauce. Wherever possible, local fresh produce is used. A liter of house wine is £4 ($9.20). There is also a good, well-thought-out wine list.

Overnight stays, including an English breakfast and dinner, will cost £30 ($69) per person, including VAT.

Lydford House Hotel, Lydford, near Okehampton (tel. Lydford 347), is a stone country house of generous proportions, set on a three-acre garden at the edge of Lydford. It was built in 1880 by the famous Dartmoor artist, William Widgery. Several of his paintings decorate the living room. Owners Ron and Ann Boulter have set the following rates: £8 ($18.40) per person nightly for bed and breakfast, £9 ($20.70) with private bath. Weekly terms are £51 ($117.30), £61 ($140.30) with private bath. Dinner, bed, and breakfast cost £71 ($163.30), £81 ($186.30) with private bath. The hotel is seven miles south of Okehampton, just off the A386, and it's on your right as you approach the hamlet of Ludford.

The **Castle Inn,** Lydford, near Okehampton (tel. Lydford 242), is a 16th-century inn next to Lydford Castle. The low inn, with its pink facade and row of rose trellises, is the hub of the village, along with the all-purpose grocery store and post office. The inn's owners, Mr. and Mrs. Red, have maintained the character of the commodious rustic lounge, with its valuable collection of old furniture and accessories, including wing chairs, a grandfather's clock, and antique prints. One room is called the "Snuggery," containing a group of high-backed oak settles arranged in a circle. Meals are served buffet style, from noon to 3 p.m., a great spread set out on a long table. The cost depends on your selection of a main course. The salads are on a help-yourself basis. Buffet salads at lunch cost about £2 ($4.60) with a main course. Snacks are available as well, and you can take your plate, along with a lager, and sneak off to an inviting nook. A three-course dinner will run about £6.50 ($14.95). For a bed and a large country-style breakfast, the charge is £10 ($23) in a single, £18 ($41.40) in a double. The bedrooms, although not large, are well planned and attractively furnished, often with mahogany and marble Victorian pieces, each room with its own color scheme.

Holne Chase Hotel (tel. Poundsgate 280) is a white-gabled country house, within sight of trout and salmon fishing waters. You can catch your lunch and take it back to the kitchen to be cooked. Although the mood of the moor predominates, Holne Chase is surrounded by trees, lawns, and pastures—a perfect setting for walks along the Dart. It's off the main Ashburton-Princetown Road, between Holne Bridge and New Bridge. Holne Chase is run by Mary and Kenneth Bromage, who have returned to their native Devon to preserve the house "as a sanctuary of peace and hospitality." Every bedroom in the house is named after a tributary of the River Dart. The best way to stay here is to take the demi-pension rate, which ranges from £22.50 ($51.75) to £29 ($66.70) in a single, from £41 ($94.30) to £47 ($108.10) in a double or twin. The more expensive tariffs are for units with private baths.

The house is furnished in period style, with a fine English 18th-century oak dresser base serving as the bar. The cooking combines the best of English fare with specialty dishes that are made all the better whenever produce from the gardens is used or fresh fish from the Dart River and Torbay. Devon beef and lamb are also featured. The old cellars hold a good selection of wines.

Leusdon Lodge Guest House, Poundsgate (tel. Poundsgate 304), is a 150-year-old stone country house, with gables, chimneys, and beyond the garden views of Dartmoor National Park. Its owners are Neelia and Denis Hutchins, who probably know more about this area than anyone else. Denis was once the chairman of the Dartmoor Tourist Association, and likes to help guide you to the best local sights, to a picnic beside a crystal-clear brook, or to tell the history of the moor and its mystical folklore. On cool nights he lights a log fire in the living room, joining guests in talks. There are seven rooms with soft beds and hot and cold water basins, budget-priced at £10 ($23) per person nightly, including VAT. Your breakfast will be abundant and varied. Dinners are English at their traditional best. The charge is £14 ($32.20) per person for half board. Meals are served in the dining room with its hand-carved paneled walls and an ornate fireplace. Specialties include steak-and-kidney pudding, Dartmoor rabbit in cider, and beefsteak casserole with dumplings. In winter there is full central heating, even a festive Christmas house party.

Old Walls Farm, Ponsworthy, near Ashburton (tel. Poundsgate 222), is a substantial, stone-colored plastered country home set remotely on a working farm and reached by very narrow lanes. Here you are comfortably in the heart of the moors, and in the safe, knowing hands of owner Bill Fursdon, an expert on the area. He is a genial, handsome, white-haired gentleman with a gracious smile who is by avocation a naturalist. He'll take you on a short walk around his farm, showing you his collection of cows, mongrel dogs, ducks, a pet goat (its milk is served at breakfast, but it's strictly optional), and a beautiful little river, lying a short distance from the house. He'll make handmade maps, pinpointing the places of interest within driving distance.

His house is a living tribute to a fast-disappearing era. He is assisted by his wife, Elizabeth, who plays the organ on Sunday at the village church, and their son who lives in a separate home close by. Guests relax around a stone fireplace in the drawing room, or else on a sunny day enjoy a crescent-shaped, all-glass sun room. From the latter, the view of the moorland is exceptional. The living room has an old grand piano, a Victorian card table, a soft arm sofa, and armchairs placed in a curving bay recess.

The bed-and-breakfast rate is about £8 ($18.40) per person. Breakfast is a special event in the dining room, and you can have as much food as you want, including mouslie, a concoction of oats, bran, wheat germ, raisins or dates, served with brown sugar, goat's milk, and a glob of clotted Devonshire cream. Old Walls Farm is reached from the A38 dual carriageway which runs between Exeter and Plymouth. Turn onto the B3357 (signposted Dartmoor) at Ashburton, then right at Poundsgate onto 984, going through the hamlet of Ponsworthy, passing the all-purpose post office and store.

4. Torbay

In April 1968, the towns of Torquay, Paignton, and Brixham combined to form the "County Borough of Torbay," as part of a plan to turn the area into one of the super three-in-one resorts of Europe. Vacationers from the factories of the Midlands find it easier to bask in the home-grown Devonshire sunshine, than to make the pilgrimage to Rimini or the Costa del Sol.

Torquay, set against a backdrop of the red cliffs of Devon, contains 11 miles of coastline, with many sheltered pebbly coves and sandy beaches. With its parks and gardens (including numerous subtropical plants and palm trees), it isn't hard to envision it as a Mediterranean-type resort (and its retired residents are fond of making this comparison, especially in postcards sent back to their cousins in Manchester). At night, concerts, productions from the West

End (the D'Oyly Carte Opera appears occasionally at the new Princess Theatre), vaudeville shows, and ballroom dancing keep the holiday-makers—and many honeymooners—regally entertained.

If you suddenly long for an old Devonshire village, you can always ride the short distance to **Cockington**—still in the same borough—which contains thatched cottages, an old mill, a forge, and a 12th-century church. Furthermore, if you want to visit one of the great homes of England, you can call on **Oldway**, in the heart of Paignton. Started by the founder of the Singer sewing-machine dynasty, Isaac Merritt Singer, and completed the year after he died (1875), the neoclassic mansion is surrounded by about 20 acres of grounds and Italian-style gardens. Inside, if you get the feeling you're at Versailles, you're almost right, as many of the rooms were copied. Open all year, Oldway may be visited weekdays from 9 a.m. to 1 p.m. and from 2 to 5:15 p.m. (on Saturday and Sunday from 2:30 to 5 p.m., May to September only). Admission is free. The gardens are always open.

WHERE TO STAY AND EAT: Rainbow House, Belgrave Road (tel. Torquay 211-161), is like a complete resort, having been enlarged and integrated with the adjoining San Remo Hotel. Facing south and open throughout the year, the hotel has been in the Marshall family for about two decades. Once a large and stately house, the hotel has expanded until now it has more than 100 bedrooms, each with bath en suite, plus a number of self-catering apartments. The peak bed-and-breakfast rate charged is £20 ($46), although half-board terms are £24 ($55.20) per person. Singles pay an additional £1.50 ($3.45) supplement.

Facilities include a heated pool and sun terraces, a Caribbean coffeeshop, an apéritif bar, plus a sauna and and solarium. Public rooms are furnished in bright, modern colors. In the hotel's nightclub, you can dance to a first-class band and often enjoy cabaret entertainment. The hotel's à la carte specialty restaurant, the Pot of Gold, serves an international menu, or else you can patronize the grill for late-night dining. In addition to that, the hotel also offers a main restaurant, serving some local specialties among its traditional repertoire.

Palm Court Hotel, Sea Front (tel. Torquay 24881), is a Victorian crescent built facing south onto the esplanade overlooking Torbay, and offers style and good living. Two lounges are wood paneled with leaded glass windows. In the dining room is a minstrels' gallery. There are two up-to-date bars and a coffeeshop, open all day. All rooms have been modernized and have color TV, tea- and coffee-making facilities, central heating, telephone, and radio. Of the bedrooms, 42 have private bathrooms. There is an elevator to two floors. From June through September, bed-and-breakfast rates are from £16.50 ($37.95) to £19.25 ($44.28), including service. With garden chairs and tables on the sun terrace outside the coffeeshop, the Palm Court becomes a social center. At night the colored floodlighting around the bay evokes a Riviera atmosphere outside the hotel.

The **Alpine Hotel,** Warren Road (tel. Torquay 27612), is a remake of one of the old homes of Torquay, on the top of the city's Rock Walk. This one was the creation of Lady Singer, of the sewing machines. (Perhaps she could see Oldway from here, where her husband had extended an invitation to Isadora Duncan). A cliff-hanging hotel, the Alpine overlooks the marina harbor. The bedrooms are pleasantly equipped with modern furnishings and are light and airy. Depending on the room, its view, its balcony, or its plumbing, the demi-pension rates range from £18 ($41.40) to £22 ($50.60) per person. A service charge and VAT are included.

Lanscombe House, Cockington Village (tel. Torquay 67556), is a Georgian house set in a two-acre garden in this beautiful village. Built nearly 200 years ago, it resembles a church rectory, with large lounges and dining rooms opening onto views. The owners, the Hayward family, have ten rooms going for around £13.50 ($31.05) in high season—April 1 to October 31—for bed and breakfast, plus an evening meal. Without dinner, the charge is £9.50 ($21.85). The furnishings are comfy English—overstuffed chairs et al. The bar-lounge has bare white walls and a beamed ceiling, the coziest place in the house (it was once the woodshed). The dinner is home-cooked, typically English fare. Readers Mr. and Mrs. Charles Aarons write, "Those who like to carry the calm and grace of a bygone age beyond the hotel grounds can take a horse-drawn carriage from the village to the beach!" Mr. Charles A. Haigh adds: ". . . a real pearl with excellent hosts, the food was just great, and it's ideal for a family."

Colindale, Rathmore Road (tel. Torquay 23947), is an exceptionally good choice. And it's about as central as you'd want, opening onto King's Garden, as well as lying within a five-minute walk of Corbyn Beach, and three minutes from the railway station. The bed-and-breakfast rate, set by Mr. and Mrs. Thomas, is £7.50 ($17.25) per person in high season. But the best arrangement in one of their nine well-kept double rooms is to take the partial board weekly rate—£60 ($138) per person. VAT is added to all tariffs. Colindale is one of a row of attached brick-built Edwardian houses, with gables and chimneys. It's set back from the road, with a tiny parking court in front. Mr. Thomas has a wine list far superior to most large hotels.

A Gourmet Cooking School (off-season only)

South Devon Technical College, Newton Road (tel. Torquay 35711), is a cooking school that serves inexpensive—but gourmet-level—lunches during the school terms (closed July, August, and the first two weeks in September, as well as on weekends). You pay a set £4 ($9.20) including coffee—and are offered the results of the day's lesson. Supervised by expert teachers, the young chefs turn out excellent meals. Lunch is served at 12:30 p.m. (you must reserve no more than seven days in advance; telephone between 10:30 a.m. and 4:30 p.m.). You leave tips at your discretion. It's pointless to give menu suggestions, as the bill of fare changes daily. It's usually in French, beginning with hors d'oeuvres and following with soup, then fish, such as filet of sole, the main course, perhaps entrecôte tyrolienne, accompanied by vegetables, and, finally dessert. The modern-looking restaurant is licensed, and offers a selection of table wines, apéritifs, and liqueurs. The linen is starched stiff white, the silver sparkling, and the copper chafing dishes shining.

5. Totnes

One of the oldest towns in the West Country, the ancient borough of Totnes rests quietly in the past, seemingly content to let the Torbay area remain in the vanguard of the building boom. On the Dart River, 12 miles upstream from Dartmouth itself, Totnes is so totally removed in character from Torquay that the two towns could be in different countries. Totnes has several old historic buildings, notably the ruins of a Norman castle, an ancient guildhall, and the 15th-century church of St. Mary, made of red sandstone. In the Middle Ages, the old cloth town was encircled by walls, and the North Gate serves as a reminder of that period.

WHERE TO STAY: **Royal Seven Stars Hotel** (tel. Totnes 862-125) is a coaching inn, rebuilt in the latter 17th century, although tracing its origins back 500 years before that. Whitewashed and severe, it stands on a street not far from the Dart at the bottom of The High. The interior courtyard, built for horses and carriages, has been enclosed in glass, with an oak staircase leading to the second-floor bedrooms, which have been upgraded with built-in furniture. In the courtyard are interesting antiques, such as a heraldic shield, hand-carved chests, and an inlaid grandfather's clock—forming the most inviting part of the inn. The rooms are in the old style—nothing fancy, but heartily recommendable for their comfortable beds, soft eiderdowns. There's hot and cold running water; half of the rooms have private baths. You pay £21 ($48.30) to £25 ($57.50) in a double room, from £14 ($32.20) to £18 ($41.40) in a single, inclusive of VAT and breakfast. A modern restaurant has replaced the old dining room. Open until 9:15 p.m., it offers a lunch from £3.75 ($8.63), dinner from £6 ($13.80), plus a choice of à la carte dishes. Olde Tyme Music Hall, dinner, dance, and cabaret are offered in the Star-lite Room every Saturday night. Reservations are necessary.

Broombrough House Farm, on the outskirts of Totnes (tel. Totnes 863-134), is a gracious 100-year-old, many-gabled stone manor house set on a hill about a ten-minute walk from Totnes. Owner Joan Veale loves to show guests around the farm. Four spacious and well-furnished bedrooms are on the first floor (two shower rooms and one bathroom are shared). They are centrally heated, each containing twin beds, innerspring mattresses, and hot and cold running water. The daily charge is £6.70 ($15.41) for bed and a farm-style breakfast, plus another £5 ($11.50) for dinner. Guest lounges are spacious and comfortable. This place is highly recommended, especially to those who have never experienced life on a farm.

WHERE TO EAT: The **Elbow Room,** 6 North St. (tel. Totnes 863-480), is a one-time cider press and adjoining cottage converted into an intimate rendezvous for diners. The original 300-year-old stone walls have been retained and decor matched to them to give a unique atmosphere. Mr. and Mrs. B. J. Sellick provide a standard of food and service which attracts gourmets. Mrs. Sellick combines technical skill with inspiration and a flair for the unusual in the selection, preparation, and presentation of her appetizers, main courses, and homemade desserts. Main courses are accompanied by, and inclusive of, fresh vegetables. The menu is restricted to a maximum of ten international dishes, ranging from truite farci de Georges Bernard (trout, boned and stuffed with salpicon of shellfish, wrapped in a pancake, and baked) at £6.60 ($15.18), to escalope de veau Maître Martino, an original of scalloped veal filled with cream cheese, chives, gherkins, mushrooms with cream and white wine at £7.50 ($17.25). Mr. Sellick presides over the restaurant with charm and unobtrusive expertise, and offers a wine list to match the food. The Elbow Room extends a warm welcome.

Ffoulkes, 30 High St. (tel. Totnes 863-853), hides behind a Tudor facade on the main street of Totnes. Have your drinks in the lounge, in front of a fireplace, before dining in the intimate Elizabethan-style restaurant. Well-prepared "Taste of England" traditional lunches and à la carte dinners are served, including sole, venison, and veal. Main dishes average £5.25 ($12.08). Desserts cost £1.40 ($3.22). Everything is cooked to order, and the service is skilled and polite. Closed on Sunday, the restaurant is open otherwise from noon to 2 p.m. Monday through Friday, and from 7:30 to midnight Monday through Saturday.

WHERE TO STAY AND EAT ON THE OUTSKIRTS: In and around this area is some of South Devon's finest scenery. The hamlets, such as **Dartington,** are especially pleasing. Here, a Yorkshireman and his American-born wife (one of the Whitneys) poured energy, courage, imagination, and money into the theory that such a village could be self-sufficient. They used historic **Dartington Hall,** built in the late 14th century and restored by them after 1925, as their center. In the surrounding acres of undulating hills and streams, several village industries were created—housing construction, advanced farming, cloth milling, and an experimental school. During the day, visitors are welcome to tour the extensive grounds and can make purchases of handmade crafts in the community store. Our food and lodgings recommendations in the village follow.

The **Cott Inn** (tel. Totnes 863-777), on the old Ashburton-Totnes turnpike, is the second-oldest inn in England, built in 1320. It is a low, rambling, two-story building of stone, cob, and plaster, with a thatched roof and walls three feet thick. The owner, Nigel Shortman, charges £12.50 ($28.75) per person, plus service and VAT, for a full English or a continental breakfast and occupancy of one of their low-ceilinged old beamed rooms upstairs, where modern conveniences, including hot and cold running water, have been skillfully installed.

The inn is a gathering place for the people of Dartington, and here you'll feel the pulse of English country life. Even though it is a lowly pub, it is sophisticated—and you'll hear good talk here. In winter, log fires keep the lounge and bar snug. You'll surely be intrigued with the tavern, perhaps wanting to take a light meal there. Eating out in restaurants today is an expensive proposition, so Mr. Shortman offers his customers a superb hot and cold buffet where prices for the numerous dishes vary between £1 ($2.30) and £4.50 ($10.35). Even if you're not staying over, at least drop in at the pub.

Stoke Gabriel

About four miles southeast of Totnes sits the little village of Stoke Gabriel, one of the loveliest in Devon. Famous as a fishing hamlet, it lies on a creek of the Dart River. Dartmouth itself is only six miles south of the village (equidistant to Torquay). Suitable as a base is:

The **Gabriel Court Hotel** (tel. Stoke Gabriel 206), is a manor house which until recently had been owned by one family since 1485. What must the ghosts have thought when Michael and Eryl Beacom acquired it and guests started to fill up the rooms, chasing away the cobwebs of the past? The gleaming white house is surrounded by gardens, hedges, and magnolia trees. A heated swimming pool has been added. Bed-and-breakfast rates are from £14 ($32.20) per person. You might get a room in the new wing, containing eight bedrooms, all with private baths. The majority of the other comfortable rooms also have private baths or shower and toilet facilities, and the remaining few feature hot and cold running water only. Gabriel Court enjoys a reputation for its well-cooked English food, enhanced all the more by fruit and vegetables from the garden, as well as trout and salmon from the Dart and poultry from nearby farms. The hotel has a bar offering moderately priced wines. It remains open all year.

Tea and Oinks on the Farm

Want to visit an English farm? **Riverford Farm** (tel. Staverton 636), Staverton, near Totnes, is the place to go. A day out on the 500-acre farm includes a tour of the fields in a 50-passenger tractor trailer, visits to the dairy herd, pig unit, harvest fields, and milking sheds, ending with light refreshments in the barn. A small exhibition is devoted to country life and farming in the past, present, and future, and there are workshops for a wood turner, violin maker, and weaver (at the last count). Visitors are welcome every afternoon April through September. The tour starts at 2:30 p.m. and costs £1.20 ($2.76) for adults, 80p ($1.84) for children. Please telephone in advance to check that there is room for you on the tour. Look for the signs to Riverford halfway between Totnes and Buckfastleigh.

6. Dartmouth

At the mouth of the Dart River, this ancient seaport is the home of the Royal Naval College. Traditionally linked to England's maritime greatness, Dartmouth sent out the young midshipmen who ensured that Britannia ruled the waves. You can take a river steamer up the Dart to Totnes (book at the kiosk at the harbor). The view along the way is of Devon's most beautiful river.

Dartmouth's 15th-century castle was built during the reign of Edward IV. The town's most noted architectural feature is The Butterwalk, lying below Tudor houses. The Flemish influence in some of the houses is pronounced.

WHERE TO STAY: The **Royal Castle Hotel**, The Quay (tel. Dartmouth 2397), has been a coaching inn since 1639, having slept a host of visitors, including Sir Francis Drake, Queen Victoria, Charles II, and Edward VII (bedrooms named after them commemorate their visits). Horse-drawn carriages (as late as 1910) would dispatch their passengers in a carriageway, now enclosed to make the reception hall. Everywhere you look, you see reminders of the inn's rich past. The glassed-in courtyard, with its winding wooden staircase, has the original coaching horn and a set of 20 antique spring bells connected to the bedrooms. Many of the rooms opening off the covered courtyard and the rambling corridors have antiques, and the beds are soft.

A single without bath costs £18 ($41.40), rising to £24 ($55.20) with bath. A double without bath is £29 ($66.70), going up to £35 ($78.20) with bath. These tariffs include breakfast and VAT. The meals are excellent, in the best of the English tradition. A set lunch goes for £4.50 ($10.35), a set dinner for £6 ($13.80). A favorite place to settle in is the Galleon Bar, once two old kitchens, with double fireplaces and large hand-hewn beams said to have been rescued from Armada ships. There are two other pub-style bars, with settles, popular with the locals. Guests lounge on the second floor in a room with a bay window overlooking the harbor.

The **Victoria Hotel**, Duke Street (tel. Dartmouth 2572), is an unheralded little hotel—just 150 yards from the harbor. However, it is a sophisticated oasis, showing excellent taste in both the hotel and restaurant. The Victoria is a favorite retreat of the officers of the Naval College (at times, you feel that Gilbert and Sullivan wrote their operettas there). For bed and breakfast, guests pay £20 ($46) in a twin, £10 ($23) in a single. A favorite place for before-dinner drinks is one of the Victorian slipper chairs in front of the lounge fireplace. The bedrooms themselves are immaculate, tidy, and personal; the beds fresh and restful. Recommended on the à la carte menu are the chef's own pâté, T-bone steak, and locally caught fish. Try Ushers Best real ale or the local cider.

WHERE TO DINE: **Taylors**, The Quay (tel. Dartmouth 2748). Almost out of place in a peaceful south coast river town, Taylors's decor is straight out of

Arabia, a huge black tent decorated with goatskins and brilliantly colored tassels. A camel comes at you through a mirage on one wall. Diana Taylor was master of horses for the film *Khartoum* and was in charge of the boats used in *A Man for All Seasons*. Her theatrical flair for the dramatic shows itself now that she has settled in rural England, and is reflected in the black chairs and tables as well as the dim lights.

Diana excels in buying fresh ingredients for the dishes, which feature plenty of fresh fish and seafood. Roger Wilson, your host, is the front man who will lead you to the bar where an open fire burns, provide your apéritif, and help you to choose your meal from such items as steak, kidney, and oyster pie, woodpigeon, or lemon sole with a rich creamy shellfish sauce. Curries are quite a feature as are mussels in season.

Desserts include homely things such as treacle tart as well as cakes and fruit dishes. There is a good cheese board. A meal will cost about £9 ($20.70) for three courses, or £12 ($27.60) if you want more. French house wine is about £5 ($11.50) a bottle. There are lovely views from the bow window down the River Dart to the sea.

The restaurant is open daily except Tuesday from noon to 2 p.m. and from 7 to 10:30 p.m. It is closed for a month from mid-January to mid-February.

The **Cherub,** Higher Street (tel. Dartmouth 2571), was built around 1380 and maintains much of its original decor, the uniqueness of the old timbered building an attraction to North Americans. The owners of this very attractive and friendly pub, John Knight and Bernard Calligan, serve bars meals at lunch for less than £2 ($4.60) each. In the evenings they offer a popular, although intimate, candlelight restaurant, seating just 20 persons. The average meal there costs about £7 ($16.10) with drinks. Every item is home-cooked, and the chef specializes in local crab and seafood dishes. Closed Sunday.

7. Plymouth

The historic seaport of Plymouth is more romantic in legend than in reality. But this was not always so. In World War II, the blitzed area of greater Plymouth lost at least 75,000 buildings. The heart of present-day Plymouth, including the municipal civic center on the Royal Parade, has been entirely rebuilt—the way that it was done the subject of much controversy.

For the old you must go to the Elizabethan section, known as the Barbican, and walk along the quay in the footsteps of Sir Francis Drake (once the mayor of Plymouth), and other Elizabethan seafarers, such as Sir John Hawkins, English naval commander and slave trader. It was from here in 1577 that Drake set sail on his round-the-world voyage. An even more famous sailing took place in 1620 when the Pilgrim Fathers left their final port in England for the New World. That fact is commemorated by a plaque at the harbor.

While playing bowls on Plymouth Hoe, Drake was told that the Spanish Armada had entered the Sound. In what must surely rank as one of the greatest displays of confidence of all time, he finished the game before taking off.

WHERE TO STAY: Still a major base for the British Navy, Plymouth makes for an interesting stopover. The pick of the lot in accommodations follows.

Duke of Cornwall, Millbay Road (tel. Plymouth 266-256), is a Gothic-Victorian monument. Spared from World War II bombings, it looms like a château. Many of its bedrooms open onto balconies with views of the harbor. Considerable modernization has enlivened the interior. The bedrooms have been successfully upgraded, with compact, streamlined furnishings. A single with bath rents for £22 ($50.60) nightly, the cost rising to £34 ($78.20) in a double, these tariffs including an English breakfast and VAT. In the paneled Clan Bar, you can order good drinks in a setting of tartan floors and country-keg stools. The dining room is contemporary, with draped walls, a circular ceiling, and banquettes for cozy dining. A set lunch costs £5 ($11.50); a set dinner, £7 ($16.10). Latecomers are drawn into the Spider's Web in the cellar.

Holiday Inn, Armada Way (tel. Plymouth 62866), would probably have upset the departure plans of our forefathers. If they'd known how luxurious the new Holiday Inn would be, they might never have sailed. It's one of the most distinguished hotels in the West Country, set beside a park, overlooking the harbor and The Hoe. Rising like a midget skyscraper, it contains 222 good-size bedrooms with long double beds. Singles go from £26.50 ($60.95), doubles from £30 ($69), plus VAT. The rooms are fashionable, with air conditioning, wide picture windows, TV, radios, telephones, and private baths. Baby-sitting is available. A covered swimming pool is on the grounds, and there's a sauna and sun terrace as well, with garden tables set up for poolside refreshments. On the top floor is the Penthouse Restaurant, and you'll find a more intimate coffee-shop and bar on the ground floor.

Mayflower Post House, The Hoe (tel. Plymouth 62828), was built in 1970 to celebrate the 350th anniversary of the Pilgrims' voyage. It's a white, nine-story building, standing high on a hill above Plymouth Hoe, commanding a view over the wide sweep of Plymouth Sound. The hotel has a resort character, with a heated outdoor swimming pool, three bars, a restaurant, and a buttery with a naval flag decor. Each of the 104 bedrooms is decorated as a bed-sitting room, with wall-wide windows, desks, armchairs, TV, telephone, and private bath, even facilities for making your own tea or coffee. Higher rates are in effect from May 25 till October, with singles costing approximately £28 ($64.40); doubles, £40 ($92). Breakfast is extra, but VAT and service are included.

The **Anchorage,** Grand Parade, West Hoe (tel. Plymouth 68645), boasts a choice location, on the Grand Parade by the sea, overlooking Plymouth Sound. Owned by Mr. and Mrs. Willmott, the hotel is simply furnished in a modified modern style. Without flair or frills, it provides its own drama. The rooms have innerspring mattresses, hot and cold running water, and electric heaters. The rate for bed and breakfast is from £6.50 ($14.95) to £7.50 ($17.25) per night. To all bills, a service charge is added.

The **Imperial Hotel,** 3 Windsor Villas, Lockyer Street (tel. Plymouth 27311), is for anyone who prefers a small, friendly place, rather than a commercial hotel. The proprietors are great characters who enjoy making guests feel at home. Mr. Brooks was a rubber planter in Malaya, but retired here and he and Mrs. Brooks bought this attractive Victorian house. The hotel is tastefully furnished, indicating the experienced travel background of its owners. The bed-and-breakfast rate is £9 ($20.70) in a single, rising to £18 ($41.40) in a double, including breakfast and service. VAT is extra. Some ground-floor rooms are offered to those who have difficulty with stairs. The cocktail bar is well stocked, and a four-course evening meal with coffee is £4 ($9.20).

WHERE TO EAT: If you're pressed for time and are only passing through, try at least to visit the Barbican—perhaps for a meal. Our dining choice is **Green Lanterns,** 31 New St., The Barbican (tel. Plymouth 60852). A 16th-century eating house, on a Tudor street, the Green Lanterns lies 200 yards from the Mayflower Steps—about as close to the Pilgrim Fathers as you can get. Even to this day, it's a good restaurant. At lunchtime only, an extensive menu of reasonably priced dishes is served from £3 ($6.90).

In the evening (you can dine until 10:30 p.m.), the price of the main dish includes fresh vegetables of the day. Two well-recommended dishes are Harriett steak at £7.25 ($16.68), and trout at £6 ($13.80). All the desserts are served with Devonshire cream. Family owned, the Green Lanterns is run by Sally M. Russell and Kenneth Pappin, who are fully aware that voyaging strangers like the Elizabethan atmosphere, traditional English fare, and personal service. The restaurant is near the municipally owned Elizabethan House. It's licensed until 11:30 p.m. and closed Sunday. Reservations for dinner are advisable.

NORTH DEVON

"Lorna, Lorna . . . Lorna Doone, my lifelong darling," is the wailing cry you'll think of as you lie abed in your North Devon farmhouse. A wildness seems to enter the air at night on the edge of the moody Doone Valley. Much of the district is already known to those who have read Victorian novelist R. D. Blackmore's romance of the West Country, *Lorna Doone*.

The bay-studded coastline itself is mysterious. Pirates and smugglers used to find havens in crooked creeks and rocky coves. The ocean crashes against the rocks, and the meadows approach so close to the cliff's edge that you wonder why they don't go spilling into the sea, sheep and all. The heather-clad uplands of Exmoor, with its red deer, extend into North Devon from Somerset —a perfect setting for an English mystery thriller. Favorite bases are Clovelly and the twin resorts of Lynton and Lynmouth. Our first stopover is the best:

8. Clovelly

This most charming of all Devon villages is overpopular in summer. Still, it remains one of the main attractions of the West Country. Starting at a great height, the village cascades down the mountainside, with its narrow, cobblestoned High which makes travel by car impossible. (You park your car at the top and make the trip by foot.) Supplies are carried down by donkeys. Every yard of the way provides views of tiny cottages, with their terraces of flowers lining the main street. The village fleet is sheltered at the stone quay at the bottom.

To avoid the climb back up the slippery, cobblestoned incline, go to the rear of the Red Lion Inn and "queue up" for a Land Rover. In summer, the line is often long, but considering the alternative, it's worth the wait. Two Land Rovers make continuous round trips, costing 25p (58¢) per person.

WHERE TO STAY: A warning: It's hard to get a room in Clovelly. Advance reservations, with a deposit, are imperative during the peak summer months, although you can always telephone in advance and just possibly get a bed.

A tip: To avoid the flock of tourists, stay out of Clovelly from around 11 in the morning till teatime. After tea, settle in your room, and have dinner— perhaps spend the night in peace and contentment. The next morning after breakfast, you can walk around the village or go for a swim in the harbor, then visit the nearby villages during the middle of the day when the congestion sets in. Bideford, incidentally, is 11 miles away.

The **New Inn** (tel. Clovelly 303), about halfway down the High Street, is the village pub, a good meeting place at sundown. It offers the best lodgings in the village, in two buildings on opposite sides of the steep street (but only a 12-foot leap between their balconies). Bed-and-breakfast ranges from £9.50 ($21.85) to £10.50 ($24.15) per person, inclusive. If you're only stopping over, then this little country inn is recommended for meals. A wide choice of moderately priced à la carte meals is offered in the oak-beamed dining room. The local faire, including genuine Devonshire cream, is featured whenever possible. Locally caught lobsters are prepared by a skilled chef exactly as you want them. The hotel is open most of the year. Motorists can park in the car park or in the garage at the top of the street. It is advisable to pack an overnight case, as the luggage has to be carried down (but is returned to the top by donkey!).

Red Lion, The Pier (tel. Clovelly 237), may well have the best location in the village—at the bottom of the steep cobbled street, right on the stone seawall of the little harbor. Rising three stories, it is an unspoiled country inn, the life centering on an antique pub where the villagers gather to satisfy their thirsts over pints of ale. Most of the bedrooms look directly onto the sea. All have hot and cold running water and adequate furnishings. The cost is £8.50 ($19.55) per person nightly, including breakfast. Other meals are available in the seaview dining room. The manager can arrange for boating in the bay, and suggests that the Red Lion is not suitable for children under 7 years of age.

On the Outskirts

Foxdown Manor, Parkham (tel. Horns Cross 221), is only five miles from Bideford, six from Clovelly. In a setting of valleys and wooded hills just a mile from the sea, this splendid Victorian house is reached by a serpentine maze of narrow lanes. Its owners and proprietors, Bruce Ross and Belinda Luxmoore, have worked to restore the manor to its original state, with suitably modern conveniences added, of course. One bedroom has a four-poster bed dating from 1760. All of the rooms are equipped with private baths or showers.

The old stone stables adjoining the main house have been converted into fully equipped cottages with two to three bedrooms in each. After a good night's sleep, guests are free to wander the ten acres of fields and woodlands or to take advantage of the manor's many facilities, including a sauna, whirlpool bath, heated pool, solarium, indoor game room, and tennis court. Other activities, such as riding, golfing, and hunting are also available in the area.

The six-course dinner menu served in the Victorian candlelit dining room is a special treat prepared by Cordon Bleu chef Ms. Luxmoore. The vegetables are home-grown, and the dairy products are obtained from the manor's own Jersey cow. Rates per person for a bed, full English breakfast, and the six-course dinner are about £18 ($41.40) per day. Special weekly rates are available for the cottages or rooms as well.

Foxdown Manor makes a particularly good center for exploring North Devon—Clovelly, Exmoor, Dartmoor, the North Cornish coastline. If you don't feel like driving, then you can enjoy rambles and walks, as Devon has miles and miles of cool, shady primrose paths. All of a sudden you'll come across masses of wildflowers, and your spirit will soar.

Foxdown lies off the A39 road. Take the first left turn after Horns Cross village or the first right after Hoops Inn.

Beaconside, Monkleigh, near Bideford (tel. Bideford 77205), was built around 1860 and still retains its high ceilings and the large rooms typical of that era. Your hosts, Thea and Andrew Brand, have brought their own personal style and a dash of humor to the running of this place which they like to think of as typical of "visiting friends in the country." They offer only nine pleasantly furnished bedrooms, each with private bath or shower, plus color TV. The daily rate peaks at £28 ($64.40) per person, which includes an imaginatively prepared, four-course dinner often featuring beef Wellington and baked sea bass with fresh fennel. The place is secluded. When you're not using the swimming pool, you might select a volume from the massive collection of books, or perhaps you'll do no more than contemplate the view from the drawing room.

READER'S HOTEL SELECTION AT BIDEFORD: "The **Royal Hotel** (tel. Bideford 2005) was a pleasant surprise. We found the staff very helpful, and the meals excellent with large portions. Kingsley wrote *Westward Ho* here, and the staff will gladly show you the Kingley Room with many antiques and a beautiful Italian ceiling. A bathless single costs £13 ($29.90), increasing to £16 ($36.80) with bath. A double room without bath goes for £21 ($48.30), rising to £24 ($55.20) with bath. These tariffs include breakfast. A four-course dinner costs £6 ($13.80), and a three-course Sunday lunch goes for £3.50 ($8.05)." (Mrs. Robert Davison, Delta, B.C., Canada).

9. Lynton-Lynmouth

The north coast of Devon is set off most dramatically in Lynton, a village some 500 feet high. It is a good center for exploring the Doone Valley and that part of Exmoor that spills into the shire from neighboring Somerset. The Valley of Rocks, west of Lynton, offers the most spectacular scenery.

The town is joined by a cliff railway to its sister, Lynmouth, about 500 feet lower. The rivers of East and West Lyn meet in Lynmouth, a popular resort with the English. For a panoramic view of the rugged coastline, you can walk on a path halfway between the two towns that runs along the cliff. From Lynton itself—or rather from Hollerday Hill—you can look out onto Lynmouth Bay, Countisbury Foreland, even Woody Bays in the west.

FOOD AND LODGING: The **Tors Hotel** (tel. Lynton 3236), set high on a cliff, opens onto a view of the coastline and the bay of Lynmouth. It was built in the fashion of a Swiss château, with more than 40 gables, Tyrolean balconies jutting out to capture the sun (or the moon), black-and-white timbered wings, and some 30 chimneys. Surrounding the hotel are a terrace and a heated swimming pool. The interior has been modernized, and much attention has been paid to the comfortable bedrooms. A single without bath is £14 ($32.20), rising to £18 ($41.40) with bath. A bathless double costs £28 ($64.40), going up to £35 ($80.50) with bath, including breakfast and VAT. Don't expect to get a room with a view of the sea if you're stopping over for only one night. A three-course luncheon costs £6 ($13.80), and a set dinner is offered for £8 ($18.40). The hotel is closed from November to March.

The **Rising Sun Hotel** (tel. Lynton 3223) is perhaps one of the most colorful thatched inns in England—especially as it's right at the end of the quay at the mouth of the Lyn River. Not only is the harbor life spread before you, but you can bask in the wonder and warmth of an inn in business for more than 600 years. In bedroom after bedroom, with crazy levels and sloping ceilings, you'll have views of the water, the changing tides, and bobbing boats. The place is owned by a restaurateur and market consultant, Mr. Wade, and his partner, Mr. Jeune, who has horticultural interests. The inn is closed in January; otherwise, they make sure that either one or the other of them is there to supervise things. They charge from £10.50 ($24.15) per person for an overnight stay, including an English breakfast and VAT. Even if you're not staying over, you may want to sample the English cuisine: dinners from £6 ($13.80). It's a delight dining at the Rising Sun, as everything is 101% British in the dining room, with its deeply set window and fireplace. See the oringinal 14th-century fireplace in the bar.

Rock House, Lynmouth (tel. Lynton 3508), stands in the Manor Grounds between the Lyn River and the shore overlooking the Bristol Channel as well as Lynmouth Harbour. Run by Paddy and Paul Green, it is reached by a bridge and occupies one of the most dramatic positions in the village. The bedrooms, each with hot and cold running water and much homelike comfort, rent for £7.50 ($17.25) per person nightly, including breakfast, VAT, and service. Meals, served in a Regency dining room with its original ceiling moldings, cost about £3 ($6.90) per person for a three-course repast. Outside is a large, sheltered garden with parking available.

Ye Olde Cottage (Spinning Wheel Restaurant) (tel. Lynton 3297) is a miniature, quayside inn, centered in this tiny resort with an unspoiled view of the harbor. Here you can get inexpensive teas and meals. For five generations, the Wakeham family has been operating the inn. Chef Peter Wakeham and his wife Heather are always to be found at the place—either in the kitchen or in the dining room looking after their guests. Peter's mother and father are called in when things get hectic. It's a favored spot for a thoroughly English Devonshire cream tea, costing £1 ($2.30), with all the trimmings. At mealtime you can order a two- or three-course meal for from £3 ($6.90), based on such traditional English "fayre" as roast beef or West Country chicken and homemade pies and tarts. From the à la carte menu you can select such delights as rainbow trout, Lyn salmon, and a full range of steaks. Expect to pay from £4 ($9.20) to £7 ($16.10) for an à la carte dinner. Peter has also introduced a line of dishes cooked in wine and cider, to his own recipes. The restaurant is open daily from 10:30 a.m. to 9:30 p.m. from March to November.

READERS' HOTEL SELECTION: "The **Bonnicott Hotel,** on Watersmeet Road, is the former vicarage of Lynmouth's Anglican church. Resting slightly back and above the sea, the Bonnicott has a beautiful dining room with large picture windows providing a wonderful view of the water. Ten cozy rooms have an equally good sea view, and the downstairs bar, with an open-hearth fire, is well stocked. The owners, Pam and George, are a husband and wife who personally execute every detail of the running of the hotel. George gives most attentive service to his guests at breakfast, dinner, and at night when he tends the bar until whatever time his guests choose to retire. Pam, who prepares all the food for breakfast and dinner, is truly a gourmet cook. Each of the five four-course dinners we were served during our stay was English cuisine at its finest, and much of it was local to Devon. From the thick clotted cream which graced the fresh homemade berry pies to the stuffed brook trout pulled from the neighboring streams, each course was different and delicious on each of our five nights there. The service did not stop with fine food and spirits, however. Pam and George were available for our every need, providing invaluable information about the best hikes, best local shopping, and best of all, local color and history, including, of course, the real-life locations of the scenes from the novel *Lorna Doone.* The cost is £8.50 ($19.55) per person for bed and breakfast, £12 ($27.60) per person for half board" (Tom and Laura Groce, Austin, Texas).

10. Combe Martin

Noted for its strawberry fields and mild climate, Combe Martin is surrounded by magnificent scenery: high, rugged cliffs, wild moors, and rocky shorelines. Among the rocks are some of Britain's favorite beaches, and local boatmen can take you to spots, impossible to reach on foot, where the scenery is breathtaking. The village itself is small, with the High Street as its shopping district. An old English church built in the Perpendicular style of architecture is the main historical structure in the town. Just six miles from Ilfracombe, Combe Martin is an ideal base for excursions into Exmoor.

WHERE TO STAY: **Saffron House,** King Street (tel. Combe Martin 3521), is an old farmhouse successfully adapted into a popular small hotel. Just a short walk from the village harbor, the house is set back from the road where it overlooks the village and surrounding countryside. The owners, Mr. and Mrs.

Chantler, are sincerely interested in your comfort, and from the moment of your friendly reception, you know you're going to enjoy your stay. The guest rooms are clean and comfortable, with the benefit of full central heating. There are also two lounges, one with color TV, the other with a well-stocked bar. Bed-and-breakfast rates are about £7 ($16.10) per person per night, including VAT. The Chantlers are only too happy to point out local areas of interest, and, if they aren't too busy, they may just accompany you on a walk through the cliff paths.

CORNWALL

The ancient Duchy of Cornwall is the extreme southwestern part of England—often called "the toe." But Cornwall is one toe that's always wanted to dance away from the foot. Although a peninsula, it is a virtual island—if not geographically, then spiritually. Encircled by coastline, it abounds with rugged cliffs, hidden bays, fishing villages, sandy beaches, and sheltered coves where smuggling was once practiced with consummate skill. Many of the little seaports with their hillside-clinging cottages resemble towns along the Mediterranean, although Cornwall retains its own distinctive flavor.

The Cornish people—except those who've married up with the "blasted foreigner" (the English)—are generally darker and shorter than the English. Their Celtic origin still lives on in superstition, folklore, and fairy tales. King Arthur, of course, is the most vital legend of all. When Cornish men speak of King Arthur and his Knights of the Round Table, they're not just handing out a line to tourists. To them, Arthur and his knights really existed, romping around Tintagel Castle, now in ruins—Norman ruins, that is—lying 300 feet above the sea, 19 miles from Bude.

The ancient land had its own language up until about 250 years ago, and some of the old words ("pol" for pool, "tre" for house) still survive. The Cornish dialect is more easily understood by the Welsh than by those who speak the Queen's English.

The Cornish men, like the Welsh, are great miners (tin and copper), and they're fond of the tall tale. Sometimes it's difficult to tell when they're serious. One resident, for example, told us that he and his wife had been walking in the woods at twilight, but had lost their way. He claimed that the former owner of the estate (in Victoria's day) appeared suddenly in a dog-carriage and guided them back to where they'd taken the wrong turn. If this really had happened, we wouldn't be surprised—at least not in Cornwall.

The English come here for their holidays in the sun. But some of the places where everybody goes, we'd recommend that you avoid. For example, there's little point in going to Land's End, the westernmost tip of England—a narrowing hunk of bleakness and crude cottages set up to peddle ice cream and souvenirs.

In lieu of such a trip, we'd suggest berthing at one of the smaller fishing villages, such as East and West Looe, Polperro, Mousehole, or Portloe—where you'll experience the true charm of the duchy. Many of the villages, such as St. Ives, have now become artists' colonies. In some of the pubs and restaurants frequented by painters, a camaraderie prevails, especially in the nontourist months. Recently, for instance, at one of the artists' hangouts (bleached wooden tables, handmade stools), three young men who had finished dining brought out guitars and spontaneously launched into folk songs for the rest of the evening. Detecting the accent of some visiting Americans, they sang (with appallingly perfect accents) several country music favorites—although it was their repertoire from Ireland and Wales that cast the greater spell.

Except for St. Ives and Port Isaac, most of our recommendations lie on the southern coast—the so-called Cornish Riviera, which strikes many foreign visitors as being the most intriguing. However, the north coast has its own peculiar charm.

A SIDE TRIP TO LIZARD: The most southerly point of England is the Lizard, an unremarkable spot with jagged rocks reaching out into the sea where cormorants and gulls fish. Down beneath the cliff, the lifeboat station is the end of the road. The boat is still launched down a ramp into the swirling sea at the one point where it is possible to sail between the rocks.

Right on the point, beneath the lighthouse, is the workshop of a man who must surely be one of the most perfect one-man cottage industries in the country. Mr. Casley runs **Lizard Point Serpentine Works** in one of the small shacks by the car park. There he turns, polishes, and fashions into pots, vases, ashtrays, and dishes, the serpentine stone found only in this part of the country. The veins in the stone can be green, gray, or sometimes red. A small vase will cost about £3 ($6.90); a larger one, £5 ($11.50).

Ornamental barometers and clocks are a lot more, but these are absolutely genuine souvenirs made by a man who is entirely at peace with himself and the country he lives in. The family, his son, and his brother assist with the quarrying of the stone which comes from under Coonhilly Down close by, the site of the country's largest radio receiving and space-tracking station. Mr. Casley's son, another blue-eyed Cornishman, is fast learning the trade so there is every hope that still in 50 years there will be someone whistling happily in the tiny workshop on the tip of the Lizard.

POLDARK MINING CO. LTD.: Wendron Forge (tel. Helston 3173), stands three miles north of Helston on the B3297 road. As you have driven around Cornwall, the old workings of the tin mines will have been evident everywhere. Here you have the chance of visiting a mine and walking through the old workings which extend for several miles beneath the surface. They have just discovered yet another cavern, and the tour of the mine will soon take longer than the present three-quarters of an hour. Above ground is a museum of mining artifacts, mining equipment, steam engines, drills, and a history of mining. There is a souvenir shop and another selling good-quality local products, a snackbar, and a children's play area if they don't want to see the exhibits. Admission is £1.20 ($2.76) for adults, 70p ($1.61) for children. The mines are open seven days a week from 10 a.m. to 6 p.m.

TALL TREES RIDING CENTRE: At Davidstow, near Camelford (tel. Otterham Station 08406/249), Mrs. Margaret Harrison, with her two daughters and various other assistants and working pupils, runs stables of 23 horses and ponies. They offer weekly courses when days are spent on long rides over majestic Bodmin Moor, through forests, and along bridle paths and country lanes. Accommodation, including breakfast and supper, is £45 ($103.50) per week for adults, £40 ($92) for children, plus VAT. If you cannot spare the time for a week, a day's riding, including lunch, is £10 ($23) or £3 ($6.90) per hour.

11. Looe

After your visit to Plymouth, about 15 miles away, you can either take the Tamar Suspension Bridge to Cornwall, or else cross by ferry from Plymouth.

You'll soon arrive in the ancient twin towns of East and West Looe, connected by a seven-arched stone bridge which spans the river. In the jaws of shrub-dotted cliffs, the fishing villages present a stark contrast to Plymouth. Houses scale the hills, stacked one on top of the other in terrace fashion.

In both fishing villages you can find good accommodations and interesting people. Fishing and sailing are two of the major sports, and the sandy coves, as well as East Looe Beach, make choice spots for seabathing. Beyond the towns are cliff paths and downs worth a ramble. In these villages you'll find varied lifestyles: the traditional Cornish fishermen landing pilchard; the sophisticates enjoying the unspoiled atmosphere; summer tourists down for a week or so; and the artists and artisans who live and work here.

Looe is noted for its shark-angling, but you may prefer simply walking the narrow, crooked medieval streets of East Looe, with its old harbor and 17th-century guildhall.

WHERE TO STAY: Space and prices are at a premium in July and August. Some hotels are so heavily booked that they can demand Saturday-to-Saturday clients only. We've not recommended such establishments, as we feel that their managers aren't interested in patronage by international visitors.

Hannafore Point Hotel, West Looe (tel. Looe 3273), is a rambling, many-gabled structure commanding an advantageous view of the harbor, overlooking miles of Cornish coastline and one of the most beautiful bays in Cornwall. In addition to the older bay-windowed chambers, newer sections of the hotel have been built with walls of glass for viewing the harbor and St. George's Island. The entrance opens onto several levels of comfortable lounges and bars, with cantilevered stairs, balconies, and birch paneling. The modern bedrooms all include either private baths or showers, and most of the front rooms have their own balconies. Bed-and-breakfast rates vary depending on the view, location of the room and the time of year. From May to October, a single or double room rents for about £24 ($55.20) per day. The panoramic view adds to the pleasure of dining in the St. George's Restaurant, where fresh, first-class ingredients are used in the fine Cornish cuisine.

Hannafore Point is situated in the main center for shark and deep-sea fishing, and is ideal for exploring either Cornwall or Devon.

The **Boscarn Hotel,** The Quay, East Looe (tel. Looe 2923). This 26-room hotel lies along a ledge, between high cliffs and beach; it's reached by walking or driving through the crooked, narrow streets of East Looe. Built more than half a century ago, it has been thoroughly modernized inside. The lounges have tall French doors opening onto a grassy terrace, adjoining the sea wall. The bedrooms have good views, soft beds, and hot and cold running water. There are enough corridor baths and toilets to prevent line-ups. Bed-and-breakfast single rates are from £10.50 ($24.15) per night. In a double with bath, the charge is £22 ($50.60). A 10% service charge, plus VAT, is added. There is one drinking lounge, a Tudor bar, with beams and natural brick walls combined with paneling. There is no restaurant, although you can order bar snacks. A good recommendation, the Boscarn is open all year.

Klymiarven Hotel, Barbican Hill, in East Looe (tel. Looe 2333), is a 180-year-old manor house, standing in its own wooded and terraced gardens above the harbor. The cellars are even older, and it is believed that smugglers made use of their dank, underground passages. The hotel is small, containing only eight bedrooms in the older part of the house plus six modern accommodations, each with a private bath and balcony. The rooms are comfortable and well appointed, costing from £10 ($23) to £13 ($29.90) per person for a bathless double or single, from £12 ($27.60) to £18 ($41.40) for a double with shower or bath. Prices include VAT and a full English breakfast. The immaculately kept house is owned by its resident proprietors Bruce and Daphne Henderson, who are known locally for their good food, served in a Regency dining room. Hot and cold bar lunches are available, served around the attractive swimming pool, weather permitting. A set dinner costs £7 ($16.10), but you get better value if you ask for demi-pension terms, when the inclusive dinner costs approximately £5 ($11.50). Guests gather in the hotel's attractively furnished lounge with French windows opening onto the garden. In addition, the hotel has a sun lounge bar and terrace, plus a second bar in the cellar houses.

The **Smugglers House,** Middle Market, near the old Guildhall (tel. Looe 2397), built in the 15th and 17th centuries, was once the headquarters of smugglers. The hotel is tucked away right in the center of the village, a few minutes' walk from the quay, the seafront, and the shops. The hotel has an original Cornish granite fireplace, and the beams in the restaurant and bar are believed to be from the ships of the Spanish Armada. There is reputed to be a tunnel in the restaurant which was used by the ancient smugglers, but attempts to find the entrance have been unsuccessful. Rooms without bath rent for £10 ($23) per person nightly, increasing to £12.50 ($28.75) per person with private bath, plus VAT. The breakfasts are super, with bacon, eggs, sausage, and tomato, all the trimmings. Your room will be immaculate, and the beds will be fresh and soft. There is also a Dungeon Restaurant (open to both residents and nonresidents), an authentic smugglers' haunt, known for its fresh English steaks and a large choice of food and wine.

The **Fisherman's Arms,** Higher Market Street (tel. Looe 2215), the main street in East Looe, is housed in a building dating from 1611. It is about 70 yards from the beach. Mr. and Mrs. Cobbing provide an array of sandwiches and locally caught crabs and shellfish. The average price for a "cutting" is from 75p ($1.73) to £1 ($2.30). The decor is provided by antique guns, spears, brass, and copper. Bed and breakfast are available from £6 ($13.80) nightly. Only double rooms are offered.

If you wish, you can strike out from Looe on the cliff walk—a distance of 4½ miles—to Polperro. The less adventurous will drive.

WHERE TO STAY AND EAT OUTSIDE LOOE: Just three miles north of East Looe on Route B3254 is the quiet country village of **Duloe,** a perfect spot for a drowsy holiday or an ideal center from which to explore Cornwall and parts of Devon. Nearby is the complete seclusion of the Bodmin Moor, while the cliffs and fishing villages of the south coast are just a short drive away. Half a mile south of the village on the road to Looe is the **Duloe Manor Hotel,** Duloe, near Liskeard (tel. Looe 2795) a lovely old Cornish house dating from around 1700. The owners, Mr. and Mrs. Hayter, like to refer to the hotel as having a "visiting friends in the country" kind of atmosphere. Indeed, the house is rich in character and warmth, from the tastefully decorated bedrooms and sitting rooms to the Victorian lounge with its carved mahogany bar and open fireplace. Guests are welcome to wander the nine acres of grounds surrounding the hotel or stroll through the 250-year-old lime tree avenue. A tennis court and heated swimming pool round out the list of amenities.

The dining room, once the kitchen of the old house, retains the cozy character of the former room with the old meat hooks and the open-hearth fireplace. Here five-course table d'hôte dinners are served daily, all prepared almost entirely from local produce. Rates at the Duloe Manor for dinner, bed, and breakfast range from £20.54 ($47.24) per person for rooms without private bath to £23.70 ($54.51) for rooms with bath. Prices include service charges and VAT.

Shutta, Stoke Climsland, near Callington (tel. Stoke Climsland 389), is a bed-and-breakfast place par excellence. Peter and Joan Davis welcome guests to their lovely 16th-century home where breakfast is served in the ancient beamed cider house of the old structure. They only have two rooms, one with two beds, the other a large double bed. Both have private bathrooms and television. They charge £7 ($16.10) per person for bed and a massive breakfast. To get there, drive on the A388 from Callington toward Bodmin Moor and, at the Swingle Tree, bear right toward Stoke Climsland. Shutta is on the right.

12. Polperro

This ancient fishing village is reached by a steep descent from the top of a hill. Motorists in summer are forbidden to take their cars down unless they are booked in a hotel. Why? Because otherwise they'd create too much of a traffic bottleneck in July and August. At one time, it was estimated that nearly every man, woman, and child in the village spent time salting down pilchards for the winter, or smuggling. Today, tourists have replaced the contraband.

You'd have to search every cove and bay in Cornwall to turn up with a village as handsome as Polperro, which looks almost as if it had been removed intact from the 17th century. The village is tucked in between some cliffs. Its houses—really no more than fishermen's cottages—are bathed in pastel-wash. A small river—actually a stream called the Pol—cuts its way through Polperro. The heart of the village is its much photographed, much painted fishing harbor, where the pilchard boats, loaded to the gunnels, used to dock.

WHERE TO STAY: Noughts and Crosses Hotel (tel. Polperro 239). One side of this 16th-century pub-hotel faces a narrow street, and the other a five-foot-wide "river" which goes through the center of the village. The Noughts and Crosses charges £8 ($18.40) per person nightly for bed and breakfast. Children are not accepted, and booking in season must be for at least three nights. Its name came from the bookkeeping habits of a baker, its one-time owner. She made a small "o" whenever she sold a small loaf of bread and a large "O" when she sold a large loaf. When the loaves were paid for, she would cross them off with an "X." The hotel has windows opening by the Pol. You may remember the crooked stairway, the time-aged beams. The quite-good bedrooms are pleasingly furnished, with hot and cold running water and beds with inner-spring mattresses. Basket meals, snacks, and chilled beer are served in the two well-equipped bars. Steaks go for £4.50 ($10.35); scampi in a basket, £3 ($6.90); and fried chicken, £2 ($4.60)—all dishes served with fried potatoes. There is a dining room upstairs in which residents of the hotel can eat their bar snacks.

WHERE TO EAT: The **Captain's Cabin,** Lansallos Street (tel. Polperro 72292), is owned by Victor S. Moore, his wife Hazel, and their son Anthony. They are pleased when Americans come by. While they don't have bedrooms for overnight guests, they have been known to give travelers tips about where to find a room. You'll surely want to dine with the Moores, among the antique furniture in their low-beamed dining room. The cuisine is very comprehensive, and Mr. Moore and his son enjoy a fine reputation for their fish dishes, from among which you may order crab mornay, £5 ($11.50); trout à la Bretonne, £4.75 ($10.93); grilled sole, £4.75 also; plus many other choices. The Moores have a table d'hôte lunch also, at £4.50 ($10.35), and a choice of six delicious snack lunches, which include a glass of beer, tea, or coffee, for £2.25 ($5.18). For dinner there is also a four-course table d'hôte menu for £7.25 ($16.68), as well as a full à la carte menu.

The **Pengelly**, near the harbor, is where locals and visitors go for their evening pints of beer and social activity; it is a large L-shaped room with a fireplace that burns brightly at night. Why don't you sit in the window seat, and listen to the talk of the villagers? That isn't really as rude as it sounds—since you probably won't be able to understand a word of their thick Cornish dialect. You may like the absence of quaint bits of decor in this honest pub, the center of life in Polperro.

WHERE TO STAY AND EAT ON THE OUTSKIRTS: If you find the busy activity of the two little harbors of Looe and Polperro too much for you, then you can live in far greater style at two of England's outstanding inns, just outside. **Pelynt,** about three miles north of Polperro, is a small, sleepy village; and **Lanreath,** lying off the road to West Looe, is another peaceful, pleasant community.

The **Jubilee Inn,** Pelynt (tel. Lanreath 312), was restored as part of a scheme to honor Queen Victoria's Jubilee, by using only the best handmade Victorian furnishings, even in the bedrooms. Today, the rate for a handsomely decorated room and big English breakfast is £14 ($32.20) per person without bath. A room with bath is £1 ($2.30) per person extra. These tariffs include breakfast, although VAT and service are extra. The food is good, with the vegetables coming fresh from the inn's own garden. The inn is a comment on, rather than monument to the past. The lounge has a hooded fireplace, with a raised hearth, Windsor armchairs, antique porcelain, and copper bowls filled with flowers cut from the garden behind the building. The dining room is elegantly Victorian, with mahogany chairs and tables. The only sound you hear is the rustling of the starched aprons of the maids. A fairly sophisticated crowd of people come here to eat and drink at the public bar. A circular, glass-enclosed staircase takes you to the bedrooms. Fitting onto the outside, the winding stairway has been built to serve as a combined tower and hothouse. The stone steps are covered with carpeting, and vines and plants grow happily in the sunlight streaming in through the glass walls.

The **Punch Bowl Inn,** at Lanreath (tel. Lanreath 218), has had a checkered past, serving in turn as a courthouse, coaching inn, and rendezvous for smugglers. Now its old fireplaces and high-backed settles, and its bedrooms with their four-posters, provide hospitality to travelers from abroad, as well as to the discriminating English. For stays of only one night, the bed-and-breakfast rate in high season, June through September, is £13.70 ($31.51) per person. A much better course is to take the partial board rate of £18.05 ($41.52) per person, inclusive. Even if you're only stopping over, you may want to sample the fare or drinks in one of the kitchens (really bars, among the few "kitchens" licensed in Britain as "bars"). In the Stable Restaurant, with its Tudor beams and fireplace, you'll be served delicious lunches from the grill menu, dinner from £6.30 ($14.49). There is a modern lounge, TV room, air-conditioned cocktail bar, and an additional bedroom wing. Many rooms have their own private bathrooms. Advance bookings of less than three nights are not accepted during the high season.

13. Fowey

Called the Dartmouth of Cornwall, Fowey is a town of historical interest (one of the most ancient seaports in the West Country). Once the Fowey Gallants sailed the seas and were considered invincible when raiding French coastal towns. However, occasional retaliation was inevitable. At the time of the Armada, Fowey sent more ships than London. With its narrow streets and whitewashed houses, it has remained unspoiled over the years, enjoying a sheltered position on a deep-water channel. Its creeks and estuary attract sailors and fishermen. If you climb to St. Catherine's Point, you'll be rewarded with a view of the harbor. Sandy beaches and coves are there to explore as well (there's also an 18-hole golf course within easy reach of Carlyon Bay).

WHERE TO STAY: Riverside, Passage Street (tel. Fowey 2275), is the all-purpose ferry-landing hotel of Fowey. Directly on the water, the hotel is at the little car-ferry station where regular crossings leave for Bodinnick. Paintings by Mrs. Featherstone, wife of the owner, decorate the walls of the hotel, and glass and china ornaments, as well as potted plants, make the place extremely warm and inviting. The 14 bedrooms are handsomely decorated in a bright, cozy, comfortable manner. Three have private bath or shower, although all have hot and cold running water. From the rooms there are views of the river, where a variety of scenery is created by the passing river craft and ferries. Rates are based on the time of the year and the view. Bed and a full English breakfast costs from £11 ($25.30) to £13 ($29.90) per person daily, plus VAT and service. Demi-pension ranges from £17 ($39.10) to £19 ($43.70) per person, the latter including private bath. The chef specializes in hot and cold salmon and lobster dishes; the produce bought locally is fresh and delicious. The hotel also offers an excellent wine list with a comprehensive choice of both English and continental wines. The menu is changed daily to ensure that variety is a key factor. If you're visiting just for dinner, the set meal goes for £8 ($18.40).

14. Truro

This ancient town on the Truro River is the only cathedral city in Cornwall. As such, it is the ecclesiastical center of Cornwall. The cathedral church of St. Mary was begun in 1880 in the Early English style (the spires are in the Norman Gothic design). The town is within 8 to 20 miles of the famed Cornish beaches. It can be used as a base to explore the countryside, which ranges from bleak Bodmin Moor to fertile farmland and the Winter Roseland of the Falmouth Estuary.

WHERE TO STAY: Pencowl Guest House, 12 Ferris Town (tel. Truro 4946), is a centrally positioned corner guest house owned by the Endacotts, who take the business of entertaining overseas guests in their home very seriously. The Endacotts charge from £6.25 ($14.36) to £7.50 ($17.25) nightly per person, including VAT. The 15 guest rooms have hot and cold running water and central heating, and all are pleasantly decorated. To keep costs trimmed, guests are accepted on a "room only" basis—that is, rooms are rented and cleaned daily, and you're supplied with an electric kettle and fresh tea or coffee. Those requiring a continental breakfast will be provided with one the evening before. However, if you want a cooked breakfast, the dining rooms open at 8 a.m., except on weekends. The cozy bar is open to all residents and friends. Free golf at the Truro Golf Club is available to all guests. Mrs. Endacott is a member of the local Family History Society, and will be happy to direct those seeking out their Cornish Family history to the nearby County Record Office and the museum.

15. Portloe

If you really want to get away from it all and go to that truly hidden-away Cornish fishing village, then Portloe is for you. On the slope of a hill, opening onto Veryan Bay, it is reached by a road suitable for cars—but chances are you may get sidetracked and spend the rest of the afternoon on byways, opening and closing gates to keep the cattle from straying.

Portloe is an ideal stopover on the south Cornish coast if you're traveling in July and August, when the popular tourist centers, such as Looe and St. Ives, are overrun with sightseers.

WHERE TO STAY: The **Lugger**, Portloe (tel. Veryan 322), is a prestigious inn, yet the narrow lane that leads the way to the establishment was obviously created by a goat. You'll find the inn fresh, sparkling clean—a good spot at the top of the harbor slip, with a bay and boats at hand. The whole picture—water dashing and pounding the nearby rocks, the sunsets, the beach, the stone walls, the crazy roofs of the houses of the fishermen—all requires that you take dozens of rolls of film with you . . . or none at all. The 17th-century establishment is managed by the Powell family. They'll put you up for from £28 ($64.40) to £32 ($73.60) per person per night for bed, an English breakfast, and a four-course dinner. The charge for an excellent bar lunch will average around £5 ($11.50). All prices are inclusive of tax. The inn, open late February to early November, is believed to have been a smugglers' hideaway, on the coast between St. Austell and St. Mawes. Guests at the Lugger can also dine at the Idle Rocks Hotel at St. Mawes, just eight miles away, on a reciprocal arrangement.

The **Rising Sun** (tel. St. Mawes 233) is a colorful inn on the seafront—made of a row of white fishermen's cottages, with a slate roof, and a flagstone terrace out front. Inside, every square inch oozes with tasteful charm. The locals gather in the pub, with its Windsor chairs grouped around the fireplace. The dining room has lush gold walls with paintings by Michael Oelman in the form of two poems, *Kubla Khan* and *Jacob's Ladder*. English gentility reigns here. The proprietor, Mrs. Campbell Marshall, sets the gracious pace, and is known for her cuisine. You can stay here for anywhere from £24 ($55.20) to £28 ($64.40) per person in rooms with bath, including an English breakfast, service, and VAT. Lunch and dinner are both à la carte, and you can expect to pay from £10.50 ($24.15), with wine extra. The dining room has become very popular, with its changing menu of imaginative dishes using local produce whenever possible. We'd particularly recommend the prawn, cheese, and cucumber mousse. Lunch is from 1 to 1:45 p.m., dinner from 7:30 to 8:45 p.m. Closed November and December.

16. St. Mawes

Overlooking the mouth of the Fal River, St. Mawes is often compared to a port on the Riviera. Because it's sheltered from northern winds, subtropical plants grow here. From the town quay, you can take a boat to Frenchman's Creek, Helford River, and other places. St. Mawes is noted for its sailing, boating, fishing, and yachting. Half a dozen sandy coves lie within 15 minutes by car from the port. The town itself, built on the Roseland Peninsula, makes for interesting walks, with its color-washed cottages and sheltered harbor. On

Castle Point, Henry VIII ordered the construction of St. Mawes Castle. Falmouth, across the water, is only two miles away.

WHERE TO STAY: Tresanton (tel. St. Mawes 544), is a member of the famous Relais de Campagne. It is really three buildings, the oldest one dating from the 18th century. One is on the roadside, another halfway up, and the third—the main part of the hotel—on top of the hill and away from the traffic noise. In the middle is an attractive cocktail lounge, with a veranda overlooking the sea. The upper level also has spacious veranda terraces—so there are a lot of places to sit outside among the flowers, looking across the bay. The bedrooms are nice and bright, furnished for the most part in the French country-house manner. In high season, May through October, singles range from £24.50 ($56.35) to £27 ($62.10), doubles or twins from £27 ($62.10) per person. The latter have private baths en suite. All the accommodations face the sea. Service and VAT are extra. The lounge has an open fireplace and comfortable chairs. The dining room, also overlooking the sea, has attractive murals and a verdant decor that is designed to carry the eye from the house to the sun terraces, the subtropical gardens, and the sea beyond. The menu is limited but good, including such dishes as caneton (duckling) à l'orange and grilled Dover sole.

The **Idle Rocks** (tel. St. Mawes 771), proudly stands on a terrace above St. Mawes Harbor, commanding views of the open sea and the mouth of the River Fal. The building itself is a bit of old Cornwall, with its mansard roof and white stucco walls. Diners at the excellent restaurant can view the sea from any table as they enjoy a blend of English and continental cuisine. The cocktail bar opens onto the 145-foot promenade where you may sip an aperitif while you take in the warm and sparkling scene.

The hotel has a total of 22 guest rooms, 15 in the main building and the remaining 7 in the annex, 50 yards away. All have private baths, and both buildings offer the comfort of central heating. Daily rates per person range from £28 ($64.40) for a double or single in the annex to £32 ($73.60) for a double in the main building overlooking the sea. Rates include bed, full English breakfast, morning and afternoon teas, and the table d'hôte dinner, as well as tax. For an evening out at no extra cost, guests at the Idle Rocks can dine at the Lugger Hotel at Portloe, just eight miles away, on a reciprocal agreement.

Braganza, Grove Hill (opposite the Catholic church), St. Mawes (tel. St. Mawes 281), is a Regency house, furnished with antiques and furniture of the period. It offers six twin-bedded rooms, three of which have private baths. All are centrally heated. Visitors gather in the lounge to watch television. The staircase is a perfect Regency one. The charge is £9.50 ($21.85) per person per night for rooms with a private bathroom, £8.50 ($19.55) per night without bath. These tariffs include an English breakfast which can be served in your room at no extra cost. The house has an extensive garden overlooking the harbor of St. Mawes where the racing of yachts takes place each Sunday and Thursday in season. Lord Byron, who stayed in Falmouth in 1809, may have visited this house, for he mentions its name in one of his poems. It's said that his limping step can be heard at Braganza.

17. Falmouth

A lot of cutthroat ship wreckers used to live in the area. In fact, when John Killigrew, a leading citizen, started to build a lighthouse on Lizard Head, they protested that the beacon in the night would deprive them of their livelihood and "take awaye God's Grace from us." Falmouth, 26 miles from Penzance, is today a favorite base for yachtsmen, who consider it one of the most beautiful harbors in Europe. On a small peninsula, Falmouth's old section overlooks the land-locked inner harbor. The newer part, center for most of the hotels, faces the bay and commands a panorama from St. Anthony's Lighthouse to Pendennis Castle. Warmed in winter by the Gulf Stream, Falmouth has become a year-round resort. Built on a promontory overlooking the estuary of the Fal, it was once occupied in part by the captains of old mail-carrying packet ships. Many find it a good center for touring the rugged Cornish coastline. It's possible, for example, to take a ferry from Falmouth to St. Mawes, a 20-minute ride.

WHERE TO STAY: **Green Bank Hotel,** Green Bank (tel. Falmouth 312-440), hangs tenaciously to the old days of the Post Office Packet Services (1688–1850). Beside the shore road, this medium-priced hotel overlooks the water with its own landing pier. Over the years, it has been expanded, but it remains traditional in every sense. The spacious lounges have views of the harbor, and the rooms are comfortably furnished. The bed-and-breakfast rate ranges from £22 ($50.60) to £26 ($59.80) in a single, from £34 ($78.20) to £40 ($92) in a double, including VAT and service. Inclusive terms are quoted for stays of three days or more. Even if you don't stay here, consider an old-fashioned English meal in the water-view dining room favored by local yachting people. Set lunches go for £4 ($9.20), dinners for £7 ($16.10).

Rosemullion, Gyllyngvase Hill (tel. Falmouth 311-019), is owned and run by Terrance and Jeanette Chambers. The private hotel stands just 200 yards from the main beach, close to the Princess Pavilion and tennis courts, lying in a favored residential area at the top of Gyllyngvase Hill. All of its 16 bedrooms are well maintained, with hot and cold running water, bedside lights, and attractive furnishings. A more modern wing has been added, with rooms opening directly onto the garden. Many baths and toilets are to be found near the bedrooms (about one to every three accommodations). Weekly terms range from £70 ($161) to £75 ($172.50) per person, including dinner, room, and breakfast. There are two lounges, one with TV.

The **Tudor Court,** Melville Road (tel. Falmouth 312-807), once part of the local manor house, is within 200 yards of the sea and offers a variety of rooms, some with private bath and a view of the bay. The hotel has a licensed bar and a comfortable lounge with color TV. All meals are prepared and cooked on the premises by the resident proprietress, Mrs. Edna Jefferys. Fresh local produce is used whenever possible. The court is open throughout the year, including Christmas. Higher rates are charged from June to the end of August, when bed, breakfast, and an evening meal cost £11 ($25.30) per person, plus VAT.

On the Outskirts

Budock Vean Hotel, Golf and Country Club, near Falmouth (tel. Mawnan Smith 250-288). Since this place lies a few miles from Falmouth, a cab will be sent to meet you at the railway station. Or else you can drive there yourself, among the pines and subtropical vegetation sloping sharply to the Helford River. You come to an old stone house with a stout front door and bright welcoming hall. There Peter, the porter, will grab your bags and hurry them to your room.

Afternoon tea is laid out on the polished table for you to help yourself; tea comes in large pots to be drunk in the depths of a chintzy armchair in the drawing room. Some bedrooms are in the old house, others in the new wing, and all have bathroom and toilet. A few units have magnificent views over the gardens and down to the distant river, and others overlook the private golf course.

The chef, John Trout, is a local man of great skill, and meals are a delicious selection of international and English dishes. Portions are large. Included in the cost of your room is the free use of the indoor, heated swimming pool. The glass walls roll back in summer to join it to the garden, and in winter an enormous log fire burns on the open grate for additional heating. The main attraction for many is the 18-hole golf course with greens fees of £2.50 ($5.75) a day, £12 ($27.60) a week. But for those who just want to walk, the gardens slope down to a private cove where sailboats lie at anchor and gulls wheel raucously above the water.

Peter Whiteside, a Canadian, owns and runs the place with the help of his son, Justin. Their boast is that a Whiteside is always on duty, and they certainly have an excellent staff to back up their efforts. Dinner, bed, and a full breakfast costs £25 ($57.50) per person, rising to £30 ($69) from mid-June until the end of September. VAT and service are extra. A buffet lunch of soup, cold meats, and a salad costs £3 ($6.90); a full lunch, £6 ($13.80).

18. Penzance

This little Gilbert and Sullivan harbor town is the end of the line for the Cornish Riviera Express. A full 280 miles southwest from London, it is noted for its equable climate (it's one of the first towns in England to blossom out with spring flowers), and summer throngs descend for fishing, sailing, and swimming. Overlooking Mount's Bay, Penzance is graced in places with subtropical plants, as well as palm trees.

The harbor is used to activity of one sort or another. *The Pirates of Penzance* were not entirely fictional. The town was raided by Barbary pirates, destroyed in part by Cromwell's troops, sacked and burnt by the Spaniards, and bombed by the Germans. In spite of its turbulent past, it offers tranquil resort living today.

The most westerly town in England, Penzance makes a good base for exploring Land's End, the Lizard Peninsula, St. Michael's Mount, the old fishing ports and artists' colonies of St. Ives, Newlyn, and Mousehole—even the Scilly Isles.

THE SIGHTS: St. Michael's Mount is reached at low tide by a causeway three miles east of Penzance. Rising about 250 feet from the sea, St. Michael's Mount is topped by a partially medieval, partially 17th-century castle. At high tide, the mount becomes an island, reached only by motor launch from Marazion. A Benedictine monastery, the gift of Edward the Confessor, stood on this spot in the 11th century. The castle, with its collections of armor and antique furniture, is open April to October on Monday, Tuesday, Wednesday, and Friday from 10:30 a.m. to 4:45 p.m. (November to March, on Monday, Wednesday, and Friday). It charges £1 ($2.30) for adults, 50p ($1.15) for children. There are conducted tours at 11 a.m. and noon, then at 2, 3, and 4 p.m., weather permitting. You can only go over when the causeway is dry. If you mistime it, they won't send a boat over to pick you up and rescue you from the island. There is, however, a tea garden and a cafe on the island, both of which are open in summer so you probably won't starve to death.

From Penzance, take bus 20, 21, or 22, then get off at Marazion, the town opposite St. Michael's Mount. To avoid disappointment, it is a good idea to telephone the office of St. Michael's Mount (tel. Marazion 710-507) to learn the state of the tides, especially during the winter months when a regular ferry service does not operate.

Craggy **Land's End** is where England comes to an end. Here you'll find the last of everything. Land's End, lying nine miles west of Penzance, is reached by bus 1 or 1B.

The **Minack Theater** in Porthcurno, nine miles from Penzance, is unique. It's carved out of the Cornish cliff-face with the Atlantic as its impressive backdrop. In tiered seating, similar to that of the theaters of Ancient Greece, 550 persons can watch the show and the rocky coast beyond the stage. The theater is generally open to visitors who come sometimes just for sightseeing, although you may want to attend an evening performance. To reach Minack, leave Penzance on the A30 heading toward Land's End. After three miles, bear left onto the B3283 and follow the signposts to Porthcurno. Or you can take buses 4 or 4A from Penzance. For details, telephone St. Buryan 471 during the season, lasting from the end of June to mid-September. Seats cost around £1.40 ($3.22) at the box office.

WHERE TO STAY: Back in Penzance, it is time to find a room.

The **Abbey Hotel**, Abbey Street (tel. Penzance 66620), is a well-preserved old place that is frequented by discerning guests. The bonus is its situation (on a narrow sidestreet, on several terraces, directly overlooking Penzance Harbor) and its budget prices. You can stay at the Abbey, having only your room and breakfast, or all of your meals in the restaurant downstairs (see dining recommendations below). The bed-and-breakfast rate per person averages around £12 ($27.60), plus VAT. Some of the larger and better appointed rooms may run higher. Behind the hotel is a tiny formal garden on two tiers, each with a view of the water. Here the herbs are grown that are used to spice the delicately flavored meats in the restaurant downstairs. The owners, the Cox family, have brought their vitality, style and charm into the hotel business.

Richmond Lodge, 61 Morrab Rd. (tel. Penzance 5560), is a small guest house just a short stroll from the Promenade. The new owners, Jean and Pat Eady, maintain the seven cheerful guest rooms, where you can stay on the bed-and-breakfast plan for £38 ($87.40) per week. Evening meals, served in the Delft blue and white dining room, cost an additional £3.50 ($8.05) per dinner.

READER'S HOTEL SELECTION: "The **Georgian House,** Chapel Street (tel. Penzance 5664), once the home of the mayors of Penzance, has been completely renovated into a cozy, intimate hotel. The proprietors, Derek and Brenda Gibbard, with their friendly manner made us feel right at home and attended to all our needs promptly and cheerfully. The relaxed atmosphere of the dining room with its sea motif goes well with the excellent Cornish menu. The hotel is centrally heated and carpeted throughout. Our room was newly furnished, well-lighted, and had a full bath. The rate in a room without a private bath is £8 ($18.40) per night, rising to £10 ($23) with bath, plus VAT. The location is a plus in that it is directly across the street from the Admiral Benbow Restaurant, and only two blocks from the town center in one direction and the harbor and Promenade in the other" (Ben N. Cox, Wabash, Ind.).

WHERE TO EAT: The **Abbey Restaurant,** Abbey Street (tel. Penzance 66620), is an ancient structure, totally unspoiled and unaltered for so many years—a restful place, almost hidden away. When you dine here, you may find that you've been admitted to the inner circle of those who know where the best food is in Penzance. The dining room takes you back several centuries. There is a bevy of women cooks who can be seen in the kitchen across the entrance hall, and their skill is revealed in the spicing of their soups, the lightness of their apple pies. A table d'hôte luncheon with three healthy-size courses costs only £3.50 ($8.05), and evening dinner goes for as little as £6 ($13.80). All prices are subject to VAT. There is a quiet atmosphere during dinner hours.

Le Tarot, 19 Quay St. (tel. Penzance 3118), brings sophistication and intimate ambience with flair to the cuisine offered in Penzance. Classic French dishes and local specialties are prepared by expert chefs under the watchful eye of the proprietors, Jolyon and Priscilla Ward, who have spent many years in different countries gathering new dishes and catering for a discerning clientele of varied tastes. Each dish is cooked to order, so plan a leisurely meal. Most main dishes cost from £4.45 ($10.24), including vegetables or salad. Count on paying £8 ($18.40) to £10 ($23) per person, plus wine. Featured are such specialties as crayfish cooked in white wine sauce with brandy, or Cornish scallops, a local delicacy. Other special dishes include frog legs poached in champagne, a brace of quail cooked in wine, saddle of venison marinated in red wine and served with sauce cassis, and many others. The wine list contains a choice of 50 different kinds, carefully selected. The restaurant is open every day for lunch, except Wednesday (open seven days a week during July and August). A Carvery serves a two-course meal for £4 ($9.20) (wine extra) and is open for lunch and dinner.

The **Admiral Benbow,** Chapel Street (tel. Penzance 3448), is a restaurant-cum-museum dedicated to the sea, that has to be experienced to be believed. What started out as a simple two-story timbered inn has grown into a showcase of nautical objects. Open every day of the week for morning coffee, lunch, and dinner, it serves meals on the lower floor with its nooks and crannies, benches and booths. On the upper level there's a lounge bar (you wait here for a table if Admiral Benbow can't take any more on board downstairs). If you prefer to eat in the bar, a hot and cold buffet luncheon is served, where for £2 ($4.60) you may choose from a wide selection of cold meats, pâtés, and quiches, all served with fresh salad. The inn is owned by Roland Morris, a professional diver who has been discovering treasures for years on old wrecks around Cornwall and the Scilly Isles.

When you get a table, consult the "Tavern Vittals Chart and Grog Log," the latter studded with everything from fine French bottled clarets to Hungarian Bull's Blood. You'll find the Cornish crab soup priced at £1 ($2.30). Among the principal à la carte selections are chicken Kiev at £3.55 ($8.17), fresh rainbow trout at £4 ($9.20), and entrecôte Tyrolienne at £4.20 ($9.66). For dessert try one of the old English standbys, such as home-cooked fruit tart for 90p ($2.07), although an order of Cornish cream would make it sparkle.

Attached to the inn is a nightclub, open from 9 p.m. till 1 a.m. It charges half price admission to the patrons of the restaurant.

On the Outskirts

Lesceave Cliff Hotel, Praa Sands, near Penzance (tel. Germoe 2325), is reached down a tiny lane, well marked off the A394 from Helston to Penzance. You drive down between high banks with nary a view of anything until you suddenly emerge with the spread of Praa Sands lying below you. The hotel owns much of the land between it and the sea, and the uninterrupted views are magnificent. A typical seaside hotel with much white paint, chintzy chairs, and bright furnishings, it charges from £11 ($25.30) per person for room and breakfast, including VAT. The whole of the Cornish peninsula is close at hand.

19. The Scilly Isles

Perhaps the most important and scenic excursion from Penzance is a day trip to the Scilly Isles, lying off the Cornish coast, about 27 miles southwest of Land's End. The granite isles are noted for their sandy beaches, palm trees, and warm climate (Gulf Stream-protected flowers bloom in December). One looks at flowers and gardens a lot in the Scillies, but the islands also have bird sanctuaries and seal colonies. **St. Mary's** is the largest inhabited island, and the site of most tourist facilities. From there, you can take a motor launch to the major sightseeing attraction—the **Tresco Abbey Gardens**, on the **Isle of Tresco**. Not only can you explore terraced gardens, but you can also duck inside the **Valhalla Ship Museum** (collection of figureheads—gleaned from wrecks in the islands). The gardens are open all year, weekdays only, including Saturday, from 10 a.m. to 4 p.m. Admission is £1.10 ($2.53).

From Penzance, the Scilly Isles may be visited by helicopter or by sea. A ship, *Scillonian III*, maintains year-round connections to St. Mary's. For details of sailings and fares, apply to **Isles of Scilly Steamship Co. Ltd.**, 16 Quay St. (tel. Penzance 2009). **British Airways Helicopters** at the Heliport in Penzance (tel. Penzance 3871) operates daily except Sunday throughout the year to the Isles of Scilly, the one-way flight taking only 20 minutes. A day return excursion fare is available for travel any day (except Saturday during May, June, July, August, and September). The day return fare is £22 ($50.60) per adult.

Incidentally, the already-mentioned Isles of Scilly Steamship Company, 16 Quay St., in Penzance, not only operates the regular service to the Scilly Islands, but also runs in-season daily cruises along the Cornish coast and to the islands, allowing four hours ashore before returning to Penzance.

Hanjague Guest House, St. Mary's (tel. Scillonia 22531), is a modern bungalow near the center of the island, offering good views stretching from the heliport in the southeast across Old Town Bay and Peninnis Headland to Buzza Mill in the southwest. Owners Dorothy and David Oxford will meet arriving guests at the heliport or quay if notified in advance. For bed, breakfast, and dinner, the Oxfords charge £15 ($34.50) per person all year. Rooms are comfortably furnished and centrally heated, containing hot and cold running water. In the studio lounge is a fine display of wildlife prints by the artist William Timym.

Tremellyn Private Hotel, St. Mary's (tel. Scillonia 22656), is a complex on one of the higher parts of St. Mary's, with views of the harbor, Tresco, Samson, and the other islands, yet it lies only a short walk from Porthcressa Beach, the old town, and the quay. The "mother house," Tremellyn, contains the dining room, lounge, TV room, and some bedrooms. Otherwise, guests are housed in private bungalows owned and looked after by Scillonian families, all lying within 100 yards of Tremellyn. All units rented out contain hot and cold running water. The bed-and-breakfast rate is £10 ($23) per person nightly. From April to September, bookings are from Wednesday to Wednesday only. Dinners are from £5.75 ($13.23).

LODGINGS AT LAND'S END: Old Success Inn, Sennen Cove, Land's End (tel. Sennen 232). Just before you reach Land's End, turn right and follow the road down to Sennen Cove. The Old Success lies at the bottom, facing the sea and wide sandy beaches. Surfing rollers come in from the Atlantic almost to the foot of the sea wall beneath the 17th-century fishermen's inn. Over the years it has been extended and modernized, now offering bright, clean rooms, many with private bath, all with radio, tea and coffee maker, electric heater, and wash basin.

Downstairs there is a lounge with color TV and fantastic panoramic views over the Atlantic, a cozy lounge bar, and Charlie's Bar where the locals and the fishermen join the residents of an evening. The chef, Don Woodward, provides bar snacks at lunch and a set three-course meal for £5 ($11.50). Fresh local fish with local fresh vegetables are featured. Try the grilled river trout or the fresh Cornish crab and salad.

For those who seek more energetic exercise than an evening walk along the sand, there is the Surf Bar by the beach which is separated from the inn by a large car park. Disco music is played on summer evenings. Gillian and Tony Webster have run the inn for the past few years. Bed and breakfast is £9 ($20.70) in low season, rising to £10.50 ($24.15) from May to September. There is an additional charge of £1.50 ($3.45) per person per night for rooms with private bath and toilet. Packed lunches can be provided. All rates are subject to VAT.

20. St. Hilary, Newlyn, and Mousehole

For even more interesting living than that described above, we turn to the outlying district of Penzance, beginning first on the eastern side of the bay at St. Hilary, then heading south to Newlyn and Mousehole.

ST. HILARY: The **Old Vicarage Country Hotel,** St. Hilary, a short drive east from Marazion (tel. St. Hilary 710572), is a secluded retreat of much charm. It will please those who respond to quiet, gentle hours spent in an old house, surrounded by woods and gardens. Once a vicarage, it is owned by Mr. and Mrs. Stoten, who accept guests for a low charge of £10 ($23) per person nightly for bed and breakfast. The dinner, bed, and breakfast rate is £13 ($29.90). Each room is individually decorated—casual, but comfortable. The beds have innersprings, and there is adequate hot and cold running water. The living room is spacious, and just right for fireside chats. Home cooking is a feature of the place. On Saturday a five-course evening dinner goes for £5 ($11.50). The main restaurant and Coach House Bar are open only in season. The house—the subject of a book entitled *Twenty Years at St. Hilary*—is about a 15-minute walk from Perranuthnoe Beach and within sight of St. Michael's Mount.

NEWLYN: From Penzance, a promenade leads to Newlyn, a mile away, another fishing village of charm on Mount's Bay. Stanhope Forbes, now dead, founded an art school in Newlyn. The village has an artists' colony, attracting both the serious painter and the amateur sketcher. From Penzance, Newlyn is reached by taking bus 1 or 1B. For a dining or overnighting recommendation, try the following.

The **Smugglers Hotel and Restaurant,** Fore Street (tel. Penzance 4207), is the central mecca for those who create in clay and paint. An artist's dream come true, this little two-story inn lies right on the roadside, across from the Newlyn Harbor. You pay £11.50 ($26.45) in a single, £19 ($43.70) in a double for a good bed and a big Cornish breakfast. The rooms are bright and sparkling clean, with innerspring mattresses and water basins. Good shore dinners are served till around 10 p.m. Conversation in the lounge or in the dining room is often most rewarding. The bar is found in the granite-walled cellars, with tables and benches made from local driftwood. The original tunnel used by smugglers, although now blocked, can still be seen.

MOUSEHOLE: Still another Cornish fishing village, Mousehole lies three miles south of Penzance (take bus 9). The hordes of tourists who flock here haven't changed it drastically: the gulls still squawk, the cottages still huddle close to the harbor wall (although they look as if they were built more to be photographed than lived in), the fishermen still bring in the day's catch, the salts sit around with their pipes talking about the good old days, and the lanes are as narrow as ever. About the most exciting thing that's occurred around here was the arrival in the latter 16th century of Spanish galleons, whose sailors sacked and burnt the village. In a sheltered cove, off Mount's Bay, Mousehole (pronounced mou-sel) has developed an artists' colony, both painters and potters. For rooms and meals, try the following recommendations, all in the village.

Old Coastguard Hotel, The Parade (tel. Mousehole 222), is a 19th-century structure, on the edge of Mousehole, with a private, unspoiled view of the bay. Open all year, it's a center for artists and others who enjoy such an atmosphere. The old inn has stairways and halls leading directly to the oddly shaped bedrooms. For a bathless double, the owners, Mrs. O. Sidoryk and Mr. S. Donnelly, charge from £12.35 ($28.41) per person nightly. This rate includes a full breakfast with, if you wish, mackerel, fresh Newlyn sole or kippers, or perhaps sausage, egg, and bacon, served with fruit juice, tea, or coffee. Dinners, served from 7 to 9:30 p.m., are exceptional, too. Every night you can select from the à la carte menu which has a wide range of seafoods, for a minimum charge of £6 ($13.80) per person. They also have two special menus which offer a three-course meal for residents only, at a charge of £6 ($13.80) per person. Also served between 6 and 9:30 p.m. is an extensive range of hot and cold bar meals. All prices are inclusive of service and VAT.

On the Outskirts

Lamorna Cove Hotel, at Lamorna Cove, near Penzance (tel. Mousehole 294). This is one of the most perfect Cornish coves, seemingly inaccessible down a winding, narrow road, dropping always toward the sea until you suddenly emerge onto the sea wall of the tiny cove. There you'll find a quayside cafe for a fresh crab salad or Cornish cream tea.

Above the cove, signposted off the approach lane, lies the Lamorna Cove Hotel. The present owners, Mr. and Mrs. Stewart Bolton, have carefully added to the old stone building, once a tiny chapel with a bell tower. They once even blasted several tons of rock from the cliff face to provide more room, a peaceful haven with views over the sea and the cove. The bar is in the chapel itself. A large dining room runs the length of the building, and there are several lounges full of comfortable chairs, with a roaring log fire against the southwesterly gales.

Accommodations are in the main hotel with bath or shower, some with balcony. There are also two cottages for rent, one suitable for four, the other for five persons. They are reached by elevator from the main house. A rocky garden clings to the cliffside and then surrounds a small swimming pool with a sun-trap terrace overlooking the sea. Bed and breakfast ranges from £24 ($55.20) per person to £30 ($69) per person in high season in double accommodation. There is also a suite available and a deluxe double room, costing £34 ($78.20) and £39 ($89.70) per person per night. From October until the end of May, prices are substantially reduced.

If you do not have the time to stay at the hotel, their bar lunches can be well recommended. On Sunday, a traditional luncheon of sirloin of beef, filet of sole, or pork chops, buttered cabbage, rutabagas, roast potatoes (fresh vegetables in season), followed by pie with Cornish cream, brandy snaps, or cheese costs around £6 ($13.80). Dinners at £8 ($18.40) are quite a feast.

21. St. Ives

This north coast fishing village, with its sandy beaches, is England's most famous art colony. Only 20 miles from Land's End, ten from Penzance, it is a village of narrow streets and well-kept cottages. The artists settled in many years ago and have integrated with the fishermen and their families.

The art colony was established long enough ago to have developed several schools or "splits," and they almost never overlap—except in a pub where the artists hang out, or where classes are held. The old battle continues between the followers of the representational and the devotees of the abstract in art, with each group recruiting young artists all the time. In addition, there are the potters, weavers, and other craftsmen—all working, exhibiting, and selling in this area. There are several galleries to visit, with such names as the Sail Loft.

A word of warning: St. Ives becomes virtually impossible to visit in August, when you're likely to be trampled underfoot by busloads of tourists, mostly the English themselves. However, in spring and early fall, the pace is much more relaxed, and a visitor can have the true experience of the art colony.

BARBARA HEPWORTH MUSEUM: At Trewyn Studio and Garden, on Barnoon Hill (tel. St. Ives 6226), the former home of Dame Barbara Hepworth contains a museum of sculpture by the artist from 1929 until her death in 1975 together with photographs, letters, and other papers documenting her life and background. The garden, too, contains sculpture and is well worth a visit. The museum is open year round from 10 a.m. to 5:30 p.m., Monday to Saturday. Closed on Sunday and bank holidays. Admission is 50p ($1.15) for adults, 25p (58¢) for children and students. There is limited parking some 200 yards away, but visitors may like to leave their cars at Lelant Station some ten miles away and use the park-and-ride service into St. Ives.

WHERE TO STAY: Tregenna Castle Hotel (tel. St. Ives 5254), standing on its own 100 acres, was once a castle. It was optimistically earmarked by Von Ribbentrop to be Hitler's British Berchtesgaden. Approached by a long driveway, it crowns a hill high above the fishing village of St. Ives. While the interior is spacious and a good background for gracious living, the grounds contain gardens and lawns, an open-air, heated swimming pool with a flagstone edging for sunbathers, three lawn tennis courts, three hard courts, a croquet lawn, a putting green, a squash court, a badminton court, and a nine-hole golf course. There is also a health room complete with Turkish baths, a Relaxatron bed, and a Vibro belt. There are riding stables situated within the grounds and arrangements can be made for shark, mackerel, and fly fishing. The bedrooms usually are of good size, handsomely maintained with contemporary furniture, and more than 80% have private bathrooms. The rates vary according to the season and the location of the room. From June 16 to September 15, the bed-and-breakfast rate, inclusive of service charge and VAT, is from £26.60 ($61.18) in a bathless single, £38 ($87.40) in a single with bath. A bathless double costs from £50 ($115), from £65 ($149.50) with bath. Tregenna has its own vegetable garden and trout pool. A set lunch goes for £6.35 ($14.59) and a set dinner for £9.80 ($22.55), inclusive of service and VAT. In addition, there is a well-stocked cellar, and an orchestra plays for dancing two nights a week in season.

Garrack Hotel, Higher Ayr (tel. St. Ives 6199), from its two-acre cliff knoll, commands a panoramic view of St. Ives and Portmeor Beach. The vine-covered little hotel, once a private home, is reached by heading up a narrow lane. It's one of the friendliest and most efficiently run small medium-priced hotels on the entire coast, with every room furnished in a warm, homey manner. The atmosphere in the living room is inviting, with a log-burning fireplace, antiques, and comfortable chairs. The Garrack belongs to Mr. and Mrs. Kilby, who are proud of their meals (see our dining recommendations). Each bedroom has an innerspring mattress and hot and cold running water (most with private baths). Prices vary because of the view, the size of the room, and the season. The bed-and-breakfast charge ranges from £8 ($18.40) to £11 ($25.30) in a single, from £8 ($18.40) to £13.50 ($31.05) per person in a double, plus VAT.

The **Trecarrell Hotel,** Carthew Terrace (tel. St. Ives 5707), is housed in a 100-year-old building in a quiet quarter of St. Ives. The restaurant and kitchen are under the personal supervision of the proprietors, who take pride in their table, using the best local produce as it becomes available. The nightly table d'hôte dinner offers such specialties as homemade pâté, coq au vin, and a delicious dessert, Somloi Delice, a Hungarian delicacy made with rum, coffee, cream, and nuts. The hotel itself, centrally heated throughout, is rather small—only 14 guest rooms in all—but each room is individually decorated and some have private en suite baths. Rents per person per week in high season, July and August, range from £81 ($186.30) to £83 ($190.90). The daily demi-pension rate in high season goes from £15.85 ($36.46) to £16.15 ($37.15) per person. The price includes full English breakfast and the four-course table d'hôte dinner. VAT is added to the bill.

WHERE TO EAT: The **Chef's Kitchen,** Halsetown (tel. St. Ives 6218), stands on a point above St. Ives on a back road to Penzance. It's in an old granite post office, very unobtrusive among the cottages. It's on the left as you come up the main street from St. Ives. Since it's so easy to miss, go slowly. The old post office has been converted into a bar lounge, plus an adjoining cottage which is the restaurant, seating 32 guests. When you reserve a table (and reservations are imperative), you have it for the evening. Orders are taken between 7 and 11 p.m. The owner/chef, Mr. Tetley, was trained in London. He cooks for pleasure and enjoys pleasing people who like good food. For starters, try oeuf (egg) en cocotte bordelaise (with bone marrow) at 65p ($1.50), or perhaps escabeche of mackerel Prunier, £1.40 ($3.22). So that he does not have to buy smoked salmon at high cost, he has a specialty all his own: marinated salmon in dill, £2.60 ($5.98). Featured are seven fish and eight meat or poultry dishes, including Dover sole filet, garnished with asparagus and coated with lobster sauce, from £4.75 ($10.93) to £5.30 ($12.19), and tournedos sauté chef's style, topped off with hollandaise sauce, £5.60 ($12.88). Desserts begin at £1.05 ($2.42). One person told us she has worked her way through the entire menu, and found everything "absolutely delicious."

The **Garrack Hotel,** Higher Ayr (tel. St. Ives 6199), the domain of Mr. and Mrs. Kilby, is outstanding, producing an excellent cuisine—using, when possible, fresh vegetables from their own garden. The hotel dining room, open to nonresidents, offers regular à la carte listings, plus cold buffet or snacks at the bar, and a £6 ($13.80) dinner from 7 to 8:30 p.m. The menu reflects some of the finest of English dishes, such as roast shoulder of lamb with mint sauce, fried filet of plaice, and a wide sampling of continental fare, such as filet of bass meunière and escalopes de veau Cordon Bleu. A 10% service charge and VAT are added. The Kilbys' son Michael has recently joined his parents in the operation of the hotel and restaurant after completing a training period with Claridges in London.

The Sloop is right on The Quay, next to the art colony on the hill. The pub has old charm, tracing its history back to 1644, but it's the life here that's important. The Lounge Bar is for daintier types, the Cellar Bar for intimate rendezvousing. But in the Public Bar, you're likely to find artists and old sea dogs mixing congenially. The local fishermen come in for their evening game of darts and to talk to the owner-bartender. Apparently, the success of the pub depends a great deal on the gift of gab of the bartender. A recent visit was memorable. Six rugged Breton sailors made room at their long table for us. Their words were unfathomable, but not their friendliness. They were in port overnight and were sampling the English beer. The youngest, the cabin boy, was tagging along, trying to imitate his older companions. The walls of the interior are covered almost entirely by the works of a master who exchanged them for his nightly ration of good English ale.

22. St. Columb Major

St. Columb Major lies about seven miles inland from the coastal town of Newquay, yet only 4½ miles from the beach at Mawganporth. It makes a good center for touring the area, especially if you find lodgings at:

The Old Rectory Hotel and Country Club (tel. St. Columb 880-656). A moated rectory, part of this Gothic-looking building dates back to the 14th century. It was restored to its original plan in 1840. It stands on two acres of grounds and gardens. The owners, Mr. and Mrs. J. C. L. van der Heiden, rent 12 bedrooms at rates ranging from £11 ($25.30) to £13 ($29.90) per person, for dinner, bed, and breakfast. The accommodations contain hot and cold running water, and corridor baths and toilets are adequate.

Ceilings are beamed, and there's even a minstrel's gallery. Guests can swim in a heated pool, and play tennis on two hard courts. Trout fishing is possible in a stream bounding one side of the property.

The Country Club bar is open to residents; the restaurant is of an extremely high standard, with an average meal costing £6 ($13.80).

23. Port Isaac

The most unspoiled fishing village on the north Cornish coastline is Port Isaac, nine miles from Wadebridge. This Atlantic coastal resort retains its original character, in spite of the intrusions of large numbers of summer visitors. By all means wander through its winding, narrow lanes, gazing at the whitewashed fishermen's cottages with their rainbow trims.

WHERE TO DRINK AND SNACK: The **Golden Lion**, Fore Street (tel. Port Isaac 336), is perhaps the most handsomely positioned pub in the old fishing harbor. Owned by Mr. and Mrs. Spry, it offers good drinks, snacks, and crab sandwiches.

For meals, try the **Harbour Café**, Fore Street (tel. Port Isaac 272), in the center of the village. It has a special fame, featured several times on British television and once in scenes from the Sherlock Holmes thriller, *The Devil's Foot*. The unique cafe is designated as a building of architectural and historic interest, and is one of several buildings on this treacherous stretch of coast that used the timber of wrecked ships in construction. The owners, Pamela and John Coulson, offer complete meals as well as snacks. In addition they have been granted a table wine license. On the menu are such local dishes as crab and mackerel salads, plus a number of other homemade specialties. Meals begin at around £5 ($11.50). Perhaps you will arrive in the afternoon, when you can have a real Cornish cream tea, and if your appetite is still unsatisfied, you may care to try a piece of homemade gâteau topped with a portion of clotted cream.

READERS' HOTEL SELECTIONS: "The **Tre-Pol-Pen Hotel** (tel. Port Isaac 232) is in the newer part of the village, just before the steep descent down into the cove and the old section. Charges are £10 ($23) per person during the main season for clean, bright rooms, a substantial breakfast (several choices), use of a lounge with color TV, and free baths. There is a large dining area where breakfast is served, and Cornish cream teas can be ordered during the afternoon. A meal at night costs £4.25 ($9.78) per person. Some of the rooms have beautiful views of the coast. There is a car park, which is necessary, as to drive down into the village is difficult in winter and virtually impossible in summer. All rooms have hot and cold water and are centrally heated. Bookings are necessary in summer" (Mr. and Mrs. David Peters, Highgate, Australia).... "The **Hathaway Guest House** (tel. Port Isaac 888-416), is beautifully situated on the cliff on the eastern side of Port Isaac harbor. The house overlooks not only the village and harbor, but also the western coastline and beyond. Resident proprietor Enid Andrews offers colorfully decorated rooms with breakfast at £7 ($16.10) per person in April, May, and June, and £8 ($18.40) in July, August, and September. Dinner is available for £4 ($9.20). It is less than a five-minute walk to the pub and shops. A two-mile cliff walk begins at the door. There's a car park and children are welcome" (A. Emerson Smith, Columbus, S.C.).

24. Tintagel

On a wild stretch of the Atlantic coast, Tintagel is forever linked with the legends of King Arthur, Lancelot, and Merlin. The Norman ruins, popularly known as "King Arthur's Castle," stand 300 feet above the sea on a rocky promontory. The colorful writing of Lord Tennyson in *Idylls of the King* greatly increased the interest in Tintagel, as did the writings of Geoffrey of Monmouth. The ruins, which date from Geoffrey's time, are what remains of a castle built on the foundations of a Celtic monastery from the sixth century.

In summer, many visitors make the ascent to Arthur's lair, 100 rock-cut steps. You can also visit Merlin's Cave and the "Old Post Office," a miniature 14th century manor in the center of the village (open May to September, weekdays, 10 a.m. to 8 p.m., and on Sunday from 1 to 5 p.m.).

If you become excited by legends of Knights of the Round Table, you can even go to **Camelford**, just five miles inland from Tintagel. The market hall there dates from 1790, but, more interestingly, the town claims to be Camelot.

The **Old Post Office** at Tintagel is a National Trust property. It was once a 14th-century manor, but since the 19th century it has had connections with the post office. In the village center, it has a genuine Victorian post room which is open, April to October, weekdays from 11 a.m. to 1 p.m. and from 2 to 5 p.m. (on Sunday from 2 to 5 p.m.). Admission is 50p ($1.15), including a guidebook.

Trebrea Lodge, Trenale, near Tintagel (tel. Tintagel 410), may appear as a dignified stately home, but in truth it looks and feels inside like an old Cornish farmhouse, although it is centrally heated. It dates back to 1315, and was lived in by the same family for more than 600 years. The house, now owned by Ann and Guy Murray, looks straight out across fields to the sea, and each bedroom has a good view. Rooms are available in many sizes, and each has hot and cold water, radio, intercom (and even a baby-listening service). Evenings are cozy in the drawing room around an open fire where guests watch color TV. You can have drinks in another lounge which is installed in an old fireplace. Dining is most informal, and all food is homemade by Mrs. Murray, who has mastered true English recipes. The cost is £11 ($25.30) per person for bed, breakfast, and dinner.

READER'S HOTEL SELECTION: "I most sincerely recommend the **Bossiney House Hotel**, just outside Tintagel as you approach from Boscastle (tel. Tintagel 240). The hotel is owned by brothers John and Reg Wrightam and their families. The Wrightams are marvelous hosts, and the whole family put themselves out to make us feel at home, telling us about the area and directing us to some of the especially lovely parts. The hotel is extremely comfortable, with a TV lounge and a well-stocked bar/lounge with a view of the surrounding meadows, which march right up to the tops of the cliffs, and a wide expanse of lawn with a putting green. Our rooms were comfortably furnished, with full bath and central heating. The meals are family prepared and delicious. The price is £16.50 ($37.95) per person per night, which includes a room with dinner, breakfast, and morning tea brought to the room" (Kathleen Martin, Englishtown, N.J.).

In our next chapter, we'll conclude our trek through the West Country by exploring Wiltshire, Somerset, and Avon.

Chapter IX

WILTSHIRE, SOMERSET, AND AVON

1. Salisbury
2. Castle Combe
3. Lacock
4. Wells
5. Bleadney
6. Glastonbury
7. The Caves of Mendip
8. Bath
9. Bristol

FOR OUR FINAL LOOK at the West Countree, we move now into Wiltshire, Somerset, and the newly created county of Avon, the most antiquity-rich shires of England. When we reach this area of woodland and pastoral scenes, London seems far removed—even divorced from the bucolic life here.

On cold, windswept nights in unrecorded times, the Druids used to steal across these plains—armed with twigs. Sheltered by boulders, they'd burn their sloe with rosemary to ward off the danger of witchcraft.

Most people seem to agree that the West Country, a loose geographical term, begins at Salisbury, with its Early English cathedral. Nearby is Stonehenge, England's oldest prehistoric monument. Both Stonehenge and Salisbury are in Wiltshire.

Somerset is even more varied—the diet richer not only in historical cities, but in wild scenic grandeur, especially in Exmoor, the home of the red deer. The legendary burial place of King Arthur at Glastonbury, and the cathedral city of Wells, also await you on your visit to Somerset. The old Roman city of Bath is the main target in the county of Avon.

WILTSHIRE

When you cross into Wiltshire, you'll be entering a county of chalky, grassy uplands and rolling plains. Most of the shire is agricultural, and a large part is devoted to pastureland. Wiltshire produces an abundance of England's dairy products, and is noted for its sheep raising. In this western shire, you'll traverse the Salisbury Plain, the Vale of Pewsey, and the Marlborough Downs (the last gobbling up the greater part of the land mass). Unquestionably, the crowning achievement of Wiltshire is:

1. Salisbury

Long before you've made the 83-mile trek from London, the spire of Salisbury Cathedral comes into view—just as John Constable painted it so many times. The 404-foot pinnacle of the Early English and Gothic cathedral is the tallest in England. But Salisbury is also a fine base for touring such sights as Stonehenge.

Salisbury, or New Sarum, lies in the valley of the Avon River. Filled with Tudor inns and tearooms, it is known to readers of Thomas Hardy as Melchester and to the Victorian fans of Anthony Trollope as Barchester.

SALISBURY CATHEDRAL: You can search all of England, but you'll find no purer example of the Early English—or pointed—style than Salisbury Cathedral. Its graceful spire has already been mentioned, but the ecclesiastical building doesn't depend totally on the tower for its appeal.

Construction began as early as 1220, then took 38 years to complete, which was jet-age speed in those days (it was customary to drag out cathedral building for three centuries at least). The spire began soaring at the end of the 13th century. Despite an ill-conceived attempt at revamping in the 18th century, the architectural harmony of the cathedral was retained.

The cathedral's octagonal Chapter House (note the fine sculpture) is especially attractive, dating from the 13th century. The Library contains one of the four copies of the Magna Carta. The cloisters enhance the beauty of the cathedral. The Close, with at least 75 buildings in its compound (some from the early 18th century, although others predate that), is exceptionally large, setting off the cathedral most fittingly.

WHERE TO STAY: The **Red Lion,** Milford Street (tel. Salisbury 23334), is too stately to roar. But since the 1300s it's been putting up wayfarers who rumbled in stagecoaches from London across the Salisbury Plain to the West Country. (A survey by the Historical Building Society has disclosed a medieval wing, built no later than 1320, making the inn one of the oldest in the British Isles.) Cross under its arch into a courtyard with a hanging and much-photographed creeper, a red lion, and a half-timbered facade—and you'll be transplanted back to the old days. The inn still maintains its rich antiques. Be sure and look at the old musical clock, with its dancing skeletons, in the entrance hall, and the large collection of Chelsea china. If possible, try to spend the night in one of the two carved double tester beds. You'll be enclosed in your private world. For the past half century, the inn has been run by the Thomas family, who charge £18.50 ($42.55) in a bathless single, £22.50 ($51.75) in a single with bath or shower, £28 ($64.40) in a bathless double, £32 ($73.60) in a double with bath or shower, all these tariffs including breakfast. The Red Lion offers one of the most sumptuous repasts in Salisbury—surprisingly inexpensive, too, considering the quality of the cuisine and the size of the portions. For £5 ($11.50) you can have a set lunch. The most recommendable dinner averages £6 ($13.80). House specialties include jugged hare with red currant jelly, roast venison, steak-and-kidney pie, and roast beef with horseradish sauce. Meals are served from noon to 2:15 p.m. and from 7 to 9 p.m.

The **Rose and Crown,** East Harnham (tel. Salisbury 27908), is an inn-collector's gem. An unspoiled, half-timbered, 13th-century hostelry, it lies at

312 DOLLARWISE GUIDE TO ENGLAND AND SCOTLAND

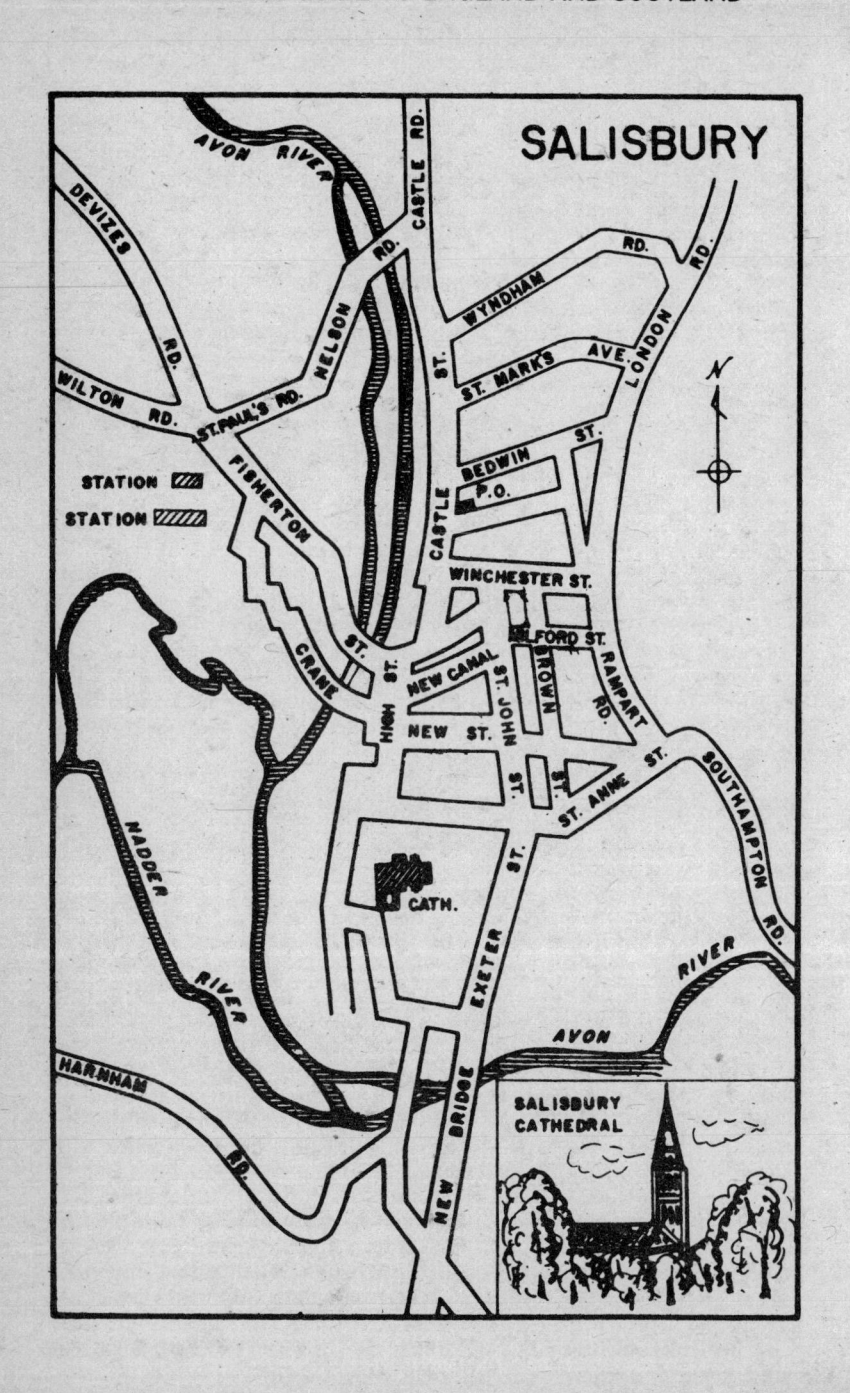

the edge of Salisbury. The Avon River winds its way within a few feet of the Rose and Crown, and beyond the water you can see the tall spire of the cathedral itself. The lawns and gardens between the inn and the river are shaded by old trees, and chairs are set out so you can enjoy the view and count the swans. The inn, part of the Grand Metropolitan Hotels chain, contains both a new and an old wing. The new wing is modern (a bath to each bedroom) and more expensive. The old wing is more appealing, with its sloping ceilings, antique fireplaces, and furniture. A single rents for £28 ($64.40), a double with bath going for £38 ($87.40), including an English breakfast, service, and VAT. You can have lunch overlooking the river. The fare is English. A set luncheon goes for £4.50 ($10.35), a set dinner for £7 ($16.10). Across the countyard (where there's free parking) are two taverns. You can easily walk over the arched stone bridge to the center of Salisbury from here in ten minutes or so.

White Hart, St. John Street (tel. Salisbury 27476), combines the best of the old and the new worlds. The White Hart has been a Salisbury landmark since Georgian times. Its classic facade is intact, with tall columns crowning a life-size effigy of a hart. The older accommodations are traditional, but a new part has been added with skill. It's in the rear, opening onto a large car park—like a motel. The new wing has 73 bedrooms, tastefully conceived and attractively decorated. The highest prices are charged from April 1 to October 31, when singles range from £20 ($46) to £24 ($55.20), doubles from £26 ($59.80) to £32 ($73.60). The higher prices are for rooms with private baths. The service charge and VAT are included. You can have your before-dinner drink in either the Elizabethan Bar or the Fountain Bar.

The **King's Arms Hotel,** St. John Street (tel. Salisbury 27629), is a former coaching inn, in black-and-white Tudor style, with leaded-glass windows, an old pub sign out front, and a covered entranceway. It is unsophisticated without being self-consciously so. The King's Arms charges from £13.30 ($30.59) in a single to £18.60 ($42.78) to £25 ($57.50) in a double or twin, the more expensive tariffs including a private bath or shower. Rates include breakfast, service, and VAT. The rooms are good, with wash basins, radios, heating, and soft beds.

No one seems to know the age of the inn, although it's generally assumed it was built around the time of the completion of the cathedral. Conspirators helping Charles II flee to France were thought to have met here in the mid-17th century. The hotel contains fine old oak beams, the original ironwork, a priest's hiding hole, the Elizabethan fireplace. Have a pint of ale in the oak-beamed pub, sitting in a high-backed settle, warming yourself in front of the flames.

The **Grange Hotel,** St. Marks Avenue, off London Road Roundabout (tel. Salisbury 25321), stands in the highest part of Salisbury, on 1½ acres of pleasant gardens. Its architecture is an example of "Victorian Mock Tudor." When constructed, the hotel incorporated the space and comforts required by wealthy Victorians. It is built of brick, with many bay windows, gables, carved fireplaces, and a dark oak central hall with an open winding staircase. The furnishings and decor are in keeping with the style of the building. Most of the bedrooms have private baths and are individually decorated, each bearing the name of a cathedral. Depending on the plumbing, rates in a single range from £15 ($34.50) to £20 ($46), in a double from £24 ($55.20) to £32 ($73.60). A three-bedded accommodation costs £36 ($82.80) without bath, £41 ($94.30) with bath. All these tariffs include an English breakfast, VAT, and service, and most rooms contain TV and telephones. Good food is served in the restaurant, a set dinner costing from £5.50 ($12.65), although if you order à la carte at either lunch or dinner expect to pay from £8 ($18.40).

WHERE TO EAT: Provençal, 14 Ox Row, Market Place (tel. Salisbury 28923), provides the most sophisticated setting of any dining place in Salisbury, and has the most ambitious French cuisine as well. This second-story restaurant overlooks the Market Place, has a sedate bistro setting, and a friendly staff to serve you. A good starter is the soupe à l'oignon. Specialties include ratatouille à la Niçoise, giant prawns grilled in garlic butter, and a sliced leg or rack of lamb roasted with rosemary and served with apricot sauce. A selection of three vegetables is available. Dessert specialties include profiteroles au chocolat and crème brulée. Of course, the menu is changed frequently, depending on the availability of produce and the season. Edward Moss, the owner, has taken Peter Barker as his assistant in the kitchen. They offer a table d'hôte luncheon for around £4.20 ($9.66), a set dinner for £5 ($11.50). If you order à la carte, expect to pay from £7 ($16.10) at lunch, from £10 ($23) at dinner. The restaurant is open from noon to 1:30 p.m. and from 6 to 10:30 p.m. (except for Saturday lunch and all day Sunday). The wine list contains a number of really good French-bottled wines, as well as an excellent carafe.

The **Haunch of Vension,** Minster Street (tel. Salisbury 22024), deserves its popularity. Right in the heart of Salisbury, this creaky-timbered, 14th-century chophouse serves some excellent dishes, especially English roasts and grills. Stick to its specialties, and you'll rarely go wrong. Diners with more adventurous palates will sample a bowl of game soup for £1.40 ($3.22). The pièce de résistance of the inn is its roast haunch of venison, with chestnut purée and red currant jelly, costing £7.90 ($18.17). All this good food and hospitality is offered in a treasured building, dating back to 1320. The centuries have given a gleam to the oak furnishings, and years of polishing have worn down the brass. Twisting steps lead to tiny, cozy rooms (there is one small room with space for about four to sit where you can saturate yourself in the best of England's yesterdays and todays). Two windows of the barroom overlook St. Thomas's cloisters (naturally, it's called the Cloisters Chamber). Dancing fires are kept burning in the old fireplace; heavy beams are overhead; antique chairs encircle the tables. Hours are from noon to 2 p.m. and from 7 to 10 p.m., except on Sunday and Monday when it's closed.

Claire's Restaurant and Coffee House, 7-9 Market Pl. (tel. Salisbury 3118), is right in the middle of the city and very convenient as a lunch stop for the tourer. It is open daily from 11:45 a.m. to 2:30 p.m. (closed Sunday). Featured are cottage pie, chicken American, deep-fried scampi, whole grilled plaice, or beef cooked in beer at prices that go from £2 ($4.60) to £3.50 ($8.05), all served with fresh vegetables and trimmings. Including a dessert or cheese, your meal will be well under £6 ($13.80). House wine is 65p ($1.50) a glass. In the coffeeshop you can also get open sandwiches at £1 ($2.30).

The Local Pub

The **New Inn,** 43 New St. (tel. Salisbury 27679), isn't new at all. Backing up to the cathedral Close wall, it's definitely part of old England. The center of the inn is the serving bar, which is a common counter for three outer rooms—one is a tiny sitting area, another a tavern with high-backed settles and a fireplace, the third a lounge with a dart board. You'll find stacks of little pork pies, to be eaten cold and washed down with pints of ale. Prices range from 35p (81¢) to £1.25 ($2.88). A half-pint of draft cider costs 52p ($1.20). The Historical Society, incidentally, once discovered several human bones in an oven behind an old doorway.

ON THE OUTSKIRTS: The **Silver Plough,** Pitton, near Salisbury (tel. Farley 266), lies just off the A30 road from London to Salisbury. It's a pretty country pub with a skillfully added restaurant. When they first came here about 17 years ago, Janice and Edward Johnson found that the pub already had a reputation for country wines and English cheeses. They increased the range even more, adding birch, elderberry, wheat and raisin, even dandelion wine. You can sup at least 17 varieties and eat home-baked cottage loaves with a wide selection of cheese for your lunch, in the beamed lounge bar, hung with tankards, coachhorns, and other country memorabilia.

There is also a dining room, where Mr. Lawley, the chef, does succulent grills and roasts for the set meals or else provides you with an à la carte dinner. The owners pride themselves in providing everything from a simple ploughman's lunch at £1 ($2.30) to a full meal, a set dinner going for £9.50 ($21.85). On the table d'hôte are featured such tempting items as roast duckling with orange and brandy sauce, chicken cooked in red wine and mushrooms, trout poached in white wine with shrimp and mushrooms. The Silver Plough has known many famous visitors, but, apart from displaying a signed letter from Queen Victoria, the management prefers to stick to its quiet country atmosphere and to concentrate on making its guests feel at home.

READER'S HOTEL SELECTION AT AMESBURY: "The **Fairlawn Hotel** (tel. Amesbury 2103) is ideally located for an in-depth visit to the archeological sites on Salisbury Plain. It is only two miles from Stonehenge and one mile from Woodhenge and Durrington Walls. The hotel is a Georgian building well into its third century. Bed and breakfast cost is £10 ($23) in a single, £18.50 ($42.55) in a double without bath, £22 ($50.60) in a double with bath, and from £25 ($57.50) to £30 ($69) in family rooms for three to four persons, these tariffs including VAT. The rooms are immaculate and sunny. The hotel also has a cocktail lounge and restaurant, serving a three-course evening meal for about £7.50 ($17.25). Gerald Hawkins, author of *Stonehenge Decoded,* stayed at the Fairlawn when he visited the area. The Tourist Information Centre in Salisbury will gladly make your reservations to assure the availability of a room before you start for Amesbury" (Edward Pasahow, San Diego, Calif.).

SIDE TRIPS FROM SALISBURY: Less than two miles north of Salisbury is **Old Sarum,** the remains of what is believed to have been an Iron Age fortification. The earthworks were known to the Romans as Sorbiodunum, and later to the Saxons. The Normans, in fact, built a cathedral and a castle in what was then a walled town of the Middle Ages. Parts of the old cathedral were disassembled to erect the cathedral at New Sarum.

Wilton House

In the small borough of Wilton, less than three miles to the west of Salisbury, is one of England's great country estates, Wilton House, the home of the Earl of Pembroke. The stately house dates from the 16th century, but has seen modifications over the years, as late as Victoria's day. It is noted for its 17th-century state rooms by Inigo Jones. Many famous personages have either lived at or visited Wilton. It is believed that Shakespeare's troupe entertained here. Plans for the D-Day landings at Normandy were laid out here by Eisenhower and his advisers, in the utmost secrecy, with only the silent Van Dycks in the Double Cube room as witnesses. The house is filled with beautifully maintained furnishings, especially a collection of Chippendale. Wilton House displays some of the finest paintings in England, including works by Rembrandt, Rubens, Reynolds, and the already-mentioned Van Dycks.

The estate lies in the midst of gardens and grounds, with cedars of Lebanon, the oldest of which were planted in 1630. The Palladian Bridge was built in 1737. Wilton House may be visited from Tuesday through Saturday, 11 a.m. to 6 p.m., April through September. Admission is £1 ($2.70) for adults, 50p ($1.15) for children. On Sunday, April through September, the historic house is open from 2 to 6 p.m. The New Restaurant here is open all day, and offers hot and cold lunches and high teas. Seating 300, the restaurant is fully licensed.

Stonehenge

Two miles west of Amesbury and about nine miles north of Salisbury is the renowned Stonehenge, believed to be anywhere from 3500 to 4000 years old. This huge oval of lintels and megalithic pillars is the most important prehistoric monument in Britain.

Some Americans have expressed their disappointment after seeing the concentric circles of stones. Admittedly, they are not the pyramids, and some imagination has to be brought to bear on them. Pyramids or not, they represent an amazing engineering feat. Many of the boulders—the bluestones in particular—were moved dozens of miles (perhaps from Southern Wales) to this site by the ancients. If you're more fanciful, you can always credit Merlin with delivering them on clouds from Ireland.

The widely held view of the 18th- and 19th-century romantics that Stonehenge was the work of the Druids is without foundation. The boulders, many weighing several tons, are believed to have predated the arrival in Britain of the Celtic cult. Recent excavations continue to bring new evidence to bear on the origin and purpose of Stonehenge. Controversy surrounds the prehistoric site especially since the publication of *Stonehenge Decoded* by Gerald S. Hawkins and John B. White, which maintains the Stonehenge was an astronomical observatory. That is, a Neolithic "computing machine" capable of predicting eclipses.

Others who discount this theory adopt Henry James's approach to Stonehenge, which regards it as "lonely in history," its origins and purposes (burial ground? sun-worshipping site? human sacrificial temple?) the secret of the silent, mysterious Salisbury Plain.

If you don't have a car, getting to Stonehenge can be difficult—unless you're athletic. First take the bus to Amesbury, then walk about 2½ miles to Stonehenge. The British do this all the time, and they don't complain. But if that is too strenuous, you'd better take one of the organized coach tours out of Salisbury.

To protect these ancient stones, Stonehenge has been fenced off.

Longleat House

Between Bath and Salisbury, Longleat House, owned by the sixth Marquess of Bath, lies four miles southwest of Warminster, 4½ miles southeast of Frome on the A362. The first view of this magnificent Elizabethan house, built in the early Renaissance style, is romantic enough, but the wealth of paintings and furnishings within its lofty rooms is enough to dazzle.

A tour of the house, from the Elizabethan Great Hall, through Libraries, the State Rooms, and the Grand Staircase, is awe inspiring in its variety and splendor. The State Dining Room is full of silver and plate, and fine tapestries and paintings adorn the walls in rich profusion. The Library represents the finest private collection in the country. The Victorian kitchens are open during the summer months, offering a glimpse of life below the stairs in a well-ordered country home. Various exhibitions are mounted in the Stable Yard. Events are staged frequently in the grounds, and the Safari Park contains a vast array of animals in open parklands.

The house is open every day, except Christmas, from 10 a.m. Admission to the house is £1.40 ($3.22) for adults, 75p ($1.73) for children. There is a toll of 30p (69¢) per person in a car at the entrance to the grounds, to a maximum of £1.25 ($2.88) per car. It costs £5 ($11.50) per car—with any number of people—to go around the Safari Park. If you wish to travel around in one of the safari buses, the cost is £2 ($4.60) for adults, £1.30 ($2.99) for children. In addition, there is a smashing 15-inch-gauge railway, costing 60p ($1.38) for adults, 40p (92¢) for children.

A maze, believed to be the largest in the world, has been added to the attractions by Lord Weymouth, son of the marquess. It has more than 1½ miles of paths among yew trees. The first part is comparatively easy, but the second part is very complicated, with bridges adding to the confusion. It knocks the Hampton Court maze into a cocked hat, as the British say.

Stourhead

After Longleat, you can drive six miles down route 3092 to Stourton, a village just off the B3092, three miles northwest of Mere (A303). Stourhead, a Palladian house, was created in the 18th century by the banking family of Hoare. The magnificent gardens became known as "le jardin anglais," in that they blended art and nature. Set around an artificial lake, the grounds are decorated with temples, bridges, islands, and grottos, as well as statuary. The gardens are open all year, daily from 8 a.m. to 7 p.m. (or until dusk if earlier). The house is open April, September, and October on Monday, Wednesday, Saturday, and Sunday, from 2 to 6 p.m. In May, June, July, and August it can be visited daily, except Friday, from 2 to 6. Picnicking in the gardens is welcomed. Admission to the house is £1 ($2.30) for adults, 50p ($1.15) for children; to the gardens, 80p ($1.84) for adults, 40p (92¢) for children.

Avebury

One of the largest prehistoric sites in Europe, Avebury lies about six miles west of Marlborough, on the Kennet River. It is gaining in popularity with visitors now that the British have had to rope off the sarsén circle at Stonehenge (see above). Explorers are able to walk the 28-acre site at Avebury, winding in and out of the circle of more than 100 stones, some weighing up to 50 tons. They are made of sarsén, a sandstone found in Wiltshire. Inside this large circle are two smaller ones, each with about 30 stones standing upright. Native Neolithic tribes are believed to have built these circles.

The village of Avebury, taken over by the National Trust, bisects the prehistoric monument, and is worth exploring. Just outside the great megalithic circle, **Avebury Manor** is Elizabethan, with gardens, a dovecote, and a herb border. The manor is noted for its plasterwork, quite beautiful, and for its paneling and furnishings. Although lived in by its owner, the Marquis of Ailesbury, it is open to the public in June, July, and August, daily from 2:30 to 5:30 p.m., charging 80p ($1.84) admission, half fare for children. In May and September it can be visited on Saturday and Sunday from 2:30 to 5:30. The manor lies a mile north of the London-Bath road at the junction of the A361 and B4003.

After sightseeing—and still in the same vicinity—you may be ready for a "cuppa."

2. Castle Combe

Once voted Britain's prettiest village, Castle Combe was used for location shots for *Dr. Doolittle*. About 9½ miles from Bath, this little Cotswold village is filled with shops selling souvenirs and antiques. The village cottages are often set beside a trout stream, and are made of stone with roofs laden with moss. The church is unremarkable except for its 15th-century tower. An old market cross and a triple-arched bridge are much photographed.

FOOD AND LODGING: The **Manor House Hotel,** Castle Combe (tel. Castle Combe 782206), is a country estate whose original manor was a 14th-century baronial seat. Set in 26 acres of gardens and parkland, it is a family-run hotel. Mr. and Mrs. Oliver Clegg are the hosts. To the south, the lawns sweep down to the trout-stocked Bybrook River where fishing is permitted for a fee. Thirty-four rooms, 29 with bath, three with shower, are offered overlooking the garden. A double with shared bath is £32 ($73.60) per night, rising to £44 ($101.20) with private bathroom. A bathless single costs £15 ($34.50), rising to £23 ($52.90) with private bath. A 12½% service charge is added, plus VAT. The bedrooms are clean and well decorated, furnished mostly with sunny yellow carpeting and light wallpaper. Some contain antiques, and two have four-posters. The garden wing annex consists of a row of genuine Cotswold stone cottages at the entrance to the grounds. These were gutted and rebuilt to provide good-size rooms with baths.

From the à la carte menu, you can order such dishes as roasts from the trolley, £6.50 ($14.95). At Sunday lunch, a table d'hôte is featured for £8 ($18.40), and on summer evenings, a cold buffet is offered. It's self-service, and you can eat as much as you like. Although casual informality prevails during the day, men in the evening should wear a jacket and tie. Jeans and denims are not acceptable. The hotel has an outdoor swimming pool for summer use only, and an all-year tennis court.

The **White Hart Inn,** at Ford, near Castle Combe (tel. Castle Combe 782-213), is run by Ken Gardner and his wife, Lily, who cater to the local population swelled during the summer months by passing tourists. The inn is a lovely old 16th-century building with gardens running down to the river. They have just added a heated swimming pool to the amenities, but the bars remain low-ceilinged with blackened beams and open fires. Various local souls help in the bars and in the dining room, where residents can dine for £8.50 ($19.55) from a vast menu, including braised venison (caught, matured, and marinated locally in port wine). If this is not enough, there is a wide à la carte menu including steaks and fresh salmon in season. Bar food includes Ken's special steak, kidney, and mushroom pie so large you receive a certificate for polishing it off at £2 ($4.60).

Bedrooms, some with four-poster beds, contain private baths, renting for £25 ($57.50) a night, including an enormous breakfast with lashings of real coffee. The honeymoon suite which includes a dressing room is £30 ($69) a night. Ken, who claims that his American-bred boxer dog is better looking than he is, reckons he must have a sense of the ludicrous. Otherwise, how would a Fleet Street man exist in a place like this? He enjoys the constantly changing stream of folk who while away the hours in the bar, and he has a marvelous store of tall stories with which to regale them when conversation falters.

The Local Pub

No accommodation but plenty of local color is offered at the **White Hart**, on the main road through the village. It's a pub painted white and built of Cotswold stone with a stone tile roof. Dating from either the 13th or 14th century, it has low ceilings (in the cellars are Norman arches). The main bar is divided into two friendly parts, with a cold buffet counter for meals. The garden is also open to visitors, and the parlor bar admits children. This is the first venture of Dennis and Cath Wheeler (she calls it "my husband's indulgence"). Den, as he is known, works in London, commuting daily, and Cath is helped by her attractive daughters. Den's specialty is a landlord's pâté, and he claims the ingredients aren't poached. Home-cooked ham or beef, with coleslaw, bread, and butter, is offered at £2 ($4.60). In winter, hot soups, chili, and toasted sandwiches are available. Traditional bitter beer from wooden barrels is popular with the locals. They have a black cat, Pussy Galore, who drinks milk with her paw from a wine glass, and a King Charles spaniel known as Jack the Ripper. This is one of the few traditional English pubs in the Cotswolds recommended for evening visits.

3. Lacock

This is a National Trust village, with a 13th-century abbey in ruins and adjoining 16th-century houses and gardens. Within an easy drive of Bath, it contains a delightful 14th-century inn, **Sign of the Angel**, Church Street (tel. Lacock 230), ideal for a meal. Mr. and Mrs. Levis run this small inn, offering gourmet meals in an atmosphere that makes one feel he or she has stepped back into Shakespeare's time, maybe even earlier. Before an open fire on nippy days, food is served under a heavily beamed ceiling. Roasts are often featured on the menu. A set luncheon or dinner runs around £12 ($27.60) per person, and a reservation is essential. Lunch is served from 1 to 1:30 and dinner from 7:30 to 8 (one sitting only). The Sign of the Angel is closed for luncheon on Saturday and for dinner on Sunday (also it shuts down for Christmas holidays).

In addition, you'll find eight "quaint" rooms, with patchwork quilts. All have private baths. Singles range from £15 ($34.50) to £18 ($41.40); doubles, £40 ($92) to £45 ($103.50). In all, it's an overnight stop that can be one of lasting memories (no guests under 12 are permitted, however).

SOMERSET

When writing about Somerset, it's difficult to avoid sounding like the editor of *The Countryside Companion*, waxing poetic over hills and valleys, dale and field. The shire embraces some of nature's most masterly scenic touches in England. Mendip's limestone hills undulate across the countryside (ever had a pot-holing holiday?). The irresistible Quantocks are the pride of the west, especially lovely in spring and fall. Here, too, is the heather-clad **Exmoor National Park**, a wooded area abounding in red deer and wild ponies—much of its moorland 1200 feet above sea level. Somerset opens onto the Bristol Channel, with Minehead the chief resort, catering primarily to the English.

Somerset is rich in legend and history—and is particularly fanciful about its associations with King Arthur and Queen Guinevere, along with Camelot and Alfred the Great. Its villages are noted for the tall towers of their parish churches. Of the many Norman castles erected in the country, the most important one remaining is **Dunster Castle**, three miles southeast of Minehead in the village of Dunster, just off the A39 (tel. Dunster 314). The National Trust owns the property and 30 acres of surrounding parkland. Terraced walks and gardens command good views of Exmoor, the Quantock Hills, and the Bristol Channel. Outstanding among the contents within are the 17th-century panels of embossed painted and gilded leather depicting the story of Antony and Cleopatra, and a remarkable 16th-century portrait of Sir John Luttrell shown wading naked through the sea with a female figure of peace and a wrecked ship in the background. The 17th-century plasterwork ceilings of the dining room and staircase and the finely carved staircase balustrade of cavorting huntsmen, hounds, and stags are also particularly noteworthy. The castle may be visited from April until the end of September every day except Friday and Saturday from 11 a.m. to 5 p.m. (last admission 4:30). In October it is open on Tuesday, Wednesday, and Sunday from 2 to 4 p.m. Admission is £1 ($2.30) for adults, 50p ($1.15) for children.

A quiet, unspoiled life characterizes Somerset. You're likely to end up in a ivy-covered old inn, talking with the regulars, and being served broiled salmon that night by the fireside. Or you may stop at a large estate that stands in a woodland setting, surrounded by bridle paths and sheep walks (Somerset was once a great wool center). Maybe you'll settle down in a 16th-century thatched stone farmhouse, set in the midst of orchards in a vale. Somerset is reputed (and we heartily concur) to have the best cider anywhere. When you lounge under a shady Somerset apple tree, downing a tankard of refreshingly chilled golden cider, all the types you've drunk in the past taste like apple juice.

Our notes on Somerset, accumulated over many a year, would easily fill a book. But because space is limited we've confined ourselves in the main to the shire's two most interesting towns—**Wells** and **Glastonbury**.

4. Wells

At the south of the Mendip Hills, the cathedral town of Wells is a medieval gem. It lies only 21 miles from Bath, 123 from London. Wells was a vital link in the Saxon kingdom of Wessex—that is, important in England long before the arrival of William the Conqueror. Once the seat of a bishopric, it was eventually toppled from its ecclesiastical hegemony by the rival city of Bath. But the subsequent loss of prestige has paid off handsomely in Wells today. After experiencing the pinnacle of prestige, it fell into a slumber—hence, much of its old look remains. Wells was named after wells in the town, which were often visited by pilgrims to Glastonbury in the hope that their gout could be eased by its supposedly curative waters. The crowning achievement of the town is:

WELLS CATHEDRAL: Dating from the 12th century, Wells Cathedral is a well-preserved example of the Early English style of architecture. The medieval sculpture (six tiers of hundreds of statues now in process of conservation) of its west front is without peer in England. The western facade was completed in and around the mid-13th century. The landmark central tower was erected in the 14th century, with its attractive fan vaulting attached later. The inverted arches were added to correct the sinking of the top-heavy structure.

Much of the stained glass dates from the 14th century. The star-vaulted Lady Chapel, also from the 14th century, is in the Decorated style. To the north is the vaulted Chapter House, built in the latter 13th century. Look also for a medieval astronomical clock (knights in armor jousting).

After a visit to the cathedral, walk along its cloisters to the moated Bishop's Palace. The swans in the moat ring a bell when summoned to eat at 11 a.m. and 4 p.m. Its former Great Hall, built in the 13th century, is in ruins.

Finally, the small lane known as the Vicars' Close is one of the most beautifully preserved streets in Europe.

FOOD AND LODGING: The **Star Hotel** (tel. Wells 73055) had its origins somewhere in the 16th century, but is best associated with the great coaching era. The cobbled carriageway is still a feature and leads to the dining room—once the stables. The hotel has been modernized, yet retains its old charm and unhurried pace. Copper and brass are used extensively for decoration, and several original stone walls and timbers have been exposed. The hotel front was restored in the Georgian period. The inclusive bed-and-breakfast rate begins at £15 ($34.50) per person. Seven rooms containing private baths cost more, of course. Five rooms have four-poster beds. Under the resident proprietors, the inn is fast gaining a reputation for good food.

The **Crown Hotel**, Market Place (tel. Wells 73457), was built in the 15th century as a coaching inn. In Elizabethan times, it witnessed a number of additions. You'll find open beams in at least one of the bedrooms. A bathless single rents for £15 ($34.50); with bath, £18.50 ($42.55). Doubles without bath cost £24 ($55.20); with bath, £28 ($64.40). These terms include a full English breakfast and VAT. Tea- or coffee-making facilities are in all the rooms. The Crown, just two minutes from Wells Cathedral, offers a pleasant "home away from home" to visitors.

The **Swan**, Saddler Street (tel. Wells 78877), enjoys an uninterrupted view of the west front of the cathedral. This 16th-century hotel blends antiquity with modern comfort. Of its 26 bedrooms, nearly all come equipped with showers or baths. A bathless single rents for £20 ($46), increasing to £23 ($52.90) with bath or shower. A double or twin with bath peaks at £38 ($87.40), these tariffs including a full English breakfast. The furnishings are of a high standard, and good service makes the atmosphere even better. Guests order lunches or dinners from the grill in the Bishop's Kitchen; light eaters are attracted to the Old Saddle Bar and its hot and cold snacks and log fire. With luck, you may meet the Mad Monk, a benevolent ghost, who over the centuries has reportedly been seen by many visitors.

The **Red Lion**, Market Place (tel. 72616), is owned by Mr. Chapman who also directs the Swan. The Red Lion is also an attractive old inn, with a wider availability of rooms in case the smaller Swan is full. Here a single with bath goes for £15 ($34.50), but only £13 ($29.90) without bath. A bathless double rents for £26 ($59.80), increasing to £30 ($69) with bath. The dining room serves a good meal for £7 ($16.10), with such English specialties as homebaked ham and steak-and-kidney pie. There is a pretty courtyard with tables and chairs for a pleasant drink in the evening.

Regency Hotel (tel. Wells 75471) is an informal, family-run hotel in a charming 230-year-old Georgian house, reputedly designed by Sir Christopher Wren. In the center of Wells, it is listed as a building of architectural merit. The hotel is under the personal supervision of its resident owners, Mr. and Mrs. Hall, who maintain a friendly atmosphere and offer good food and lodgings. All their bedrooms have hot and cold running water, and some are equipped with shower cabinets and color TV. With breakfast included, doubles rent for £21 ($48.30), and singles go for £14 ($32.20), including VAT and service. In the licensed restaurant, à la carte meals cost around £6 ($13.80), plus VAT, although you can order a table d'hôte menu at £4.75 ($10.93). Outside you'll find a large free car park.

The **Ancient Gate House,** across from the cathedral (tel. Wells 72029), is ideal year-round for good English meals or slumber, Tudor style. Part of the

Great West Gate, called Browne's Gate, it overlooks the stunning west front of the cathedral. In fact, it is part of the ecclesiastical precincts. Three of its handsomely furnished bedrooms have intricately carved four-poster beds. One, for example, was carved by a craftsman who specialized in Tudor roses and monstrous dream-haunting figures which appear on the headboard. The oak-beamed rooms have lovely furniture. Modern facilities, such as electric heaters and water basins, have been installed without wrecking the spirit of the building.

The hosts, Mr. and Mrs. Rossi, charge from £12 ($27.60) per person for bed and breakfast. The price for bed, breakfast, and evening dinner is from £18.50 ($42.55), plus VAT.

If you can't stay here, at least stop in for lunch, noon to 2 p.m. For a typical English luncheon of three courses you'll pay from £5 ($11.50), plus service charge. It is a mystic and moving experience to sit on the lawn, 60 feet of frontage on the cathedral green, and take afternoon tea in the shade of the limes.

The **City Arms,** 69 High St. (tel. Wells 73916), is the former city jail, but now it's been converted into a local pub and restaurant. It has a high beamed ceiling, and around the dining tables are dark-oak Windsor chairs. On the ground floor is a pub, with an open-air courtyard and umbrella-crowned tables, a popular gathering place for the youth of Wells, who order snacks for around £1.20 ($2.76). The restaurant upstairs offers mainly grills, homemade soups, and desserts. A grilled sirloin and salad will cost about £3.50 ($8.05); fish and chips, £2 ($4.60). Even if you're not hungry, drop in for a pint and soak up the atmosphere.

5. Bleadney

The unspoiled character of the West Country has been preserved in the quiet rural village of Bleadney, just four miles west of Wells on the B3139. Overlooking the moors toward the Cheddar Valley and the Mendip Hills, the village is a convenient center for the exploration of the beauty and history of Somerset with its medieval castles and cathedrals as well as its serene countryside and miles of coastline.

WHERE TO STAY: Threeways Country Guest House (tel. Wells 72817) stands on five acres of garden and paddock through which flows the Axe River. Guests can waken to a refreshing view of the moors and valleys surrounding the village. The inn provides clean, comfortable double or twin-bedded rooms with hot and cold running water and central heating. A double costs about £12.50 ($28.75), going up to £15 ($34.50) for a room with a private shower. Prices include a continental breakfast, but you can have a full English breakfast for another £1.25 ($2.88). VAT is added to all charges.

In summer, the restaurant at Threeways is open seven days a week, serving snacks from £1 ($2.30), although the more adventurous may prefer trout or one of the inn's succulent filet steaks.

6. Glastonbury

The goal of the medieval pilgrim, **Glastonbury Abbey,** once one of the wealthiest and most prestigious monasteries in England, is no more than a ruined sanctuary today. But it provides Glastonbury's claim to historical greatness, an assertion augmented by legendary links to such figures as Joseph of Arimathea, King Arthur, Queen Guinevere, even St. Patrick.

It is said that Joseph of Arimathea journeyed to what was then the Isle of Avalon, with the Holy Grail in his possession. According to tradition, he buried the chalice at the foot of the conically shaped Glastonbury Tor, and a stream of blood burst forth. (You can scale this more than 500-foot-high hill today, on which rests a 15th-century tower.)

At one point, the saint is said to have leaned against his staff, which immediately was transformed into a fully blossoming tree. A cutting alleged to have survived from the Holy Thorn can be seen on the abbey grounds today. It blooms at Christmastime. Some historians have traced this particular story back to Tudor times.

Joseph, so it goes, erected a church of wattle in Glastonbury. The town, in fact, may have had the oldest church in England, as excavations have shown.

The most famous link—fanned for Arthurian fans in the Victorian era by Tennyson—concerns the burial of King Arthur and Queen Guinevere on the abbey grounds. In 1191, the monks dug up the skeletons of two bodies on the south side of the Lady Chapel, said to be those of the king and queen. In 1278, in the presence of Edward I, the bodies were removed and transferred to a black marble tomb in the choir. Both the burial spot and the shrine are marked today.

A large Benedictine Abbey of St. Mary grew out of the early wattle church. St. Dunstan, who was born nearby, was the abbot in the tenth century, later becoming archbishop of Canterbury. Edmund, Edgar, and Edmund "Ironside" —three early English kings—were buried at the abbey.

In 1184 a fire destroyed most of the abbey and its vast treasures. It was eventually rebuilt after much difficulty, only to be dissolved by Henry VIII. Its last abbot, Richard Whiting, was hanged by the neck at Glastonbury Tor. Like the Roman forum, the abbey for years later was used as a stone quarry.

The modern-day pilgrim to Glastonbury can visit the ruins of the Lady Chapel, linked by an Early English "Galilee" to the nave of the abbey. The best preserved building on the grounds is a 14th-century octagonal Abbot's Kitchen, where oxen were once roasted whole to feed the wealthier of the pilgrims (that is, the biggest donors). You can visit the ruins from 9:30 a.m. till dusk for 40p (92¢) for adults, 20p (46¢) for children under 16.

Glastonbury may be one of the oldest inhabited sites in Britain. Excavations have revealed Iron Age lakeside villages on its periphery. Some of the discoveries dug up may be viewed in a little museum in the High Street.

After the destruction of its once-great abbey, the town lost prestige. It is a market town today. The ancient gatehouse entry to the abbey, by the way, is a museum, its principal exhibit a scale model of the abbey and its community buildings as they stood in 1539, at the time of the dissolution. The above fees include entry to the abbey museum.

SOMERSET RURAL LIFE MUSEUM: Abbey Farm, Chilkwell Street (tel. Glastonbury 32903). To have a title like "Keeper of Rural Life" must give Martyn C. Brown an edge over most of us. What a charming person to run such an attractive museum. The main part of the exhibition is Abbey Barn, the home barn of the abbey, built in 1370. The magnificent timbered roof, the stone tiles, and the sculptures outside, including the head of Edward III, make it special. There are also a Victorian farmhouse and various other exhibits illustrating farming in Somerset during the "horse age" and domestic and social life in Victorian times. In summer they have demonstrations of butter making, weaving, basketwork—anything which has reference to the rural life of the country, now rapidly disappearing with the invention of the engine, the freezer, and the instant meal. The museum is open daily from 10 a.m. to around sunset (on

Sunday from around 2 p.m. to sunset). Admission is 35p (81¢) for adults, 10p (23¢) for children. There is a snackbar for light meals and soft drinks.

WHERE TO STAY: If you're one of the lucky few who can stay over in this town rich in history, you can lodge where the wealthy pilgrim of yore did.

The **George & Pilgrims Inn,** High Street (tel. Glastonbury 31146), is one of the few pre-Reformation hostelries still left in England. Once it offered hospitality to Glastonbury pilgrims; now it accepts modern travelers. In the center of town, the inn has a facade that looks like a medieval castle, with stone-mullioned windows with leaded glass. Some of the bedrooms are former monk cells, others have four-posters, carved monuments of oak. You may be given the Henry VIII Room, where the king watched the burning of the abbey in 1539. Prices start at £18 ($41.40) for a single room, £15.50 ($35.65) per person in a double, VAT and an English breakfast included. A well-worn spiral staircase was in use by the monks for centuries, and if your dressing robe looks anything like a monk's robe, you may stir up the ghosts of the past as you walk along the corridors. You could be drawn to the old kitchen which is now the Pilgrim's Bar with its old oak beams. Even if you don't stay over, you may want to stop in for lunch or dinner in the Regency Restaurant to enjoy the excellent à la carte or table d'hôte menus, both of which feature traditional local dishes, or homemade fare in the snackbar. A set luncheon goes for £4.50 ($10.35), a dinner for £7 ($16.10).

Chalice Hill House, Dod Lane (tel. Glastonbury 32459), is not only a place to stay—it may open doors to new spiritual worlds! Chalice Hill House is a honey-colored, 200-year-old Georgian manor, standing at the rear of the abbey ruins, at the foot of Chalice Hill and also close to the legendary Tor. Its youthful owners, David and Anne Jevons, have opened the manor to paying guests, who are likely to be everybody from Seventh-Day Adventists to rabbis, Catholic priests, atheists, soothsayers, doctors, lawyers, and Indian chiefs. It's impressive, yet in no sense foreboding or overpowering, and it's surrounded by lawns and has a true English garden, with well-tended vegetable patches. Dominating all is a towering oak tree.

At the rear of a wide reception hall is a graciously curved staircase with an overscale rare stained-glass window. On your right is a tall and magnificent drawing room, divided by a pair of huge black marble pillars. The lounge side has a comfortable couch and armchairs grouped around a marble fireplace with its elaborate Venetian gilt mirror. At the far end, a 12-foot pine refectory table surrounded by Glastonbury Abbey chairs is set in front of French doors opening onto an orangerie converted into an enclosed swimming pool area. The house furnishings are mostly luxurious, with marquetry chests and tables, and the bedrooms are individually decorated. There are no private baths, however.

Slim, bearded Mr. Jevons is most idealistic. He's an airline captain and flies planes all over the world, but looks forward to returning to his special home at Glastonbury. Mrs. Jevons is vivacious and forthright, an attractive wife and mother with seemingly unlimited sources of energy. She not only runs the house with its multitude of details, but prepares unusual and bountiful meals. She does not serve meat, but she's very adept at making special dishes, such as quiches and casseroles. Dinners usually consist of at least five steamed and lightly cooked vegetables, a tremendous salad with two homemade dressings, all fresh from the garden, and a choice of desserts.

Mrs. Jevons charges £7 ($16.10) per person nightly for bed and breakfast. By arrangement, an evening meal can be had for £4 ($9.20). Reservations are advised in summer months. Guests who smoke are given a corner in the

GLASTONBURY/MENDIP CAVES

swimming pool terrace with ashtrays where they can indulge their habit, as the Jevonses like to keep the rest of their rooms fresh and airy.

The Jevoneses have written a metaphysical book, and he has finished a short booklet, "The Living Legend of Glastonbury," which, although mystical and spiritual, is yet practical for the visitor. You'll be invited to a good audio-visual of Mystical Glastonbury, and, in addition, can meditate in a 12-sided, dome-shaped sanctuary under the oak tree. The whole structure is birch and pine.

LIVING IN THE ENVIRONS: Hayvatt Manor Guest House, Hayvatt (tel. Glastonbury 32330), is an attractive stone house, set back from the road, with true English gardens, even a hothouse where grapes are grown for making wine. The manor house is three miles from Glastonbury via Shepton Mallet Road. The owners, Mr. and Mrs. E. N. Collins, quickly become Norman and Molly, they are so down-to-earth and hospitable. They have three double, and one single room, for which they charge £6.50 ($14.95) per person for bed and breakfast, plus £5 ($11.50) for an evening dinner of three courses and coffee. They grow their own vegetables and fruits for their meals. Families may want to inquire about one of their attached apartments, where you can cook meals for yourself. These go for a weekly rate of £6 ($149.50) and for that you get a sitting room, two bedrooms, and bath, plus a folding bed and cot. Besides making his own wine, Norman has many hobbies, including playing a Hammond organ in the living room and doing special woodwork on boats. The Collinses are justly proud of their house, which has been designated by the government as worth preserving.

7. The Caves of Mendip

The Caves of Mendip are two exciting natural sightseeing attractions in Somerset—the great caves of Cheddar and Wookey Hole, both easily reached by heading west out of Wells. After leaving Wells, you'll first come to **Wookey Hole** (less than two miles away), the source of the Ax River. In the first chamber of the caves, you can see—as legend has it—the Witch of Wookey turned to stone. These caves were believed to have been inhabited by prehistoric man at least 60,000 years ago. Even in those days there was a housing problem, with hyenas moving in and upsetting real-estate values! A museum nearby exhibits prehistoric relics.

In 1973 Madame Tussaud's bought the ravine and a mill where paper has been made since the 17th century. In Madame Tussaud's storage room, more than 2000 molds of the famous and the infamous have been brought to Wookey Hole for safekeeping. Adults pay £1.50 ($3.45); children under 16, 75p ($1.73). Wookey Hole is open every day from 10 a.m. The last visitors are admitted at 6 p.m. from April to September, and at 4:30 p.m. from October to March.

At **Cheddar**, eight miles from Wells, you'll find an attractive village, famous for its cheese and an underground river (the Ax), powerful enough to hollow out the spectacular Cheddar Gorge, a two-mile-long pass through 450-foot-high limestone cliffs. It's unlawful to try to mount the cliffs, except by way of Jacob's Ladder, an exhausting 322 steps to the top. Your "heavenly" reward will be panoramic views of the Mendip Hills and the Somerset moors. The cost of the climb is 20p (46¢) for adults, 10p (23¢) for children. The main attractions of the gorge, however, are below the limestone cliffs, in **Gough's Cave** and **Cox's Cave**, with their stalactites and unique rock formations. The museum contains exhibits of prehistoric man taken from the caves and dating as far back as 8000 B.C. Gough's Cave, with an admission price of 40p (92¢), is open year round, every day, from 10 a.m. to 6 p.m. Cox's Cave, with an admission price of 50p ($1.15), is open from Easter to mid-October, also from 10 a.m. to 6 p.m. Parking is free.

WHERE TO STAY: In and around this area, you'll find some interesting accommodations, as typified by the **George Hotel** (tel. Wedmore 712-264) which lies three miles south of the Cheddar Gorge in the modest village of Wedmore. Here, King Alfred made peace with the Danes and their ruler Guthrum in 878 A.D., forcing him to be baptized. Faced with such antiquity, nothing but an old-world coaching inn will do. The George, part of which dates back to the 1350s, has for centuries been giving strangers a refreshing pint of ale and a restful night's sleep in one of the 12 upstairs bedrooms. The bed-and-breakfast rate is £11 ($25.30) per person nightly. Lunches are available for around £3 ($6.90), dinners from £5 ($11.50).

Behind the cellar bar are barrels of ales and beer, and rows of mugs hang from an overhead, time-blackened beam. Everywhere there is a sense of living in the past. It was in 1926 that the custom of holding "court leet of Wedmore" (a special type of manorial court) was abandoned, but the inn still functions as the center of village life.

THE CHEESE TOUR: **Chewton Cheese Dairy,** Priory Farm, Chewton Mendip (tel. Chewton Mendip 560), is one of the six remaining dairies in England still making cheddar in the traditional way. Visitors are welcome to watch the cheesemaking process, which takes place every morning. Mid-morning is the best time to arrive. After the tour, you may wish to purchase a "truckle" (or wheel) of mature cheddar to send home. A six-pound wheel costs about £11.90 ($27.37), including shipping. The knowledge that Prince Charles is also a customer adds even more flavor to one of England's unique products.

AN INN NEAR MINEHEAD: The **Ship Inn,** Porlock Weir, near Minehead (tel. Porlock 862-753). As you drive along the A39 road from Bridgewater, through the Quantock Hills and toward North Devon and Exmoor, signs on your right will lead you down from Porlock to Porlock Weir, a tiny little port on the Bristol Channel backed by the Exmoor foothills. The Ship Inn is very old—almost 1000 years of history may have swept past it. Typical of many hard-working seaside harbors, timbers dragged from the sea have been used in the construction of the inn. Ceilings are low and windows are small.

None of the rooms has a private bathroom but there are adequate facilities available. Overnight, including a large English breakfast, will cost you around £15 ($34.50), plus VAT and service. Dinner costs from £6 ($13.80) per person, and lunches are somewhat cheaper, about £4 ($9.20) for three courses.

The Sechiari family, who have run the hotel for many years, will do all they can to make you welcome, although they do not cater to small children.

AVON

Avon is the name that has been given to the area around the old port of Bristol—an area that used to be in Somerset.

8. Bath

Victoria didn't start everything. In 1702, Queen Anne made the 115-mile trek from London to the mineral springs of Bath, thereby launching a fad that was to make the city the most celebrated spa in England. Of course, Victoria-come-lately eventually hiked up, too, to sample a medicinal cocktail (which you can still do today), but Bath by then had passed its zenith.

The most famous personage connected with Bath's scaling the pinnacle of fashion was the 18th-century dandy, Beau Nash. He was the final arbiter of taste and manners (one example: he made dueling déclassé). The master of ceremonies of Bath, he cut a striking figure as he made his way across the city, with all the plumage of a bird of paradise. While dispensing (at a price) trinkets to the courtiers and aspirant gentlemen of his day, Beau was carted around in a liveried carriage.

The gambler was given the proper setting for his considerable social talents by the 18th-century architects John Wood the Elder and his son. These architects designed a city of stone from the nearby hills, a feat so substantial and lasting that Bath today is the most harmoniously laid out city in England.

Their work done, the Georgian city on a bend of the Avon River was to attract a following among leading political and literary figures—Dickens, Thackeray, Nelson, Pitt. Canadians may already know that General Wolfe lived on Trim Street, and Australians may want to visit the house at 19 Bennett St. where their founding father, Admiral Philip, lived. Even Henry Fielding came this way, observing in *Tom Jones* that the ladies of Bath "endeavour to appear as ugly as possible in the morning, in order to set off that beauty which they intend to show you in the evening."

Bath has had two lives. Long before its Queen Anne, Georgian, and Victorian popularity, it was known to the Romans as Aquae Sulis. The foreign legions founded their baths here (which may be visited today), so they might ease rheumatism in the curative mineral springs.

Remarkable restoration and careful planning have ensured that Bath retains its handsome look today. The city suffered devastating destruction from the infamous Baedeker air raids of 1942, when Luftwaffe pilots seemed more bent on bombing historical buildings, such as the Assembly Rooms, than in hitting any military target.

The major sights today are the rebuilt Assembly Rooms, the abbey, and the Pump Room and Roman Baths. But if you're intrigued by architecture and city planning, you may want to visit some of the buildings, crescents, and squares. The North Parade, where Goldsmith lived, and the South Parade, where Fanny Burney (English novelist and diarist) once resided, represent harmony—the work of John Wood the Elder. The younger Wood, on the other hand, designed the Royal Crescent, an elegant half-moon row of town houses copied by Astor architects for their colonnade in New York City in the 1830s. Queen Square is one of the most beautiful (Jane Austen and Wordsworth used to live here—but hardly together), showing off quite well the work of Wood the Elder. And, don't miss his Circus, built in 1754, as well as the shop-flanked Pulteney Bridge, designed by Robert Adam and compared aptly to the Ponte Vecchio of Florence.

BATH ABBEY: Built on the site of a much larger Norman cathedral, the present-day abbey is a fine example of the late Perpendicular style. When Queen Elisabeth I came to Bath in 1574, she ordered that a national fund be set up to restore the abbey. The west front is the sculptural embodiment of a Jacob's Ladder dream of a 15th-century bishop. When you go inside and see its many windows, you'll understand why the abbey is called the "Lantern of the West." Note the superb fan vaulting, achieving at times a scalloped effect. Beau Nash was buried in the nave and is honored by a simple monument totally out of keeping with his flamboyant character.

PUMP ROOM AND ROMAN BATHS: In 75 A.D., the Romans founded their baths, dedicated to the goddess Sul (similar to Minerva). Like many of their other baths, the one in Bath was in its day an engineering feat and even today, it is considered one of the finest Roman remains in the country. It is still fed by the only hot spring water in Britain. The Baths decayed, and were buried until mid-18th century, although it was late in Victoria's day before major excavations were undertaken. A museum connected to the baths contains the most interesting objects from the digs (look for the head of Minerva). You can have coffee in the 18th century Pump Room or a drink at the licensed restaurant on the terrace. The Pump Room and the Roman Baths and Museum are open daily in summer from 9 a.m. to 6 p.m. In winter weekday hours are from 9 a.m. to 5 p.m., on Sunday from 11 a.m. to 5 p.m. Admission is 80p ($1.84).

THE ASSEMBLY ROOMS: Lying right off the Circus, the Assembly Rooms were originally designed by John Wood the Younger in 1769. Partly destroyed by 1942 air raids, the rooms have been restored to the height of their 18th-century elegance, when the fashionable dandies and their ladies paraded about. Today they house a Costume Museum, founded on the collection of Mrs. Doris Langley-Moore, and greatly enlarged and enriched by donations from many sources. The display of clothes covers more than 300 years of fashion history—Madame Recamier's lounging ladies, Jane Austen's upper-middle-class look, styles right out of Watteau paintings, the Alice B. Toklas post–World War I garb, up to Dior haute couture and a mini by Mary Quant.

Men's apparel isn't neglected in the exhibition, and there are embroidered silk suits of the 18th century, tailored coats worn by Victorian gentlemen, and outfits brought up to the present day by some of the world's leading fashion designers. There are also several dresses belonging to the British royal family, children's clothes, underwear, jewelry, and dolls. Head first for the Card Room, known to Dickens readers from the descriptions in *Pickwick Papers*. The museum is open weekdays in summer from 9:30 a.m. to 6 p.m., on Sunday from 10 a.m. to 6 p.m. Winter hours are 10 a.m. to 5 p.m. weekdays, 11 a.m. to 5 p.m. on Sunday. Admission is 90p ($2.07) for adults, 40p (92¢) for children.

BATH FESTIVAL: This annual festival of the performing arts lasts 17 days and takes place at the end of May and beginning of June. Essentially it's a festival of music under the artistic direction of Sir William Glock. Concerts are held in the Assembly Rooms, the Guildhall, the Theatre Royal, the abbey, Wells Cathedral, and many other historic houses and churches in the area. The varied program includes concerts by the major British choirs and orchestras, an international line-up of soloists and chamber groups, exhibitions, lectures, garden and church tours. All information can be obtained from the Bath Festival Office, 1 Pierrepont Pl., Bath, BA1, 1JY (tel. Bath 62231). Finally, on the outskirts of Bath stands this leading attraction:

A GEORGIAN HOUSE: No. 1 Royal Crescent (tel. Bath 28126), is a Georgian House as it was. By the generosity of Major Cayzer, the house was bought and handed over to the Bath Preservation Trust in 1968 for the fulfillment of a long-cherished idea—the creation of an authentic Georgian interior—so that people could see for themselves what the inside of a Bath house looked like in its heyday. It is open the first Tuesday in March to the last Sunday in October, inclusive, Tuesday to Saturday from 11 a.m. to 5 p.m., Sunday from 2 to 5 p.m. Admission is 40p (92¢) for adults and 30p (69¢) for children and students.

CLAVERTON MANOR: Some 2½ miles outside Bath, you get a glimpse of life as lived by a diversified segment of American settlers until Lincoln's day. It was the first American museum established outside the United States. A Greek Revival house, designed by a Georgian architect, Claverton Manor sits proudly in its own extensive grounds in the Avon valley. Among the authentic exhibits—shipped over from the States—are a Rio Grande room, a Conestoga wagon, an early American fireplace (ever had gingerbread baked from the recipe of George Washington's mother?), the parlor of a New York town house of the early 19th century, and (on the grounds) a copy of Washington's flower garden at Mount Vernon. You can visit the museum from March 29 to November 2, daily except Monday, from 2 to 5 p.m. Adults pay £1.20 ($2.76); children, £1 ($2.30).

READER'S SIGHTSEEING TIP: "The mayor's **Corps of Honorary Guides** conducts free walking tours of the City of Bath every day during the summer, bank holidays and every Sunday throughout the year. Guides are also available for private parties at other times if required. These guides are unpaid and act in a purely honorary capacity: they do not accept gratuities. A tour lasts approximately 1½ hours and visitors see the main points of historical and architectural interest within the city. For further information, write to Mr. J. Clifton, Assistant Director, Department of Leisure and Tourist Services, Pump Room, Bath, BA1 1LZ, Avon" (R. Alter, Lexington, Ky.).

WHERE TO STAY: In accommodations, Bath offers a wide choice—some in architectural landmarks.

Landsdown Grove Hotel, Landsdown Road (tel. Bath 315891), is a well-run hotel outside the center of the city, set on the northern slopes with magnificent views, 600 feet above sea level. Its drawing room is informal, with flowering chintz draperies, a large gilt and marble console, and comfortable armchairs. A modernization program has produced not only carpeting and fresh paint, but full central heating throughout and private bathrooms and showers and color TV in all the cheerful, comfortable bedrooms. Single rooms with bath cost from £25 ($57.50); doubles with bath, from £38 ($87.40). All rates are inclusive of service and VAT, but a full English breakfast costs from £3 ($6.90) per person. It's a pleasure to eat in the sunny dining room, with its bay window that opens onto the garden. Before-dinner drinks are available in the cocktail bar, which is decorated with delightful murals of Edwardian fairground scenes, while a bar annex is adorned with illustrations of oldtime music halls, bringing a uniquely charming atmosphere. Bathonians as well as visitors to the hotel patronize this place. There is an area for parking your car, as well as a covered garage.

Royal York Hotel, George Street (tel. Bath 61541), was a coaching inn in Georgian days, and now provides moderate comfort at a location within easy walking distance of the abbey. Every room is centrally heated, and there are elevators to all floors. Each room contains a radio, telephone, and razor outlet —and is furnished with tasteful, traditional pieces, appropriate to the genteel character of the hotel. Some rooms have private baths. In high season (April to October), the rate in a single ranges from £18 ($41.40) to £24 ($55.20), the latter with private bath. Doubles range from £28 ($64.40) to £36 ($82.80). Try to get an accommodation in the rear, as these rooms are much quieter.

Royal Crescent Hotel, 15-16 Royal Crescent (tel. Bath 319-090), is a special place for special people. It stands proudly in the center of the famed Royal Crescent, a Georgian colonnade of town houses designed by John Wood the Younger in 1767. The owners are continuing the tradition that has made this hotel a comfortable and pleasant place to stay. The 29 bedrooms—all with private bath, telephone, color TV, and radio—vary greatly in size, but all are nicely furnished and well equipped. The hall, lounges, and main staircases are said by eminent architects to represent the 18th century at its peak. Everything is furnished with a high standard of luxury and comfort. Central heating runs throughout.

An excellent cuisine is provided by the chef and his staff. The hotel has a good wine cellar and attractive bar. An elevator runs to all floors. In addition to the facilities, the hotel has a courteous and friendly staff. Attractive gardens lead to garages. The bed-and-breakfast rate is £31.75 ($72.80) in a single, £18.75 ($42.90) to £26.75 ($61.30) per person in a double. These prices include a continental breakfast, service, and VAT. Dinner is from £10 ($23) per person.

Jane's Hotel, Manvers Street (tel. Bath 65966), is central, a short walk from the main railroad and bus stations and near the abbey and the Roman Baths. Ample parking space is available in the multistory car park behind the hotel. The hotel is a Victorian building created from a row of terraced houses. It provides clean, comfortable bedrooms, with plenty of hot water, tea- and coffee-making facilities, and color TV, at a cost ranging between £13.50 ($31.05) and £15 ($34.50) per person, including tax. Jane's is managed by Adrian Leonards, a Cornishman, who, along with his staff, has spent the last few years refurbishing, repainting, and improving the hotel.

Nosebags Bistrotheque offers disco-dining facilities from 8 p.m. to 1 a.m., offering exotic cocktails. Recently opened is the French-style Crêperie and Wine Bar, created in a separate section of the hotel. This is the innovation of Christopher Bradshaw, son of the proprietor. Open from 10 a.m. to 11 p.m., it offers excellent value for money, along with good music. One of the West Country's most popular nightclubs is beneath the hotel. It's the Beau Nash Disco, which opens at 8 p.m. and closes late. Entrance is free to hotel guests. Otherwise, visitors pay £1.50 ($3.45) per person.

Villa Magdala, Henrietta Road (tel. Bath 25836), is a "country" guest house just a five-minute walk from the center of Bath. In a quiet residential area across the Avon from the Parade Gardens and overlooking Henrietta Park, the villa was completed in 1868 and named after the Battle of Magdala which was fought the same year. The stone and gabled structure offers many features of a residential hotel, including refrigerators, baths or showers, TVs, hotplates, and baby-listening services. A few of the rooms are even furnished with deluxe four-poster beds. Rates range from approximately £18 ($41.40) for a single room with private shower to £25 ($57.50) for a double room with four-poster and bath. Price per night includes VAT and a full English breakfast. Ample car parking is provided on the grounds. The Villa Magdala is open for guests from February to November. You get real personal attention from the hosts, George and Sally Fuller, who show what they can do at breakfast. Mr. Fuller himself is the cook, buying bacon and sausages from Trowbridge. He simmers his ham in stock and offers it, carefully curled, with eggs poached to perfection. Mrs. Fuller even takes care to see that the prunes are just right, as she soaks them and then simmers them for hours with lemon.

Christopher Hotel, High Street (tel. Bath 60029), is an attractive, well-run hotel, with an 18th-century facade, one of Bath's oldest coaching inns. Opposite a side of the abbey and overlooking the Grand Parade, it is only a one-minute walk from the Roman Baths. The residents' lounge combines traditional and modern elements. The bedrooms are utilitarian and well kept; a double with bath costs £16 ($36.80) per person nightly. The rates include an English breakfast. You can order good food in the restaurant, which has both a table d'hôte and an à la carte menu. The hotel has two bars but no elevator. A multistory car park is nearby.

The **Old Mill**, Tollbridge Road (tel. Bath 858-476), is right on the Avon, beside a stone bridge in Batheaston, about 2½ miles from Bath on the A4 to Chippenham. Nearly every bedroom has a view of the river, with its willows, punting boats, and towering trees. The Mill (and its annex) is not as ancient as the name implies; rather, it's boxy modern, with a new dining room and a drinking lounge. Even if you can't stay overnight, you can reserve a table for a meal here. The cooking is excellent. The "Taste of England" menu features such dishes as guinea fowl in season, £6.80 ($15.65); Severn River salmon, £6.70 ($15.42); baked ham in sauce, £5.25 ($12.08); and kidney-and-mushroom pie, £5.20 ($11.96). The bedrooms are furnished modestly, but are comfortable. A single room costs £18 ($41.40); doubles with bathroom, £24 ($55.20). In the annex, singles without bath are £10 ($23); doubles without bath, £21 ($48.30). All tariffs include an English breakfast, service, and VAT.

The **Kingsley House**, Upper Oldfield Park (tel. Bath 25749), is a Victorian mansion refurbished in excellent taste by its owners, Jon and Mary Hillary. With only six guest rooms, the hotel has an intimate atmosphere, and the live-in owners encourage the air of genuine friendliness. Five of the rooms are equipped with private bath or shower and toilet, and all have radio and television. There's also a sauna on the premises. Rates begin at about £21 ($48.30) for a double room without private bath and go up to £24 ($55.20) for the best room, furnished with wing chairs and a handsome colonial bed. Tariffs include breakfast and VAT. Kingsley House is renowned for its breakfasts.

WHERE TO DINE: Bath is increasingly gaining a reputation as a gourmet citadel.

Popjoy's, Beau Nash House, Sawclose (tel. Bath 60494), is housed in a 1720 Regency building which was once the home of the notorious Beau Nash, the "King of Bath." The restaurant is named after Juliana Popjoy, Nash's one-time mistress and a prominent Bath society figure in her own right. When Nash died in 1761, Juliana vowed to never again sleep in a bed, and spent the rest of her life gathering herbs and living in a hollow tree in Wiltshire.

With such a background, Popjoy's is certain to be something more than the run-of-the-mill restaurant. Its food, decor, and service all add up to making this one of the best restaurants in the West Country. You'll be greeted at the door by a charming young lady in a pinafore who will lead you to a sitting room on the second floor. Here you may contentedly sip an apéritif while your table is prepared in the small cozy dining room. In the winter, the fireplaces all glow with the friendly warmth of crackling fires.

A prix-fixe menu, offered on Saturday only, includes service, VAT, and coffee, going for £15.75 ($36). Otherwise, à la carte meals run from £18 ($41.40) at dinner. Appetizers include terrine of sole and salmon, a delicate watercress mousse, or a rich fish soup afloat with tiny fish quenelles. For the main course, you might choose the suprême de volaille stuffed with apricots, deliciously tender chicken breasts stuffed with fruit, or veal braised in herbs imported fresh from Provence. For dessert you might try a rich chocolate mousse or a truly English gooseberry fool. Popjoy's is open for dinner each evening Monday through Saturday. From April to October the restaurant also serves a remarkable lunch.

The Hole in the Wall, 16 George St. (tel. Bath 25242), may give you one of your finest gourmet experiences in Avon. You enter what looks like the living room of a Georgian town house, where a hostess greets you, takes your name and order for a drink, and presents you with the impressive menu. She'll even help you plan your meal if you prefer. All the selections are especially prepared for you. When your table is ready, you descend into a colorful, old-world dining room, with an attractive decor that includes a great "dungeon" fireplace. The benches, tables, and chairs are antiques.

To start the meal, you face a choice of both "cold and hot beginnings," which are likely to include fish soup with wine, saffron, and herbs. Main courses include the fish specialty of the day, depending on what the market has to offer. The menu is changed frequently, but you may be lucky enough to find such items as baked ham with mead and spiced peaches and chicken braised with eggplant in wine. For dessert, the homemade fruit sorbets are delicious, as is the chilled rum mousse. Count on spending at least £15 ($34.50) for dinner, exclusive of wine.

The restaurant has a selection of more than 120 wines, including a number of "bin ends," usually older vintages, which are offered at reasonable prices. The Hole in the Wall is open daily, except Sunday, for lunch from noon to 2 p.m., and for dinner from 7 to 10:30 p.m.

Beaujolais, 5 Chapel Row (tel. Bath 23417), is run by French proprietors, Jean-Pierre Auge and Philippe Wall, on true bistro lines. You enter through the undistinguished front door and find a seat in one of the three rooms of brightly clad tables. Then you're greeted by a member of the friendly and knowledgeable staff. Call in advance for a reservation, as this cheerful place has become very popular. You'll definitely need to give notice if you want one of the more private tables for four with settles, as fresh materials are used in the dishes served. Appetizers cost around £1.20 ($2.76), and main courses begin at £4 ($9.20). However, there is rarely a main course costing more than £6 ($13.80), which is what you are likely to pay for specialties like sea bass, half a roast pheasant, or venison. A new menu is offered every day, and it attaches importance to fish. Among the most popular appetizers are crêpe au camembert, fish soup, and piperade, to be followed by poulet en croûte Napoléon, coquilles St. Jacques à la Provençale, and entrecôte steak moscovite. The Beaujolais is open daily, except Sunday and bank holidays, from 12:30 to 2:30 p.m. and from 7:30 to 11:30 p.m. Faint music plays in the background, and the atmosphere is informal, the value excellent.

Brunos Restaurant, 2 George St. (tel. Bath 63341), opposite the prestigious Hole in the Wall, is an intimate bistro where you can order a predinner drink while charting your way through the à la carte menu. The friendly staff will advise and help should you need it. You can start with pâté made by the chef or one of the many other starters, followed by a choice of half a dozen or more main dishes, including fish, meat, poultry, and game in season. Brunos is open six days a week from Monday through Saturday. An excellent cold table is available at lunchtime, as well as hot casseroles, and last orders are accepted at 2. The à la carte menu is available at all times, last orders being taken in the evening at 10:15. You may eat well at lunch for from £3 ($6.90), and à la carte from about £8.50 ($19.55) per person at any time. Specialties include brace of local wood pigeon casserole and Wiltshire venison with juniperberries casserole. A very good house wine is available, together with a varied selection of reasonably priced specialty wines. The restaurant is closed all day Sunday and for lunch Monday.

Clarets Wine Bar, Kingsmead Square (tel. Bath 66688), is a cellar with whitewashed walls beneath one of Bath's Georgian houses. Simple slate and pinewood tables and benches and a plain decor show that David Tearle and his wife Lisa are experienced restaurateurs who offer simple surroundings and high-quality food. Casseroles of lamb and eggplant, pork and cucumber, or meatless vegetables and cheese are around £2.50 ($5.75). Interesting salads, chicken pie, and fish and garlic pie go from £1.75 ($4.03) to £2.25 ($5.18). There is soup served with French bread and homemade desserts. Try the St. Emilion au chocolat. A good meal will cost about £4 ($9.20) to £5 ($11.50), washed down with wine by the glass at 75p ($1.73) or from £3 ($6.90) a bottle. In summer they go really "bistro" and have tables outside for al fresco eating. It is open from 10 a.m. to 12:30 p.m. and from 6:30 to 11 p.m., Monday to Saturday; on Sunday from 7 to 10:30 p.m. only.

Sally Lunns House, North Parade Passage, is a tiny gabled stone coffeeshop, with a Georgian bay window, original early Tudor fireplaces, and "bow and arrow" cupboards. The house is a landmark in Bath, built in 1482 and considered the oldest structure in the city. Sally Lunn was known by legend to all Bathonians for her buns baked in the cellars here in 1680. The same tradition of good cakes is carried on today (also salads and light meals are served all day). Take your coffee, tea, or hot chocolate at a natural wood tavern table, or while seated in a settle. Coffee with a Sally Lunn bun costs only 45p ($1.04). You can have toasted sandwiches at 90p ($2.07), chocolate gateau at 65p ($1.50). In addition, the owner has opened a Salad Bowl on the first floor which serves from Easter until Christmas, between noon and 2 p.m. This is a help-yourself plate which costs from £2 ($4.60), depending on which salads or dishes you select. You can eat as much as you like, although soups, coffee, and desserts are extra. A small gift shop on the second floor features the work of local crafts people. The house is easy to spot—near the abbey, off Church Street.

9. Bristol

Bristol, the largest city in the West Country, is a good center for touring western Britain. Its location is 10 miles west of Bath, just across the Bristol Channel from Wales, 20 miles from the Cotswolds, and 30 miles from Stonehenge. This historic inland port is linked to the sea by seven miles of the navigable Avon River. Bristol has long been rich in seafaring traditions and has many links with the early colonization of America. In fact, some claim that the new continent was named after a Bristol town clerk, Richard Ameryke! In 1497 John Cabot sailed from Bristol, which led to the discovery of the northern half of the New World.

In Bristol, the world's first iron steamship and luxury liner has been restored to her 1840 glory. She's the 3000-ton S.S. *Great Britain,* and was created by Isambard Brunel, a Victorian engineer. Visitors can go aboard this "floating palace" between 10 a.m. and 5 p.m. for an admission of $1 (half price for children).

At the age of 25 in 1831, Brunel began a Bristol landmark, a suspension bridge over the 250-foot-deep Avon Gorge at Clifton.

Bristol Cathedral was begun in the 14th century on the site of a Norman abbey. The central tower was added in 1466. The Chapter House and Gatehouse are good examples of late Norman architecture, and the choir is magnificent.

Another church, **St. Mary Redcliffe,** was called "the fairest, the goodliest, and most famous parish church in England" by such an authority as Elizabeth I. Built in the 14th century, it has been carefully restored.

Cobbled King Street is known for its Theatre Royal, the smallest English playhouse and the oldest in continuous operation. Many old taverns line this quayside area, principally the 17th-century Llandoger Trow, once the haunt of pirates.

FOOD AND LODGING: Holiday Inn, Lower Castle Street (tel. Bristol 294-281), is a modern city-center hotel, ideal for the business traveler, but also suitable to the tourist who makes it to this part of the West Country. The heated swimming pool is impressive, and the foyer is spacious. Public areas are well groomed, comfortable, and stylish, in the tradition of this popular chain. You have a choice of several bars, and there's a coffeeshop as well, serving moderately priced light meals. Bedrooms are uniformly furnished, bright, and cheerful, with double beds (doubles have two) and good tiled bathrooms. Singles cost £26 ($59.80) nightly, and the double tariff ranges from £29 ($66.70) to £34 ($78.20). There's also disco action nightly except Sunday.

Among the restaurants, the most creative cookery is found at **Michael's,** 129 Hotwell Rd. (tel. Bristol 26190), run by Michael McGowen. His charming and well-patronized restaurant is near Clifton, on a highway leading toward the piers. In his pleasant bar, decorated like an Edwardian parlor, an open fire burns. The dining room is also bright and inviting. Michael's menu is imaginative, and he likes to change it, depending on the availability of seasonal produce. Service is informal and enthusiastic. Lunch is offered daily except Monday and Sunday, costing from £5 ($11.50). Dinner is served until midnight (on Saturday till 1 a.m.) every night except Monday. Expect to pay about £12 ($27.60) per person. Always call for a table and to make sure Michael hasn't taken a summer vacation.

Chapter X

THE COTSWOLDS

1. Burford
2. Clanfield
3. Minster Lovell
4. Bibury
5. Cirencester
6. Painswick
7. Cheltenham
8. Royal Sudeley Castle
9. Malmesbury
10. Tetbury
11. Wotton-under-Edge
12. Shipton-under-Wychwood
13. Chipping Norton
14. Bourton-on-the-Water
15. Lower Swell
16. Upper and Lower Slaughter
17. Stow-on-the-Wold
18. Moreton-in-Marsh
19. Broadway
20. Chipping Campden

THE COTSWOLDS, the once-great wool center of the 13th century, lie mainly in the county of Gloucestershire, although parts dip into Oxfordshire, Warwickshire, and Worcestershire. If possible, try to explore the area by car. That way, you can spend hours surveying the land of winding goat paths, rolling hills, and sleepy hamlets, with names such as Stow-on-the-Wold, Wotton-under-Edge, Moreton-in-Marsh, Old Sodbury, Chipping Campden, Shipton-under-Wychwood, Upper and Lower Swell, even Upper and Lower Slaughter, often called "The Slaughters." These most beautiful of English villages keep popping up on book jackets and calendars.

Cotswold lambs used to produce so much wool they made their owners very rich—wealth they invested in some of the finest domestic architecture in Europe, made out of the honeybrown Cotswold stone. The wool-rich gentry didn't neglect their church contributions either. Often the simplest of villages will have a church that in style and architectural detail seems to rank far beyond the means of the hamlet.

Picture yourself as part of the life of these hills:

"Come on in through the kitchen" is all you need hear to know that you've found a homelike place where naturalness and friendliness prevail. Many readers will want to seek out comfortable (although decidedly unchic) accommodations in little stone inns that survive among the well-known and sophisticated hotels that advertise heavily. Perhaps you'll be served tea in front of a two-way fireplace, its walls made of natural Cotswold stone. Taking your long pieces of thick toasted bread, saturated with fresh butter, you'll find the flavor so good you won't resist putting on more chunky cherry jam.

Or maybe you'll go down a narrow lane to a stately Elizabethan stone manor, with thick walls and a moss-covered slate roof. Perhaps you'll arrive at haying time and watch the men at work in the fields beyond, as well as the cows and goats milked to produce the rich "double cheese" you'll be served later. Your dinner that night? Naturally, a roast leg of Cotswold lamb.

Or you may want to settle down in and around Cheltenham, where the view from your bedroom window of the Severn Valley to the Malvern Hills to the Welsh mountains is so spectacular that old King George III himself came for a look. The open stretches of common, woodlands, fields, and country lanes provide the right setting for picnics. Life inside your guest house may be devoted to comfort and good eating—baskets of fresh eggs, Guernsey milk, cream, poultry, and a variety of vegetables from the garden.

If your tastes are slightly more expensive, you may seek out a classical Cotswold manor (and there are dozens of them), with creamy field stone, high-pitched roofs, large and small gables, towering chimneys, stone-mullioned windows, a drawing room with antique furnishings, a great lounge hall, and ancient staircase, flagstone floors. Such Cotswold estates represent England at its best, with clipped hedges, rose gardens, terraces, stone steps, sweeping lawns, old trees, and spring flowers. Here you can revel in a fast-disappearing English country life.

The adventure begins in:

1. Burford

In Oxfordshire, Burford is the gateway to the Cotswolds. This unspoiled medieval town, built of Cotswold stone, is 19 miles to the west of Oxford, 31 miles from Stratford-upon-Avon, 14 miles from Blenheim Palace, and 75 miles from London. Its fame rests largely on its early Norman church (c. 1116) and its High Street, lined with coaching inns. Oliver Cromwell passed this way, as did Charles II and Nell Gwynne. Burford was one of the last of the great wool centers, the industry surviving into Victoria's reign. You may want to photograph the bridge across the Windrush River, where Queen Elizabeth I once stood. Burford is definitely equipped for tourists, as the antique shops along The High will testify.

WHERE TO STAY: Whether you're staying over or simply stopping off for lunch, there's a choice of some romantic old inns.

The **Bay Tree Hotel,** Sheep Street (tel. Burford 3137), would astonish the former owner of this 400-year-old, stone-gabled home. Surely Sir Lawrence Tanfield would never have predicted that this stately old house would become a quiet and peaceful setting for retreat-seekers. In his time, he was the unpopular Lord Chief Baron of the Exchequer to Elizabeth I—and was not noted for his hospitality! But time has erased the bad memory, and the splendor of this Cotswold manor house remains.

For a stay of three days (the minimum full-board requirement), you are charged £20 ($46) per person daily in a bathless double. If you prefer bed and breakfast only, the rate is from £14 ($32.20) per person (higher in a room with bath).

This is one of the showplaces of England. The house has oak-paneled rooms with huge stone fireplaces, where logs burn in chilly weather. There is a high-beamed hall with a minstrel's gallery. Room after room is furnished tastefully with antiques. The 20th-century comforts, such as central heating and a large number of bathrooms, have been discreetly installed. And the beds are a far cry from the old rope-bottom contraptions of the days of Queen Elizabeth I. You will sleep peacefully on soft mattresses.

Try to get one of the rooms overlooking the terraced gardens at the rear of the house. As the season changes, new flowers come into bloom against the old stone walls. Flagstone walks, tidy lawns, and comfortable garden furniture will lure you into a lazy afternoon. A servant will bring you a tray at teatime.

You dine at night by candlelight: the meals are first class, some of the finest you'll be served in the Cotswolds. A recent lunch for £3.95 ($9.09) consisted of a smoked salmon omelet, served with string beans and potatoes, and a spicy hot mince pie with brandy butter for dessert. Dinner is £6 ($13.80), and the big Sunday lunch costs the same.

Have after-dinner coffee on the terrace and experience twilight. Slowly the soft shadows grow darker and longer: this is the moment of enchantment in England. You may even hear a meadow lark.

The **Lamb Inn**, Sheep Street (tel. Burford 3155), is a thoroughbred Cotswold house, built solidly in 1430 of thick stones, with mullioned and leaded windows, many chimneys and gables, and a slate roof mossy with age. On a quiet street, it opens onto a stone-paved rear garden, with espalier fruit trees, a rose-lined walk, and a shaded lawn. Mrs. Nancy North Lewis is the owner; a most gracious hostess, she is joined by her son, Commander North Lewis. Some members of their staff have been with the inn for 20 years. The chef is Cordon Bleu oriented, and the meals, served in the beamed dining room with a garden view, attract nonresidents, who pay £15 ($11.50) for a set luncheon, £6 ($13.80) on Sundays. A set dinner goes for £6 also. If you're dining here in the right season, you can feast on treats of the river or forest, such as salmon, venison, trout, game, roast capon.

While there is a per-person bed-and-breakfast rate of £15.50 ($35.65) to £18.50 ($42.55)—the latter with a private bath—most dollarwise visitors stay for at least three days so they can take advantage of the full-board rates, ranging from £24 ($55.20) to £28 ($64.40) per person daily. The bedrooms are a mixture of today's comforts, such as soft beds and plentiful hot water, and yesterday's antiques. The public living rooms contain heavy oak beams, stone floors, window seats, oriental rugs, and fine antiques (Chippendale, Tudor, Adam, Georgian, Jacobean). In the drinking lounge, a special beer, made in an adjoining brewery, is served. In addition, a four o'clock tea is offered in front of the fireplaces, or else—weather permitting—out on the flagstoned courtyard.

2. Clanfield

Clanfield lies at the foot of the Cotswolds, near the upper reaches of the Thames. In the heart of "hunting country," it is convenient to Cheltenham and the Newbury race courses. Golf and fishing are available nearby. Clanfield lies 20 miles from Oxford, eight miles from our last stopover in Burford, and 16 miles from Swindon, and also makes a center for visits to Blenheim Palace, Stratford-upon-Avon, Henley-on-Thames, and the Cotswold Wild Life Park, only a ten-minute drive from the following recommendation.

WHERE TO STAY: The **Plough Hotel and Restaurant,** Clanfield, (tel. Clanfield 222), is a perfect example of a mid-16th-century Elizabethan manor house. Throughout the summer, climbing roses cover the honey-colored Cotswold stone walls. Its attractive gardens just opposite the village green offer a peaceful spot for meditation. Under protection as a landmark building, the Plough maintains an air of authenticity inside as well, with cloistered halls, massive fireplaces, and fine antiques and tapestries.

The restaurant has become internationally recognized, having won various awards for its cuisine every year since 1970. Dinners are served in the Knights' and Tapestry Rooms with their authentic period furnishings. During the summer months, luncheon is frequently served in the small walled garden. Drinks are available in the beamed lounge with its magnificent Elizabethan fireplace. The Plough is open seven days a week, with luncheon prices beginning at £8 ($18.40) and the à la carte dinner from £10 ($23). VAT is added to the tab.

For those desiring overnight accommodations, the Plough offers several small but attractively furnished rooms. A double without bath costs £30 ($69) nightly, rising to £33 ($75.90) with bath. A bathless single goes for £21 ($48.30), increasing to £23 ($52.90) with bath.

3. Minster Lovell

From Oxford along the A40, you pass through Witney. Soon after, you turn right at the Minster Lovell signpost, about half a mile off the highway between Witney and Burford. The village's main attraction is **Minster Lovell Hall,** the remains of a moated house where an early Lovell supposedly hid out and starved to death after a battle in the area.

By the Windrush River, Minster Lovell is mainly built of Cotswold stone, with thatch or stone-slate roofs. It's rather a pity there is a forest of TV aerials, but the place is still attractive to photographers.

The **Old Swan Hotel,** Minster Lovell (tel. Asthall Leigh 614), was built in the 14th century and visited by Richard III in the 15th. It is still run in the traditional English manner. The lawns and gardens are dominated by centuries-old horse chestnuts. In winter a warm, relaxed atmosphere is created by the chintz-covered armchairs and the log fires in the inglenooks. The hotel's unusual sign is that of a flying swan. The food is good, and the restaurant offers both continental and traditional English dishes prepared by a team of enthusiastic young chefs. The headwaiter has served the hotel for more than 30 years. A timbered ceiling, candlelight, and real oil lamps make for a memorable dinner. A table d'hôte luncheon costs from £5 ($11.50) on weekdays, £6 ($13.80) on Sunday. Dinner tabs are, of course, more expensive. Garlic mushrooms followed by chicken Cotswold or tournedos Stilton, with fresh vegetables and a light gâteau from the trolley, will be about £10 ($23). The five bedrooms are centrally heated and double- or twin-bedded accommodations, costing £25 ($57.50) for two persons per night. This includes a full English breakfast and VAT. Service is extra.

4. Bibury

On the road from Burford to Cirencester, Bibury is one of the loveliest spots in the Cotswolds. In fact, the utopian romancer of Victoria's day, poet

William Morris, called it England's most beautiful village. On the banks of the tiny Coln River, Bibury is noted for **Arlington Row**, a gabled group of 15th-century cottages, its biggest and most-photographed drawing card. The row is protected by the National Trust.

Arlington Mill dates from the 17th century and was in use until the outbreak of World War I. It contains a collection of 19th-century mill machinery, along with Peter Waals furniture, Victorian costumes and furniture, and Staffordshire china. The mill is open March to October and most winter weekends from 11 a.m. to 7 p.m., and charges 50p ($1.15) admission for adults, 20p (46¢) for children. They also have pottery for sale.

WHERE TO STAY: Bibury is a good base for touring the old wool towns of the North Cotswolds. For those who prefer a secluded roadside oasis, we have the following recommendations:

Bibury Court Hotel (tel. Bibury 337) is a Jacobean manor house built by Sir Thomas Sackville in 1633 (parts of it date from Tudor times). Its eight acres of grounds are approached through a large gateway, the lawn extending to the encircling Coln River. The famous house was privately owned until it was turned into a medium-priced hotel in 1968. The structure is built of Cotswold stone, with many gables, huge chimneys, leaded-glass stone-mullioned windows, and a formal graveled entryway. Inside there are many country manor furnishings, and antiques, as well as an open stone log-burning fireplace. In a double, the inclusive bed-and-breakfast rate is £22 ($50.60), dropping to £13 ($29.90) in a single. Many of the rooms have four-poster beds, original oak paneling, and antiques. Meals are an event in the stately dining room, where lunches and dinners start at £6 ($13.80). After tea and biscuits in the drawing room, walk across the lawn along the river where you find a doorway leading to a little church. On your return, head for one of the coaching houses which has been converted into a drinking lounge, a restful place for a glass of stout.

The **Swan Hotel** (tel. Bibury 204) is a scene-stealer. Before you cross over the arched stone bridge spanning the Coln, pause and look at the vine-covered facade. Yes, it's the same view that has appeared on many a calendar. The former coaching inn will bed you down for the night in one of its handsomely appointed chambers, all with bath or shower, charging £16 ($36.80) per person nightly. A traditional English breakfast and VAT are included. All of the rooms have been modernized, and there are many comforts. The special feature of the Swan is the small stretch of trout stream reserved for guests. If you're just passing through for the day, you may want to stop over and order the £6 ($13.80) lunch or the £8 ($18.40) dinner.

When you see the gardens at the Swan, your exploring days may be over.

5. Cirencester

Don't worry about how to pronounce the name of the town. Even the English are in disagreement. Just say "siren-sess-ter," and you won't go too far wrong. Cirencester is often considered the unofficial capital of the Cotswolds, probably a throwback to its reputation in the Middle Ages when it flourished as the center of the great wool industry.

But even in Roman Britain, five roads converged on Cirencester, which was called Corinium in those days. In size, it ranged second only to London. Today, it is chiefly a market town, a good base for touring, as it lies 34 miles from Bath, 16 from the former Regency spa at Cheltenham, 17 from Gloucester, 36 from Oxford, and 38 from Stratford-upon-Avon. The trip from London is 89 miles. In the heart of the town itself are two important sights:

Corinium Museum on Park Street houses archeological remains left from the Roman occupation of Cirencester. The mosaic pavements found on Dyer Street in Cirencester in 1849 are the most important exhibit. And the provincial Roman sculpture (Minerva, Mercury), the pottery, the bits and pieces salvaged from long-decayed buildings, provide a remote link with the civilization that once flourished here. The museum has been completely redeveloped and modernized. It's open from 10 a.m. to 6 p.m. weekdays, 2 to 6 p.m. on Sunday. Admission is 30p (68¢) for adults, 20p (46¢) for senior citizens, 10p (23¢) for children. The museum is closed on Wednesday from October to April.

Cirencester Parish Church, dating back to Norman times and Henry I, is the Church of John the Baptist, overlooking the Market Square. (Actually, a church may have stood on this spot in Saxon times.) In size, the Cirencester church appears to be a cathedral—not a mere parish church. The present building represents a variety of styles, largely Perpendicular, as in the early 15th-century tower. Among the treasures inside are a 15th-century pulpit and a silver-gilt cup given to Queen Anne Boleyn two years before her execution.

WHERE TO STAY: Stratton House Hotel, Gloucester Road (tel. Cirencester 61761), on the outskirts of town, has a delightful country-house atmosphere in buildings that date, in part, from the 17th century. The owners, Mr. and Mrs. Manley Walker, have much improved this mellow old house, built of Cotswold stone and standing on secluded grounds that have some towering trees and a walled garden with herbaceous borders. Some of their bedrooms are quite large, and many have private baths en suite. The more modern units are found in the new wing. The demi-pension rate ranges from £24 ($55.20) to £25.50 ($58.65) per person, including an English breakfast and a well-served dinner of good British food. In the older part of the restaurant are fine oil paintings, although many guests prefer the more modern wing, with its picture-window view of the garden. There's also a smoke room bar with timbered beams and, in winter, a blazing log fire.

Fleece Hotel, Market Place (tel. Cirencester 2680), appropriately honors the wool trade of yore in its name. Associated with the days of Henry VIII, it is right in the heart of town, close to the parish church. The inn is twin-gabled, with a black and white timbered facade. A single costs £20 ($46) if bathless, but £22 ($50.60) with shower. A bathless double rents for £26 ($59.80), going up to £30 ($69) with bath, these tariffs including breakfast, service, and VAT.

If you don't want to stay at a hotel, you might try **La Ronde Guest House/Restaurant,** 52–54 Ashcroft Rd. (tel. Cirencester 4611), run by Mr. and Mrs. N. E. Shales, who charge approximately £10 ($23) per person for bed and breakfast. They have family rooms, as well as doubles and twins. In the town center, within walking distance of Cirencester Park, the Abbey Grounds, and the museum and parish church, the small hotel is licensed. The dining room offers a varied menu and an extensive wine list. Dinner is from £6 ($13.80). The hotel offers central heating, hot and cold running water in all the rooms, and has a color TV lounge as well.

WHERE TO DINE: The Crown, West Market Place (tel. Cirencester 3811), has been a coaching inn since the 14th century. Its position is perfect, opposite the lovely old parish church. Many of the Crown's original architectural features have been preserved, and the old beams tell a story of long ago. A large buffet table comprising hot and cold homemade dishes is available each day. Prices range from 75p ($1.73) to £3 ($6.90).

The Crown also operates a restaurant, dating from the 14th century. It is open for traditional English meals all day, and is operated as a steakhouse in the evening until late. In addition, the Crown also has a medieval ballroom, where occasionally medieval-style banquets are held.

6. Painswick

The sleepy little town of Painswick, four miles northeast of Stroud, is considered a model village. All of its houses, while erected at different periods, blend harmoniously, as the villagers used only Cotswold stone as their building material. The one distinctive feature on the Painswick skyline is the spire of its 15th-century parish church. The church is linked with the legend of 99 yew trees, as well as its annual Clipping Feast (not the yew trees—rather, the congregation joins hands and circles around the church as if it were a Maypole, singing hymns as they do). Ancient tombstones dot the churchyard. Finally, you may want to visit **Court House,** a private Cotswold manor (see the court room of Charles I), open to the public for 20p (46¢) on Thursday only, June to mid-September, from 2 to 5 p.m. It is also open by special appointment (tel. Painswick 813689).

WHERE TO STAY: For accommodation, try the **Painswick Hotel** (formerly the Cranham Wood Hotel), Kemps Lane, at the rear of the church (tel. Painswick 812-160). Completely refurnished, this beautiful Georgian house was once a royal vicarage and is encircled by terraces of formal gardens. The hotel reception area was once the private chapel. There are rooms both with and without private bathrooms, and the rates for bed and continental breakfast start at £18 ($41.40) per person, including VAT. The hotel has high standards of cuisine and service. It is managed by resident proprietors, who give particular attention to their North American guests.

WHERE TO DINE: The **Country Elephant** (tel. Painswick 813564) is an excellent restaurant serving fine, English country-style cuisine. Owned and operated by Michael and Jane Medforth, the restaurant has a distinct personal touch. Mrs. Medforth does the cooking, keeping the menu limited so that only the freshest ingredients are used. In the simple dining room done in modern style, you may dine on steak-and-mushroom pie with bacon and red wine, pork chops stuffed with apricots, almonds, and raisins and baked in cider and herbs, or a fresh grilled trout with cream and chives. Appetizers may include a homemade cream of watercress soup or an individual prawn and cheese quiche. The menu changes twice a week and sometimes even more often depending on what is available at the local markets. A meal will cost about £10 ($23) per person, plus 10% for service. Although they offer the finest California wines in their cellar, an inexpensive French wine will cost from £4.50 ($10.35) a bottle. The restaurant is open Tuesday through Saturday from 7 to 11 p.m., and also for Sunday lunch from 12:30 to 2:30 p.m.

ON THE OUTSKIRTS: **Edge Farm Cottage,** Edge, near Stroud in Gloucestershire (tel. Painswick 81-2476), is a carter's dwelling dating from 1800, nestled in what has been called "a secret part of the Cotswolds." Aside from the charm of the house, what makes Edge Farm Cottage special is its owner, Barbara Blatchley, who, along with her doctor husband, welcomes guests. They've modernized their spacious house and have centrally heated it. Available are two guest bedrooms, each with twin beds, basin, and shower. Preferred are parties of two, three, or four persons.

The cost is about £30 ($69) per person per day, including not only the bed and a full breakfast, but a delicious dinner with wine. Mrs. Blatchley offers personalized home cooking, good British food, including roasts, game such as pheasant and venison, and salmon when in season. Guests eat together in a dining room with an old bread oven, enjoying the conversation.

As a qualified guide for the Heart of England Tourist Board, Mrs. Blatchley will also offer her services with a car, charging about £50 ($115) for a full day's tour.

7. Cheltenham

In a sheltered area between the Cotswolds and the Severn Vale, a mineral spring was discovered by chance. Legend has it that the Cheltenham villagers noticed pigeons drinking from a spring, and observed how healthy they were. The pigeon has therefore been incorporated into the town's crest.

Always seeking a new spa, George III arrived in 1788 and launched the town. The Duke of Wellington also came to ease his liver disorder. Even Lord Byron came this way, too, proposing marriage to Miss Millbanke.

Some 100 miles from London, Cheltenham is one of England's most fashionable spas. Its architecture is mainly Regency, with lots of ironwork, balconies, and verandas. Attractive parks and open spaces of greenery make the town especially inviting.

The main street, the Promenade, has been called "the most beautiful thoroughfare in Britain." Rather similar are such thoroughfares as Lansdowne Place and Montpellier Parade. The design for the dome of the Rotunda was based on the Pantheon in Rome. Montpellier Walk, with its shops separated by caryatids, is one of the most interesting shopping centers in England.

You can take guided tours of Cheltenham on foot by checking in at the Tourist Information Centre on the Promenade. A one-hour tour costs about £1.50 ($3.45) and is well worth it, especially if you're interested in Regency architecture. However, an advance notice of at least two days is required.

WHERE TO STAY: **Queens Hotel**, Promenade (tel. Cheltenham 514-724), can be safely considered the best hotel at the spa. At the head of the Regency Promenade, this upper bracket hotel looks down on the gardens. Architecturally, it is imposing, built in 1838 in the style of the Roman temple of Jupiter. This distinguished hotel has a Regency decor and an unusually fine staircase. There are 77 bedrooms, all with private baths, radios, and color televisions. Accommodations at the back are quieter. Everything is well furnished, although decidedly old-fashioned. A single rents for £28 ($64.40), a double for £40 ($92), including service and VAT. The restaurant serves a table d'hôte luncheon at £5.75 ($13.23). The budget-conscious can enjoy a Queen's Table lunch from £2.20 ($5.06). A complete set dinner is £6.25 ($14.36).

Malvern View Hotel, Cleeve Hill (tel. Bishops Cleeve 2017), thinks of itself justifiably as a "restaurant avec chambres." It offers only seven double bedrooms, with central heating, color TV, and private baths or showers (one chamber has a four-poster bed). These rent for £15 ($34.50) per person, with an extra £10.50 ($24.15) charged for dinner. The hotel's reputation for food

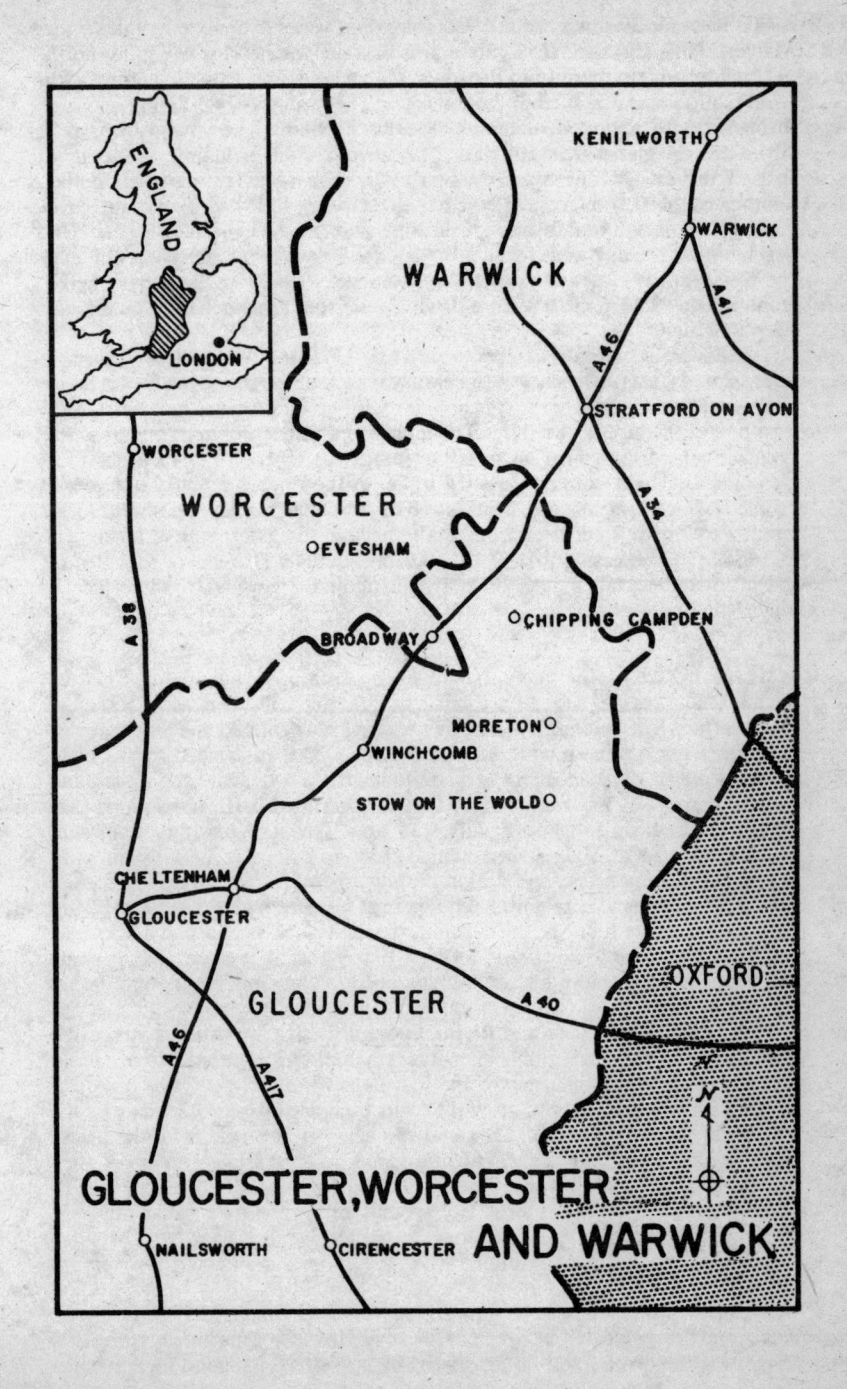

CHELTENHAM

GLOUCESTER, WORCESTER AND WARWICK

is the finest for 20 miles around. Commanding views over Severn Vale to the Malvern Hills and the Welsh mountains beyond, the hotel is five miles north of Cheltenham, on the A46 to Broadway. It's a long, low, stone structure, with white shutters and a surrounding garden. The country-style dining room is furnished with antiques, including wheelback chairs. The silverware is real silver, and the glassware is cut glass. The menu is wide, including various good French dishes. On our most recent rounds, one of us ordered ratatouille; another, smoked trout pâté. These appetizers were followed by a giant quail stuffed with pâté in brandy and mushrooms and carré d'agneau en croûte. The vegetables of the day were fresh, a luxury these days. No lunch is served, and the restaurant is closed Sunday to nonresidents. Otherwise, dinner is offered from 7:30 to 9:30 p.m. If you're driving out from Cheltenham, you should telephone first.

Lilleybrook Hotel, Cirencester Road, Charlton Kings (tel. Charlton Kings 25861), was formerly a 19th-century mansion, five miles outside Cheltenham, set in a nine-acre park. It is popular with golfers, as its course is considered one of the best in the shire. The interior has fluted columns and an open fireplace where logs burn on frosty evenings (or where you can order four o'clock tea). The decor enhances the image of the English country house. All rooms have central heating, a private bath or shower, telephones, and large windows with views of the gardens. The bed-and-breakfast rate in a single is £23 ($52.90), increasing to £32 ($73.60) in a double. Drinks are provided in the intimate cocktail lounge or in the intriguing Ziggy's Bar where jazz is played on Sunday.

WHERE TO EAT: Aubergine, Belgrave House, Imperial Square (tel. Cheltenham 31402), provides a creative English and French cuisine in a semibasement bistro setting. The cooking is by the owner and his wife, Iñaki and Sue Beguiristain (she's responsible mainly for the desserts). The atmosphere ranks high. Coconut matting is placed on the plain floors, the wood chairs and tables; and the walls are red—an overall effect that is cheerful. Mr. Beguiristain speaks almost no English, but his friendly staff does. The French onion soup and gazpacho are good. Main dishes include steak au poivre, trout with almonds, tongue in Madeira sauce, and veal in brandy cream. All the dishes are cooked to order, so patience is required. You can eat here for as little as £8 ($18.40). Or if you finish with one of the delicious desserts, such as chocolat à la crème, and have a bottle of Rioja wine at £4.50 ($10.35), the bill is more likely to come to £12 ($27.60) a head, plus service. It's open for lunch from noon to 2 p.m. and for dinner from 7 to 10 p.m., except Sunday.

Montpelier Wine Bar and Bistro, Bayshill Lodge, Montpelier Street (tel. Cheltenham 27774), is an imposing Regency building converted from an old established shop to a cellar bistro and first-floor wine bar. Very busy at lunchtime, but worth the effort to get in, it offers a choice of some 12 wines by the glass at around 60p ($1.38). Then you can select a hot meal from the blackboard menu. A hot soup is always featured among the various appetizers, then cold meats and salad, hot meat pies, smoked fish, lasagne, interesting salads, and a good selection of desserts. Pay around £3 ($6.90) for a satisfying meal either in the cellar or, in good weather, on the terrace. It is open from Monday to Saturday, noon to 2:30 p.m. and 6 to 10:30 p.m., on Sunday from noon to 2 p.m. only.

That Sandwich Place, Regent Street (tel. Cheltenham 29575), is a good luncheon choice, located in back of Cavenish House, a department store. Mr. Curtoys is the owner, and he is assisted by several very helpful local women who know how to make at least 200 different kinds of sandwiches, costing from 45p ($1.04) to 85p ($1.96), plus an additional 20p (46¢) if you request salad garnishes such as lettuce and tomato. The repertoire uses such ingredients as peanut butter, cheese, prawns, pâté, beef, even bananas. Milkshakes, tea, and coffee are sold as well at 50p ($1.15) to 75p ($1.73) a drink. You have a choice of eating on the premises or else ordering from the take-away service.

Forrests Wine House, Imperial Lane (tel. Cheltenham 38001), is an extraordinarily economical place to eat. It's a small wine bar in an old bakery with tables given some intimacy by stall seats which divide the room. Presiding is Mrs. Henry Forrest Hampson (a true Cheltenham name if ever there was one). She provides a super menu with a daily homemade soup, then quiche or pizza with a dressed salad, spaghetti bolognaise, or a continental ploughman's lunch at around £1 ($2.30) to £1.50 ($3.45) each. Daily hot dishes are about £1.50 ($3.45) to £3 ($6.90). Upward of 20 different wines are available by the glass, so you can conduct your own tasting if you don't have to drive further. Prices range from about 65p ($1.50). The house is open daily except Sunday from 12:30 to 2:30 p.m. and 7 to 10 p.m. (to 11 p.m. on Friday and Saturday).

On the Outskirts

The Mill Inn and the **Mill House Restaurant,** Withington, near Cheltenham (tel. Withington 204), have charm and hearthside comfort. The inn itself, until fairly recently a corn or grist mill, has a small number of pleasantly decorated bedrooms, some of which have private baths, renting anywhere from £19 ($43.70) to £23 ($42.90) per person nightly, including sherry and a fruit bowl upon arrival, a full English breakfast, and the service charge, but not VAT. The units open onto the river and a lake beyond. In winter guests enjoy the log fires, and, in summer they retreat to the riverside garden to enjoy lunch.

The restaurant itself, where you can dine for around £10 ($23) per person, is decorated with flagstones, and oak furniture, as well as an open grill which was built into one of the original fireplaces. The well-prepared menu consists of a limited, although well-chosen, selection of English and continental dishes, mostly meat and poultry, including steak-and-oyster pie or else lamb kidneys Marechand du Vin. Charcoal grills are also a feature, and, for dessert, a choice of puddings is offered. The appetizers are especially imaginative, everything from smoked eel to stuffed eggplant with crab. Specialty coffees, costing another £1.50 ($3.45), are extra.

The village of Withington itself lies at the head of the Coln Valley, one of the most attractive spots in the Cotswolds.

8. Royal Sudeley Castle

In 1962 Elizabeth Chipps of Lexington, Kentucky, met and married Mark Dent-Brocklehurst, the wedding taking place in the 16th-century chapel of Royal Sudeley Castle. In 1970 her husband died, and Elizabeth inherited the 15th-century castle in the Cotswold village of Winchcombe, six miles northeast of Cheltenham (tel. Winchcombe 602-308). The history of the castle dates back to Saxon times, when the village was the capital of the Mercian kings.

Elizabeth Dent-Brocklehurst first opened the castle to visitors shortly after her husband's death, to enable people to share the treasures of royal relics, stained glass, tapestries, and paneling. The gardens are formal and surrounded by rolling farm and parkland. The herb garden dates from the time when Catherine Parr, sixth wife of Henry VIII, lived and died at Sudeley. There are several permanent exhibitions, some magnificent pictures and furniture, and peacocks that strut on the grounds.

The castle also has a restaurant good enough to participate in the "Taste of Britain" scheme, offering particularly good local recipes of an international standard, including roast beef and Yorkshire pudding and roast lamb with mint sauce.

The castle is open daily from noon to 5:30 p.m., March 1 to October 31. The grounds are open from 11 a.m. Admission prices are £1.10 ($2.76) for adults, 60p ($1.38) for children.

9. Malmesbury

At the southern tip of the Cotswolds, the old hill town of Malmesbury is encircled by the Avon River. In the center of England's "Middle West," it makes a good base for touring the Cotswolds. Cirencester is just 12 miles away; Bibury, 19 miles; and Cheltenham, 28 miles, Malmesbury is a market town, with a fine market cross. Its historical fame is reflected by the Norman abbey built there on the site of King Athelstan's grave.

Malmesbury is considered the oldest "borough" in England, as it was granted its charter by Alfred the Great in 880. In 1980 it celebrated its 1300th anniversary. Some 400 years ago the Washington family lived there, leaving their star-and-stripe coat-of-arms on the church wall. In addition, Nancy Hanks, Abraham Lincoln's mother, came from Malmesbury. The town still has members of the family, noted for their lean features and tallness. The Penns of Pennsylvania also originally came from Malmesbury.

WHERE TO STAY: The **Old Bell,** Abbey Row (tel. Malmesbury 2344), is an unusual place—once a monastic retreat—to use as a touring center. It sits in the heart of the town, adjoining the Norman abbey. Its facade is wisteria-covered stone, with six gables and two towering chimneys; an iron picket fence guards the flowers and shrubbery. The inn opens onto a formal garden, with graveled monks' walks leading to the rear back wall, with its little stone gazebo bordering the Avon below. Architecturally, much remains of the original building, including a 13th-century window and a medieval spiral staircase. There are 19 centrally heated bedrooms, nine of them with private baths (otherwise hot and cold running water). Singles range from £15.50 ($35.65) to £20 ($46), and doubles range from £26 ($59.80) to £29 ($66.70), including VAT. Open year round, the inn is often used by sportsmen, especially during Saturday hunts. Guests congregate in the dining room, and in either of the two informal lounges and bars. The dining room is more modern (Regency), serving lunch for £5 ($11.50), although dinner is à la carte.

WHERE TO DINE: Apostle Spoon, 6 Malmesbury Cross (tel. Malmesbury 3129), is run by Mr. and Mrs. Smalley, who serve delicious food. The restaurant stands facing the octagonal market cross, adjoining the abbey. A two-course meal is featured for anywhere from £6 ($13.80) to £7.50 ($17.25). Included in this set meal are such main dishes as sirloin on the bone, kidneys in wine, pepper steak, venison, tournedos Rossini, and grilled ham. Appetizers begin at £1 ($2.30). The restaurant is open daily in summer; in winter it is closed on Sunday and Monday.

10. Tetbury

Tetbury, in South Gloucestershire, is a sleepy Cotswold town, with old stone houses, some fine medium-priced inns, and an antique market hall.

WHERE TO STAY: The Close, Long Street (tel. Tetbury 52272), dates from 1695 and takes its name from a Cistercian monastery to which it was linked. It was once the home of a wealthy Cotswold wool merchant. Architecturally, it is built of warm honey-brown Cotswold stone, with gables and stone-mullioned windows. The ecclesiastical-style windows in the rear overlook a garden with a reflection pool, a haven for doves. Inside, you'll find a Georgian room with a domed ceiling (once it was an open courtyard), where predinner drinks are served and you can peruse the menu. Dining is in one of two rooms. Owners Jean-Marie and Sue Lauzier have spared none of their attractive antiques and silver, proudly sharing their treasures with guests. Candlelight on winter evenings, floral arrangements, sparkling silver and glass are just the background for the fine food.

The cooking is superb, and an à la carte menu offers specialty dishes. At lunch or dinner appetizers might include homemade soup at £1 ($2.30). Main dishes, from £5.20 ($11.96), feature chicken cooked in champagne and encased in light pastry; steaks, beef, and fish at £7 ($16.10); even an exotic guinea fowl for two persons at £12 ($27.60). Desserts from the trolley are priced at £1.25 ($2.88). From November to March, except at Cheltenham week and Christmas, they offer three nights or more at a daily cost of £18 ($41.40), including a full breakfast and an £8 ($18.40) allowance for either lunch or dinner.

Most of the 12 bedrooms (all contain private baths) are spacious and handsomely furnished with antiques. A single room ranges in price from £16.50 ($37.95) to £26 ($59.80), a double from £22 ($50.60) to £48 ($110.40), including a continental breakfast, service, and VAT.

The **White Hart Hotel,** Market Place (tel. Tetbury 52436), is a village center hotel, a remake of an attractive Jacobean stone house, which provides sophisticated surroundings for a Cotswold stay. In its present incarnation, it has respected the past. The lounge, for example, has bare stone walls, comfortable armchairs around a raised fireplace, with a high tapered copper hood. The dining room is elaborate, with restored beamed ceilings, strong colors, and fine china and chairs—a proper background for the French-English cuisine. Sunday dinner costs £5.25 ($12.08), and many feature roast Norfolk turkey with stuffing and cranberries. Bar snacks are in the 65p ($1.50) to £1.50 ($3.45) range. A luncheon is offered daily, except Sunday, for £3.75 ($8.63). You help yourself to cold meats and salads. The bedrooms contain private baths, with doubles renting from £28 ($64.40) to £36 ($82.80); singles go for £20 ($46) to £22 ($50.60), including an English breakfast, service, and VAT. Many amenities come with your room, including color TV, central heating, and a telephone.

11. Wotton-under-Edge

At the western edge of the Cotswolds, in Gloucestershire, Wotton-under-Edge is in the rural triangle of Bath (23 miles), Bristol (20 miles), and Gloucester (20 miles). Many of its old buildings indicate its former prosperity as a wool town. One of its obscure claims to fame is that it was the home of Sir Isaac Pitman, who invented shorthand. Its grammar school is one of the oldest in England, founded in 1834 and once attended by Dr. Edward Jenner, discoverer of the smallpox vaccine.

WHERE TO STAY: The **Swan Hotel**, Market Street (tel. Wotton-under-Edge 2329), lures with its Georgian facade, painted a distinctive blue. It offers comfortable rooms with and without private bath, but it is the fine French cuisine that attracts locals and visitors alike. Premeal drinks are taken in either the Lounge or Tudor Bars, both with open fireplaces. Meals are served in the restaurant, with its heavy beams, Windsor chairs, polished tables, and fireplace. Meals in the restaurant, à la carte only, cost around £10 ($23). Specialties include beef Stroganoff and steak Diane maison. On Saturday nights, there's a dinner-dance for which you pay a £1 ($2.30) cover charge. In the Buttery, you can order anything from a sandwich to a full meal, a three-course repast costing £5 ($11.50). Bathless singles cost £18 ($41.40), £22 ($50.60) with bath. Doubles are £26 ($59.80) without bath, £30 ($69) with. These rates include service and VAT. Breakfast is extra.

12. Shipton-under-Wychwood

Taking the A361 road, en route from Burford to Chipping Norton, you arrive after a turn-off at the little village of Shipton-under-Wychwood in Oxfordshire. It's about four miles north of Burford; but don't blink—or you'll pass it right by. The monks of Bruern Abbey used to run a hospice in the village. That hospice is now an inn, and even it has some serious competition today.

WHERE TO STAY: The **Shaven Crown,** High Street (tel. Shipton-under-Wychwood 830-330), was originally a hospice operated by monks as part of Bruern Abbey. In the 13th century, it served as a center for dispensing aid to the poor. Built of rugged Cotswold stone during the reign of Queen Elizabeth I, it is on the main village road, and opens onto a triangular village green in the shadow of a church (you'll either love or hate the bell ringing). Most of the rooms overlook a cobblestoned courtyard and garden, and have attractive antiques. Hot and cold running water have been installed in every bedroom, and there are adequate hallway baths and toilets, and two of the bedrooms have private baths. The charge is £26 ($59.80) nightly for bed and breakfast in a double room with private bath, although this is lowered to £24 ($55.20) in a bathless double. Tariffs include a full English breakfast. Singles are charged £13 ($29.90) nightly on the bed-and-breakfast arrangement.

The **Lamb Inn,** High Street (tel. Shipton-under-Wychwood 830-465), is a small stone Cotswold house, turned into an inn and perfect if you're seeking a simple village stopover serving a superior cuisine. It's owned by Mr. Benstead, who gives a cordial welcome. Twins and doubles with bath cost from £20 ($46) to £24 ($55.20) per night, including a continental breakfast and service but not VAT. The inn also has a number of cottages in the village which are fully furnished and rented at a cost of about £22 ($50.60) per night. Each room in the main inn is country style, with antiques and inviting views of the village and garden.

A five-course dinner goes for around £10 ($23). Main dishes are based on the season and the day's buying, but are likely to include roast pheasant, grilled trout with almonds, and coq au vin. The house specialty is filet Wychwood, filet steak in a cream sauce. At Sunday lunch the traditional roast beef or lamb is offered, with all the trimmings, £5.50 ($12.65). Locals like this. At lunch a hot and cold buffet is available in the bar and you eat very well for around £5 ($11.50), or you can get something for as little as £2 ($4.60). The inn is closed on Sunday evenings.

Mr. Benstead is an expert snail breeder, and so snails (the edible sort) are featured on his menu. Don't, however, write with snail-breeding questions, as this is his business, and he only answers questions from his guests and not his competitors.

On the Outskirts

The **Wychwood Arms Hotel,** Ascott-under-Wychwood (tel. Shipton-under-Wychwood 830-271). Until recently the Wychwood Arms was a local pub, a Cotswold-stone building among many. But Tim Randall and his wife Miranda have converted the upper floor to provide five comfortable double bedrooms, all with private bathroom, telephone and color TV. The rate for a room and continental breakfast, including VAT and service, is £30 ($69) in a double, £21 ($48.30) in a single. The furnishings are those of a country pub, and the pictures and prints which adorn the walls follow a sport theme. There is central heating throughout, and the atmosphere is friendly.

At lunch, apart from a thriving bar trade, they provide a simple menu of ploughman's lunch at £1 ($2.30), or a rump steak, £5.50 ($12.65). In the evening, all items on the dinner menu are cooked to order, so you must expect a small delay before tucking into French onion or oxtail soup, 80p ($1.84), or local game pâté, £1.20 ($2.76). Main dishes include local roast pheasant, £5.50 ($12.65), or baked trout, £4 ($9.20). Vegetables accompanying each dish are fresh and tasty. The meal is rounded off with a light dessert and coffee. The good location is only 18 miles from Oxford, 26 miles from Stratford-upon-Avon.

13. Chipping Norton

Just inside the Oxfordshire border is Chipping Norton, another gateway town to the Cotswolds. Since the days of Henry IV, it has been an important market town, and its main street is a curiosity as it's built on a slope, making one side higher than the other.

Chipping Norton has long been noted for its tweed mills; also seek out its Guildhall, its church, and its handsome almshouses. If you're touring, you can search for the nearby prehistoric Rollright Stones, more than 75 stones forming a circle 100 feet in diameter—the "Stonehenge of the Cotswolds." Chipping Norton lies 11 miles from Burford, 20 miles from Oxford, and 21 miles from Stratford-upon-Avon.

WHERE TO STAY: The **Crown and Cushion Hotel,** The High (tel. Chipping Norton 2533), dates back to 1497 and was originally a coaching inn. Half of the bedrooms are equipped with private shower baths, phones, and television sets, and all are centrally heated. Rates are £15.50 ($35.65) per person in a room without bath, rising to £21.50 ($49.45) per person with bath, these tariffs including breakfast and VAT. The bar can provide hot and cold snacks morning and evening. The restaurant is à la carte. There's a color TV lounge, plus a residents' reading room. This is an ideal center for touring the Cotswolds, and it's close to Oxford, Stratford-upon-Avon, Cheltenham, and Silverstone. Resident proprietors are Pamela and Archie Rollinson.

An Old Mill on the Outskirts

The **Mill Hotel,** Kingham, Oxfordshire (tel. Kingham 255), five miles south of Chipping Norton, provides an up-to-date budget-range accommodation in an old stone mill, with its original bakehouse and open stone fireplaces. The stone water ducts at the rear are being converted into a formal garden, and in the front there is a rose arbor and a lawn with benches for those who want to enjoy the views and the sun. The Mill is owned by Mr. and Mrs. Barnett. All of the bedrooms have hot and cold running water (most contain private baths), and the furnishings are modern and streamlined. The bed-and-breakfast rate in a single is £12 ($27.60), £19.50 ($44.85) in a double. A double with private bath is £22.50 ($51.75). Specialties include rainbow trout and roast duckling. There are several lounges, one opening onto another; all have their original beams. Guests congregate in either the tiny sitting room, with its inglenook and wood-burning fireplace, or in the tavern with its Windsor chairs and wine-barrel bar.

FOOD AT AN OLD INN: On the B4450 across country from Chipping Norton to Stow-on-the-Wold, right on the village green at Bledington, lies the **King's Head,** Bledington, Oxfordshire (tel. Kingham 365). This lovely 16th-century inn has been catering to travelers for more years than it's possible to remember. Nowadays, Ann Ellse, wife of the indomitable Wally (of the Turf Tavern in Oxford and now the Golden Ball at Burford), provides real ale to be quaffed in the beer garden or in the low-ceilinged bars. Lunchtime and in the evenings a buffet provides an ample meal of smoked mackerel, scotch eggs, steak-and-wine pie, and pâtés which complement the usual bar snacks. There is always a steaming pot of soup going, and chocolate and cream cakes are there if you don't want cheese. You can eat for as little as 75p ($1.73), or the most extravagant dish will cost around £3 ($6.90).

14. Bourton-on-the-Water

In this most scenic Cotswold village, you can be like Gulliver, voyaging first to Brobdingnag, then to Lilliput. Brobdingnag is Burton-on-the-Water, lying 85 miles from London, on the banks of the tiny Windrush River.

To see Lilliput, you have to visit the Old New Inn. In the garden is a near-perfect and most realistic model village. It is open daily from 8:30 a.m. till dusk, and costs 40p (92¢) for adults, 25p (58¢) for children.

If you're coming to the Cotswold by train from London, you'll find the nearest rail station is in Moreton-on-Marsh, eight miles away. Buses make connections with the trains, however.

READERS' SIGHTSEEING SUGGESTION: "Tourists should visit **Birdland** nearby. It consists of a beautifully designed garden of 4½ acres, a veritable paradise for some 600 birds of 158 different species. The macaws (each named) are particularly interesting and colorful—they love entertaining visitors with their antics and chatter. There is an exquisite group of flamingoes and a large collection of penguins with an eye-level pool so that they can be seen feeding, which is a rare sight. Also there are hummingbirds and others in a tropical house. A wildlife art gallery, opened by Sir Peter Scott, is part of the attraction. Admission is 70p ($1.61) for adults, and 35p (81¢) for children and old-age pensioners." (D. and R. Hosie, Balwyn, Victoria, Australia).

WHERE TO STAY: Bourton-on-the-Water offers a handful of quite-good accommodations, all of them inexpensive in spite of its reputation as a tourist attraction.

The **Old New Inn** (tel. Bourton-on-the-Water 20467) can lay claim to being the leading hostelry in the village. Right in the center, overlooking the river, it's a good example of Queen Anne design. But it is mostly visited because of the miniature model village in its garden (referred to earlier). Hungry or tired travelers are drawn to the old-fashioned comforts and cuisine of this most English inn. The bed-and-breakfast rate is £12.10 ($27.83) per person nightly, including service charge and VAT. The rooms are comfortable, with homey furnishings, soft beds, and hot and cold running water. Packed lunches at £1.75 ($4.03) will be provided for your excursion jaunts. You may want to spend evenings in the pub lounge, playing darts or chatting with the villagers. Non-residents may also want to stop in for a meal, with lunches at £5 ($11.50), dinners at £6.50 ($14.95).

The **Old Manse Hotel** (tel. Bourton-on-the-Water 20642) is reminiscent of the setting of Nathaniel Hawthorne's *Mosses from an Old Manse.* A gem architecturally, the hotel is by the slow-moving river that wanders through the village green. Built of ivy-covered Cotswold stone, with chimneys, dormers, and small-paned windows, it has been modernized inside, and all rooms have radio, color TV, and central heating. The proprietor, Mrs. Wendy Parkes, charges from £24.50 ($56.35) for two persons in a twin with private bath, a continental breakfast included. Rates are lowered off-season. The inn's best feature is the stone fireplace in the dining room, as well as the wood-paneled bar. Dining is a treat here. A three-course lunch costs about £4.75 ($10.93); a set dinner, £5 ($11.50)—but you can order from an à la carte menu as well.

Chester House Hotel & Motel (tel. Bourton-on-the-Water 20286) is a weathered, 300-year-old Cotswold stone house, built on the banks of the Windrush River. Owned and managed by Mr. and Mrs. J. Davies, the hotel is a convenient place at which to stay. A double room without bath rents for £24 ($55.20), increasing to £28 ($64.40) with bath and TV.

15. Lower Swell

Near Stow-on-the-Wold, Lower Swell is a twin. Both it and Upper Swell, its sister, are small villages of the Cotswolds. The hamlets are not to be confused with Upper and Lower Slaughter.

WHERE TO STAY: You may want to anchor in for the night or stop for a meal at the following recommendation:

Old Farmhouse Hotel (tel. Stow-on-the-Wold 30232) is a small, intimate, 16th-century hotel in the heart of the Cotswolds. It is owned by David and Ann Gladstone, who have built up a reputation for excellent food and a warm, friendly atmosphere. The hotel is pleasantly furnished, and the cocktail bar (which only has a restaurant-and-residential license) and restaurant are popular with locals and visitors alike.

The bedrooms are comfortable and have central heating. A bathless double, inclusive of a full English breakfast and early morning tea, costs from £14 ($32.20) per person nightly. Light lunches (soup, smoked salmon, chicken-in-the-basket, sandwiches, ice cream, etc.) are served à la carte from Monday to Saturday, from 12:15 to 2:15 p.m., while on Sunday a traditional English lunch is featured. Dinner is served from 7:30 p.m. Monday through Saturday, and is likely to be a mouthwatering, filling repast from around £9 ($20.70) per person.

16. Upper and Lower Slaughter

Midway between Bourton-on-the-Water and Stow-on-the-Wold are the twin villages of Upper and Lower Slaughter. Don't be put off by the name because these are two of the prettiest villages in the Cotswolds. Actually the name "Slaughter" was a corruption of "de Sclotre," the original Norman landowner. The houses are constructed of honey-colored Cotswold stone, and a stream meanders right through the street, providing a home for the ducks which wander freely about, begging scraps from kindly visitors. In Upper Slaughter you can visit a fine example of a 17th-century Cotswold manor house.

WHERE TO STAY: Lords of the Manor Hotel, in Upper Slaughter (tel. Bourton-on-the-Water 20243), is a rambling 17th-century house standing on several acres of rolling fields and gardens which include a lovely trout pond. Completely modernized in its amenities, the hotel has still been successful in maintaining the quiet country-house atmosphere of 300 years ago.

Twelve of the 16 guest rooms are equipped with private bath, and many rooms have pleasant views of the Cotswold hills. The walls in the lounge bar are hung with family portraits of the original Lords of the Manor. Another bar overlooks the garden, and chintz and antiques are everywhere.

The country atmosphere is carried into the dining room as well, with its antiques and mullioned windows. All the well-prepared dishes are fresh and home-cooked. You'll pay an average of about £10 ($23) for a meal which may consist of leek and potato soup or broiled scallops wrapped in bacon for an appetizer, grilled rainbow trout with almonds, or chicken Kiev for the main course, and a selection of rich homemade sweets from the trolley for dessert. Room rates, which include breakfast, VAT, and service charge, range from £40 ($92) to £57.50 ($132.25) for a double room, depending on facilities.

17. Stow-on-the-Wold

This is an unspoiled Cotswold market town, in spite of the busloads of tourists who stop off en route to Broadway and Chipping Campden, about ten miles away. The town is the highest in the Cotswolds, built on a wold about 800 feet above sea level. In its open market square, you can still see the stocks where offenders in days gone by were jeered at and punished by the townspeople with a rotten egg in the face. The final battle between the Roundheads and the Royalists took place in Stow-on-the-Wold. The town, which is really like a village, is used by many not only for exploring the Cotswold wool towns, but Stratford-upon-Avon, 21 miles away. The nearest rail station is at Moreton-in-Marsh, four miles away.

WHERE TO STAY: A wealth of old inns is to be found here.

Stow Lodge Hotel (tel. Stow-on-the-Wold 30485) dominates the Market Place, but is set back far enough to maintain its aloofness. Its gardens, honeysuckle growing over the stone walls, diamond-shaped windows, gables and many chimneys, capture the best of country living, while letting you anchor right into the heart of town. Mr. and Mrs. Jux, the owners, who are partners with their daughter and son-in-law, Mr. and Mrs. Hartley, offer 22 ample, well-furnished bedrooms, all with private baths, radio, TV, and central heating. The bed-and-breakfast rate ranges from £14 ($32.20). Arrange to have your afternoon tea out back by the flower garden. The owners recently discovered an old (approximately 1770) open stone fireplace in their lounge, so they now offer log fires as an added attraction.

Unicorn Hotel (tel. Stow-on-the-Wold 30257) was a posting house and staging inn, putting up wayfarers on the old Fosse Way. Nowadays run as a hotel, it is built of the local stone—low and sprawling with miniature dormers. While there is a nicely furnished residents' lounge, even two pubs, the emphasis

STOW-ON-THE-WOLD/MORETON-IN-MARSH 353

is placed on the dining room and the bedrooms overhead. Offered are 20 rooms, all with private bath or shower and toilet, color TV, radio, telephone, trouser presser, and tea- and coffee-making facilities. The rate for a double- or twin-bedded room is £34 ($78.20), including service charge and VAT. The rooms are pleasant, excellent for sleeping, especially the chambers away from the road. The dining room provides table d'hôte and à la carte menus specializing in old English cooking with dishes of local color. Summer season luncheon is available from the chef's table. There is an excellent choice of table wines. This heart of England hotel offers walks and historic places of interest within easy reach.

The **Kings Arms Hotel** (tel. Stow-on-the-Wold 30602) is a 500-year-old posting house, opening onto the Market Square. The much-traveled Charles I slept here, on May 8, 1645. You can, too, surrounded by some fine old antiques, for £11 ($25.30) per person nightly for bed and breakfast or £17 ($39.10) nightly for bed, breakfast, and a three-course dinner, plus VAT. The lucky ones get the King Charles room itself, with its carved bed and open fireplace. The other bedrooms are all comfortably furnished with all modern comforts—innerspring mattresse, bedside lamp, TV, and wash basin. In the dining room, dinner averages £6.50 ($14.95). Hot and cold snacks are served in the new lounge-bar at lunchtime and in the evening, from as little as 95p ($2.19).

The **Talbot Hotel,** The Square (tel. Stow-on-the-Wold 30631), is an old house on the main square overlooking the church, the village stocks, and the bustling life of the small country town. The hotel has a lot of very comfortable bedrooms, mostly with bath or shower, in the main building and in the annex across the road which go for £25 ($57.50) to £30 ($69) per night for two, including an English breakfast and VAT. However, it is perhaps more for the excellence of the bar snacks that we include the Talbot here.

The lounges and bars are warm and cheerful, with open log fires burning, fresh flowers, and cozy chairs. Snack lunches are served daily and include such things as prawns in cheese sauce, jacket potatoes filled with cheese and onions, Welsh rarebit, cottage pie, and chicken and ham vol-au-vent. You can hardly spend more than 95p ($2.19) unless you get carried away and decide to try more than one dish.

For those who stay at the hotel or passersby who require a more substantial and leisurely meal, the dining room specializes in many traditional dishes made from fresh local ingredients and accompanied by fresh vegetables. The manager, Mr. Curwen-Reed, has run the place for several years and takes great pride in the excellence of his menus, a meal costing from £6 ($13.80).

READER'S RESTAURANT SUGGESTION: "I would like to recommend a new restaurant opened in Stow-on-the-Wold, **Country Style Restaurant,** 5 Park St. (tel. Stow-on-the-Wold 30000). As I recall, complete dinners are £7.50 ($17.25), prix fixe, which is rather expensive, but all the food is prepared to order and of gourmet quality. The owners, Andie and Juliette Broadhurst, are a young couple just starting out in the restaurant business, and they are most hospitable. The menu is quite small, and thus the quality can remain high" (Stanley W. Kallmann, East Orange, N.J.).

18. Moreton-in-Marsh

As it's connected by rail to Paddington Station in London (83 miles away), Moreton-in-Marsh is an important center for train passengers headed for the Cotswolds. It is very near many of the villages of interest—Bourton-on-the-Water, 8 miles; Stow-on-the-Wold, 4 miles; Broadway, 8 miles; Chipping Campden, 7 miles; Stratford-upon-Avon, 17 miles away.

354 DOLLARWISE GUIDE TO ENGLAND AND SCOTLAND

Each of the Cotswold towns has its distinctive characteristics. In Moreton-in-Marsh, look for the 17th-century Market Hall and its old Curfew Tower, and then walk down its High, where Roman legions trudged centuries ago (the town once lay on the ancient Fosse Way). Incidentally, if you base here, don't take the name, Moreton-in-Marsh, too literally. Marsh derives from an old word meaning border.

WHERE TO STAY: For accommodations, seek out the following:

Manor House Hotel (tel. Moreton-in-Marsh 50501) is a 300-year-old stone manor—complete with its own ghost, a priest's hiding hole, a secret passage, and a Moot Room used centuries ago by local merchants to settle arguments over wool exchanges. Placed prominently on the main village street, it is formal, yet gracious, and its rear portions reveal varying architectural periods of design. Here, the vine-covered walls protect the garden, a tranquil retreat. Inside are many living rooms, one especially intimate with leather chairs and a fireplace-within-a-fireplace—ideal for drinks and the exchange of "bump-in-the-night" stories. Servants are instructed to keep the log fires burning—"never spare the woodpile."

You can't miss on most of the bedrooms, as they are tastefully furnished, often with antiques or fine reproductions. Many have fine old desks set in front of window ledges, with a view of the garden and ornamental pond. The centrally heated rooms have hot and cold running water or else private baths. All contain color TV sets. A single without bath costs £18.50 ($42.55), increasing to £24.50 ($56.35) with bath. In a bathless double, the tariff is £33 ($75.90), going up to £45 ($103.50) with bath, including breakfast, VAT, and service. A favorite nook is the bar-lounge, with its garden view through leaded Gothic windows. Evening meals in the two-level dining room are candlelit. A table d'hôte lunch goes for £5.50 ($12.65), dinner for £7.50 ($17.25).

The **Redesdale Arms** (tel. Moreton-in-Marsh 50308) is an old coaching inn, on the main village street, its original Cotswold stone features intact. Guests gravitate to the bar-lounge, where drinks are served in front of a six-foot-high stone fireplace. In warmer months, the rear paved terrace is the focal point, with tables set out for refreshments. The bedrooms are simply furnished, with soft beds, dressing tables with three-way mirrors, and hot and cold running water. A single without bath costs £14.70 ($33.81); a double or twin without bath goes for £25.50 ($58.65), and a double or twin with bath, £31.60 ($63.20). These charges include service and VAT. The inn is also well known for its meals. A three-course dinner goes for £7.25 ($16.68), although a full à la carte menu is available as well. A superb Cotswold buffet luncheon is offered for £4 ($9.20), including homemade soup.

White Hart Royal Hotel, High Street (tel. Moreton-in-Marsh 50731), is one of the Trust Houses Forte hotels. It's also another one of the hostelries graced by Charles I (in 1644), who did a lot of sleeping around. The inn provides the amenities of today without compromising the personality of yesteryear. There are two dozen well-furnished bedrooms, with hot and cold running water (some with private bath), innerspring mattresses, and a few antiques intermixed with basic 20th-century pieces. A single goes for £19 ($43.70) without bath, £24 ($55.20) with bath. A bathless double is £26 ($59.80), increasing to £38 ($87.40) with bath. All rates include service and VAT. The old hallway is romantic, as is the bar lounge, built of irregular Cotswold stone. You can have drinks in front of the ten-foot open fireplace. Over the bar and on the walls is a good collection of swords, pewter, and copper warming pans.

19. Broadway

This is the best known Cotswold village. Its wide and beautiful High Street is flanked with honey-colored stone buildings with mullioned windows—remarkable for the harmony of their style and design. Overlooking the Vale of Evesham, Broadway is virtually mobbed with tourists in summer, a major stopover for bus tours. That it retains its charm in spite of the invasion is a credit to its character.

Broadway lies near Evesham at the southern tip of Worcestershire—more than just a sauce familiar to steak lovers. Many of the prime attractions of the Cotswolds as well as Shakespeare Country lie within easy reach of Broadway. Stratford-upon-Avon is only 15 miles away. The nearest rail stations are at Evesham and Moreton-in-Marsh.

WHERE TO STAY: For lodgings, Broadway has the dubious distinction of sheltering the most expensive inn in the Cotswolds. Even the guest houses can command a good price—and get it.

The Upper Bracket

The **Lygon Arms** (tel. Broadway 2255) basks in its well-deserved reputation as one of the greatest old English inns. Sitting sedately in the center of the village, it opens onto a private garden in the rear, with three acres of lawns, trees, and borders of flowers, stone walls with roses, and nooks for tea or sherry. The oldest portions, built of fieldstone with a mossy slate roof, date from the 16th century. But builders in each century have made their additions. There seems to be some basis to the claim that Oliver Cromwell slept here on the night before the Battle of Worecester.

In 1904, the inn was acquired by S. B. Russell and has remained in his family. The Russells are experts in antiques—in fact, some of their collection appears in *The Dictionary of English Furniture*. The various lounges are appropriately decorated; there are smaller ones with tall and wide fireplaces where logs burn on chilly days. For example, an inglenook lounge, made from the original kitchen, has a 12-foot-wide fireplace, with a carved beam, a collection of wood, copper, and pewter artifacts.

The bedrooms vary in size and importance, their prices including a full English breakfast, early-morning tea brought to your room, and an English newspaper. Rates range from £21.30 ($42.60) to £28.70 ($66.01) per person. There are a few private sitting rooms such as the one used by Cromwell, with its ornate plaster ceiling frieze, Tudor fireplace, and Cromwellian chairs.

You dine by candlelight in the oak-paneled Great Hall, with a Tudor fireplace, a cove ceiling, and a Minstrels' Gallery. The cuisine is international (even American specialties). A fixed-price luncheon begins at £6 ($13.80), and a fixed-price dinner starts at £8.20 ($18.86) and goes up.

Even if you aren't spending the night, a meal or afternoon tea at the Lygon Arms is a way to savor the fine flavor of this historic inn.

The Medium-Priced Range

The **Broadway Hotel**, The Green (tel. Broadway 852-401), is right on the village green, perhaps one of the most colorful houses in Broadway. It is a converted 15th-century house, formerly used by the abbots of Pershore, combining the half-timbered look of the Vale of Evesham with the stone of the Cotswolds. While keeping its old-world charm, the hotel has been modernized and converted to provide comforts. It recently was refurbished, with more private baths being added. There is hot and cold running water in the bedrooms, as well as central heating and bedside telephones. A bathless single costs £18 ($41.40), rising to £21 ($48.30) with bath; and bathless doubles go for £32 ($73.60), increasing to £37 ($85.10) with bath, these tariffs including a full English breakfast, service, and VAT. The cooking is fine; the service personal; the dining room attractive; the bedrooms pleasantly furnished. The attractive, comfortable cocktail bar is well stocked.

The **Dormy House Hotel,** Willersey Hill, near Broadway (tel. Broadway 852-711), is a manor farmhouse, standing high on a hill above the village of Broadway, with views in all directions. Its spectacular position has made it a favorite place for those who desire either a meal, afternoon tea, or lodgings. Halfway between Broadway and Chipping Campden, it was created from a sheep farm. The owners have transformed it, remaking an old adjoining timbered barn into studio-style rooms, with open-beamed ceilings, window seats, a few antiques, good soft beds, and full central heating. All the rooms have private baths. A single goes for £19 ($43.70), increasing to £35 ($80.50) in a double, these tariffs including a continental breakfast and VAT.

The tavern meals in the bar have become popular, as the word is out that you get the most for your money here. Only fresh foods—nothing canned—are used. The breads and cakes are baked right on the premises in the farm kitchen. The dining room is gaining a reputation for haute cuisine second to none in the Cotswolds. There is also a fine cellar. In the lounge is a pleasant mixture of old pieces, comfortable armchairs, and a cozy fireplace. A feature of Dormy is the ingeniously decorated tavern lounge.

The Budget Range

Bankside House, 140 High St. (tel. Broadway 852-450), is in the exclusive residential area of Broadway—and isn't allowed to put out a sign—but it accepts bed-and-breakfast guests, who want to live in the atmosphere of a private home. Its owner, Elizabeth B. Oldham, tells the story quite aptly: "My bacon is crisp and my toast is hot! And I'm an American doing bed and breakfast in Broadway." Double rooms go for £8 ($18.40) per person nightly, with extra-wide twin beds and a large breakfast. The house dates from the 15th and 16th centuries, and is said to have belonged to Catherine Parr, one of the wives of Henry VIII. It is a honey, with its low beams, huge fireplaces, and garden. But it is the geniality and helpfulness of Mrs. Oldham that makes a stopover here a highlight of your Cotswold jaunt.

WHERE TO DINE: **Hunter's Lodge Restaurant** (tel. Broadway 3247) is set back quietly from the long High Street, surrounded by its own lawns, flower beds, shady trees, and flowering shrubs. The stone gables are partially covered with ivy, and the windows are deep-set with mullions and leaded panes. There is a formal entrance, with a circular drive and a small foyer furnished with antiques. The restaurant serves outstanding food, prepared by its chef-patron of international reputation. The menu, which is changed every month, features high-quality seasonal food and fresh vegetables. Also, delicious homemade sweets and chocolates are available. The cost is about £20 ($46) for two persons at dinner. Lunches, for £3 ($6.90) to £6 ($13.80), are served from 12:30 to 2 p.m., and dinners from 7:30 to 10 p.m. The Lodge is closed on Sunday nights and all day Monday.

20. Chipping Campden

The English themselves, regardless of how often they visit the Cotswolds, are attracted in great numbers to this town. It's neither too large nor too small. Off the main road, it's easily accessible to major points of interest, and double-decker buses frequently run through here on their way to Oxford (36 miles away) or Stratford-upon-Avon (12 miles away).

Chipping Campden is the winner of the "Best Kept Village Award" in the Bledisloe Cup competition. Rich merchants built homes of Cotswold stone along its model High Street. They have been so well preserved that Chipping Campden to this day remains a gem of the Middle Ages. Its church dates from the 15th century, and its old Market Hall is the loveliest of the Cotswolds. Look also for its almshouses.

WHERE TO STAY: Here are several good choices, all in the medium-priced range:

The **Noel Arms,** High Street (tel. Evesham 840-317), may make you a snob. You just may assume a title for the night, dreaming that this is your personal manor house, with its staff of servants. Dating back to the 14th century, the Noel Arms is a famous establishment. It charges £12.50 ($28.75) for a bathless single, £14.50 ($33.35) for a single with bath. Bathless doubles go for £23.50 ($54.05), doubles with bath for £26 ($59.80), plus VAT, for a bed and a full English breakfast. You can drive your car under the covered archway and into the old posting yard, where parking is private.

Mr. and Mrs. R. P. Sargent, the owners, have had much experience in running hotels, and they offer a warm welcome to their visitors from overseas. Their food always draws praise. Lunch averages £4.25 ($9.78), and a dinner costs as little as £6 ($13.80), if you order from the à la carte menus. The food is traditional English: poached salmon, roast sirloin of beef with Yorkshire pudding, roast leg of lamb with onion sauce, steak hollandaise, apple and loganberry pie.

There's a private sitting room for residents, but you may prefer the lounge, with its 12-foot-wide fireplace. The adjoining room is the public tavern—public in the sense that it's frequented by the locals. It's almost too quaint: old worn curved settles where you can drink beer from mugs of pewter, and soak up an atmosphere enhanced by racks of copper, brass pans, medallions, and oak chairs worn from centuries of use.

The **Cotswold House Hotel** (tel. Evesham 840-330) is a stately, formal Regency house, dating from 1800. Right in the heart of the village, opposite the old wool market, it is run by two gentlemen partners, Graeme Black and Geoffrey Douglass. They have teamed up to bring a high taste level to this handsome old house, and are rightfully proud of the winding Regency staircase in the reception hall. All of the bedrooms have been renovated and two medieval cottages in the garden have been turned into very comfortable bedrooms with bathrooms. Each bedroom has its own personality, enhanced in some cases by antiques. A bathless single goes for £16.45 ($37.84), a double for £28.50 ($65.55). A double with private bath rents for £35.25 ($81.08). VAT is extra.

Taking your meals in the elegant Adam dining room is one of the pleasures of stopping over. The food is prepared with imagination and skill, a set dinner going for £6.70 ($15.41). A typical meal might include cream of celery soup, baked rainbow trout with almonds or roast leg of pork with apple sauce, along with fresh vegetables, followed by a wide selection of desserts. Set lunches are served in the dining room on Sunday. They begin with the largest table of hors d'oeuvres outside Claridge's. Otherwise bar lunches, snacks, salads, sandwiches, and soups fill the public need, judging by their popularity. Both guests and nonresidents are welcomed in this elegant background of fluted columns, an ornate ceiling, and three arched windows opening onto the garden in the rear. The front drawing room is homelike and informal, with a fine collection of framed needlework. Fires burn during the winter months, and the drinking lounge is a cozy spot on a cold day. The friendly management will do much to try to provide tickets for the Shakespeare performances and will offer after-theater suppers if you arrange them in advance.

Kings Arm Hotel, Chipping Campden (tel. Evesham 840-256), stands right by the Market Square. It is partly Georgian, partly much older, a pretty house with a large garden in which you can wander and whence come the fresh vegetables for your delicious dinner. Bathless singles rent for £10.30 ($23.69); bathless doubles, £19.60 ($45.08); doubles with bath, £21.75 ($50.23)—plus VAT and service. All the accommodations are well furnished and spotlessly clean. Snacks for lunch start at £1.20 ($2.76), and a Sunday lunch in the traditional English style is served for about £5.50 ($12.65). A table d'hôte dinner is a good meal with interesting dishes, costing about £6.50 ($14.95).

TIME OUT FOR TEA: Bantam Tea Rooms, Chipping Campden (tel. Evesham 840-386). Real old-fashioned English afternoon teas are served in this lovely bay-windowed 17th-century stone house. You can almost feel the warmth from the much-used oven when you enter to be greeted by Judith McKay and her staff of cheerful local women. Tea can be just a pot of tea and a teacake for 70p ($1.61), or you can indulge in homemade scones, crumpets, sandwiches, and delicious homemade pastries and cakes. Tea is served from 2 to 5:15 p.m. Tuesday through Sunday. It is almost an anticlimax to say that they also serve lunches Tuesday through Saturday with a selection of quiches and salad, cold game pie, pâtés, omelets, and salads (apple, date and nut?) for around £1.50 ($3.45). This is the brainchild of a famous cookery writer and her husband, but you can rely on Judith McKay to see that everything is in "apple pie order."

Chapter XI

STRATFORD AND THE HEART OF ENGLAND

1. Stratford-upon-Avon
2. Warwick
3. Kenilworth Castle
4. Coventry
5. Hereford and Worcester
6. Salop (Shropshire)
7. Staffordshire

SO CLOSE TO LONDON, so rich in fascination, the Shakespeare Country in the heart of England is that district most visited by North Americans (other than London, of course). Many who don't recognize the county name, Warwickshire, know its foremost tourist town, Stratford-upon-Avon, the birthplace of England's greatest writer.

The county and its neighboring shires form a land of industrial cities, green fields, and sleepy market towns—dotted with buildings, some of which have changed little since Shakespeare's time. Here are many of the places that have magic for overseas visitors, not only Stratford-upon-Avon, but also Warwick and Kenilworth Castles, as well as Coventry Cathedral.

Those who have time to penetrate deeper into the chapter will find elegant spa towns, such as Great Malvern, historic cathedral cities such as Hereford and Worcester, and industrial archeology at Stoke-on-Trent (the famous potteries). Scenery in Salop ranges from untamed borderlands to gentle plains which give way in the north to wooded areas and meres.

HEART OF ENGLAND COUNTRY TOURS: These tours, booked at Yew Tree House, Ombersley, Hereford and Worcester (tel. Worcester 0905/620848), are the brainchild of Jane Moyle, a housewife and mother who started the venture as a hobby and is now an international concern. Jane and her partner, Caroline Clist, invite visitors to take a journey through the familiar sights of the Cotswolds and Stratford-upon-Avon, as well as the little-known countryside of Hereford and Worcester, Salop, and the Welsh Borders, lunching and staying overnight in private homes or country inns.

If you opt for a tour, your charming guide will meet you at the railway station and look after you throughout your tour. Lunch will vary from a quick

...storic pub to Sunday lunch en famille in a Georgian manor house. ...nay be spent in a restored 17th-century water mill or a 12th-century ...everywhere you will be treated as an honored family guest instead ...ist a "room number."

...night stays—including drinks, bed, breakfast, and your own bathroom in a private house, inclusive of all reasonable private comforts—cost about £70 ($161) for two people. Lunch in private houses (you can opt for just this if you are touring self-drive) is £8.50 ($19.55) per person, including wine. Add £65 ($149.50) a day for two people, plus £20 ($46) a day per person over two to cover the cost of your guide, transportation, and afternoon tea.

1. Stratford-upon-Avon

This town has a phenomenal tourist trade. Actor David Garrick really got it launched in 1769 when he organized the first of the Bard's birthday celebrations. It is no secret by now, of course, that William Shakespeare was born in Stratford-upon-Avon on April 23, 1564.

Surprisingly little is known about his early life, as the frankest of his biographers concede. Perhaps because documentation is so lacking about the writer, much useless conjecture has arisen (did Elizabeth I really write the plays?). But the view that Francis Bacon wrote all of Shakespeare's work would certainly stir up *The Tempest,* if suggested to the innkeepers of Stratford-upon-Avon. Admittedly, however, some of the stories and legends connected with Shakespeare's days in Stratford are largely fanciful, invented belatedly to amuse and entertain the vast number of literary fans making the pilgrimage.

Today's magnet, in addition to Shakespeare's birthplace, is the Royal Shakespeare Theatre, where Britain's foremost actors perform during a long season that lasts from Easter until January. Stratford-upon-Avon is also a good center for trips to Warwick Castle, Kenilworth Castle, Sulgrave Manor (ancestral home of George Washington), Compton Wynyates, even Coventry Cathedral. The market town lies 92 miles from London, 40 from Oxford, and 8 from Warwick.

THE SIGHTS: Besides the attractions on the periphery of Stratford, there are many Elizabethan and Jacobean buildings in this colorful town—many of them administered by the Shakespeare Birthplace Trust Properties. One ticket—costing £1.80 ($4.14) for adults, 75p ($1.73) for children—will permit you to visit the five most important sights. You should pick up the ticket if you're planning to do much sightseeing (obtainable at your first stopover at any one of the Trust properties). The houses are open from 9 a.m. to 6 p.m. weekdays (on Sunday from 2 to 6 p.m.), from April through October; Shakespeare's birthplace and Anne Hathaway's Cottage open at 10 a.m. on Sunday during the summer. Off-season, the houses are open from 9 a.m. to 4 p.m. On winter Sundays, only Shakespeare's birthplace and Anne Hathaway's Cottage are open, from 1:30 to 4:30. On weekdays in summer and on Thursday and Saturday during April, May and October, both remain open until 7 p.m.

Shakespeare's Birthplace

On Henley Street, the son of a glover and whittawer was born on St. George's day (April 23) in 1564, and died 52 years later on the same day. Filled with Shakespeare memorabilia, including a portrait, and furnishings of the writer's time, the Trust property is a half-timbered structure, dating from the early years of the 16th century. The house was finally bought by public donors in 1847 and preserved as a national shrine. You can visit the oak-beamed living room, the bedroom where Shakespeare was born, a fully equipped kitchen of the period (look for the "baby-minder"), and a Shakespeare Museum, illustrating his life and times. Later, you can walk through the garden out back. It is estimated that some 660,000 visitors pass through the house annually. If visited separately, admission is 70p ($1.61) for adults, 30p (69¢) for children. Next door to the birthplace is the modern Shakespeare Center, built to commemorate the 400th anniversary of the Bard's birth. It serves both as the administrative headquarters of the Birthplace Trust and as a library and study center.

Anne Hathaway's Cottage

One mile from Stratford in the hamlet of Shottery is the thatched, wattle-and-daub cottage where Anne Hathaway lived before her marriage to the poet. In sheer charm, it is the most interesting and most photographed, it would seem, of the Trust properties. The Hathaways were yeoman farmers, and—aside from its historical interest—the cottage provides a rare insight into the life of a family of Shakespeare's day. If the poet came a-courtin', he must have been treated as a mere teenager, as he married Miss Hathaway when he was only 18 years old and she much older. Much of the original furnishings—including the courting settle—and utensils are preserved inside the house, which was occupied by descendants of Shakespeare's wife until late in Victoria's day. After a visit through the farmhouse, you'll surely want to linger in the garden and orchard. You can either walk across the meadow to Shottery from Evesham Place in Stratford (pathway marked), or else take a bus from Bridge Street. The admission is 70p ($1.61) for adults, 30p (69¢) for children.

New Place

This site is on Chapel Street, where Shakespeare retired in 1610—a prosperous man to judge from the standards of his day. He died there six years later, at the age of 52. Regrettably, only the site of his former home remains today, as the house was torn down. You enter the gardens through Nash's House (Thomas Nash married Elizabeth Hall, a granddaughter of the poet). Nash's House has 16th-century period rooms and an exhibition illustrating the archeology and later history of Stratford. The heavily visited Knott Garden adjoins the site, and represents the style of a fashionable Elizabethan garden. New Place itself has its own Great Garden, which once belonged to Shakespeare. Here, the Bard planted a mulberry tree, so popular with latter-day visitors to Stratford that the cantankerous owner of the garden chopped it down. The mulberry tree that grows there today is said to have been planted from a cutting of the original tree. But that doesn't mean we have to believe it. The admission is 45p ($1.04) for adults, 20p (46¢) for children.

Mary Arden's House

A crooked-timbered Tudor farm, this is the house where Shakespeare's mother, the daughter of a yeoman farmer, lived. The farmstead lies in the village of Wilmcote, three miles from Stratford-upon-Avon. Look for the stone dovecote out back, and the farming museum in the barns. The admission is 45p ($1.04) for adults, 20p (46¢) for children.

By now, you will have seen the Trust properties, except for Hall's Croft (see "Where to Eat" further on). Other interesting sights not administered by the Trust foundation include the following:

Harvard House

Not just of interest to Harvard men, Harvard House on High Street is a fine example of an Elizabethan town house. Rebuilt in 1596, it was once the home of Katherine Rogers, mother of John Harvard, founder of Harvard University. In 1909, the house was purchased by a Chicago millionaire, Edward Morris, who presented it as a gift to the American university. Its present furnishings are not original, although they are of the period when Miss Rogers lived in the house. But the floors, made of the local flagstone, are authentic. Look for the Bible Chair, used for hiding the Bible during the days of Tudor persecution. Harvard House, charging admission of 40p (92¢) for adults, 20p (46¢) for children, is open April through September, 9 a.m. to 1 p.m. and 2 to 6 p.m. weekdays, 2 to 6 p.m. on Sunday; October through March, 10 a.m. to 1 p.m. and 2 to 4 p.m. weekdays, closed Sunday. Finally, you may want to visit the:

Holy Trinity Church

In an attractive setting near the Avon, the parish church of Stratford-upon-Avon is distinguished mainly because Shakespeare was buried in the chancel ("and curst be he who moves my bones"). The Parish Register records his birth and death (copies of the original, of course). No charge is made for entry into the church, described as "one of the most beautiful parish churches in the world," but visitors wishing to view Shakespeare's tomb are asked to donate a small sum, at present 10p (23¢) for students, 20p (46¢) for adults, toward the restoration fund.

AN ELIZABETHAN SHOW: The new **Heritage Theatre**, Waterside (tel. Stratford-upon-Avon 69190), presents a full-time show, an Elizabethan pageant which tries to recreate the time of Shakespeare. The theater stands near the Royal Shakespeare Theatre. Its presentation tells the story of the great pageant which Lord Leicester scheduled for Queen Elizabeth in the summer of 1575. After a Royal Progress across the country, it culminated in several days of dances, songs, plays, and pomp at Kenilworth Castle. As a young man, Shakespeare is believed to have witnessed and been influenced by this pageant. The Heritage uses music, an eight-track sound tape, lights, costumes, and scenery, and dialogue is spoken by members of the Royal Shakespeare Theatre. Fourteen shows are presented daily, 9:30 a.m. to 8:30 p.m., April to September; 10:30 a.m. to 5 p.m., October to March. Admission is £1.20 ($2.76) for adults, 80p ($1.84) for students and children over 6 (no charge for children under 6).

TOURS: Guide Friday Ltd., 32 Henley St. (tel. Stratford-upon-Avon 69888), just past Shakespeare's Birthplace on the left, is a young company with a London office. In Stratford, it is run by Roger Thompson. The company's intention is to further establish Stratford, in the heart of England, as the center to tour from, rather than just to. Tours operate throughout the year from Guide Friday's Stratford office and the main hotels, including: Stratford and Shakespeare Lecture Tours (these not only teach but save a 13-mile walk), £3 ($6.90) per person; Warwick and Kenilworth Castles, at 2 p.m., £3.50 ($8.05) per person; the Cotswold Hills and Country Villages, at 11 a.m., £4 ($9.20) per person. During the summer months, tours by open-top double-decker bus operate making stops at Anne Hathaway's Cottage and at Mary Arden's House, four miles from Stratford, with a general look at the town, included in the price of £1.50 ($3.45) per person. The Cotswolds and Country Pubs Tour operates every evening during the summer by double-decker bus for the scenic drive (if the weather is good), at a cost of £3 ($6.90), including your first pint of Real Ale. It makes a superb alternative to the theater, and you visit some four or five pubs in the attractive villages, with time for a game of darts with the locals, a pint of ale, and perhaps a late pub-snack supper. The tour departs at 7:30 p.m. from Guide Friday's office. Booking arrangements can be made for all tours after your arrival in Stratford-upon-Avon, and all tours are accompanied by qualified guides.

In conjunction with British Rail, a new service has been started by Guide Friday, **The Shakespeare Connection,** a combined road/rail ticket from London Euston Station to Stratford-upon-Avon. The cost is £10.20 ($23) per person, second class, for the round trip to Coventry Station and coach from Coventry to right outside Shakespeare's Birthplace. It's now possible to be standing by the Bard's bed in Stratford in less than two hours from the time you leave London. You can leave Euston at 8:40 a.m. and arrive in Stratford at 10:30 a.m., returning to Euston at 5:40 p.m., or if you wish, go to the theater or take Guide Friday's Pub Tour, catching the train back to London at 11:40 p.m., arriving in the capital in the early hours. Ask for your ticket at Euston for the Shakespeare Connection.

The services of Guide Friday also include car rental (you can avoid the drive out of London and "start from the heart"). Car tours of the region with driver guides are arranged, as well as assistance with theater tickets. Guide Friday operates the Scene Setter Package, the cheapest and easiest method of visiting Stratford, giving you accommodation and theater seats combined. Telephone the Stratford office for information.

CAUGHT WITHOUT A ROOM?: During the long theater season, the hotels in Stratford-upon-Avon are jam-packed, and you may run into difficulty if you arrive without a reservation. However, if you should visit from April to October during regular office hours (9 a.m. to 5:30 p.m. weekdays, 2 to 5 p.m. on Sunday) you can go to the **Information Centre** at the Judith Shakespeare House, 1 High St. (tel. 293-127).

Here a staff person, who has had much experience with travelers on all budgets, will get on the telephone and try to book a room for you in the price range you are seeking.

It is also possible to reserve accommodations if you write well enough in advance. By writing to the Information Centre, you'll be spared having to get in touch with several hotels on your own and running the risk of getting turned down. If you do write, specify the price range and the number of beds required. The centre often gets vague letters, and the staff doesn't know whether to book you into a private suite at the Shakespeare Hotel, or else lend you a cot to put in front of the Royal Shakespeare Theatre. Don't be surprised. Stratford-upon-Avon visitors are a varied group. Recently a young man not only slept in front of the theater, but was seen frying an egg there over an open fire the next morning.

WHERE TO STAY: For our hotel recommendations, we'll lead off with the most expensive in:

The Upper Bracket

Alveston Manor Hotel, Clopton Bridge (tel. Stratford-upon-Avon 4581), is a black-and-white timbered manor, conveniently placed for attending the theater, just a two-minute walk from the Avon. It has more chimneys and gables that one can count—a hodgepodge of styles, everything from an Elizabethan gazebo to Queen Anne windows. Tracing the building's ancestry involves one in early English history, as its origins predate the arrival of William the Conqueror. A ping-pong game of ownership has been played with Alveston, mentioned, by the way, in the Domesday Book. Perhaps any other manor would have become frayed at the edges, but under the Trust House management, a well-directed program of expansion is being carried out, making for a top-level accommodation that combines the past with the comfort of today.

Rooms in the Manor House are for those who enjoy an atmosphere of old slanted floors, overhead beams, and antique furnishings. However, in the new block, attached by a covered walk through the rear garden, rooms are fully modernized with skillfully designed built-in pieces, baths with showers, heated towel racks, telephones, radios, bedside lamps, dressing tables, and a color-coordinated decor. The price of lodgings varies according to the season, peaking from June through September. In a single room, the rate is £26 ($59.80), increasing to £38 ($87.40) in a double or twin. Breakfast is extra, but service charge and VAT are included. In the new block, a number of large rooms are rented to three or four persons.

The lounges are in the manor; and guests gather in the Cedar Room for relaxation, enjoying the view of the centuries-old tree at the top of the garden—said to have been the background for the first presentation of *A Midsummer Night's Dream*. In the main living room, with its well-preserved linenfold paneling, logs burn in the Tudor fireplace. The bar-lounge is another cozy spot, with its stone fireplace, Tudor bench, and Windsor armchairs. Good food is served in the softly lit Tudor Restaurant, with its oak beams and leaded-glass windows.

Stratford Hilton, Bridgefoot (tel. Stratford-upon-Avon 67511). It had to happen: a Hilton in Stratford! On five landscaped acres of lawns and gardens, laid out in a semi-Tudor style, this complex of red brick and stone stands right on the Avon, within walking distance of the theater. In fact, not since the construction of the theater back in the 1930s has a building sparked such controversy, and attracted so many defenders and detractors. It's only four stories high—the top floor semidisguised by a mansard roof—and it's spread out, much like a hospital. Each of its 253 rooms contains individually controlled heating and air conditioning, plus views of the river, the theater, and the surrounding countryside. Each has a private bath and shower, with direct-dial telephones, taped music, color TV. High-season rates apply from April 1 to October 1; singles range from £28 ($64.40) to £31 ($71.30), doubles from £34 ($78.20) to £38 ($87.40). Tax and service are included in the tariffs. The hotel has an Actors Bar, an unusual octagonal-shaped cocktail lounge, with windows overlooking the gardens and the Avon. A live group plays for dancing here from 10 p.m. to 2 a.m. It is joined to the main building by an enclosed walkway. Guests can reach the theater via a ten-minute boat ride on a barge docked in front on the canal. The Tavern restaurant is a coffeeshop open for lunch and dinner, serving a buffet of cold meats, salads, and desserts, plus at least two hot dishes, costing from £5 ($11.50) per head. The Warwick Grill, the prestige restaurant of the hotel, offers a wide range of international and English cuisine. A specialty is roast rib of Scottish beef.

Welcombe Hotel, Warwick Road (tel. Stratford-upon-Avon 295-252), is one of England's great Jacobean country houses, placed about a ten-minute ride from the heart of Stratford-upon-Avon. The home once belonged to Sir Archibald Flower, the philanthropic brewer who helped create the Shakespeare Memorial Theatre. Converted into a hotel, and run by the British Transport

Hotels Ltd., it is surrounded by 120 acres of grounds. It is reached by a formal entrance on Warwick Road, a winding driveway leading to the main hall. There's even an 18-hole, 6300-yard course on the estate. Guests gather on fair days for afternoon tea or drinks on the rear terrace, with its Italian-style garden and steps leading down to flower beds. The public rooms are heroic in size, with high mullioned windows providing views of the park. Although the antiques have been removed, the furnishings are suitable. The bedrooms—some big enough for tennis matches—have pleasant pieces. A single room with bath rents for £36 ($82.80). A double with bath costs £55 ($126.50), including a full breakfast, service charge, and VAT. There is an elaborate à la carte menu, plus a good wine list. The management tries to provide tickets for theater performances and serves pretheater suppers.

The **Shakespeare Hotel,** Chapel Street (tel. Stratford-upon-Avon 294-771), a 16th-century building, now redecorated and run as a Trust House, lies within a few minutes of the theater, the poet's grammar school, and New Place, where the Bard died. It's easy to spot, with its nine gables, black-and-white timbering, leaded diamond windows, bays, and hanging baskets of red geraniums. In 1769, David Garrick, the famous actor, named most of the lounges and bedrooms after plays or characters of Shakespeare. You may be assigned the Ophelia Bedroom or the Romeo and Juliet Bedroom. There's even a private Hamlet suite. Room rates are higher between April 1 and November 1, with a single going for £28 ($64.40). Double rooms rent for an inclusive £38 ($87.40). All meals are extra. The rooms are centrally heated, and all have private bath, radio, and TV.

Meals are served in the "As You Like It" dining room, where the old beams have been preserved. You dine on red leather and brass-studded chairs. While there is an extensive à la carte menu and a fine wine list, the bargain is the table d'hôte dinner starting at £7 ($16.10). The table d'hôte luncheon starts at £5.50 ($12.65). "The Measure for Measure" bar, with its Windsor chairs and pine settles, and Frank's Bar, with its winged chairs and open fireplace, lure one to the Shakespeare.

The Medium-Priced Range

The **Falcon,** Chapel Street (tel. Stratford-upon-Avon 5777), is a blending of the very old and the very new. At the rear of a black-and-white timbered inn, licensed a quarter of a century after Shakespeare's death, is a contemporary bedroom extension, joined by a glass-covered passageway. In the heart of Stratford, the Falcon faces the Guild Chapel and the New Place Gardens. The bedrooms in the mellowed part have oak beams, diamond leaded-glass windows, antique furnishings, and good reproductions. One arrives at the rear portion to unload luggage, just as horse-drawn coaches once dispatched their passengers. All bedrooms have private bathrooms, radio, television, telephone, electric trouser press, and tea- and coffee-making equipment. Rates include accommodation, full English breakfast, space for your car, and service charge, although VAT is extra. A single with bath is around £24 ($55.20); a double or twin with bath, £34 ($78.20).

The social lounges are tasteful and comfortable—some of the finest in the Midlands. In the intimate Merlin Lounge is an open copper-hooded fireplace where coal and log fires are kept burning under beams salvaged from old ships (the walls are a good example of wattle and daub, typical of Shakespeare's day). The Oak Lounge Bar is a forest of weathered beams, and on either side of the stone fireplace is the paneling removed from the poet's last home, New Place.

The **Arden Hotel,** Waterside (tel. Stratford-upon-Avon 294-949), is frankly your best choice if you're really devoted to the Shakespeare theater. A Regency brick house, with its own acre garden right on the Avon, the hotel sits diagonally across from the theater. The management knows how to spell hospitality, going out of their way to obtain seats for guests, providing tea and refreshments in their English garden, with its arbor of white roses, fruit trees, and views of the swan-studded river. Constantly returning guests have created a space problem, which has been solved by building a 20-bedroom wing. All the rooms contain private baths and overlook the Avon and the garden. There is a residents' lounge, opening onto the herb garden, plus a TV room. The rooms are pleasant, all with central heating and hot and cold running water. Bathless singles rent for £15 ($34.50), increasing to £22 ($50.60) with bath. Bathless doubles cost £28 ($64.40), the price going up to £36 ($82.80) with bath, these tariffs including an English breakfast, service, and VAT. Meals are served in the front dining room, where two large bay windows open toward the river. Nonresidents should note the inexpensive and good-tasting meals here: lunches are served carvery style and you pay only for what roast you select, around £5 ($11.50) per head. Dinners are available at £7 ($16.10). The food is typical English fare, and includes boiled York ham with a parsley sauce, stuffed Norfolk turkey, roast beef with Yorkshire pudding, and fresh Wye salmon. The latest addition is an open-air terrace overlooking the river where one can eat or drink.

Haytor, Avenue Road (tel. Stratford-upon-Avon 297-799), is the domain of Mr. and Mrs. Hockerston Tagg, whose Edwardian-style house at the edge of a residential sector is an offbeat private hotel. Planned by a French architect in Edwardian times, it's surrounded by a garden, scheduled under the National Gardens Scheme. Most rooms contain private baths. The cost is from £11.90 ($27.37) per person in a bathless room, £13.25 ($30.48) in a room with bath or shower and toilet. A full English breakfast is included, and so is service, but not VAT. The Taggs will give you many gardening tips and information on sightseeing possibilities. In addition, Mr. Tagg offers a free theater-booking service for guests.

Grosvenor House Hotel, Warwick Road (tel. Stratford-upon-Avon 69213), is a Georgian residence converted into a hotel of 61 bedrooms (42 with private shower or bath), run by the Adcock family and friendly staff. Lawns and gardens to the front and rear of the hotel lend additional character. In high season (March through October), singles rent from £16 ($36.80) to £19 ($43.70); doubles, £25 ($57.50) to £31 ($71.30)—including service, VAT, and a big English breakfast. Rooms are centrally heated, and all have radio, telephone, and color TV. There are two comfortable bars, open till midnight.

Stratford House, Sheep Street (tel. Stratford-upon-Avon 68288), is a pleasant Georgian house 100 yards from the Avon River and the Royal Shakespeare Theatre. A new small hotel of only ten bedrooms (seven of which have private baths or showers), the agreeable bed-and-breakfast establishment is run by Peter and Pamela Wade, who extend a fond welcome for their North American clients. The house is furnished tastefully and with style, somewhat like a private home, with books and pictures along with a scattering of antiques. Everything is spotlessly maintained. On the side is a small walled courtyard, with flowering plants. A double with private bath rents for £16.25 ($37.38), only £14.25 ($32.78) if bathless. Families can rent a room for four with private bath at a cost of £13 ($29.90) per adult. Singles, however, are charged from £22 ($50.60). No service charge is included. Rates quoted include a full English breakfast, VAT, and early morning tea. Color TV, incidentally, is provided in every bedroom.

The Budget Range

Stratheden Hotel, Chapel Street (tel. Stratford-upon-Avon 2837), is a small, tuck-away hotel, in a weathered building dating back to 1673, with a tiny rear garden and top-floor rooms with slanted, beamed ceilings. Owned by Mr. and Mrs. Wells (she's from Northern Ireland, he's a native of Warwickshire), the house has improved in both decor and comfort, with fresh paint, new curtains, and good beds. The charge for bed and breakfast ranges from £6.75 ($15.33) to £7.75 ($17.83) per person, plus VAT. Some rooms have private showers and toilets.

The entry hallway has a glass cupboard, holding family heirlooms and collector tidbits. The house itself is sprinkled with old pieces. The dining room, with a bay window, has an overscale sideboard that once belonged to the "insanely vain" Marie Corelli, the eccentric novelist, poet, and mystic who wrote a series of seven books, beginning with *A Romance of Two Worlds* and ending with *Spirit and Power and Universal Love.* Queen Victoria was one of her avid readers. The Victorian novelist (1855-1924) was noted for her passion for pastoral paintings and objets d'art. In Room 4 you can see an example of her taste in bedchamber furniture: a massive mahogany tester bed.

WHERE TO EAT: The **Box Tree Restaurant,** the Royal Shakespeare Theatre, Waterside (tel. Stratford-upon-Avon 293-226), has dibs on the best position in town, in the theater, with walls of glass providing an unobstructed view of the Avon and its swans. You can also dine on the outer terrace where tables are placed in fair weather. The meals and service are worthy of its unique position. The restaurant is open on matinee days and Sunday from 12:30 p.m. to 2 p.m., and in the evenings from 6 to 11 p.m. A three-course pretheater dinner begins at £7.50 ($17.25), going up to £10 ($23). Lunches start at £5 ($11.50). After each evening's performance, you can dine by flickering candlelight. Such items are featured as duckling à l'orange, grilled sirloin steak, coq au vin, escalope of veal. Be sure to book your table in advance, especially on the days of performances (there's a special phone for reservations in the theater lobby).

In the **River Terrace Restaurant,** an assortment of snack meals, homemade pizzas, quiches, pâtés, pies, soups, and hamburgers, all with salads, is offered. With dessert to finish off your meal, expect to pay around £5 ($11.50).

Marianne, 3 Greenhill St. (tel. Stratford-upon-Avon 293-563), is a bistro-like restaurant, providing an authentic French cuisine. The small two-story dining room has an open wooden staircase leading to additional tables on the mezzanine. The best value here is the table d'hôte dinner, which includes an appetizer, main course, and cheese or dessert, and costs £3.50 ($8.05). On the à la carte menu, appetizers include gratinée lyonnaise, a tasty onion soup for £1.20 ($2.76), or perhaps escargots in sauce with hazelnuts, £2 ($4.60). The menu selections vary according to the season since the owner, Pierre Denervaux, makes every effort to obtain only fresh ingredients for his dishes. When you visit, you may find such items listed as scampi à l'estragon, a savory shrimp dish in a delicate tarragon sauce, or caneton au cassis, duckling served with a fragrant cassis glaze. Entrees range from £4 ($9.20) to £5.50 ($12.65). For dessert, you might like to sample one of the delicious pastries prepared by the chef and costing about £1 ($2.30). Marianne's is open Monday through Saturday for dinner, and also offers a daily set lunch from 12:30 to 2 p.m.

Christophi's, 21-23 Sheep Street (tel. Stratford-upon-Avon 293-546), is a bit of old Athens set down in the middle of Shakespeare's hometown. Owned by Nicos Christophi, the restaurant is laid out in Greek fashion, with an indoor courtyard. You may dine on both Greek and Cypriot dishes while live Greek music plays in the background. A number of items of standard British fare are included on the menu for the less adventurous. To begin your meal you might try the dolmadakia, a meat and rice ball wrapped in vine leaves, for £2.25 ($5.18), or the popular avgolemono, a chicken soup heavily laced with lemon juice, for £1.20 ($2.76). The entree portion of the menu includes moussaka, a casserole of chopped beef, eggplant, and potatoes, crowned with a wonderful cheese-flavored cream sauce, and priced at £5 ($11.50). Christophi's features the meze, a typical Greek "taverna" dinner, consisting of a variety of individual dishes, including various hors d'oeuvres and a main course "to satisfy the most adventurous palate." The restaurant is open for dinner from 5:30 p.m. to midnight. Closed Sunday.

Mr. Christophi also operates the **Bancroft Garden Hotel and Restaurant,** Waterside (tel. Stratford-upon-Avon 0789), just opposite the Royal Shakespeare Theatre. Here single rooms rent for £15 ($34.50) and doubles for £25 ($57.50). All rooms are equipped with private shower and toilet. Rates include a continental breakfast, VAT, and service.

Da Giovanni, 8 Ely St. (tel. Stratford-upon-Avon 293-528), is an intimate spot, favored by actors at the theater. The yellow brick cottage is graced with white bay windows. Up front is a sophisticated cocktail lounge with antiques. Da Giovanni is in the true trattoria style, its cuisine beginning fittingly enough with minestrone. The classic Italian menu includes such pasta dishes as lasagne and cannelloni, and such main dishes as escalope Pietmontese and spezzato di pollo alla casalinga (casserole of chicken cooked in wine with tomatoes and mushrooms). A good Italian dessert is the zabaglione, although at least two persons must order it. A selection of excellent continental ices is also featured, everything from Italian cassata to mela Stregata. Expect to pay from £10 ($23) for a complete dinner. A 10% service charge is added. It's closed on Sunday, but open other days from 12:30 to 2 p.m. and from 6 to 11:30 p.m.

Cobweb Restaurant & Confectionery, 12 Sheep St. (tel. Stratford-upon-Avon 292-554), is a black-and-white timbered building, with a high gabled wing, dating from the early 16th century. It's steeped in associations with the days of Shakespeare. On the ground floor are cases of goodies for sale, but you may want to go to the second floor, where there's a maze of three rooms filled with antique oak tables, Windsor chairs, and settles. The shop is noted as one of the finest in England for its cakes, pastries, cream gâteaux (especially chocolate and sherry gâteau), meringues, apple strudel, and cheesecake.

The light luncheons are excellent, and the kitchen provides the traditional English roasts. The soups are most tasty—each costing 60p ($1.38). A full lunch of three courses costs from £4 ($9.20). After morning coffee and luncheon, the next major event is teatime. A good-size pot of tea is 60p ($1.38) and the Cobweb offers at least 60 varieties of English and continental cakes from 30p (69¢) upward. The Cobweb is also open for teas on Sunday from 3 to 6 p.m.

The Dirty Duck, Waterside Street, was formerly known as the Black Swan. By whatever bird it's called, it's been popular since the 18th century as a hangout for Stratford players. The autographed photographs of its patrons, such as Lord Laurence Olivier, line the wall. The front lounge and bar crackles with intense conversation. In the spring and fall an open fire burns moodily.

In the Dirty Duck Grill Room meals are served from noon to 2:30 p.m. and from 6 to midnight. An à la carte menu is offered. Typical English grills are featured from £4 ($9.20). In fair weather, you can drink while sitting in the front garden, and watching the swans on the Avon glide by.

The **Garrick Inn**, High Street, is a black-and-white timbered Elizabethan pub named after one of England's greatest actors, David Garrick. It has its own kind of unpretentious charm. The front bar is decked out with tapestry-covered settles, an old oak refectory table, and an open fireplace where the locals gravitate. The back bar has a circular fireplace with a copper hood—plus a buffet bar serving "ploughman's lunches."

The **Hall's Croft Festival Club,** in the Old Town, makes an ideal headquarters during your stay in Stratford-upon-Avon. This skillfully preserved, timbered Elizabethan building can become your private club, where you can congregate with fellow Shakespeare enthusiasts, and dine inexpensively. Hall's Croft was the original town house of Susanna, daughter of William Shakespeare, and her husband, Dr. John Hall. Parts of the authentically furnished house may be visited on your £1.80 ($4.14) ticket which admits you to five Shakespeare Trust Properties. The house lies about two blocks from the Royal Shakespeare Theatre, and a block from the Avon.

The cost of membership is £1.50 ($3.25) weekly. As a member, you'll be entitled to use the facilities of the club, including the comfortable rooms for lounging, lunching, or reading, as well as the garden. Lectures and poetry readings are held; books and pamphlets sold—and you can even get your mail here.

Eating at the club is inexpensive, and the food is quite good. A typical luncheon selection might include oxtail soup, roast lamb with mint sauce, roast potatoes, carrots, cabbage, followed by apple crumble and custard—all for approximately £4 ($9.20) including coffee. Luncheon is served from noon to 2 p.m. After these hours, snacks are available. The club is open from April till the end of October, six days a week, from 10:30 a.m. till 6 p.m. (later in the summer).

ATTENDING THE THEATER: The **Royal Shakespeare Theatre** on the banks of the Avon is the number one theater for Shakespearean productions. The season runs for nine months from March to January, with a winter festival of music and ballet in February. The present theater was opened in 1932, after the old Shakespeare Memorial Theatre, erected in Victoria's day, burned down in 1926. The theater employs the finest actors and actresses on the British stage. In an average season, five Shakespearean plays rotate in repertory.

Usually, you'll need reservations: there are three successive booking periods, each one opening about two months in advance. You can best pick these up from a North American or an English travel agent. If you wait until your arrival in Stratford, it may be too late to get a good seat. In summer the stall (orchestra) seats range in price from £6 ($13.80) to £10 ($23), and if you're not subject to nosebleed, you may want to anchor in the high-altitude balcony in a seat that goes for £3 ($6.90) to £4 ($9.20).

Tip: Don't despair completely if you should arrive in Stratford without a ticket. The theater box office always holds back a block of £4 ($9.20) stall seats that go on sale the day of each performance at 10:30 a.m. An alternative course is to buy standing room at the same time for £1 ($2.30).

In the Victorian wing of the old Memorial Theatre—spared by the fire—is a Picture Gallery and Museum, filled with portraits of the Bard, oils of performances from his various classics showing 18th- and 19th-century costume designs, portraits of actors in memorable characterizations of Shakespearean roles, such as Lord Laurence Olivier as Macbeth and Dame Edith Evans as Volumnia. The gallery is open April to October weekdays 10 a.m. to 1 p.m. and 2 to 6 p.m.; matinee days, 10 a.m. to 6 p.m.; Sunday, 2 to 6 p.m. December to March, open Sunday only. Admission is 45p ($1.04) for adults, 25p (58¢) for children.

BOOK BROWSING: Although it seems ironic to call this shop at 21 Chapel St. the **Chaucer Head Bookshop,** it is still an interesting place to visit—offering both new and secondhand editions. A friend of Shakespeare's, Julius Shaw, who was one of the executors of his will, lived at this address from 1597 to 1629. It is owned and run by Dorothy Withey, who has opened a second-floor art gallery, displaying the work of living artists, but setting aside a room for prints and engravings as well.

STAYING AT WILMCOTE: **Swan House Hotel,** The Green (tel. Stratford-upon-Avon 67030), lies in the heart of the tiny hamlet of Wilmcote, where Shakespeare's mother, Mary Arden, lived. Really an upgraded village pub-hotel, the white-painted Swan is tranquil, restful, and gracious, offering not only attractive and fresh bedrooms at low prices, but good meals as well. It's owned by Mr. and Mrs. Paul Knight, who have made the little inn homelike. You'll find bright colors and antiques, as well as an attractive staff. Bathless singles rent for £12 ($27.60), bathless doubles for £22 ($50.60). The charge is £25 ($57.50) in a double with private bath, VAT and service included. Drinks are offered in the little bar, with its log-burning fireplace, a bay window with a view of the Mary Arden cottage which you can visit, and tiny rear courtyard and old well.

The beamed dining room at the rear provides a good setting for an excellent English cuisine with some French overtones. You might start with an apple filled with a creamy mixture of Stilton cheese. Lunch is from noon till 2 p.m. and dinner from 7:30 to 9:30 p.m. At Sunday dinner, only residents are served.

Most travelers approach our next stopover, Warwick, via route A46 from Stratford-upon-Avon, eight miles away. The town is 92 miles from London, and is on the Avon.

2. Warwick

Visitors seem to rush through Warwick to see Warwick Castle; then they're off on their next adventure, traditionally to the ruins of Kenilworth Castle. But the historic center of medieval Warwick deserves to be treated with greater respect. It has far more to offer than a castle.

In 1694, a fire swept through Warwick, destroying large segments of the town, but it still retains a number of Elizabethan and medieval buildings—along with some fine Georgian structures. (Very few traces remain, though, of the town walls, except the East and West Gates.) Warwick looks to Ethelfleda, daughter of Alfred the Great, as its founder. But most of its history is associated with the Earls of Warwick, a title created by the son of William the Conqueror in 1088. The story of those earls—the Beaumonts, the Beauchamps (such figures as "Kingmaker" Richard Neville)—makes for an exciting episode in English history, but is too detailed to document here.

WARWICK CASTLE: Perched on a rocky cliff above the Avon, this magnificent 14th-century fortress encloses a stately mansion in the grandest late 17th-century style.

The importance of the site has been recognized from earliest times. The first defense works of importance at Warwick were built by Ethelfleda, daughter of Alfred the Great, in 915 A.D. Her fortifications were further developed by the construction of a motte and bailey castle on the orders of William the Conqueror in 1068, two years after the Norman Conquest. There are now no remains of the Norman castle, as this was sacked by Simon de Montfort in the Barons War of 1264.

The Beauchamp family, the most illustrious medieval Earls of Warwick, are responsible for most of the castle as it is seen today, and much of the external structure remains unchanged from the mid-14th century. When the castle was granted to Sir Fulke Greville by James I in 1604, he spent £20,000 (an enormous sum in those days) converting the existing castle buildings into a luxurious mansion. The Grevilles have held the Earl of Warwick title since 1759, when it passed from the Rich family.

The State Rooms and Great Hall house fine collections of paintings, furniture, arms, and armor. The armory, dungeon, torture chamber, ghost tower, clock tower, and Guy's tower give vivid insights into the castle's turbulent past and its important part in the history of England. Surrounded by gardens, lawns, and woodland, where peacocks roam freely, and skirted by the Avon, Warwick Castle was described by Sir Walter Scott in 1828 as "that fairest monument of ancient and chivalrous splendor which yet remains uninjured by time."

The castle is open daily, except Christmas Day, March 1 to October 31, 10 a.m. to 5:30 p.m.; November 1 to February 28, 10 a.m. to 4:30 p.m. Admission is £1.65 ($3.80) for adults, 90p ($2.07) for children.

OTHER SIGHTS: Other nearby sights worth exploring include the following:

St. Mary's Church

Destroyed, in part, by the fire of 1694, this church with its rebuilt battlemented tower and nave is considered among the finest examples of the work of the late 17th and early 18th centuries. The Beauchamp Chapel, spared from the flames, encases the Purbeck marble tomb of Richard Beauchamp, a well-known Earl of Warwick who died in 1439 and is commemorated by a gilded bronze effigy. The most powerful man in the kingdom, not excepting Henry V. Beauchamp has a tomb considered one of the finest remaining examples of Perpendicular-Gothic as practiced in England in the mid-15th century. The tomb of Robert Dudley, Earl of Leicester, a favorite of Elizabeth I, is against the north wall. The Perpendicular-Gothic choir dates from the 14th century. The Norman crypt and the 14th-century Chapter House are also fine examples of this period.

Lord Leycester Hospital

At the West Gate, this group of half-timbered almshouses was also spared from the Great Fire. The buildings were erected in about 1400, and the hospital was founded in 1571 by Robert Dudley, the Earl of Leicester, as a place for old soldiers. It is still in use by ex-servicemen today. On top of the West Gate is the attractive little chapel of St. James, dating from the 12th century, although much restored. The hospital may be visited weekdays from 10 a.m. to 5:30 p.m. (closed Sunday) for 50p ($1.15) for adults, 30p (69¢) for children. Off-season, it closes at 4 p.m.

Warwickshire Museum

At the Market Place, this museum was established in 1836 to house a collection of geological remains, fossils, and a fine collection of British amphibians from the Triassic period. There are also displays illustrating the history, archeology, and natural history of the county, including the famous Sheldon tapestry map. It is open weekdays from 10 a.m. to 5:30 p.m., and on Sunday in summer from 2:30 to 5 p.m.

St. John's House

At Coten End, not far from the castle gates, there is a display of folk life, craft, and costumes, and the house in which these exhibitions are displayed is a fund of beauty itself, dating from the early 17th century. A Victorian schoolroom, recently opened, is furnished with original 19th-century school furniture and equipment. During term time, Warwickshire children, dressed in replica costumes, can be seen enjoying Victorian-style lessons. An important collection of musical instruments is on view, including a Tabel harpsichord and three Stanesby recorders dating from the 18th century and a 16th-century lute by Hans Frei. On the first floor is a military exhibition, tracing the history of the Royal Warwickshire Regiment from 1674 to the present day.

Warwick Doll Museum

Housed in one of the most charming Elizabethan buildings in Warwick, Oken's House, the Warwick Doll Museum keeps alive the memory of childhood. It contains an extensive collection of dolls—be they wood, wax, or porcelain. Of particular interest is a swivel-necked, double-headed doll that moves from tears to smiles. The house is on Castle Street, near St. Mary's Church. It was the birthplace of Thomas Oken, a bailiff in Warwick in Tudor days, whose reputation rests largely on his philanthropic work. The dolls, however, are from the collection of Joy Robinson. The house is open weekdays from 10 a.m. to 6 p.m. (on Sunday from 2:30 to 5 p.m.), for 50p ($1.15) for adults, 25p (58¢) for children.

WHERE TO STAY: Many prefer to seek lodgings in Warwick, then commute to Stratford-upon-Avon. If you're one of them, then here are our hotel recommendations:

Tudor House Inn & Restaurant, West Street (tel. Warwick 45447), was built in 1472. It's at the edge of town, on the main road from Stratford-upon-Avon leading to Warwick Castle. It is a stunning black-and-white timbered inn, one of the few buildings to escape the fire that destroyed the High Street in 1694. Off the central hall are two large rooms, each of which could be the setting for an Elizabethan play. In the corner of the lounge is an open turning staircase, waiting for the entrance of a minstrel player. The minstrels' gallery is dominated by a large inglenook. A regular meal in the restaurant and steak bar costs about £8 ($18.40). The inn has nine bedrooms, all with wash basins, although some have baths en suite. The cost ranges from £9 ($20.70) to £20 ($46) per room nightly. Two of the rooms have doors only four feet high! There's the usual resident ghost—an old man who gets up early in the morning, leaving the front door open and heading toward Stratford-upon-Avon, without paying his bill. In addition, the old priest's hiding hole has become the Priest Hole Bar.

Lord Leycester Hotel, Jury Street (tel. Warwick 41481), is a remake of what was once the country house of the Earl of Leicester. Extensively renovated, it now accommodates guests comfortably in its 50 bedrooms, some of which have private baths. Its position is most central, within walking distance of the castle and other historic buildings of Warwick. A bathless single goes for £16 ($36.80), £19 ($43.70) with bath. In a bathless double or twin, the price is £25 ($57.50), £29 ($66.70) with bath. Prices include a full English breakfast, service, and VAT. A nicety is the inclusion of early-morning tea and a newspaper (if you state your preference the night before to the porter). The bedrooms are furnished with moderately modern pieces, neat and attractive. Lord Leicester's former stables have been transformed into the Stable Bar, where imbibers sit on cobblers' stools at trestle tables. In the dining room a table d'hôte lunch is £4.20 ($9.66); a set dinner, £5 ($11.50).

WHERE TO EAT: The **Saxon Mill,** Guy's Cliffe, Kenilworth Road (tel. Warwick 42255). On the outskirts of Warwick, the mill predates the Norman Conquest and was in use up until the year before World War II. The setting basks in its legendary associations with Sir Guy of Warwick, unlucky in love with Felice, but a dangerous man to all dragons and giants. Now converted into a restaurant, with two drinking taverns, it is one of the best spots for dining in the Midlands.

You can drink in the lower tavern, with its old timbers and milling equipment, and make selections from an elaborate menu. Hopefully, you'll be ushered upstairs to a table with a view of the Avon, where you can order roast joints, sole, duck à l'anglaise, whitebait, steaks, and chicken dishes, perhaps crêpes suzette for dessert. An average meal should run about £10 ($23) plus service. Half a liter of the French house wine costs £2.50 ($5.75). A set three-course lunch goes for £4.30 ($9.89), plus service and VAT. Hours are noon to 2 p.m. and 7 to 10 p.m. The mill shuts down on Sunday evenings and all day on Monday.

3. Kenilworth Castle

In magnificent ruins, this castle—the subject of Sir Walter Scott's romance *Kenilworth*—once had walls that enclosed an area of seven acres. It lies five miles north of Warwick, 13 from Stratford-upon-Avon. In 1957, Lord Kenilworth presented the decaying castle to England, and limited restoration has since been carried out.

The castle dates back to the days of Henry I, having been built by one of his lieutenants, Geoffrey de Clinton. Of the original castle, only Caesar's Tower, with its 16-foot-thick walls, remains. Edward II was forced to abdicate at Kenilworth in 1327, before being carried off to Berkeley Castle in Gloucestershire, where he was undoubtedly murdered. Elizabeth I in 1563 gave the castle to her favorite, Robert Dudley, Earl of Leicester. The earl built the Gatehouse, which was visited on several occasions by the queen. After the Civil War, the Roundheads were responsible for breaching the outer wall and towers, and blowing up the north wall of the keep. This was the only damage caused following the Earl of Monmouth's plea that it be "Slighted with as little spoil to the dwellinghouse as might be."

In March, April, and October, weekday hours are from 9:30 a.m. to 5:30 p.m. (on Sunday from 2 to 5:30 p.m.). From May to September, weekday hours are from 9:30 a.m. to 7 p.m. (on Sunday from 2 to 7 p.m.). From November to April, weekday hours are from 9:30 a.m. to 4 p.m. (on Sunday from 2 to 4 p.m.). Admission charges are 40p (92¢) for adults, 20p (46¢) for children under 16.

FOOD AND LODGING: The **Clarendon House Hotel,** High Street (tel. Kenilworth 54694), is a family-run hotel and restaurant in the old part of Kenilworth. The oak tree around which the original ale house was built in 1538 is still supporting the roof of the building today. The present owners, the Lea family, welcome guests to spend the night in any of the 14 bedrooms, all of which are tastefully decorated. Prices range from £14.50 ($33.35) for a single with shower to £25 ($57.50) for a double with private shower, toilet, and four-poster bed. Tariffs include a full English breakfast and VAT.

Before the evening meal, guests gather in the timbered lounge. The hotel's restaurant is housed in what was once the inn stable. The oddly timbered room is decorated with antique maps and armor, constant reminders that a Cromwellian garrison once stayed at the inn during a seige of Kenilworth Castle.

Game is a specialty at the Clarendon House, and in season you may dine on such specialties as pigeon Normandy, casseroled in cider with onions, venison casserole, and mallard (wild duck cooked in red wine) are other specialties. A complete meal, inclusive of VAT, is available for around £6 ($13.80) per head. The restaurant is open for dinner from 7 to 9:30 p.m., on Sunday from 6:30 to 8:30 p.m. The Leas also have an interesting collection of small antiques and old maps for sale.

Restaurant Bosquet, Warwick Road (tel. Kenilworth 52463), is a tiny restaurant—only eight tables—run by Noreen Groves and her daughter Marian. The cooking is done by David Groves, Noreen's husband, who is a skillful master of French cuisine. The impressive à la carte menu features game and a number of meat and fish dishes. Included are chevrenil forestière, local venison marinated in red wine and sautéed with mushrooms and bacon, or sauté d'agneau Romarin, a lamb steak sauteed with fresh rosemary and served in a white wine sauce. Fish dishes include two poached salmon dishes, one served with a delectable hollandaise sauce and the other poached in white wine and tomato and served with sour cream. You may begin with an hors d'oeuvres assortment or a "petite entree." Desserts feature such delightful specialties as banana soufflé and a delicate Bavarian cream laced with Curaçao. The average meal here will run about £10 ($23) per head, plus another £4.50 ($10.35) for a bottle of wine. Restaurant Bosquet is open for dinner from 7 to 10 p.m. daily, except Sunday and Monday. It is closed during the first three weeks in August. Reservations here are absolutely essential.

Tudor Cottage (tel. Kenilworth 56702), is a 450-year-old half-timbered structure right across the street from the castle. Its little restaurant is a delightful spot for a refreshing afternoon tea following a tour of Kenilworth. The friendly owner, Frank Hart, is happy to share his wealth of knowledge about the interesting history and the sights of the area. If you decide to spend the night, bed and breakfast will cost you a modest, all-inclusive £7 ($16.10). Both lunch and dinner are served in his tiny restaurant which is open for coffee at 10:30 a.m., then for lunch between 12:30 and 2:30 p.m., and for dinner from 7:30 p.m. "until the last person leaves." Simple dishes are accompanied by fresh vegetables. Homemade soup, for example, is followed by roast beef and Yorkshire pudding, then a dessert from the trolley at a cost of about £5 ($11.50) per head. The restaurant is closed on Monday.

4: Coventry

Although the Midlands city of Coventry, home of motorcar and cycle manufacturing, is principally industrial, you'll want to pay it a visit to see Sir Basil Spence's controversial **Coventry Cathedral,** consecrated in 1962. The city was partially destroyed during the blitz in the early '40s, but the rebuilding was miraculous. No city more than Coventry seems to symbolize England's power to bounce back from adversity.

Before the war, Coventry was noted in legend as the ancient market town through which Lady Godiva made her famous ride, giving birth to a new name in English: Peeping Tom. The Lady Godiva story is clouded in such obscurity that the truth has probably been lost forever. It has been suggested that the good lady never appeared in the nude, but was the victim of scandalmongers, who, in their attempt to tarnish her image, unknowingly immortalized her.

The cathedral itself grew up on the same site as the 14th-century Perpendicular building. Many Coventry residents have maintained that the foreign visitor is more likely to admire the structure than the Britisher, who perhaps is more attached to traditional cathedral design.

Outside is Sir Jacob Epstein's bronze masterpiece, St. Michael slaying the Devil. Inside, the outstanding feature is the 70-foot-high altar tapestry by Graham Sutherland, said to be the largest in the world. The floor-to-ceiling abstract stained-glass windows are the work of the Royal College of Art. The West Window is most interesting, with its engraved glass, rows of stylized saints and monarchs with jazzy angels flying around between them.

Coventry is 19 miles from Stratford-upon-Avon, and only 11 from Warwick and 6 from Kenilworth.

FOOD AND LODGING: De Vere Hotel, Cathedral Square (tel. Coventry 51851), is strikingly modern, designed to relate architecturally to the adjoining cathedral. Just off the Coventry inner ring road, it stands in the center of the city. For such a provincial hotel, it has an international first-class standard of comfort and service. Attracting a large business clientele, the hotel sounds an elegant tone in its public rooms, including the Terrace Room, a coffeeshop-restaurant where, in summer, glass doors slide back to give access to the terrace forming one side of Cathedral Square. In addition, the Taverna, the hotel's biggest bar, is decorated in an Italianate style, and the Three Spires Restaurant specializes in classical British and continental cookery, with prime Scottish beef a specialty. Bedrooms are spacious and equipped with rosewood furnishings, and each unit was designed as a twin-bedded studio with private baths and double-glazed windows to keep out traffic noises. Twins range in price from £50 ($115) to £68 ($156.40), and singles pay from £40 ($92) to £58 ($133.40), including breakfast and VAT.

Leofric, Broadgate (tel. Coventry 21371), named for Lady Godiva's husband, is the major hotel in the city, attracting, we suspect, far more business people than tourists. However, if you're overnighting in Coventry, it's the best choice, lying only two or three minutes from the cathedral, overlooking the famous statue of Lady Godiva. Each of the 90 bedrooms has a private bath, TV, phone, and central heating. The regular rate in a single is $58 (U.S.), increasing to $76 in a double or twin. Tariffs include a continental breakfast, service, and VAT. The Leofric's French Restaurant is perhaps the finest dining spot in Coventry. In spite of its name, the restaurant has a traditional English atmosphere. A table d'hôte luncheon—very British-type cooking—is offered for $14. The coffeeshop, Peep-in Tom's, is named after the legendary figure who took a look at Lady Godiva. For a predinner drink, we'd recommend one of the specials in Ray's Bar.

The **Post House,** Rye Hill, Allesley, near Coventry (tel. Allesley 402-151), is a motor hotel, built in rural surroundings three miles to the west of the center of Coventry, overlooking the main A45 road. There are nine floors and 200 bedrooms, each with wide-view window, private bath, radio, telephone, color

TV, and central heating, as well as tea- and coffee-making facilities. You pay £26 ($59.80) in a single, £35 ($80.50) in a double, including service and VAT. Meals are rapid in the Buttery, more leisurely in the restaurant.

5. Hereford and Worcester

The Wye Valley contains some of the most beautiful river scenery in Europe. The river cuts through agricultural country, and there is no population explosion in the sleepy villages. Wool used to be its staple business, although fruit growing and dairy farming are important today.

The old county of Herefordshire has now combined with Worcestershire to form "Hereford and Worcester"-shire. Worcestershire's name, of course, has become famous around the world because of its sauce familiar to gourmets. It is one of the most charming of Midland counties, covering a portion of the rich valleys of the Severn and Avon.

Herefordshire's Black Mountains border the Welsh Brecon Beacons National Park, and between the two cathedral cities of Hereford and Worcester the ridge of the Malverns rises from the Severn Plain.

HEREFORD: One of the most colorful old towns of England, the ancient Saxon city of Hereford, on the Wye River, was the birthplace of both David Garrick and Nell Gwynne. Dating from 1070, the red sandstone **Hereford Cathedral** contains all styles of architecture, from Norman to Perpendicular. One of its most interesting features is a library of chained books—more than 1600 copies—as well as one of the oldest maps in existence, the Mappa Mundi from 1314.

Hereford is surrounded by both orchards and rich pasturelands. Hence, it has some of the finest cider in the world, best sampled in one of the city's mellow pubs. Hereford cattle sold here are some of the finest in the world, too.

The Old House, High Town, is preserved as a Jacobean period museum, with the appropriate furnishings. The completely restored half-timbered structure, built in 1621, has a brass rubbing center installed on the second floor during July and August. It's open, April to September, weekdays from 10 a.m. to 1 p.m. and 2 to 5:30 p.m. (October to March, Monday to Friday, 10 to 1 and 2 to 5:30; on Saturday 10 to 1). Admission is 15p (35¢) for adults, 5p (12¢) for children.

Food and Lodging

Green Dragon, Broad Street (tel. Hereford 2506), hides behind an 18th-century Georgian facade, although the former coaching inn is considerably older. Convenient to the cathedral, the inn has a large, pillared main hall. It's warm and inviting, made especially so by the traditional old features which remain, including some early 17th-century paneling of Herefordshire oak. Next to the restaurant is a paneled cocktail bar, and there's also the Offa Bar on the ground floor.

Many of the bedrooms are spacious, and all are pleasantly decorated—93 units in all, mainly with private baths. Depending on the plumbing, singles range in price from £22 ($50.60) to £24 ($55.20), and doubles go from £26 ($59.80) to £30 ($69), including VAT, service, and breakfast. The paneled restaurant is a room of character. Good food, including both English and continental dishes, are featured by the chef. Expect to pay about £5 ($11.50) for lunch, from £8 ($18.40) for dinner.

WORCESTER: This historic cathedral city, famous for its gloves and porcelain, stands 27 miles from Birmingham and 26 miles from Stratford-upon-Avon.

Offering views of the Malvern Hills, **Worcester Cathedral** stands on the banks of the Severn River. Dating from 1084, it contains the Quire (rebuilt in 1224) which shelters King John's Tomb from 1216. The Chapter House, with its massive central supporting column, is considered one of the finest in England. The cathedral is open from 7:30 a.m. to 6 p.m. daily (in summer until 7:30 p.m.).

A visit to the **Royal Worcester Porcelain Factory** (tel. Worcester 23221) is worthwhile. At the factory, a two-hour tour, including an introductory talk by a member of the staff, a souvenir guidebook, and tea or coffee, costs £4 ($9.20). For the more hurried visitor, there is a shorter tour for £1 ($2.30) for adults, 40p (92¢) for children, allowing you to see the crafts people at work. Unfortunately it's necessary to book ahead if you wish to take a tour, but everyone can enjoy browsing in the shop at the factory. There you can buy examples of their craft. Many pieces are "seconds," all marked as such and sold at low prices. Most of the time you won't be able to tell why! There is a magnificent museum as well.

The city is rich in other sights as well, including the **Commandery,** a fine 15th-century timber-framed structure which was originally founded about 1085 as a hospital. Purchased by the City of Worcester in 1973, it contains a great hall with a hammer-beam ceiling and oriel window. It features displays on the city's history from Roman times. It's open Tuesday to Saturday, 10:30 a.m. to 5 p.m. (Sunday from April 1 to October 1 only, 2:30 to 5 p.m.) Admission is 50p ($1.15) for adults, 20p (46¢) for children.

If time remains, see **King Charles' House,** where Charles II hid after his defeat; **Queen Elizabeth's House,** and the **Queen Anne Guildhall,** built in 1723 (inside, the Royalists honored Charles I and II with statues, but a death mask of Cromwell is hung by its ears over the door); and **St. Helen's,** the nation's oldest church, dating back to 680.

Guided walking tours leave every Sunday from the Giffard Hotel (tel. Worcester 24153 for information and times). You can also ask at the tourist office about how to rent rowboats or canoes for trips on the Severn.

Food and Lodging

Giffard Hotel, High Street (tel. Worcester 27155), is a modern hotel in the center of the city, built in a new shopping district, which contains a multistory car park. In the lounge, guests can gaze through picture windows which frame a view of the cathedral. Often used as a conference center, the hotel has more than 100 well-furnished bedrooms, each with private bath, radio, TV, phone, and coffee-making equipment. The cost is from £24 ($55.20) in a single, from £34 ($78.20) in a double, including both service and VAT. The pleasantly efficient staff will make your stay comfortable. Adjoining the Royal Worcester Room, the elegantly furnished restaurant, is a cocktail bar. The hotel is easily accessible from the M5 Motorway (exit 7).

For meals, we'd suggest the **King Charles II,** 29 New St. (tel. Worcester 22449), a mellow old half-timbered building where Charles II was believed to have hidden out following the Battle of Worcester. The paneled dining room is elegantly decorated with two open fireplaces. The specialties—continental with mainly Italian dishes—are enjoyably prepared from good ingredients. Expect to pay about £12 ($27.60) per person for dinner. The restaurant, however, serves a set lunch for £4 ($9.20). It is closed on Sunday and for the last three weeks in July.

Bottle's Wine Bar & Bistro, 5 Friar St. (tel. Worcester 21958), is a favored rendezvous right in the historic center, particularly among young people. The decor is handsomely subdued, with black painted wickerwork tables, and the selection of cold foods is very good. We prefer the clove-studded freshly baked ham, along with a nice crisp salad, costing £2 ($4.60) per platter. In addition, the good-tasting soups are also homemade, going for 35p (81¢) a bowl. The roast joints, seafood dishes, and at least one hot specialty every day are also recommended. You might end your meal with cheesecake or gâteau, or even with brie or Stilton cheese at 65p ($1.50). The wine bar is open from noon to 2:30 p.m. (last orders are taken at 2 p.m.) and from 6:30 to 10:30 p.m. (until 11 p.m. on Friday and Saturday; last orders a half hour before closing). Closed Sunday.

A Museum on the Outskirts

Avoncroft Museum of Buildings, Stoke Heath, Bromsgrove, Worcester (tel. Bromsgrove 31886), is 11 miles from Worcester and 21 miles from Stratford-upon-Avon. It is open daily from March 1 to November 30 from 10:30 a.m. to 5:30 p.m. Admission is 90p ($2.07) for adults, 45p ($1.04) for children. You can hire a guide for £3 ($6.90) per party. The museum's cafeteria is open from 11 a.m. for coffee, lunch, and afternoon tea. Lunch includes quiches, pâtés, and a selection of salads with cold meats for around £2 ($4.60), and snacks are available from 75p ($1.73) upward. Tea or coffee costs 30p (69¢). The museum is an open-air site where a number of historic buildings have been saved from destruction and reconstructed. There is a windmill in working order, a timber-framed merchant's house from the 15th century, an Elizabethan house, a chain-making workshop, and a shop where nails were once made by hand. This gives one a fascinating insight into the construction of those buildings as done by our forefathers. The 14th-century Guesten Hall roof from Worcester has been reconstructed at ground level so that you can see how the joints were made by the skill of craftsmen of the past. Recent additions include an 18th-century building in which cockfighting once took place, and a blacksmith's forge. These are just a few of the things on display at this ten-acre site. Free car parking is available, and also a picnic area.

GREAT MALVERN: A holiday spa and splendid walking center, Great Malvern is the best spot for your headquarters if you want to tour the beautiful, historic Malverns, once part of the ancient kingdom of Mercia. Great Malvern became important in the 19th century as a spa town, and much of the Victorian splendor remains. The Malvern Hills themselves stretch for nine miles, with six townships lying along their line.

A Farm Cottage Holiday

Whitewells Farm Cottages, Ridgeway Cross, near Malvern (tel. Ridgway Cross 607), are just one example of the country cottages offered in the heart of England. Leslie and Mavis Gordon have turned their farm buildings into unique holiday accommodations. The old hop kiln has a circular kitchen and bedroom; saddlestones and haywain have bedrooms on the ground floor, a lounge and kitchen in the old hayloft. The cottages have antique oak beams and country-style furnishings. The old pony stables act as the reception. Milk, bread, and newspapers are delivered here, and you'll find a telephone, a library of books, and local information. All cottages are well furnished with refrigerator, cooker, central heating, color TV, and electric blankets, plus little extras such as hair-driers, toasters, and irons. They will willingly tell you where to buy provisions and will make you welcome to their part of the country. Prices range from £80 ($184) per week for two, £100 ($230) for four to £105 ($241.50) for six persons. During the early spring, winter, and autumn, shorter rentals are possible.

LODGINGS NEAR EVESHAM: Salford Hall, Abbots Salford, near Evesham (tel. Evesham 870-561). Part of the original building dates back to the 15th century but, as with so many country houses of those times, it has been added to in the 17th century and later restored to provide ten bedrooms, six with baths. The Abbots Bar (this was once a nunnery) is oak paneled, and the lounge is full of comfortable chairs. The restaurant provides a lunchtime carvery on Sunday for £5.50 ($12.65). At other times an ample three-course meal will cost around £8 ($18.40) per person. A single room with bath is £15 ($34.50) a night, a double or twin renting from £24 ($55.20) to £26 ($59.80) a night, including a full breakfast. All rooms have tea and coffeemakers. Service and VAT are included.

WEOBLEY: This small medieval village of old timbered houses lies west of the A49 Hereford–Ludlow road, only a few miles east of the border of Wales.

Red Lion Hotel (tel. Weobley 220) is a charming village inn, more than 500 years old, which has been carefully restored to offer seven rooms, all with private bath or shower, color TV, warm furnishings, and comfortable beds.

Mrs. McIlwrick runs the place most efficiently, and everything is kept spotlessly clean. Rooms go for £20 ($46) in a single, from £26 ($59.80) in a double, including service and VAT. Breakfast, featuring cooked dishes, is included. Dinner will cost about £8 ($18.40). A daily set luncheon is featured for £3.75 ($8.63). On Sunday, the traditional English luncheon of roast meats and vegetables with all the trimmings goes for £4.25 ($9.78). Lunch is served from 12:30 to 2 p.m., dinner from 7 to 10 p.m. (till 9 p.m. on Sunday). Aside from the bar occupied in the evenings by locals, there is a cozy lounge with a roaring fire and soft armchairs where your orders for dinner are taken. You dine in the elegant dining room, selecting your choice from a wide menu of soup, pâté, and other appetizers, followed by chicken, steak dishes, and the day's specialty, then delicious homemade desserts such as apple pie and trifle. Service is good and friendly, and passersby are welcomed.

6. Salop (Shropshire)

Immortalized by A. E. Housman's "A Shropshire Lad," this hilly county borders Wales, which accounts for its turbulent history. The bloody battles are over today, and the towns of Salop, with their black-and-white timbered houses, are peaceful and quiet. Salop makes a good base for touring in the Welsh mountains.

SHREWSBURY: Lying within a horseshoe bend of the Severn River, Shrewsbury is the capital of Salop. The river almost encloses the town. Known for its cakes and ale, Shrewsbury contains one of the bestknown schools in England. It was also the birthplace of Charles Darwin.

Considered the finest Tudor town in England, Shrewsbury is noted for its black-and-white buildings of timber and plaster, including Abbot's House from 1450 and the tall gabled Ireland's Mansion from 1575 standing on High Street. It also has a number of Georgian and Regency mansions, some old bridges, and handsome churches, including the Abbey Church of Saint Peter and St. Mary's Church.

Shrewsbury Castle is 900 years old and was saved from destruction in 1790 when an engineer, Thomas Telford, had it restored as a private house. Built of red sandstone on a hill dominating the town, it is now the headquarters of the local government.

Rowley's House on Barker Street has a fine collection of Roman artifacts from Viroconium (Wroxeter), and is open weekdays from 10 a.m. to 1 p.m. and 2 to 5 p.m.

Food and Lodging

Prince Rupert Hotel, Butcher Row (tel. Shrewsbury 52461), is a hotel of character—part of it dating from the 15th century—right on a quiet side street in the center of town. Its front has four peaked gables and, in summer, a wealth of flower boxes full of petunias and geraniums. The facade is characterized by peaked gables on the Old Church Street entrance. Even though the interior has been modernized, it still has exposed beams and uneven floors. A favorite gathering spot is the lounge, which is tapestried. There are three restaurants in all, including the Cavalier. The rooms are bright and fresh, with compact, well-maintained baths found in 47 of the 66 units. Singles range in price from £16 ($36.80) to £19 ($43.70); doubles or twins go from £24 ($55.20) to £29 ($66.70).

Lion Hotel, Wyle Cop (tel. Shrewsbury 53107), is a simple red brick structure, once a well-known posting inn, standing on the outskirts of town on the Telford Road. In part the hotel dates from the 15th century, and oak beams and paneling from that period remain. Many famous people have stayed here, including Dickens, Jenny Lind, and De Quincey, who described the hotel's Adam-style ballroom in his *Confessions of an Opium Eater*. Bedrooms are simply furnished, and many are quite small. Depending on the plumbing, singles range from £19 ($43.70) to £23 ($52.90), and doubles cost from £26 ($59.80) to £30 ($69), including both VAT and service. Forty-four of the 64 bedrooms contain private baths. The Dickens Suite boasts a "half-tester" bed in which the Victorian novelist is reputed to have slept. The restaurant with its Victorian decor is named after him, and it serves both table d'hôte and à la carte meals. The hotel has two bars, the Tudor one featuring a buffet at lunchtime.

OSWESTRY: Near the Welsh border, this interesting old market town has some Yale monuments in its St. Oswald's Church and a 17th-century Griddle Gate nearby. At Old Owestry, an Iron Age hill fort with multiple ramparts can be seen.

LUDLOW: Looking down on the Teme River, this is a mellow old town with a historic Norman castle. Many Georgian and Jacobean timbered buildings stand on its quiet lanes and courts. The most colorful street is known as "Broad," rising from the old Ludford Bridge to Broadgate, the one remaining gateway from walls erected in the Middle Ages. See, in particular, the Church of St. Laurence, Butter Cross, and Reader's House.

Food and Lodging

The Feathers, Bullring (tel. Ludlow 2919), is one of England's most famous Elizabethan inns. Built in 1603 as a private residence, it is characterized by its half-timbered front and richly decorated interior. Bedrooms are bright and cheerful, and most of them contain private baths or showers, as well as phones, radios, television sets, and coffee-making facilities. Colors are in perfect harmony, with Welsh tapestry bedspreads. Singles range in price from £19 ($43.70) to £23 ($52.90), and doubles cost from £18 ($41.40) to £22 ($50.60) per person, including an English breakfast. If possible, ask for one of the units with a four-poster bed. The Richard III restaurant, with its original fireplace, is in the old-world style, serving good food and drink. There are also two fully licensed bars, and polished brass and copper set the right decorative tone. In the James I lounge, you can enjoy a carved mantelpiece and an elaborately ornamented plaster ceiling.

For lunch, we'd suggest the **Bull Hotel,** Corve Street (tel. Ludlow 2962). Close to the castle, it's an old coaching inn which you enter under a typical arch into the courtyard. The oldest parts of the building are early Tudor. There is a large bar with roaring open fire where bar snacks are served, including the day's special hot soup at 15p (35¢) or salads at £1 ($2.30). In summer you can take your drink and food into the courtyard, but in winter, far better to hog the fire.

TUTBURY: Once a stronghold of the Anglo-Saxon kings of Mercia, and mentioned in the Domesday Book, Tutbury is a small town on the Dove River, lying four miles north of Burton-upon-Trent. It has a fine Norman church and the ruins of Tutbury Castle.

Ye Olde Dog and Partridge, High Street (tel. Tutbury 813-030), has been a colorful village inn for so long there is no clear record of its beginnings. Charming in appearance, it has an ornate black-and-white timbered facade, bay windows, and leaded glass, surviving elements from the 15th century. A popular coaching house in the 18th and 19th centuries, it offers a more modernized hospitality today. New baths have been installed for each bedroom, and singles rent for £24 ($55.20) a night, doubles going for £30 ($69), including a full English breakfast.

Inside, the inn still has a wealth of old timbering and fireplaces, maintaining a traditional character. On a more incongruous note, it has a French restaurant which is open from Monday evening through Saturday evening (Saturday lunches excepted). The à la carte menu, costing about £8 ($18.40) for a meal, is changed weekly. In addition, the inn also has a wine bar and carvery open seven days a week.

7. Staffordshire

Staffordshire is known throughout the world for its excellence in the ancient craft of pottery, eventually made famous by Josiah Wedgwood, who is properly eulogized in these parts. The county embraces the "Black Country," with its steel and iron works, coal mines, and smoky, dirty towns, yet there are features here worth exploring.

In the north is the land of the **Potteries,** the Five Towns of Arnold Bennett's novels. **Stoke-on-Trent** now encompasses these towns, whose cone-shaped kilns dot the skyline. Within easy reach of the industrial town of **Dovedale** is a valley with some of England's most beautiful scenery, forming part of the Peak District National Park.

STAFFORD: The county town was the birthplace of Izaak Walton, the British writer and celebrated fisherman. Its main industry is boot making, and it contains many historic buildings, notably St. Chad's, the town's oldest church; St. Mary's, with its unusual octagonal tower; and the William Salt Library, with its interesting collection of folklore.

Food and Lodging
Tillington Hall Hotel, Eccleshall Road (tel. Stafford 53531), which has been extensively remodeled and renovated, stands in its own grounds just a mile from the center of the county town, yet less than half a mile from the M6 Motorway (junction 14). The attractive paneled reception lounge, where you are likely to stand next to Midlands business people checking in, leads to a modern bar and a lounge with an open fire on nippy nights. Eighty bedrooms, each furnished in a contemporary idiom, come equipped with private bath, radio, phone, color TV set, and coffee-making equipment. The cost is £32 ($73.60) nightly in a single, £38 ($87.40) in a double, including a full English breakfast. Good food is served in the Izaak Walton Restaurant, where meals begin at £7 ($16.10).

LICHFIELD: Fans of Samuel Johnson pay a pilgrimage here to this historic city where he was born in 1709, son of an unsuccessful bookseller and parchment maker. The city is noted for its **cathedral,** whose three spires are known as "Ladies of the Vale." The tallest spire rises more than 250 feet, and the west front of the cathedral was built from about 1280.

Dr. Johnson's Birthplace on Breadmarket Street contains mementos and pictures of the author and his contemporaries. It is open from 10 a.m. to 5 p.m., closing at 4 p.m. off-season and Sunday afternoons in the summer. The admission charged is 35p (81¢) for adults, 15p (35¢) for children.

READER'S TOURING SUGGESTION: "We took the day bus trip run by Windsorian Bus Line to the **Wedgwood Factory,** which is in Barlaston near Stoke-on-Trent. The trip took 3½ hours, and the factory has a nice program for visitors. We were shown a film on the making of Wedgwood, after which we could browse through their museum and then through a craft demonstration area showing the making and painting of pottery and china. We enjoyed the day very much. To go by car you would take the M1 to the M6 from London going northwest" (Rosemary Baginski, Brooklyn, N.Y.).

Chapter XII

CAMBRIDGE AND EAST ANGLIA

    1. Cambridge
    2. Ely
    3. Thaxted
    4. Saffron Walden
    5. Finchingfield
    6. Dedham
    7. Clare
    8. Long Melford
    9. Lavenham
    10. Woodbridge
    11. Aldeburgh
    12. East Bergholt
    13. Norwich
    14. Tottenhill
    15. North Norfolk
    16. English Country Cottages

"WE ARE FARMERS—great animal lovers," say two sisters who run a small farm in Essex. They delight in receiving paying guests at their old farm, feeding them fresh vegetables and home-grown fruit. They are not atypical of the East Anglians. The four counties of East Anglia—Essex, Suffolk, Norfolk, and Cambridgeshire—are essentially low-lying areas, where the bucolic life still reigns supreme.

East Anglia was an ancient Anglo-Saxon kingdom—under heavy domination of the Danes for many a year. Beginning in the 12th century, it was the center of a great cloth industry that brought it prosperity, as the spires of some of its churches testify to this day. Essentially, it is a land of heathland, fens, marshes, and broads in Norfolk.

Cambridge is the most visited city in East Anglia, but don't neglect to pass through Suffolk and Essex, Constable country, containing some of the finest landscapes in England. Norwich, the seat of the Duke of Norfolk, is less visited, but the fortunate few who go that far toward the North Sea will be rewarded.

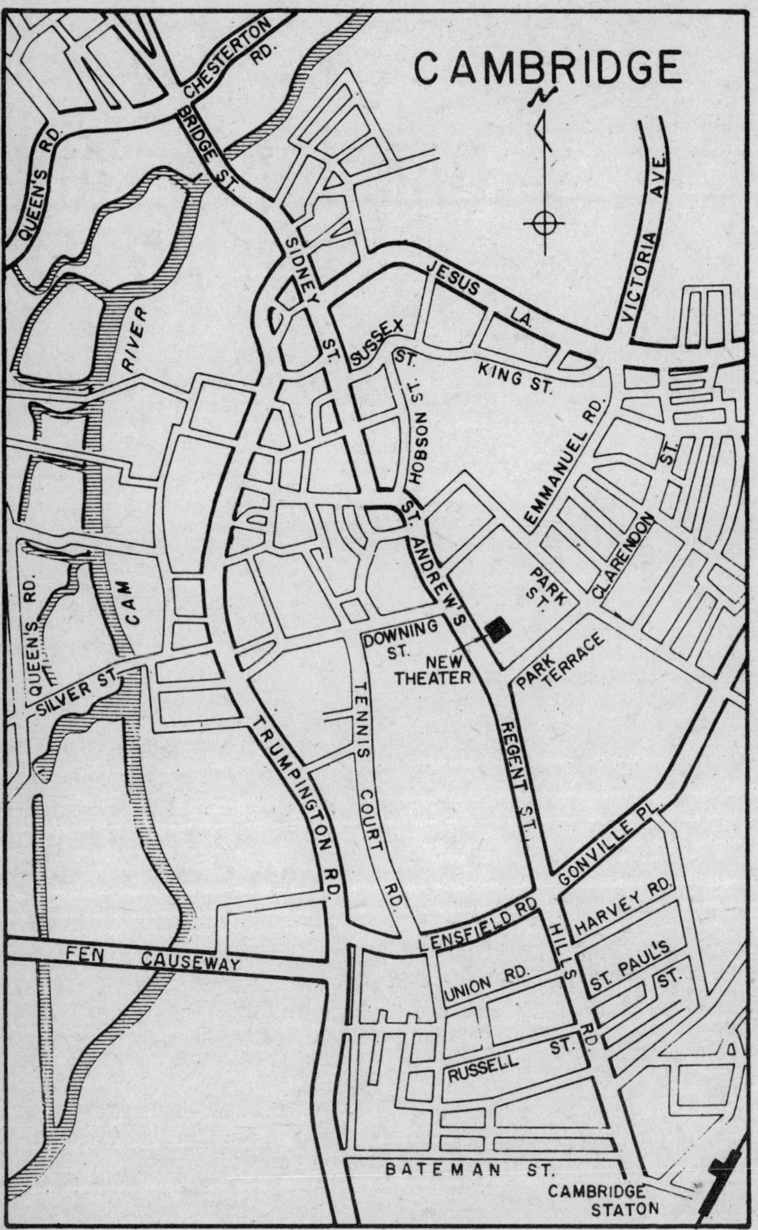
CAMBRIDGE
N
CHESTERTON RD.
QUEEN'S RD.
BRIDGE ST.
SIDNEY ST.
JESUS LA.
VICTORIA AVE.
RIVER
SUSSEX ST.
KING ST.
HOBSON ST.
EMMANUEL RD.
ST.
ST. ANDREW'S
CLARENDON
PARK ST.
QUEEN'S RD.
CAM
DOWNING ST.
NEW THEATER
PARK TERRACE
SILVER ST.
TENNIS COURT RD.
TRUMPINGTON RD.
REGENT ST.
GONVILLE PL.
HARVEY RD.
LENSFIELD RD
HILLS RD.
FEN CAUSEWAY
UNION RD.
ST. PAUL'S ST.
RUSSELL ST.
BATEMAN ST.
CAMBRIDGE STATON

1. Cambridge

A young couple lying in an open green space between colleges, reading the Romantic poets . . . rowing under the Bridge of Sighs . . . spires and turrets . . . drooping willows that witness much punting . . . dusty secondhand bookshops . . . daffodils swaying in the meadows . . . carol singing on Christmas Eve in King's College Chapel . . . dancing till sunrise at the May balls . . . the sound of Elizabethan madrigals . . . the purchase of horse brasses at the corner stall in the open market . . . narrow lanes where Darwin, Newton, and Cromwell once trod . . . The Backs, where the lawns of the colleges sweep down to the Cam River . . . the tattered black robe of an upperclassman, rebelliously hanging by a thread to his shoulder as it flies in the wind.

We're in the university city of Cambridge, which, along with Oxford, is one of the ancient seats of learning in Britain. The city on the banks of the Cam River is also the county town of Cambridgeshire, 55 miles northeast of London, 80 miles from Oxford. In many ways, the stories of Oxford and Cambridge are similar—particularly the age-old conflict between town and gown (impoverished scholars vs. rent-gouging landlords). But Oxford is an industrial city, sheltering a thriving life beyond the campus. Cambridge has some industry, but if the university were removed, we suspect it would revert to an unpretentious market town.

There is much to see and explore in Cambridge—so give yourself time to wander, even aimlessly. For those pressed, we'll offer more specific direction.

CAMBRIDGE UNIVERSITY: Oxford University predates the one at Cambridge. But in the early 13th century scholars began coming up to Cambridge, as opposed to being "sent down." The choice of the market town as a seat of learning just happened—perhaps coming about as a result of a core of important masters, dissatisfied with Oxford, electing to live near the fens. Eventually, Cambridge won partial recognition from Henry III, rising and slumping with the approval or disdain of subsequent English monarchs. Cambridge consists of 18 colleges for men, five for women, and six for both men and women. If you have time for only one sight, then make it:

King's College Chapel

The teenaged Henry VI founded the college on King's Parade in 1441. But most of its buildings today are from the 19th century. It is the Perpendicular Chapel which is not only the crowning glory, but one of the architectural gems in England inherited from the Middle Ages. The chapel, owing to the chaotic vicissitudes of English kings, wasn't completed until the early years of the 16th century. Its most characteristic features are its magnificent fan vaulting—all of stone—and its Great Windows, most of which were fashioned by Flemish artisans between 1515 and 1531 (the west window, however, dates from the late Victorian period). The stained glass, in hues of blues, reds, and ambers, reflects biblical stories. The long range of the windows, reading from the first on the north side at the west end right around the chapel back to the first on the south side, tell the story of the Birth of the Virgin, the Annunciation, the Birth of Christ, the Life, Ministry, and Death of Christ, the Resurrection, the Ascension, the Acts of the Apostles, and the Assumption. The upper range contains Old Testament parallels to these New Testament stories. The rood screen is from the early 16th century. Henry James called King's College Chapel "the most beautiful in England." It is open during vacation time on weekdays from 9 a.m. to 5 p.m., and on Sunday from 10:30 a.m. to 5 p.m. During term time the public is welcome to choral services which are at 5:30 p.m. on weekdays (service said on Monday), and at 10:30 a.m. and 3:30 p.m. on Sunday. In "term" the chapel is open to visitors from 9 a.m. to 3:45 p.m. on weekdays, from 2 to 3 p.m. and from 4:30 to 5:45 p.m. on Sunday. Closed December 26 to January 1. It may be closed at other times for recording sessions.

Peterhouse

This college on Trumpington Street is visited largely because it is the oldest Cambridge college, having been founded as early as 1284. The founding father was Hugh de Balsham, the bishop of Ely. Of the original buildings, only the Hall remains, but this was restored in the 19th century and now contains stained-glass windows by William Morris. Old Court was constructed in the 15th century, but refaced in 1754, and the chapel dates from 1632. Ask permission to enter at the porter's desk.

Trinity College

On Trinity Street, Trinity College—the largest at Cambridge (not to be confused with Trinity Hall)—was founded in 1546 by Henry VIII from a number of smaller colleges that had existed on the site. The courtyard is the most spacious one in Cambridge, built when Thomas Nevile was master. Sir Christopher Wren designed the Library. For opening times, inquire at the porter's lodge.

Emmanuel College

On St. Andrew's Street, Emmanuel was founded in 1584 by Sir Walter Mildmay, a chancellor of the exchequer to Elizabeth I. It is of interest at least to Harvard men, as John Harvard, founder of that university, studied here. With its attractive gardens, it makes for a good stroll. You might even visit the chapel designed by Sir Christopher Wren and consecrated in 1677. Both the chapel and college are open daily from 9:30 a.m. to 12:15 p.m. and from 2 to 6 p.m.

Queens' College

On Queens' Lane, Queens' College is considered by some old Cambridgeites as the loveliest in the architectural galaxy. Dating back to 1448, it was founded, then "refounded" by two English queens—one the wife of Henry VI, the other the wife of Edward IV. Its second cloisters are the most interesting—flanked with the half-timbered President's Lodge, dating from the first half of the 16th century. The college is open to visitors during the day. Individual visitors are admitted between 2 and 4:30 p.m. only. Entry and exit is by the Old Porters' Lodge in Queens' Lane only. The college is closed between May 11 and June 14 and on June 20. The Old Hall and chapel are normally open to the public when not in use.

St. John's College

On St. John's Street, the college was founded in 1511 by Lady Margaret Beaufort, mother of Henry VII. A few years earlier she had founded Christ's College. Before her intervention, an old monk-run hospital had stood on the site of St. John's. The impressive gateway bears the Tudor coat-of-arms, and the dining room, one of the largest in Cambridge, is handsome, dating from the early 16th century. But its best known feature is the Bridge of Sighs, crossing the Cam, built as late as the 19th century and named after the bridge in Venice. It connects the more dated part of the college with New Court—a Gothic revival—on the opposite bank. Wordsworth was an alumnus. The college may be visited any time before dusk, except during the summer examination period, May to early June.

The above are only a representative selection of some of the more interesting colleges. **Magdalen College** on Magdalene Street was founded in 1542; **Pembroke College** on Trumpington Street was founded in 1347; **Christ's College** in St. Andrew's Street was founded in 1505; and **Corpus Christi College** on Trumpington Street dates from 1352. Only someone planning to stop in Cambridge for a long time will get around to them.

A Word of Warning: Unfortunately, because of the disturbances caused by the influx of tourists to the university, Cambridge has regretfully had to limit visitors, and even exclude them from various parts of the university altogether, and, in some cases, even charge a small fee for entrance. Small groups of up to six persons are generally admitted with no problem, and you can inquire from your local tourist office about visiting hours here.

OTHER SIGHTS: However, colleges aren't the only thing to see in Cambridge, as you'll assuredly agree if you explore the following attractions.

The Fitzwilliam Museum

On Trumpington Street, near Peterhouse, this museum was the gift of the Viscount Fitzwilliam, who in 1816 gave Cambridge University his paintings and rare books—along with £100,000 to build the house in which to display them. He thereby knowingly or unknowingly immortalized himself. Other gifts have since been bequeathed to the museum, and now it is one of the finest in England. It is noted for its porcelain, old prints, archeological relics, and oils (works by Titian and Rembrandt).

The museum is open weekdays from 10 a.m. to 5 p.m., Sunday from 2:15 till 5 p.m. Closed Monday, Good Friday, December 24 to 31, and New Year's Day. Admission is free.

St. Mary the Great

St. Mary the Great, opposite King's College Chapel on King's Parade, is the university church. It is built on the site of an 11th-century church, but the present building dates largely from 1478. It was closely associated with events of the Reformation. The cloth which covered the hearse of King Henry VII is on display in the church. A fine view of Cambridge may be obtained from the top of the tower.

BOAT RENTALS: Scudamore's, at Granta Place adjacent to the Anchor Pub, has been in business since 1910. Costs are by the hour—£2.40 ($5.52) for a punt, £2 ($4.60) for a rowboat, or £1.80 ($4.14) for a canoe. A deposit of £10 ($23) is required, and it is refundable if you don't wreck the boat. Upriver you can go all the way to Grantchester, about a distance of two miles, made so famous by Rupert Brooke. Downstream, you pass along the Backs behind the colleges of the university.

PERSONALIZED TOURS: The person to know if you're in the Cambridge area is **Mrs. Isobel Bryant,** who runs Heritage Tours from her 200-year-old cottage, Manor Cottage, Swaffham Prior, Cambridge (tel. Newmarket 741-440). A highly qualified expert on the area, she will arrange tours, starting from your Cambridge hotel to, say, Saffron Walden, Thaxted, and Audley End, for example, or to the U.S. military cemetery at Madingley, then Ely, and Anglesey Abbey, or to the charming timbered houses of Lavenham. Lunch is often organized in beautifully furnished private manor houses, so that you have the change of meeting local people. The day's trip costs around £30 ($69) for three people. Lunch and admission charges are extra—probably about £5 ($11.50) per person more.

Mrs. Bryant can also arrange accommodations with local families in their lovely country houses. The charges range from £13 ($29.90) to £16 ($36.80) for two persons per night in double rooms with private baths, these tariffs including a full English breakfast. Often dinner with the family can be arranged at around £5 ($11.50) per person, including wine.

There are also walking tours around the colleges of Cambridge and, if you can make up a party of 15 or more persons, a fascinating tour of Newmarket, center of the horse-racing industry. On that tour, you visit two racecourses, a sales paddock and a bloodstock agency, as well as the workshops where saddlery and racing silks are made. In addition, you can watch a training gallop and visit stables and a stud farm. A whole day costs £10 ($23) per person; a half day, £6 ($13.80). If you want lunch arranged at a private house with Cordon Bleu cookery, the cost is around £4 ($9.20) per person. All prices include VAT.

A SELF-GUIDED TOUR: The center of Cambridge is closed to cars. There is good parking at the Anchor Pub in Silver Street, so why not leave your car there and then go for a walk around to some of the colleges?

Cross Silver Street Bridge, and you'll see the entrance to Queens College. Go into the college, crossing over the mathematical wooden bridge, so called because of its geometrical design. Then enter the older part of the college into the center of a quadrangle, and you'll see much of the beautiful Elizabethan architecture and also the doors around the quad, leading to the "staircases" of tiny studies and bedrooms for undergraduates within the college itself. Those who cannot get an accommodation here are boarded out around the city.

Leave through the fine Elizabethan arch into the new part of the college; turn right and, just past the chapel, take the doorway open to the road. Turn left and at the end of the road the archway leads to King's College Chapel and the college itself. Just inside is a very well-defined "staircase." This is also a beautiful college with lawns sweeping to the Cam. Visit the chapel to see the *Adoration of the Magi* by Reubens hanging over the High Altar. You can attend evensong at King's most every night at 5:30 p.m. There are services every Sunday at 10:30 a.m., 3:30 p.m., and again at 6 p.m.

Leave by the Porter's Lodge and walk to the Church Tower of the 800-year-old parish church of St. Edward Saint and Martyr. Within its walls the reformers of the 16th century preached and ministered the gospel. Turn right into the main Market Square where there is a daily market for fruit, vegetables, and other produce.

Leave on Wheeler Street, leading on to Benet Street. Opposite St. Benet's Church in St. Benet's Lane you will see two doors leading to a passage which will bring you to the **Eagle Pub** on the grounds of Corpus Christi—arguably the only galleried inn in Cambridge. It is little known by tourists but much frequented by locals. The usual bar snacks are provided to mop up the beer.

Totter back to Benet Street and you'll be back where you started at the Anchor where you left your car. Without stopovers, this walk will take you about one hour of leisurely observation.

WHERE TO STAY: Accommodations are limited in scope and facilities, although generally adequate for the purpose. Much of the overload in summer is siphoned off by little guest houses, filled at term time with scholars, but otherwise freed when most visitors arrive in July and August. We'll begin with a general survey of the best hotels in:

The Medium-Priced Range

University Arms Hotel, Regent Street (tel. Cambridge 51241), is a successful blending of the old and new. It originated late in Victoria's day as an inn operated by Marcus Dennis Bradford, grandfather of the present manager, William Bradford. One portion is traditionally designed, although a new wing was added in 1965, offering 58 ultramodern bedrooms, all with private bath and tasteful decorations. Sliding glass doors open onto private balconies, with views of the cricket grounds of Parker's Place, known for its associations with cricketer Sir Jack Hobbs. The rooms opening onto Regent Street have sound-proofed double-glass windows.

Each bedroom has its own telephone, central heating, private bath, electric razor outlets, radio, and color TV. The single rate is £19 ($43.70), and a twin-bedded room is £28.50 ($65.55). These rates include service, VAT, and a full English breakfast. Meals are served in the wood-paneled dining room, opening toward the lawn and trees. The charge for a table d'hôte luncheon is from £4.50 ($10.35), rising to £5.20 ($11.96) for a set dinner. The older octagonal lounge, with its stained-glass dome, is still the best place to gather at teatime. Tip: The hall porter can arrange for a guide to show you the nearby colleges.

The **Royal Cambridge Hotel,** Trumpington Street (tel. Cambridge 51631), may be the answer to England's hotel problem. The facade of a row of town houses has been preserved, but the inside has been gutted and redesigned in a tasteful modern way. The 86 rooms are compact and handsomely appointed. The bedrooms use many of the built-in techniques of motel design. Rates depend on the season, plumbing, and floor. Singles range from £15 ($34.50) to £19 ($43.70); twins, £24 ($55.20) to £29 ($66.70)—including service and VAT. Each room is centrally heated, and has both radio and telephone. A lot of extras are found here, including a hairdressing salon. Meals are à la carte.

Cambridgeshire Hotel, Bar Hill (tel. Crafts Hill 80-555), is four miles from the city itself, a resort hotel with a heated indoor swimming pool, a sauna bath, three squash and two tennis courts, plus an 18-hole golf course being created on the grounds. Most rooms are spacious and furnished in a functional, streamlined way. Singles go for £24 ($55.20), increasing to £35 ($80.50) in a double, plus all the extras. The entrance lobby is styled after an English coaching inn. The main dining room with its hammer-beamed ceiling is overlooked by the coffee lounge in the Minstrels' Gallery. The food is traditionally English, including such selections as roast pork and apple sauce or grilled Dover sole. Bar snacks are offered daily.

Blue Boar Hotel, Trinity Street (tel. Cambridge 63121), has an innkeeping fame that stretches back at least to the late 17th century. The most central of all our recommendations, it is run by Trust Houses Forte, attracting international visitors as well as parents of Cambridge students. Since its early days, it has been considerably modernized, with hot and cold running water added to every room (eight with private baths), as well as central heating and well-maintained furnishings. A pleasant brick building, directly opposite the Trinity Great Gate, it still keeps its original Blue Boar inn sign hanging over the arched doorway. Room prices are £20 ($46) for a single, from £27 ($62.10) to £34 ($78.20) in a double, including VAT and service, although breakfast is extra. Being a small inn, the hotel offers a limited lounge area with a small cocktail bar. There is also the Athene Bar, drawing an interesting crowd of people. It couldn't be handier for visiting the colleges, and there's a public car park a few blocks away.

Gonville Hotel, Gonville Place (tel. Cambridge 66611), stands on its own grounds, opposite Parkers Place, only a five-minute walk from the center of the city. It's not unlike a country house—ivy covered, with shade trees and a formal car entry. In 1973 it was gutted and rebuilt as a commercial hotel, intending to attract business people as well as tourists in summer. Singles go for £24 ($55.20), doubles for £34 ($78.20). Prices include VAT, service charge, and an English breakfast. Special three-bedded family rooms rent for £40 ($92). Central heating is provided throughout, plus air conditioning in the restaurant, where you can get a set lunch or dinner for about £6 ($13.80). The quality of comforts is good, the furnishings stylish.

WHERE TO EAT: **The Pentagon,** 6 St. Edwards Passage (tel. Cambridge 355-246), is in the center of Cambridge, overlooking medieval cottages and the historic churchyard. Cold buffet meals and four hot specialties are served daily, the price per dish being about £2.50 ($5.75). There is a fine wine list, and fully licensed bar. Connected to and run by the Arts Theatre, the restaurant has a strong artistic atmosphere and is patronized by many stars of the English stage. It's open for lunch from noon to 2 p.m. and for supper from 6 to 10:30 p.m.

The **Arts Roof Garden Buffet,** perched above the theater, is popular in summer as it offers alfresco meals, self-service lunch, afternoon tea and supper, with a view of the Cambridge spires. You select from an array of hot and cold dishes, with meals averaging around £2 ($4.60). Wines are available by the glass, and there's a fully licensed bar. Local artists, incidentally, exhibit their work upstairs. It's open from 9:30 a.m. to 8 p.m.

Nettles, 6 St. Edward's Passage, is a small and cheerful vegetarian health-food bar, offering a delicious variety of homemade soups, a wide range of tossed salads, served with crusty whole-meal rolls, and a ploughman's lunch with cheese. Live yogurts are on the menu, as well as muesli and fresh orange juice and a wide range of herbal and Oriental teas. Whole-wheat spaghetti and nut roasts add to the existing menu of pizzas. Nettles is run by Miss Marks, who came from Cranks in London, and has brought renewed life to this popular place. The dish of the day costs £1.50 ($3.45), and you can eat well and healthily for under £2.50 ($5.75). Hours are from 10 a.m. to 3 p.m. Monday to Saturday. The food bar is busy with undergraduates at term time.

Just off St. Benet Street in Free School Lane, a narrow passage past Friar's House Gift Shop, is the **Eros Restaurant,** 25 Petty Cury (tel. Cambridge 63420), fully licensed and offering an interesting menu. Specialties include roast duckling with stuffing and orange sauce, roast lamb peperoni with cream cheese, kebab indienne with ginger and curry, marinated lamb and rice, all served with vegetables and a salad. There are many good appetizers, and crème caramel, cheesecake, and sorbets finish off the menu. The Greek coffee is thick and sweet. A three-course Greek meal costs about £5 ($11.50), and the Cypriot, Italian, and English dinners go for about the same price. Hours are from noon to 3 p.m. and from 5:30 to 11 p.m. Monday to Friday, from noon to 11:30 p.m. on Saturday and Sunday. It's very popular with undergraduates who know they are getting good value for their money and who enjoy listening to the Greek music on weekends.

Shades Wine Bar & Restaurant, opposite King's College on Kings Parade (tel. Cambridge 54907 for the restaurant), gives you a choice of having either a full meal or else bar snacks. The wine bar itself does pâtés, salads, quiches, and well-filled rolls (sandwiches), to be washed down with a selection of excellent wines. It's open Monday to Saturday from noon to 2:30 p.m. and from 6 to 10 p.m. It's closed on Sunday and bank holidays.

The restaurant, on the other hand, is open from 7 to 10 p.m. daily except Sunday. It's wise to book a table. Homemade soup is usually good, followed by prawns in a shell with garlic mayonnaise, escargots, Mediterranean chicken casserole, sukiyaki, or cold beef or smoked ham with a choice of a variety of salads. There is as well a tasty selection of desserts or fresh fruit. The menu is not only good but imaginative, and the portions are ample. A meal costs around £4 ($9.20), including wine, although the dish of the day usually goes for £2 ($4.60).

The **Anchor Pub,** Silver Street, right beside the Silver Street Bridge, has a bar and terrace right on the waterside, where you can get snacks—a ploughman's lunch, French bread and pâté, ham salad, and various cold meats in sandwiches.

Upstairs is a restaurant where you can enjoy a prawn cocktail, soups, lamb cutlets with mint sauce, peas, jacket potato, plus vanilla meringue surprise, or grilled rump steak with potatoes, followed by dessert. A beefburger is another popular item. A meal will cost about £5 ($11.50) per person. Below the pub is the Rock Revival snackbar where you can buy the makings of a picnic lunch to be taken on a boat on the River Cam. The pub is by Scudamore's where you rent boats.

READER'S RESTAURANT SELECTION: "**La Taverna,** 72 Regent St. (tel. Cambridge 53942), is at the top of our list for agreeable atmosphere, prompt and friendly service, fresh, well-seasoned food, and reasonable prices. The menu offers a wide choice, but we often took the daily special for £1.70 ($3.91) and were never disappointed. One example: A dish listed as steak and vegetables—a wonderful Italian beef stew—lives on in memory. We especially appreciated the variety of vegetables served with entrees from day to day. Desserts are Italian and luscious, but one should not overlook the ice creams. And Taverna's coffee, with a fluff of cream and a shake of powdered chocolate, is a special way to end your meal. Closed Sunday, it is fully licensed" (L. Davidson, Charlottesville, Va.).

THE ARTS THEATRE: The outstanding attraction in Cambridge is the Arts Theatre, with its entrance on Peas Hill, squeezed among lodging houses and shops. It provides Cambridge and the surrounding area with its most important theatrical events. Almost all the leading stars of the British stage have performed here at one time or another. Call Cambridge 352-000 to find out what's playing. The cheapest seats cost £2.10 ($4.83); the most expensive ones range from £2.35 ($5.41) to £3.70 ($8.51).

Nearby, on Market Passage, you'll find the principal **movie house,** the **Arts Cinema,** which usually has separate showings daily. Seats for the evening performances are "bookable" by telephoning Cambridge 352-001.

2. Ely

The top attraction in the fen country, outside of Cambridge, is Ely Cathedral. The small city of Ely lies 70 miles from London, only 16 miles north of Cambridge. Ely used to be known as the Isle of Ely, until the surrounding marshes and meres were drained. The last stronghold of Saxon England, Ely was defended by Hereward the Wake, until his capitulation to the Normans in 1071.

ELY CATHEDRAL: The near-legendary founder of the cathedral was Etheldreda, the wife of a Northumbrian king, who established a monastery on the spot in 673. The present structure dates from 1083. Seen for miles around, the landmark octagonal lantern tower is the crowning glory of the cathedral. It was erected in 1322, following the collapse of the old tower, and represents a remarkable engineering achievement.

You enter the cathedral through the Galilee West Door, a good example of the Early English style of architecture. The already-mentioned lantern tower and the Octagon are the most notable features inside, but visit the Lady Chapel. Although it's lost much of its decoration over the centuries, it still is a handsome example of the Perpendicular style, having been completed in the mid-14th century.

The city, really a market town, is interesting—at least momentarily so—as it seems to be living in the past. If you choose to lodge or dine at Ely, here are our recommendations.

WHERE TO STAY AND EAT: The **Lamb Hotel** (tel. Ely 3574), right in the center of Ely, with ample car parking space available and in the shadows of Ely Cathedral, is a Grand Metropolitan hotel offering all bedrooms with private baths and showers, televisions, and tea- and coffee-making facilities. The bed-and-breakfast rate in a double or twin is £25 ($57.50), £20 ($46) in a single. Tariffs are inclusive of an English breakfast and VAT. Both table d'hôte and à la carte menus are offered.

The Old Fire Engine House, St. Mary's Street (tel. Ely 2582), opposite St. Mary's Church, is one of the finer restaurants in East Anglia, worth a detour. It enjoys an interesting setting, in a complex of buildings with an art gallery. The restaurant itself was converted from a fire station. It has a walled garden. It is open for lunch from 12:30 to 2 p.m. and for dinner from 7:30 till 9 p.m. (closed Sunday). Reservations are required.

All the good English cooking is the result of the staff, a harmonious combination of unusual people who really care about food preparation. Food materials are all fresh. Soups are served in huge bowls, and accompanying the soups is a coarse-grained crusty bread. Main dishes include duck with orange sauce, jugged hare, and steak-and-kidney pie. Main courses cost from £3.75 ($8.63) with vegetables at lunchtime, and from £4.80 ($11.04) at dinner. The soups mentioned go from 75p ($1.73), and appetizers such as pâtés begin at £1.15 ($2.65). Desserts, costing from 75p ($1.73), include fruit pie and cream, although we'd recommend the syllabub at £1.10 ($2.53). In summer, you can dine outside in the garden, even order a cream tea. The young and attractive Anne Ford owns the place, and not only cooks and serves but still has time to talk to customers.

A TOUR TO GRIME'S GRAVES: On the B1108, off the main A1065 from Swaffham to Mildenhall road east of Ely, you can visit **Grime's Graves.** This is well worth the short detour, as it is the largest group of Neolithic flintmines in the country. This is fir-wooded country with little population, and it's easy to imagine oneself transported back to ancient times.

The mines are well signposted, and you soon find yourself at a small parking lot presided over by a bearded enthusiast and his aging labrador. Because the mines have no head machinery and are spread around a common area, they are all securely enclosed. But, on your arrival, the custodian will open up one or several of the shafts, allowing you to enter ancient Britain.

Climb down the ladder of the pit and imagine what must have been going on even before the time of the Anglo-Saxons. Restoration has been carried out during the intervening years, and it is now possible to see where work took place and, if you're lucky, you may find a worked flint of your own to present to the custodian. He has a vast knowledge of the working methods and the implements used in those far-off days.

The location is close to the air force bases so well known to countless American air crews during World War II.

The place is open for most of the year from 9:30 a.m. to 4 p.m. (longer in summer), charging adults an admission of 30p (69¢); children, 15p (35¢).

AN AIRCRAFT MUSEUM: The **Imperial War Museum** (tel. Cambridge 833-963), on the A505 Newmarket–Royston Road, is housed appropriately at Duxford Airfield, the former Battle of Britain station. In airport hangars which date from World War I, you'll find a huge collection of historic civil and military aircraft, including the B17 Flying Fortress, the Super Sabre and Concord 01, Britain's preproduction specimen of the controversial jet. Other exhibits include midget submarines, British and German tanks, and a variety of field artillery pieces. The museum is open daily from March 15 to November 2 from 11 a.m. to 5 p.m. (dusk if earlier). Admission is 80p ($1.84) for adults, 40p (92¢) for children. Parking is free.

ESSEX

Even though it borders London, and is heavily industrialized in places, Essex still contains unspoiled rural areas and villages. Most tourists pass through it on the way to Cambridge. What they find, after leaving Greater London, is a land of rolling fields. In the east are many seaside towns and villages, as Essex opens onto the North Sea.

The major city is **Colchester,** in the east, known for its oysters and roses. Fifty miles from London, it was the first Roman city in Britain, the oldest recorded town in the kingdom. It's a rather dull-appearing city today, although parts of its Roman fortifications remain. A Norman castle has been turned into a museum, containing a fine collection of Roman Britain. Among the former residents of Colchester were King Cole, immortalized in the nursery rhyme, and Cunobelinus, the warrior king, known to Shakespearean scholars as Cymbeline.

However, Colchester is not the pathway of most visitors—so we have concentrated instead on three tiny villages in the western part of Essex: **Saffron Walden, Thaxted,** and **Finchingfield,** all three representative of the best of the shire. You can explore all of them quite easily on your way to Cambridge or on your return trip to London. Roughly, they lie from 25 to 30 miles south of Cambridge.

A BASE OUTSIDE LONDON: Moat House, London Road, Brentwood (tel. Brentwood 225-252), stands on the London side of Brentwood, about three-quarters of a mile from the center of town and only 22 miles from London's West End. A remarkably well-preserved and modernized country mansion, this early 16th-century hotel claims associations with Henry VIII and Catherine of Aragon.

It's a handsome black-and-white timbered structure with a great hall for dining and a minstrels' gallery. Nowadays modern extensions give you a wide choice of accommodations, although traditionalists will gravitate to one of the original Tudor bedrooms which have maintained their character, complete with four-poster beds. These latter units rent for £24.50 ($56.35) in a single, from £30 ($69) in a double. Garden suites with private baths go for £27.50 ($63.25) in a single, from £34.50 ($79.35) in a double.

Bargains are the house rooms, which, true to their original Tudor character, have no baths, costing from £22.50 ($51.75) in a single, from £28 ($64.40) in a double, including VAT and service, although breakfast is extra. The restoration of the public rooms has been skillful, and you're invited to enter a world of heavy old beams, oak paneling, inglenooks, and ceilings of carved plasterwork.

3. Thaxted

Some 43 miles north of London, the Saxon town of Thaxted sits on the crest of a hill. It contains the most beautiful small church in England, whose graceful spire can be seen for miles around. Its bells are heard throughout the day, ringing out special chimes to parishioners who attend their church seriously. Dating back to 1340, the church is a nearly perfect example of religious architecture.

Thaxted is well known to newspaper and magazine readers because of the late iconoclastic Conrad Noel, the Red Vicar, whose son-in-law, the Rev. Jack Putterill, carries on in the traditions of the elder.

The Rev. Putterill has brought back to the church a sense of drama, which he feels has been gradually eliminated elsewhere. The parishioners often enter the church in a processional, carrying a banner or a long branch of leaves. Gay and colorful flags hang from the heights of the church; flowers are everywhere; the rare and ancient chairs are meant to be used. There are candles in great brass stands, and incense billows up as the purple-robed vicar and his assistants proceed with the ceremony. The choir kneels and sings at the rear of the church, near the bell tower. On a banner you'll see Picasso's dove of peace.

During the summer, folk dancing is performed by the townspeople, both in and out of the church. The London Philharmonic Orchestra comes down to play. The vicar has encouraged the church to use music, and you can hear both the old and the experimental. The denizens of Thaxted are divided about the activities of the church, but one thing they like: their town is alive and flourishing because of it.

Thaxted also has a number of well-preserved Elizabethan houses and a wooded-pillared Jacobean guildhall.

WHERE TO STAY AND EAT: The **Swan Hotel,** Watling Street (tel. Thaxted 832-321), is a 14th-century coaching inn, right in the middle of everything. From several of the bedroom windows you can see the church—even have a box seat if a processional should pass by. For many centuries, the townspeople have patronized the Swan for drinks and gossip. It is owned by Alma and Sam

Carter, who respect the heritage of the inn. Their bed-and-breakfast rate is £12.50 ($28.75) for two persons, plus service and VAT, based on double occupancy. If you're just passing through for the day, you may want to consider the three-course lunch for £4.25 ($9.78), plus service and VAT, consisting, say, of cream of mushroom soup, roast leg of pork with apple sauce, and a lemon mousse with cream for dessert. You can also have a three-course dinner from £5.25 ($12.08), plus service and VAT.

4. Saffron Walden

In the northern corner of Essex, a short drive from Thaxted, is the ancient market town of Walden, renamed Saffron Walden because of the fields of autumn crocus that used to grow around it. Although it lies only 44 miles from London, it still hasn't succumbed to heavy tourist traffic. Residents of Cambridge, 15 miles to the north, escape to this old borough for their weekends.

One mile west of Saffron Walden (on the A11 road) is **Audley End House**, considered one of the finest mansions in all of East Anglia. This Jacobean estate was begun in 1603, built on the foundation of a monastery. It is open from April to early October daily, except bank holidays and on Good Friday, from 10 a.m. to 5:30 p.m., for an admission of £1 ($2.30) for adults, 50p ($1.15) for children. The grounds close at 6:30 p.m. James I is reported to have said, "Audley End is too large for a king, though it might do for a lord treasurer." At the north end of the hall is a screen dating from the early 17th century and considered one of the most ornamental in England.

Many of the houses in Saffron Walden are distinctive in England, in that the 16th- and 17th-century builders faced their houses with parget—a kind of plasterwork (sometimes made with cow dung) used for ornamental facades.

WHERE TO STAY: The **Saffron Hotel,** 10 High St. (tel. Saffron Walden 23286), was once an old coaching inn, with a driveway leading to an inner courtyard, catering to simple wayfarers. Nowadays, it's found a new lease on life through the sophistication and style of its two owners, Mr. Wakefield and Mr. Brown. They have brought a personal style to their innkeeping—based on the theory of providing the same elegance they might in their own home. The lounge bar has rose swag draperies across a front bay window, a group of red Victorian chairs, and a grandfather clock—all telltale clues as to the general ambience. Each bedroom is personalized, with bits of old beams utilized. The bed-and-breakfast rate ranges from £20 ($46) to £32 ($73.60) in a double, the latter with private bath. A single room (bathless) rents for £16 ($36.80) to £19 ($43.70) with a shower added. The hotel does not cater to children under the age of 10. Rates include a continental breakfast, service, and VAT.

The same thoughtfulness, care, and distinction reflected in the running of the hotel go into the good meals, which include a set lunch or dinner for from £6 ($13.80). A typical noonday repast might include an appetizer followed by either a seafood omelet or braised lamb kidneys, plus a dessert.

5. Finchingfield

This little village, only a short drive east of Thaxted, puts in a serious claim for being the model village of England. Even though you may have another personal favorite, you still must admit it's a dream village, surrounded by the quiet life of the countryside. If you're staying in either Saffron Walden or Thaxted, you might want to motor over here. It makes for an interesting jaunt.

WHERE TO STAY: The **Fox Inn** (tel. Great Dunmow 810306), two hours from London airport, stands near the edge of the pond on the village green. It's an attractive old pub, run more or less as an inn by Joe King. Note the authentic pargeting (raised plaster) design on the facade. Mr. King is enthusiastic about his food, especially his steak-and-kidney pie and other English dishes. Lunches are served every day from noon to 2 p.m., providing a real fill-up for £3 ($6.90), including coffee. His homemade soups are excellent, as is his homemade fruit pie. Near to the Fox, he runs the little eight-room **Old Manse**, all accommodations with central heating, wall-to-wall carpeting, hot and cold running water, and shaving points. Two rooms have private baths, and most of them overlook the village pond. There is a lounge with color TV, plus a large garden as well. Terms, including a full English breakfast consisting of farm produce, are £11 ($25.30) in a single, £20 ($46) in a double, including an English breakfast, VAT, and service.

6. Dedham

Remember Constable's *Vale of Dedham?* In this little Essex village on the Stour River, you're in the heart of Constable country. Flatford Mill is only a mile further down the river. The village, with its Tudor, Georgian, and Regency house, is set in the midst of the water meadows of the Stour. Constable immortalized its church and tower. Dedham itself is right on the Essex-Suffolk border, and makes a good center for exploring both North Essex and the Suffolk border country.

In the village is **Castle House**, home of Sir Alfred Munnings, the president of the Royal Academy and painter extraordinaire of racehorses and animals. The house contains sketches and other works, and is open from May to October, Wednesday and Sunday from 2 to 5 p.m., charging adults an admission of 50p ($1.15); children, 15p (35¢).

WHERE TO STAY: **Maison Talbooth** (tel. Colchester 322-367), is small and exclusive, each of its ten bedrooms really a spacious suite. This Victorian country house has been given a facelift, and each accommodation has been distinctively furnished by one of England's best known decorators. High-fashion colors abound; antiques are mixed discreetly with reproductions—and the original architectural beauty has been preserved. The super-luxury suite, with a sunken bath, goes for £65 ($149.50) nightly, and has a draped bed. Other suites, each with its own theme, start as low as £45 ($103.50) for two. One person pays from £32 ($73.60) to £50 ($115). When you arrive, you're greeted with a bowl of fresh fruit and an array of soft and hard drinks on the mantelpiece, even a bowl of ice cubes. A continental or cooked breakfast is brought in the morning. In an informal, yet stylish, drawing room, guests mingle with the hostess making you feel as if you're a guest in her country home. Although the Maison Talbooth doesn't have a restaurant on its premises, it does own one nearby. **Le Talbooth** (tel. Colchester 323-150 for reservations), a 16th-century timbered weaver's house set in beautiful gardens on the banks of the River Stour in Constable country. The owner, Gerald Milsom, has brought a high standard of international cooking, backed by good wines. Dinner is served from 7:30 to 9 p.m.

Dedham Vale, Gun Hill (tel. Colchester 322-273), is a handsome, Virginia-creeper-covered 19th-century residence, with tall windows overlooking spacious lawns, flowerbeds, and trees, plus a view of the Stour River. Mr. and Mrs. Milsom run it graciously and well. Even though the house isn't furnished with fabulous antiques, it is pleasant and comfortable, each bedroom different in character. A single room with breakfast rents for £14.50 ($33.35), increasing to £22 ($50.60) with bath. Doubles begin at £24.50 ($56.35) if bathless, going up to £31 ($71.30) with bath. You will be served a set luncheon for £6 ($13.80), dinner for £10 ($23). Some of the specialties are cooked at your table. The hotel is within easy reach of Felixstowe and Harwich for journeys to the continent.

SUFFOLK

The easternmost county of England—a link in the four-county chain of East Anglia—Suffolk is a refuge for artists, just as it was in the day of its famous native sons, Constable and Gainsborough. Through them many of the Suffolk landscapes have ended up in museums on canvas.

A fast train can make it from London to East Suffolk in approximately an hour and a half. Still, its fishing villages, dozens of flint churches, historic homes, and national monuments remain relatively unvisited by overseas visitors.

The major towns of Suffolk are **Bury St. Edmunds,** the capital of West Suffolk, and **Ipswich** in the east, a port city on the Orwell River. But to capture the true charm of Suffolk, you must explore its little market towns and villages. Beginning at the Essex border, we'll strike out toward the North Sea—highlighting the most scenic villages as we move easterly across the shire.

7. Clare

Lying 58 miles from London, but only 26 east from Cambridge, the small town of Clare holds to the old ways of East Anglia. Many of its houses are bathed in Suffolk pink, the facades of a few demonstrating the 16th- and 17th-century plasterwork technique of pargeting, discussed previously. The Stour River, which has its source a few miles away, flows by, marking the boundary of Suffolk and Essex. The little rail station has fallen to the economy axe. The nearest station is now at Sudbury, where Gainsborough was born. The journey by road from London takes about two hours—unless you succumb to the scenery and the countryside along the way. For accommodations in Clare, we have the following recommendations in the budget range.

FOOD AND LODGING: The **Bell Hotel** (tel. Clare 430) is considered one of the oldest inns in England. Once known as the Green Dragon, it served the soldiers of Richard de Clare, one of William the Conqueror's barons. Later it became a posting house, but in time the old stable gave way to a car park. Its owners, Hugh and Daphne Jones, are responsible for its recent facelift. Both of them maintain a friendly give-and-take with their guests. Bed-and-breakfast rates range from £26 ($59.80) for a single, £34 ($78.20) for a double, plus service and tax. The rooms have a fresh, pleasant style to them, and the beds are soft. The beamed dining room, with its high-back chairs and large brick fireplace, is ideal for winter dining. Lunch costs £5.50 ($12.65); dinner, around £7.50 ($17.25).

READERS' SIGHTSEEING TIP: "You might mention the **Ancient House Museum,** directly across from the churchyard. The house itself is a splendid example of pargeting and has many notable architectural features and numerous fascinating exhibits. One comes away from the Ancient House with a deeper understanding and appreciation of the rural life of Suffolk" (David and Jackie Allswang, Oakland, Calif.).

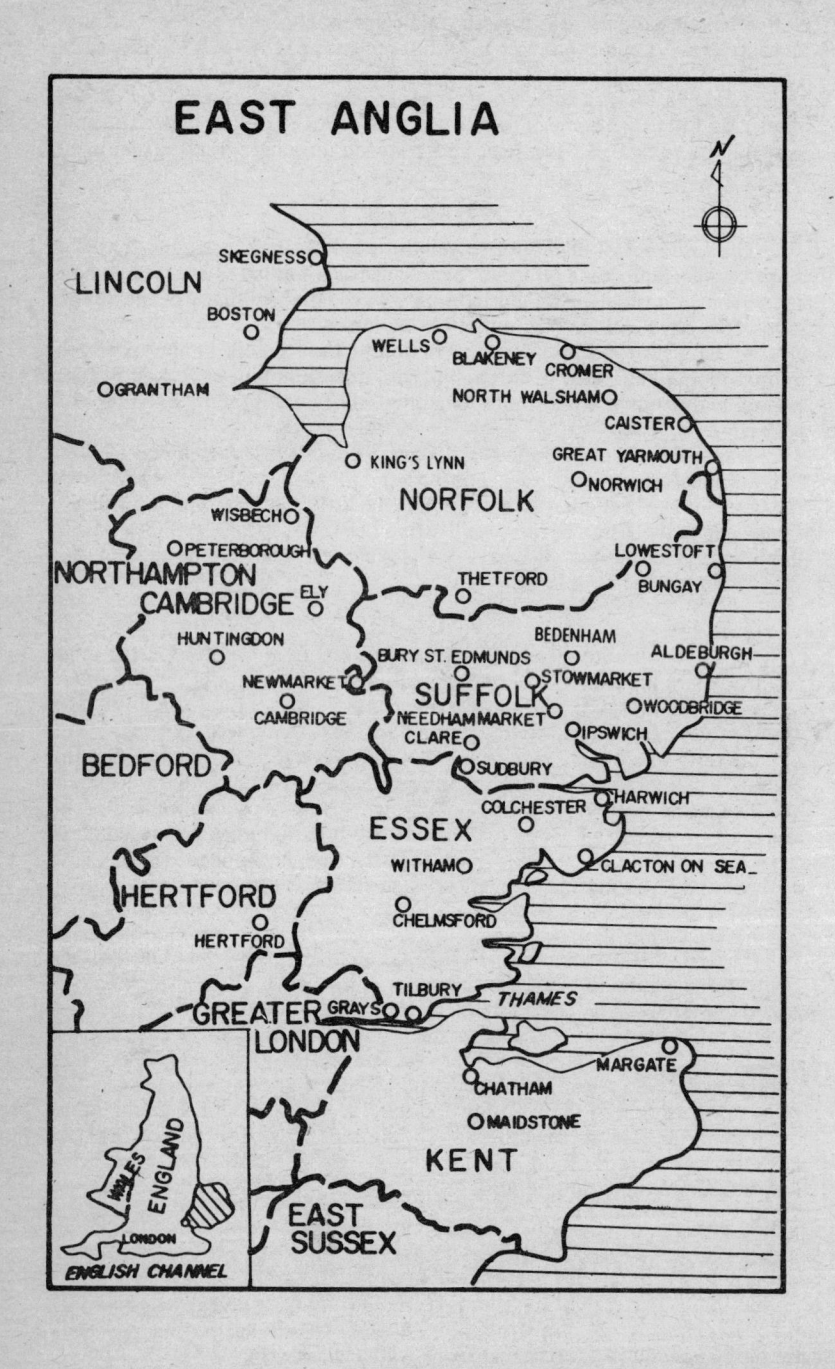

EAST ANGLIA

8. Long Melford

Long Melford has been famous since the days of the early clothmakers. Like its sister, Lavenham (coming up), it grew in prestige and importance in the Middle Ages. Of the old buildings remaining, the village church is often called "one of the glories of the shire." Along its High Street are many private homes erected by wealthy wool merchants of yore. While London seems far removed here, it is only 61 miles to the south.

WHERE TO STAY: Bull Hotel (tel. Long Melford 494) provides another fortunate opportunity to experience life in one of the great old inns of East Anglia. Built by a wool merchant, it probably is Long Melford's finest and best preserved building, dating back to 1450. The improvements and interior modernization have been undertaken by Trust Houses Forte Ltd., who have shown a tasteful respect for the beauty of the old beams. Incorporated into the general hotel is a medieval weavers' gallery and the open hearth with its Elizabethan brickwork. The bedrooms are a goodly mixture of the old and new—each centrally heated, with telephones and radios—a nice ambience. A single room with bath rents for £26 ($59.80), a double with bath for £34 ($78.20). The dining room is the outstanding part of the Bull, with its high beamed ceilings, trestle tables, settles, and handmade chairs, as well as a ten-foot fireplace. You can order a set three-course lunch for £4.50 ($10.35), a table d'hôte dinner for £8 ($18.40).

WHERE TO EAT: Jason's Carving Room, Hall Street (tel. Long Melford 226), is housed in a converted 15th-century building, warmed with oak beams, natural wood tables, flowers, and copper pots. At a set price, you dine bountifully: all the roast beef, lamb, or pork you want, and as many vegetables and salads as you wish. The carving room is run by Marius Signorini. Lunch weekdays costs £3 ($6.90), going up to £3.70 ($8.51) on Sunday. The weekday dinner tab is £5 ($11.50). It's closed on Sunday evenings.

9. Lavenham

Once a great wool center, Lavenham is considered a model village of East Anglia. It is filled with a number of half-timbered Tudor houses, washed in the characteristic Suffolk pink. Be sure to visit its church, with its landmark tower, built in the Perpendicular style. Lavenham lies only seven miles from Sudbury, 11 from Bury St. Edmunds. For accommodations or meals, there is the following medium-priced recommendation.

WHERE TO STAY AND EAT: Swan Hotel, High Street (tel. Lavenham 247-477), is linked to the Middle Ages—a lavishly timbered inn, probably one of the oldest and best preserved buildings in this relatively unmarred village. Its success has necessitated incorporating an adjoining ancient Wool Hall, which provides a high-ceilinged and timbered guest house and additional raftered, second-story bedrooms, opening onto a tiny cloistered garden. The Garden Bar opens onto yet another garden, with old stone walls and flowerbeds. Londoners often visit on September-to-March weekends for dinner and chamber music concerts. All the accommodations contain private baths. A single rents for £25 ($57.50), doubles from £38 ($87.40). The bedrooms vary greatly in size, according to the eccentricities of the architecture. Most have beamed ceilings and a mixture of traditional pieces which blend well with the old. There are nearly enough lounges for guests to try a different one every night of the week.

Meals in the raftered, two-story-high dining room have their own drama, as you sit on leather and oak chairs with brass studding. Even if you're not spending the night, you can sample the three-course luncheon priced at £6 ($13.80). Evening dinners go for £8 ($18.40). From the à la carte menu, you can order such specialties as Norfolk duckling in a sauce with almonds and raisins or boned English saddle of lamb with artichokes. In World War II, Allied pilots (who made the Swan their second home) carved their signatures in the bar, a longish room with a timbered ceiling and a fine weapon collection —with placards advertising everything from the Huntingdon Steeplechase to a wine and cheese party for the Young Conservatives.

READER'S GUEST HOUSE SELECTION: "It was our last night on the road when we luckily stumbled across our gem accommodation of the trip. It was New Year's Day, and we were in Lavenham. In desperation we resorted to the little card on the notice board in town. It referred us to the home of Mrs. Yvonne Green, **The White House,** 1 The Glebe, Brent Eleigh, Sudbury (tel. Lavenham 247-170). Brent Eleigh is only two miles from Lavenham, and when we telephoned Mrs. Green, in spite of being in the midst of holiday merrymaking with her children and grandchildren, she asked us to give her a half hour and then come along. Upon our arrival we were greeted by a charming and handsome couple and led into a beautiful, modern house that was exquisitely decorated. The house was full of fine drawings and etchings, and every corner was pleasant to the eye. Mr. and Mrs. Green are a retired couple who have moved to Suffolk from Sussex after leaving their jobs in London. In spite of the fact that they were seeing their son off to a long-term teaching position in New Zealand, they welcomed us into their family gathering with the ultimate in warmth and hospitality. For breakfast we were offered whatever we wanted and received some longed-for scrambled eggs and fine Russian tea, all served on lovely china among fresh-cut flowers and good modern paintings. We lingered over breakfast chatting with our hosts before tearing ourselves away to continue our journey. We paid £6 ($13.80) each for bed and breakfast. Although we did not sample one of Mrs. Green's evening meals for £3.75 ($8.63), there is no doubt in our minds that it would be well worth having. For summer visitors there is a garden around the house" (Kathy Greve Moriarty, Townshend, Vt.).

A Dining Event in Hintlesham

Hintlesham Hall (tel. Hintlesham 268) is the personal statement of Robert Carrier, of cookbook fame. After a smash success with his London restaurant (Carrier's), he decided to tackle the country, and selected one of England's fine old estates in East Anglia. The hall was begun in the reign of Henry VIII and completed during that of Elizabeth I. There are two ghosts—a Lady in Gray and a crying baby. Two moats are all that remain of the original medieval structure, dating from the 13th century, and laurel hedges lead to a Queen Anne orangery.

Mr. Carrier has not only found a stylish background for his creative cookery, but he's tied it in with a music and art festival—all in the same old brick manor house. Concerts, piano recitals, and opera give the Hintlesham Festival a certain renown. But on any night of the week, dining itself is a dramatic event. You're ushered into the Red Room or the Blue Room, where you can order an apéritif and make your selections from the menu. Meals are served in either the China Room, the Justice Room, or the Great Saloon with its trompe-l'oeil decorations. A set lunch costs £10.75 ($24.73), a set dinner from £12.50 ($28.75), certainly one of the finest values in East Anglia, considering the quality of the cuisine. Specialties of the house—carrying supplements—include Mr. Carrier's super sirloin, with a béarnaise sauce; charcoal-grilled guinea fowl with juniper berries; a paupiette of sole with champagne sauce. A not-so-simple starter is a brandade of smoked mackerel, and "your just desserts" include Elizabeth Moxon's lemon posset.

Hintlesham Hall stands in 18 acres of parkland just off the A12, 5 miles from Ipswich, 15 miles from Colchester, and 50 miles from Cambridge.

Truly, this is one of Britain's exciting restaurants.

10. Woodbridge

A yachting center, 12 miles from the North Sea, Woodbridge is a market town on a branch of the Deben River. Its best known resident was Edward FitzGerald, the Victorian poet and translator of the *Rubáiyát* of Omar Khayyám (some critics consider the Englishman's version better than the original). The poet died in 1883 and was buried four miles away at Boulge.

Woodbridge is a good base for exploring the East Suffolk coastline and excursions to Constable's Flatford Mill, coming up. But first, a look at our medium-priced accommodations and dining recommendation, which is some 1½ miles from the Woodbridge rail station.

WHERE TO STAY: Seckford Hall, A12 Road near Woodbridge (tel. Woodbridge 5678), captures the spirit of the days of Henry VIII and his strong-willed daughter Elizabeth (the latter may have held court here). The estate is built of brick, now ivy covered, and adorned with crow stepped gables, mullioned windows, and ornate chimneys—pure Tudor. The hall was built in 1530 by Sir Thomas Seckford, a member of one of Suffolk's first families. You enter through a heavy studded Tudor door into a flagstone hallway with antiques. The butler will show you to your bedroom. Owners Mr. and Mrs. M. S. Bunn have seen to it that your stay is like a house party. A single room rents for £18 ($41.40) nightly, increasing to £21 ($48.30) with bath. A double or twin without bath costs £30 ($69) per night, increasing to £35 ($80.50) with bath. At least one room is high-ceilinged with a monumental four-poster, costing from £37 ($85.10). In summer, reservations are helpful for those desiring bed, breakfast and evening dinner. (Nonguests can stop by for dinner, which is à la carte. Best to phone first.)

If you arrive before sundown, you may want to stroll through a portion of the 34-acre gardens. As you proceed to the side and rear, you'll come upon a rose garden, herbaceous borders, and greenhouses. At the bottom of the garden is an ornamental lake, complete with weeping willows and paddling ducks. At four o'clock, you can have a complete tea in the Great Hall. Sip your brew slowly, savoring the atmosphere of heavy beams and a simple stone fireplace. Your chair may be Queen Anne, your table Elizabethan. Dinner will be announced by the butler. Good English meals are served in a setting of linenfold paneling and Chippendale and Hepplewhite chairs. After-dinner coffee and brandy are featured in the Tudor Bar.

FOOD AND DRINK: Sherlock's Wine Bar, 17 The Thoroughfare. The owner, Douglas Wilmer, who portrayed Holmes in a B.B.C. TV series, littered his upstairs wine bar with memorabilia of the famous detective. His homemade vegetable broth is 55p ($1.27); pâté, 65p ($1.50); quiche Lorraine and salad, £1.75 ($4.03); and a whole host of homemade goodies such as beef in Guinness go for £1.75 also. Chili con carne is £1.20 ($2.76), and ravioli, £1.10 ($2.53). Cakes and flans are around 65p ($1.50). A glass of good wine from France, Germany, Italy, or Spain goes for 75p ($1.73). Food is served from noon to 2:30 p.m. and 7:30 to 11 p.m. daily, except Sunday and Monday.

11. Aldeburgh

Pressed against the North Sea, Aldeburgh is a favorite retreat of the in-the-know traveler, even attracting some Dutch tourists who make the sea crossing via Harwich, the British entry port for those coming from the Hook of Holland. The late composer Benjamin Britten *(Peter Grimes, The Rape of Lucretia)*, used to live in the area. But the festival he started at Aldeburgh in 1948 is held at Snape in June, a short drive to the north.

Less than 100 miles from London, the resort was founded in Roman times, but legionnaires have been replaced by fishermen, boatmen, and fanciers of wildfowl. A bird sanctuary, Havergate Island, lies about ten miles offshore. Some take time out from their sporting activities (a golf course stretches 3½ miles) to visit the 16th-century **Moot Hall**.

WHERE TO STAY AND EAT: In August, the time of the regatta, accommodations tend to be fully booked. We'll survey the pick of the lot:

Brudenell Hotel, The Parade (tel. Aldeburgh 2071), is Aldeburgh's prestige hotel, right on the waterfront. Built at the beginning of the 20th century, it was remodeled and decorated by its owner, Trust Houses Forte Ltd. An attractive and comfortable accommodation awaits the visitor exploring the East Anglian seacoast. The interior is most successful and pleasant, and from many of the bedrooms there's a view of the churning sea. All of the rooms contain private baths. A single begins at £22 ($50.60), a double at £34 ($78.20) to £38 ($87.40). During the months of October to May, many bargain-break offers are available, with golfing breaks a specialty. Every room has TV, telephone, radio, tea and coffee makers, and central heating, as well as good, soft beds. The dining room with an all-glass wall overlooking the coast is an ideal spot for a three-course luncheon costing £4.50 ($10.35). A dinner costs £8 ($18.40). There are à la carte selections also. Excellent bar snacks featuring local fish are available, at a price range starting at £1.25 ($2.88).

Uplands Hotel, Victorian Road (tel. Aldeburgh 2420), is as untouristy a retreat as you're apt to find. It's more like a private home run by good friends (Mr. and Mrs. Forge and Mr. Ashworth) who take in paying guests. The inn dates from the 18th century; at one time it was the childhood home of Elizabeth Garrett Anderson, the first woman doctor in England. Uplands provides personally decorated bedrooms and excellently planned and well-served meals. Once inside the living room, you sense the informality and charm. They have furnished it with some good antiques, a few comfortable upholstered chairs, paintings, and books. The prices range from £10 ($23) to £14 ($32.20) per person for an overnight stopover. There are seven twin-bedded chalets in the garden, with TV and private bathrooms. The chef, with a stack of cooking awards, offers an à la carte dinner for approximately £6 ($13.80). A typical offering might include escalope de veau Uplands and roast Aylesbury duck. You can have coffee in front of the fireplace or, in fair weather, in the garden.

The Local Pub

Ye Olde Crosse Keys, Crabbe Street, is a genuine 15th-century pub, with the real atmopshere of a Suffolk seaside local. In the summertime, everyone takes his or her real English ale or lager out and sits on the seawall, sipping, talking, and thinking. The pub itself is rustic—favored by local artists, who in the cooler months sit beside an old brick fireplace and eat plates of oysters or smoked salmon. Sandwiches—and very good ones—are available at from 55p

($1.27). Ye Olde Crosse Keys is easy to spot, a short walk from Ye Olde Curiosity Shoppe.

12. East Bergholt

The English landscape painter, John Constable (1776–1837), was born at East Bergholt. Near the village is **Flatford Mill**, subject of one of his most renowned canvases. The mill, in a scenic setting, was given to the National Trust in 1943, and since has been leased to the Fields Studies Council for use as a residential college. Weekly courses are arranged on all aspects of the countryside and the environment. None of the buildings contains relics of Constable, nor are they open to the general public, but students of all ages and capabilities are welcome to courses. Details may be obtained from the warden, Flatford Mill Field Centre, East Bergholt, near Colchester. Beside a bridge nearby sits a 16th-century cottage, where you can have drinks and sandwiches.

THE LOCAL PUB: Red Lion Inn, Gaston Street (tel. Colchester 298-332), traces its ancestry back to around 1500. Numerous authors have written of the Red Lion, citing it as one of the unmarred inns of East Anglia.

The hosts keep an immaculate, friendly place. Bowls of soup are available in the bar, along with a ploughman's lunch. Also offered are scampi, sausages with fried potatoes, and fruit pie. Snacks are in the £1 ($2.30) to £ ($4.60) range. A short stroll from Flatford Mill, the inn is reached by turning off the A12, the Colchester–Ipswich road. An Eastern National Coach, no. 87 or 87A, comes here from Colchester.

NORFOLK

Bounded by the North Sea, Norfolk is the biggest of the East Anglian counties. It's a low-lying area, with fens, heaths, and salt marshes. An occasional dike or windmill makes you think you've been delivered to the Netherlands. One of the features of Norfolk is its network of Broads, miles and miles of lagoons—shallow in parts—connected by streams.

Summer sports people flock to Norfolk to hire boats for sailing or fishing. From Norwich itself, **Wroxham,** the so-called capital of the Broads, is easily reached, only eight miles to the northeast. Motorboats regularly leave from this resort, taking parties on short trips. Some of the best scenery of the Broads is to be found on the periphery of Wroxham.

EN ROUTE TO NORWICH: If you're searching for a place to dine near the Suffolk/Norfolk border, before driving on to Norwich, you'll find none better than the recommendation below.

The Fox and Goose, Fressingfield, near Diss, Norfolk (tel. Fressingfield 247), is a charming old building with a wide gravel courtyard and a pond with ducks. It was the old guildhall, and is the only remaining inn we could find in England still owned by the church and originally provided by the church for the refreshment of parishoners instead of their eating in the nave after services. The place is a delight. It's open daily from noon to 1:30 p.m. and from 7 to 9 p.m., except Tuesday and from December 21 to December 25.

The Clarke family runs it, and its members have been here for longer than a decade, serving lunches and dinners to locals (London is only 80 miles of fast road away so some come from there) and passersby.

If you can plan ahead, telephone and reserve a table. The Clarkes will send you the menu and you can select your meal in advance. The kitchen staff prefers one party to order the same entree if possible, as this place is very much a family concern. The selection is made from a wide variety of fresh fish and local meat dishes. Featured are smoked eel, mackerel, salmon and trout, sole normande, coquille St. Jacques, king prawns, lobster, and crab, followed by beef or pork en croûte, five sorts of steak, tournedos provençale, three duck dishes, venison in season or game, all served with a variety of vegetables. Desserts include fresh fruit dishes and delicious sorbets and ices laced with liqueurs.

Mr. Clarke used to be a wholesale butcher, and the quality of the meat reflects his interest. Adrian, his young son, hated school but had a knack for cooking. He presides in the kitchen, but Mrs. Clarke oversees everything, and her influence is evident in the gleaming tablecloths and fresh flowers. The kitchen staff bakes its own whole-meal crusty bread to serve with masses of yellow butter.

The dining room only seats 26 "at a pinch," and punctuality is essential. But, once you're there, the table is yours to enjoy your meal in comfort. Start in the bar with an apéritif. The wine list is long and excellent, although you can order a bottle of the house wine for £4 ($9.20). Service is unobtrusive in the simple dining room, with its low ceiling and wooden tables and chairs. A meal, not including wine, will cost from £10 ($23) to £15 ($34.50).

13. Norwich

Some 20 miles from the North Sea, Norwich still holds to its claim as the capital city of East Anglia. The county town of Norfolk, Norwich is a charming and historic city, despite encroachments by industry and its position as a market town for the shire. Besides its cathedral, the city has more than 30 parish churches, some of which were built in the 15th century of flint.

Norwich is a city of narrow and cobbled streets, with endless baffling one-ways. The big open-air market place, with stalls with canvas roofs, comes alive with fruit, vegetable, and trinket peddlers on Wednesday and Saturday. The city also boasts a thriving art colony: the Norwich Players long ago revived the 18th-century Maddermarket Theatre (built in the style of an Elizabethan playhouse), whose predecessor had been ordered shut down by Cromwell. In addition the Norwich School of Painting is a good rallying center for East Anglian artists.

THE CASTLE: In the center of Norwich, on an artificial mound, sits the castle, formerly the county gaol (jail). Its huge 12th-century Norman keep and the later prison buildings are used as a civic museum and headquarters of the county-wide Norfolk Museums Service. The museum houses an impressive collection of pictures by artists of the Norwich School, of whom the most distinguished were John Crome, born 1768, and John Sell Cotman, born 1782. The Castle Museum also contains a fine collection of Lowestoft porcelain and Norwich silver. These are shown in the new rotunda. There are two sets of dioramas, one showing Norfolk wildlife in its natural setting, the other illustrating scenes of Norfolk life from the Old Stone Age to the early days of Norwich Castle.

The Castle Museum is open weekdays from 10 a.m. to 5 p.m. (on Sunday from 2 to 5 p.m.). Charges from the spring bank holiday until September are 50p ($1.15) for adults, 10p (23¢) for children, and 25p (58¢) for students. The rest of the year, adults pay 25p (58¢); children, 10p (23¢); and students, 15p

(35¢). There's a coffee bar, and the licensed Buttery is open from 10:30 a.m. to 2:30 p.m.

THE CATHEDRAL: Principally of Norman design, the cathedral dates back to 1096. It is noted primarily for its long nave, with its lofty columns. Its spire, built in the late Perpendicular style, rises 315 feet, and shares distinction with the keep of the castle as the significant landmarks on the Norwich skyline. On the vaulted ceiling are more than 300 bosses (knoblike ornamental projections) depicting biblical scenes. The impressive choir stalls with the handsome misereres date from the 15th century. Edith Cavell—"Patriotism is not enough"— the English nurse executed by the Germans in World War I, was buried on the cathedral's Life's Green. The quadrangular Cloisters go back to the 13th century, and are among the most spacious in England.

The cathedral Visitors' Centre includes a refreshment area and an exhibition and film room with tape/slide shows about the cathedral. Admission is free.

A short walk from the cathedral will take you to **Tombland,** one of the most interesting old squares in Norwich.

SAINSBURY ART CENTRE: In 1973, Sir Robert and Lady Sainsbury, and their son David, gave their private art collection and an endowment to the University of East Anglia. The money was used to build the Art Centre, an umbrella-like roof which can be transformed in minutes from solid to glass, and to extend the existing collection of paintings and sculpture. Today, this is one of the foremost collections in the country, including the original Sainsbury collection of modern, ancient, and classical pieces, the Reserve Collections of art nouveau and 20th-century nonfigurative art, and a special exhibition of art, sculpture, and needlework.

The center is open from noon to 5 p.m. Tuesday to Sunday; admission is free, except for the Sainsbury collection which charges a fee of 25p (58¢).

A buffet is open, Monday to Friday only, from 10:30 a.m. to 2:30 p.m. Ham, fish, or chicken with salad costs around 75p ($1.73). There is always a hot dish of the day and salads at 32p (74¢) a helping. Desserts go from 35p (81¢). The Conservatory Coffee Bar is open Monday to Friday from 2:30 to 4:30 p.m., on Saturday and Sunday from 2 to 4:30 p.m.

WHERE TO STAY: The **Post House,** Ipswich Road (tel. Norwich 56431), is built in the motel style, two miles from the center of the city on the A140 Ipswich Road and one mile from the A11 London Road. Free parking space is provided for 200 cars. Run as a Trust House Forte hotel, it charges £27 ($62.10) in a single, £38 ($87.40) in a double, VAT and service charge included. Each of the 120 bedrooms has a private bath, telephone, TV, radio, central heating, tea- and coffee-making equipment, and a small refrigerated bar. The rooms have combined sitting areas, with sofas and armchairs. The Yeoman Buttery, which stays open till 10:30 p.m., reflects Norfolk's ties with agriculture (sturdy farming tools decorating the walls); the main restaurant specializes in traditional English fare, such as game in season, smoked fish, and potted meats. The modern Punch Bar is decorated with early *Punch* cartoons and drawings.

The **Maid's Head Hotel,** Tombland (tel. Norwich 28821), claims to be the oldest continuously operated inn in England, circa 1272. Opposite the cathedral, in the most interesting district of Norwich, it has a dual personality architecturally: one portion an Elizabethan black-and-white timbered inn with four gables, the other a modernized Georgian section with a prim white entry and small-paned windows. The interior—83 bedrooms with private baths—is joined by a glassed-in courtyard, with many flowering and hanging plants and vines.

The resident general manager, Derek B. Cooke, charges £25 ($57.50) in a single, £30 ($69) in a double, including service. The bedrooms vary according to their location—some are contemporary, some traditional, others in between. The lucky ones get the Queen Elizabeth I bedroom, where the Tudor monarch allegedly slept. It is furnished with an ornate carved four-poster. Meals, basically English with continental influences, are served in the formal paneled dining room, where you can have a set lunch for £5.75 ($13.23), dinner for £6 ($13.80).

Santa Lucia Hotel and Foundry House Hotel, 38–40 Yarmouth Rd. (tel. Norwich 33207), is one of the best for value of the hotels outside Norwich, only 1½ miles from the center. The combined hotel and guest house offers not only inexpensive rooms, but an attractive setting and a friendly atmosphere.

You pay £6.50 ($14.95) nightly for bed and breakfast. The food is quite good, too, costing £3.20 ($7.36) for a dinner. Each of the rooms has running water and a radio. There are sun terraces for relaxing, modern bathrooms, and plenty of parking space. Three buses pass by the door heading for the center of the city.

WHERE TO EAT: The **Assembly House,** Theatre Street (tel. Norwich 26402), is a good example of Georgian architecture. You enter the building through a large front courtyard, which leads to the central hall, with its columns, find paneling, and crystal chandelier. The restaurant is administered by H. J. Sexton Norwich Arts Trust.

On your left is a high-ceilinged room, with paneling, fine paintings, and a long buffet table—ready for self-service. After making your selection, take your plate to any one of the many tables. Often you'll share—perhaps with an artist, or else a woman who owns an estate in the country. You'll find an unusually varied selection of hors d'oeuvres. A big bowl of homemade soup is nutritious. Hot entrees are homemade, too, prepared with fresh ingredients. The prices, like the food, are simple. For example, a home-cured ham and salad meal goes for £1.50 ($3.45), an omelet for £1 ($2.30). The restaurant is open from 10:30 a.m. to 2 p.m. and from 3:30 to 8 p.m.

After dining, you may want to stroll through the rest of the building. Art exhibits are usually held regularly in the Ivory and Hobart Rooms, open from 10:30 a.m. to 5:30 p.m. Concerts are sponsored in the Music Room, with its chandeliers and sconces. There's even a small movie house.

The **Britons Arms Coffee House,** 9 Elm Hill (tel. Norwich 23367), overlooks the most beautiful cobbled street in Norwich, in the heart of the old city. Over the years, it's had several names, and traces its history back to the days of Edward III. Now it's one of the least expensive eating places in Norwich—certainly the most intimate and informal. The coffeehouse has several rooms, including a back one with an inglenook. You'll find old beamed ceilings, Tudor benches, and pink-washed walls.

It's open every day except Sunday, Thursday afternoons, and evenings, serving mostly lunches and coffee. Lunch begins at 12:15 p.m. (the staff is strict about that!), ending at 2:30 p.m. Generally, you can have tea from 3:30 until 5 p.m.

The procedure here is to go to the little counter, where you purchase your lunch and bring it to the table of your choice. Everything we've tried was delicious—and the items are homemade. In summertime the food is cold; in winter, hot. You'll find an assortment of soups, quiches, flans, fruit pies, and cheeses, a meal costing around £3 ($6.90). It's a good place to stop after your inspection of the cathedral, only a block away.

14. Tottenhill

This village can be a center for exploring some stately homes and gardens, the seaside resorts and fens and broads of East Anglia. Within a day's drive are the historic old port of King's Lynn, the country home of Queen Elizabeth (Sandringham), the lavender fields of Heacham, the tulip fields of Spalding, as well as the large man-made forest at Thetford and the neolithic flint mines at Grime's Graves. The following private hotel is recommended as a stopover.

Oakwood House, on Route A10 in Tottenhill, just four miles south of King's Lynn (tel. King's Lynn 810-256), is a country house of Tudor origin with all the amenities of a modern hotel. The house was enlarged some 200 years ago and refaced with a typical Georgian exterior. Within a short drive of the Norfolk coast, Oakwood House offers visitors a peaceful alternative to the bustling seaside resorts and market towns.

Nestled in its own two acres of gardens, the hotel has guest rooms with color TV, tea- and coffee-making facilities, hot and cold running water, individually controlled heating, and pleasant views over the Norfolk countryside and the gardens. Some rooms are equipped with private showers en suite. The comfortably furnished guest lounge contains a color TV and the spacious dining room adjoins the well-stocked period bar.

The menu is carefully chosen to make the best use of local and homegrown produce whenever possible, and all cooking is under the personal supervision of Julie Hollinger, who, with her husband Philip, sees that the needs of their guests are attended to. Rates per person for bed and breakfast begin at £10.50 ($24.15). The four-course dinner will cost you an additional £5 ($11.50). VAT is included in the price, and no service charge is made. Ample parking facilities are maintained within the grounds.

15. North Norfolk

This part is already well known by members of the American Eighth Air Force, for many Liberators and Flying Fortresses took off and landed from this corner of the country. Their captains and crews sampled most of the local hostelries at one time or another. Now it is just feathered birds that fly overhead, and the countryside is quiet and peaceful.

THE SIGHTS: This area is of considerable scenic interest, having some very good value in its offering of accommodations and food. Norfolk especially provides an alternative to the vastly overcrowded West Country in summer, and it's extremely convenient for a weekend out of London, as it lies only a three-hour drive away.

Sandringham

Some 110 miles northeast of London, Sandringham has been the country home of four generations of British monarchs, ever since the Prince of Wales (later King Edward VII) purchased it in 1861. The son of Queen Victoria, along with his Danish wife, Princess Alexandra, rebuilt the house, standing on 7000 acres of grounds, and, in time, it became a fashionable rendezvous of British society.

The red brick Victorian Tudor mansion consists of more than 200 rooms, and in recent times some of these rooms have been opened to the public, including two drawing rooms and a dining room. Sandringham joins Windsor Castle and the Palace of Holyroodhouse in Edinburgh as the only British royal residences which can be examined by the public. Guests can also visit a lofty saloon with a minstrels' gallery.

A group of former coach houses has been converted into a museum of big-game trophies, plus a collection of cars, including the first vehicle purchased by a royal, in 1900 Daimler Tonneau that belonged to Edward VII. The house and grounds are open Tuesday to Thursday from Easter to May 1. After that, they are open Sunday through Thursday until about the end of September, except for a period in late July and early August when members of the royal family are likely to be in residence.

The house visiting hours are from 11 a.m. (from noon on Sunday) to about 5 p.m., although the grounds are open from 10:30 a.m. (11:30 a.m. on Sunday) to 5 p.m. Admission to both the house and gardens is £1 ($2.30) for adults, 50p ($1.15) for children. If you want to be admitted just to the gardens, expect to pay 65p ($1.50) for adults, 40p (92¢) for children. The 70-acre gardens, incidentally, are richly planted with azaleas, rhododendrons, hydrangeas, and camellias.

Sandringham lies 50 miles from Cambridge and 10 miles from King's Lynn. There is bus service between King's Lynn and Sandringham.

Blickling Hall

A long drive, bordered by massive yew hedges towering above and framing your first view of this lovely old house, leads you to Blickling Hall, at Aylsham. A great Jacobean house built in the early 17th century, it is, perhaps, one of the finest examples of such architecture in the country. The Long Gallery has an elaborate 17th-century ceiling, and the Peter the Great Room, decorated later, has a fine tapestry on the wall. The house is set in ornamental parkland with a formal garden and an orangery. Meals and snacks are available. It is open from April 1 until the beginning of October, except Monday, from 2 to 5:30 p.m. The house is also open from 11 a.m. to 1 p.m. daily, except Monday, from June to September. Admission £1.10 ($2.53) for adults, 55p ($1.27) for children.

Norfolk Lavender Ltd.

At Caley Mill at Heacham (tel. Heacham 70384), you can see how lavender is grown, the flowers harvested, and the essence distilled before appearing prettily packaged as perfume, aftershave, potpourri, and old-fashioned lavender bags to slip between your hankies. Much of the lavender is grown on the nearby Sandringham royal estate, so you may end up with a regal product. The mills are open from 10 a.m. to 6 p.m. May to September, from 9 a.m. to dusk in winter. Admission is 20p (46¢) for adults, 10p (23¢) for children. The Miller's Cottage Tearoom serves delicious cream teas with homemade cakes, scones, and buns, as well as light lunches. The best time to see the lavender in bloom is mid-July to early August. You will be able to discuss the merits of the various varieties and their suitability for your own particular garden.

Alby Crafts Ltd.

This brainchild of Valerie Alston, on Cromer Road, Erpingham (tel. Nanworth 590-226), is open from Easter to Christmas, daily, except Monday, from 10 a.m. to 5 p.m. The craft center is housed in an old Norfolk stone farmhouse and its outbuildings. Mrs. Alston scours the country to find genuine articles of country craft, including leatherword, woodcarving, and ceramics. A rocking chair model, perfect in every detail, yet only four inches high, costs £16 ($36.80). A woodcarving of a Bedfordshire farmer and his pig goes for £55 ($126.50). Bronze and wrought-iron work can be made to order, a piece costing from £2 ($4.60) to £500 ($1140). There are sometimes demonstrations and specialist exhibitions, and several of the workshops are made available to local craftspeople. The delight of this place is that the articles come from all over the country and are entirely genuine craftware. Homemade dishes and cakes are served throughout the day in the tearoom.

Sutton Windmill

At Sutton (1½ miles south east of Stalham off the A149) is the tallest mill in the country. But its main claim to fame, in a county where many windmills still work, is the exceptional quality and interest of the working machinery. Chris Nunn, the young man who owns the mill, decided it was time he put something back into the country instead of taking it out. So he left the construction business and now devotes his days to restoring the mill. When money runs short, he works on the North Sea oil rigs for a time. He hopes shortly to be grinding corn again, but the lower floors—there are nine in all—house a collection of tools and bygones reflecting the mill's 100 years of history. The mill is open from the beginning of April until the end of September, from 9:30 a.m. to 6 p.m. Admission is 30p (69¢) for adults, 15p (35¢) for children. There is a telescope on the top floor, and the view over the countryside is magnificent. Crafts, pottery, books, and gifts are on sale.

The Thursford Collection

Just off the A148 which runs from Kings Lynn to Cromer, at Laurel Farm, Thursford Green, Thursford, near Fakenham (tel. Thursford 238), George Cushing has been collecting and restoring steam engines and organs for more years than you'd care to remember. His collection is now a trust, and the lovely old painted giants are on display, a paradise of traction engines with impeccable pedigrees such as Burrells, Garretts, and Ruston Proctors. There are some static engines, the sort that run merry-go-rounds at funfairs, but the most flamboyant exhibits are the showman's organs, the Wurlitzers and concert organs with their brilliant decoration, moving figures, and mass of windpipes. The organs play at 4 p.m. There is a children's play area, and a Savages Venetian Gondola switchback ride with Gavoili organ, which operates daily. It was built at nearby Kings Lynn, and Disneyland has been after it for years. On many days during the summer, the two-foot gauge steam railway, the Cackler, will take you around the wooded grounds of the museum. There is a refreshment cafe and a souvenir shop to buy your Thursford T-shirt, as well as photographs, books, and records of the steam-organ music. The collection is open daily from 2 to 5:30 p.m. from the beginning of April until the end of October. On Sunday it is open throughout the year. Admission is 80p ($1.84) for adults, 45p ($1.04) for children.

The North Norfolk Railway

This steam railway plies from Sheringham to Weybourne. The station at Sheringham is open daily from 10 a.m. from Easter to October. Admission is 30p (69¢) for adults; children pay 15p (35¢). There are two museums of railway paraphernalia, steam locomotives, and historic rolling stock. The round trip to Weybourne by steam train takes about 45 minutes through most attractive countryside. Days and times of departures vary so you should telephone Sheringham 0263/822-045 between 10 a.m. and 5 p.m. before you go there. The return journey will cost 90p ($2.07) for adults; children, 45p ($1.04).

FOOD AND LODGING: The **Maltings,** Weybourne, near Holt (tel. Weybourne 275). Almost on the edge of the sea but protected from its worst ravages, the Maltings is a delightfully friendly, family-run country "pub" in the best tradition. It is under the watchful eye of Chris Trueman and his wife Elizabeth, who are aided and abetted by James and Lillian, Chris's mother and father. Bedrooms are simple and comfortable with color TV and radio. They go from £13.50 ($31.05) to £18 ($41.40) in a single, and from £26 ($59.80) to £30 ($69) in a double, depending on whether or not you have a private bath. Rates include a large breakfast, VAT, and service.

The original building dates back to the 16th century, and the flint walls and stout plain exterior bear witness to those times. The elegant restaurant has a surprisingly sophisticated à la carte menu, including most of those haute cuisine dishes that you crave—coquilles St. Jacques frites, veal escalope with rosemary, beef filet with parsley butter—along with a Taste of England menu when a succulent three courses will cost you £6 ($13.80). There are some interesting variations such as jugged hare cooked in red wine.

If you feel unable to sustain a whole meal, drift down the yard to the Inn and the Buttery where, in another solid old stone building, you can sup off a variety of salads complemented by fresh-caught seafoods, home-cooked meats, and, the main attraction, hot baked jacket potatoes, with an amazing variety of fillings. John Byle rules over the kitchens, but he has a superb team of chefs with him. To crown it all, Myles Nolan, headwaiter of the restaurant, and the Trueman family make absolutely sure that you will be greeted with a smile.

The **Blakeney Hotel,** The Quay, Blakeney, near Holt (tel. Cley 740797). As its address indicates, the hotel is right on the quay overlooking the harbor and across the flats from Blakeney Point where migrating birds rest on their way south. The village and neighboring Cley built many of the Elizabethan sailing ships, and the hotel bars are named for them—Jacob, Revenge, and Mayflower. Rooms are cozy, have tea- and coffee-making facilities, as well as telephones and radios. Most have baths and color TVs. Singles are from £12 ($27.60) in low season, going up to £20 ($46) in high season. Doubles are £22 ($50.60) to £28 ($64.40). These rates include service and breakfast, but VAT is added. For half board add £10 ($23) per person per day.

There is an indoor swimming pool, and the lounge has panoramic windows with superb views over the flats to the sea. Table d'hôte meals are offered: £5 ($11.50) for lunch. £7 ($16.10) for dinner, both with three courses. There is a good à la carte menu, but if you just want a snack, the Blakeney Bar offers real ale with which to wash down your selection. A meal will cost as little as £1.50 ($3.45) or, if you indulge yourself, £4 ($9.20).

The **Buckinghamshire Arms Hotel,** Blickling, near Aylsham (tel. Aylsham 2133), is a very pleasant 17th-century village inn with roaring fires in the bars. Offered are comfortable rooms—some with four-poster beds, others with half-tester beds (the canopy reaches over the sleeper's head only). Some come with just ordinary divans, although all have TV and coffee- and tea-making trays. The charge for the night, plus a large and satisfying breakfast, is £20 ($46) for two, VAT and service extra. A real country-style dinner will cost about £8 ($18.40). The soup comes from an aromatic stockpot, and Norfolk duckling and chicken are served with fresh vegetables. During the winter they hold special feasts once or twice a month with lobster, venison, and pheasant among the main dishes. Robert Dawson-Smith leases the inn from the National Trust, which owns the nearby Blickling Hall. Real ale, featured in the bar, is often so strong that it only comes in "nips."

The **Old Rectory,** Great Snoring, Fakenham (tel. Walsingham 597). The history of this old house is shrouded in mystery, but in 1500 it was believed to be hexagonal with stone-mullioned windows and heraldic shields of the then owners, the Shelton family, carved on the oaken front door. The Victorians did their bit to restore the house, but it still remains a solid part of medieval village life.

Rosamond Scoles and her family have six comfortable and elegantly furnished rooms for guests. Overnight is £15 ($34.50) to £18 ($41.40) per person for a room with bathroom, including a leisurely and substantial breakfast. There is a large lounge for guests, where a huge log fire burns, and the light flickers on antique woodwork.

Dinner is three courses, cheese, and coffee for £6 ($13.80) per person. Picnic hampers are provided for luncheon alfresco if you wish. The Old Rectory has a residential license so you can enjoy a sherry before dinner or a nightcap by the fire before retiring to your bed. It's an entirely elegant, relaxed experience, an insight into comfortable country life.

Gasche's Swiss Restaurant, Weybourne (tel. Weybourne 220), has been going on for about 30 years. These days it is run by Edgar Steiner, nephew of the original Herr Gasche, now retired and living peacefully in the village. Nigel Massingham, the chef, trained here and has picked up those Swiss touches in the preparation of the dishes. The beamed dining room of the flint and thatch cottage is warmed by a log fire, you will be greeted as warmly by the staff as you partake of the set lunch, costing £5 ($11.50) for three courses. You have a choice of seven appetizers, a delicious homemade soup, and eight main courses including wienerschnitzel. Dinner for £8 ($18.40) is chosen from a similarly large menu, including roast Norfolk duckling. There is an à la carte menu where a meal will cost around £12 ($27.60), but we think you will find enough choices on the set menus to satisfy all tastes. The restaurant is open daily except Monday throughout the year (except for dinner on Sunday).

16. English Country Cottages

"England's most exclusive and individual self-catering holiday homes," the blurb says, and it could well be so. Mainly in Norfolk, "the big county," these cottages are the dream-child of Major Bowlby who has controlled the operation for the past 15 years from Vere Lodge, tucked away in the Norfolk village of South Raynham. The major lives with his charming wife and pretty daughter at the lodge surrounded by gardens in which peacocks strut.

Three years ago, the cottages at Vere Lodge were the only ones owned and rented as self-catering properties by Major Bowlby. Since then, English Country Cottages has expanded beyond all expectations, and now offers a choice of some 500 properties, which range from a mini-apartment to a converted boathouse, farmhouses, and stately homes in most parts of England and Wales, with one outstanding property in Scotland.

Visitors therefore have a choice not only of a wide range of types but also of a variety of locations. They can choose to take their holiday either in the upland moorland of Yorkshire; in the spacious corn-growing country of East Anglia; in Dorset, where Thomas Hardy lived and wrote; or in the lush pastureland of Devon and Cornwall, with their tall, bright-red cliffs, narrow lanes, the high banks of which are bright with wildflowers, and hundreds of pretty fishing villages. This part of England is the mecca of vacationers and provides everything one could possibly want—surfing, sailing, pony trekking, riding, old-world inns, high-class restaurants—all in a climate which is the kindest and softest England has to offer.

The cottages sleep from 2 to 14 persons. A brochure provides full details of all the properties available, with a color photograph of each. Prices range from £60 ($138) per week in low season (April 1 to May 24) to £390 ($897) for the high season (July and August). The interior appointments range from the simple to the luxurious. Prices, of course, depend not only on the quality of the decor but also on the location of the property and the amenities which accompany it, such as a heated swimming pool, a hard tennis court, or a barbecue patio.

The great advantage of this type of holiday is that visitors can do their own thing in their own way in their own time. They can get up when they like, eat when they like, wear what they like. A self-catering vacation with English Country Cottages offers outstanding value for the money, complete freedom from all restrictions, and an opportunity of sampling English country life in its many and varied aspects.

A word of advice: Most cottages are in villages or else on the grounds of mansions and farms. Most are quite difficult to find. Don't worry, however. When you reserve, the major will send you detailed instructions on how to get there. The head office is Vere Lodge, South Raynham, Fakenham, Norfolk, and the telephone is Weasenham Saint Peter 395 or 411 (from London, dial 032-874).

Chapter XIII

EAST MIDLANDS

1. Northamptonshire
2. Leicestershire
3. Derbyshire
4. Nottinghamshire
5. Lincolnshire

THE EAST MIDLANDS contains several widely varied counties, both in character and scenery. This part of central England, for instance, offers miles of dreary industrial sections and their offspring row-type Victorian houses, yet the district is intermixed with some of Britain's noblest scenery, such as the Peak District National Park, centered in Derbyshire. Byron said that scenes there rivaled those of Switzerland and Greece. There are, in short, many pleasant surprises in store for you, from the tulip land of Lincoln to the 18th-century spa of Buxton in Derbyshire, from George Washington's ancestral home at Sulgrave Manor in Northamptonshire to what remains of Sherwood Forest.

1. Northamptonshire

This sprawling county in the middle of England is rather undistinguished in scenery, although its meadows are pleasant in summer. The county town is—

NORTHAMPTON: This has long been an important shoe-making center, and the **Central Museum** on Guildhall Road commemorates that fact. In its collection it traces footwear through the ages, some of which dates back to Roman times. It can be visited from Monday to Saturday, 10 a.m. to 6 p.m. Admission is 15p (35¢). Most visitors pass through here en route to Sulgrave Manor, previewed below.

Food and Lodging

Saxon Inn, Silver Street (tel. Northampton 22441), is a concrete-and-glass structure, attracting mainly the business client, drawn to its good location just off the Inner Ring Road (West). A first-class motor hotel, it checks you in and out smoothly and efficiently. The atmosphere isn't stiff at all—in fact, it's rather informal, and the public lounges are attractively decorated. Portraits of sporting personalities decorate the the Sportsman Bar, and light meals are served in the Little Mermaid coffeeshop. Or else you can dine in a coaching-house atmosphere in the Saddle Room, with its large stone fireplace and heavy beams.

The menu is international, and guests dine by candlelight, enjoying soft music from a piano player. A resident band entertains on Saturday nights. Rooms are well furnished and comfortable, each with private bath, shower, and toilet en suite, along with color TV, radio, phone, and wall-to-wall carpeting. Singles range in price from £22 ($50.60), and doubles cost from £32 ($73.60).

Westone Hotel, Ashley Way, Weston Favell (tel. Northampton 406-262), is a big 19th-century mansion that has seen much modernization. Our favorite spot here is the cocktail lounge, which has a calm elegance, its windows opening onto the terrace and grounds. Most of the bedrooms have private baths, at least those in the more contemporary section, although traditionalists may prefer the comfortable older rooms. Depending on the facilities, singles range from £20 ($46) to £24 ($55.20) nightly, with twins costing from £25 ($57.50) to £31 ($71.30). Provincial French dishes are among the offerings in the restaurant which has good food, fine service, and a bright, cheery decor.

SULGRAVE MANOR: On your way from Oxford to Stratford-upon-Avon, you can visit Sulgrave Manor, the ancestral home of George Washington. First, you'll come to **Banbury,** a market town famed in the nursery rhyme, immortalizing the lady upon the white horse. The old Banbury Cross was destroyed by the Roundheads, but was replaced in Victoria's day. Eight miles northeast of Banbury will take you to Sulgrave Manor, a small Tudor manorial house, built in about the mid-16th century. Follow the A422 east from Banbury toward Brackley. Go left on the B4525 toward Northampton until you pick up the signs to Sulgrave.

As part of Henry VIII's plan to dissolve monasteries, he sold the priory-owned manor in 1539 to Lawrence Washington, who had been mayor of Northampton. George Washington was a direct descendant of Lawrence (seven generations removed). The Washington family occupied Sulgrave for more than a century. In 1656, Col. John Washington left for the New World.

In 1914 the manor was purchased by a group of English people in honor of the friendship between Britain and America. Over the years, major restoration has taken place (a whole new wing had to be added), with an eye toward returning it as much as possible to its original state. The Colonial Dames have been largely responsible for raising the money. From both sides of the Atlantic the appropriate furnishings were donated, including a number of portraits—even a Gilbert Stuart original of the first president. On the main doorway is the Washington family coat-of-arms—two bars and a trio of mullets—which is believed to have been the inspiration for the "Stars and Stripes."

The manor is open daily except Wednesday from April 1 to September 30, 10:30 a.m. to 1 p.m. and from 2 to 5:30 p.m. From October to March the hours are from 10:30 a.m. to 1 p.m. and from 2 to 4 p.m. It's closed in January. Admission is 50p ($1.15) for adults, 25p (58¢) for children.

Food and Lodging

Across from Sulgrave Manor is the **Thatched House Hotel** (tel. Sulgrave 232), a long, low group of thatched 17th-century cottages, with a front garden full of flowers. It's a good place to stop for afternoon tea, served at a table in either the beamed living or dining room, furnished with antiques. You'll get a pot of tea with homemade scones, jam, thick cream, and cakes, £1.35 ($3.11). In season, a tea with strawberries and thick cream may be served for an additional cost.

The owners, Eileen and Ron Walpole, offer delicious lunches in the £4.50 ($10.35) to £8 ($18.40) price range, and dinners from £6.50 ($14.95) to £11 ($25.30). A former hotel consultant, Mr. Walpole will rent you one of his well-furnished singles for £12 ($27.60) or a double with bath for £22.50 ($51.75) to £25 ($57.50) price range, including an English breakfast and VAT.

OUNDLE: A good stopover after Cambridge, if you're driving north, is Oundle in Northamptonshire, 80 miles from London. It's a pleasant old stone town with a fine church dating back to the 14th century. Its Latham almshouses date from 1611. Those motorists moving between East Anglia and Northeastern England will find a warm welcome at—

The **Talbot Hotel,** Oundle, Northamptonshire (tel. Oundle 3621), an ancient inn last reconstructed in 1626. An arch from the street leads to the yard and a pleasant garden in the rear. At this busy country-town pub, with its many beams and old pictures, the oak staircase is reputed to have come from Fotheringhay Castle where Mary Queen of Scots was imprisoned and then executed in 1587. Most of the bedrooms have private bath, color TV, and radio. Singles without bath rent for £18.50 ($42.55), that rate going up to £23.50 ($54.05) with bath. Bathless doubles are priced at £28 ($64.40), that rate going up to £33 ($75.90) with bath, these tariffs including breakfast and VAT. The hotel is warm and well furnished. Meals are quickly and efficiently provided from a wide menu of grills and roasts. This is a typical country-town inn, catering to local business people, but welcoming strangers, too, in their long tradition as a coaching inn.

AT WEEDON: The **Crossroads Hotel,** High Street, Weedon (tel. Weedon 40354), is a true crossroad hotel, off the M1, the A5, and A45. The owners, Richard and Wendy Amos, have created a little nook where imagination and good taste reign. The clock tower of the hotel, standing in the garden, is a sign of hospitality. Inside there is a fascinating collection of old clocks throughout the dining room and lounges. The antique collection in the dining room is enhanced with stuffed fish, horse prints, birds in cages, a Victorian carved sideboard, old bicycles hanging from the ceiling, and etched mirrors. There's a large brick oven, and, best of all, excellent meals are offered. The house specialty is "Wendy's famous steak, kidney, and mushroom pie," served with vegetables for £4.35 ($10.01). The bedrooms, with color TV sets, are handsomely decorated, singles renting for £16.75 ($38.53) bathless, £20.50 ($47.15) with bath. Bathless doubles are £25.90 ($59.57), going up to £30 ($69) with bath. Included is a continental breakfast.

2. Leicestershire

Virtually ignored by most North American tourists, this eastern Midland county was the home of King Lear and is rich in historical associations.

LEICESTER: Although the county town is a busy industrial center, it was once a Roman settlement and has a forum and other sites that remind one of those days.

It also has a Norman castle-hall, a period museum, a 15th-century Guildhall (Shakespeare is said to have played here), and many interesting gardens. On its abbey park and grounds are the remains of Leicester Abbey, Cardinal

Wolsey's grave, a boating lake, paddling pool, riverside walks, a miniature railway, ornamental gardens, and an aviary.

You can ask at the Information Bureau on Bishop Street (tel. Leicester 20644) for details of guided walks around the city or inquire of the **City Transport** on Rutland Street (tel. Leicester 24326) about double-decker bus tours.

Food and Lodging

Grand Hotel, Granby Street (tel. Leicester 56222), is aptly named, a grandiose Victorian pile in the heart of Leicester. Greatly improved in recent years, it is modernized period piece that retains its oak and mahogany paneling in profusion, particularly in a quartet of bars. The grand staircase still calls for an entrance. Its Kings Hall banqueting suite has for decades enjoyed a reputation for dining in the grand manner. The completely refurbished bedrooms have a bright, cheery decor, and all have been equipped with private baths. Singles cost from £28 ($64.40), doubles from £34 ($78.20).

Holiday Inn, St. Nicholas Circle (tel. Leicester 51161), is smart and stylish, much warmer on its interior than its rather plain facade would suggest. Its enclosed swimming pool is a special feature, and plants and flowers throughout the hotel soften the modernity. Bedrooms, for the most part, are well furnished, with good, large beds, carpeting, private baths, radios, color TV sets, direct-dial phones, and individually controlled air conditioning. Rates begin at £26 ($59.80) in a single, going up to £34 ($78.20) in a double. We'd suggest a meal in the Hayloft Restaurant, with its collection of rustically decorated small lofts. The menu is wide ranging, and the dishes are well prepared and presented, a complete dinner costing about £12 ($27.60) per person.

TOURING THE COUNTRY: As long as people continue to read Sir Walter Scott's *Ivanhoe*, they will remember **Ashby-de-la-Zouch,** a town that retains a pleasant country atmosphere. Mary Queen of Scots was imprisoned in an ancient castle here.

If you're in the area, you might want to dine at the **Fallen Knight Restaurant,** 16 Kilwardby St. (tel. Ashby-de-la-Zouch 2230), a small place that takes its name from a resident suit of armor. A rustic decor is created by the plain wooden tables and ladderback chairs. The menu is like a "taste of England," with some good, country-style cookery and some imaginative dishes. The hospitable staff adds to the pleasant stopover—lunch till 2 and dinner from 7 to 10:30 p.m. No lunch is served on Saturday, no dinner on Sunday. Meals are from £7 ($16.10) per person.

On the northern border of Leicestershire, **Belvoir Castle** has been the seat of the Dukes of Rutland since Henry VIII's time, overlooking the Vale of Belvoir. Rebuilt by Wyatt in 1816, the castle contains paintings by Holbein, Poussin, and Gainsborough, as well as tapestries in its magnificent state rooms. The location is seven miles west-southwest of Grantham, between the A607 to Melton Mowbray and the A52 to Nottingham. It is open from Easter to the end of September on Wednesday, Thursday, and Saturday from noon to 6 p.m., on Sunday from 2 to 7 p.m. (except in June, July, and August when Sunday hours are noon to 7 p.m.), and bank holiday Mondays from 11 a.m. to 7 p.m. Special events, such as medieval jousting tournaments, mock battles, and hawking and falconry displays, are held most Sundays throughout the summer months.

Other interesting towns to visit in Leicestershire include **Melton Mowbray**, a famous fox-hunting center and market town which claims to be the original home of Stilton cheese and is renowned for its delicious pork pies.

For a sample of this town's gastronomy, we'd recommend **Dickinson & Morris Ltd.**, 10 Nottingham St., in Melton Mowbray, which is an unlicensed cafe in a 17th-century structure. By tradition, the first Melton pork pie was baked here, and you can sample it today, based on an old recipe, costing from £1.20 ($2.76). The Melton Hunt cake (rich fruit) is made in the bakery shop to the rear, going for 35p (81¢) a serving. The cafe, called also Ye Olde Pork Pie Shop, serves from 8:30 a.m. to 5 p.m. only. Closed Sunday and public holidays.

3. Derbyshire

The most magnificent scenery in the Midlands is found within the borders of this county, lying between Nottinghamshire and Staffordshire. Derbyshire has been less defaced by industry than its neighbors. The north of the county, containing the **Peak District National Park,** is by far the most exciting for touring, as it contains waterfalls, hills, moors, green valleys, and dales. In the south the land is more level, and the look becomes, in places, one of pastoral meadows.

Some tourists avoid this part of the country, because it is ringed by the industrial sprawl of Manchester, Leeds, Sheffield, and Derby. To do so, however, would be a pity, and this part of England contains the rugged peaks and leafy dales which merit a substantial detour, especially Dovedale, Chee Dale, and Millers Dale.

Chatsworth House, home of the Dukes of Devonshire, and **Haddon Hall,** home of the Duke of Rutland, are worth a visit. Melbourne Hall, Kedlestone, and Hardwick Hall are also open to view.

OTHER PLACES TO SEE: In addition to majestic scenery, you may want to seek out the following specific sights.

Tramway Museum, Crich, near Matlock (tel. Ambergate 2565). One young 65-year-old whom we know spends as much of his free time as his wife will allow in the paradise of trams—electric, steam, and horse-drawn. Your admission ticket is £1 ($2.30) for adults, 50p ($1.15) for children. This ticket allows you to ride on the tram which makes a round trip to Glory mine with scenic views over the Derwent Valley, then back through Wakebridge where a stop is made to visit the Peak District Mines Historical Society display of lead mining. It also includes admission to the tramway exhibition and museum. It is open every Saturday and Sunday from April to October, and daily, except Monday and Friday, from mid-May to the end of August (also open Monday from the end of July to mid-August). Hours are from 10 a.m. until some time in the late afternoon.

Peak District Mining Museum, The Pavilion, Matlock Bath (tel. Matlock 3834), is open year round, daily (except for Christmas Day) from 11 a.m. to 4 p.m. Admission is 60p ($1.38) for adults, 30p (69¢) for children. The main exhibit of this display of 2000 years of Derbyshire lead mining is a giant water pressure engine, used to pump water from the mines and itself rescued from 360 feet underground by members of the society before being brought to the museum.

Magpie Mine, at Sheldon, near Bakewell, has been the site of much desperate toil, murders, vendettas, and enormous financial losses. In summer the surface remains of the lead mine (the underground workings are dangerous) are open to view from 2:30 to 4 p.m. The cost is 30p (69¢) for adults, 20p (46¢) for children. This is definitely a specialist tour, but it is representative of conditions which existed in the 18th- and 19th-century English countryside.

The **Red House Stables,** Old Road, Darley Dale, near Matlock (tel. Darley Dale 3583). Caroline Dale's father collected coaches and carriages as a hobby, restored them, and used them for his own pleasure, driving through the Peakland countryside. Today, the carriages and horses are available for the pleasure of anyone who wants to learn to drive a four-in-hand (as Prince Philip does), a pair or a tandem. An introductory course of three days costs £70 ($161), but if you already have some experience in driving, tuition is available by the hour or day, ranging from £8 ($18.40) an hour for a single, £32 ($73.60) an hour for a four-in-hand. A four-hour day with a pair or a tandem is £60 ($138).

If you would rather someone else drove so that you could enjoy the scenery, Mrs. Dale operates special drives through Chatsworth Park with halts at local inns for refreshment in traditional style. A stagecoach—yes, a real one—or a four-in-hand which seats 14 people costs £120 ($276). Or, if you require your coach to wait while you have lunch, £140 ($320). For a party of four, a landau and pair is more suitable at £40 ($92), or £50 ($115) if you stop for lunch. These prices include the use of the coach and the services of the coachman, but your meal and drinks are at your own expense.

Two or three times a year, a luxury three-day tour of the Peak District in the stagecoach Gay Gordon leaves the stables with a fanfare of posthorns. Overnights are spent in traditional coaching inns, and meals during the day, plus your overnight accommodations, will cost £200 ($460) per person.

These tours are very popular, and the coaches are often busy with film and television work, weddings, and private parties, so it is worth booking early. Mrs. Dale also has riding horses at livery. An hour will cost £4 ($9.20); a day's trek, £20 ($46) (bring your own picnic basket and bad-weather clothing).

BUXTON: One of the loveliest towns in Britain, Buxton was built in the 18th century to rival the spa at Bath. Although it eventually fell into a decline, it is now being considerably revived. The 18th-century opera house, for years the local movie palace, is being restored, and will be the centerpiece for a festival featuring Britain's National Theatre. Buxton is 20 miles southeast of Manchester and 163 miles northwest of London.

Of its old buildings, the finest is the Crescent, built by the fifth Duke of Devonshire between 1780 and 1784. The Pump Room, opened in 1894, now houses the Tourist Information Centre, in which you may drink the water from Buxton's natural springs.

ASHBOURNE: This old market town has a 13th-century church, a 16th-century grammar school, and ancient almshouses.

For accommodations, we recommend—

Green Man Hotel (tel. Ashbourne 3861), in the town center, has many historical connections going back to 1710. In 1777, Dr. Samuel Johnson and his biographer, James Boswell, stayed at the inn, and Boswell writes, "I took my post-chaise from the Green Man, a very good inn." In the Tap Room you can still see the chairs of Boswell and Johnson. Even Princess Victoria and her widowed mother, the Duchess of Kent, halted here and gave the inn the right to add "Royal" to its name. This red brick posting inn has retained its tradition-

DERBYSHIRE: BUXTON/DOVEDALE

al character, although modern amenities have been added. You can get a bathless double for £22.50 ($51.75); with bath, £24 ($55.20). Bathless singles are £15.50 ($35.65); with bath, £17 ($39.10). There are 17 rooms, each well decorated, and all tariffs include breakfast, early-morning coffee, and VAT. Service is extra. Luncheons and evening dinners are offered in the Shrovetide Restaurants, selections made from an à la carte menu.

On the Outskirts

Pervil of the Peak, Thorpe, near Ashbourne (tel. Thorpe Cloud 333), is a low, rambling hotel which may have been the Thorpe rectory. Offering 29 handsomely furnished bedrooms, it stands at the foot of Thorpe Cloud, a 900-foot peak guarding the gateway to Dovedale, an area preserved by the National Trust which incorporates 5000 acres of the Peak District. A Trust Houses Forte hotel, it charges from £21.50 ($49.45) daily in a bathless single, from £25.40 ($58.42) in a single with bath, including breakfast, service, and VAT. Doubles go for £28 ($64.40) if bathless, rising to £30 ($69) with bath. Most units have private plumbing.

The interior is paneled in natural pine, combined with local stone walls, and large picture windows open onto the big country garden, where a hard tennis court is situated. The attractively decorated hotel restaurant offers both table d'hôte and à la carte meals, a set luncheon going from £5.70 ($13.11), a set dinner costing from £7 ($16.10).

DOVEDALE: Overhung by limestone crags, this beautiful wooded valley forms part of the Peak District National Park, with its views of Thorpe Cloud, a conical hill 900 feet high. It's best explored on foot. Fishermen know of its River Dove trout stream, because of its associations with such famous anglers as Izaak Walton and Charles Cotton. One is honored by the hotel named after him (previewed below).

The **Izaak Walton Hotel,** Dovedale (tel. Thorpe Cloud 261). Even the telephone exchange—Thorpe Cloud—has a romantic ring about it. This is a very comfortable hotel in what was originally a 17th-century farmhouse. Most of the rooms have private bathrooms, and the views over the dales and peaks of Derbyshire are unsurpassed. This is ideal rambling country, with Dovedale spreading before you.

A single room will cost £25 ($57.50); a double, £24 ($78.20)—including service and VAT. A massive breakfast is £3 ($6.90); luncheon, £6 ($13.80). A set dinner at £9 ($20.70) offers an excellent variety of appetizers, three entrees, and a cold buffet, followed by dessert and coffee. Or else you can make selections from a pleasant country menu where a meal will cost around £10 ($23).

This is the country for the fisherman, as the name implies, but if that is not your scene, it is an excellent center for touring, with Haddon Hall, Chatsworth House, and Hardwick Hall, to name but a few, lying within easy reach.

FOOD AND LODGING ELSEWHERE IN DERBYSHIRE:
The **Howard Hotel,** Friar Gate, Derby (tel. Derby 43455), is a small elegant city house run by Charles Price as a pleasant hotel, ideally situated for visitors to the peaks and dales or those just passing along the M1 from London to Scotland. Bedrooms are warm and comfortable, with radio and wash basin, and go for £12 ($27.60) in a single, £15 ($34.50) in a double. There is a TV in the small lounge. Room rates include a full English breakfast, and there is a pleasant dining room where a set meal costs £5 ($11.50). In the cellars, reputedly part of the old

Derby jail, lurks or burgeons the Secret Place, with music and dancing nightly until 2 a.m. Meals in the basket are served until 11 p.m.

Peacock Hotel, Rowsley, near Matlock (tel. Darley Dale 833518), is a charming old house with a creeper covering the front door, where fishermen gather with tales of catches in the nearby Wye and Derwent Rivers. Just up the valley is Chatsworth House and down the road is Bakewell, where the tarts (a sort of maccaroon with jam) come from. Accommodations reflect the informal country atmosphere, with patterned curtains, deep beds, and well-appointed baths. The lounge and dining room gleam with well-polished woods. The reception area is informal, decorated with trophies from bygone battles. A single room will cost £15 ($34.50), £23 ($52.90) in a double. Lunch is £4 ($9.20); dinner, £8 ($18.40). Meals are served beneath low beams in the dining room by friendly local waitresses. Details of local walks and other attractions are available, and the hotel has fishing rights on local waters.

Rutland Arms, The Square, Bakewell (tel. Bakewell 2812), is a lovely old hotel on the edge of town, offering comfort and good food. There are a comfortable lounge and bar, plus a dining room that has an excellent local reputation. Dinner includes such delicacies as chicken suprême, wienerschnitzel, fresh seafood from the East Coast, and scotch roast beef, costing around £8 ($18.40) per person. Rooms are well equipped and have private bathrooms. To keep costs down, there is no porterage or room service. Overnight will cost £18 ($41.40) in a single, £26 ($59.80) in a double, including VAT and an English breakfast.

Cavendish Hotel, Baslow, near Bakewell (tel. Baslow 2311), is the most select choice for food and hotel accommodations in the entire Peak District. It's a well-preserved Georgian stone manor house, part of the estate of the Dukes of Devonshire. Under the supervision of the Duchess, this gem of a house was completely redecorated. The hotel is small, only 13 rooms, and it's owned and managed by Eric Marsh and a small team of professional colleagues. The style and standard are comparable to the most highly rated of British inns, including Chewton Glen and Gravetye Manor. Some of the furnishings of the house came from Chatsworth, home of the Cavendish family for four centuries.

All guest bedrooms face due south, with a wide view of the park and encircling hills. Twin- or double-bedded rooms rent for £30 ($69) nightly. Singles aren't available; however, sole occupancy of a double costs from £25 ($57.50). All units feature an en suite private bath with shower, phone, color TV, and a mini-bar. The Park Top cocktail bar is a sophisticated rendezvous, and after a drink you can go to the Paxton Room where classical cookery, beautifully served, is presented. The menu includes many unusual dishes such as game specialties.

4. Nottinghamshire

"Notts," as it is called, was the county of Robin Hood and Lord Byron. It is also Lawrence country, as the English novelist, author of *Sons and Lovers* and *Lady Chatterley's Lover,* was also from here, born at Eastwood. Although Sherwood Forest isn't the green wood paradise it used to be, it did provide in its time excellent cover for its world-famous bandit and his band, including Friar Tuck and Little John.

Nottinghamshire is so rarely visited by foreign tourists that its beautiful landscapes could almost be called "undiscovered," although British trippers know of its hidden villages and numerous parks.

NOTTINGHAM: The county town is a busy industrial city, 121 miles north of London. On the north bank of the Trent, Nottingham is one of the most pleasant cities in the Midlands.

Overlooking the city, **Nottingham Castle** was built by the Duke of Newcastle on the site of a Norman fortress in 1679. After restoration in 1878, it was opened as a provincial museum, surrounded by a charmingly laid-out garden. See, in particular, the collection of medieval Nottingham alabaster carvings. The works of Nottingham-born artists are displayed in the first-floor gallery. The admission-free castle is open from April to September, daily from 10 a.m. to 6:45 p.m. (Friday until 6, Sunday till 5). Otherwise, its hours are daily from 10 to 4:45.

For 25p (58¢), 10p (23¢) on Sunday and bank holidays, you'll be taken on a conducted tour at the castle of **Mortimer's Hole** and underground passages. King Edward III is said to have led a band of noblemen through these secret passages, surprising Roger Mortimer and the queen, killing Mortimer, and putting his lady in prison. A statue of Robin Hood stands at the base of the castle.

More recently opened, the **Brewhouse Yard Museum** consists of five 17th-century cottages at the foot of Castle Rock, presenting a panorama of Nottingham life in a series of furnished rooms. Some of them, open from cellar to garret, have much local history material on open display, and visitors are encouraged to handle these exhibits. The most interesting features are in a series of cellars cut into the rock of the castle itself instead of below the houses. This is not a typical folk museum, but attempts to be as lively as possible, involving both visitors and the Nottingham community in expanding displays and altering exhibitions on a bimonthly basis.

An elegant row of Georgian terraced houses, the **Museum of Costume and Textiles** at Castle Gate, presents lace, textile, and costume collections of one of the city's great industries. You'll see everything from the 1632 Eyre map tapestries of Nottingham to "fallals and frippery." The admission-free museum is open daily from 10 a.m. to 5 p.m.

On the outskirts of Nottingham, at Linby, **Newstead Abbey** was once Lord Byron's home. It lies 11 miles north of Nottingham on the A60 (the Mansfield Road). Some of the original Augustinian priory, bought by Sir John Byron in 1540, still survives. In the 19th century the mansion was given a neo-Gothic restoration. The poet's bedroom is somewhat as he left it. Mementos, including first editions and manuscripts, are displayed inside, and, later, you can explore a parkland of some 300 acres, with waterfalls, rose gardens, a Monk's Stew Pond, and a Japanese water garden.

The gardens are open all year from 10 a.m. to dusk. Adults are charged 40p (92¢) for admission; children pay 12p (28¢). The abbey is open from Easter to October, daily from 2 to 6 p.m. adults pay an admission of 30p (69¢); children, 10p (23¢). There is a tearoom open during the summer.

Also on the outskirts of Nottingham, **Wollaton Hall** is a well-preserved Elizabethan mansion, housing a natural history museum, with lots of insects, invertebrates, and British mammals, along with reptiles and crustaceans, some a long way from their former home in the South Seas. The mansion is open, April to September, on Wednesday and Friday from 10 a.m. to 5:30 p.m., on Thursday and Saturday from 10 to 7, and on Sunday from 2 to 5. From October to March its hours are 10 a.m. to 4:30 p.m. on Thursday and Saturday, 1:30 to 4 on Sunday. Admission is free. The hall is surrounded by a deer park and gardens.

Food and Lodging

Albany Hotel, St James's Street (tel. Nottingham 40131), a Trust Houses Forte hotel, is a large tower block of 160 bedrooms in the heart of the city. Flanked by multistory car parks, it offers good rooms, each with private bath, double-glazed windows, air conditioning, and central heating, as well as a color TV, radio, direct-dial phone, and coffee-making facilities. Singles rent for £38 ($87.40) nightly, doubles going for £50 ($115).

In the hotel's Carvery, guests can carve as much as they wish from prime hot and cold joints, or else patronize the more elegant Four Seasons, which, in honor of its namesake, changes its menu and floral decorations quarterly. Along with seasonal specialties, continental dishes are featured. The Forum, the lounge and cocktail bar, is a sleek rendezvous.

Savoy Hotel, Mansfield Road (tel. Nottingham 602-621), stands on the A60 Nottingham–Mansfield Road, a little less than a mile from the city center. A bustling, modern hotel, it is immaculately maintained and efficiently run, and there's plenty of room to park your car. Attracting business people (and likely to be heavily booked on weekdays), it offers well-furnished, streamlined rooms for £24 ($55.20) daily in a single, £31 ($71.30) in a double, including private baths (some have showers), color TVs, radios, and phones. Have a predinner drink in Fagin's Bar, its decor inspired by the Dickensian atmosphere of the 19th century, before dining in one of two steak bars or else the Colonial Restaurant.

Strathdon Hotel, 44 Derby Rd. (tel. Nottingham 48501), a favorite of traveling business people, lies about five miles from the M1, in the center of the city. Of the 67 bedrooms (the majority of which are singles), 23 come with private and pleasant tiled bath, the rest with shower, although all have color TV, phone, radio, and coffee-making facilities. The rate for either a twin- or double-bedded room is £37 ($85.10) from Monday to Thursday, the tariff lowered to £30 ($69) from Friday to Sunday. Breakfast is extra. Drinks are ordered in the dark-paneled Jacobite Lounge, its swords and shields giving it a Highland manor-house aura. In the hotel's restaurant, a good table d'hôte evening meal goes from £7 ($16.10). The cookery is acceptable, and some international dishes are featured along with traditional English fare.

The **Bridgford Hotel,** Trent Bridge (tel. Nottingham 868-661), attracts not only the business person, but the sports lover as well, as it lies near cricket and football grounds. Sleek modernity is the keynote in the standard bedroom units which have private baths, paneling, and modern appointments. The cost is £30 ($69) nightly in a double, £35 ($80.50) in a double or twin, or £40 ($92) in a triple, these tariffs including a full English breakfast. The Riverside Restaurant opens onto views of the Trent River and the embankment beyond, serving both table d'hôte and à la carte menus. The hotel, which has its own car park and disco, lies about ten miles from the center of Nottingham, about nine miles from the M1 motorway (A52 south of A610 north).

Farmhouse Dining on the Outskirts

Grange Farm, Toton (tel. Long Eaton 69426), is an old English farmhouse, built in 1691, serving traditional English fare and run by the Ackroyd family. This busy Nottinghamshire restaurant serves lunch Monday to Saturday from noon to 2 p.m., a set meal costing £5 ($11.50), inclusive of VAT, service charge, and coffee. The chefs prepare an excellent choice of interesting starters and many homemade English dishes—for example, steak-and-kidney pudding, venison pie, braised steak in Burgundy sauce, followed by a large variety of desserts and cheeses. Dinner is served in two sittings, 7 and 8:30 p.m., a set meal costing £8 ($18.40), inclusive. Dinner is similar to lunch with an addition of an extra course. For example, you may also enjoy battered mushrooms in sweet-and-sour sauce or fried whitebait. It is advisable to telephone for a reservation to avoid disappointment. Saturday nights, the restaurant has a dinner-dance, which is popular. There is a fine collection of porcelain and ivories in the lounges which should be seen. Grange Farm has excellent car parking facilities and is six easy miles from Nottingham.

About a half-hour's drive from Lord Byron's Newstead Abbey leads to—

SOUTHWELL: This ancient market town is a good center for exploring the Robin Hood country. Byron once belonged to a local amateur dramatic society here. An unexpected gem is the old twin-spired cathedral, **Southwell Minster,** which many consider the most beautiful church in England. James I found that it held up with "any other kirk in Christendom." Look for the well-proportioned Georgian houses across from the cathedral.

Saracen's Head, Market Place (tel. Southwell 681-2701), is a historic coaching inn, where both Charles I and James I dined. In fact, Charles I was made a prisoner here before the Scots handed him over to the Parliamentarians. After he was beheaded, the name of the inn was changed from King's Arms to Saracen's Head. Commanding the junction of the main ancient thoroughfares of the town, the old hostelry also frequently entertained Byron. Today, your hosts are Joanna and René Koomen, who are proud of its old atmosphere, such as cozy bars with exposed beams and fine old paneling. The bedrooms are up-to-date, however, each containing a private bath, TV, radio, and phone. Doubles cost from £24 ($55.20), and singles begin at £16 ($36.80). From the well-stocked cellar emerges a good selection of wines to complement a meal, with both an à la carte and a table d'hôte menu.

East of Southwell, near the Lincolnshire border—

NEWARK-ON-TRENT: Here is an ancient riverside market town, on the Roman Fosse Way, lying about 15 miles across flatlands from Nottingham. King John died at **Newark Castle** in 1216. Constructed between the 12th and 15th centuries, the castle—now in ruins—survived three sieges by Cromwell's troops before falling into ruin in 1646. From its parapet, you can look down on the Trent River and across to Nottingham. The delicately detailed parish church here is said to be the finest in the country. The town contains many ancient inns, reflecting its long history.

THE DUKERIES: In the Dukeries, portions of Sherwood Forest, legendarily associated with Robin Hood, are still preserved. These are vast country estates on the edge of industrial towns. Most of the estates have disappeared, but the part at **Clumber**—covering some 4000 acres—is administered by the National Trust, which has preserved its 18th-century beauty, as exemplified by Lime Tree Avenue. Rolling heaths and a peaceful lake add to the charm. You can visit Clumber Chapel, built in 1886-1889 as a chapel for the seventh Duke of Newcastle. It is open April 5 to September 30 Monday to Friday from 2 to 7 p.m. On weekends its hours are noon to 7 p.m. Off-season hours are daily, 1 to 4. There is no admission charge, but car entry charge to the park is 90p ($2.07). The location is at Clumber Park, five miles southeast of Worksop.

A few miles south of Clumber stands the greatest Victorian house in the Midlands, **Thoresby Hall.** Built by Salvin in 1864, it is the only mansion in the Dukeries still occupied as the home of the original owners. Barton & Skills run tours from Nottingham. The hall is open to the public during June, July, and August. It lies four miles north of Ollerton, just west of the Bawtry Road (A614).

EASTWOOD: Because of the increased interest in D. H. Lawrence these days, many literary fans like to make a pilgrimage to Eastwood, his hometown. The English novelist was born there on September 11, 1885. Mrs. Brown, a member of the D. H. Lawrence Society, conducts parties of visitors around the "Lawrence country." Hopefully, at the end, you'll make a donation to the society. If you're interested in taking a tour, write her in advance—Mrs. M. Brown, D. H. Lawrence Society, c/o 8A Victoria St., Eastwood, Nottingham (tel. Langley Mill 68139).

5. Lincolnshire

This large East Midlands county is bordered on one side by the North Sea. Its most interesting section is Holland, in the southeast, a land known for its fields of tulips, its marshes and fens, and windmills reminiscent of the Netherlands. Although much of the shire is interesting to explore, time is too important for most visitors to linger long. Foreign tourists, particularly North Americans, generally cross the tulip fields, scheduling stopovers in the busy port of Boston before making the swing north to the cathedral city of Lincoln, lying inland.

BOSTON: This old seaport in the riding of Holland has a namesake that has gone on to greater glory, and perhaps for this reason it is visited by New Englanders. At Scotia Creek, on a river bank near Boston, is a memorial to the early Pilgrims who made an unsuccessful attempt in 1607 to reach the promised land. They were imprisoned in the Guildhall in cells that can be visited today. A company left again in 1620—and fared better, as anybody who has ever been to Massachusetts will testify. Part of the ritual here is climbing the Boston Stump, a church lantern tower with a view for miles around of the all-encircling fens. In the 1930s, the people of Boston, U.S.A., paid for the restoration of the tower, known officially as St. Botolph's Tower. Actually, it's not recommended that you climb the tower, as the stairs aren't in good shape. The tower, as it stands, was finished in 1460. The city fathers were going to add a spire, making it the tallest in England. But because of the wind and the weight, they feared the tower would collapse. Therefore, the tower became known as "the Boston Stump." An elderly gentleman at the tower assured us it was the tallest in England—that is, 272½ feet tall. Boston is 116 miles north from London, and 34 miles southeast of Lincoln.

Food and Lodging

White Hart Hotel, High Street (tel. Boston 64877), is a gleaming white hotel, built against the high wall of a canal embankment. A bathless single rents for £12 ($27.60); a bathless double is priced at £21 ($48.30), going up to £24 ($55.20), with bath. These tariffs include a full breakfast, service, and VAT. Rooms are pleasantly furnished, with central or electrical heating and a radio, and are kept immaculate. A bonus is the free car park at the rear of the hotel (you drive through an old coaching alleyway).

The White Hart contains half a dozen bars, each one decorated differently, serving draft sherries and beer, as well as spirits and food. Of the two restaurants, one features duck and steak dishes; the other, fish and chicken specialties. A meal costs around £6 ($13.80) to £7 ($16.10), and hours are from noon to 2:30 p.m. and 6 to 11 p.m.

LINCOLN: One of the most ancient cities of England, and only 135 miles north of London, Lincoln was known to the Romans as Lindum. Some of the architectural glory of the Roman Empire still stands to charm the present-day visitor. The renowned Newport Arch (the North Gate) is the last remaining arch left in Britain that still spans a principal highway. For a look at the Roman relics excavated in and around Lincoln, head for the **City and County Museum,** Broadgate—open daily from 10 a.m. to 5:30 p.m. (2:30 to 5 p.m. on Sunday).

Two years after the Battle of Hastings, William the Conqueror built a castle on the site of a Roman fortress. Used for administrative purposes, parts of the castle still remain, including the walls, the 12th-century keep, and fragments of the gateway tower. In addition, you can visit the high bridge over the Witham River, with its half-timbered houses (you can have a meal in one of them). This is one of the few medieval bridges left in England that has buildings nestling on it.

Lincoln Cathedral

Towering over the ancient city, the Minster forms a grand sight, with its three towers. The central one is 271 feet tall, making it the second tallest in England, ranking under the Boston Stump, mentioned earlier. However, the central tower at Lincoln was once the tallest spire in the world (525 feet) until it blew down in 1549. There are regular summer trips up the tower on weekdays, costing 60p ($1.38) for adults, 35p (81¢) for children. The Norman cathedral was consecrated in 1092, but only the west front remains. The cathedral represents the Gothic style, particularly the Early English and decorated periods. The nave, in its present form, was built in the early 13th century. In the Early English Great Transept, you can see a rose medallion window, known as the Dean's Eye. The rose window at the opposite end of the transept—in the decorated style—is known as the Bishop's Eye. The Angel Choir, in the eastern end, consecrated on October 6, 1280, is named after the sculptured angels displayed in it. The exquisite carving in the choir dates from the 14th century. The black font of Tournai marble is from the 11th century.

In the Seamen's Chapel is a window commemorating Lincolnshire-born Capt. John Smith, one of the pioneers of early settlement in America and the first governor of Virginia.

The Library, in the Cloister, was built in 1674 by Sir Christopher Wren. It contains many fine books and manuscripts, some of which are on view in the adjoining Medieval Library (1422), together with one of the four remaining original copies of the Magna Carta of 1215, the Cathedral Charter of 1072, and the Foresters' Charter of 1225. The Library is open Monday through Saturday, 10:30 a.m. to 4:30 p.m. Easter through September, and in winter by appointment (tel. Lincoln 21089).

In the Treasury (open weekdays 2:30 to 4:30 p.m., Easter through September), there is fine gold and silver plate from churches in the diocese.

Admission to the cathedral is 60p ($1.38) for adults, 35p (81¢) for children.

Where to Stay

Eastgate Hotel, Eastgate (tel. Lincoln 20341), should put to shame those critics who resist contemporary architecture, especially in old English cathedral cities. A hotel attached to a Victorian mansion (now the Eastgate Bar), the Trust House occupies a historic site: in fact, when workmen were digging its foundations in the mid-'60s, they discovered the remnants of the north tower of the East Gate of Roman Lincoln. Many of the large bedrooms, 16 with balconies, offer unimpaired views of the cathedral. The airy main lounge, with its high slat ceiling and overscale windows, is spacious, furnished with compact, tasteful pieces. The modern bedrooms, each with a private bath, telephone, radio, picture window, and Nordic-style appurtenances, are inviting and rent for £26 ($59.80) in a single, from £36 ($82.80) in a double, all with private baths. The rates include service and VAT. The wood-paneled dining room, warmed by vibrant colors, offers an extensive à la carte menu, plus a set lunch for £6 ($13.80), a set dinner for £7 ($16.10). In addition, the Eastgate runs a good coffeeshop, serving the usual grilled and fried dishes, plus one specialty every day. A coffeeshop meal averages around £4 ($9.20), and you get a fine view of the cathedral as well.

The **White Hart,** Bailgate (tel. Lincoln 26222), is a red brick Georgian inn, with its corner clock and miniature figure of a white hart, right in the shadow of the cathedral, within the range of its chimes. On Lincoln's historic mile, the inn is unpretentious, and skillfully operated by a well-trained staff. Oldtimers respect the ambience, as reflected in the large living room opening onto a hothouse and patio garden. High mahogany cabinets hold a collection of old silver and porcelain; overstuffed chairs are set around tables for after-dinner coffee; and there are antiques in the reception lounges and corridors, including the more intimate upstairs residents' lounge. The bedrooms have nice old furnishings, with such pieces as a pedestal swivel mirror or a mahogany table. Each has a telephone and radio, and many have private baths.

Depending on the facilities, singles range in price from £21 ($48.30) to £26 ($59.80), and doubles go from £28 ($64.40) to £41 ($94.30). In the olive and red dining room, you'll be served some of the finest English fare in Lincoln, a meal costing from £6 ($13.80) to £8 ($18.40). Very good sandwiches are served with coffee or tea in the lounge throughout the day, and you can also enjoy the same in a patio and garden bar known as the Orangery.

Grand Hotel, St. Mary Street (tel. Lincoln 24211), is a good bet for the seeker of economy, as it's an extensively remodeled hotel, top-heavy with contemporary amenities and a cooperative staff. It offers bathless doubles for £31 ($71.30). But you'll pay around £33 ($75.90) for a double with a private bath. Singles go for £19 ($43.70) without bath, £21 ($48.30) with bath. The Grand's program of redecorating has given it a pleasant, spacious look. The West Bar and the lounges are streamlined, but the Tudor Bar pays homage to the past. The bedrooms are compact, with many built-in features and coordinated colors. The Grand is easy to spot, as it lies opposite the bus depot. It's a long walk to the cathedral, however, but you can hop a bus. Its food is a top-notch bargain, both in price and taste. From 6:30 to 8:30 p.m., a table d'hôte dinner is offered for £5.20 ($11.96). Meals are inclusive, priced according to the entree. The food is not only good and typically English, but the portions are ample. You can also lunch at the Grand from noon to 2 p.m. A buttery is open from 11 a.m. to 10 p.m.

Where to Eat

Harveys Cathedral Restaurant, 1 Exchequergate, Castle Square (tel. Lincoln 21886), lies in the heart of the old town, a short walk from the cathedral and the castle. Our favored dining spot in the city, it is run by Adrianne and Bob Harvey, whose children may occasionally be glimpsed helping in the background. It is housed in a stately Georgian building which, until recently, was reputed to be haunted, but the cozy modern decor has routed any dismal spirits. The motto of the Harveys is "Simple lunches—superb dinners," and they live up to this with a lunch menu offering traditional English dishes such as farmhouse chicken pie for £2.20 ($5.06) and beef in Guinness, £2.50 ($5.75), followed by Victorian sherry trifle, 85p ($1.96). Coffee is good value at 45p ($1.04) for a bottomless cup. Start with Bob's homemade pâté at 85p ($1.96), or warming soup, always freshly made, 65p ($1.50).

In the evenings the restaurant is candlelit and bubbles with a romantic atmosphere (reservations are essential on weekends). The Harveys offer a table d'hôte gourmet menu at £10 ($23), fully inclusive. This consists of a special soup or fruit dish, followed by the appetizer course, with a choice of fish, savory dishes, or pâté. Then there is a selection of seven main dishes, including French and "Taste of England" specialties. A massive choice of cheeses follows, with a finale of diet-beating homemade desserts and ice creams, plus the bottomless coffee cup and mints. Almost everything the Harveys serve is homemade, and all ingredients are fresh.

Finally, if you're in Lincoln over a weekend, take in a traditional Sunday lunch here. You won't taste better roast beef anywhere, but remember to book your table. The restaurant is open for lunch daily except Monday in winter, from noon to 1:45 p.m. Dinners are from 7:30 to 9:30 p.m. Tuesday through Saturday. **Green Dragon,** Broadgate (tel. Lincoln 24950), near the river, about a block from The High, is one of Lincoln's most attractive buildings, sheltering both pubs and a dining room. Actually, it is comprised of a row of 16th-century houses, black-and-white timbered, joined together and heavily reconstructed to create an inviting ambience. On the ground floor, the Gateway Bar is made cozy by a beamed ceiling and relaxed drinking nooks. The Garret Grill on the top floor is a forest of time-blackened oak beams and a cathedral ceiling, opening onto an excellent view of the nearby river and the bridge spanning it. The second floor attracts with its wide, walk-in fireplace.

A set lunch is featured for £3 ($6.90). If you're ordering à la carte, you'll find a wide menu selection, with main dishes costing up to £7 ($16.10). Otherwise, you can enjoy a simple meal, perhaps prawns, followed by sirloin steak in a cream sauce, vegetables, dessert, and coffee for about £5.50 ($12.65), VAT and service included. Many bar snacks are available, including toasted sandwiches at 55p ($1.27) or meat and potato pie, £2 ($4.60).

Chapter XIV

CHESHIRE, LIVERPOOL, AND THE LAKES

1. Chester
2. Nantwich
3. Liverpool
4. Kendal
5. Windermere
6. Ambleside
7. Rydal
8. Grasmere
9. Hawkshead and Coniston
10. Keswick
11. Bassenthwaite
12. Ullswater

ONE OF ENGLAND'S most popular summer retreats in Victoria's day was the Lake District in the northwest. It enjoyed vogue during the flowering of the Lake Poets, including Wordsworth, who was ecstatically moved by the rugged beauty of this area. In its time, the district has lured such writers as S. T. Coleridge, Charles Lamb, Shelley, Keats, Alfred Lord Tennyson, Matthew Arnold, and Charlotte Brontë.

The Lake District is a miniature Switzerland condensed into about 32 miles, principally in Cumbria, although it begins in the northern part of Lancashire.

As an added bonus, we've included Liverpool, plus Cheshire, a county that lies south of Lancashire. We suggest that you make a pilgrimage to the ancient city of Chester, with its medieval walls, near the border of Wales.

The northwest of England is one of the special parts of the country, yet it is rarely visited by the agenda-loaded foreigner, who considers it too far removed. In many ways, however, its remoteness is part of its charm. Have you ever seen one of those English-made films depicting the life of the Lake District? A soft mist hovers over the hills and dells, sheep graze silently on the slope of the pasture—and a foggy enchantment fills the air.

But first—

CHESHIRE

This county is low lying and largely agricultural. The name it gave to a cheese (Cheshire) has spread across the world. This northwestern county borders Wales, which accounts for its turbulent history. The towns and villages of Chesire are peaceful and quiet—forming a good base for touring North Wales, the most beautiful part of that little country. For our headquarters in Cheshire, we'll locate at:

1. Chester

Chester is ancient, having been founded by a Roman legion on the Dee River in the first century A.D. It reached its pinnacle as a bustling port in the 13th and 14th centuries, declining thereafter following the gradual silting up of the river. The upstart Liverpudlians captured the sea-trafficking business. The other walled medieval cities of England were either torn down or badly fragmented, but Chester still retains two miles of fortified city walls intact.

The main entrance into Chester is Eastgate, itself dating back to only the 18th century. Within the walls are half-timbered houses and shops. Of course, not all of them came from the days of the Tudors. Chester is freakish architecturally in that some of its builders kept to the black-and-white timbered facades —even when erecting buildings during the Georgian and Victorian periods, with their radically different tastes.

The Rows are double-decker layers of shops—one tier on the street level, the other stacked on top and connected by a footway. The upper tier is like a continuous galleried balcony. Shopping upstairs is much more adventurous than down on the street. Rain is never a problem. Thriving establishments operate in this traffic-free paradise: tobacco shops, restaurants, department stores, china shops, jewelers, even antique dealers. For the most representative look, take an arcaded walk on Watergate Street.

At noon and at 3 p.m. daily at the City Cross, the world's champion town crier issues his news (local stuff on sales, exhibitions, and attractions in the city) at the top of his not-inconsiderable voice, to the accompaniment of a hand bell—at the junction of Watergate(!), Northgate, and Bridge Streets.

After exploring The Rows, focus your attention on:

CHESTER CATHEDRAL: Representing a medley of architectural styles— all fairly harmonious—the Cathedral of Chester grew out of a Benedictine abbey, which was dissolved under Henry VIII. The abbey was founded after the Norman Conquest, although little of that period in its development remains today, excepting the North Transept. The ecclesiastical center owes much of its present look to the 19th-century architect, Sir Gilbert Scott, who rescued it from decay. Architecturally distorted, the South Transept, from the 14th century is large, but the North Transept—prevented from expansion by other, crowded buildings—remains small. Look for the elegantly carved misericords in the choir, the earliest of which go back to the 14th century.

HERITAGE CENTER: The **British Heritage Centre,** Bridge Street Row (tel. Chester 317-948), is open from April to September, weekdays from 10 a.m. to 5 p.m. (on Sunday from 2 to 5 p.m.), and from October to March it is open daily except Wednesday from 2 to 5 p.m. Admission for adults is 40p (92¢); children pay 20p (46¢). The center contains an exhibition of pictures and models depicting Chester's history from Roman times and a reproduction of an old street of 150 years ago (life-size), with storefronts such as "Miss Smith,

Dressmaker and Milliner," "A. Yates, Seedsman"; and a tableau of a blacksmith's and cooper's shop. An audio-visual theater is included in the complex with a well-presented history of Chester. Also offered here is a place where you can do your own brass rubbings from 50p ($1.15) to £3 ($6.90), depending on size. The price includes the special paper needed and wax crayons, plus some basic instructions.

Private guides can be arranged at the center for a tour around Chester city at £3 ($6.90) per hour.

For about £3 ($6.90) per person, you can join a Ghost Tour of Chester which starts in the cobbled Victorian street in the center and takes you through haunted buildings and streets in the city.

WHERE TO STAY: Grosvenor Hotel, Eastgate Street (tel. Chester 24024), is rightly considered a leading first-class hotel in the upper-bracket price range. A well-organized establishment, it offers a bathroom and color TV in every bedroom (more than 100), an excellent dining room (open to nonresidents and providing à la carte meals), and a much-favored Arkle Bar, named after the well-known steeplechaser. In 1784, when the hotel was first established, it was known as the Royal, and accommodated wayfarers on the London-to-Holyhead run. Although its interior was rejuvenated, the facade remains in the traditional Chester style, with gables and black-and-white beams. The lobby is spacious, with a chandelier and an encircling staircase. Each bedroom has its own personality with coordinated wallpaper, paint, and fabric. A single room goes for £35 ($80.50), a double- or twin-bedded room for £55 ($126.50), inclusive of VAT. In the cellars is the Grosvenor Bar, popular with shoppers seeking a quick snack.

Blossoms Hotel, St. John Street (tel. Chester 23186), has been in business since the mid-17th century, although the present structure was rebuilt late in Victoria's day. Each of the 77 traditionally furnished bedrooms is equipped with central heating and 57 have private baths. Each room has a telephone and radio, as well as color TV and coffee maker. The price for bed and breakfast in a single is from £26 ($59.80); in a twin or double, from £40 ($92). The old open staircase in the reception room sets the tone of the hotel. Dinner is served in the Egerton Room from 6:30 to 9:30 p.m., both table d'hôte at £7 ($16.10) and à la carte. The Snooty Fox coffeeshop offers salads and seafoods in the 75p ($1.73) to £2.50 ($5.75) price range.

Rowton Hall, Whitchurch Road (tel. Chester 35262), is a stately home, two miles from the city center, which offers overnight accommodation for motorists. The gracious house, built in 1797, with a later wing added, is nearly covered with green ivy, and stands on its own eight-acre garden, with a formal driveway entrance. The Hall has comfortable traditional and semicontemporary pieces. A bathless single goes for £20 ($46), for £24 ($55.20) with bath. A bathless double is £30 ($69), £34 ($78.20) with bath. Breakfast, service, and VAT are included. A set lunch or dinner costs from £5.50 ($12.65), although you are likely to spend more than £8 ($18.40) if you order from the à la carte menu. The good English meals are served in the oak-paneled dining room, with its Tudor fireplace. On Saturday nights, a dinner dance is staged, costing £8 ($18.40) per person. The hotel stands on the site of the battle of Rowton Moor, which was fought in 1643 between the Roundheads and the Cavaliers.

Ye Olde King's Head, Lower Bridge Street (tel. Chester 24855), is a 17th-century museum piece of black-and-white architecture. From 1598 to 1707, it was occupied by the well-known Randle Holme family of Chester, noted heraldic painters and genealogists (some of their manuscripts have made it to the British Museum). Since 1717, the King's Head has been a licensed inn. The host rents out a dozen handsome bedrooms at £15 ($34.50) for a single room, from £10.50 ($24.15) per person in a double, for bed and breakfast, VAT, and service. The bedchambers are linked with the past; many of the walls and ceilings are sloped and highly pitched, with exposed beams.

The residents' lounge, with its massive beams overhead, boasts a Tudor fireplace, and authentic furnishings, including an elaborate grandfather clock, an octagonal card table, high-backed Jacobean oak chairs, and soft upholstered pieces. The main lounge has a number of wall settles, barrel tables, wood paneling, and a Tudor fireplace. The 17th-century dining room is also a showcase of timberwork, with old furnishings, such as a Welsh cupboard and pewter and copper pieces. A set lunch costs £5 ($11.50). Dinner is served from 6:30 to 9 p.m. every day, costing from £7 ($16.10).

The **Belgrave Hotel,** City Road (tel. Chester 312-138). Derek and Alma Wood have concentrated on friendly service in their Victorian-era hotel, within a stone's throw of the railway station and within easy walking distance of the city center. They charge around £9 ($20.70) a night for a bed and breakfast.

WHERE TO EAT: The Courtyard, 13 St. Werburgh St. (tel. Chester 21447), was originally a stable courtyard, opposite the south transept of the cathedral. Today, it's been turned into one of the finest dining spots in Chester. The narrow entrance, with its black-and-white decorative motif, sets the stage for a two-in-one restaurant. Opening into the inner courtyard is the ingeniously designed split-level bistro, which offers a luncheon buffet from noon to 2:30 p.m.

A smörgåsbord lunch is individually priced with hot dishes, cold meats, and salads. Prices range from 55p ($1.27) per helping. From 6 to 10 p.m., the restaurant offers a bistro dinner where one serves one's self for an inclusive price of £6.60 ($15.18). It's good value. A more elaborate à la carte menu is available from 7 to 10 p.m., including items such as veal in orange and rum sauce at £8.50 ($19.55). A specialty appetizer is Raymond's homemade pâté at £1.50 ($3.45), or you might try mushroom Armenienne cooked in red wine, bacon, and garlic at £1.70 ($3.91). The chef's desserts include walnut fudge at £1.20 ($2.76).

The Courtyard cellar is open nightly for dancing Monday to Friday. The restaurant is open Monday to Saturday and is closed on bank holidays.

The Witch's Kitchen, Frodsham Street (tel. Chester 311-836), is in the center of town, just a short walk from the station. It seats 100 and has old-world charm and good service. The ground-floor restaurant is 15 yards from the city walls and Chester Cathedral. It is open every day for morning coffee (10 a.m.), luncheon (11:30 a.m. till 5:30 p.m.), high tea (5 to 6:30 p.m.), afternoon tea (3 to 5 p.m.) and dinner (7 to 10:30 p.m.). À la carte meals are served all day, and the Kitchen is open seven days a week. Luncheon is a three-course meal for £3 ($6.90) beginning with juice or soup, a choice of three different roasts (beef, pork, or chicken), fried filet of plaice or a salad, vegetables, and a choice of potatoes, ending with a dessert or coffee. And for £3.50 ($8.05) a traditional three-course Sunday luncheon is served which includes soup or fruit juice, roast beef and Yorkshire pudding with horseradish sauce, vegetables, and a choice of dessert. For a nightly three-course dinner by candlelight, the price is £4 ($9.20).

Jean's Kitchen, 1 Newtown Close, St. Anne Street (tel. Chester 24239). Jean Lacey runs this red-checked kitchen with the help of her husband, Tom. She offers a table d'hôte luncheon that continues up to 7 p.m. at a cost of

£3.50 ($8.05). Dinner from their à la carte menu will cost about £10 ($23) per person. Specialties include mushrooms cooked in wine, seafood salad with rice, veal cutlets smothered in a cheese and tomato sauce, or lamb provençale, followed by the richest desserts in Chester, if not the United Kingdom. Wine is Spanish, a small bottle costing from £2 ($4.60).

The **Royal Oak,** Foregate Street (tel. Chester 314-336), is a 17th-century building with a nice old paneled dining room where a set three-course lunch with two or three choices for each course will cost £3 ($6.90). Or else a meal chosen from the à la carte menu will go for £5 ($11.50). Choose from spicy tomato soup with cream, then chicken schnitzel with sweet corn relish, a jacket potato and vegetables, or lamb cutlets with peas and fried potatoes, grilled plaice with chips, followed by a large slice of Black Forest cake. Steaks, grilled to your specification and served with jacket or fried potatoes, peas, and tomato, run from about £4 ($9.20) to £5 ($11.50). Peter and Anne Flaig supervise everything and also provide bar snacks in the Long Bar if you don't have time to stop for a meal.

Some Local Pubs

The **Bear & Billet Inn,** Lower Bridge Street (tel. Chester 21272), with its intricately timbered and highly decorative facade from the mid-17th century, is one of the most famous buildings in Chester. The well-preserved pub—once a city house belonging to the Earls of Shrewsbury—still preserves its traditional atmosphere. Snacks available include a ploughman's lunch, ham and pineapple salad, cheese and beetroot salad, homemade soup, and fresh Dee salmon in season.

An alternative for drinking is the **Boot Inn,** Eastgate Street, established in 1643, making it even older than the Bear & Billet. It's the smallest and most unspoiled pub in Chester. Only oldtimers and those on the "in" know about it. It's reached by entering a passageway along the upper Rows of Eastgate Street. The publican has a multitude of mementos cluttering the walls—horse brasses, steins, curios from everywhere, even brass crocodiles and castanets!

2. Nantwich

The old market town on the Weaver River lies only 15 miles southeast of the county town of Chester, and can easily be tied in with a visit to that city. The town is particularly outstanding because of its black-and-white timbered houses. The most spectacular one, Churche's Mansion, is one of our dining recommendations.

WHERE TO STAY: Crown Hotel and Restaurant, High Street (tel. Nantwich 65283), is a black-and-white timbered structure, with leaded windows and an archway for carriages. The hotel was rebuilt in 1583 after a fire. Most attractive, the Crown offers guest rooms where you can immerse yourself in the charm of old England for £10 ($23) in a bathless single, £20 ($46) in a bathless double, £24 ($55.20) in a double with bath, these tariffs including breakfast, VAT, and service. The plank floors are so slanted you have to be careful not to lose your balance! The tavern and lounge blend antiquity with charm. The unique Georgian Assembly Room attached to the Crown has been restored, redecorated, and refurnished in the style of the period, and is now used as a dining and ballroom. Lunch at the Chef's Table runs from £2.50 ($5.75). You make your selection from a choice of three hot dishes with accompaniments which are then plated and served to you. Dinner is à la carte, costing a minimum of £6 ($13.80) but ranging up to £12 ($27.60) if you insist on having fresh lobster. If you only want a light snack, try the fully licensed Lounge Bar.

WHERE TO EAT: Churche's Mansion Restaurant, Hospital Street, is the most enchanting old restaurant in Cheshire, lying in Nantwich at the junction of Newcastle Road and the Chester bypass. Many years ago, Dr. and Mrs. E. C. Myott learned that this historic home of a wealthy Elizabethan merchant had been advertised for sale in America, and asked the town council to step in and save it. Alas, no English housewife wanted such a gloomy and dark home, so the Myotts attended the sale and outbid the American syndicate who wanted to transport it to the United States. Dr. Myott said that "our friends thought we were mad." They sought out the mysteries of the house: a window in the side wall, inlaid initials, a Tudor well in the garden, a long-ago love knot with a central heart (a token of Richard Churche's affection for his young wife). Today the house is widely known and recommended for its quality meals. A table d'hôte luncheon is offered for £5 ($11.50), and a set dinner for £10 ($23). You need to reserve a table, especially for dinner (tel. Nantwich 65933). Guests dine at candlelit tables. The mansion is "open to view" throughout the day for 35p (81¢), and refreshments are available.

CONWY CASTLE (WALES): Conwy, the home of Welsh harpmaking, on the northwestern coast of Wales, is some 48 miles from Chester. On an estuary of the Conwy River, this medieval fortress town has as its treasure the 13th-century Conwy Castle, reputedly one of the finest in Wales. It stands at the harbor where the river finds its way to the sea. Edward I ordered its walls built with their half-moon towers.

From these ancient walls you can see the small fishing fleet at anchor in the sheltered harbor. Fishermen bring in their catch of mussels and Conwy dabs here.

The castle is open, May to September, daily from 9:30 a.m. to 7 p.m.; March and October, 9:30 to 5:30, Monday to Saturday, and from 2 to 5:30 on Sunday. In April, hours are daily from 9:30 to 5:30; and November to February, the openings are weekdays from 9:30 to 4 and on Sunday from 2 to 4. Admission is 50p ($1.15); 30p (69¢) in winter.

The town contains many interesting old buildings, including the National Trust property of Aberconwy, Plas Mawr, and what is said to be the smallest house in Britain.

Sunnybanks Guest House, Woodlands, Conway, Gwynedd (tel. Conwy 3845). The owner, Peter Nissen, welcomes you into a world of old-fashioned good manners and homelike hospitality. He carries in your luggage before you can protest, turns down your bedspread at night, and brings you a cup of hot tea and cookies. Each meal prepared offers true home-cooking. He has set a per-person rate of £8 ($18.40) per night, and this includes a large breakfast, plus a three-course dinner finished off with coffee, as well as VAT and service. Without the evening meal, the bed-and-breakfast price is £6 ($13.80). Sunnybanks is a five-minute run from Conwy Castle. Readers Dr. and Mrs. Garry Lee Guilloud, Houston, Texas, write: "It is an immaculately clean place with an excellent cuisine. The gardens are lovely with a charming view. A place for a special memory."

3. Liverpool

Liverpool, with its famous waterfront on the Mersey River, is a great shipping port and industrial center that gave the world everybody from Fannie Hill to the Beatles. King John launched it on its road to glory when he granted it a charter in 1207, and it quickly became a port for shipping men and materials to Ireland. At the time Victoria came to the throne, Liverpool had become Britain's biggest port.

Liverpudlians, as they are called, are rightly proud of their city, with its new hotels, two cathedrals, shopping and entertainment complexes (as exemplified by St. John's Centre, a modern pedestrian precinct), and the parks and open spaces (2400 acres in and around the city, including Sefton Park with its Palm House). Liverpool's main shopping street, Church, is traffic free for most of the day.

Consecrated in 1967, the **Metropolitan Cathedral of Christ the King** contains more stained glass than any other, 25,000 square feet in 300 shades. It was built in only four years.

Among Liverpool's historic buildings, **St. George's Hall,** designed by a 24-year-old architect who never saw it realized, was completed in 1854. It has been called "England's finest public building." It contains law courts, and in the rear are pleasantly laid-out gardens.

Many visitors head for Liverpool these days just to see one attraction, the great new Anglican edifice, the **Cathedral Church of Christ,** completed 74 years after it was begun in 1903. On a rocky eminence overlooking the Mersey River, the cathedral might possibly be the last Gothic-style one to be built on earth. Dedicated to Queen Elizabeth in 1979, it is the largest church in the country (the fifth largest in the world). England's poet laureate, Sir John Betjeman, hailed it as "one of the great buildings of the world." Its vaulting under the tower is 175 feet high, the highest in the world, and its length of 619 feet is second only to that of St. Peter's in Rome. The architect who won a competition in 1903 for the building's design was Giles Scott. He later went on to rebuild the House of Commons, gutted by bombs after World War II. He personally laid the last stone on the highest tower pinnacle.

Want to visit the early Liverpool beginnings of the Beatles? Go to the Liverpool Travel Information Centre, 187 St. John's Centre, Elliot Street, and the staff will tell you what to see. If you want a guide, they'll arrange for you to join a tour run by Alan Williams, who takes a carload for about $25 U.S. on a tour. He can be found at 20 Tithebarn St.

WHERE TO STAY: Adelphi Hotel, Ranelagh Place (tel. Liverpool 709-7200), a British Transport hotel, is "the grand hotel" of Liverpool, known for its good rooms and fine cuisine. Past the elegant entrance, you enter a world of marble corridors, molded ceilings, and dark polished wood. However, these traditional features are complemented by a range of modern facilities, including a swimming pool.

In the basement are the modern Zodiac Coffee Shop and the Sporting Life Bar. The service and food are superb in the Sefton Restaurant, which is open daily, serving lunch and dinner (closed for lunch on Saturday and all day Sunday). The restaurant has all the elements associated with luxury, such as rich paneling, chandeliers, and deep carpeting. For a dinner here, expect to pay about £30 ($69) for two persons. The large rooms themselves are well furnished and attractively maintained, costing from £24 ($55.20) to £31 ($71.30) in a single, from £36 ($82.80) to £38 ($87.40) in a twin or double, the more expensive tabs for units with private baths.

Holiday Inn, Paradise Street (tel. Liverpool 709-0181), is large and modern, just what you'd expect. In the center of the city, it is one of the most comfortable hotels in Liverpool, if you like its particular brand of plush modernity. Close to the shopping and commercial area, the hotel offers 273 bedrooms, each with private tiled bath, color TV (showing free in-house movies), radio, and direct-dial phone, plus individually controlled heating and air conditioning. Each of the roomy bedrooms has two double beds. Rates are £25 ($57.50) in a single, from £32 ($73.60) in a double. There's a spacious lounge bar that is most inviting, and, in addition, guests can enjoy a heated indoor pool, complete with its own mini-gymnasium and sauna. Guests gravitate to either the Spyglass or the Warehouse for a drink before dinner in the well-appointed London Pride Restaurant.

St. George's Hotel, Lime Street (tel. Liverpool 709-7090), a Trust Houses Forte hotel, was opened in the early 1970s in a modern shopping district, known as the St. John's Precinct development scheme, directly opposite Lime Street Station. In the heart of Liverpool, it is well run and of an international high standard, with color-coordinated bedrooms, 155 in all, each with a private bath, color TV, razor socket, phone, and coffeemaker. Singles range in price from £28 ($64.40), and doubles go from £36 ($82.80). The large restaurant on the second floor has a modern look and an impressive menu of international dishes. There's also a Buttery for quick snacks or grills.

WHERE TO EAT: In food, **Jenny's Seafood Restaurant,** the Old Ropery, Fenwick Street (tel. Liverpool 236-0332), is consistently good. In the vicinity of the harbor, it has a basement room that is both pleasantly decorated and softly illuminated. All this forms a backdrop for the good-tasting fresh seafood which is brought in daily. Everything we've sampled has been of fine quality and well prepared. The service, on our latest rounds, was excellent. Expect to pay about £10 ($23) to £12 ($27.60) per person. The restaurant is closed for lunch on Saturday and all day on Sunday, but is open otherwise until 2:30 p.m. for lunch, serving dinner from 6 to 9:30 p.m.

In a much more elegant, luxurious bracket, the **Oriel,** Oriel Building, Water Street (tel. Liverpool 236-4664), presents a large menu of superb dishes, mainly fish, but with some excellent game and meat dishes as well. Good ingredients are competently cooked, and the service is attentive. The backdrop consists of silver silk-textured wallpaper and a water garden lit at night. A set luncheon costs £8 (18.40), but in the evening you can expect to pay from £15 ($34.50) per person. The Oriel doesn't service lunch on Saturday, and is closed all day on Sunday and for three weeks in August. Otherwise, it is open for lunch until 2 p.m., serving dinner until 10 p.m.

CUMBRIA

Driving in the wilds of this northwestern shire is fine for a start, but the best activity is walking, which is an art—practiced here by both young and old with a crooked stick. Don't go out without a warning, though. There is a great deal of rain and heavy mist. Sunny days are few. When the mist starts to fall, try to be near an old inn or pub, where you can drop in for a visit and warm yourself beside an open fireplace. You'll be carried back to the good old days, as many places in Cumbria have valiantly resisted change. If you strike up a conversation with a local, just make sure you know something about hounds.

The far northwestern part of the shire, bordering Scotland, used to be called Cumberland. Now part of Cumbria, it is generally divided geographically into a trio of segments: the Pennines dominating the eastern sector (loftiest point at Cross Fell, nearly 3000 feet high); the Valley of Eden; and the lakes and secluded valleys of the west—by far the most interesting. The area, so beautifully described by the Romantic Lake Poets, enjoys many literary associations. Wordsworth ("when all at once I saw... a host of golden daffodils") was a native son, having been born at Cockermouth.

The largest town is Carlisle in the north—not a very interesting tourist center, but possible as a base for explorations to **Hadrian's Wall.** The wall stretches from Wallsend in the east to Bowness on the Solway, a distance of about 75 miles. It was built in the second century A.D. by the Romans.

4. Kendal

A simple market town, Kendal contains the ruins of a castle where Catherine Parr, the last wife of Henry VIII, was born. With its 13th-century parish church, Kendal makes for a good stopover en route to the lakeside resort of Windermere, about nine miles away. Kendal is 270 miles from London.

The town was also associated with George Romney, the 18th-century portrait painter (Lady Hamilton his favorite subject) who used to travel all over the Lake District trying to get someone to sit for him. He held his first exhibition in Kendal, married and had children there. He deserted them in 1762, not returning until the end of his life. He died at Kendal in 1802.

WHERE TO STAY: Woolpack Hotel, Stricklandgate (tel. Kendal 23852), offers every modern convenience in this sprawling, motel-like establishment. Many of the 67 rooms are equipped with private bath, and some are suits which are ideal for families of three or more. Children under 12 are accommodated at no charge when sharing their parents' rooms. All the rooms are decorated in bright colors to add to the already cheerful atmosphere. Convenient parking is provided just outside. Singles range upward from £22 ($50.60), while doubles begin at £34 ($78.20). VAT, service, and a full English breakfast are included in the tab.

5. Windermere

The grandest of the lakes is Windermere, the largest one in England, whose shores wash up against the adjoining towns of **Bowness** and **Windermere.** Both of these lakeside resorts lie on the eastern shore of Windermere. A ferry service connects Hawkshead and Bowness. Windermere, the resort, is the end of the railway line. From either town, you can climb up Orrest Head in less than an hour for a panoramic view of England's lakeland. From that vantage point, you can even see Scafell Pike, rising to a height of 3210 feet—the peak pinnacle in all of England.

WHERE TO STAY AND DINE: Miller Howe Hotel, Rayrigg Road (tel. Windermere 2536), serves theatrically presented meals with dramatic flourish. This inn bears the unique imprint of its creator, former actor John Tovey. At the beginning of the 1970s, he selected a country estate overlooking Lake Windermere, with views of the Langdale Peaks, and converted it to provide stylish accommodations and an exquisite cuisine.

His large, graciously furnished rooms have names—no number—and he treats each guest as if he or she were invited to a house party. Each accommodation is provided with binoculars to help absorb the view better, and even copies

THE LAKE DISTRICT

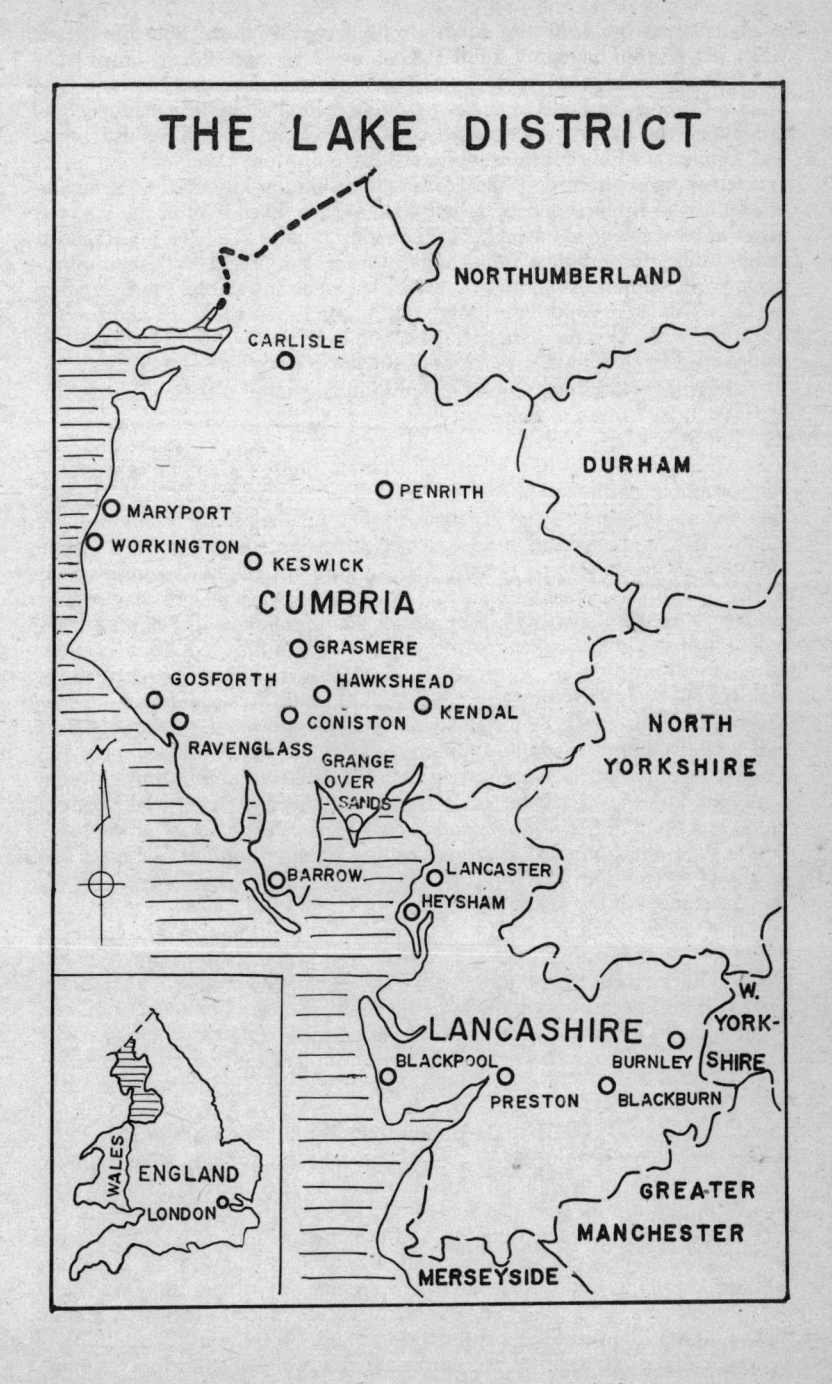

of *Punch* from the 1890s. Antiques are used lavishly throughout the house. Rates per person, including a full English breakfast and dinner, range from £32 ($73.60) to £52 ($119.60), depending on the plumbing and the view. The hotel is closed from mid-December to mid-March. The public rooms, such as the lounge and library, are lushly decorated, evoking London sophistication.

Dinner at Miller Howe is worth the drive up from London. It's a joyful and satisfying experience. While Tovey is famed as a pastry chef, he is equally known for his original appetizers and main dishes. Even if you can't stay the night, at least consider a meal here. The set meal costs £15 ($34.50). Regional dishes using local produce are a special feature. You might try Lake District lamb, fresh salmon, game pies (in season), Lancashire cheese, and Cumbria sausage. The lettuce and fennel soup with bacon is superb. Coats and ties are worn in the dining room. Dinners are served at 8:30 only; at 7:30 and 9:30 on Saturday. You're allowed half an hour for menu selections and apéritifs.

Overnight guests can request a picnic lunch, packed with goodies, including homemade rolls and quiches.

Langdale Chase Hotel, on the A591 between Windermere and Ambleside (tel. Ambleside 2201), is a great old lakeside house—built for grandeur—comparable to a villa on Lake Como, Italy. The story goes back to 1930 when the dynamic Ms. Dalzell and her mother took over the country estate, with its handsomely landscaped gardens, and decided to accept paying guests while retaining an uncommercial house-party atmosphere. The hotel is owned and run by Mrs. Buckley and her family. Waterskiing, rowing, lake bathing, tennis, croquet on the grounds, and fishing attract the sports-minded. The per-person rate for bed and breakfast ranges from £17 ($39.10) to £24 ($55.20), or else you can take half-board terms, costing from £26 ($59.80) to £32 ($73.60) per person nightly. The bedrooms are skillfully furnished, with excellent pieces.

The interior of the Victorian stone château, with its many gables, balconies, large mullioned windows, and terraces, is a treasure house of antiques. The main lounge hall looks like a setting for one of those English drawing-room comedies. The house itself was built in part with bits and pieces salvaged from the destruction of a nearby abbey and castle—hence, the ecclesiastical paneling. On the walls are distinctive paintings, mostly Italian primitives, although one is alleged to be a Van Dyck.

The dining room ranks among the finest in the Lake District—with guests selecting tables which are good vantage points for lake viewing. The cuisine is highly personal, mostly a liberated English fare, supported by a fine wine list. Open to nonresidents, the dining room charges £5.50 ($12.65) for a set lunch, £10 ($23) for a set six-course dinner. Next to the dining room is a cocktail bar, opening onto the terrace through two French windows. In this room are some old prints of the Lake District which have been collected over the years.

LAKE DISTRICT TOURS: Mountain Goat Tours, Victoria Street, Windermere (tel. Windermere 5161), is one of the most enterprising ideas we have come across. Begun in 1972 by Chris Taylor, who had a strong desire to start his own business after spending some years in Australia, it has become firmly established in the Lake District as the fell-walking tours. For the less energetic, Mountain Goat has minibus tours that take you to many of the otherwise inaccessible beauty spots of the area. For the one-day tripper, they provide a visit to Duddon Valley, as a picnic tour. A half-day tour to this wild, remote area going via Coniston Water and Broughton in Furness costs £5 ($11.50) per person. You picnic beside the river, surrounded by woodlands. Before returning over the Wrynose Pass to Windermere, you can wander around the rock pools and waterfalls.

Another trip, the Stately Homes of Lakeland Tour, visits three houses during the day's outing and costs £6 ($13.80) per person, which includes entrance fees, and you will have time out for lunch (which costs extra).

For a full day's tour to the homes of the poet Wordsworth, the cost is £6.50 ($14.95) per person and includes the entrance fees. You retrace the poet's life and places he has lived. This is called the In the Steps of Wordsworth Tour.

For £5.50 ($12.65) for a full day, you can go into the hills and tiny valleys of Cartmell Fell, descending Gummers How with its wonderful views over Windermere and the mountains beyond. You then go along the east side of Coniston Water to see Brantwood, home of John Ruskin, before heading to Tarn Hows.

Another possibility for the more energetic is the tour up Hardknott and Wrynose Passes to Eskdale, following the old Roman route to Hardknott Roman Fort, where a pub lunch can be had in Eskdale. You can take a ride on the miniature Ravenglass-Eskdale railway before having tea at Ravenglass and returning over the fells to Duddon Bridge, Coniston, and Windermere. The cost is £6 ($13.80) per person.

Mountain Goat Tours will also arrange two- or three-night stopovers in the Lakes, including a special discount rail ticket from London or wherever. Excluding travel to the Lakes, the cost of two nights in a guest house, a full-day tour by minibus, a boat trip on Windermere, and taxis to and from Windermere coach or bus station is £51.50 ($118.45) per person, including bed and breakfast. An experienced guide can be hired for this tour. For a hotel with a bath or shower, the cost is £70.50 ($162.15) per person.

There are also week-long walking tours available, providing you are properly clad and reasonably fit, from £115 ($264.50). Required equipment can be hired locally. However, if you arrive without a suitable kit for this tour they will not take you out, for it is an area that calls for proper equipment. We suggest you inquire about what you will need for these specialized tours directly from Mountain Goat.

6. Ambleside

A good and idyllic retreat, Ambleside is one of the major centers attracting pony-trekkers, fell-hikers, and rock-scalers. The charms are essentially there year round, even in late autumn when it's fashionable to sport a mackintosh. Ambleside is superbly perched, at the top of Lake Windermere. Traditions are entrenched, especially at the Rushbearing Festival, an annual event.

WHERE TO STAY AND DINE: Rothay Manor, Rothay Bridge (tel. Ambleside 3605), at the edge of Ambleside, is like a French country inn, where the sparkling star is the cuisine, combined with a dedicated chef in the kitchen, well-selected French wines, and 12 comfortable, centrally heated bedrooms (nine with bath or shower), all with phones and color TVs. All this is possible because of a very special person, Mrs. Bronwen M.G. Nixon, who has installed herself in this gracious Regency house, bringing her energy, imagination, and taste to bear on its operation. She charges from £21 ($48.30) to £24 ($55.20) per person for bed and breakfast. The rooms are individually decorated, with a free use of vibrant colors. Most of them have shuttered French doors opening onto a sun balcony, with a mountain view. Throughout the estate you'll find an eclectic combination of antiques (some Georgian blended harmoniously with Victorian), flowers, and "get-lost" armchairs.

The manor is also a restaurant open to nonresidents. Mrs. Nixon's spacious dining room is decked with antique tables and chairs. Her appointments are flawless, and incorporate fine crystal, silver, and china. At night candles burn in silver holders. Lunches seven days a week feature soup, cold meats, a variety of salads, sweets, cheeses, and coffee.

Dinners, from 7:30 till 9 p.m., are more ambitious, costing £12 ($27.60). Here is a typical selection: homemade chicken liver pâté laced with brandy, celery and almond soup, filet Talleyrand (beef filet rolled in a mirepoix of vegetables, baked in a flaky pastry case and served with a rich Espagnole sauce), an exciting selection of homemade desserts, fresh fruit, and a cheese trolley. Afterward good coffee awaits you in the lounges. All prices include VAT.

In the kitchen Mrs. Nixon directs everything herself with a wise and loving eye, and has trained a friendly young staff to produce delicious meals. We've saved the best news for last: that is, Mrs. Nixon herself, a forthright conversationalist and (that rarity) a sensitive listener—a winning combination.

Riverside Hotel, Gilbert Scar, Under Loughrigg (tel. Ambleside 2395). The River Rothay foams along in front of the old stone house, and it's difficult to imagine that you are only minutes by car from the center of Ambleside. Loughrigg Fell climbs behind the hotel, providing excellent walking for the enthusiast. Simple bedrooms go for £12.50 ($28.75) to £15 ($34.50) per person, including dinner and breakfast. In the Gilbert Scar Cottage, alongside the hotel, are two bedrooms which share a bathroom for a small additional charge. Breakfast is a communal meal at 9 a.m., dinner at 7 p.m. Gillian Rhone who, with her husband Alan, owns and runs the hotel, does the cooking, serving ample portions. There are two lounges, one with TV, and in the bar snacks can be produced throughout the day.

READERS' GUEST HOUSE SELECTION: "We were treated to the finest hospitality we've found throughout our entire six-month visit to Europe, when we discovered a truly fantastic place to stay with John and Sue Horne at **Horseshoe Guest House**, Rothay Road (tel. Ambleside 2000). An architect from London by profession, John has left the big city life behind and is creating an enviable lifestyle for Sue and himself in the Lake Country. For £15 ($34.50) per night for a double, you can stay in a large and immaculate room, bath down the hall, in a former church-owned residence which is undergoing a complete restoration by the Hornes. John, an avid outdoorsman and member of the local Mountain Rescue Squad, has a complete knowledge of the surrounding area and he will gladly direct you to places of interest. Sue was up bright and early in the morning to fix us a delicious breakfast of eggs, bacon, and sausage, all included in the room cost" (Phil Pritulsky and Pauline Dainty, Norfolk, Va.).

7. Rydal

Between Ambleside and Wordsworth's former retreat at Grasmere is Rydal, a small village on one of the smallest lakes, Rydal Water. Wordsworth selected a spot overlooking the lake for his home in later years. The village itself is noted for its sheepdog trials at the end of summer.

WHERE TO STAY: Rydal Lodge (tel. Ambleside 3208), beside the roadway between Ambleside and Grasmere, is a good center for walking and touring the whole of the Lake District. The Rothay River runs beside the pleasant and secluded gardens; and Rydal Water, a beautiful lake, is at the end of the garden. Mr. and Mrs. Warren provide meals of high quality, and the menus are well planned. Strawberries and other fruit from the garden are provided in season, and the lodge has a license to serve wine with main meals. The bedrooms are equipped with hot and cold running water, shaving points, electric blankets, heaters, and innerspring mattresses. There are two bathrooms as well as a private car park. Terms are from £10 ($23) for bed and breakfast, with dinner costing from £6 ($13.80), including VAT and service. Rydal Lodge is of historical interest. Matthew Arnold stayed here, and it is connected with Harriet Martineau. The older part of the house was an inn in 1655.

8. Grasmere

On a lake that bears its name, Grasmere was the home of Wordsworth from 1799 to 1808. The nature poet lived with his sister, Dorothy (the English writer and diarist) at **Dove Cottage,** which is now a museum administered by Dove Cottage Trust. Wordsworth, who followed Southey as poet laureate, died in the spring of 1850, and was buried in the graveyard of the village church at Grasmere. The other tenant of Dove Cottage was Thomas De Quincey *(Confessions of an English Opium Eater).* For a combined ticket costing 90p ($2.07) for adults, 40p (92¢) for children, you can visit both Dove Cottage and the **Wordsworth Museum,** with its collection of his manuscripts and memorabilia, as well as a collection of portraits of the Wordsworth Circle, including Lamb, Coleridge, Keats, and Hazlitt, from the National Portrait Gallery. The trust property is open weekdays from 9:30 a.m. to 1 p.m. and from 2 to 5 p.m., Easter to October. Off-season, the properties open at 10 a.m. and close at 4:30 p.m. and remain shut entirely from mid-November to March 1.

A SHOPPING RECOMMENDATION: It isn't often that you get the opportunity to watch the material that you will later purchase being made. But at **Chris Reekie's,** in the Old Coach House at Grasmere (tel. Grasmere 221), you can see Mr. Reekie or one of his sons, perhaps young apprentices, working at the traditional fly-shuttle loom which Mr. Reekie brought from his own apprenticeship employers in Selkirk. For about the last 30 years, he has been weaving tartans and fine woolens for direct sale, thus keeping the prices down. His charges are below those in Scotland. Apart from a vast range of ready-made cloths and clothing, he will make to measure a garment within seven days. If that is too long to wait, he will send articles anywhere in the world—so you can buy for relatives and friends.

FOOD AND LODGING: In this hiking and rock-scaling center, you'll find the following recommendations, beginning first with the most expensive, then descending in price level.

Michael's Nook, outside Grasmere (turn off the A591 at the Swan Hotel; tel. Grasmere 496), is a country-house hotel, once a private residence, standing in its own secluded garden of three acres. A lakeside home of stone, it contains much fine mahogany woodwork and paneling, exemplified by its elegant staircase. Throughout the house, owned by Mr. R. S. E. Gifford, are many fine antiques, which are only enhanced by the mellow glow of log fires or the discreetly placed vases of flowers.

The handsomely decorated bedrooms, ten in all, are individually furnished with grace and care. All are equipped with phones, private baths or showers, and TV sets. The minimum booking is usually three nights. The tariffs range from £34 ($78.20) to £43 ($98.90) per person per night and include a five-course dinner, bed, early-morning tea, and an English or a continental breakfast, service, and VAT. After only a few hours here, guests become acquainted with Mr. Gifford's cats and other pets. The feeling is very much that of living in a private home.

A limited number of guests can be accommodated in the dining room, and advance reservations are essential. Great care and an attention to detail go into the excellent English cooking, and the best of fresh ingredients are used whenever available. An attractive young staff serves the fine food, which costs from £7.50 ($17.25) for lunch, £15 ($34.50) for dinner, service and VAT included. The menus change, but you might have an appetizer of quiche of guinea fowl and asparagus, a first for us! Main courses include such dishes as homebaked Cumberland ham with mustard sauce, loin of lamb with green-pepper stuffing, and poached Loch trout with hollandaise sauce.

If Michael's Nook is full, we hear that **Mrs. Butterworth**, at White Moss House, Rydal Water (tel. Grasmere 295), one mile from Grasmere, is building a big reputation for her hospitality and cookery. An overnight stay with her, including a large breakfast and dinner, is about £28 ($64.40) per person nightly. If you're a nonresident, dinner costs about £15 ($34.50), but you must book well in advance.

Red Lion Hotel (tel. Grasmere 456) is a 200-year-old coaching inn in the heart of the village, owned by the Fawthrops, Mr. John and Mr. Stewart. It's only a short stroll to the waterside cottage once occupied by Wordsworth, and it's assumed that the poet often stopped in for a meal, a drink, or to warm himself by the fire. A rambling informal structure, it is imbued with a sophisticated rustic decor. In the spacious residents' lounge, the rugged stone fireplace is two-sided. Two of the three bars are paneled in mahogany, with refectory tables and chairs. In the dining room, you will be served some of the finest fare in the district: a set meal from £18 ($41.40), increasing to £24 ($55.20) with bath. A twin ranges from £32 ($73.60) without bath, from £36 ($82.80) with bath. Breakfast is included in the room rates, as are VAT and service. There is an elevator serving all 36 bedrooms, 21 of which contain private baths. As a family-run hotel, the Grasmere Red Lion maintains a personal atmosphere.

Swan Hotel (tel. Grasmere 551) has been renovated so that only the shell of the old building remains. However, there have been inns on this site for 300 years. Wordsworth mentioned it in *The Waggoner*. In fact, in one of the lounges is the poet's tapestry chair. The 31 rooms contain built-in furniture and good beds. Singles without bath rent for £19 ($43.70), going up to £23 ($52.90) with bath. Bathless doubles cost £27 ($62.10), rising to £32 ($73.60) with bath, these tariffs including service and VAT. The restaurant provides both table d'hôte and à la carte meals. A set luncheon goes for £5.50 ($12.65); dinner, £8.50 ($19.55).

Meadow Brow (tel. Grasmere 275) is an old country house perched halfway up a hillside just a mile from the center of the village. Commanding superb views of the surrounding hills, the stone-and-timber building stands in two acres of secluded gardens nourished by a tiny stream. The house itself is furnished with antiques, and on cooler evenings you can relax by the open fire in the sitting room. The small library is stacked with books on the history and geology of the Lake District. All the bedrooms are comfortably and thoughtfully furnished, right down to the electric blankets for those colder nights. Every evening except Wednesday, the hosts, Mr. and Mrs. Bateman, serve a four-course dinner, along with good conversation and enjoyable wines. The cost for dinner, bed, and breakfast is £18 ($41.40) per person per night.

The **Cumbria Carvery** (tel. Grasmere 515) offers lunches and dinners until 9 p.m. It's a cheerful, friendly place, and the food is simple, the prices reasonable. Appetizers, including soup, pâté, or prawn cocktail, are in the 65p ($1.50) to £1.75 ($4.03) range. Scampi, filet of plaice, or halibut with tartar sauce cost from £2.25 ($5.18) to £3 ($6.90). Meat dishes begin at £2.50 ($5.75) for liver and bacon, ranging up to £5 ($11.50) for a steak with garnish. The kitchen, under the direction of Elaine and Louis Diomedous, who also own and run the place, does roast joints with the usual accompaniments for around £2.60 ($5.98). Desserts begin at 60p ($1.38), ranging upward to £1.20 ($2.76).

9. Hawkshead and Coniston

Discover for yourself the village of Hawkshead, with its 15th-century grammar school where Wordsworth went to school for eight years (he carved his name on a desk that still remains). Near Hawkshead, in the vicinity of Esthwaite Water, is the 17th-century **Hill Top Farm,** former home of Beatrix Potter, the author of the Peter Rabbit books, who died during World War II.

At **Coniston,** four miles away from Hawkshead, you can visit the village famously associated with John Ruskin. Coniston is a good base for rock climbing. The Coniston "Old Man" towers in the background at 2633 feet, giving mountain climbers one of the finest views of the Lake District.

Ruskin moved to his home, **Brantwood,** on the east side of Coniston Water in 1872 and lived there until his death in 1900. The house today is open for visitors to view much Ruskiniana, including some 175 pictures by him. Also displayed is his coach and boat, the *Jumping Jenny.* The house is owned and managed by the Education Trust, a self-supporting registered charity. It is open Easter to October, Sunday to Friday, from 11 a.m. to 5:30 p.m., charging an admission of 75p ($1.73) for adults, 35p (81¢) for children. Part of the 250-acre estate is also open as a nature trail at 40p (92¢) for adults, 20p (46¢) for children. A special £2 ($4.60) family day ticket covers house, nature trail, and a guidebook. Tea, coffee, and light refreshments are available.

Literary fans should pay a pilgrimage to the graveyard of the village church, where Ruskin was buried; his family turned down a chance to have him interred at Westminster Abbey.

ACCOMMODATIONS: Ivy House Hotel, Main Street (tel. Hawkshead 204), is a friendly Georgian house that warms the austere Lake District. It's an ideal headquarters from which to branch out for visits on Lake Windermere. If you stay anywhere from one to three days, the bed-and-breakfast rate is £9 ($20.70) per person daily. Cheaper terms are quoted for longer stays. Dinner, bed, and breakfast cost £13.50 ($31.05). The hospitable proprietors, Mr. and Mrs. Williams, are used to welcoming overseas visitors, and Mrs. Williams tries to take a personal interest in all her lodgers. But because of her charming house and lovely situation, she is heavily booked—so it's imperative that you reserve well in advance. Some other points worth noting: All the rooms are centrally heated and have hot and cold running water. A modern, motel-type annex, with unrestricted electric heating, handles overflow guests. The house is open March to October only.

10. Keswick

Lying 22 miles north of Windermere, Keswick opens onto Derwentwater, one of the loveliest lakes in the district. Robert Southey, poet laureate, lived for four decades at Greta Hall, and was buried at Crosthwaite Church. Coleridge lived here, too, depending on Southey for financial aid. Sir Hugh Walpole, the novelist, in a different era also resided near Keswick. Keswick is a good center for touring the northern Lake District.

WHERE TO STAY: Royal Oak Hotel (tel. Keswick 72965) dates back to the days of Queen Elizabeth I, although the present building more accurately reflects the architecture of the 18th century. As a posting house, it was a favored lakeland retreat of Sir Walter Scott, who is said to have written a section of *Bridal of Triermain* here. The famous hunter, John Peel, and authors Alfred Lord Tennyson and Robert Louis Stevenson also patronized the inn. Now redecorated and modernized under Trust House Forte auspices, the hotel is a cheerful and atmospheric place at which to stay. Rates are £14.50 ($33.35) for a bathless single, £21 ($48.30) for a single with bath. A bathless double or twin-bedded room costs £24 ($55.20), £30 ($69) with bath. Breakfast is extra, but service and VAT are included.

Borrowdale, Borrowdale, near Keswick (tel. Borrowdale 224), is a typical lakeside stone building with log fires—even in summer—to welcome you. Its rooms are comfortable, many opening onto lovely views. All have private baths and showers, going for £22 ($50.06) per person, including dinner, bed, breakfast, service and VAT. The management likes you to stay just one or two nights or for more than a week; otherwise, the charges are increased a little.

The main attraction of Borrowdale is its restaurant. Lunches are offered only on Sunday, costing from £5.50 ($12.65); and on other days you can order bar snacks in the £1.50 ($3.45) to £3 ($6.90) range. Dinner at £9 ($20.70) might begin with avocado and crab salad, then local roast pheasant or a specialty dish such as wienerschnitzel, piccata milanese, or marha gulyas, all served with the appropriate vegetables or a salad, and potatoes. For dessert, the choice is bewildering—French peach flan, chilled Bavarian cream, profiteroles, to name only a few. You dine by candlelight on silver service, attended to by an efficient, friendly staff. The restaurant is run by Gunter Fidrmuc and his wife, Jean.

Skiddaw Hotel (tel. Keswick 72071) has a bone-white, clean-cut facade, and is built right onto the sidewalk in the heart of Keswick. The owners, Mr. and Mrs. Kitchin, have used natural elements in the interiors with walls of simple pine or rugged fieldstone. The meals are totally English, well prepared. The bedrooms are compact and eye-catching, renting at prices that vary according to the season and the view. The bed-and-breakfast rate is £13 ($29.90) in a single, £26 ($59.80) in a double, including service and VAT. Twelve different dishes are featured on the breakfast menu. Every room has hot and cold running water; the beds are bouncy soft, and the linen as clean as the lake air. Guests gather in the stone-walled lounge, or else in the pine-paneled cocktail bar.

The **George Hotel,** St. John Street (tel. Keswick 72076), is a wayside tavern that has bedded down many a traveler who pulled in on a horse-drawn coach. Once associated with Coleridge, it brings a comfort and pleasure to the modern pilgrim. Guests still gather for a warming hot punch in the bar where Wordsworth and Southey met for quiet talks in high-backed settles in front of the fireplace. Modern amenities have been sneaked in, including central heating, electric razor outlets, and hot and cold running water. Six have private baths. For £13.50 ($31.05), including VAT, you can get bed and breakfast, but for £20.30 ($46.69) you can take the demi-pension arrangement. Throughout the inn, modern furniture is blended harmoniously with well-chosen antiques.

WHERE TO DINE: The Cellar Restaurant, Lake Road (tel. Keswick 72990), is run by Stewart Lietch who offers a simple menu with ample portions. Morning coffee and lunch are served, and dinner is available from 6 p.m. Deep-fried plaice, roast chicken, ham and pineapple, steaks, and veal escalopes are served with vegetables, garnishes, and potatoes, costing in the £2 ($4.60) to £6 ($13.80) range. Specialties such as roast pheasant or duckling with orange sauce go for anywhere from £3.50 ($8.05) to £5.50 ($12.65). Appetizers are modest, including soup at 55p ($1.27) or pâté at £1 ($2.30), and there is a selection of desserts, cheese, or fresh fruit at 75p ($1.73). Wine by the glass is 65p ($1.50).

READERS' RESTAURANT SELECTION: "While in Keswick, we chanced upon the **Yan, Tyan, Tethera,** 70 Main St., where we not only had a tasty meal, but a delightful time as well. Simone Boddington is the owner of this small, cozy place, and the feeling is one of being a guest in her house rather than a customer in a restaurant. The cooking and preparing of food is done out in the open; and Simone herself cuts up and prepares a fresh salad for your table right before your eyes, all the while chatting, joking, and bantering with customers, during the summer, May to October, from 6:30 to 10 p.m. daily, except Monday (Thursday through Saturday only in winter). The specialty of the house is shrimp. There are several delicious sauces to accompany it, as well as rolls and that crispy salad already referred to. Featured is casserole of local venison. A typical à la carte dinner, which might include an appetizer of pâté, jumbo shrimp, tossed salad, rolls, cherry pie, and beverage, costs about £8 ($18.40) per person. From 11 a.m. to 3 p.m. daily, the restaurant serves delightful dishes to satisfy either large or small appetites. Weight watchers and vegetarians will find many satisfying dishes also. Especially popular specialties include savory cheese and prawn platters at 50p ($1.15) or a stockpot soup and roll, 50p also. Draft sherry, lager, and wines are sold at reasonable prices. Reservations for the evening are advisable by telephoning Keswick 0596/72033" (Dave and Jan Gelman, East Longmeadow, Mass.).

11. Bassenthwaite

With its fine stretch of water in the shadow of the 3053-foot Skiddaw, Bassenthwaite makes a good center for exploring the western Lakeland. In the village we have a choice recommendation.

The **Pheasant Inn,** Bassenthwaite Lake, Cockermouth (tel. Bassenthwaite Lake 234), is a 16th-century inn with a neat exterior set against a wooded mountain backdrop. Inside, the bar is wood-paneled and smoke-mellowed. Old hunting prints dot the walls, and real ale is on tap. The beamed dining room is bright and cheerful, with spotless white tablecloths and a menu of good-quality roasts, fish, and poultry with fresh vegetables. A set lunch is £5 ($11.50), a set dinner is £8 ($18.40), and the staff will pack you a lunch for £2.50 ($5.75). There are three pleasant lounges with an open log fire, and fresh flowers abound. The bedrooms are spotless and bright with chintz. Eleven have a bath or shower room attached, and there are electric blankets on the beds. There are also three bedrooms in the annex, which is a bungalow on the grounds. Bed and breakfast starts at £13 ($29.90) per person, including VAT and a service charge. With a private bathroom, the charge is £15 ($34.50). A double room costs £26 ($59.80); with bath, £28 ($64.40).

12. Ullswater

A seven-mile sheet of water, stretching from Pooley Bridge to Patterdale, Ullswater is the second-largest lake in the district. Incidentally, it was on the shores of Ullswater that Wordsworth saw his "host of golden daffodils." The market town of Penrith lies seven miles to the east, and while housed in the area it is easy to explore several places of archeological interest, such as Hadrian's Wall, east of Carlisle, or Long Meg stone circle near Penrith.

WHERE TO STAY AND EAT: Sharrow Bay Country House Hotel, Howtown, Lake Ullswater, near Penrith (tel. Pooley Bridge 301). Francis Coulson rules in the kitchen, Brian Sack in the dining room. Mr. Coulson bought this unusual Victorian house in 1949, and, up to then, it'd been a private house, similar to those one might find on Lake Maggiore, with a low angled roof and wide eaves. Sleeping on the floor during restoration work, he had the place rebuilt, turning it into one of England's finest country dining places, and offering accommodations as well, with daily terms in the range of £35 ($80.50) to £48 ($110.40) per person for room, dinner, breakfast, service, and VAT.

The atmosphere is relaxed, the lounges comfortable and handsomely decorated. From the picture window in the drawing room, a view opens across the lake to the Martindale Fells.

The five-course, £16 ($36.80) set menu contains a formidable list of choices. We recently counted 28 appetizers, including the chef's specialty, mousseline of fresh salmon with hollandaise sauce. The carefully chosen main courses seemed designed to make the best of home-grown food items, including roast Lancashire guinea fowl, a roast stuffed shoulder of young English lamb, or even a Cumberland ham from a cold table selection. The dessert selections are among the best you'll find in northwest England, including a fresh strawberry hazelnut brandy cream roulade. A feature as well is the Sharrow homemade cream ices, including prune and armagnac.

Brian Sack is a delightful host, and his staff is friendly and efficient which makes Mr. Coulson's food all the more delectable.

If you're motoring through the area, and not stopping over for the night, we suggest you call in advance and make a reservation for the £14 ($32.20) set luncheon. On one recent occasion, a delicious carrot and orange soup was featured, along with roast leg and loin of Cumberland pork cooked with rosemary grown on the hotel grounds, and served with a sweet-and-sour sauce and a sage and onion stuffing. For dessert, try one of the hot puddings, such as plum pie with a creamy egg custard.

The hotel offers 29 antique-filled bedrooms, 17 of them in the lodge annex and cottages. In the main hotel, seven rooms have private baths, and 13 of the bedrooms in the cottages have private baths as well. Some rooms open onto views of the lakes, others onto fells and trees. Each of the individually decorated bedrooms has been given a name rather than a number, a nice touch.

Also write or telephone in advance, either for a meal or a room. Closed December, January, and February.

READER'S SIGHTSEEING TIP: "Driving west on the A67 toward Carlisle, one is close to the Roman wall and passes through rolling hills, and tiny ancient stone villages, with Norse and Danish names, settled by the Vikings. There are several Norman towers still standing, and some were turned into houses in the 17th century, when England and Scotland were united and the Border warfare stopped (more or less). We found **Armathwaite Castle,** one of the Tower Houses (built in the 14th century and 'modernized' in the 17th), in the tiny village of Armathwaite, just off the M6, between Penrith and Carlisle. The castle is still a private house, but the present owner has decided to open it to guests. If you can't stay over, at least stop by for a delicious and lavish tea. Address inquiries regarding accommodations to the owner, Charles Francis, Armathwaite Castle, Cumbria, England (tel. Armathwaite 287)" (Elizabeth S. Paltz, Wayland, Mass.).

Chapter XV

YORKSHIRE AND NORTHUMBRIA

1. York
2. North Yorkshire
3. West Yorkshire
4. Durham
5. Tyne and Wear
6. Northumberland

UNLESS YOU ENJOY untamed scenery and perhaps a visit to an ancient city or two, such as York, then this huge hunk of northeastern England may hold little interest for you. Many of its towns carry the taint of the Industrial Revolution, but once you've bypassed them, you'll discover heather-covered moors, comprising some of the most dramatic scenery England has to offer.

Let's begin our travels through this area of northeast England in its major historical and ecclesiastical center—

1. York

Few cities in England are as rich in history as York. It is still encircled by its 13th- and 14th-century city walls—about 2½ miles long—with four gates. One of these, Micklegate, once grimly greeted visitors coming up from the south with the heads of traitors. To this day, you can walk on the footpath of the walls of the Middle Ages.

The crowning achievement of York is its Minster or cathedral, which makes the city an ecclesiastical center topped only by Canterbury. In spite of this, York is one of the most overlooked cities on the cathedral circuit. Perhaps foreign visitors are intimidated by the feeling that the great city of northeastern England is too far north. Actually, it lies about 195 miles north of London on the Ouse River, and can easily be tied in with a motor trip to Edinburgh. Or, after visiting Cambridge, a motorist can make a swing through a too-often-neglected cathedral circuit: Ely, Lincoln, then York.

There was a Roman York (Hadrian came this way), then a Saxon York, a Danish York, a Norman York (William the Conqueror slept here), a medieval York, a Georgian York, a Victorian York (the center of a flourishing rail business), even a 20th-century York. A surprising amount of 18th-century York remains, including Richard Boyle's restored Assembly Rooms.

THE SIGHTS: The best way to see York is to go to the **Tourist Information Centre,** DeGrey Rooms, Exhibition Square (tel. York 21756) at 10:15 a.m. and 2:15 p.m. daily from Good Friday to the end of October, where you'll be met by a voluntary guide who will take you on an 1½-hour walking tour of the city, revealing its history and lore through numerous intriguing stories. There is no charge. Additional tours are made at 7:15 p.m. daily during June, July, and August.

At some point in your exploration, you may want to visit **The Shambles,** once the meat-butchering center of York, dating back before the Norman Conquest. But this messy business has given way, and the ancient street survives. It is filled with jewelry stores, cafes, and buildings that huddle so closely together you can practically stand in the middle of the pavement, arms outstretched, and touch the houses on both sides of the street.

York Minster

One of the great cathedrals of the world, York Minster traces its origins back to the early seventh century. The present building, however, dates mainly from the 13th century. Like the minster at Lincoln, York Cathedral is characterized by three towers, all built in the 15th century. The central tower is lantern shaped, in the Perpendicular style.

Perhaps the distinguishing characteristic of the cathedral is its medley of stained glass from the Middle Ages—in glorious Angelico blues, ruby reds, forest greens, and ambers. See in particular the large east window, the work of a 15th-century Coventry glass painter. In the north transept is an architectural gem of the mid-13th century, the "Five Sisters," with its lancets. The choir screen, from the late 15th century, has an impressive line-up—everybody from William the Conqueror to the overthrown Henry VI.

The undercroft is open Monday to Saturday from 10 a.m. to dusk (on Sunday from 1 to 4 p.m.), charging adults 40p (92¢) for admission; children 20p (46¢). The central tower is open Monday to Saturday, April to September, from 10:30 a.m. to 7 p.m. (October to March, 10:30 a.m. to 3:30 p.m.), costing adults and children 50p ($1.15). The chapter house is open Monday to Saturday, May to October, from 10 a.m., costing adults 10p (23¢); children, 5p (12¢). The crypt is shown during conducted tours only. At an Information Desk in the south aisle of the Minster parties can be put in touch with a guide, if one is available, for a conducted tour. No charge is made, and the guides do not accept gratuities. Gifts toward the maintenance of the Minster are, however, always welcome.

York Castle Museum

On Tower Street, the York Castle Museum is one of the finest folk museums in the country. Its unique feature is the shop-flanked Kirkgate, the recreation of a cobbled street, with authentic facades moved to the site (including a silversmith). The present exhibition was inspired mainly by a Dr. Kirk who on his travels through Yorkshire acquired a large collection of antiques and old relics.

Upstairs rooms range from a formal, neoclassic Georgian interior to an overstuffed and heavily adorned Victorian living room. In the debtors' prison, former prison cells have been converted into workshops, such as one cubicle where a blacksmith plies his trade.

On the main floor, a collection of costumes ranges from a gown a Georgian debutante would have worn to a fancy-dress ball all the way to the grandmother of the mini in the post-World War I era. Firearms and armor are also displayed.

Part of the debtors' prison is the Half-Moon Court, a recreation of an Edwardian street, with a gypsy caravan, a sheriff's coach, and a pub that would have attracted the eye of Dickens. Finally, you can visit a mill powered by the water of the Foss River. The museum is open April to September, Monday to Saturday, 9:30 a.m. to 6 p.m.; Sunday, 10 a.m. to 6 p.m. From October to March, hours are from 9:30 to 4:30 p.m. weekdays, 10 a.m. to 4:30 p.m. on Sunday. Admission is 85p ($1.96) for adults, 45p ($1.04) for children.

National Railway Museum

The first national museum to be built away from London, the National Railway Museum has attracted more than seven million visitors in five years of operation. Adapted from an original steam locomotive depot, the museum gives visitors a chance to look under and inside steam locomotives or see how Queen Victoria traveled in luxury. In addition, there's a full-size collection of railway memorabilia, including an early 19th-century clock and penny machines for purchasing tickets to the railway platform. On display are more than 20 full-size locomotives. One, the *Agenoria*, dates from 1829, and is a contemporary of Stephenson's well-known *Rocket*. It's almost identical to the first American locomotive, the *Stourbridge Lion*, brought over from England in 1828. The last steam locomotive made in Britain, the *Evening Star*, is from 1960. Of several royal coaches, the most interesting is the century-old Royal Saloon, in which Queen Victoria rode until her death. It's like a small hotel, with polished wood, silk, brocade, and silver accessories. The museum, on Leeman Road, can be visited weekdays from 10 a.m. to 6 p.m. and on Sunday from 2:30 to 6. Admission is free.

Theatre Royal

Finally, Theatre Royal, St. Leonard's Place (tel. York 23568), is an old traditional theater building with modern additions to house the box office bars and restaurant. It is worth inquiring about the current production as the Royal Shakespeare Company includes York in its tours, the Arts Council presents dance, drama, and opera, and visiting celebrities appear in classics. There is also an excellent resident repertory company.

Seats go from around £1.50 ($3.45) to about £5 ($11.50) when there are visiting celebrities. The glass-walled, ground-floor restaurant does pre- and postperformance meals, and a hot dish costs about £1.25 ($2.88). Sandwiches and burgers, cakes, and pies go at about 95p ($2.19). You don't have to buy a seat to eat here, and it's quite a relaxing experience to sit inside with your drink and a snack, looking out on the world passing by.

A Horse-Drawn Carriage Tour

While in York, what about a 15-minute trip in a horse-drawn Danish carriage around the city? One or two horses pull up to five persons, and an umbrella protects you in case it rains. The cost is 80p ($1.84) for adults and 40p (92¢) for children. Call Mr. B. W. Calam (tel. York 769-490) for more information, or else just turn up at the cathedral's west doors where he is likely to be found. He's also available for private rentals, including day country trips for four to six persons, costing about £24 ($55.20) per person up to eight hours. You can stop at country pubs for drinks and farmhouses for tea. He also takes visitors on evening trips, with lantern lights, the price depending on the time.

WHERE TO STAY: Our recommendations for rooms and meals follow.

The Upper Bracket

Viking Hotel, North Street (tel. York 59822), is a nine-floor, ultramodern hotel, built in 1968. It takes its name from the Viking kingdom of York of 867, but that's the only thing ancient about it. Borrowing some of the best of Scandinavian design concepts, it is perhaps the most tastefully contemporary hotel in northeastern England, utilizing such features as natural pine, brick, wool, and ceramic glass. On the river's edge, its public rooms (and all double bedrooms) face not only the water, but the minster in the distance.

Steve Tavener, the general manager, has set the following rates: £26 ($59.80) to £30 ($69) for a single room, £37 ($85.10) to £41 ($94.30) in a double, including breakfast and service charge, plus tax. The bedrooms—all with private bath—have built-in furniture, dressing tables, wardrobes (with luggage space), and headboards with buttons to turn on music, radio, lights, TV, or else to summon the maid. Each room—114 in all—is decorated in vibrant, primary colors, contrasting with the white brick walls and wood paneling. The baths have showers and a lot of amenities too often overlooked, including facial tissues and heated towel racks. Off the airy, light, and lofty reception area is Longboat Bar, in natural wood and red brick, with corner nooks for relaxed drinking. In the Regatta Restaurant, luncheon and dinner are served.

The Judges Lodging, 9 Lendal (tel. York 23587). The earliest historical fact about this charming house is that it was the home of a certain Dr. Wintringham in 1710. At the beginning of the 19th century it is listed as having been a judges' lodging, used when they traveled north from the London Inns of Justice. In 1979 it was bought by Geoffrey Mason, Her Majesty's consul in Biarritz, and his delightful Hungarian countess wife. Mme. la Comtesse was brought up in Paris and has had a very wide experience of hotels. Her touch is evident throughout the elegant building. Drive around the sweeping drive, then up the broad stone steps to the stout front door. You will be greeted by the butler who will register your name and then lead you up a magnificent circular wooden staircase, the only one of its type in the United Kingdom, to one of the bedrooms. Many have four-poster beds; others, large doubles and twins. Hand-embroidered sheets and French embroidered linen in the bathrooms are an additional elegant touch. Each room has a different decor and is named accordingly. One is known as the Queen Mother Room and, in fact, it is with her blessing that the coffee cups you will use at dinner come from Clarence House.

There are two dining rooms, where candles flicker and the carefully trained French staff will attend to your every need. Dinner will cost around £12 ($27.60) for four courses, but the experience is worth it. All meat, fish, and vegetables are brought in fresh, and the countess does much of the selecting and cooking. The menu is a mouthwatering selection. Down in the old cellars where they found all sorts of bits of Roman pottery, antique pieces of glass, and other relics of the house's varied past, there is the Cocktail Bar, open to the public. Bar snacks at lunchtime include quiche Lorraine and smoked salmon with brown bread, from 85p ($1.96) to £2.50 ($5.75). Tuesday is always Pancake Day, when two large pancakes with varied fillings will cost £1.50 ($3.45). Your room will go from £50 ($115) a night for two, to £55 ($126.50) for two in a room with a four-poster, including breakfast and VAT. You may be lucky enough to see one of the three ghosts—the countess has—that of Elizabeth Wintringham who was shut in to stop her eloping with her lover.

Royal Station Hotel (tel. York 53681), outside the city, was built when it was fashionable to stop for the night at a railway station hotel. Owned by British Transport Hotels, it is a mammoth building, not unlike a palace. Most of its 118 bedrooms have private baths. The most expensive rates apply from May 1 to September 30, when a bathless single rents for £24 ($55.20), a bathless double for £36 ($82.80). With bath, a single goes for £32 ($73.60), a double for £40 ($92), including a full breakfast, service, and VAT. The rooms are generally spacious, well furnished, and comfortable. There's an elaborate garden with a central fountain, and surrounding woods. York Minster is only a five-minute walk from the hotel. The public rooms were designed for Victorian grandeur, with high ceilings and miles of carpeting. In the lofty dining room, you can order an à la carte dinner at £10 ($23), including VAT and service. With a separate entrance at the side of the hotel, Bess's Coffee Shop offers steaks, omelets, curries, hamburgers, and salads, a good meal costing under £5 ($11.50).

The Medium-Priced Range

The **Post House,** Tadcaster Road (tel. York 67921), is a Trust Houses Forte enterprise, built on the grounds of a former manor house. Only a mile and a half south of the center of York, it is on the A1036, the main approach to York from the A1 and the south. Although contemporary in design, with picture windows in each bedroom, there are many traditional touches as well. The entrance hall and living room, for example, have authentic York flagstones and a montage of old prints and local family crests. A single in summer rents for £26 ($59.80), a double for £38 ($87.40). Service and tax are included, but breakfast is extra. Each room has a single color theme, with such amenities as air conditioning, color TV, radio, tea- and coffee-making facilities. The Cedar Restaurant has wide-view windows overlooking a magnificent cedar of Lebanon planted many years ago. An international cuisine is offered. Light meals and snacks, as well as breakfasts, are served in the York Highflyer buttery. Predinner drinks are to be had in the bar, where the wall cabinets are filled with heavy leather-bound books, such as one finds in a country house.

Mount Royale Hotel, The Mount (tel. York 56261), is excellent value for the money, and the food is good, too. Run by Richard and Christine Oxtoby, the Mount Royale is only minutes from the city center. Built in 1833, it is carefully furnished with some beautiful antiques blended with modern pieces. They have taken over the house next door, increasing their bedroom capacity to 18 units, each with bath, costing from £30 ($69) for two persons, including VAT and a large breakfast. The hotel has a swimming pool. The menu consists of roast joints with interesting accompaniments—grilled York ham with eggs and spinach, fresh halibut with mushroom sauce, roast duckling with black cherry and brandy sauce, duckling with green pepper and corn sauce. The extensive set menu, costing £9 ($20.70), carries supplements for such items as fresh out-of-season asparagus or strawberries. The dining room opens onto an attractive garden.

Justifiably popular with locals, the restaurant requires advance booking. As one local habitué told us, "I suppose that now my son is a week old, it's too late to book for his 21st birthday!" It's still worth the effort trying to get in, however.

Dean Court Hotel, Duncombe Place (tel. York 25082), is an ancient building lying right beneath the towers of the minster. All rooms have bathroom or shower, telephone, radio, and color TV. Ian Washington, the owner, has done a lot recently to bring facilities up to the standards expected these days. Bed and breakfast is £22 ($50.60) per person nightly. Lunch will cost £6 ($13.80); dinner, £7.50 ($17.25), for a meal from a well-chosen table d'hôte. VAT and service are included in all prices. There is a coffee lounge where snacks are served from 10 a.m. to 10 p.m. A salad will cost around £2 ($4.60), or there are sandwiches at about 65p ($1.50) a serving.

The Budget Range

Beechwood Close Hotel, 19 Shipton Rd. (tel. York 58378). On the A19, north of the city, Beechwood is a large house surrounded by trees, a garden with a putting green, and free parking space. Mr. and Mrs. Bulmer have converted it into a hotel, with all modern comforts, such as hot and cold running water in the rooms (most with showers) and central heating. The charge for a bed and a good Yorkshire breakfast is £13.50 ($31.05) to £14.50 ($33.35), including VAT and service. With its friendly atmosphere, Beechwood attracts many North Americans. It's a 15-minute walk to the minster, either by road or along the river. However, a bus stop is close by.

The **White Swan Hotel**, Piccadilly (tel. York 28851), is a large corner building, fashioned in the Elizabethan style and lying within easy walking distance of the Shambles. It has 30 bedrooms, pleasantly furnished and immaculately maintained, with a relatively large number of single rooms. The rate for bed and breakfast is £15.25 ($35.08) in a single, £25 ($57.50) in a double, VAT included. The rooms are adequately equipped, with innerspring mattresses, hot and cold running water, radio, telephone, and facilities for making tea and coffee. Breakfast is served in a modern dining room on the ground floor.

Galtres Lodge, Low Petergate (tel. York 22478), is a Georgian brick building, presided over by Mr. and Mrs. Adams, who have completely redecorated it, and, in so doing, found three priest holes, one Adam fireplace, and two beautiful Georgian fireplaces which have greatly added to the charm of the hotel. The tariff is £10 ($23) per person for bed and breakfast, including VAT. Some of the rooms open onto a view of the rose window of the cathedral. Lunch is offered à la carte from noon to 2 p.m. The location of the Galtres is faultless, lying only a hop from the minster, and in the vicinity of the railway station. Incidentally, the name of the street (Petergate) is a holdover from the Danish occupation in pre-Norman days. Gate is not used in the English sense, but in the Scandinavian way, meaning street. Historical note: There is a plaque attached to the wall outside the hotel, showing that the street was once the "via principalis" of the old Roman fortress of Eboracum.

Bootham Bar Hotel, 4 High Petergate (tel. York 58516), is a charming place, a scrupulously clean, 18th-century house with bedroom views over various city sights. Right by the minster, it is well situated for walking in the evening. Mr. and Mrs. M. Warren offer ten bedrooms at a rate of £8.25 ($18.98) per person nightly, including an English breakfast, although VAT is extra. A £5 ($11.50) deposit will secure a room. All the accommodations, incidentally, are heated and contain wash basins and radios. There is a small lounge with TV. Mrs. Warren's tiny staff is pleasant and helpful.

Granby Lodge Hotel, Scarcroft Road (tel. York 53291), is a family-run hotel lying about a ten-minute walk from the historical "downtown" of York. Centrally heated, the hotel, run by the Jacksons, offers 57 pleasantly furnished bedrooms which contain hot and cold running water, shaver points, radios, and tea- or coffee-making facilities. Some of the units are equipped with private baths or showers. The cost is £12 ($27.60) per person nightly, including VAT, although you'll pay a small supplement for private plumbing. The licensed restaurant, seating 120 diners, offers good English food, a reasonably priced dinner served between 6 and 7 p.m. A full English breakfast is included in the tariff quoted. The cozy cocktail bar provides an attractive old-world atmosphere, and there is a separate TV lounge. Private parking is available.

On the Outskirts

Lady Anne Middleton's Hotel, Skeldergate House, Skeldergate (tel. York 32257), is a delightful 17th-century house, originally built as a hostel for the widows of York's freemen. On the river right opposite the Castle Museum is the main hotel with 21 rooms, mostly with shower. The restaurant is converted from an old sawmill, and across the way is Cromwell House with a further 16 bedrooms. Although recently built, it was very carefully constructed to keep the tone of its ancient surroundings.

Andrew Clark and his wife Kathe have lovingly restored the buildings and created a very comfortable overnight hostelry. They charge £7.50 ($17.25) to £9.50 ($21.85) per person for a room and a continental breakfast. There is good car parking, and close by is the world's largest "O" railway exhibition. And in the nearby Quaker burial ground lie John Woolman and Linley Murray, the founders of the American Quaker movement.

WHERE TO EAT: Betty's Restaurant, St. Helen's Square (tel. York 22323), is a good all-around eating house in York, regardless of the price range in which you travel. First, at its second-floor self-service restaurant, well-prepared luncheons are served from 11:30 a.m. till 2 p.m., averaging £2 ($4.60) for a meal consisting of a main course, including vegetables, plus dessert for 50p ($1.15). The food is traditionally English, including roast pork with stuffing and steak-and-kidney pie. All dishes are attractively served. There's no skimping on the portions either, and the restaurant is licensed.

In the Oak Room in the basement, with bar and waitress service, a set lunch is featured for £3.50 ($8.05). Dinner is à la carte only. Main courses average around £3.50 also, and desserts are priced from 75p ($1.73). On the ground floor is a confectionery, gift section, and coffee lounge. The restaurant is closed on Sunday.

Aquarius, 108 Fishergate (tel. York 54750), is a "New Age" restaurant, run by Joanna Rayes, and specializing in vegetarian whole-food cookery, deep frying, and fish dishes. Except for the fish, the health-food restaurant does not use any animal produce or sugar in its cuisine. The setting is modest, and the cooking is done to order. A bowl of homemade soup with bread is featured daily, along with two or three specials which might include deep-fried rice balls, savory bean bake, or cauliflower tempura with noodles. The average price of a meal is £2.50 ($5.75). However, the most expensive dish, with coffee, will only cost around £4 ($9.20). The restaurant is open daily, except Sunday and Monday, from 12:30 to 3 p.m. and from 6 to 11 p.m.

Lew's Place, Kings Staithe (tel. York 28167), is an old wharfside gathering place, run with sprightly charm by Lewis Speight, who admits, "We try to cater for most tastes." Even some of his rival restaurant and cafe owners drop in whenever they're free. It's that relaxed and friendly. The food is good, too, certainly hardy. The menu changes daily. Main-course lunch prices average £2.80 ($6.44), increasing to £3.50 ($8.05) in the evening. The fare is likely to include a homemade moussaka, a savory seafood crêpe, a lamb steak (marinated in red wine, herbs, and garlic), even chili con carne. Usually a homemade soup is offered for a beginning course. Meals are served Monday to Saturday from noon to 2 p.m. and from 7 to 10 p.m.

Restaurant Bari, 15 The Shambles (tel. York 33807), is run by Giovanni and Helen Santorsola. It takes its name from the city of Bari, the hometown of Mr. Santorsola. The setting is modest, and the menu offers pizzas in the £1.50 ($3.45) to £2.20 ($5.06) range, the latter price for the chef's special concoction. The pasta dishes are good, especially the cannelloni at £2.20 ($5.06). Of course, there is homemade minestrone at 75p ($1.73). A main dish meat specialty is scalloppe Sophia Loren (filet of pork with brandy and cheese in a tomato sauce), £4 ($9.20). Lunchtime meals cost from as little as £1.50 ($3.45). The restaurant is open seven days a week from 11:30 a.m. to 2:30 p.m. and from 6 to 11 p.m.

Thomas's Wine Bar and Bistro, Museum Street (tel. York 54494). On a site where in the 1870s Eldrige's Royal Hotel was offering "a high standard of comfort and service to the nobility and county gentry," Thomas's now offers very good, economical meals or just a snack to sustain anyone who wants to stop. Downstairs, the wine bar has bare wooden floors and country-style wooden furniture; wine and sherry are dispensed from casks behind the bar. Pâtés, cheeses, pies, and salads are available at lunchtime. The bar is open seven days a week from noon to 2:30 p.m. and from 7 to 10:30 p.m.

Upstairs, the Bistro dispenses a set luncheon at £3.50 ($8.05) with a choice of three dishes. A more ambitious menu is offered at £5.50 ($12.65). There is also quite a large menu of dishes at around £6 ($13.80), including duck with orange, poached turbot, or veal escalope. The cost entitles you to an appetizer and dessert. The very pleasant atmosphere is created by Pam and Ian Postlethwaite, who run the place.

Plunkets, 9 High Petergate, is a bright, cheerful, busy place right beneath the shadow of the minster yet seeming to fit in with its ancient surroundings. Hamburgers are served with french fries, salad with choice of dressing, and the relish tray. All the usual ones are there from plain quarter-pounder at £1.80 ($4.14) to Plunket Burger, a half-pounder with cheese or chili topping. A large club sandwich is £1.70 ($3.91), and a T-bone steak goes for £5 ($11.50). There are milkshakes, ice creams, cheesecake, chocolate fudge cake, and banana splits, all costing around 90p ($2.07). At peak hours—lunch and suppertime—you must eat, but at other times just a coffee or milkshake is all you need have. There are several smaller rooms upstairs where you cannot hear the musak and be a little more intimate if you wish to. The place is open from 11 a.m. to 11 p.m. daily, although in winter they close from 3 to 5 p.m.

The Kings Arms, King Street, started life as a hostelry in 1534 when the cobbled street was called Kergate. Right beside Ouse Bridge and the river, the place has flood marks in the bar recording times when the whole place must have been under water for days at a time. On less damp days you can watch coasters unloading their cargo at the wharfs opposite the pub. Your host is Derick Bragg, and most of the beer he sells is brewed in local breweries. He features some very strong real ales. Bar snacks include a Highwayman's Platter, black pudding (a dark, spicy sausage) with onions, gravy peas, and chips, for £1.50 ($3.45). There are less filling hot dishes and interesting salads, such as sardine and apple, from 75p ($1.73) to £1.30 ($2.99).

LODGINGS IN THE ENVIRONS: Just about 30 miles southeast of York lies a small market town, Beverley, in North Humberside. There are several medieval buildings in the town, and many travelers prefer to stay here instead of in York proper.

The **Beverley Arms Hotel,** North Bar Within, Beverley, North Humberside (tel. Hull 885-241), is, in part, more than 300 years old. A wing has been added to provide bedrooms with bath, radio, phone, TV, and tea- and coffee-making equipment. A double room costs £30 ($69) a night, including VAT and service. Breakfast, and all other meals, are extra. The restaurant features many seafood and fish dishes, using produce caught daily in the North Sea and landed at Hull. There is also the Ridings Buttery, a coffeeshop constructed in the old kitchens, with a stone-flagged floor and high-backed chairs where snacks and light meals are served from 9:20 a.m. to 10:30 p.m. The North Bar serves traditional ales, and there are good bar snacks.

Kings Head Hotel, Market Place, Beverley, North Humberside (tel. Hull 883-103), is a Georgian inn where a double room will cost you £21 ($48.30); a single, £11 ($25.30)—including a full Yorkshire breakfast. This is a typical small-town place where standards have to be kept up otherwise you lose your regular customers. Lunch at £3 ($6.90) includes a choice of three appetizers, then from two roasts, steak-and-kidney pie, or several other hot dishes, plus dessert. Dinner at £5 ($11.50) includes such substantial dishes as lamb cutlets and braised steak with carrots and onions. There is also an à la carte menu with dishes, grills, and salads at around £7 ($16.10). But who wants it when such succulent local dishes are available?

A SIDE TRIP FROM YORK: The most interesting day trip from York is a trip to:

Castle Howard

In its dramatic setting of lakes, fountains, and extensive gardens, the 18th-century palace designed by Sir John Vanbrugh is undoubtedly the finest private residence in Yorkshire. The first major achievement of the architect who later created the lavish Blenheim Palace near Oxford, Castle Howard was begun in 1699 for the third Earl of Carlisle, Charles Howard, whose descendants still call the place "home." The striking facade is topped by a painted and gilded dome, reaching more than 80 feet into the air. The interior boasts a 192-foot "Long Gallery," as well as a chapel with a magnificent stained-glass window by the 19th-century artist, Sir Edward Burne-Jones. Besides the collections of antique furniture, tapestries, porcelains, and sculpture, the castle contains a number of important paintings, including a portrait of Henry VIII by Holbein, and works by Rubens, Reynolds, and Gainsborough.

The seemingly endless grounds around the palace also offer the visitor some memorable sights, including the domed Temple of the Four Winds, by Vanbrugh, and the richly designed family mausoleum by Hawksmoor. There are two rose gardens, one with old-fashioned roses, the other featuring modern creations. The stable court houses the Costume Galleries, the largest private collection of 18th- to 20th-century costumes in Britain. The authentically dressed mannequins are exhibited in period settings. Castle Howard is just 15 miles northeast of York. The grounds are open from 11 a.m., and the hours for the house and Costume Gallery are from 11:30 a.m. to 5 p.m. Admission is £1.50 ($3.45) for adults, 75p ($1.73) for children, including entrances to both the house gallery and grounds.

2. North Yorkshire

Yorkshire, known to readers of *Wuthering Heights* around the world, is now divided into three counties—West Yorkshire, South Yorkshire, and North Yorkshire. For those seeking legendary untamed scenery, we'd recommend a tour of North Yorkshire, which also takes in the historic cathedral city of York.

North Yorkshire contains England's most varied landscape. Its history has been turbulent, often bloody, and many relics of its rich past are still standing, including ruined abbeys. Yorkshire is little known to the average North American visitor, but many an English traveler knows of its haunting moors, serene valleys, and windswept dales.

The hospitality of the people of Yorkshire is world renowned, and if a pudding which originated there doesn't accompany a slab of roast beef, the plate looks naked to the British. The people of Yorkshire, who speak an original twang often imitated in English cinema, are, in general, hard-working and industrious, perhaps a little contemptuous of the easy living of the south. But they are decidedly open and friendly to strangers, providing you speak to them first.

HARROGATE: If you head northeast from York for 20 miles, you reach Harrogate, North Yorkshire's second-largest town after York itself. In the 19th century, Harrogate was a fashionable spa. Most of its town center is surrounded by a 200-acre lawn called "The Stray." Boutiques and antique shops—which Queen Mary used to frequent—make Harrogate a shopping center of excellence, particularly along Montpellier Parade. Harrogate is called England's floral resort, deserving such a reputation because of its gardens, including Harlow Car Gardens and Valley Gardens. The former spa has an abundance of guest houses and hotels, including the expensive Swan where Agatha Christie hid out during her mysterious disappearance—still unexplained—in the 1920s.

Food and Lodging

The Old Swan, Swan Road (tel. Harrogate 504-051). This is the spot where the late mystery writer, Agatha Christie, suddenly surfaced after a mysterious 11-day disappearance that was the subject of the film *Agatha*, starring Dustin Hoffman. One of the most famous hotels in northern England, the Old Swan commemorates that long-ago event by naming its restaurant the Agatha Christie Library, which, incidentally, serves a chocolate cake known as "Delicious Death" which was featured in one of her novels. The Old Swan certainly predates Ms. Christie—in fact, it goes back to 1700.

Its 140 rooms are well furnished, and each has a private bath. The basic tariff for a twin-bedded room is £45 ($103.50) per night, and in a single, £30 ($69), both rates including VAT and an English breakfast. The public rooms are spacious and pleasantly grand, often with Victorian design.

Yorke Arms Hotel, Ramsgill, near Harrogate (tel. Harrogate 75243), is surrounded by moody moorland scenery, and is an ideal center for excursions. It's a widely spread manor house, with many well-preserved architectural features, plus a selection of antiques. The dining hall, for example, with its black oak sideboard, holds a collection of pewter, and you dine on Windsor armchairs in front of a time-blackened fireplace. The lounge has tufted velvet sofas drawn up around a stone fireplace. The exterior is stately, built of stone, with creeping ivy covering part of its gables and mullioned windows. The rooms are comfortably furnished and well maintained, and some contain private baths. The cost of half board here is about £27 ($62.10) per person nightly.

In this attractively furnished town house, built back in Victoria's day, **Number Six,** 6 Ripon Rd. (tel. Harrogate 502-908), is one of the finest dining rooms at the spa, and we recommend that you skip a meal at your hotel to patronize this fine and well-run establishment. Mr. Di Silvestro and Mr.

McClure have hired a well-trained staff to serve their beautifully prepared dishes, which are likely to include such delicacies as poached Tay salmon, chicken Kiev, roast duckling in orange sauce, lobster thermidor, and quails in cocotte.

As you enter the restaurant you can head for the intimate bar to enjoy an apéritif, and, while sipping it, make menu selections from an imaginative choice of dishes, mostly continental in flavor and presentation. Ingredients are well chosen, and the wine list is above average. The price of most dishes, beginning at £8.25 ($18.98) and going up, includes appetizer, soup, and dessert, the latter most often a mouthwatering, rich concoction. Expect to pay at least £11 ($25.30) per person. Only dinner is served, except Monday, and hours are from 7 to 10 p.m., when reservations are essential.

MOORS AND DALES: The rural landscape is pierced with ruins of once-great abbeys and castles. North Yorkshire is a land of green hills, valleys, and purple moors. Both the Yorkshire Dales and the Moors are wide open spaces, two of Britain's finest national parks, with a combined area of some 1200 square miles. However, the term "national" can be misleading, as the land is managed by foresters, farmers, and private landowners. In fact, more than 90% of the land is in private ownership. The Dales rise toward Cumbria and Lancashire to the east, and the Moors stretch to the eastern coastline.

Of course, York, the major center, has already been previewed. But those with the time may want to explore deeper into the rural roots of England. From Harrogate, our last stopover, you can enjoy the wildest scenery of the region by heading out on day trips, anchoring at one of the inns coming up if you don't want to return to the old spa.

After leaving Harrogate, you can discover white limestone crags, drystone walls, fast-rushing rivers, and isolated sheep farms or else clusters of sandstone cottages.

Malhamdale receives more visitors annually than any dale in Yorkshire. Of the priories and castles to visit, two of the most interesting are the 12th-century ruins of **Bolton Priory,** and a 14th-century pile, **Castle Bolton,** to the north in Wensleydale.

Richmond, the most frequently used town name in the world, stands here at the head of the Dales as the mother of them all. Here the Norman towers of Richmond Castle, the county's best known fortress, dominate the cobbled market town.

In contrast, the Moors, on the other side of the Vale of York, have a wild beauty all their own, quite different from that of the Dales. They are bounded by the Cleveland and Hambleton Hills. The white horse of Kilburn can be seen hewn out of the landscape.

Both **Pickering** and **Northallerton,** two market towns, serve as gateways to the Moors. Across the Moors are seen primordial burial grounds and stone crosses. The best known trek in moorland is the 40-mile hike over bog, heather, and stream from Mount Grace Priory inland to Ravenscar on the seacoast. It's known as **Lyke Wake Walk.**

In your tour of the Moors, a good center is **Helmsley,** the key to Ryedale and the mother town of the district, standing as it does at the junction of the roads from York, Pickering, Malton, Stokesley, and Thirsk. Beyond the main square at Helmsley are the ruins of the castle with its impressive keep. This castle was built between 1186 and 1227.

Three miles to the north of Helmsley, the ruins of **Rievaulx Abbey** are among the most impressive in England, charging an admission of 50p ($1.15) for visits. Rievaulx was the first large Cistercian church to be built in England. Construction began in 1131, and work continued until its completion in 1175. In its heyday, it was a stunning example of the English Gothic style.

Coxwold is on the southern border of the park, one of the most attractive villages in the Moors.

Along North Yorkshire's 45 miles of coastline are such traditional seaside resorts as **Filey, Whitby,** and **Scarborough,** the latter claiming to be the oldest seaside spa in Britain, standing on the site of a Roman signaling station. It was founded in 1622, following the discovery of mineral springs with medicinal properties. In the 19th century, its Grand Hotel, a Victorian structure, was acclaimed "as the best in Europe." The Norman castle on big cliffs overlooks the twin bays.

At Helmsley

The **Black Swan** (tel. Helmsley 466) has stood since the 16th century overlooking the marketplace. Part Tudor, part Georgian, part modern, this Trust House Forte hotel offers 38 well-furnished bedrooms, each with private bath, radio, TV, phone, and coffee-making facilities. These rent from £26 ($59.80) in a single, from £32.50 ($74.75) in a double, including service, breakfast, and VAT. A new wing of bedrooms has been added at the rear. Public rooms are full of character, with open fires, paneling, and time-aged beams. In the traditionally furnished restaurant, you can enjoy unusual Yorkshire dishes, such as Wensley fowl stuffed with dale cheese or jugged venison, a dinner costing from £8 ($18.40) per head. The hotel also has three bars.

Crown Hotel, Market Square (tel. Helmsley 297), is of undetermined age, but quite old and colorful. It's built of stone, standing at the edge of the village square, and the walls are covered by creepers, giving it charm. The owners, Mr. and Mrs. Mander, have spared no effort to make every room not only attractive, but comfortable. Seven of their bedrooms now have showers, all have hot and cold running water, and, wherever possible, in the restoration old beams have been left exposed. The dining room is well furnished; there are two bars, one public and one better furnished for residents. In addition, there are two living rooms. Bed and breakfast are priced according to the plumbing you get, £11 ($25.30) to £12 ($27.60) per person, including VAT. For dinner, bed, and breakfast, the cost is £14 ($32.20) to £15 ($34.50). Set lunches are from £4 ($9.20), dinners from £7 ($16.10), and the food is typically English.

Near Skipton

Devonshire Arms, Bolton Abbey, near Skipton (tel. Bolton Abbey 265), is a home of old-world charm, a riverside inn which is furnished in part with antiques and old furniture. The owners are Mr. and Mrs. Hodgson, who give you a hearty welcome and will point out ways of reaching nearby attractions, including Haworth and the Brontë country. The hotel itself is in Wharfedale, with a view across to the river, and Bolton Priory is less than a mile away. Guests can also enjoy North Country trouting at its best.

After warming yourself by the open fire, you're shown to one of a dozen rooms, only one of which has a private bath (a double), that one going for £33 ($75.90) nightly, breakfast extra. A standard bathless double costs £27.50 ($63.25), dropping to £21 ($48.30) in a single.

The restaurant, filled with antiques, opens onto views of the garden. Well-chosen ingredients are used in the traditional English fare, and service is polite and efficient. A table d'hôte dinner begins at £12 ($27.60), although lunches are served from £5 ($11.50).

The **Buck Inn,** Malham, near Skipton (tel. Airton 317), is a Victorian stone inn where Dale explorers can find excellent ale, a comfortable and cozy room, and a good breakfast and dinner. There are two bars, one especially for hikers, the other for residents. The inn offers ten centrally heated bedrooms, each with a wash basin, only one with a private bath, which costs £1 ($2.30) extra per night. The cost is £10 ($23) for bed and breakfast, £15 ($34.50) for half board, including VAT, between July 1 and mid-October, and after that, tariffs are reduced. You can order bar lunches noon and evenings if you don't want a full meal.

At Thornton-le-Dale

The **Hall,** Thornton-le-Dale, near Pickering (tel. Thornton-le-Dale 254), is a stately 16th-century manor house with a formal facade and an informal rear garden. A fully licensed residential hotel, it stands in the center of what had been called "the prettiest village in Yorkshire," on the main Pickering–Scarborough Road. The interior has been adapted for modern comfort, and many of the comfortable bedrooms have private baths. For the most part, antiques have given way to modern furnishings. The bed-and-breakfast tariff ranges from £20 ($48.30) per night in a single to £30 ($69) in a double. Dinner costs yet another £7 ($16.10). A riding school is attached to the hotel.

Ripon

A cathedral city on the Ure River, Ripon is the second oldest incorporated community in the country, dating from 886 A.D. It still maintains the ancient custom of the "Sounding of the Horn" at 9 o'clock every evening. The Curfew Bell and the Corn Bell are also still used.

Of its many fine old buildings, none is better known than its cathedral, with its fine Saxon crypt dating from 674 A.D. Across from the Market Square is the Wakeman's House, one of the oldest and most interesting buildings of its kind in England, containing a tiny museum.

The **Unicorn Hotel,** Market Place (tel. Ripon 2202), is a coaching and posting inn that has been putting up wayfarers for some 400 years. It's directly on the market square, in full view of the cathedral. The facade of the inn is decorated rather elaborately, with a cluster of five bay windows and an ornate front entrance. Of the 25 well-appointed bedrooms, 13 are equipped with private baths en suite. Singles rent from £15 ($34.50), and doubles or twins peak at £24 ($55.20), these tariffs including VAT and a full English breakfast. Guests can dine either in the Pykestolle restaurant, with a wide choice of mainly British dishes, or else in the Cornucoppia coffee bar, serving light snacks or grills.

The **Nordale,** 1 North Parade, Ripon (tel. Ripon 3557), is a bargain at the daily per-person rate of £7.25 ($16.68), which includes not only a complete full-course breakfast but VAT. There are no "private facilities" except the hot and cold running water in your room. However, adequate baths are in the halls. Consider having a Yorkshire dinner as well, and this costs £10.50 ($24.15) per person, including your room and breakfast. Mrs. Richmond, the owner, will pack a picnic lunch for you if you are making a day trip. All her bedrooms are attractively furnished, with twins and doubles, according to your wish. Children can stay at reduced rates. The Nordale is a good center for exploring the Yorkshire Dales.

Black-a-Moor Inn, Risplith, near Ripon (tel. Sawley 214), is a stone country inn well known for its hospitality and convivial atmosphere. It's on the Ripon to Pateley Bridge road, the B6265, five miles from Ripon, just perfect for visits to Fountains Abbey, the Brimham Rocks, and the Dales. Owners Peter and Elisabeth James have decorated the three bedrooms with taste, installing central heating as well as hot and cold running water. They charge £8.50 ($19.55) per person daily for bed and breakfast, including VAT and the service charge. Their breakfasts are "as you want it." In addition, Elisabeth can prepare evening meals—simple country fare—such as homemade steak-and-kidney pie.

3. West Yorkshire

HAWORTH: In West Yorkshire, this ancient stone village lying on the high moors of the Pennines—45 miles west of York via Leeds and 21 miles west of Leeds itself—is world famous as the home of the Brontë family. The three sisters—Charlotte, Emily, and Anne—distinguished themselves as English novelists. They lived a life of imagination at a lonely parsonage at Haworth.

Anne wrote two novels, *The Tenant of Wildfell Hall* and *Agnes Grey,* and Charlotte's masterpiece was *Jane Eyre,* which depicted her experiences as a governess and enjoyed popular success in its day.

But, of course, it was Emily's fierce and tragic *Wuthering Heights* which made her surpass her sisters, as she created a novel of such passion, intensity, and primitive power, with its scenes of unforgettable, haunting melancholy, that the book has survived to this day, appreciated by later generations far more than those she'd written it for.

From Haworth, you can walk to Withens, the "Wuthering Heights" of the immortal novel. In Haworth, Charlotte and Emily are buried in the family vault under the church of St. Michael's.

The parsonage where they lived has been preserved as the **Brontë Parsonage Museum.** Emily and Charlotte died there. It may be visited daily from April 1 to September 30 on weekdays from 11 a.m. to 5:30 p.m., and on Sunday from 2 to 5:30 p.m. In winter it is open from 11 a.m. to 4:30 p.m. weekdays and on Sunday from 2 to 4:30 p.m. The admission is 40p (92¢) for adults, 20p (46¢) for children.

On the Haworth Moor stands a Brontë landmark, **Ponden Hall,** reputedly the model for Thrushcross Grange, Catherine's home after her marriage to Edgar Linton. Nestling in moorland in the middle of Pennine Way, this is, in fact, a private home (circa 1800). However, it sells hand-loomed rugs to visitors, and offers teas and lunches, all very typically English fare, costing from $4 to $7 for a meal.

For a tour of the many sights of the Brontë country—far too numerous to mention here—you can get in touch with Norman Raistrick, curator of the Parsonage Museum, or the U.S. representative of the Brontë Society, Katherine Reise, 335 Grove St., Oradell, NJ 07649.

Food and Lodging

The **Tourist Information Centre,** at Mill Hey in Haworth (tel. Haworth 42329), offers an accommodation-booking service, and the office is open daily from 11:30 a.m. to 5:30 p.m. from Easter until the end of October. Otherwise, you might stay at one of the recommendations below.

The **Old White Lion Hotel** (tel. Haworth 42313) stands at the top of a cobbled street. It was built around 1700 with a solid stone roof almost next door to the church where the Reverend Brontë preached and to the parsonage where the family lived. June and Ken Cousins welcome Brontë buffs in their warm, cheerful, and comfortable inn. They charge them £10 ($23) per person in a double, £11 ($25.30) in a single. For an additional £1.50 ($3.45) per person, you'll be given a room with a bath or shower. VAT and service are extra. Dinners, except Sunday, are à la carte, and good local meats and fresh vegetables are used at a cost of £5 ($11.50), per person. A set Sunday lunch costs £4 ($9.20), usually featuring a roast. Bar snacks include the usual favorites—ploughman's lunch, hot pies, and sandwiches at 85p ($1.96) a portion.

The Black Bull, Main Street (tel. Haworth 42249), owned by Ron and Kath Bennett, stands close to the parish church where Patrick Brontë was incumbent for 41 years and is closely associated with the son, Branwell Brontë. Although renovated and improved since Branwell's day, it is still interesting to spend time within the walls that drew him so strongly and even to sit in the chair which he occupied on his many visits to the place, still on the premises. Today the Black Bull is as comfortable an inn as you will find.

Conversion of the restaurant, which seats 40, has made use of a thick stone wall in forming a central arch. This is the room where Branwell's chair sits and here is the original bell pull and bell which he used to ring for his many drinks. Luncheon and bar snacks are served from noon until 2:30 p.m. A three-course lunch with roast beef and Yorkshire pudding costs around £4 ($9.20). Snacks and assorted sandwiches are served in the lounge area. Chicken, scampi, and haddock with chips and peas or homemade steak pie are offered for around £2 ($4.60). Dinner is served from 7 until 10:30 p.m. The cuisine is excellent, and the à la carte menu, with a good supporting wine list, gives an ample choice. Morning coffee and high tea are served on Sunday. The Bennetts charge £18 ($41.40) for a double room, including a good breakfast.

Keepers Restaurant, The Fold, Haworth, near Keighley (tel. Haworth 42919). Four cottages make up this delightful place presided over by Mrs. Starr, while her daughter, a qualified chef, and her husband do all the cooking. Although the present structure is not all that old (just a couple of hundred years), the original cottages date from the 15th century, and the decor reflects the period. More than 300 watercolor paintings decorate the walls, and they serve a variety of simple dishes, such as roast beef and Yorkshire pudding, but they also do Korma or hot Bengal curry with sambals (side dishes of relish). The dessert specialty of the house is a chocolate brandy cake made with fresh cream. A meal will cost around £4 ($9.20).

In the evenings, they like to have warning of your arrival for dinner (from 8 p.m.). A homemade soup followed by sirloin steak, beef Stroganoff, or chicken cooked with a sauce of cream, asparagus, and sherry, dessert, and coffee costs around £9 ($20.70). They bake all their own cakes and pastries, and are open from 11:30 a.m. to 7 p.m. daily in summer, noon to 6 p.m. in winter, when they also close on Friday. They do not have a liquor license, but will happily provide glasses without a corkage charge if you produce your own bottles. They also have a couple of rooms available in their cottage next door and charge £7 ($16.10) per person for bed and breakfast (you have to come along to the restaurant). The units are spotlessly clean and comfortable.

The Brontë Bookshop, 1 Church St. (tel. Haworth 42243), was the post office in the Brontës' time. Today, Mrs. Tricia Richmond runs a spotlessly clean bed-and-breakfast accommodation at the address, charging £7 ($16.10) per person, including a truly enormous Yorkshire breakfast. She and her husband spent many years in Africa before returning to Haworth. Mrs. Richmond admits to being from Lancashire, but "as my father was from Yorkshire, they let me in."

HAREWOOD HOUSE: In West Yorkshire, eight miles north of Leeds on the Leeds–Harrogate Road (A61), stands Harewood House, home of the Earl and Countess of Harewood. It's one of the "magnificent seven" homes of England, which includes Blenheim Palace and Beaulieu Abbey. The 18th-century house was designed by Robert Adam and John Carr. It contains superb plasterwork, beautiful Chippendale furnishings, and a fine private art collection. See also its collection of Sèvres and Chinese porcelain, and of English and Italian paintings.

Harewood Bird Garden borders the lake and blends successfully with the fine landscape, created by Capability Brown. It houses some 180 exotic species from all over the world, including penguins, macaws, snowy owls, and flamingos. The extensive grounds offer terrace and lakeside walks, shops, a cafeteria, a picnic area, occasional exhibitions, and an Adventure Playground for the children.

Harewood is open daily from April 1 to October 31. Gates open at 10 a.m. The house, bird garden, and playground are also open on Tuesday, Wednesday, Thursday, and Sunday in November, February, and March. There is a special holiday opening of the bird garden and playground only, daily from Boxing Day to January 3. Admission rates vary, but a Summer Freedom ticket costs approximately £1.60 ($3.68) for adults. In winter, it's £1.25 ($2.88). Reductions are given for children under 14. For information, you can call Harewood 0532/886-225 (24 hours a day).

Incidentally, although Harewood is on a regular bus route, the stop is about a one-mile walk from the house. There are excursions from York, Harrogate, and Leeds on varying days in the summer.

4. Durham

This densely populated county of northeast England is too often pictured as a dismal, foreboding place, with coalfields, ironworks, mining towns, and shipyards. Yet it contains valleys of quiet charm and a region of wild moors in the west.

DURHAM: The county town is built around a sandstone peninsule. It possesses a Norman **cathedral** which ranks as one of the most important in England. Adjoining the cathedral is **Durham Castle,** a Norman structure of the prince bishops which has been used by Durham University since 1832. Except on the occasion of university or other functions, the castle is open to visitors from 10 a.m. to noon and 2 to 4:30 p.m., daily during the first three weeks in April and during all of July, August, and September; 2 to 4 p.m. on Monday, Wednesday, and Saturday the rest of the year. Admission is 60p ($1.38) for adults, 30p (69¢) for children.

Food and Lodging

The **Royal County Hotel,** Old Elvet (tel. Durham 66821), is a Georgian hotel tracing its origins back to Cromwellian times. In its well-conceived modernization program, this antique riverside coaching inn blends yesteryear with modern design, and does so effectively. The owner has decorated the public rooms with mementoes depicting the checkered history of the place. There are 126 bedrooms in the hotel, most of them in contemporary design, and you're given a choice of accommodations in the older building, with its traditional furnishings, or else in the new block of rooms overlooking the river. Most units are fully equipped with private bath and shower, toilet, TV set, radio, phone, and coffee-making facilities. Food is served in the Light Infantryman Restaurant, and the coffeeshop provides light snacks. Rates range from £22.35 ($53.71) to £27.50 ($63.25) in a single, from £30 ($69) to £33 ($75.90) in a double. In the foyer is an aviary, and there is sunken seating in the bar.

Ramside Hall Hotel, Belmont (tel. Durham 65282), complete with towers and turrets (but no moat), was built as the country home of a prominent family, standing in 80 acres of parkland, just half a mile from the A1M on the A690. The castellated mansion is known both as a hotel of first-class accommodations and a superb eating house. The handsomely decorated public rooms are spacious and gracious, and the bedrooms are pleasantly appointed as well, the majority of which contain their own private baths. Depending on the facilities, singles range in price from £20 ($46) to £22.50 ($51.75), and doubles pay anywhere from £28 ($64.40) to £32 ($73.60), these tariffs including breakfast. Guests can dine either in the restaurant or grill room, selecting from either an à la carte or a table d'hôte menu, a dinner costing from £8 ($18.40).

BARNARD CASTLE: Near the Tees River, in the town of Barnard Castle, stands the **Bowes Museum,** at the eastern end of town. It was built in 1869 by John Bowes and his wife, the Countess of Montalbo, to house and display their art collection. Here you'll find masterpieces by Goya and El Greco, plus many fine tapestries and porcelains. There are also collections of French and English furniture, superb costumes, musical instruments, a children's gallery, and many other things of interest. A tearoom and ample parking are found on the premises. It is open all year, weekdays from 10 a.m. to 5:30 p.m., on Sunday from 2 to 5 p.m., charging 50p ($1.15) for adults, 10p (23¢) for children. It closes at 4 p.m. from November to February.

Where to Dine

Blagraves House Restaurant, The Bank (tel. Teesdale 37668), occupies a 15th-century house with a dining room which has been richly, warmly decorated by Mr. and Mrs. Davidson. They invite you to come by and "taste our food," which we've found to be excellently prepared and very wholesome. Fresh local produce and friendly service characterize the establishment. The price of the main dish determines the cost of your meal. Main dishes usually start at £8 ($18.40), and are likely to include rounds of filet of beef with a roquefort herb butter, duckling with peach and lemon sauce, or else chicken breasts stuffed with asparagus in a white wine and cheese sauce. Our favorite beginning, if featured, is a "very fine fish soup," made with lobsters, crab, prawns, plaice, cream, and brandy. Only dinner is served, and it's offered nightly from 7 to 9, except Sunday. Call for a reservation.

5. Tyne and Wear

In the newly created county of Tyne and Wear, industrial Newcastle upon Tyne is the dominant focus, yet outside the city there is much natural beauty. Cattle graze on many a grassed-over mining shaft. There is such scenic beauty as moors and hills of purple-blue. The rugged coastline is beautiful. Americans like to pass through because of their interest in the ancestral home of George Washington (see below), and Newcastle itself also merits a stopover, particularly from motorists heading to Scotland.

The National Trust administers two sights in the region surrounding Newcastle:

Gibside Chapel, built in the classical style of James Paine in 1760, is an outstanding example of Georgian church architecture. A stately oak-lined avenue leads to the door of the chapel, which is the mausoleum of the Bowes family. The interior is decorated in delicate plasterwork and is furnished with panelled pews of cherrywood and a rare mahogany three-tiered pulpit. Visitors are welcomed at any reasonable time. Just call the custodian at Rowlands Gill 2255. There is no charge for admission, but you'll pay 20p (46¢) to leave your car at the car park. The location is six miles southwest of Gateshead and 20 miles northwest of Durham between Rowlands Gill and Burnopfield.

Washington Old Hall is the ancestral home of the first president of the United States, and the place from which the family took its name. President Carter visited the manor house in 1977. The interior of the house, whose origins date back to 1183, is furnished with period antiques and a collection of Delft ware. Relics of the Washingtons are also on display. The hall is open from March to October daily, except Thursday, from 1 to 6 p.m. From November to February, it is open on Saturday and Sunday, and by appointment, from 2 to 5 p.m. Admission is 50p ($1.15) for adults, 25p (58¢) for children. The location is in Washington on the east side of the A182, five miles west of Sunderland (two miles from the A1). South of Tyne Tunnel, follow signs for Washington New Town District 4 and then Washington Village.

READERS' SIGHTSEEING SUGGESTION: "At Stanley, just a few miles south of Newcastle upon Tyne, is **Beamish,** the north of England open-air museum. Here a collection of buildings, machinery, and transportation has been assembled to recreate the northern way of life. Ride behind a working copy of an 1825 steam locomotive or in an open-top trolley car. The pub still functions, too" (Peter, Susan, and Eric Wildman, Lexington, Mass.).

NEWCASTLE UPON TYNE: Although an industrial city, Newcastle is graced with some fine streets and parks, as well as many old buildings. After crossing its best known landmark, the Tyne Bridge, you enter a steep city which sweeps down to the Tyne, usually on narrow lanes called "chares." Once wealthy merchants built their town houses right on the quayside, and some of them remain.

For years Newcastle has been known as a shipbuilding and coal-exporting center, and gave rise to the expression of suggesting the absurdity of shipping coals to Newcastle.

Dominating the skyline, the **Cathedral of Newcastle** rises to a beautiful Scottish crown spire. It is England's most northerly cathedral, lying on a downward sweep between the Central Station and the quay. Its provost admits, "We're not on the cathedral circuit, like York Minster and Lincoln, but foreigners still seek us out." The cathedral's date of construction is unknown, although its recorded history predates 1122. The church was rebuilt in the 14th century, and John Knox preached from its pulpit.

The keep of the so-called New Castle, built by Henry II in 1170, contains the **Keep Museum,** on St. Nicholas Street, with a collection of medieval relics. It's open April to September, Monday from 2 to 5 p.m.; Tuesday to Saturday, 10 a.m. to 5 p.m. From October to March, its Monday hours are from 2 to 4 p.m.; Tuesday to Saturday, 10 a.m. to 4 p.m.

Food and Lodging

Royal Station Hotel, Neville Street (tel. Newcastle 20781), was built back in the days when the big, grand hotels were connected to the railway station by a covered way. This well-kept hotel has two restaurants, the main one called the Victoria, where an expensive à la carte menu is served. Otherwise, you can dine slightly cheaper at their Oscar's Viking Restaurant, which specializes in Scandinavian food and seafood. Of the three bars, the Black Barrel attracts a youthful crowd, done as it is in red and black. Most of the bedrooms have been kept up to date with the times, although some of the more spacious older ones still have their heavy Victorian-style furniture. Bathless singles rent for £20 ($46), the rate increasing to £26 ($59.80) with bath, and bathless doubles or twins cost only £28 ($64.40), rising to £36 ($82.80) with bath. On weekends, prices are reduced slightly, and the tariffs quoted include a full English breakfast, service, and VAT.

6. Northumberland

Most motorists zip through this far-northern county on their way to Scotland. Because it lies so close to Scotland, Northumberland was the scene of many a skirmish. The county now displays a number of fortified castles which saw action in those battles.

Wallington, at Cambo, 12 miles west of Morpeth (take the A696 north from Newcastle), dates from 1688, but the present building reflects the great changes brought about in the 1740s when Daniel Garrett completely refashioned the exterior of the house. The interior is decorated with rococo plasterwork and furnished with fine porcelains, antiques, and paintings. Visitors may also visit the museum and enjoy an extensive display of doll houses. The West Coach House contains an exhibit of ornate carriages. The main building itself sits on 100 acres of woodlands and lakes, including a beautifully terraced garden and a conservatory. The grounds are open all year; the house, from April 1 to the end of September, daily except Tuesday, from 2 to 6 p.m. Admission to the grounds is 50p ($1.15) for adults, 25p (58¢) for children. A combined ticket to the hall and grounds costs adults £1.20 ($2.76); children, 60p ($1.38).

The **Farne Islands** are a group of small islands off the Northumbria coast, which provide a summer home for at least 20 species of sea birds as well as for one of the largest British colonies of gray seals. St. Cuthbert died here in 687, and a chapel built in the 14th century is thought to be on the site of his original cell. Only Inner Farne and Staple Island are open to the public. Visiting season extends from April through September, but access is more controlled during the breeding season, from mid-May to the end of July. Admission is 80p ($1.84), going up to £1.20 ($2.76) during the breeding season.

The best way to get to this most famous bird and animal sanctuary in the British Isles is to telephone or write Billy Shiel, the Farne Islands boatman at 4 Southfield Ave., Seahouses, Northumberland (tel. Seahouses 720-308). He has been taking people in his licensed boat for the past 40 years, so he knows the tides and the best places to film seals, puffins, and guillemots. He runs 2½-hour trips in his 40-passenger craft at a cost of £2.50 ($5.75) per person.

Incidentally, these are the islands where Grace Darling and her father made their famous rescue of men from a foundered ship.

HOLY ISLAND: The site of the Lindisfarne religious community during the Dark Ages, Holy Island is only accessible for ten hours of the day, high tides covering the causeway at other times. For crossing times, check with local information centers.

Lindisfarne Castle, built on the island about 1550, is open from April until the end of September, daily, except Friday, from 11 a.m. to 1 p.m. and from 2 to 5 p.m., charging an admission of £1 ($2.30).

At Lindisfarne, you can stay at the **Lindisfarne Private Hotel** (tel. Holy Island 89273). This is a fine, substantial frame building with a trio of tall chimneys. It's run by members of the Massey family, who conduct it more like a private home than a hotel. Centrally heated bedrooms contain hot and cold running water (a few with private baths) and are decorated with personality, providing a homelike atmosphere. The charge ranges from £13 ($29.90) to £16 ($36.80) per person daily for bed, breakfast, and evening dinner. Boating excursions can be arranged to the Farnes.

READERS' SIGHTSEEING TIPS: "**Bamburgh Castle** guards the British shore along the North Sea. Legend has it that Lancelot and Guinevere fled here. It is open Easter until the end of October, daily at 1 p.m. Admission is 90p ($2.07) for adults, 40p (92¢) for children. For more information, telephone Bamburgh 208" (Paul W. Ware, New Providence, Pa.).

"**Seaton Delaval,** the enormous country house off Whitley Bay, Northumberland, represents the architecture of Sir John Vanbrugh at its most forbidding. It looks like the stage settings for 14 Roman tragedies piled one on top of another. Walk over and look through a window in the east wing. Knights and wenches are feasting at long tables and drinking mead. You will find the guests assembled in the Presence Chamber, waiting to be summoned to the banquet. Stewards show the guests to their places at great refectory tables, which are laid with pewter plates and goblets, fresh rough bread, and dishes of butter and salt. Small daggers are the only cutlery provided. The drink is mead, the potent honey wine invented by the Norsemen. As fast as you drain the goblets, serving wenches refill them. The first remove is Delaval broth, a steaming soup drunk from the bowl and helped down with torn chunks of brown bread. The second remove is a great dish of Northumbrian spare ribbes, succulent pieces of roast lamb. Ypocras is served with them, a spiced burgundy that has the effect of making one long to seize a lute and break into a roundelay. The third and most substantial remove is chikeyn in browet with salumgundy. This means half a chicken, basted in honey until it is so tender that daggers are hardly needed to help it fall apart. The fourth remove, for those with any room left, is rastons, or fruit tarts, fat and swimming in cream. By the time you have been feasting for three hours, your soul may cry out for some 20th-century coffee. The price of a medieval banquet is about £10 ($23) during the week, rising to £12 ($27.60) on weekends. It's best to inquire locally, as banquets are not staged every day or even every week" (Andrew L. Glaze, New York, N.Y.).

Authors' Note: The house may be visited on just a sightseeing expedition on Wednesday and Saturday from May to September, from 2 to 6 p.m., for an admission of 40p (92¢) for adults, 20p (46¢) for children.

HADRIAN'S WALL: This wall, which extends across the north of England for 73 miles, from the North Sea to the Irish Sea, is particularly interesting for a stretch of 3½ miles west of Housesteads. Only the lower courses of the wall are preserved intact; the rest were reconstructed in the 19th century with the original stones. From several vantage points along the wall, you have incomparable views north to the Cheviot Hills along the Scottish border, and south to the Durham moors.

At Housesteads you can visit a **Roman fort,** built about A.D. 130 to house an infantry of 1000 men. Called Vercovicium in Latin, the fort housed a full-scale military encampment, the remains of which can be seen today. The fort is open in April daily from 9:30 a.m. to 5:30 p.m., from May to September the hours are 9:30 a.m. to 7 p.m. daily, and in October it is open weekdays from 9:30 a.m. to 5:30 p.m. (on Sunday from 2 p.m. to 5:30 p.m.); in November through February, the hours are 9:30 a.m. to 4 p.m. weekdays (on Sunday from

2 p.m. to 4 p.m.). Price of admission in summer is 60p ($1.38) for adults, 30p (69¢) for children; in winter it costs 40p (92¢) for adults and 20p (46¢) for children.

HALTWHISTLE: About 20 miles east of Carlisle lies the town of Haltwhistle. There the **Grey Bull Hotel** (tel. Haltwhistle 20298) would be a good base of operations for seeing the best section of Hadrian's Wall and its Roman garrisons. These include Housesteads, Vindolanda (the largest site in Europe), and the Chesters—all are within 15 minutes' drive from the hotel. The Grey Bull has been modernized and reequipped. There are 11 bedrooms, each with its own wash basin with hot and cold running water. The inclusive price is £8.50 ($19.55) per person, including an English breakfast, service, and VAT. Packed lunches are available on request. The bar at the hotel is a lively gathering place for the local people.

ALLENDALE: In the southwestern sector of the shire, this unspoiled country village is the geographic center of Great Britain. It is well known for its ancient Fire Festival on New York's Eve in the Market Place. From a base here, some of the finest scenery of Northumbria—heather-clad hills, moor, and woodland —unfolds.

For accommodations, the **Dale Hotel,** Allendale, near Hexham (tel. Allendale 212), is a village hotel built in 1870 and covered with green vines. Mr. and Mrs. W. A. Thompson have provided many facilities and considerations for their guests, including electric blankets and stoves in addition to oil-fired central heating throughout. The daily bed-and-breakfast rate is £7.50 ($17.25) per person, and half board is £9.50 ($21.85) per person daily, plus VAT. There are two large lounges and two dining rooms on the ground floor. In back is a large garden with a putting green and a summer house overlooking the Allen River. Guests are welcome to visit the grounds of the owners' private residence, a short distance from the village. Called Heathcote, the home is set in a three-acre garden with a lily pond.

HEXHAM: Above the Tyne River, this historic old market town is characterized by its narrow streets, old Market Square, a fine abbey church, and its Moot Hall. It makes a good base for exploring Hadrian's Wall and the Roman supply base of Corstopitum at Corbridge-on-Tyne, the ancient capital of Northumberland.

For accommodations, try the **Beaumont Hotel,** Beaumont Street (tel. Hexham 2331), a family-run place across from the village park. It offers excellent facilities, including handsomely furnished and pleasantly decorated bedrooms, which are in the modern style, the effect livened by bright colors. Nearly all 20 bedrooms have private baths or shower units tucked in. A bathless single room costs £11.50 ($26.45), rising to £12.75 ($29.33) with bath. Doubles or twins with baths or showers rent from £20.50 ($47.15). Tariffs include VAT, but not the service charge. Guests have a choice of two bars, and can dine either in the grill or the main dining room. Lunch is from £4.50 ($10.35), and dinner is à la carte.

The **Hadrian Inn,** Wall, near Hexham (tel. Humshaugh 232), is the ideal place to stay when visiting Hadrian's Wall. It's an ivy-covered building built of stones taken from the wall itself. The lounge has a collection of antiques and curios, excellent for after-dinner coffee in front of the blazing fire. The dining room with three window walls has red tablecloths with white lace overcloths.

You can look across the meadow toward the wall. The lounge has many curiosities—a flower-filled cradle and collection of silver button hooks, old china, ancient clocks, copperware, an Indian carved ivory, and an Indian tray table for coffee. There are eight bedrooms, all with hot and cold running water, innerspring mattresses, and electric blankets. The daily tariff in a single room is £14.50 ($33.35), from £24 ($55.20) in a double. From June until September, these prices go up to £18 ($41.40) in a single, £28 ($64.40) in a double. Lunches are table d'hôte, costing from £5 ($11.50), and dinners begin at £7 ($16.10).

On the Outskirts

The **George Hotel,** Chollerford, Humshaugh, near Hexham (tel. Humshaugh 446), stands on the banks of the Tyne, an ingratiating, creeper-covered country hotel with well-tended gardens leading down to the riverbank. The age of the hotel is unknown, and its drawing room maintains a true country-house style, with ornate white woodwork including an original fireplace. Brightly colored chintz armchairs are drawn up for after-dinner coffee. Out the bay window you can see the river at the bottom of the garden. The bedrooms are small, nicely equipped, and come with private baths or showers and TV sets. Many of the units have been recently modernized, refurnished, and decorated. Adjoining the restaurant is a cocktail bar and lounge, and locals gather in the Fisherman's Bar, which has the atmosphere of a country inn. A single rents for £22.70 ($52.21) nightly, a double or twin for £29.50 ($67.85).

OTTERBURN: This mellowed old village on the Rede River was the scene of the famous Battle of Otterburn in 1388. It makes a good base for touring the Cheviot Hills.

The **Otterburn Tower Hotel** (tel. Otterburn 673) stands in a quiet, tree-edged hollow in the hills. It's reached by crossing over a tiny bridge, past the Otterburn Mill. Once Sir Walter Scott was a guest at the tower in 1812, and the hotel still retains many fine architectural details, including 16th-century paneling in the dining room as well as stained-glass family crests. Guests dine while seated on Windsor chairs, and in the dining lounge is an Italian marble fireplace. The bedrooms are large and traditionally furnished. A single rents for £14 ($32.20), rising to anywhere from £20 ($46) in a bathless double to £28 ($64.40) in a twin with private bath. All tariffs include VAT and a full English breakfast. A dinner costs from £6 ($13.80).

ALNMOUTH: A seaside resort on the Aln estuary, Alnmouth attracts sporting people who fish for salmon and trout in the Coquet River or else play on its good golf course.

The **Schooner Hotel,** Northumberland Street (tel. Alnmouth 216), is a well-preserved Georgian coaching inn, only a few minutes' walk to the water. The hotel is adjacent to the nine-hole Village Golf Course, the second oldest in the country. A single room with breakfast is £11.20 ($25.76), £10 ($23) per person in a double, including VAT. Guests count on the delicious meals prepared and served at low prices. Set luncheons are £4 ($9.20); set dinners, £7 ($16.10); or you can also stay here on the full-board rate of £18 ($41.40) per person daily, which includes either a packed picnic or bar luncheon. There are 24 bedrooms, a grill room, dining room, the Sea Hunter bar, the Chase Bar, and the Long Bar, as well as a resident's lounge with color TV.

On the outskirts, the **Dunes Hotel,** Seahouses (tel. Seahouses 720-378), is a 30-bedroom establishment, from which you can view the Farne Islands with their bird and seal sanctuaries, Bamburgh Castle, and the sand dunes and Seahouses Harbour. Rooms are well kept and pleasantly furnished, and five doubles contain private baths. In a double or twin with bath, the bed-and-breakfast rate is £15 ($34.50) per person, dropping to £12.50 ($28.75) per person without bath. Singles go for £12 ($27.60), and all these tariffs include breakfast. There are three large lounges and a sun parlor overlooking the front lawn, plus a bright, sunny smoking room opening onto a flower garden. In the paneled restaurant, a good and varied cuisine is served. The Dunes Hotel is an excellent center for exploring the Farne Islands, Holy Island, the Roman Wall, and the Border Country. The hotel lies just half a mile from Seahouses itself, 14 miles from Alnmouth.

ALNWICK: Set in the peaceful countryside of Northumberland, this ancient market town has had a colorful history. A good center for touring an area of scenic beauty, Alnwick is visited chiefly today by travelers wanting to see—

Alnwick Castle

In the town of Alnwick, 30 miles north of Newcastle, Alnwick Castle is the seat of the Duke of Northumberland. This border fortress dates from the 11th century, when the earliest parts of the present castle were constructed by Yvo de Vescy, the first Norman Baron of Alnwick. A major restoration was undertaken by the fourth duke in the mid-19th century, and Alnwick remains relatively unchanged to this day. The rugged medieval outer walls do not prepare the first-time visitor for the richness of the interior, decorated mainly in the style of the Italian Renaissance.

Most of the castle is open to the public during visiting hours. You can tour the principal apartments, including the armory, guard chamber, and library, where you can view portraits and landscapes painted by such masters as Titian, Canaletto, and Van Dyck. You may also visit the dungeons and the interesting Museum of Early British and Roman Relics. From the terraces within the castle's outer walls, you can look across the broad landscape stretching over the River Aln.

Alnwick is open to the public daily, except Saturday from 1 to 5 p.m. from May to September. Admission is 80p ($1.84) for adults and 40p (92¢) for children. For an additional 10p (23¢) you can also visit the Regimental Museum of the Royal Northumberland Fusiliers, within the castle grounds.

Cragside, designed in the late 19th century by architect Richard Norman Shaw for the first Lord Armstrong, is a grand estate stretching across 900 acres on the southern edge of the Alnwick Moor. Here groves of magnificent trees and fields of rhododendrons frequently give way to peaceful ponds and lakes. The Victorian house itself is open only for part of the season, but the grounds alone are well worth the visit. At Rothbury, the house is just 13 miles southwest of Alnwick. The park is open April to October from 10:30 a.m. to 6 p.m. (or sunset). Admission to the park is 50p ($1.15). The house is open from April to September. Admission to both the park and house is £1.20 ($2.76). For more information, telephone Rothbury 20333.

Dunstanburgh Castle, on the coast nine miles northeast of Alnwick, was begun in 1316 by Thomas, Earl of Lancaster, and enlarged in the 14th century by John of Gaunt. The dramatic ruins of the gatehouse, towers, and curtain wall stand on a promontory high above the sea. You can reach the castle on foot only, either walking from Craster in the south or across the Dunstanburgh Golf Course from Embleton and Dunstan Steads in the north. The castle is open daily from 9:30 a.m. to 4 p.m. with longer hours during the summer months. Admission is 50p ($1.15).

Food and Lodging

White Swan, Bondgate Within (tel. Alnwick 2109), has a history going back to medieval days when it entertained highwaymen and passengers on the Edinburgh to London stagecoaches. A neoclassic-style coaching inn, just inside an ancient town gate, the Hotspur, it has also become the permanent home of the music room of the S.S. *Olympic,* sister ship of the *Titanic.* This beautiful paneled room was removed from the ship and completely reconstructed at the hotel. The hotel has 40 bedrooms, with bath and shower, and some of these are in a modern block and others in the older, more traditional part of the inn. Singles begin at £24 ($55.20), and doubles peak at £30 ($69), including a full breakfast, service, and VAT. The pleasant restaurant offers traditional dishes from a large table d'hôte menu.

CORNHILL-ON-TWEED: This border village, on the Tweed River, faces Coldstream on the Scottish shore.

Tillmouth Park Hotel (tel. Coldstream 2255), built in 1882, is an imposing Victorian mansion, occupying a secluded position in its own parkland gardens overlooking the Till River at the heart of a 1000-acre estate. It stands about nine miles from Berwick, three miles from Cornhill-on-Tweed, and four miles from Coldstream. Monumental and impressive, it rises four stories high, with many wings, gables, and chimneys, including a porch emblazoned with heraldic devices.

In spite of its size, there are only 14 bedrooms, each one exceptionally comfortable, seven containing private baths. Ask for the Sir Walter Scott room, with its stunning four-poster and private bath. Often Edwardian furnishings grace the private chambers. It's best to stay here on a half-board arrangement, at tariffs of £26 ($59.80) to £29 ($66.70) per person nightly.

Modernity, as reflected by a cocktail bar, has been blended with tradition, as represented by a galleried lounge with a massive stone fireplace. Spacious lawns adjoin the hotel.

Chapter XVI

SCOTLAND

1. The Border Country
2. Edinburgh
3. Day Trips from Edinburgh
4. The Kingdom of Fife
5. Exploring Tayside
6. The Trossachs and Loch Lomond
7. Aberdeen and Royal Deeside
8. Aviemore, Speyside, and Elgin
9. Inverness and Loch Ness
10. Fort William and Lochaber
11. Kyle of Lochalsh and Skye
12. Oban, Mull, and District
13. Kintyre, Arran, and Islay
14. Glasgow and the Clyde
15. Ayr, Prestwick, and District
16. Dumfries and Galloway

HIGHLANDS AND LOWLANDS... clans and bagpipes... lochs and glens... heather-covered moors... twirling kilts and tam o'shanters... pastel-bathed houses and gray-stone cottages... mountains and rivers and sea monsters... the sound of Gaelic... Shetland ponies... scotch whiskey... misty blue hills. This is Scotland, where you'll find some of the most dramatic scenery in Europe.

Most motorists approach Edinburgh after a stopover in the York area of England. That way, they can start in the east with Edinburgh, then go up through Deeside and on to Inverness, cross over and down the west side to Glasgow, emerging at Gretna Green, near Carlisle in England's Lake District.

1. The Border Country

Castles in romantic ruins and Gothic skeletons of abbeys stand as reminders, in this ballad-rich land of plunder and destruction, of interminable battles that raged between England and the proud Scots. For a long time, the so-called Border Country was a no-man's land. And this is also the land of Sir Walter Scott, that master of romantic adventure in a panoramic setting, who died in

472 DOLLARWISE GUIDE TO ENGLAND AND SCOTLAND

SCOTLAND

This map is taken from *Historic Houses, Castles & Gardens* with permission of ABC Historic Publications, a Division of ABC Travel Guides Ltd., Oldhill London Road, Dunstable LU6 3EB

1832. Today he is remembered for such works as *Rob Roy, Kenilworth, Ivanhoe,* and *The Bride of Lammermoor.*

Southeast Scotland contains the remains of the four great abbeys built by David I in the mid-12th century: Dryburgh (where Scott was buried) Melrose, Jedburgh, and Kelso. "The Borders" are also home of the famous "Common Riding" gatherings celebrating major events in the past.

From York you can drive straight up to Edinburgh via Jedburgh and then the Lauderdale Valley—which is what we shall proceed to do.

JEDBURGH: Jedburgh lies 325 miles from London, 48 from Edinburgh. This royal burgh and border town is famous for its ruined **abbey,** founded by King David in 1147, and considered one of the finest abbeys in Scotland. The town lies on the River Jed. The abbey is open daily from April to September, charging 25p (58¢) for adults, 15p (35¢) for children.

On Queen Street, you can visit the **Mary Queen of Scots House,** where she stayed and almost died after a tiring ride visiting her beloved Bothwell at Hermitage Castle in 1566. The house, containing articles dealing with her life, paintings, and engravings, is open from April to September only, weekdays from 10 a.m. to noon and 1 to 5 p.m., on Sunday from 1 to 5 p.m. Admission is 20p (46¢) for adults, 10p (23¢) for children.

Food and Lodging

Mrs. A. Richardson, 124 Bongate (tel. Jedburgh 2480), is more of a private home than a guest house—in fact, it's an apartment in a block of buildings. The Richardsons have two bedrooms, one with double bed, the other with a double and single, which is classified as a family room. The per-person cost for an adult is £6 ($13.80) nightly. Mrs. Richardson gives you a hot beverage and cookies before you go to bed, and in the morning, a big breakfast. She'll also cook an evening meal, if asked beforehand, which she serves at 6:30 ("so I can go for a walk afterward").

The Carters' Restaurant (tel. Jedburgh 3414) is a pub with downstairs dining room built of old abbey stones. The building has had a colorful history— a local grammar school from 1779, before finding its present role. This is the favorite gathering place of the people of Jedburgh who know that its owner, Michael Wares, serves good food and drink. Soups, bar snacks, and coffee are served daily in the lounge bar. The restaurant itself offers either British or continental dishes daily from £4 ($9.20). Lunches are served Monday to Saturday from noon to 2 p.m. Dinners are more elaborate, served Monday to Thursday from 6 to 9 p.m. (till 10 on Friday and Saturday). Fish is fresh from Eyemouth, and plates begin at £2.50 ($5.75), accompanied, if you wish, by a tomato and cole slaw salad at £1 ($2.30).

If you follow the A698 northeast of Jedburgh, the road will lead to:

KELSO: Another typical historic border town, Kelso lies at the point where the Teviot meets the Tweed. **Kelso Abbey,** now in ruins, was the earliest and probably the largest of the border abbeys. In the town's marketplace, the "Old Pretender," James Stewart, was proclaimed king, designated James VIII.

Kelso is also the home of the Duke of Roxburghe, who lives at **Floors Castle,** built in 1721 by William Adam. Part of this border castle is on view to the public, which is allowed to tour through it, admiring the tapestries, French antiques, Chinese porcelain, and paintings by such artists as Gainsborough, Reynolds, and Landi. Afternoon tea is served in the Courtyard Restaurant. Floors is open daily, except Friday and Saturday, from early May to late September. The house is open at 1:30 p.m., the last guests shown through at 4:45 p.m. The grounds and gardens may be visited from 12:30 to 5:30 p.m. The Garden Centre is open daily from 10:30 a.m. to 4:30 p.m.

Food and Lodging

Kelso makes a good base if you're planning to overnight in the Borders. There you'll find the **Woodside Hotel,** Edenside Road (tel. Kelso 2152), a mansion standing on its own immaculately kept grounds. Some guests find that the best bedrooms are the modern ones, with showers, in a converted stable. However, we prefer the comfortably fitted bedrooms in the main house. Singles range in price from £18 ($41.40), doubles from £24 ($55.20). The restaurant is particularly recommendable. Many guests visit from all over "Scott country" to enjoy the fine continental dishes. A set dinner costs £7 ($16.10), served from 7 to 9:30 p.m. The pleasantly traditional dining room overlooks the garden.

Ednam House Hotel (tel. Kelso 2168) is a delightful conversion of a Georgian house into a 34-room hotel often referred to as "that lovely place beside the river." The hotel, lying on the fringe of Kelso, has a good atmosphere, and the bedrooms are well kept, some with river views. Built in 1761, the hotel was purchased by the Brooks family from the Duke of Roxburghe in 1928, and it is one of the finest examples of Georgian architecture in the Border Country. Still family owned, the hotel at present is managed by R. Alastair Brooks, grandson of the original purchaser.

A few of the bedrooms are spacious and airy, although late arrivals might be given the more cramped quarters. At least half the accommodations come equipped with private baths, and you pay more for these, of course. Singles range in price from £14.50 ($33.35) to £18 ($41.40), doubles from £25 ($57.50) to £32 ($73.60), the latter the price charged for the James I room with its two double beds, including a full Scottish breakfast and VAT, although service is extra. For those wanting to chance it with the highly unreliable Scottish sun, there is a terrace.

From Kelso, it is only a short drive on the A699 to—

DRYBURGH: Scott himself is buried at **Dryburgh Abbey.** These Gothic ruins are surrounded by gnarled yew trees and cedar of Lebanon, said to have been planted there by knights returning from the Holy Land during the years of the Crusades. Near Dryburgh is "Scott's View," over the Tweed to his beloved Eildon Hills, considered one of the most beautiful views in the region.

The adjoining town is—

ST. BOSWELLS: This old village, 40 miles from Edinburgh, stands on the Selkirk–Kelso road, near Dryburgh Abbey. It lies four miles from Melrose and 14 miles from Kelso. Because of the following hotel, many motorists prefer to make St. Boswells their headquarters for touring "the Borders."

Dryburgh Abbey Hotel (tel. 2261) actually stands beside the ruins from which it takes its name. On the outskirts of St. Boswells, the red sandstone hotel is surrounded by lovely grounds, made all the more so by the gently flowing Tweed River. Built in the Scottish baronial manor, the abbey hotel has all the amenities associated with the traditional country house hotel, including large, extensive grounds. Modern conveniences have been slipped in, however. About 30 rooms are offered, with singles renting for £22 ($50.60), doubles from £25 ($57.50), these tariffs including a full English breakfast. You have a choice of several lounges and a handsome dining room, plus a cocktail bar. The hotel is open all year.

Four miles from Dryburgh Abbey is—

MELROSE: Lying 37 miles from Edinburgh, Melrose enjoys many associations with Scott. This border town, as mentioned, is also famous for its ruined **Melrose Abbey,** in the Valley of the Tweed. You can visit the ruins of the abbey in which the heart of Robert Bruce is said to have been buried. Look for the beautiful carvings and the tombs of other famous Scotsmen buried in the chancel. In Scott's *The Lay of the Last Minstrel,* the abbey's east window received rhapsodic treatment, and in *The Abbot* and *The Monastery,* Melrose appears as "Kennaquhair." It is open Monday to Saturday from 9:30 a.m. to 4 p.m. (from 2 to 5 p.m. on Sunday), charging an admission of 25p (58¢) for adults, 12p (28¢) for children.

The leading hotel in Melrose is **George & Abbotsford,** High Street (tel. Melrose 2308), a 19th-century coaching inn built overlooking the ruins of Melrose Abbey. The hotel is unpretentious, with well-equipped bedrooms, about half of which contain private baths. Singles range in price from £21 ($48.30) to £23.50 ($54.05), and doubles rent from £27.50 ($63.25) to £30.50 ($70.15). Breakfast is extra. In the garden you can admire the roses—and think about the brave heart of the Scottish hero, Robert Bruce. Later on, you can fortify yourself for another day's exploration in one of the two lounges or bar, meeting a congenial blend of tourists and locals.

At sunset you can stroll along the banks of the River Tweed, perhaps walk along a public footpath on a hill overlooking the town.

The next morning, you can drive three miles to—

ABBOTSFORD: This was the home of Sir Walter Scott that he built and lived in from 1812 until he died. It contains many relics collected by the famous author. Especially interesting is his study, with his writing desk and chair. In 1935 two secret drawers were found in the desk. One of them contained 57 letters, part of the correspondence between Sir Walter and his wife-to-be. The Scott home is open from March 20 to October 31, weekdays from 10 a.m. to 5 p.m., on Sunday from 2 to 5 p.m., charging 80p ($1.84) for adults, 40p (92¢) for children.

After leaving Scott's house, you can continue along the Tweed to—

TRAQUAIR HOUSE: At Innerleithen, a few miles east of Peebles, Traquair is considered the oldest inhabited and most romantic house in Scotland. Dating back to the tenth century, it is rich in associations with Mary Queen of Scots and the Jacobite risings. Its treasures include glass, embroideries, silver, manuscripts, and paintings. Of particular interest is a brewhouse equipped as it was two centuries ago. The great house is still lived in by the Stuarts of Traquair.

The house and grounds are open from Easter Saturday until the first week in October, daily from 1:30 to 5:30 p.m. In July and August, hours are from 10:30 a.m. to 5:30 p.m. Rates (subject to change) are 90p ($2.07) for adults, 45p ($1.04) for children.

From Innerleithen, it's only a six-mile ride to—

PEEBLES: This royal burgh and county town, 23 miles from Edinburgh, is a market center in the Valley of the Tweed. Scottish kings used to come here when they went to hunt in Ettrick Forest. The town is noted for its large woolen mills. In fact, you can visit the **Scottish Museum of Wool Textiles,** where you can see how tartans and fine woolens are dyed and spun, and where you can buy lengths of cloth and garments to take home.

Peebles is also known as a "writer's town." John Buchan Tweedsmuir, the Scottish author and statesman who died in 1940 and is remembered chiefly for writing the Stevensonian adventure story *Prester John* in 1910, lived here. He was also the author of *The Thirty-Nine Steps* (1915), the first of a highly successful series of secret-service thrillers. In 1935 he was appointed governor-general of Canada. Robert Louis Stevenson once lived at Peebles, and drew upon the surrounding countryside in *Kidnapped,* which was published first in 1886.

On the north bank of the Tweed stands **Neidpath Castle,** its peel (tower) dating from the 13th century. Cromwell besieged and took it in 1650.

Food and Lodging

If you'd like to spend the night instead of heading on to Edinburgh, a good bet is the **Tontine Hotel,** High Street (tel. Peebles 20892), which has a Scottish lion on a fountain in its forecourt. The hotel was built in 1808 by subscription—hence its name. It has been recently redecorated and restyled, and in the comfortable main lounge is a fine display of silver belonging to the hotel. An extension has been added, housing a block of modern, studio-style rooms, all equipped with private baths. Singles rent for £21 ($48.30), doubles for £32 ($73.60). The staff is efficient and friendly. The restaurant, the Adam Room, has good views overlooking Glensax Hills. One bar is known as the Tweeddale Shoot Bar, named after the long-established Shooting Club of Peebles. The second bar, the Beltane, is decorated in pine and named after a local festival. It has one of the finest displays of working-horse harnesses in the country.

The **Cringletie House Hotel,** at Eddleston, near Peebles (tel. Eddleston 233), is an imposing country hotel, with towers and turrets, standing on 28 acres of private grounds. It's like a small French château, built of red sandstone and lying slightly more than two miles from the center of Peebles, set back from the A703. Your hosts, Mr. and Mrs. Maguire, receive you as if you were a private guest in their baronial mansion.

Most of the bedrooms, 16 in all, are spacious, and all of them are comfortably appointed. Nine have private baths. Singles range in price from £15.50 ($35.65), and doubles go from £16.50 ($37.95) per person with private bath. Top-floor bedrooms without private baths cost £12.50 ($28.75) per person. The public rooms are rich in character and style, as befits a Victorian mansion. There was, to our surprise, an elevator as well. The bar is well stocked, and guests gather there before dinner, exchanging introductions.

Mrs. Maguire is in charge of the hotel's restaurant. In elegant surroundings, you are given a limited but extremely well-selected choice of dishes. The food is made even more enjoyable by the attentive service. In season the vegetables come fresh from Mrs. Maguire's garden. She has her own style of cooking, and her special dishes include a delectable smoked haddock mousse. A set luncheon is offered from 1 to 1:45 at £5.50 ($12.75), and dinner is from 7:30 to 8:30, going for £8.50 ($19.55). You must be punctual, because of the limited staff and short hours of serving, and you'll need a reservation, of course, particularly if you aren't a guest of the hotel. The restaurant and hotel are closed from mid-November to mid-March.

MELLERSTAIN: Seat of the Lord Binning, Mellerstain lies in "the Borders," although it is most often visited on a day trip from Edinburgh, 37 miles away. One of Scotland's famous Adam mansions, it lies near Gordon, nine miles northeast of Melrose and seven miles northwest of Kelso (tel. Gordon 225). It's open from May to September daily, except Saturday, from 1:30 to 5:30 p.m.

Mellerstain enjoys associations with Lady Grisel Baillie, the Scottish heroine, and Lord Binning is her descendant. William Adam built two wings of the house in 1725, although the main building was designed by his more famous son, Robert, some 40 years later.

You're shown through the interior, with its decorations and ceilings by Robert Adam, and are allowed to view the impressive library as well as paintings by old masters and antique furniture. Later, from the garden terrace, you can look south to the lake, with the Cheviot Hills in the distance, a panoramic view. Afternoon tea is served, and tweeds and souvenir gifts are on sale.

2. Edinburgh

Scotland's capital city is Edinburgh, off the beaten path for those doing the mad whirlwind tour of Europe, as it lies 373 miles north of London.

The city is associated with John Knox, Mary Queen of Scots, Robert Louis Stevenson, Sir Arthur Conan Doyle (creater of Sherlock Holmes), David Hume, Alexander Graham Bell, Sir Walter Scott, and Bonnie Prince Charlie—to name-drop only a bit.

From the elegant Georgian crescents of the New Town, to the dark medieval "wynds" of the Old Town, down the wide, magnificent Princes Street (Stevenson's "liveliest and brightest thoroughfare"), Edinburgh lives up to its reputation as one of the fairest cities in Europe. Of course, it's not as sophisticated as Paris, nor as fast-paced as London. And it's banal to call it the Athens of the North, although the Greek revival movement of the 19th century made many of the buildings look like pagan temples.

What Edinburgh has to offer is unique. It's Scottish (scotch is a drink—so play it safe and refer to the hearty, ruddy-faced people as Scots)—and that means it's different from English. It wasn't sameness that made these two countries fight many a bloody border skirmish.

Most travelers know that since World War II Edinburgh has been the scene of an ever-growing International Festival, with its action-packed list of cultural events. But that shouldn't be your only reason for visiting the ancient seat of Scottish royalty. Its treasures are available all year. In fact, the pace the rest of the time—when the festival-hoppers have gone south—is more relaxed. The prices are lowered, and the people themselves, under less pressure as hosts, return to their traditional hospitable nature.

If you can't make it to Edinburgh for the festival, be relieved to know that you've missed the time of the worst rainy season in Scotland. Since many visitors arrive during the three wet weeks of the festival, they go away spreading the news that the weather up north is disgraceful. However, the late spring, early summer, and autumn can be a fine time to visit; you may even see green grass in many places at Christmastime.

Before looking closer at the attractions of Edinburgh, we'll tackle the question of finding a hotel. In the Scottish capital that doesn't have to be a problem.

WHERE TO STAY: Searching for a suitable hotel isn't too difficult in Edinburgh, as the city offers a full range of accommodations at different price levels

478 □ **DOLLARWISE GUIDE TO ENGLAND AND SCOTLAND**

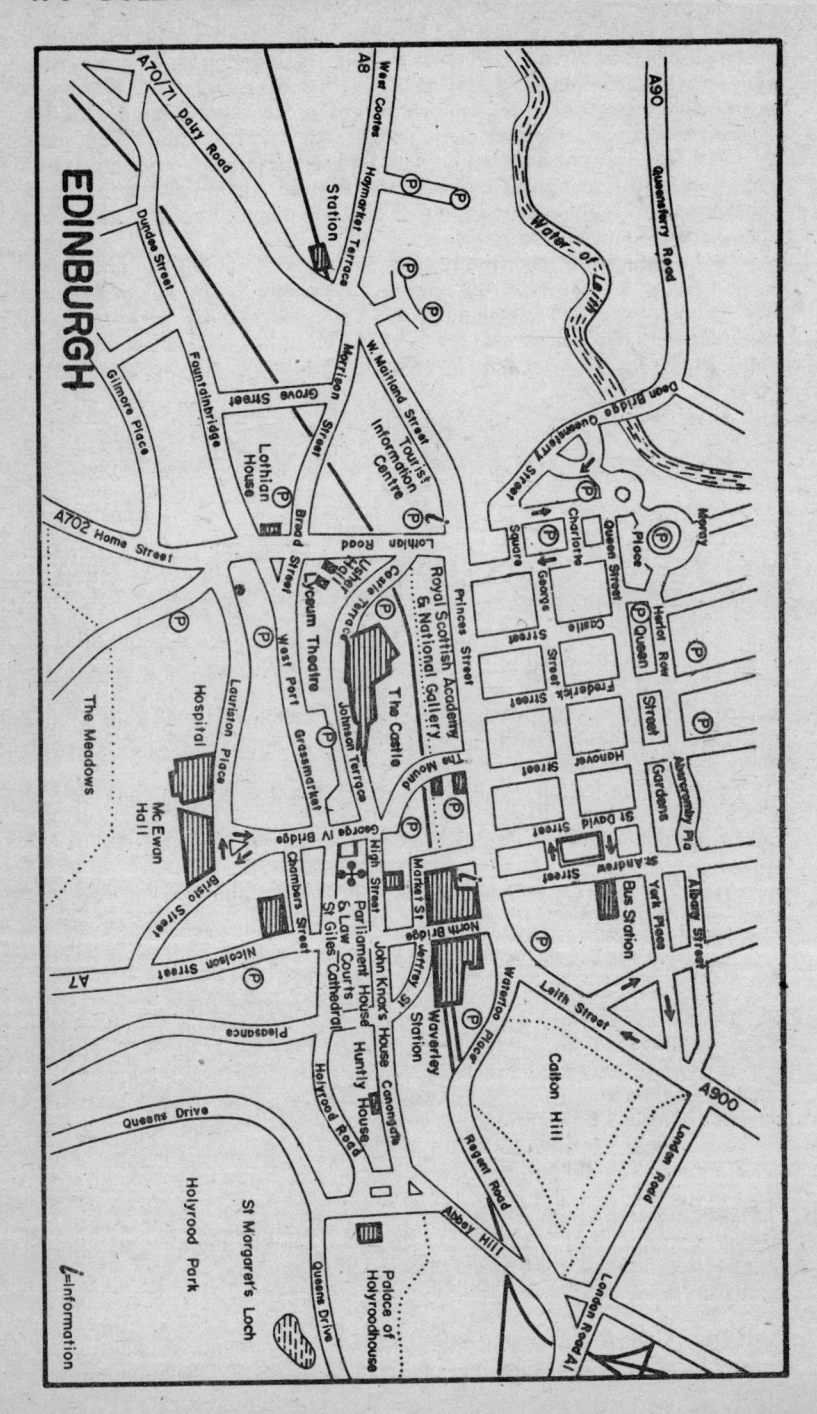

throughout the year. However, during the three-week period of the festival, the establishments fill up with international visitors, so it's prudent to reserve in advance. To take care of emergency lodging 360 days a year, the **Edinburgh Tourist Information & Accommodation Service,** at 5 Waverley Bridge (tel. 226-6591), compiles a well-investigated and lengthy list of small hotels, guest houses, and private homes that provide bed and breakfast for as little as £5 ($11.50) per person. Homes in this latter category may have only one to three bedrooms per household to rent though. The bureau's hours of opening during the peak season, May 1 to September 30, are from 8:30 a.m. to 8 p.m. Monday through Saturday, and from 11 a.m. to 8 p.m. on Sunday (open till 9 p.m. during July and August). A 40p (92¢) booking fee is charged.

Assuming you arrive in Edinburgh when the hotels aren't fully booked or that you will reserve a room in advance, we've prepared a representative sampling of the leading candidates, from the upper bracket to the budget range.

The Upper Bracket

The **Caledonian,** Prince Street and Lothian Road (tel. 225-2433), is the king of the hotels in Edinburgh, standing opposite its queen, the North British, at the other end of Princes Gardens. A British Transport hotel, it is the first choice for those who demand the best against an elegant background where service is keyed to personal tastes. It occupies the entire end of a block, with views of the castle and the parklike grounds. The interior is prestigious, drawing on some of the classic decorative and architectural features of both France and Scotland. The entrance hall achieves dignity with oyster-white paneled walls and desks, brass chandeliers, and a vibrant ceiling mural; and the main lounge is graced with neoclassic columns, a grand staircase, and chandelier.

The rates at the hotel in high season—May 1 to October 31—range from £35 ($80.50) in a single room with shower to £60 ($138) in a twin-bedded room with bath. A full breakfast is included. The bedrooms are freshly decorated and pleasantly furnished.

For drinks, try the cavelike American Bar, with a curvy ceiling of cedar and walls of marble, spiked with flame-red accents. The Caledonia's Pompadour Restaurant, with its bona fide French cuisine, is such a highlight of the Edinburgh scene that we've featured it separately in our dining section, coming up. The most recent addition is Laird's Lodge Coffee House, featuring such items as Arbroath smokie mousse at £1.10 ($2.53), grills and griddles from £1.70 ($3.91). All prices quoted are inclusive of service and VAT.

North British Hotel, Princes Street (tel. 556-2414), is the queen of Edinburgh's hotels, at the eastern end of Princes Street, opposite the Caledonian. It's a great old structure, designed for grand living and administered by British Transport Hotels. It is constantly being renewed and freshly decorated. Its lounges are impressively 18th and 19th century, the basic architecture classic. The finest is the residents' lounge, all in soft aqua and white, with a tall, formal fireplace, an elaborately carved ceiling and woodwork, and sky-high windows draped in gold. The cost of staying here is £25 ($57.50) in a bathless single, £35 ($80.50) with a private bath. In a bathless double, the rate is £35 ($80.50); it's £60 ($138) for two persons in a room with bath. Off-season reductions are granted. Most rooms are furnished with a combination of traditional and modern—most comfortable.

The main dining room, with its blue tile columns, is neoclassic—just right for your best bib and tucker. Guests usually take advantage of the £8.50 ($19.55) table d'hôte luncheon or set dinner. A typical meal might include crème longchamps, salmon véronique, roast turkey and stuffing with vegetables, followed by lemon pancakes.

On the lower floor, you'll find the Cleikum, featuring many national dishes. Ever had cock-a-leekie soup? Scottish trout fried in oatmeal? Haggis and champit neeps? Collops in the pan (rump beef, with onion, butter, and walnut catsup)? A good meal averages around £7 ($16.10). At one recent meal, we resisted the "Piggy Wigglies"! If you have the courage, you can order "stovies" and "rumbledethumps" as vegetables. Overlooking the castle, the Gourmet Restaurant is open in summer only. A meal here will cost around £18 ($41.40) or even more on the à la carte menu, but it will be quite an experience.

The **Roxburghe Hotel,** Charlotte Square (tel. 225-3921), is an Adam building of dove-gray stone, trimmed in white, with a stately town house opening directly onto a tree-filled square. While not elaborately equipped, and only four floors high (including a row of dormered mansard windows), it is, nevertheless, the first choice for a number of discriminating people who prefer a dignified place at which to stay. Within five minutes of the British Airways Terminal, the hotel is central, a short walk from Princes Street. The atmosphere is genteel and traditional, as reflected in the drawing room, with its ornate ceiling and woodwork, and tall arched windows opening toward the park. The furnishings are mostly antique, with groups of Chippendale chairs.

Most of the 75 bedrooms, reached by elevator, have private baths or showers. The rooms are handsomely traditional, a favorite scheme being Wedgwood blue-and-white Adam-style paneling. There are a few bathless singles for £24 ($55.20); with shower or bath, it's £28 ($64.40). The bathless doubles go for £45 ($103.50) for two persons, the price rising to £50 ($115) with bath, service and VAT included. A smart place to congregate for drinks is the Consort Bar, with its festive decor of chinoiserie and bistro tables. A modern dining room serves not only good meals, but gives diners a view of the square. For a description of the Consort Restaurant, see our dining section coming up.

The **George Hotel,** George Street (tel. 225-1251), is concentrated quality. A great deal is compressed into a comparatively small space. A member of the Grand Metropolitan chain, the George is only two short blocks from Princes Street, in the midst of a number of boutiques, bus, rail, and air terminals. Between April 1 and October 1 the highest rates are in effect: £34 ($78.20) in a single with bath, £42 ($96.60) in a twin or double-bedded room, also with bath. Most of the bedrooms have been refurnished and redecorated, but the public rooms have retained the old-fashioned comfort of a country house. The George Buttery serves a good grill-type menu, charging £8.50 ($19.55) for a three-course meal. And the George is also known for its Restaurant des Ambassadeurs (refer to our dining recommendations).

The Medium-Priced Range

Carlton Hotel, North Bridge (tel. 556-7277), is in a unique position, just off the Royal Mile at the entrance to the North Bridge, with views of Princes Gardens. It's pure Victorian, with brick towers and turrets, reached by an unimpressive entrance from North Bridge. Even the public lounges give no clue to the quite up-to-date bedrooms that evoke Scandinavia in their design. Each pleasant bedroom has its own bath and costs £25 ($57.50) single, £40 ($92) for a twin, including a full breakfast, service, and tax. In the Carving Room, you can carve as much as you want, either at lunch or dinner, for £8 ($18.40). The hotel is 100 yards from Waverley Station (you can enter via a station-level doorway in Jeffrey Street).

The **Old Waverley Hotel**, 43 Princes St. (tel. 556-4648), can be an ideal stopover for those desiring a central, clean, and comfortable establishment. The Old Waverley's world is that of the turn of the century, although a great deal of modernization has made it serviceable and fairly streamlined inside, with a friendly personnel providing efficient service. All of the bedrooms have hot and cold running water, and only a few are fitted with private baths. The bed-and-breakfast rate in a bathless single is £14 ($32.20), £23 ($52.90) with a private bath. In a bathless double, the bed-and-breakfast charge is £23 ($52.90), rising to £37 ($85.10) with bath. The lounges on the second floor have been given that contemporary look. The Waverley is a pleasant place to unwind after a day of sightseeing across loch and dale. Some of the rooms look onto Princes Street and at night the floodlit castle. The Waverley has a good restaurant serving à la carte meals at around £8 ($18.40) for a lunch or dinner.

The **Mount Royal Hotel**, Princes Street (tel. 225-7161), is right in the middle of the famed thoroughfare, complete with exclusive shops. A modern world emerges as you climb the spiral staircase or take an elevator to the second floor, with its reception rooms and lounges, and ceiling-to-floor windows opening onto views of the Old Town. In reality, Mount Royal is a remake of an old hotel, providing streamlined bedrooms with a view. The emphasis is utilitarian —not on frills, although the comfort is genuine. In summer, singles with bath go for £26 ($59.80) and up; twins with bath begin at £36 ($82.80). Prices include a continental breakfast, service, and VAT. The main dining room serves reasonably priced lunches and dinners.

The lounge on the second floor, with floor-to-ceiling windows offering views over the Scot Memorial and Princes Street, provides a wide variety of sandwiches and snacks throughout the day and night. The penthouse Harlequin Room offers dancing and cabaret with dinner.

King James Hotel, 107 St. James Centre (tel. 556-0111), at the end of Princes Street, is a large modern hotel with functional bedrooms, each equipped with bath, color TV, radio, telephone, and double-glazed windows to protect against the roar of traffic. Singles rent for £30 ($69), doubles for £42 ($96.60), including VAT and service, although breakfast is extra. The hotel, well run by Mr. McAngus, is directly connected to the St. James Centre, with its wide variety of shops and good parking for cars.

The Budget Range

Belmont Hotel, 10 Carlton Terrace (tel. 556-6146), is right in the midst of a row of classic town houses, dating from the 18th and 19th centuries. A 15-minute walk from the center of Edinburgh, with views of the parks and rooftops from most of the windows, it is really two houses joined together by Mr. and Mrs. Stanley, who accept paying guests year round, charging them £9.50 ($21.95) per person in a double, £10 ($23) in a single in high season. These rooms are bathless. If you want a double or twin with bath, the rate increases to £12 ($27.60) nightly, plus VAT. The price includes breakfast. Your bed will be soft, the sheets freshly laundered, the furnishings comfortable. The dining room is as old-fashioned as the rest of the place, in typical Georgian style. The hotel was awarded a commendation prize by the Edinburgh New Town Conservation Committee for the extensive renovations to the dining room, restoring it to its natural Georgian splendor. The Belmont is ideal for those who want a simple, uncluttered life in a homelike atmosphere.

Georgian Hotel, Dean Terrace (tel. 332-4520), is a small, family-run hotel in central Edinburgh, and from it you can walk alongside the Water of Leith to historic Dean Village or to the Botanical Gardens. This Georgian house, under the direction of Mr. and Mrs. Frank Tomney, has many fine Adam architectural features and tall, wide windows. The owners have a variety of nicely decorated bedrooms, renting from £17 ($39.10) in a single, from £15 ($34.50) per person in a double or twin. Many of the units have their own shower and toilet en suite, and all have TV, radio, intercom, and a baby-listening service. Guests can enjoy drinks and the company in the hotel's bar, later going to the hotel's dining room which serves a dinner for £5.50 ($12.65).

Golf View Hotel, Marchhall Road (tel. 667-4812); along Dalkeith Road, just past Commonwealth Swimming Pool, turn down Marchhall Place into Marchhall Road. There, Joseph and Margaret d'Ambrosio have run a spotlessly kept, comfortable guest house for the past 12 years. Most of their bedrooms have private baths or showers, and some have views over the golf course. The accommodations are well furnished, and there is a lounge with TV for a peaceful evening. The d'Ambrosios have been in catering for many years, and their breakfast is large and well cooked. They also provide a door key so that you can come and go at will. They offer singles, twins, and doubles, and all their twins have both a double bed and a single bed, making them ideal as family rooms. The charge is £8.50 ($19.55) per person nightly, including VAT and breakfast. There is no service charge.

Hotels on the Outskirts

These hotels in the environs might be useful if Edinburgh gets heavily booked—at festival time and during the summer. Both are in the medium-priced range.

The **Royal Scot Hotel,** 111 Glasgow Rd. (tel. 334-9191), is close to EDI airport to the west of the city. It's a modern hotel with its own helicopter pad and good parking, yet it lies within easy reach of the city center. Large lounges and bars lead to your pleasant room, where you have tea- or coffee-making facilities, color TV, and phone, plus private bath and shower. Singles rent for £30 ($69), doubles for £42 ($96.60), including a traditional cooked breakfast, VAT, and service.

Kings Manor Hotel, 100 Milton Rd. East (tel. 669-0444), is owned and run by the Solley family. The hotel lies within a ten-minute walk of the beach on the Firth of Forth, but still is within easy reach of the city center. It's a pleasant old building, comfortably modernized to provide most rooms with private baths. There is a bar and a lounge with a roaring fire. Rooms have color TV, radio, and phone. Singles rent for £12.50 ($28.75) without bath, £21 ($48.30) with bath. Bathless doubles are priced at £18 ($41.40), rising to £31 ($71.30) with bath, including VAT and service. A set luncheon is provided for £3.50 ($8.05), a table d'hôte dinner costing from £5.50 ($12.65), giving you a choice of 15 main dishes. However, if you want a filet steak, you'll pay slightly more.

Castle Hotels

To fulfill your fantasy, you might want to spend your first night in Scotland in a real castle surrounded by gardens and spacious grounds. If so, we have the following recommendations.

Dalhousie Castle, Bonnyrigg (tel. Gorebridge 20153), dates back to the 12th century. It lies off the A7 Carlisle-to-Edinburgh road, just outside the village of Bonnyrigg, only nine miles from Edinburgh. It is now run by Miss McIlroy, who welcomes guests to this historic old castle. A turreted and fortified house, with ramparted terraces and battlements, it offers such delights as a dungeon lounge and restaurant where delicous meals are served, including many local Scottish dishes. The rooms themselves are large and traditionally furnished, with private baths and plenty of space to sit and relax. One of the suites has a four-poster bed. The cost per night ranges from £35 ($80.50) to £40 ($92), depending on the room's location and including breakfast for one or two persons. The suites go for £45 ($103.50) to £60 ($138) per night, plus service and VAT.

Borthwick Castle, North Middleton (tel. Gorebridge 20514), lies 12 miles south of Edinburgh on the A7. Guests can be met at Edinburgh airport or railway station by arrangement. This 15th-century structure has just celebrated its 550th anniversary and was the last refuge of Mary Queen of Scots and the Earl of Bothwell in 1567. Her apartments, the small chapel where she prayed, and the bedchamber once occupied by Bothwell are available to guests. Both bedchambers have four-poster beds. All the bedrooms have shower and toilet en suite and are centrally heated. Guests dine in the magnificent stone-vaulted Great Hall by roaring log fire and candlelight. On special evenings, pipers, dancers, and traditional entertainment are enjoyed. Borthwick Castle has become internationally famous for the excellence of its cuisine and personal service, its authentic medieval ambience, and the recreation of a gracious lifestyle which is unrepeatable. Miss Helen Bailey, the chatelaine of the castle, and the members of her household provide warm hospitality to all who enter this stately home. The rates are: £45 ($103.50) for a twin or double, £35 ($80.50) for single occupancy (no single rooms), including a full Scottish breakfast. VAT and service are extra. A five-course menu is available for £15 ($34.50).

WHERE TO DINE: The Scots are hearty eaters—and you'll like the sizes of their portions as well as the quality of their fare, with choices from river, sea, and loch. You can dine on a cock-a-leekie soup, fresh Tay salmon, haggis, neeps, tatties, and whiskey, Aberdeen Angus filet steak, potted hough, poacher's soup, and good old stovies and rumbledethumps. If none of the above tempts you, you'll find that the French cuisine has made an inroad at some of the first-class hotels.

The Upper Bracket

Prestonfield House, Priestfield Road (tel. 667-8055), offers gourmet meals in the setting of a Jacobean country estate, in the midst of a 17-acre garden. King James II often visited before students burned down the house. Rebuilt, it was later to host Benjamin Franklin, then American ambassador, as well as Boswell and Johnson. The architect was William Bruce, who designed the Palace of Holyroodhouse. No matter which room you enter, you'll find fine furnishings and paintings, including two Ramsays over the dining room fireplace. Have a predinner toast in the Old Bar (drinks served from a Sheraton bookcase), while perusing the menu. If you arrive early enough, you can stroll through the gardens and pay your respects to the peacocks. The manager will guide you to one of the early 19th-century candlelit dining rooms, with their exquisite table settings.

All meals are à la carte, and the cuisine is essentially French. With so many fine dishes to recommend, we hesitate to point out a small group. Nevertheless, specialties include smoked haddock mousse for £1.80 ($4.14), or pâté maison, £2.60 ($5.98). The Scottish national soup, cock-a-leekie, is featured for £1 ($2.30). Another local treat is trout fried in oatmeal, £4.75 ($10.93). Main courses are likely to include escalope of pork, £7.30 ($16.79). You can have after-dinner coffee in the second floor Mortlake Tapestry Room, with its ornate ceiling, Persian carpets, and antiques, or in the Leather Room, with its panels from Córdoba. There is a £1.25 ($2.88) cover charge. Meals are served between 12:30 and 3 p.m. and between 7 and 10:30 p.m., including Sunday. It's essential to call ahead for a reservation.

Five bedrooms are available for those who book well in advance. The rooms are large and well furnished, with pieces from the 18th and 19th centuries. The rate for bed and breakfast, including VAT and service, is £34 ($78.20) for a single, £45 ($103.50) for a double. Two rooms have shower units, and the others have baths within easy reach. The breakfast is most generous, complete with Scottish oatmeal.

Pompadour Restaurant, Caledonian Hotel, Princes Street (tel. 225-2433), serves the haute French cuisine. At least 60 classic Gallic specialties are offered, augmented by an extensive wine list. The setting is convincing, in a drawing room atmosphere of pale blue and white, with ornate bas-relief plaster paneling, fruitwood provincial armchairs, cerise draperies, and half-moon windows overlooking Princes Street. For your à la carte opening you might prefer escargots at £4 ($9.20) or smoked trout at £4.20 ($9.66). Main dishes start from £5.75 ($13.23) for the chicken maréchal to £10 ($23) for sole Caledonian. Various specialty dishes are also offered, including filet d'angus chemise au poivre at £10.30 ($23.69). Desserts range from ices at £1.20 ($2.76) to crêpes suzette at £3.80 ($8.74).

Restaurant des Ambassadeurs, George Hotel, George Street (tel. 225-1215), provides a top-level French cuisine in a glamorous setting—a classical impressive 19th-century room, with ornate ceilings, marble columns, Adam paneling, and silver chandeliers. To assist your wooing, a musician plays every night, and on Friday and Saturday evenings, the resident quartet plays for dancing. Between 12:30 and 2:30 p.m. you can order from three different menus, costing £6.50 ($14.95), £7.50 ($17.25), and £8.50 ($19.55), including unlimited wine. There is always a roast joint.

In the evening, guests select wines from a wide assortment. A set dinner is offered for £9 ($20.70), plus wine. The à la carte menu is impressively balanced, with a wide-ranging offering of hors d'oeuvres and soups, followed by fish such as saumon grillée, and grilled Dover sole. Main-dish specialties include rib of prime Scottish beef, as well as a wide range of other beef, pork, lamb, veal, and poultry dishes. Vegetables are fresh when in season. On the à la carte menu, you can pay as much as £14 ($32.20) for a dish.

Café Royal, 17 West Register St. (tel. 556-1884), is the most famous of Edinburgh's seafood restaurants. It's at the east end of Princes Street. Surely it would have been Oscar Wilde's choice. A turn-of-the-century palace, with an abundance of Victorian curlicues, cut-out wood, brass, and stained-glass windows, it offers some of the best food in the city.

Specialties in the second-floor restaurant include river trout meunière and shrimp Newburg. If you want to be daring, try the Scots haggis and neeps (turnips). Appetizers include poacher's broth. The dessert listing is varied, with sorbets being favored. A set lunch is provided for £5 ($11.50); however, if you order dinner from the à la carte menu, expect to pay about £12 ($27.60). The house wine begins at £3.50 ($8.05) a bottle. The dining rooms are open from noon to 2:30 p.m. and 6 to 10:15 p.m. The restaurant is closed all day Sunday and on Saturday at lunch.

The lower-floor pub is not to be overlooked—especially for the privilege of having a lager in one of the Victorian booths.

The Medium-Priced and Budget Range

The Consort, Roxburghe Hotel, Charlotte Square (tel. 225-3921), provides intimate dining in a plush atmosphere at one of Edinburgh's leading hotels. It and its adjoining cocktail bar attract sophisticated residents, artists during the festival weeks. Through its separate entrance on George Street, you descend a stairway into an almost theatrical setting. Lunch is served between 12:15 and 2:30 p.m., dinner from 7 to 10:30 p.m. (Sunday till 10 p.m.). For appetizers, you might prefer either smoked Scottish salmon or escargots bourgignon. Many attractive prepared main dishes are offered, including the mixed grill and steak Diane. Three different set menus are featured—at £4 ($9.20), £5.50 ($12.65), and £7 ($16.10).

Henderson's Salad Table, 94 Hanover St., is a Shangri-la for healthfood lovers as well as those who want an array of rich, nutritious salads—some of the most imaginative and original we've known. It's self-service, and you can pick and choose at 45p ($1.04) per mammoth dollop, or pay a flat £1.50 ($3.45) for a representative plate. The ingredients are combined ingeniously—eggs, carrots, grapes, nuts, yogurts, cheese, potatoes, cabbage, watercress, you name it. A variety of cosmopolitan international dishes is served on request, including a Spanish omelet for £1.20 ($2.76). For around £1 ($2.30), you can have a number of hot plates, such as stuffed peppers with rice and pimiento. The soups are fabulous, costing 45p ($1.04). Desserts are homemade, so rich and pure you'll strain trying to choose between them. Settle for a fresh fruit salad or a gâteau with double whipped cream and chocolate sauce. Average price is 60p ($1.38).

Henderson's is open regularly from 8 a.m. to 11 p.m. Monday through Saturday. The scene takes place in a semibasement; and the furnishings are appropriate: pine-wood tables (often shared) and crude box-stools. The Vegetarian Society raises a provocative question: "Have you ever thought that killing for food is not necessary?" At Henderson's it certainly isn't. The Sherry Bar serves Spanish tapas (hors d'oeuvres). The wine cellar provides a choice of 50 wines, some 20 of which may be had by the glass. Live classical music is played most evenings. The bar may be reached by the same entrance as the Salad Table.

Casa Espanola, 61–65 Rose St. (tel. 225-5979), is a Spanish restaurant, the best of its type in Edinburgh. Its owners, Mrs. Pascual and Mr. Hernanz, specialize in paella, a savory offering, costing £10 ($23) for two persons. Or perhaps you'd have their fish stew, zarzuela, going for £10 also, for two persons. The gazpacho is very tasty and strongly flavored, £1.20 ($2.76). A shrimp cocktail with garlic at £1.80 ($4.14) is another appetizing opener. The best bargain is a three-course luncheon offered for £3.50 ($8.05). Matador capes, bullfight posters, and wine bottles enliven the decor. Lunch is served until 2 p.m., and dinner is from 7 to 11 p.m. Closed Sunday.

Denzler's, 80 Queen St. (tel. 226-5467), offers appetizing Swiss dishes, skillfully prepared, using high-quality ingredients. Portions are generous, and service is efficient, although informal, the waiters contributing to the relaxed atmosphere. Air-dried Swiss ham with melon is the most enticing opener, costing £2.10 ($4.83). For a main course, choose from slices of venison at £4 ($9.20), or else the pièce de résistance, fondue bourguignonne, £10 ($23) for two persons. For dessert, we'd endorse the apfelstrudel at £1.10 ($2.53). Dinner is served nightly, except Sunday, from 6:30 to 10. At lunch, offered from noon to 2 p.m., main dishes range in price from £2.25 ($5.18) to £4.50 ($10.35). The brown onion soup is especially good at 75p ($1.73).

Madogs, 38a George St. (tel. 225-3408), evokes a touch of American sophistication and flair in the Scottish capital. With its menu and movie posters (heavy on Bogart), it suggests someplace in California. Although English beer is very good, it's chicer here to order an American variety, such as Budweiser. The New England clam chowder at £1.20 ($2.76) is often very good, and better than you're likely to get at many places in New England these days. The kosher pastrami at £2.20 ($5.06) is popular, however most guests prefer the hamburger with french fries and a salad at £3 ($6.90). Chili con carne at £1.45 ($3.34) is another favorite. Eggs Benedict (the menu writer has to translate this for local diners) costs £2.10 ($4.83). At dinner the menu has a continental range—teriyaki steak at £4.60 ($10.58); Long Island duck, £4.60 also; even Bahamian grouper, £4.20 ($9.66). The split-level restaurant is graced with hanging baskets and potted palms, and the slim-hipped waitresses are attired in jeans. Lunch is until 3 p.m., and dinner is from 6 to 11:30. Closed Sunday.

Cosmo, 58a North Castle St. (tel. 226-6743), is one of the most heavily patronized Italian restaurants in the Scottish capital. Courtesy, efficiency, and good cookery are featured here. Cosmo Tamburro is your host. In season you can ask for mussels as an appetizer, costing £2 ($4.60). Soups and pastas are in the £1.10 ($2.53) to £2 ($4.60) range. However, remember that the cost of your pasta is doubled if you order it as a main course. We've found the veal dishes the best cooked, and good value at that, ranging from £4.80 ($11.04) although you may be attracted to the seafood at £4.90 ($11.27). The cassata Siciliana, 90p ($2.07), is well made and not unbearably sweet. Closed Sunday and Monday, the restaurant serves otherwise until 2:15 p.m. for lunch and until 10:30 p.m. for dinner.

Luckpenny Salad Restaurant, 30 Grassmarket. Pamela Fowler, the owner, welcomes you to her very well-run little restaurant which specializes in homebaking and freshly made salads using crisp ingredients. University students, musicians, and actors—all on limited budgets—are attracted to her precincts, enjoying rich, nutritious soups at 32p (74¢) a serving. Vol-au-vents, stuffed with everything from seafood to poultry, are featured occasionally, costing from £1.50 ($3.45). The quiches are good, too, going for 75p ($1.73). For dessert, we'd suggest you finish with a homemade cheesecake at 75p also. The restaurant is open from 9 a.m. (you can drop in for breakfast) until 6 p.m. It is closed on Sunday.

The Best of the Pubs

Deacon Brodie's Tavern, 435 Lawnmarket, is the neighborhood pub along the Royal Mile. It perpetuates the memory of Deacon Brodie, good citizen by day, robber by night. Mr. Brodie, it is believed, was the inspiration for Robert Louis Stevenson's *The Strange Case of Dr. Jekyll and Mr. Hyde.* Brodie ended up on the gallows on October 1, 1788. The tavern and wine cellars contain a cocktail and lounge bar—decked out in Jacobean and tartan decor. It offers a traditional pub setting and lots of atmosphere, making it popular with visitors and locals alike. The tavern provides inexpensive snacks between 11 a.m. and 2:30 p.m. (every day except Sunday), with prices averaging around 75p ($1.73). Among the selection: cottage pie, Scottish eggs, cheese, and the ploughman's special.

The **Guildford Arms,** West Register Street, dates back to the "mauve era" of the 1890s. This Victorian-Italianesque corner pub, still harboring its oldtime memories, has one of the most intriguing decors of any pub in Edinburgh—or Scotland for that matter. Next door to the world-famed Café Royal, it lies near the King James Hotel. It still has seven arched windows with etched glass, plus an ornate ceiling, as well as a central bar and around-the-wall se... and bustling, with plenty of character.

READERS' RESTAURANT SELECTION: "We chanced upon a charming res... **Lyceum Apéritif Restaurant,** in the Royal Lyceum Theatre. It is open to the garden motif with beautiful plants is used in the decor. A delicious meal for £6 complete, with a choice of about four main dishes is served before the theater. theater, a supper is offered for £6.50 ($14.95). Not only is the food good, but we f...nd it most convenient, as we do not like to rush but much prefer eating before attending the theater" (Phil and Eileen Hoffman, Winnetka, Ill.).

Restaurants on the Outskirts

At least once you should get out into the countryside surrounding Edinburgh. One way to do this is to take bus 41 for about five miles from the West End to the little Scottish village of Cramond. Few visible traces remain today of its Roman occupation.

Quietly nestling on a sloping street is the **Cramond Inn,** on Cramond Glebe Road, which has been serving food and drinks to wayfarers for 300 years (it was known to Robert Louis Stevenson). Picture upholstered booths, opera-red carpeting, some beerbarrel upholstered chairs, a collection of local watercolors, a low ceiling, large foot-square old beams, dark oak and creamy-colored walls, recessed windows, a small stone fireplace—and you'll begin to get the feel of the inn.

The restaurant can serve 60 diners, but you'd better call in advance (tel. 336-2035), as it's most popular. The prices are quite reasonable, considering the quality of food—some of the finest of Scottish dishes. The steak-and-kidney pie is delicious, costing £3 ($6.90), but we're drawn to the haggis, the famed dish of Scotland, made with an assortment of chopped meats, oatmeal, and spices—going for £2.50 ($5.75) for an individual serving. For starters, the Scottish game soup at £1 ($2.30) is a favorite. A specialty of the house is roast duck for £4 ($9.20). Desserts average around 95p ($2.19). The inn serves lunch from noon to 2:30 p.m., dinner till 10:30 p.m. The minimum charge is £2 ($4.60), and Cramond Inn is closed Sunday.

THE TOP SIGHTS: Before leaving the Scottish capital, you'll want to take a look at both the Old Town and the New Town. Both have their different attractions—the Old Town's largely medieval; the New Town, Georgian. We'll begin our exploration on the Royal Mile of the Old Town, a collective term for Canongate, Lawnmarket, and The High. At one end on Castle Rock sits—

Edinburgh Castle

It is believed that the ancient city grew up on the seat of the dead volcano, Castle Rock. History is vague on possible settlements, although it is known that in the 11th century Malcolm III (Canmore), and his Saxon queen, Margaret, founded a castle on this spot. The good Margaret was later venerated as a saint. The only fragment left of their original castle—in fact, the oldest structure in Edinburgh—was established by her. It is St. Margaret's Chapel, built in the Norman style, the present oblong structure dating principally from the 12th century. Outside the tiny chapel sits the five-ton Mons Meg, a 15th-century cannon.

Inside the castle you can visit the State Apartments—particularly Queen Mary's Bedroom—where Mary Queen of Scots gave birth to James VI of Scotland (later James I of England). The Great Hall with its hammer-beam ceiling was built by James IV. It displays armaments and armor, although Scottish Parliaments used to convene in this hall.

The highlight, however, is the Crown Chamber, which houses the Honours of Scotland, used at the coronation of James VI, along with the sceptre and the sword of state of Scotland. Unseen by the public for 15 years, the French prisons have been reopened. Turned into a prison in the 18th century, these great storerooms housed hundreds of Napoleonic soldiers during the early 19th century. Many of them made wall carvings which you can see today. The castle may be visited weekdays from 9:30 a.m. to 5:05 p.m. (on Sunday from 12:30 to 4:20 p.m.) November through April. From May 1 to October 31, hours are 9:30 a.m. to 6 p.m. weekdays (11 a.m. to 6 p.m. on Sunday). The last admission tickets are sold 45 minutes before closing times. Admission November through April is 40p (92¢) for adults, 20p (46¢) for children; May through October it's 70p ($1.61) for adults, 30p (69¢) for children.

In addition, you may want to visit the **Scottish United Services Museum** on the premises, which displays an admirable collection of Highland weapons and uniforms, some of which were the type worn by the men under Bonnie Prince Charlie in their victory over the English in the battle of Prestonpans. It is open weekdays, 9:30 a.m. to 6 p.m. in season (closes at 5:05 otherwise). Your ticket to the State Apartments includes a visit to the Services Museum. The War Memorial and precincts are free.

Along the Royal Mile

Ideally, if you have the time, you should walk the full length of the Royal Mile—all the way to the Palace of Holyroodhouse at the opposite end. Along the way, you'll see some of the most interesting old structures in Edinburgh, with their turrets, gables, and towering chimneys. Of all the buildings that may intrigue you, the most visited are John Knox's House and **St. Giles Cathedral.**

The cathedral is known as the High Kirk. Inside, one outstanding feature is its Thistle Chapel, designed by Sir Robert Lorimer and housing beautiful stalls and notable heraldic stained-glass windows. The chapel is open from 10 a.m. to 5 p.m. and may be visited for 15p (35¢). John Knox, the leader of the Reformation in Scotland, was minister of St. Giles from 1560 to 1572.

Further down the street at 45 High St. is **John Knox's House,** whose history goes back to the late 15th century. Even if you're not interested in the reformer who founded the Scottish Presbyterian Church, you may want to visit his house, as it is characteristic of the "lands" that used to flank the Royal Mile. All of them are gone now, except Knox's house, with its timbered gallery. Inside, you'll see the tempera ceiling in the Oak Room, along with exhibitions of Knox memorabilia. The house may be visited daily (except Sunday) from 10 a.m. to 5 p.m. for 30p (69¢) for adults, 15p (35¢) for children.

READERS' SIGHTSEEING TIPS: "An unusual attraction is the **Museum of Childhood,** 38 High St., on the Royal Mile, opposite John Knox's House. Three floors are devoted to every facet of childhood, ranging from antique toys and games to penny arcade machines, juvenile 'arsenals,' and many other items representing the childhood experience of different nationalities and periods" (Ralph M. Stein, Flushing, N.Y.).

Authors' Note: The museum is open weekdays from 10 a.m. to 5 p.m. (to 6 p.m. from June through September), charging 30p (69¢) for adults, 10p (23¢) for children.

"I'd like to recommend the **Scottish Craft Centre** in the Acheson House on the Royal Mile. There's no pressure to buy anything—you can browse to your heart's content. It's rather like an exhibition of local crafts, not so much a store. Some things are quite reasonable, such as beautiful buttons made of horn. Other items are more expensive" (Hazel Blumberg, Utica, N.Y.).

The Palace of Holyroodhouse

At the eastern end of the Royal Mile, the palace was built adjacent to an Augustinian abbey, established by David I in the 12th century. The nave, now in ruins, remains today. James IV founded the palace nearby in the early part of the 16th century, but, of his palace, only the north tower is left. Much of what you see today was ordered built by Charles II.

In the old wing occurred one of the most epic moments in the history of Holyroodhouse, when Mary Queen of Scots was in residence. Mary, who had been Queen of France and widowed while still a teenager, decided to return to her native Scotland. She eventually entered into an unsuccessful marriage with Lord Darnley but spent more time and settled affairs of state with her secretary, David Rizzio. Darnley plotted to kill the Italian, and he and his accomplices marched into Mary's supper room, grabbed Rizzio over her protests, then carried him to the Audience Chamber, where he was murdered by 56 stab wounds. A plaque marks the spot of his death on March 9, 1566.

Darnley himself was to live less than a year after, dying mysteriously in a gunpowder explosion. Mary, of course, was eventually executed on the order of her cousin, Elizabeth I. One of the most curious exhibits in Holyroodhouse is a piece of needlework by Mary, depicting a cat-and-mouse scene (Elizabeth's the cat!).

The State Apartments also contain some fine 18th-century Flemish tapestries, especially a whole series devoted to Diana, as well as some Gobelins. In the Great Gallery are 89 portraits, depicting Scottish kings, including Macbeth, painted by a Dutchman, de Wet.

The palace suffered long periods of neglect, although it basked in glory at the ball in the mid-18th century thrown by Bonnie Prince Charlie. The present Queen and Prince Philip live at Holyroodhouse whenever they visit Edinburgh. When they're not in residence, you can visit the palace weekdays from 9:30 a.m. to 5:15 p.m. (on Sunday from 12:30 to 4:30 p.m.). In the off-season, the palace is closed on Sunday. Adults pay 60p ($1.38) to enter, and children are charged 30p (69¢) in summer; 45p ($1.04) for adults and 20p (46¢) for children in winter. When the rest of the palace is closed, admission to the historical apartments is only 30p (69¢). Light refreshments are available only in the summer months.

The New Town

At some point, the Old Town became too small. The burghers decided to build a whole new town across the valley, the marsh being drained and eventually turned into public gardens. Princes Street is the most striking boulevard. Architecturally, the most interesting district of the New Town is the north side of Charlotte Square, designed by Robert Adam. It was young architect James Craig who shaped much of the Georgian style of the New Town, with its crescents and squares.

At No. 7 Charlotte Square, a part of the northern facade, is the restored building known simply as the **Georgian House** (tel. 226-5922). It is a prime example of Scottish architecture and interior design in the zenith of the New Town. Originally the home of John Lamont XVII, known as "the last of the patriarchs and the first of the moderns," the house has recently been refurbished and reopened to the public by Scotland's National Trust. The furniture in this Robert Adam house is mainly Hepplewhite, Chippendale, and Sheraton, all dating from the 18th century. In a ground-floor bedroom is a sturdy old four-poster with an original 18th-century canopy. The dining room table is set for a dinner on fine Wedgwood china, and the kitchen is stocked with gleaming copper pots and pans. The house is open April to October from 10 a.m. to 5 p.m. (on Sunday from 2 to 5 p.m.). In winter its hours are from 10 to 5 weekdays (on Sunday from 2 to 5 p.m.). Admission is 75p ($1.73) for adults, 35p (81¢) for children.

As an Old Town complement to the New Town Georgian House, the National Trust has opened in a 1620 tenement in the Royal Mile, **Gladstone's Land,** an upstairs apartment of four rooms furnished as it might have been in the 17th century. On the ground floor, reconstructed shop booths display replicas of goods of the period. It is open April through October, Monday through Saturday from 10 a.m. to 5 p.m. (on Sunday from 2 to 5 p.m.). Admission is 50p ($1.15) for adults, 25p (58¢) for children.

The Gothic-inspired **Scott Monument** lies in the **East Princes Street Gardens.** It is the most famous landmark of Edinburgh, completed in the mid-19th century. Sir Walter Scott's heroes are honored by small figures in the monument. You can climb the tower weekdays in summer from 9 a.m. to 6 p.m. for 25p (58¢). Off-season, you must scale the monument before 3 p.m. At **West Princes Street Gardens** is the first ever **Floral Clock,** which was constructed in 1904.

ART TREASURES: For the art lover, Edinburgh has a number of masterpieces, and many visitors come here just to look at the galleries. Of course, the principal museum is the **National Gallery of Scotland,** on The Mound, in the center of Princes Street Gardens. Although the gallery is small as national galleries go, the collection came about with great care and was expanded considerably by bequests and loans. A few paintings are of exceptional merit. We'll highlight a representative sampling.

Among recent acquisitions is Guido Reni's *Moses and Pharoah's Crown.* Other Italian paintings are Andrea del Sarto's *Portrait of a Man* and Domenichino's *Adoration of the Shepherds.* However, perhaps the most acclaimed among them is Tiepolo's *The Finding of Moses.*

The Spanish masters are less well represented but shine forth in El Greco's *Saviour,* Velázquez's *Old Woman Cooking Eggs,* an early work by that great master, and *Immaculate Conception* by Zurbarán, his friend and contemporary.

The Flemish School emerges notably in Rubens's *The Feast of Herod* and the Dutch in Rembrandt's *A Women in Bed.*

Among the paintings on loan to the gallery since World War II, from the Duke of Sutherland, are two Raphaels: *The Holy Family with a Palm Tree* and *The Bridgewater Madonna.* Titian gives us his favorite subject, Venus, this time rising from the sea, but he's even more masterly in his Diana canvases. A rare feature of the gallery: the *Seven Sacraments* paintings by Poussin, the 17th-century French painter, are also on loan.

The most valuable gift to the gallery since its foundation, the Maitland Collection, includes Cézanne's *Mont St. Victoire,* as well as works by Degas, Van Gogh, Renoir, Gauguin and Seurat, among others.

The great English painters are represented by excellent examples—Gainsborough's *The Hon. Mrs. Graham,* Constable's *Dedham Vale,* along with works by Turner, Reynolds, and Hogarth. Naturally, the work of Scottish painters decks the walls, none finer than Henry Raeburn, at his best in the whimsical *The Rev. Robert Walker Skating on Duddingston Loch.*

The gallery is open from 10 a.m. to 5 p.m. weekdays (2 to 5 on Sunday). During the festival, hours are from 10 a.m. to 6 p.m. weekdays and from 11 a.m. to 6 p.m. on Sunday. Admission is free.

SCOTLAND: EDINB[URGH]

It may be typical of Edinburgh that it houses the only museum coll[ection] in Britain solely of 20th-century art, the **Scottish National Gallery of Moder[n] Art**, in an 18th-century house, Inverleith House, on an eminence in the Royal Botanic Garden looking up to the skyline of the old city, a uniquely beautiful situation. But it is too small, and the gallery will move early in the 1980s to a much larger but still old building, the former John Watson's School. Meanwhile, in the garden outside the gallery are major sculptures by Bourdelle, Epstein, Marini, Moore, Hepworth, Reg Butler, and William Turnbull, and a sundial by Ian Hamilton Finlay. The galleries contain works by Picasso, Matisse, Braque, Léger, Rouault, Derain, Miro, Magritte, Kirchner, Nolde, Kokoschka, Giacometti, Arp, Schwitters, Popova, and many others of the major creators' of the 20th century, with a sound representation of English and, particularly, Scottish modern art. Bus routes passing the Royal Botanic Garden are 8, 9, 19, 23, and 27. Hours are from 10 a.m. to 5 p.m. (or dusk if earlier) on weekdays, and 2 to 5 p.m. (or dusk if earlier; opening at 11 a.m. during the Edinburgh Festival) on Sunday.

THE FESTIVAL: The highlight of Edinburgh's year—and the time of the greatest tourist invasion—is when the world-famous Edinburgh International Festival takes place. The annual festival is usually staged around mid-August to mid-September. Artists in all fields—music, drama, opera, ballet, painting—contribute their talents, and "Auld Reekie" takes on a cosmopolitan air.

One of the best attended spectacles is the military tattoo on the floodlit Esplanade in front of Edinburgh Castle. This is a chance for the spectator to witness some Highland dancing of the Scots and to watch a parade of Scottish Regiments. In addition to operatic presentations, choral and orchestral concerts, soloists, chamber concerts, and recitals (expect at least half a dozen every evening), there is a large number of dramatic shows and, to top it off, a widely attended film festival.

During these busy days, it's smart to make your headquarters at the **Festival Club**, a rendezvous for people participating in and witnessing the events. The club's headquarters are in the Assembly Rooms and Music Hall at 54 George St. The licensed club operates a reasonably priced restaurant, snackbar, and disco. The daily membership costs 50p ($1.15), or £2 ($4.60) weekly. Season membership is £5 ($11.50).

For festival tickets, write to Festival Box Office, 21 Market St., Edinburgh E41 1BW (tel. 226-4001). For accommodations, write to Tourist Accommodation Service, 9 Cockburn St., Edinburgh E41 1BR.

LOW-COST TOURS: If you want a quick introduction to the principal attractions in and around the capital, then consider one or more of the inexpensive tours offered by the **Lothian Region Transport.** You won't find a cheaper way to hit the highlights, and, later, you can go back on your own if you want a deeper experience. The luxury-type coaches leave from Waverley Bridge, near the Scott Monument. The tours start in April and run through late October. A winter program is also offered. A half-day coach tour (which takes about 3½ hours) leaves daily at 9:30 a.m. and 1:30 p.m. (Sunday at 1:30 p.m. only), costing £4 ($9.20) and visiting the castle, the Palace of Holyroodhouse, and St. Giles Cathedral. Operating throughout the day are half a dozen shorter tours that show you some of the environs—such as Scott and Stevenson Country. These tours are priced from £1 ($2.30). One of the more recent additions to the program is a daily excursion to South Queensferry to view the world-

...E GUIDE TO ENGLAND AND SCOTLAND

...d and Rail Bridges. For more information, telephone 556-

... Pipers, 23 Lothian Rd. (tel. 229-8291), provides a pleasant ...ing of food and entertainment. The underground restaurant is ...ith warm red walls, glinting woodwork, and tartan floor coverings. You ... eeted by a kilted lassie, who offers a welcoming whiskey or sherry, and you then find your table where you can enjoy a meal of kipper pâté, Scottish broth, then Aberdeen angus prime beef with Ayrshire potatoes and vegetables, followed by Scottish cake. The master of ceremonies, Steve John MacGregor, makes the traditional speech and festivities commence. Featured are singers, sword-dancers (the audience is invited to join in this hazardous activity), a comedian and then dancing to the band. For a thoroughly good evening out for the family, the fully inclusive cost is £15 ($34.50) per person. The cabaret is likely to feature Jimmy Millar, the Scottish tenor, and Jimmy Blue, the country's top accordionist. Pipers is open seven nights a week from 7:30 to 10:30 p.m.

The **White Cockade**, 55 Rose St. (tel. 225-5944), is a popular place that offers live groups on selected weeknights and on Saturday afternoons. The pub is open 11 a.m. to 11 p.m. and serves good-quality reasonably priced lunches. It can get quite crowded at nights, so you should try to get there early. All you need to pay is for drink and food.

3. Day Trips from Edinburgh

Within easy reach of Edinburgh lie some of the most interesting castles and mansions in Scotland, the most important of which follow.

STIRLING: Almost equidistant from Glasgow and Edinburgh, Stirling is dominated by its impressive castle, perched on a 250-foot basalt rock. From Edinburgh, a bus takes about an hour and a half, traveling a distance of 37 miles.

This ancient town, with its turbulent history, was the scene of several battles, notably the Battle of Bannockburn in 1314, in which the Scots routed the army of Edward II. On the right bank of the Forth, the castle dates from an unknown age, although its main gateway was built by James III. At one time the castle was considered the "key to the Highlands," and is today the headquarters of the Argyle and Sutherland Highlanders, one of Britain's most famous regiments.

The castle is open daily in April, May, and September from 9:30 a.m. to 6:15 p.m. (on Sunday from 11 to 6); June, July, and August, daily from 9:30 a.m. to 8 p.m. (on Sunday from 11 to 7); and October to March, daily from 9:30 a.m. to 4 p.m. (on Sunday from 1 to 4), charging adults 30p ($69¢); children, 15p (35¢).

Other places of interest to visit in Stirling include the 15th-century **Church of the Holy Rude**, in which Mary Queen of Scots was crowned in 1543 at the age of nine months; the **Auld Brig** over the Forth, dating from the 14th century; and the **palace** built by James V in the 16th century.

Just outside the town is the **Robert Bruce Memorial and Museum**. Admission is 15p (35¢) for a continual audio-visual presentation of stories of Bruce's times and history.

Food and Lodging

Portcullis Hotel, Castle/Wynd (tel. Stirling 2290), is our favorite place to stay in the area. It's a tall, 14th-century, rugged stone building hugging the walls of the castle. You enter through a lower courtyard of shrubbery and trees, protected by a high old stone wall. The inviting bar, which is colorful itself, is on the ground floor. You ascend to the second-floor lounge with stone walls, a cathedral ceiling, and a fireplace at one end. It's furnished with a mixture of antiques and comfortable chairs. The dining room has encircling windows offering a spectacular view. The finest Scottish china is used for meals. Snacks include "mince and mash" at £1.50 ($3.45), although upstairs a meal will cost from £5 ($11.50) to £7 ($16.10). The bedrooms are highly personal, each furnished informally and comfortably. The per-person rate is £12.50 ($28.75), plus VAT and service.

If you're a Scottish history buff and would like to spend the night in this historic town, creaking with memories of time gone by, you might try to find a room at the tiny **Heritage Hotel,** containing only four bedrooms, all of which have private baths and showers.

It's at 16 Allan Park (tel. Stirling 3660). You're welcomed by the owner, Monsieur Marquetty, a Frenchman who married "a Scottish lassie" and settled in this unlikely spot. Their "hotel" is really like a private residence, and they have outfitted it as such, discreetly using antiques, paintings, and personal objects to make it warm and homelike. Their single rate is £14 ($32.20) per night, and two persons are charged from £28 ($64.40).

Monsieur Marquetty also offers a good cuisine in his adjoining restaurant, which features a set lunch at £4.50 ($10.35), served between noon and 3, and a table d'hôte dinner, four courses, for £8.50 ($19.55), offered between 6:30 and 11 p.m., the latter a surprisingly late hour for provincial Stirling.

La Romantica, 4 Viewfield Pl. (tel. Stirling 64521), is a trattoria with a good bar, Valentino's Lounge, near the Royal Hotel. It offers well-prepared, familiar, and enjoyable Italian dishes, including the chef's pasta specialty, spaghetti Romantica at £2.50 ($5.75). All pasta dishes, ordered as a main course, cost £3 ($6.90). Instead of pasta, you might begin with minestrone at 75p ($1.73). Recommendable main courses include chicken suprême "Romeo and Juliet," £4.25 ($9.78), or else veal alla Romantica, £4.30 ($9.89). The smoothest finish is the zabaglione at £1.10 ($2.53). The restaurant is closed on Sunday, although open otherwise until 11 p.m.

DOUNE CASTLE: At Doune, on the banks of the Teith River, four miles west of Dunblane, stands this 14th-century castle, once a royal palace. Now owned by the Earl of Moray, it was restored in 1883, making it one of the best preserved of the medieval castles of Scotland. It is open daily from April through October, charging adults 50p ($1.15) for admission; children, 30p (69¢). It's closed on Thursday in April, May, September, and October.

After visiting the castle, guests can drive 1½ miles to the **Doune Motor Museum,** which charges £1 ($2.30) for adults, 20p (46¢) for children. The motor museum contains about 35 vintage and postvintage motor cars, including the second-oldest Rolls-Royce in the world. It is open daily from April 1 to October 31. In April and May, the last admissions are at 4:30 p.m. From June to August, the hours are from 10 a.m. to 6 p.m., and in September and October, the last admissions are again at 4:30 p.m.

South of Doune is the highly popular **Blair Drummond Safari Park.** It's open from mid-March to the last Sunday in October, from 10 a.m. (tel. Doune 456). Apart from the zebras, you are likely to meet the typical safari-park cast of lions, giraffes, elephants, and Highland cattle, and there's even a pet's corner. Meals are offered in the Ranch Kitchen, and free picnic areas are provided. Cars are admitted for £3.30 ($7.59), including a guidebook. Safari buses, costing £1 ($2.30) for adults, 70p ($1.61) for children, are available for those without their own transport. A Safari boat trip is offered at a cost of 40p (92¢) for adults, 25p (58¢) for children.

Food and Lodging

The Woodside (tel. Doune 237) is a pleasant stone structure standing on the A84 main Stirling–Oban Road. In the heart of Perthshire, the family-run hotel can be useful either as a luncheon stopover or for an overnight stay. It contains 15 well-furnished bedrooms, most of which private baths or showers. Singles rent for £15 ($34.50), doubles going for £25 ($57.50). The lounge is brightened by red plush seating, and there are, in addition, two simply decorated bars. The dining room overlooks the garden, and you sit in high-backed carved Edwardian chairs, enjoying such standard Scottish dishes as roast gigot of lamb, roast shoulder of pork, and grilled rainbow trout. You are likely to find these items on the luncheon menu, costing from £4.50 ($10.35) for a meal. At dinner, which is likely to run about £6 ($13.80), you might enjoy such specialties as venison, lobster, and Aberdeen angus filet steaks.

Deanston House Hotel (tel. Doune 248) is a Georgian building dating from 1820 and standing on 56 acres of private woodland and park, with the River Teith running along one side of the property. The manor was later given an Italianate style, and a three-story tower and conservatory were added. Owned by Denzil S. Crawford, the hotel has a wide variety of rooms, with and without private baths. The decor honors the era, and there are many fine antiques and paintings. A double or twin rents from £14 ($32.20) per person nightly without private bath, increasing to £20 ($46) per person with private bath (these latter rooms often contain four-poster beds). Singles without bath rent from £15 ($34.50) nightly. Good Scottish food is served, a dinner costing from £6 ($13.80). Before your meal, you may want to have a drink in the ornate Ormonde cocktail bar, with its interesting and original wooden ceiling.

LINLITHGOW: In this royal burgh, a county town in West Lothian, 18 miles west of Edinburgh, Mary Queen of Scots was born. The roofless **Palace of Linlithgow,** site of her birth in 1542, can still be viewed here today, although it is but a shell of its former self. Once a favorite residence of Scottish kings, the palace was built square-shaped. In the center are the remains of a royal fountain erected by James V. The queen's suite was in the north quarter, but this was rebuilt for the homecoming of James VI in 1617. The Great Hall is on the first floor. Gen. Henry Hawley's dragoons burned the palace in 1746, destroying one of the gems in the Scottish architectural crown. It is open daily from 10 a.m. to 5 p.m. (on Sunday from 2 to 5 p.m.), charging an admission of 25p (58¢) for adults, 15p (35¢) for children.

South of the palace stands the medieval kirk of **St. Michael the Archangel.**

From Linlithgow, it is but a 3½-mile drive east on the Queensferry Road (A904) to the **House of the Binns,** the historic home of the Dalyells. The mansion, with its fine Jacobean plaster ceilings, portraits, and panoramic vistas, receives visitors Easter Week and then from May 1 to September 30—daily, except Friday, from 2 to 5:30 p.m. The parkland is open from 10 to 7. Admission is 75p ($1.73) for adults, 35p (81¢) for children.

For dining, **Champany**, on the A904, three miles northeast of Linlithgow (tel. Philpstoun 532), was once a farmhouse built of stone, but it has been handsomely converted into one of the finest places for dining in the area. The dining room is circular, with a steep hexagonal ceiling. Victorian mahogany furniture adds a sedate touch. Our happiest experience was discovering the chef's specialty, a chicken breast suprême, made royal with its clever use of hazelnuts, port, and tasty apples. It's a remarkable dish and we recommend it highly, although the escalope of veal, prepared in the Roman style, is almost as good. All in all, it's personal cookery at reasonable prices. The set luncheon goes for £6.80 ($15.65), and a complete dinner on an à la carte menu runs around £12 ($27.60) per head. The menu changes twice yearly. The restaurant is open daily except Sunday from 12:30 to 2:15 p.m. and from 7 to 10 p.m.

HOPETOUN HOUSE: This is Scotland's greatest Adam mansion, that fine example of 18th-century architecture. It is the seat of the Marquess of Linlithgow, whose ancestors were once the governor general of Australia and the viceroy of India. Set in the midst of beautifully landscaped grounds, laid out along the lines of Versailles, the mansion lies near the Forth Road Bridge at South Queensferry, off the A904. On a tour you're shown through splendid reception rooms filled with 18th-century tapestries, unique Cullen furniture, paintings, statuary, and other works of art. From a rooftop viewing platform, you look out over a panoramic view of the Firth of Forth. Even more enjoyable, perhaps, is to take the Nature Trail, explore the Deer Parks, investigate the Stables' Museum, or stroll through the formal gardens, all on the grounds. In the Ballroom Suite is the gift shop, and a licensed restaurant serves coffee, lunch, afternoon tea, and high tea. Hopetoun is open Easter weekend, then daily from May to the end of September, from 11 a.m. to 5:30 p.m.

If, instead of the Ballroom at Hopetoun, you want to have lunch in less grand surroundings, you may want to seek out the 300-year-old **Hawes Inn**, South Queensferry (tel. 331-1990), in which Robert Louis Stevenson wrote parts of *Kidnapped*. Beneath the Forth Railway Bridge, the inn specializes in Scottish dishes, but also offers a number of continental temptations, such as escalope Marsala and steak Diane. Prices of these dishes begin at £5.50 ($12.65). A set luncheon is featured for £4.50 ($10.35), and it's served from 12:30 to 2:30 p.m. Dinner, if you should be in the area, will run about £12 ($27.60) on the à la carte menu. After enjoying the view of the garden, you may find the inn so peaceful you'll want to spend the night. If so, there are nine rooms, two of which contain private baths. Everybody requests no. 13, in which Stevenson stayed. A single goes for £15 ($34.50), a double from £21 ($48.30) to £28 ($64.40). The accommodations with bath and color TV are in an annex, but why come all the way here for that?

NORTH BERWICK: This royal burgh, created in the 14th century, was once an important Scottish port. In East Lothian, 24 miles east from Edinburgh, it is today a holiday resort popular with the Scots themselves and an increasing horde of foreigners just discovering the place. Visitors are drawn to its golf courses, beach sands, and colorful harbor life on the Firth of Forth. You can climb the rocky shoreline or else enjoy the heated outdoor swimming pool in July and August.

At the tourist office (tel. North Berwick 2197), you can pick up information on how to take boat trips to the offshore islands, including **Bass Rock**, a famous breeding ground inhabited by about 10,000 gannets and one or two crusty lighthouse keepers. The volcanic island is one mile in circumference. It's possible to see the rock from the harbor. The viewing is even better at Berwick Law, a volcanic lookout point surmounted by the jawbones of a whale.

Some three miles east of the resort stand the dramatic ruins of the 14th-century diked and rose-colored **Tantallon Castle,** rising magnificently on cliffs. This was the ancient stronghold of the Douglasses.

The favorite choice for accommodations in North Berwick is the **Marine Hotel,** Cromwell Road (tel. North Berwick 2406), one of those grand seaside resort establishments, standing in its own garden looking across the West Link golf course to the Firth of Forth. After a slumber, it has now blossomed out into a summer holiday hotel of the finest standing, ideal for families. In its modernization, all 85 of its bedrooms now contain private baths. An airiness and freshness prevail. Singles rent for £21 ($48.30), doubles from £34 ($78.20). Tennis courts and a putting green are on the hotel's grounds. A resident orchestra plays for dancing on Saturday evening. The public rooms are spacious and nicely furnished. The hotel also has a heated outdoor pool in use from May to September, as well as squash courts, tennis courts, a putting green, and a sauna.

If you're seeking something less expensive, **Blenheim House** (tel. North Berwick 2385), is, we understand from readers' reports, a good bet, although we've never stayed there. It's tiny, offering only two singles (and these go fast), eight doubles, and a couple of family rooms. Rates are £11.50 ($26.45) in a single, from £21 ($48.30) in a double. The food—again, according to reports—is also good. Service is until 9 p.m. The hotel is very popular in summer, so reservations will be essential. In addition, Mr. and Mrs. Wight rent a garden flat, consisting of two double bedrooms and one single room at a rate of £110 ($253) per week.

DIRLETON: Another popular excursion from North Berwick is to the rose-tinted **Dirleton Castle,** with its surrounding gardens, at Dirleton on the Edinburgh-North Berwick Road (A198). This 13th-century castle is well preserved, receiving visitors from April to September—weekdays from 9:30 to 7 (on Sunday from 2 to 7 p.m.). Dirleton itself vies for the title of "the prettiest village in Scotland."

For dining at Dirleton, the **Open Arms** (tel. Dirleton 241), will receive you in keeping with the promise of its name. This old stone hostelry has been transformed into a handsome restaurant, serving the finest food in the area. It lies off the A198, 2½ miles southwest of North Berwick. Overlooking the castle ruins, the hotel is owned by Arthur Neil, who has built up an enormous local reputation for serving Scottish dishes. Try, for example, cranachan (served with shortbread, this is a concoction of oatmeal, heavy cream, and brambles). Cold Scottish salmon is served encased in pastry, and is one of the inn's specialties. Another specialty is a stew made of fresh mussels and onions. The people who serve are quiet, informed, and skillful. Try to be adventuresome and sample the Scottish dishes. A table d'hôte luncheon is offered for £5 ($11.50), although you can order à la carte as well. Hours are from 12:30 to 2:15 p.m. In the evening, between 7 and 10, a three-course set dinner is offered for £10 ($23), plus service.

DUNBAR: In East Lothian, southeast of North Berwick, Dunbar, another royal burgh, is a popular seaside resort at the foot of the Lammermuir Hills. On a rock above the harbor are the remains of **Dunbar Castle,** built on the site of an earlier castle that dated from 856. Mary Queen of Scots fled there with

Darnley in 1566, immediately after the murder of her secretary, Rizzio. Today the kittiwakes live where once the "Black Angus of Dunbar," the Countess of March, held off the English. The famous Battle of Dunbar was fought in 1650 between Cromwell's army and the Scots led by David Leslie. The Scots, fighting valiantly, lost and nearly 3000 were killed in one day.

Roxburghe Hotel, Queen's Road (tel. Dunbar 62755), is a rather old-fashioned hotel of much comfort. A large, 40-bedroom establishment, it stands in a sheltered position on the seafront, adjoining the Dunbar golf course. Bedrooms are often roomy and most comfortable, a large proportion containing private baths. Bed and breakfast, depending on the plumbing, ranges from £15 ($34.50) to £20 ($46) per person. The public rooms are furnished in a homey fashion, often with open fires. The cocktail bar is modernized, and in the sea-view dining room the good food, using fresh produce, is supervised by Mr. Marcel, a well-known chef de cuisine.

The **Battleblent Hotel** (tel. Dunbar 62234) lies just outside Dunbar on the road to Edinburgh, 26 miles away. Jim and Faye Ferguson own the castle-like home set on a hill surrounded by three acres of their own land overlooking the Balhaven Bay on the Firth of Forth. The bedrooms are large, high-ceilinged, and comfortable, with electric heaters and facilities for making tea and coffee. Assisted by their sons, Martin and Kevin, the Fergusons have a disco and lounge bar downstairs, and a small, charming, bright dining room on the first floor. The bar and disco are popular with the people of Dunbar, so you can get acquainted with the local affairs of the day. Get Mr. Ferguson to show you his collection of international coins in the downstairs lounge bar. The tariff is £10 ($23) for bed and a continental breakfast, or £11 ($25.30) for bed and a big Scottish breakfast.

DALKEITH: This small burgh in Midlothian, seven miles southeast of Edinburgh, is the site of **Dalkeith Palace**, rebuilt and redesigned by Sir John Vanbrugh, circa 1700. Such monarchs as George IV, Victoria, and Edward VII have stayed here during visits to Edinburgh.

Visitors flock here for **Dalkeith Park**, to explore the woodland and riverside walks in and around the extensive grounds of the palace. Luring guests are natural trails and an adventure woodland play area, a tunnel walk, and an Adam bridge. The park is open daily from 11 a.m. to 6 p.m., April 2 to October 1. To reach the park, go seven miles south of Edinburgh on the A68. The price of admission is 50p ($1.15) for adults, 30p (69¢) for children.

On the same tour, it's easy to explore—

HADDINGTON: Created as a royal burgh by David I, this small town of East Lothian lies on the Tyne River, about 17 miles east of Edinburgh. In the 15th century it was Scotland's largest town, but its fortunes declined thereafter.

On the right bank of the river, in the industrial suburb of Giffordgate, the Scottish reformer, John Knox, was believed to have been born in 1505. Much to the chagrin of the Catholic Mary Queen of Scots, he rose from these dire origins to found the Scottish Presbyterian Church.

St. Mary's Church, built in the 14th century, in red and gray sandstone, contains the tomb of Jane Welsh, who was born in the town. She married the historian, Thomas Carlyle.

Browns Hotel, West Road (tel. Haddington 082-2254), is owned and run by the Brown family. Theirs is a distinctive, rather stately Georgian-style house, situated where you can enjoy an uninterrupted view of the rolling

Lammermuir Hills, just 19 miles east of Edinburgh and a mile off the A1. The Browns charge £18 ($41.40) per person for dinner, bed, and breakfast without a private bath. With your own bath, it's £19 ($43.70). The Browns feel rather proud of their table d'hôte dinner, and welcome nonresidents to sample it.

4. The Kingdom of Fife

North of Forth from Edinburgh, the county of Fife still likes to call itself a "kingdom." Its name, even today, suggests the romantic episodes and pageantry during the reign of the early Stuart kings. Fourteen of Scotland's 66 royal burghs lay within this shire. Many of the former royal palaces and castles, either restored or in colorful ruins, can be visited today, and we've previewed the most important ones coming up.

As Edinburgh is so near, the temptation is to set up headquarters in one of the city's many elegant hotels or bed-and-breakfast houses and explore Fife from that base. However, serious golfers may want to stay at one of our recommended hotels in St. Andrews.

DUNFERMLINE: This ancient town was once the capital of Scotland. It is easily reached by ferry or by the railway crossing the famous Forth Bridge. Dunfermline lies five miles northwest of the Forth Bridge, a distance of 14 miles northwest of Edinburgh.

In **Dunfermline Abbey** lie many of Scotland's royal dead, including Robert the Bruce, who gave the town its charter in 1322. His skeleton was rediscovered in 1818 during excavations. Queen Victoria herself commanded that the tomb of St. Margaret be restored.

The **Royal Palace** witnessed the birth of Kings Charles I and James I. Only the southwest wall remains of this once-gargantuan edifice. The last king to reside here was Charles II in 1651.

Andrew Carnegie, the American industrialist and philanthropist, was born here in 1835. The **Andrew Carnegie Birthplace,** a former weaver's cottage, lies at the junction of Priory Lane and Moodie Street and may be visited weekdays, May to August, from 11 a.m. to 1 p.m. and 2 to 5 p.m. From September, it's open 11 a.m. to 1 p.m. and 2 to 4 p.m.; on Sunday from 2 to 6 p.m. all year.

After he retired from steelmaking and finance, Carnegie gave away $400 million for charitable purposes, mainly in Britain and America. Dunfermline received the first free library of many thousands, public baths, and the magnificent **Pittencrieff Park,** rich in history and natural charm. Run by the trust which still provides extra benefits for his native town, the birthplace museum gives a fascinating glimpse of his humble origins and his enormous benefactions.

From Dunfermline, you can take an excursion six miles west to—

Culross

This old royal burgh has been renovated by the Scottish National Trust, and is one of the most beautiful in the country. As you walk its cobbled streets, admiring its charming whitewashed houses, you'll feel you're taking a stroll back into the 17th century. Many of the cottages have crow-stepped gables and red pantiled roofs.

Set in tranquil walled gardens, **Culross Palace** was built in the village between 1597 and 1611, containing a most beautiful series of paintings on its wooden walls and ceilings. It has been handsomely restored and may be visited,

SCOTLAND: DUNFERMLINE/FALKLAND

April to September, daily from 9:30 a.m. to 7 p.m. (on Sunday From October to March, it's open daily from 9:30 to 4 (on Su 4). Admission is 30p (69¢) for adults, 15p (35¢) for children.

For food and lodging, the **Red Lion Inn** (tel. Newmills 225) north side of the Forth River midway between Forth Road Bridge dine Road Bridge. Both ancient and modern, the little pub has rooms which owner Findlays Sinclair rents out at £8 ($18.40) per person per day, including breakfast. There is a pine-paneled pub and a lounge with a fireplace, where you can have bar snacks. The pub is easy to spot, a blue and stucco building with a slate roof in the center of the village. There's parking in the rear—next to the stone wall, overlooking the river. A mixed crowd frequents the Red Lion, the rich, the poor, locals blending with tourists. The cooking is above average, and you'll have a wide choice of whiskeys, including Royal Culross.

FALKLAND PALACE: Now owned by Queen Elizabeth, Falkland was once the hunting retreat of the Stuart kings. This royal burgh of cobbled streets and crooked houses lies at the northern base of the hill of East Lomond, 21 miles north of Edinburgh.

Since the 12th century, it has been connected with Scottish kings. Originally a castle stood on the site of today's palace, but it was replaced in the 16th century. Falkland then became a favorite seat of the Scottish court. A grief-stricken James V died here. Mary Queen of Scots used to come to Falkland for "hunting and hawking." It was also here that the Earl of Bothwell was arrested, accused of a plot against her. Cromwell's forces occupied Falkland in 1654.

The royal chapel and apartments are open from April 1 to October 31, weekdays from 10 a.m. to 6 p.m. and on Sunday from 2 to 6. The gardens, incidentally, have been laid out to the original royal plans. At Falkland is the oldest royal tennis court in Scotland. For a ticket to both the palace and gardens, adults pay £1 ($2.30); children, 50p ($1.15).

Food and Lodging

Covenanter Hotel (tel. Falkland 224) has been a popular inn since the early 18th century. With modest modernization, it offers a good standard of accommodation. It's built ruggedly of local stone, with high chimneys, wooden shutters, and a modest Georgian entry. The location is on a tiny plaza, opposite the church and castle. You enter a gleaming white entry hall with a circular staircase leading to the lounges and bedrooms. The dining room is strictly "old style" and for predinner drinks there is an intimate pub, the Covenanter Cocktail Bar. Bed and breakfast costs £9 ($20.70) per person, including service and VAT, and luncheons go for £4.50 ($10.35). Evening meals are à la carte.

Kind Kyttock's Kitchen, Cross Wynd, stands right near the palace and welcomes you most of the year with a stone fireplace where logs burn brightly. The "kitchen" is also an art gallery, displaying local crafts and paintings. A specialty is four homemade oatcakes with cheese at 80p ($1.84). The bread is always homemade, very fresh tasting, as you'll discover if you order an open sandwich at 90p ($2.07). For a tea, we'd suggest the homemade pancake with fruit and fresh cream at 55p ($1.27). Even better, however, are the homemade tarts with fresh cream, costing 60p ($1.38). Salads are good tasting, costing from £1.20 ($2.76) a plate. A cup of Scottish broth, served with a slice of home-baked whole-meal bread, goes for 45p ($1.04). The women who run the place serve from 10 a.m. to 6 p.m. Off-season, it is open only on weekends.

Back at Dunfermline you can connect with the costal road, heading east

Largo

Alexander Selkirk, the original Robinson Crusoe, was born here in 1676. This famous Scottish sailor, son of a shoemaker and tanner, was once charged with "indecent behavior in church," but he never had to pay the penalty, whatever it was, as he was away at sea. He disappeared in the South Seas, but was discovered in 1709. He returned to Largo in 1712. A statue in the village honors this hometown boy, who was clearly the inspiration for the Daniel Defoe classic. A house Selkirk purchased for his father is still standing.

THE EAST NEUK: Within a half hour's drive of St. Andrews are some of the most beautiful and unspoiled fishing villages of eastern Scotland:

Pittenweem

If you're here in the morning, try to get caught up in the action at the fish auction held under a large shed (except Sunday). The actual time depends on the tides. Afterward you can go for a walk through the village, taking in the sturdy stone homes, some of which have been preserved by Scotland's National Trust people.

Anstruther

This is an important fishing port and a summer resort, with the **Scottish Fisheries Museum** down by the harbor. Tracing the history of the fishing industry in Scotland, it charges 50p ($1.15) admission for adults, 25p (58¢) for children. The museum is open from April 1 to October 31, Monday to Saturday, from 10 a.m. to 12:30 p.m., and from 2 to 6 p.m. (on Sunday from 2 to 5). From November 1 to March 31, it may be visited every day, except Tuesday from 2 to 5 p.m. The museum also has a tearoom and a marine aquarium. It has restored two large sail fishing boats in Anstruther Harbor. One, the 70-foot *Fifie*, is open to the public. From the museum, you can walk to the tiny hamlet of Cellardyke which is really Old Anstruther, with many charming stone houses.

The **Craw's Nest Hotel,** Bankwell Road (tel. Anstruther 310-691), was originally an old Scottish manse before its conversion to a popular hotel, with beautiful views over the Firth of Forth and May Island. To the original building, many extensions were added under the direction of the owners, Mr. and Mrs. Edward Clarke, and their son-in-law, Ian Birrel. The black-and-white building is step-gabled, standing behind a high stone wall. Bedrooms are handsomely equipped and well appointed, costing from £20 ($46) per person nightly for bed and breakfast. Each of the units contains a private bath. Public areas are simply decorated and cozy, including a lounge bar as well as a bustling public bar. The food is good, and the wine is priced reasonably in the hotel's dining room.

Smuggler's Inn, High Street (tel. Anstruther 310-506), stands in the heart of town, a warmly inviting inn that evokes memories of smuggling days around here. The original inn that stood on this spot dates back to 1300. In Queen Anne's day, it was a well-known tavern. The ceilings are low, the floors uneven, and, of course, the stairways are winding. Overlooking the harbor, rooms are rented for £11.50 ($26.45) per person if bathless, rising to £13 ($29.90) with bath. Again, depending on the plumbing, the demi-pension rate ranges from £16 ($36.80) to £18 ($41.40) per person. If featured, ask for the local Pittenweem prawns. Mr. and Mrs. McSharry offer a set lunch for £3.75 ($8.63) and an à la carte dinner, served from 7 to 9:30 p.m., from £10 ($23).

Elie

With its step-gabled houses and little harbor, this is our favorite village along the coast. Nearby is a good golf course, and there are rock-ribbed sands for bathing.

If you're passing this way, we'd suggest you drop in at the **Ship Inn** on the Toft, there to enjoy a pint of lager. In summer you can sit out in fair weather, overlooking the water. In colder months, a fireplace burns brightly. The pub has a nautical atmosphere, and doesn't do much in the way of food, but the friendly woman who runs it will prepare a sandwich if you're hungry.

For more substantial dining, we'd suggest **Upstairs/Downstairs**, 51 High St. (tel. Elie 330-374), a pleasant little place to eat, opposite a small triangular park. For a menu of standard dishes, you are charged £6 ($13.80) for an evening's dinner. During the day, snacks and bar lunches are also offered, followed by high teas and suppers. The restaurant, incidentally, is licensed. A bar lunch averages around £2 ($4.60), and wine by the glass goes for 55p ($1.27). If you'd like to stay overnight, you can request one of the simple, pleasant bedrooms, costing only £6 ($13.80) per person nightly.

Mrs. Barbara Walker, Dalmore, The Toft (tel. Elie 330-583), is the village librarian. She wisely began to accept guests so she could afford to keep her bayfront home. Since then, she's won all sorts of new friends, especially among Americans, and she feels she's expanded her own horizons. "We feel less isolated—now we are a part of the world," Mrs. Walker told us. Her Tudoresque, tall and stylish 19th-century villa is on a grassy terrace, just 20 steps up from the harbor. It's still a private-seeming home, with many antiques in the sitting-breakfast room, the entry, and bedrooms. She personalizes the breakfasts, and charges £6 ($13.80) per person nightly. She also serves a beverage and cookies around 9 p.m. If you ask, she'll serve an evening meal for £3 ($6.90).

Crail

Considered the pearl of the East Neuk of Fife, Crail is an artists' colony, and many painters have found cottages around this little harbor. Natural bathing facilities are found at Roome Bay, and there are many beaches nearby. The Balcomie Golf Course, in good condition, is one of the oldest in the world.

Croma Hotel (tel. Crail 239) is near the harbor with ten bedrooms. It's the "home base" of famed all-American ball player Jack Healy and his attractive wife Rosemarie, originally from Ireland. Brooklyn-born Jack is a strapping, handsome former Pan Am executive. From Samoa he brought handicrafts and trinkets, and has hung them against the wall-size geographic maps from Pan Am. This, the Chart Room, is fully licensed, and it's Jack's domain. Rosemarie, who does the cooking for their guests, has decorated the dining room in green and white and used Windsor chairs set in front of the bay window. Many of the artists who live in this little fishing village come here for drinks and evening meals. The Healys charge £10 ($23) per person for bed and breakfast. They serve a table d'hôte lunch for £2.50 ($5.75), and an evening meal for £6.50 ($14.95).

ARWISE GUIDE TO ENGLAND AND SCOTLAND

EWS: On a bay of the North Sea, St. Andrews is sometimes known ...ford of Scotland." Founded in 1411, the **University of St. Andrews** ...est in Scotland and the third oldest in Britain. At term time you can ... students in their characteristic red gowns.

...he university's most interesting buildings include the tower and church of St. Salvator's College and the courtyard of St. Mary's College, dating from 1338. An ancient thorn tree, said to have been planted by Mary Queen of Scots, stands near the college's chapel. The church of St. Leonard's College is also from medieval days. The Scottish Parliament in 1645 met in the University Library, now containing nearly half a million books, with many rare and ancient volumes.

The historic sea town in northeast Fife is also known as the home of golf in Britain. The world's leading golf club, the **Royal & Ancient,** was founded here in 1754. All of St. Andrews's four golf courses—the Old, the New, the Jubilee, and the Eden—are open to the public, charging modest fees. Of course, the hallowed turf of the Old Course is the sentimental favorite.

The old gray royal burgh of St. Andrews is filled with many monastic ruins and ancient houses; regrettably, they represent but a few mere skeletons of medieval St. Andrews.

The **St. Andrews Cathedral and Priory** was begun in 1127, although in 1160 a much bigger cathedral was launched, finally consecrated in 1318. Built in both the Norman and Gothic styles, it was the largest church in Scotland, establishing St. Andrews as the ecclesiastical capital of the country. Today the ruins can only suggest the former beauty and importance of the cathedral. The east and west gables and a part of the south wall remain, and standing still is "the Pends," part of the old main gateway of the priory.

The **St. Andrews Cathedral Museum** contains a collection of early Christian and medieval monuments, as well as artifacts discovered on the cathedral site. It is open April to September—daily from 9:30 a.m. to 7 p.m. (on Sunday from 2 to 7). From October to March, hours are daily from 9:30 a.m. to 4 p.m. (on Sunday from 2 to 4). Admission is 20p (46¢) for adults, 10p (23¢) for children.

The **Holy Trinity Church,** dating from 1410, was much altered in 1799 and was restored in Edwardian times. In 1559 it had been sacked by Knox iconoclasts. The 12th-century tower of St. Regulus stands within its precincts, and visitors can climb this 108-foot structure.

You can also visit the 13th-century, ruined **Castle of St. Andrews,** with its bottle dungeon and secret passages.

Food and Lodging

In hotels, many dedicated golfers prefer the **Old Course Hotel** (tel. St. Andrews 4371), as it stands right in the middle of this legendary 17th-century fairway—hence, the protective net covering the hotel's entrance. Fortified by finnan haddie and porridge, a real old-fashioned Scottish breakfast, you can face that diabolical stretch of greenery where nearly all of the world's golfing greats have played and the Scots themselves have been whacking away since early in the 15th century.

The hotel itself is not ancient—far from it; it's bandbox modern, its balconies affording top preview seats at all tournaments. The bedrooms themselves are well equipped and always spotlessly maintained, renting for £35 ($80.50) in a single, from £45 ($103.50) in a double. All 80 bedrooms contain private baths.

Try to pay a predinner visit to the Jigger Inn adjoining the hotel. In a former stationmaster's house, this pub quaintly evokes days of yore in sharp contrast to the modernity of the hotel. However, if you're in a rush, a cofeeshop at the hotel serves snacks and light meals until 6 p.m.

The main dining room on the top floor opens onto views of the links. The menu is continental although many Scottish specialties are featured. A set lunch is offered for £7 ($16.10), a table d'hôte dinner for £9 ($20.70). Fresh produce is used whenever possible. The restaurant serves lunch from 12:30 to 2 p.m. and dinner from 7:30 to 9:30 p.m.

Other golfers prefer the cozier retreat of **Rufflets Hotel,** on the B939, about a mile and a half from St. Andrews (tel. St. Andrews 72594). Of the 22 bedrooms, 18 are equipped with private baths or showers, and all are well furnished in a warm, homelike way. Set in a garden of about ten acres, this is a substantial country house. The furnishings throughout are tasteful, as is the decor. The more modern bedrooms are in an annex, although traditionalists request space in the handsome main building, and those in the know reserve well in advance, as Rufflets is very popular with the British themselves. Singles rent from £16 ($36.80) to £18 ($41.40), doubles from £16 ($36.80) to £17 ($39.10) per person. The hotel is closed from mid-January to mid-February.

Even if you aren't staying here, you may want to call and reserve a table at the Rufflets Hotel Restaurant, a trio of dining rooms overlooking a well-laid-out garden. Excellent, fresh ingredients are used in the continental and British dishes, and everything we've sampled here has been accurately cooked and delicious. The service, too, is polite and friendly. A set luncheon costs £4 ($9.20), a table d'hôte dinner from £6 ($13.80). Lunch is served from 12:30 to 2 p.m. and dinner from 7 to 9 p.m. Like the hotel itself, the restaurant shuts down from mid-January to mid-February.

If you're seeking less formality, a favorite eating spot for years has been the **Grange Inn,** at Grange, about a mile and a half from St. Andrews on the A959 (tel. St. Andrews 2670). In this country cottage, with its charming garden, an old-fashioned hospitality prevails. In such a homey atmosphere, tempting dishes are served, some of them continental in flavor, but all of them well cooked and pleasantly served. The fresh produce tastes homegrown. The proprietors are justly proud of the reputation they have acquired for food. Lunch is served from 12:30 to 2 p.m. and dinner from 7 to 10 p.m. Be sure to reserve and expect to pay about £10 ($23) per head for a very large meal, everything included.

Argyle House Hotel, 127 North St. (tel. St. Andrews 73387), is a substantial renovated hotel in the center of town. While it has the rates of a simpler guest house, it offers many of the amenities of a larger hotel. There are three lounges—one for watching color TV, another where you can have a predinner drink, and the third for games such as chess, "snakes and ladders," backgammon, and bridge. Owners Tom and Joan Dowie and their courteous staff can make this an excellent stay. Their rooms have hot and cold water, good firm beds, and if you waken early you'll find each room has an electric kettle for making your own coffee. The rate per person, including VAT, for bed and breakfast is £7 ($16.10) to £8 ($18.40). Evening meals are offered for £4.50 ($10.35).

Number Ten, 10 Hope St. (tel. St. Andrews 74601), is run by Mr. and Mrs. Featherstone who have set reasonable rates per person for bed and breakfast—£7.50 ($17.25). With an evening meal, which we strongly recommend, it's £10.50 ($24.15). They invite parents to bring their children along, as they charge half price for them, providing they share their parents' room and are under 12. Prices include VAT, and there is no service charge. Every room has hot and cold water, and you are invited to watch the color TV set in the lounge.

5. Exploring Tayside

The trouble with exploring Tayside is you may find it so fascinating in scenery you'll never make it on to the Highlands. Carved out of the old counties of Perth and Angus, Tayside is named for its major river, the 119-mile Tay. Its tributaries and dozens of lochans and highland streams are some of the best salmon and trout waters in Europe. One of the loveliest regions of Scotland, Tayside is filled with heatherclad Highland hills, long blue lochs under tree-clad banks, and miles and miles of walking trails.

It is a region dear to the Scots, a symbol of their desire for independence, as exemplified by the Declaration of Arbroath and the ancient coronation ritual of the "Stone of Destiny" at Scone. In cities, Perth and Dundee are among the leading six centers of Scotland.

Tayside also provided the backdrop for many novels by Sir Walter Scott, including *The Fair Maid of Perth, Waverley,* and *The Abbot.*

Its golf courses are world famous, ranging from the trio of 18-hole courses at Gleneagles to the open championships links at Carnoustie.

We'll begin our trip in an offshoot southern pocket of the county at Loch Leven, then take in Perth and its environs, heading east to Dundee, and later along the fishing villages of the North Sea, cutting west again to visit Glamis Castle, and, finally, ending our journey of exploration even further west in the lochs and glens of the Perthshire Highlands.

LOCH LEVEN: "Those never got luck who came to Loch Leven." This proverbial saying sums up the history of the ruined **Loch Leven Castle,** on Castle Island, dating from the late 14th century. Among its more ill-fated prisoners, none was more notable than Mary Queen of Scots. Within its forbidding walls, she signed her abdication on July 24, 1567. However, she effected her escape from Loch Leven on May 2, 1568. Thomas Percy, seventh Earl of Northumberland, supported her cause. For his efforts, he, too, was imprisoned and lodged in the castle for three years until he was handed over to the English, who beheaded him at York.

Lying to the north of Dunfermline (head toward Kinross), the loch has seven islands. Loch Leven Castle, of course, is in ruins. So is the **Priory of Loch Leven,** built on the site of one of the oldest Culdee establishments in Scotland, and lying on St. Serf's, the largest of the islands in the loch.

In Kinross, 25 miles north of Edinburgh, you can make arrangements to visit Loch Leven Castle by boat, the only means of access.

For dining or lodgings, we offer **Nivingston House,** on the B9097, two miles south of Kinross at Cleish (tel. Cleish Hills 216), which serves some of the finest food in Tayside. The hotel's chef, Bill Kerr, was voted the best Scottish chef of the year in 1977, and in the time since then he seems to have gotten even better. The place is run by Mr. and Mrs. Scott-Smith, who offer only three bedrooms for £15 ($34.50) per person nightly for bed and breakfast.

However, most visitors arrive to sample the wares of the kitchen. We've never had the same meal here twice, as one must depend on the inspiration of the chef. But that's hardly a problem. A thick piece of lamb here was not only tasty but tender, one of the most exquisitely flavored cuts we've ever enjoyed of that meat.

A set lunch costs £6.50 ($14.95); a four-course dinner. £14 ($32.20). Dinner offers a choice of ten appetizers, at least three homemade soups, then 12 main dishes, plus a dessert from the trolley. Hours are from 12:30 to 2 p.m. and from 7:30 to 9 p.m. The hotel shuts down on Monday and is closed sometime in the autumn for vacations. Always reserve a table, and men should wear a jacket and tie in the evening. The hotel stands on ten acres of grounds.

Hawthorn Vale (tel. Kinross 63117) has a picture-postcard look to it, a small stone house set in a garden, with a stone wall along the road, overlooking Loch Leven. It's the private home of Mrs. P. Warder, who has three double rooms, one with twins, which she rents reasonably at £7 ($16.10) per person. Each of her rooms is acceptably attractive and comfortable, with hot and cold running water. Along the hall is a separate toilet. In Mrs. Warder's guest lounge is a TV set and a radio at your disposal. Two of her rooms overlook her garden (and she's rightly proud of how well kept it is). Her breakfasts are filling and done as you like them, and although she doesn't provide dinners (snacks are quite possible), she'll guide you to nearby restaurants.

Kirklands Hotel, High Street (tel. Kinross 63313), is a village hotel, all glistening white with bright shutters and a modernized interior. It has Georgian touches in its entry, and the pillars in the residents' lounge. Warm colors have been used throughout; even the bedrooms carry out the autumnal theme. Each bedroom is pleasant, with hot and cold water. The owner, Mrs. Cawley, has set the rate for bed and breakfast, including VAT, at £10 ($23) per person, and if you wish there are tasty bar lunches. In the evening you can have a choice of two set meals, £4 ($9.20) and £5 ($11.50), which include Scottish dishes. The hotel is 30 minutes from Gleaneagles and St. Andrews golf courses.

PERTH: From its majestic position on the Tay, the ancient city of Perth was the capital of Scotland until the middle of the 15th century. Here the Highland meets the Lowland. Sir Walter Scott immortalized the royal burgh in *The Fair Maid of Perth*. On Curfew Road you can still see the house of Catherine Glover, the fair maid herself.

The main sightseeing attraction of "the fair city" is the **Church of St. John the Baptist,** of which the original foundation, it is believed, dates from Pictish times. However, the present choir dates from 1440 and the nave from 1490. In 1559 John Knox preached his famous sermon here attacking idolatry, and it caused a turbulent wave of iconoclasm to sweep across the land. The church was restored as a World War I memorial in the late 1920s. In the church is the tombstone of James I, who was murdered by Sir Robert Graham.

Food and Lodging

Royal George, Tay Street (tel. Perth 24455), is royal because it once listed on its guest list the illustrious name of Queen Victoria. But since that monarch's day, the hotel has been considerably updated with the latest amenities. Now run by Trust Houses Forte, the Royal George opens onto views of the River Tay and the Bridge of Perth. All of its roomy, solidly furnished bedrooms contain private baths, renting for £23 ($52.90) to £26 ($59.80) in a single, from £32 ($73.60) to £36 ($82.80) in a double. The lounges are still large enough to evoke if not Victoria's day, then Edward's. The food is—well, solid. The Ox and Claret restaurant serves à la carte meals, costing from £7 ($16.10), and the Riverside Buffet features a set three-course meal for £4.50 ($10.35).

The **Station Hotel,** Leonard Street (tel. Perth 24141), also evokes Queen Victoria, although she never, to our knowledge, stayed there. However, like the

Royal George, it has been considerably updated, and its bedrooms are well equipped and maintained. Some of the bathrooms, at least the one we had, would have pleased Lily Langtry at least, as it was as large as most bedrooms in many modern hotels. The lounge is faithful to the old style, and the drinks in the bar seem generous if you order enough of them. You can even stroll in the garden, inspecting the lime trees. Singles pay from £18 ($41.40) to £26 ($59.80), doubles from £27 ($62.10) to £45 ($103.50). All units have color TV and bedside controls. A set lunch is offered for £7.50 ($17.25), and dinner costs the same.

Another good choice is the **City Mills Hotel,** West Mill Street (tel. Perth 28281), which is so named because it was once an oldtime watermill. It has been cleverly adapted to its present function, that of a modern hotel in the center, containing 40 rooms, all with private baths. Singles range from £22 ($50.60), doubles from £35 ($80.50), including VAT. The rooms, although not large, are well furnished, conservative in tone, and warm and comfortable if you're not planning to stay too long. Again, the City Mill has a garden for your pleasure. As for the millstream, you're given a view through panels of glass. On Saturday nights, the merchants of Perth bring their wives, or whomever, here for dancing.

For dining, we recommend **Timothy's,** 24 St. John St. (tel. Perth 26641), which has a convivial informality, and also serves the best food in this ancient city, far superior to that we've encountered in the dining rooms of the staid Victorian hotels. Ever had a Scottish smörgasbord? If not, then try the table offered by the owner, Timothy Norman. Roast beef (served rare and tender), smoked trout, tasty sausages, crabmeat wrapped in smoked salmon, and truly delicious homemade soups are well prepared and pleasantly served here. Meals are from noon to 2:30 p.m. and from 7 to 10 p.m., and it's necessary to call for a reservation, as the restaurant can fill up rapidly, particularly in summer. For a complete meal, expect to pay £5 ($11.50) per head. Closed Sunday and Monday.

SCONE: On the River Tay, Old Scone was the ancient capital of the Picts. On a lump of granite, the "Stone of Destiny," the monarchs of the Dark Ages were enthroned. The British sovereign to this day is still crowned on the stone, but in Westminster Abbey. Edward I removed the stone there in 1296. Charles II was the last king crowned at Scone; the year: 1651.

Scone Palace, the seat of the Earl of Mansfield, was largely rebuilt in 1803, incorporating the old palace of 1580. Inside is an impressive collection of French furniture, china, ivories, and 16th-century needlework; including bed hangings executed by Mary Queen of Scots. A fine collection of rare conifers is found on the grounds in the Pinetum. Rhododendrons and azaleas grow profusely in the gardens and woodlands around the palace. To reach the palace, head north of Perth on the A93. It lies half a mile west of Old Scone. The site is open April 27 to October 13 on weekdays from 10 a.m. to 6 p.m. (on Sunday from 2 to 6), charging an admission of £1.20 ($2.76) for adults, 80p ($1.84) for children, including entrance to both the house and grounds.

GLENEAGLES: This is a famous golfing center on a moor between Strath Earn and Strath Allan, and, in addition, it provides a good, although lethal in expense, base from which to explore the major attractions of Central Scotland. The center gets its name from the Gaelic Gleann-an-Eaglias, "glen of the church." The golf courses here are said to be unrivaled anywhere in the world.

SCOTLAND: SCONE/GLENEAGLES/CRIEFF

If you are prepared to stay in one of the greatest hotels in Britain—and can afford it—then we endorse—

Gleneagles Hotel Restaurant, Gleneagles, Auchterarder (tel. Auchterarder 2231), is one of the showcases of Scotland. From golfers to gourmets, the hotel has catered to everybody from the Duke of Edinburgh to Richard Burton to the late Noel Coward. Opened in 1924 in the Scottish hills, this wonder of the society world is a self-contained resort, with three 18-hole golf courses, one nine-holer, plus a swimming pool, sauna, and tennis courts. Gleneagles even has its own bank and post office.

The location is 37 miles out in the country northwest of Edinburgh. The stone monument to the good life offers 210 luxuriously appointed rooms, costing sky-high prices: from £75 ($172.50) to £100 ($230) in a double, from £45 ($103.50) to £50 ($115) in a single, including service and VAT.

An orchestra plays nightly for dancing. A superb chef from France keeps the cuisine standards high. In an elegantly proper dining room, with tall windows opening onto views of greenery, you are served traditionally fine, rich, and quite subtle food. The service—considerate, polished, and affable. The Gleneagles must surely be the high place of French gastronomy in Scotland, everything offered in a quiet, princely, and refined atmosphere. A set luncheon costs around £12 ($27.60); a table d'hôte dinner, £15 ($34.50). However, if you want to order from the à la carte menu, enjoying the specialties, then expect to pay around £20 ($46) per person. Hours are from 12:30 to 2:30 p.m. and from 7:30 to 10 p.m. The hotel is closed from the end of October until mid-April.

CRIEFF: At the edge of the Perthshire Highlands, Crieff makes for a pleasant stopover, what with its possibilities for fishing and golf. This small burgh, 18 miles from Perth, was the seat of the court of the Earls of Strathearn until 1747. Once gallows in its marketplace were used to execute Highland cattle rustlers.

Three miles south of Crieff, you can visit the gardens of **Drummond Castle,** the seat of the Earl of Ancaster. The second Earl of Perth laid out these ten-acre gardens in 1662 along continental lines. The grounds are open from April 1 to October 31 on Wednesday and Sunday from 2 to 6 p.m. Admission is 50p ($1.15) for adults, 25p (58¢) for children.

In accommodations, we recommend the following:

If you're like most people and can't afford the tariffs at the nearby Gleneagles Hotel, you might prefer to anchor instead at Crieff's **Murraypark Hotel,** Connaught Terrace (tel. Crieff 3731). It's small, offering only 15 rooms, but its standards are first rate. Each year the hotel seems to improve a bit. The bedrooms have a pleasing decor and are comfortably furnished. Singles rent for £13 ($29.90) for bed and breakfast, doubles going for £26 ($59.80). Before dinner you can meet in one of two bars, after having strolled around the hotel, enjoying views across Strathearn. Meals are based on country-house fare, costing from £8 ($18.40) for four courses.

Gwydyr, Comrie Road (tel. Crieff 3277), now a century old, is a fine house about a five-minute walk from the center of the burgh. David and Kay Marris, along with their warm and hospitable staff, welcome you to this friendly and gracious hotel. The bed-and-breakfast charge is about £7.50 ($17.25) per person nightly, and all of their accommodations contain hot and cold running water. The beds are comfortable, and, as an added convenience, you're given facilities for making tea or coffee. The dining room serves well-prepared food, using local ingredients whenever possible. They offer a selection of dishes, all reasonably priced. The dining room is open from 7 to 10:30 p.m. Prices range from about £6 ($13.80) for a set dinner. The cellar is well stocked with wines, beers, and liquors. In the residents' lounge, guests gather around a color television. Gwydyr stands on its own grounds, more than an acre of charming garden overlooking MacRosty Park. You'll have an uninterrupted view of Ben Vorlich and Glen Artney to the south.

COMRIE: An attractive little village in Strathearn, 25 miles from Perth, Comrie stands at the confluence of the Earn, Ruchill, and Lednock Rivers. The A85 runs through the village to Lochearnhead, Crianlarich, Oban, and the Hebrides in the west. It's convenient as an overnight stop for travelers crossing Scotland. Waterskiing, boating, and sailing are available on Loch Earn.

The **Royal Hotel**, Melville Square (tel. Comrie 200), was awarded the "royal" after the visit of Her Majesty, Queen Victoria. It's not, as you might imagine, a Victorian hotel, but rather an L-shaped stone inn dating back to 1765, with white trim and six bedroom dormers. Its cocktail bar with copper-top tables, furnished and decorated in the proprietor's own Gordon tartan, is noted for its selection of malt whiskeys and on the walls are framed prints and photographs with signatures of numerous famous guests who have stayed here over the years, including that of "Monty," Lloyd George, actress Sarah Bernhardt, and Queen Victoria's faithful servant, John Brown. The dining room is equally attractive, with an open log fire and autumnal colors. The bedrooms are most comfortable, consisting of a three-room suite with one four-poster bed, plus 13 bedrooms of which 10 have private bathroom or shower, and all have telephone, radio, tea- and coffee-making facilities, electric blanket, and self-selection heating control. The lounge offers color television in comfortable and well-appointed surroundings. The charge per person nightly for bed and breakfast is £12.35 ($28.41), rising to £13.50 ($31.05) per person with private bath. Dinner prices start at £7.60 ($17.48), although you can also choose à la carte.

DUNDEE: This royal burgh and old seaport is an industrial city, one of the largest in Scotland, lying on the north shore of the Firth of Tay. It's noted for its flax, jute, and marmalade. Spanning the Firth, the famous Tay Railway Bridge was opened in 1888. It's nearly two miles long, one of the longest in Europe.

In the suburbs, at **Broughty Ferry**, 3½ miles from Dundee, the **castle** dates from 1498. For a spectacular view, go to **Dundee Law,** a 572-foot hill just a mile north of the city.

Most tourists pass through Dundee en route to Glamis Castle, 12 miles north. However, if you'd like to stop for the night, there is the—

Angus Hotel, 101 Market Gait (tel. Dundee 26874), the best equipped hotel in the heart of town, a glass-and-concrete structure. On our most recent stopover, we encountered a number of businessmen from Pakistan who export raw materials to Dundee used in making jute. Don't stay here seeking historical romance. But if you want a comfortable accommodation, you'll find all the amenities. The furnishings throughout are well maintained, and most bedrooms contain private baths. In a single the rate ranges from £24 ($55.20) to £28 ($64.40), depending on the plumbing. A double with bath rents for £27 ($62.10) to £24 ($78.20), plus breakfast and VAT. The hotel also possesses three bars and a main dining room serving a standard cuisine.

CARNOUSTIE: This seaside resort, 61 miles northeast of Edinburgh, is celebrated for its championship golf course. Lying between Dundee and Arbroath (eight miles away), Carnoustie opens onto the North Sea. In summer its five miles of sand give plenty of beach space to its visitors.

The **Bruce Hotel**, 1 Links Parade (tel. Carnoustie 52364), is preferred by golfers, who book up its most desired accommodations in peak season. Mr. Hamish Martin, who heads a dynamic, hearty staff, welcomes you to one of the well-kept, clean bedrooms which vary in size and furnishings as well as plumbing. The hotel comfortably evokes Edwardian seaside days, and from its windows you can look out onto views of the North Sea—rather rugged the last time we stopped by. The hotel also offers views of the already-mentioned golf course. Bed and breakfast is £22 ($50.40) in a single, from £38 ($87.40) in a double, including service and VAT. Be duly warned that only 17 of the 38 rooms contain private baths. We've found the food quite good, and the portions are so ample that few leave the dining room hungry.

ARBROATH: Samuel Johnson wasn't that much impressed with Scotland on his jaunt there, but he did say that the view of Arbroath repaid him for some of the hardships suffered in his journey. Arbroath is a popular coastal resort with a colorful fishing harbor and rugged, red sandstone cliffs weathered into grotesque shapes. Smugglers once used the sandstone caves along the coast. Arbroath "smokies" (smoked haddock) are one of the fish delicacies along the east coast of Scotland.

The "Fairport" of Sir Walter Scott's *The Antiquary,* the royal burgh of Arbroath lies 17 miles northeast of Dundee. On its High Street are the ruins of a red sandstone abbey, once the richest in Scotland. It was founded by William the Lion in 1178, and the king was buried in its precincts in 1214. The Scottish Parliament met there in 1320 and sent the pope a famous letter asserting the independence of their country. In the abbey a historical pageant is presented every year.

Two miles to the west stands **Kellie Castle,** Arbroath, built in 1170 and restored in 1679. Of pink sandstone, the castle is noted for its unique courtyard and left-handed spiral stairway. Robert the Bruce once came into possession of it, during the "Black Parliament." It is open from May until the end of December, daily except Tuesday, from 10:30 a.m. to 5:30 p.m., charging adults 60p ($1.38) for admission to both the castle and grounds, although children pay only 30p (69¢).

Hotel Seaforth (tel. Arbroath 72232) has been modernized and refurnished, a stone structure that is made inviting by the pleasant staff, the fine service, and the good food. The hotel overlooks the sea with a southern exposure, standing some 200 yards from the beach and within minutes of the center of town. Roomy, comfortable bedrooms rent for £15 ($34.50) in a single, from £25 ($57.50) in a double if bathless; increasing to £18 ($41.40) in a single and £28 ($64.40) in a double with private bath. The cuisine consists of a concise, balanced range of popular standard dishes, a dinner costing from £5 ($11.50). Good, fresh ingredients are used.

MONTROSE: Instead of heading immediately for Glamis Castle, we suggest you continue along the coastal road from Arbroath toward Montrose. Along the way you'll pass stretches of rugged beauty. Sandstone cliffs rise sharply out of the water, and little slate-roofed cottages house the families who make their living from the often turbulent sea.

Montrose itself stands on a bottleneck of Montrose Basin, a broad estuary inhabited by hundreds of wild birds, notably pink-footed geese. This harbor town, with its well-known golf links, is a North Sea coastal resort for holiday makers. Its spired church and town hall date from the 18th century. David I granted Montrose its charter, and in 1352 it became one of Scotland's many royal burghs. Montrose lies 30 miles northeast of Dundee by road.

The Links Hotel (tel. Montrose 2288) is modern and attractive, the successful adaptation of a grand old house with interesting stained glass. Modern additions have been made, and central heating has been added. The bedrooms are brightly furnished and spotlessly kept, and the service provided by the friendly, helpful staff is excellent. A single room costs about £20 ($46) per night, a double goes for £28 ($64.40), and a triple for £34 ($78.20), these prices including a private bath en suite and breakfast as well. Lunch is served from a table d'hôte menu, costing from £5 ($11.50), and dinner from £6 ($13.80) is likely to include veal Cordon Bleu, steaks, salmon, and trout. There is entertainment every evening in the Spanish bar, and disco dancing to local groups. Private fishing is available from the hotel.

Central Hotel, High Street (tel. Montrose 2152), is one of the Welcome Inn chain which gives one assurance of a well-run hostelry. It's in the heart of town, where you can get all the necessities and sleep in peace. A bathless single with breakfast is £9.50 ($21.85), and a double or twin is £16 ($36.80) to £19 ($43.70) nightly. If you want a private bath, the tariff rises to £20.50 ($47.15). In the Steakhouse, lunch starts at £3 ($6.90), high tea from £2 ($4.60), and dinners from £4 ($9.20). When in the bar, you can have a simple lunch at a low tab. All prices include VAT.

KIRRIEMUIR: This town of narrow streets is the famous birthplace of Sir James Barrie, the "Thrums" of his novels. The Scottish dramatist and novelist, whose best-loved play is *Peter Pan,* was born here in 1860, the son of a father who was employed as a hand-loom weaver of linen. **Barrie's Birthplace** contains manuscripts and mementos of the writer, and is open May 1 to September 30 on weekdays from 10 a.m. to 12:30 p.m. and from 2 to 6 p.m. (2 to 6 p.m.), charging 40p (92¢) for admission for adults, 20p (46¢) for children. For information, telephone Kirriemuir 2646.

If you'd like to stay over, we'd recommend the following:

Park House, Gordon Park (tel. Kirriemuir 2425), is one of the best buys around, if you can adjust to certain regulations such as being in by 11 p.m. and dining promptly. Because of the high cost of heating water, baths are also limited. The cost for bed and breakfast daily is £5.50 ($12.65) per person. Evening meals cost only £3 ($6.90), and this includes three courses with a beverage. After dinner, tea and cookies are provided. Children up to 9 years of age are charged a half rate.

From Kirriemuir, it's a four-mile drive south to—

GLAMIS CASTLE: After Balmoral Castle, most visitors to Scotland want to see Glamis Castle at Glamis (pronounced Glaams), for its architecture, its Shakespearian link (Macbeth was Thane of Glamis at the beginning of the play), and its link with the crown. For ten centuries it has been connected to British royalty. Her Majesty, Queen Elizabeth, the Queen Mother, was brought up here; her daughter, now Queen Elizabeth II, spent a good deal of her childhood here; and Princess Margaret, the Queen's sister, was born here, becoming the first royal princess born in Scotland in three centuries. The existing castle dates in part from the middle of the 15th century, but there are records of a castle having been in existence in the 11th century, at which time it was one of the hunting lodges of the kings of Scotland. King Malcolm II was carried there mortally wounded in 1034 after having been attacked by his enemies while hunting in a nearby forest.

Glamis Castle has been in the possession of the Lyon family since 1372, when it formed part of the dowry of Princess Joanna, daughter of King Robert II, when she married John Lyon, secretary to the king. The castle was altered in the 16th century and restored and enlarged in the 17th, 18th, and 19th centuries. It contains some fine plaster ceilings, furniture, and paintings.

The present owner, the Queen's cousin, is the 17th Earl of Strathmore and Kinghorne. He lives at the castle with his wife and three children. He is the direct descendant of the first Earl.

The castle is open to the public, who have access to the Royal Apartments and many other rooms, and also to the fine gardens, May to September, Sunday through Thursday (also Friday from June 1 to September), at £1.20 ($2.76) for adults, 60p ($1.38) for children. If you wish to visit only the grounds, laid out by Capability Brown, the charge is 50p ($1.15).

Also in Glamis, you may want to visit the **Angus Folk Museum,** Kirkwynd Cottages, run by the National Trust of Scotland. From the former county of Angus, rich in folklore, were collected domestic utensils, agricultural implements, furniture, and clothing. The museum is open May 1 to September 30 from 1 to 6 p.m., charging adults 45p ($1.04); children, 20p (46¢). Last entry is at 5:30 p.m.

DUNKELD: A cathedral town, Dunkeld lies in a thickly wooded valley of the Tay River, at the edge of the Perthshire Highlands. Once a major ecclesiastical center, it is one of the seats of ancient Scottish history. It was an important center of the Celtic church, for example.

The National Trust of Scotland has been effective in restoring many of the old houses and shops around the marketplace and cathedral that had fallen into decay.

The **Cathedral of Dunkeld** was founded in 815. David I converted the church into a cathedral in 1127. The 14th and 15th centuries witnessed subsequent additions. The cathedral was first restored in 1815, and at that time traces of the 12th-century structure clearly remained, as they do to this day.

Finally, Shakespeare fans may want to seek out the oak and sycamore in front of the destroyed **Birnam House,** a mile to the south. This was believed to be a remnant of the Birnam wood to which the Bard gave everlasting literary fame in *Macbeth*. In Shakespeare's drama, you may recall, the "woods of Birnam came to Dunsinane."

The **Dunkeld House Hotel** (tel. Dunkeld 243) offers the quiet dignity of life in a Scottish country house. Built for the seventh Duke of Atholl in the 19th century, the house was erected on the banks of the Tay, and the surrounding grounds were planted with trees and flowering bushes, making for a parklike setting. You reach the house by going down a long drive. Guests can fish for trout and salmon on the grounds.

The house is well preserved and beautifully kept, and, as befits such a place, accommodations come in a wide range of styles, space, and furnishings. The bed-and-breakfast rate ranges from £15 ($34.50) to £27 ($62.10) per person daily.

The people of Dunkeld come here on Saturday nights for dancing. The dining room opens onto a Tayside vista, and the owners have established a reputation for continental dishes, including some original offerings, plus good wines from their cellar. Service is exemplary. Lunch is served from 12:30 to 2 p.m., costing £5.50 ($12.65) for a table d'hôte, and dinner is from 7 to 9 p.m. It closes half an hour earlier on Sunday, when a buffet dinner goes for £10 ($23). The price for the set evening meal is £8.50 ($19.55). The hotel and restaurant are closed from the first of November to mid-January.

Cardney House (tel. Butterstone 222) is an elegant 18th-century manor on a private estate outside Dunkeld, three miles from the town on the A923 Blair Gowrie Road. The house is surrounded by hills, forests, and lochs, and on the grounds rare and beautiful shrubs are grown, as well as orchids, stephanotis, and lemon and orange trees. Here you are received like the guest at a private party at a country home by the charming and hospitable hosts, Lieutenant Commander (retired) and Mrs. MacGregor, who because of "crippling taxes" now receive paying guests. The gracious home is well furnished, often with antiques, and the atmosphere is one of refinement and tranquility, a style set so admirably by the proprietors.

They have available now only two singles and six doubles, charging £18 ($41.40) for the singles, £29 ($66.70) for the doubles. Dinner, often a Cordon Bleu cuisine, is served until 8 in the evening, and you definitely feel you are dining family style. The food is well prepared and beautifully served, and meals are complemented by a first-class wine cellar. Guests relax freely in the lounges, which are furnished with family treasures, often antiques. Surprisingly, there's an elevator. During the day, shooting and fishing expeditions can be arranged. Mrs. MacGregor is an active concert singer, and musical evenings are given regularly at Cardney.

PITLOCHRY: After leaving Edinburgh, many motorists stop here for the night before continuing on the Highland road to Inverness. However, once they discover the charms of Pitlochry, they want to linger. This popular holiday resort center is a touring headquarters for the Valley of the Tummel.

It is particularly renowned for its **Pitlochry Festival Theatre,** Scotland's "theater in the hills." Telephone Pitlochry 0796/2680 for information. Founded in 1951, the festival theater draws people from all over the world to its repertoire of plays, usually presented from early May until early October. Performances in the evening begin at 8 p.m., and on Wednesday and Saturday there is a matinee at 2:15 p.m. A new theater is going up next to Pitlochry's famous salmon ladder and is expected to be ready for the 1981 season.

The **Pitlochry Dam** was created because a new power station was needed, but in effect the engineers created a new loch. The famous "Salmon Ladder" was built to help the struggling salmon upstream. An underwater portion of the ladder—a salmon observation chamber—has been enclosed in glass to give fascinated sightseers a look.

Pitlochry doesn't just entertain tourists, although it would appear that way in summer. It also produces scotch whiskey and tweeds.

Food and Lodging

Green Park (tel. Pitlochry 2537) lies about half a mile from the center, at the northwest end of Pitlochry, and it's one of the best hotels in the area, the preferred choice of many. Against a backdrop of woodland, the white-painted mansion with its carved eaves enjoys a top scenic position, its lawns reaching to the shores of Loch Faskally, the only hotel so situated. Visitors who reserve well in advance get one of the half dozen or so snappy modern rooms in the garden wing, each with a private bath and all enjoying a view of loch and woodland. The more antiquated rooms, however, are still good, with old-fashioned furniture. Depending on where you anchor, singles range from £18 ($41.40) to £20 ($46), doubles from £32 ($73.60) to £34 ($78.20) nightly. Guests enjoy drinks in a half-moon-shaped lounge overlooking the water. Many diners come here during festival season to enjoy not only the good food and wine, but the panoramic views. The hotel is closely supervised by Anne and Graham Brown. Dinner is served until 8 p.m., and many traditional Scottish dishes are featured. The Green Park is open from mid-March until November 1.

Hydro Hotel, Knockard Road (tel. Pitlochry 2666), was originally known by the English gentry who came here in summer to enjoy the fresh air of the Perthshire Highlands. Built in the Scottish baronial mansion style, the hotel has kept up with much needed modern improvements, and now ranks with Green Park as the preferred choice of accommodations in Pitlochry. The hotel stands on large, well-manicured grounds, offering tennis and a nine-hole golf course. The merchants of Pitlochry and their wives come here on Saturday nights for dancing.

At our latest count, the hotel had nearly 70 rooms and at least 40 of them contained private baths. Hopefully, you'll be given one of the turreted corner rooms, although you should request such space when making a reservation. Depending on the perch you're given, rates in a single range from £18 ($41.40) to £23 ($52.90), and in a double from £26 ($59.80) to £35 ($80.50), plus VAT.

The lounges have been considerably improved since we first stayed there in 1973. The Hydro shuts down from September 30 to the middle of April.

The Pine Trees, Strathview Terrace (tel. Pitlochry 2121), is a mansion built in the 1890s and now converted into a charming country-house hotel, located high above the main Pitlochry Road. Deer and squirrels roam the tranquil grounds, 14 acres of bucolic bliss, about a ten-minute walk from the center. Mr. White owns this fine Scottish home of character and charm, and he and his staff are most hospitable. Of the roomy 30 bedrooms offered, 25 have private baths, for which you pay extra, of course. The high-season rates are £16 ($36.80) in a single, £30 ($69) in a double, including breakfast. It's best to take the demi-pension rate of £22 ($50.60) per person nightly. Nonresidents are welcome to drop in for dinner, enjoying not only the bountiful cuisine, but a view of the Valley of Tummel. For guests, Mr. White can also provide exclusive salmon fishing.

Moulin Hotel (tel. Pitlochry 2196) is an old Highland coaching inn converted to a comfortable hotel, lying less than a mile from the center of Pitlochry in the attractive old-world village of Moulin. It is within easy reach of the theater and all the attractions of Pitlochry. A detached annex at the Moulin contains more modern rooms. Nine of the pleasantly furnished bedrooms contain private baths. For bed and breakfast, one person pays £12.50 ($28.75) to £16.50 ($37.95); two persons, from £23 ($52.90) to £31 ($71.30). The food is good, so you might want to request the bed, breakfast, and evening meal tariff of £16.50 ($37.95) to £21 ($48.30) per person. The dining room opens onto beautiful views of the hills. In summer umbrella-shaded tables are set out for drinks, although when the wind blows, patrons prefer the modern lounge bar, where they can also order snacks and sandwiches. The hotel is open April to October.

Excursions from Pitlochry

From the town you can take excursions in almost any direction. Heading northwest for four miles, you come to the **Pass of Killiecrankie,** where "Bonnie Dundee" and his Jacobites won their famous victory over the armies of General

Mackay fighting for King William in 1689. This is one of the scenic highlights of the area.

If time remains, try to see another attraction, **Queen's View**, where Victoria herself picnicked. The view is reached by taking the road alongside Loch Tummel. At the eastern end, Victoria looked down the length of the loch toward Schiehallion.

BLAIR ATHOLL: Eight miles to the northwest of Pitlochry stands the gleaming white **Blair Castle,** the home of the Duke of Atholl, on the A9. Built in the Scottish baronial style, and dating from 1269, the castle allows you to view some 30 rooms. Inside is an impressive collection of Jacobite relics, china, lace, and armor, along with many family portraits. It is open Easter weekend, then Sunday and Monday in April, and then again daily from the first Sunday in May until the second Sunday in October. Hours are weekdays from 10 a.m. to 6 p.m. (on Sunday from 2 to 6).

For both food and lodging, you might prefer a stopover in Blair Atholl to Pitlochry. If so, we'd recommend **Atholl Arms** (tel. Blair Atholl 205). Once lords and ladies who couldn't find room at Blair Castle stayed here, and some of the grand balls of old Perthshire were held here. Now the Atholl Arms is a roadside inn, built of stone and gabled with large bays, attracting motorists en route to Inverness. A cocktail lounge has been redecorated, and there's a public bar as well, attracting the locals. The ballroom has been turned into an arched-roof restaurant, complete with a minstrels' gallery. There's also a more intimate dining room with antiques and mahogany chairs. Both rooms offer a substantial menu. The bedrooms are individually styled and well fitted, and each one we inspected had a completely different character. The bed-and-breakfast price is £8.50 ($19.55) per person, or else you can take half board for £14 ($32.20) per person daily.

ABERFELDY: The "Birks o' Aberfeldy" is one of the beauty spots made famous by Robert Burns. Once a Pictish center, this small town makes a fine base for touring Perthshire's glens and lochs. Loch Tay lies 6 miles to the west; Glen Lyon, 15 miles west; and Kinloch Rannoch, 18 miles northwest.

In Aberfeldy, the famous **Round Tower** dates from the 11th century. General Wade in 1733 built the bridge spanning the Tay. In the town's shops you'll find good buys in tweeds and tartans, plus other items of Highland dress.

The **Cruachan Hotel,** Kenmore Street (tel. Aberfeldy 545), stands at the edge of town in about three acres of flowery gardens and greenery. The hotel is small and immaculately kept, renting out only three singles, six doubles, and one family room, each containing hot and cold running water. The rate is £9.50 ($21.85) per night per person, £2 ($4.60) per person extra if a private bath is required. Evening meals, and well-prepared ones at that, are served from 7 to 8 p.m. It's best to take the half-board arrangement, costing from £14 ($32.20) per person daily. The centrally heated, fully licensed, private hotel is closed in December, January, and February. On the grounds is a nine-hole putting green for the use of guests.

KILLIN: Just over the border from Tayside in the Central Region, Killin is a village on the Dochart at the lower end of Loch Tay. Lying 45 miles west of Perth by road, Killin is both a summer holiday resort and a winter sports center. The **Falls of Dochart** are world famous, but the town itself is noted for beauty spots, and there are sights of historical interest as well.

Killin Church contains a font more than 1000 years old. Less than a quarter of a mile from the church stands an upright stone, said to mark the grave of Fingal. An island in the Dochart was the ancient burial place of the MacNab Clan.

The ruins of **Finlarig Castle** contain a beheading pit near the castle gate which was written about in Scott's *The Fair Maid of Perth*. Perched 1000 feet above the loch, the castle was the seat of "Black Duncan of the Cowl," a notoriously ruthless chieftain of the Campbell Clan.

For accommodations or meals, we recommend **Bridge of Lochay** (tel. Killin 272), which retains some of its 16th-century character, although it has seen many alterations and additions since that time. Half a mile from Killin itself, the "bridge"—an attractive, rambling, white-painted building—lies on the banks of the Lochay River, at the tip of Loch Tay. A. G. Symon, the owner, welcomes you to one of his 17 bedrooms, simply but comfortably furnished, each containing hot and cold running water. The overnight charge is £10 ($23) per person for a bed and a large Scottish breakfast. Guests can enjoy good drinks in the bar or else sit in front of peat and log fires in the lounges. The food is plain Scottish cooking, quite good. If you stay at least three nights, you'll be quoted a half-board tariff of £16 ($36.80) per person daily. The hotel is open from April to October.

Morenish Lodge (tel. Killin 258) is now a small Highland hotel, although formerly it was the shooting lodge of an earl, lying 200 feet above Loch Tay and less than three miles from Killin itself (on the A827 Aberfeldy Road). The hotel offers only a dozen bedrooms, with hot and cold running water. Furnishings are comfortable and old-fashioned. It's best to stay here on a half-board arrangement, costing from £20 ($46) per person nightly. Many of the public rooms face the loch, and you can enjoy a good meal with wine in the Tay View room; and in the Laird's Bar, scotch whiskey, both blended and malt, is served.

Dall Lodge Hotel (tel. Killin 217) is a 19th-century stone house with ornate white Victorian trim on its many gables. It stands opposite the church, on the main road, with a well-tended garden. Across the road is frontage on the Lochay River where guests have fishing rights. The heart, the core of everything here, is Mrs. Wilson, who does the cooking herself. She prepares superb oatmeal porridge, giving you brown sugar to sweeten it. She also prepares good evening meals. The tariff, VAT included, for bed and breakfast is £12 ($27.60) per person, and Mrs. Wilson's dinners go for £5.50 ($12.65). After dinner, Mrs. Wilson serves coffee in the lounge. She uses her garden produce whenever possible. Her ten bedrooms have hot and cold water. The views outside the bedrooms are memorable—black Angus cattle, and the hills beyond.

6. The Trossachs and Loch Lomond

"The Trossachs" is the collective name given that wild Highland area lying east and northeast of Loch Lomond. Both the Trossachs and Loch Lomond are said to contain Scotland's finest scenery in moor, mountain, and loch. The area is famed in history and romance ever since Sir Walter Scott included vivid descriptive passages in *The Lady of the Lake* and *Rob Roy*.

In Gaelic, the Trossachs means "the bristled country," an allusion to its luxuriant vegetation. The thickly wooded valley contains three lochs—Vennachar, Achray, and Katrine. The best centers for exploring are the village of the Trossachs and the "gateways" of Callander and Aberfoyle.

Legendary Loch Lomond, the largest and most beautiful of Scottish lakes, is famed for its "bonnie banks." Lying within easy reach of Glasgow, the loch is about 24 miles long. At its widest point, it stretches for five miles. At Balloch in the south the lake is a Lowland loch of gentle hills and islands. But as it moves north, the loch changes to a narrow lake of Highland character, with moody cloud formations and rugged steep hillsides.

CALLANDER: For many, this small burgh, 16 miles northwest of Stirling by road, makes the best base for exploring the Trossachs and Loch Katrine, Loch Achray, and Loch Vernachar. For years, motorists—and before them passengers traveling by bumpy coach—stopped here to rest up on the once-difficult journey between Edinburgh and Oban.

Callander stands at the entrance to the **Pass of Leny** in the shadow of the Callander Crags. The Teith and Leny Rivers meet to the west of the town. British TV viewers know of Callander as the "Tannochbrae" of the popular B.B.C. "Dr. Finlay's Casebook."

Four miles beyond the Pass of Leny, with its beautiful falls, lies **Loch Lubnaig** ("the crooked lake"), divided into two reaches by a rock and considered fine fishing waters. Nearby is **Little Leny**, the ancestral burial ground of the Buchanans.

More falls are found at **Bracklinn**, 1½ miles northeast of Callander. In a gorge above the town, Bracklinn is considered one of the most scenic of the local beauty spots. Other places of interest include the **Roman Camp**, the **Caledonian Fort**, and the **Foundations of St. Bride's Chapel**. The tourist office will give you a map pinpointing the above-recommended sights. While there, you can also get directions for one of the most interesting excursions from Callander, to **Balquhidder Church**, 13 miles to the northwest, the burial place of Rob Roy.

The leading hotel is **Roman Camp** (tel. Callander 30003), once a 17th-century hunting lodge with pink walls and small gray-roofed towers, built on the site of what was believed to have been a Roman camp. The Dukes of Perth once came to this turreted establishment, lodging here for "hunting and hawking." Entering through a gate, the modern-day traveler drives up a splendid driveway, enjoying the gardens along the way with their well-manicured yew hedges. The setting, as in the cliché, is like a picture postcard, with peacocks roaming the grounds. Naturally, a river runs through the 20-acre estate. Inside a walled garden, vegetables and fruit—used in the hotel's kitchen—are grown. In summer flowerbeds are in full bloom.

Once inside, you are welcomed to a country house furnished in a gracious manor. The hotel contains 11 bedrooms, most of which have their own baths, as well as another five bedrooms in the cottage standing on the grounds. Depending on your room assignment, singles range in price from £20 ($46) to £24 ($55.20), doubles from £30 ($69) to £36 ($82.80), plus service and VAT. The bedrooms vary in size and furnishings, but all are comfortable, spotless, and cozy. We prefer the rooms in the main house to those in the annex across the drive.

The hotel has added a small cocktail bar, but the library, with its plasterwork and paneling, remains undisturbed. The meals—"Scottish country-house fare," as one reader described them—are served until 9 in the evening.

For the tradition-minded, the Roman Camp is one of the finest choices in the Trossachs, and, by all means, treat yourself to "tea and scones" in the afternoon. The hotel closes down from November to Easter.

ABERFOYLE: Looking like an Alpine village, in the heart of the Rob Roy country, this small holiday resort is the gateway to the Trossachs, near Loch Ard. A large crafts center contains a wealth of gift items related to the Highlands.

Bailie Nicol Jarvie Hotel (tel. Aberfoyle 202) is an old-fashioned hotel on the road between Loch Ard and Aberfoyle. If you're passing through the Trossachs, it makes a suitable overnight stopover. The hotel takes its name from Nicol Jarvie, the Glasgow magistrate who used to visit the outlaw, Rob Roy, at a former inn on this site. The hotel is one of character, somewhat dated in appeal.

Many of the rooms have high ceilings and are furnished in "comfy" pieces. The bed-and-breakfast rate is £11.50 ($26.45) per person nightly, increasing to £15 ($34.50) per person for half board. Private bathrooms carry a £1.50 ($3.45) per-person daily supplement. Lovers of antiquity are drawn to Bailie Bar, a cocktail lounge hung with weaponry. The hotel serves good country meals, using farm produce when available. It's open from April to October.

THE TROSSACHS: The Duke's Road (A821) north from Aberfoyle climbs through the Achray Forest, past the **David Marshall Lodge** information center, operated by the Forestry Commission, where you can stop for snacks and a breathtaking view of the Forth Valley. The road runs to the Trossachs—the "bristly country"—between Lochs Achray and Katrine.

Loch Katrine, at the head of which Rob Roy was born, owes its fame to Sir Walter Scott who set his poem *The Lady of the Lake* there. The loch is the principal reservoir of the city of Glasgow. A small steamer, S.S. *Sir Walter Scott,* plies the waters of the loch which has submerged the Silver Strand of the romantic poet.

Sailings are between May 14 and September 24, between Trossachs Pier and Stronachlachar at a round-trip fare of £1 ($23) for adults, 50p ($1.15) for children. Complete information as to the sailing schedules is available from the Strathclyde Water Department, Lower Clyde Division, 419 Balmore Rd., Glasgow, Scotland G22 6NU.

Trossachs Hotel, Trossachs (tel. Trossachs 232), became famous in Victoria's heyday. Built on the site of one of the old posting inns of Scotland which dated from the 18th century, it was erected by Lady Willoughby as a castle in 1826, converting to a hotel in 1852. After a long career, the hotel, now mellowed with time, is still going strong. Rooms come in a variety of styles with a wide range of plumbing, costing about £17 ($39.10) per person for bed and breakfast. Usually you pay another small supplement for a single room or for the privilege of private bath. The Shield Hung Dining Room is draped with the plaids of the ancient clans and has a timbered ceiling, serving dinners for about £6 ($13.80). The location is right in the heart of the Trossachs, two miles from Loch Katrine where you can sail on the loch steamship *Sir Walter Scott.*

On Loch Achray, lying between Lochs Venachar and Katrine, stands the **Loch Achray Hotel,** Trossachs (tel. Trossachs 229), run by Mr. Penny and Mr. MacDonald. The hotel stands in an estate of 45 acres between Callender and Aberfoyle on the A821. From the hotel you can step directly into the Achray Forest, part of the vast Queen Elizabeth National Park, which abounds in wildlife, including roe deer. The original building of the hotel dates from Jacobean times. The Achray Burn is an overflow of Loch Katrine and runs through the hotel grounds. This hotel is a good stopping place for a two-day tour out of Edinburgh or for those on their way north. A pleasant hotel, it offers lovely views over the loch. Rooms are comfortable—only two have private baths—and the first-floor lounge is well furnished, opening onto views of the famous Trossachs Hotel, resembling a French château. They charge from £10.50 ($24.15) per person for bed and breakfast, or else you can stay here on half-board terms of £15.50 ($35.65) per person nightly.

DRYMEN: This peaceful village—still in the Rob Roy country—makes a good base for exploring Loch Lomond. Many hunters and fishermen from Glasgow like to come here for the weekend.

Buchanan Arms (tel. Drymen 588) may trace its origins back to the 13th century, but it has been completely modernized, its corridors carpeted in tartans, its dining room enlarged, and its bedrooms equipped for your comfort. From the entrance of the hotel you can see the gardens from which come the flowers that decorate the hotel. Of the 20 rooms, nine contain private baths. Tariffs range from £12.70 ($29.21) to £21 ($48.30) in a single, from £23 ($52.90) to £43 ($98.90) in a double. So close to Loch Lomond (5 miles) and to Glasgow (36 miles), the hotel makes a good base for exploring the area. Its food is good, a set dinner costing from £8 ($18.40) for three courses. The sun lounge is an attractive oasis, even in winter, and the lounge bar is decorated in a Scottish baronial style. The hotel remains open year round.

LOCH LOMOND: This largest of Scotland's lochs was the center of the ancient district of Lennox, in the possession of the branch of the Stewart family from which sprang Lord Darnley, second husband of Mary Queen of Scots and father of James VI of Scotland, who was also James I of England. The ruins of Lennox Castle are on Inchmurrin, one of the 30 islands of the loch—one having ecclesiastical ruins, one noted for its yew trees planted by King Robert the Bruce to ensure a suitable supply of wood for the bows of his archers. The loch is fed by at least ten rivers from west, east, and north. On the eastern side is Ben Lomond, rising to a height of 3192 feet.

The song "Loch Lomond" is supposed to have been composed by one of Bonnie Prince Charlie's captured followers on the eve of his execution in Carlisle Jail. The "low road" of the song is the path through the underworld which his spirit will follow to his native land after death, more quickly than his friends can travel to Scotland by the ordinary high road.

The road from Dumbarton to Crianlarich runs along the western shore of the loch, but the paddle steamer *Maid of the Loch* is an interesting, if slower, way to see the "banks and braes." It sails daily during the summer from Balloch Pier which is reached by the railway. There is a large car park serving the pier.

On the western shore of Loch Lomond is **Rossdhu**, chosen as the family home of the chiefs of Clan Colquhoun in the 12th century. There are ruins of the 15th-century Chapel of St. Mary of Rossdhu and one wall of the 15th-century castle. Its lochside grounds, with a park, picnic area, and bathing beach, are open daily from May to mid-October. The house is open daily from 10:30 a.m. to 5:30 p.m. (last admission at 5 p.m.). Admission to the house and grounds is 90p ($2.07) for adults, 45p ($1.04) for children; to the grounds only, 60p ($1.38) for adults, 30p (69¢) for children.

Traveling around Loch Lomond from the east, you'll find:

LUSS: This village on the western side of Loch Lomond is the traditional home of the Colquhouns. Among its picturesque stone cottages, on the water's edge, is a branch of the Highland Arts Studios of Seil. Cruises on the loch or boat rentals may be arrnaged at the nearby jetty.

For accommodations or meals, we'd recommend the **Colquhoun Arms Hotel**, Luss, Alexandria (tel. Luss 225), on the A82, 25 miles northwest of Glasgow, commanding a view of the village and the loch. The hotel is centrally heated, fully licensed, and charmingly furnished in the Scottish tradition. It makes a fine center for touring the Western Highlands. A single room costs £18 ($41.40); a twin or double without bath, £26 ($59.80), £30 ($69) with bath. Plaid carpets are used throughout, and you can enjoy drinks in the comfortable lounge, where a large fireplace crackles on cool days. Good Scottish dishes are served in the dining room.

TARBET: On the western shores of Loch Lomond, Tarbet is not to be confused with the larger center of Tarbert, headquarters of the Loch Fyne herring industry. Loch Lomond's Tarbet is merely a village and a summer holiday base with limited accommodations.

Ben Cruach Lodge, Tarbet, on Loch Lomond (tel. Arrochar 301), run by Mrs. P. V. L. Watson, wife of an engineer on Polaris submarines, offers bed and breakfast for £9.50 ($21.85) nightly per person, in her two-story house overlooking the loch. An evening meal costs £5 ($11.50), and all costs include V.A.T. Mrs. Watson will also provide you with a packed lunch or fix you a special diet if given sufficient time. There is an open fire, television, and a lounge which serves supper in the evening. All bills have the personal touch of the owner, with "Haste Ye Back" written in her own hand at the bottom. You can arrange for a boat rental on the loch for the day, as well as fishing, waterskiing, hill climbing, and walking.

ARDLUI: This small holiday resort is at the head of Loch Lomond, commanding splendid views of Highland scenery and serving as a base for loch steamer cruises. Again, its accommodations are extremely limited.

Ardlui Hotel (tel. Inveruglas 243) stands on the banks of Loch Lomond, offering a panoramic view from the hotel's landscaped front garden. The owners, Cyril P. Squires and D. Brian Squires, welcome you to their comfortable bedrooms, providing facilities for fishing for salmon, trout, pike, or perch in the local waters. Sportsmen are especially fond of the hotel, booking up its well-equipped double rooms, which rent for about £28 ($64.40). The hotel, open all year, offers fine cooking, and fellow guests who meet before dinner in the cocktail bar usually create a convivial atmosphere. Music each evening makes the place festive, an oasis of Highland hospitality. The hotel has its own privately stocked Pike Loch, where permits go for £1 ($2.30) per day.

ARROCHAR: At the head of the sea-arm of Loch Long, 1½ miles west of Loch Lomond, this tourist village, easily reached by road and railway from Glasgow, is a center for climbers.

A pleasant accommodation is the **Lochside Guest House** (tel. Arrochar 467), a small guest house with a garden overlooking the shores of Loch Long. There Mrs. Bishop will welcome you to one of her singles for £7.50 ($17.25), or in a double for £14 ($32.20), including breakfast. For £10.50 ($24.15) per person, she'll include not only your room and breakfast, but a good, hearty dinner as well, quite a bargain. Receiving guests year round, Mrs. Bishop can arrange for a small-boat rental (also chartered sea fishing). Naturally, anglers flock to Lochside.

Heading west from Loch Long and Loch Lomond on the A83 toward Inveraray, at the summit of the pass from Glen Croe to Loch Fyne stands a rough stone seat inscribed "Rest and Be Thankful." The road is on the military route from Dumbarton to Inveraray, completed in 1748.

Near the head of Loch Fyne is:

CAIRNDOW: Barely visible from the main highway, the A83, this little town nestles between a hill and Loch Fyne, on the loch's eastern shore. It is a peaceful haven with a view of the loch and the high mountains. **Strone Gardens,** open on Sunday from April 1 to September 30 and by arrangement otherwise, has in its pine forest the tallest tree in Great Britain.

The **Cairndow Inn** (tel. Cairndow 286) is a fully licensed, stone gem of an old stagecoach inn overlooking the loch. The present building is only about 200 years old, the original having been destroyed by fire in the 1700s. There's a residents' lounge with a piano for sing-alongs and a bar. The stone staircase, with a low ceiling, leads to nine immaculate and cozy bedrooms on the second and third floors, one with private bath. You'll pay £7.65 ($17.60) per person daily, plus VAT, for bed and breakfast. Lunch is £3 ($6.90); dinner, £4.60 ($10.58). The hosts, Mr. and Mrs. Fraser, will arrange for you to ride in their jaunting cart. The poet, John Keats, made a stay at the inn in 1818. It's open all year.

7. Aberdeen and Royal Deeside

Traveling north from the lochs—previewed in the section above—heading toward Royal Deeside, you can't help but go through Glen Shee and Glen Clunie, a most spectacular route which will give you your first taste of Highland scenery.

As you journey across uncrowded roads into Scotland's northeast, you'll pass heather-covered moorland and peaty lochs, wood glens and salmon-filled rivers, granite-stone villages and fishing harbors, even North Sea beach resorts.

This is the Grampian region, with such centers as Aberdeen and Braemar, and such sights as Balmoral Castle and the "Whiskey Trail." Even the Queen herself comes here for holidays.

BRAEMAR: This little Deeside resort is famous as the site of the **Royal Highland Gathering,** which takes place there annually, either in late August or early September. It is usually attended by Queen Elizabeth. The "royal link" dates from the 1840s when Queen Victoria first attended the games.

The capital of the Deeside Highlands, Braemar is overrun with foreign visitors, as well as the British themselves, during the gathering. Anyone thinking of attending would be wise to make application for accommodation anywhere within a 20-mile radius of Braemar not later than early April.

The gathering in Braemar is the most famous of the many Highland games. The spectacular occasion is held in the **Princess Royal and Duke of Fife Memorial Park.** Competitions include tossing the caber, throwing the hammer, sprinting, vaulting, a tug-o'-war, the long leap, Highland dancing, putting a 16-pound ball, sword dancing, relay races, and, naturally, a bagpiping contest. At a vast refreshment tent, Scottish lassies serve tea, coffee, buns, and other refreshments.

The romantic 17th-century **Braemar Castle** lies half a mile northeast of Braemar on the A93. A private residence of architectural grace, scenic charm, and historical interest, it is the seat of Capt. A. A. Farquharson of Invercauld. It can be visited from early May until the first Monday in October—daily from 10 a.m. to 6 p.m., costing adults 60p ($1.38); children under 13, 25p (58¢).

Food and Lodging

Invercauld Arms Hotel, Braemar (tel. Braemar 605), is a lovely old stone Highlands house converted to welcome guests. Its main building dates back to the 18th century. In cool weather they're greeted by a roaring fire in the hearth and shown to a comfortable armchair. In this friendly atmosphere one can really relax. This is a perfect part of the country for walking and fishing, and, in winter in nearby Glenshee, skiing. When you return to the hotel, you can have a dram in the bar called Colonel's Bed, named after a local gentleman who escaped the Battle of Killiecrankie with his mistress and hid out near the hotel. A single room goes for £12 ($27.60) without bath, going up to £18 ($41.50) with bath. Bathless doubles rent for £22 ($50.60); with bath, £40 ($92)—including a full Scottish breakfast. Lunch goes for £6.50 ($14.95); dinner, about £8 ($18.40). You'll sample a taste of Scotland here in the salmon and trout fresh from the River Dee, or perhaps succulent Angus beef, Highland venison, and grouse. For breakfast you might dare to order kippers and porridge, and you can even try haggis. The staff will pack a lunch for you if you're going on a walking trip. This is a thoroughly pleasant place, well run by Mr. Lock, the owner.

Fife Arms Hotel, Mar Road, near the center of Braemar (tel. Braemar 644), is a pleasant stone building surrounded by gardens. It contains a comfortable lounge with two bars to slake your thirst. Many bedrooms have baths and go for £28.50 ($65.55) to £35 ($80.50) for two persons. Singles with bath rent for £24 ($55.20) nightly, the tariff lowered to £18 ($41.40) without bath, including VAT, service, and a full breakfast. Dinner from the set menu costs around £5.50 ($12.65), including VAT. The menu offers two or three choices for each course. The Fife Arms is a busy, bustling place.

Braemar Lodge Hotel (tel. Braemar 617) is run by the delightful Mrs. McKay, who is frightfully apologetic that on bookings in advance she must insist on a £5 ($11.50) deposit. The house is an old hunting lodge but has been converted into a friendly hotel with a small lounge for guests. The bedrooms are warm and neat, and there are adequate bathroom facilities. Bed and breakfast costs £9 ($20.70). Dinner, served at 7 p.m. (and don't be late), costs £6 ($13.80). You can sit afterward in the lounge, ordering coffee and Drambuie if you wish. Local information is willingly given, and the small staff will go out of their way to make you feel at home. Mrs. McKay spends a lot of time in the kitchen, and the food is plain and excellent, served by attractive young women. When booking, say whether you plan to be there for dinner, as that helps Mrs. McKay plan the meals. Opposite the hotel is the cottage where Robert Louis Stevenson wrote *Treasure Island.*

THE WHISKEY TRAIL: Extending north from Braemar, from Grantown and Dufftown to Elgin, are many distilleries of scotch whiskey. Many are open for visits only by appointment—collect the list of telephone numbers from the local toursit office at Braemar. However, **Glenfiddich Distillery** in **Dufftown** is open Monday to Friday from 10 a.m. to 12:30 p.m. and from 2 to 4:30 p.m. Visitors are shown around the plant, and the process of distilling is explained by charming young women in tartans. At the finish of the tour, you're given a free dram of malt whiskey—and the whole tour is free! There is a souvenir shop where you can buy glasses, tankards, and hip flasks, plus other tokens of your visit to what is, perhaps, the only malt distillery left in Scotland which is still owned by the founding family and not by a combine.

BALLATER: On the Dee River, with the Grampian mountains in the background, Ballater is a holiday resort center where visitors flock to attend one of Scotland's most popular sightseeing attractions, Balmoral Castle (see below).

The town still centers around its **Station Square,** where the royal family used to be photographed as they arrived to spend holidays. The railway has since been closed.

From Ballater you can drive west to view the magnificent scenery of **Glen Muick** and **Lochnagar,** where you'll see herds of deer.

Food and Lodging

Tullich Lodge, on the A93, 1½ miles east of Ballater (tel. Ballater 406), is a turreted country house built in the Scottish baronial style, standing in five acres of its own gardens and woods above Royal Deeside and Ballater. The attractive hotel is tastefully decorated and furnished, often with antiques, its brass fittings and wood paneling providing the traditional touches. Your pleasant hosts, Hector Macdonald and Neil Bannister, offer only ten bedrooms, but they're of generous size and are beautifully furnished. At least eight contain private baths, the rest showers. Rates are £23 ($52.90) in a single, from £20 ($46) per person in a double. The lodge closes from January to March.

Its restaurant, commanding panoramic views of the "royal valley," serves some of the finest food along Royal Deeside. One of the chef's specialties is cuisine minceur casseroles, although he does all the standard dishes with above-average flair, including versions of locally caught trout and salmon, game and especially venison in season, as well as crab and lobster. The homemade soups are particularly enjoyable. A table d'hôte luncheon served at 1 p.m. costs £6.50 ($14.95) per person. Dinner, from 7:30 to 9 p.m., goes for about £9 ($20.70). It's essential to make a reservation. In an amusing bar, with a model railway, you can order from a good selection of malt whiskeys.

The **Invercauld Arms** (tel. Ballater 417) is a whitewashed Victorian hotel right in the heart of Royal Deeside. Queen Victoria used to visit it when at court at Balmoral. Col. and Mrs. Charles Napier, the owners, will welcome you most kindly, offering good food, comfortable bedrooms, and solid service. He is a colonel in the Gordon Highlanders, and served in Vietnam. The atmosphere is informal, and visitors quickly get to know each other. Nearly half the bedrooms contain private baths. The peak bed-and-breakfast rate is £15 ($34.50), in high season. In some of the more traditionally furnished bedrooms the antiques were made by Victoria's cabinetmaker.

The fully licensed hotel is long established, offering a wide range of pursuits such as game fishing, tennis, bowling, and golf. The hotel's spacious restaurant is especially fine, not only opening onto beautiful views, but serving a country-house fare of standard dishes that are well prepared, using fresh ingredients. The roasts are especially good. Lunch is served from noon to 2:30 p.m., dinner from 7 to 8:30 p.m. Expect to pay about £7.50 ($17.25) for a four-course dinner. Lunch served in the bar is from a cold buffet table, with the hot dish of the day priced at £3 ($6.90). The hotel closes from mid-November to mid-March.

Glen Lui (tel. Ballater 402) stands on two acres of private grounds overlooking the golf course at Ballater (access from the grounds). An ideal center for a holiday in Royal Deeside, Glen Lui is run by Mr. and Mrs. M. G. Fraser. Their hotel is small, with only one single and seven double rooms, but their welcome is big. Careful consideration has gone into the planning of the bedrooms, with such thoughtful touches as razor points. Each accommodation contains hot and cold running water.

What sets Glen Lui above the standard small hotel along the Deeside is their cuisine, reinforced by a good wine cellar and lounge bar. Mr. and Mrs. Fraser are even recommended by hoteliers in the area who might be full. However, it's important to reserve, as Glen Lui, owing to its size, can fill up quickly. The bed-and-breakfast rate is £12.50 ($28.75) per person nightly. For bed, breakfast, and an evening meal, the charge is around £18 ($41.40) per person. The hotel is open only from April to October.

Balmoral Castle

"This dear paradise" is how Queen Victoria described this castle, rebuilt in the Scottish baronial style by her beloved Albert. It was completed in 1855. Today Balmoral, eight miles west of Ballater, is still a private residence of the British sovereign. Albert, the prince consort, acquired the property in 1847, and the royal family first arrived there in 1848. As the small castle left by the Farquharsons proved too small, the present castle was rebuilt. Its principal feature is a 100-foot tower. On the grounds are many memorials to the royal family. Only the grounds, incidentally, can be visited—daily, except Sunday in May, June, and July from 10 a.m. to 5 p.m. However, no visits are allowed if the royal family is in residence. Admission is 50p ($1.15) for adults, 20p (46¢) for children.

BANCHORY: On lower Deeside, this pleasant resort is rich in woodland and river scenery. From this base, you can take excursions to two of the most popular castles in the Grampian region.

The Sights

Crathes Castle and Gardens, (tel. Crathes 525) two miles east of Banchory, is a fine early Jacobean building which is celebrated for its gardens, its sculptured yews dating from 1702. Just north of the A93 on the north bank of the Dee, this baronial castle contains remarkable painted ceilings. Gardens and grounds are open all year from 9:30 a.m. to dusk, charging an admission of 40p (92¢) for adults, 20p (46¢) for children. The castle is open from May 1 until the end of September—weekdays from 11 a.m. to 6 p.m., on Sunday from 2 to 6 p.m., charging an admission of 75p ($1.73) for adults, 35p (81¢) for children. There is a restaurant serving light meals during the hours the castle is open.

Structurally unchanged since its completion in 1626, **Craigievar Castle** (tel. Lumphanan 635) is an example of Scottish baronial architecture at its greatest height. Original molded plaster ceilings are to be seen in most rooms. The castle has been continually inhabited by the descendants of the builder, William Forbes, and is now preserved by the National Trust for Scotland. It is open daily except Friday from May to September, from 2 to 7 p.m., charging an admission of 60p ($1.38) for adults, 40p (92¢) for children. The grounds are open all year from 9:30 a.m. to dusk, and admission is by donation.

A mile from the castle is **Macbeth's Cairn,** where, according to legend, Macduff put an end to Macbeth.

Food and Lodging

Raemoir House (tel. Banchory 2846) is an 18th-century manor standing on 3500 acres of grounds with such sporting attractions as shooting, fishing, and riding. It is a journey into nostalgia, with its ballroom, antiques, and fine

tapestries, and log fires burning in the colder months. Sometimes overflow
guests of the Queen at Balmoral have been discreetly tucked in here. The rooms
are handsomely decorated, most of them quite large, and at least 17 of the 23
bedchambers contain private baths. What is so lovely about Scotland is its
curious mixtures—in this case, an 18th-century manor house with its own
helipad! This place is run by two of the most charming ladies you could find
anywhere. Mrs. Kit Sabin and Mrs. Peggy Jordan have been there since 1942,
and they and the house have grown together. Meals are served in an attractive
Georgian dining room, featuring a standard repertoire of familiar dishes, rather
well done. Service is informal and prompt. A double room without bath costs
£21 ($48.30), rising to £23 ($52.90) with a private bath, including a full Scottish
breakfast. Dinner is £8 ($18.40) per person. Lunch is usually £4 ($9.20),
although the bigger traditional Sunday meal goes for £6 ($3.80). Full-board
terms are £150 ($345) per week in a room with bath.

Tor-Na-Coille, Inchmarlo Road (tel. Banchory 2242), is a country house
hotel—really a Victorian mansion—standing on its own wooded grounds of
about six acres. Public rooms are suitably spacious, most comfortable, and the
whiskey always tastes better in the modern bar. If you're on your way to see
Balmoral Castle or else to attend the Highland gathering at Braemar, you will
be able to relax here, enjoying the gracious hospitality of Mr. Parkinson. The
bedrooms, many quite large, are restful, 60% of them have private baths, and
all of them have color TV, radio, phone, and coffee-making equipment. Bathless singles cost from £18 ($41.40), rising to £23 ($52.90) with private bath; and
bathless doubles begin at £31 ($71.30), going up to £39 ($89.70) with private
bath, including a full breakfast and VAT. A half-board rate applies for stays
of more than three nights. The hotel is interesting architecturally, and the room
you may be assigned could have much character.

Lunches are light meals in the bar, including smoked venison sausage
blended with rum and red wine. Prices range from £2 ($4.60) to £3.50 ($8.05)
for a steak and fried potatoes. Sunday lunch is a grander affair, when the main
dishes include roast beef, turkey, and leg of pork. A meal then costs around
£4.50 ($10.35), coffee extra. Food at night is by candlelight, and here might be
your chance to try real Scottish salmon (the salmon leap at the Falls of Feugh
nearby). Dinner costs from £7 ($16.10), and is likely to feature the chef's special
pheasant.

Banchory Lodge Hotel (tel. Banchory 2625). Built in 1738, this lodge was
once the home of a well-known Deeside family. But when Maggie and Dugald
Jaffray took it over, it was almost derelict. With dedication and hard work, they
transformed it into the charming country-house place it is today, with much
Georgian charm. On its own grounds, on the bank of the Dee, where it is joined
by the Water of Feugh, the lodge is open all year, accommodating 40 guests
in some 21 bedrooms, many of which overlook the river. Ten have private
baths. The bed-and-breakfast rate is about £20 ($46) per person, increasing to
£26 ($59.80) for half board. In the dining room, overlooking the river, furnish-
ings and decor are in period style. Maggie Jaffray supervises the kitchen, where
specialties include fresh Deeside salmon and Aberdeen Angus roast beef.
Guests can fish from the lawn or in one of the hotel's boats.

ABERDEEN: The harbor in this seaport in the northeast of Scotland is one
of the largest fishing ports in the country, literally infested with kipper and
deep-sea trawlers. The **Fish Market** is well worth a visit, as it's the liveliest in
Britain.

SCOTLAND: ABERDEEN

Bordered by fine sandy beaches (delightful if you're a polar bear), Scotland's third city is often called "the granite city," as its buildings are constructed largely of granite, in pink or gray, hewn from the Rubislaw quarries.

Aberdeen has become the capital of the oil workers pouring into northeast Scotland to help harvest the riches from six North Sea oilfields. The city lies on the banks of the salmon- and trout-filled Don and Dee Rivers. Spanning the Don is the world-famous **Brig o' Balgownie,** a steep Gothic arch, begun in 1285.

In Castlegate is the **Mercat Cross,** a hexagonally shaped structure, built in 1686, and considered the most handsome of the old crosses in Scotland.

Aberdeen University is a fusion of two separate colleges. King's College is older, dating from 1483, and it contains the oldest school of medicine in Great Britain. The chapel of King's College is crowned by a stately tower from 1505. Marischal College, founded in 1593, is recognized as one of the finest granite buildings in the world.

The university is in Old Aberdeen, as is the **Cathedral of St. Machar,** founded in 1136, although the present structure dates from the 13th century. Its splendid heraldic ceiling contains three rows of shields representing the kings and princes of Europe along with the Scottish ecclesiastical and aristocratic hierarchy. The modern stained-glass windows are magnificent, the work of Douglas Strachan, an Aberdonian.

Provost Skene's House, 45 Guestrow, is named for a rich merchant who was Lord Provost of Aberdeen during 1676–85. Off Broad Street, it is now a museum with period rooms and artifacts of domestic life. Admission is 20p (46¢) for adults, 5p (12¢) for children, and it can be visited Monday to Saturday from 10 a.m. to 5 p.m.

Provost Ross's House, in Shiprow, is the oldest house in Aberdeen, built in 1593 and recently restored. It is open to the public on Monday and Friday from 2:30 to 4:30 p.m.

Food and Lodging

Because of the increasing numbers of tourists and business visitors to the Granite City, now established as Europe's Offshore Oil Capital, hotels are likely to be heavily booked any time of the year. In that case, it's best to go to the **Tourist Bureau,** St. Nicholas House, Broad Street (tel. Aberdeen 23456). A member of the staff there will assist with hotel or guest house reservations. If you're calling on a Saturday, use a different telephone number (tel. Aberdeen 24890).

For those willing to reserve in advance, here are our favorite selections:

Holiday Inn, Oldmeldrum Road, Bucksburn (tel. Bucksburn 3911), is especially popular with business people from the oil-related concerns flocking to Aberdeen. Even though Laird's Bar is done up in a Highland baronial flavor, you're likely to hear customers ordering Jack Daniels and Old Grand-Dad as much as malt scotch. The 99-unit Holiday Inn is a fresh package, all accommodations containing fully tiled private baths. In decor the tone is traditional rather than modern. Singles rent for £30 ($69), doubles for £34 ($78.20), and breakfast is extra. The Mariner Restaurant, serving until 10:30 p.m., evokes the nostalgia for the days of the Aberdeen clipper ships. The Holiday Inn's food is much improved, the service prompt. Amenities include an indoor swimming pool. The chain hotel lies about three miles from the heart of Aberdeen, but only two from the airport.

Prince Regent Hotel, Waverley Place (tel. Aberdeen 55071), is a small, attractive, and well-kept hotel run by Mr. and Mrs. W. G. Wilson. Their little oasis lies only yards from the West End of Union Street. The public rooms have a Regency decor, and the bedrooms, although simply furnished, have all the necessities, and most of them come with private baths. Singles begin at £17 ($39.10), and doubles or twins rent for about £30 ($69). The cookery is quite fine and is handsomely presented, the hotel offering both table d'hôte and à la carte menus. Guests can enjoy apéritifs in the Regency Buck or drinks in the Jug.

Malacca Hotel, 349 Great Western Rd. (tel. Aberdeen 28901), is one of the best of the small hotels of Aberdeen. Actually, it offers only eight bedrooms, seven of which contain private baths and showers. Singles rent for £27 ($62.10) nightly, doubles going for £36 ($82.80). The granite town-house hotel, with its surrounding stone wall and trees, is much better known for its restaurant, an attractively decorated dining room with bentwood coned chairs, a sophisticated setting for the international dishes served here, everything from bouillabaisse to chicken jubilee to duck in orange sauce. You can dine here for about £15 ($34.50) per person. Lunch is served until 2 p.m. and dinner until 10:30 p.m.

The **Struan Hotel,** 239 Great Western Rd. (Aberdeen 574-484), at the western end of Aberdeen, is run by Mr. and Mrs. Milne. Their hotel has been modernized and attractively furnished, and they rent out 16 double bedrooms, all but three of which have private baths and color TV. Bathless twins cost £28 ($64.40), the tariff rising to £33 ($75.90) in a twin with bath. This is a corner stone building, with a garden and a stone wall. The hotel also has a good dining room.

In nearby Cults, the **Royal Darroch,** North Deeside Road (tel. Aberdeen 48811), might be a more attractive and tranquil choice for motorists. Four miles west of Aberdeen, the low-lying Royal Darroch, a Reo Stakis hotel, is built on the Dee River. Unlike most country hotels of Scotland, this one is modern, offering 67 streamlined rooms on three floors, each with functional furnishings and private bath, color TV, radio, and telephone. The single bed-and-breakfast rate is £30 ($69), rising to £38 ($87.40) in a double. The Royal Darroch is popular as a restaurant, its dining room feeding at least a hundred patrons a first-class cuisine. All the amenities, such as a cocktail bar, TV lounge, and elevator, await you.

If you're seeking the less expensive tariffs of a bed-and-breakfast house, we'd suggest the **Valley Hotel,** 145 Crown St. (tel. Aberdeen 20-034), run by the delightful Sandy Bruce and his wife Frances. You can get a spacious double room and a big Scottish breakfast for only £6 ($13.80). After a day at the beach, guests gather in the attractive lounge to watch color television.

The **Myrtle Mill Restaurant,** North Deeside Road, Bieldside (tel. Aberdeen 48877), is a recently converted 17th-century mill, given a sophisticated style, and has some of the best food of the area. On the walls you'll find a collection of old Scottish prints, tartans, and memorabilia. Just five minutes from the center, the restaurant makes for a pleasant stopover on your way to Royal Deeside. Appetizers are large in selection, including such unusual items as smoked cod's roe pâté at £2.50 ($5.75), and smoked duckling and smoked trout served with chopped cucumber, £3.25 ($7.48). The chef specializes in Angus beef, a nine-ounce sirloin steak going for £6.50 ($14.95). Main courses are international in scope, including Caribbean chicken, with prices beginning at £5 ($11.50). For dessert, we'd suggest the lemon pancakes at £2.25 ($5.18).

What's Cookin', 18 Holborn St. (tel. Aberdeen 575-685), is a bright, sophisticated, bistro-style restaurant, offering some imaginative dishes, a refreshing change of pace from the standard Aberdeen cuisine repertoire. For example, you might get your repast started by ordering either the Catalan seafood soup at £1.20p ($2.76) or else a delicious duck and orange pâté, £2

($4.60). Continental specialties are prepared with flair—pork with fruits, £4.25 ($9.78); or else seafood vol-au-vent, £4.50 ($10.35). A cheerful little place, it offers friendly service.

On the outskirts, if you're heading for Royal Deeside, we'd suggest a dining stopover at **Marycutler House** (tel. Aberdeen 732-124), about six miles from Aberdeen on the South Deeside Road. World traveler Mrs. Martin purchased this 17th-century house beside the river, imaginatively decorating the dining rooms with treasures brought back from her trips. The baronial bar has an eclectic collection—an African mask, an Early English settle, a Victorian sofa, and Adam bar. In addition to the bar are two handsome dining rooms as well as one with a glass roof, evoking memories of Marrakesh. The menu is likely to change by the time of your visit, but it's international in scope— soupe au pistou, £1.80 ($4.14); oxtail stew, £6 ($13.80); chicken cardamon, £6 also, with a side helping of ratatouille, £85p ($1.96), followed by a creamy apple pie, £1.80 ($4.14). Lunch is until 2, and dinner (make a reservation) is from 7:30 to 9:30 p.m. If you're stopping in for lunch, you can have a light pub meal in front of the fireplace. Closed Sunday.

Excursions in "Castle Country"

Aberdeen is the center of "castle country," as 40 inhabited castles lie within a 40-mile radius. Two of the most popular castle excursions are previewed below. For others, refer above to Banchory.

Drum Castle: The handsome mansion (tel. Drumoak 204) was added in 1619, but the great square tower dates from the late 13th century, making it one of the three oldest tower houses in the country. Historic Drum lies ten miles west of Aberdeen, off the A93. The castle is open May to September, Monday to Saturday from 11 a.m. to 6 p.m. (on Sunday from 2 to 6), charging adults 75p ($1.73) for admission; children pay 35p (81¢). The grounds are open all year from 9:30 a.m. to dusk, and admission is by donation.

Muchalls Castle: Built by the Burnetts of Leys in 1619, this castle is now lived in by Mr. and Mrs. Maurice A. Simpson. It is noted for its elaborate plasterwork ceilings and fireplaces. The castle itself lies five miles north of Stonehaven, nine miles south of Aberdeen. It is open May to September on Tuesday and Sunday from 3 to 5 p.m., charging adults 30p (69¢); children, 20p (46¢).

8. Aviemore, Speyside, and Elgin

Aviemore is the winter sports capital of Britain, but it also enjoys mass popularity in summer, too. Aviemore Centre, previewed below, is Scotland's most modern holiday resort, an all-year, all-weather center, endowed with a multitude of outdoor pursuits, such as golfing, angling, skiing, or ice skating.

Those seeking a more traditional Scottish ambience will gravitate to one of the many Speyside villages, each with its own attractions and atmosphere. Ranking next to Aviemore, Grantown-on-Spey is another major center.

The Spey itself is the fastest flowing river in the British Isles, famed not only for its scenery, but its salmon and ski slopes.

Finally, on your way to Inverness, you might care to stop off at the old cathedral city of Elgin.

Our first stop up the Spey follows.

NEWTONMORE: This Highland resort on Speyside is a good center for the Grampian and Monadhliath Mountains, and it offers excellent fishing, golf, pony trekking, and hill walking. Most motorists zip through it on the way to Aviemore, but sightseers may want to stop off and visit the **Clan MacPherson House & Museum** (tel. Newtonmore 332), at the south end of the village. Displayed are clan relics and memorials, including the Black Chanter and Green Banner as well as a "charmed sword," and the broken fiddle of the freebooter James MacPherson—a Scottish Robin Hood. Sentenced to death in 1700, he is said to have played the dirge "MacPherson's Rant" on his fiddle as he stood on the gallows at Banff. He then offered the instrument to anyone who would think well of him. There were no takers, so he smashed it. The museum is open from May to September on weekdays from 10 a.m. to noon and from 2 to 6 p.m.

A track from the village climbs past the Calder River to Loch Dubh and the massive Carn Ban (3087 feet), where eagles fly. Castle Cluny, ancient seat of the MacPherson chiefs, is six miles west of Newtonmore.

A good place to stay is the **Pines Hotel,** Station Road (tel. Newtonmore 271), on a hill overlooking the Spey Valley, with the Cairngorms, the Grampians, and the Monadhliath Mountains all in view. The resident proprietors, Mike and Betty Wood, offer seven rooms in their attractive stone house, all with heaters and hot and cold running water, and some with TV available. They charge £7.50 ($17.25) for bed and breakfast per person in low season, £8.50 ($19.55) in high season (June, July, and August). We recommend taking the dinner, bed, and breakfast at £11 ($25.30) per person in low season, £12 ($25.60) in high season, because of the excellent cuisine. Such choices as trout, salmon, venison, beef, and lamb are offered, all locally supplied. Mr. Wood sees to it that trout is served once a week, catching it himself. All the food is home-cooked, and a substantial wine list is offered. The hotel has a pleasant residents' lounge where guests enjoy malt whiskey and fine liqueurs. Every Saturday evening from the middle of May, a piper plays in the garden which overlooks the valley. As its name implies, the hotel is in the middle of a pine grove. Closed in November.

KINGUSSIE: Your next stop along the Spey might be at this little summer holiday resort and winter ski center (it's pronounced King-youcie), the so-called capital of Badenoch, a district known as "the drowned land" because the Spey can flood the valley when the snows of a severe winter melt in the spring. There you can visit the six-acre **Highland Folk Museum,** on Duke Street, just off High Street, with its comprehensive collection of artifacts, including weaponry, bagpipes, and fiddles illustrating more than two centuries of Highland customs, plus the work of crafts people. Naturally, there are tartans. A furnished cottage with a mill and a farming shed stand on the museum grounds. It is open all year from 10 a.m. to 3 p.m. It closes on Friday, and keeps slightly longer hours in summer. The admission is 50p ($1.15) for adults, 10p (23¢) for children.

If you'd like to stop here instead of at Aviemore, we'd recommend the following establishments.

Scott's Hotel (tel. Kingussie 351) is more personal than the leading hotel at Kingussie, the Duke of Gordon. Scott's is really more of a bed-and-breakfast house, under the personal supervision of its resident proprietors, Mr. and Mrs. Patrick John Cook, who are most hospitable. Rooms are comfortable and well appointed. One reader wrote, "Our stay here was the happiest in Scotland." The hotel has mostly double rooms, charging £25 ($57.50) for two persons for an overnight's stay off-season, this tariff including a good dinner and a mammoth breakfast. In high season, the rate rises to £35 ($80.50) for two, but that price is still good value. The hotel has a residential license, and its cuisine is home cooking, family style.

If you're not dining at a hotel, try the **Wood'n Spoon,** 3 High St. (tel. Kingussie 488), on the A9, run by Mr. and Mrs. David Russell. It is considered by some the only "real pub" in the Highlands, and it serves excellent home-cooked food. For lunch (11:30 a.m. to 2:30 p.m.) there is a delicious cold display and numerous hot dishes made to order. In the evening from 5:30 to 9:30 p.m. (Highland dining is early), a more extensive selection is available. Dishes offered are, as much as possible, made from local produce including fish from the Spey and venison from the nearby glens. The Russells also offer a large selection of homemade jams and chutneys for sale. Expect to pay £7 ($16.10) for a meal.

AVIEMORE CENTRE: This year-round holiday complex on the Spey was opened in 1966 in the heart of the Highlands, at the foot of the historic rock of Craigellachie. This rock was the rallying place for Clan Grant.

In winter, ski runs are available for both beginners and experts (four chair lifts and seven T-bar tows). Après-ski activities include swimming in a heated indoor pool 82 feet long, folk singing, table tennis, or else just relaxing and drinking in one of the many bars in the complex.

The ice rink is the second-largest indoor ice rink in Britain, with seven curling lanes and ice skating on a separate 4000-square-foot pad. At night younger people are attracted to the discos, although others seek out one of the Scottish nights, country dancing, supper dances, or else dancing in the large Osprey Ballroom with a sprung maple floor.

In summer, sailing, canoeing, pony trekking, hill walking, and mountain climbing, as well as golf and fishing, are just some of the many activities. The **Speyside Theatre,** seating 720, changes its film programs every day, and often is host to live shows and concerts. The center's shopping precincts cover a wide range of services, ranging from banking to hairdressing to car-rental offices.

Children always like to visit **Santa Claus Land,** set on a six-acre site, with a log cabin, toy factory, doll house, and a permanently frozen "North Pole" in peppermint colors. It also includes pony rides, cowboy trail, veteran cars, and a gingerbread house. Since it's Scotland, there is also Santa Shortbread.

Adjacent to Santa Claus Land is the **Highland Craft Centre,** where woodcarvers, potters, jewelers, weavers, blacksmiths, and engravers maintain the ancient skills and crafts of the Highlands. Their products are offered for sale.

Later, you can visit **Alan Keegan's Craft Shop,** where you can see 135 different kinds of scotch whiskey from 65 different distileries. He doesn't sell drinks. Collecting scotch whiskey is his hobby. He's good at it, too, as his collection is considered the largest in Scotland. The most expensive is a Springbank whiskey. Only one cask was ever produced.

Food and Lodging

The following hotels in the complex are recommended.

Strathspey (tel. Aviemore Centre 810-681). The tower block of this hotel recalls the design of the traditional Scottish keep. The 90-bedroom, six-story hotel dominates the approach to Aviemore Centre. This well-organized hotel was built with a purpose—to provide a comfortable nest in both summer and winter for sports-minded holidaymakers. Its public lounges are large, with picture windows opening onto views of the Cairngorms.

Bedrooms come in a variety of styles and amenities, containing private bath and color TV. Some rooms, for example, are booked by families, as they contain bunk beds for children. Others are large, airy, and pleasantly decorated. Singles rent for £26 ($59.80), twins for £20 ($46) per person, plus VAT. Coffee makers are provided, and there is suitable storage space for sports equipment. In addition, the hotel offers bars, a restaurant, plus a sauna bath, and there is, as well, ski instruction in winter.

Post House (tel. Aviemore Centre 810-771) is one of the increasingly popular post houses belonging to Trust House Forte. (At a post house, you don't get room service, but every other amenity seems to be there.) The hotel is spread informally over a hillside, which often causes a split-level effect. The style here is most casual and informal, a holiday atmosphere. The spacious layout is balanced effectively by a warm color scheme. Picture windows and terraces open onto country views. The staff is most helpful and friendly. The bedrooms are all equipped with private baths, and some family rooms are available. Singles rent for £26 ($59.80) the tariff increasing to £35 ($80.50) in a double.

You can drink in the Illicit Still Bar, with its shiny copper-topped tables and a copper whiskey still, or else in the White Lady Bar, named after one of the Cairngorm ski runs. The Crystal Buttery is for light meals, and the main restaurant is crowned by a tall pyramidal ceiling, from which a quartet of chandeliers hangs. The service and the food are first class. We'd highly recommend the roast ribs of Scottish beef. In the game room is a resident nanny—so, if you have children, you're free to hit the slopes without them.

Badenoch Hotel (tel. Aviemore Centre 810-261) overlooks the Craigellachie Nature Reserve and its famous rock. The hotel gives summer and winter holidaymakers a choice of both luxury and economy rooms. In this starkly modern Highland building, 60 rooms are streamlined and functional, all large sized, all with the modern amenities. For these you pay £17 ($39.10) in a single, from £23.50 ($54.05) in a twin. But there are as well about 16 more "rawboned" accommodations, with bunk-type beds and adjacent bathrooms and showers, going for £14 ($32.20) in a single, from £13.60 ($31.17) in a twin. The hotel is well stocked with facilities—a nursery, cocktail bar, disco, a game room, ski equipment, rover touring, a Norseman bar, even an attractive restaurant with a view of heather-covered grounds in summer or snow caps in winter.

Aviemore Chalets Motel (tel. Aviemore Centre 810-618) offers comfortable, moderately priced double-story chalets with four units on each floor. Each chalet is centrally heated, carpeted, and adequately furnished with double-tiered bunks, two wash basins with hot and cold running water, private showers, toilets, and heated drying cupboards. Based on four persons in a room, the rate is from £6.60 ($15.07) per person. The reception chalet offers a snackbar, large lounge, and an attractive licensed lounge bar, the Craigellachie. For meals, the Pinewood is a cafeteria (self-service) restaurant, but in Das Stübel, an Austrian-style grillroom, friendly waitresses serve your meals. There are also four self-catering apartments, each sleeping six, with cooking facilities and color television.

The Rank organization has the following offering.

Coylumbridge Hotel, Rothiemurchus (tel. Aviemore Centre 810-661), suggests northern Sweden rather than northern Scotland. Christened by the Duke of Edinburgh, the Coylumbridge stands on 65 acres of tree-studded grounds, facing the slopes of the Cairngorms. The bedroom decor is chalet-style, with pinewood used profusely. Cheerful appointments evoke both a summer and a winter holiday atmosphere. All rooms have private bathroom, color TV, radio, telephone, and coffee maker. Singles are £23 ($52.90) and doubles go for £38 ($87.40), including VAT.

The Coylumbridge is geared for the winter skier, with instruction and equipment available. In summer, pony-trekkers, fishermen, and golfers check in. On some nights there is disco dancing. It's really a self-contained unit, with a game room, hairdresser, 24-hour coffeeshop, plus a pleasant modern restaurant, the Epicure, offering a continental cuisine in the evening, a set dinner costing £7 ($16.10). As well as the restaurant, the hotel has a Chieftain Grill, open seven days a week.

Another leading hotel in the area is the **High Range** (tel. Aviemore Centre 810-636), standing above the main Perth-Inverness road. This chalet hotel enjoys a wooded setting of natural birch. From the windows of the single-story chalets, you look out onto the Rothiemurchus Forest and the snow- or else heather-covered slopes of the Cairngorms.

In the main block, built of western red cedar, are housed a restaurant, a cocktail bar, and public lounges, all evoking the atmosphere of a ski lodge. The rooms themselves are pleasantly and attractively decorated, offering single, double, twin, and family bedded rooms, each with bath or shower and the majority with bidet. For half board, the charge ranges from £18 ($41.40) to £22 ($50.60) per person nightly, according to the time of the year.

The restaurant at High Range is one of the best at Aviemore, serving dinner only, from 7:30 to 10:30 p.m. The attractive modern dining room draws a lively, youthful crowd to its capable bistro cooking. On our last visit, in summer, the vegetables were garden fresh, and the fish, salmon from the Spey, was exquisitely tender. The soups were interesting, too, and the service alert and efficient but definitely not rushed. Expect to pay £5 ($11.50) for the set dinner, or perhaps £12 ($27.60) if you're ordering à la carte and selecting some good-tasting French specialties (the chef, Peter Morris, does lamb especially well).

Fish 'n' Chips

At the **Happy Haggis Chip Shop,** Grampian Road (tel. Aviemore Centre 810-430), you can get fish and chips to take out.

Know Your Clan

It took Alex Haley 12 years to track down Kunta Kinte and his ancestors in Africa. Now visitors with clan names arriving in Aviemore can track down their roots in three seconds. Aviemore Center is the site of the **Clan Tartan Centre** where a computer holds research done by a team of experts on 8000 Scottish names. The visitor simply finds if his or her name is on the list, and the machine automatically puts out all the Scottish background laboriously programmed into it. You can also follow the history of the clans and the development of tartans and Highland dress through a continuous film program in the auditorium.

GRANTOWN-ON-SPEY: This holiday resort, with its gray granite buildings, stands in a wooded valley and commands splendid views of the Cairngorm mountains. It is a key center of winter sports in Scotland. Fishermen are also attracted to its setting, because the Spey is renowned for its salmon. Lying 34 miles southeast of Inverness by road, it was one of Scotland's many 18th-century planned towns, founded on a heather-covered moor in 1765 by Sir James Grant of Grant, becoming the seat of that ancient family. Grantown became famous in the 19th century as a Highland tourist center, enticing visitors with its planned concept, the beauty of surrounding pine forests, the Spey River, and the mountains around it.

From a base here you can explore the valleys of the Don and Dee, the already-mentioned Cairngorms, and Culloden Moor, scene of the historic battle in 1746.

In hotels, the leading recommendations follow.

Grant Arms, The Square (tel. Grantown-on-Spey 2526). When Queen Victoria stayed here in 1860, she is reported to have said, "My bed was hard, but at least it was clean." Her old room with its four-poster is still there—and still clean—although not at all hard. Into its second century of hospitality, the Grant Arms is still the best place to stay at the resort. The hotel has been considerably modernized, yet it retains traditional touches. The color-coordinated bedrooms are well maintained, and some of them are deluxe in their appointments. At least 40 of the 55 units contain private baths, and another 15 come equipped with showers. In the peak season, the overnight charge ranges from £20 ($46) per person, based on double occupancy, this rate including a full Scottish breakfast. The inclusive daily rate, with all meals, begins at £32 ($73.60) per person daily. There's about a £3 ($6.90) daily supplement for single rooms.

At the Grant Arms a former ballroom has been converted into the Balmoral Restaurant, where tour groups often dine. It serves what is perhaps the best food in Grantown-on-Spey, not only the national dishes of Scotland, but fresh salmon and trout and venison in season. The service is expert even when the Balmoral seems crowded. Lunch is from noon to 2:30 p.m. and dinner from 7 to 8:45 p.m.

Craiglynne, Woodland Terrace (tel. Grantown-on-Spey 2597), is spacious and sprawling, standing on its own grounds overlooking the wooded valley and the hills beyond. Resident ski instructors—and equipment for renting—are on hand in winter, and in summer pony-trekkers check in. Accommodations come in a variety of styles, plumbing, and space. Only 14 of the 60 rooms contain private baths, however. The bedrooms are pleasant and bright, well maintained, although some are somewhat spartan in decor. The charge is £16.50 ($37.95) per person in a room without bath, the cost rising to £18 ($41.40) per person with bath, these tariffs including a full breakfast, VAT, and service. The tartan bar with its peat fire is the center of après-ski life. In season there is entertainment every evening. The dining room is light and airy, serving good country fare, including such Scottish dishes as haggis and malt gravy.

ROTHES: A Speyside town with five distilleries, Rothes lies just to the south of the lovely Glen of Rothes. You can stay in Rothes and explore "The Whiskey Trail," detailed earlier. It is but a short ride from here to **Dufftown,** containing at least seven distilleries, including **William Grant's Glenfiddich Distillery,** operating a reception room from March to October and showing visitors how malt whiskey is produced.

After your career up "The Whiskey Trail," **Rothes Glen Hotel** in Rothes (tel. Rothes 254) may appear to be a mirage. The old turreted house, with many of its original pieces of furniture, stands back from the road, surrounded by about 40 acres of fields with grazing Highland cattle—how can they see to eat with all that shaggy hair? This historic castle-like building was designed by the architect who built Balmoral. Inside the house a warm fire greets you. Bedrooms are well furnished and relaxing. Depending on the plumbing, the bed-and-breakfast rate ranges from £20 ($46) to £21 ($48.30) per person. The dining room is paneled in wood, and good wholesome meals are served in true Scottish tradition. Lunch is from 12:30 to 2 p.m. and dinner from 7 to 8:30 p.m. A set luncheon costs £4.50 ($10.35) and a table d'hôte dinner is £10 ($23). The hotel shuts down from mid-November to March 1.

FOCHABERS: This village, on the Inverness-Aberdeen road, dates from 1776 and was created as one of the early planned towns by John Baxter, for the fourth Duke of Gordon. Most of the buildings along High Street are protected and have not been changed much in 200 years. On the Spey, Fochabers is distinguished by its **Market Cross** and **Tower of Gordon Castle.**

The **Gordon Arms** (tel. Fochabers 820-508) is a well-known 18th-century coaching inn, run by Mr. and Mrs. Pern, who are justing proud of the hospitality they offer wayfarers of today. Bedrooms are both traditional and modern, either in the old wing or the new. Singles without bath cost £28 ($64.40), rising to £31 ($71.30) with bath, and doubles cost from £29 ($66.70) to £34 ($78.20), including a full breakfast and VAT. Only 7 of the 17 rooms contain private baths. Fishermen are fond of the place, as revealed by the "salmon house" for the storing of rods and tackle.

The Perns are noted for their catering, and their food is some of the best along Speyside, including many national dishes Mrs. Pern herself cooks for her visitors, such as herring rolled in oatmeal and grilled. The Moray beef and salmon are rarely equaled. Sometimes continental dishes appear on the menu. A table d'hôte luncheon goes for £4.20 ($9.66), a set dinner for £10 ($23). Meals are served from 12:30 to 2 p.m. and from 7 to 9:30 p.m. It's important to make a reservation, incidentally. On the wall are paintings by local artists. If you're stopping on a summer afternoon, you might have tea in the garden.

ELGIN: The center of local government in the Moray district, an ancient royal burgh, this cathedral city lies on the Lossie River, 38 miles from Inverness by road. Once called the "lantern of the north," the **Cathedral of Moray** is now in ruins. It was founded in 1224 but almost destroyed in 1390 by the "wolf of Badenoch," the natural son of Robert II. After its destruction, the citizens of Elgin rebuilt their beloved cathedral, turning it into one of the most attractive and graceful buildings in Scotland. The architect's plan was that of a Jerusalem cross. However, when the central tower fell in 1711, the cathedral was allowed to fall into decay. But a faithful cobbler still respected its grandeur, and he became the caretaker of it. At his death, in 1841, he had removed most of the debris that had fallen. Today tourists wander among its ruins, snapping pictures. Best preserved is the 15th-century chapter house.

Samuel Johnson and Boswell came this way on their Highland tour, reporting a "vile dinner" at the Red Lion Inn in 1773.

Hopefully, you'll fare better at the **Eight Acres Hotel,** Sheriffmill (tel. Elgin 3077), a modern, low-lying, motel-type unit, all 40 of its streamlined, functionally furnished rooms offering a private bath or shower. Standing on spacious grounds, the hotel lies on the western approaches to Elgin on the main A96 Inverness Road. The public rooms are spacious, and the restaurant attracts a lot of motorists bound for Inverness. Rates in a single are £22 ($50.60), rising to £38 ($87.40) in a double, including breakfast. The hotel offers quite a bit of entertainment at various times of the year, not only a disco and dinner/dancing to a live band, but occasional Scottish folk evenings.

Less expensive is the **Royal Hotel,** corner of Station Road and Moss Street (tel. Elgin 2320), a pleasant, privately owned hotel standing on its own grounds about a four-minute walk from the center of Elgin. It lies in the vicinity of the railway station and in close proximity to golf and tennis courts. The owner, Miss McKee, asks £8.50 ($19.55) per person for bed and a big Scottish breakfast. She offers only one single but eight double rooms, all comfortably furnished and containing hot and cold running water. You can get a two-course lunch for £2.50 ($5.75), with dishes such as roast chicken and two vegetables, plus a dessert. The owner also serves a high tea at £2.50 ($5.75) at 6 p.m., offering such items as braised steak and vegetables or poached eggs and ham, followed by a dessert. Guests are invited to enjoy the cozy TV lounge, with a fireplace in which either peat or wood is burned on cool days. The house is rich in antiques, with a beautiful double staircase with wrought-iron banisters and a mahogany rail. The house was built in 1865 by James Grant, the founder of the Glen Grant Distillery, who also built all the railways in northwest Scotland north to Wick. A three-story structure, it was originally called Dalehaple.

FINDHORN: As you travel westward from Elgin to Forres, a turn to the right and then to the left will bring you to Findhorn, a tiny village whose name has become internationally known through its connection with the University of Light in Forres and as a gathering place for persons seeking a place where communal living and creativity have burgeoned. Actually, a caravan park just before you arrive in Findhorn is the center of these activities. Findhorn itself is on a unique tidal bay at the mouth of the River Findhorn, which makes it ideal for yacht racing, sailing, and waterskiing. Across the bay from Findhorn is the Culbin Sands, under which lies a buried village.

In Findhorn, a good place to stay is the **Culbin Sands Hotel** (tel. Findhorn 252), which has panoramic views of Moray Firth, Findhorn Bay, and Culbin Forest, and is within two minutes' walk of sandy beaches. The hotel has 14 bedrooms, all with hot and cold running water, renting for £10.45 ($24.03) to £18.90 ($43.47) in a single, £14.60 ($33.58) per person in a double, for bed and breakfast, VAT included. Extra cots can be supplied in rooms for £1.75 ($4.03) each per night. Half price is charged for children under 8. The hotel boasts two well-stocked bars, a pleasant dining room, and a color TV lounge. An extensive buffet, with one hot dish, is offered in the evenings. Bar lunches are served in both the cocktail and public bars Monday through Saturday, and a buffet lunch on Sunday. Ample parking facilities are offered. It's best to reserve well in advance if you plan to visit Findhorn in the high season.

FORRES: This ancient burgh, mainly residential in character, stands on the Aberdeen–Inverness Road, between Elgin and Nairn (ten miles to the east). Near the mouth of the Findhorn, it is one of Scotland's oldest towns. Once a castle associated with Duncan and Macbeth stood here. Nearby is **Sueno's Stone,** a 23-foot sandstone monolith containing 10th- and 11th-century Celtic carvings with intricate figures of men. The **Witches' Stone,** in the same vicinity, marks the site of the burnings of persons accused of witchcraft.

The best hotels include the **Ramnee,** Victoria Road (tel. Forres 72410), a charming house set back from the road and entered through well-kept gardens. Mrs. Jill Martini personally supervises the day-to-day running of the place, keeping it spotless. There is a lounge plus a pleasant dining room with wood panels and gleaming napery where meals are served. A full breakfast is included in the overnight cost, and dinner consists of simple grills, steak, and fish. There is as well a bar for the use of residents. The bedrooms are large and, where bathrooms have been added, the workmanship has been professional—

you don't feel that your toilet has been carved out of a corner of your room. The charge is £14 ($32.20) per person, £2 ($4.60) extra for a room with bath. A set dinner goes for from £7.50 ($17.25).

Built in an informal 19th-century style, the hotel is sited within a garden in the Laigh of Moray. To reach it, pull off the A96 Aberdeen–Inverness Road on a clearly marked driveway leading to the hotel. The view from the front of the hotel is the richly wooded Cluny Hill of *Macbeth* witches fame. To the rear the view stretches out many miles over Findhorn Bay and the Culbin Sands Forest.

Nearby, the **Park Hotel,** Victoria Road (tel. Forres 72328), is very much the same sort of house. Set on spacious, well-kept grounds, it overlooks Findhorn Bay and the Moray Firth. The bedrooms are comfortable and well appointed, containing hot and cold running water. In season fresh fruit and vegetables come from the garden, the produce used in the hotel's kitchen. Mr. and Mrs. Leslie welcome guests, charging them £10 ($23), (plus VAT and service, for bed and breakfast. Bar lunches are served. The hotel also has a cocktail bar, drawing room, and television lounge.

9. Inverness and Loch Ness

After Glasgow, most motorists wanting to explore the Highlands head for Inverness, its ancient capital. From its doorstep, one can explore a romantic land of hills, lochs, and lots of myths.

Of course, the most popular excursion is to Loch Ness, where one sets up an observation point to await the appearance of "Nessie," the Loch Ness monster. But even if the monster doesn't put in an appearance, the loch itself has splendid scenery. We have a scattering of recommendations around the loch for those wanting to base there.

Finally, visitors going east may want to explore the old town of Nairn, and those adventurous readers wanting to venture into the forlorn and relatively uninhabited section of northwest Scotland may want to do so from a base at the old spa of Strathpeffer.

INVERNESS: The capital of the Highlands, Inverness is a royal burgh and seaport, at the north end of Great Glen, lying on both sides of the Ness River. It is considered the best base for touring the north. At the Highland Games, with their festive balls, the season in Inverness reaches its social peak.

The city has a new and luxurious theater complex on the bank of the Ness, the **Eden Court Theatre,** Bishops Road, which has a superb restaurant, bars, and an art gallery. Included in the repertoire are variety shows, drama, ballet, pop music, movies, opera, rock and folk concerts, and a summer-season traditional Scottish show with top stars. The theater, which opened in 1976, was constructed with an ingenious use of hexagonal shapes and has a horseshoe-shaped auditorium. Programs are advertised in most hotels and guest houses. The box office is open 10:30 a.m. to 8 p.m., Monday through Saturday (tel. Inverness 221-718).

Inverness is one of the oldest inhabited localities in Scotland.

On **Craig Phadrig** are the remains of a vitrified fort, believed to date from the fourth century B.C., where the Pictish King Brude is said to have been visited by St. Columba in A.D. 565. The old castle of Inverness stood to the east of the present Castlehill, the site still retaining the name **Auld Castlehill.** Because of the somewhat shaky geography of Shakespeare in dramatizing the crime of Macbeth by murdering King Duncan, some scholars claim that the deed was done in the old castle of Inverness while others say it happened at Cawdor Castle, 4½ miles to the south where Macbeth held forth as Thane of Cawdor.

King David built the first stone castle in Inverness around 1141. The **Clock Tower** is all that remains of a fort erected by Cromwell's army between 1652 and 1657. The 16th-century **Abertarff House** is now the headquarters of An Comunn Gaidhealach, the Highland association which preserves the Gaelic language and culture.

Inverness today has a castle, but it's a "modern" one—that is, dating from 1835. Crowning a low cliff of the east bank of the Ness, the **Castle of Inverness** occupies the site of an ancient fortress blown up by the Jacobites in 1746. Today the castle houses county offices and law courts. Mary Queen of Scots was denied admission to the castle in 1562, and she subsequently occupied a house on Bridge Street. From the window of this house, she witnessed the execution of her cousin, Sir John Gordon. For not gaining admission to the castle, she took reprisals, taking the fortress and hanging the governor.

Opposite the town hall is the **Old Mercat Cross**, with its **Stone of the Tubs**, an Inverness landmark said to be where women rested their washtubs as they ascended from the river. Known as "Clachnacudainn," the lozenge-shaped stone was the spot where the early kings were crowned.

The **Inverness Museum and Art Gallery**, at Castle Wynd (tel. Inverness 37114), contains displays of the culture of the Highlands, including silver and an exhibition called "The Life of the Clans." Hours are weekdays, 9 a.m. to 5 p.m.

West of the river rises the wooded hill of **Tomnahurich**, known as "the hill of the fairies." It is now a cemetery, and from here the views are magnificent.

In the Ness are wooded islands, linked to Inverness by suspension bridges and turned into parks.

From Inverness, you can visit **Culloden Battlefield**, six miles to the east. This is the spot where Bonnie Prince Charlie and the Jacobite army were finally crushed at the battle on April 16, 1746. A cairn marks the site on Drummossie Moor where the battle raged. **Leanach Cottage**, around which the battle took place, still stands and was inhabited until 1912. A path from the cottage leads through the Field of the English, where 76 men of the Duke of Cumberland's forces who died during the battle are said to be buried. Features of interest include the **Graves of the Clans**, communal burial places with simple stones bearing individual clan names alongside the main road and through the woodland; the great memorial cairn, erected in 1881; the **Well of the Dead**, a single stone with the inscription: "The English Were Buried Here"; and the huge **Cumberland Stone** from which the victorious "Butcher" Cumberland is said to have reviewed the scene. The battle lasted only 40 minutes; the prince's army lost some 1200 men out of 5000 and the king's army 310. A visitors' center and museum are open all year.

Between Inverness and Nairn, also about six miles to the east of Inverness, are the **Stones of Clava,** one of the most important prehistoric monuments in the north. These cairns and standing stones are from the Bronze Age.

Back in Inverness, we'll investigate—

Food and Lodging

Culloden House, at Culloden Moor, six miles from Inverness (tel. Culloden Moor 461), is a Georgian mansion with extensive gardens and parkland. It stands on the ruins of the Renaissance castle in which Bonnie Prince Charlie

SCOTLAND: INVERNESS

slept the night before the last great battle on British soil, the Battle of Culloden. Superbly isolated, it is perfect for a relaxed Highland holiday. Public rooms, furnished in the grand style, are suitably spacious and comfortable. The bedrooms are cheerful, cozy, and agreeably furnished. All 21 of them contain private baths. Depending on your room assignment, singles pay from £38 ($87.40); doubles, from £45 ($103.50) to £60 ($138), the latter double tariff for a suite—plus service and VAT.

The hotel maintains pleasantly traditional ideas of personal service. The food, in our opinion, is of exceptional quality, and it's served against an impressive backdrop of refinement and elegance. Simple and complex dishes are virtually flawless, and the finest of fresh local ingredients are used. Ordering à la carte, expect to pay about £15 ($34.50) per person.

Station Hotel, Academy Street (tel. Inverness 31926), adjacent to the railway station, offers a high standard of first-class service, comfortable accommodations, and well-prepared food. The occupants of those baronial Highland mansions like to stop here when they're in Inverness on shopping or social expeditions, gathering for somewhat lively chats in the conservatory lounge, there ordering their tea and scones. Grandly Victorian, the bedrooms are tastefully decorated and welcoming, costing from £25 ($57.50) to £30 ($69) in a single, from £35 ($80.50) to £43 ($98.90) in a double. The majority of rooms contain fully equipped private baths.

The dining room is one of the finest in Inverness, serving good-quality Scottish dishes, plus some excellently cooked continental favorites. Courteous waiters create a friendly atmosphere. Lunch is served from 12:30 to 2 p.m. and dinner from 7 to 9 p.m. A table d'hôte evening meal costs £6.50 ($14.95), but expect to pay £15 ($34.50) if you're ordering à la carte, sampling the French specialties.

Dunain Park, 2½ miles southwest of Inverness (tel. Inverness 30512), stands in six acres of garden and woods, between Loch Ness and Inverness. This 18th-century house was opened as a hotel in 1974, and is furnished with fine antiques, china, and clocks, allowing it to retain its atmosphere of a private country house. Although Dunain Park was won its fame mainly as a restaurant, it does offer six bedrooms, four of which contain private baths and one of which has an antique four-poster bed. The rates range from £25 ($57.50) to £40 ($92) in a double or twin, plus VAT and service. A host of thoughtful details and pretty, soft furnishings have gone into the bedrooms. The breakfast served here is exceptional—in fact, the homemade marmalade was the best we've ever tasted, and you can buy some to take with you.

You can order a simple lunch (in the garden, if you prefer). Snack meals are served from 12:30 to 1:30 p.m. But it is at dinner that the chef really delivers, offering a set meal for about £14 ($32.20), fully inclusive. This menu changes daily, depending on the availability of high-quality produce, fish, and meat. The chicken with ginger and honey and cod's-roe pâté are particular favorites. The restaurant and hotel are closed from mid-November until mid-March.

Kingsmills Hotel, Damfield Road (tel. Inverness 37166), is an 18th-century house of much charm that lies only a mile from the center of Inverness. Once a private mansion, it stands adjacent to an 18-hole golf course, and the hotel has its own private squash courts. Angus and Lillian MacLeod have carefully maintained a country-house atmosphere, with a small, pleasantly informal, and most hospitable Highland staff. They've added a modern wing of rooms with twin beds, each with private bath and color TV. Well-fitted bed-sitting rooms and large family rooms are available. You can get a bathless single here in low season for £22.50 ($51.75), although expect to pay £28

($64.40) for a single with bath in high season. The low-season bathless double rate is also £28 ($64.40), that tariff rising to £38 ($87.40) in high season for a double with bath, these prices including a full breakfast, service, and VAT. The food is good and pleasantly served, dinner offered nightly from 7 to 9 p.m., costing from £7.75 ($17.83). The fish dishes always taste exceptionally fresh. In addition, bar lunches feature the usual array of items, and a large Sunday lunch with a roast costs from £4.75 ($10.93). Centrally heated, the hotel remains open all year.

Mercury Motor Inn, Nairn Road, at the junction of the A9 and the A96 (tel. Inverness 39666), is without surprises, each uniform room well furnished with a high degree of comfort, an ideal center for those who want to tour the Highlands. Accommodations come with private baths, toilets, color TV, radio, and tea-or coffee-making facilities. In all, 84 rooms are offered, ranging in price from £20 ($46) to £26 ($59.80) in a single from £30 ($69) to £38 ($87.40) in a double. Breakfast is extra. The inn offers a conically shaped grill and two fully licensed bars. There's even a garden.

Glen Mhor, 10 Ness Bank (tel. Inverness 34308), looks out onto the River Ness. A house of gables and bay windows, it is a hospitable, family-run hotel with an enduring charm in spite of its creaky quality. From many of the individually styled bedrooms, you have views of the river. The staff is informal and friendly. The hotel offers seven single rooms and 20 doubles. The bed-and-breakfast rate in a single is £18 ($41.40), rising to £22 ($50.60) in a double. The bed, breakfast, and dinner tariff is £24 ($55.20) per person. The hotel is a good center for angling, horseback riding, and hunting.

Redcliffe, 1 Gordon Terrace (tel. Inverness 32767), is a small hotel set on its own grounds, commanding a peaceful perch above the Ness and the castle, yet lying within a three-minute walk of the main shopping district. Your hosts, Mr. and Mrs. West, have completely modernized the interior, but have kept the traditional stone facade intact. The bedrooms are pleasantly decorated and have hot and cold running water. The bed-and-breakfast rate is £10.50 ($24.15) per person, increasing to £12 ($27.60) if you request a private bath. VAT is extra. In a spacious, comfortable lounge, guests gather to watch TV. At the hotel is a permanent exhibition of the work of local artists, with all works for sale. The hotel also serves excellent Highland dinners with pheasant, haggis, venison, and salmon (the latter should be requested in advance when making a reservation). Our latest à la carte meal, including coffee later in the lounge, cost about £6.50 ($14.95) per person.

In the Environs

North of Inverness is a fertile peninsula known as the **Black Isle** because it is seldom whitened by snow. Here tropical plants flourish, and **Cromarty,** at the northeast tip, has fine sandy beaches. The cottage there where Hugh Miller, noted geologist, was born in 1802 is now a geological museum. **Fortrose,** an ancient town facing the Moray Firth, has a sheltered bay for yachting.

Dingwall is a town in Easter Ross district near the mouth of the River Conon. The town arms, a starfish, are displayed on the tolbooth (originally a booth for collecting tolls), dating from 1730. In front of this is the shaft of a former Mercat Cross, and beside it is an iron gate of the old town jail.

Strathpeffer, about six miles west of Dingwall, is a good center for touring Easter Ross, where the countryside is dominated by the 3433-foot summit of Ben Wyvis. If you'd like to stop over, we have the following recommendation:

Rosslyn Lodge (tel. Strathpeffer 281) is a stone hotel dating from 1898 and standing on its own well-maintained grounds. Family run, it is personally supervised by the MacLeods. Comfort, good food, and a friendly atmosphere attract clients to its 15 well-furnished bedrooms, each with hot and cold running water. A reader, G. O. Beckwith of Mount Waverley, Australia, wrote: "Deathly quiet, tremendously respectable, and with a somewhat older clientele—it was hard to believe it wasn't 1920." Bed and breakfast are provided for £8.50 ($19.55) per person, including VAT. One of the owners, Patricia MacLeod, does the cooking, serving local game and meat produce whenever possible, and vegetables fresh from the garden. Dinner is £5 ($11.50).

Heading back toward Inverness, an interesting stop is at **Beauly**, 12 miles west of the city, where you can visit the ruins of a Valliscaulian priory built in 1230. On the south bank of the River Beauly southwest of the town is **Beaufort Castle,** a 19th-century baronial mansion which is the seat of the Frasers of Lovat whose ancestor was the "Lovat of the Forty-five." The original seat of the Lovats was Castle Dounie, built about 1400, but it was destroyed by "Butcher" Cumberland after his victory at Culloden.

ULLAPOOL: Northwest of Inverness, on an arm of the sea called Loch Broom, the little town of Ullapool is an embarkation point for travelers crossing The Minch, a section of the North Atlantic separating Scotland from the Outer Hebrides. The road from Inverness takes you through the wild Northwest Highlands, and a car-ferry from Ullapool will deposit you in Stornaway on Lewis, one of the Western Isles.

Altanaharrie Inn, at Ullapool, Wester Ross (tel. Dundonnell 230), is one of those places that you feel you should not tell anyone about, as it is small (only three bedrooms). But it is one of those places which calls for inclusion because of its uniqueness and total integration into the life of the region. The Altanaharrie was once a drovers' inn on the banks of Loch Broom. There is no access by road so guests are brought over the loch by private launch. Tell them what time you are arriving at Ullapool, and they'll come and meet you.

Once you're landed, Fred Brown greets you with a warm log fire in a bar for a dram before dinner which is likely to consist of locally caught seafood. Much meat, local venison, and fish such as trout and lobster are obtained locally. They make their own bread, and they like to know beforehand if you are eating "in" so that they can cater accordingly.

Overnight will cost you £20 ($46) per person in winter, including dinner, VAT, and breakfast, £25 ($57.50) per person in summer.

Fred also has canoes and small dinghies available free, or else motorized dinghies and sailing craft for rent at £10 ($23) a day. He also operates Summer Isles Charters for cruising among the offshore islands or, for the more ambitious, to Skye or the Outer Hebrides, with or without skipper. This is a serious business, and you should write to Fred before you embark on such a venture, giving details of your experience. Otherwise he may not let you take a boat out.

NAIRN: A favorite family seaside resort on the sheltered Moray Firth, Nairn is a royal burgh, lying at the mouth of the Nairn River. Its fishing harbor was constructed in 1820, and golf has been played here since 1672, as it still is today. A large uncrowded beach, tennis, and angling draw a horde of middle-class vacationers in summer.

At **Cawdor Castle,** to the south of Nairn, you encounter 600 years of Highland history. Since the early 14th century it's been the home of the Thanes of Cawdor. The castle has all the architectural ingredients you associate with the medieval: a drawbridge, an ancient tower (this one built around a tree), and fortified walls. The severity is softened by the handsome gardens, flowers, trees, and rolling lawns. As we mentioned earlier, even the Scots can't agree as to where Macbeth, who actually was made Thane of Cawdor by King Duncan, committed his foul deed of murdering the king—at Cawdor or in the castle which once stood on Auld Castlehill in Inverness, if at all. The castle is open to the public from 10 a.m. to 5:30 p.m. every day from May 1 to September 30. Admission is £1.25 ($2.88) for adults, 70p ($1.61) for children. It's a member of "The Grand Tour of Scotland" group of Historic Houses.

Food and Lodging

Clifton, Viewfield Street (tel. Nairn 53119), reflects the dynamic personality of J. Gordon MacIntyre, the owner of this battleship-gray, vine-covered Victorian mansion. The Clifton has been owned by the same family longer than any other hotel in Nairn. Fully licensed, it stands on the seafront, three minutes from the beach and golf links.

Both Mr. and Mrs. MacIntyre have spent a lot of time, trouble, and money in decorating the house, often with interesting prints, and in selecting the furnishings, as exemplified by the Clifton's old-fashioned parlor. The bedrooms do not have the same appeal, though. For example, those on the first floor are better equipped, each pleasantly appointed, while those on the second floor are more spartan, yet the view from this higher perch seems to compensate. Singles rent for £14.50 ($33.35), doubles from £28 ($64.40). Musical and theatrical performances are often staged here.

The Clifton also serves the best food in Nairn, and you're allowed to take as much as you want from an artistically presented array of appetizers, including mousses and terrines. The cooking is often in the hearty Highland tradition—that is, game pie, pigeons in wine, lamb in a mustard sauce—although French specialties also tempt. The bar serves snacks at lunchtime. Dinner hours are from 7 to 9:30, when an à la carte order is likely to run between £6 ($13.80) and £8.50 ($19.55). Bar snacks at lunchtime go for around £2.50 ($5.75) for an ample plateful. The hotel and restaurant are shuttered from November until February.

Newton, Inverness Road (tel. Nairn 53144), a castle-like hotel, stands just outside town in an attractive park of 35 acres, offering views across sweeping lawns and the golf course to the sea. Considered one of the finest of the "manor house" hotels of Scotland, it is spacious and sumptuous, drawing a clientele likely to include everybody from a prime minister to a Glasgow industrialist. Prices have a pedigree, too: from £31 ($71.30) per person for bed and breakfast. The public rooms are furnished with taste, and the Moray Firth, viewed on a day when the sun is shining brightly, forms a spectacle of beauty from many of the Newton's windows. The bedrooms have many fine appointments—sedate, comfortable, although unpretentious. All 34 of them contain private baths. There is a high standard of maintenance and personal service.

The **Windsor Hotel,** Albert Street (tel. Nairn 53108), is a fine sandstone building which has been renovated and refurbished to good effect. The resident proprietors, Mr. and Mrs. Charles Woolley, see to it that the hotel provides a comfortable family atmosphere and first-class cuisine. The hotel is centrally heated, and each bedroom contains its own basin with hot and cold running water. There are numerous bathrooms, showers, and toilets throughout the hotel. The color TV lounge, residents' lounge, and fully licensed cocktail bar add to the guests' enjoyment. Daily rates for bed and breakfast are £12.35 ($28.41) to £14.65 ($33.70) per person in high season, slightly lower in low season. Special rates are allowed for children. Dinner costs £6.75 ($15.53). The hotel is close to centers of transportation and sports facilities. It is open all year.

DRUMNADROCHIT: This pleasant little hamlet lies about a mile from Loch Ness at the entrance to Glen Urquhart. The ruined **Urquhart Castle,** one of Scotland's largest castles, is a mile and a half southeast on a promontory overlooking Loch Ness. The chief of Clan Grant owned the castle in 1509, and most of the existing building dates from that period. In 1692, the castle was blown up by the Grants to prevent its becoming a Jacobite stronghold. It is here at Urquhart Castle that sightings of the Loch Ness monster are most often reported.

In the vicinity stands the **Lewiston Arms,** Lewiston, near Drumnadrochit (tel. Drumnadrochit 225), an old whitewashed coaching inn, lying just off the principal road in the village of Lewiston. Many motorists prefer to stop off here instead of going on to Inverness. The inn offers only one single and seven doubles, none with private bath. The tariffs are £10 ($23) in a single, £18 ($41.40) in a double. You might ask for the dinner, bed, and breakfast rate of £16 ($36.80) per person. Bedrooms are simply but adequately furnished. Outside is an attractive garden. In all, it's a good center for exploring the Loch Ness district. The place is owned and run by Nicholas and Helen Quinn, a team with a spotless little inn off the fast A82, right beside the castle.

FORT AUGUSTUS: This Highland touring center stands at the head (the southernmost end) of Loch Ness. The town took its name from a fort named for the Duke of Cumberland. Built after the 1715 Rising, the present Benedictine Abbey stands on its site.

In accommodations, it offers the **Inchnacardoch Lodge** (tel. Fort Augustus 6258), a family-run, two-star hotel in a beautiful setting overlooking Loch Ness. From one of the bedroom windows, you can monster-watch. The old-fashioned house of many gables offers comfortable and well-equipped bedrooms, charging £12 ($27.60) to £15 ($34.50) per person, including a full breakfast, service, and VAT. None of the rooms contains a private bath, however. You can enjoy mellow scotch whiskey in the lounge bar and then succulent Scottish steak in the fully licensed Highland restaurant, where a dinner with some choices averages about £6 ($13.80). Open all year, the hotel is owned and run by a former London architect, Alan Anderson, and his wife, Val, who enjoy meeting their guests as much as they hope their guests enjoy their stay.

INVERGARRY: A Highland center for fishing and deer stalking, Invergarry is noted for its fine scenery. It, too, is a good center for exploring Glen More and Loch Ness. At Invergarry is the beginning of the road through the West Highland glens and mountains, forming one famous "Road to the Isles" that terminates at Kyle of Lochalsh.

Near Invergarry, you can visit the **Well of the Heads,** on the west side of Loch Oich near its southern tip, erected in 1812 by MacDonnell of Glengarry to commemorate the decapitation by the family bard of seven brothers who had murdered the two sons of a 17th-century chief of Clan Keppoch, a branch of the MacDonnell Clan. The seven heads were washed in the well before being presented to the chief of the MacDonnells at Glengarry.

The **Glengarry Castle Hotel,** at Invergarry (tel. 254), stands on the River Garry, which runs into Loch Oich. The castle hotel is privately owned and run by Mr. and Mrs. MacCallum and Mrs. Paterson. Their 100-year-old house lies on extensive grounds and has recently been modernized to provide comfort to the passerby or to be pleasant base for a week or so of country holiday with fishing, tennis, walking, and rowing. On the grounds are the ruins of **Glengarry Castle,** the historic seat of the MacDonnells.

There are two spacious lounges where drinks can be served to residents, and the dining room offers excellent meals made from local produce. They charge £12 ($27.60) per person in a bathless room, £13.70 ($31.51) per person with bath. Lunch costs from £4.25 ($10.93); dinner, from £5.25 ($12.08); and tariffs quoted include VAT and service.

SPEAN BRIDGE: This village is a busy intersection of the Fort William-Perth and Fort William-Inverness roads, as well as having daily train service to Fort William, Glasgow, and London, and bus service to Inverness and Fort William. Two miles outside the town, in Glen Spean, is the striking **Commando Memorial** by Scott Sutherland which the Queen Mother unveiled in 1952. In this area many commandos were trained during World War II. Numerous war movies have been filmed here.

On the outskirts of the village on the A86 going toward Newtonmore and Perth is **Coire Glas** (tel. Spean Bridge 272), a motel-style guest house with 15 bedrooms. Mr. and Mrs. MacFarlane have added onto the back of their one-story home, to come up with an attractive and convenient place for visitors to stay overnight or for long periods. All the rooms are equipped with hot and cold running water, and ample bathroom facilities are provided. The MacFarlanes charge £6.75 ($15.53) per person per night for bed and breakfast. Dinner is £4 ($9.20). A lunch will be packed for you upon request. Spean Bridge is a central area for touring the loch country, and from Coire Glas, looking across a wide, grassy lawn, you can see Ben Gurry, which is a part of the Ben Nevis range.

10. Fort William and Lochaber

Fort William, the capital of Lochaber, is the major touring center for the western Highlands. Wildly beautiful Lochaber, the area around Fort William, has been called "the land of bens, glens, and heroes."

Dominating the area is **Ben Nevis,** Britain's highest mountain, rising 4418 feet. In summer when it's clear of snow, there's a safe path to the summit. Fort William stands on the site of a fort built by General Monk in 1655, which was pulled down to make way for the railroad. This district is the western end of what is known as Glen Mor—the Great Glen, geologically a fissure which divides the northwest of Scotland from the southeast and contains Loch Lochy, Loch Oich, and Loch Ness. The Caledonian Canal, opened in 1847, linked these lochs, the River Ness, and Moray Firth. It provided sailing boats a safe alternative to the stormy route around the north of Scotland. Larger steamships made the canal out of date commercially, but fishing boats and pleasure steamers still use it. Good roads run the length of the Great Glen, partly following the line of General Wade's military road. From Fort William you can take steamer trips to Staffa and Iona.

The ruins of **Old Inverlochy Castle,** scene of the famous battle in 1645, can be reached by driving on the A82 two miles north of Fort William. At a point just one mile north of Fort William is **Glen Nevis,** one of the most beautiful in Scotland.

About 15 miles west of Fort William, on the A830 toward Mallaig, at Glenfinnan at the head of Loch Shiel is the **Glenfinnan Monument,** which marks the spot where Bonnie Prince Charlie unfurled his proud red-and-white silk banner on August 19, 1745, in the ill-fated attempt to restore the Stuarts to the British throne. The monument is topped by the figure of a kilted Highlander. At a new Visitors' Centre one may learn of the prince's campaign from Glenfinnan to Derby and back to the final defeat at Culloden.

FORT WILLIAM: The name evokes redcoats billeted in rough barracks to keep the Highlanders of Lochaber under control. Fort William today is a busy tourist town on the shores of Loch Linnhe. Although it stands in the shadow of Ben Nevis, the mountain can't be seen from town. While the town is most often used as a touring center, in Fort William itself you can visit the **West Highland Museum,** on Cameron Square, containing all aspects of local history, expecially the 1745 Jacobite rising, plus sections on tartans and folk life. The museum is open Monday to Saturday, September to June, from 9:30 a.m. to 1 p.m. and from 2 to 5 p.m.; in July and August its hours are from 9:30 a.m. to 9 p.m. Admission costs 20p (46¢) for adults, 10p (23¢) for children.

Where to Stay

In Fort William, we'd recommend the following accommodations, beginning first with a deluxe suggestion:

Inverlochy Castle (tel. Fort William 2177) is another one of the places where Queen Victoria stayed. In her time it was newly built (1863), a Scottish baronial mansion belonging to Lord Abinger. The monarch claimed in her diary, "I never saw a lovelier or more romantic spot." We do not wish to detract from that long-ago sentiment. In fact, Inverlochy Castle today remains one of the premier places of Scotland for food and accommodations.

Against the scenic backdrop of Ben Nevis, the castle hotel has a mood inside of elegance and refinement, luxurious appointments and antiques, artwork and crystal, plus a profusion of flowers. Danish-born Mrs. Hobbs, the owner, is a delight, equally at home in welcoming a prime minister or an American couple from the Midwest.

Only 14 bedrooms, each with private bath, are offered, and all of them are beautifully furnished. The prices reflect the opulence, however—from £50 ($115) in a single, from £70 ($161) in a double, plus VAT and service, which can run up the tab considerably, of course.

The cuisine is one of the finest in all of Scotland. Every dish emerging from the kitchen of Miss Mary Shaw is cooked to order and served on silver platters. Sparkling crystal and fine china are placed on hand-carved polished tables where the fortunate guests enjoy such fare as salmon from the Spean or crayfish from Loch Linnhe, even produce from the hotel's own garden. Miss Shaw is a natural-born cook, an unusually gifted one at that, adding a creative touch to food yet instinctively preserving its natural flavor. Her orange soufflé Grand Marnier makes for spectacular dining. Only dinner is served, and reservations are mandatory. It is likely you'll spend about £17 ($39.10) per person, plus tax and service charge, before leaving the table a most satisfied diner. The hotel and restaurant are closed from mid-November to March.

Alexandra (tel. Fort William 2241) is a familiar sight, a hotel with tall gables and formidable granite walls, so common in this part of the Highlands. But the hotel is no antiquated mansion—rather, it has been completely modernized, offering 76 double rooms and 11 singles that are pleasantly and attractively furnished. The per-person rate in a bathless double or twin is £16.80 ($38.64), rising to £20.80 ($47.84) in a double or twin with bath, with dinner costing another £8.50 ($19.55). Service and housekeeping standards are good. The chef makes excellent use of fresh fish, and the wine cellar is amply endowed. The vegetables are simply cooked with enjoyable results.

Croit Anna (tel. Fort William 2268) lies on the A82, the Inverness-Glasgow Road, 2½ miles southwest of Fort William. Somewhat like a Scottish motel, it commands views of loch and hills. Croit Anna is a good-size establishment, containing a total of 115 bedrooms, and is owned and run by the same Watt family which designed and built it on a croft that was in the family's possession for more than 250 years. At present it's run by Mr. Watt's married daughter, Elizabeth Morgan, and her family. The rooms are pleasant, the service competent. Don't come here expecting luxury, just a good "average standard."

In the low season, a single without bath costs £15 ($34.50), rising to £26 ($59.80) in a double. The high-season rate in a single with bath is £19 ($43.70), rising to £35 ($80.50) in a double, including a full breakfast, VAT, and service.

Open all year, the hotel offers a large dining room serving good food, plus a lounge bar, a resident's lounge, and even a first-floor panoramic lounge with a dance floor. A set dinner costs £7 ($16.10), although a four-course à la carte meal is likely to run about £9 ($20.70).

Where to Dine

Like its counterpart in Oban, **McTavish's Kitchen** and the **Tweeddale Restaurant**, under the same management, on the High Street (tel. Fort William 2406), is dedicated to preserving the hearty Scottish cuisine. The kitchen is a self-service cafeteria, which is open from mid-May until the end of October. Light meals are served throughout the day and evening. A homemade soup of the day is offered, although you may prefer poacher's broth or even pheasant consommé with burgundy. Main courses include Scottish crab with hot cheese and smoked salmon with chips and brown bread. Smoked fish, traditionally cooked in milk, is always featured. You can dine well for around £4 ($9.20).

If you'd prefer waitress service, try the Tweeddale, but first have a drink at the adjoining Laird's Bar, a snug tavern with photographs of a Scottish laird. The licensed restaurant is open from mid-May until the end of September, seven days a week. Specialties include haggis and neeps, Scotland's national dish, at £2 ($4.60); Loch Fyne kippers (smoked herring), £3.50 ($8.05) for two; Scottish crab with hot cheese sauce and duchesse potatoes, £4.50 ($10.35, when available); and a deep-dish apple pie with thick cream, 65p ($1.50).

A feature of the restaurant is folk cabaret, offered Easter and every evening from mid-May until the end of September from 9 to 11 p.m., with singers, a piper, and a Highland dancer. Children are welcome. Admission is £1.05 ($2.42) for adults, 60p ($1.38) for children.

ONICH: On the shores of Loch Linnhe, this charming little village lies to the north of the Ballachulish Bridge. It's a good center if you're taking the western route to Inverness, or going to Skye and Fort William. Our favorite hotels in the area follow.

Creagdhu Hotel (tel. Onich 238) was once the country home of Lady McPherson and takes its name from the rallying cry of her clan. Now a family-run hotel, it lies between Ben Nevis and Glencoe, with expansive lochside and mountain views. The loch views are of prawn-filled Linnhe and Leven.

Creagdhu is an imposing country home with modern additions; the hotel is congenial without being luxurious. More than half the rooms contain private baths. Rates range from £12 ($27.60) per person in low season to £15 ($34.50) per person in high season, plus another £2 ($4.60) supplement for each room with a private bath. The half-board rate runs from £18 ($41.40) per person in low season to £22 ($50.60) in high season, including a full breakfast, service, and VAT. Receiving guests from April to October, the hotel has a loyal repeat clientele.

Onich Hotel (tel. Onich 214) is handsomely perched on the shores of Loch Linnhe, commanding views of the Ardgour and Glencoe Mountains and the Firth of Lorne. Its gardens slope down to the water. Under family management, the hotel definitely reflects a personal touch, both in its welcome of real Highland hospitality and in the appointments of its bedrooms and lounges. The hotel is owned by Ian and Ronald Young, brothers who have run the inn since 1964. They have a very loyal band of guests who return over and over again. Their cookery enjoys a good reputation for its consistency. Ronald cooks, incidentally, and Ian looks after the administration of the hotel. The bright, airy bedrooms have been modernized—25 in all, renting for £11.50 ($26.45) per person for bed and breakfast. The bed, breakfast, and evening meal rate is £18 ($41.40) per person. Rooms do not contain private baths, however. The hotel attracts the athletic-minded, as it's a center for walking, climbing, loch bathing, putting, fishing, sailing, and pony-trekking. The cuisine is of a good standard, backed up by a fine wine list. Guests gather either in the Clan cocktail bar or the Deerstalker lounge bar. The hotel is open only from April to October.

Allt-Nan-Ross (tel. Onich 210) is a family hotel which draws a faithful coterie to its hospitality, good food, and old-fashioned comfort. A Scottish house of many gables and chimneys, the hotel has a cheery, bright aura. Over the years it's been considerably improved and brought up to date from what it was when we first stopped by years ago. The sun lounge on a fair day is a magnet for guests, and is attractively furnished. The hotel stands on ample grounds, with views south across the loch to the hills. Don't expect a private bath in the pleasant but simply furnished rooms. The bed, breakfast, and dinner rate is £14 ($32.20) per person nightly. There is ample parking, plus a putting green and a sheltered garden. Guests are accepted from April to October.

BALLACHULISH: This small village enjoys a splendid scenic position on the shores of Loch Leven at the entrance to Glencoe. The Ballachulish Bridge now links North and South Ballachulish. A good center for touring the Western Highlands, the village has the following recommended hotel:

Ballachulish Hotel (tel. Ballachulish 239) stands right on the shores of Loch Leven, at the point where hills split Leven from Loch Linnhe. Built in the style of a Scottish manor house, it offers hospitality, warmth, relaxation—just what you're seeking in a Highland hotel. The bedrooms have a high standard of comfort and convenience, although they vary considerably in style and plumbing. The bed-and-breakfast rate ranges from £14.50 ($33.35) to £16.50 ($37.95) per person nightly, inclusive of VAT and service. Half-board rates, ranging from £18.50 ($42.55) to £20.50 ($47.15), are quoted for a stay of four nights or more. Receiving guests from April to October, the hotel also serves good food, handsomely presented, with fresh ingredients. Residents from nearby gather in the hotel's bars, mingling with foreign visitors, and by that we mean the English. From the windows of the hotel you can look out onto views of hill and loch. The staff will arrange boat trips on the lochs or else fishing expeditions.

GLENCOE: On the shores of Loch Leven, near where it joins Loch Linnhe, the Ballachulish Bridge now links the villages of North and South Ballachulish, at the entrance to Glencoe. The bridge saves a long drive to the head of the loch if you are coming from the north, but many visitors enjoy the scenic drive to Kinlochleven to come upon the wild and celebrated Glencoe from the east.

Glencoe runs from Rannoch Moor to Loch Leven between some magnificent mountains, including 3766-foot Bidean nam Bian. Known as the "Glen of Weeping," Glencoe is where, on February 13, 1692, Campbells massacred MacDonalds—men, women and children—who had been their hosts for 12 days. Although massacres were not uncommon in those times, this one shocked even the Highlanders because of the breach of hospitality. When the killing was done, the crime of "murder under trust" was regarded by law as an aggravated form of murder, and carried the same penalties as treason.

The glen, much of which now belongs to the Scottish National Trust, is full of history and legend. A tiny lochan is known as "the pool of blood" because by its side some men are said to have quarreled over a piece of cheese, and all were killed.

This is an area of massive splendor, with towering peaks and mysterious glens where you can well imagine the fierce battle among the kilted Highlanders to the skirl of the pipes and the beat of the drums.

Splurge into History

Almost where Glen Etive joins Glencoe, under the jagged peak of Buchaille Etive Mor dominating the road (A82), lies the **King's House Hotel** (tel. King's House 259), several miles from the village of Glencoe. A building has stood here since the time of the Jacobite Rising of 1745, when it was required to accommodate troops on their way south from Fort William. It is now a center for skiing and attracts thousands from far and near.

Believed to be the oldest licensed inn in Scotland, **King's House Hotel** has now been enlarged and modernized by its present laird, Robin Fleming of Black Mount. Provided are warm, well-furnished rooms, many with private baths, and, of course, views of the majestic scenery. The lounge, too, has views, and the dining room relies on a lot of good fresh produce for its appetizing meals. There is a fine wine cellar, plus a bar. Such pleasant amenities as a drying room are provided for those who want to walk, fish, or go climbing. The charge is £13 ($29.90) a night for bed and breakfast, going up to £14 ($32.20) for those requesting a private bath. Dinner is from £7 ($16.10), and the staff will provide an excellent packed lunch for £1.75 ($4.03).

A ski lift is almost opposite the hotel. The Buachaille Etive Mor guards Glencoe's eastern end. This mountain provides a challenge for climbers and was the training ground for Sir John Hunt and the party he took to the top of Everest in Coronation year. This is great climbing and walking country, and rescue techniques evolved and taught here have been widely used.

Besides access from the Glasgow–Inverness highway, guests at the King's House Hotel can be met at the Bridge of Orchy railway station by arrangement. **Glen Orchy,** to the south, is well worth a visit, too, with the wild river and mountain scenery being beautiful and photogenic. It was the birthplace of the Gaelic bard Duncan Ban MacIntyre, whose song, "In Praise of Ben Doran," is considered a masterpiece.

In Glencoe Village

As you turn away from Loch Leven to enter the historic glen, you will find a number of accommodations available in the village of Glencoe, including—

Glencoe Hotel (tel. Ballachulish 245) is a spruce and stucco building with a slate mansard roof, dominating its area. In the hotel itself are 14 rooms, including one with a double bed and a private bathroom, one twin-bedded with a private bath, while the other doubles, twins, and singles have hot and cold running water. A bungalow annex contains an additional five bedrooms. The hotel charges £13 ($29.90) per person for bed and breakfast in a room in the main building, £12 ($27.60) in the annex. Lunch costs from £3.50 ($8.05); dinner, from £5 ($11.50). VAT is included in all charges. The hotel is open all year.

MALLAIG: This small fishing village is a good touring center for the Western Highlands and the islands. Steamers call here for the Kyle of Lochalsh, the Isle of Skye, the Outer Hebrides, and the sea lochs of the northwest coast. At the tip of a peninsula, Mallaig itself is a busting little fishing village, and it is surrounded by moody lochs and hills. The distance between Morar and Mallaig is just three miles.

In the village you can find food and lodging at the **West Highland Hotel** (tel. Mallaig 2210), Mallaig's major hotel, situated above the port, its bedroom windows looking upon the harbor and the Isle of Skye. The hotel is antiquated, but it offers good old-fashioned comfort and pleasant Highland hospitality. Only a handful of rooms contain private baths, however. Depending on room assignment, singles rent for £14.50 ($33.35) to £18.50 ($42.55), doubles for £23 ($52.90) to £33 ($75.90), including breakfast. The bed, breakfast, and evening meal rate is £22.50 ($51.75) to £25 ($57.50) per person. The hotel is open from May to September.

Less expensive is the **Marine Hotel** (tel. Mallaig 2217), a family-owned operation which is about to pass to the third generation. The hotel has been brought up to date, offering rooms with ordinary bedroom facilities, hot and cold running water in all rooms, heaters, shaving points, and tea- and coffee-making facilities. The cost is £11 ($25.30) in a single, £18 ($41.40) in a double, although you'll pay £2 ($4.60) extra for a private bath. Unlike the West Highland, the Marine is open all year. There is a small garden below. The location is above shops and a bank.

11. Kyle of Lochalsh and Skye

From the Kyle of Lochalsh you can take a ferry to the mystical Isle of Skye, off the northwest coast of Scotland. The island has inspired many of the best loved and best known of Scottish ballads such as "Over the Sea to Skye" and "Will Ye Not Come Back Again." On the 48-mile-long island, you can explore castle ruins, duns, and brochs, enjoying a Highland welcome. For the Scots, the island will forever evoke images of Flora Macdonald, who conducted Bonnie Prince Charlie to Skye. She disguised him as Betty Burke after the Culloden defeat.

Once on Skye, you'll find ferry service back to Kyle or to Mallaig from Armadale. The Armadale ferry transports cars, but the service is less frequent than the one to Kyle. If you're planning to take your car, reservations are recommended.

Caledonian MacBrayne, The Pier, Gourock, near Glasgow (tel. Gourock 33950), runs ferry services to Skye, as well as to Mull and the Shetland Islands.

The company also offers inclusive tours for people and cars to "island-hop," using their services between islands. This is an ideal opportunity to visit places well away from the beaten track. The information office at Gourock is most helpful, and someone there will assist you in planning a trip if you wish to make up your own journey.

The largest island of the Inner Hebrides, Skye is separated from the mainland by the Sound of Sleat on its southeastern side. At Kyleakin, on the eastern end, the channel is only a quarter of a mile wide and thus the ferry docks there. Dominating the land of summer seas, streams, woodland glens, mountain passes, cliffs, and waterfalls are the Cuillin Hills, a range of jagged black mountains. The Peninsula of Sleat, the island's southernmost arm, is known as "The Garden of Skye."

DORNIE: This small crofting village on the road to the Isle of Skye is the meeting place of three lochs—Duich, Long, and Alsh. On a rocky islet stands **Eilean Donan Castle,** Wester Ross at Dornie, eight miles east of Kyle of Lochalsh on the A87. This romantic castle was built in 1220 as a defense against the Danes. In 1719 it was shelled by the British frigate, *Worcester*. In ruins for 200 years, it was restored by Colonel MacRae of Clan MacRae in 1932 and is now a clan war memorial and museum, containing Jacobite relics, mostly with clan connections. It is open April to September 30—daily, including Sunday, from 10 a.m. to 12:30 p.m. and from 2 to 6 p.m., charging 50p ($1.15) for admission.

South of Dornie and Eilean Donan Castle is Shiel Bridge. From here, an "unclassified road" leads to **Glenelg,** after a twisting climb over Ratagan Pass with a fine view of the mountain range known as the **Five Sisters of Kintail,** which is dominated by Sgurr Fhuaran, 3505 feet high. In summer a car-ferry crosses the Sound of Sleat to Skye. It was from Glenelg that Dr. Johnson and James Boswell crossed to Skye in 1773. In Gleann Beag, two miles to the southeast, stand two of the best preserved Iron Age brochs on the Scottish mainland—**Dun Telve** and **Dun Troddan.** Brochs are stone towers with double walls, probably built more than 2000 years ago by the Picts for protection against raiders. The walls of the two brochs are more than 30 feet high.

Just outside Dornie, across Loch Long and at the end of Loch Duich, is the **Loch Duich Hotel,** Ardelve, near Kyle of Lochalsh (tel. Dornie 213). A long white house, it is set back from the road overlooking fields and then down Loch Duich to Eilean Donan Castle, surely one of the most attractive vistas in the country. In the other direction you'll see the Cuillins on Skye. Mr. and Mrs. Snowie will greet you warmly and show you to your pretty, simply furnished room. Some of the accommodations are tiny and under the eaves. Many have wonderful views of the already-mentioned castle. Bed and breakfast costs £10 ($23) per person.

Downstairs there is a cozy lounge and a dining room where Mrs. Snowie, who does most of the cooking, provides a wonderful breakfast. It's enormous, including, for example, kippers. Dinner costs from £5 ($11.50). Again, you can rely on Mrs. Snowie for a good meal. A luncheon in the dining room will cost £3 ($6.90), a packed lunch from £1.50 ($3.45), all tariffs plus service and VAT. Mr. Snowie runs the bar. Since he used to be in the wine business, he knows what he's talking about. Loch Duich is a thoroughly pleasant and informal place at which to stay.

From Dornie, it is a short drive to the—

SCOTLAND: KYLE OF LOCHALSH/SKYE

KYLE OF LOCHALSH: This popular center for touring the Western Highlands is also a good jumping-off point to the islands. A car-ferry leaves for Kyleakin on the Isle of Skye. There is no need to book in advance. The journey is only ten minutes, costing 25p (58¢) for each person, £2 ($4.60) for a standard car. The ferry shuttles back and forth all day, and you will have plenty of time to drive the length of Skye in a day, returning to the mainland by night if you want to. If that is your intent, you might register at:

Lochalsh Hotel (tel. Kyle 4204), a British Transport hotel, is mainly a place to stay overnight, embracing Scottish scenery of pinewood and moors from its waterside perch. It lies right on the loch, near the ferry—convenience itself. The hotel has been modernized by its owners, who have shown a healthy respect for Scottish tradition. The choice of fabrics and appointments give it a definite Highland flavor. It's important to reserve well in advance because of the hotel's popularity with those on the "Road to the Isles." Rooms with private bath are quite expensive, from £30 ($69) in a single, a peak £50 ($115) in a twin, including breakfast. Economy seekers will request a bathless single at £14 ($32.20) or a bathless twin or double at £23 ($52.90). The food is good, too, and dinner is served from 7 to 10:30 p.m. The dining room is handsomely decorated, its tables overlooking the loch.

BALMACARA: Those planning to stay in the Kyle of Lochalsh district, taking the car and passenger ferry to Skye, may prefer a more remote oasis for a day or two. Near the Balmacara estate, now the property of the National Trust, the **Balmacara Hotel** (tel. Balmacara 283) is a quiet, unassuming choice. On the road along Balmacara Bay, facing the Cuillins of Skye, it has been preferred by many readers, although we personally have not stayed there. Guests are received all year and charged from £10.75 ($24.73) to £12.75 ($29.33) in a single, from £19.50 ($44.85) to £23.50 ($54.05) in a double, including breakfast. An evening meal will cost from £8 ($18.40). A fishing party can be arranged.

ISLE OF SKYE: Skye is the largest of the Inner Hebrides, 48 miles long and between 3 and 25 miles wide. It is separated from the mainland by the Sound of Sleat (pronounced Slate). There are many stories as to the origin of the name, Skye. Some believe it is from the Norse "ski," meaning a cloud, while others say it is from the Gaelic word for winged. There are Norse names on the island, however, as the Norsemen held sway for four centuries before 1263. Overlooking the Kyle is the ruined Castle Maol, once the home of a Norwegian princess.

For those who want to overnight or else spend a longer holiday on the Isle of Skye itself, we offer the following suggestions, scattered in the island's various hamlets. However, in summer be sure to reserve in advance, as accommodations are extremely limited.

Kyleakin

The ferry from Kyle of Lochalsh docks at this tiny waterfront village. For those seeking a quiet, well-kept place to stay, we'd recommend:

Dunringell Hotel (tel. Kyle 4180) sits in 4½ acres of extensive lawns in which rhododendrons, azaleas, and other flowering shrubs provide a riot of color from March to July. Dunringell is a spacious structure, built in 1912, with large bedrooms and public rooms. Mr. and Mrs. MacPherson charge £8 ($18.40) for bed and breakfast per person in high season, £7 ($16.10) in low. For dinner, bed, and breakfast, the tariff is £11.50 ($26.45) in high season,

£10.20 ($23.46) in low. Both a smoking and nonsmoking lounge are maintained for guests. For those who wish to participate, the MacPhersons hold a short worship service in one of the lounges each evening. Some of the bedrooms are in the lodge, a stone building about 100 yards from the main house.

Broadford

This town is the meeting point for the ports of Armadale, Kylerhea, and Kyleakin.

Broadford Hotel (tel. Broadford 204) is a venerated old inn dating from 1611, when it was established by Sir Lauchlin MacKinnon. It was here that a descendant of his first came up with the secret recipe for Drambuie liqueur, now a symbol throughout the world of Highland hospitality.

The Broadford has seen a lot of changes since those days, and it's been completely modernized and brought up to date, both in its bedrooms and public facilities. The inn lies by the waters of Broadford River, and guests are allowed to fish for salmon and trout. If you'd like this congenial center for exploring the southern part of Skye, you can request a double room for £34 ($78.20) or a single for £19 ($43.70). Rooms are comfortable, and unpretentious.

The old inn offers good Scottish cooking, making fine use of the local produce. You can stop in for a drink in the cocktail bar. The inn lies four minutes from the Skye airfield, where there is direct daily service to Glasgow. Nearby are the famous ruins of the farmhouse where Samuel Johnson and his companion, Boswell, spent a night on their tour of the Highlands.

Sligachan

Sligachan Hotel (tel. Sligachan 204) stands in the middle of the island on its own moorland at the head of a beautiful loch, affording views of water and hills. As such, the hotel is the most convenient center from which to explore the entire island. Climbers who love "to go up in the heather" book its 23 simply furnished bedrooms, only nine of which contain private baths. From April to October, they cost from £16 ($36.80) to £17.50 ($40.25), including a big Scottish breakfast that often features kippers and porridge. The meals are excellent, comprising, for example, homemade soups, steak-and-kidney pie with a flaky crust, salmon, followed by fresh fruit and cream, ending with good coffee. A complete dinner costs from £9.20 ($21.16). At Sligachan guests in their classic tweeds (which have been well broken in) mingle freely in good companionship, and the talk is of fishing for trout and salmon and of motorboat excursions through the Outer Hebrides.

Portree

Skye's capital, Portree, is the port for steamers making trips around the island and linking Skye with the 15-mile-long island Raasay. Sligachan, nine miles south, and Glenbrittle, seven miles further southwest, are centers for climbing the Cuillin (Coolin) Hills.

Royal Hotel (tel. Portree 2525) is the leading hotel in Portree. Standing on a hill facing the water, it was said to have offered hospitality to Bonnie Prince Charles during his flight in 1746. In less dramatic and rushed circumstances, you can book one of its comfortable bedrooms, the preferred ones opening onto the sea. Of the inn's 29 rooms, 16 contain private baths. A double- or twin-bedded room costs £15.50 ($35.65) if bathless, increasing to £17.50 ($40.25) with private bath. All singles are bathless, renting from £15 ($34.50) nightly, these tariffs including VAT, service, and a full Scottish breakfast. The hotel is open all year.

The **Rosedale Hotel,** Beaumont Crescent (tel. Portree 2531), appeals to those seeking a homelike atmosphere. Its owners give you one of the biggest welcomes on Skye. Reader Nicky Riddle, Lenoir, North Carolina, writes: "It's one of the best spots on the island, set in the midst of fishermen's cottages that flank a rock-strewn path along the water. A festive, holiday atmosphere pervades." The Rosedale is open only from May to October, and most of its rooms are bathless, costing from £11.50 ($26.45), including a big Scottish breakfast. If you request one of the eight chambers with bath, the charge is from £14 ($32.20) per person. The owners offer very tasty food.

Uig

This village is on Trotternish, the largest Skye peninsula, and ferry port for Harris and Uist in the Outer Hebrides. It is 15 miles north of Portree and 49 miles from Kyle of Lochalsh. **Monkstadt House,** a mile and a half north, is where Flora MacDonald brought Prince Charles, in the guise of a girl named Betty Burke, after their the escape flight from Benbecula. In **Kilmuir** churchyard, five miles north, Flora was buried, wrapped in a sheet used by the prince. Her grave is marked by a Celtic cross.

Uig Hotel (tel. Uig 205) has been furnished with warmth, imagination, and creativity. In homelike comfort, guests are welcomed and shown to the lounge with its pleasant, harmonious colors. The hotel stands on a hillside overlooking a small bay and a tiny fishing harbor. The food, excellently prepared Scottish fare, is served in a cheerful dining room with a view of the bay. The 24-room hotel comes equipped with private bath or shower in every chamber. Rates range from £17.50 ($40.25) to £19.50 ($44.85) for singles, £35 ($80.50) to £39 ($89.70) for doubles, including a full Scottish breakfast and VAT. Dinner, bed, and breakfast rates go from £23.85 ($54.86) to £25.85 ($59.46) per person. The hotel is open from April to the end of September.

Dunvegan

The village of Dunvegan grew up around **Dunvegan Castle,** the principal man-made sight on the Isle of Skye, seat of the chiefs of Clan MacLeod who have lived there for 700 years. The castle, which stands on a rocky promontory, was once accessible only by boat, but now the moat is bridged and the castle open to the public. It holds many fascinating relics, including a "fairy flag." It is reputed to be the oldest inhabited castle in Britain. It is open from March 31 to mid-May from 2 to 5 p.m.; from mid-May to the end of September, from 10:30 a.m. to 5 p.m.; and for most of October from 2 to 5 p.m. It is closed all day Sunday. Adults pay £1 ($2.30) for admission; children, 50p ($1.15).

The **Black House museum,** four miles from Dunvegan on the Glendale Road (tel. Glendale 291), contains implements and furniture of bygone days and has a peat fire burning throughout the day. A replica of an illicit whiskey still can be seen behind the museum. Open daily 10 a.m. to 7 p.m.

At **Trumpan,** nine miles north of Dunvegan, are the remains of a church which was set afire in 1597 by MacDonald raiders while the congregation, all MacLeods, were inside at worship. Only one woman survived. The MacLeods of Dunvegan rushed to the defense, and only two MacDonalds escaped death.

Atholl House Hotel (tel. Dunvegan 219) lies right in the village of Dunvegan, only half a mile from Skye's most popular sightseeing attraction, Dunvegan Castle. The owner of Atholl House, Ena McPhie, a Gaelic singer, welcomes guests seeking a bed-and-breakfast accommodation from April to October. She charges from £7 ($16.10) per person, including a hearty Scottish breakfast that will fortify you for the day. She offers only 12 rooms, including a trio rented to families. The rooms themselves are clean and pleasantly furnished. There is a spacious, comfortable lounge which adds to the comfort of Atholl House.

Skeabost Bridge

Eastward from Dunvegan is Skeabost Bridge, with an island cemetery of great antiquity. The graves of four Crusaders are here.

Nearby is the **Skeabost House Hotel** (tel. Skeabost Bridge 202), one of the most comfortable, refreshing, and inviting country homes of Skye, receiving paying guests from May 1 to mid-October. Thoroughly modernized, it is interesting architecturally with its dormers, chimneys, tower, and gables, everything a weather-worn beige. Inside the taste level is high, with wood paneling and carpets. Once a private estate, it has been converted into a lochside hotel, standing on beautiful grounds that in summer are studded with flowering bushes. The location is 35 miles from Kyle of Lochalsh and 5 miles from Portree.

Sportsmen are attracted to the hotel, gathering in the firelit lounge for a mellow scotch whiskey. The atmosphere is of hardy tweeds with the distinctive aroma of a good cigar. The loch outside is well stocked with salmon and trout.

Of the 27 handsomely furnished rooms, 11 contain private baths. Singles are accepted at a rate of £9.50 ($21.85) to £15 ($34.50), doubles from £19 ($43.70) to £31 ($71.30), including a big Scottish breakfast. The Scottish fare, including smoked salmon, is served on fine china and elegant silver, a dinner costing from £7.50 ($17.25).

12. Oban, Mull, and District

Oban (meaning "small bay") is the great port for the Western Isles and a center of Gaelic culture. It is the gateway to Mull, largest of the Inner Hebrides; to the island of Iona, the cradle of Scottish Christianity; and to Staffa, where Fingal's Cave inspired Mendelssohn to write his Hebridean overture. The ferries to the offshore islands run only twice a day until summer; then there are cruises to Iona from early June to late September. For information about island ferry services to Mull, Iona, and the Outer Hebrides, get in touch with **MacBraynes Steamers** at their office in Oban (tel. Oban 2285).

Back on the mainland, we'll include a number of colorful sites, such as Fort Appin and Inveraray, for those who prefer to soak up atmosphere away from the major towns.

OBAN: One of Scotland's leading coastal resorts, the bustling port town of Oban is set in a sheltered bay that is almost landlocked by the island of Kerrera. A yachting center and small burgh, it lies about 50 miles south of Fort William.

From Pulpit Hill in Oban there is a fine view across the Firth of Lorn and the Sound of Mull. Overlooking the town is an unfinished replica of the Colosseum of Rome, built by a banker, John Stuart McCaig, in 1897–1900 as a memorial to his family and to try to curb local unemployment during a slump. Its walls are two feet thick and from 37 to 40 feet high. The courtyard within is landscaped and the tower is floodlit at night. It is known locally as **McCaig's Folly**.

In September the Oban Highland Games are held, with massed pipe bands marching through the streets. The Oban Pipe Band plays regularly throughout the summer, parading up and down main street. Paul W. Ware, New Providence, Pennsylvania, writes: "During evening, the promenade is traversed by little dogs pulling their masters who are wearing tweed jackets and smoking pipes. But the town also attracts young people."

On the island of Kerrera stands **Gylen Castle,** home of the MacDougalls, dating back to 1587.

Near the little granite **Cathedral of the Isles,** one mile north of the end of the bay, is the ruin of the 13th-century **Dunollie Castle,** seat of the Lords of Lorn who once owned a third of Scotland.

You can visit **Dunstaffnage Castle,** 3½ miles to the north, which was believed to have been the royal seat of the Dalriadic monarchy in the eighth century. The present castle was probably built in 1263. "The Stone of Destiny," now in Westminster Abbey, was kept here before its removal to Scone.

In Oban, Gaelic is taught in schools as a "leaving certificate subject."

Where to Stay

As a holiday resort, Oban has a number of good hotels and guest houses within easy reach of the seafront and the piers from which cruises to the offshore islands can be booked.

Alexandra, Esplanade (tel. Oban 2381), is a stone hotel with gables and a tower, plus a Regency-style front veranda, enjoying a sunny perch on the promenade. From its public rooms, you can look out onto lovely Oban Bay. Two sun lounges overlook the seafront. The bedrooms are substantial and pleasing, offering comfort and conveniences at a rate in a single that ranges from £16 ($36.80) to £20 ($46), in a double from £26 ($59.80) to £34 ($78.20), plus VAT. Of the 60 bedrooms, nearly half contain private baths. The restaurant, serving good food, also opens onto the panorama. Bar lunches are available for around £2.50 ($5.75), a complete dinner in the evening averaging around £8 ($18.40). The hotel is open from April to October.

Lancaster, Esplanade (tel. Oban 2587), is distinguished by its attractive pseudo-Tudor facade. On the crescent of the bay, it commands views from its public rooms of the islands of Lismore and Kerrera, even the more distant peaks of Mull. Open all year, the hotel is managed by its resident owners, Mr. and Mrs. J. T. Ramage, who welcome you to one of their well-furnished bedrooms, charging from £13 ($29.90) in a single, from £13 also per person in a double, including breakfast. For bed, breakfast, and evening meal, the charge is £18 ($41.40) per person nightly. A number of rooms offer central heating, and a few have private baths or showers. The fully licensed Lancaster is the only hotel in Oban featuring a heated indoor swimming pool, a sauna bath, and a solarium.

Wellpark Hotel (tel. Oban 2948) is a substantial stone house with a gabled bay window, positioned on the seafront and commanding views of the bay and the islands of Kerrera, Mull, and Lismore. It's also one of the best bargains in Oban. Mr. and Mrs. R. B. Dickison welcome you, charging £12 ($27.60) per person nightly for bed, dinner, and a full Scottish breakfast, based on double occupancy. Their rooms—simple, pleasantly comfortable—contain hot and cold running water and are equipped with electric blankets. Only demi-pension bookings are accepted. The hotel receives guests from April to October. There is full central heating for the colder days.

Where to Dine

McTavish's Kitchens, George Street (tel. Oban 3064), like its cousin in Fort William, is dedicated to preserving the local cuisine. Downstairs is a self-service restaurant providing à la carte breakfasts from 9 to 11:30 a.m., and light meals starting at 11:30 a.m. and served throughout the day and evening, seven days a week. There are, in addition, Laird's Bar, opening onto a beautiful view over Oban Bay, and the Mantrap Bar with a "real Mantrap."

The licensed second-floor restaurant has a more ambitious Scottish and continental menu with higher prices. It's open only from mid-May until the end of September, from 9 to 11 p.m. Specialties include a poacher's broth at 60p ($1.38) and haggis and neeps (Scotland's national dish) at £2 ($4.60). Main courses are genuinely Scottish, too—smoked salmon with brown bread, £3.50 ($8.05); Scottish crab with hot cheese sauce and duchesse potatoes, £4 ($9.20); and Loch Fyne kippers (smoked herring), £4 ($9.20) for two. Deep-dish apple pie with thick cream tallies up at 65p ($1.50).

A feature of the restaurant is folk cabaret, with singers, a piper, and a Highland dancer, 9 to 11 p.m., offered at Easter and each evening from mid-May to the end of September. Children are welcome. Admission is £1.05 ($2.42) for adults, 60p ($1.38) for children. Some of the best folk and contemporary music in Scotland is heard here. Recordings of these concerts are available at the restaurant. The bagpipes provide haunting melodies, new and old.

MULL: The largest island in the Inner Hebrides, Mull is rich in legend and folklore, a land of ghosts, monsters, and the wee folk. Over log fires that burn on cold winter evenings, the talk is of myths and ancient times. The island itself is wild and mountainous, characterized by sea lochs and sandy bars.

The capital is **Tobermory,** lying on a bay guarded by **Duart Castle,** restored in 1912 and still the seat of the once-fiery MacLeans, who shed much blood in and around the castle during their battles with the Lords of the Isles. In the bay—somewhere—lies the *Florencia,* the Spanish galleon that went down laden with treasure. Many attempts have been made to bring it up, but so far all of them have failed.

To the southeast, near Salen, are the ruins of **Aros Castle,** once the stronghold of the Lords of the Isles.

On the far south coast at Lochbuie, **Moy Castle** has a water-filled dungeon. The wild countryside of Mull was the scene of many of David Balfour's adventures in *Kidnapped* by Robert Louis Stevenson.

Roads on Mull are few and can be quite rough. If you're taking a bus tour, the driver often has to stop to let sheep and cattle cross.

From Oban you can take one of the car-ferry services to Mull, operated by **Caledonian MacBrayne.** For information in Oban, telephone 2285. In Tobermory, on Mull, you can reach the steamer office by telephoning 2017.

Always make a reservation if you're planning to spend the night on Mull.

We'll follow with a selection of hotels scattered across the island, beginning first at—

Tobermory

Western Isles (tel. Tobermory 2012) has a beautiful location above the harbor, looking out upon the bay. The hotel itself is plain and simple, rather conventional, although the atmosphere is made most gracious by the hospitality and helpfulness of the owners. Singles go from £16 ($36.80), doubles from £23 ($52.90) to £31 ($71.30), including a full Scottish breakfast. Here you get good meals with excellent fish, the chef equally adept at both Scottish and French cuisine. Lunches in the bar range from £2 ($4.60) to £3.50 ($8.05), and a three-course dinner goes for £7 ($16.10). The hotel receives guests only from April to October, and advance reservations in season cannot be accepted just for bed-and-breakfast bookings.

Carnaberg Hotel, 55 Main St. (tel. Tobermory 2479), lies right on the quay, overlooking the harbor and the Sound of Mull. The house has been pleasantly redecorated, and the rooms are comfortable. Mrs. MacLean charges £6.50 ($14.95) per person nightly—small reductions for children—this tariff including a Scottish breakfast. The dinner, bed, and breakfast rate is £9.50 ($21.85) per person. If you're there on a cold night, you might be given a hot water bottle to take to bed with you, but only after you've been offered a snack before retiring. And what a snack! On one recent occasion, it consisted of four different kinds of cake, including chocolate, and three types of cookies (the oatmeal ones were delicious).

Mishnish Hotel (tel. Tobermory 2009) is a personal favorite. It's small, only 15 rooms, but its owners, the "MacCleod clan," have run it for four generations, giving island hospitality and creating a congenial atmosphere for guests. They never seem too busy that they can't stop and give advice and directions for exploring both Mull and Iona. Open all year, the Mishnish charges from from £15 ($34.50) to £18 ($41.40) per person nightly, including a full Scottish breakfast, service, and VAT. The food is simple but the portions are ample, the ingredients fresh. The hotel contains many low ceilings and narrow passageways, and many of its furnishings have been polished with years of loving care. Residents can ask about boats for rent. In all, the Mishnish is a plain, simple, and friendly choice.

Suidhe Hotel, 59 Main St. (tel. Tobermory 2209), was originally recommended by readers Joseph and Elizabeth Mooney, and we agree fully with their point of view. Suidhe is Gaelic for "sit, rest, or a break in a journey," and that's exactly what this place is. Jim and Christine Scott, delightful people, run this clean, friendly little hotel charging £15 ($34.50) per person nightly, including bed, breakfast, and evening dinner. The meals are well prepared and delicious. All rooms have hot and cold water. Trout fishing, sea angling, and pony trekking are available locally. Suidhe is in a village off the western coast, right on the harbor, facing mountains covered with all shades of rhododendron in spring. In the village is a very good craft shop in a former church.

Craignure

Isle of Mull (tel. Craignure 351) is a first-class hotel which opened in 1971. It stands near the ferry and the meeting point of the Sound of Mull and Loch Linnhe. From the picture windows of its public rooms you'll have panoramic vistas of mountains and the island of Lismore. Each of its 60 bedrooms, all handsomely furnished, comes equipped with private bath and good views. The single rate is £20 ($46), increasing to £36 ($82.80) in a double, plus VAT. The food is good and pleasantly served in the attractive dining room, which faces both sea and hills. The chef does both British and continental dishes. The sea trout is superb. Hopefully, you'll be there on a night when the specialty is roast haunch of venison with gooseberry sauce. A set lunch costs about £5 ($11.50), a dinner going for around £8 ($18.40). Other facilities include a cocktail bar and a residents' television lounge. The hotel is open from the first of May until the end of September.

Dervaig

Bellachroy (tel. Dervaig 225) is a small hotel, consisting of only eight rooms. But it remains open all year, welcoming visitors and charging them £9.50 ($21.85) per person nightly for a comfortable bed and a hearty Scottish breakfast the next morning. You can also stay here on demi-pension terms of £15 ($34.50) per person nightly. The Bellachroy is run by farmers, David and Jean Haworth, and their breakfast consists of farm-fresh eggs and produce. You can hire a boat to go fishing on Loch Frisa.

IONA: Iona has been known as a place of spiritual power and pilgrimage for centuries. It was the site of the first Christian settlement in Scotland. A remote, low-lying, and treeless island now owned by the National Trust of Scotland, Iona lies off the southwestern coast of Mull and is only one mile by 3½ miles in size. It is accessible only by passenger ferry from the Isle of Mull (cars must remain on Mull). The ferry to Iona is run by local fishermen, and it's very informal in service, depending in large part on the weather.

Iona is known for its **"graves of the kings."** A total of 48 Scottish kings, including Macbeth and his victim Duncan, were buried on Iona, as were four Irish kings and eight Norwegian kings.

Today the island attracts nearly 1000 visitors a week in high season. Most of them come here mainly to see the **Abbey of Iona,** part of which dates back to the 13th century. But they also visit relics of the settlement founded there by St. Columba in 563, from which Celtic Christianity spread through Scotland. The abbey has been restored by an ecumenical group called the Iona Community, which conducts workshops on Christianity, sponsors a youth camp, offers tours of the abbey, and leads a seven-mile hike to the various holy and historic spots on the island each Wednesday.

Although there are many visitors to the abbey, the atmosphere on the island remains very rare, peaceful, and spiritual. It's possible to walk off among the sheep that wander freely everywhere to the top of Dun-I, a small mountain, and contemplate the ocean and the landscape as if you were the only person on earth.

There is much to do on Iona, but perhaps best of all, you can simply do nothing and absorb the kind of atmosphere that has drawn people on pilgrimages here for centuries.

One reader, Capt. Robert Haggart, Laguna, California, described his experience this way: "I was enchanted by the place. It really has a mystic atmosphere—one *feels* something ancient here, something spiritual, sacred, long struggles and wonderment about the strength of religion."

Most of the islanders live by crofting and fishing. In addition, they supplement their income by taking in paying guests in season, charging usually very low or at least fair prices. You can, of course, check into the hotel recommended below, but a stay here in a private home may be an altogether rewarding travel adventure. If you don't stay on Iona, you must catch one of the ferries back to Mull, and they rarely leave after 5 p.m.

The **St. Columba Hotel** (tel. Iona 304) stands right outside the village, in the vicinity of the cathedral. Offering a total of 29 simply furnished rooms (only two of which have private baths), the hotel accepts guests from March to October. Singles range in price from £15 ($34.50) to £22 ($50.60), doubles from £11.50 ($26.45) to £14 ($32.20) per person including a full Scottish breakfast. The demi-pension rate ranges from £18 ($41.40) to £30 ($69) per person. The food is good, especially the fish dishes, but, remember, the last order for dinner is taken at 7 p.m. People turn in early on Iona. Try to get a room overlooking the sea, but know that it's virtually impossible to secure an accommodation here in season without a reservation made well in advance.

STAFFA: Fingal's Cave, on Staffa, a 75-acre island in the Hebrides off Scotland's west coast, has been attracting visitors for more than 200 years. It has been the inspiration for music, poetry, paintings, and prose. No less a personage than Queen Victoria visited the cave in the 19th century and wrote: "The effect is splendid, like a great entrance into a vaulted hall. The sea is immensely deep in the cave. The rocks under water were all colors—pink, blue and green." The sound of the crashing waves and swirling waters caused Mendelssohn to write the "Fingal's Cave Overture." Turner painted the cave on canvas, and Keats, Wordsworth, and Tennyson all praised it in their poetry.

The cave is unique in that it is the only known cave in the world formed of basalt columns. Over the centuries, the sea has carved a huge cavern in the basalt, leaving massive hexagonal columns to create the "vaulted hall" effect which enchanted Queen Victoria.

The Gaelic name of the cave is An Uamh Ehinn or the musical cave.

Although the island of Staffa itself has not been inhabited for more than 160 years, visitors can still explore the cave, thanks to the Laird of Staffa, Alastair de Watteville. In his hydrojet-equipped boat, *Fulmar*, the laird makes three trips a day from the quay at Ulva Ferry on the Isle of Mull to the rocky shores of Staffa. After docking, visitors are led along the basalt path and into Fingal's Cave. Inside, the noise of the pounding sea is deafening.

Another cave, **Clamshell Cave**, can also be visited, but only at low tide. Appropriately named, **Boat Cave** is accessible only by water.

Staffa Marine Limited operates a range of excursions, cruises, and tours from Oban, Argyle, and the nearby Isle of Mull. There are daily sailings in summer (May 7 to September 24) to Staffa, Iona, Mull, and a variety of beauty spots on the Argyll coast. Visits to Staffa include opportunities to land on this unique island, explore Fingal's Cave, and study the remarkable sea caves formed in the hexagonal basalt. All trips present views of dramatic, beautiful scenery and sights of varied marine and seabird life. Puffins, cormorants, gannets, kittiwakes, fulmars, and many kinds of gull are frequently seen, as are seals and porpoises.

Staffa Marine Excursion Centre is at 13 Stafford St., Oban (tel. Oban 4747).

PORT APPIN: To the north of Oban lies a beautiful lochside district, including Lismore Island. On an islet nearby is a famous landmark, **Castle Stalker**, the ancient seat of the Stewarts of Appin, built in the 15th century by Duncan Stewart, son of the first chief of Appin. Dugald, the ninth chief, was forced to sell the estate in 1765, and the castle slowly fell into ruin. It was recently restored and is once again inhabited. According to myth, there's a subterranean undersea passage at Port Appin where a piper supposedly entered with his dog. Only the dog returned, and he was hairless. Port Appin itself is a small hamlet of stone cottages.

Airds Hotel (tel. Appin 236) is an old ferry inn dating from 1700, in one of the most beautiful spots in the historic district of Appin. You're assured of serenity if you take a room at this tranquil choice on Loch Linnhe, midway between Oban and Fort William. The hotel overlooks not only Loch Linnhe, but the island of Lismore and the mountains of Morvern, an ideal center for touring this historic area of the country. You can take forest walks in many directions, or else go pony trekking, sea angling, or trout fishing. Boats can be rented and trips arranged to see the seals and to visit the island of Lismore.

The resident proprietors, Mr. and Mrs. Allen, welcome you to one of their comfortably furnished bedrooms, five of which contain private baths (in the new addition). Depending on your room assignment and plumbing, rates range from £12 ($27.60) to £14 ($32.20), including a full Scottish breakfast, featuring eggs from the hotel's own farm. Dinner costs from £8 ($18.40). The food is excellent, using fresh produce when possible. By all means try to return to the inn for a bountiful Scottish tea in the late afternoon, with home-baked scones and cakes. Guests are received from March to October. The hotel has both a cocktail bar and a public bar, plus a TV and residents' lounge.

SEIL: Those seeking a truly hidden oasis in the district south of Oban can leave town on the 816, turning west at Kilninver on the 844 until you reach Clachan Bridge. The locals claim, somewhat whimsically, that this is "the only bridge across the Atlantic Ocean." Easdale is an attractive, tiny slate village, nestling under the cliffs of Seil Island, with a view of Mull. Here you have complete serenity.

The **Dunmor House,** Seil, near Easdale (tel. Balvicar 203), is a licensed country-house hotel, enjoying a beautiful setting on its own 1000-acre hill farm, with panoramic views over the Atlantic and Hebridean islands. The house was built by a steward of the Bredalbane Campbells, who considered it much too big for a steward and promptly fired him. Today, the resident owners, Lieutenant Commander and Mrs. H. D. Campbell-Gibson, welcome you to one of their simply furnished, but comfortable, rooms, for which they charge £17 ($39.10) in a single, from £16 ($36.80) in a double, including breakfast.

The real reason for recommending such an out-of-the-way place is the cookery of Mrs. Campbell-Gibson, who uses produce from her own garden. She even grows her own fresh herbs. At lunch typical Scottish pub fare is featured from 1 to 2 p.m., and you are likely to spend no more than £2.50 ($5.75) for food and a bottled beer. However, at dinner, from 8 to 9 nightly, any array of delectable continental dishes is offered. The ingredients are fresh, the results enjoyable. Easdale salmon is a specialty. Your tab is likely to run around £9 ($20.70). Dunmor shuts down the third week of October, reopening on May 1. Trout fishing in 12 lochs is available, and special day excursions by boat to offshore islands are available.

LOCH AWE: Twenty-two miles long and in most places only about a mile wide, Loch Awe for years acted as a natural moat protecting the Campbells of Inveraray from their enemies to the north. Along its banks and on its islands are many reminders of its fortified past. There is a ruined castle at Fincharn, at the southern end of the loch, and another on the island of Fraoch Eilean. The **Isle of Inishail** has an ancient chapel and burial ground, and at the northern end of the loch are the ruins of **Kilchurn Castle,** built by Sir Colin Campbell in 1440. The bulk of Ben Cruachan, 3689 feet, dominates Loch Awe at its northern end and attracts climbers. On the ben is the world's second-largest hydroelectric power station, which pumps water from Loch Awe to a reservoir high up the mountain. Below the mountain are the **Falls of Cruachan** and the wild **Pass of Brander,** where Robert the Bruce routed the Clan MacDougall in 1308.

In this area, the Forestry Commission has vast forests, and a new road now makes it possible to travel around Loch Awe, so that it is more than ever a popular angling center. Sharp-eyed James Bond fans may even recognize some scenes which appeared in one of the films.

The Pass of Brander where Loch Awe narrows was the scene of many a fierce battle in bygone times, and something of that bloody past seems to brood over the narrow defile. Through it the waters of the Awe flow on their way to Loch Etive. This winding sealoch is 19 miles long, stretching from Dun Dunstaffnage Bay at Oban to Glen Etive, reaching into the Moor of Rannoch at the foot of the 3000-foot Buachaille Etive (the Shepherd of Etive), into which Glencoe also reaches.

Taychreggan Hotel, Lochaweside, near Taynuilt (tel. Kilchrenan 211), is a delightful old house nestling in firs beside the loch. John Taylor and Tove, his Danish wife, have furnished the place with great simplicity, skillfully joining the old with the new by using pinewood and stonework. They have created a friendly country-house atmosphere, providing comfortable, warm rooms, soft armchairs to sink into in the lounge, and dinner cooked from local produce, including freshly caught fish. This is an excellent center for walking and relaxing, but there are many interesting things to do in this area, where good hotels are few and far between. The charge is £18 ($41.40) per person with bath. Without bath, the per-person rate ranges from £16.50 ($37.95), including a large breakfast. Most guests prefer to take the half-board arrangement, costing from £23 ($52.90) to £25 ($57.50) per person nightly. A high tea can be provided for children who do not stay up for dinner. Lunch at £4.50 ($10.35) is a smashing Danish cold table. Packed lunches are available as a matter of course, and afternoon tea or coffee, with crackers, goes for £1 ($2.30). You can hire a boat for the day for £5 ($11.50).

THE CRINAN CANAL: The nine-mile-long canal, constructed during 1793-1801, was designed to provide water communication between the Firth of Clyde, Argyll, the western Highlands, and the islands. It runs roughly north from Ardrishaig and curves gradually to the west before reaching Loch Crinan on the Sound of Jura. Four miles north of **Cairnbaan,** on the canal, is the ruined hill-fort of **Dunadd,** once capital of Dalriada, kingdom of the Scots. There are numerous Bronze Age stone circles in the vicinity, and **Kilmartin churchyard,** five miles north of Cairnbaan, has a carved cross dating from the 16th century. **Carnasserie Castle,** also to the north of the canal, built in the late 16th century, was the home of John Carswell, the first post-Reformation bishop of the isles, whose translation of John Knox's liturgy into Gaelic was the first book to be published in that language.

Crinan, a yachtsman's haven on the Sound of Jura, is overlooked by the early 11th-century **Duntrune Castle,** one of the oldest castles in Scotland, and still inhabited by the descendants of the original owners, the Clan Malcolm. Crinan itself is a charming little village.

Lochgilphead, a pleasant little town sitting just where the canal turns westward, is the address of our recommendation for a stopover in this area:

The **Cairnbaan Motor Inn** (tel. Lochgilphead 2488). Formerly an old coach inn and now a privately owned hotel, this is an excellent base for touring Argyll and the islands. Nearby are safe beaches, and for the sportsman there is loch fishing, sea angling, and salmon fishing on the River Add. The motor inn has comfortable, modern bedrooms, some with private bathrooms and verandas. All bedrooms have built-in wardrobes, wash basins, razor sockets, radios, intercoms, and baby-listerning service. The tariff in a twin-bedded room without bath is £10.50 ($24.15)—with bath, £12 ($27.60)—per person, the same charges holding in a single room.

The split-level dining room has a superb view southward down the busy canal. Emphasis for the cuisine is on Scottish dishes. There is a handsome cocktail bar and a comfortable sun lounge with a patio beyond.

Crinan Hotel (tel. Crinan 235), off the B841, seven miles northwest of Lochgilphead, is an inn with a bright, attractive decor and modern comforts and conveniences. Because of its location on a canal and yacht basin, it is naturally a favorite with yachtsmen, who book its 24 rooms with private bath in July and August, the peak sailing months. If you're reserving (and we highly recommend that you do), ask for one of the rooms with private balconies opening onto mountains and lochside sunsets.

The hotel is managed by Nicolas Ryan, who once worked as a bellboy on the old *Queen Mary*, later rising rapidly within the Cunard organization. Bedrooms rent for £18.50 ($42.55) in a single, from £28 ($64.40) to £31 ($71.30) in a double, including a breakfast that often features oatcakes and hot croissants.

Open all year, the hotel serves exceptionally good food—dishes such as fresh salmon, Crinan clams mornay, roast duckling in black cherry sauce, and Scottish sirloin. Meals are served from noon to 2 p.m. and from 7 to 9 p.m. A table d'hôte luncheon goes for £5 ($11.50), a set dinner for £9.50 ($21.85), although you are likely to pay £12 ($27.60) if you order from the à la carte menu. Luncheon in fair weather is served alfresco. The hotel is one of the best run in the area. As efficient as Mr. Ryan's staff is, they never overlook Scottish hospitality and friendliness.

INVERARAY: This small resort and royal burgh occupies a splendid Highland setting on the upper shores of Loch Fyne. The hereditary seat of the Dukes of Argyll, **Inveraray Castle** has been headquarters of the Clan Campbell since the earth 15th century. In 1644, the original village was burned by the Royalist Marquess of Montrose. The third Duke of Argyll built a new town and castle between 1744 and 1788. The castle was badly damaged by fire in 1975, but it is being restored. The present laird, the 12th Duke of Argyll and 26th MacCailein Mor, chief of the Clan Campbell, has opened the castle to the public, with a special welcome for anyone who is related to Clan Campbell. The castle is among the earliest examples of Gothic revival in Britain, and offers a fine collection of pictures and 18th-century French furniture, old English and continental porcelain, and a magnificent Armoury Hall, which alone contains 1300 pieces. There is a castle shop for souvenirs and a tearoom where home-made cakes and scones are served. The castle is open daily from April 5 to September 30, charging £1.50 ($3.45) for adults, 75p ($1.73) for children. The castle is closed on Friday from the opening date until the end of June each year.

At one end of the main street of the town is a Celtic burial cross from Iona. The parish church is divided by a wall enabling services to be held in Gaelic and English at the same time.

Auchindrain, six miles southwest of Inveraray, is a museum of farming life over the past 200 years. It is a unique survival of the past, whose origins are so far back as to be a subject for archeology. The farming township stands more or less as it was in the late 1800s, but studies are showing at least two centuries before that. One description states, "Auchindrain avoided progress." Open daily during the summer, Auchindrain and mid-Argyll are in an area crammed with things and places of interest for historians, antiquarians, and archeologists.

A fine woodland garden may be visited at **Crarae Lodge,** four miles southwest of the village.

Vacationing fishing enthusiasts may want to visit the **Castle Fisheries**, two miles north past the castle on the Oban Road. Primarily a farm providing trout for the table, facilities are set up so that visitors can try their luck in one of the trout ponds, while the children play in the playground area or enjoy snacks from the refreshment stand. Other facilities include a baby deer park and even a hospital for sick fish. Admission is 50p ($1.15) for adults, 25p (58¢) for children, with an additional charge to those who go fishing. It's open 10 a.m. to 6 p.m., from April to October (fishing all year).

For food and accommodations in Inveraray, we'd suggest the **George**, Main Street (tel. Inveraray 2111), which is a small inn, open all year. The overnight rate is £10 ($23) to £12 ($27.60) per person, including a full Scottish breakfast, service, and VAT. The rooms are simply furnished, with a minimum of plumbing, decidedly old-fashioned. The dining room, however, is attractively modern with bright furnishings. A four-course dinner costs from £5 ($11.50), and bar snacks for lunch range from bacon rolls at 45p ($1.04) to fresh salmon salad at £2.50 ($5.75). Downstairs there's a public bar with stone walls and a flagstone floor, a part of which was connected with the stables when the George was a stagecoach inn. Here you can order snacks at lunch along with your lager. The George also owns the cheaper Loch Fyne Guest House, 500 yards up the road.

13. Kintyre, Arran, and Islay

For many foreign visitors, the Atlantic seaboard of the old county of Argyll will represent a journey into the unknown. For those who want to sample a bygone age, this is one of the most rewarding trips off the coastline of western Scotland. Our recommendations lie on islands, easily reached by ferries—except the Kintyre Peninsula which is a virtual island in itself. You'll soon discover that the Gaelic traditions of the islands endure. Peace and tranquility prevail.

ISLE OF ARRAN: At the mouth of the Firth of Clyde, this island is often described as Scotland in miniature, because of its wild and varied scenery, containing an assortment of glens, moors, lochs, sandy bays, and rocky coasts that have made the country famous. Ferry services, making the 50-minute crossing, operate from Ardrossan to Brodick, the major village of Arran, lying on the eastern shore. There are also ferry connections linking the northern part of Arran with the Kintyre Peninsula and the Highlands. Once on Arran, you'll find buses take you to the various villages, each with its own character. A coast road, 60 miles long, runs the length of the island.

Arran contains some splendid mountain scenery, notably the conical peak of **Goatfell** in the north, reaching a height of 2866 feet. It's called "the mountain of the winds."

Students of geology flock to Arran to study igneous rocks of the Tertiary Age. Cairns and standing stones at **Tormore** intrigue archeologists as well.

Arran is also filled with beautiful glens, especially **Glen Sannox** in the northeast and **Glen Rosa**, directly north of Brodick. In one day you can see a lot, as the island is only 25 miles long, 10 miles wide.

After the ferry docks at Brodick, you may want to head for Arran's major sight—**Brodick Castle**, 1½ miles north of the Brodick pierhead. The historic home of the Dukes of Hamilton, the castle dates from the 13th century and contains antiques, portraits, and objets d'art. It is open in April after Easter on Monday, Wednesday, and Saturday from 1 to 5 p.m. From May 1 to

September 30, hours are weekdays, 1 to 5 p.m.; Sunday from 2 to 5 p.m. The gardens are open all year, daily from 10 a.m. to 5 p.m. Admission to both the castle and gardens is 85p ($1.96) for adults, 40p (92¢) for children.

South from Brodick lies the village and holiday resort of **Lamlash,** opening onto Lamlash Bay. From here a ferry takes visitors over to **Holy Island,** with its 1000-foot peak. A disciple of St. Columba founded a church on this island.

One of the best known centers on the western coast is **Blackwater Foot,** which offers pony trekking and golfing.

Finally, in the north, **Lochranza** is a village with unique appeal. It opens onto a bay of pebbles and sand, and in the backdrop lie the ruins of a castle that reputedly was the hunting seat of Robert Bruce.

Brodick

Glenartney (tel. Brodick 2220) is a two-story, 20-bedroom rough-cast hotel commanding a hilltop perch overlooking the bay. The hotel offers comfortable rooms and good food, plus a congenial atmosphere. Singles peak at £10 ($23); doubles, £14 ($32.20)—including breakfast. A lunch goes for £3.50 ($8.05), a complete dinner costing from £5 ($11.50). None of the rooms contains a private bath, and you have to get to the dining room between 7 and 7:30 p.m. The hotel is closed from October to February. Bookings for just bed and breakfast can't be accepted in high season.

Whiting Bay

Whiting Bay Hotel (tel. Whiting Bay 247) is a substantial, well-heated hotel, its windows looking out over the bay and the Firth of Clyde. The hotel is immaculately maintained, and the staff is most hospitable. They will welcome you all year in one of their comfortable bedrooms, of which only 6 out of 22 contain private baths. Rates range from £12.75 ($29.33) to £14 ($32.20) in a single, from £22.50 ($51.75) to £26 ($59.80) in a double, including a full Scottish breakfast. The demi-pension rate goes from £16.50 ($37.95) to £20 ($46) per person nightly. The cook prepares Scottish specialties, among other dishes, quite well. The hotel is fully licensed, and it has ample parking as well as a cocktail bar, lounge bar, and a ballroom with regular entertainment. A piper pipes guests to dinner most evenings.

Kildonan

Kildonan Hotel (tel. Kildonan 207) stands on the tip of a headland on the southern seashore of the island, commanding beautiful views from its spacious sun lounges which front the sea. It looks out onto Pladda Island and its lighthouse. Unlike many hotels on Arran, the Kildonan has a full license for serving alcoholic beverages. There is both a bar and a bar lounge, and, even if you're not staying over, you might want to drop in to its fine restaurant, serving good food and wine which comes from a well-stocked cellar. The hotel has its own tennis court and putting green, plus separate game rooms. Nearby is a sandy beach suitable for bathing. Golf, fishing, and "stalking" are the major sports. Receiving visitors from April to October, the hotel charges from £11.50 ($26.45) per person, including breakfast. Dinner is an additional £6 ($13.80) per head. Rooms are pleasantly and attractively furnished, most comfortable, and there is central heating and log or electric fires.

Lamlash

Although we missed this on our latest rounds, the **Carraig Mhor**, Lamlash, Arran (tel. Lamlash 453), continues to get accolades by food writers and has been awarded rosettes. This highly spoken-of restaurant is open nightly except Sunday and Monday, and you can expect to pay from £12 ($27.60) for a meal. Always telephone ahead for a reservation, however.

KINTYRE PENINSULA: The longest peninsula in Scotland, Kintyre is more than 60 miles in length, containing much beautiful scenery, pleasant villages, and magnificent gardens on the Isle of Gigha, which lies off its western shores. The largest center on Kintyre is Campbeltown, although Tarbert in the north is also popular. In the evening you just might hear the music of the "ceilidhs" in hotels and village halls.

The major sight is an excursion to Gigha's famous gardens. They're called **Achamore** and are located a quarter of a mile from Ardminish on the Isle of Gigha. The island is reached by ferry boat which picks up passengers at the Tayinloan jetty on Kintyre. Weather permitting, sailings are about every 20 minutes.

These extensive gardens contain roses, hydrangeas, rhododendrons, camellias, and azaleas. They are open March to October from 10 a.m. to dusk, charging adults 40p (94¢); children, 20p (46¢).

At Carradale, near the ruins of Aird Castle on the eastern coast, you can visit the **Carradale Forest Centre** and the gardens of Carradale House.

TARBERT: A sheltered harbor protects this fishing port and yachting center which lies on a narrow neck of the northern tip of the Kintyre Peninsula, between West Loch Tarbert and the head of herring-filled Loch Fyne. Nearby is the finest accommodation on the Kintyre Peninsula.

Stonefield Castle Hotel (tel. Tarbert 207), occupying a commanding position, is a luxuriously appointed and magnificent hotel on 100 acres of wooded grounds and parklike gardens on Loch Fyne, two miles outside Tarbert. The grounds are studded with rare shrubs, and from the gardens come the flowers for the exquisite arrangements inside the house. Extended from the central square tower are tall step-gabled wings, with highly pitched windows and rows of dormers. From this impressively handsome building are seemingly unlimited views. Older readers especially find it a tranquil oasis. The castle was formerly owned by a member of the Campbell clan. Its public rooms are lofty, decorated, in part, with antiques.

Try to get one of the well-furnished bedrooms in the main building, although you may be assigned an accommodation in the more modern wing. In all, there are 34 rooms, 29 with private bath. Singles range from £16 ($36.80) to £21 ($48.30), doubles from £26 ($59.80) to £40 ($92), including a full Scottish breakfast, service, and VAT. Meals utilize produce from the hotel's own garden. In the kitchen the staff does their own baking. The paneled dining room is decorated in a formal style, and the service is superb.

Lunch in the bar costs about £2.50 ($5.75), and dinner ranges from £7.50 ($17.25) to £10.50 ($24.15), the difference in cost depending on your selection of a main dish. The hotel has many excellent facilities, including a spacious drawing room overlooking the loch, a cocktail bar, tennis court, putting green, a large library, an outdoor swimming pool, a sauna, even yacht anchorage. Sea fishing can be arranged. It's imperative to book well in advance, as Stonefield has a large repeat clientele. It remains open all year.

Considerably less expensive, the **Tarbert Hotel** (tel. Tarbert 264) stands on the quayside where the Kintyre fishermen anchor with their herring-filled boats. The hotel is really like a pub, painted in white, and the frugal Scots themselves book the comfortable and simply furnished rooms which cost from £10 ($23) per person. Dinner is an additional £7.50 ($17.25) per person. If you don't dine in the main room, you'll find a goodly assortment of snacks. The lounge bar is usually well stuffed with the local people themselves, enjoying their Scottish & Newcastle.

The **West Loch Hotel** (tel. Tarbert 283), a small, family-managed hotel, is also good, although it contains only six bedrooms, renting for £16 ($36.80) in a single, from £24 ($55.20) in a double, including a full breakfast. The rooms are immaculately maintained, furnished in an old style. The main building dates back to old coaching days. You really should take the demi-pension rate of £21 ($48.30) per person, or else drop in for a meal, because the cookery is first rate. Fresh ingredients are used whenever available, and the fish dishes are superb. In season game is featured. Hot and cold snacks are served both in the bar and dining room at noon. The black-and-white inn overlooks West Loch—hence its name. It lies one mile south of the village on the Campbeltown Road. It's popular with yachtsmen from the east harbor. The hotel is conveniently situated for ferries sailing to Arran, Islay, and Jura. A nine-hole golf course, pony trekking, forestry walks, and the sandy West Coast beaches are all within easy reach.

CAMPBELTOWN: This is a fishing port and resort with a shingle beach at the southern tip of the Kintyre peninsula. A mile to the southeast stands the ruins of Kilkerran Castle. You can ask in town about excursions to St. Kieran's Cave and the Islands of Davaar, which lie in the Campbeltown Loch.

Argyll Arms (tel. Campbeltown 3431) is the largest hotel in town, containing 42 bedrooms, none of which offers a private bath. Centrally heated throughout, the hotel has plain but adequate accommodations that go for £11 ($25.30) in a single, rising to £19 ($43.70) in a double, including breakfast and VAT. Open all year, the hotel is fully licensed, containing a garage and a TV lounge. It's near golf and sandy beaches at Machrihanish (five miles away) and Southend (ten miles). Arrangements can be made for loch and river fishing.

SOUTHEND: This is a tiny village that lies at the tip of the Kintyre peninsula, near the Mull of Kintyre. It offers golf and bathing. It's reached by going first to Campeltown on the 83. Shortly after leaving Campeltown, 83 becomes 842 as it continues south to Southend.

Keil Hotel (tel. Southend 253) is the best bet if you've made the long trip the entire length of the Kintyre Peninsula. At the tip stands this fine hotel, a modern block opening onto views of Brunerican Bay, Sanda Island, tennis courts, and verdant pastures. Rooms are plain and simply furnished. They have five rooms with private baths. Daily terms begin at £11.30 ($25.99) per person for bed and breakfast, and dinner costs another £6 ($13.80). You must get there by 8 p.m. for dinner. The Keil is open from Easter until mid-October.

ISLE OF ISLAY: The southernmost island of the Inner Hebrides, Islay lies 16 miles west of the Kintyre Peninsula and less than a mile southwest of Jura, from which it is separated only by a narrow sound. At its maximum breadth, Islay is only 15 miles wide (25 miles long).

Called "the Queen of the Hebrides," it is a peaceful unspoiled island of moors, salmon-filled lochs, sandy bays, and wild rocky cliffs. Islay was the ancient seat of the Lords of the Isles, and today you'll see the ruins of two castles and several Celtic crosses.

Near Port Charlotte are the graves of the U.S. seamen and army troops who lost their lives in 1918 when their carriers, the *Tuscania* and *Otranto,* were torpedoed off the shores of Islay. There's a memorial tower on the Mull of Oa, eight miles from Port Ellen.

The island is noted for its distilleries producing single-malt Highland whiskeys by the antiquated pot-still method.

MacBrayne Steamers operate a daily service to Islay—you leave West Tarbert on the Kintyre Peninsula, arriving at Port Askaig on Islay.

The island's capital is Bowmore, on the coast across from Port Askaig. There you can see a fascinating round church—no corners for the devil. But the most important town is Port Ellen, on the south coast, a holiday and golfing resort as well as Islay's principal port.

As accommodations are limited on Islay, always arrive with a reservation in your pocket.

Port Askaig

Port Askaig Hotel (tel. Port Askaig 245) is a genuine old island inn, dating from the 18th century, built on the site of an even older inn. It stands on the Sound of Islay overlooking the pier where a MacBrayne steamer berths daily. The hotel is quite charming, offering island hospitality and Scottish fare, including broiled trout, cock-a-leekie soup, roast pheasant, smoked Scottish salmon, and, of course, haggis. The hotel is a major destination for anglers on Islay, and the bar at the inn is popular with local fishermen. All year the friendly staff welcomes you to one of its modestly furnished bedrooms, costing from £14.55 ($33.47) in a single and from £23.40 ($53.82) in a double, including a continental breakfast. Dinner costs from £6.50 ($14.95). The hotel, incidentally, offers only nine rooms, half of which contain private baths.

Port Ellen

White Hart (tel. Port Ellen 2311) is modest, but pleasantly situated, standing on a tiny promenade on the skirttails of Port Ellen. The furnishings are in good taste, offering unassuming comfort. The hotel rents out 19 rooms, of which only 5 contain private baths. All year singles cost from £12.50 ($28.75); doubles, £36 ($82.80), including a full breakfast. The demi-pension rate is £23 ($52.90) per person. Meals are good, although simple, and are served in a dining room opening onto a view of the water. Log fires burn in the attractive lounge. If given proper notice, the staff will arrange fishing expeditions for guests.

Bridgend

Bridgend Hotel (tel. Bowmore 212) is a good base if you're crossing Islay, making your headquarters around the capital at Bowmore. All year the resident owners of this hotel will welcome you to their quiet retreat, opening onto Loch Indaal. The hotel itself is plainly furnished, although a nice touch is added by the pictures of wild bird life on Islay and the seascape paintings of local artists. The Bridgend offers only nine rooms, none of which contains a private bath. For these, you pay from £15 ($34.50) per person, including breakfast. The demi-pension tariff is £22 ($50.60) per person. Meals—good, simple, unassuming cookery—are served between 7 and 7:30 p.m. The hotel also has a fully licensed cocktail bar.

ISLE OF JURA: This is the fourth-largest island in the Inner Hebrides. It perhaps takes its name from the Norse "Jura," meaning "deer island." The red deer on Jura outnumber the people by about 20 to 1. At four feet high, the deer are the largest wild animals roaming Scotland. The hearty islanders themselves number only about 250 brave souls, and most of them live along the east coast. The west coast is virtually uninhabited.

The capital, **Craighouse,** is hardly more than a hamlet. It is connected by steamer to West Loch Tarbert on the Kintyre Peninsula. If you're already on Islay, you can journey to Jura by taking a five-minute ferry ride from Port Askaig, docking at the Feolin Ferry berth.

The breadth of Jura varies from two to eight miles, and at its maximum length it is 27 miles long. The island's landscape is dominated by the **Paps of Jura,** reaching a peak of 2571 feet at Beinn-an-Oir. An arm of the sea, **Loch Tarbert** nearly divides the island, cutting into it for nearly six miles.

As islands go, Jura is relatively little known and explored, although its mountains, soaring cliffs, snug coves, and moors make it an inviting paradise—nowhere is there overcrowding. The island has actually lost population drastically.

The square tower of **Claig Castle** is now in ruins, but once it was the stronghold of the MacDonalds until they were subdued by the Campbells in the 17th century.

Literary historians may be interested to know that George Orwell in the bitter postwar winters of 1946 and 1947 lived at Jura. Even then a sick and dying man, he wrote his masterpiece, *1984,* a satire on modern politics. He almost lost his life on Jura when he and his adopted son ventured too close to the famous whirlpool in the Gulf of Corryvreckan. Orwell and his son were saved by local fishermen, and he went on to finish *1984,* only to die in London of tuberculosis in 1950. His life span hardly matched that of Gillouir MacCrain, said to have been 180 when he died on Jura in the days of Charles I.

In accommodations, the **Jura Hotel** (tel. 243) at Craighouse is the only licensed premises on the island. Overlooking the sea, it actually has palms growing on its grounds, thanks to the benevolence of the Gulf Stream. All year it rents 18 bedrooms, four of which contain private baths. The single tariff is £15 ($34.50); the double rate, £31 ($71.30)—including breakfast. The demi-pension terms are from £18 ($41.40) per person daily. Rooms are simply although agreeably furnished. However, bring along some mosquito repellant to deal with the pest of the islands. Your kilted host will dispense the local single-malt in a cozy little bar opening onto the bay. The peaty whiskey is distilled right near the hotel. During the day guests go fishing, sailing, hill climbing, and, of course, deer stalking.

14. Glasgow and the Clyde

Forty miles west of Edinburgh, Scotland's largest city stands on the banks of the River Clyde, which was the birthplace of the *Queen Mary* and *Queen Elizabeth,* plus many other ocean-going liners. Here is housed half of Scotland's population. The Firth of Clyde itself is one of the loveliest waterways in the world, with its long sea lochs, islands, and hills.

SCOTLAND: ISLE OF JURA/GLASGOW

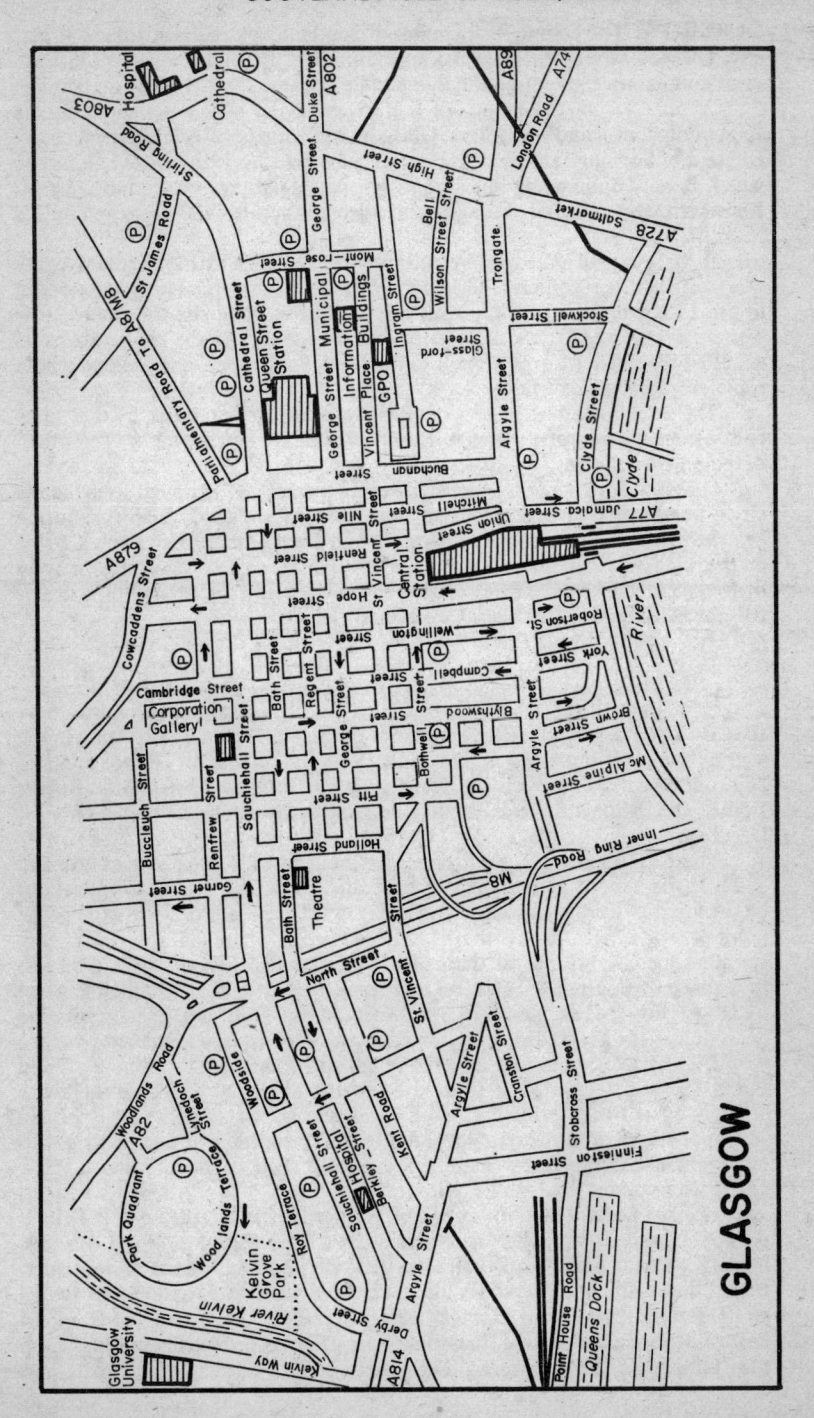

GLASGOW

GLASGOW: The commercial capital of Scotland, and Britain's third-largest city, Glasgow is very ancient, making Edinburgh, for all its wealth of history, seem comparatively young. The village that became the city grew up beside a ford 20 miles from the mouth of the River Clyde, which is famous for its shipbuilding, iron and steelworks. Glasgow was a medieval ecclesiastical center and seat of learning. The ancient city is buried beneath 19th-century Glasgow, which is now undergoing vast urban renewal. Glasgow was founded by St. Kentigern, also called St. Mungo, who selected the site 1400 years ago for his church.

In 1136 a cathedral was erected over his remains; in 1451 the university was started—the second established in Scotland. Commercial prosperity began in the 17th century when its merchants set out to dominate the trade of the western seas. The Clyde was widened and deepened, and the city's expansion engulfed the smaller towns of Ardrie, Renfrew, Rutherglen, and Paisley, whose roots are deep in the Middle Ages.

The smoking industrial city of Glasgow is blighted, in parts, by the "Gorbals," some of the worst slums in Europe which are now giving way to urban development schemes.

Glasgow does contain some sightseeing attractions—enough to make the city a worthy goal for many tourists. But mainly it's a good center for touring central Scotland. For example, you can sail on Loch Lomond and Loch Katrine on the same day, and the resorts along the Ayrshire coast are only an hour away by frequent train service. From Glasgow you can also explore the Burns Country, the Stirling area, Culzean Castle, and the Trossachs.

The Sights

In Glasgow itself, the center of the city is **George Square,** dominated by the City Chambers which Queen Victoria opened in 1888. Of the statues in the square, the most imposing is that of Sir Walter Scott on an 80-foot column. Naturally, you'll find Victoria along with her beloved Albert, plus Robert Burns. The Banqueting Hall, lavishly decorated, is open to the public on most weekdays.

The **Cathedral of St. Kentigern,** first built in 1136, was burned down in 1192. It was rebuilt soon after, and the Laigh Kirk, the vaulted crypt said to be the finest in Europe, remains to this day. Visit the tomb of St. Mungo in the crypt where a light always burns. The edifice is mainland Scotland's only complete medieval cathedral, dating from the 12th and 13th centuries. Formerly a place of pilgrimage, 16th-century zeal purged it of all "monuments of idolatry." For the best view of the cathedral, cross the Bridge of Sighs into the necropolis—the graveyard containing almost every type of architecture in the world. The graveyard is built on a rocky hill and dominated by a statue of John Knox. It was first opened in 1832, and the first person to be buried there was a Jew—typical of the mixing of all races in this cosmopolitan city where tolerance reigns until the rival local football teams meet. The necropolis is full of monuments to Glasgow merchants, among them William Miller (1810–1872) who wrote "Wee Willie Winkie."

The **Art Gallery and Museum,** at Kelvingrove Park, is the finest in Britain outside London. The gallery contains such a fine collection of old masters, including Dutch and French painters, that one first-time woman visitor questioned their authenticity—she could not believe her eyes. Displayed are works by Giorgione (*Adulteress Brought before Christ*), Rembrandt (*Man in Armour*), Rubens, and Bellini, including four galleries of British paintings from the 16th century to the present. The gallery of 19th-century French paintings includes all the famous names. Even Salvador Dali gets in on the act with his *Christ of St. John of the Cross*. Scottish painting, of course, is also well represented.

In 1944 Sir William Burrell presented a splendid collection of paintings, tapestries, and other objets d'art. The Burrell collection is to be housed separately, but may still be at Kelvingrove during your visit. One highlight of the Burrell bequest are nearly two dozen drawings and paintings by Degas.

The museum has an outstanding collection of European arms and armor, displays from the ethnography collections featuring the Eskimo peoples, Africa, and Polynesia, as well as a large section devoted to natural history. There are also small, regularly changing displays from the decorative art collections of silver (especially Scottish), ceramics, glass, and jewelry. The museum and gallery are open weekdays from 10 a.m. to 5 p.m., on Sunday from 2 to 5 p.m. On the premises is a restaurant and coffee bar.

Haggs Castle is a branch museum for children, with displays showing the history of the castle, temporary exhibitions, and a workshop for activities.

St. Enoch Exhibition Centre is a gallery for temporary exhibitions of contemporary film and decorative arts.

If time remains, **Provands Lordship,** 3 Castle St., is the oldest house in Glasgow, built in 1471. Mary Queen of Scots is said to have written the notorious "Casket letters" there. The house contains 17th- and 18th-century furniture and domestic utensils. It is now in the care of Glasgow Museums and Art Galleries. Entrance is 15p (35¢) for adults, 5p (12¢) for children; open Monday through Saturday from 11 a.m. to 4 p.m., Sunday from 2 to 4 p.m.; closed Christmas and New Year's Day.

Glasgow also offers a number of branch museums, including the **Museum of Transport,** 25 Albert Dr. (tel. 423-8000). Once Glasgow's trams were famous. You can see seven displayed here, dating from 1894. Many Scottish-built vintage cars are also exhibited, along with railway locomotives. The most recent extensions house a magnificent display of nearly 200 ship models and a reconstruction of the old Glasgow underground. Hours are weekdays from 10 a.m. to 5 p.m., on Sunday from 2 to 5 p.m.

Pollok House, in Pollok Park, is an Adam house built circa 1752, with later additions. The interior is in the rococo style, with displays of British furniture from the years 1750–1820, Spanish and English glass, and the important Stirling Maxwell collection of Spanish paintings. In a wooded park, the house may be visited weekdays from 10 a.m. to 5 p.m., Sunday from 2 to 5 p.m.

Finally, **People's Palace,** Glasgow Green, provides a visual record of the rise of Glasgow. The palace was built originally as a cultural center for the people of the East End of Glasgow, and it was constructed between 1895 and 1897. Exhibitions trace the foundation of the city in 1175–8. Such turbulent interludes as the reign of Mary Queen of Scots are represented by the personal relics of the queen herself. The bulk of the collections are from the 19th century, representing Victorian Glasgow, including posters, programs, and props from the music hall era. The city museum may be visited weekdays from 10 a.m. to 5 p.m., on Sunday from 2 to 5 p.m.

The park in which the palace is situated, **Glasgow Green,** is the oldest public park in the city. Once a common pasture for the early town, it has witnessed much history. Seek out, in particular, Nelson's monument, the first of its kind in Britain; the Saracen Fountain, opposite the palace; and Templeton's Carpet Factory, modeled on the Doge's Palace in Venice.

The principal shopping district is **Sauchiehall Street,** Glasgow's fashion center, containing many shops and department stores where you'll often find quite good bargains, particularly in woolen goods. The major shopping area—about three blocks long—has been made into a pedestrian mall.

Although it's blighted by much industry and stark commercial areas, Glasgow contains many gardens and open spaces.

Chief among these is **Bellahouston Park,** Paisley Road West, 171 acres of beauty with a sunken wall and rock gardens as well as wildlife. It's open all year—daily from 8 a.m. to dusk.

Glasgow's **Botanic Gardens,** Great Western Road, covers 40 acres—an extensive collection of tropical plants and herb gardens. It, too, is open all year, daily, including Sunday, from 7 a.m. to dusk.

Linn Park, on Clarkston Road, is 212 acres of pine and woodland, with many lovely walks along the river. There's also a nature trail. The park is open all year, daily from 8 a.m. to dusk.

Greenock is an important industrial and shipbuilding town on the Clyde Estuary a few miles west of the center of Glasgow. It was the birthplace in 1736 of James Watt, inventor of the steam engine. A huge Cross of Lorraine on Lyle Hill above the town commemorates Free French sailors who died in the Battle of the Atlantic during World War II.

Past Greenock, sea lochs strike into the Strathclyde hills—Gareloch, Loch Long, and Loch Goil—with Holy Loch pointing more to the west. This was once a holiday region, but that was changed by the World War. Holy Loch was its Polaris base, and British atomic subs are stationed in these waters. There are new seaports on Loch Long and the Gareloch. Loch Long is long, but its name derives from the Gaelic word meaning "a ship," and the name really means the "loch of the ships." Long before the Clyde was world famous for shipbuilding, the galleys of the old chieftains sheltered in these waters. Vikings hauled their boats overland from Loch Long to raid the country around Loch Lomond.

Gourock, three miles west of Greenock, is a resort and yachting center. On the cliff side of Gourock is **"Granny Kempock,"** a six-foot-high stone of gray schist which was probably significant in prehistoric times. In past centuries it was used by fishermen in rites to ensure fair weather. Couples planning marriage used to circle Granny to get her blessing and to ensure fertility in their marriage.

From Gourock, car-ferries take travelers to Dunoon on the Cowal peninsula.

Upper-Bracket Hotels

Albany, Bothwell Street (tel. 248-2656), is a contemporary tower block hotel in the heart of Glasgow, rising nine stories and offering a total of 250 well-furnished rooms, all with private baths. The rate in a single is £32 ($73.60), rising to £45 ($103.50), including a full breakfast, service, and VAT. Windows are double glazed against the noise, and air conditioning and color TV sets are what you'd expect in a hotel of this standing. However, in spite of its modernity, the Albany is efficiently and beautifully run in the grand tradition of Scottish hospitality. The staff extends a friendly welcome, and you don't feel part of a computer. The restaurant, Four Seasons, exudes formality, offering a well-chosen French menu, although you may prefer the Carvery, typical of such places already recommended in London. At any hour of the day, you can order drinks and sandwiches brought to your room. The public rooms are well appointed, of a first-class international standard, and there are ample bars, including a Scandinavian-style Cabin Bar if you want to sneak away to the cellar for a light snack.

The **North British Hotel,** George Square (tel. 332-6711), is an old-fashioned and handsome hotel looking out over the green trees and lawns of the square in the center of this busy, commercial city. It is close to the Queen Street Station where trains depart for the north of Scotland. There is a comfortable lounge bar for a quiet rest or the Devil's Elbow, a bright and lively pub. The addition of a new wing means that you will alalmost certainly get an accommodation with private bath. Singles go for £20.50 ($47.15) to £26 ($59.80), and doubles or twins from £36 ($82.80) to £43 ($98.90). Over the weekends the rates are often cheaper—by about a pound or so. The dining room is enormous and discreet, and the food is standard, although quite good.

Central Hotel, Gordon Street (tel. 221-9680), still retains its Victorian aura, although it has been completely updated to meet modern demands. Owned by British Railways, the hotel stands at the Central Station where it has been welcoming train travelers for more than a century. Its rooms, some of which are cavernous, are comfortable and well appointed, and of the 211 accommodations available, at least 150 contain their own private baths. Singles range in price from £35 ($80.50), and doubles go from £46 ($105.80). We've saved the best for last—the Malmaison Restaurant, serving what, in our opinion, is the finest food in Glasgow (see our dining recommendations, immediately following).

Excelsior Hotel, Glasgow Airport (tel. 887-1212), stands at the Glasgow Airport at Abbotsinch, and is not to be confused with the international Prestwick Airport. The Excelsior is modern, and, like many other concrete-and-glass buildings these days, is absolutely geared to the needs of today's traveler. All rooms, for example, contain private baths with shower, and there are radio and TV sets as well. The 24-hour room service promised by the hotel really works. We asked for sandwiches and drinks at 3 a.m. and got them promptly and cheerfully. In the rooms are coffee- and tea-making equipment for do-it-yourselfers. Singles rent for £30 ($69) and doubles for £45 ($103.50), including VAT and service. There are the usual lounges and bars, plus a well-designed and pleasantly paneled dining room with quite a wide menu of international and Scottish dishes, as well as a cut-and-come-again Carvery. All meals are extra, but not expensive.

The Middle Bracket

Tinto Firs, 470 Kilmarnock Rd. (tel. 637-2353), is a modern, two-story building in a residential sector away from the city center. It's small, only 30 rooms, of which 25 contain private baths. It is efficiently run, but the welcome from the staff is almost old-fashioned and personal. The bedrooms are well designed and compact—pleasantly, although not lavishly, decorated, costing from £25 ($57.50) to £30.50 ($70.15) in a single, from £35 ($80.50) in a double, but you must pay extra for breakfast. The food is of a good standard, competently served.

Lorne, 923 Sauchiehall St. (tel. 334-4891), is a modern hotel, with compact, functional bedrooms that are, nevertheless, attractively decorated and most comfortable. It's best suited for a stay of only one or two nights. Of its 86 chambers, only 50 contain private baths. Singles rent for £20 ($46) to £25 ($57.50), going up to £28 ($64.40) to £34 ($78.20) in a double. The hotel serves dinner till around 9:30 p.m., offering such specialties as chicken Devonshire and steak tartare. One of the Lorne's bars stays open till 1 a.m., and is most popular.

Bellahouston, 517 Paisley Rd. (tel. 427-3146), a modern, three-story hotel, is especially preferred by business people, as it's convenient to the Glasgow

Airport, although about a ten-minute ride from the center of the city. It is also quite near Bellahouston Park, from which it takes its name. There's plenty of parking which makes the hotel even more alluring. Each of its 50 functional bedrooms contains a private bath, renting for £19 ($43.70) in a single, from £25 ($57.50) in a double, including a full breakfast. The fully licensed hotel has central heating, an elevator, TV lounge, and cocktail bar, as well as a restaurant. In winter there is dancing on Saturday nights.

The **Glasgow Centre Hotel,** Argyle Street (tel. 248-2355), is a modern block of 120 bedrooms, all with bath, standing in the heart of the city, within easy reach of the main railway stations. Somewhat stark in appearance, it offers rooms which have been equipped with many conveniences, such as auto-dial telephone, electric alarm clocks, and individually controlled central heating. Opened in 1974, the hotel charges £25 ($57.50) in a single, from £32 ($73.60) in a double, these tariffs including a continental breakfast, although a full Scottish breakfast costs extra. The Centre (not to be confused with the Central) also features a specialty restaurant, plus two bars.

The Budget Hotels

The **Burnbank Hotel,** 67–85 West Princes St. (tel. 332-4400), sits on a quiet crescent just a few steps from the nearest public transportation—and only a ten-minute walk from the center of Glasgow. Yet the large hotel and its peaceful street exude a leisurely atmosphere of an earlier era. The two lounges are furnished with antiques in keeping with the spirit of the hotel. Many of the 36 bedrooms have private baths or showers. Bed-and-breakfast rates range from £9.50 ($21.85) to £10.50 ($24.15) per person, inclusive of VAT. The full Scottish breakfast is a hearty meal served in the relaxed atmosphere of the comfortable hotel dining room. The droll wit of Mr. Lind, proprietor, captivates his guests. He is happy to explain all sorts of things about his antiques, Glasgow, whiskey, or whatever you'd like to ask about.

Hazelcourt Hotel, 232 Renfrew St. (tel. 332-7737), is small and quiet, a pleasantly furnished hotel in the heart of the city, convenient to bus depots, the rail and air terminals, plus shops and theaters, even the Kelvin Hall and Art Galleries. The comfortable rooms are centrally heated, containing hot and cold running water, shaver sockets, and electric radiators. The Hazelcourt contains only seven bedrooms, none with private bath, charging from £9 ($20.70) in a single, from £16 ($36.80) in a double, these tariffs including breakfast. Dinner, served between 6 and 7 p.m., can also be ordered if requested in advance.

Kelvin Hotel, 15 Buckingham Terrace (tel. 339-7143), stands at the west end of Glasgow, off Great Western Road on the road to Loch Lomond, about a ten-minute drive from the heart of Glasgow. Near the university, it is also convenient to the Botanic Gardens and the BBC. The rooms are comfortable, although simply furnished—14 in all, ranging in price from £10 ($23) in a single to £16 ($36.80) in a double, including breakfast.

The Leading Restaurant

Malmaison Restaurant, Gordon Street (tel. 221-9680), takes its name from the villa that once housed Josephine and Napoleon outside Paris. The Malmaison in Scotland is actually in the previously recommended Central Hotel, that Victorian building that forms part of one of the city's principal railway stations.

Of course, you dine here in your best jacket and tie (if you're a man), because the Malmaison is clearly the most luxurious dining choice in town—the aura enhanced by the fresh flowers, the soft piano music, and the stern portraits.

Both simple and complex dishes are virtually without flaw, and the sauces are light and well balanced. In addition to the decor, the lavishness is evident in the presentation. On one recent occasion, the highly trained waiter gave us a veritable lesson in cookery when we inquired about a particular dish.

The food is perhaps the best in Scotland of an international nature. Chef Stuart Cameron is a past master. His specialties are a dream, including surprise de sole, avocat fourré écossaise, soup de poissons Ondine, broccoli with hollandaise sauce, délices de turbot la Rochelle, and ris de veau Jacoulet.

Over the years we've had some of our finest meals in Scotland here, including, on one memorable night, grouse. Although chefs have come and gone, the standards have remained consistent.

Lunch is from 12:30 to 2:30 p.m. and dinner from 7 to 10:30 p.m. A set luncheon goes for £9 ($20.70), and an à la carte dinner for £20 ($46) and up. It is essential to make a reservation. The restaurant is closed for lunch on Saturday, shuts down all day on Sunday, and is closed for all of August.

Other Favorites for Dining

Fountain, 2 Woodside Crescent, Charing Cross (tel. 332-6396), attracts a clientele of gourmets and Glasgow's most fashionable people. Although it doesn't have the standards of Malmaison, already recommended, it is, nevertheless, sophisticated and formal. The cookery is almost invariably good.

Against an attractive backdrop, with a subdued piano player performing nightly, you can enjoy some fine French cooking between the hours of noon and 2:30 p.m. and 7 and 10 p.m. One of the all-time favorite dishes here is crayfish tails. Ever had a "casserole des gourmets"?

The restaurant shuts for lunch on Saturday and all day on Sunday. The table d'hôte luncheon costs about £6 ($13.80), although you can easily pay as much as £17 ($39.10) per person in the evening. The wine list is excellent, and it's most atmospheric. For some reason, it seems out of place in Glasgow, but that's part of its charm.

Ambassador, 19 Blythswood Sq. (tel. 221-2034), is a cellar restaurant specializing in continental dishes, including such specialties as scampi Ambassadeur (in a white sauce served with rice), tender escalope de veau, and, of course, the finest rib of roast Angus beef on the bone. The licensed restaurant features dancing to a live band, and the service by the waiters is polite and attentive. Lunch is from 12:30 to 2:30 p.m., costing £5 ($11.50) if you order from the set menu. A special lure of the Ambassador is its pretheater set meal, costing the same price as the lunch. However, if you dine à la carte, any time before 11 p.m., expect to pay about £12 ($27.60) per person. The restaurant closes on Sunday and bank holidays.

Rogano Restaurant, 11 South Exchange Pl. (tel. 248-6687), is famous for its seafood and crustaceans, serving some of the most superbly prepared and fresh-tasting fish dishes in Glasgow. The oysters (if you're there on the right night) are superb. Most definitely, Rogano is one of the best known eating places in Scotland, and night after night you'll see some of the same customers pondering the long, varied menu, which also has steak, veal, and chicken dishes. For a complete meal, expect to pay as much as £15 ($34.50) per head, although you can dine much cheaper, of course. Lunch is from noon to 2:30

p.m. and dinner from 6 to 10:30 p.m. It's advisable to reserve a table. Closed Sunday and bank holidays.

Vesuvio, 15 St. Vincent Pl. (tel. 221-0355), seems run pretty much like an Italian family business. It is a praiseworthy, unassuming restaurant, where the service is brisk and efficient. The feature of the place is its dinner dancing to a live orchestra about six nights a week. Although Italian cookery is the attraction, the chef does not limit himself to the cuisine of that country, but offers a full range of continental dishes. Specialties include chicken Vesuviana, prepared in a tomato sauce with green peppers, and saltimbocca, a veal and ham dish, and, for dessert, a delectable zabaglione. If you visit for lunch, you can order a set meal, costing £5.25 ($12.07) per person, although your à la carte tab in the evening is more likely to tally up to £12 ($27.60). Closed Sunday. Hours are from noon to 3 p.m. and from 5:30 p.m. to 1 a.m.

Danish Food Centre, 56 St. Vincent St. (tel. 221-0518), offers what you'd expect, the famous Danish cold table and those delectable open-face sandwiches known as smørrebrød. You are rarely disappointed here. The smoked fish, in particular, is fresh and most reliable—so good, in fact, we've often made an entire meal of it. If you have the appetite for it, a hot "plat du jour" is featured daily. The service is friendly and efficient. Arrive between noon and 2:30 p.m. and between 6 and 10:30 p.m. and expect to pay about £6.50 ($14.95) per person for a really filling menu and a change of pace from typically Scottish fare. Closed on bank holidays.

A Few Pubs

The **Horseshoe Bar and Restaurant,** 17 Drury St., is worth taking a look at even if you don't stop for a drink or a pub lunch or dinner. Drury is a narrow, short street, probably little changed for a century or so. There's lots of highly polished brass edging the door, and frosted glass door panels. The pub has dark wood paneling and a real pub flavor. You can have high teas upstairs in the restaurant from 5 to 7:30 p.m.

Amphora, 410 Sauchiehall St., and **Saints and Sinners,** 278 St. Vincent St., cater especially to young people, with rock and disco music.

Ingram Lounge, 138 Queen St., has wood-paneled walls and a modern air. There's a bar upstairs and a lounge downstairs, where you can relax after sightseeing all around George Square.

15. Ayr, Prestwick, and District

As Sir Walter Scott dominates the Borders, so does Robert Burns the country around Ayr and Prestwick. There are, in addition, a string of famous seaside resorts stretching from Girvan to Largs. Some of the greatest golf courses in Britain, including Turnberry, are found here, and Prestwick, of course, is one of the major airports of Europe.

AYR: Ayr is the most popular resort on Scotland's west coast. A busy market town, it offers 2½ miles of sands and makes for a good center for touring the Burns Country. This royal burgh is also noted for its manufacture of fabrics and carpets, so you may want to allow time to browse through its shops. With its steamer cruises, fishing, golf, and racing, it faces the Isle of Arran and the Firth of Clyde.

Ayr is full of Burns associations. The 13th-century **Auld Brig o' Ayr,** the poet's "poor narrow footpath of a street,/ Where two wheelbarrows tremble when they meet," was renovated in 1910. A Burns museum is housed in the thatched **Tam o'Shanter Inn** in Ayr High Street, an alehouse in Rabbie's day.

The **Auld Kirk** of Ayr dates from 1654 when it replaced the 12th-century Church of St. John. Burns was baptized in the kirk.

Ayr is also the birthplace of the famous road builder, John L. MacAdam, whose name was immortalized in road surfacing.

In Tarbolton village, 7½ miles northeast of Ayr, is the **Bachelors' Club**, a 17th-century house where in 1780 Burns and his friends founded a literary and debating society, now a property of the National Trust for Scotland. In 1779 Burns attended dancing lessons there, against the wishes of his father. There also, in 1781, he was initiated as a Freemason in the Lodge St. David. Eleven months later, he became a member of Lodge St. James, which continues today in the village. Samuel Hay, 7 Croft St. (tel. Tarbolton 424), says the Bachelors' Club is open for visitors any time of day from April until October, and he will arrange to show it at other times if you telephone. Admission is 30p (69¢) for adults, 15p (35¢) for children. Tarbolton is six miles from Prestwick Airport.

For centuries, Ayr has been associated with horse racing, and it now has the top racecourse in Scotland. One of the main streets of the town is named Racecourse Road for a stretch near the town center.

Where to Stay

Pickwick Hotel, 19 Racecourse Rd. (tel. Ayr 60111). It may seem ironic to have a hotel commemorating a character in a Charles Dickens novel in a town noted for its memories of Rabbie Burns. But this early Victorian hotel—set on its own grounds—does just that. The Pickwick itself is really a large-size house, renting out 15 well-furnished private bedrooms which contain either a private shower or else a complete bath. The bed-and-breakfast rate is £18 ($41.40) per person, including a full breakfast, VAT, and service. Each room bears a Dickensian title. In the paneled Pickwick Club you can soak up much Dickensian atmosphere. The food itself is simple but well prepared, a dinner costing from £7 ($16.10). Both hot and cold snacks are available in the Eatanswill lounge. Dickensian fans, of course, will recall that Eatanswill was where Mr. Pickwick got involved in the Parliamentary election.

Caledonian Hotel, Dalblair Road (tel. Ayr 69331), occupies a convenient central location, offering comfortable although certainly not luxurious bedrooms, all 122 of which contain functional, compact private baths. Singles rent for £25 ($57.50), doubles for £38 ($87.40). Flight crews from various international carriers stay here, a fact acknowledged by the Flight Deck Bar. The food is good, particularly in the hotel's theme restaurant, Chaplin's. There is also a sauna, souvenir shop, and a disco which is open five nights a week. A dinner-dance is held every Saturday night.

Marine Court, Fairfield Road (tel. Ayr 67461), has long been a favorite with travelers. A substantial building, in a cul-de-sac, it offers good, solid comfort, and many of its rooms open onto a sweeping view of the Firth of Clyde. The hotel also lies about 200 yards from the beach, and it makes for a charming oasis, especially as you wander through its garden. The bedrooms are well furnished and immaculately maintained, and almost all of them come equipped with private bath. Singles peak at £15.50 ($35.65), and doubles are rented for a top £28 ($64.40), including a full breakfast. The food is well prepared and handsomely served. The demi-pension rate is about £21 ($48.30) per person nightly.

The Local Pub

By all means, pay your respects to Burns by going to **Rabbie's Bar,** Burns Statute Square (tel. Ayr 69200), right in the heart of town. A colorfully decorated pub, this place is, of course, dedicated to the memory of the poet. On the walls you'll find a selection of some of his most famous lines. In addition to the good drink which Burns himself enjoyed, you can also order simple fare such as snacks and grills. Guests sit near a thatched bar counter.

ALLOWAY: Some three miles from the center of Ayr is where Robert Burns, Scotland's national poet, was born on January 25, 1759, in the gardener's cottage—the "auld clay biggin"—his father, William Burns, built in 1757. More than 100,000 people visit the **Burns Cottage** annually, and it still retains some of its original furniture, including the bed in which the poet was born. Chairs displayed here were said to have been used by Tam O'Shanter and Souter Johnnie. Beside the cottage in which the poet lived is a museum, open all year from 11 a.m. to 7 p.m. or dusk. Admission to the cottage and the Burns Monument is 30p (69¢) for adults, 15p (35¢) for children.

The Auld Brig over the Ayr, mentioned in "Tam o'Shanter," still spans the river, and Alloway Auld Kirk, also mentioned in the poem, stands roofless and "haunted" not far away. The poet's father is buried in the graveyard of the kirk.

The **Land o' Burns Centre** near the monument is a good place to stop. You can watch a multiscreen presentation of highlights of Burn's life, his friends, and his poetry. Information is available from the friendly personnel, and a well-stocked gift shop is there. The Russians are particularly fond of Burns and his poetry, and many come annually to visit the cottage and pore over his original manuscripts.

Where to Stay

The **Burns Monument Hotel** (tel. Alloway 42466), is an 185-year-old inn which looks out onto the Doon River and the bridge, "Brig o'Doon," immortalized in "Tam O'Shanter." The inn is an attractive, historical place, with riverside gardens. The rooms are pleasantly and attractively decorated, bright and cheerful, opening onto river views. There are only nine rooms, each with hot and cold running water, some with private bathroom or shower. Terms are £15.50 ($35.65) per person per night for bed and a full breakfast, inclusive of VAT. In the bar you can order such simple fare as sandwiches and grills.

The **Balgarth Hotel,** Dunure Road, at Doonfoot (tel. Alloway 43418), lies two miles south of Ayr on the A719, a coastal road at the estuary of the Doon River, about half a mile from the village of Alloway. The hotel stands on its own grounds of pleasant gardens and woods, opening onto views of the Firth of Clyde and the Carrick Hills. Many motorists stop here en route to Ireland from the ferry station at Stranraer. Rooms are comfortably and pleasantly furnished—ten in all, three of which contain private baths. The overnight charge is £11 ($25.30) per person in a room without bath, £11.50 ($26.45) per person with bath, these tariffs including a full breakfast, VAT, and service. A set dinner costs £6 ($13.80). The hotel is open all year.

CULZEAN CASTLE: One of Robert Adam's most notable creations, although built around an ancient tower of the Kennedys, Culzean (pronounced Cullane), 12 miles south-southwest of Ayr, dates mainly from 1777 and is considered one of the finest Adam houses in Scotland. The castle, with a view of Ailsa Craig to the south and overlooking the Firth of Clyde, is well worth a visit and is of special interest to Americans because of General Eisenhower's connection with it and its National Guest Flat. In 1946 the guest flat was given to the general for his lifetime in gratitude for his services as Supreme Commander of Allied Forces in World War II. Culzean stands near the famous golf courses of Turnberry and Troon, a fact which particularly pleased the golf-loving Eisenhower.

An exhibition of Eisenhower memorabilia includes sound and audio-visual spectacles, and is seen by more than 100,000 people a year. The exhibition is sponsored by the Scottish Heritage U.S.A., Inc., and Mobil Oil. To illustrate his career, there is a capsule history of World War II demonstrated with wall maps. Mementos of Eisenhower include his North African campaign desk and a replica of the Steuben glass bowl given him by his cabinet when he retired from the presidency.

The castle is open April 1 through September daily, 10 a.m. to 6 p.m. (last admission at 5:30 p.m.); October 1 through October 31 daily, 10 a.m. to 4 p.m. Admission to the castle is £1.20 ($2.76) for adults, 60p ($1.38) for children.

In the castle grounds is **Culzean Country Park**, which in 1970 became the first such park in Scotland. It has an exhibition center in farm buildings by Adam. The 565-acre grounds include a walled garden, an aviary, a swan park, a camellia house, and an orangery. Cars can drive through the Culzean Country Park at a cost of 80p ($1.84).

After leaving Culzean Castle, you might want to take a short drive to **Kirkoswald** near Maybole. This is the thatched cottage which was the home of the village cobbler, John Davidson (Souter Johnnie), at the end of the 18th century. Davidson and his friend Douglas Graham of Shanter Farm were immortalized by Burns in his poem "Tam o' Shanter." The cottage contains Burnsiana and contemporary cobblers' tools. In the churchyard are the graves of Tam O'Shanter and Souter Johnnie, two of his best known characters. The cottage is open April 1 to September 30, daily except Friday, noon to 5 p.m. (other times by appointment). Admission is 30p (69¢) for adults, 15p (35¢) for children.

GIRVAN: About eight miles south of Culzean Castle on the A77, Girvan is the leading coastal resort of southwest Scotland, with sandy beaches and good fishing. A whiskey distillery offers guided tours (and samples) for visitors.

In summer entertainment is offered at the **Beach Pavilion**, featuring music, dancing, children's shows, variety shows, and concerts.

Ailsa Craig, a 1110-foot-high, rounded rock ten miles offshore, is a nesting ground and sanctuary for seabirds and formerly provided granite for stones used in the Scottish game of curling. You can sail out to the rock for a modest charge.

Three miles northeast of Girvan is the 16th-century **Kilochan Castle**, stronghold of the Cathcarts of Carleton in the valley of the Water of Girvan.

Six miles north of Girvan are the scant remains of **Turnberry Castle**, where many historians believe Robert the Bruce was born in 1274.

The **Westcliffe Hotel**, Louisa Drive (tel. Girvan 2128), is on the seafront and overlooks the Promenade, putting greens, and a children's boating lake. This is a family hotel, and the resident proprietors, Mr. and Mrs. Robert Jardine, have carried out extensive alterations, adding six ground-floor bedrooms, all with private bathrooms, at the back. Some bedrooms in the original building have showers. All bedrooms have hot and cold water and electric shaving points, and are carpeted. Rooms without bath rent for £8 ($18.40) per person for bed and breakfast. With bath, the rent is £9 ($20.70). The Westcliffe is licensed, with a small service bar at the end of the dining room which looks out over the seafront and Ailsa Craig. Mrs. Jardine personally supervises preparation of the food, which is very good. There are tea- and coffee- making facilities in the reception area.

PRESTWICK: Prestwick is the oldest recorded baronial burgh in Scotland. But most visitors today aren't concerned with that ancient fact—rather, they fly in, landing at Prestwick's International Airport, which is, in itself, a popular sightseeing attraction, as spectators gather to watch planes take off and land from all over the world.

Behind St. Ninian's Episcopal Church is **Bruce's Well,** the water from which is reputed to have cured Robert the Bruce of leprosy. The **Mercat Cross** still stands outside what used to be the Registry Office and marks the center of the oldest part of Prestwick, whose existence goes back to at least 983. Prestwick is a popular holiday town, and is considered one of Scotland's most attractive resorts, with its splendid sands and famous golf courses. Prestwick opens onto views of Ayr Bay and the Isle of Arran.

Where to Stay

Carlton Motor Hotel, 187 Ayr Rd. (tel. Prestwick 76811), is a good stopover point if you're waiting for your plane at Prestwick. On the Prestwick–Ayr Road, right in the vicinity of the international airport, the hotel is built in a straightforward modern design which offers all the amenities you'd expect in such a place—coffee-making equipment, full baths with all rooms, color TV, and attractive furnishings. Singles begin at £18 ($41.40), and doubles rent for £26 ($59.80), including breakfast, service, and VAT. A trio of bars is offered, and there are plenty of lounges in which to relax. Some of the windows open onto a garden. A set dinner costs £5 ($11.50), and you can dance to a live band on Friday and Saturday nights at no extra charge.

Adamton House Hotel, Monkton, near Prestwick (tel. Prestwick 70678), is an 18th-century, 30-bedroom hotel with views of the Isle of Arran and Ailsa Craig. As it lies only a few miles from Prestwick Airport, it provides an excellent opportunity to get over jet-lag. All rooms have bath or shower, tea-making equipment, and TV and radio. The beautiful curved wooden staircase leads down again to a quiet, comfortable lounge, the restaurant, and the cocktail bar. In the Secret Room beneath the house, the hotel stages nightly a historical banquet with candlelight and medieval entertainment. Singles with shower are £28 ($64.40), and doubles and twins with bath cost from £40 ($92), including breakfast and service, although VAT is extra.

Towans Hotel, Prestwick Airport (tel. Prestwick 79691). The original building faces a side lawn and then looks out over the Firth of Clyde to the Isle of Arran. Much of the accommodation is in a new hotel/motel block which blends very successfully with the old. The Martin family, conscious of the needs of international travelers passing through Prestwick Airport, are geared to catering for early and late arrivals. Rooms have private baths, and tea and coffee makers. Breakfast is served from 4 a.m., and the dining room has a good local reputation for well-cooked meals. A bed will cost you from £12 ($27.60). All meals are extra, but you can make as much tea and coffee as you want in your room.

The Parkstone, Esplanade (tel. Prestwick 77286), is more suited for a beach holiday center, as it opens onto the sea. Catering to families, it is handsomely perched, receiving guests all year in one of its many bedrooms, none of which contains a private bath. The single tariff is £11.75 ($27.03), rising to £24 ($55.20) in a double, including a full breakfast, VAT, and service. Rooms are comfortably and pleasantly furnished. A two-course luncheon goes for £3.50 ($8.05), a set dinner for £6.50 ($14.95).

TROON: This holiday resort looks out across the Firth of Clyde to the Isle of Arran. It offers several golf links, including the "Old Troon" course. Bathers in summer find plenty of room on its two miles of sandy beaches, stretching from both sides of its harbor. The broad sands and shallow waters make it a safe haven also. From here you can take steamer trips to Arran and the Kyles of Bute.

Troon is mostly a 20th-century town, its earlier history having gone unrecorded. It takes its name from the curiously shaped promontory that juts out into the Clyde estuary on which the old town and the harbor stand. The promontory was called "Trwyn," the Cymric word for nose, and later this became the Trone and then Troon.

Fullarton Estate, on the edge of Troon beyond the municipal golf course, is the ancestral seat of the Dukes of Portland.

A massive statue of **Britannia** stands on the seafront as a memorial to the dead of the two World Wars. On her breastplate is the lion of Scotland emerging from the sea.

Where to Stay

Marine Hotel, Crosbie Road (tel. Troon 31-4444), is a large deluxe hotel which is enveloped by about 20 miles of seaside golf courses. One of the principal hotels along the Clyde coast, it offers a wide range of accommodations —70 rooms in all, each with bath, and each differing in style, space, and furnishings. The single rate is £28 ($64.40), rising to £45 ($103.50) in a double, including VAT. Not only are the views from the windows spectacular, but the hotel is most agreeable and makes a good base for touring the Burns Country. The helpful staff gives personal attention—if you come back a second time they'll know your name. The noise from Prestwick—three miles away—is kept out by double-glazed windows.

The hotel's restaurants offer excellent fare, although we prefer L'Auberge de Provence, where the French cookery is superb, as is the selection of fine burgundies. The auberge is decorated in a rustic style, serving dinner only, from 7:30 to 10:30 p.m. daily, except Sunday and Monday, charging about £12 ($27.60) per person. The lounges are spacious, and there are two stylish bars.

Sun Court, Crosbie Road (tel. Troon 312727), was once the home of an industrialist, and it offers all the grand style of the Edwardian era. Like the Marine, it looks out onto golf courses and the sea. Its most delightful feature is a conservatory filled with flowers. The hotel also contains a Real Tennis Court, one of the few in Britain. A sandy beach along the Firth of Clyde is about a 100-yard walk away.

Open all year, the Sun Court offers 20 handsome bedrooms, 17 of which contain private baths. The single tariff ranges from £20 ($46) to £22 ($50.60), the double rate going from £23 ($52.90) to £28 ($64.40). There is as well a beautiful walled garden. The lounges are stylish and decorated in a conservative idiom. Try to get one of the more old-fashioned bedrooms, although you may be assigned a more modernized one. From a well-stocked cellar emerges a fine collection of wine, and the food at Sun Court is well prepared and served.

KILMARNOCK: This inland town is the site of the largest whiskey-bottling concern in the world. Johnnie Walker, a grocer in King Street, started to blend whiskey in Kilmarnock in 1820, and the product is known all over the world today.

The town also has Burns associations. The first edition of his poems was printed here in 1786. Burns published the poems to raise money to emigrate to Jamaica, but they were so successful he decided to remain in Scotland. In Kay Park, the **Burns Monument** is a red sandstone temple surmounted by a tower, which contains a good museum of Burnsiana.

Dundonald Castle, 4½ miles southwest of Kilmarnock, is a notable landmark high on an isolated hill. It was built by Robert II, the first Stuart king, who died there in 1390, as did Robert III in 1406. East along the River Irvine are the three lace-making towns of Galston, Newmilns, and Darvel where Dutch and Huguenot immigrants settled in the 17th century.

16. Dumfries and Galloway

Southwestern Scotland is often overlooked by motorists rushing north. But this country of Burns is filled with many rewarding targets—a land of unspoiled countryside, fishing harbors, artists' colonies of color-washed houses, and romantically ruined abbeys and castles dating from the days of the border wars.

It's a fine touring country, and the hotels are generally small—of the Scottish provincial variety—but that usually means a friendly reception from a smiling staff and good traditional Scottish cookery, using the local produce.

We've documented the most important centers below, but have included some offbeat places for those seeking a more esoteric trip.

LOCKERBIE: A border market town, Lockerbie lies in the beautiful valley of Annandale, offering much fishing and golf. It's a good center for exploring some sightseeing attractions in its environs.

Lockerbie was the scene in 1593 of a battle which ended one of the last great Border family feuds. The Johnstones routed the Maxwells, killing Lord Maxwell and 700 of his men. Many of the victims had their ears cut off with a cleaver—a method of mutilation which became known throughout the Border Country as the "Lockerbie Nick."

Of interest are the remains of **Lochmaben Castle,** 3½ miles west of Lockerbie, said to have been the boyhood home (some historians say the birthplace) of Robert the Bruce. This castle, on the south shore of Castle Loch, was captured and recaptured 12 times and also withstood six attacks and sieges. James IV was a frequent visitor, and Mary Queen of Scots was here in 1565. The ruin of the early 14th-century castle is on the site of a castle of the de Brus family, ancestors of Robert the Bruce. However, the charming little hamlet of Lochmaben, with its five lochs, is reason enough to visit, regardless of who was or was not born there.

Rammerscales lies five miles west of Lockerbie and 2½ miles south of Lochmaben on the B7020. It can easily be visited on your tour of Lochmaben and its lakes. Rammerscales is a Georgian manor house, dating from 1760. Set on high ground, it offers beautiful views of the Valley of Annandale. You can visit a walled garden of the period. It is open from June 5 to September 16 on Tuesday and Thursday (also alternate Sundays from June 8), from 2 to 5 p.m., charging an admission of 60p ($1.38) for adults, 35p (81¢) for children.

SCOTLAND: LOCKERBIE/MOFFAT

If you're heading north to Lockerbie on the A74, we'd suggest a stopover in the village of Ecclefechan. There you can visit **Carlyle's House**, five miles southeast of Lockerbie on the Lockerbie–Carlisle Road. Even though the historian, critic, and essayist Thomas Carlyle isn't much read these days, the "arched house" in which he was born in 1795 is interesting in itself, containing mementoes and manuscripts of the author. It's open from April until the end of October, daily except Sunday, from 10 a.m. to 6 p.m., charging an admission of 25p (58¢) for adults, 15p (35¢) for children. For more information, telephone Ecclefechan 666.

In Lockerbie itself, you'll find the best accommodations at the **Dryfesdale** (tel. Lockerbie 2427), an 18th-century inn, replacing an earlier one which dated from the 17th century. The hotel offers traditional comfort and cleanliness, presenting you with a choice of 15 bedrooms, seven of which contain private plumbing. Several of the bedrooms are quite spacious, and you can stay either in the main building or in an annex. Singles range from £15.50 ($35.65) to £18.50 ($42.55), and doubles go from £23 ($52.90) to £30 ($69). The bar is done in a modern style, and a sun lounge opens onto good views. The management is most obliging and will direct you to nearby points of interest.

MOFFAT: An Annandale town, Moffat thrives as a center of a sheep-farming area, symbolized by a statue of a ram in the wide High Street, and has been a holiday resort since the mid-17th century, because of the curative properties of its water. It was here that Robert Burns composed the drinking song "O Willie Brew'd a Peck o' Maut." Today people visit this border town on the banks of the Annan River for its good fishing and golf.

North of Moffat is spectacular hill scenery. Five miles northwest is a huge, sheer-sided 500-foot-deep hollow in the hills called the **Devil's Beef Tub**, where Border cattle thieves, called reivers, hid cattle lifted in their raids.

Northeast along Moffat Water, past White Coomb, which stands 2696 feet high, is the **Grey Mare's Tail**, a 200-foot hanging waterfall formed by the Tail Burn dropping from Loch Skene. It is under the National Trust for Scotland.

Food and Lodgings

Annandale Hotel, High Street (tel. Moffat 20013), has been a coaching inn since the 18th century, housing travelers who crossed through the Border Country en route to Glasgow. However, the inn has been modernized and the amenities provided around here have improved considerably since the old days. Still, only five of the nearly 30 bedrooms contain private baths, and none of these has a shower. But the rates in the bathless rooms, to compensate, are low—from £12 ($27.60) in a single, from £23 ($52.90) in a double. In the more expensive chambers, expect to pay £19 ($43.70) in a single, from £29 ($66.70) in a double. The rooms, including the public ones, are kept immaculately. The proprietors have built up a good reputation for their cuisine which includes both British and German specialties. The last dinner is served at 8:30 p.m., and the cost is from £8 ($18.40). Although it's in the center of town, Annandale provides ample car parking on its own grounds.

Beechwood Country House Hotel & Restaurant, off Harthope Place (tel. Moffat 20210), has built its reputation more as a restaurant than a hotel. However, it does offer eight rooms, four of which contain private baths. The bedrooms are adequate for a short stay, costing from £9.50 ($21.85) in a single, from £19 ($43.70) in a double, although the best doubles go for £23.50 ($54.05).

The owner, Mrs. McIlwrick, is from New Zealand, and she serves some of the finest food in the area where good restaurants are few.

A set luncheon is offered from 1 to 2 p.m. for just £4.20 ($9.66), and it usually features a good-tasting, homemade soup, including, on one occasion, curried apple. When weather permits, you can take your coffee in the garden. Dinner is served between 7:30 and 9:30 p.m., when reserving a table is essential. Mrs. McIlwrick sparkles as the chef. A set meal will run £6.50 ($14.95), although you will more likely spend about £9.75 ($22.43). The dinner offers four courses, and the dishes are nearly always imaginative, certainly well prepared, and everything is made more enjoyable by the staff which sometimes lacks experience but always shows much enthusiasm. The freshly caught sea trout is a favorite, but if you arrive at the right season you are likely to find venison, even guinea-fowl, on the menu. The produce is fresh, our vegetables tasting as if they had just been picked in the garden. For breakfast the next morning, we were served oatcakes. Closed in January.

Mercury Motor Inn (tel. Moffat 20464) makes a good place to stop off for the night as you're traveling through the Border Country. At the southern end of town, each of its compact, functional bedrooms contains a private bath, toilet, and coffee-making equipment. Some rooms open onto a public park with a boating pond. Bunk beds for children can also be rented, and there is ample car parking. The staff is helpful and friendly, and you'll be charged from £18 ($41.40) to £21 ($48.30) in a single, from £26 ($59.80) to £31 ($71.30) in a double, including a full breakfast and VAT. The charming licensed bar is bedecked in an 1890s mauve, and the grill room provides good and reasonably priced meals—including such treats as grilled Scottish trout—until about 10 p.m. Dinner costs from £7 ($16.10).

READER'S SHOPPING RECOMMENDATION: "We visited the Moffat weavers at **Ladyknowe Mill**, High Street, a perfect place to purchase the least expensive tweeds, tartans, kilts, and knitwear that can be found in Britain. Wool kilts can be found for as little as £14 ($32.20). At the mill you can also watch the kiltmakers busy at work" (Anita T. Taylor, Hartsdale, N.Y.).

A Castle Hotel at Beattock

On the outskirts of Moffat, near the village of Beattock, the most luxurious accommodations in the area are found at **Auchen Castle Hotel** (tel. Beattock 407), a Victorian mock-castle, really a charming country house, built on the site of Auchen Castle. It's one of the most tranquil oases in the Scottish Lowlands, with terraced gardens, a trout-filled loch, and vistas from its windows. Beginning with your arrival at the reception desk, you are treated with graciousness and courtesy, and much effort is extended to make your stay a pleasant one.

The bedrooms, although lacking in fanciful decor, are often spacious and invariably comfortable, and each has a private bath or shower. Rates are £18 ($41.40) in a single, from £28 ($64.40) in a double, including a full breakfast, VAT, and service. The rooms in the main building are preferred over those in the annex.

The lofty dining room is exceptional for the area, its windows looking out over flowering ornamental grounds in late spring. Simple dishes are appetizingly good because of the excellent materials used. Roast Scottish beef is superb. The well-appointed tables and efficient staff complement the atmosphere of the peaceful country house. Lunch is from 12:30 to 2 p.m. and dinner from 7 to 8:30 p.m. The set luncheon goes for £5.50 ($12.65), the table d'hôte dinner for £8 ($18.40). Closed mid-December until mid-February.

DUMFRIES: A county town and royal burgh, this Scottish Lowland center enjoys associations with Robert Burns and James Barrie. In a sense it rivals Ayr as a mecca for admirers of Burns. He lived in Dumfries from 1791 until his death in 1796, and it was here that he wrote some of his most famous songs, including "Auld Lang Syne" and "Ye Banks and Braes of Bonnie Doon."

In **St. Michael's Churchyard,** a burial place for at least 900 years, stands the **Burns Mausoleum.** The poet was buried there along with his wife, Jean Armour, as well as five of their children. Burns dies in 1796, although his remains weren't removed to the tomb until 1815. In the 18th-century church of St. Michael's you can still see the pew used by the Burns family.

The poet died at what is now called the **Robert Burns House,** a simple, unpretentious stone structure, which can be visited by the public, as it contains personal relics and mementoes relating to Burns. His death may have been hastened by icy dips in well water which his doctor prescribed. The house is on Burns Street (formerly Mill Vennel). The **Town Museum,** the **Globe Inn,** and the **Hole in the Wa' Tavern** all contain Burns relics, and a statue of him stands in the High Street. You can stroll along **Burns' Walk** on the banks of the River Nith.

St. Michael's is the original parish church of Dumfries and its founding is of great antiquity. The site was probably sacred before the advent of Christianity. It appears that a Christian church has stood there for more than 1300 years. The earliest written records date from the reign of William the Lion (1165–1214). The church and the churchyard are interesting to visit because of all its connections with Scottish history, continuing through World War II.

From St. Michael's, it's a short walk to the Whitesands, where four bridges span the Nith. The earliest of these was built by Devorgilla Balliol, widow of John Balliol, father of a Scottish king. The bridge originally had nine arches but now has six and is still in constant use as a footbridge.

The Tourist Information Office is near the bridge. The wide esplanade was once the scene of horse and hiring fairs and now is a fine place to park your car and explore the town. Tour buses park here.

The **Mid Steeple** was built in 1707 as municipal buildings, courthouse, and prison. The old Scots "ell" measure of 37 inches is carved on the front of the building. A table of distances on the building includes the mileage to Huntingdon, England, which in the 18th century was the destination for Scottish cattle drovers driving their beasts south for the markets of London.

At the **Academy,** Barrie was a pupil, and he later wrote that he got the idea for *Peter Pan* from his games in the nearby garden.

Where to Stay

Cairndale Hotel, English Street (tel. Dumfries 4111), is most reliable, a fine and substantial choice. Its bedrooms have been attractively decorated, with special care paid to modern amenities (at least the ones we inspected). Most of the color-coordinated chambers contain private baths, although there are a few bathless bargains offered. Depending on the plumbing, singles range from £16.50 ($37.95) to £21 ($48.30), and doubles go from £28 ($64.40) to £32 ($73.60), plus service. You have a choice of a trio of bars, and guests quickly decide which one they'll make their local. The public lounges are handsomely decorated, and you can select your own favorite nook, perhaps a comfortable chair upholstered in velvet. Dinner, served until 9 p.m., is generally quite good, including such dishes as Galloway beef and grilled scampi.

Station Hotel, 49 Lovers Walk (tel. Dumfries 4316), has been improved in recent years and now offers one of the best of the moderately priced accommodations in Dumfries. Rooms come in a variety of styles with differences in plumbing. The atmosphere is modest, although pleasant, and the hosts are most agreeable. Nearly 15 of their rooms contain private baths. Singles range from £16 ($36.80) to £18 ($41.40), and doubles go from £21 ($48.30) to £24 ($55.20). Meals, at £7 ($16.10), are well prepared, and the service is efficient and polite.

County Hotel, High Street (tel. Dumfries 5401), was converted into a hotel in the early 19th century by a niece of John Paul Jones. In 1745 Bonnie Prince Charlie set up his headquarters here, a fact commemorated today by the Prince's Restaurant. Guests can see the room where he held a council during the Jacobite Rising. The inn offers 45 modernized bedrooms, nine of which contain private baths and several of which have color TV. Most of the bedrooms are of generous size, and all of them seem quite adequate and are spotlessly clean. Singles cost £15 ($34.50) if bathless, rising to £18 ($41.40) with bath, and bathless doubles go for £24 ($55.20), increasing to £28 ($64.40) with bath, these tariffs including a full breakfast. Bar snacks, and good ones at that, are available in the Georgian Bar, and late grills are offered in the intimate Regent Grill. The already-mentioned Prince's Restaurant offers both a table d'hôte, at £7.50 ($17.25), as well as an à la carte menu (typical Scottish fare), or you may prefer a quick lunch in The Tavern.

Newall House, 22 Newall Terrace (tel. Dumfries 2676), is owned by Charlie and Sheila Cowie. Together they run a friendly place, and do so cheerfully and well. Their rooms are clean and comfortable and include tea- and coffee-making facilities. They charge £7 ($16.10) for a single and £6.50 ($14.95) per person for double occupancy. The tariffs include a well-cooked breakfast. Mrs. Cowie will also prepare an appetizing dinner, if given fair warning, for just £3 ($6.90).

Fulwood Private Hotel, Lovers Walk (tel. Dumfries 2262), is run by congenial, friendly hosts, Mr. and Mrs. J. B. Rowland, who believe in giving wayfarers pleasure, cleanliness, and comfort in their tiny home, containing only five bedrooms (the bath must be shared). They have a wealth of information about touring in the area, and, on one occasion, Mr. Rowland drove a reader from San Jose, California, to some scenic spots. Their rate is £7.50 ($17.25) per person, including breakfast, VAT, and service.

The **Mayfair Hotel,** St. Mary's Street, top of English Street (tel. Dumfries 4588), is another good bargain, close to the station, about a five-minute walk to the center of town. It's small, but fully licensed, and there is central heating. The owners, Jan and Gloria Stradmeyer, offer 15 bedrooms, with hot and cold running water, shaving points, electric blankets, and floor lamps. Some family rooms are available and there is a reduction for children sharing their parents' room. Singles cost £10 ($23), and doubles are rented for £18 ($41.40), including VAT and a full breakfast. Drinks can be enjoyed in the Windmill Cellar Bar, and you can also order dinner, selecting from a well-chosen menu, a set meal costing only £4 ($9.20). Everything tastes homemade in the attractively decorated, although petite, dining room.

Where to Eat

Bruno's, 5 Balmoral Rd. (tel. Dumfries 5757). It may seem ironic to recommend an Italian restaurant in the seat of Rabbie Burns, but Bruno's serves some of the best food in town. It is most unassuming, but that is part of its charm. Its minestrone is first rate, and its pastas such as lasagne are homemade. The chef doesn't serve the most imaginative Italian dishes ever sampled—in fact, the repertoire is most familiar, such as saltimbocca alla Romana and pollo alla diavola, but it's done with flair. The veal is particularly tender, and the tomato sauce well spiced and blended. Steak au poivre is also excellent. The waiters are friendly and skillful and offer good advice. Bruno's serves only dinner, from 6:30 to 10 p.m. nightly except Tuesday and it will cost you about £10 ($23) per person, but it's worth it.

If you're looking for a place to have lunch or tea, go to **Barbour's Department Store,** Buccleuch Street, where you can get tasty dishes in the dining room on the second floor, for prices ranging from 30p (69¢) for a bowl of soup to £1.10 ($2.53) for a meat pie. The dining room is licensed, and there's an elevator to take you up. Open only during store hours.

Several carry-out delicatessens are along the street across from the Tourist Information Office. The **Merry Chef,** for one, has a variety of goodies if you're in a hurry.

The Local Pub

The **Globe Tavern** was a favorite haunt of Burns. It was one of the "howffs" (taverns) where he imbibed. The location is on a little side street, so ask at your hotel for directions before heading out for your nightly game of "skittles."

Excursions from Dumfries

Based in Dumfries, you can set out on treks in all directions to some of the most intriguing sightseeing goals in the Scottish Lowlands.

South on the 710 leads to the village of **New Abbey,** dominated by the red sandstone ruins of the Cistercian abbey founded in 1273 by Devorgilla, mother of John Balliol, the "vassal King." When her husband, John Balliol the Elder, died, she became one of the richest women in Europe. Most of Galloway, with estates and castles in England and land in Normandy, belonged to her. Devorgilla founded Balliol College, Oxford, in her husband's memory. She kept his embalmed heart in a silver and ivory casket by her side for 21 years until her death in 1289 at the age of 80, when she and the casket were buried beside Balliol in the front of the abbey altar. So the abbey gained the name of "Dulce Cor," Latin for "sweet heart," which has since become a part of the English language.

Built into a wall of a cottage in the village is a rough piece of sculpture showing three women rowing a boat—an allusion to the bringing of sandstone across the Nith to build the abbey.

Directly south from New Abbey on the 710 to Southerness leads to the **Arbigland Gardens and Cottage** at Kirkbean, 15 miles southwest of Dumfries. This is where John Paul Jones, one of the founders of the American navy, was born. You can visit the woodland with its water gardens arranged around a secluded bay, walking in the pathways where the great admiral once worked as a boy. The gardens are open, May to September on Tuesday, Thursday, and Sunday from 2 to 6 p.m., charging adults 40p (92¢); children, 20p (46¢).

Or, alternatively, you can head south from Dumfries on the 725 to **Caerlaverock Castle,** near the mouth of the River Nith, two miles south from Glencaple. Once the seat of the Maxwell family, this impressive ruined fortress dates back to 1220. In 1300 Edward I laid siege to it. In 1638 it yielded to Covenanters after a 13-week siege. The castle is triangular with round towers. The interior was reconstructed in the 17th century as a Renaissance mansion, with fine carving. Near the castle is the Caerlaverock National Nature Reserve between the River Nith and Lochar Water. It is a noted winter haunt of wildfowl, including barnacle geese.

After leaving the castle, continue east along the 725 to the village of **Ruthwell,** about ten miles southeast of Dumfries. There at the early 19th-century Ruthwell Church, you'll see one of the most outstanding crosses of the Dark Ages. Standing 18 feet high, the cross is believed to date from the eighth century. Engraved with carvings, it bears the earliest known specimen of written English (a Christian poem in Runic characters).

North from Dumfries on the A76 takes you to **Lincluden College,** two miles away. This is the richly decorated remains of a 15th-century collegiate church.

Four miles away, still following the A76, leads to **Ellisland Farm,** where Robert Burns made his last attempt at farming, renting the spread from 1788 to 1791. The present occupants of the house will show you through the Burns Room. It was at this farm that Burns wrote "Tam O'Shanter."

Continuing north, still on the A76, you reach **Thornhill,** a country resort —familiar to Burns—overlooking the River Nith. From here, it's possible to branch out for excursions in many directions.

The main target is **Drumlanrig Castle,** the seat of the Dukes of Buccleuch and Queensberry, built between 1679 and 1689. It lies three miles north of Thornhill, off the A76. This exquisite pink castle contains some celebrated paintings, including a famous Rembrandt and a Holbein. In addition, it is further enriched by Louis XIV antiques, silver, porcelain, and relics related to Bonnie Prince Charlie. The castle stands in a parkland ringed by wild hills, and there's even an "Adventure Woodland Playground." The house is open daily from noon to 6 p.m. from April 30 to the end of August. The grounds can be visited from noon to 6 p.m. Admission is £1 ($2.30) for adults, 50p ($1.15) for children.

Of almost equal interest, **Maxwelton House** (tel. Moniave 384) lies three miles south of Moniaive and 13 miles north of Dumfries on the B729. It was the stronghold of the Earls of Glencairn in the 14th and 15th centuries. But it is more remembered today as the birthplace (1682) of Annie Laurie of the famous Scottish ballad. From Maxwelton you can see that the braes are just as bonnie as ever. The braes, of course, refer to the neighboring hills. The house, garden, chapel, and an agricultural museum can be visited from May to September on Wednesday and Thursday from 2 to 5 p.m. and every fourth Sunday of those same months. Admission is 80p ($1.84) for adults, 20p (46¢) for children.

Back on the A76, you can branch northwest on the B797, heading in the direction of Mennock Pass. There, at **Wanlockhead,** you'll be in the highest village in Scotland. Once this village was a gold-mining center and known as "God's Treasure House." Gold was mined here for the Scottish crown jewels.

CASTLE DOUGLAS: A cattle and sheep market town, Castle Douglas makes a good touring center for Galloway. It lies about eight miles southwest of Dumfries, at the northern tip of Carlingwark Loch. On one of the islets in the loch is an ancient lake dwelling known as a "crannog."

The favorite excursion is to **Threave Castle,** 1½ miles west on an islet in the River Dee west of town, the ruined 14th-century stronghold of the Black Douglases. The four-story tower was built between 1639 and 1690 by Archibald the Grim, Lord of Galloway. In 1455 Threave Castle was the last Douglas stronghold to surrender to James II, who employed "Mons Meg" (the famous cannon now in Edinburgh Castle) in its subjection. Over the doorway projects the "gallows knob" from which the Douglases hanged their enemies. The castle was captured by the Covenanters in 1640 and dismantled. Owned by the

National Trust, the site must be reached by a *lengthy* walk through farmlands and then by small boat across the Dee.

Threave Gardens, around Threave House, a Scottish baronial mansion 1½ miles west of Castle Douglas, off the A75, is under the protection of the National Trust for Scotland which uses it as a school for gardening and a wildlife refuge. The gardens are open daily from 9 a.m. to 5 p.m. From April 1 to October 31, a Visitor Centre is also open. Admission is 75p ($1.73) for adults, 35p (81¢) for children.

Back in Castle Douglas, we'd recommend the follwoing selections for food and lodging.

Douglas Arms, King Street (tel. Castle Douglas 2231), was once an old coaching inn, but it has been turned into a modernized hotel, right in the center of this hamlet, situated at a busy crossroads. Therefore, it's not the most tranquil choice, but it is still inviting—made all the more so by the gracious hospitality extended by management. Behind a rather stark, two-story facade, the public rooms are bright and cheerful, giving you a toasty feeling on a cold night. Bedrooms have color-coordinated schemes, and such new gadgets as razor sockets. At least 11 out of the 27 rooms contain private baths. Single rates go from £14.50 ($33.35) to £18 ($41.40), and doubles from £25 ($57.50) to £31 ($71.30), including VAT and service. Dinner is served until 9 p.m., and, of course, trout and salmon are featured along with good beef and lamb, of which the hamlet has plenty.

King's Arms, St. Andrew's Street (tel. Castle Douglas 2097), is a good place at which to stop over, enjoying either a room or a meal or drink in the trio of tartan-clad bars, featuring the malt whiskey collection of Mr. Iain MacDonald. The restaurant serves good, simple meals, using the freshest of fish and tender beef, a meal costing from £7 ($16.10). It is attractively decorated, and the staff is most helpful. Bedrooms are comfortable, although modest, and only a couple contain private baths. For these, the rate is £18 ($41.40) per person daily. However, in a bathless chamber, the tariff is £12.50 ($28.75) per person. Everything is maintained immaculately, and parking is provided.

An excellent hotel choice lies south of Castle Douglas, near Dalbeattie, in the hamlet of—

ROCKCLIFFE: An attractive seaside village, Rockcliffe has a bird sanctuary on its offshore Rough Island. From its sand and rock beach, you can look out to the Lake District mountains on the distant horizon.

Baron's Craig Hotel (tel. Rockcliffe 225) is a stately country home, built of granite, and set back from the shoreline of Solway Firth. Because of its sheltered position from the cold north wind, its gardens bloom profusely in season. Lawns and grounds—nearly 20 acres—are well manicured. The public rooms are spacious and airy, brightly decorated and most welcoming. In the modern bar you can select at leisure your favorite whiskey. The owners have paid special attention to the bedrooms, decorating them in warm, pleasing colors to suggest in summer a holiday atmosphere. From April to October, it rents singles (bathless) for £18.20 ($41.86), going up to £23.50 ($54.05) with bath. A bathless double costs £18 ($41.40), rising to £21 ($48.30) with bath, including breakfast. At least 21 of the rooms contain private baths, which are spotlessly clean.

Even if you're not staying here, you might want to drive down to enjoy the hotel's fine cookery. The dining room overlooks the water, and table appointments have flair and style. At lunch the menu is considerably shortened, but still quite good, a set meal costing £6.50 ($14.95). A cold table is invariably featured. In the evening, however, a four-course table d'hôte is offered at £10 ($23) between the hours of 7 and 9 p.m. The menu is based on good local ingredients, and all dishes are acceptably prepared. The service is exceptional.

KIRKCUDBRIGHT: Stewartry's most ancient burgh, Kirkcudbright (pronounced Kir-coo-bree) lies at the head of Kirkcudbright Bay on the Dee Estuary. This intriguing old town contains color-washed houses inhabited, in part, by artists. In fact, Kirkcudbright has been called the "St. Ives (Cornwall) of Scotland."

In the old town graveyard are memorials to Covenanters and to Billy Marshall, the tinker king who died in 1792 at the age of 120, reportedly having fathered four children after the age of 100.

Maclellan's Castle, built in 1582 for the town's provost, Sir Thomas Maclellan, easily dominates the center of town. Kirkcudbright is an attractive town which is the center of a lively group of weavers, potters, and painters who work in the 18th-century streets and lanes.

The **Tolbooth,** a large building, dates back to the 16th and 17th centuries, and in front of it is a **Mercat Cross** of 1610. The Tolbooth is a memorial to John Paul Jones (1747–1792), the gardener's son from Kirkbean who became a slave trader, a privateer, and in due course one of the founders of the American navy. For a time, before his emigration, he was imprisoned for murder in the Tolbooth.

Art exhibitions are regularly sponsored at **Broughton House,** a 17th-century mansion which once belonged to E. A. Hornel, the artist. The house contains a large reference library with a valuable Burns collection, along with pictures by Hornel and other artists, plus antiques and other works of art. You can stroll through its beautiful garden. Broughton is open April to October seven days a week, from 11 a.m. to 1 p.m. and 2 to 5 p.m.; and November to March on Saturday, Sunday, and Monday, 2 to 5 p.m.

In addition, the **Stewartry Museum** contains a fascinating collection of antiquities, depicting the history and culture of Galloway. It is open daily, except Sunday, from 10 a.m. to 5 p.m., charging adults 30p (69¢) and children 10p (23¢). It's open from Easter to October.

North of town is the ruined **Tongland Abbey,** one of whose abbots, John Damian, once tried to fly from the battlements of Stirling Castle wearing wings of bird feathers, in the presence of James IV. He landed in a manure pile.

Dundrennan Abbey, seven miles southeast of Kirkcudbright, the ruins of a rich Cistercian house founded in 1142, include much late Norman and Transitional work. Dundrennan is a daughter abbey of Rievaulx Abbey in Yorkshire and the mother abbey of Glenluce and Sweetheart Abbeys. The small village is partly built of stones "quarried" from the abbey. Mary Queen of Scots, after escaping from Loch Leven and being defeated at the Battle of Langside, spent her last night in Scotland at the abbey in May 1568. She went to England to seek help from Elizabeth who imprisoned her instead. The transept and choir—a unique example of the Early Pointed style—remain.

In accommodations, we'd suggest the **Selkirk Arms,** Old High Street (tel. Kirkcudbright 30402), where Robert Burns stayed when he composed the celebrated Selkirk Grace. (The grace was actually given on St. Mary's isle, the seat of the Douglases, Earls of Selkirk, and, in part, it went as follows: "But we ha'e meat, and we can eat, And sae the Lord be thankit.") The hotel is fairly small, and its appointments are simple, yet it is colorful staying in such charming surroundings. The neighborhood evokes memories of John Paul Jones, and there are little art galleries displaying the works of local painters. In all, you'll enjoy a restful, tranquil atmosphere. You have a choice of rooms in the main building or in the annex. Depending on the plumbing, singles range from £12.50 ($28.75) to £15 ($34.50) and doubles from £21 ($48.30) to £24 ($55.20), including breakfast. Dinner costs £7.50 ($17.25). The hotel is open all year. It has both a TV lounge and a cocktail bar, and there is ample parking.

GATEHOUSE-OF-FLEET: This sleepy former cotton town, on the Water of Fleet, was the **Kippletringan** in Sir Walter Scott's *Guy Mannering,* and Burns composed "Scots Wha Hae wi' Wallace Bled" on the moors nearby and wrote it down in the Murray Arms Hotel there.

The town's name probably dates from 1642 when the English government opened the first military road through Galloway to assist the passage of troops to Ireland. In 1661 Richard Murray of Cally was authorized by Parliament to widen the bridge and to erect beside it an inn which was to serve as a tollhouse, with the innkeeper responsible for the maintenance of a 12-mile stretch of road. This is believed to have been the original house on the "gait," or road, which later became known as the "gait house of Fleet," and by 1790 it was being written in its present form and spelling. This ancient "gait house" is now part of the Murray Arms Hotel, used as a coffeeroom, and is therefore probably the oldest building still in existence in the town.

West of Gatehouse, on the road to Creetown, is the well-preserved 15th-century tower of the McCullochs, with its sinister "murder hole" over the entrance passage. Through this trapdoor, boiling pitch was poured onto attackers. **Cardoness Castle** was originally the seat of the McCulloch family, one of whom, Sir Godfrey McCulloch, was the last person in Scotland to be executed, at Edinburgh in 1697, by the "Maiden," the Scots version of the guillotine.

For accommodations, we recommend the following:

Cally Hotel (tel. Gatehouse 341) is a large 18th-century mansion standing in 100 acres of beautiful gardens and wooded parkland. Especially popular with more mature readers, it is an oasis of peace and quiet—most comfortable, more suited for someone who wishes to spend a few days in Galloway than the fleeting overnight motorist. The public lounges are overscale with some fine period pieces, and a sun patio looks out onto a swimming pool. Amenities include two bars, table tennis, billiards, in addition to a hard tennis court, putting, croquet, a sauna, game fishing, loch boating, and dancing at certain times of the year. All of its 90 rooms contain private baths or showers, costing from £24 ($55.20) in a single, from £38 ($87.40) in a double. Some of the bedrooms have balconies opening onto the grounds. Rooms come in widely varying styles and sizes, but all have color TV and tea- and coffee-making facilities.

Murray Arms (tel. Gatehouse 207) is a long, low, white-painted building that was once a posting inn in the 18th century, its coffeehouse dating back even earlier, 1642. Burns wrote his stirring song, "Scots Wha' Ha'e" while staying at the inn, the occasion still commemorated to this day by the Burns room with its Leitch pictures. The inn has been considerably updated and modernized by the laird of the Cally Estate, and that is as it should be, since it was James Murray of Cally who made the Murray Arms into a coaching inn so long ago. Now it's back in the same family after a long departure.

Standing by an old clock tower, the inn has long been known for its food and hospitality. In addition to three bars, the house has a sun lounge opening onto a roof terrace. The rooms are modestly furnished, and singles range from £14 ($32.20) to £21 ($48.30), doubles from £26 ($59.80) to £42 ($96.60), plus VAT. Nearly half of the rooms contain private baths.

You can stop in for a complete dinner in its attractively decorated restaurant opening onto the garden. Between 12:30 and 2 p.m. typical bar lunches are offered. But at dinner, from 7:30 to 9 p.m., you can order a table d'hôte meal for £8 ($18.40). Specialties include Galloway beef and fresh Solway Firth salmon.

CREETOWN: "The Ferry Toon," as Creetown is called, lies west of Gatehouse-on-Fleet, on the road to Newton Steward. There are two ruined 16th-century castles about midway along the road, **Carsluith** and **Barholm.** Up the Kirkdale Burn from Barholm are the 4000-year-old standing stones and chambered tombs of Cairn Holy.

NEWTON STEWART: Sometimes called "the gateway to Galloway" and the "heart of Galloway," this small town on the River Cree was made a burgh or barony in 1677 after a son of the second Earl of Galloway built some houses beside the ford across the river and gave the hamlet its present name. When the estate was later purchased by William Douglas, he changed the name to Newton Douglas, but it didn't stick. The town has a livestock market and woolen mills. Cree Bridge, built of granite in 1813 to replace one swept away by a flood, links the town with **Minnigaff** where there is an old church with interesting carved stones and some quaint memorials.

Newton Stewart is associated with Scott, Stevenson, and Burns. Today it is chiefly a center for touring, especially north for nine miles to the famous beauty spot of **Loch Troolin** in the Glen Trool Forest Park, 200 square miles of magnificently preserved splendor. On the way to Loch Trool, you go through the village of Glentrool where you'll find the first car park for those wanting to take the Stroan Bridge walk, a distance of 3½ miles. The hearty Scots, of course, walk the entire loch, all 4½ miles of it.

Food and Lodging

Newton Stewart itself has a wide range of accommodations, making it one of the best bases for touring Galloway.

Bruce, Queen Street (tel. Newton Stewart 2294), is an exemplary up-to-date hotel. Although not lavish in appointments, it is completely modern and efficiently run, maintaining a high standard of comfort, but keeping its prices low—from £12 ($27.60) in a single, from £22 ($50.60) in a double. The decor is bright, and the bedrooms well designed. All of the 20 bedrooms contain either private baths or showers. Guests enjoy a pleasant bar, with a jukebox, and congenial company, composed mainly of locals who frequent the Bruce. Dancing in summer is a feature of the hotel. The restaurant, also in the modern style, offers a delicious cold table at lunch from 12:30 to 2 p.m., costing £3 ($6.90). Dinners, when the menu is more varied, is quite interesting, and everything tastes as if it were home cooked from fresh produce. A table d'hôte, served from 7:30 to 9 p.m., goes for £6 ($13.80).

Kirroughtree, (tel. Newton Stewart 2141) is an impressive manor house, once the seat of the Herons of Galloway, built in 1719 and full of traditional character. Lying about a mile east of the town, it borders a gold course. The hotel is ideal for those who want complete peace and quiet, as it is surrounded by some nine acres of private grounds with beautiful views of the Galloway countryside and Solway Firth. The hotel is fully licensed with two cocktail bars and an extensive wine list, central heating, and many amenities. The 26 bedrooms (12 with private bath) all have color TV, radio, and tea- and coffee-making facilities. Rates range from £11.50 ($26.45) to £14 ($32.20) per person for bed and breakfast. The demi-pension tariffs go from £20 ($46) to £22.50 ($51.75), including VAT. There are golf courses nearby, pony trekking, and beautiful walks. Permits for salmon or trout fishing are available at the hotel.

Creebridge (tel. Newton Stewart 2121) is a two-story, vine-covered stone building on its own grounds. Fully licensed, it is set in the midst of beautiful gardens, and is perhaps the pleasantest and most comfortable hotel in Newton Stewart. It is secluded enough to be a peaceful oasis, yet it is also near the center of town. It overlooks the River Cree where it's possible to fish. Both the public rooms and bedrooms have been modernized without destroying the charm of the house. Open all year, the hotel offers a total of 29 rooms, with hot and cold running water. Rates are low, from £15 ($34.50) in a single room for bed and breakfast, £28 ($64.40) for the same accommodations in a double. The hotel is licensed. The food is very good, consisting of roast Galloway beef, local produce, and fresh salmon and trout.

Galloway Arms, Victoria Street (tel. Newton Stewart 2282), was once known simply as "The Inn." Built of granite and flint—some of its walls almost 25 feet thick—it is somewhat like a three-story pub hotel, with fully equipped modern bedrooms, 23 in all, of which 15 come equipped with private bath. Rates are £11.50 ($26.45) in a single and from £20 ($46) in a double, including a full breakfast, service, and VAT. Locals gather in the Bruce Bar, and there is, as well, a dining room, serving simple, well-cooked dishes, mainly grills, costing about £5.50 ($12.65) a dish.

WIGTOWN: This former county town of the district is still a center for fishing and wildfowling although its harbor is silted up. Two market crosses, an 18th-century one topped by a sundial and another which was erected in 1816, stand in the town's central square. In 1685 two women, Margaret Maclauchlan and Margaret Wilson, Covenanters who were accused of attending meetings of their sect, were tied to stakes at the mouth of the River Bladnoch and drowned by the rising tide after refusing to give up their beliefs. An obelisk marks the traditional site of their martyrdom. A monument to all Covenanters stands on Windy Hill back of the town.

Three miles northwest of Wigtown, near Torhouskie Farm, are the Bronze Age **Stones of Torhouse,** 19 standing stones in a circle with three in the center.

The remains of **Baldoon Castle** are one mile from Wigtown. This was the setting for Sir Walter Scott's *The Bride of Lammermoor.* It was the home of David Dunbar and his wife, supposed to be the principal characters of the *Bride.* The castle was captured by Wallace in 1297.

WHITHORN: Ten miles south of Wigtown, you come upon Whithorn, a modern town with a museum containing ancient crosses and tombstones, including the fifth-century **Latinus Stone,** the earliest Christian memorial in Scotland. St. Ninian, the son of a local chieftain, founded a monastery here in A.D. 397 and built his "Candida Casa" or "White House," probably the first Christian church in Scotland. In the 12th century Fergus, Lord of Galloway, built a priory. The church and monastery were destroyed in the 16th century. Excavations in the ruins have revealed fragments of wall covered in pale plaster believed to be from Ninian's Candida Casa. The ruins are entered through the Pend, a 17th-century arch on which are carved the Royal Arms of Scotland.

A moorland walk to the west coast 2½ miles away leads to **St. Ninian's Cave** in Port Castle Bay, used by the missionary as a retreat.

The **Isle of Whithorn,** three miles southeast of the town, is where St. Ninian landed about A.D. 395 on his return from studying in Rome; to bring Christianity to Scotland. The ruins of a plain 13th-century chapel are here but no signs of an earlier church. On the point of the promontory are the remains of an Iron Age fort and a late 17th-century tower.

Chapel Finian, near the shore road on the way from Whithorn to Glenluce, is a small chapel or oratory probably dating from the 10th or 11th century, in an enclosure about 50 feet wide.

An excellent place to stay just outside Whithorn is the **Castlewigg Hotel** (tel. Whithorn 213), a small licensed country hotel under the personal supervision of its owners, Sam and Bett Christie. Castlewigg is two miles north of Whithorn on the A746, with views to the north toward Newton Stewart and to the east to Fleet Bay. More than 200 years old, the hotel building was the dower house of Castle Wigg, which lies in ruins, not open to the public, a mile or so off the road. The hotel has two singles, two doubles, and one family room, which rent for £11 ($25.30) for bed and breakfast per person. Guests may enjoy the resident's lounge with color TV, the spacious, colorful dining room, and the lounge bar. Dinner costs from £5 ($11.50). From the à la carte menu you can order such delicacies as prawn cocktail, venison in red wine and port, rainbow trout. The Castlewigg sits in seven acres of grounds, about 150 yards from the main road, so there's ample parking. It's open all year.

GARLIESTON: When you're traveling around Wigtown Bay, passing through the hamlet of Isle of Whithorn to the little villages along Luce Bay, you're fortunate to find almost any suitable stopover for food and lodgings. Garlieston itself once had an active fishing harbor, but nowadays it is known more to artists.

Nearby, at Sorbie, the **Pheasant Inn** (tel. Garlieston 223) is very petite, six rooms in all, two with bath, but it is such a warm, welcome spot after a long day on the road. The proprietors, Mr. and Mrs. Montgomery, take pride, and well they should, in their unpretentious little inn, and they are known in these parts for their friendly reception and hospitality. They have furnished the rooms in an attractive, comfortable way, and the rates are £8.50 ($19.55) in a single, and from £16 ($36.80) in a double, plus VAT. You have a choice of a couple of bars, or, instead, you may prefer to retreat to the lounge up the steps to watch some British television. The food consists of simple Scottish specialties, everything reasonably priced. Bar lunches are available, and evening dinners cost from £4.50 ($10.35).

PORT WILLIAM: On Luce Bay, this little holiday resort is a center for tennis, golf, and swimming.

By taking the 714 west, you'll reach **Drumtrodden Stones,** a cluster of ring and cup markings from the Bronze Age on a rock face. Just 400 yards to the south is an alignment of three adjacent surviving stones. Hardly Stonehenge, but interesting, nevertheless.

While still on an antiquity search, you can drive directly south of Port William a short distance to **Barsalloch Fort,** the remains of a fort dating from the Iron Age.

In the pleasant village, you can stay at the **Monreith Arms Hotel** (tel. Port William 206), a big stone building at the roundabout where you will find immaculate bedrooms, innerspring mattresses, and comfortable public rooms, as well as a good garage accommodation for your car. Mr. and Mrs. A. R.

Jardine, in their fully licensed hostelry, offer bed and breakfast for £9.70 ($22.31) per night per person. Dinner costs from £5 ($11.50). All prices include VAT and service charge. The hotel is open all year.

GLENLUCE: Lying on the Water of Luce near its estuary in Luce Bay, Glenluce is another attractive village. **Glenluce Abbey,** one mile northwest, is a ruined Cistercian house founded about 1190, which has intact a 15th-century vaulted chapter house of architectural interest. The border "wizard," Michael Scott, is said to have lured the plague to the abbey in the 13th century and shut it in a vault. **Castle of Park,** a 16th-century mansion, overlooks the village from the brow of a hill across the river.

A convenient and pleasant place to stay in Glenluce is the **Judge's Keep,** in the center of town (tel. Glenluce 203), where Mrs. Jean Buchanan receives guests in her fully licensed hotel for £9 ($20.70) per person for bed and breakfast. Dinner, prepared under Mrs. Buchanan's close supervision in the immaculate kitchen on the ground floor, costs £6 ($13.80), and it's well worth it. There is a TV lounge for guests, as well as public and lounge bars and ample car parking. The hotel is open April to October.

PORTPATRICK: Until 1849 steamers sailed the 21 miles from Donaghdee in Northern Ireland to Portpatrick, which became a "Gretna Green" for the Irish. Couples would land on Saturday, have the banns called on Sunday, and marry on Monday. When the harbor became silted up, Portpatrick was replaced by Stranraer as a port.

Commanding a clifftop to the south are the ruins of **Dunskey Castle,** a grim keep built in 1510 by John Adair.

Ten miles south of Portpatrick is the quiet little hamlet of **Port Logan.** In the vicinity is **Logan House,** the seat of the McDouall family, which could trace their ancestry so far back that it was claimed they were as "old as the sun itself." This family laid out the world-famous gardens at Logan which are visited by people from all over the world. **Logan Botanic Garden,** an annex of the Royal Botanic Garden, Edinburgh, contains a wide range of plants from the temperate regions of the world. Cordylines, palms, tree ferns, and tender rhododendrons grow well in the mild climate of southwest Scotland. The garden is open from 10 a.m. to 5 p.m. Admission is around 50p ($1.15). The site is 14 miles south of Stranraer off the B7065 road.

Nearby is **Ardwell House,** with gardens which are at their best in April and May.

The ancient church site of **Kirkmadrine** lies in the parish of Stoneykirk, south of Portpatrick. The site now has a modern church but there is an ancient graveyard and early inscribed stones and crosses, including three of the earliest Christian monuments in Britain, showing the chi-rho symbol and inscriptions dating from the fifth or early sixth century. There was an early Christian monastery and in the Middle Ages a parish church.

Instead of going north to the larger town, Stranraer, you might stay at the **Knockinaam Lodge** (tel. Portpatrick 471), a Victorian house with view looking out to Northern Ireland. People come to Knockinaam for the peace and relaxation, as the lodge stands in 30 secluded acres of private grounds right on the sea. It's run in the best country-house tradition by the resident owners. In the heat of World War II, Churchill came here to escape from some of the pressure, enjoying a long hot bath (in a tub which remains) while smoking a cigar. The hotel contains only ten rooms, most of which have private bath or shower. The rate is £16 ($36.80) per person, including VAT, although you must pay extra for a full Scottish breakfast. The lodge serves the best food in Portpatrick, with a surprising array of continental dishes. The standard of cuisine is very high. All ingredients used in the kitchen by the chefs are fresh, and dishes on both the à la carte and table d'hôte menus are cooked to order. Service is polite and efficient, and the views open onto the water. Lunch from noon to 2 p.m. is offered, along with dinner from 7 to 9 p.m., when a set meals costs £8.50 ($19.55), including VAT. The lodge is closed from mid-January to mid-March.

STRANRAER: The largest town in Wigtownshire, Stranraer is the terminal of the 35-mile ferry crossing from Larne, Northern Ireland. An early chapel, built by a member of the Adair family near the 16th century **Castle of St. John** in the heart of town, gave the settlement its original name of Chapel, later changed to Chapel of Stranrawer and then shortened to Stranraer. The name is supposed to have referred to the row or "raw" of original houses on the "strand" or burn, now largely buried beneath the town's streets. The Castle of St. John became the town jail and in the late 17th century held Covenanters during Graham of Claverhouse's campaigns of religious persecution.

To the east is **Lochinch Castle,** a late 19th-century Scots baronial mansion. In the grounds are White and Black Lochs and the ruins of **Castle Kennedy,** built during the reign of James IV, but burned down in 1716. Restored in the middle of the 19th century, the gardens contain the finest pinetum in Scotland. Go in the right season and you can wander among rhododendrons, azaleas, and magnolias. The gardens are open daily, except Saturday from April to September—10 a.m. to 5 p.m., charging adults 50p ($1.15) for admission; children, 30p (69¢).

An island in Black Loch has a crannog which was partly excavated in the last century.

The leading hotels are as follows.

North West Castle, Royal Crescent (tel. Stranraer 4413), overlooks Loch Ryan and the departure quay for Northern Ireland. The oldest part of the house was built in 1820 by Capt. Sir John Ross, R.N., the Arctic explorer. Of course, to honor the brave man, your bedroom window should face northwest, an allusion to his search for the "North West Passage." The hotel owners will give you a brochure in which are related the exploits and disappointments of the explorer. The original building has been altered and extended to meet the hotel's increasing popularity. At last count, a total of 79 rooms are offered, all with private bath. Singles go from £14 ($32.20) and doubles from a low of £20 ($46) to a high of £26 ($59.80) for the well-appointed suites. Many of the best rooms are in the two more modern wings.

The lounges are cozy and pleasantly furnished, and the dining room is impressive, serving mainly continental fare with Scottish overtones. Fresh local ingredients are used. The bars downstairs are well stocked—we prefer the Explorers' Lounge with its views of the harbor. Further amenities include a garden, a sauna, and a solarium, plus a curling rink, game room, buttery, indoor swimming pool, and dancing to a live band on Saturday night.

George Hotel, George Street (tel. Stranraer 24878), stands right in the heart of town. We first stayed there many, many years ago, and, on our most recent visit, found it considerably improved, a lot of money spent, in fact, to provide the latest up-to-date comforts for its guests, many of whom are embarking for Northern Ireland in the morning. Less than half the bedrooms contain private baths. Singles cost £18 ($41.40) nightly, and doubles go for £34 ($71.30). Most of the rooms contain such amenities as razor sockets, TV, and radio. Color-coordinated schemes are used in the bedrooms, and the baths are spotlessly clean. A friendly, cooperative staff is expert at giving touring advice. The hotel's restaurant is also good, the cooking and service quite acceptable. The lighting is subdued and the ingredients fresh, the emphasis placed on Scottish dishes. You must arrive there before 9 p.m. to dine with any sort of relaxation.

Appendix

CURRENCY EXCHANGE

The Dollar and the Pound

AS WE GO TO PRESS, Britain's pound sterling is worth about $2.30, and the price conversions in this book have been computed at that exchange rate. Since the pound is far from stable, however, it's always wise to check with a bank before you set off for Britain.

Each pound breaks down into 100 pence, making each penny worth just over 2¢ U.S. Here are some approximate conversions:

Pence	U.S. $	Pounds	U.S. $
1	.02	1	2.30
2	.05	2	4.60
5	.12	3	6.90
10	.23	4	9.20
20	.46	5	11.50
25	.58	6	13.80
50	1.15	7	16.10
75	1.73	8	18.40
100	2.30	9	20.70
		10	23.00
		20	46.00

FROMMER/PASMANTIER PUBLISHERS
380 MADISON AVE., NEW YORK, NY 10017   Date _____

Friends, please send me (postpaid) the books checked below:

$-A-DAY GUIDES
(In-depth guides to low-cost tourist accommodations and facilities.)

- ☐ Europe on $20 a Day $7.95
- ☐ Australia on $15 & $20 a Day $4.95
- ☐ England and Scotland on $20 a Day $5.95
- ☐ Greece and Yugoslavia on $15 & $20 a Day $4.95
- ☐ Hawaii on $25 a Day $5.95
- ☐ Ireland on $25 a Day $5.95
- ☐ Israel on $15 & $20 a Day $4.95
- ☐ Mexico and Guatemala on $15 & $20 a Day $6.95
- ☐ New Zealand on $15 & $20 a Day $4.95
- ☐ New York on $20 a Day $4.95
- ☐ Scandinavia on $25 a Day $5.95
- ☐ South America on $15 & $20 a Day $5.95
- ☐ Spain and Morocco (plus the Canary Is.) on $15 & $20 a Day $5.95
- ☐ Washington, D.C. on $25 a Day $4.95

DOLLARWISE GUIDES
(Guides to tourist accommodations and facilities from budget to deluxe, with emphasis on the medium-priced.)

- ☐ Egypt $4.95
- ☐ England & Scotland $6.95
- ☐ France $6.95
- ☐ Germany $4.95
- ☐ Italy $5.95
- ☐ Portugal $4.95
- ☐ Canada $6.95
- ☐ Caribbean (incl. Bermuda & the Bahamas) $6.95
- ☐ California & Las Vegas ... $5.95
- ☐ New England $4.95
- ☐ Southeast & New Orleans .. $4.95

THE ARTHUR FROMMER GUIDES
(Pocket-size guides to tourist accommodations and facilities in all price ranges.)

- ☐ Amsterdam/Holland $2.95
- ☐ Athens $2.95
- ☐ Boston $2.95
- ☐ Hawaii $2.95
- ☐ Dublin/Ireland $2.95
- ☐ Las Vegas $2.95
- ☐ Lisbon/Madrid/Costa del Sol $2.95
- ☐ London $2.95
- ☐ Los Angeles $2.95
- ☐ Mexico City/Acapulco ... $2.95
- ☐ New Orleans $2.95
- ☐ New York $2.95
- ☐ Paris $2.95
- ☐ Philadelphia/Atlantic City .. $2.95
- ☐ Rome $2.95
- ☐ San Francisco $2.95
- ☐ Washington, D.C $2.95

SPECIAL EDITIONS

- ☐ The Caribbean Bargain Book. $6.95 (Guide to resorts that slash rates 20% to 60% mid April to December.)
- ☐ Where to Stay USA .... $4.95 (Guide to accommodations in all 50 states, from $2 to $20 per night.)
- ☐ Alternative Guide to China .. $8.95 (Guide to the latest opportunities for China travel; includes complete phrase section; avail. April 1981.)
- ☐ How to Live in Florida on $10,000 a Year $8.95

Include 85¢ post. & hdlg. for 1st book over $3; 60¢ for books under $3. $1.25 for shipment of 1st book over $3 outside U.S.; 60¢ under $3.   25¢ any add'l book.

Enclosed is my check or money order for $ _____

NAME _____

ADDRESS _____

CITY _____ STATE _____ ZIP _____